Europe

The most in-depth campsite guides

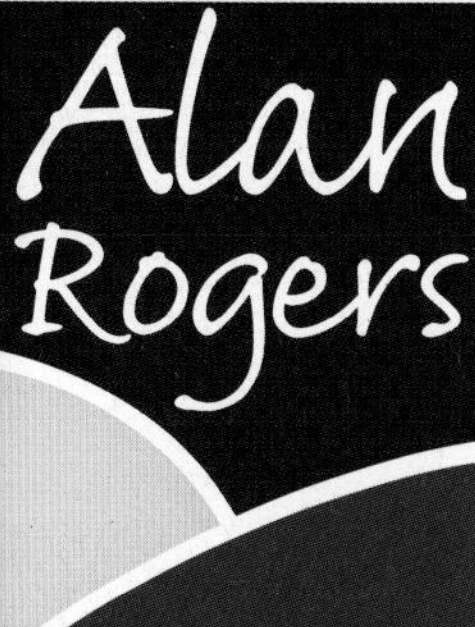

INSPECTED & SELECTED CAMPSITES

Compiled by: Alan Rogers Guides Ltd

Designed by: Paul Effenberg, Vine Design Ltd

Additional photography: T Lambelin, www.lambelin.com
Maps created by Customised Mapping (01769 540044)
contain background data provided by GisDATA Ltd

Published by: Alan Rogers Guides Ltd,
Spelmonden Old Oast, Goudhurst, Kent TN17 1HE
www.alanrogers.com Tel: 01580 214000

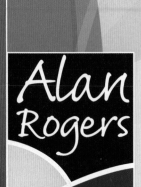

British Library Cataloguing-in-Publication Data:
A catalogue record for this book is available
from the British Library.

ISBN-978-1-906215-14-9

Printed in Great Britain by J H Haynes & Co Ltd

Contents

The Alan Rogers approach

Alan Rogers Guides were first published over 40 years ago. Since Alan Rogers published the first campsite guide that bore his name, the range has expanded and now covers 27 countries in five separate guides. No fewer than 20 of the campsites selected by Alan for the first guide are still featured in our 2009 editions.

There are many thousands of campsites in Europe of varying quality: this guide contains impartially written reports on over 950 of the very finest, in no less than 22 countries. Each one is individually inspected and selected. This guide does not include sites in Britain and Ireland, for which we publish a separate guide, and it contains only a limited selection of sites in France, Italy and Spain & Portugal as we also publish separate guides for these destinations. All the usual maps and indexes are also included, designed to help you find the choice of campsite that's right for you. We hope you enjoy some happy and safe travels – and some pleasurable 'armchair touring' in the meantime!

A question of quality

The criteria we use when inspecting and selecting sites are numerous, but the most important by far is the question of good quality. People want different things from their choice of campsite so we try to include a range of campsite 'styles' to cater for a wide variety of preferences: from those seeking a small peaceful campsite in the heart of the countryside, to visitors looking for an 'all singing, all dancing' site in a popular seaside resort. Those with more specific interests, such as sporting facilities, cultural events or historical attractions, are also catered for.

The size of the site, whether it's part of a chain or privately owned, makes no difference in terms of it being required to meet our exacting standards in respect of its quality and it being 'fit for purpose'. In other words, irrespective of the size of the site, or the number of facilities it offers, we consider and evaluate the welcome, the pitches, the sanitary facilities, the cleanliness, the general maintenance and even the location.

" ...the campsites included in this book have been chosen entirely on merit, and no payment of any sort is made by them for their inclusion."

Alan Rogers, 1968

Expert opinions

We rely on our dedicated team of Site Assessors, all of whom are experienced campers, caravanners or motorcaravanners, to visit and recommend sites. Each year they travel some 100,000 miles around Europe inspecting new campsites for the guide and re-inspecting the existing ones. Our thanks are due to them for their enthusiastic efforts, their diligence and integrity.

We also appreciate the feedback we receive from many of our readers and we always make a point of following up complaints, suggestions or recommendations for possible new sites. Of course we get a few grumbles too – but it really is a few, and those we do receive usually relate to overcrowding or to poor maintenance during the peak school holiday period. Please bear in mind that, although we are interested to hear about any complaints, we have no contractual relationship with the campsites featured in our guides and are therefore not in a position to intervene in any dispute between a reader and a campsite.

Independent and honest

Whilst the content and scope of the Alan Rogers guides have expanded considerably since the early editions, our selection of campsites still employs exactly the same philosophy and criteria as defined by Alan Rogers in 1968.

'telling it how it is'

Firstly, and most importantly, our selection is based entirely on our own rigorous and independent inspection and selection process. Campsites cannot buy their way into our guides – indeed the extensive Site Report which is written by us, not by the site owner, is provided free of charge so we are free to say what we think and to provide an honest, 'warts and all' description. This is written in plain English and without the use of confusing icons or symbols.

HIGHLY RESPECTED BY SITE OWNERS AND READERS ALIKE, THERE IS NO BETTER GUIDE WHEN IT COMES TO FORMING AN INDEPENDENT VIEW OF A CAMPSITE'S QUALITY. WHEN YOU NEED TO BE CONFIDENT IN YOUR CHOICE OF CAMPSITE, YOU NEED THE ALAN ROGERS GUIDE.

- SITES ONLY INCLUDED ON MERIT
- SITES CANNOT PAY TO BE INCLUDED
- INDEPENDENTLY INSPECTED, RIGOROUSLY ASSESSED
- IMPARTIAL REVIEWS
- OVER 40 YEARS OF EXPERTISE

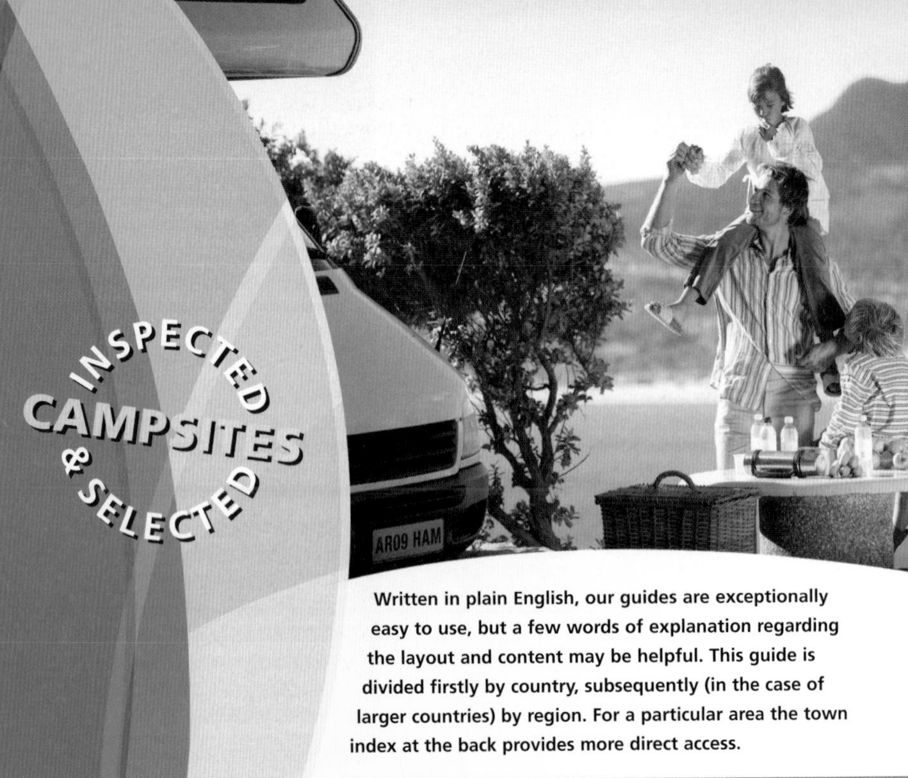

Written in plain English, our guides are exceptionally easy to use, but a few words of explanation regarding the layout and content may be helpful. This guide is divided firstly by country, subsequently (in the case of larger countries) by region. For a particular area the town index at the back provides more direct access.

The Site Reports – *Example of an entry*

Country

Site Number **Site name**

Postal address (including county)

Telephone number. Email address

alanrogers.com web address

A description of the site in which we try to give an idea of its general features – its size, its situation, its strengths and its weaknesses. This section should provide a picture of the site itself with reference to the facilities that are provided and if they impact on its appearance or character. We include details on pitch numbers, electricity (with amperage), hardstandings etc. in this section, as pitch design, planning and terracing affect the site's overall appearance. Similarly we include reference to pitches used for caravan holiday homes, chalets, and the like. Importantly at the end of this column we indicate if there are any restrictions, e.g. no tents, no children, naturist sites.

Facilities

Lists more specific information on the site's facilities and amenities and, where available, the dates when these facilities are open (if not for the whole season). Off site: here we give distances to various local amenities, for example, local shops, the nearest beach, plus our featured activities (bicycle hire, fishing, horse riding, boat launching). Where we have space we list suggestions for activities and local tourist attractions.

Open: Site opening dates.

Directions

Separated from the main text in order that they may be read and assimilated more easily by a navigator en-route. Bear in mind that road improvement schemes can result in road numbers being altered. GPS: references are provided for satellite navigation systems (in degrees and minutes) as we obtain them.

Charges 2009 (or a general guide)

Indexes

Our three indexes allow you to find sites by country, site number and name, by country and site name (alphabetically) or by the town or village where the site is situated. See also the handy Quick Reference sections at the back.

Campsite Maps

The maps of each country are designed to show the country in relation to others and will help you to identify the approximate position of each campsite. The colour of the campsite number (in red) indicates whether it is open all year or not. You will certainly need more detailed maps and we have found the Michelin atlas to be particularly useful.

Facilities

Toilet blocks

We assume that toilet blocks will be equipped with a reasonable amount of British style WCs, washbasins with hot and cold water and hot showers with dividers or curtains, and will have all necessary shelves, hooks, plugs and mirrors. We also assume that there will be an identified chemical toilet disposal point, and that the campsite will provide water and waste water drainage points and bin areas. If not the case, we comment. We do mention certain features that some readers find important: washbasins in cubicles, facilities for babies, facilities for those with disabilities and motorcaravan service points. Readers with disabilities are advised to contact the site of their choice to ensure that facilities are appropriate to their needs.

Shop

Basic or fully supplied, and opening dates.

Bars, restaurants, takeaway facilities and entertainment

We try hard to supply opening and closing dates (if other than the campsite opening dates) and to identify if there are discos or other entertainment.

Children's play areas

Fenced and with safety surface (e.g. sand, bark or pea-gravel).

Swimming pools

If particularly special, we cover in detail in our main campsite description but reference is always included under our Facilities listings. We will also indicate the existence of water slides, sunbathing areas and other features. Opening dates, charges and levels of supervision are provided where we have been notified. There is a regulation whereby Bermuda shorts may not be worn in swimming pools (for health reasons). It is worth ensuring that you do take 'proper' swimming trunks with you.

Leisure facilities

For example, playing fields, bicycle hire, organised activities and entertainment.

Dogs

If dogs are not accepted or restrictions apply, we state it here. Check the quick reference list at the back of the guide.

Off site

This briefly covers leisure facilities, tourist attractions, restaurants etc. nearby.

Charges

These are the latest provided to us by the sites. In those cases where 2009 prices are not given, we try to give a general guide.

Reservations

Necessary for high season (roughly mid-July to mid-August) in popular holiday areas (ie beach resorts). You can reserve many sites via our own Alan Rogers Travel Service or through other tour operators. Or be wholly independent and contact the campsite(s) of your choice direct, using the phone or e-mail numbers shown in the site reports, but please bear in mind that many sites are closed all winter.

Telephone numbers

The numbers given assume you are actually IN the country concerned. If you are phoning from the UK remember that the first '0' is usually disregarded and replaced by the appropriate country code. For the latest details you should refer to an up-to-date telephone directory.

Opening dates

Are those advised to us during the early autumn of the previous year – sites can, and sometimes do, alter these dates before the start of the following season, often for good reasons. If you intend to visit shortly after a published opening date, or shortly before the closing date, it is wise to check that it will actually be open at the time required. Similarly some parks operate a restricted service during the low season, only opening some of their facilities (e.g. swimming pools) during the main season; where we know about this, and have the relevant dates, we indicate it – again if you are at all doubtful it is wise to check.

Sometimes, campsite amenities may be dependent on there being enough customers on site to justify their opening and, for this reason, actual opening dates may vary from those indicated.

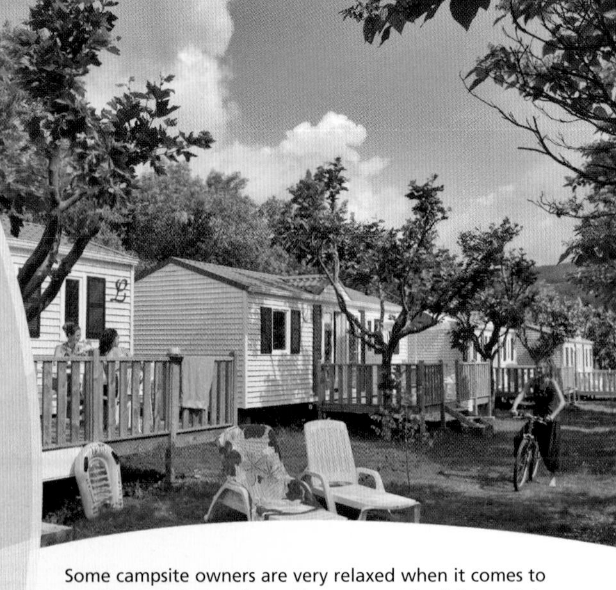

Some campsite owners are very relaxed when it comes to opening and closing dates. They may not be fully ready by their stated opening dates – grass and hedges may not all be cut or perhaps only limited sanitary facilities open. At the end of the season they also tend to close down some facilities and generally wind down prior to the closing date. Bear this in mind if you are travelling early or late in the season – it is worth phoning ahead.

The Camping Cheque low season touring system goes some way to addressing this in that participating campsites are encouraged to have all key facilities open and running by the opening date and to remain fully operational until the closing date.

Whether you're an 'old hand' in terms of camping and caravanning or are contemplating your first trip, a regular reader of our Guides or a new 'convert', we wish you well in your travels and hope we have been able to help in some way.

We are, of course, also out and about ourselves, visiting sites, talking to owners and readers, and generally checking on standards and new developments.

Win a holiday in Luxembourg

In this Alan Rogers Guide you will find quality campsites from across Europe. As a special reader benefit, we have teamed up with Topcamp Luxemburg to give you a chance of winning a campsite holiday. This is a group of 4 ideally situated campsites in Luxembourg, all offering high standards of quality and service. The only thing you need to do is answer the question for a chance of winning.

How many official languages does Luxembourg have?

For a chance of winning, visit www.alanrogers.com/topcamp
Terms and conditions are stated on line.

We wish all our readers thoroughly enjoyable Camping and Caravanning in 2009 – favoured by good weather of course!

THE ALAN ROGERS TEAM

Countries

Finland
Norway
Sweden
Denmark
Netherlands
Belgium
Czech Republic
Luxembourg
Slovakia
Germany
Austria
France
Hungary
Switzerland
Liechtenstein
Slovenia
Croatia
Andorra
Portugal
Italy
Greece
Spain

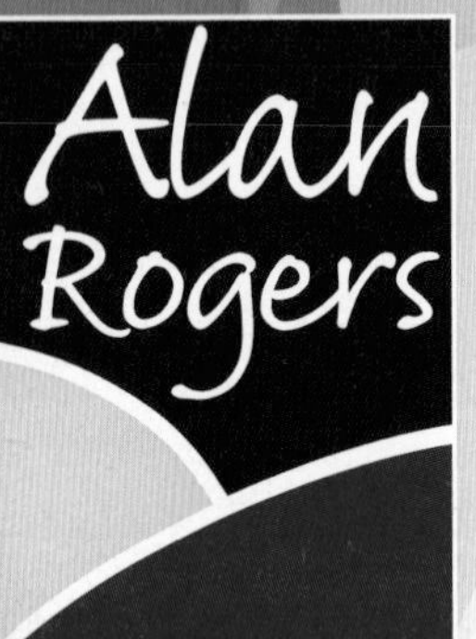

The Alan Rogers Awards

The Alan Rogers Campsite Awards were launched in 2004 and have proved a great success.

Our awards have a broad scope and before committing to our winners, we carefully consider more than 2,000 campsites featured in our guides, taking into account comments from our site assessors, our head office team and, of course, our readers.

Our award winners come from the four corners of Europe, from southern Portugal to Slovenia, and this year we are making awards to campsites in 13 different countries.

Needless to say, it's an extremely difficult task to choose our eventual winners, but we believe that we have identified a number of campsites with truly outstanding characteristics.

In each case, we have selected an outright winner, along with two highly commended runners-up.

Listed below are full details of each of our award categories and our winners for 2008.

Our warmest congratulations to all our award winners and our commiserations to all those not having won an award on this occasion.

THE ALAN ROGERS TEAM

Alan Rogers Progress Award 2008

This award reflects the hard work and commitment undertaken by particular site owners to improve and upgrade their site.

WINNER

PO8202	Turiscampo, Portugal

RUNNERS-UP

DE3202	Grav-Insel, Germany
IT60450	Marina di Venezia, Italy

Alan Rogers Welcome Award 2008

This award takes account of sites offering a particularly friendly welcome and maintaining a friendly ambience throughout reader's holidays.

WINNER

FR05000	Princes d'Orange, France

RUNNERS-UP

FR71110	Du Lac, France
DK2022	Vikær Diernæs, Denmark

Alan Rogers Active Holiday Award 2008

This award reflects sites in outstanding locations which are ideally suited for active holidays, notably walking or cycling, but which could extend to include such activities as winter sports or water sports

WINNER

FR07120 L'Ardéchois, France

RUNNERS-UP

SV4210 Sobec, Slovenia
AU0265 Park Grubhof, Austria

Alan Rogers Motorhome Award 2008

Motorhome sales are increasing and this award acknowledges sites which, in our opinion, have made outstanding efforts to welcome motorhome clients.

WINNER

UK0220 Trevornick, England

RUNNERS-UP

BE0655 De Lilse Bergen, Belgium
CZ4840 Oase Praha, Czech Republic

Alan Rogers 4 Seasons Award 2008

This award is made to outstanding sites with extended opening dates and which welcome clients to a uniformly high standard throughout the year.

WINNER

AU0440 Schluga, Austria

RUNNERS-UP

NL6520 BreeBronne, Netherlands
ES92950 Don Cactus, Spain

Alan Rogers Seaside Award 2008

This award is made for sites which we feel are outstandingly suitable for a really excellent seaside holiday.

WINNER

NL5735 Tempelhof, Netherlands

RUNNERS-UP

UK1070 Woolacombe Bay, England
CR6732 Polari, Croatia

Alan Rogers Country Award 2008

This award contrasts with our former award and acknowledges sites which are attractively located in delightful, rural locations.

WINNER

FR23030 Creuse Nature, France

RUNNERS-UP

ES90260 El Burro Blanco, Spain
IT62090 Vidor, Italy

Alan Rogers Rented Accommodation Award 2008

Given the increasing importance of rented accommodation on many campsites, we feel that it is important to acknowledge sites which have made a particular effort in creating a high quality 'rented accommodation' park.

WINNER

IT60370 Jesolo International, Italy

RUNNERS-UP

FR33300 La Jenny, France
NL5560 De Wijde Blick, Netherlands

Alan Rogers Unique Site Award 2008

This award acknowledges sites with unique, outstanding features – something which simply cannot be found elsewhere and which is an important attraction of the site.

WINNER

FR34070 Sérignan, France

RUNNERS-UP

IT60030 Pra' delle Torri, Italy
DE3182 Teutoburger Wald, Germany

Alan Rogers Family Site Award 2008

Many sites claim to be child friendly but this award acknowledges the sites we feel to be the very best in this respect.

WINNER

FR32010 Camp de Florence, France

RUNNERS-UP

ES80350 L'Amfora, Spain
IT62630 Bella Italia, Italy

Alan Rogers Readers' Award 2008

We believe our Readers' Award to be the most important. We simply invite our readers (by means of an on-line poll at **www.alanrogers.com**) to nominate the site they enjoyed most.

The outright winner for 2008 is:

WINNER

IT60200 Union Lido, Italy

Alan Rogers Special Award 2008

A special award is made to acknowledge sites which we feel have overcome a very significant setback, and have, not only returned to their former condition, but has added extra amenities and can therefore be fairly considered to be even better than before. In 2008 we acknowledged two campsites, which have undergone major problems and have made highly impressive recoveries.

UK2885 Warner Farm, England
FR32080 Le Talouch, France

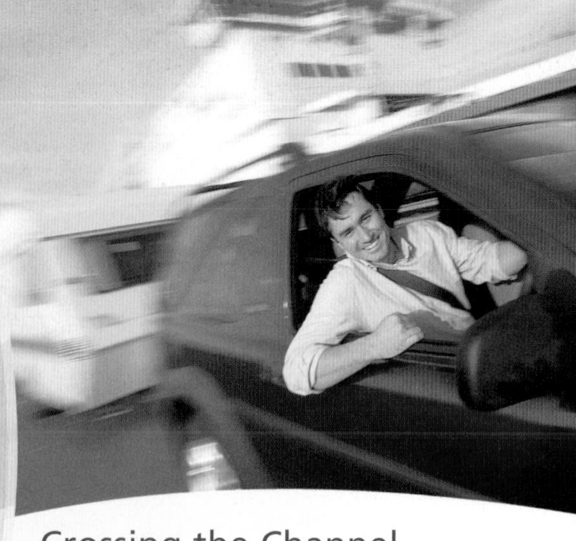

Alan Rogers

Crossing the Channel

One of the great advantages of booking your ferry-inclusive holiday with the Alan Rogers Travel Service is the tremendous value we offer. Our money-saving Ferry Deals have become legendary. As agents for all major cross-Channel operators we can book all your travel arrangements with the minimum of fuss and at the best possible rates.

Just call us for an instant quote

01580 214000

or visit

www.**alanrogers.com/travel**

Let us price your holiday for you

instantly!

The quickest and easiest way is to call us for advice and an instant quote. We can take details of your vehicle and party and, using our direct computer link to all the operators' reservations systems, can give you an instant price. We can even check availability for you and book a crossing while you're on the phone!

Please note we can only book ferry crossings in conjunction with a campsite holiday reservation.

Whether you book on-line or book by phone, you will be allocated an experienced Personal Travel Consultant to provide you with personal advice and manage every stage of your booking. Our Personal Travel Consultants have first-hand experience of many of our campsites and access to a wealth of information. They can 'paint a picture' of individual campsites, check availability, provide a competitive price and tailor your holiday arrangements to your specific needs.

- Discuss your holiday plans with a friendly person with first-hand experience
- Let us reassure you that your holiday arrangements really are taken care of
- Tell us about your special requests and allow us to pass these on
- Benefit from advice which will save you money – the latest ferry deals and more
- Remember, our offices are in Kent not overseas and we do NOT operate a queuing system!

The aims of the Travel Service are simple

- To provide convenience - a one-stop shop to make life easier.
- To provide peace of mind - when you need it most.
- To provide a friendly, knowledgeable, efficient service – when this can be hard to find.
- To provide a low cost means of organising your holiday – when prices can be so complicated.

HOW IT WORKS

1. Choose your campsite(s) – we can book around 500 across Europe. Look for the yellow coloured campsite entries in this book. You'll find more info and images at www.alanrogers.travel.

   Please note: the list of campsites we can book for you varies from time to time.

2. Choose your dates – choose when you arrive, when you leave.

3. Choose your ferry crossing – we can book most routes with most operators at extremely competitive rates.

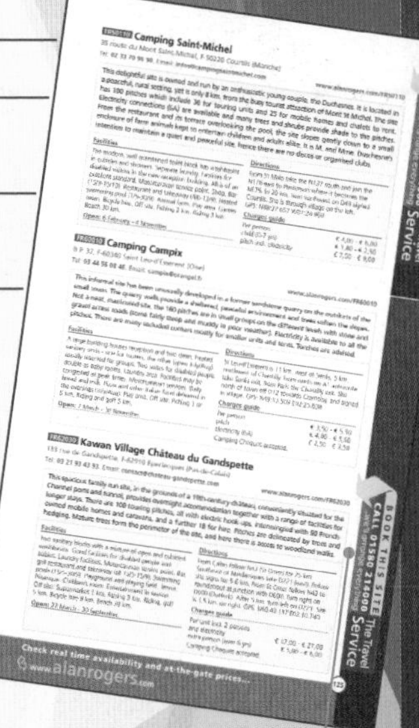

LOOK FOR A CAMPSITE ENTRY LIKE THIS TO INDICATE WHICH CAMPSITES WE CAN BOOK FOR YOU.

THE LIST IS GROWING SO PLEASE CALL FOR UP TO THE MINUTE INFORMATION.

Then just call us for an instant quote

01580 214000

or visit

www.**alanrogers.com/travel**

INSPECTED
CAMPSITES
& SELECTED

The tiny independent principality of Andorra is situated high in the Pyrenees between France and Spain. With a diverse landscape of mountains, valleys, forests, lakes and hot springs, it is probably best known for skiing and duty-free shopping.

CAPITAL: ANDORRA LA VELLA

Tourist Office

Embassy of the Principality of Andorra
63 Westover Road, London SW18 2RF
Tel/Fax: 020 8874 4806 (visits by appointment only)
Internet: www.andorra.com

Shopping and skiing aside, Andorra has plenty to offer the visitor in terms of leisure activities. One of the most unspoilt areas of the country is the hamlet of Llorts. Set amidst fields of tobacco overlooked by mountains, it's a great place for hiking. The enormous spa complex in Caldea offers the perfect place to relax. Fed by natural thermal springs, it houses lots of pools, hot tubs and saunas. Village festivals are a popular event with many Andorran towns and hamlets celebrating their heritage with music, dancing, wine and feasts. Most fall in the high season.

Administratively Andorra is divided up into seven parishes: Canillo, Encamp, Ordino, La Massana, Andorra la Vella, Sant Julià de Lòria and Escaldes-Engordany. The Principality of Andorra can be accessed by road from France through Pas de la Casa and the Envalira Pass and from Spain via Sant Julià de Lòria. The nearest main cities are Barcelona (185 km) and Lleida (151 km) on the Spanish side and Toulouse (187 km) and Perpignan (169 km) on the French side.

Population

72,400

Climate

The climate is temperate, with cold winters with a lot of snow and warm summers. The country's mountain peaks often remain snowcapped until July.

Language

The official language is Catalan, with French and Spanish widely spoken.

Telephone

The country code is 00 376.

Money

Currency: The Euro
Banks: Mon-Fri 09.00-13.00 and 15.00-17.00, Sat 09.00-12.00.

Shops

Mon-Sat 09.00-20.00, Sun 09.00-19.00.

Public Holidays

New Year's Day; Epiphany; Constitution Day, Mar 14; Holy Thursday to Easter Monday; Labour Day; Ascension; Whit Sunday; Whit Monday; St John's Day Jun 24; Assumption Aug 15; National Day Sep 8; All Saints' Day Nov 1; St Charles' Day; Nov 4; Immaculate Conception; Dec 8; Christmas Dec 24-26; New Year's Eve.

Motoring

There are no motorways in Andorra. Main roads are prefixed 'N' and side roads 'V'. Certain mountain passes may prove difficult in winter and heavy snowfalls could cause road closures. Expect traffic queues in the summer, with a high volume of motorists coming to and from France.

AN7143 Camping Xixerella

Ctra de Pals, Xixerella, AD400 La Massana

Tel: **836 613**. Email: **c-xixerella@campingxixerella.com** **www.alanrogers.com/AN7143**

Andorra is a country of narrow valleys and pine and birch forested mountains. Xixerella is attractively situated in just such a valley below towering mountains and beside a river. The site is made up of several sections of gently sloping grass, accessed by tarmac or gravel roads which lead to informal pitching. Electricity (3/6A) is available for most of the 150 places. There are barbecues and a picnic area with bridge access to walks in the woods. A pleasant bar and restaurant have a poolside terrace. The site can be very busy from mid July to mid August, but otherwise it is usually quite peaceful.

Facilities

The satisfactory main sanitary building is fully equipped, including British style WCs (no paper), some washbasins in cabins, showers with curtains. Laundry facilities. Further modern facilities in novel round building by the pool. Small shop, bar and restaurant (closed Oct). Swimming and paddling pools (15/6-15/9). Play area. Minigolf. Electronic games. Disco in season. Torch useful.
Off site: Riding 3 km. Skiing at Arinsal (5 km) or Pal (6 km).

Open: All year.

Directions

Site is 8 km. from Andorra la Vella on the road to Pal (this road can only be accessed on the north side of town), via La Massana. GPS: N42:33.194 E01:29.330

Charges guide

Per person	€ 5,00
child	€ 4,80
pitch	€ 9,80
electricity (3A)	€ 5,00

AN7145 Camping Valira

Avenida Salou s/n, AD500 Andorra la Vella

Tel: **722 384**. Email: **campvalira@andorra.ad** **www.alanrogers.com/AN7145**

This small and unusual site is named after the river in the town of Andorra La Vella. It has a steep curving entrance which can become congested at peak times. You pass the pleasant restaurant and bar and the heated indoor pool as you enter the site. Maximum use has been made of space here and it is worth looking at the picture of the site in reception as it was in 1969. The 150 medium sized pitches are mostly level on terraces with some shading. All pitches have access to electricity, although some may need long leads, and there are drinking water points around the site.

Facilities

The facilities are modern and spotless, with provision for disabled campers, plus separate room with toddlers' toilet and good baby room. Two washing machines and dryer. The two blocks can be heated in winter. Bar/restaurant with good menu at realistic prices. Well stocked small shop. Small heated indoor pool. Paddling pool. Jacuzzi. Play area. Barrier closed 23.00-07.00. WiFi. Off site: Town shops 10 minutes walk.

Open: All year.

Directions

Site is on the south side of Andorra La Vella, on left travelling south behind sports stadium. It is well signed off the N145. Watch signs carefully - an error with a diversion round town will cost you dear at rush hour. GPS: N42:30.149 E01:30.896

Charges guide

Per person	€ 5,75
child (1-10 yrs)	€ 4,75
pitch	€ 11,50
electricity (3-10A)	€ 3,50 - € 6,00

MAP 1

Austria is primarily known for two contrasting attractions: the capital Vienna with its fading Imperial glories, and the variety of its Alpine hinterland. It is an ideal place to visit year round, whether you want to admire the spectacular scenery and participate in winter sports or to visit historical sites and cultural attractions.

Alan Rogers

CAPITAL: VIENNA

Tourist Office

Austrian National Tourist Office
PO Box 2363, London W1A 2QB
Tel: 0845 101 1818
Fax: 0845 101 1819
Email: holiday@austria.info
Internet: www.austria.info/uk

Perhaps the best known area and the most easily accessible part of the country is the Tirol in the west. A charming region with picturesque valleys to explore, you'll be able to enjoy folk-lore entertainment year round. Situated in the centre are the Lake District and Salzburg. With its ancient castles, curative spas and salt mines to visit, Salzburg also has plenty of music, art and drama festivals to enjoy. Vienna, too, offers plenty of cultural pursuits with its museums, opera and famous choirs. The neighbouring provinces of Lower Austria, Burgenland and Styria, land of vineyards, mountains and farmland, are off the tourist routes, but provide good walking territory. Further south, in the Carinthia region, lakes and mountains dominate the landscape. The beautiful scenery and rural way of life offers a quieter retreat. There are a few large towns to explore, lots of pleasant villages and good, often uncrowded roads.

Population

8.3 million

Climate

Temperate, with moderately hot summers, cold winters and snow in the mountains.

Language

German

Telephone

The country code is 0043.

Money

Currency: The Euro
Banks: Mon, Tues, Wed & Fri 08.00-12.30 and 13.30-15.00. Thurs 08.00-12.30 and 13.30-17.30.

Shops

Mon-Fri 08.00-18.30, some close 12.00-14.00; Sat 08.00-17.00.

Public Holidays

New Year; Epiphany; Easter Mon; Labour Day; Ascension; Whit Mon; Corpus Christi; Assumption 15 Aug; National Day 26 Oct; All Saints 1 Nov; Immaculate Conception 8 Dec; Christmas 25, 26 Dec.

Motoring

Visitors using Austrian motorways and 'A' roads must display a Motorway Vignette on their vehicle as they enter Austria. Failure to have one will mean a heavy, on-the-spot fine. Vignettes are obtained at all major border crossings into Austria and at larger petrol stations. All vehicles above 3.5 tonnes maximum permitted laden weight are required to use a small device called the 'GO-Box' - see page 22.

AU0010 Alpencamping Nenzing

Garfrenga 1, A-6710 Nenzing (Vorarlberg)

Tel: **055 256 2491**. Email: **office@alpencamping.at** **www.alanrogers.com/AU0010**

Although best known for its skiing resorts, the forests and mountains of the Vorarlberg province make it equally suitable for a peaceful summer visit. Alpencamping Nenzing, is some 690 m. above sea level, set in a natural bowl surrounded by trees with some views across the pleasant countryside. You wind your way up from the main road or motorway, following a narrow road (you leave by a different route). Some of the 162 level, but small, touring pitches are in a flat area with others on neat terraces beyond. All have electricity (12-16A) and 105 also have water, drainage, sewerage, TV, gas and phone connections. On the left of the entrance is a large building with the reception and restaurant, and in front an old farm cart loaded with brightly coloured flowers. These are repeated around the site in hanging baskets and borders. The site provides comprehensive entertainment for children and adults during the peak season. Being open all year, this could be a base from which to ski in winter. The site is owned and run by the English speaking Morik family.

Facilities

The newer facilities are 'state of the art' and contain 20 free private bathrooms. Two older blocks remain and provide good facilities. Excellent children's washroom. Baby room. Facilities for disabled visitors. Motorcaravan service point. Small shop. Bar. Restaurant with terrace. Heated swimming pool (20 x 8 m). Small play area with another larger one on the top terrace. Practice climbing wall. Sauna, solarium, massage and relax room. Internet access. Off site: Bicycle hire, riding, tennis and fishing nearby.

Open: All year excl. week after Easter - 30 April.

Directions

From A14 Feldkirch - Bludenz motorway take exit for Nenzing on B190 road and then follow small 'Camping' signs which have the site logo, a butterfly. GPS: N47:10.965 E09:40.929

Charges guide

Per unit incl. 2 persons	€ 19,30 - € 29,00
extra person	€ 5,90 - € 9,00
child	€ 4,00
electricity per kWh	€ 0,65
dog	€ 2,50 - € 3,60

No credit cards.

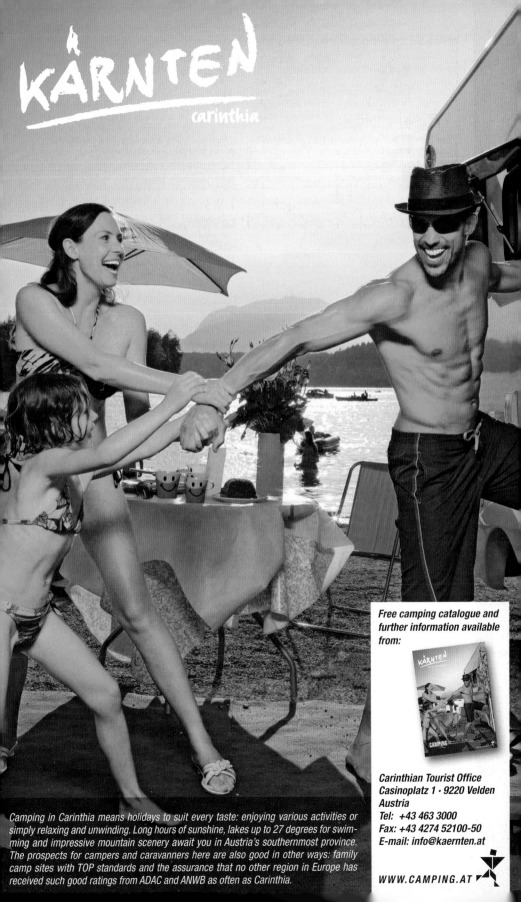

AU0005 Camping Salzmann Rohrspitz

Rohrspitz Yachting Salzmann GmbH, Rohr 1, A-6972 Fussach am Bodensee (Vorarlberg)
Tel: **055 787 5708**. Email: **office@salzmann.at** **www.alanrogers.com/AU0005**

Camping Salzmann is a part of the large Rohrspitz holiday and leisure complex on Lake Constance's southern bank. There are 45 grassy touring pitches here, of varying sizes each with an electrical connection. The complex comprises many leisure facilities and a club card system enables campers to use these. The same card is also used for access to the washblocks. The lakeside restaurant has fine views across the lake to the distant mountains of the Vorarlberg, and is a far cry from the humble kiosk which was the origin of the complex back in 1954. The Salzmann harbour is at the heart of the complex and has moorings for 190 boats, as well as good maintenance facilities. This is excellent walking and cycling country, with direct access to the Lake Constance cycle network. Cycle hire is available on site. There is direct access to a sandy beach and water sports are understandably popular here. The site runs regular wakeboard courses, as well as windsurfing and waterskiing.

Facilities

Shop. Snack bar (kiosk). Playground. Games room. Restaurant. Bar. Bicycle hire. Direct beach access. Canoe hire. Watersports courses. Activity and entertainment programme. Off site: Cycle and walking routes. Sailing. Boat trips on the MS Elisa.

Open: 1 April - 15 October.

Directions

Approaching from the north and Germany (A96) leave at the Bregenz exit. From here head west on the B202 as far as Fussach and the site is well signposted from here. GPS: N47:29.833 E09:37.850

Charges guide

Per unit incl. 2 persons and electricity	€ 14,50 - € 34,50
extra person	€ 4,00
child (under 14 yrs)	€ 2,00

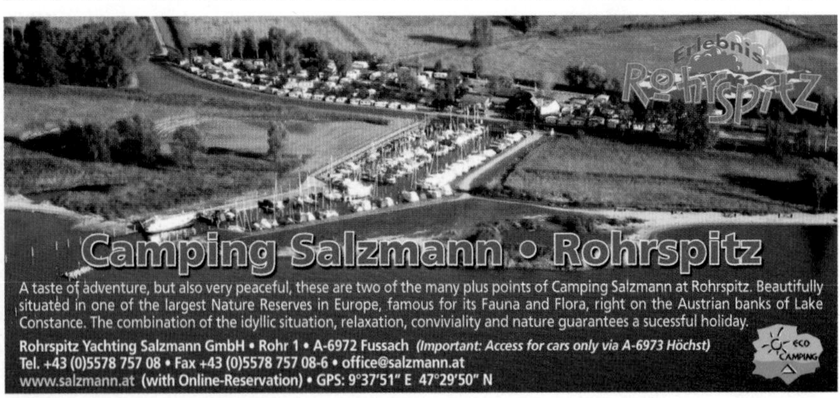
Erlebnis Rohrspitz
Camping Salzmann • Rohrspitz
A taste of adventure, but also very peaceful, these are two of the many plus points of Camping Salzmann at Rohrspitz. Beautifully situated in one of the largest Nature Reserves in Europe, famous for its Fauna and Flora, right on the Austrian banks of Lake Constance. The combination of the idyllic situation, relaxation, conviviality and nature guarantees a sucessful holiday.
Rohrspitz Yachting Salzmann GmbH • Rohr 1 • A-6972 Fussach (Important: Access for cars only via A-6973 Höchst)
Tel. +43 (0)5578 757 08 • Fax +43 (0)5578 757 08-6 • office@salzmann.at
www.salzmann.at (with Online-Reservation) • GPS: 9°37'51" E 47°29'50" N
eco CAMPING

AU0015 Camping Grosswalsertal

Plazera 21, A-6741 Raggal (Vorarlberg)
Tel: **055 532 09**. Email: **info@camping-austria.info** **www.alanrogers.com/AU0015**

As we climbed up to this site we seemed to be above the clouds. We then descended into a beautiful green valley and saw the site on a flat plateau below. From almost every pitch there are the most fantastic views down the valley. On open grass, there are 55 slightly sloping, un-numbered and unmarked pitches all with 10A electricity. Plenty of sporting activities are available locally and many places to visit, as well as walks and bike rides in the immediate area. Alternatively, just rest on the site and watch the clouds roll by. The site is very popular with Dutch visitors.

Facilities

The modern sanitary block has ample and clean toilets, hot showers and washbasins. Washing machine and dryer. Small shop with essential supplies. Swimming pool (1/6-15/9). Play area. Bicycle hire. Off site: Fishing 2 km. Riding 2 km. Golf 14 km.

Open: 15 May - 30 September.

Directions

From the A14 take exit for Nenzing and Gr. Walsertal and proceed to Ludesch. Turn right toward Raggal where you take the left fork, pass a Spa supermarket and 2 km. downhill to the site.
GPS: N47:12.951 E09:51.222

Charges guide

Per unit incl. 2 persons	€ 14,50 - € 17,00
incl. electricity	€ 16,00 - € 18,50
extra person	€ 4,00
child (0-13 yrs)	€ 2,00 - € 3,00
dog	€ 2,00

No credit cards.

AU0232 Terrassencamping Sonnenberg

Hinteroferst 12, A-6714 Nüziders bei Bludenz (Vorarlberg)

Tel: **055 526 4035**. Email: **sonnencamp@aon.at** **www.alanrogers.com/AU0232**

A friendly welcome awaits you at this well equipped site on the western end of Austria, at the junction of five alpine valleys. The views are captivating and ever changing. The site is mostly terraced with pitches for longer stay units having gravel hardstandings at one side of the site, while shorter stay units have an area closer to the entrance. A large car park area reduces the traffic congestion at peak times, and there are eight pitches designated for motorcaravans. There are 120 good sized pitches, all with electricity, 40 are fully serviced.

Facilities

A superb new building contains high quality facilities providing WCs, hot showers, washbasins (some in cubicles), and a baby room. Drying room and laundry. Motorcaravan service point. TV and cinema room, and a sleeping loft for four campers. Shop. Baker calls daily in July/August. Playground. Only one dog per unit is allowed. Internet access. Secure bicycle storage. Seven studio apartments. Off site: Village with shops 500 m. Fishing 3 km. Riding and bicycle hire 4 km. Golf 8 km.

Open: 1 May - 4 October.

Directions

Nüziders is about 25 km. southeast of Feldkirch. From A14 exit 57 (Bludenz - Nüziders) turn north on road 190 and left at roundabout into village. Follow camping signs through village to site.
GPS: N47:10.191 E09:48.448

Charges 2009

Per unit incl. 2 persons and electricity (13A)	€ 17,90 - € 26,90
extra person	€ 5,00 - € 6,00

No credit cards.

AU0040 Ferienanlage Tiroler Zugspitze

Obermoos 1, A-6632 Ehrwald (Tirol)

Tel: **056 732 309**. Email: **camping@zugspitze.at** **www.alanrogers.com/AU0040**

Although Ehrwald is in Austria, it is from the entrance of Zugspitzcamping that the cable car runs to the summit of Germany's highest mountain. Standing at 1,200 feet above sea level at the foot of the mountain, the 200 pitches (120 for tourists), mainly of grass over stones, are on flat terraces with fine panoramic views in parts. All have electricity connections (16A). The modern reception building at the entrance also houses a fine restaurant with a terrace.

Facilities

Two good sanitary blocks (cleaning may be variable) provide some washbasins in cabins and 20 private bathrooms for rent. Separate children's unit. Baby room. Unit for disabled people. Laundry facilities. Drying rooms. Motorcaravan service point. Shop. Bar. Restaurant. Indoor pool with sauna, whirlpool and fitness centre with solarium and massage room. Outdoor pool and children's pool with slide. Internet access. Bicycle hire. Play area. Organised activities in season. Off site: Hotel, souvenir shop and cable car station 100 m. Ehrwald 5 km.

Open: All year.

Directions

Follow signs in Ehrwald to Tiroler Zugspitzbahn and then signs to site. GPS: N47:25.595 E10:56.486

Charges guide

Per person	€ 10,00 - € 12,00
child (4-15 yrs)	€ 7,50 - € 8,50
pitch	€ 6,00 - € 8,00
electricity per kWh	€ 0,80
dog	€ 4,00

Special seasonal weekly offers.
Mastercard accepted.

AU0045 Campingplatz Øtztal

Unterlangenfeld 220, A-6444 Längenfeld (Tirol)

Tel: **052 535 348**. Email: **info@camping-oetztal.com** **www.alanrogers.com/AU0045**

Camping Øtztal, a family run site, is situated some 400 metres from the pretty village of Längenfeld, at the edge of a forest. Next door are the local sports centre and swimming pool and a restaurant. In summer the campsite is ideal for walking and cycling, as well as mountaineering tours. In the winter you can enjoy cross-country skiing right from the doorstep and a free bus shuttle operates to the Øtztal Ski arena. The site provides 200 level grass pitches of which 170 are for tourers. All pitches have electricity and 100 have also gas, water, drainage and TV point.

Facilities

Excellent sanitary facilities include 4 bathrooms to rent for private use. Baby room. Facilities for disabled people. Female hairdressing room. Dog shower. Washing machines and dryer. Ski room. Motorcaravan service point. Restaurant serves breakfast and takeaway. Sauna and solarium. WiFi. Bicycle hire. Off site: Längenfeld and Aqua Dome thermal spa facility.

Open: All year.

Directions

From the A12 take exit 123 and follow the 186 along the Øtztal Valley towards Sölden for about 20 km. Site entrance is at the top of the hill in the centre of Längenfeld, to the right.
GPS: N47:04.337 E10:57.859

Charges guide

Per person	€ 5,60 - € 7,40
pitch	€ 6,70 - € 11,60
electricity	€ 1,90

No credit cards.

AU0060 Ferienparadies Natterer See

Natterer See 1, A-6161 Natters (Tirol)

Tel: **051 254 6732**. Email: **info@natterersee.com** **www.alanrogers.com/AU0060**

Above Innsbruck, 7 km. southwest of the town, this excellent site is in a quiet and isolated location around two small lakes. Founded in 1930, the site is renowned as one of Austria's finest campsites and in 2007 the owners embarked on an ambitious improvement project with 40 large new 'super' pitches. Each with a minimum size of 110 sq.m, these pitches are equipped with water, drainage, electricity and cable TV connection. There are a further 235 individual pitches of varying sizes (60-150 sq.m), either on flat ground by the lake or on higher, level terraces. The standard pitches have 6A electricity. Many are reinforced by gravel. Other projects include new roads, reception, café/bistro and an ultramodern toilet block with private family bathrooms. There are many fine mountain views and a wide variety of scenic excursions. For the more active, signed walks start from the site. One of the lakes is used for swimming with a long 67 m. slide (free to campers, on payment to day visitors.) For winter camping the site offers ski and drying rooms and a free ski-bus service. A toboggan run and langlauf have been developed with ice skating, ice hockey and curling on the lake. The excellent restaurant with a bar and a large terrace overlooking the lake has a good menu. Very good English is spoken at this site.

Facilities

The large sanitary blocks have underfloor heating, some washbasins in cabins, plus excellent facilities for babies, children and disabled people. Laundry facilities. Motorcaravan services. Fridge box hire. Bar/restaurant. Pizzeria and takeaway. Good shop. Playgrounds. Children's activity programme. Child minding (day nursery) in high season. Sports field. Archery. Youth room with games, pool and billiards. TV room with Sky. Internet point and WiFi. Open air cinema. Mountain bike hire. 'Aquapark' (1/5-30/9). Surf bikes and wind-glider. Canoes and mini sailboats for rent. Extensive daily entertainment programme (mid May - mid Oct). Dogs are not accepted in high season (July/Aug). Off site: Tennis and minigolf nearby. Riding 6 km. Golf 12 km.

Open: All year excl. 1 November - 14 December.

Directions

From Inntal autobahn (A12) take Brenner autobahn (A13) as far as Innsbruck-sud/Natters exit (no. 3) without payment. Turn left by Shell petrol station onto the B182 to Natters. At roundabout take first exit and immediately right again and follow signs to site 4 km. GPS: N47:14.258 E11:20.557

Charges 2009

Per person	€ 5,70 - € 7,80
child (under 13 yrs)	€ 11,30 - € 20,00
pitch incl. electricity	€ 4,40 - € 5,40
dog (excl. July/Aug)	€ 9,80 - € 14,00

Special weekly, winter, summer or Christmas packages. Camping Cheques accepted.

AU0055 Camping Arlberg

A-6574 Pettneu am Arlberg (Tirol)

Tel: **054 482 2266-0**. Email: **info@camping-arlberg.at** **www.alanrogers.com/AU0055**

This is an unusual site, located alongside, and lower than, the S16 autobahn, just a few kilometres to the east of the 13 km. long Arlberg toll tunnel. Inevitably there is some traffic noise. The site is unusual because it offers 145 pitches (out of 185) that are provided with an on-pitch wooden cabin housing the sanitary facilities, TV connection and 16A electricity. The grass and hardcore pitches are of medium size, fairly level and offer some views of the surrounding mountains. The other 40 pitches are near the reception building and offer electricity with a prepayment meter only (€ 1 coins).

Facilities

145 private bathrooms in wooden cabins, electrically heated with WC, washbasin and shower (electricity is metered). Motorcaravan service point. Shop. Bar. Restaurant. Indoor pool. Play area. Fishing. Bicycle hire. Off site: Pettneu, swimming pool and the Tyrol. Skiing; ski bus operates in the season.

Open: All year.

Directions

From S16 (B316) take exit to Pettneu (not St Anton). Just at the end of the slip road between a swimming complex and a play area is the site entrance. GPS: N47:08.705 E10:20.295

Charges 2009

Per unit incl. 2 persons	€ 25,00 - € 37,00
extra person	€ 9,00 - € 10,00
child (4-14 yrs)	€ 5,00
electricity per kWh	€ 0,45

No credit cards.

NOTE: From 1 January 2004, all vehicles above 3.5 tonnes maximum permitted laden weight using the Austrian network of motorways and expressways are required to attach a small device called the 'Go-Box' to their windscreen. The Go-Box uses the high frequency range to communicate with the around 400 fixed-installation toll points covering Austria, making it possible to effect an automatic toll deduction without slowing the flow of traffic. The on-board devices can be obtained for a one-off handling fee of Euro 5.00 at about 220 sales centres in Austria and in neighbouring countries or via the Internet. For further information visit the website at http://www.austria.info

AU0070 Camping Hofer

Gerlosstrasse 33, A-6280 Zell-am-Ziller (Tirol)

Tel: **052 822 248**. Email: **info@campingdorf.at** **www.alanrogers.com/AU0070**

Zell-am-Ziller is in the heart of the Zillertal valley at the junction of the B169 and B165 Gerlos Pass road and nestles round the unusual 18th-century church noted for its paintings. Camping Hofer, owned by the same family for over 50 years, is on the edge of the village just five minutes walk from the centre on a quiet side road. The 100 pitches, all with electricity (6/10A), (long long leads may be needed) are grass on gravel. A few trees decorate the site and offer some shade. A pleasant development provides a bar/restaurant, games and TV room and a small heated pool.

Facilities

Good quality, heated sanitary provision is on the ground floor of the apartment building and has some washbasins in cabins. Baby room. Laundry facilities. Motorcaravan services. Restaurant with bar (closed 1/11-10/12 and 30/4-31/5), offers special themed weeks with international dishes. Shop opposite. Swimming pool (1/4-31/10). WiFi internet. Free organised entertainment and activities in high season. Guided walks, cycle tours, barbecues, biking, skiing. Ski room. Youth room. Apartments to rent. Off site: Town and supermarket within walking distance.

Open: All year.

Directions

Site is well signed from the main B169 road at Zell-am-Ziller. Site is at southern end of town close to the junction of the B169 and B165. GPS: N47:13.724 E11:53.157

Charges 2009

Per unit incl. 2 persons and electricity (plus meter in winter)	€ 21,60 - € 26,50
extra person	€ 5,80 - € 8,50
child (under 14 yrs)	€ 3,50 - € 5,50

No credit cards.
Camping Cheques accepted.

AU0085 Mountain Camp Pitztal

Niederhof 206, A-6474 Jerzens (Tirol)

Tel: **054 148 7571**. Email: **mountain-camp@aon.at** **www.alanrogers.com/AU0085**

Mountain Camp Pitztal was opened in 2002 by Tobias Eiter and his wife and is the only site in the Pitztal valley. It is an ideal base for walks in the Tiroler Mountains or for mountain bike tours on the numerous paths through the woods and on the Schotterpiste or Wildspitze, the highest mountain in Tirol. Being a new site, the pitches are in the open, but all 38 have 13A electricity, water, waste water and gas supplies. The pitches are laid out on level, rectangular fields on a grass and gravel base.

Facilities

One new, centrally located toilet block (heated) with toilets, washbasins (open style and in cabins) and free, controllable hot showers. Bathroom. Free washing machine. Dryer. Restaurant with bar and covered terrace. Fishing. Bicycle hire. Skate ramp. Swimming pond with small beach. Full activity programme for all in high season. Off site: Riding 2 km. Golf 25 km.

Open: All year excl. 2 May - 9 June.

Directions

From the A12, take exit 132 at Imst and continue south on minor road. Site is on the right, just before entering Jerzens. GPS: N47:08.552 E10:44.789

Charges guide

Per unit incl. 2 persons	€ 18,00 - € 24,00
extra person	€ 4,00 - € 5,00
child (4-14 yrs)	€ 3,00 - € 3,50
electricity (per kWh on meter)	€ 0,50

AU0090 Camping Zillertal-Hell

Gragering 212b, A-6263 Fügen (Tirol)

Tel: **052 886 2203**. Email: **info@zillertal-camping.at** **www.alanrogers.com/AU0090**

The village of Fügen lies about six kilometres from the A12 autobahn at the start of the Zillertal, so is well placed for exploring the valley and the area around Schwaz. Easy to reach, Zillertal-Hell is an attractive small site with excellent facilities and 170 marked pitches (140 for touring units) on flat grass. All have electricity (16A), 80 also have water and drainage and there are some hardstandings for motorcaravans. The site could make a good overnight stop or for a longer stay but, being on a main road, there is a little daytime road noise.

Facilities

New modern heated sanitary block of top quality has some washbasins in cabins, a children's wash room, and private bathrooms for hire. Unit for disabled campers. Laundry facilities. Motorcaravan service point. Bar and small restaurant. Small shop. Heated swimming pool (20 x 10 m, 1/5-15/10). Solarium, sauna and steam room. Games room with TV. Children's activity room. Playground. Internet point. Organised games, activities and entertainment. Bicycle hire. Dogs are not accepted in high season. Off site: Shops and restaurants in the village 800 m. Fishing 500 m. Riding 2 km. Golf 15 km.

Open: All year.

Directions

From the A12 Innsbruck - Worgl motorway take exit 39 and turn south on B169 towards Mayrhofen for 5 km. Turn into service road (on right) 1 km. north of Fugen (signed Gagering and site) and site entrance is on right. Note: this is a fast road, care is needed exiting site. GPS: N47:21.576 E11:51.128

Charges 2009

Per pitch incl. 2 persons and electricity	€ 22,40 - € 35,50
extra person	€ 4,20 - € 8,00
child (2-13 yrs)	€ 3,00 - € 6,00

AU0035 Camp Alpin Seefeld

Leutascherstrasse 810, A-6100 Seefeld (Tirol)

Tel: **052 124 848**. Email: **info@camp-alpin.at** **www.alanrogers.com/AU0035**

Alpin Seefeld is a pleasant, modern campsite with very good facilities in an attractive setting some 1,200 metres high. With excellent views of the surrounding mountains and forests there are 140 large, individual pitches mainly on flat grass (plus a few hardstandings), all with gas, TV, electricity (16A) and waste water, with ten water points around, but no shade. Some pitches at the back and edge of the site are terraced. This is a good base for both summer and winter activity, whether you wish to take a gentle stroll or participate in something more demanding, including skiing direct from the site.

Facilities

Excellent heated sanitary facilities include nine private bathrooms for hire, some private cabins. Washing machines and dryer. Sauna, Turkish bath and solarium. Infra-red cabin. Shop. Bar, snack bar and takeaway. Fishing. Play area. Bicycle hire. Off site: Sports centre with heated indoor and outdoor pools and restaurant are close. The popular Tirolean village of Seefeld 1 km. Golf 1.5 km.

Open: All year.

Directions

Seefeld is about 17 km. northwest of Innsbruck. The site is 2 km. from Seefeld on the road signed to Leutasch. It is well signed as you approach the town. GPS: N47:20.241 E11:10.716

Charges guide

Per person	€ 4,00 - € 9,90
child (3-14 yrs)	€ 3,00 - € 7,90
electricity	€ 0,70 - € 3,80
pitch	€ 5,00 - € 12,90

AU0080 Schloß-Camping

A-6111 Volders (Tirol)

Tel: **052 245 2333**. Email: **campingvolders@utanet.at** **www.alanrogers.com/AU0080**

The Inn valley is not only central to the Tirol, but is a very beautiful and popular part of Austria. Volders, some 15 km. from Innsbruck, is one of the little villages on the banks of the Inn river and is perhaps best known for its 17th-century Baroque Servite Church and monastery. Conveniently situated here is the very pleasant Schloss-Camping, dominated by the castle from which it gets its name, that towers at the back of the site with mountains beyond. The 160 numbered grass pitches are on level or slightly sloping ground. Electricity connections throughout (16A, long leads may be necessary).

Facilities

The small, sanitary block of old design is near the entrance and has some washbasins in cabins. Washing machine. Motorcaravan service point. Bar/restaurant. Snack bar with terrace. Shop for basics (all May - end Sept). Fenced and heated swimming pool (mid May - mid Sept). Minigolf. Playground. Car wash. Games and entertainment for children in high season. Off site: Supermarket 400 m. Bicycle hire 500 m. Golf and riding 7 km.

Open: 15 April - 15 October.

Directions

From A12 motorway, travelling east, leave at exit 68 for Hall, going west, take exit 61 for Wattens and follow the B171 and signs for Volders where site is signed. GPS: N47:17.231 E11:34.352

Charges guide

Per person	€ 5,60 - € 6,50
child (2-14 yrs)	€ 3,40 - € 4,00
pitch incl. car and electricity	€ 9,30 - € 10,50
dog	€ 2,50

No credit cards. Reductions for stays of 3 nights or more in low season.

AU0100 Camping Seeblick Toni

Reintalersee, Moosen 46, A-6233 Kramsach (Tirol)

Tel: **053 376 3544**. Email: **info@camping-seeblick.at** **www.alanrogers.com/AU0100**

Austria has some of the finest sites in Europe and Seeblick Toni is one of the best. In a quiet, rural situation on the edge of the small Reintalersee lake, it is well worth considering for holidays in the Tirol with many excursions possible. The 243 level pitches (215 for touring) are in regular rows off hard access roads and are of good size with grass and hardstanding. All pitches have electricity, 150 are fully serviced including cable TV and phone connections.

Facilities

Two outstanding sanitary blocks (heated in cool weather). One includes en-suite toilet/basin/shower rooms, the other also has individual bathrooms to let. Facilities for disabled visitors. New facilities for children. Baby room. Laundry facilities. Drying rooms. Freezer. Motorcaravan services. Restaurant. Bar. Snack kiosk. Shop. Fitness centre. Playground. Indoor play area. 'Topi' club, kindergarten and organised activities for children in high season. Youth room. Fishing. Bicycle hire. Riding. Internet point (July/Aug only). Off site: Kramsach 3 km.

Open: All year.

Directions

Take exit 32 for Kramsach from A12 autobahn and turn right at roundabout, then immediately left following signs 'Zu den Seen' in village. After 3 km. turn right at site sign. There are two sites side by side at the lake – ignore the first and continue through to Seeblick Toni. GPS: N47:27.673 E11:54.396

Charges 2009

Per unit incl. 2 persons and electricity (10A)	€ 22,50 - € 30,50
extra person	€ 5,50 - € 8,00

Camping Cheques accepted.

AU0102 Seen Camping Stadlerhof

Seebühel 14, A-6233 Kramsach (Tirol)

Tel: **053 376 3371**. Email: **camping.stadlerhof@chello.at** **www.alanrogers.com/AU0102**

This child friendly family run site is in a beautiful location near the Krummsee. There are 130 sensibly sized pitches (99 for touring units) all with electricity (10A). Many are individual and divided by hedges and shrubs, and some mature trees offer shade in parts. 50 multi-serviced pitches are available. The site has its own small lake, a panorama walk and a dog walk. Reasonable English is spoken. A 'Quickstop' facility with electric hook-up for overnighting is also offered.

Facilities

Spacious sanitary facilities include showers, some washbasins in cubicles, and five family bathrooms for rent. Laundry facilities. No dedicated facilities for disabled people. Small restaurant and bar. Basic provisions available. 'Wellness Centre', an outdoor heated stainless steel swimming pool (12.5 x 6 m. and open in winter) with spa pool and children's pool, and a café. Playground. TV room. Drying room, ski room. Off site: Kramsach is within walking distance. Reintalersee 3 km.

Open: All year.

Directions

Kramsach is about mid-way between Innsbruck and Kufstein. From A12 exit 32 turn right at roundabout and immediately left following signs for 'Zu den Seen' in village. Site is just outside village on left, after a right hand bend. GPS: N47:27.402 E11:52.850

Charges guide

Per person	€ 4,60 - € 5,80
child (under 14 yrs)	€ 2,95 - € 4,00
electricity per kWh	€ 0,65

No credit cards.

AU0110 Tirol Camp

Lindau 20, A-6391 Fieberbrunn (Tirol)

Tel: **053 545 6666**. Email: **office@tirol-camp.at** **www.alanrogers.com/AU0110**

This is one of many Tirol campsites that cater equally for summer and winter (here seemingly more for winter, when reservation is essential and prices are 50% higher). Tirol Camp is in a quiet and attractive mountain situation and has 280 pitches all on wide flat terraces, set on a gentle slope (193 for touring units). Marked out mainly by the electricity boxes or low hedges, they are said to be 80-100 sq.m. and all have electricity (10A), gas, water/drainage, TV and telephone connections.

Facilities

A refurbished toilet block is excellent with some washbasins in cabins and some private bathrooms on payment. A modern heated block has spacious showers and washbasins in cabins. Facilities for disabled visitors. Laundry facilities. Motorcaravan services. Self-service shop and snacks. Restaurant (closed Oct, Nov and May). Outdoor swimming pool (12 x 8 m; 1/6-30/9). Indoor pool and wellness centre. Sauna. Tennis. Lake fishing. Riding. Bicycle hire. Playground and children's zoo. Entertainment and activity programmes (July/Aug). Internet point.

Open: All year excl. 16 April - 16 May, 8 Nov. - 9 Dec.

Directions

Site is on the east side of Fieberbrunn, which is on the B164 St Johann - Saalfelden road. Turn south off the B164, 2 km. east of Fieberbrunn. Follow signs up the hill to the site. GPS: N47:28.095 E12:33.237

Charges 2009

Per unit incl. 2 persons (electricity on meter)	€ 24,00 - € 26,50
with private sanitary facility	€ 37,00 - € 41,00
extra person	€ 8,50

Winter charges higher. No credit cards. Camping Cheques accepted.

AU0065 Camping Seehof

Reintalersee, Moosen 42, A-6233 Kramsach (Tirol)

Tel: **053 376 3541**. Email: **info@camping-seehof.com** **www.alanrogers.com/AU0065**

Camping Seehof, an excellent site in every respect, is situated in a marvellous, sunny and peaceful location on the eastern shores of the Reintalersee lake. Add to this that it is very much a family run site for families and you have almost perfection itself. It separates into two areas: a small area next to the lake, good for sunbathing, and a larger one nearer the excellent, large sanitary block. All the large pitches are served by good access roads and have electricity and TV point and many have waste water drainage including 40 new fully serviced pitches. Seehof provides an ideal starting point for walking, cycling or riding (with a riding stable nearby), and in the winter for cross-country skiing, ice-skating and curling. A free shuttle bus operates from the site during the skiing season.

Facilities

New and refurbished sanitary facilities are first class and include ten bathrooms to rent for private use. Baby room. Facilities for disabled visitors. Dog shower. Washing machine and dryer. Ski room. Motorcaravan service point. Small shop. Good restaurant. Playground and play room. WiFi. Bicycle hire. Fishing. Off site: Kramsach. Kristallwelten and the Swarovski Factory.

Open: All year.

Directions

From the A12 take exit 32 to Kramsach. At roundabout turn right and immediately turn left following signs for 'Zu den Seen' in village. After 3 km. turn right at site sign.
GPS: N47:27.712 E11:54.429

Charges guide

Per unit incl. 2 persons and electricity	€ 17,30 - € 25,30
extra person	€ 4,50 - € 6,50
child (2-14 yrs)	€ 3,00 - € 4,50
dog	€ 3,00

AU0120 Erlebnis-Comfort-Camping Aufenfeld

Aufenfeldweg 10, A-6274 Aschau im Zillertal (Tirol)

Tel: **052 822 9160**. Email: **info@camping-zillertal.at** **www.alanrogers.com/AU0120**

This site is attractively situated in a mountain region with fine views and good facilities. The main area of the site itself is flat with pitches of 100 sq.m. on grass between hard access roads, with further pitches on terraces at the rear. There are around 350 pitches (240 for touring units with 6A electricity) including around 40 with individual sanitary cubicles. The site can become full mid July until mid August and at Christmas. A splendid indoor swimming pool has been added and there is a heated outdoor pool and paddling pool for summer use. Member of 'Leading Campings Group'.

Facilities

Four well kept, heated sanitary blocks of excellent quality and size, each with a few washbasins in cabins for each sex, baby rooms and units for disabled people. Additional units provide 40 private cabins for luxury pitches and family bathrooms for rent. Laundry and drying room. Ski room. Motorcaravan services. New supermarket. Restaurant. TV. Indoor pool, sauna and sunbeds. Wellness centre. Outdoor pool. Playground. Multisport court. Tennis. Riding. Fishing. Skateboard and rollerblade facilities. Bicycle hire. Western village. Mineral museum. Entertainment in high season. Off site: Walking and cycling in the Zillertall valley. Cross-country skiing (winter).

Open: All year excl. 3 November - 8 December.

Directions

From A12 Inntal motorway, take Zillertal exit 39, 32 km. northeast of Innsbruck. Follow road no. 169 to village of Aschau from which site is well signed. GPS: N47:15.800 E11:53.960

Charges 2009

Per unit incl. 2 persons (electricity on meter)	€ 19,00 - € 36,00
incl. private sanitary cabin	€ 27,00 - € 51,00
extra person	€ 6,00 - € 12,00
child (2-12 yrs)	€ 4,50 - € 8,00
dog	€ 5,00

Winter prices are higher.

AU0170 Camping Innsbruck-Kranebitten

Kranebitter Allee 214, A-6020 Innsbruck (Tirol)

Tel: **051 228 4180**. Email: **campinnsbruck@hotmail.com** **www.alanrogers.com/AU0170**

This basic site is in a pleasant situation just outside Innsbruck. The 120 pitches are numbered, but not marked out, on mostly sloping grass, with good shade cover. There are three separate terraces for caravans and motorcaravans and all pitches have electricity (6A with some more installed in 2008, long leads are on loan for some). By the side of the site, with access to it, is a large open field with a good playground and plenty of space for ball games. Being so near the attractive town of Innsbruck, the site makes an excellent base from which to visit the ancient city and also to explore the many attractions nearby. The 'Innsbruck-Card', available from the site, gives all-inclusive attractions in the city, plus free travel on public transport (park-and-ride from the site, even if you don't stay overnight). A private taxi also runs a shuttle service to and from the city for € 5. Some road and aircraft noise may be heard. Good English is spoken.

Facilities

The large, toilet block shows signs of age, but is heated, clean and acceptable, with some washbasins in cabins and renovated showers. Washing machines and dryers. Motorcaravan services. Bar/restaurant (all year, but open times may vary). Small shop. Playground with large play field adjoining. Games for children and barbecues in summer. Free mountain hiking and cycling tours in summer, free ski bus in winter. Bicycle hire. WiFi.
Off site: Swimming pool 2 km.

Open: All year.

Directions

From A12 Innsbruck - Arlberg motorway, take Innsbruck-Kranebitten exit 83 from where site is well signed, directly on B171 (Telfs - Innsbruck non-toll road). GPS: N47:15.821 E11:19.579

Charges guide

Per unit incl. 2 persons and electricity	€ 20,70 - € 25,30
extra person	€ 5,40 - € 6,80
child (4-14 yrs)	€ 3,50

Less 10% for stays over 10 days.
Special offers for sporting groups.

AU0130 Terrassen-Camping Schloßberg Itter

Brixentaler Straße 11, A-6305 Itter bei Hopfgarten (Tirol)

Tel: **053 352 181**. Email: **info@camping-itter.at** **www.alanrogers.com/AU0130**

This well kept site with 200 pitches and good facilities is suitable as a base for longer stays and also for overnight stops, as it lies right by a main road west of Kitzbühel. It is on a slight slope but most of the 200 numbered pitches are on level terraces. Some pitches are individual and divided by hedges and have electricity (8/10A) and cable TV connections, 150 have water and drainage. Space is usually available. There is a free ski lift from the site in winter, especially suitable for beginners and children, and a toboggan run. There is some road and rail noise.

Facilities

The main sanitary facilities are heated and of very high standard. The newest section has a large room with private cubicles. Some of these have vanity style washbasins, others have baths, one a 'body wash' type brush or showers. Two slightly larger units for families, with baby baths. Facilities for disabled visitors. Washing machines and dryers. Motorcaravan services. Cooking facilities. Fridge. Small shop, bar/restaurant (both closed Nov). Solar heated swimming pool (16 x 8 m) and paddling pool (1/5-30/9). Sauna and solarium. Excellent playground and indoor playroom for wet weather. Youth room. Full animation programme. WiFi internet. Dog shower. Ski and drying rooms. Good English spoken.
Off site: Tennis, fishing, riding, skiing, bicycle hire within 2 km. Golf 10 km.

Open: All year excl. 16 - 30 November.

Directions

Site is 2 km. northwest of Hopfgarten. From A12 exit 17 (Worgl-Ost) turn right on B178 towards St Johann for 5 km. then take the B170 towards Hopfgarten for 2 km. Site is signed to left on a right hand bend opposite a Peugeot/Talbot garage.
GPS: N47:28.013 E12:08.607

Charges 2009

Per unit incl. 2 persons and electricity (meter in winter)	€ 16,00 - € 29,00
extra person	€ 4,50 - € 8,50
child (1-13 yrs)	€ 2,50 - € 6,50
dog	€ 3,00 - € 3,50

Prices higher for winter.
Less 50% on pitch fee in mid-seasons.
No credit cards.

AU0140 Euro Camp Wilder Kaiser

Kranebittau 18, A-6345 Kössen (Tirol)

Tel: **05375 6444**. Email: **info@eurocamp-koessen.com** **www.alanrogers.com/AU0140**

The village of Kössen lies to the south of the A8 Munich - Salzburg autobahn and east of the A93/A12 motorway near Kufstein. It is well situated for overnight stops but even more for longer stays. Wilder Kaiser is located at the foot of the Unterberg with views of the Kaisergebirge and surrounded by forests. Being about 2 km. south of the village, it is in a quiet location. About 130 of the 190 pitches are available for touring units, plus an area for tents and a new area for motorcaravans.

Facilities

The heated, central sanitary block is of good quality with spacious showers, some washbasins in cubicles and a baby room. Washing machines and dryers. Motorcaravan services. Shop. Large restaurant/bar (closed Nov). Snack bar (high season). Club room with TV and play station. Heated swimming pool (May - Sept). Youth room. Sauna and solarium. Tennis. Large adventure playground. Club for children and other activities for all (high season). Off site: Bicycle hire 1 km. Golf 2 km. Fishing and Riding 4 km. Beach and boat launching 6 km.

Open: 8 December - 8 November.

Directions

From A8 (München - Salzburg), take Grabenstatt exit 109 and go south on B307/B176 to Kössen. Cross the river and at roundabout follow signs for Bergbahnen and Euro Camp. After 600 m. follow signs to site. From A93 (Rosenheim - Kufstein) take Oberaudorf exit and go east on B172 to Walchsee and Kössen. GPS: N47:39.222 E12:24.915

Charges guide

Per unit incl. 2 persons and TV	€ 18,70 - € 22,70
extra person	€ 6,20 - € 7,20
electricity per kWh	€ 0,65

AU0150 Camping Riffler

Bruggenfeldstraße 2, A-6500 Landeck (Tirol)

Tel: **054 426 4898**. Email: **lorenz.schimpfoessl@aon.at** **www.alanrogers.com/AU0150**

This small, pretty site is almost in the centre of the small town of Landeck and, being on the main through route from the Vorarlberg to the Tirol, would serve as a good overnight stop. Square in shape with the main road on one side and the fast flowing River Sanna on the other edge, it has just 40 pitches on either side of hard access roads on level grass. Trees and flowers adorn the site giving good shade and all pitches have electricity (10A). Activities in the area include walking, mountain biking, paragliding, kite flying, rafting, canoeing and climbing.

Facilities

The small toilet block has been rebuilt to a good standard. Washing machine and dryer. Basic motorcaravan services. Shop. Small general room with TV. Fishing. Off site: Supermarket just outside the gate, other shops 100 m. Restaurants about 100 m. Bicycle hire and swimming pool 500 m. Reshen and Arlberg mountain passes within easy driving distance. Opportunities for watersports and hang-gliding.

Open: All year excl. May.

Directions

Site is at the western end of Landeck. Take exit for Landeck-West from the A12 and turn left towards Landeck. Site is on the left (sharp left bend) just before entering the town centre. GPS: N47:08.525 E10:33.665

Charges 2009

Per unit incl. 2 persons and electricity	€ 20,80 - € 30,00
extra person	€ 5,00 - € 7,40

Winter prices slightly higher. No credit cards.

AU0155 Aktiv-Camping Prutz

Beim Sauerbrunn, A-6522 Prutz (Tirol)

Tel: **054 722 648**. Email: **info@aktiv-camping.at** **www.alanrogers.com/AU0155**

Aktiv-Camping is a long site which lies beside, and is fenced off from, the River Inn. Most of the 110 individual level pitches are for touring and range in size from 70 to 90 sq.m. They all have 6A electrical connections and in the larger area fit together sideways and back to back. As a result, the site can sometimes have the appearance of being quite crowded. There is a separate overnight area for motorcaravans. This is an attractive area with many activities in both summer and winter.

Facilities

The sanitary facilities are of a high standard, with private cabins and good facilities for disabled visitors. Baby room. Washing machine. Dog shower. Small shop. Bar. Takeaway. Play room. Ski room. Skating rink. Internet point. Children's entertainment. Guided walks, skiing (free shuttle service). WiFi. Off site: Indoor pool at Feichten, Pilgrim's Church at Kaltenbrunn. Kaunertaler Glacier.

Open: All year.

Directions

Travelling west from Innsbruck on the E60/A12 for about 65 km. turn south onto the B180 signed Bregenz, Arlberg, Innsbruck and Fernpass for 11 km. to Prutz. Site is signed from the B180 over the bridge. GPS: N47:04.807 E10:39.564

Charges guide

Per unit (summer) incl. electricity and 2 persons	€ 21,50 - € 29,00
winter price (plus electricity on meter)	€ 21,00 - € 28,50
extra person	€ 7,00 - € 9,40

AU0185 Campingplatz Seewiese

Tristachersee 2, A-9900 Lienz (Tirol)

Tel: **048 526 9767**. Email: **seewiese@hotmail.com** **www.alanrogers.com/AU0185**

High above the village of Tristach and 5 km. from Lienz, this is a perfect location for a good campsite. When we arrived the owner said, 'This is a green paradise at the gateway to the Dolomites' – it did not take us long to agree. The 110 pitches all have 6A electricity (long leads may be necessary) and the 11 pitches for motorcaravans each have electricity, water and internet access. Caravans are sited on a gently sloping field which has level areas although pitches are unmarked and unnumbered.

Facilities

Toilet facilities are clean, heated and modern with free showers. Washing machine and dryer. Motorcaravan service point. Excellent restaurant/bar. Small play area. Internet access. Swimming in adjoining lake.
Off site: Lienz 5 km.

Open: 11 May - 25 September.

Directions

In Lienz initially follow signs for Spittal and at traffic lights turn right towards Tristach. Go under railway and over a small bridge then turn left, still towards Tristach. Go through village of Tristach and after 1.5 km. turn right up to site at the top of a 1 km, 1:10 climb. GPS: N46:48.098 E12:48.172

Charges guide

Per unit incl. 2 persons and electricity	€ 24,90 - € 29,00
extra person	€ 6,30

No credit cards. Camping Cheques accepted.

AU0220 Øtztal Arena Camp Krismer

A-6441 Umhausen (Tirol)

Tel: **052 555 390**. Email: **info@oetztal-camping.at** **www.alanrogers.com/AU0220**

This is a delightful site with lovely views, in the beautiful Øtz valley, on the edge of the village of Umhausen. Situated on a gentle slope in an open valley, it has an air of peace and tranquillity and makes an excellent base for mountain walking in spring and autumn, skiing in winter or a relaxing holiday. The 98 pitches, some on individual terraces, are all marked and numbered and have electrical connections (12A); charges relate to the area available, long leads may be necessary.

Facilities

With underfloor heating, open washbasins, hairdressing room and showers on payment, the toilet facilities are of good quality. A small toilet/wash block at the far end of the site is used in summer. Baby room. Laundry facilities. Basic motorcaravan services. Bar/restaurant (May-Sept, Dec-April). No shop, but bread can be ordered. Sauna. TV room. Ski room. Fishing. Bicycle hire. Basic playground. Off site: Swimming pool and tennis 100 m. Shops in village 200 m. Boat launching 6 km. Riding 10 km.

Open: All year.

Directions

Take Øtztal Valley exit 123 from Imst - Innsbruck A12 motorway, and Umhausen is 13 km. towards Solden on the B186; site is well signed to south of village. GPS: N47:08.122 E10:55.951

Charges 2009

Per unit incl. 2 persons	€ 14,40 - € 20,00
electricity (per kWh)	€ 0,75
extra person	€ 6,00
child (2-13 yrs)	€ 4,30
dog	€ 2,60

AU0225 Romantik Camping Schloß Fernsteinsee

Am Fernpaß Tirol, A-6465 Nassereith (Tirol)

Tel: **052 655 210**. Email: **hotel@fernsteinsee.at** **www.alanrogers.com/AU0225**

This is a secluded and attractive site in a sheltered location in the protected area of the Fernstein Lakes and part of the Schloss Fernsteinsee estate. There are 125 pitches, all for touring units, in two separate areas and 80 have electricity (4/13A), water and waste water. The pitches are on level grass on four shallow terraces divided by low rails or shrubs. A new area with flat, gravel pitches and all services has been developed at the bottom of the site. There is good shade and gravel access roads.

Facilities

Modern heated facilities with a generous supply of controllable hot showers, washbasins (open style and in cabins) and facilities for disabled visitors. Laundry room. Boules. Small playground. Games room. Drinks machine. Communal barbecue facility. Sauna and solarium. Fishing and boating on the lake. Off site: Hotel Schloss Fernsteinsee with bar and restaurant 500 m. Nassereith village, shops and indoor swimming pool 1.5 km. The Fern Pass and alpine road.

Open: 15 April - 26 October.

Directions

Nassereith is 15 km. north of Imst, just south of the Fern Pass. From Imst take road 189 north for 13 km, then left on road 179 and continue past Nassereith, taking a tarmac entry road 500 m. before the river bridge. From the north: pass hotel entrance, cross bridge, first entrance is off car park, but second entry after 500 m. is better. GPS: N47:20.258 E10:49.092

Charges guide

Per unit incl. 2 persons	€ 18,00 - € 24,00
extra person	€ 5,60
electricity (plus meter)	€ 2,80

AU0180 Sportcamp Woferlgut

Kroessenbach 40, A-5671 Bruck (Salzburg)

Tel: **065 457 3030**. Email: **info@sportcamp.at** **www.alanrogers.com/AU0180**

The village of Bruck lies at the junction of the B311 and the Grossglocknerstrasse in the Hohe Tauern National Park. Sportcamp Woferlgut, a family run site, is one of the best in Austria. Although surrounded by mountains, the site is quite flat with pleasant views. The 350 level, grass pitches are marked out by shrubs (300 for touring units) and each has electricity (16A), water, drainage, cable TV socket and gas point. A high grass bank separates the site and the road. The site's own lake, used for swimming and fishing, is surrounded by a landscaped sunbathing area. The fitness centre has a fully equipped gym, whilst the other building contains a sauna and cold dip, Turkish bath, solarium (all free) massage on payment and a bar. In summer there is a free activity programme, live music evenings, children's club, weekly barbecues and guided cycle and mountain tours. In winter a cross-country skiing trail and toboggan run lead from the site and a free bus service is provided to nearby skiing facilities. With Salzburg to the north and Innsbruck to the northwest, the management is pleased to advise on local attractions and tours, making this a splendid base for a family holiday. Good English is spoken. Used by tour operators (45 pitches).

Facilities

Three modern sanitary blocks (the newest in a class of its own) have excellent facilities, including private cabins, underfloor heating and music. Washing machines and dryers. Facilities for disabled visitors. Family bathrooms for hire. Motorcaravan services. Well stocked shop. Bar, restaurant and takeaway. Small, heated outdoor pool and children's pool (28/4-30/9). Fitness centre. Two playgrounds, indoor play room and children's cinema. Tennis. Bicycle hire. Fishing. Watersports and lake swimming. Collection of small animals with pony rides for young children. Off site: ATM 500 m. Skiing 2.5 km. Golf 3 km. Boat launching and sailing 3.5 km. Hiking and skiing (all year) nearby.

Open: All year.

Directions

Site is southwest of Bruck. From road B311, Bruck by-pass, take southern exit (Grossglockner) and site is signed from the junction of B311 and B107 roads (small signs). GPS: N47:17.028 E12:49.016

Charges guide

Per person	€ 4,90 - € 7,90
child (under 10 yrs)	€ 4,00 - € 5,90
pitch incl. electricity	€ 9,40 - € 12,30
dog	€ 3,10 - € 4,30

Special offers for low season, longer stays.

AU0227 Comfort Camp Grän

Engetalstr. 13, A-6673 Grän (Tirol)

Tel: **056 756 570**. Email: **comfortcamp@aon.at** **www.alanrogers.com/AU0227**

In a village location in the Tannheimer Tal, with panoramic mountain scenery, Comfort Camp Grän is a family run site with excellent heated sanitary facilities and a stylish modern indoor pool complex. It makes a good base for exploring this border region of Austria and Germany. The site has 210 pitches of 80-100 sq.m. (170 for touring units) all with 16A electricity, water (only for summer use) and waste water on fairly level grass, over gravel terrain with some shallow terraces. There are 14 private sanitary cabins for rent. The main services are grouped at the entrance.

Facilities

The main sanitary unit has superb facilities: controllable hot showers, washbasins in cubicles, a children's section in the ladies, a baby room and many family bathrooms for rent. The second smaller unit at one end of the site is equally good. Indoor pool complex, sauna and steam room. Solarium. Shop. Restaurant and bar. Small playground. Indoor playroom. Internet. Teenagers' room. Off site: Beach 2 km. Fishing 2 km. Haldensee (lake) 3 km. Riding 6 km. German Border 10 km. Ski runs.

Open: 23 May - 2 November; 15 December - 18 April.

Directions

Grän is close to the German border, southwest of Füssen. From Germany on the autobahn A7, turn off at exit 137, and turn south on road 310 to Oberjoch, then take road 308 (road 199 in Austria) east to Grän. At eastern end of village turn north signed Pfronten, and site is 1.5 km. on left. GPS: N47:30.610 E10:33.050

Charges guide

Per person	€ 7,00 - € 10,00
pitch (electricity on meter)	€ 8,00 - € 12,50

AU0250 Alpencamping Mark

Bundesstraße 12, Maholmhof, A-6114 Weer bei Schwaz (Tirol)

Tel: **052 246 8146**. Email: **alpcamp.mark@aon.at** **www.alanrogers.com/AU0250**

This pleasant Tirol site is neat and friendly with family owners who offer a warm welcome. Formerly a farm, they now breed horses, giving a free ride each day to youngsters and organising treks. Herr Mark junior (a certified alpine ski guide and ski instructor) runs courses in climbing, rafting, mountain bike riding, trekking, hiking, etc. Set in the Inn valley, between mountain ranges, the site has 96 flat, grass pitches (71 for touring) on either side of gravel roads, with electricity connections.

Facilities

Good quality, modern, heated sanitary facilities are provided in the old farm buildings. Washing machines and dryer. Freezer. Motorcaravan services. Small, cheerful bar/restaurant and shop (1/6-1/9). Small heated pool (15/5-15/9). Activity programme with instruction. Bicycle hire. Riding (free for children). Glacier tours. Large play area. Barn for use by children in wet weather. Off site: Imtal Valley, good for mountain biking.

Open: 1 April - 31 October.

Directions

Site is 200 m. east of the village of Weer on Wattens - Schwaz road no. B171 which runs parallel to the A12, just 10 km. east of Innsbruck. (If using A12 take exit 61 from west or 53 from east). GPS: N47:18.446 E11:38.875

Charges guide

Per unit incl. 2 persons and electricity (10A)	€ 16,70 - € 26,25
extra person	€ 4,50 - € 6,00

AU0160 Seecamp Zell am See

Thumersbacherstrasse 34, A-5700 Zell-am-See (Salzburg)

Tel: **065 427 2115**. Email: **zell@seecamp.at** **www.alanrogers.com/AU0160**

Zellersee, delightfully situated in the south of Salzburg province and near the start of the Grossglocknerstrasse, is ideally placed for enjoying the splendid southern Austrian countryside. Seecamp is right by the water about 3 km. from the town of Zell and with fine views to the south end of the lake. One is immediately struck by the order and neat appearance of the site, with 176 good level, mainly grass-on-gravel pitches of average size, all with electricity (10/16A). About half have water, drainage and TV connections. Units can be close together in peak season.

Facilities

Excellent, heated sanitary facilities include facilities for disabled visitors and a baby room. Laundry facilities. Motorcaravan services (access difficult for larger units). Restaurant (15/12-30/9). Shop (1/7-31/8 and 15/12-6/1). Play area. Play room. Fishing. Bicycle hire. 'Topi' Club and summer entertainment for children. Activity programme. Winter ski packages and free ski bus. Glacier skiing possible in summer. Off site: Lake beach, indoor pool and ice skating rink. Nearby Schloss Prielau and villages along the eastern side of lake. Skiing 1.8 km. Golf, riding 2 km.

Open: All year.

Directions

Approaching from the north on the B311 take the Thumersbach exit just before tunnel entrance (2 km. north of Zell-am-See town). After 500 m. turn left and site entrance is 750 m. on the right. Note: 3.5 ton weight restriction but it is the only access to site. GPS: N47:20.384 E12:48.536

Charges 2009

Per person	€ 6,70 - € 8,40
pitch	€ 4,00 - € 12,20
electricity (plus meter)	€ 2,50
Gas on meter.	

AU0265 Park Grubhof

A-5092 Saint Martin bei Lofer (Salzburg)

Tel: **065 888 237**. Email: **camping@lofer.net** **www.alanrogers.com/AU0265**

Park Grubhof is a well organised, spacious site in a very scenic riverside location, once the pleasure park of the adjacent Schloss (now a hotel). The 200 pitches all with electricity (10A), have been carefully divided into separate areas for different types of visitor – dog owners, campers without children, young people, families and groups. There are now 150 very large pitches, all with electricity, water and drainage, along the bank of the Saalach river. Parents of small children should be aware that the site is adjacent to the fast flowing river which is unfenced. The site will open all year round from winter 2009. Some areas are wooded with plenty of shade, others are more open and there are some very attractive log cabins which have been rescued from the old logging camps. Many of the possible activities are based around the river, where you will find barbecue areas, canoeing and white water rafting, fishing and swimming (when the river level reduces). Bordering the National Park of Berchtesgaden, The area is renowned for hiking, mountain climbing and cycling (the site is on the Tauernradweg cycling trail). Good English is spoken.

Facilities

Two attractive, modern sanitary units built with plenty of glass and wood, give a good provision of all facilities. Large showers. Some washbasins in cubicles. Separate facilities for canoeists. Motorcaravan service point. Shop, restaurant and bar. Playground. Games room. Watersports. Cabins to rent. Off site: Lofer 1 km. Gorges and caves 5-7 km. Salzburg 40 minutes drive. Many marked walking and cycling trails. Mountain climbing.

Open: All year, commencing on 25 April 2009.

Directions

From A12 exit 17 (south of Kufstein) take B178 east to St Johann in Tyrol, then continue on the B178 northwest to Lofer, and finally south on B311. Just past Schloss Grubhof at the northern edge of St Martin, turn left (site signed) and follow lane to site. GPS: N47:34.474 E12:42.391

Charges guide

Per unit incl. 2 persons	€ 19,20 - € 21,60
extra person	€ 5,60 - € 6,40
child (under 15 yrs)	€ 3,60 - € 3,90

No credit cards.

AU0212 Panoramacamping Stadtblick

Rauchenbichl, Rauchenbichler Straße 21, A-5020 Salzburg (Salzburg)

Tel: **066 245 0652**. Email: **info@panorama-camping.at** **www.alanrogers.com/AU0212**

With a panoramic view over the city of Salzburg this site is well named, and you can be sure of a warm welcome from the multilingual owner, Herr Wörndl. The site has 70 pitches all with electricity (4A) and water points, on grass over gravel terraces, plus 10 grassy tent pitches. They are reasonably sized for a city site location, and the view and the good value restaurant amply compensate for any shortcomings. This is an ideal site for a short stay to see all the sights of the city.

Facilities

The single sanitary unit is in the older style, but is clean and well maintained. It provides some washbasins in cabins and controllable hot showers. No facilities for babies or disabled visitors. Laundry. Motorcaravan service point. Shop for basics and souvenirs. Restaurant (May-Sept). TV lounge. Small playground. Off site: Bicycle hire 3 km. Swimming pool 3 km. Golf 3 km. or 10 km.

Open: 20 March - 5 November; 5-15 December and 28 December - 10 January.

Directions

From A1 exit 288 (Salzburg-Nord) turn south towards city. Approaching the first set of traffic lights get into the right hand lane, turn right here on a minor road (site signed) and continue to top of hill, and follow site signs. GPS: N47:49.708 E13:03.145

Charges guide

Per unit incl. 2 persons and electricity	€ 24,00 - € 26,00
extra person	€ 8,00

AU0262 Oberwötzlhof Camp

Erlfeld 37, A-5441 Abtenau (Salzburg)

Tel: **062 432 698**. Email: **oberwoetzlhof@sbg.at** **www.alanrogers.com/AU0262**

High up in the Lammertal Valley is this small farm site with amazing views of the surrounding mountains. Part of a working farm, it has a total of 70 pitches, of which 30 are for long stay units, leaving 40 places for tourers. All are serviced with electricity (10A), water and drainage. Amateur astronomers will appreciate the lack of site lighting, but campers may find a torch useful. The small fenced swimming pool (10 x 5 m) is unheated, and has paved surrounds. Despite the slightly dated facilities, we think that the atmosphere and stunning location compensate for any shortcomings.

Facilities

New sanitary building. No special facilities for babies or disabled visitors. A new unit is under construction but it could be some time before it is finished. Laundry facilities and drying room. Solarium. Restaurant (winter only). Swimming pool. Internet terminal. Off site: Abtenau 2.5 km. (about 25 minutes walk). Skiing 2.5 km. Riding 8 km. Hallstättersee and salt mines 30 km.

Open: All year.

Directions

Abtenau is southeast of Salzburg. From A10 exit 28 (Golling), take B162 east for 14 km. and site is signed to the left about 2.5 km. before Abtenau. GPS: N47:35.171 E13:19.474

Charges guide

Per person	€ 6,00
pitch (plus electricity on meter)	€ 9,00 - € 11,00
electricity	€ 0,70

No credit cards.

AU0340 Camping am See

Winkl 77, A-4831 Obertraun (Upper Austria)

Tel: **061 31265**. Email: **camping.am.see@chello.at** **www.alanrogers.com/AU0340**

It is unusual to locate a campsite so deep in the heart of spectacular mountain scenery, yet with such easy access. Directly on the shores of Halstattersee, near Obertraun and the Dachstein range of mountains, this 2.5 hectare, flat site, with 70 pitches is an excellent, peaceful holiday base which has been upgraded. The grass site has a shady area for tents, whilst caravans and motorcaravans are more in the open. There are no specific pitches although the owners, within reason, control where you place your unit. At the time of our visit there were only 36 electricity hook-ups.

Facilities

Completely refurbished, fully equipped and modern, the toilet block includes a small baby room. Washing machine. Area with purpose built barbecues, seating and tables. Bar and limited restaurant. Basic daily provisions kept such as bread and milk. Small playground.
Off site: Activities nearby include walking, bird watching, fishing, mountain biking, rock climbing, scuba diving and much more. For naturists, 100 m. from the site there is a delightful popular area designated as an FKK strand (naturist beach).

Open: 1 May - 30 September.

Directions

Due south from Bad Ischl on road B145, take road B166 to Hallstatt. After single carriageway tunnel, site is 4 km. on left on entering village of Winkl. Note: Road is a little narrow in places so care is needed. GPS: N47:32.927 E13:40.661

Charges guide

Per unit incl. 2 persons	€ 21,80 - € 25,30
electricity	€ 3,00
small tent incl. 2 persons	€ 5,20

No credit cards.

AU0350 Camp Mond See Land

Punz Au 21, A-5310 Mondsee (Upper Austria)

Tel: **062 322 600**. Email: **austria@campmondsee.at** **www.alanrogers.com/AU0350**

Mond See Land was upgraded in 2000 and now offers excellent facilities in a pleasant part of Austria, to the east of Salzburg, between the lakes of Mondsee and Irrsee. It is peacefully situated in a natural setting with mountain views, yet less than 10 minutes drive from the autobahn. There are 60 good sized, level touring pitches (80 long stay), set amongst the trees at the lower level and on terraces, each with water, waste water and 16A electricity. The heated swimming pool is covered and has a sunbathing terrace. There is a small fishing lake (unfenced) and a small playground for children.

Facilities

The sanitary facilities are in the reception and pool complex and offer first class facilities including some washbasins in cabins and a suite for disabled visitors. Laundry with washing machines and dryer. Kitchen with cooking and dishwashing. Motorcaravan service point. Shop and restaurant. Swimming pool (free). Playground. Riding. Off site: Mondsee is a popular large lake with many sporting opportunities. Golf 5 km.

Open: 1 April - 31 October.

Directions

From A1/E55 exit 265 (signed Straßwalchen) turn north onto B154. In 1.5 m. turn left at crossroads (by glassworks) and then 2 km. to site (signed). Note: Signs can be difficult to spot. GPS: N47:51.993 E13:18.394

Charges guide

Per person	€ 4,90 - € 5,50
child (6-15 yrs)	€ 3,50 - € 3,80
pitch incl. electricity	€ 9,40 - € 10,40

AU0345 Seecamping Gruber

Dorfstrasse 63, A-4865 Nußdorf am Attersee (Upper Austria)

Tel: **076 668 0450**. Email: **office@camping-gruber.at** **www.alanrogers.com/AU0345**

The Attersee is the largest of a group of lakes just to the east of Salzburg in the very attractive Salzkammergut area. Seecamping Gruber is a small, often crowded site halfway up the western side of the lake. There are 150 individual pitches, with an increasing number of seasonal units taking the larger pitches. There are still some 60 pitches for tourers, all with 16A electricity and many with shade. Pitches tend to be small to medium size and the access roads are narrow making entrance and exit difficult and this is not helped by the seasonal visitors erecting fences to utilise every last inch of their pitches. Sadly views across the lake to the hills beyond can only be enjoyed from the 25 metre swimming pool, the shallow children's play pool (both heated to 26 degrees) and the surrounding sunbathing areas.

Facilities

Modern sanitary facilities offer some private cabins, washing machine and dryer, good unit for disabled visitors, and baby room. Restaurant and takeaway. Shop. Play area. Swimming and paddling pools. Sauna, solarium and gym. Fishing. Off site: Windsurfing, sailing, both with courses. Mountain bikes, diving and balloon rides all available locally.

Open: 15 April - 15 October.

Directions

From the A1/E55/E60 between Salzburg and Linz, take exit 243 to Attersee and then south on the B151 to Nußdorf. Site is on the southern edge of the village. GPS: N47:52.779 E13:31.466

Charges guide

Per unit incl. 2 persons and electricity	€ 23,40 - € 29,20
dog	€ 3,50

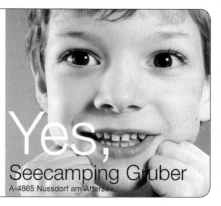

AU0240 Camping Appesbach

Au 99, A-5360 Saint Wolfgang (Upper Austria)

Tel: **061 382 206**. Email: **camping@appesbach.at** **www.alanrogers.com/AU0240**

St Wolfgang, a pretty little village on the lake of the same name which was made famous by the operetta 'White Horse Inn', is ringed round by hills in a delightful situation. The location of Appesbach, on the banks of the lake with a good frontage, is one of its main assets. The site has 170 pitches, with 100 for touring units (including 20 tent pitches) with some in regular rows and the rest on open meadows that could become full in high season. Pitches near the lakeside have higher charges. All have electricity (10A) with a mix of German and European sockets.

Facilities

The two toilet blocks have been combined into one, extended and refurbished to a good standard. Motorcaravan service point. Good shop. Bar (1/5-31/8). Restaurant with TV (Easter-30/9). Snack bar with terrace (Easter-30/9). Small playground. Off site: Tennis nearby. Village 1 km. Many excursions possible including Salzburg 50 km.

Open: Easter - 31 October.

Directions

From B158 Salzburg - Bad Ischl road, turn towards St Wolfgang just east of Strobl and site is on the left 1 km. before St Wolfgang.
GPS: N47:43.947 E13:27.826

Charges guide

Per person	€ 4,10 - € 6,10
child (3-15 yrs)	€ 2,55 - € 3,55
pitch	€ 5,00 - € 13,00
electricity	€ 2,80
dog	€ 2,00

AU0280 Camping Stumpfer

A-3392 Schönbühel (Lower Austria)

Tel: **027 528 510**. Email: **office@stumpfer.com** **www.alanrogers.com/AU0280**

This small, well appointed site with just 60 pitches is directly on the River Danube, near the small town of Schönbühel, and could make a convenient night stop being near the Salzburg - Vienna autobahn. The 50 unmarked pitches for touring units, all with electricity (16A), are on flat grass and the site is lit at night. There is shade in most parts and a landing stage for boat trips on the Danube.

Facilities

Part of the main building, the toilet block is of good quality with hot water on payment. Facilities for disabled visitors include ramps by the side of steps up to the block. Washing machine and dryer. Motorcaravan services. Small shop. Playground. Fishing. The main building also houses a Gasthof, with a bar/restaurant of the same name, that can be used by campers. Off site: Swimming pool, bicycle hire or riding within 5 km.

Open: 1 April - 31 October.

Directions

Leave Salzburg - Vienna autobahn at Melk exit. Drive towards Melk, but continue towards Melk Nord. Just before bridge turn right (Schönbühel and St Polten), at T-junction turn right again and continue down hill. Turn right just before BP filling station (signed Schönbühel) and site is 3 km. on left with narrow entrance, next to the Gasthof Stumpfer.
GPS: N48:15.240 E15:22.264

Charges 2009

Per unit incl. 2 persons and electricity	€ 21,40
extra person	€ 6,00

Less 2% for cash payment, 5% after 7th day.

AU0290 Donaupark Camping Tulln

Donoulande 76, A-3430 Tulln (Lower Austria)

Tel: **022 726 5200**. Email: **camptulln@oeamtc.at** **www.alanrogers.com/AU0290**

Donaupark Camping, owned and run by the Austrian Motor Club (OAMTC), is imaginatively laid out village style with unmarked grass pitches grouped around six circular gravel areas. Further pitches are to the side of the hard road which links the circles and these include some with grill facilities for tents; 100 of the 120 touring pitches have electricity (3/6A) and cable TV sockets. Tall trees surrounding the site offer shade in parts. Tucked neatly away at the back of the site are 120 long stay caravans. Activities are organised in high season with guided tours around Tulln.

Facilities

Three identical, modern, octagonal sanitary blocks can be heated. One is at reception (next to the touring area), the other two are at the far end of the site. Facilities for disabled visitors. Washing machines and dryers. Cooking rings. Gas supplies. Bar and restaurant (1/5-15/9). Shop (1/5-30/9). Play areas. Tennis. Bicycle and canoe hire. Excursion programme. Internet access. Off site: Lake swimming in adjacent park (entry free for campers). Fishing 500 m. Bus service into Vienna (May - Sept). Train service to Vienna. Steamer excursions.

Open: 25 March - 15 October.

Directions

From Vienna follow south bank of the Danube on B14; from the west, leave the A1 autobahn at either St Christophen or Altenbach exits and go north on B19 to Tulln. Site is on the east side of Tulln and well signed. GPS: N48:19.943 E16:04.365

Charges 2009

Per unit incl. 2 persons and electricity	€ 24,50 - € 29,50
extra person	€ 7,00
child (5-14 yrs)	€ 3,00

Camping Cheques accepted.

AU0302 Aktiv Camping Wien Neue Donau

Am Kaisermuhlendamm 119, A-1220 Wien-Ost (Vienna)

Tel: **012 024 010**. Email: **neuedonau@campingwien.at** **www.alanrogers.com/AU0302**

This is the sister site of Camping Wien-Sud and closer to Vienna. Near two busy motorways there is inevitably traffic noise. However it is perhaps easier to find and has similar facilities and standards. With 254 level touring pitches with electricity and a further 12 with water and drainage also, the site has a large and changing population. The site is close to the 'Donauinsel', a popular recreation area. The Neue Donau (New Danube), a 20 km. long artificial side arm of the Danube provides swimming, sports and play areas, while the Danube bicycle trail runs past the site.

Facilities

Modern toilet facilities are clean, and well maintained with free showers. Facilities for disabled visitors. Washing machines and dryers. Motorcaravan service point. Campers' kitchen with cooking, fridges, freezers and TV. Shop. Small restaurant. Play area. Internet access. Barbecue areas. Bicycle hire and free guided bicycle tours. Off site: Vienna city centre 5 km. Prater Park 1 km.

Open: Easter - 15 September.

Directions

Site is close to the A23 and A22. From A23 heading east turn off at first exit after crossing the Donau (signed Lobau). At first traffic lights, near Shell station, turn left and after 200 m. turn right into site. GPS: N48:12.555 E16:26.669

Charges guide

Per person	€ 5,90 - € 6,90
pitch	€ 5,50 - € 12,00

AU0306 Camping Wien West

Hüttelbergstrasse 80, A-1140 Wien (Vienna)
Tel: **019 142 314**. Email: **west@campingwien.at** **www.alanrogers.com/AU0306**

Opera, classical music, museums, shopping and the Danube; whatever it is you want in Vienna you are spoilt for choice. Wien West is an all year round site with good transport links to the city centre. It is the parent site of Wien Sud and Neue Donau and is inevitably busier. The site is located on the edge of the Vienna Woods with direct access to walking and mountain bike trails. There are 202 level and numbered pitches, all with 13A electricity. Buses to the metro stop right outside the gates and you can be in the centre in 35 minutes. For somewhere different try the 'Black Camel' for a light lunch – it is easy to find from Stephensplatz – or perhaps the Danube cruise that will introduce you to the architecture of Freiderreich Hundertwasser. Whatever you do it will be a memorable visit to the Austrian capital.

Facilities

Three modern toilet blocks provide ample and clean toilets, hot showers and washbasins. Washing machine and dryer. Kitchen facilities. Motorcaravan services. Small shop for essentials. Restaurant (1/4-1/10). WiFi (free) and internet point. Games room. Playground. Bicycle hire. Off site: Vienna centre 8 km. Schönbrunn palace. Bicycle and walking trails. Tennis.

Open: All year excl. February.

Directions

From the city centre follow signs to autobahn west and Linz. Site is well signed from the main roads. Coming from the A1 (Salzburg - Vienna) drive over the Bergmillergasse (bridge). Stay on this road to Huttelbergstraße after the first traffic lights. GPS: N48:12.859 E16:15.011

Charges guide

Per person	€ 5,90 - € 6,90
child (4-15 yrs)	€ 3,50 - € 4,00
pitch	€ 5,50 - € 9,50
electricity	€ 3,00 - € 4,00

AU0304 Camping Wien-Sud

Breitenfursterstrasse 269, A-1230 Wien-Atzgersdorf (Vienna)
Tel: **018 673 649**. Email: **sued@campingwien.at** **www.alanrogers.com/AU0304**

This site, which is in a former Palace park and was closed for some years, reopened in 2003 with new facilities and new management. It is now probably the best site in the greater Vienna area, with good public transport links to the city centre and a friendly and welcoming atmosphere. With 154 touring pitches with electricity (16A) and 42 with water and drainage, the site provides a good base for city sightseeing. With many mature trees and some shade you will find this a peaceful and quiet site. Walking and cycling are popular in the nearby Vienna woods. Right next door is a Merkur supermarket which is well worth a visit for stocking up, whichever way you are heading.

Facilities

Excellent modern toilet facilities are clean and well maintained with free showers. Facilities for disabled visitors. Washing machine and dryer. Some cooking facilities. Motorcaravan service point. Small play area. Tickets for Schloss Schönbrunn and other attractions sold at reception. Off site: Vienna 6 km.

Open: 1 June - 31 August.

Directions

From the A2 turn onto the A21 towards Linz (if you're heading north the slip is just past IKEA). Turn off the A21 at first exit (Brunn am Gebirge) and head north. Keep going on this road to site (well signed) on the right in Atzgersdorf. From the A23 (Süd-Ost Tangene) take Altmannsdorf exit and follow the signs. GPS: N48:08.984 E16:18.024

Charges guide

Per person	€ 5,90 - € 6,90
child (4-15 yrs)	€ 3,50 - € 4,00
pitch	€ 5,10 - € 17,00

AU0300 Camping Rodaun

Breitenfurter Straße 487, An der Au 2, A-1230 Wien-Südwest-Rodaun (Vienna)

Tel: **018 884 154** **www.alanrogers.com/AU0300**

This good little site is within the Vienna city boundary and is a pleasant base for visiting this old, interesting and world famous city. Just 9 km. from the centre, there is an excellent public transport system for viewing the sights as car parking is almost impossible in the city. Situated in a southern suburb, it has space for about 40 units on flat grass pitches or on concrete bases and an additional area for about 20 tents. With little shade, the pitches are not numbered or marked, either in the centre or outside the circular tarmac, with electricity provided (6A).

Facilities

The toilet block has some washbasins in cabins and hot showers for which a token is needed (purchased at reception). Laundry service provided by Frau Deihs. Off site: Supermarket and restaurant within 250 m. Swimming pool 2 km.

Open: 15 June - 20 October.

Directions

Take Pressbaum exit from Westautobahn or Vosendorf exit from Sudautobahn and follow signs. Site is at An der Au 2, which is a small side street leading off from Breitenfurter Strasse (a 16 km. long road). An der Au is opposite house number 487 Breitenfurter Strasse. GPS: N48:06.996 E16:16.998

Charges guide

Per person	€ 6,50
pitch incl. car	€ 7,50 - € 9,00
electricity per kWh	€ 0,80

AU0330 Camping Central

Martinhofstraße 3, A-8054 Graz (Steiermark)

Tel: **067 637 85102**. Email: **guenther_walter@utanet.at** **www.alanrogers.com/AU0330**

Although not as well known as Vienna, Salzburg and Innsbruck, Graz in the southern province of Styria, is Austria's second largest city. Camping Central is a quiet place, ideal as a base from which to explore the region. It is situated in the southwest of the town in the Strassgang district, some 6 km. from the centre. The 136 level touring pitches are either in regular rows either side of tarmac roads under a cover of tall trees or unmarked in an open meadow. All have electricity (6A).

Facilities

The new, well built toilet block is of good quality and the other two blocks have been refurbished. Each can be heated in cool weather. Facilities for disabled visitors. Laundry facilities. Swimming pool with facilities including a special entry to the water for disabled people. Small restaurant at the pool. Tennis. Playground. Jogging track. Limited animation during high season. Off site: Two other restaurants within 300 m. Good shop about 400 m.

Open: 1 April - 31 October.

Directions

From the west take Graz-west exit, from Salzburg the Graz-sud exit and follow signs to Central and Strassgang and turn right just past traffic lights for site (signed). GPS: N47:01.227 E15:23.552

Charges guide

Per unit incl. 2 persons and electricity	€ 24,00 - € 28,00
extra person	€ 5,00 - € 8,00

No credit cards.

AU0502 Camping Im Thermenland

Bairisch Kölldorf 240, A-8344 Bairisch Kölldorf (Steiermark)

Tel: **031 593 941**. Email: **gemeinde@bairisch-koelldorf.at** **www.alanrogers.com/AU0502**

Near both the Slovenian and Hungarian borders and set in the rolling countryside of southeast Austria, this is a real hidden gem. Not shown on many maps, but well worth the trip, if you want a good quiet site with modern amenities and excellent standards then come right here. There are 100 pitches of which 70 are for touring and all have electricity, water and drainage. The site is near numerous spas and thermal baths and close to Styrassic Park, a must for younger campers.

Facilities

Excellent toilet facilities are clean, well maintained and include free showers. Facilities for disabled visitors. Washing machine and dryer. Dog shower. Restaurant. Unheated outdoor, but covered, swimming pool (May - Sept). Small play area. Off site: Fishing 100 m. Golf 3 km. Styrassic Park 4 km.

Open: All year.

Directions

Southeast of Graz, but you're unlikely to find Bairisch Kolldorf on any map. Leave A2 at exit 157 and head towards Feldbach on the 68. Continue on the 66 to Bad Gleichenberg, go straight over first roundabout and turn left at the second. After 2.8 km. (just past fire station) turn left by a chapel and immediately right to site in 600 m. GPS: N46:52.535 E15:56.067

Charges guide

Per person	€ 6,15
pitch	€ 7,25
electricity per kWh	€ 0,50

Camping Cheques accepted.

AU0505 Camping Leibnitz

Rudolf Hans Bartsch-Gasse 33, A-8430 Leibnitz (Steiermark)

Tel: **034 528 2463**. Email: **stadtgemeinde@leibnitz.at** **www.alanrogers.com/AU0505**

Near the Slovenian border, close to the small town of Leibnitz, this site is set in the rolling wine-growing countryside of southeast Austria. A small site with only 52 pitches, it is set in a lovely park area and close to an excellent swimming pool complex which is available for campers' use (with access arrangements for disabled visitors). Minigolf and tennis facilities are nearby. All the pitches are of a good size, level and with 16A electricity connections, and some have shade.

Facilities

Excellent toilet facilities are clean and well maintained. Showers cost € 0.50. Facilities for disabled visitors. Washing machine. Small restaurant but many more within walking distance. Small play area. Off site: Leibnitz 500 m. Town has shops and restaurants with weekly events held at the Jazz Club. Leisure centre with two heated outdoor swimming pools 100 m.

Open: 1 May - 30 September.

Directions

From the A9 take exit for Leibnitz, go straight over two roundabouts (through factory outlet centre), over traffic lights and after 300 m. turn left (site signed). Go straight over roundabout and enter Leibnitz, turn right and site is 500 m. on the left, set in the park next to the pool complex. GPS: N46:46.733 E15:31.863

Charges guide

Per person	€ 4,50
pitch incl. car	€ 6,50
electricity	€ 1,80

AU0515 Katschtal Camping

Peterdorf 100, A-8842 Peterdorf (Steiermark)

Tel: **035 842 2813**. Email: **katschtalcamping@yahoo.de** **www.alanrogers.com/AU0515**

The small, quiet campsite with only 48 pitches is ideally located for exploring southwest Styria and the beautiful Mur valley, and the Niedere Tauern alps (highest point Greimberg 2,472 m). To the north, snowcapped Greimberg sits high above the site whilst in other directions you can see pine clad slopes and alpine pastures. Not too far away is Turracher Hohe, the small ski resort that nestles at an altitude of 1,700 m. in the Nocky mountains, one of Austria's most scenic Alpine ranges between Styria and Carinthia. The level, unmarked pitches all have access to 6A electricity.

Facilities

The modern sanitary block provides ample and clean facilities including toilets, hot showers and washbasins. Washing machine. Kitchen facilities.

Open: All year.

Directions

From the Murau - Scheifling 96 road, turn north towards Katsch just west of Frojach. Follow this road up the valley towards and through Peterdorf to the site on the right set back from the road but clearly signed. GPS: N47:10.848 E14:13.003

Charges guide

Per unit incl. 2 persons	€ 13,50
extra person	€ 3,50
electricity per kWh	€ 0,55

AU0520 Camping am Badesee

Hitzmannsdorf 28, A-8822 Mühlen (Steiermark)

Tel: **035 862 418**. Email: **office@camping-am-badesee.at** **www.alanrogers.com/AU0520**

Set in a beautiful open alpine valley alongside a lake in the southern part of the Steiermark region, this family run site will provide you with a warm welcome and a relaxing holiday. The 60 good sized pitches are well spaced on open grassy terraces, and with only 15 long stay units, there should be around 45 available for touring units. All have electricity hook-ups. From reception you can order bread, milk, eggs and basic provisions. A small cafe/snack bar with terrace overlooks the lake.

Facilities

A modern heated sanitary unit provides spacious hot showers, some washbasins in cubicles, with child size showers and basins. Hairdressing and shaving areas. Laundry room also has a baby bath and changing facility. No dedicated facilities for disabled persons. Communal barbecue. Playground. Pets corner. Trampoline. Lake for swimming, fishing and boating. Bicycle hire. Off site: Two restaurants and services in Mühlen (15 minutes walk). Riding 1 km. Neumarkt (6 km.) has more comprehensive shopping facilities. Golf 14 km.

Open: 30 April - 30 September.

Directions

Mühlen is southwest of Judenburg. From the west using the A10, take exit 104 (St Michael im Lungau) and head east on road 96 through Murau to Scheiffling. Turn right (south) on B317 to Neumarkt and, towards the end of village, turn left on B92 to Mühlen. Site is 5.8 km. on the right. GPS: N47:02.244 E14:29.256

Charges 2009

Per unit incl. 2 persons and electricity	€ 16,00 - € 18,90
extra person	€ 5,00
child (3-14 yrs)	€ 2,50

AU0525 50plus Campingpark Fisching

Fisching 9, A-8741 Weißkirchen (Steiermark)

Tel: **03577 82284**. Email: **campingpark@fisching.at** **www.alanrogers.com/AU0525**

This small site is unusual in that it only accepts clients over 50 years of age. It is a high quality site with an attractive setting in the Steiermark region, east of Graz. There are 42 large, level pitches (100-130 sq.m), all equipped with electricity (6A), water, drainage and cable TV connections. Most pitches are on hardstanding. A number of chalets and holiday apartments are also available for rent. There is a small swimming lake which is surrounded by a garden and sunbathing area.

Facilities

Bar and snack bar with a selection of homemade dishes. Shop. Swimming lake. Tennis. Bicycle hire. Activity programme. Chalets and appartments for rent. Off site: Walking and cycle tracks. Golf (Murtal). Graz 70 km.

Open: 1 April - 15 October.

Directions

From the north (A9 motorway), head for Graz and join the westbound S36 at Sant Michael in Obersteiermark. Continue on this road as far as Aichdorf. Then head south on B78 to Weisskirchen then follow signs to Fisching, from where site is clearly signed. GPS: N47:09.791 E14:44.297

Charges 2009

Per unit incl. 2 persons and electricity € 20,00 - € 22,50
extra person € 5,50

AU0415 Camping Rosental Roz

Gotschuchen 34, A-9173 Saint Margareten im Rosental (Carinthia)

Tel: **042 268 1000**. Email: **camping.rosental@roz.at** **www.alanrogers.com/AU0415**

In the picturesque Drau valley, southeast of Flagenfurt, Rosental Roz has magnificent views along the valley and of the cliffs that form the Austrian southern border with Slovakia. The site is also close to Italy. With 430 pitches (all for touring) and ten mobile homes to rent around a small swimming lake, all pitches have 6A electricity and 50 pitches have water and drainage. An active children's club provides lots to occupy the youngsters and guided walks for adults are organised from the campsite.

Facilities

Toilet facilities are clean and modern with free showers, 10 family washrooms and a large shower facility for young children. Washing machine and dryer. Facilities for disabled visitors. Restaurant/bar (1/5-30/9). Shop (1/6-15/9). Children's club (1/6-30/8). Playgrounds and large games area. Water slide. WiFi. Off site: Fishing 1 km. Riding 2 km. Many walks. Cycle rides.

Open: Easter - 15 October.

Directions

Site is southeast of Klagenfurt. From the 91 road turn onto the 85 towards Feriach. Before reaching Saint Margareten, in the centre of the small hamlet of Gotschuchen turn left towards site. It is 1.5 km. but well signed (watch for overhanging gutters especially when passing another vehicle). GPS: N46:32.618 E14:23.453

Charges guide

Per person € 7,10
pitch € 8,20 - € 10,40

AU0410 Strandcamping Turnersee Breznik

A-9123 Saint Primus (Carinthia)

Tel: **042 392 350**. Email: **info@breznik.at** **www.alanrogers.com/AU0410**

This neat and tidy site is situated in a valley with views of the surrounding mountains. The 260 marked and numbered pitches for touring units vary in size, on level grass terraces. Although there are many trees, not all parts have shade. All pitches have electricity (6A) and 50 also have water, drainage, TV and phone connections. At the lakeside is a large, well kept grass area for sunbathing, with a wooden deck area right next to the water providing steps for swimming in the lake. It is very much a site for families where children really are catered for and it has a pleasant atmosphere.

Facilities

Four modern sanitary blocks include provision for young children and babies in the largest block. Facilities for disabled people. Large, central building housing well stocked shop. Pleasant restaurant with terrace, takeaway (16/5-6/9) and play room for small children. Good play areas and small zoo with goats and rabbits. 'Topi' club and organised activities for adults and children. Games room. Bicycle hire. Watersports. Internet access. Off site: Fishing and golf 1.5 km. Riding 3 km. Boat launching 5 km.

Open: 11 April - 4 October.

Directions

Site is 20 km. east-southeast of Klagenfurt. Leave A2 motorway at exit 298 signed Grafenstien. Go east on road 70 for 5 km. and turn right for Tainach and St Kanzian. In St Kanzian keep bearing to the right, St Primas is signed. Site is on left before St Primus. GPS: N46:35.141 E14:33.959

Charges guide

Per unit incl. 2 persons and electricity € 16,10 - € 26,30
extra person € 4,80 - € 8,10

Special deals for families.
Camping Cheques accepted.

www.camping.woerthersee.com

Wörthersee • 4-Seental Keutschach

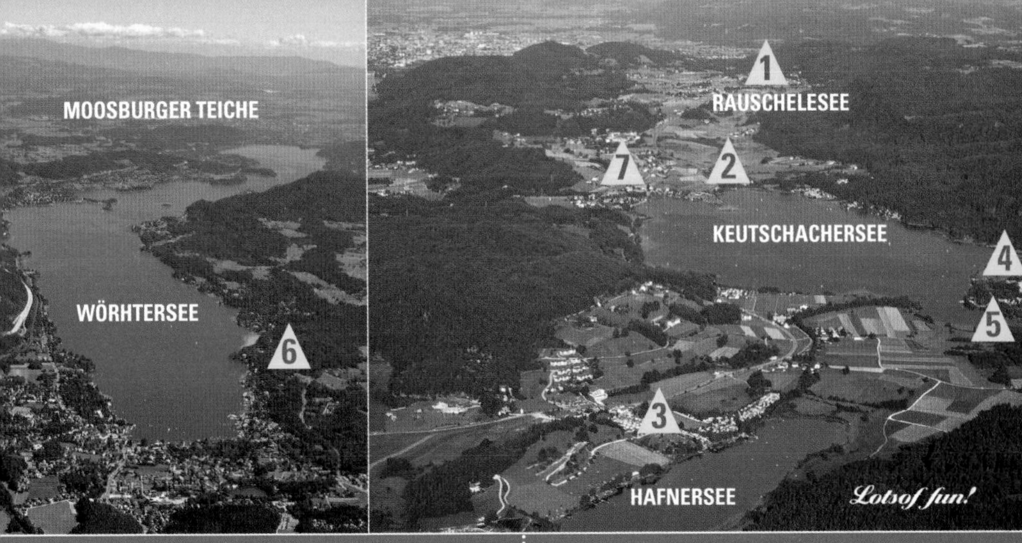

Textilcamping Reichmann

ichter Günter Hassler, Reauz 5, A-9074 Seental Keutschach,
l. 00 43/664/14 30 437 od. 00 43/699/15 00 00 57
Mail: info@camping-reichmann.at,
ww.camping-reichmann.at; Family run campsite, 12.000 m², quietly located the heart of unspoiled nature, located on the eastern bank of Lake auschelesee, Ideal site for families with children. Very good restaurant.

Strandcamping Süd

elga Hannelore Seger, A-9074 Seental Keutschach, Tel. 00 43/42 73/27 73,
x 00 43/42 73/27 73-4, Mobile phone from 6 pm: 00 43/699/12424403,
Mail: info@strandcampingsued.at, www.keutschachsued.at
eautiful family campsite, with direct lake access and at the forest edge, xurious facilities, large bathing area and play area, restaurant and Kidsclub.

Family-Camping Hafnersee

otour Kärntner Seen Hotelbetriebs GmbH, Plescherken 5,
-9074 Seental Keutschach, Tel. 00 43/42 73/23 75-0, Fax 00 43/42 73/23 75-16,
Mail: info@hafnersee.at, www.hafnersee.at
odern and well equipped campsite, very child friendly, ith direct lake access, large pitches and play area.

Sabotnik Naturist campsite

wner Kaufitsch, Dobein 9, A-9074 Seental Keutschach,
l. 00 43/42 73/25 09, Fax 00 43/42 73/26 05,
Mail: info@fkk-sabotnik.at, www.fkk-sabotnik.at
amily friendly campsite in a tranquil setting, direct lake access, ntertainment programme, activities for children of all ages, sport nd play areas, several spots for swimming, massage, mobile homes r hire, dog area, childrens' farm, internet café and wireless lan.

5 FKK-Camping Müllerhof, Familie Safron

Dobein 10, A-9074 Seental Keutschach,
Tel. 00 43/42 73/25 17, Fax 25 17-5, Mobile phone: 00 43/664/33 55 425,
E-Mail: muellerhof@fkk-camping.at , www.fkk-camping.at . Very well maintained family campsite at the south banks of the Keutschacher See. Recommended by ÖNV, DFK, NFN, ANWB, ECC. Wireless internet access on the whole campsite. Sports facilities, massage, restaurant, shop, play area. Mobil homes to rent at: Fa. Gebetsroither GmbH., A-8940 Weißenbach/Liezen, Hauptstraße 6,
Tel. 00 43/3612/26300, Fax: 00 43/3612/26300 4,
E-Mail: office@gebetsroither.com, www.gebetsroither.com

6 Camping Weisses Rössl

Wörthersee-Süd, A-9220 Velden-Auen, Auenstr. 47,
Tel. 00 43/42 74/28 98, Fax 00 43/42 74/28 98-4,
E-Mail: weisses.roessl@aon.at, http://members.aon.at/weisses.roessl
Idyllic and quiet, located in an especially beautiful spot between Velden and Maria Wörth. Private lake beach , two sanitary blocks with free hot water in the showers and wash cabins. Children's play areas, Children's play camp.

7 Strandcamping Brückler Nord

Gerhard Seger, A-9074 Seental Keutschach, Tel. 00 43/42 73/23 84,
Fax 00 43/42 73/210 80, E-Mail: camp.brueckler@aon.at,
www.brueckler.co.at
Family friendly campsite, direct at the bank of Lake Keutschach.
We accept camping cheques.

nformation: Wörthersee-Tourismus
-9220 Velden, Villacher Straße 19

Tel. 00 43/42 74/38 288
Fax 00 43/42 74/38 288-19

E-mail: info@woerthersee.com
woerthersee.com

AU0400 Camping Arneitz

Seeuferlandesstrasse 53, A-9583 Faak am See (Carinthia)

Tel: **042 542 137**. Email: **camping@arneitz.at** **www.alanrogers.com/AU0400**

Directly on Faakersee, Camping Arneitz is one of the best sites in this area, central for the attractions of the region, watersports and walking. Family run, Arneitz led the way with good quality and comprehensive facilities. A newly built reception building at the entrance reflects the quality of the site and apart from reception facilities, has a good collection of tourist literature and three desks with telephones for guests to use. The 400 level, marked pitches are mainly of gravel, off hard roads, with electricity available. Some have good shade from mature trees. Grass pitches are available for tents. There is a delightfully appointed restaurant at the entrance where there is entertainment in high season. Day trips can be made to Venice and many other parts of northern Italy.

Facilities

Splendid family washroom, large, heated and airy, with family cubicles around the walls and in the centre, washbasins at child height in a circle with a working carousel in the middle. Extra, small toilet block nearer the lake. Laundry facilities. Motorcaravan services. Supermarket. Self-service restaurant, bar and terrace. General room with TV. Small cinema for children's films. Beauty salon. Massage and back therapy. Large sauna/solarium. Minigolf. Well equipped playground. Fishing. Bicycle hire. Off site: Riding 3 km. Golf 10 km.

Open: 30 April - 30 September.

Directions

Site is southeast of Villach, southwest of Veldon. Follow signs for Faakersee and Egg rather than for Faak village. From A11 take exit 3 and head towards Egg, turn left at T-junction and go through Egg village. Just after leaving village, site is on right. GPS: N46:34.511 E13:55.996

Charges guide

Per unit incl. 2 persons and electricity	€ 24,10 - € 28,50
extra person	€ 6,80 - € 7,50
child (3-10 yrs)	€ 6,40 - € 7,00

AU0440 Schluga Camping

Obervellach 15, A-9620 Hermagor-Pressegger See (Carinthia)

Tel: **042 822 051**. Email: **camping@schluga.com** **www.alanrogers.com/AU0440**

Schluga Camping is under the same ownership as Schluga Seecamping, some 4 km. to the west of that site in a flat valley with views of the surrounding mountains. The 243 touring pitches are of varying size, 142 with water, drainage and satellite TV connections. Electricity connections are available throughout (10-16A). Mainly on grass covered gravel on either side of tarmac surfaced access roads, they are divided by shrubs and hedges. The site is open all year, to include the winter sports season, and has a well kept tidy appearance, although it may be busy in high season. English is spoken. The site reports a new artificial swimming lake and 23 new pitches for motorcaravans. A new bar and terrace have been added by the lake. Entertainment in high season includes a disco and cinema and a weekly programme sheet details events at both Schluga sites and in the local area.

Facilities

Four sanitary blocks (a splendid new one, plus one modern and two good older ones) are heated in cold weather. Most washbasins in cabins and good showers. Family washrooms for rent. Baby rooms and suite for disabled people. Laundry facilities. Drying rooms and ski rooms. Motorcaravan services. Shop (1/5-30/9). Bar/restaurant (closed Nov). Heated swimming pool (12 x 7 m; 1/5-30/9). Playground. Games room. Bicycle hire. Sauna. Solarium. Fitness centre. Internet.

Open: All year.

Directions

Site is on the B111 Villach - Hermagor road (which is better quality than it appears on most maps) just east of Hermagor town. GPS: N46:37.871 E13:23.749

Charges 2009

Per unit incl. 2 persons and electricity	€ 17,95 - € 27,20
extra person	€ 5,40 - € 8,40
child (5-14 yrs)	€ 3,80 - € 5,70
dog	€ 2,20 - € 2,80

AU0450 Naturpark Schluga Seecamping

A-9620 Hermagor (Carinthia)

Tel: **042 822 051**. Email: **camping@schluga.com** **www.alanrogers.com/AU0450**

This site is pleasantly situated on natural wooded hillside. It is about 300 m. from a small lake with clean water, where the site has a beach of coarse sand and a large grassy meadow where inflatable boats can be kept. It also has a sunbathing area for naturists although this is not a naturist site. The 250 pitches for touring units are on individual, level terraces, many with light shade and all with electricity (10-16A). 124 pitches also have water, drainage and satellite TV and a further 47 pitches are occupied by a tour operator. English is spoken. This part of Carinthia is a little off the beaten track but the site still becomes full in season. Close by is Schluga Camping, under the same ownership, which is open all year. Many walks and attractive car drives are available in the area.

Facilities

Four heated modern toilet blocks are well constructed, with some washbasins in cabins and family washrooms for rent. Facilities for disabled people. Washing machines and dryer. Motorcaravan services. Shop (20/5-10/9). Restaurant/bar by entrance and takeaway (all 20/5-10/9). Playground. Room for young people and children. Films. Kiosk and bar with terrace at beach. Surf school. Pedalo and canoe hire. Aqua jump and Iceberg. Pony rides. Bicycle hire. Fishing. Weekly activity programme with mountain walks and climbs. Internet point. Off site: Tennis (indoor and outdoor).

Open: 10 May - 20 September.

Directions

Site is on the B111 road (Villach - Hermagor) 6 km. east of Hermagor town.
GPS: N46:37.910 E13:26.792

Charges 2009

Per unit incl. 2 persons and electricity	€ 17,95 - € 27,20
extra person	€ 5,40 - € 8,40
child (5-14 yrs)	€ 3,80 - € 5,70
dog	€ 2,20 - € 2,80

Camping Cheques accepted.

AU0475 Camping Brunner am See

Glanzerstraße 108, A-9873 Döbriach (Carinthia)

Tel: **042 467 189**. Email: **office@camping-brunner.at** **www.alanrogers.com/AU0475**

This well appointed site at the eastern end of the Millstätter See, is the only site in the area with its own private beach directly accessible from the site. Consisting of fairly coarse sand, it is regularly cleaned. The 236 marked pitches (60-95 sq.m), all for touring units, are nearly all serviced with water, drainage and electric hook-ups (6A), and are in rows on level grass, with tarmac access roads. The site is fairly open with some shade from bushes and trees. The site owns land on the opposite side of the road, which includes forest walks, a dog walk, a parking area and one of the playgrounds.

Facilities

A new building behind reception houses the well appointed sanitary unit. Good facilities for disabled campers, especially handicapped children, plus a children's room with low level showers, basins, baby baths, changing deck etc. Family bathrooms (some for rent), some washbasins in cubicles, laundry facilities. Motorcaravan service point. Site owned supermarket adjacent. Communal barbecue. Internet access. WiFi. Fishing. Watersports. Off site: Supermarket (May - Oct). Several restaurants (some open all year). Tennis 100 m. Bicycle hire 300 m. with access to cycle route around Millstätter See. Riding 1.5 km. Golf 10 km. Skiing area 11 km.

Open: All year.

Directions

Döbriach is at the eastern end of the Millstätter See, about 15 km. southwest of Spittal. Leave A10, exit 139 (Spittal, Millstätter), then proceed alongside northern shore of lake through Millstatt towards Döbriach. Just before Döbriach turn right and after 1.5 km. turn right at roundabout. Site is on right after 100 m. GPS: N46:46.056 E13:38.910

Charges guide

Per unit incl. 2 persons and electricity	€ 19,00 - € 35,70
extra person	€ 6,00 - € 8,10
child (4-18 yrs)	€ 4,00 - € 7,50
dog	€ 2,20 - € 3,50

Discounts for senior citizens in low season.

AU0480 Komfort-Campingpark Burgstaller

Seefeldstrasse 16, A-9873 Döbriach (Carinthia)

Tel: **042 467 774**. Email: **info@burgstaller.co.at** **www.alanrogers.com/AU0480**

This is one of Austria's top sites in a beautiful location and with all the amenities you could want. You can always tell a true family run site by the attention to detail and this site oozes perfection. This is an excellent family site with a very friendly atmosphere, particularly in the restaurant in the evenings. Good English is spoken. The 600 pitches (560 for tourists) are on flat, well drained grass, backing onto hedges on either side of access roads. All fully serviced (including WiFi), they vary in size (45-120 sq.m.) and there are special pitches for motorcaravans. One pitch actually rotates and follows the sun during the course of the day! The latest sanitary block warrants an architectural award; all toilets have a TV and a pirate ship on the first floor of the children's area sounds its guns every hour. The site entrance is directly opposite the park leading to the bathing lido, to which campers have free access. There is also a heated swimming pool. Much activity is organised here, including games and competitions for children and there are special Easter and autumn events.

Facilities

Three exceptionally good quality toilet blocks include washbasins in cabins, facilities for children and disabled visitors, dishwashers and underfloor heating for cool weather. Seven private rooms for rent (3 with jacuzzi baths). Motorcaravan services. Good restaurant with terrace (May-Oct). Shop (May-Sept). Bowling alley. Disco (July/Aug). TV room. Sauna and solarium. Two play areas (one for under 6s, the other for 6-12 yrs). Bathing and boating in lake. Special entrance rate for lake attractions. Fishing. Bicycle hire. Mountain bike area. Riding. Comprehensive entertainment programmes. Covered stage and outdoor arena provide for church services (Protestant and Catholic, in German) and folk and modern music concerts. Off site: Mountain walks, climbing and farm visits all in local area.

Open: 4 April - 5 November.

Directions

Döbriach is at the eastern end of the Millstätter See about 15 km. southeast of Spittal. Leave A10 at exit 139 (Spittal, Millstätter) then proceed alongside northern shore of lake through Millstätter towards Döbriach. Just before Döbriach turn right and after 1 km. site is on left. GPS: N46:46.208 E13:38.875

Charges guide

Per unit incl. 2 persons and electricity	€ 20,40 - € 32,50
extra person	€ 7,00 - € 10,00
child (4-14 yrs)	€ 5,00 - € 7,50
dog	€ 2,50 - € 3,00

Discounts for retired people in low season.

AU0445 Alpencamp Kötschach Mauthen

A 9640 Kötschach Mauthen (Carinthia)

Tel: **047 154 29**. Email: **info@alpencamp.at** **www.alanrogers.com/AU0445**

Materials hundreds of millions of years old, centuries old crafts and practices, together with the very latest technology have been combined in the construction of this environmental award winning site. Four years in the planning, Alpencamp is a showplace of how using techniques available today, comfortable, attractive and environmentally friendly accommodation can be realised. Set against an impressive panorama of mountains in the beautiful Lesactal, this quiet family run site has 85 pitches all with electricity; they are level, on grass with some tree shade.

Facilities

Modern well maintained sanitary facilities. Free hot showers, washbasins in cabins. Laundry. Motorcaravan service point. Shop with fresh bread each morning. Comfortable and bright restaurant with bar. Playground and playroom for children. Free internet terminal in reception, WiFi over site. Off site: Walking, cycling, mountain bike trails, climbing, riding. Aquarena, swimming pool, wellness centre. Rafting, canoeing, fishing. During winter, skiing and other winter sports.

Open: All year excl. 1 November - 14 December.

Directions

Coming from Villach on the 111, in town at the junction with the 110 turn left then after 200 m. turn right and continue along the 111 towards Lesachtal. After 500 m. site is to the left. GPS: N46:40.185 E12:59.477

Charges guide

Per unit incl. 2 persons and electricity	€ 14,90 - € 22,20
extra person	€ 4,10 - € 6,40
child (3-13 yrs)	€ 2,50 - € 3,90

AU0425 Seecamping Berghof

Ossiachersee Süduferstraße 241, A-9523 Villach Landskron (Carinthia)

Tel: **042 424 1133**. Email: **office@seecamping-berghof.at** **www.alanrogers.com/AU0425**

This surely must be the ultimate camping experience: a perfect location, excellent facilities, great pitches and a welcome to match. The Ertl family and their staff manage this 480 pitch site to perfection. Use of the natural topography means that you actually think you are in a small site wherever you camp. Constant improvements mean that the number of pitches slowly reduces as larger and more equipped places are provided. There are 190 pitches with water, electricity and drainage and many pitches have access to the internet.

Facilities

Five modern toilet blocks spread around the site, provide the usual facilities including special provision for young children and babies in two blocks. Facilities for disabled people. Supermarket. Restaurant with terrace, takeaway and games room for older children. Play area. Daily club (ages 4-11 yrs). Bicycle hire. Watersports, boat hire and windsurfing school. Minigolf. Swimming possible in the lake. Skateboard park. Off site: Fishing. Villach 5 km.

Open: 1 April - 20 October.

Directions

From A10 take exit 178, which travelling south is just after the tunnel. Head towards Ossiacher See and after 1 km. turn right towards Ossiacher See Sud. At traffic lights turn left and site is 3.5 km. on the left just after entering hamlet of Heiligengestade. GPS: N46:39.272 E13:55.768

Charges guide

Per person	€ 5,00 - € 8,00
pitch	€ 7,50 - € 12,50

AU0405 Sommer & Winter Camping Ramsbacher

Gries 53, A-9863 Rennweg (Carinthia)

Tel: **047 346 63** **www.alanrogers.com/AU0405**

This is a beautiful small site set in a high alpine valley with great views in every direction. With 72 touring pitches, all with electricity, this is a great site for those seeking peace and quiet and the opportunity to explore the local area either by bike or on foot. The site is well placed in the Katschberg Mountains and close to the Pölital nature reserve. Cars are not allowed in the national park in the summer so entry is via a small 'train'. In winter the site is very well placed for local skiing.

Facilities

Toilet facilities are clean, heated and modern with free showers but a communal changing area. Washing machine, dryer and drying area. Attractive restaurant/bar. Small play area. Off site: Swimming pool, minigolf, tennis, rollerskating and play area 25 m. Winter skiing with free shuttle bus.

Open: All year.

Directions

From A10 take exit 113 (just south of the Katschberg toll tunnel) and turn towards Rennweg. Turn right a little later into the village and then right again towards Oberdorf where site is well signed. Alternatively from the A10 exit, climb the hill from the junction and then turn left down towards Oberdorf. GPS: N47:01.560 E13:35.430

Charges guide

Per person	€ 5,20 - € 5,50
pitch	€ 6,50 - € 7,00
electricity	€ 2,00

AU0490 Camping Terrassen Maltatal

Malta 6, A-9854 Maltatal (Carinthia)

Tel: **047 332 34**. Email: **info@maltacamp.at** **www.alanrogers.com/AU0490**

Situated between two national parks in a valley between the mountains, this site offers spectacular views over the surrounding area especially from the pool which is over 300 sq.m. with a grassy sunbathing area and is open to all (free for campers). There are 220 grass pitches on narrow terraces (70-100 sq.m) and mostly in rows on either side of narrow access roads. Numbered and marked, some separated with low hedges, all have electricity and 90 have water and drainage (the electric boxes are often inconveniently located on the next terrace). The 'Kärnten-card' is available to purchase from the site, giving free travel on public transport and free entry to many attractions.

Facilities

Two toilet blocks, one with underfloor heating, have about half the washbasins in cabins and 10 family wash cabins. Facilities for babies and children. Laundry facilities. Motorcaravan services. Only basic provisions kept. Restaurant. Swimming pool (20/5-15/9). Sauna. Playground. Bicycle hire. Riding. Entertainment programme and many walks and excursions.
Off site: Village 500 m. Fishing or golf 6 km. Malta High alpine road, Reisseck mountain railways and The Porsche Museum in Gmund are all nearby.

Open: Easter - 31 October.

Directions

Site is 15 km. north of Spittal. Leave A10 at exit 129 Gmund. Pass through Gmund towards Malta. Site is on right 6 km. from autobahn exit.
GPS: N46:56.990 E13:30.576

Charges guide

Per person	€ 4,70 - € 6,90
child (2-14 yrs)	€ 3,40 - € 4,50
pitch incl. electricity	€ 6,20 - € 9,10
incl. water and drainage	€ 8,80 - € 10,90
dog	€ 2,20 - € 2,60

Electricity included. Less for longer stays.
Camping Cheques accepted.

MALTATAL
The campsite at 800 m altitude between the «Hohe Tauern» and «Nockberge» national parks, with amazing panoramic views.
Terrassencamping Maltatal
A-9854 Malta 5-6, Kärnten • Tel. 0043-4733-234 • Fax 0043-4733-23416 • www.maltacamp.at • info@maltacamp.at

AU0460 Terrassen Camping Ossiacher See

Ostriach 67, A-9570 Ossiach (Carinthia)

Tel: **042 434 36**. Email: **martinz@camping.at** **www.alanrogers.com/AU0460**

This gently sloping site has been partly terraced to provide good, level pitches. The site is protected by rising hills and enjoys lovely views across the lake to the mountains beyond. Trees, flowers, hedges and bushes abound, adding atmosphere to this neat, tidy site. The 530 pitches (429 with electricity) are in rows on the level grass terraces, separated by hard roads and some marked by hedges. There is shade in parts and electricity connections (4/6A) throughout. A separate area (25 pitches only) is provided for campers with dogs. Used by tour operators (28 pitches). Good English is spoken.

Facilities

Five well maintained sanitary blocks are heated in cool weather, and some with washbasins in cabins. 10 family washrooms (charged), baby rooms and facilities for disabled campers. Laundry facilities. Motorcaravan services. Restaurant (15/5-15/9). Well stocked supermarket. ATM. High season entertainment programme. Playgrounds, games rooms and disco courtyard. Waterskiing and windsurfing schools and boats for hire. Tennis. Bicycle and moped hire. Fishing. Riding.
Off site: Cycle path around lake. Hang-gliding possibilities in area.

Open: 1 May - 30 September.

Directions

Site is directly on the lake shore, 1.5 km. southwest of Ossiach village. Leave the A10 at exit 178 for Ossiacher See, turn left on road B94 towards Feldkirchen and shortly right to Ossiach Sud. The site is shortly before Ossiach.
GPS: N46:39.825 E13:58.495

Charges 2009

Per unit incl. 2 persons and electricity	€ 22,10 - € 33,20
extra person	€ 5,60 - € 8,30
child (3-12 yrs)	free - € 5,60
dog	€ 3,00

MAP 2

A small country divided into three regions, Flanders in the north, Wallonia in the south and Brussels the capital. Belgium is rich in scenic countryside, culture and history, notably the great forest of Ardennes, the historic cities of Bruges and Ghent and the western coastline with its sandy beaches.

CAPITAL: BRUSSELS

Tourist Office

Belgian Tourist Office Brussels & Wallonia,
217 Marsh Wall, London E14 9FJ
Tel: 020 7537 1132 Fax: 020 7531 0393
Email: info@belgiumtheplaceto.be
Internet: www.belgiumtheplaceto.be

Tourism Flanders-Brussels,
Flanders House, 1a Cavendish Square,
London W1G 0LD
Tel: 020 7307 7738
Email: info@visitflanders.co.uk

Brussels is at the very heart of Europe and doubles as the capital of the European Union. A multi-cultural and multi-lingual city full of remarkable monuments, interesting museums and highly acclaimed restaurants. In the French speaking region of Wallonia lies the mountainous Ardennes, an area famous for its forests, lakes, streams and grottoes, making it a popular holiday destination, especially for those who like nature and walking. The safe, sandy beaches on the west coast run for forty miles. Here lies Ostend, a popular seaside resort with an eight kilometre long beach and a promenade coupled with a bustling harbour and shops. Bruges is Europe's best preserved medieval city and is certainly one of the most attractive, whether you want to relax on a boat trip along the canals, explore the narrow streets or visit one of the many churches and art museums.

Population

10.6 million

Climate

Temperate climate similar to Britain.

Language

There are three official languages. French is spoken in the south, Flemish in the north, and German is the predominant language in the eastern provinces.

Telephone

The country code is 00 32.

Money

Currency: The Euro
Banks: Mon-Fri 09.00-15.30.
Some banks open Sat 09.00-12.00.

Shops

Mon-Sat 09.00-17.30/18.00 hrs - later on Thurs/Fri; closed Sundays.

Public Holidays

New Year's Day; Easter Mon; Labour Day; Ascension; Whit Monday; Flemish Day 11 July; National Day 21 July; Assumption 15 Aug; French Day 27 Sept; All Saints 1, 2 Nov; Armistice Day 11 Nov; King's Birthday 15 Nov; Christmas 25, 26 Dec.

Motoring

For cars with a caravan or trailer, motorways are toll free except for the Liefenshoek Tunnel in Antwerp. Maximum permitted overall length of vehicle/trailer or caravan combination is 18 m. Blue Zone parking areas exist in Brussels, Ostend, Bruges, Liège, Antwerp and Gent. Parking discs can be obtained from police stations, garages, some shops.

CAMPING IN
BELGIAN LIMBURG.
ENJOYMENT IS IN OUR NATURE.

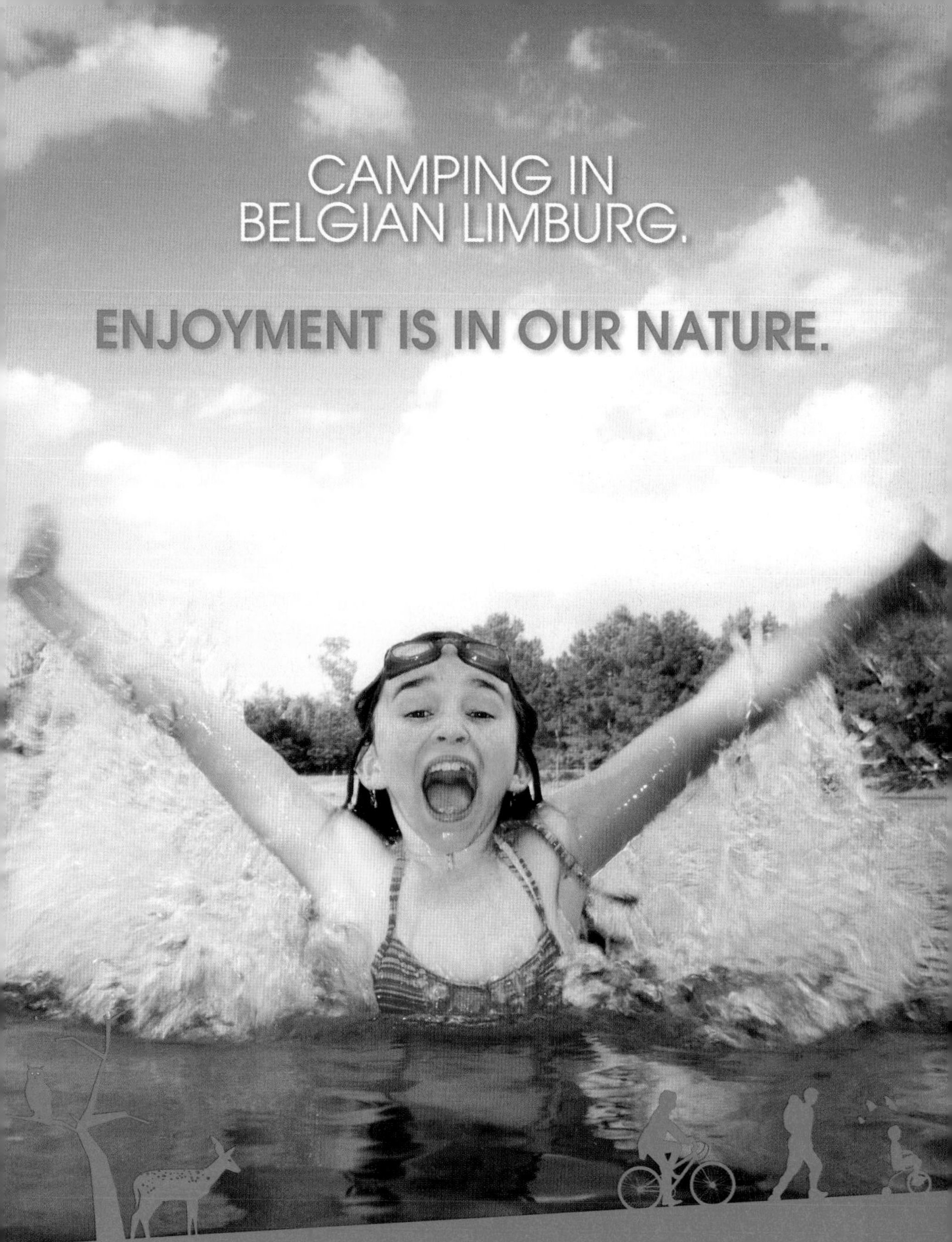

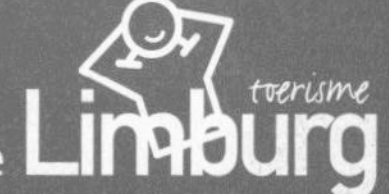

BE0650 Camping Floréal-Club Het Veen

Eekhoornlaan 1, B-2960 Sint Job in't Goor (Antwerp)

Tel: **036 361 327**. Email: **het.veen@florealclub.be** **www.alanrogers.com/BE0650**

Floréal Club Het Veen can be found 20 km. north of Antwerp in a woodland area, and with many sports facilities. There are 345 marked pitches (60 for tourists) on level grass, most with some shade and electricity (10A, long leads in some places) and also seven hardstandings. Amenities include an indoor sports hall (charged per hour) and courts for tennis, football, basketball and softball are outside. Good cycling and walking opportunities exist in the area. English is spoken.

Facilities

Four spacious toilet blocks include a few washbasins in cubicles (only two are close to touring pitches). Facilities for disabled people. Laundry facilities. Motorcaravan services. Shop. Restaurant, bar, café and takeaway (daily July/Aug. weekends only at other times). Tennis. Badminton. Boules. Playgrounds and entertainment for children in season. Fishing. Canoeing. Bicycle hire. Wooden chalets for rent. Off site: Riding and golf 8 km.

Open: 1 March - 31 October.

Directions

Sint Job In't Goor is northeast of Antwerp. From A1 (E19) exit 4, turn southeast towards Sint Job in't Goor, straight on at traffic lights and, immediately after canal bridge, turn left at campsite sign. Continue straight on for about 1.5 km. to site. GPS: N51:18.307 E04:35.173

Charges guide

Per person	€ 3,80
child (3-11 yrs)	€ 2,80
pitch incl. electricity	€ 9,40
hiker/cyclist and tent	€ 5,70

BE0530 Camping du Waux-Hall

Avenue Saint-Pierre 17, B-7000 Mons (Hainault)

Tel: **065 337 923**. Email: **ot1@ville.mons.be** **www.alanrogers.com/BE0530**

Waux-Hall is a useful and convenient site for a longer look at historic Mons and the surrounding area. It is a well laid out municipal site, close to the town centre and E42 motorway. The 75 pitches, most with electricity (10A), are arranged on either side of an oval road, on grass and divided by beds of small shrubs; the landscape maintenance is excellent. The pitches are small and manoeuvring could be difficult for larger units. A large public park with refreshment bar, tennis, a playground and a lake are adjacent, with direct access from the site when the gate is unlocked.

Facilities

A single, heated toilet block is of older style, basic but clean, with most washbasins in cubicles for ladies. Washing machine and dryer. Soft drinks machine and ice cream. Bicycle hire. Tennis. Playground. Off site: Public park adjacent. Town centre shops and restaurants within easy walking distance. Fishing 300 m. Riding 2 km. Golf 4 km.

Open: All year.

Directions

From Mons inner ring road, follow signs for Charleroi, La Louviere, Binche, Beaumont. When turning off the ring road, keep to right hand lane, turning for site is immediately first right (signed Waux-Hall and camping). GPS: N50:28.082 E03:57.777

Charges guide

Per unit incl. 1 person	€ 5,20 - € 6,10
extra adult	€ 3,35
child (0-12 yrs)	€ 2,15
electricity after 2 nights (per kWh)	€ 0,15

No credit cards.

BE0550 Kompas Camping Nieuwpoort

Brugsesteenweg 49, B-8620 Nieuwpoort (West Flanders)

Tel: **058 236 037**. Email: **nieuwpoort@kompascamping.be** **www.alanrogers.com/BE0550**

Near Ostend, this large site with 952 pitches caters particularly for families. There are many on-site amenities including a heated pool complex with two pools, a children's pool and a water slide, many sporting activities, and a children's farm. The numbered pitches, all with electricity, are in regular rows on flat grass. With 386 seasonal units and 71 caravan holiday homes, the site becomes full during Belgian holidays and in July/August. A network of footpaths links all areas of the site, gates to the rear lead to a reservoir reserved for sailing, windsurfing and canoeing (canoes for hire) during certain hours only. The site is well fenced, with a card operated barrier and a night guard.

Facilities

Seven functional, clean and well maintained toilet blocks include washbasins in cubicles. The blocks are accessible to disabled people. Motorcaravan services. Supermarket, bakery, restaurant and café/bar (weekends and Belgian holidays outside July/Aug). Takeaway. Swimming pools with slide and pool games (21/5-13/9). Tennis. Adventure playground. Minigolf. Entertainment programme July/Aug. Off site: Fishing and bicycle hire within 500 m. Riding 3 km. Golf driving range 5 km. Nearest village is 2 km. Beach 4 km.

Open: 27 March - 11 November.

Directions

From E40 take exit 4 (Middelkerke - Diksmuide). Turn towards Diksmuide following signs to Nieuwport. Pass through Sint-Joris and IC-Camping is on the right. GPS: N51:07.778 E02:46.333

Charges 2009

Per family (max 6 persons) in Jul/Aug and B.Hs	€ 22,50 - € 33,50
electricity	€ 2,40
dog	€ 2,40

Largest unit accepted 2.5 x 8 m.
Less 10% with camping carnet.
Camping Cheques accepted.

BE0595 Kompas Camping Oudenaarde

Kortrijkstraat 342, B-9700 Oudenaarde (East Flanders)

Tel: **055 315 473**. Email: **oudenaarde@kompascamping.be** **www.alanrogers.com/BE0595**

This is an extensive holiday site with 381 pitches, 179 of which are for touring. The remainder are occupied by 190 seasonal units, rental or private chalets, and a few pitches for a tour operator. Pitches are generally on grass, all with 10A electricity (31 also with water) and are of a reasonable size, some divided by hedges. A separate area for motorcaravans is close to the main entrance with a drive-over service point adjacent (tokens from reception). The majority of the services are grouped around a central square close to reception, but some of the sporting facilities are at the far end of the site by the pool complex.

Facilities

Four toilet blocks all of a similar design include some facilities for babies and disabled campers. Block E has some washbasins in cubicles. Bar/restaurant and takeaway (30/3-11/11, weekends only outside July/August, public holidays). Shop. Swimming pool. Indoor playroom and several playgrounds for children. Boules. Tennis. Bicycle hire. Fishing. Children's entertainment and activities programme in July/August. Off site: Golf 3 km. Shops and other services in Oudenaarde 4 km. Riding 7 km.

Open: 27 March - 11 November.

Directions

Oudenaarde is 25 km. south of Ghent. From main N60 (Ghent-Ronse) road, take exit to Avelgem on N453. (just north of River Schelde). Continue west for 2.5 km. and follow rather small site signs to your right. GPS: N50:50.459 E03:34.476

Charges 2009

Per unit incl. 4 persons	€ 21,50 - € 30,50
electricity	€ 2,40
dog	€ 2,40

Camping Cheques accepted.

BE0565 Kompas Camping Westende

Bassevillestraat 141, B-8434 Westende (West Flanders)
Tel: **058 223 025**. Email: **westende@kompascamping.be** **www.alanrogers.com/BE0565**

Part of the Kompas chain, Camping Westende is another large holiday site with 422 pitches. Of these 130 are taken by seasonal units and five chalets, leaving around 300 touring pitches. These are generally individual, on grass and with 10A electricity. There are 39 multi service pitches with water, waste water drainage and electricity. When we visited, some pitches were looking rather well worn and untidy and would have benefited from a good clean up and re-seeding. The rigid pitching policy dictates that caravans have to be placed on a specific side of the pitch, which may mean that you have to manhandle your UK-built van into a nose in situation.

Facilities

Four main toilet blocks are in modern style but suffer from heavy use and variable maintenance and cleaning. Facilities for children and disabled people at each block. Shop, bar, restaurant and takeaway (Easter - 14/11, but weekends only outside July/Aug. and certain public holidays). Adventure playground. Tennis. Boules. Children's entertainment and activities programme (July/Aug). Off site: Fishing 20 m. Golf 100 m. Beach 800 m. Bicycle hire 500 m. Riding and sailing 5 km. Markets in Nieuwpoort Friday, Middelkerke Thursday.

Open: Easter - 14 November.

Directions

Westende is 15 km. southwest of Ostende. From A18 (E40) take exit 3 to Nieuwpoort, turn right at traffic lights in town centre, and follow road round to the left, turning right at American War Memorial, and almost immediately left towards Westende. In Westende continue along the main street, passing two sites on the right, turn left into Hovenierstraat (site sign is very small). Site entrance is straight ahead at far end of street. GPS: N51:09.487 E02:45.628

Charges 2009

Per unit incl. 4 persons	€ 22,50 - € 33,50
electricity	€ 2,40
dog	€ 2,40

Camping Cheques accepted.

BE0555 Recreatiepark Klein Strand

Varsenareweg 29, B-8490 Jabbeke (West Flanders)
Tel: **050 811 440**. Email: **info@kleinstrand.be** **www.alanrogers.com/BE0555**

In a convenient location, only 10 km. from Bruges, this site is in two distinct areas divided by an access road. The touring half of the campsite has 128 large pitches on flat grass and all with electricity. This central block of touring pitches is surrounded by semi-permanent caravans on the outer edges and it is a surprisingly relaxing area. The static half is closer to the lake and this area has most of the amenities. These include the main reception building, two restaurants, takeaways, bar, minimarket, and most of the sports facilities. This is a family holiday site with plenty of activities. A comprehensive programme of activities and entertainment is provided in July/August. Water-ski shows take place on the lake (every Sunday in July/August at 5pm), and there is a water-ski school (charged for). The lake also has a swimming area with a slide (lifeguard) and beach volleyball area. In low season the site would also make a good base for sightseeing.

Facilities

A single modern, heated, toilet block in the touring area provides the usual facilities including good sized showers (charged) and vanity style open washbasins. Facilities for disabled campers. Laundry. Additional toilet facilities are located behind the touring field reception building and are opened for July/August. Motorcaravan service point. In high season a fun pool for small children. Barrier card deposit € 25. Off site: Golf 10 km. Riding 5 km.

Open: All year.

Directions

From Dunkirk take A10, then exit 6B signed Jabbeke. At roundabout take first exit signed for site. If missed, there is a second turn after a further 200 m. GPS: N51:11.071 E03:06.268

Charges guide

Per unit incl. up to 6 persons and electricity	€ 16,00 - € 31,00
dog	€ 2,00

BE0520 Camping de Blekker

Jachtwakersstraat 12, B-8670 Koksijde aan Zee (West Flanders)

Tel: **058 511 633**. Email: **camping.deblekker@belgacom.net** **www.alanrogers.com/BE0520**

This family owned site, adjacent to a 186 hectare nature reserve on the Belgium coast, is divided into two sections: de Blekker and Blekkerdal. De Blekker has 178 pitches with 75 allocated for touring units, all with 10A electricity. The pitches are grassy with some dividing hedges and trees. Visitors should drive to the de Blekker reception but will be given a choice of where to park. Local attractions include the Koksijde annual Flower Market and Floral Pageant, National Fishery Museum and horseback shrimp fishing in Oostduinkerke, and Plopsaland (a small theme park) or Clown City in De Panne.

Facilities

Each section has a single modern sanitary unit including washbasins in cubicles. Facilities for babies and disabled persons (other than for washbasins, hot water is on payment throughout). Laundry. Small infirmary with bed. Bicycle hire. Internet access (in reception). English is spoken. Barbecues are not permitted in hot weather. Off site: Shop in nearest village 300 m. Restaurant and bars 0.4-3 km. Riding 1 km. Fishing and boat launching 1.5 km.

Open: 1 April - 15 November.

Directions

From A16 (E40) take junction 1A, then the N8 towards Koksijde. At roundabout take N396 towards Koksijde Dorp and then turn towards Koksijde-aan-zee. Follow small yellow site signs. Site entrance road is on the right.
GPS: N51:06.685 E02:39.141

Charges guide

Per unit incl. 4 persons € 19,00 - € 27,00

Special rates for Ascension, Pentecost and Easter weekends. 10% discount on production of Alan Rogers Guide. Camping Cheques accepted.

BE0560 Camping De Lombarde

Elisabethlaan 4, B-8434 Lombardsijde Middelkerke (West Flanders)

Tel: **058 236 839**. Email: **info@delombarde.be** **www.alanrogers.com/BE0560**

De Lombarde is a spacious, good value holiday site, between Lombardsijde and the coast. It has a pleasant atmosphere and modern buildings. The 380 pitches are set out in level, grassy bays surrounded by shrubs, all with electricity (16/20A), long leads may be needed. Vehicles are parked in separate car parks. There are many seasonal units and 22 holiday homes, leaving 180 touring pitches. There is a range of activities (listed below) and an entertainment programme in season. This is a popular holiday area and the site becomes full at peak times. A pleasant stroll takes you into Lombardsijde. There is a tram service to the town or the beach.

Facilities

Three modern heated, clean sanitary units are of an acceptable standard, with some washbasins in cubicles. Facilities for disabled people. Large laundry. Motorcaravan services. Shop (1/4-31/8). Restaurant/bar and takeaway (July/Aug. plus weekends and holidays 21/3-11/11). Tennis. Boules. Fishing lake. TV lounge. Animation programme for children. Playground. Internet access (in the bar). Torch useful. Off site: Beach 400 m. Riding and golf 500 m. Bicycle hire 1 km.

Open: All year.

Directions

Coming from Westende, follow the tramlines. From traffic lights in Lombardsijde, turn left following tramlines into Zeelaan. Continue following tramlines until crossroads and tram stop, turn left into Elisabethlaan. Site is on right after 200 m.
GPS: N51:09.381 E02:45.222

Charges guide

Per unit incl. 1-6 persons and electricity	€ 16,50 - € 29,50
dog (1 per pitch)	€ 2,60

No credit cards.

BE0580 Camping Memling

Veltemweg 109, B-8310 Brugge (West Flanders)

Tel: **050 355 845**. Email: **info@campingmemling.be** **www.alanrogers.com/BE0580**

This traditional site is ideal for visiting Brugge. The 100 unmarked pitches (60 for touring units) are on slightly undulating grass, with gravel roads and trees and hedges providing some shade. Electricity (6A) is available to 40 pitches. There is a separate area for tents. Bars, restaurants, local shops and supermarkets are within walking distance. Brugge itself has a network of cycle ways and for those on foot a bus runs into the centre from the campsite. Reservation in July and August is necessary. Visitors with large units should always telephone in advance to ensure an adequate pitch.

Facilities

Heated toilet facilities are clean and tidy, including some washbasins in cubicles. Facilities for disabled visitors. Laundry with washing machine and dryer. Freezer. Club/TV room for 30 persons. Bicycle hire. Internet access. Off site: Municipal swimming pool (open all year) and park nearby. Supermarkets 250 m. The Maldegem Steam Centre and narrow gauge railway are 12 km. To the southwest of the town is the Boudewijn park and dolphinarium.

Open: All year.

Directions

From R30 Brugge ring road take exit 6 onto N9 towards Maldegem. At Sint-Kruis turn right at traffic lights, where site signed (close to garage and supermarket, opposite MacDonald's).
GPS: N51:12.415 E03:15.776

Charges guide

Per person	€ 5,00
child (under 15 yrs)	€ 4,00
pitch	€ 11,00 - € 25,00
electricity	€ 2,00
dog	€ 2,00

BE0740 Camping l'Eau Rouge

Cheneux 25, B-4970 Stavelot (Liège)

Tel: **080 863 075** **www.alanrogers.com/BE0740**

A popular, lively and attractively situated site, L'Eau Rouge is in a sheltered valley close to Spa and the Grand Prix circuit. There are 180 grassy pitches of 110 sq.m. on sloping ground either side of a central road (speed bumps) – 60 are taken by permanent units and 120 for touring units. The main building houses the busy reception, shop, bar and the main sanitary facilities. There are plenty of sporting activities in the area including skiing and luge in winter. The site is close to the motor race circuit at Spa Francorchamps and is within walking distance for the fit. The site's Dutch owners have embarked on a five year programme upgrading the infrastructure and have other ideas in the pipeline.

Facilities

There is a main block but a smaller unit serves the touring area. Good numbers of British WCs, mostly open washbasins, but rather fewer hot showers (free) which could be stretched at times. Additional facilities should be available in the near future. Shop. Baker calls daily at 08.30 (in season). Takeaway (in summer). Bar. Boules. Archery (free lessons in high season). Playground. Entertainment in season. Off site: Bicycle hire 6 km. Riding 10 km. Spa Francorchamps motor racing circuit.

Open: All year.

Directions

Site is 1 km. east of Stavelot on the road to the race circuit. Leave E42 exit 11 Malmédy, at roundabout follow signs for Stavelot. At end of road at T-junction turn right, then first right.
GPS: N50:24.722 E05:57.190

Charges guide

Per unit incl. 2 persons and electricity	€ 17,50
extra person	€ 2,25
child (4-15 yrs)	€ 2,00
dog	€ 1,00

BE0735 Panoramacamping Petite Suisse

Al Bounire 27, B-6960 Dochamps (Luxembourg)

Tel: **084 444 030**. Email: **info@petitesuisse.be** **www.alanrogers.com/BE0735**

This quiet site is set in the picturesque countryside of the Belgium Ardennes, a region in which rivers flow through valleys bordered by vast forests where horses are still usefully employed. Set on a southerly slope, the site is mostly open and offers wide views of the surrounding countryside. The 205 touring pitches, all with 10A electricity, are either on open sloping ground or in terraced rows with hedges between the rows and with trees providing some separation. Gravel roads provide access around the site. To the right of the entrance barrier a large wooden building houses reception, a bar and a restaurant. Close by is an attractive outdoor pool with wide terraces surrounded by grass. Behind this is a large children's play area adjoining a small terrace. Although the site has many activities on offer the opportunity should not be missed to make excursions into the countryside with its hills and forests. The villages are filled with houses built from the local stone, and small inviting bars and restaurants. Member of the 'Ardenne and Gaume Group'.

Facilities

All the facilities that one would expect of a large site are available. Showers are free, washbasins both open and in cabins. Baby room. Laundry room with washing machines and dryers. Shop. Restaurant, bar and takeaway. Swimming pool, paddling pool and slide. Sports field. Tennis. Bicycle hire. Playground and club for children. Entertainment programme (24/4-1/11). Varied activity programme, including archery, canoeing, climbing, abseiling and walking. WiFi (free). Off site: La Roche en Ardennes 10 km. Baraque de Fraiture (ski resort) 10 km. Golf 20 km.

Open: All year.

Directions

From E25/A26 autoroute (Liège - Luxembourg) take exit 50 then the N89 southwest towards La Roche. After 8 km. turn right (north) on N841 to Dochamps where site is signed. GPS: N50:13.832 E05:37.549

Charges 2009

Per pitch incl. 2 persons and electricity	€ 19,50 - € 27,00
extra person (over 4 yrs)	€ 4,25 - € 5,00
dog	€ 4,00 - € 5,00

Camping Cheques accepted.

BE0570 Camping Jeugdstadion

Bolwerkstraat 1, B-8900 Ieper (West Flanders)

Tel: **057 217 282**. Email: **info@jeugdstadion.be** **www.alanrogers.com/BE0570**

Camping Jeugdstadion is a small municipal close to the historic old town. At present there are only 21 caravan pitches, 12 on hardstandings and all with electricity (6A), plus a separate area for 15 tents. At the end of Leopold III Laan is the Menin Gate built in 1927, which bears the names of British and Commonwealth soldiers who lost their lives between 1914-1918. The last post is sounded beneath the gate at 8 pm. every evening in their honour.

Facilities

The modern, heated but fairly basic toilet block can struggle to cope in busy periods. It has cold water to washbasins and three sinks for dishwashing outside. Bicycle hire. Minigolf. Boules. Barrier key deposit € 24.79 or £20. Off site: Sports complex adjacent. Indoor and outdoor swimming pools 500 m. Very large comprehensive playground. Minigolf. During school holidays these facilities are extensively used by local children and can therefore be fairly busy and lively.

Open: 16 March - 31 October.

Directions

Site is southeast of the city centre. From N336 (Lille) at roundabout by the Lille Gate, turn left on Picanolaan and first right into Leopold III laan. Jeugdstadion entrance is on the right. Use roadside parking and book in at 'Kantine' inside gates, or go straight to vehicle gate and walk through the site to book in. GPS: N50:51.059 E02:53.400

Charges guide

Per person	€ 3,00
caravan pitch incl. electricity	€ 4,50

BE0578 Camping Ter Duinen

Wenduinsesteenweg 143, B-8421 De Haan (West Flanders)

Tel: **050 413 593**. Email: **infolawrence.sansens@scarlet.com** **www.alanrogers.com/BE0578**

Ter Duinen is a large, seaside holiday site with 120 touring pitches and over 700 privately owned static holiday caravans. The pitches are laid out in straight lines each side of tarmac roads and the site has three immaculate toilet blocks. Other than a bar, and a playing field, the site has little else to offer, but it is only a 400 m. walk to the sea and next door to the site is a large sports complex with a sub-tropical pool and several sporting facilities. Opportunities for riding and golf (18-hole course) are close by. It is possible to hire bicycles in the town. Best places to visit for a daytrip are Oostende with the Atlantic Wall from WWII, Knokke (which holds many summer festivals) and Brugge.

Facilities

Three modern toilet blocks have good fittings, washbasins in cubicles (hot and cold water) and showers (€ 1.20). Baby bath. Facilities for disabled visitors. Two launderettes with two washing machines and a dryer, irons and ironing boards. Motorcaravan service point. Shop (closed Wed). Snack bar. Off site: Sea with sandy beach 400 m. Bicycle hire 400 m. Riding 1 km. Golf 3 km. Boat launching 6 km. A bus for Brugge stops 200 m. from the site, a tram for the coast 400 m.

Open: 16 March - 15 October.

Directions

On E40 in either direction take exit for De Haan/Jabbeke. In De Haan drive through centre and turn right in front of the station (don't cross the tramlines). Follow the Wenduinsesteenweg to the site on the right. GPS: N51:16.319 E03:01.979

Charges guide

Per unit incl. 2 persons and electricity	€ 17,00 - € 23,00
extra person	€ 2,50
child (under 10 yrs)	€ 2,00

Camping Cheques accepted.

BE0778 Vakantiepark Mooi Zutendaal

Roelerweg 13, B-3690 Zutendaal (Limburg)

Tel: **089 715527**. Email: **info@mooi-zutendaal.be** **www.alanrogers.com/BE0778**

This family site in Belgian Limburg is situated at the edge of the National Park Hoge Kempen which offers 6,000 hectares of nature. The beautiful landscape of valleys, moors and pine forests provides an ideal opportunity for walking or cycling tours. There are 130 comfort pitches available for touring on flat grass and separated by good hedges. There is a wide range of bungalows (6-12 persons) to rent. Swimming is possible all year as there are both outdoor and indoor pools. The interesting Dutch towns of Valkenburg and Maastricht are close by, as is the friendly Belgian town of Hasselt.

Facilities

The modern toilet block includes facilities for disabled visitors. Laundry. Supermarket. Restaurant. Café/bar. Snack bar. Takeaway. Outdoor and indoor swimming pools. Paddling pool. Animation programmes. Indoor playground. Play areas. Sports field. Boules. Bicycle and go-kart hire. Off site: National Park Hoge Kempen with many walking and cycle paths. Cities of Hasselt, Maastricht and Valkenburg.

Open: 21 March - 25 October.

Directions

From A2 take exit for Lanaken at Stein and follow direction Lanaken. Turn right at roundabout Rekem, after 6 km. at T-junction turn right and immediately left. Site is 1 km. and well signed. GPS: N50:54.831 E05:35.844

Charges guide

Per unit incl. up to 6 persons, electricity and water	€ 16,00 - € 36,00
dog	€ 3,00

BE0670 Camping Parc La Clusure

Chemin de la Clusure 30, B-6927 Bure-Tellin (Luxembourg)

Tel: **084 360 050**. Email: **info@parclaclusure.be** **www.alanrogers.com/BE0670**

Set in a river valley in the lovely wooded uplands of the Ardennes, known as the L'Homme Valley touring area, Parc La Clusure has 425 large marked, grassy pitches (350 for touring). All have access to electricity, cable TV and water taps and are mostly in avenues off a central, tarmac road. There is some noise from the nearby railway. There is a very pleasant riverside walk (the river is shallow in summer and popular for children to play in). The site's heated swimming pool and children's pool have a pool-side bar and terrace. The site is used by a tour operator (number of pitches varies). The famous Grottoes of Han are nearby, also the Eurospace center and Lavaux St. Anne castle. Those preferring quieter entertainment might enjoy the Topiary Park at Durbuy.

Facilities

Three sanitary units (one heated in winter) include some washbasins in cubicles, facilities for babies and family bathrooms. Facilities for disabled persons. Motorcaravan services. Well stocked shop, bar, restaurant, snack bar and takeaway (all 27/3-1/11). Swimming pools (25/4-13/9). Bicycle hire. Tennis. New playgrounds. Organised activity programme including canoeing, archery, abseiling, mountain biking and climbing (summer). Caving. Fishing (licence essential). WiFi. Barrier card deposit (€ 20). Off site: Riding 7 km. Golf 25 km.

Open: All year.

Directions

Site is signed north at the roundabout off the N803 Rochefort - St Hubert road at Bure, 8 km. southeast of Rochefort with a narrow, fairly steep, winding descent to site. GPS: N50:05.788 E05:17.230

Charges 2009

Per pitch incl. 2 persons	€ 17,00 - € 28,50
extra person	€ 4,00 - € 5,50
electricity (16A)	€ 4,00 - € 5,00
dog	€ 4,00

Camping Cheques accepted.

BE0782 Camping Jocomo Park

Maastrichterweg 1a, B-3620 Lanaken (Limburg)

Tel: **089 722884**. Email: **info@jocomo.be** **www.alanrogers.com/BE0782**

Situated in dense pine forest this is a peaceful site but lively enough to keep young children happy. There are 127 pitches with 37 available for touring units, all with electricity (4A) and water. The touring pitches are arranged around an open field in the middle of the site. Children's entertainment is provided in high season and is centred around a small lake. A pleasant heated outdoor pool also has a separate pool for children (fenced).

Facilities

One modern toilet block serves the touring pitches. Preset showers with controllable hot and cold water to open washbasins. Baby bath. No facilities for disabled visitors. No shop but basics are available in reception. Small taverna type bar with simple takeaway menu (all year). Several small playgrounds throughout site. Off site: Riding 1 km. Fishing and bicycle hire 1.5 km.

Open: All year.

Directions

From Lanaken follow the N77 towards Zutendaal. About 2.5 km after leaving Lanaken look for a small gravel road on the right. The site is not signed and is very difficult to find. GPS: N50:54.383 E05:37.691

Charges guide

Per unit incl. 2 persons and electricity	€ 15,00
extra person	€ 3,75
child (2-9 yrs)	€ 2,50
dog	€ 1,00

BE0760 Goolderheide Vakantiepark

Bosstraat 1, B-3950 Bocholt (Limburg)

Tel: **089 469 640**. Email: **info@goolderheide.be** **www.alanrogers.com/BE0760**

A large family holiday site with 900 individual pitches, Goolderheide has been owned and operated by the same family for many years and has an excellent pool complex and playgrounds. There are many seasonal and rental units, plus around 300 tourist pitches with 4/6A electricity, all in a forest setting. The pitches are of variable size and access roads are quite narrow. The outdoor pool complex has two large pools (one Olympic size), a slide and a paddling pool. There is also a fishing lake, and a lake with a small sandy beach. An enormous area is devoted to a comprehensive play area with a vast range of equipment. During the main season there is also a weekly supervised 'assault' course complete with aerial ropeways, etc., a soundproofed over-16s disco, plus a 'younger kids' disco, and an extensive programme of varied activities to keep children and adults occupied. There are no extra charges for most of these activities.

Facilities

Four sanitary buildings provide an ample supply of WCs and washbasins, but rather fewer showers. Baby areas. Laundry facilities. Two suites for disabled people. Bar. Shop (daily in July/Aug, w/ends and public holidays in low season). Takeaway. Swimming pools. Tennis. Fishing. Boules. Minigolf. Play area and 'assault' course. Children's discos. Programme of activities. Night security staff (main season). Off site: Bicycle hire 1 km.

Open: 1 April - 30 September.

Directions

From A13 (E313, Antwerp - Liege) take exit 25 and N141 to Leopoldsburg, then N73 through Peer, to outskirts of Bree (35 km). Take N76 north for 3 km, turn left at large roundabout into Bocholt, and towards Kaulille. Site road is on left towards edge of town. GPS: N51:10.406 E05:32.341

Charges guide

Per person	€ 5,50
child (up to 12 yrs)	€ 3,00
pitch incl. 4A electricity	€ 16,50 - € 25,00
extra 2A electricity	€ 3,00
dog	€ 4,00

No credit cards.

BE0784 Recreatieoord Kikmolen

Kikmolenstraat 3, B-3630 Opgrimbie/Maasmechelen (Limburg)

Tel: **089 770 900** **www.alanrogers.com/BE0784**

This is a large and very lively site situated around a large, man-made lake which also serves as the site swimming pool. The site is very much targeted at a teenage clientèle. Regular discos continue until around 03.00 and sometimes later. Large pitches are spread throughout the site and are mixed with the 680 seasonal and rental units. The pitches are on grass and all have electricity (4A) and water. Dogs are officially not accepted but when we visited there were many dogs on the site. Two water slides run into the large artificial lake (not fenced and unsuitable for young children).

Facilities

Eight modern blocks are spread throughout the site. All have good facilities with some washbasins in cabins but we suspect would be under pressure when the site is full. All hot water is charged through a prepaid SEP key system. One disabled toilet per block which is unlocked and used by all. Two restaurants and bars. Takeaway food. Well stocked shop. Games room. Lake swimming with water slides. Sports field. Lively activity and entertainment programme. Off site: Fishing 1 km. Golf and riding 15 km. Sailing 3 km.

Open: 1 April - 31 October.

Directions

From A76 Antwerpen - Koln motorway take exit 33 towards Maasmachelen. Follow the N78 from 1km and the site is well signed on the right. GPS: N50:57.232 E05:39.719

Charges guide

Per unit incl. 2 persons and electricity	€ 15,00 - € 17,00
extra person	€ 4,25 - € 5,00
child (4-15 yrs)	€ 2,00 - € 2,25

BE0780 Family Camping Wilhelm Tell

Hoeverweg 87, B-3660 Opglabbeek (Limburg)

Tel: **089 854 444**. Email: **receptie@wilhelmtell.com** **www.alanrogers.com/BE0780**

Wilhelm Tell is a family run site that caters particularly well for children with its indoor and outdoor pools and lots of entertainment throughout the season. There is a total of 128 pitches with 70 available for touring units, some separated, others on open fields. There are 60 electricity connections (10A) and, for winter use, 20 hardstandings. The super bar/restaurant has access for wheelchair users. M. Lode Nulmans has a very special attitude towards his customers and tries to ensure they leave satisfied and want to return. For example, in his restaurant he says 'it serves until you are full'. The Limburg region is a relaxing area with much to do, including shopping or touring the historic towns with a very enjoyable choice of food and drink!

Facilities

Toilet facilities are adequate. Facilities around the pool supplement at busy times. Baby room in reception area. Two en-suite units for disabled visitors. Laundry facilities. Motorcaravan service point. Fridge hire. Bar/restaurant and snack bar (times vary acc. to season). Outdoor heated pool with slide and wave machine (1/7-31/8) and indoor pool (all year), both well supervised. Play area. WiFi.

Open: All year.

Directions

From E314 take exit 32 for Maaseik and follow 730 road towards As. From As follow signs to Opglabbeek. In Opglabbeek take first right at roundabout (Weg van Niel) then first left (Kasterstraat) to site. GPS: N51:01.711 E05:35.888

Charges 2009

Per person	€ 8,00
child	€ 4,00
pitch incl. electricity	€ 15,00

Less 30% in low season.
Camping Cheques accepted.

BE0785 Recreatiepark Blauwe Meer

Kattenbos 169, B-3920 Lommel (Limburg)

Tel: **011 544 523**. Email: **info@blauwemeer.be** **www.alanrogers.com/BE0785**

Surrounded by woodland, and with shade from tall pines, this large site has 976 pitches, of which 277 are for touring units. The touring pitches are attractively arranged around a large man-made lake with a surrounding it (safe for children). Each pitch has electricity (10A), water, drainage and television connections. There is a whole range of activities including a disco and a heated outdoor pool with slide. There are two additional small pools for children. A bar offers takeaway food and a good supermarket is on the site. This is a popular and lively site with a extensive entertainment programme which is varied to suit all age groups.

Facilities

Good clean toilet blocks are located throughout the site. Free hot showers, washbasins in cabins. Facilities for babies and children. Good facilities for disabled people. Laundry room. Supermarket. Bar. Takeaway. Heated outdoor swimming pool, two smaller ones for children (May - Aug). Several adventure style playgrounds. Children's zoo. Minigolf. WiFi (charged). Only one dog per pitch. Off site: Forest Park adjacent for walking and cycling. Golf 10 km. Riding 7 or 12 km.

Open: Easter - 30 October.

Directions

Lommel is 35 km. north of Hasselt. From the N71 at Lommel, turn south at traffic lights on N746 (signed Leopoldsburg), for 2 km. to Kattenbos, and site entrance is on southern side of village on left. GPS: N51:11.644 E05:18.193

Charges guide

Per unit incl. up to 4 persons	€ 25,00 - € 33,00

Minimum stays apply (1 week in high season, 3 or 4 nights on public holidays. American RVs, 12 metres max. in high season, larger at other times).

BE0788 Camping Hengelhoef

Tulpenstraat 141, B-3530 Houthalen/Helchteren (Limburg)

Tel: **089 382500**. Email: **info@hengelhoef.nl** **www.alanrogers.com/BE0788**

This attractive and well cared for site would suit families with younger children. Situated in a forest it has 478 pitches of which 368 are for touring units. The pitches are large and laid out in avenues with plenty of shade and all have electricity (10A), water and drainage. At the centre of the site is a large, man-made lake surrounded by sand which is safe for children. A good subtropical style pool complex offers a range of slides and water based activities. With a range of activities on offer there is little need to leave the site. There is a large supermarket and a good restaurant and bars.

Facilities

Several good quality toilet blocks throughout the site provide very good facilities including hot showers, washbasins in cabins and good facilites for babies and disabled visitors. Laundry facilities. Motorcaravan services. Supermarket. Restaurant. Bar. Takeaway. Lake with beach. Indoor pool complex. Multisports court. Dogs accepted in certain areas. Off site: Bicycle hire 1 km. Riding 3 km.

Open: All year.

Directions

From the E314/A2 motorway take exit towards Houthalen Centrum Zuid. The site is well signed from the centre. GPS: N51:00.863 E05:27.993

Charges guide

Per unit incl. 3-4 persons and electricity	€ 14,00 - € 39,00
extra person	€ 5,00 - € 7,50
child (4-15 yrs)	€ 2,50 - € 5,00
dog	free

BE0792 Camping Zavelbos

Kattebeekstraat 1, B-3680 Opoeteren (Limburg)

Tel: **089 758146**. Email: **receptie@zavelbos.com** **www.alanrogers.com/BE0792**

Camping Zavelbos lies between woods and moors in a nature park of 2,000 hectares and is a pleasant spot for nature lovers and those who love peace and quiet. There are many cycle and walking routes to enjoy in this beautiful region, alternatively you can simply relax in the peaceful campsite grounds complete with fishpond. There is no swimming pool but guests have free use of the pool complex at Wilhelm Tell Holiday Park (6 km). The 35 touring pitches (80-100 sq.m) all have electricity and water. Bungalows and chalets are available to rent.

Facilities

New sanitary facilities include family bathrooms, baths with jacuzzi and jetstream. Snack bar. Tavern. Fishpond. Playground. Boules. Free WiFi. Off site: Cycle and walking routes. National Park Hoge Kempen. Bobbejaanland. Maastricht. Hasselt. Genk.

Open: All year.

Directions

Take the Maaseik exit from the A2 (Eindhoven - Maastricht) motorway and drive via Neerpoeteren to Opoeteren. The site is on the right heading to Opglabbeek. GPS: N51:03.498 E05:37.728

Charges guide

Per unit inc. 2 persons and electricity	€ 24,00
extra person	€ 7,00
child (under 12 yrs)	€ 4,00
dog	€ 4,00

BE0794 Camping Molenheide

Molenheidestraat 7, B-3530 Houthalen - Helchteren (Limburg)

Tel: **011 521044**. Email: **info@molenheide.be** **www.alanrogers.com/BE0794**

In the centre of a naturally beautiful area, Park Molenheide is predominantly a high class bungalow park. However, it does have 61 large touring pitches which are located in a flat grass field with easy access. All the pitches have electricity (6A). What sets this site aside from others in the area is its amazing range of activities and high class facilities. All manner of recreational activities are housed indoors with a large tropical style swimming pool with slides and an excellent Disney themed children's pool, all supervised. There are numerous high quality bars and restaurants, all housed under the same roof.

Facilities

One single well equipped, modern toilet block (bring your own paper) with large free controllable showers. Fully equipped en-suite unit for disabled visitors. Excellent bars and restaurants. Outstanding leisure facilites with tropical indoor heated swimming pool, bowling, incredible children's indoor play area and unique indoor crazy golf course. Dogs allowed on the campsite but in none of the facilites.

Open: All year.

Directions

Follow the E314 motorway towards Aken and take exit 29. Follow the N74 for 8 km. and site well signed on the right. GPS: N51:04.746 E05:23.730

Charges guide

Per unit incl. up to 4 persons (per week)	€ 210,00 - € 325,00
extra person	€ 56,00
electricity	€ 14,00

BE0786 Camping Holsteenbron

Hengelhoefseweg 9, B-3520 Zonhoven (Limburg)
Tel: **011 817 140**. Email: **camping.holsteenbron@skynet.be** www.alanrogers.com/BE0786

Situated in the heart of the Park Midden-Limburg, this is a delightful site. There are 91 pitches with 60 for touring units, numbered and arranged in rows that are separated by hedges. All have easy access and electricity (6A). Water is provided by a single supply at the toilet block, but being such a small site, this is not a problem. A pretty lake is at the centre of the site and is well stocked with fish for the exclusive use of the camping guests. The site is situated only 500 m. from the start of a network of cycle tracks that stretches for 1,600 km. throughout the National Park. There is a pleasant restaurant and bar which is full of local character. Look for the owner's collection of egg cups! For relaxing or cycling this is a fine site in a beautiful situation. The owners live on site and provide a personal touch to all that happens. The site is highly recommended.

Facilities

One single well equipped toilet block with large token operated showers. Laundry room. Excellent bar and restaurant with limited but good menu (all season). Playground. Sports field. Fishing. TV in bar. Off site: Riding 3 km.

Open: Easter - 31 October.

Directions

Site is situated on the N29 Eindhoven - Hasselt road and is well signed from Zohoven.
GPS: N50:59.896 E05:25.471

Charges guide

Per unit incl. electricity	€ 17,00 - € 19,00
dog	€ 1,00

BE0796 Vakantiecentrum De Lage Kempen

Kiefhoekstraat 19, B-3941 Hechtel-Eksel (Limburg)
Tel: **011 402243**. Email: **info@lagekempen.be** www.alanrogers.com/BE0796

This is a small, good quality site of which the owners are rightly proud. There are 100 pitches with 62 available for touring units. The pitches are large, all with electricity (6/10A) and are laid out in rows. A pleasant swimming pool complex has three heated pools, two for children and one with a large slide, and they are supervised in high season. A traditional bar also provides a limited menu and serves as a popular meeting point for relaxation. Entertainment is provided daily in high season. This is a pleasant site with a good atmosphere. The owners have found the right balance of entertainment and time for relaxation.

Facilities

A single, high quality toilet block provides very good facilities including hot showers, washbasins in cabins and good facilites for babies and disabled people. Laundry facilities. Motorcaravan services. Bar/restaurant. Takeaway. Outdoor heated pool complex (May-Sept). Large adventure playground. Off site: Bicycle hire 1 km. Riding 3 km. Fishing 5 km.

Open: Easter - 30 October.

Directions

From the E314/A2 motorway take exit for Houthalen and follow signs to Hechtel. Shortly after passing through Hechtel look for campsite signs on the left.
GPS: N51:09.655 E05:18.860

Charges 2009

Per unit incl. 2 persons and electricity	€ 23,00
extra person	€ 4,00
dog (max. 1)	€ 2,00

BE0798 Recreatiepark Parelstrand

Luikersteenweg 313A, B-3920 Lommel (Limburg)

Tel: **011 649 349**. Email: **info@parelstrand.be** **www.alanrogers.com/BE0798**

This large, attractive site is situated alongside the Bocholt - Herentals canal and the Lommel yacht marina. It has 800 pitches of which 250 are for touring units. Each pitch has electricity (10A), water and drainage. The site fronts onto a large lake with a safe beach and there are two smaller lakes within the site, one of which is used for fishing (well stocked but all fish must be returned). There is an Olympic size, outdoor pool with a large slide and a small pool for children (not supervised).

Facilities

All the facilities that one would expect from a large site are available. Free hot showers, some washbasins in cabins. Facilities for babies and children. Good facilities for disabled visitors. Laundry room. Supermarket. Bar. Takeaway. Outdoor swimming pools, one for children. WiFi (charged). Only one dog per pitch. Off site: Boat launching 1 km. Riding 5 km.

Open: Easter - 30 October.

Directions

Take the N712 from Lommel and after 3 km. turn left on the N715. After a further 3 km. the site is on the right hand side. It is well signed from Lommel. GPS: N51:14.586 E05:22.746

Charges guide

Per unit incl. 3-4 persons and electricity	€ 25,00 - € 33,00

BE0590 Camping De Gavers

Onkerzelestraat 280, B-9500 Geraardsbergen (East Flanders)

Tel: **054 416 324**. Email: **gavers@oost-vlaanderen.be** **www.alanrogers.com/BE0590**

Domein de Gavers is a modern, well organised holiday site in a peaceful location adjacent to a large sports complex, about 5 km. outside Geraardsbergen. A busy site in season, there is good security and a card operated barrier. Most of the 448 grassy, level pitches are taken by seasonal units but about 80 are left for touring units. Pitches are arranged on either side of surfaced access roads with some hedges and few trees to provide shade in parts, with electricity available to most. The site offers an extensive range of sporting activities and a full entertainment programme over a long season.

Facilities

Six modern, heated and well equipped sanitary buildings provide hot showers on payment (€ 0.50). Modern rooms for disabled people, and babies. Launderette. No motorcaravan services. Shop (July/Aug). Restaurant and takeaway. Cafeteria and bars (daily 1/4-30/9, otherwise weekends). Heated indoor pool (all year). Outdoor pool (1/5-31/8). Excellent playground. Tennis. Boules. Minigolf. Fishing. Sailing. Canoes, windsurfers, pedaloes, yachts and rowing boats for hire. Bicycle hire. Tourist train. Swimming and beach area at lake. Climbing. Off site: Bars and restaurants within 1.5 km.

Open: All year.

Directions

From E429/A8 exit 26 towards Edingen, take N255 and N495 to Geraardsbergen. Down a steep hill, then left at site sign towards Onkerzele, through village and turn north to site. From E40/A10, exit at junction 17 on to N42, turn left on to N495 and follow as above. GPS: N50:47.459 E03:55.422

Charges guide

Per unit incl. electricity	€ 10,00 - € 20,00
tent pitch	€ 10,00 - € 16,00

Discounts of 5-30% for longer stays.

BE0600 Camping Groeneveld

Groeneveldreef, Bachte-Maria-Leerne, B-9800 Deinze (East Flanders)

Tel: **093 801 014**. Email: **info@campinggroeneveld.be** **www.alanrogers.com/BE0600**

Quiet and clean is how Rene Kuys describes his campsite. Groeneveld is a traditional site in a small village within easy reach of Gent. It has a friendly atmosphere and is also open over a long season. Although this site has 108 pitches, there are a fair number of seasonal units, leaving around 50 large touring pitches with electricity (10A). Hedges and borders divide the grassy area, access roads are gravel and there is an area for tents. Family entertainment and activities organised in high season include themed, musical evenings, barbecues, pétanque matches, etc.

Facilities

Two clean sanitary units of differing ages and designs provide British style WCs, washbasins and free hot showers (new facilities are planned). Motorcaravan services. Freezer (free). Bar/café (July/Aug. and weekends) with snacks, and a comprehensive range of speciality and local beers. Small coarse fishing lake. Floodlit petanque court. Adventure style play area. TV room. Internet access (at reception). Off site: Shops and restaurants nearby. Golf 3 km. Swimming pool 5 km. Kayaking 5 km.

Open: 26 March - 12 November.

Directions

From A10 (E40) exit 13, turn south on N466. After 3 km. continue straight on at roundabout and site is on left on entering village (opposite a large factory). Note: yellow signs are very small.
GPS: N51:00.305 E03:34.337

Charges guide

Per unit incl. 2 persons and car	€ 17,50 - € 23,00
2 persons and tent	€ 13,00 - € 15,00

No credit cards.

X p. 63 cc.c

BE0610 Camping Blaarmeersen

Zuiderlaan 12, B-9000 Gent (East Flanders)

Tel: **092 668 160**. Email: **camping.blaarmeersen@gent.be** **www.alanrogers.com/BE0610**

Belgium

Blaarmeersen is a comfortable, well managed municipal site in the west of the city. It adjoins a sports complex and a fair sized lake which together provide facilities for a variety of watersports, tennis, squash, minigolf, football, athletics track, roller skating and a playground. The 250 individual, flat, grassy touring pitches are separated by tall hedges and mostly arranged in circular groups, with electricity to 228. There are 40 hardstandings for motorcaravans, plus a separate area for tents with barbecue facilities. Some noise is possible as the city ring road is close.

Facilities

Five sanitary units of a decent standard vary in size. Showers and toilets for disabled people. Laundry. Motorcaravan services. Shop, café/bar (both daily March - Oct). Takeaway. Sports facilities. Playground. Fishing on site in winter, otherwise 500 m. Lake swimming. Off site: Good network of paths and cycle routes around the city. Bicycle hire 5 km. Riding and golf 10 km.

Open: 1 March - 15 October.

Directions

From E40 take exit 13 (Gent-West) and follow dual carriageway for 5 km. Cross second bridge and look for Blaarmeersen sign, turning sharp right and following signs to leisure complex. In city avoid overpasses - most signs are on the lower levels. GPS: N51:02.833 E03:41.000

Charges guide

Per person	€ 3,50 - € 4,50
pitch	€ 5,50 - € 7,00
electricity	€ 1,25

BE0630 Camping Grimbergen

Veldkantstraat 64, B-1850 Grimbergen (Brabant)

Tel: **022 709 597**. Email: **camping.grimbergen@telenet.be** **www.alanrogers.com/BE0630**

A popular little municipal site with a friendly atmosphere, Camping Grimbergen has 90 pitches on fairly level grass, of which around 50 have electricity (10A). The site is not really suitable for large units, although four pitches for motorcaravans have been added. The municipal sports facilities are adjacent and the site is well placed for visiting Brussels. The bus station is by the traffic lights at the junction of N202 and N211, as well as 150 m. from the campsite and buses run into the city centre every 15 minutes.

Facilities

Immaculate new sanitary facilities are heated in colder months. Separate facilities for disabled people. Motorcaravan services. Adventure playground. Off site: Fishing 800 m. Grimbergen with Norbertine Abbey, St Servaas church and Sunday morning market.

Open: 1 April - 31 October.

Directions

From Brussels ring road take exit 7 (N202) to Grimbergen. After 2.5 km, turn right at traffic lights on N211 towards Vilvoorde (site signed), then left at second set of lights (slightly oblique turn). Site entrance is on right in 500 m. (watch for blue and white sign 'Lammekenshoeve'). GPS: N50:56.091 E04:22.954

Charges guide

Per person	€ 4,50
pitch incl. electricity	€ 5,00 - € 10,00
caravan or tent	€ 3,00

No credit cards.

BE0640 Camping Druivenland

Nijvelsebaan 80, B-3090 Overijse (Brabant)

Tel: **026 879 368**. Email: **info@campingdruivenland.be** **www.alanrogers.com/BE0640**

This small, peaceful site is within easy reach of Brussels and also close to 25,000 hectares of woodland where you can enjoy some of the best Belgian countryside on foot or bicycle. Neat and mature, the site is well looked after and family run. It has a large open touring field and further pitches available in the sheltered area of the static park. The pitches are slightly sloping but almost all have views over the countryside. In total there are 120 pitches, with 40 for touring units, all with electricity (16A).

Facilities

Fully equipped toilet block with some washbasins in cabins and toilets for children. Well laid out provision for disabled visitors (shower room and toilet/washroom). Washing machine and dryer. Kept extremely clean at all times, it is of a very high standard. Limited shop with some fresh food. Boules. Off site: Golf 3 km.

Open: 15 March - 15 October.

Directions

From E411 Brussels - Namur road take exit 3 to Overijse (not exit 2). After 1 km. turn right signed Tombeek, Waver and Terlanen. Site is 1 km. on right. GPS: N50:45.712 E04:32.821

Charges guide

Per unit incl. 2 persons	€ 15,00 - € 17,00
extra person	€ 2,00
electricity	€ 2,00

Runner up Alan Rogers Awards 2008

BE0655 Camping De Lilse Bergen

Strandweg 6, Gierle, B-2275 Lille (Antwerp)

Tel: **014 557 901**. Email: **info@lilsebergen.be** **www.alanrogers.com/BE0655**

This attractive, quietly located holiday site has 503 shady pitches, of which 241 (all with electricity) are for touring units. Set on sandy soil among pine trees and rhododendrons and arranged around a large lake, the site has a Mediterranean feel. It is well fenced, with a night guard and well labelled, fire fighting equipment. Cars are parked away from units. The site is really child-friendly with each access road labelled with a different animal symbol to enable children to find their own unit easily. An entertainment programme is organised in high season. The lake has marked swimming and diving areas (for adults), a sandy beach, an area for watersports, plus a separate children's pool complex (depth 60 cm) with a most imaginative playground. There are lifeguards and the water meets 'Blue Flag' standards. A building by the lake houses changing rooms, extra toilets and showers and a baby room. There are picnic areas and lakeside or woodland walks.

Facilities

Five of the six main toilet blocks have been fully refitted to a good standard and can be heated. Some washbasins in cubicles and good hot showers (on payment). Well equipped baby rooms. Facilities for disabled campers. Laundry. Barrier 'keys' can be charged up with units for operating showers, washing machine etc. First aid post. Motorcaravan service point. Restaurant (all year, weekends only in winter), takeaway and well stocked shop (Easter - 30/9; weekends only outside July/Aug). Tennis. Minigolf. Boules. Climbing wall. Playground, trampolines and skateboard ramp. Pedaloes, kayaks and bicycles for hire. Children's electric cars and pedal kart tracks (charged for). Off site: Golf 1 km.

Open: All year.

Directions

From E34 Antwerp - Eindhoven take exit 22. On the roundabout take the exit for 'Lilse Bergen' and follow forest road to site entrance.
GPS: N51:17.345 E04:51.305

Charges 2009

Per unit incl. electricity (10A)	€ 19,00 - € 25,00
dog	€ 4,00

BE0700 Camping Spa d'Or

Stockay 17, B-4845 Sart-lez-Spa (Liège)

Tel: **087 474 400**. Email: **info@campingspador.be** **www.alanrogers.com/BE0700**

Camping Spa d'Or is set in a beautiful area of woodlands and picturesque villages, 4 km. from the town of Spa (the 'Pearl of the Ardennes'). The site is on the banks of a small river and is an ideal starting point for walks and bicycle trips through the forests. The Dutch owners have long-term plans to upgrade the site which had been rather neglected. With 310 pitches in total, 240 are for touring (40 places are reserved for tents). The touring pitches have an open aspect, most are slightly sloping and all have 10A electricity connections.

Facilities

One new large, bright and cheerful sanitary block and one new smaller block (portacabin) both with all the usual facilities. Room for visitors with disabilities. Laundry. Shop (1/4-24/10). Bar, restaurant and takeaway (1/4-24/10). Outdoor heated swimming pool (1/5-15/9). Play area with good equipment. TV in bar. Goal posts and two boules courts. Entertainment during July and August. Off site: Fishing 2 km. Golf and riding 5 km. Maps for cycling and walking on sale at reception. Spa 4 km.

Open: All year.

Directions

From E42 take exit 9 and follow the signs to Spa d'Or. GPS: N50:30.455 E05:55.171

Charges guide

Per unit incl. 2 persons	€ 17,50 - € 22,50
extra person (over 3 yrs)	€ 4,25 - € 4,75
tent incl. 2 persons	€ 12,50 - € 15,50
electricity	€ 3,25
dog	€ 4,00 - € 5,00

BE0660 Camping Baalse Hei

Roodhuisstraat 10, B-2300 Turnhout (Antwerp)

Tel: **014 448 470**. Email: **info@baalsehei.be** www.alanrogers.com/BE0660

The 'Campine' is an area covering three quarters of the Province of Antwerp, noted for its nature reserves, pine forests, meadows and streams and is ideal for walking and cycling, while Turnhout itself is an interesting old town. Baalse Hei, a long established, friendly site, is a recent Benelux award winner. It has 459 pitches including a separate touring area of 70 large pitches (all with 16A electricity, TV connections and shared water point) on a large grass field, thoughtfully developed with young trees and bushes. Cars are parked away from the pitches. Large motorcaravans can be accommodated (phone first to check availability). There is also a fully equiped bungalow for rent. It is 100 m. from the edge of the field to the modern, heated, sanitary building. There is a small lake for swimming with a beach, a boating lake and a large fishing lake (on payment). Entertainment and activities are organised in July/Aug. Walk in the woods and you will undoubtedly come across some of the many red squirrels or take the pleasant 1.5 km. riverside walk to the next village. Arrival after 4 pm. departure before 12 noon.

Facilities

The toilet block provides hot showers on payment (€ 0.50), some washbasins in cabins and facilities for disabled visitors. Dishwashing facilities (hot water € 0.12), Launderette. Motorcaravan services. Café/restaurant (daily 1/4-31/10, w/ends only other times, closed 16/11-25/1). Breakfast served in high season. Shop (all year). Club/TV room. Lake swimming. Fishing. Two tennis courts. Boules. Adventure play area. Bicycle hire. English is spoken. Off site: Riding 1.5 km. Golf 15 km.

Open: 16 January - 15 December.

Directions

Site is northeast of Turnhout off the N119. Approaching from Antwerp on E34/A12 take Turnhout ring road to the end (not a complete ring) and turn right. There is a small site sign to right in 1.5 km. then a country lane.
GPS: N51:21.280 E04:57.300

Charges guide

Per unit all inclusive	€ 16,00 - € 24,00
electricity	€ 1,00
2 cyclists and tent	€ 10,00 - € 13,00
dog	€ 1,25

No credit cards.

BE0770 Camping le Vieux Moulin

Petite Strument 62, B-6980 La Roche-en-Ardenne (Luxembourg)

Tel: **084 411 380**. Email: **info@strument.com** www.alanrogers.com/BE0770

Located in one of the most beautiful valleys in the heart of the Ardennes, Le Vieux Moulin has 183 pitches and, although there are 127 long stay units at the far end of the site, the 60 touring pitches do have their own space. Some are separated by hedges, others for tents and smaller units are more open, all are on grass, and there are 50 electric hook-ups (6A). The 19th-century water mill has been owned and operated by the owner's family for many years, but has now been converted into a small hotel and a fascinating mill museum.

Facilities

A newly constructed, centrally located toilet block is between the touring and long stay areas. It can be heated in cool weather and provides washbasins in cubicles and controllable hot showers on payment. Washing machine. No facilities for disabled persons. A further older unit is at the end of the mill building. Restaurant and bar with hotel (8 rooms). Mill museum. Off site: Town facilities 800 m.

Open: 1 April - 11 November.

Directions

From town centre take N89 south towards St Hubert, turning right towards Hives where site is signed. Site is 800 m. from the town centre.
GPS: N50:10.417 E05:34.650

Charges 2009

Per unit incl. 2 persons and electricity	€ 16,00 - € 18,50
extra person	€ 2,50
dog	€ 2,00

BE0675 Camping Spineuse

Rue de Malome 7, B-6840 Neufchâteau (Luxembourg)

Tel: **061 277 320**. Email: **info@camping-spineuse.be** **www.alanrogers.com/BE0675**

This Dutch owned site lies about 2 km. from the town centre. It is on low lying, level grass, bordered by a river, with trees and shrubs dotted around the 87 pitches. The main gravel access road can be dusty in dry weather. Seasonal units take 25 pitches leaving 62 for touring units, all with 10/15A electricity. There is also a separate area for tents. Parents of small children should be aware that there is unfenced water on site and a footbridge over the river with no guard rails.

Facilities

Toilet facilities are in the central building and are looking dated with some cubicles rather small. Preset showers and open washbasins. However the building can be heated and was reasonably clean when seen. No facilities for disabled campers. Washing machine and dryer. Extra facilities are in a portacabin (July/Aug). Motorcaravan service point. Bistro/bar (1/4-31/10). Small inflatable children's pool (1/6-30/9). Tennis. Boules. Small playground. Fishing. Off site: Riding 10 km. Golf 30 km.

Open: All year.

Directions

Site is 2 km. southwest of Neufchâteau on the N15 towards Florenville. There are 3 sites fairly close together, this is the last one on the left hand side. GPS: N49:49.899 E05:25.045

Charges guide

Per person	€ 3,10
child (0-6 yrs)	€ 2,00
pitch	€ 9,00
incl. electricity	€ 11,25

BE0680 Camping Sud

Voie de la Liberté 75, B-6717 Attert (Luxembourg)

Tel: **063 223 715**. Email: **info@campingsudattert.com** **www.alanrogers.com/BE0680**

This is a pleasant family run site which would make a good base for a short stay and is also well sited for use as an overnight halt. The 86 touring pitches are on level grass with 6A electricity hook-ups and are arranged around an oval loop access road. There are 11 drive-through pitches especially for one-nighters, plus four hardstandings for motorcaravans and a tent area. The far end of the site is close to the N4 and may suffer from some road noise. On-site facilities include a small restaurant/bar with takeaway, a shop for basics, an outdoor swimming pool and separate paddling pool.

Facilities

A single building provides modern sanitary facilities including some washbasins in cubicles and baby areas. Showers are free in low season (€ 0.50 July/Aug). No facilities for disabled campers. Small bar/restaurant and takeaway (1/4-25/10). TV in bar. Swimming pool (May-Sept). Small playground. Children's entertainment (4-12 yrs) three afternoons per week during July/Aug. Off site: Attert village has two churches and a museum and the Liberation Route passes the site. Internet café and Roman Museum in Arlon 8 km. Local nature parks. Supermarket, riding 5 km. Golf 8 km.

Open: 1 April - 25 October.

Directions

Attert is 8 km. north of Arlon. From N4 take Attert exit, continue east for 1 km. to Attert village, site entrance is immediately on your left as you join the main street. GPS: N49:44.894 E05:47.219

Charges guide

Per person	€ 4,00
child (2-12 yrs)	€ 2,25
pitch incl. electricity	€ 10,25
dog	€ 1,50

No credit cards.

BE0710 Camping Colline de Rabais

Rue de Bonlieu, B-6760 Virton (Luxembourg)

Tel: **063 571 195**. Email: **info@collinederabais.be** **www.alanrogers.com/BE0710**

Colline de Rabais is a large site with an unusual layout. This comprises a circular road with smaller roads leading to circular pads with wedge shaped pitches. In a hill top setting, the site is surrounded by forest. The present Dutch owners took over in 1997 and are slowly revamping the site. There are around 250 pitches for touring units, all with 16A electricity (some long leads needed), plus 43 mobile homes and bungalows for rent and 22 tour operator tents. Various activities are organised throughout the season.

Facilities

Three toilet blocks, one modernised with shower/washbasin cubicles and an en-suite room for disabled people. Cleaning and maintenance can be variable. Not all blocks are open in low season. Laundry facilities. Motorcaravan service point. Bar/restaurant and shop (opening times vary). Small outdoor swimming pool (1/5-1/10) with wood decking for sunbathing. Bicycle hire. Off site: Fishing 1 km. Riding 3 km.

Open: All year.

Directions

From E25/E411 take exit 29 towards Etalle and Virton. Follow signs for Vallée de Rabais. Turn right at sports complex. At crossroads (with phone box) turn right and uphill to site at end of road. GPS: N49:34.809 E05:32.864

Charges guide

Per unit incl. 2 persons	€ 17,50 - € 23,00
extra person (over 2 yrs)	€ 4,00 - € 4,50
electricity (16A)	€ 3,00

BE0705 Camping L'Hirondelle

Rue de la Burdinale 76a, B-4210 Oteppe (Liège)

Tel: **085 711 131**. Email: **info@lhirondelle.be** **www.alanrogers.com/BE0705**

This site is set in 20 hectares of woodland in the grounds of a castle that dates back to the 14th century. From the entrance one gets a glimpse of the restaurant in one part of the castle. There are 800 pitches with 300 for tourers, all with 6A electricity. The pitches are arranged around a huge playground, basketball court and a building housing a games room, a supermarket and a bar. In high season the site offers a full programme of entertainment with sports tournaments, discos and contests. This is a pleasant site which has a lot to offer for children and teenagers. The large open air pool (15 x 25 m) will accommodate both youngsters and teenagers. A video circuit in all the buildings advertises and informs about the activity programmes.

Facilities

The two toilet blocks for tourers provide some washbasins in cabins, children's toilets and basins and a unisex baby room. Washing machine and dryer. Good provision for disabled visitors. Shop. Bar. Restaurant. Swimming pool (15 x 25 m). Huge adventure type playground. Boules. Playing field. Entertainment (10/7-22/8). Games room.

Open: 1 April - 31 October.

Directions

From Namen on the E42 take exit 10 towards Biewart then continue on the 80 to Burdinne. In Burdinne follow signs for Oteppe. The site is signed just before entering Oteppe.
GPS: N50:34.055 E05:07.031

Charges guide

Per unit incl. 2 persons and electricity	€ 13,75 - € 21,00
extra person	€ 2,75 - € 4,00
dog	€ 2,50

BE0711 Ardennen Camping Bertrix

Route de Mortehan, B-6880 Bertrix (Luxembourg)

Tel: **061 412 281**. Email: **info@campingbertrix.be** **www.alanrogers.com/BE0711**

Bertrix is located at the heart of the Belgian Ardennes, between the towns of Bastogne and Bouillon and overlooking the hills of the Semois valley. The 498 pitches are terraced, giving an open aspect and views for everyone. The 138 level touring pitches are scattered amongst a variety of seasonal caravans and there is a friendly feel to the area. All have electricity and are near amenities. The activities, particularly for children, are of a high standard and well supervised. A visit to the nearby ruined castle at Bouillon is a must.

Facilities

Five well appointed toilet blocks, each with facilities for disabled visitors. The central one has a large laundry and a special brightly decorated unit for children, with basins, toilets, showers of varying heights and baby baths in cubicles. Motorcaravan service point. Shop for basics and bread. Excellent restaurant and bar (closed low season Mon/Thur only), with satellite TV and internet access and a terrace overlooking pool. Large heated swimming and paddling pools (supervised high season). Tennis. Bicycle hire. Children's games room. Ardennes chalets and holiday homes for rent. Off site: Canoeing. Fishing. Walking and cycle trails. Shops, banks and restaurants in Bertrix.

Open: 27 March - 12 November.

Directions

Take exit 25 from the E411 motorway and join the N89 towards Bertrix. After 6.5 km. join the N884 to Bertrix and upon arrival in the town, follow yellow signs to site. GPS: N49:50.316 E05:15.145

Charges guide

Per unit incl. 2 persons	€ 17,00 - € 22,00
extra person (over 2 yrs)	€ 4,00 - € 4,50
electricity (10A)	€ 3,50

Camping Cheques accepted.

BE0720 Camping Tonny

Tonny 35, B-6680 Amberloup (Luxembourg)
Tel: **061 688 285**. Email: **camping.tonny@belgacom.net** **www.alanrogers.com/BE0720**

With a friendly atmosphere, this family campsite is in a pleasant valley by the River Ourthe. It is an attractive small site with 75 grass touring pitches, with wooden chalet buildings giving a Tyrolean feel. The pitches (80-100 sq.m) are separated by small shrubs and fir trees, electricity (4/6A) is available. Cars are parked away from the units and there is a separate meadow for tents. Surrounded by natural woodland, Camping Tonny is an ideal base for outdoor activities. The main chalet has a café/bar, freestanding fireplace and a shady terrace for relaxing outside and is open all year (according to demand). Nearby St Hubert has a Basilica, the St Michel Furnace Industrial Museum and a wildlife park, with wild boar, deer and other native species – all worth a visit.

Facilities

Two fully equipped sanitary units (both heated in cool weather) include dishwashing and laundry sinks (all hot water is on payment). Baby area and laundry. Freezer for campers' use. Small shop. Cafe/bar. TV lounge and library. Sports field. Boules. Games room. Playgrounds. Bowling alley. Bicycle hire. Fishing. Canoeing. Cross-country skiing.

Open: 15 February - 15 November.

Directions

From N4 take exit for Libramont at km. 131 (N826), then to Amberloup (4 km.) where site is signed just outside of the southwest town boundary. GPS: N50:01.594 E05:30.770

Charges guide

Per person	€ 4,00
child (0-12 yrs)	€ 2,50
pitch incl. electricity (4A)	€ 10,40 - € 10,90
dog	€ 2,00

Off season discounts for over 55s and longer stays.

BE0712 Camping Ile de Faigneul

Rue de la Cherizelle 54, B-6830 Poupehan-sur-Semois (Luxembourg)
Tel: **061 466 894**. Email: **iledefaigneul@belgacom.net** **www.alanrogers.com/BE0712**

Few campsites are in sole possession of an island, and when that island lies in a beautiful tree lined valley the site is likely to be something special. Camping Ile de Faigneul is! This quiet, peaceful site, surrounded by the River Semois, is near the small village of Poupehan in the picturesque Belgium Ardennes. The 130 level pitches, all with electricity, on this grass covered island are all for touring units. The site's friendly owners, Alouis and Daniella van Zon-Berkes, who speak good English, took over the site a few years ago and have worked hard to return it to its present state of natural beauty.

Facilities

The well appointed sanitary block is new and maintained to the highest standard. Ultra modern, it has preset showers operated by key (deposit € 25) and some washbasins in cabins. Facilities for disabled visitors, family shower room, baby changing area. Laundry room. Shop. Bar and restaurant. Canoe rental. Fishing. Playground. Special area beside river for campfires.

Open: 1 April - 30 September.

Directions

From A4/E411 towards Luxembourg take exit 25 (Libramont/Bouillon) then N89 southwest to Bouillon. In Bouillon follow signs for Poupehan. The twisting road passes through the forests and ends up alongside the Semois just before Poupehan. Left over the stone bridge and immediately right (site signed) and follow road to is end, site is over bridge to the right. GPS: N49:48.963 E05:00.940

Charges guide

Per unit incl. 2 persons and electricity	€ 24,65
extra person	€ 3,00
child (4-13 yrs)	€ 2,20
dog	€ 2,20

BE0725 Camping Le Val de L'Aisne

Rue du TTA 1, B-6997 Erezee (Luxembourg)

Tel: **086 470 067**. Email: **info@levaldelaisne.be** **www.alanrogers.com/BE0725**

From a nearby hill Château de Blier overlooks Camping Le Val de L'Aisne, a large site attractively laid out around a 1.5 hectare lake in the Belgium Ardennes. The site has 450 grass pitches with 150 for touring units, on level ground and with 10A electricity. Tarmac roads circle the site providing easy access. Trees provide some shade although the site is fairly open. Activities play a large part on this site, ranging from quiet fishing in the lake to hectic quad bike tours in the surrounding hills.

Facilities

Three toilet blocks provide showers (paid for by token) and mainly open washbasins. Facilities for disabled people. Baby room. Washing machines and dryers. Motorcaravan service point. Bar/restaurant and snack bar with takeaway. Bread can be ordered in reception. On the lake: fishing, swimming, kayaks and pedal boats (to hire). Quad bike hire and tours arranged. Kayaks and mountain bike hire. Play area. Entertainment programme during summer and adventure games in the nearby wooded area. Off site: Riding, cycle and walking trails in the Ardennes woods.

Open: All year.

Directions

Leave the E411/A4 (Brussels - Luxembourg) motorway at exit 18 (Courière, Marche en Famenne), then southeast on the N4 to Marche. At Marche head northeast on N86 to Hotton, crossing bridge over river. In Hotton follow signs (Soy/Erezée). Just west of Erezée at roundabout follow signs (La Roche). Site is 900 m. on left. GPS: N50:16.890 E05:33.030

Charges guide

Per pitch incl. 2 persons and car	€ 18,00
extra person (over 3 yrs)	€ 3,00
electricity (3A)	€ 3,00

No credit cards.

BE0730 Camping Moulin de Malempré

1 Malempre, B-6960 Manhay (Luxembourg)

Tel: **086 455 504**. Email: **camping.malempre@cybernet.be** **www.alanrogers.com/BE0730**

This pleasant countryside site, very close to the E25, is well worth a visit and the Dutch owners will make you very welcome (English is spoken). The reception building houses the office and a small shop, above which is an attractive bar and restaurant with open fireplace. The 140 marked touring pitches are separated by small shrubs and gravel roads on sloping terrain. All have electricity (10A), 40 have water and drainage as well and the site is well lit. There is a little traffic noise from the nearby E25 (not too intrusive).

Facilities

Modern toilet facilities include some washbasins in cubicles and family bathrooms on payment. The unisex unit can be heated and has a family shower room. Unit for disabled people. Baby room. Laundry. Motorcaravan services. Shop for basics (15/5-31/8). Baker calls daily. Restaurant and bar (both 15/5-15/9 and weekends). Takeaway (15/5-15/9). Heated swimming pool and children's pools (15/5-15/9). TV. Boules. Playground. Off site: Bicycle hire 3 km. Riding 6 km. Fishing 10 km.

Open: 1 April - 31 October.

Directions

From E25/A26 (Liege - Bastogne) exit 49. Turn onto N651 (southwest) towards Manhay. After 220 m. turn sharp left (east) towards Lierneux. Follow signs for Malempré and site. GPS: N50:17.699 E05:43.390

Charges guide

Per unit incl. 2 persons	€ 18,50 - € 22,00
extra adult	€ 4,00
child (3-12 yrs)	€ 2,75
electricity	€ 2,85
dog	€ 2,85

BE0732 Camping Floreal La Roche

Route de Houffalize 18, B-6980 La Roche-en-Ardenne (Luxembourg)

Tel: **084 219 467**. Email: **camping.laroche@florealclub.be** **www.alanrogers.com/BE0732**

Maintained to very high standards, this site is set in a beautiful wooded valley bordering the Ourthe river. Open all year, the site is located on the outskirts of the attractive small town of La Roche-en-Ardenne in an area understandably popular with tourists. The site is large with 600 grass pitches, of which 280 are for touring units. The pitches are on level ground and all have electricity. There are plenty of opportunities for walking, mountain biking, rafting and canoeing.

Facilities

Six modern, well maintained sanitary blocks provide washbasins (open and in cabins), free preset showers. Facilities for disabled visitors. Baby room. Laundry facilities. Motorcaravan service point. Shop. Bar, restaurant, snack bar and takeaway. At Camping Floreal 1: outdoor heated swimming pool. Sports field. Tennis. Minigolf. Pétanque. Kayaks to rent. Off site: Indoor pool 800 m. Golf, riding and bicycle hire 1 km. Skiing 15 km.

Open: All year.

Directions

From E25/A26 take exit 50 and follow N89 southwest to La Roche. In La Roche follow signs for Houffalize (beside Ourthe river). Floral Club Camping 1 is 1.5 km. along this road. N.B. Go to camping 1 not 2. GPS: N50:10.560 E05:35.160

Charges guide

Per unit incl. 2 persons and electricity	€ 13,50 - € 17,45
extra person	€ 3,25

MAP 11

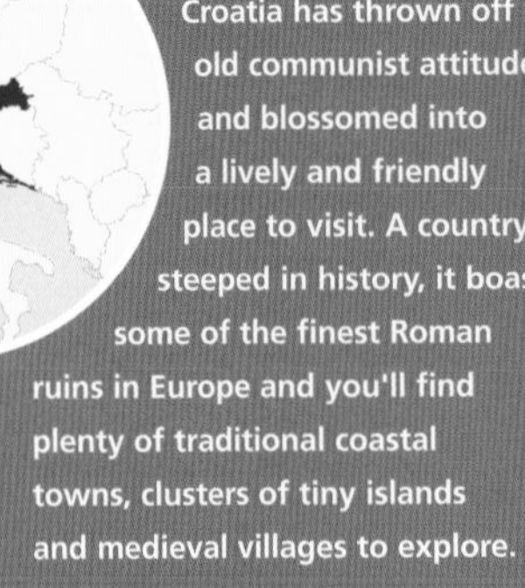

Croatia has thrown off old communist attitude and blossomed into a lively and friendly place to visit. A country steeped in history, it boas some of the finest Roman ruins in Europe and you'll find plenty of traditional coastal towns, clusters of tiny islands and medieval villages to explore.

CAPITAL: ZAGREB

Tourist Office

Croatian National Tourist Office
2 The Lanchesters
162-164 Fulham Palace Road
London W6 9ER
Tel: 020 8563 7979 Fax: 020 8563 2616
Email: info@cnto.freeserve.co.uk
Internet: www.croatia.hr

The heart-shaped peninsula of Istria, located in the north, is among the most developed tourist regions in Croatia. Here you can visit the preserved Roman amphitheatre in Pula, the beautiful town of Rovinj with its cobbled streets and wooded hills, and the resort of Umag, well known for its recreational activities, most notably tennis. Islands are studded all around the coast, making it ideal for sailing and diving enthusiasts. Istria also has the highest concentration of campsites.

Further south, in the province of Dalmatia, Split is the largest city on the Adriatic coast and home to the impressive Diolectian's Palace. From here the islands of Brac, Hvar, Vis and Korcula, renowned for their lively fishing villages and pristine beaches, are easily accessible by ferry. The old walled city of Dubrovnik is 150 km south. At over 2 km. long and 25 m. high, with 16 towers, a walk along the city walls affords spectacular views.

Population

4.4 million

Climate

Predominantly warm and hot in summer with temperatures of up to 40°C.

Language

Croat

Telephone

The country code is 00 385.

Money

Currency: Kuna
Banks: Mon-Fri 08.00 - 19.00.

Shops

Mainly Mon-Sat 08.00-20.00, although some close on Monday.

Public Holidays

New Year's Day; Epiphany 6 Jan; Good Friday; Easter Monday; Labour Day 1 May; Parliament Day 30 May; Day of Anti-Fascist Victory 22 June; Statehood Day 25 June; Thanksgiving Day 5 Aug; Assumption 15 Aug; Independence Day 8 Oct; All Sain 1 Nov; Christmas 25, 26 Dec.

Motoring

Croatia is proceeding with a vast road improvement programme. There are still some roads which leave a lot to be desired but things have improved dramatically. Roads along the coast can become heavily congested in summer and queues are possible at border crossings. Tolls: some motorways, bridges and tunnels. Cars towing a caravan or trailer must carry two warning triangles. It is illegal to overtake military convoys.

Croatian
Camping
Union

CROATIA
CAMPING

CR6716 Camping Lanterna

Lanterna, HR-52440 Porec (Istria)

Tel: **052 404 500**. Email: **lanterna@valamar.com** **www.alanrogers.com/CR6716**

This is one of the largest sites in Croatia with an amazing selection of activities and high standards and is part of the 'Camping on the Adriatic' group. Reception is buzzing in high season as around 10,000 guests are on site. Set in 90 hectares with over 3 km. of beach, there are 3,000 pitches of which 2,600 are for touring units. Pitches are 60-120 sq.m. with some superb locations right on the sea, although these tend to be taken first so it is advisable to book ahead. Some of the better pitches are in a 'reserved booking' area. Terracing has improved the view in many areas. Electrical connections are 10A. Facilities at Lanterna are impressive with the whole operation running smoothly for the campers. The land is sloping in parts and terraced in others. There is a large pool and pretty bay with rocky beaches and buoyed safety areas. Some of the marked and numbered pitches are shaded and arranged to take advantage of the topography. Many activities and quality entertainment for all are available both on and off site – you are spoilt for choice here, including a vast choice of places to eat. Prices tend to be higher than other sites in the area but you get value for money with the supporting facilities.

Facilities

The fourteen sanitary blocks (many refurbished in 2007) are clean and good quality. Children's facilities and baby care areas, some Turkish style WCs, hot showers with some blocks providing facilities for disabled people. Three supermarkets sell most everyday requirements. Fresh fish shop. Four restaurants, bars and snack bars and fast food outlets. Swimming pool and two paddling pools. Sand-pit and play areas, with animation for all in high season. Tennis. Bicycle hire. Watersports. Boats hire. Minigolf. Riding. Internet café. Jetty and ramp for boats. Dogs are restricted to a certain area. Off site: Nearest large supermarket in Novigrad, 9 km. Hourly bus service from the reception area. Fishing. Riding 500 m.

Open: 1 April - 15 October.

Directions

The turn to Laterna is well signed off the Novigrad to Porec road about 8 km. south of Novigrad. Continue for about 2 km. down the turn off road towards the coast and the campsite is difficult to miss on the right hand side. GPS: N45:17.803 E13:35.665

Charges guide

Per person	€ 3,85 - € 6,60
child (4-10 yrs)	free - € 4,65
pitch incl. electricity	€ 6,60 - € 12,25
incl. water	€ 8,35 - € 14,95

Prices for pitches by the sea are higher.

CR6727 Camping Valkanela

Valkanela, HR-52450 Vrsar (Istria)

Tel: **052 445 216**. Email: **valkanela@maistra.hr** **www.alanrogers.com/CR6727**

Camping Valkanela is located in a beautiful green bay, right on the Adriatic Sea, between the villages of Vrsar and Funtana. It offers 1200 pitches, all with 6A electricity. Pitches near the beach are numbered, have shade from mature trees and are slightly sloping towards the sea. Those towards the back of the site are on open fields without much shade and are not marked or numbered. Unfortunately the number of pitches has increased dramatically over the years, many are occupied by seasonal campers and statics of every description, and parts of the site resemble a shanty town. Most numbered pitches have water points close by, but the back pitches have to go to the toilet blocks for water. Access roads are gravel. For those who like activity, Valkanela has four gravel tennis courts, beach volleyball and opportunities for diving, water skiing and boat rental. There is a little marina for mooring small boats and a long rock and pebble private beach, with some grass lawns for sunbathing. It is a short stroll to the surrounding villages with their bars, restaurants and shops. There may be some noise nuisance from the disco outside the entrance and compared to most the site looks rather overcrowded and depressing.

Facilities

Fifteen toilet blocks of varying styles and ages provide toilets, open style washbasins and controllable hot showers. Bathroom (free). Facilities for disabled visitors. Laundry with sinks and washing machines. Supermarkets. Souvenir shops and newspaper kiosk. Bars and restaurants with dance floor and stage. Pâtisserie. Tennis. Minigolf. Fishing. Bicycle hire. Games room. Marina with boat launching. Boat and pedalo hire. Daily entertainment for children up to 12 yrs. Off site: Riding 2 km.

Open: 25 April - 3 October.

Directions

Follow campsite signs from Vrsar.
GPS: N45:09.913 E13:36.434

Charges 2009

Per person	€ 4,50 - € 7,00
child (5-11 yrs)	free - € 3,50
child (12-18 yrs)	€ 3,40 - € 5,30
pitch incl. electricity	€ 6,50 - € 18,00
dog	€ 2,50 - € 6,00

CR6720 Naturist Centre Ulika

Cervar, HR-52440 Porec (Istria)

Tel: **052 436 325**. Email: **mail@plavalaguna.hr** **www.alanrogers.com/CR6720**

One of the many naturist campsites in Croatia, Ulika is run by the same concern as Zelena Laguna (CR6722) and Bijela Uvala (CR6724) and offers similar facilities. The site is well located, occupying a small peninsula of some 15 hectares. This means that there is only a short walk to the sea from anywhere on the site. The ground is mostly gently sloping with a covering of rough grass and there are 388 pitches with electricity connections. One side of the site is shaded with mature trees but the other side is almost devoid of shade and could become very hot. Single men are not accepted.

Facilities

Six toilet blocks provide mostly British style WCs, washbasins (half with hot water) and showers (around a third with controllable hot water). Facilities for disabled visitors. Laundry. Motorcaravan services. Supermarket. Restaurant, pizzeria and snacks. Bicycle hire. Swimming pool. Tennis. Watersports. Boating. Off site: Bicycle hire 3 km. Riding 15 km. Porec the nearest town is 6 km.

Open: 19 March - 7 October.

Directions

Site is about 3 km. off the main Novigrad - Porec road, signed in village of Cevar.
GPS: N45:15.424 E13:35.027

Charges guide

Per person	€ 3,80 - € 7,00
child (4-10 yrs)	free - € 4,90
pitch	€ 5,60 - € 13,20
electricity	€ 2,30 - € 3,20

CR6725 Camping Porto Sole

Petalon 1, HR-52450 Vrsar (Istria)

Tel: **052 426 500**. Email: **petalon-portosole@maistra.hr** **www.alanrogers.com/CR6725**

Located near the pretty town of Vrsar and its charming marina, Porto Sole is a large campsite with 800 pitches and is part of the Maistra Group. The pitches vary; some are in the open with semi shade and are fairly flat, others are under a heavy canopy of pines on undulating land. There is some terracing near the small number of water frontage pitches. The site could be described as almost a clover leaf shape with one area for rental accommodation and natural woods, another for sporting facilities and the other two for pitches. There is a large water frontage and two tiny bays provide delightful sheltered rocky swimming areas. In peak season the site is buzzing with activity and the hub of the site is the pools, disco and shopping arcade area where there is also a pub and both formal and informal eating areas. The food available is varied but simple with a tiny terrace restaurant by the water.

Facilities

Five completely renovated toilet blocks have mostly British style WCs and are clean and well maintained. The low numbers of showers (common to most Croatian sites) result in long queues. Facilities for disabled visitors and children. Washing machines and dryers. Large well stocked supermarket (1/5-15/9). Small shopping centre. Pub. Pizzeria. Formal and informal restaurants. Swimming pools (1/5-29/9). Play area (alongside beach). Boules. Tennis. Minigolf. Massage. Disco. Entertainment in season. Miniclub. Scuba-diving courses. Boat launching. Off site: Marina, sailing 1 km. Vrsar 2 km. Riding 3 km.

Open: 25 April - 3 October.

Directions

Follow signs towards Vrsar and take turn towards Koversada, then follow campsite signs. GPS: N45:08.527 E13:36.136

Charges 2009

Per person	€ 5,00 - € 7,40
child (5-12 yrs)	free - € 4,30
pitch	€ 7,50 - € 23,50
dog	€ 3,10 - € 6,50

Camping Cheques accepted.

CR6722 Autokamp Zelena Laguna

HR-52440 Porec (Istria)

Tel: **052 410 101**. Email: **mail@plavalaguna.hr** **www.alanrogers.com/CR6722**

A busy medium sized site (by Croatian standards), Zelena Laguna (green lagoon) is very popular with families and boat owners. Part of the Plava Laguna Leisure group that has eight other campsites and seven hotels in the vicinity, it is long established and is improved and modernised each year as finances permit. The 1,100 pitches (540 for touring units) are a mixture of level, moderately sloping and terraced ground and range in size from 40-120 sq.m. There are plenty of electrical hook-ups (10A). 42 super pitches are very popular. Some quite steep slopes will be encountered on the site.

Facilities

The sanitary blocks are good and some have been refurbished. The washbasins have hot water and there are free hot controllable showers. Toilets are mostly British style and there are facilities for disabled campers. Supermarket and shop. Several restaurants and snack bars. Swimming pool. Sub-aqua diving. Tennis. Bicycle hire. Boat hire. Riding. Entertainment programme. Off site: Small market and shops outside site. Riding 300 m. Supermarkets in Porec 4 km. Fishing 5 km.

Open: 19 March - 7 October.

Directions

Site is between the coast road and the sea with turning 2 km. from Porec towards Vrsar. It is very well signed and is part of a large multiple hotel complex. GPS: N45:11.717 E13:35.356

Charges guide

Per person	€ 3,80 - € 7,00
child (4-9 yrs)	free - € 4,90
pitch	€ 5,60 - € 13,20
electricity	€ 2,30 - € 3,20

CR6729 Naturist Camping Koversada

Koversada, HR-52450 Vrsar (Istria)

Tel: **052 441 378**. Email: **koversada-camp@maistra.hr** **www.alanrogers.com/CR6729**

According to history, the first naturist on Koversada was the famous adventurer Casanova. Today Koversada is an enclosed holiday park for naturists with bungalows, 1,700 pitches (1,438 for tourers, all with 6/8A electricity), a shopping centre and its own island. The main attraction of this site is the Koversada island, connected to the mainland by a small bridge. It is only suitable for tents, but has a restaurant and two toilet blocks. Between the island and the mainland is an enclosed, shallow section of water for swimming and, on the other side of the bridge, an area for mooring small boats. The pitches are of average size on grass and gravel ground and slightly sloping. Pitches on the mainland are numbered and partly terraced under mature pine and olive trees. Pitching on the island is haphazard, but there is also shade from mature trees. The bottom row of pitches on the mainland has views over the island and the sea. The site is surrounded by a long beach, part sand, part paved.

Facilities

Seventeen toilet blocks provide British and Turkish style toilets, washbasins and controllable hot showers. Child-size toilets and basins. Family bathroom (free). Facilities for disabled visitors. Laundry service. Supermarket. Kiosks with newspapers and tobacco. Several bars and restaurants. Tennis. Minigolf. Fishing. Boats, surf boards, canoes and kayaks for hire. Paragliding. 'Tweety club' for children. Live music. Sports tournaments. Off site: Riding 2 km.

Open: 25 April - 3 October.

Directions

Site is just south from Vrsar. From Vrsar, follow site signs. GPS: N45:08.573 E13:36.316

Charges 2009

Per person	€ 5,00 - € 7,00
child (5-11 yrs)	free - € 3,50
child (12-18 yrs)	€ 3,75 - € 5,25
pitch	€ 8,00 - € 18,00
dog	€ 3,10 - € 5,50

Camping Cheques accepted.

Naturist park Koversada Vrsar
Istria
Green Mediterranean.
New seaside lots! Children's clubs and playgrounds!
ONLINE BOOKING
A Mediterranean paradise in a superb natural setting; the gentle climate and clean seas have made this a favourite summer holiday destination for many generations of naturists.
tel:+385(0)52 800200 / fax:800215 / koversada-camp@maistra.hr
www.maistra.hr

CR6724 Camping Bijela Uvala

Bijela Uvala, Zelena Laguna, HR-52440 Porec (Istria)

Tel: **052 410 551**. Email: **mail@plavalaguna.hr** **www.alanrogers.com/CR6724**

Bijela Uvala is part of the Plava Laguna Leisure group and is a large friendly campsite with an extensive range of facilities. The direct sea access makes the site very popular in high season. The 2,000 pitches, 1,476 for touring, are compact and due to the terrain some have excellent sea views and breezes, however as usual these are the most sought after so book early. They range from 60-120 sq.m. and all have electricity, 400 also have water connections. Some are formal with hedging, some are terraced and most have good shade from established trees or wooded areas. There are also very informal areas where unmarked pitches are on generally uneven ground.

Facilities

Eight sanitary blocks are clean and well equipped with mainly British style WCs. Free hot showers. Washing machines. Facilities for disabled visitors. Motorcaravan service point. Two restaurants, three fast food cafés, two bars and a bakery. Large supermarket and a shop. Two swimming pool complexes, one with a medium size pool and the other a larger lagoon style with fountains. Tennis. Playground. Amusements. TV room. Entertainment centre for children. Off site: Zelena Laguna campsite facilities. Sports complex 100 m. Naturist beach 25 m.

Open: 19 March - 7 October.

Directions

The site adjoins Zelena Laguna. From the main Porec to Vrsar coast road turn off towards coast and the town of Zelena Laguna about 4 km. south of Porec and follow campsite signs.
GPS: N45:11.489 E13:35.812

Charges guide

Per person	€ 3,80 - € 7,00
child (4-9 yrs)	free - € 4,90
pitch	€ 5,60 - € 13,20
electricity	€ 2,30 - € 3,20

CR6730 Camping Amarin

Monsena bb, HR-52210 Rovinj (Istria)

Tel: **052 802 000**. Email: **ac-amarin@maistra.hr** **www.alanrogers.com/CR6730**

Situated 4 km. from the centre of the lovely old port town of Rovinj this site has much to offer. The complex is part of the Maistra Group. It has 12.6 hectares of land and is adjacent to the Amarin bungalow complex. Campers can take advantage of the facilities afforded by both areas. There are 670 pitches for touring units on various types of ground and between 80-120 sq.m. Most are separated by foliage, 10A electricity is available. A rocky beach backed by a grassy sunbathing area is very popular, but the site has its own superb, supervised round pool with corkscrew slide plus a splash pool for children. Boat owners have a mooring area and launching ramp and a breakwater is popular with sunbathers. The port of Rovinj contains many delights, particularly if you are able to contend with the hundreds of steps which lead to the church above the town from where the views are well worth the climb.

Facilities

Thirteen respectable toilet blocks have a mixture of British style and Turkish toilets. Half the washbasins have hot water. Some showers have hot water, the rest have cold and are outside. Some blocks have a unit for disabled visitors. Fridge box hire. Washing machines. Security boxes. Motorcaravan service point. Supermarket. Small market. Two restaurants, taverna, pizzeria and terrace grill. Swimming pool. Flume and splash pool. Watersports. Bicycle hire. Fishing (permit). Daily entertainment. Hairdresser. Massage. Barbecues are not permitted. Dogs are not allowed on beach. Off site: Hourly minibus service to Rovinj. Excursions from site including day trips to Venice. Riding 2 km.

Open: 25 April - 27 September.

Directions

Follow signs towards Rovinj and if approaching from the north turn off about 2 km. before the town towards Amarin and Valalta. Then follow signs to Amarin and the campsite. Watch for a left turn after about 3 km. where signs are difficult to see.
GPS: N45:06.526 E13:37.193

Charges 2009

Per person	€ 4,50 - € 7,80
child (5-12 yrs)	free - € 4,80
pitch incl. electricity	€ 6,50 - € 13,00
dog	€ 4,00 - € 7,00

For stays less than 3 nights in high season add 10%.

CR6728 Camping Orsera

Sv. Martin 2/1, HR-52450 Vrsar (Istria)

Tel: **052 441 330**. Email: **valamar@riviera.hr** **www.alanrogers.com/CR6728**

This 30 hectare site is very close to the fishing port of Vrsar, to which it has direct access. The site has 833 pitches of which 593 are available to touring units. Marked and numbered, the pitches vary in size with 90 sq.m. being the average. The sand and grass ground slopes towards the sea and there is some terracing. Ample shade is provided by mature trees. Over 200 pitches have electricity and water and 60 also have waste water drainage. Part of the 'Camping on the Adriatic' group.

Facilities

Many of the toilet blocks have been renovated and one completely new block provides very good facilities. Mainly British style WCs, washbasins and showers, mostly with hot water. Some have facilities for disabled campers. Facilities for babies and children. Laundry. Supermarket (1/5-15/9). Bar/restaurant (1/5-15/9). Sports centre. Cinema. Bicycle hire. Fishing. Watersports (no jet skis). Only gas barbecues are permitted. Off site: Golf 7 km.

Open: 1 April - 8 October.

Directions

Site is on the main Porec (7 km) - Vrsar (1 km) road, well signed. GPS: N45:09.329 E13:36.619

Charges guide

Per person	€ 3,45 - € 6,15
child (4-10 yrs)	free - € 4,50
pitch incl. electricity (16A)	€ 5,75 - € 13,65
incl. water	€ 8,55 - € 14,65

Prices for pitches by the sea are higher.

Runner up Alan Rogers Awards 2008

CR6732 Camping Polari

Polari bb, HR-52210 Rovinj (Istria)

Tel: **052 801 501**. Email: **polari@maistra.hr** **www.alanrogers.com/CR6732**

This 60 hectare site has excellent facilities for both textile and naturist campers, the latter having a reserved area of 12 hectares called Punta Eva. Prime places are taken by permanent customers but there are some numbered pitches which are very good. Many of the pitches have been thoughtfully upgraded and now a new pitch (100 sq.m) is offered with full facilities. Pitches are clean, neat and level and there will be shade when the young trees grow. There is something for everyone here to enjoy or you may prefer just to relax. An impressive swimming pool complex is child friendly with large paddling areas. The site, which is part of the 'Maistia Group', has undergone a massive improvement programme and the result makes it a very attractive option. Enjoy a meal on the huge restaurant terrace with panoramic views of the sea.

Facilities

All the sanitary facilities have been renovated to a high standard with plenty of hot water and good showers. Washing machines and dryers. Laundry service including ironing. Motorcaravan service point. Two shops, one large and one small, one restaurant and snack bar. Tennis. Minigolf. Children's entertainment with all major European languages spoken. Bicycle hire. Watersports. Sailing school. Off site: Riding 1 km. Five buses daily to and from Rovinj (3 km).

Open: 4 April - 10 October.

Directions

From any access road to Rovinj look for red signs to AC Polari (amongst other destinations). The site is about 3 km. south of Rovinj.
GPS: N45:03.772 E13:40.493

Charges 2009

Per person	€ 5,00 - € 8,50
children and seniors according to age	free - € 8,50
pitch incl. electricity	€ 8,00 - € 21,50

For stays less than 3 nights in high season add 20%. Camping Cheques accepted.

CR6731 Naturist Camping Valalta

Cesta Valalta-Lim bb, HR-52210 Rovinj (Istria)

Tel: **052 804 800**. Email: **valalta@valalta.hr** **www.alanrogers.com/CR6731**

This is a most impressive site for up to 6,000 naturist campers, which has a pleasant, open feel. The passage through reception is efficient and this feeling is maintained around the well organised site. A friendly, family atmosphere is to be found here. Valalta is a family oriented campsite. All pitches are the same price with 16A electricity, although they vary in size and surroundings. The variations include shade, views, sand, grass, sea frontage, level ground, slopes and terracing. It is not possible to reserve a particular pitch and campers do move pitches at will. The impressive pool is in lagoon style with water features and cascades.

Facilities

Twenty high quality new or refurbished sanitary blocks of which four are smaller units of plastic 'pod' construction. Hot showers (coin operated). Facilities for disabled campers. Washing machines and dryers. Supermarket. Four restaurants (one specialising in seafood). Pizzeria. Two bars. Large lagoon style pool complex. Beauty saloon. Fitness club. Massage. Minigolf. Tennis. Sailing. Play area. Bicycle hire. Beach. Marina with full services. Internet. Animation all season. Kindergarten. Dogs are not accepted. Off site: Riding 7 km.

Open: 25 April - 27 September.

Directions

Site is on the coast 8 km. north of Rovinj. If approaching from the north turn inland (follow signs to Rovinj) to drive around the Limski Kanal. Then follow signs towards Valalta about 2 km. east of Rovinj. Site is at the end of the road and is well signed. GPS: N45:07.334 E13:37.848

Charges 2009

Per person	€ 5,00 - € 9,50
child (4-14 yrs)	€ 2,50 - € 4,75
pitch incl. electricity	€ 8,00 - € 14,50

CR6733 Camping Vestar

Vestar b.b., HR-52210 Rovinj (Istria)

Tel: **052 829 150**. Email: **vestar@maistra.hr** **www.alanrogers.com/CR6733**

Camping Vestar, just 5 km. from the historic harbour town of Rovinj, is one of the rare sites in Croatia with a partly sandy beach. Right behind the beach is a large area, attractively landscaped with young trees and shrubs, with grass for sunbathing. The site has 670 large pitches, of which 550 are for tourers, all with 6/10A electricity (the rest being taken by seasonal units and 14 pitches for tour operators). It is largely wooded with good shade and from the bottom row of pitches there are views of the sea. Pitching is on two separate fields, one for free camping, the other with numbered pitches. The pitches at the beach are in a half circle around the shallow bay, making it safe for children to swim. Vestar has a small marina and a jetty for mooring small boats and excursions to the islands are arranged. There is a miniclub and live music with dancing at one of the two bar/restaurants in the evenings. The restaurants all have open air terraces, one covered with vines to protect you from the hot sun.

Facilities

Five modern and one refurbished toilet block with mainly Turkish style toilets and some British style, open washbasins and controllable hot showers. Child-size basins. Family bathroom. Facilities for disabled people. Laundry service. Fridge box hire. Motorcaravan services. Shop. Two bar/restaurants. Large swimming pool. Playground. Tennis. Fishing. Boat and pedalo hire. Miniclub (5-11 yrs). Excursions. Off site: Riding 2 km. Rovinj 5 km.

Open: 25 April - 3 October.

Directions

Follow site signs from Rovinj.
GPS: N45:03.259 E13:41.141

Charges 2009

Per person	€ 5,00 - € 9,20
child (5-12 yrs)	free - € 6,90
pitch incl. electricity	€ 7,00 - € 22,00
dog	€ 3,10 - € 6,20

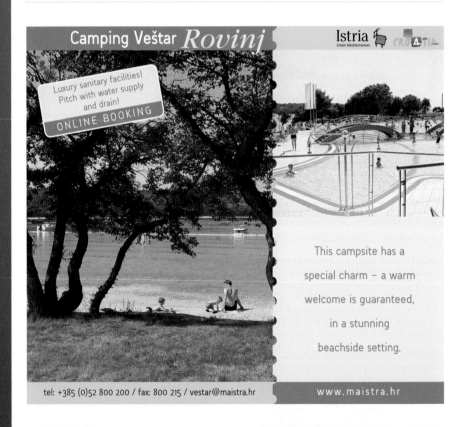

CR6745 Camping Bi-Village

Dragonja 115, HR-52212 Fazana (Istria)

Tel: **052 300 300** www.alanrogers.com/CR6745

Camping Bi-Village is large holiday village, close to the historic town of Pula and opposite the Brioni National Park. The location is excellent and there are some superb sunsets. The site is landscaped with many flowers, shrubs and rock walls and offers over 1,000 pitches for touring units (the remainder taken by bungalows and chalets). The campsite is separated from the holiday bungalows by the main site road which runs from the entrance to the beach. Pitches are set in long rows accessed by gravel lanes, slightly sloping towards the sea, with only the bottom rows having shade from mature trees and good views over the Adriatic.

Facilities

Four modern toilet blocks with toilets, open plan washbasins and controllable hot showers. Child-size washbasins. Baby room. Facilities for disabled visitors. Washing machine. Shopping centre (1/5-11/10). Bars (1/5-30/9) and restaurants. Bazaar. Gelateria. Pastry shop. Three swimming pools. Playground on gravel. Playing field. Trampolines. Minigolf. Jet skis, motorboats and pedaloes for hire. Boat launching. Games hall. Sports tournaments and entertainment organised. Massage. Internet point. Off site: Historic towns of Pula and Rovinj are close. Fishing 3 km. Riding 15 km.

Open: 5 March - 31 October.

Directions

Follow no. 2 road south from Rijeka to Pula. In Pula follow site signs. Site is close to Fazana.
GPS: N44:55.030 E13:48.663

Charges guide

Per person	€ 4,00 - € 8,50
child	free - € 4,50
pitch incl. electricity and water	€ 5,50 - € 16,00
dog	€ 2,00 - € 3,00

Camping Cheques accepted.

CR6650 Autocamp Korana

Rakovica, HR-47246 Plitvicka Jezera (Central)

Tel: **053 751 888**. Email: **info@np-plitvicka-jezera.hr** www.alanrogers.com/CR6650

For a visit to the famous Plitvice lakes in the far eastern part of the country, this site is a totally acceptable option for spending a night nearby. In a large, park-like environment, caravans and motorcaravans are placed on one of 540 unmarked tarmac hardstandings, with electricity available (16A). The toilet facilities are adequate and clean but other facilities are entirely missing: no washing machine, fridges, internet, pools, sports or other forms of entertainment. Most people stay here for only one or two nights, so every morning and afternoon serious traffic jams arise. Leave early. A huge restaurant in the centre of the site tries hard to suggest it caters for groups only, but individual guests may find something here.

Facilities

The toilet blocks include facilities for disabled persons. Chemical disposal and motorcaravan service point. Shop is opened in the morning and afternoon and information about the national park can be found here. Off site: The wonderful (and expensive) National Park, but not much else.

Open: May - end September.

Directions

Along the main road, pass entrances 1 and 2 of the National Park. Site is north of the park area just beyond the village of Seliste on the right (eastern) side and is signed. GPS: N44:57.026 E15:38.468

Charges guide

Per person	€ 9,00
child (7-12 yrs)	€ 6,30
pitch incl. electricity	€ 6,00
dog	€ 3,00

Camping Cheques accepted.

CR6765 Camping Kovacine

Helin I/20, HR-51557 Cres (Kvarner)

Tel: **051 573 150**. Email: **campkovacine@kovacine.com** **www.alanrogers.com/CR6765**

Camping Kovacine is located on a peninsula on the beautiful Dalmatian island of Cres, just 2 km. from the town of the same name. The site has 750 numbered, mostly level pitches, of which 632 are for tourers (300 with 12A electricity). On sloping ground, partially shaded by mature olive and pine trees, pitching is on the large, open spaces between the trees. Some places have views of the Valun lagoon. Kovacine is partly an FKK (naturist) site, which is quite common in Croatia, and has a pleasant atmosphere. Here one can enjoy local live music on a stage close to the pebble beach (Blue Flag), where there is also a restaurant and bar. The site has its own private beach, part concrete, part pebbles, and a jetty for mooring boats and fishing. A swimming pool has been added recently. It is close to the historic town of Cres, the main town on the island, which offers a rich history of fishing, shipyards and authentic Dalmatian-style houses. There are also several bars, restaurants and shops.

Facilities

Five modern, comfortable toilet blocks (two refurbished) offer British style toilets, open plan washbasins (some cabins for ladies) and hot showers. Bathroom for hire. Facilities for disabled people (although access is difficult). Washing machine. Fridge box hire. Motorcaravan services. Car wash. Supermarket. Bar, restaurant and pizzeria. New swimming pool. Playground. Daily children's club. Evening shows with live music. Boat launching. Fishing. Diving. Motorboat hire. WiFi. Airport transfers. Off site: Historic town of Cres with bars, restaurants and shops 2 km.

Open: 16 April - 15 October.

Directions

From Rijeka take no. 2 road south towards Labin and take ferry to Cres at Brestova. Continue to Cres and follow site signs. GPS: N44:57.713 E14:23.790

Charges guide

Per person	€ 4,80 - € 9,60
child (3-11 yrs)	€ 2,30 - € 3,50
pitch	€ 4,60 - € 8,40
dog	€ 1,00 - € 3,00

CR6757 Camping Jezevac

HR-51500 Krk (Kvarner)

Tel: **052 465 010**. Email: **camping@valamar.com** **www.alanrogers.com/CR6757**

Camping Jezevac is a seaside site, close to the pretty town of Krk. This is a large site extending over 11 hectares with 670 pitches (80-120 sq.m). In high season the atmosphere is lively and the site's 800 m. private beach is a focal point. Jezevac has benefited from some renovation work in recent years. The reception area has been modernised and a quantity of mobile homes was added in 2008. A children's club is run for most of the season with a varied programme of activities. A good sports centre can be found 300 m. away.

Facilities

Heated toilet block with hot showers. Washing machines. Shops (1/4-15/10). Restaurants (1/5-1/10) and bars. Takeaway (1/5-30/9). Tennis. Playground. Activity and entertainment programmes and club for children (May - Sept). Fishing. Bicycle hire. Boat launching and sailing. Off site: Sports centre 300 m.

Open: 18 April - 15 October.

Directions

From Ostrovica: Upon entering Krk, follow signs to the town centre. Take the second right turn and continue ahead for 2.2 km. At the first roundabout take the second exit. Continue for 600 m. following signs to Camp Jezevac. GPS: N45:01.178 E14:34.243

Charges guide

Per unit incl. 2 persons	€ 18,10 - € 27,70
extra person	€ 4,40 - € 6,10

CR6758 Naturist Camping Politin

HR-51500 Krk (Kvarner)

Tel: **052 465 010**. Email: **camping@valamar.com** **www.alanrogers.com/CR6758**

Politin is an attractive naturist site on the wooded peninsula of Prniba, quite close to the centre of Krk. There are 250 touring pitches here, not all with electricity, and ranging in size from 70-110 sq.m. The site has its own 'blue flag' accredited private beach. There is an activity programme for children during the high season. On-site amenities include a shop, renovated toilet blocks and a restaurant. Boat trips to the neighbouring islands of Rab and Cres are possible and can be arranged on site.

Facilities

Restaurant, bar and shop (all 1/5-30/9). Tennis. Play area. Children's activity programme (May - Sept). Fishing. Boat launching. Sailing. Free WiFi internet access. Off site: Fitness centre 1.5 km. Sports centre 2 km. Krk town centre.

Open: 15 April - 30 September.

Directions

Head for the island's capital, Krk (around 28 km). On arrival head to first junction and turn right. After 500 m. turn left (beyond petrol station). Continue for 800 m. to site. GPS: N45:01.464 E14:35.568

Charges guide

Per unit incl. 2 persons	€ 18,10 - € 32,20
extra person	€ 4,40 - € 6,35

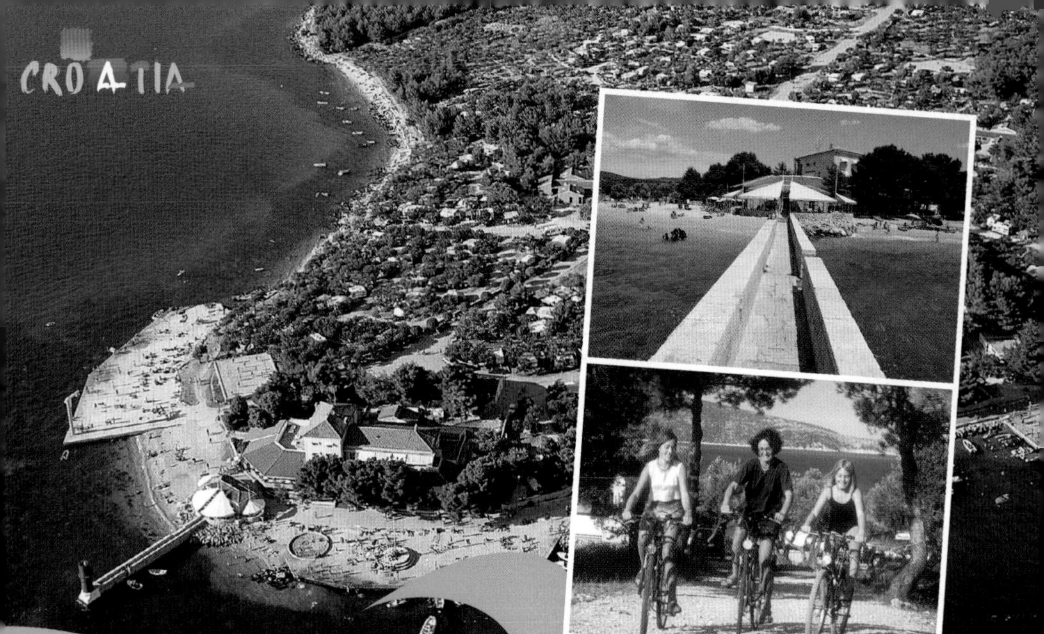

The freedom of camping with all the comforts of home.

A crystal clear sea, beautiful beaches and pine and olive trees which provide plenty of shade: visitors are guaranteed a unique atmosphere. Camping Kovacine is situated on a peninsula and is close to the fishing town of Cres. There are 850 well appointed, modern pitches.

WE OFFER YOU

- **New, modern sanitary facilities (solar energy)**
- **Bar, buffet, restaurant, self service shop**
- **Mini marina and boat crane**
- **First aid service**
- **Animation for children**
- **Sport facilities**
- **Diving and diving school**
- **New mobile homes for 2 and 4-6 persons**
- **Rooms directly on the beach with breakfast**
- **Free WiFi**
- **Airport transfer Rijeka – Cres vice versa only € 25 pp**
- **Ferry costs refunded for 7 or 14 nights stay**
- **Special offers in low season: 7=6, 14=12 nights**

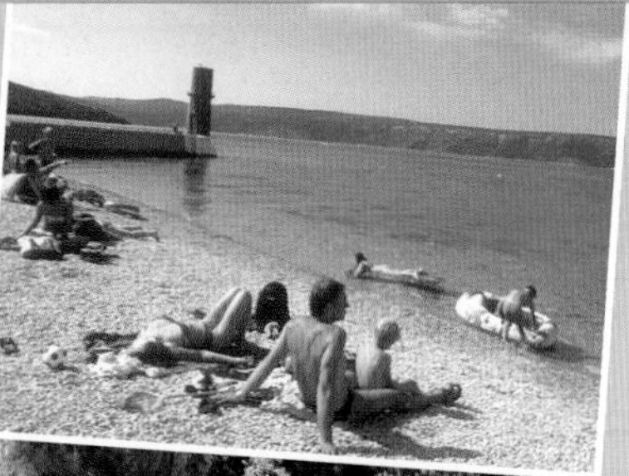

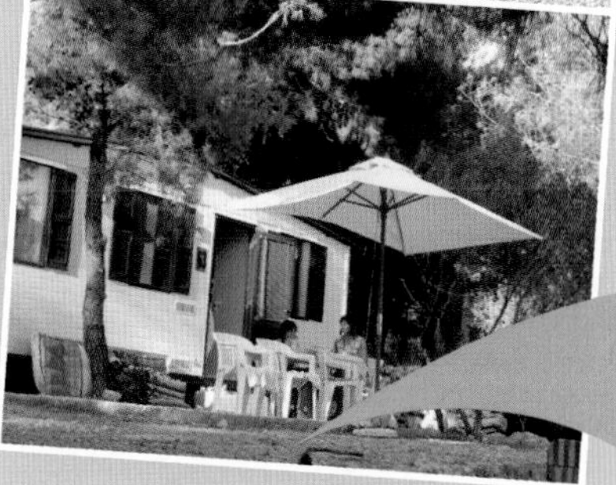

Camping Kovačine Cres
HR-51557 Cres
Tel. 00-385/51/573-150
Fax 00-385/51/571-086
campkovacine@kovacine.com

CAMP KOVAČINE
CRES

W W W . C A M P - K O V A C I N E . C O M

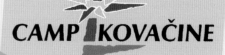

CR6736 Camping Valdaliso

Monsena bb, HR-52210 Rovinj (Istria)

Tel: **052 805 505**. Email: **info@rovinjturist.hr** **www.alanrogers.com/CR6736**

Unusually Camping Valdaliso has its affiliated hotel in the centre of the site. The pitches are mostly flat with shade from pine trees and the site is divided into three sections all with 16A electricity. The choice of formal numbered pitches, informal camping or proximity to the sea impacts on the prices. The kilometre plus of pebble beach has crystal clear water. The entertainment programme is extremely professional and there is a lot to do at Valdaliso, which is aimed primarily at families. The variety of activities here and the bonus of the use of the hotel make this a great choice for campers. The fine Barabiga restaurant within the hotel offers superb Istrian and fish cuisine and the pool is also within the hotel. You are close to the beautiful old town of Rovinj and parts of this site enjoy views of the town. A water taxi makes exploring Rovinj very easy, compared with the impossible parking for private cars. A bus service is also provided but this involves considerable walking. Dogs are not accepted.

Facilities

Two large clean sanitary blocks have hot showers (coin operated). The northeastern block has facilities for disabled campers. Hotel facilities. Shop. Pizzeria. Restaurant. Tennis. Fitness centre. Bicycle hire. Games room. Children's games. Summer painting courses. Exchange. Boat rental. Watersports. Boat launching. Fishing. Diving school. Internet in both receptions. Water taxi. Bus service. No animals allowed. Off site: Town 1 km.

Open: 4 April - 3 October.

Directions

Site is 7 km. north of Rovinj on the main coast road between Vsrar and Rovinj. Watch for the signs to Monsena and the site. GPS: N45:06.256 E13:37.511

Charges 2009

Per person	€ 4,50 - € 7,80
child (5-12 yrs)	free - € 4,80
pitch	€ 6,50 - € 15,00

CR6761 Camping Zablace

E Geistlicha 38, HR-51523 Baska (Kvarner)

Tel: **051 856 909**. Email: **campzablace@hotelibaslea.hr** **www.alanrogers.com/CR6761**

Camping Zablace is at the southern end of the beautiful island of Krk, in the ancient ferry port of Baska. Like most sites in Croatia it has direct access to a large, pebble beach and from the bottom row of pitches one has views over the Adriatic islands. The site has 500 pitches with 400 used for touring units. Zone 1 (nearest the beach) provides 100 individual pitches with electricity and water. The quietest zone, if further away (and across a public road that splits the site in two) has electricity and water taps. There is not much shade anywhere. There are not many amenities on the site, but it is an easy five minute walk along the promenade to the centre of Baska where there are bars, restaurants and pizzerias.

Facilities

Five toilet blocks with toilets, open plan basins and controllable hot showers (key access for the toilets nearest the beach). Facilities for disabled visitors. Motorcaravan service point. Shop. Kiosks with fruit, cold drinks, tobacco, newspapers and beach wear. Off site: Giant slide and games hall. Tennis and minigolf 200 m. Windsurfing. Diving. Marked hiking and cycle routes.

Open: 19 April - 15 October.

Directions

On Krk follow the no. 29 road south to Baska, then good signs to site. GPS: N44:58.001 E14:44.707

Charges guide

Per person	Kn 30,00 - 45,00
child (7-11 yrs)	Kn 15,00 - 22,00
pitch incl. electricity	Kn 75,00 - 130,00
dog	free - Kn 25,00

Camping Cheques accepted.

CR6845 Camp Adriatic

Huljerat bb, HR-22202 Primosten (Dalmatia)

Tel: **022 571 223**. Email: **info@camp-adriatic.hr** **www.alanrogers.com/CR6845**

As we drove south down the Dalmatian coast road, we looked across a clear turquoise bay and saw a few tents, caravans and motorcaravans camped under some trees. A short distance later we were at the entrance of Camping Adriatic. With 530 pitches that slope down to the sea, the site is deceptive and enjoys a one kilometre beach frontage which is ideal for snorkelling and diving. Most pitches are level and have shade from pine trees. There are 212 numbered pitches and 288 unnumbered, all with 10/16A electricity. Close to the delightful town of Primosten (with a taxi boat service in high season) the site boasts good modern amenities and a fantastic location.

Facilities

Four modern sanitary blocks provide clean toilets, hot showers and washbasins. Facilities for disabled visitors. Bathroom for children. Washing machine and dryer. Kitchen facilities. Small supermarket (15/5-30/9). Restaurant and bar (all season). Sports centre. Miniclub. Beach. Diving school. Sailing school and boat hire. Entertainment programme in July/Aug. Internet point.

Open: 1 May - 15 October.

Directions

Take the new A1 motorway south and leave at the Sibenik exit. Follow the 33 road into Sibenik and then go south along the coast road (no. 8), signed Primosten. Site is 2.5 km. north of Primosten.
GPS: N43:36.391 E15:55.257

Charges guide

Per person	Kn 31,00 - 43,00
child (5-12 yrs)	Kn 22,00 - 28,00
pitch	Kn 30,00 - 60,00

Camping Cheques accepted.

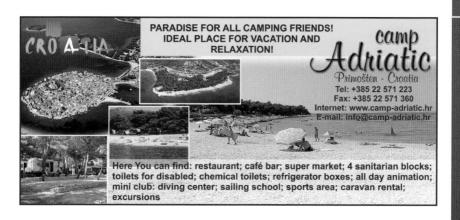

CR6850 Camp Seget

Hrvatskih zrtava 121, HR-21218 Trogir Seget Donji (Dalmatia)

Tel: **021 880 394**. Email: **kamp@kamp-seget.hr** **www.alanrogers.com/CR6850**

Seget is a simple site which is pleasant and quiet with only 120 pitches, just 2 km. from the interesting old harbour town of Trogir. The site is set up on both sides of a tarmac access lane that runs down to the sea. Pitches to the left are arranged off three separate, gravel lanes. They are fairly level and from most there are views of the sea. Pitches to the right are slightly sloping and mostly used for tents. Of varying sizes (60-100 sq.m) the pitches are on grass and gravel (firm tent pegs may be needed), mostly in the shade of mature fig and palm trees and some are numbered.

Facilities

Two sanitary blocks (one half remaining a portacabin style). British style toilets, washbasins and controllable, hot showers (free). Facilities for disabled visitors. Campers' kitchen. Fridge box hire. Shop (1/5-31/10). Bicycle hire. Beach. Fishing. Boat rental. Barbecues permitted only on communal area. Off site: Bus at gate for touring. Golf 1 km. Boat launching 500 m.

Open: 15 April - 15 October.

Directions

Follow no. 8 coastal road south from Zadar towards Split and in Trogir look for prominent site signs, finishing in a sharp right turn.
GPS: N43:31.116 E16:13.450

Charges guide

Per person	Kn 33,00 - 47,00
child (5-12 yrs)	Kn 33,00 - 31,00
pitch incl. car	Kn 60,00 - 95,00
electricity	Kn 20,00

CR6865 Camp Vira

HR-21450 Hvar (Dalmatia)

Tel: **021 741 803**. Email: **viracamp@suncanihvar.com** **www.alanrogers.com/CR6865**

Camp Vira has been recommended to us by our Croatia agent and we plan to undertake a full inspection next year. Located only 4 km. from the town of Hvar, it is said to be a nature lover's paradise that combines Hvar's natural beauty and clean sea with an environmentally friendly array of modern amenities. Solar powered units supply the bulk of the campsite's energy needs, while pine trees provide natural shade for the 90 pitches and 72 camping places. Vira's private cove has a pebble beach making it ideal for sunbathing, swimming and variety of water activities.

Facilities

Amenities include newly renovated shower and bathroom facilities. Laundry and ironing services. Grocery shop and souvenir shop. Aloe Vera bar and grill. Playground. Recreation rentals and beach shop. Fridge hire. Tent hire. Off site: Bus service to Hvar.

Open: 15 May - 31 October.

Directions

Site is 4 km. northwest from the town of Hvar. From Hvar go forward leaving the central car park on the left and follow roadside directions to site. GPS: N43:11.452 E16:25.819

Charges guide

Per person	€ 6,00 - € 7,00
child (3-11 yrs)	€ 3,00 - € 4,00
pitch	€ 11,00 - € 22,00
dog	€ 4,00 - € 5,00

Camping Cheques accepted.

MAP 6

The Czech Republic is a land full of fascinating castles, romantic lakes and valleys, picturesque medieval squares and famous spas. It is divided into two main regions, Bohemia to the west and Moravia in the east.

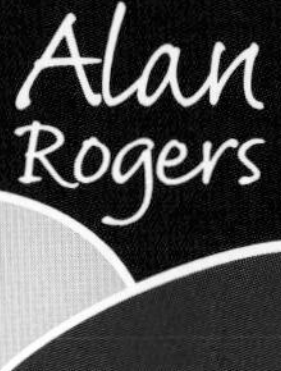

CAPITAL: PRAGUE

Tourist Office

Czech Tourist Authority
13 Harley Street, London W1G 9QG
Tel: 020 7631 0427 Fax: 020 7631 0419
Email: info-uk@czechtourism.com
Internet: www.visitczech.cz

Although small, the Czech Republic is crammed with attractive places to explore. Indeed, since the new country first appeared on the map in 1993, Prague has become one the most popular cities to visit in Europe. Steeped in history with museums, architectural sights, art galleries, and theatres, it is an enchanting place. The beautiful region of Bohemia, known for its Giant Mountains, is popular for skiing, hiking and other sports. The town of Karlovy Vary, world famous for its regenerative waters, is Bohemia's oldest Spa town, with 12 hot springs containing elements that are said to treat digestive and metabolic ailments. It also has many picturesque streets to meander through and peaceful riverside walks. Moravia is quieter, the most favoured area Brno and from here it is easy to explore historical towns such as Olomouc and Kromeriz. North of Brno is the Moravian Karst, with around 400 caves created by the underground Punkya River. Some caves are open to the public, with boat trips along the river and out of the caves.

Population

10.3 million

Climate

Temperate, continental climate with four distinct seasons. Warm in summer with cold, snowy winters.

Language

The official language is Czech.

Telephone

The country code is 00420.

Money

Currency: The Koruna
Banks: Mon-Fri 08.30-16.30.

Shops

Mon-Fri 08.00-18.00, some close at lunchtime. Sat 09.00 until midday.

Public Holidays

New Year; Easter Mon; May Day; Prague Uprising 5 May; National Day 8 May; Saints Day 5 July; Festival (John Huss) Day 6 July; Independence Day 28 Oct; Democracy Day 17 Nov; Christmas 24-26 Dec.

Motoring

There is a good and well signposted road network throughout the Republic and, although stretches of cobbles still exist, surfaces are generally good. An annual road tax is levied on all vehicles using Czech motorways and express roads, and a disc can be purchased at border crossings, post offices and filling stations. Do not drink any alcohol before driving. Dipped headlights are compulsory throughout winter months. Always give way to trams and buses.

CZ4640 Autocamping Areal Jadran

Jezerni 84/12, CZ-35101 Frantiskovy Lazne (Zapadocesky)

Tel: **354 542 412**. Email: **atc.jadran@centrum.cz** **www.alanrogers.com/CZ4640**

Autocamping Areal Jadran is on the outskirts of the spa town of Frantiskovy Lázné and is the perfect base to visit the many restored spa baths and tour the beautiful West Bohemian countryside. Marie Novotny with her husband Jiri, owner of the site, welcomed us warmly and are busy making many improvements. There should now be 90 new 'super' pitches available. There are 180 pitches for tourers, all with 16A electricity, and the site has its own lake for cooling down in the hot summer months. The pitches are partly shaded and some are of at least 120 sq.m. Adjacent to the site is Hotel Jadran which serves fine meals for very reasonable prices and has a pleasant bar.

Facilities

The heated toilet blocks (two older, one refurbished) are simple, but are clean and tidy. They include toilets, washbasins with hot and cold water, controllable showers. Washing machines and sinks with free hot water. Restaurant (1/4-31/10). No shop but fresh bread available every morning in the restaurant. Giant chess, draughts and other games. Russian bowling. Fishing. Riding. Bicycle hire. Inflatables allowed on the lake. Off site: Riding 400 m. Fishing 6 km.

Open: All year.

Directions

Frantiskovy Lazne is north of Cheb. Stay on the 21 road to the north of route 6 and leave by the first slip road to the village. Turn sharp left at the Hotel Bohemia and then right. Follow the lakeside road for 2 km. and then turn right to the site.
GPS: N50:07.022 E12:19.801

Charges guide

Per person	€ 4,10
child (3-12 yrs)	€ 2,10
pitch incl. electricity	€ 4,10 - € 6,20

CZ4650 Autocamping Luxor

Plzenska, CZ-35301 Velká Hledsebe (Zapadocesky)

Tel: **354 623 504**. Email: **autocamping.luxor@seznam.cz** **www.alanrogers.com/CZ4650**

An orderly site, near the German border, Luxor is adequate as a stopover for a couple of days. Now under new management, it is in a quiet location by a small lake on the edge of the village of Velká Hledsebe, 4 km. from Marianbad. The 100 pitches (60 for touring units) are in the open on one side of the entrance road (cars stand on a tarmac park opposite the caravans) or in a clearing under tall trees away from the road. All pitches have access to electricity (10A) but connection in the clearings section may require long leads.

Facilities

Toilet buildings are old and should be refurbished, but the provision is more than adequate. Cleaning could be better. No chemical disposal point. Restaurant with self-service terrace (1/5-30/9). Rest room with TV, kitchen and dining area. Small playground. Fishing. Bicycle hire. Off site: Very good motel restaurant and shops 500 m. in village. Riding 5 km. Golf 8 km.

Open: 1 May - 30 September.

Directions

Site is directly by the Stribo - Cheb road no. 21, 500 m. south of Velká Hledsebe.
GPS: N49:57.145 E12:40.100

Charges guide

Per unit incl. 2 persons and electricity	CZK 160 - 250
extra person	CZK 60
child (under 10 yrs)	CZK 40

No credit cards.

CZ4750 Camping Bilá Hora

Ul. 28.rijna 49, CZ-30162 Plzen (Zapadocesky)

Tel: **377 562 225** **www.alanrogers.com/CZ4750**

Even non-drinkers probably know that Pilsen is famous for its beer (Pils) and as the home of the Skoda car factory. Camping Bilá Hora is a suitable site and is situated amidst trees in the suburb of Bilá Hora, about three kilometres north of the city centre on the edge of town. The 50 pitches are on a slope in a clearing, but level concrete tracks have been made for caravans and motorcaravans, with electricity available at 30 pitches. It is a pleasant, quiet site with its own restaurant. Bungalows are quite separate from the camping area.

Facilities

The toilet block in the camping area has British style WCs, bath and a laundry, and there is another with the bungalows – they are good by Czech standards. Washing machine and iron. Motorcaravan services. Kitchen. Restaurant. Kiosk with small terrace (all year). Bicycle hire. Playground. Off site: Bus stop at site entrance. Shops 200 m. Fishing 500 m. Swimming and tennis near.

Open: 15 May - 30 September.

Directions

Site is to the north of the town on the Plzen (Pilsen) - Zruc no. 231 road where it is signed.
GPS: N49:46.719 E13:24.548

Charges guide

Per person	CZK 50
child (10-15 yrs)	CZK 70
pitch	CZK 215
electricity	CZK 70

CZ4780 Autocamping Konopiste

CZ-25601 Benesov u Prahy (Stredocesky)

Tel: **317 729 083**. Email: **reserve@cckonopiste.cz** www.alanrogers.com/CZ4780

Benesov's chief claim to fame is the Konopiste Palace, the last home of Archduke Franz Ferdinand whose assassination in Sarajevo sparked off the First World War in 1914. Autocamp Konopiste, now under new ownership, is part of a motel complex with excellent facilities situated in a very quiet, tranquil location south of Prague. On a hillside, rows of terraces separated by hedges provide 65 grassy pitches of average size, 50 with electricity (10A). However, 34 are occupied all year by a tour operator's tents. One of the best Czech campsites, Konopiste has many different varieties of trees and much to offer.

Facilities

The good quality sanitary block is central to the caravan pitches. Washing machine and irons. Kitchen. Site's own bar/buffet (high season) with simple meals and basic food items. Motel bar and two restaurants (all year). Swimming pool (1/6-31/8). Tennis. Minigolf. Bicycle hire. Badminton. Fitness centre. Playground. Club room with TV. Château and park. Off site: Shop 200 m. Fishing 1.5 km. Riding 5 km. Prague 48 km. (public transport available).

Open: 1 May - 30 September.

Directions

Site is signed near the village of Benesov on the main Prague - Ceske Budejovic road no. 3/E55.
GPS: N49:46.560 E14:40.140

Charges guide

Per person	CZK 90 - 120
child (6-15 yrs)	CZK 60 - 90
pitch	CZK 100 - 390
dog	CZK 50

Electricity included.

CZ4785 Camp Drusus

K Reporyjim 4, CZ-15500 Praha 5 Trebonice (Prague)

Tel: **235 514 391**. Email: **drusus@drusus.com** www.alanrogers.com/CZ4785

Camp Drusus is a friendly, family site on the western edge of Prague. It provides a good base from which to explore this beautiful city with the metro station only 15 minutes walk away. The site has 70 level pitches (all for tourers), 66 with 10A electricity and varying in size (60-90 sq.m), with access off a circular, grass and gravel road. There is no shop here but basics can be ordered at reception and one of the biggest shopping areas in Prague is only 2 km. You could enjoy a real Czech breakfast in the restaurant which also opens for dinner and serves as a bar. This is a pleasant, well kept and quiet site with good connections to the Czech capital.

Facilities

Portacabin style toilet facilities that look basic but are clean, contain British style toilets, open washbasins and free, controllable hot showers. Laundry facilities. Kitchen. Motorcaravan service point. No shop, but basics to order at reception. Bar/restaurant. Small fitness centre. Playground. Games room with billiards. Riding. Off site: Shops 2 km. Metro station for Prague 15 minutes. Golf 12 km.

Open: 15 April - 15 October.

Directions

On E50/E48 from Pilsen to Brno take exit 19 for Reporyje, from Brno to Pilsen take exit 23a. In the centre turn left on K Trebonicum to site on the right.
GPS: N50:02.645 E14:17.053

Charges guide

Per person	CZK 100 - 120
child (6-14 yrs)	CZK 50 - 60
pitch incl. electricity	CZK 150 - 290
dog	free
electricity	CZK 90

CZ4795 Cisarska Louka Caravan Park

Cisarska Louka 599, CZ-15000 Praha 5 (Prague)

Tel: **257 318 681**. Email: **convoy@volny.cz** **www.alanrogers.com/CZ4795**

This city site on the Cisarská Louka Island is about the closest campsite you can get to the centre of Prague. Right behind the site, which is on the premises of the local Yacht Club, a ferry takes you across the Moldau River to the nearest metro station for the city centre (hourly until 22.00). This is a useful site for a visit to Prague if you can cope with the basic toilet facilities. The site is arranged on one large, well fenced field providing 50 touring pitches, 25 with electricity (10A). Pitching is rather haphazard off a gravel access road running half way up the site.

Facilities

Basic toilet facilities with British style toilets, open washbasins and controllable hot showers (on payment). Facilities for disabled people. Motorcaravan service point. River fishing. Boat launching. Off site: Two bar/restaurants nearby.

Open: All year.

Directions

Coming in from the west on the E50 continue alongside the river towards the town centre. Take a sharp right bend just before Shell petrol station. Site is the second site on the Cisacská Louka Island in the Moldau River. GPS: N50:03.781 E14:24.783

Charges guide

Per person	CZK 950
pitch incl. electricity	CZK 265 - 325

CZ4820 Caravan Camp Valek

Chrustenice 155, CZ-26712 Lodenice (Stredocesky)

Tel: **311 672 147**. Email: **info@campvalek.cz** **www.alanrogers.com/CZ4820**

Only 2.5 km. from the E50 motorway, this well maintained, family owned site creates a peaceful, friendly base enjoyed by families. Surrounded by delightful countryside, it is possible to visit Prague even though it is about 28 km. from the city centre. The medium sized, gently sloping grass site is divided in two by a row of well established trees, offering some shade, and the toilet block. Most pitches are relatively flat, in the open and not specifically marked. However this does not appear to cause overcrowding and generally there is plenty of space. Electricity (10A) is available.

Facilities

The single clean toilet block has limited numbers of toilets and showers, but during our visit in high season coped well. Small shop with fresh rolls daily. Waiter service restaurant with terrace has an extensive menu. Natural swimming pool (20 x 60 m; June - Sept) with constantly changing water checked regularly by the authorities to ensure its purity. Extensive games room with arcade machines and internet. Live musical nights on Saturday. Tennis. Off site: Prague 28 km. Plzen 69 km.

Open: 1 May - 30 September.

Directions

From E50 (D5) motorway take exit 10 for Lodenice. Follow camping signs and or Chrustenice. Site is 300 m. on right on leaving Chrustenice. GPS: N50:00.687 E14:09.033

Charges guide

Per unit incl. 2 persons and electricity	CZK 480
extra person	CZK 115
electricity	CZK 95

CZ4825 Camping Bucek

Tratice 170, CZ-27101 Nové Straseci (Stredocesky)

Tel: **313 564 212**. Email: **info@campingbucek.cz** **www.alanrogers.com/CZ4825**

Camping Bucek is a pleasant Dutch owned site 40 km. west of Prague. Its proprietors also own Camping Frymburk (CZ4720). Bucek is located on the edge of woodland and has direct access to a small lake – canoes and rowing boats are available for hire, as well as sun loungers on the site's private beach. There are 100 pitches here, many with pleasant views over the lake, and all with electrical connections (6A). Shade is quite limited. Nearby, Revnicov is a pleasant small town with a range of shops and restaurants.

Facilities

Renovated toilet blocks with free hot showers. Washing and drying machine. Direct lake access. Swimming pool. Pedaloes, canoes, lounger hire. Minigolf. Play area. Off site: Revnicov 2 km. with shops (including a supermarket), bars and restaurants. Prague 40 km. Karlovy Vary 10 km. Koniprusy caves.

Open: 24 April - 15 September.

Directions

From the west, take no. 6/E48 express road towards Prague. Site is close to this road, about 3 km. after the Revnicov exit and is clearly signed from this point. Coming from the east, ignore other camping signs and continue until Bucek is signed (to the north). GPS: N50:10.210 E13:50.350

Charges guide

Per person	CZK 85
pitch incl. electricity	CZK 350

Reductions in low season. No credit cards.

See advertisement on page 93

Runner up Alan Rogers Awards 2008

CZ4840 Camping Oase Praha

Zlatniky-Liben, CZ-25241 Dolni Brezany (Prague)

Tel: **241 932 044**. Email: **info@campingoase.cz**

www.alanrogers.com/CZ4840

Camping Oase Praha is an exceptional site, only five kilometres from Prague and with easy access. You can take the bus (from outside the site) or drive to the underground stop (10 minutes). The site has 110 pitches, all around 100 sq.m, with 6A electricity and 55 with water and drainage, on level, well kept fields. The site is very well kept and has just everything one may expect, including a new Western style toilet block, a well maintained, heated swimming pool and separate paddling pool, a restaurant and a bar. Children can amuse themselves with trampolines, the new playground or volleyball and basketball. The main attraction here is, of course, the Czech capital. However, this site will provide a relaxing environment to return to and another advantage is that Mr Hess, the helpful owner, speaks English.

Facilities

An outstanding, new toilet block includes washbasins (open style and in cabins) with hot and cold water, spacious, controllable showers and child size toilets. Facilities for disabled visitors. Laundry facilities. Campers' kitchen with hob, fridge and freezer. Motorcaravan services. Restaurant and bar. Basic groceries are available in the shop. Swimming pool (9 x 15 m) and separate paddling pool with slide (both 15/5-20/9). New adventure style playgrounds. Trampolines. Football. Minigolf. Internet point and WiFi. TV and video. Board games. Bicycle hire. Closed circuit security cameras. Barbecues are permitted. Off site: Fishing 2 km. Riding 3 km. Golf 10 km. Boat launching 15 km.

Open: 20 April - 20 September.

Directions

Go southeast from Prague on the D1 towards Brno and take exit 11 to Jesenice via road 101. At Jesenice turn right then immediately left, following camping signs to the site in Zlatniky where you turn left at the roundabout. Site is 700 m. after the village. GPS: N49:57.087 E14:28.510

Charges guide

Per person	CZK 120
child (under 12 yrs)	CZK 90
pitch incl. electricity	CZK 220 - 650
dog	free - CZK 60

Less 20% discount 15/4-31/5 and 1/9-30/9.
Less 3% discount for payment in cash.
Camping Cheques accepted.

CZ4845 Camping Busek Praha

U parku 6, CZ-18200 Praha 8 Brezineves (Prague)

Tel: **283 910 254**. Email: **campbusekprag@volny.cz**

www.alanrogers.com/CZ4845

No trip to the Czech Republic would be complete without a visit to the capital, Prague. At this site you can do just that without getting tangled up with the city traffic. Just about 8 km. from the centre, there is an excellent bus link from the site to the new metro station at Ladvi that is a part of the new integrated transport system. The site is on the edge of a small, rural village and is part of a small motel complex and provides 20 level and unnumbered pitches, all with 10A electricity.

Facilities

Modern sanitary block with clean toilets, hot showers and washbasins. Washing machine and dryer. Kitchen and dishwashing facilities. Small restaurant (all year). Off site: Prague city centre only a bus and metro ride away. Outdoor swimming pool.

Open: All year.

Directions

From the Prague - Teplice (Dresden) motorway, the D8/E55, take exit to Brezineves and head towards the village. The site is before the village on the right. Turn towards the small fire station and the site is on the right. GPS: N50:09.844 E14:29.118

Charges guide

Per person	CZK 80
pitch	CZK 60 - 170
electricity	CZK 50

No credit cards.

CZ4850 Camp Sokol Troja

Trojská 171A, CZ-17100 Praha (Prague)

Tel: **233 542 908** www.alanrogers.com/CZ4850

This site is very close to the Vltava river although you cannot see it. It was subject to heavy flooding in 2002 and some of the facilities were washed away. There are 75 touring pitches (10 with 16A electricity). The pitches are small (80-90 sq.m) and can become muddy with rain. The access road is narrow and manoeuvring space is limited so the site may be less suitable for large caravans and motorcaravans. There is clearly a continuing risk of flooding so care is needed when visiting this site. Nevertheless, it is only a 15 or 20 minute journey to the centre of the city by bus. There is a bus stop in front of the site or a tram (no. 17) a 300 m. walk away. Unlike many of the municipal sites near Prague, this site has few facilities and little entertainment. The site restaurant serves real Czech meals at very reasonable prices (many locals eat here) – you don't have to go to town for good value meals.

Facilities

The single, refurbished toilet block is a good provision with toilets, washbasins with hot and cold water and preset showers in cabins without curtain or door. Cleaning can be variable. Facilities for disabled people. Campers' kitchen with hob. Good restaurant.
Off site: Fishing 1 km.

Open: All year.

Directions

From Dresden or Teplice, follow signs to the centre and turn right before the first bridge over the Moldau into the Kozlovka Pátkova, in the Troja district. Site is well signed from here.
GPS: N50:07.010 E14:25.500

Charges guide

Per person	CZK 105 - 120
child (under 18 yrs)	CZK 70 - 80
caravan	CZK 120 - 190
motorcaravan	CZK 170 - 200
electricity	CZK 100

CZ4685 Slavoj Autocamp Litomerice

Strerelecky Ostrov, CZ-41201 Litomerice (Severocesky)

Tel: **416 734 481**. Email: **kemp.litomerice@post.cz** www.alanrogers.com/CZ4685

Slavoj is a pleasant, small site with a friendly atmosphere and welcoming people. The site was totally destroyed during the flood of 2002 and has been rebuilt with help from many camp guests from all over Europe. For example, an American visitor painted the little landscape on the restaurant. Located centrally, the bar/restaurant is the main focus on the site and here you can enjoy a good value breakfast, as well as lunch and dinner. The site is on level ground, with 50 unmarked pitches, all for tourers. Some look out over the river Laba which is well fenced. Around 24 electricity connections (8/16A) are available. In high season the site can become rather crowded.

Facilities

The basic but clean toilet block has British style toilets, open washbasins and free, controllable hot showers. Laundry facilities. Kitchen. Motorcaravan service point. Basics from restaurant. Bar/restaurant with covered and open-air terrace. River fishing. Canoeing. Off site: Tennis adjacent. Boat launching 500 m.

Open: 1 May - 30 September.

Directions

On E55 from either direction, take exit 45 towards Litomerice. Cross the river, the railway bridge and turn left. Take first left and go left again. Cross under railway bridge and continue to site.
GPS: N50:31.920 E14:08.320

Charges guide

Per person	CZK 75 - 80
child (6-12 yrs)	CZK 45 - 50
pitch incl. car	CZK 90 - 150
electricity	CZK 65
dog	CZK 30

CZ4590 Holiday Park Lisci Farma

Dolni Branna 350, CZ-54362 Vrchlabi (Vychodocesky)

Tel: **499 421 473**. Email: **info@liscifarma.cz** **www.alanrogers.com/CZ4590**

This is truly an excellent site that could be in Western Europe considering its amenities, pitches and welcome. However, Lisci Farma retains a pleasant Czech atmosphere. The helpful young manager welcomes many Dutch visitors throughout the year. In the winter months, when local skiing is available, snow chains are essential. The 260 pitches are fairly flat, although the terrain is slightly sloping and some pitches are terraced. There is shade. The site is well equipped for the whole family to enjoy with its adventure playground offering trampolines for children, archery, beach volleyball, Russian bowling and an outdoor bowling court for older youngsters. A beautiful sandy, lakeside beach is 800 m. from the entrance. The more active amongst you can go paragliding or rock climbing, with experienced people to guide you. This site is very suitable for relaxing or exploring the culture of the area. Excursions to Prague are organised and, if all the sporting possibilities are not enough, the children can take part in the activities of the entertainment team, while you are walking or cycling or enjoying live music at the Fox Saloon. The site reports the addition of completely new electrical connections, restaurant, games room and mini-market.

Facilities

Two good sanitary blocks, one new in 2005 near the entrance and another modern block next to the hotel, both include toilets, washbasins and spacious, controllable showers (on payment). Child size toilets and baby room. Toilet for disabled visitors. Launderette with a washing machine. Shop (15/6-15/9). Bar/snack bar. Games room. Swimming pool (6 x 12 m). Adventure style playground on grass. Trampolines. Tennis. Minigolf. Archery. Russian bowling. Bowling. Paragliding. Bicycle hire. Excursions to Prague. Shuttle bus for skiing. Off site: Fishing and beach 800 m. Riding 2 km. Golf 5 km.

Open: 1 December - 31 March, 1 May - 31 October.

Directions

Follow road no. 14 from Liberec to Vrchlabi. At the roundabout turn in the direction of Prague and site is about 1 mile on the right.
GPS: N50:36.622 E15:36.158

Charges guide

Per person	CZK 115
child (4-12 yrs)	CZK 90
pitch incl. electricity	CZK 410 - 570
dog	CZK 90

Various discounts available in low season.

CZ4690 Camping Slunce

CZ-47107 Zandov (Severocesky)

Tel: **487 861 116** **www.alanrogers.com/CZ4690**

Away from larger towns, near the border with the former East Germany, this is pleasant countryside with a wealth of Gothic and Renaissance castles. Zandov has nothing of particular interest but Camping Slunce is a popular campsite with local Czech people. There is room for about 50 touring units with 35 electrical connections (12A) on the level, circular camping area. Outside this circle are wooden bungalows and tall trees. This is a fairly basic site, but value for money.

Facilities

The satisfactory toilet block is good by Czech standards. Kitchen. Restaurant (under separate management) has live music during high season. Kiosk for basics (May - Sept). Tennis. Swimming pool. Mountain bike hire. Playground. Large club room for games and TV. No barbecues. Dogs are not accepted. Off site: Fishing 1 km. Riding 2 km.

Open: 15 May - 28 August.

Directions

Zandov is 20 km. from Decin and 12 km. from Ceske Lipa on the 262 road. Signed in the centre of Zandov village. GPS: N50:43.278 E14:24.179

Charges guide

Per person	CZK 64
pitch incl. car	CZK 82 - 125
electricity per kWh	CZK 8

CZ4700 Autokemp Paulovice Jaroslav Kohoutek

Ul. Letná - Pavlovice, CZ-46001 Liberec (Severocesky)

Tel: **485 123 468**. Email: **info@autocamp-liberec.cz** **www.alanrogers.com/CZ4700**

Autocamp Kohoutek is a good site, nicely situated on the edge of the town near the sports ground. Just outside the entrance are the inevitable drab multi-storey flats, but trees screen these from view on the site. The Jested mountain at 1,012 m. dominates the distant sky line and is accessible by cable way for winter skiing and summer sightseeing. There are 130 touring pitches, 80 with electricity, between the excellent bungalows and trees which give a peaceful air. Some caravan pitches are divided by low hedges on the edge of the site with views across open countryside.

Facilities

The single, good quality sanitary block has toilets, washbasins and good hot showers (on payment) plus a kitchen with electric rings. Restaurant, with café, snack bar and raised terrace. Good size swimming pool (1/7-31/8). Tennis. Playground. Off site: Shops outside entrance. 'Centrum Babylon' leisure park nearby. Fishing, golf, riding and bicycle hire within 5 km.

Open: All year.

Directions

Coming from the south on the E442 to Liberec, ignore exit for Liberec and take exit for Frydlant Pavlovice shopping centre instead. Keep right at first roundabout, and at second roundabout follow sign for Pavlovic. Pass shopping centre and immediately after footbridge turn left to site.
GPS: N50:47.050 E15:02.556

Charges guide

Per person	CZK 60 - 80
pitch incl. electricity (10A)	CZK 170 - 210
electricity	CZK 70

CZ4880 Camping Roznov

Horni Paseky 940, CZ-75661 Roznov pod Radhostem (Severomoravsky)

Tel: **571 648 001**. Email: **info@camproznov.cz** **www.alanrogers.com/CZ4880**

Roznov pod Radhostem is halfway up the Roznovska Becva valley amidst the Beskydy hills which extend from North Moravia into Poland in the extreme east of the Republic. It is a busy tourist centre which attracts visitors to the Wallachian open-air museum and those who enjoy hill walking. There are 300 pitches (200 for touring units), some of which are rather small, although there are some new landscaped pitches of 90-100 sq.m. Arranged on flat grass and set amidst a variety of fruit and other trees, there are 120 electrical connections (16A) and shade in some parts.

Facilities

The good quality central toilet block has hot water in showers, washbasins and sinks. This block also has a large, comfortable TV lounge/meeting room. A further well equipped toilet block has washbasins and WCs en-suite for ladies and a washing machine. Only very basic food items available in shop (not always open). Swimming pool (25 m. open July/Aug). Tennis. Trampolines.
Off site: Restaurant or snack-bar night club at the modern Europlan Hotel some 300 m. towards the town. Fishing and golf 1 km. Riding 4 km.

Open: All year.

Directions

Site is at eastern end of Roznov on the main 35/E442 Zilina - Olomouc road opposite sports stadium. GPS: N49:27.977 E18:09.840

Charges guide

Per person	CZK 55 - 90
child (3-15 yrs)	CZK 45 - 70
pitch	CZK 95 - 175
electricity	CZK 60 - 80

CZ4890 Eurocamping Bojkovice S.R.O.

Stefanikova ATC, CZ-68771 Bojkovice (Jihormoravsky)

Tel: **604 236 631**. Email: **eurocamping@iol.cz** **www.alanrogers.com/CZ4890**

This family site in Bojkovice, close to the Slovak border, is one of the better Czech sites. It is on hilly ground with tarmac access roads connecting the 40 pitches. These are all for touring units on grassy fields taking six or eight units, but the manager will try to fit you in wherever possible. Mostly on terraces in the shade of mature birch trees, all have 6A electricity. A footpath connects the three toilet blocks which offer a more than adequate provision and are cleaned twice daily.

Facilities

Three toilet blocks (one refurbished) are a good, clean provisions, including British style toilets, open washbasins and controllable, hot showers (free). Washing machine. Campers' kitchen. Bar/restaurant with open air terrace (breakfast and dinner served). Outdoor swimming pool (15 x 8 m, unfenced). Fishing. Bicycle hire. Off site: Riding 3 km.

Open: 1 May - 30 September.

Directions

From Brno take E50 road southeast towards the Slovakian border. Exit onto the 495 road towards Uhersky Brod and follow signs for Bojkovice. In town, turn left uphill and follow the green signs.
GPS: N49:02.250 E17:47.835

Charges guide

Per unit incl. 2 persons, and electricity	€ 12,00 - € 16,15
extra person	€ 2,50 - € 3,05

CZ4720 Camping Frymburk

Frymburk 184, CZ-38279 Frymburk (Jihocesky)

Tel: **380 735 284**. Email: **info@campingfrymburk.cz**

www.alanrogers.com/CZ4720

Camping Frymburk is beautifully located on the Lipno lake in southern Bohemia and is an ideal site. From this site, activities could include walking, cycling, swimming, sailing, canoeing or rowing and afterwards you could relax in the small, cosy bar. You could enjoy a real Czech meal in one of the restaurants in Frymburk. The site has 170 level pitches on terraces (all with 6A electricity) and from the lower terraces on the edge of the lake there are lovely views over the water to the woods on the opposite side. A ferry crosses the lake from Frymburk where one can walk or cycle in the woods. The Dutch owner, Mr Wilzing, will welcome the whole family, personally siting your caravan. Children will be entertained by 'Kidstown' and the site has a small beach.

Facilities

Two new toilet blocks are immaculate with toilets, washbasins (open style and in cabins) with cold water only, preset showers on payment (with curtain) and an en-suite bathroom with toilet, basin and shower. Launderette. Bar (15/5-30/9). Takeaway (1/5-15/9). Playground. Canoe, bicycle, pedalo, rowing boat and surfboard hire. Kidstown. Volleyball competitions. Rafting. Bus trips to Prague. Torches useful. Off site: Shops and restaurants in the village 900 m. from reception. Golf 7 km. Riding 20 km.

Open: 25 April - 1 October.

Directions

Take exit 114 at Passau in Germany (near the Austrian border) towards Freyung in the Czech Republic. Continue on this road till Philipsreut and from there follow the no. 4 road towards Vimperk. Turn right a few kilometres after the border towards Volary on no. 141 road. From Volary follow the no. 163 road to Horni Plana, Cerna and Frymburk. Site is on the 163 road, right after the village.
GPS: N48:39.960 E14:10.980

Charges guide

Per unit incl. 2 persons and electricity	CZK 416 - 580
extra person	CZK 72 - 90
child (under 12 yrs)	CZK 48 - 60
dog	CZK 48 - 60

No credit cards.
Less 20% 15/4-15/6 and 1/9-1/10.

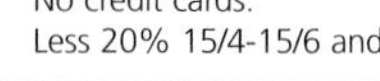

CZ4770 Camping Dlouhá Louka

Stromovka 8, CZ-37001 Céske Budejovice (Jihocesky)

Tel: **387 203 601**. Email: **motel@dlouhalouka.cz** **www.alanrogers.com/CZ4770**

The medieval city of Céske Budejovice is the home of Budweiser beer and is also an industrial centre. It lies on the River Vltava with mountains and pleasant scenery nearby. Dlouhá Louka is a motel and camping complex two kilometres south of the town on the Céske Budejovice - Cesky Krumlov road. The camping part is a flat, rectangular meadow surrounded by trees which give some shade around the edges. There are some marked, hedged pitches and hardstanding, but many of the grass pitches are not marked or numbered so pitching can be rather haphazard. In total, 100 units are taken and there are 50 electricity connections (10A).

Facilities

The single sanitary block, with British style WCs, is at one end making a fair walk for some. Washing machine and irons. Kitchen with electric rings. Very pleasant restaurant (1/6-31/8). Tennis. Playground. Off site: Shops 200 m. Bicycle hire 2 km. Fishing and golf 10 km.

Open: All year.

Directions

From town follow signs for Cesky Krumlov. After leaving ring road, turn right at Motel sign. Take this small road and turn right 60 m. before Camp Stromovky. Campsite name cannot be seen from the entrance - only the word Motel.
GPS: N48:57.984 E14:27.630

Charges guide

Per person	CZK 50 - 70
pitch	CZK 120 - 140
electricity	CZK 80

No credit cards.

CZ4895 Camping Hana

Dlouha 135, CZ-66471 Veverska Bityska (Jihormoravsky)

Tel: **549 420 331**. Email: **camping.hana@quick.cz** **www.alanrogers.com/CZ4895**

The caves of the Moravian Karst, the site of the battle of Austerlitz and the castles of Veveri, Pertstejn and Spillberk are all within easy reach of this pleasant, small and quiet campsite. Hana Musilova runs the site to very high standards, speaks excellent English and Dutch and is keen to provide lots of local information. There are 55 level, numbered pitches with 10A electricity. Brno, the capital of Moravia and the Czech Republic's second largest city, is a short boat or bus ride away and the village of Veverska Bityska has shops, restaurants, bars and an ATM plus a reasonable small supermarket.

Facilities

The modern sanitary block provides ample and clean toilets, hot showers (token, 1st free per person then CZK 5) and washbasins. Washing machine and dryer. Kitchen and dishwashing facilities. Small shop with essential supplies. Off site: Fishing 1 km. Golf 10 km. Riding 4 km. Boat cruise to Brno 500 m. Veversak Bityska village 1 km.

Open: 1 May - 30 September.

Directions

From the D1 Prague - Brno autoroute, turn off at Ostrovacice and head towards Tisnov. The site is at Veverska Bityska on the road to Chudcice. From the 43 turn off south of Lipuvka towards Kurim and then follow the signs to Veverska Bityska where the site is on the right before entering the village.
GPS: N49:16.594 E16:27.158

Charges guide

Per person	CZK 80
pitch incl. electricity	CZK 180 - 220

CZ4896 Camping Country

Hluboke Masuvky 257, CZ-67152 Hluboke Masuvky (Jihormoravsky)

Tel: **515 255 249**. Email: **camping-country@cbox.cz** **www.alanrogers.com/CZ4896**

Camping Country is a well cared for and attractively landscaped site, close to the historical town of Znojmo. It is a rural location close to a National Park and close to the Austrian border which would make it ideal either as a stopover on your way south and for a longer stay to enjoy the new cycling routes which have been set out. Camping Country has 60 touring pitches, 30 with electricity, on two fields – one behind the main house taking 6 or 8 units, the other one larger with a gravel access road.

Facilities

Modern and comfortable toilet facilities provide British style toilets, open washbasins (cold water only) and free, controllable hot showers. Campers' kitchen. Bar/restaurant with one meal served daily. Play area. Tennis. Minigolf. Riding. Some live music nights in high season. Internet access. Tours to Vienna, Brno and wine cellars. Torch useful. Off site: Fishing and beach 10 km.

Open: 1 May - 31 October.

Directions

Coming from the northwest on the E59 road exit to the east at Kasarna onto the 408 road and continue north on the 361 road towards Hluboké Masuvky. Site is well signed. GPS: N48:55.240 E16:01.600

Charges guide

Per person	CZK 120
pitch incl. car	CZK 120 - 170
electricity (6A)	CZK 80

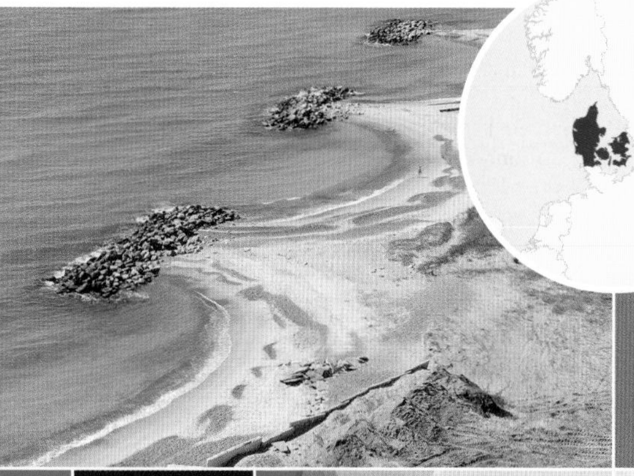

Denmark offers a diverse landscape all within a relatively short distance. The countryside is green and varied with flat plains, rolling hills, fertile farmland, many lakes and fjords, wild moors and long beaches, interrupted by pretty villages and towns.

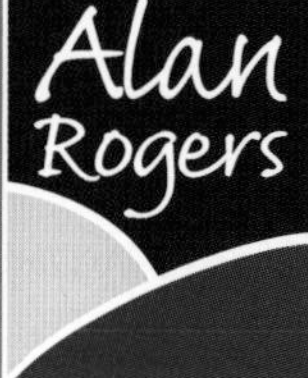

CAPITAL: COPENHAGEN

Tourist Office

Danish Tourist Board
55 Sloane Street, London SW1X 9SY
Tel: 020 7259 5958
Fax: 020 7259 5955
Email: london@visitdenmark.com
Internet: www.visitdenmark.com

Denmark is the easiest of the Scandinavian countries to visit, both in terms of cost and distance. There are many small islands but the main land masses that make up the country are the islands of Zeeland and Funen and the peninsula of Jutland, which extends northwards from the German border. Zeeland is the most visited region, its main draw being the capital, Copenhagen. This vibrant city has a beautiful old centre, an array of museums and art galleries plus a boisterous night life. Funen is the smaller of the two main islands and is known as the Garden of Denmark, with its neat green fields and fruit and vegetable plots. Sandy beaches and quaint villages can be found here. Jutland has the most varied landscape ranging from heather-clad moors, dense forests to plunging gorges. It's also home to one of the most popular attractions in Denmark, Legoland, and the oldest town in Scandinavia, Ribe.

Population

5.4 million

Climate

Generally mild although changeable throughout the year.

Language

Danish, but English is widely spoken.

Telephone

The dialling code for Denmark is 00 45.

Money

Currency: Danish Krone
Banks: Mon-Wed & Fri 09.30-16.00, Thurs to 18.00. Closed Sat. In the provinces opening hours vary.

Shops

Hours may vary in the main cities. Regular openings are Mon-Thu 09.00-17.30, Fri 09.00-19.00/20.00, and Sat 09.00-13.00/14.00.

Public Holidays

New Year's Day; Three Kings Day 6 Jan; April Fools Day 1 April; Maundy Thursday; Good Friday; Easter Monday; Queen's Birthday 16 April; Flag Day 18 April; Ascension; Whit Mon; Constitution Day 5 Jun; Valdemars 15 June; Mortens Day 11 Nov; Christmas 24-26 Dec; New Year's Eve

Motoring

Driving is much easier than at home as roads are much quieter. Driving is on the right. Do not drink and drive. Dipped headlights are compulsory at all times. Strong measures are taken against unauthorised parking on beaches, with on the spot fines.

DK2015 Ådalens Camping

Gudenåvej 20, DK-6710 Esbjerg V-Sædding (Ribe)

Tel: **75 15 88 22**. Email: **info@adal.dk** **www.alanrogers.com/DK2015**

Owned and run by Britta and Peter Andersen, this superb site is in the northeast of Esbjerg and is a great starting point from which to tour the city with its harbour, museums and sea water aquarium. It is also convenient for those arriving on the ferry from Harwich (16 hours). From the attractive, tree lined drive, gravel lanes lead to large fields with well mown grass and good services. Ådalens has 193 pitches for touring visitors and 30 seasonal places. The pitches are split into groups of 5 or 10 by mature trees that provide some shade.

Facilities

Two modern toilet blocks with free hot showers. Special children's section in bright colours and family shower rooms (for rent). Excellent facilities for disabled visitors. Baby room. Laundry. Motorcaravan services. Basics from reception (bread to order). Outdoor pool (15 x 10 m) with slide, waterfall, flume and paddling pool (1/6-1/9). Two new playgrounds. Animal farm. Minigolf. Internet access. TV room with library. Off site: Fishing, golf, bicycle hire and boat launching 5 km. City centre 5 km.

Open: All year.

Directions

From Esbjerg, take the 447 road northeast and continue along the coast. Turn right at sign for site and follow the signs. GPS: N55:30.778 E08:23.349

Charges 2009

Per person	DKK 73
child (1-11 yrs)	DKK 45
pitch	DKK 35
electricity (10A)	DKK 30

Camping Cheques accepted.

DK2010 Hvidbjerg Strand Camping

Hvidbjerg Strandvej 27, DK-6857 Blavand (Ribe)

Tel: **75 27 90 40**. Email: **info@hvidbjerg.dk** **www.alanrogers.com/DK2010**

A family owned, 'TopCamp' holiday site, Hvidbjerg Strand is on the west coast near Blåvands Huk, 43 km. from Esbjerg. It is a high quality, seaside site with a wide range of amenities. Most of the 570 pitches have electricity (6/10A) and the 130 'comfort' pitches also have water, drainage and satellite TV. To the rear of the site 70 new fully serviced pitches have been developed, some up to 250 sq.m. and 16 with private sanitary facilities. Most pitches are individual and divided by hedges, in rows on flat sandy grass, with areas also divided by small trees and hedges. Member of 'Leading Campings Group'.

Facilities

Five superb toilet units include washbasins (many in cubicles), roomy showers, spa baths, suites for disabled visitors, family bathrooms, kitchens and laundry facilities. The most recent units include a children's bathroom and baby baths. Motorcaravan services. Supermarket. Café/restaurant. TV rooms. Pool complex, solarium and sauna. Play areas. Supervised play rooms (09.00-16.00 daily). Barbecue areas. Minigolf. Riding (Western style). Fishing. Dog showers. Off site: Legoland 70 km.

Open: 31 March - 22 October.

Directions

From Varde take roads 181/431 to Blåvand. Site is signed left on entering the town (mind speed bump on town boundary). GPS: N55:32.760 E08:08.104

Charges guide

Per person	€ 10,34
child (0-11 yrs)	€ 7,59
pitch	€ 3,45 - € 16,55
electricity (6/10A)	€ 4,41 - € 4,97
dog	€ 3,72

DK2020 Mogeltonder Camping

Sonderstregsvej 2, Mogeltonder, DK-6270 Tonder (Sønderjylland)

Tel: **74 73 84 60**. Email: **moegeltoender.camping@post.tele.dk** **www.alanrogers.com/DK2020**

This site is only five minutes walk from one of Denmark's oldest villages and ten minutes drive from Tønder with its well preserved old buildings and magnificent pedestrian shopping street. A quiet family site, Møgeltønder has 285 large, level, numbered pitches on grass, most with electricity (10A), divided up by new plantings of shrubs and small hedges. Only 35 pitches are occupied by long stay units, the remainder solely for touring units, and there are 15 cabins. The site also has an excellent outdoor heated swimming pool and children's pool.

Facilities

Two superb, modern, heated sanitary units include roomy showers (on payment), washbasins with either divider/curtain or in private cubicles, plus bathrooms for families and disabled visitors. Baby room. Two kitchens. Laundry. Motorcaravan services. Shop for essentials (bread ordered daily). Swimming pool (10 x 5 m) and paddling pool. Minigolf. Playground. TV and games rooms. Internet access. Off site: Golf and bicycle hire 10 km.

Open: All year.

Directions

Turn left off no. 419 Tønder - Højer road, 4 km. from Tønder. Drive through Møgeltønder village and past the church where site is signed. The main street is cobbled so drive slowly. GPS: N54:56.296 E08:47.964

Charges guide

Per person	DKK 56
child (0-12 yrs)	DKK 29
electricity	DKK 22

DK2140 Jesperhus Feriecenter & Camping

Legindvej 30, DK-7900 Nykobing Mors (Viborg)

Tel: **96 70 14 00**. Email: **jesperhus@jesperhus.dk** **www.alanrogers.com/DK2140**

Jesperhus is an extensive, well organised and busy site with many leisure activities, adjacent to Blomsterpark (flower park). It is a 'TopCamp' site with 662 numbered pitches, mostly in rows with some terracing, divided by shrubs and trees and with shade in parts. Many pitches are taken by seasonal, tour operator or rental units, so advance booking is advised for peak periods. Electricity (6A) is available on all pitches and water points are in all areas. An excellent centre for touring.

Facilities

Four good sanitary units are cleaned three times daily. Facilities include washbasins in cubicles or with divider/curtain, family and whirlpool bathrooms (on payment), suites for babies and disabled visitors. Sauna. Kitchens and laundry. Supermarket (1/4-1/11). Restaurant. Bar. Café, takeaway. Pool complex with spa facilities. Bowling. Minigolf. Tennis. Go-karts and other outdoor sports. Children's 'play-world'. Playgrounds. Pets corner. Golf. Fishing pond. Practice golf (3 holes). Off site: Riding 2 km. Bicycle hire 6 km. Beach 2 km.

Open: All year.

Directions

From south or north, take road no. 26 to Salling Sund bridge, site is signed Jesperhus, just north of the bridge. GPS: N56:45.049 E08:48.948

Charges guide

Per person	DKK 75
child (1-11 yrs)	DKK 55
pitch	free - DKK 50
electricity	DKK 40

Runner up Alan Rogers Awards 2008

DK2022 Vikær Diernæs Strand Camping

Dundelum 29, Diernæs, DK-6100 Haderslev (Sønderjylland)

Tel: **74 57 54 64**. Email: **info@vikaercamp.dk** **www.alanrogers.com/DK2022**

The warm welcome at Vikær Diernæs will start your holiday off in the right way. This family site in Southern Jutland lies in beautiful surroundings, right on the Diernæs Bugt beaches – ideal for both active campers and relaxation seekers. The attractively laid out site has 330 grass pitches (210 for touring units), all with 10/16A electricity and separated by low hedges. Access is from long, gravel lanes. The upper part of the site provides 40 newly developed, fully serviced pitches with electricity, water, sewerage, TV aerial point and internet. From some pitches there are marvellous views.

Facilities

Three modern toilet blocks with washbasins in cabins and controllable hot showers. Family shower rooms. Children's section. Baby room. En-suite facilities for disabled visitors. Laundry. Campers' kitchen. Motorcaravan services. Shop (Thursday-Sunday 07.30-21.00). Playground. Minigolf. Fishing. Archery. Watersports and boat launching. Pétanque. TV room. Play house. Daily activities for children in high season. Torch useful. English is spoken. Off site: Golf 30 minutes. Riding 2 km.

Open: Week before Easter - mid October.

Directions

From German/Danish border follow E45 north. Take exit 69 and follow to Hoptrup. From Hoptrup follow to Diernæs and Diernæs Strand.
GPS: N55:09.017 E9:29.814

Charges guide

Per person	DKK 67
child (under 12 yrs)	DKK 45
pitch	DKK 25 - 60
electricity	DKK 28

DK2030 Sandersvig Camping & Tropeland

Espagervej 15-17, DK-6100 Haderslev (Sønderjylland)

Tel: **74 56 62 25**. Email: **sandersvig@dk-camp.dk** **www.alanrogers.com/DK2030**

An attractively laid out, family run site, Sandersvig offers the very best of modern facilities in a peaceful and beautiful countryside location, 300 metres from the beach. The 470 very large grassy pitches (270 for tourers) are divided by hedges, shrubs and small trees into small enclosures, many housing only four units, most with electricity (10A). The site is well lit, very quiet at night and there are water taps close to most pitches. The playground boasts Denmark's largest bouncing cushion!

Facilities

Four heated sanitary blocks offer some washbasins in cubicles and roomy showers (on payment). Suites for disabled visitors, 14 family bathrooms and baby rooms. Excellent kitchens. Laundry. Motorcaravan services. Supermarket and fast food service, with dining room (Easter - 13/9). Takeaway (15/6-15/8). Indoor heated pool with sauna, solarium, jacuzzi, whirlpool and slide (DKK 12.50). Solarium. Playground. Games room. TV lounge. Tennis. Boat launching. Off site: Riding 4 km. Bicycle hire 6 km. Fishing 7 km. Golf 16 km.

Open: 3 April - 13 September.

Directions

Leave E45 at exit 66 and turn towards Christianfeld. Turn right at roundabout onto 170 and follow signs for Fjelstrup and Knud village, turning right 1 km. east of the village from where site is signed.
GPS: N55:20.054 E9:37.891

Charges 2009

Per person	DKK 70
child (0-11 yrs)	DKK 40
pitch	DKK 20 - 50
electricity (10A)	DKK 30

DK2036 Gammelmark Strand Camping

Gammelmark 16, DK-6310 Broager (Sønderjylland)

Tel: **74 44 17 42**. Email: **info@gammelmark.dk** **www.alanrogers.com/DK2036**

The Siegers, a Danish/Dutch couple, have owned this site since 2001. Gammelmark has 289 level, grass pitches (200 for tourers), all with 13A electricity. From the new fully serviced pitches on the top terraces there are some great views of the Flensburger Förde. This site combines Danish hospitality with historical interest. In 1864 war was waged between the Danes and the Germans over the Flensburger Förde and this site organises excursions to the war museum in Dybbøl Banke.

Facilities

Modern, heated sanitary facilities include toilets, washbasins (open and in cabins), controllable showers. Facilities for children and disabled visitors. Baby room. Private facilities to rent. Laundry facilities. Motorcaravan services. Shop. Snacks. Heated swimming pool. Play area. Children's farm. Fishing. Riding. Sailing. Diving. Beach. Daily activity programme (high season). TV room. Internet access. Torches advised. English spoken. Off site: Bar and restaurant 2 km. Bicycle hire 6 km. Golf 10 km.

Open: Easter - 22 October.

Directions

From Flensburg take no. 7 road north and at exit 75 turn east towards Sønderborg. Take exit Dynt and follow site signs. GPS: N54:53.127 E9:43.726

Charges guide

Per person	€ 9,03
child (1-11 yrs)	€ 4,44
pitch	€ 2,08 - € 5,76
electricity (plus meter)	€ 2,08

DK2040 TopCamp Riis

Osterhovedvej 43, DK-7323 Give (Vejle)

Tel: **75 73 14 33**. Email: **info@topcampriis.dk** **www.alanrogers.com/DK2040**

TopCamp Riis is a good quality touring site ideal for visiting Legoland (18 km) and Givskov Zoo (3 km). It is a friendly, family run 'TopCamp' site with 235 large touring pitches on sheltered, gently sloping, well tended lawns surrounded by trees and shrubs. Electricity (13A) is available to all pitches, ten comfort pitches have electricity, water and waste water and there are 61 site owned cabins. The outdoor heated pool and water-slide complex and the adjacent small bar that serves beer, ice cream, soft drinks and snacks are only open in main season.

Facilities

Two excellent sanitary units (the older one now refurbished) include washbasins with divider/curtain and controllable showers (on payment). Suites for babies and disabled visitors, family bathrooms (one with whirlpool bath, on payment) and solarium. New kitchen. Sitting room with TV, plus new barbecue grill house. Laundry. Motorcaravan services. Shop. Pool complex (30/5-6/9). Café/bar (high season). Minigolf. New playground. Animal farm. Bicycle hire. WiFi. Off site: Fishing and golf 4 km.

Open: 4 April - 27 September.

Directions

Turn onto Osterhovedvej southeast of Give town centre (near Shell Garage) at sign to Riis and site. After 4 km. turn left into tarmac drive which runs through the forest to the site. Alternatively, turn off the 442 Brande-Jelling road at Riis village north of Givskud. GPS: N55:49.870 E9:18.046

Charges guide

Per person	€ 9,90
pitch	free - € 11
electricity	€ 4,10

DK2044 Hampen Sø Camping

Hovedgaden 31, DK-7362 Hampen (Vejle)

Tel: **75 77 52 55**. Email: **info@hampen-soe-camping.dk** **www.alanrogers.com/DK2044**

If you are heading up towards Denmark to cross to Norway or Sweden, then this site in a natural setting close to lakes and moors could be a useful stopover. There are 230 pitches in total, with 80 seasonal units plus 34 cabins, but there will always be space for touring units. The pitches are arranged in large grassy bays taking around 15 units, and there are 10A electric hook-ups (some long leads may be needed). The nearby Hampen See lake is a pleasant walk through the forest and is said to be one of the cleanest lakes for swimming in Denmark.

Facilities

Three toilet blocks, one basic near the entrance, one central on the site with new laundry, new children's room and new kitchen, and one to far end with two family shower rooms. En-suite facilities for disabled people. Laundry. Supermarket. Restaurant open all year (weekends in winter). Takeaway. Kitchen. Games and TV rooms. Small outdoor pool (15/6-1/9). Covered minigolf. New play equipment. Race track for mini cars. WiFi. Off site: Riding 500 m. Fishing 3 km. Golf 18 km.

Open: All year.

Directions

Site lies on road no.176, 500 m. southwest of its junction with road no.13 between Vejle and Viborg (around 50 km. south of Viborg). Look for Spar supermarket and camping signs. GPS: N56:00.855 E09:21.856

Charges guide

Per person	€ 8,97
electricity	€ 3,86

No credit cards.
Camping Cheques accepted.

DK2046 Trelde Næs Colorcamp

Trelde Næsvej 297, Trelde, DK-7000 Fredericia (Vejle)

Tel: **75 95 71 83**. Email: **trelde@colorcamp.dk**

www.alanrogers.com/DK2046

Trelde Næs Color Camp is one of Denmark's larger sites with 500 level and numbered pitches. The 400 touring pitches all have 10A electricity and there are 37 fully serviced pitches with electricity, water, drainage and internet access. Seasonal units take up the remaining pitches. Pitching is off tarmac access roads on well kept, grassy fields with some shade from bushes at the rear. At the front of the site is a heated, open air, fun pool with large slide, jacuzzi and play island.

Facilities

Four traditional toilet blocks have washbasins in cabins and controllable hot showers (card operated). Child size toilets and basins. Family shower room. Baby room. Laundry. Fun pool (10 x 20 m). Turkish bath, solarium and sauna. Shop. Takeaway. Playgrounds. Minigolf. Fishing. Watersports. Entertainment programme for children (high season). TV room. WiFi. Cabins and rooms to rent. Off site: Boat launching 7 km. Golf 6 km.

Open: All year.

Directions

From Fredericia follow road no. 28 north and take Trelde exit. Follow signs for Trelde and Trelde Næs. GPS: N55:37.493 E9:50.000

Charges guide

Per unit incl. 2 persons and electricity	DKK 148 - 208
extra person	DKK 60

Camping Cheques accepted.

DK2048 Fårup Sø Camping

Fårupvej 58, DK-7300 Jelling (Vejle)

Tel: **75 87 13 44**. Email: **faarup-soe@dk-camp.dk**

www.alanrogers.com/DK2048

This site was originally set up on the woodlands of Jelling Skov where local farmers each had their own plot. Owned since January 2004 by the Dutch/Danish Albring family, this is a rural location on the Fårup Lake. Many trees have been removed to give the site an open feel. Fårup Sø Camping has 250 grassy pitches, mostly on terraces (from top to bottom the height difference is 53 m). The 35 newest terraced pitches provide beautiful views of the countryside and the Fårup lake. There are 200 pitches for touring units, most with 10A electricity, and some tent pitches without electricity.

Facilities

One modern and one older toilet block have British style toilets, open style washbasins and controllable hot showers. Family shower rooms. Baby room. Facilities for disabled visitors. Laundry. Campers' kitchen. Motorcaravan services. Shop (bread to order). Outdoor swimming pool (15 x 5 m). New playgrounds. Minigolf. Games room. Pony riding. Lake with fishing. Watersports. Activities for children (high season). Internet. Off site: Golf and riding 2 km. Lion Park 8 km. Legoland 20 km.

Open: 1 April - 30 September.

Directions

From Vejle take the 28 road towards Billund. In Skibet turn right towards Fårup Sø, Jennum and Jelling and follow the signs to Fårup Sô. GPS: N55:44.159 E09:25.063

Charges guide

Per person	DKK 61
child (3-11 yrs)	DKK 35
pitch	DKK 15 - 35
electricity	DKK 28

DK2050 Terrassen Camping

Himmelbjergvej 9A, Laven, DK-8600 Silkeborg (Århus)

Tel: **86 84 13 01**. Email: **info@terrassen.dk**

www.alanrogers.com/DK2050

Terrassen Camping is a family run site arranged on terraces, overlooking Lake Julso and the local countryside. There are 260 pitches with good views, most with electricity (6/10A) and three hardstanding pitches for motorcaravans. A small area for tents (without electricity) is at the top of the site where torches may be required. There are also 29 seasonal units, and some site owned cabins. The solar heated swimming pool has a paved terrace and is fenced. This is a comfortable base from which to explore this area of Denmark where a warm welcome and good English will greet you.

Facilities

The main modern sanitary unit is heated and includes many washbasins in cubicles. Controllable showers (on payment). Family bathrooms. Baby room. Facilities for disabled visitors. Kitchen. An older refurbished unit contains another kitchen, plus 4 more shower cubicles with external access. Motorcaravan services. Shop. Swimming pool (8 x 16 m; 15/5-31/8). Games/TV rooms with internet. Adventure playground. Indoor play room. Pets corner. Covered barbecue area. Canoe hire. Bicycle hire. Riding. Off site: Fishing 200 m. Golf, sailing and boat launching 5 km. Tudstrup Kro for a real Danish meal.

Open: 18 March - 18 September.

Directions

From the harbour in the centre of Silkeborg follow signs and minor road towards Sejs (5 km.) and Ry (20 km). Site lies on the northern side of the road at village of Laven (13 km). Height restriction of 3 m. on railway bridge over this road. GPS: N56:07.445 E9:42.622

Charges guide

Per person	DKK 72
child (1-11 yrs)	DKK 48
pitch	free - DKK 40
electricity	DKK 30

DK2070 Fornæs Camping

Stensmarkvej 36, DK-8500 Grenå (Århus)

Tel: **86 33 23 30**. Email: **fornaes@1031.inord.dk** **www.alanrogers.com/DK2070**

In the grounds of a former farm, Fornæs Camping is about 5 km. from Grenå. From reception a wide, gravel access road descends through a large grassy field to the sea. Pitches to the left are mostly level, to the right slightly sloping with some terracing and views of the Kattegat. The rows of pitches are divided into separate areas by colourful bushes and each row is marked by a concrete tub containing a young tree and colourful flowers. Fornæs has 320 pitches of which 240 are for tourers, the others being used for seasonal visitors. All touring pitches have 10A electricity.

Facilities

Two toilet blocks have British style toilets, washbasins in cabins and controllable hot showers (on payment). Child-size toilets. Family shower rooms. Baby room. Facilities for disabled people. Laundry. Campers' kitchen. Motorcaravan service point. Shop. Café/grill with bar and takeaway (evenings). Swimming pool (80 sq.m) with paddling pool. Sauna and solarium. Play area. Adventure playground. Games room with satellite TV. Minigolf. Fishing. Watersports. Off site: Golf and riding 5 km.

Open: 15 March - 20 September.

Directions

From Århus follow the 15 road towards Grenå and then the 16 road towards town centre. Turn north and follow signs for Fornæs and the site.
GPS: N56:27.361 E10:56.464

Charges guide

Per person	DKK 67 - 75
child (1-12 yrs)	DKK 38 - 42
electricity (10A)	DKK 28

Credit cards 5% surcharge.

DK2080 Holmens Camping

Klostervej 148, DK-8680 Ry (Århus)

Tel: **86 89 17 62**. Email: **info@holmens-camping.dk** **www.alanrogers.com/DK2080**

Holmens Camping lies between Silkeborg and Skanderborg in a very beautiful part of Denmark. The site is close to the waters of the Gudensø and Rye Møllesø lakes which are used for boating and canoeing. Walking and cycling are also popular activities. Holmens has 225 grass touring pitches, partly terraced and divided by young trees and shrubs. The site itself is surrounded by mature trees. Almost all the pitches have 6A electricity and vary in size between 70-100 sq.m. A small tent field is close to the lake which is suitable for swimming but the site also has an attractive pool complex.

Facilities

One traditional and one modern toilet block have washbasins (open and in cabins) and controllable hot showers (on payment). En-suite facilities with toilet, basin, shower. Baby room. Facilities for disabled visitors. Laundry. Kitchen. Small shop. Covered pool with jet stream. Paddling pool with water canon. Finnish sauna, solarium, massage and fitness facilities. Pool bar. Games room. Playground. Tennis. Minigolf. Fishing. Bicycle hire. Boat rental. Large units are not accepted. Off site: Riding 2 km.

Open: 16 March - 29 September.

Directions

Going north on E45, take exit 52 at Skanderborg turning west on 445 road towards Ry. In Ry follow the site signs. GPS: N56:04.568 E09:45.601

Charges guide

Per person	DKK 62 - 73
child (3-11 yrs)	DKK 35 - 40
pitch	DKK 20

DK2100 Blushoj Camping

Elsegårdevej 55, DK-8400 Ebeltoft (Århus)

Tel: **86 34 12 38**. Email: **blushoj@mail.dk** **www.alanrogers.com/DK2100**

This is a traditional type of site where the owners are making a conscious effort to keep mainly to touring units – there are only six seasonal units and four rental cabins. The site has 250 pitches on levelled grassy terraces surrounded by mature hedging and shrubs. Some have glorious views of the Kattegat and others overlook peaceful rural countryside. Most pitches have electricity (10A), but long leads may be required. There is a heated and fenced swimming pool (14 x 7 m) with a slide and terrace. The beach below the site provides opportunities for swimming, windsurfing and sea fishing.

Facilities

One toilet unit includes washbasins with dividers and showers with divider and seat (on payment). The other unit has a new kitchen, dining/TV room, laundry and baby facilities. An extension provides six family bathrooms, and additional WCs and washbasins. Motorcaravan service point. Shop. Swimming pool (20/5-20/8). Minigolf. Play area. Games room. Beach. Fishing. Internet access.
Off site: Riding, bicycle hire, boat launching and golf 5 km.

Open: 1 April - 15 September.

Directions

From road 21 northwest of Ebeltoft turn off at junction where several sites are signed towards Dråby. Follow signs through the outskirts of Ebeltoft turning southeast to Elsegårde village. Turn left for Blushøj. Follow signs. GPS: N56:10.066 E10:43.843

Charges guide

Per person	DKK 68 - 77
electricity	DKK 25

No credit cards.

DK2130 Hobro Camping Gattenborg

Skivevej 35, DK-9500 Hobro (Nordjylland)

Tel: **98 52 32 88**. Email: **hobro@dk-camp.dk**

www.alanrogers.com/DK2130

This neat and very well tended municipal site is imaginatively landscaped and has 139 pitches on terraces arranged around a bowl shaped central activity area. Most pitches (100 for touring units) have electricity (10A) and there are many trees and shrubs. Footpaths connect the various terraces and activity areas. There are 30 seasonal units and ten cabins. The reception building with a small shop and tourist information, has a covered picnic terrace behind, and houses a large TV lounge. The small, heated, outdoor swimming pool with water slide is open in high season, weather permitting.

Facilities

The main heated sanitary building includes washbasins in cubicles and hot showers (on payment). Two family bathrooms. Facilities for disabled people. Baby room. Kitchen. Laundry facilities. Tiny unit in the centre of the site has two unisex WCs and basins (cold water only) and a small kitchen. Motorcaravan services. Shop (order bread before 9 pm). Swimming pool (high season). Play areas. Minigolf. TV lounge with board games and library. Bicycle hire. Internet access. Off site: Town 500 m. Beach 1 km.

Open: 4 April - 27 September.

Directions

From E45 exit 35, take road 579 towards Hobro Centrum. Site is well signed to the right, just after railway bridge. GPS: N56:38.083 E09:46.953

Charges 2009

Per person	DKK 65
child (0-11 yrs)	DKK 35
electricity	DKK 28
dog	DKK 10

DK2150 Sølyst Camping

Logstorvej 2, DK-9240 Nibe (Nordjylland)

Tel: **98 35 10 62**. Email: **soelyst@dk-camp.dk**

www.alanrogers.com/DK2150

You will always be near the water in Denmark, either open sea or, as here, alongside the more sheltered waters of a fjord – Limfjord. Sølyst is a family run site providing 170 numbered pitches, of which 120 are for touring units. All have electricity (6A) and are arranged on gently sloping grass in fairly narrow rows separated by hedges. There are facilities for watersports and swimming in the fjord. The site also has a small heated swimming pool, slide and splash pool, and a children's pool.

Facilities

A central sanitary unit includes washbasins in cubicles, four family bathrooms, a baby room and facilities for disabled visitors. Good kitchen and small dining area. Fully equipped laundry. A second unit provides extra facilities. Hot water (except in washbasins) is charged for. Motorcaravan services. Shop. Snack bar and takeaway (main season). Swimming pool. Solarium. Play area. Minigolf. TV room. Games room. Fishing. Bicycle hire. Boat launching. Beach. Off site: Riding 1 km. Nibe 1 km.

Open: All year.

Directions

Site is clearly signed from the no. 187 road west of Nibe town, with a wide entrance. GPS: N56:58.332 E09:37.475

Charges guide

Per person	DKK 67
child (under 12 yrs)	DKK 35
pitch	DKK 20
electricity	DKK 27

DK2165 Skiveren Camping

Niels Skiverenrej 5-7, DK-9982 Skiveren/Aalbæk (Nordjylland)

Tel: **98 93 22 00**. Email: **info@skiveren.dk**

www.alanrogers.com/DK2165

This friendly seaside site, a member of the Danish 'TopCamp' organisation, is set up in maritime style with the pitches separated by low wooden poles connected by a sailor's rope. Skiveren Camping has 595 pitches (510 for tourers), almost all with 10/16A electricity. Around the site are different varieties of low spruce and fir which give the site a pleasing appearance and atmosphere. The level pitches are of a good size (up to 120 sq.m), some having a picnic table and all are separated from the main tarmac access road by the low wooden fences.

Facilities

Three immaculate toilet blocks include family showers and private facilities with shower, toilet and basin for rent (Dkr. 40-60). Facilities for disabled visitors. Laundry. Campers' kitchen. Motorcaravan services. Supermarket. Strand Café for meals and takeaway (1/5-15/8). Outdoor pool (15 x 8 m) with whirlpool and sauna. Playground. New indoor play hall. Multisport court. Tennis. Games room with TV. Bicycle hire. Children's club. Live music and dancing. Off site: Fishing 14 km. Golf 7 km. Riding 10 km.

Open: 3 April - 30 September.

Directions

From the no. 40 road going north from Ålbæk, turn left at sign for 'Skiveren'. Follow this road all the way to the end. GPS: N57:36.997 E10:16.803

Charges 2009

Per person	DKK 78
child (1-11 yrs)	DKK 55
pitch	DKK 40 - 135
electricity	DKK 32 - 37

Credit cards 4% surcharge.
Low season discount 10-30%.

DK2170 Klim Strand Camping

Havvejen 167, Klim Strand, DK-9690 Fjerritslev (Nordjylland)

Tel: **98 22 53 40**. Email: **ksc@klim-strand.dk** **www.alanrogers.com/DK2170**

A large family holiday site right beside the sea, Klim Strand is a paradise for children. It is a privately owned 'TopCamp' site with a full complement of quality facilities. The site has 560 numbered touring pitches, all with electricity (10A), laid out in rows, many divided by trees and hedges and shade in parts. Some 220 of these are fully serviced with electricity, water, drainage and TV hook-up. A 'Wellness' spa centre is a recent addition. Member of 'Leading Campings Group'.

Facilities

Two good, large, heated toilet blocks are central, with spacious showers and some washbasins in cubicles. Separate children's room. Baby rooms. Bathrooms for families and disabled visitors. Laundry. Kitchens. TV lounges. Motorcaravan services. Pizzeria. Supermarket. Restaurant and bar. Pool complex. Sauna, solariums, whirlpool bath, fitness room. Wellness centre. Internet café. TV rental. Play areas. Crèche. Bicycle hire. Cabins to rent. Off site: Golf 10 km. Boat launching 25 km.

Open: 1 April - 31 December.

Directions

Turn off Thisted - Fjerritslev no. 11 road to Klim from where site is signed. GPS: N57:08.000 E09:10.140

Charges 2009

Per person	DKK 75
child (1-11 yrs)	DKK 55
pitch with electricity	DKK 145 - 195

DK2180 Nordstrand Camping

Apholmenvej 40, DK-9900 Frederikshaven (Nordjylland)

Tel: **98 42 93 50**. Email: **info@nordstrand-camping.dk** **www.alanrogers.com/DK2180**

An excellent site, Nordstrand is 2 km. from Frederikshaven and the ferries to Sweden and Norway. It is another 'TopCamp' site and provides all the comforts one could possibly need with all the attractions of the nearby beach, town and port. The 430 large pitches are attractively arranged in small enclosures of 9-13 units surrounded by hedges and trees. 250 pitches have electricity (10A) and drainage, a further 20 have water and there are 16 on hardstandings. There are 64 seasonal units and 23 site owned cabins.

Facilities

Centrally located, large, clean toilet blocks provide spacious showers (on payment) and washbasins in cubicles, together with some family bathrooms, rooms for disabled visitors and babies. Laundry. Good kitchens. Motorcaravan services. Supermarket. Café (15/6-15/8). Pizza service. Indoor swimming pool. Sauna. Solarium. 'Short' golf course. Minigolf. Tennis. Bicycle hire. Play areas. Internet access. Off site: Beach 200 m. Shops 2 km.

Open: 1 April - 20 October.

Directions

Turn off the main no. 40 road 2 km. north of Frederikshaven at roundabout just north of railway bridge. Site is signed. GPS: N57:27.853 E10:31.653

Charges guide

Per person	DKK 70
child (0-11 yrs)	DKK 50
pitch	DKK 50
electricity	DKK 29

DK2200 Bøjden Strand Ferie Park

Bøjden Landevej 12, Bøjden, DK-5600 Fåborg (Fyn)

Tel: **63 60 63 60**. Email: **info@bojden.dk** **www.alanrogers.com/DK2200**

Bøjden is located in one of the most beautiful corners of southwest Fyn (Funen in English) known as the 'Garden of Denmark'. This is a well equipped site separated from the beach only by a hedge. Bøjden is a delightful site for an entire holiday, while remaining a very good centre for excursions. Arranged in rows on mainly level grassy terraces and divided into groups by hedges and trees, many pitches have sea views as the site slopes gently down from the road. The 295 pitches (210 for touring units) all have electricity and include 65 new fully serviced pitches.

Facilities

The superb quality, central toilet block includes washbasins in cubicles, controllable showers, family bathrooms (some with whirlpools and double showers), baby room and excellent facilities for disabled people. Kitchen and laundry. A new unit serves a recent extension to the site. Motorcaravan services. Supermarket. Licenced restaurant. Takeaway. Indoor and outdoor swimming pools. Solarium. Fenced toddler play area. Adventure playground. TV and games rooms. Internet café and WiFi. Barbecue area. Fishing. Minigolf. Off site: Beach adjacent. Bicycle hire and riding 10 km. Golf 12 km.

Open: 14 March - 20 October.

Directions

From Faaborg follow road no. 8 to Bøjden and site is on right 500 m. before ferry terminal (from Fynshav). GPS: N55:06.317 E10:06.765

Charges guide

Per person	DKK 67
child (0-11 yrs)	DKK 45
pitch	DKK 10 - 100
electricity (10A)	DKK 31

Credit cards accepted with 5% surcharge.

DK2205 Løgismosestrand Camping

Løgismoseskov 7, DK-5683 Hårby (Fyn)

Tel: **64 77 12 50**. Email: **info@logismose.dk** **www.alanrogers.com/DK2205**

A countryside site with its own beach and pool, Løgismosestrand is surrounded by picturesque villages and the owners are a friendly young couple. The 220 pitches here are arranged in rows and groups divided by hedges and small trees which provide a little shade. All the 221 pitches for touring units have 6/10A electricity points. A barbecue area has been developed with gas grills and there are swimming (8 x 14 m.) and paddling pools for which there is a small charge. Recent additions include an Asian restaurant, a new football pitch and ten cabins to rent.

Facilities

Heated toilet units, kept very clean, include washbasins in cubicles, roomy showers (on payment), baby room, bathrooms for families and disabled people. Good laundry with washing machine and dryer. Excellent fully fitted kitchen (cooking charged). Motorcaravan services. Well stocked shop. Asian restaurant. Takeaway (high season). Swimming pool (1/6-1/9). Minigolf. Bicycle and boat hire. Adventure playground. Large undercover games room. Play field. Off site: Riding 2 km. Golf 8 km.

Open: 20 March - 22 September.

Directions

Southwest of Hårby via Sarup and Nellemose to Løgismose Skov, site is well signed. Lanes are narrow, large units should take care.
GPS: N55:10.763 E10:04.434

Charges guide

Per person	DKK 59
pitch	free - DKK 40
electricity	DKK 26

Credit cards accepted with 4% surcharge.

DK2210 Bøsøre Strand Feriepark

Bøsørevej 16, DK-5874 Hesselager (Fyn)

Tel: **62 25 11 45**. Email: **info@bosore.dk** **www.alanrogers.com/DK2210**

A themed holiday site on the eastern coast of Fyn, the tales of Hans Christian Andersen are evident in the design of the indoor pool complex and the main outdoor play area at this site. The former has two pools on different levels, two hot tubs and a sauna and features characters from the stories; the latter has a fairytale castle with moat as its centrepiece. There are 300 pitches in total, and with only 25 seasonal units there should always be room for touring units out of the main season. All have 10A electricity, there are 124 multi-serviced pitches and 20 hardstandings.

Facilities

Sanitary facilities are in one main central block and a smaller unit close to reception. They provide all usual facilities plus some family bathrooms, special children's section, baby rooms, facilities for disabled visitors. They could be stretched in high season. Laundry. Motorcaravan service point. Shop, bar/restaurant, pizzeria, takeaway. Kitchen. Solarium. Indoor pool complex. Games and TV rooms. Playground with moat. Animal farm. Internet access and WiFi. Bicycle hire. Entertainment (main season). Boat launching with jetty. Off site: Golf 20 km.

Open: Easter - 22 October.

Directions

Site is on the coast about midway between Nyborg and Svendborg. From road no. 163 just north of Hesselager, turn towards coast signed Bøsøre Strand (5 km). GPS: N55:11.572 E10:48.318

Charges guide

Per person	DKK 64
child (0-11 yrs)	DKK 43
pitch	DKK 25 - 70
electricity	DKK 28

Camping Cheques accepted.

DK2215 DCU Camping Odense

Odensevej 102, DK-5260 Odense (Fyn)

Tel: **66 11 47 02**. Email: **odense@dcu.dk** **www.alanrogers.com/DK2215**

Although within the confines of the city, this site is hidden away amongst mature trees and is therefore fairly quiet and an ideal base from which to explore the fairy-tale city of Odense. The 225 pitches, of which 200 have electricity (10A), are on level grass with small hedges and shrubs dividing the area into bays. There is a number of seasonal units on site, together with 13 cabins. A good network of cycle paths lead into the city. The Odense Adventure Pass (available at the site) allows unrestricted free travel on public transport within the city limits.

Facilities

Large sanitary unit provides modern facilities including washbasins in cubicles, family bathrooms, baby room and excellent suite for disabled visitors. Well equipped kitchen with gas hobs. Laundry. Motorcaravan services. Shop. Small swimming and paddling pools. Games marquee. Large playground. Minigolf. WiFi. Off site: Cycle track through the zoo to city centre. Hans Christian Andersen's house. Bicycle hire 700 m. Golf 4 km. Fishing 10 km.

Open: All year.

Directions

From E20 exit 50, turn towards Odense Centrum, site entrance is 3 km. on left immediately beside the Hydro-Texaco garage. GPS: N55:22.182 E10:23.578

Charges guide

Per person	DKK 65 - 68
child (0-11 yrs)	DKK 33 - 34
pitch	DKK 20 - 40
electricity	DKK 25 - 30

DK2220 Helnæs Camping

Strandbakken 21, Helnæs, DK-5631 Ebberup (Fyn)
Tel: **64 77 13 39**. Email: **info@helnaes-camping.dk** **www.alanrogers.com/DK2220**

Helnæs Camping is on the remote Helnæs peninsula to the southeast of Fyn, connected to the mainland by a small road. The site is adjacent to a nature reserve making it ideal for walkers, cyclists and birdwatchers, or for those who enjoy sea fishing (this is a great location for sea trout). The road to the site takes you through a breathtaking environment with colourful flowerbeds on the Bobakkerne Wall to the north and large outer marches in the south. Helnæs Camping has 160 pitches, some terraced, on grassy fields sloping down towards to the sea.

Facilities

Two toilet blocks, one brand new, with washbasins in cabins and controllable showers. Baby room (heated). Facilities for disabled visitors. Laundry with washing machines and dryers. Campers' kitchen. Shop. Takeaway. Adventure type playground. Minigolf. Bicycle hire. Canoe hire. Watersports. In high season small circus for children. TV lounge. Internet access. Covered barbecue area. Off site: Sea fishing.

Open: 15 March - 1 September.

Directions

From Nørre Åby follow 313 road south to Ebberup. In Ebberup turn south to Helnæs and follow signs for Helnæs Strand. GPS: N55:07.970 E10:02.140

Charges guide

Per person	DKK 55 - 67
child	DKK 30 - 36
electricity	DKK 25

No credit cards.
Camping Cheques accepted.

DK2235 Sakskøbing Grøn Camping

Saxes Allé 15, DK-4990 Sakskøbing (Lolland)
Tel: **54 70 47 57**. Email: **sax.groen.camp@mail.dk** **www.alanrogers.com/DK2235**

This small, traditional style site provides a useful stopover on the route from Germany to Sweden, within easy reach of the Puttgarden - Rødby ferry. There are 125 level grass pitches, most with electricity (10A) and, although there are a fair number of seasonal units, one can usually find space. There is a pool at a nearby sports centre. The site has a well stocked shop, which is open long hours, and the semi-pedestrianised town centre has a good range of shops and a supermarket. The town is noted for its unusual 'smiling' water tower, which you pass on the way to the site.

Facilities

Two sanitary units provide basic, older style facilities, including push-button free hot showers, some curtained washbasin cubicles and a baby room. Cooking and laundry facilities. Motorcaravan services. Shop. New play area. Off site: Town 100 m.

Open: 1 April - 30 September.

Directions

From E47, exit 46, turn towards town on road 9. Turn right at crossroads towards town centre (site is signed), cross railway and then turn right again, and site entrance is 250 m. on left. GPS: N54:47.905 E11:38.456

Charges 2009

Per person	DKK 67
child (0-14 yrs)	DKK 35
electricity	DKK 35

DK2257 Vesterlyng Camping

Ravnholtvej 3, DK-4591 Føllenslev (Sjælland)
Tel: **59 20 00 66**. Email: **info@vesterlyng-camping.dk** **www.alanrogers.com/DK2257**

Vesterlyng is a pleasant, quiet site, close to Føllenslev and Havnsø on Sjælland. The ground slopes towards the sea and there are good views from some pitches. It is an open site but some mature trees provide shade. Vesterlyng has 181 mostly level touring pitches, 150 with 6/13A electricity. A further 100 pitches are used by mostly elderly, seasonal units. The pitches are on long, grassy meadows each taking 16-20 units, off tarmac access roads. Facilities on this site are basic, but clean. The local beaches are ideal for swimming and a relaxing beach holiday.

Facilities

Two traditional style toilet blocks include washbasins (open style and in cabins) and controllable hot showers. Family shower rooms. Basic facilities for disabled people. Washing machine and dryer. Small shop. Bar. Swimming pool complex. Minigolf. Fishing. Riding. Bicycle hire. Watersports. WiFi. Boules. Animal enclosure. Live music nights. Off site: Fishing 1 km. Golf 15 km. Boat launching 1 km.

Open: 22 March - 21 October.

Directions

From Kalundborg follow road no. 23 east and exit on no. 155 road towards Svinninge. At Snertinge, continue north on road no. 255 for 2 km. Follow signs to site (6 km). From the west exit on road no. 225 towards Snertinge and follow signs after 2 km. GPS: N55:44.504 E11:18.540

Charges guide

Per person	DKK 67
pitch	DKK 10 - 40
electricity	DKK 27

No credit cards.

DK2250 Hillerød Camping

Blytækkervej 18, DK-3400 Hillerød (Sjælland)

Tel: **48 26 48 54**. Email: **info@hillerodcamping.dk** **www.alanrogers.com/DK2250**

The northernmost corner of Sjælland is packed with interest, based not only on fascinating periods of Denmark's history but also its attractive scenery. Hillerød is also a fine base for visiting Copenhagen and is only 25 km. from the ferries at Helsingør and the crossing to Sweden. Centrally situated, this neat campsite has a park-like setting in a residential area with five acres of well kept grass and some attractive trees. There are 100 pitches, of which 70 have electricity (10A) and these are marked.

Facilities

The bright, airy toilet block is older in style and includes washbasins with partitions and curtain. Facilities for babies can be used by disabled visitors. Campers' kitchen. Laundry room. Motorcaravan services. Small shop. Club room with TV. Play area. Bicycle hire. Off site: Tennis and indoor pool 1 km. Riding 2 km. Golf 3 km. Excellent new electric train service every 10 minutes (20 minutes walk) to Copenhagen. The site sells the Copenhagen card.

Open: Easter - 16 September.

Directions

Follow road no. 6 bypassing road to south until sign for Hillerød S. Turn towards town at sign for 'Centrum' on Roskildvej road no. 233 and site is signed to the right. GPS: N55:55.436 E12:17.722

Charges guide

Per person	DKK 60 - 67
child (2-11 yrs)	DKK 30 - 35
electricity	DKK 25 - 30

DK2255 Topcamp Feddet

Feddet 12, DK-4640 Faxe (Sjælland)

Tel: **56 72 52 06**. Email: **info@feddetcamping.dk** **www.alanrogers.com/DK2255**

This interesting spacious site with ecological principles is located on the Baltic coast. It has a fine, white, sandy beach (Blue Flag) which runs the full length of one side, with the Præstø fjord on the opposite side of the peninsula. There are 413 pitches for touring units, generally on sandy grass, with mature pine trees giving adequate shade. All have 10/13A electricity and 20 are fully serviced. Two specially designed sanitary buildings have been recently constructed.

Facilities

Both sanitary buildings are impressive, equipped to a very high standard. Family bathrooms (with twin showers), complete suites for small children and babies. Facilities for disabled visitors. Laundry. Kitchens, dining room and TV lounge. Motorcaravan service point. Licensed shop. Licensed bistro and takeaway (1/5-20/10 but weekends only outside peak season). Minigolf. Games room. Indoor playroom. Playgrounds. Event camp for children. Pet zoo. Bungee jump. WiFi. Gym, massage, reflexology and sun beds. Watersports. Fishing. Off site: Land Rover safaris, abseiling, Icelandic pony riding, educational courses, ocean kayaking, and seal watching in Fakse Bay.

Open: All year.

Directions

From south on E47/55 take exit 38 towards Præsto. Turn north on 209 road towards Fakse and from Vindbyholt follow site signs. From the north on E47/55 take exit 37 east towards Fakse. Just before Fakse turn south on 209 road and from Vindbyholt, site signs. GPS: N55:10.498 E12:06.122

Charges 2009

Per person	DKK 72
child (0-11 yrs)	DKK 50
pitch	DKK 37 - 105
electricity	DKK 35
dog	DKK 15

DK2265 Camping Charlottenlund Fort

Strandvejen 144B, DK-2920 Charlottenlund (Sjælland)

Tel: **39 62 36 88**. Email: **info@campingcopenhagen.dk** **www.alanrogers.com/DK2265**

On the northern outskirts of Copenhagen, this unique site is within the walls of an old fort which still retains its main armament of twelve 29 cm. howitzers (disabled, of course). There are 100 pitches on grass, all with 10A electricity. The obvious limitation on the space available means that pitches are relatively close together, but many are quite deep. The site is very popular and is usually full every night, so we suggest that you either reserve or arrive well before mid-day.

Facilities

Sanitary facilities located in the old armoury are newly rebuilt, well maintained and heated. Free showers. Kitchen facilities include gas hobs and a dining area. Laundry. Motorcaravan service point. Small shop in reception. Bicycle hire. WiFi. Beach. Off site: Riding 1.5 km. Golf 2 km. Copenhagen town centre 20 minutes by bus.

Open: 1 May - 14 September.

Directions

Leave E47/E55 at exit 17, and turn southeast on Jægersborgvej. After a short distance turn left (east) on Jægersborg Allé, following signs for Charlottenlund (5 km.) and follow all the way to the end. Finally turn right (south) on to Strandvejen, and site entrance is on left after 500 m.
GPS: N55:44.688 E12:35.123

Charges guide

Per person	DKK 80
pitch	DKK 25 - 45
electricity	DKK 5

MAP 8

Situated in the far north, Finland is a long and mainly flat county, dominated by huge dense forests and glorious lakes. The unspoilt wilderness of this country makes it a perfect place for relaxing in natural, peaceful surroundings.

CAPITAL: HELSINKI

Tourist Office

Finnish Tourist Board
PO Box 33213, London W6 8JX
Tel: 020 7365 2512
Fax: 020 8600 5681
Email: finlandinfo.lon@mek.fi
Internet: www.visitfinland.com

There is a considerable difference in the landscape between north and south, with the gently rolling, rural landscape of the south giving way to the hills and vast forests of the north and treeless fells and peat-lands of Lapland, where reindeer and moose run free. Forests of spruce, pine and birch cover three quarters of the country's surface and are inhabited by hares, elks and occasional wolves and bears.

The other outstanding feature of Finland is its thousands of post-glacial lakes and islands. The main Lake District is centred on the beautiful Lake Saimaa in the south east, where you can swim, sail and fish. In the south, the capital Helsinki retains a small town feel, with open air cafes, green parks, waterways and a busy market square surrounded by 19th-century architecture and museums. The flat western coastal regions include Turku and the Åland islands, ideal for sailing and fishing.

Population

5.2 million

Climate

Temperate climate, but with considerable variations. Summer is warm, winter is very cold.

Language

Finnish

Telephone

The country code is 00 358.

Money

Currency: The Euro
Banks: Mon-Fri 09.15-16.15
(regional variations may occur).

Shops

Mon-Fri 09.00-17.00/18.00.
Sat 09.00-14.00/15.00, department stores usually remain open to 18.00. Supermarket usually open to 20.00 Mon-Fri.

Public Holidays

New Year; Epiphany; Saints Day 16 Mar; Language Day 9 April; Good Friday; Easter Mon; May Day 30 Apr/1 May; All Saints Da 1 Nov; Independence Day 6 Dec; Christmas 25, 26 Dec.

Motoring

Main roads are excellent and relatively uncrowded outside city limits. Traffic drives on the right. Horn blowing is frowned upon. There are many road signs warning motorists of the danger of elk dashing out on the road. If you are unfortunate enough to hit one, it must be reported to police. Do not drink and drive, penalties are severe if any alcohol is detected.

FI2850 Rastila Camping

Karavaanikatu 4, FIN-00980 Helsinki (Uusimaa)

Tel: **093 216 551**. Email: **rastilacamping@hel.fi** **www.alanrogers.com/FI2850**

No trip to Finland would be complete without a few days stay in Helsinki, the capital since 1812. This all year round site has exceptional transport links with the metro, only five minutes walk from the campsite gates. It provides 165 pitches with electrical hook-ups, plus an additional small field for tent campers. Shrubs have been planted between the tarmac and grass pitches. All visitors will want to spend time in the Capital and a 24-hour bus, tram and metro pass can be bought at the metro station. Once on the metro you are in the city centre within 20 minutes on this regular fast train service. Essential visits will include Senate Square, in the heart of the city, and Suomenlinna, a marine fortress built on six islands in the 1700s. This garrison town is one of the most popular sights in Finland and is the world's largest maritime fortress. Helsinki, on the other hand, is one of Europe's smallest capitals and walking around the centre and port is popular as well as visiting the market square alongside the ferry port. The city also has a wide variety of art galleries and museums, many of which are free with the Helsinki card.

Facilities

Four sanitary blocks (two heated) provide toilets and showers. Kitchens with cooking rings and sinks. Facilities for disabled visitors and babies. Laundry room. Saunas. Motorcaravan service point. Fully licensed restaurant. Playground. Games and TV room. Bicycles and kayaks for hire. Off site: Small beach adjacent. Golf 5 km. Tallinn the capital of Estonia is only 90 minutes away from Helsinki by fast jetliner ferry.

Open: All year.

Directions

Well signed from 170 or Ring I. From the 170, turn at Itakeskus shopping complex towards Vuosaari. After crossing bridge go up slip road to Rastila. At top of road turn left. Site is directly ahead.
GPS: N60:12.395 E25:07.279

Charges guide

Per pitch incl. 2 persons	€ 9,00 - € 15,00
electricity	€ 4,50

Discounts for weekly or monthly bookings.

FI2820 Tampere Camping Härmälä

Leirintäkatu 8, FIN-33900 Tampere (Häme)

Tel: **032 651 355**. Email: **harmala@lomaliitto.fi** **www.alanrogers.com/FI2820**

Härmelä is a lively campsite near Lake Pyhäjärvi. It is situated only 4 km. from Tampere city centre. You can chose from a large, unspecified number of unmarked pitches (about 180). The site has 111 cabins of various sizes and facilities. Amenities include a beach, saunas, playgrounds for children, a small shop and a pizzeria. The site seems a little run down but is acceptable for a couple of nights. Tampere is beautifully situated beside Lake Näsijärvi. A stroll along the harbour with its yachts and through the parks is a pleasant experience.

Facilities

There are four sanitary blocks, one block is new, three are rather basic. Washbasins and showers have free hot water. Facilities for disabled visitors. Laundry room. Campers' kitchen with cooking rings, microwave. Motorcaravan service point. Small shop. Pizzeria. Off site: Golf and riding 5 km.

Open: 17 May - 27 August.

Directions

Turn off the E12 and follow signs.
GPS: N61:28.318 E23:44.367

Charges guide

Per person	€ 4,00
child (0-14 yrs)	€ 2,00
pitch	€ 10,00 - € 11,50
electricity	€ 4,00

FI2830 Camping Lakari

Lakarintie 405, FIN-34800 Virrat (Häme)

Tel: **034 758 639**. Email: **virtain.matkailu@phpoint.fi** **www.alanrogers.com/FI2830**

The peace and tranquillity of the beautiful natural surroundings are the main attractions at this vast (18 hectares) campsite which is located on a narrow piece of land between two lakes. This site is a must if you want to get away from it all. There is a variety of cabins to rent, some with their own beach and jetty! Marked pitches for tents and caravans are beside the beach or in little meadows in the forest. You pick your own place. Site amenities include a café and a beach sauna. This is a spectacular landscape with deep gorges and steep lakeside cliffs.

Facilities

Two toilet blocks, basic but clean and well kept include toilets, washbasins and showers. Free hot water. Chemical disposal and motorcaravan service point. Covered camper's kitchen with fridge, cooking rings and oven. Washing machine. Small shop and cafeteria. TV. Fishing. Bicycle hire. Off site: Golf 1 km. Riding 5 km.

Open: 1 May - 30 September.

Directions

Site is 7 km. south of Virrat on road 66. Follow signs. GPS: N62:12.589 E23:50.266

Charges guide

Per person	€ 2,00
child	€ 1,00
pitch	€ 12,00
electricity	€ 2,00

FI2960 Koljonvirta Camping

Ylemmäisentie 6, FIN-74120 Iisalmi (Kuopio)

Tel: **017 825 252**. Email: **info@campingkoljonvirta.fi** **www.alanrogers.com/FI2960**

Koljonvirta Camping is a large but quiet site located about 5 km. from the centre of Iisalmi. There are 200 marked grass pitches, 120 with electricity (16A). The site adjoins a lake and has a small beach and facilities for boating and fishing. Iisalmi town itself is on the northern edge of the Finnish Lake District and provides a good variety of shops and an interesting variety of events during June, July and August. These vary from the world famous 'Wife Carrying' World Championships to the Lapinlahti 'Cattle Calling' Competition and the International Midnight Marathon.

Facilities

The sanitary blocks provide showers, toilets and a sauna in one block. Launderette. Shop. Snack bar. Fully licenced restaurant. Motorcaravan service point. Lake and small beach with facilities for boating and fishing. The site exhibits large wooden sculptures of animals.
Off site: Riding 100 m. Golf 5 km.

Open: May - September.

Directions

From road 5 turn onto the 88 (towards Oulu) just north of Iisalmi. Go straight over the roundabout and the site is about 1 km. on the left. Follow signs. GPS: N63:35.649 E27:09.646

Charges guide

Per person	€ 4,00
child	€ 1,00
pitch incl. electricity	€ 12,50

FI2970 Nallikari Camping

PL 55, FIN-90015 Oulun Kaupunki (Oulu)

Tel: **085 586 1350**. Email: **nallikari.camping@ouka.fi** **www.alanrogers.com/FI2970**

This is probably one of the best sites in Scandinavia, set in a recreational wooded area alongside a sandy beach on the banks of the Baltic Sea, with the added bonus of the adjacent Eden Spa complex. Nallikari provides 200 pitches with electricity (some also have water supply and drainage), plus an additional 79 cottages to rent, 28 of which are suitable for winter occupation. Oulu is a modern town about 100 miles south of the Arctic Circle that enjoys long, sunny and dry summer days. The Baltic however is frozen for many weeks in the winter and then the sun barely rises for two months. In early June the days are very long with the sun setting at about 11.30pm and rising at 1.30 am! Nallikari, to the west of Oulu, is 3 km. along cycle paths and the town has much to offer.

Facilities

The modern shower/WC blocks also provide male and female saunas, kitchen and launderette facilities. Facilities for disabled visitors. Motorcaravan service point. Playground. Reception with café/restaurant, souvenir and grocery shop. TV room. WiFi. Bicycle hire. Off site: The adjacent Eden centre provides excellent modern spa facilities where you can enjoy a day under the glass-roofed pool with its jacuzzis, saunas, Turkish baths and an Irish bath. Fishing 5 km. Golf 15 km.

Open: All year.

Directions

Leave route 4/E75 at junction with route 20 and head west down Kiertotie. Site well signed, Nallikari Eden, but continue on, just after traffic lights, cross a bridge and take the second on the right. Just before the Eden Complex turn right towards Lerike and reception. GPS: N65:01.784 E25:25.076

Charges guide

Per pitch incl. 2 persons	€ 9,00 - € 18,00
extra person	€ 4,00
child (under 15 yrs)	€ 1,00
electricity	€ 4,00 - € 6,00

FI2975 Manamansalo Camping

Teeriniemientie 156, FIN-88340 Manamansalo (Oulu)

Tel: **088 741 38**. Email: **manamansalo@kainuunmatkailu.fi** **www.alanrogers.com/FI2975**

Manamansalo is a top class, 'Wild North' tourist centre on the island of Manamansalo in Lake Oulojärvi. You arrive by ferry or via a bridge from the mainland. This site is a real find if you are looking for peace and quiet and is also very good for families. It has 200 pitches, 140 with electricity, very attractively laid out in the forest with natural dividers of pine trees. The site stretches along the lake and has a long, narrow sandy beach. Nature lovers will appreciate the network of trails in the pine forest. Choose between walking and cycling or even skiing in spring.

Facilities

Three toilet blocks have toilets, washbasins and showers in cubicles with free hot water. Washing machines and dryers. Kitchen with sinks, cooking rings and ovens. Motorcaravan service point. Fully licensed restaurant and small shop (from May). Playground. Canoes, pedaloes and rowing boats for hire. Fishing. WiFi.

Open: 1 March - 30 September.

Directions

Coming from the south on road 5/E63 turn at Mainau on road 28. At Vuottolahti turn on road 879 and follow signs to Manamansalo and site. From road 22 turn at Liminpuro or Melaillahti and follow signs. GPS: N64:23.365 E27:01.565

Charges guide

Per person	€ 4,00
child (0-15 yrs)	€ 1,00
pitch	€ 12,00 - € 14,00
electricity	€ 3,50

FI2980 Ounaskoski Camping

Jäämerentie 1, FIN-96200 Rovaniemi (Lapland)

Tel: **016 345 304** **www.alanrogers.com/FI2980**

Ounaskoski Camping is situated almost exactly on the Arctic Circle, 66 degrees north and just 8 km. south of the Santa Claus post office and village, on the banks of the Kemijoki River. The site has 153 marked touring pitches, (68 with electricity), plus a further small area for tents. Rovaniemi attracts many visitors each year, especially in the weeks leading up to Christmas, who fly direct to the local airport and pay Santa Claus a visit. The town has much to offer with a good selection of shops and some restaurants. Reindeer meat is well worth trying!

Facilities

There are two sanitary buildings each providing toilets, showers, laundry and kitchen. One also houses a sauna. Facilities for disabled visitors. Motorcaravan service point. Café. Small shop. Playground. TV room. Fishing. Bicycle hire. Organised coach trips. Off site: Ranua Zoo. The Kemijoki, Finland's largest river, offers numerous opportunities for sightseeing by boat. Santa Claus village and Santa Park.

Open: 1 June - 15 September.

Directions

Ounaskoski Camping is on the banks of the Kemijoki River in the middle of Rovaniemi. From the 4/E75 go via the centre across the river and turn right. Site is between the Jatkankynttilasilta Bridge and the Rautatiesilta Bridge. GPS: N66:29.847 E25:44.594

Charges guide

Per person	€ 5,00
child (under 15 yrs)	€ 2,50
pitch	€ 14,00
electricity (16A)	€ 4,00

FI2985 Camping Sodankylä Nilimella

Kelukoskentie 4, FIN-99600 Sodankylä (Lapland)

Tel: **016 612 181**. Email: **antti.rintala@naturex-ventures.fi** **www.alanrogers.com/FI2985**

Camping Sodankylä Nilimella is a small, peaceful site situated alongside the Kitinen River, just one kilometre from the centre of Sodankylä. The site is split into two areas by a small, relatively quiet, public road. The 80 good sized pitches are clearly marked with hedges and 40 have 16A electricity. The reception area also serves drinks and snacks. Sodankylä town itself, at the junction of routes 4 and 5, is home to a small Sami community and is an important trading post, so you will find some shops and supermarkets. The town is also home to the Geophysical Observatory, which constantly surveys the earth's magnetic field and measures earthquakes using seismic recordings.

Facilities

Two good sanitary blocks with toilets, hot showers and saunas. Facilities for disabled visitors. Campers' kitchen. Motorcaravan service point. Playground. Bicycle hire. River swimming, canoeing and water skiing. Off site: Shops and supermarkets in Sodankylä town.

Open: 1 June - 30 September.

Directions

Turn off route 4 onto route 5. Site is on the left just after crossing the river. It is well signed and easy to find. GPS: N67:25.053 E26:36.482

Charges guide

Per unit incl. 2 persons and electricity	€ 22,00
extra person	€ 4,00
child	€ 2,00

FI2990 Camping Tenorinne

FIN-99950 Karigasniemi (Lapland)

Tel: **016 676 113**. Email: **camping@tenorinne.com** **www.alanrogers.com/FI2990**

This is probably the most northerly campsite in Finland and makes an excellent stopover on route to North Cape. This is a small site with space for 30 units, on three levels with a small access road sloping down to the river. Electricity points (16A) are available throughout the site but the pitches are unmarked. This area is still largely unpopulated, scattered with only small Sami communities and herds of reindeer. Karigasniemi is a slightly larger town as it is a border post with Norway and is close to both the Kevo Nature reserve and the Lemmenjoki National Park.

Facilities

Sanitary block includes showers, toilets and sauna. Launderette. Kitchen. Reception with TV.

Open: 1 June - 20 September.

Directions

If travelling south on the 970, site is on right as you enter town. If travelling west on the 92, turn right immediately before Norwegian customs point. Site is shortly on left past petrol station. Entrance is quite steep. GPS: N69:24.020 E25:50.670

Charges guide

Per person	€ 3,00
pitch	€ 12,00
incl. electricity	€ 16,00

FI2995 Ukonjärvi Camping

Ukonjärventi 141, FIN-99801 Ivalo (Lapland)

Tel: **016 667 501**. Email: **nuttu@ukolo.fi** **www.alanrogers.com/FI2995**

Ukonjärvi Camping lies on the banks of Lake Inari, situated in a forested area alongside a nature reserve. It is a quiet, peaceful site, ideal for rest and relaxation. 30 touring pitches have electricity and are surrounded by pine and beech trees. Cottages are available to rent. A bar and restaurant are located at reception; a range of local dishes is produced including reindeer casserole. There is also a barbecue hut, located in the centre of the site, if you prefer to cook your own food. A climb up to the nearby viewpoint offers spectacular views over the lake – you can even see over to Russia.

Facilities

Sanitary block includes toilets and showers. Laundry and campers' kitchen. Lakeside sauna (extra cost). Bar and restaurant. Barbecue hut with logs. Small beach. Fishing and boating on lake. TV room. WiFi. Off site: Tankavaaran Kansainvalinen Kulamuseo, a gold mining experience where you can try gold panning, keeping what you find! The Northern Lapland Centre and the Sami Museum, displaying cultural and natural history exhibitions.

Open: May - September.

Directions

Ukonjärvi Camping is 11 km. north of Ivalo on route 4. Look for signs to Lake Inari viewpoint; site is about 1 km. down the narrow road (signed). GPS: N68:44.212 E27:28.612

Charges guide

Per person	€ 3,50
child	€ 2,50
pitch incl. electricity	€ 19,00

From the hot sunny climate of the Mediterranean to the more northerly and cooler regions of Normandy and Brittany, with the Châteaux of the Loire and the lush valleys of the Dordogne, France offers holidaymakers a huge choice of destinations to suit all tastes.

CAPITAL: PARIS

Tourist Office

French Government Tourist Office
Maison de la France
178 Piccadilly, London W1J 9AL
Tel: 020 7399 3520
Fax: 020 7493 6594
Email: info.uk@franceguide.com
Internet: www.franceguide.com

France boasts every type of landscape imaginable ranging from the wooded valleys of the Dordogne to the volcanic uplands of the Massif Central, the rocky coast of Brittany to the lavender covered hills of Provence and snow-capped peaks of the Alps. Each region is different and this is reflected in the local customs, cuisine, architecture and dialect. Many rural villages hold festivals to celebrate the local saints and you can also find museums devoted to the rural arts and crafts of the regions.

France has a rich architectural heritage with a huge variety of Gothic cathedrals, châteaux, Roman remains, fortresses and Romanesque churches to visit. Given the varied landscape and climate there is also great scope for outdoor pursuits with plenty of hiking and cycling opportunities across the country, and rock-climbing and skiing in the mountains. And of course a trip to France wouldn't be complete without sampling the local food and wine.

Population

60.7 million

Climate

France has a temperate climate but this varies considerably from region to region.

Language

French

Telephone

The country code is 00 33.

Money

Currency: The Euro
Banks: Mon-Fri 09.00-12.00 and 14.00-16.00.

Shops

Mon-Sat 09.00-18.30. Some are closed between 12.00-14.30. Food shops are open 07.00-18.30/19.30. Some food shops (particularly bakers) are open Sunday mornings. Many shops close Mondays.

Public Holidays

New Year; Easter Mon; Labour Day; VE Day 8 May; Ascension; Whit Mon; Bastille Day 14 July; Assumption 15 Aug; All Saints 1 Nov; Armistice Day 11 Nov; Christmas Day.

Motoring

France has a comprehensive road system from motorways (Autoroutes), Routes Nationales (N roads), Routes Départmentales (D roads) down to purely local C class roads. Tolls are payable on the autoroute network which is extensive but expensive, and also on certain bridges.

FR29080 Camping le Panoramic

Route de la Plage-Penker, F-29560 Telgruc-sur-Mer (Finistère)

Tel: **02 98 27 78 41**. Email: **info@camping-panoramic.com** **www.alanrogers.com/FR29080**

This medium sized traditional site is situated on quite a steep, ten acre hillside with fine views. It is personally run by M. Jacq and his family who all speak good English. The 200 pitches are arranged on flat, shady terraces, in small groups with hedges and flowering shrubs and 20 pitches have services for motorcaravans. Divided into two parts, the main upper site is where most of the facilities are located, with the swimming pool, its terrace and a playground located with the lower pitches across the road. Some up-and-down walking is therefore necessary, but this is a small price to pay for such pleasant and comfortable surroundings. This area provides lovely coastal footpaths to enjoy. A 'Sites et Paysages' member.

Facilities

The main site has two well kept toilet blocks with another very good block opened for main season across the road. All three include British and Turkish style WCs, washbasins in cubicles, facilities for disabled people, baby baths, plus laundry facilities. Motorcaravan services. Small shop (1/7-31/8). Refurbished bar/restaurant with takeaway (1/7-31/8). Barbecue area. Heated pool, paddling pool and jacuzzi (1/6-15/9). Playground. Games and TV rooms. Tennis. Bicycle hire. WiFi. Off site: Beach and fishing 700 m. Riding 6 km. Golf 14 km. Sailing school nearby.

Open: 1 June - 15 September.

Directions

Site is just south of Telgruc-sur-Mer. On D887 pass through Ste Marie du Ménez Horn. Turn left on D208 signed Telgruc-sur-Mer. Continue straight on through town and site is on right within 1 km. GPS: N48:13.428 W04:22.382

Charges guide

Per person	€ 5,00
child (under 7 yrs)	€ 3,00
pitch	€ 12,00
electricity (6/10A)	€ 3,10 - € 4,50
dog	€ 1,60

Less 20% outside July/August.

FR22090 Castel Camping le Château de Galinée

La Galinée, F-22380 Saint Cast-le-Guildo (Côtes d'Armor)

Tel: **02 96 41 10 56**. Email: **chateaugalinee@wanadoo.fr** **www.alanrogers.com/FR22090**

Situated a few kilometres back from St Cast and owned and managed by the Vervel family, Galinée is in a parkland setting on level grass with numerous and varied mature trees. It has 273 pitches, all with electricity, water and drainage and separated by many mature shrubs and bushes. The top section is mostly for mobile homes. An attractive outdoor pool complex has swimming and paddling pools and two pools with a water slide and a 'magic stream'. A new indoor complex has now also been added and includes a swimming pool, bar, restaurant and large entertainment hall.

Facilities

The large modern sanitary block includes washbasins in private cabins, facilities for babies and a good unit for disabled people. Laundry room. Shop for basics, bar and excellent takeaway menu (all 1/7-26/8). Attractive heated pool complex (12/5-7/9). New covered complex with heated pool, bar, restaurant, entertainment hall and internet access. Outside terrace with large play area. Tennis. Fishing. Field for ball games. Off site: Beach and golf 3.5 km. Riding 6 km.

Open: 7 May - 12 September.

Directions

From D168 Ploubalay - Plancoet road turn onto D786 towards Matignon and St Cast. Site is very well signed 1 km. after leaving Notre Dame de Guildo. GPS: N48:35.067 W02:15.438

Charges 2009

Per person	€ 4,00 - € 6,50
child (under 7 yrs)	€ 2,50 - € 4,50
pitch with electricity	€ 13,50 - € 23,50
animal	€ 4,00

Camping Cheques accepted.

FR29090 Camping le Raguenès-Plage

19 rue des Iles, F-29920 Névez (Finistère)

Tel: **02 98 06 80 69**. Email: **info@camping-le-raguenes-plage.com** **www.alanrogers.com/FR29090**

Mme. Guyader and her family will ensure you receive a warm welcome on arrival at this well kept and pleasant site. Le Raguenès-Plage is an attractive and well laid out campsite with many shrubs and trees. The 287 pitches are a good size, flat and grassy, separated by trees and hedges. All have electricity, water and drainage. The site is used by one tour operator (60 pitches), and has 46 mobile homes of its own. A pool complex complete with water toboggan is a key feature and is close to the friendly bar, restaurant, shop and takeaway. From the far end of the campsite a delightful five minutes' walk along a path and through a cornfield takes you down to a pleasant, sandy beach looking out towards the Ile Verte and the Presqu'île de Raguenès.

Facilities

Two clean, well maintained sanitary blocks include mixed style toilets, washbasins in cabins, baby baths and facilities for disabled visitors. Laundry room. Motorcaravan service point. Small shop (from 15/5). Bar and restaurant (from 1/6) with outside terrace and takeaway. Reading and TV room, internet access point. Heated pool with sun terrace and paddling pool. Sauna (charged). Play areas. Games room. Various activities are organised in July/Aug. Off site: Beach, fishing and watersports 300 m. Supermarket 3 km. Riding 4 km.

Open: 1 April - 30 September.

Directions

From N165 take D24 Kerampaou exit. After 3 km. turn right towards Nizon and bear right at church in village following signs to Névez (D77). Continue through Névez, following signs to Raguenès. Continue for 3 km. to site on left. GPS: N47:47.607 W03:48.040

Charges 2009

Per unit incl. 2 persons and electricity	€ 20,00 - € 36,80
extra person	€ 4,40 - € 5,70
child (under 7 yrs)	€ 2,20 - € 3,40

FR22110 Camping les Madières

Le Vau Madec, F-22590 Pordic (Côtes d'Armor)

Tel: **02 96 79 02 48**. Email: **campinglesmadieres@wanadoo.fr** **www.alanrogers.com/FR22110**

Les Madières is well placed for exploring the Goëlo coast with its seaside resorts of St Quay-Portrieux, Binic and Etables-sur-Mer, ports used in the past by fishing schooners and now used by pleasure boats and a few coastal fishing boats. The young and enthusiastic owners here have already made their mark on this quiet campsite. With plenty of open spaces and set in the countryside, yet near the sea (800 m), it has 93 pitches of which ten are used for mobile homes. There are no tour operators. Only 800 m. away is the Vau Madec beach for swimming, fishing and collecting shellfish. This is linked to the beach at Binic by the GR34 coastal path (3 km.) where there are sandy beaches and holiday activities such as sailing, minigolf and tennis.

Facilities

Two refurbished heated toilet blocks include private cabins and facilities for disabled visitors. Laundry facilities. Motorcaravan services. Gas. Simple shop (all season). Bar, restaurant and takeaway (all season). Swimming pool (1/6-20/9). Games room. Play area. Some entertainment (high season). Mobile home rental. Caravan storage. Off site: Beach 800 m. Bus service nearby. Riding 2.5 km. Bicycle hire 3 km.

Open: 1 April - 30 October.

Directions

From St Brieuc ring-road (N12), turn north on D786 signed Paimpol (by the coast). Les Madières is at Pordic, 3 km. from the ring-road. Site is well signed from the D786. GPS: N48:34.944 W02:48.288

Charges guide

Per person	€ 4,80
child (0-10 yrs)	€ 3,00
pitch incl. electricity (10A)	€ 11,00
dog	€ 2,00

Discounts outside July and August.

FR29010 Castel Camping le Ty-Nadan

Route d'Arzano, F-29310 Locunolé (Finistère)

Tel: **02 98 71 75 47**. Email: **infos@camping-ty-nadan.fr** **www.alanrogers.com/FR29010**

Ty-Nadan is a well organised site set amongst wooded countryside along the bank of the River Elle. The 183 pitches for touring units are grassy, many with shade and 99 are fully serviced. The pool complex with slides and paddling pool is very popular as are the large indoor pool complex and indoor games area with a climbing wall. There is also an adventure play park and a 'Minikids' park for 5-8 year olds, not to mention tennis courts, table tennis, pool tables, archery and trampolines. This is a wonderful site for families with children. Several tour operators use the site. An exciting and varied programme of activities is offered throughout the season – canoe and sea kayaking expeditions, rock climbing, mountain biking, aquagym, paintball, riding or walking – all supervised by qualified staff. A full programme of entertainment for all ages is provided in high season including concerts, Breton evenings with pig roasts, dancing, etc. (be warned, you will be actively encouraged to join in!)

Facilities

Two older, split-level toilet blocks are of fair quality and include washbasins in cabins and baby rooms. A newer block provides easier access for disabled people. Washing machines and dryers. Restaurant, takeaway, bar and well stocked shop. Crêperie (July/Aug). Heated outdoor pool (17 x 8 m). New indoor pool. Small river beach (unfenced). Indoor badminton and rock climbing facility. Activity and entertainment programmes (high season). Bicycle hire. Boat hire. Fishing. Off site: Beaches 20 minutes by car. Golf 12 km.

Open: 3 April - 7 September.

Directions

Make for Arzano which is northeast of Quimperlé on the Pontivy road and turn off D22 just west of village at site sign. Site is about 3 km.
GPS: N47:54.284 W03:28.457

Charges guide

Per unit incl. 2 persons and electricity	€ 19,90 - € 45,90
child (under 7 yrs)	€ 1,70 - € 5,40
dog	€ 1,70 - € 5,40

Less 15-20% outside July/Aug.
Camping Cheques accepted.

FR29050 Castel Camping l'Orangerie de Lanniron

Château de Lanniron, F-29336 Quimper (Finistère)

Tel: **02 98 90 62 02**. Email: **camping@lanniron.com** **www.alanrogers.com/FR29050**

L'Orangerie is a beautiful and peaceful family site set in ten acres of a 17th-century, 42 acre country estate on the banks of the Odet river, formerly the home of the Bishops of Quimper. The site has 199 grassy pitches (156 for touring units) of three types varying in size and services. They are on flat ground laid out in rows alongside access roads with shrubs and bushes providing pleasant pitches. All have electricity and 88 have all three services. The original outbuildings have been attractively converted around a walled courtyard. With lovely walks within the grounds, the restaurant and the gardens are both open to the public and in spring the rhododendrons and azaleas are magnificent. The site is just to the south of Quimper and about 15 km. from the sea and beaches at Bénodet. The restoration of the park, including the original canal, fountains, ornamental 'Bassin de Neptune', the boathouse and the gardens is now complete. Recent additions are a new reception and restaurant, plus a nine-hole golf course and driving range. Used by tour operators (30 pitches).

Facilities

Excellent heated block in the courtyard and second modern block serving the top areas of the site. Facilities for disabled people and babies. Washing machines and dryers. Motorcaravan services. Shop (15/5-9/9). Gas supplies. Bar, snacks and takeaway, plus new restaurant (open daily). Swimming pool (144 sq. m) with paddling pool. Small play area. Tennis. Minigolf. Golf course (9 holes) and driving range. Fishing. Archery. Bicycle hire. General reading, games and billiards rooms. TV/video room. Karaoke. Outdoor activities. Large room for indoor activities. Pony rides and tree climbing (high season). Internet access and WiFi. Off site: Two hypermarkets 1 km. Historic town of Quimper under 3 km. Activities in the area include golf, cycling, walking, fishing, canoeing, surfing and sailing. Beach 15 km.

Open: 15 May - 15 September.

Directions

From Quimper follow Quimper Sud signs, then 'Toutes Directions' and general camping signs, finally signs for Lanniron. GPS: N47:58.630 W04:06.655

Charges guide

Per person	€ 4,25 - € 7,10
child (2-9 yrs)	€ 2,75 - € 4,50
pitch (100 sq.m)	€ 10,25 - € 17,70
incl. electricity (10A)	€ 13,25 - € 22,20
special pitch (120/150 sq.m) incl. water and electricity	€ 17,00 - € 27,70

Less 15% outside July/Aug.
Camping Cheques accepted.

BOOK THIS SITE CALL 01580 214000 ...we'll arrange everything The Travel Service

FR29180 Camping les Embruns

Rue du philosophe Alain, le Pouldu, F-29360 Clohars-Carnoët (Finistère)

Tel: **02 98 39 91 07**. Email: **camping-les-embruns@wanadoo.fr** **www.alanrogers.com/FR29180**

This site is unusual in that it is located in the heart of a village, yet is only 250 metres from a sandy cove. The entrance with its code operated barrier and wonderful floral displays, is the first indication that this is a well tended and well organised site, and the owners have won numerous regional and national awards for its superb presentation. The 180 pitches (100 occupied by mobile homes) are separated by trees, shrubs and bushes, and most have electricity (10A), water and drainage. There is a covered, heated swimming pool, a circular paddling pool and a water play pool. It is only a short walk to the village centre with all its attractions and services. It is also close to beautiful countryside and the Carnoët Forest which are good for walking and cycling.

Facilities

Two modern sanitary blocks, recently completely renewed and heated in winter, include mainly British style toilets, some washbasins in cubicles, baby baths and good facilities for disabled visitors. Family bathrooms. Laundry facilities. Motorcaravan service point. Shop and restaurant by entrance. Bar and terrace (1/7-31/8). Takeaway (20/6-5/9). Covered, heated swimming and paddling pools. Large games hall. Play area. Minigolf. Communal barbecue area. Activities for children and adults organised in July/Aug. Bicycle hire. Off site: Nearby sea and river fishing and watersports. Beach 250 m. Riding 2 km.

Open: 3 April - 19 September.

Directions

From N165 take either 'Kervidanou, Quimperlé Ouest' exit or 'Kergostiou, Quimperlé Centre, Clohars Carnoët' exit and follow D16 to Clohars Carnoët. Then take D24 for Le Pouldu and follow site signs in village. GPS: N47:46.119 W03:32.716

Charges 2009

Per unit incl. 2 persons and electricity	€ 14,50 - € 33,90
extra person	€ 3,95 - € 5,50
child (under 7 yrs)	€ 2,60 - € 3,50
animal	€ 2,00 - € 2,50

FR29030 Camping du Letty

F-29950 Bénodet (Finistère)

Tel: **02 98 57 04 69**. Email: **reception@campingduletty.com** **www.alanrogers.com/FR29030**

The Guyader family have ensured that this excellent and attractive site has plenty to offer for all the family. With a charming ambience, the site on the outskirts of the popular resort of Bénodet spreads over 22 acres with 493 pitches, all for touring units. Groups of four to eight pitches are set in cul-de-sacs with mature hedging and trees to divide each group. Most pitches have electricity, water and drainage. Although there is no swimming pool here, the site has direct access to a small sandy beach, and has provided a floating pontoon (safe bathing depends on the tides).

Facilities

Six well placed toilet blocks are of good quality and include mixed style WCs, washbasins in large cabins and controllable hot showers (charged). Baby rooms. Separate facility for disabled visitors. Launderette. Motorcaravan services. Well stocked shop. Extensive snack bar and takeaway (21/6-31/8). Bar with games room and night club. Reading room with four computer stations. Entertainment room with satellite TV. Fitness centre (no charge). Saunas, jacuzzi and solarium (all on payment). Tennis and squash (charged). Boules. Well equipped play area. Entertainment and activities (July/Aug).

Open: 15 June - 6 September.

Directions

From N165 take D70 Concarneau exit. At first roundabout take D44 to Fouesnant. Turn right at T-junction. After 2 km. turn left to Fouesnant (still D44). Continue through La Forêt Fouesnant and Fouesnant, picking up signs for Bénodet. Shortly before Bénodet at roundabout turn left (signed Le Letty). Turn right at next mini-roundabout and site is 500 m. on left. GPS: N47:52.020 W04:05.270

Charges 2009

Per person	€ 4,00 - € 6,50
child (1-6 yrs)	€ 2,00 - € 3,25
pitch incl. electricity	€ 12,50 - € 15,00

FR35000 Camping le Vieux Chêne

Baguer-Pican, F-35120 Dol-de-Bretagne (Ille-et-Vilaine)
Tel: **02 99 48 09 55**. Email: **vieux.chene@wanadoo.fr** www.alanrogers.com/FR35000

This attractive, family owned site is situated between Saint Malo and Mont Saint-Michel. Developed in the grounds of a country farmhouse dating from 1638, its young and enthusiastic owner has created a really pleasant, traditional atmosphere. In spacious, rural surroundings it offers 199 good sized pitches on gently sloping grass, most with 10A electricity, water tap and light. They are separated by bushes and flowers, with mature trees for shade. A very attractive tenting area (without electricity) is in the orchard. There are three lakes in the grounds and centrally located leisure facilities include a restaurant with a terrace overlooking an attractive pool complex. In high season, some entertainment is provided, which is free for children. The site is used by a Dutch tour operator (20 pitches).

Facilities

Three very good, unisex toilet blocks, which can be heated, include washbasins in cabins, a baby room and facilities for disabled people. Small laundry. Motorcaravan services. Shop, takeaway and restaurant (15/5-15/9). Heated swimming pool, paddling pool, slides (15/5-15/9; lifeguard July/Aug). TV room (satellite). Games room. Tennis. Minigolf. Giant chess. Play area. Riding in July/Aug. Fishing. Off site: Supermarket in Dol 3 km. Golf 12 km. Beach 20 km.

Open: 31 March - 22 September.

Directions

Site is by the D576 Dol-de-Bretagne - Pontorson road, just east of Baguer-Pican. It can be reached from the new N176 taking exit for Dol-Est and Baguer-Pican. GPS: N48:32.972 W01:41.050

Charges guide

Per person	€ 4,50 - € 5,75
child (under 13 yrs)	free - € 3,90
pitch incl. electricity	€ 10,00 - € 21,50
dog	€ 1,50

FR29340 Camping de la Côte des Légendes

B.P. 36 Keravezan, F-29890 Brignogan-Plages (Finistère)
Tel: **02 98 83 41 65**. Email: **camping-cote-des-legendes@wanadoo.fr** www.alanrogers.com/FR29340

Located just behind a safe, sandy beach on the Bay of Brignogan and adjacent to a Centre Nautique (sailing, windsurfing, kayaking), this site is ideal for a family seaside holiday. It is a quiet site with 147 level pitches arranged in rows and protected by hedges. There are a few mobile homes and chalets for rent but no tour operators. A shop, bar and takeaway are open in high season when activities are arranged for adults and children by the helpful owner (good English is spoken). The beach of fine sand can be reached directly from the site.

Facilities

Main toilet facilities are at the rear of the site in a large block that provides washbasins in cubicles, baby baths and facilities for disabled visitors. The upper floor provides a games room with views of the sea. Further toilet facilities are at the reception building, also a laundry. Motorcaravan service point. Bar, small shop and takeaway (July/Aug). Playground and playing field. Off site: Watersports centre adjacent. Village services 700 m. Bicycle hire 1 km. Riding 6 km.

Open: Easter - 1 November.

Directions

From Roscoff take the D58 towards Morlaix and after 6 km. turn right on the D10 towards Plouescat and then Plouguerneau. Turn right on the D770 to Brignogan-Plages. In the main street go straight on following signs for site and Club Nautique.
GPS: N48:40.367 W04:19.757

Charges guide

Per unit incl. 2 persons	€ 9,90 - € 12,50
extra person	€ 3,05 - € 3,75
electricity	€ 1,00 - € 3,10

FR44090 Kawan Village du Deffay

B.P. 18 Le Deffay, Sainte Reine-de-Bretagne, F-44160 Pontchâteau (Loire-Atlantique)
Tel: **02 40 88 00 57**. Email: **campingdudeffay@wanadoo.fr** **www.alanrogers.com/FR44090**

A family managed site, Château du Deffay is a refreshing departure from the usual formula in that it is not over organised or supervised and has no tour operator units. The 142 good sized, fairly level pitches have pleasant views and are either on open grass, on shallow terraces divided by hedges, or informally arranged in a central, slightly sloping wooded area. Most have electricity. The facilities are located within the old courtyard area of the smaller château (that dates from before 1400). With the temptation of free pedaloes and the fairly deep, unfenced lake, parents should ensure that children are supervised. The landscape is natural right down to the molehills, and the site blends well with the rural environment of the estate, lake and farmland which surround it. For these reasons it is enjoyed by many. The larger château (built 1880) and another lake stand away from this area providing pleasant walking. The reception has been built separately to contain the camping area. Alpine type chalets overlook the lake and fit in well with the environment. The site is close to the Brière Regional Park, the Guérande Peninsula, and La Baule with its magnificent beach (20 km).

Facilities

The main toilet block could do with some updating but is well equipped including washbasins in cabins, provision for disabled people and a baby bathroom. Laundry facilities. Maintenance can be variable and hot water can take time to reach temperature in low season. Shop, bar, small restaurant with takeaway (1/5-20/9) and solar heated swimming pool and paddling pool (all season). Play area. TV. Animation in season including miniclub. Torches useful. Off site: Golf and riding 5 km.

Open: 1 May - 18 September.

Directions

Site is signed from D33 Pontchâteau - Herbignac road near Ste Reine. Also signed from the D773 and N165-E60 (exit 13). GPS: N47:26.270 W02:09.350

Charges guide

Per person	€ 3,20 - € 5,10
child (2-12 yrs)	€ 2,15 - € 3,50
pitch	€ 7,60 - € 11,60
incl. electricity (6A)	€ 11,00 - € 15,60
incl. 3 services	€ 12,90 - € 17,70

Camping Cheques accepted.

FR44190 Camping le Fief

57 chemin du Fief, F-44250 Saint Brévin-les-Pins (Loire-Atlantique)

Tel: **02 40 27 23 86**. Email: **camping@lefief.com** **www.alanrogers.com/FR44190**

If you are a family with young children or lively teenagers, this could be the campsite for you. Le Fief is a well established site only 800 metres from sandy beaches on the southern Brittany coast. It has a magnificent 'aqua park' with outdoor and covered swimming pools, paddling pools, slides, river rapids, fountains, jets and more. The site has 220 pitches for touring units (out of 413). Whilst these all have electricity (5A), they vary in size and many are worn and may be untidy. There are also 143 mobile homes and chalets to rent and 55 privately owned units. This is a lively site in high season with a variety of entertainment and organised activity for all ages. This ranges from a miniclub for 5-12 year olds, to 'Tonic Days' with aquagym, jogging and sports competitions, and to evening events which include karaoke, themed dinners and cabaret. There are plenty of sporting facilities for active youngsters.

Facilities

One excellent new toilet block and three others of a lower standard. Laundry facilities. Shop (15/5-15/9). Bar, restaurant and takeaway (15/4-15/9) with terrace overlooking the pool complex. Outdoor pools, etc. (15/5-15/9). Covered pool (all season). Play area. Tennis. Volleyball. Basketball. Pétanque. Table tennis. Archery. Games room. Internet access. Organised entertainment and activities (July/Aug). Off site: Beach, bicycle hire 800 m. Bus stop 1 km. Riding 1 km. Golf 15 km. Planète Sauvage safari park.

Open: 1 April - 15 October.

Directions

From the St Nazaire bridge take the fourth exit from the D213 signed St Brévin - L'Océan. Continue over first roundabout and bear right at the second to join chemin du Fief. The site is on the right, well signed. GPS: N47:14.188 W02:10.109

Charges guide

Per pitch incl. 2 persons	€ 17,00 - € 37,00
extra person	€ 5,00 - € 9,00
child (0-7 yrs)	€ 2,50 - € 4,50
electricity	€ 5,00 - € 6,00
dog	€ 2,00 - € 5,00

FR44180 Camping de la Boutinardière

Rue de la Plage de la Boutinardière, F-44210 Pornic (Loire-Atlantique)

Tel: **02 40 82 05 68**. Email: **info@laboutinardiere.com** **www.alanrogers.com/FR44180**

This is truly a holiday site to suit all the family whatever their ages, just 200 m. from the beach. It has 250 individual good sized pitches, 100-120 sq.m. in size, many bordered by three metre high, well maintained hedges for shade and privacy. All pitches have electricity available. It is a family owned site and English is spoken by the helpful, obliging reception staff. Beside reception is the excellent site shop and across the road is a complex of indoor and outdoor pools, paddling pool and a twin toboggan water slide. On site there are sports and entertainment areas. Facing the water complex, the bar, restaurant and terraces are new and serve excellent food, be it a snack, a restaurant meal or perhaps a takeaway. This campsite has it all – 2 km. from the beautiful harbour town of Pornic and 200 metres from the sea, together with the very best of amenities and facilities.

Facilities

Toilet facilities are in three good blocks, one large and centrally situated and two supporting blocks. Washbasins are in cabins. Laundry facilities. Shop. New complex of bar, restaurant, terraces. Three heated swimming pools, one indoor, a paddling pool and water slides (15/5-22/9). Games room. Sports and activity area. Playground. Minigolf. Fitness equipment and sauna. Off site: Sandy cove 200 m. Golf, riding, sea fishing, restaurants, cafés, fishing harbour, sailing and windsurfing, all within 5 km.

Open: 5 April - 30 September.

Directions

From north or south on D213, take Nantes D751 exit. At roundabout (with McDonalds) take D13 (Bemarie-en-Retz). After 4 km. site is signed to right. Note: do NOT exit from D213 at Pomic Ouest or Centre. GPS: N47:05.490 W02:03.080

Charges guide

Per unit incl. 2 persons	€ 15,00 - € 34,00
extra person	€ 3,00 - € 7,50
child (under 8 yrs)	€ 2,00 - € 5,50
electricity (6/10A)	€ 4,00 - € 5,50

FR44210 Camping de l'Océan

F-44490 Le Croisic (Loire-Atlantique)

Tel: **02 40 23 07 69**. Email: **camping-ocean@wanadoo.fr** **www.alanrogers.com/FR44210**

Camping de l'Océan is situated on the Le Croisic peninsula, an attractive part of the Brittany coastline. Out of a total of 400 pitches, just 80 are available for tourers with the remainder being taken by mobile homes either privately owned or for rent. The pitches are level and 80-100 sq.m. in size (they were rather worn when we visited). This site, probably more suitable for families with young teenagers, can be very lively in high season with a wealth of activities and entertainment. The leisure facilities, which include a restaurant, bar and pool complex are of an excellent standard. Sports are well catered for and there are tournaments in high season. The site is within walking distance of the Atlantic Ocean and white sandy beaches just 150 m. away.

Facilities

Five adequate toilet blocks include facilities for disabled visitors. Washing machines and dryers. Good restaurant and bar. Takeaway. Shop. Motorcaravan service point. Indoor pool, outdoor pool and paddling pool. Basketball. Tennis. Off site: Market (most days). Le Croisic for shops, bars and restaurants. Sailing, riding and golf.

Open: 5 April - 30 September.

Directions

From Le Pouliguen, travel west on N171 to Le Croisic. Site is well signed from here and found in about 1.5 km. GPS: N47:17.520 W02:32.090

Charges guide

Per unit incl. 2 persons	€ 16,50 - € 36,50
extra person	€ 3,00 - € 7,00
electricity (10A)	€ 1,00 - € 3,00

FR44220 Camping Parc de Léveno

Route de Sandun, F-44350 Guérande (Loire-Atlantique)

Tel: **02 40 24 79 30**. Email: **domaine.leveno@wanadoo.fr** **www.alanrogers.com/FR44220**

There have been many changes to this extensive site over the past three years and considerable investment has been made to provide some excellent new facilities. The number of mobile homes and chalets has increased considerably, leaving just 47 touring pitches. Pitches are divided by hedges and trees providing good shade and all have electricity (10A). Access is tricky to some and the site is not recommended for larger units. Twin axle caravans and American motorhomes are not accepted.

Facilities

Main refurbished toilet block offers preset showers, washbasins in cubicles and facilities for disabled visitors. Laundry facilities. Shop for basics and snacks. Restaurant, bar with TV (July/Aug). Indoor pool. Heated outdoor pool complex (15/5-15/9). Fitness room. Play area. Multisport court. Activities (high season). Off site: Hypermarket 1 km. Fishing 2 km. Beach, golf and riding all 5 km.

Open: 4 April - 30 September.

Directions

From D774 and from D99/N171 take D99E Guérande by-pass. Turn east for Villejames and Leclerc hypermarket and continue on D247 to site on right. GPS: N47:19.987 W02:23.478

Charges 2009

Per unit incl. 2 persons, electricity and water	€ 18,00 - € 35,00
extra person	€ 4,00 - € 7,00

FR44100 Camping le Patisseau

29 rue du Patisseau, F-44210 Pornic (Loire-Atlantique)

Tel: **02 40 82 10 39**. Email: **contact@lepatisseau.com** **www.alanrogers.com/FR44100**

Le Patisseau is situated in the countryside just a short drive from the fishing village of Pornic. It is a relaxed site with a large number of mobile homes and chalets, and popular with young families and teenagers. The 120 touring pitches, all with electrical connections (6A), are divided between the attractive 'forest' area with plenty of shade from mature trees, and the more open 'prairie' area. Some are on a slight slope and access to others might be tricky for larger units. A railway runs along the bottom half of the site with trains several times a day, (none overnight) and the noise is minimal.

Facilities

The modern heated toilet block is very spacious and well fitted; most washbasins are open style, but the controllable showers are all in large cubicles which have washbasins; these are very popular, so it is best to avoid busy times! Also good facilities for disabled visitors and babies. Laundry rooms. Shop (15/5-8/9). Bar, restaurant and takeaway (1/7-31/9). Indoor heated pool with sauna, jacuzzi and spa (all season). Small heated outdoor pools and water slides (15/5-3/9). Play area. Multisport court. Bicycle hire. Off site: Fishing and beach 2.5 km. Riding, golf, sailing and boat launching all 5 km.

Open: 4 April - 11 November.

Directions

Pornic is 19 km. south of the St Nazaire bridge. Access to site is at junction of D751 Nantes - Pornic road with the D213 St Nazaire - Noirmoutier 'Route Bleue'. From north take exit for D751 Nantes. From south follow D751 Clion-sur-Mer. At roundabout north of D213 take exit for Le Patisseau and follow signs to site. Avoid Pornic town centre.
GPS: N47:07.183 W02:04.397

Charges 2009

Per unit incl. 2 persons and electricity (6A)	€ 25,00 - € 39,00
extra person	€ 3,00 - € 7,00

FR44150 Camping la Tabardière

F-44770 La Plaine-sur-Mer (Loire-Atlantique)

Tel: **02 40 21 58 83**. Email: **info@camping-la-tabardiere.com** **www.alanrogers.com/FR44150**

Owned and managed by the Barre family, this campsite lies next to the family farm. Pleasant, peaceful and immaculate, it will suit those who want to enjoy the local coast and towns but return to an 'oasis' for relaxation. It still, however, provides activities and fun for those with energy remaining. The pitches are mostly terraced and care needs to be taken in manoeuvring caravans into position. Pitches have access to electricity and water taps are conveniently situated nearby. The site is probably not suitable for wheelchair users. A 'Sites et Paysages' member.

Facilities

Two good, clean toilet blocks are well equipped and include laundry facilities. Motorcaravan service point. Shop, bar, snacks and takeaway (high season). Good sized covered swimming pool, paddling pool and slides (supervised). Playground. Minigolf. Half size tennis courts. Boules. Fitness programme. Overnight area for motorcaravans (€ 13 per night). Off site: Beach, sea fishing 3 km. Golf, riding and bicycle hire all 5 km.

Open: 4 April - 27 September.

Directions

Site is well signed, situated inland off the D13 Pornic - La Plaine-sur-Mer road.
GPS: N47:08.280 W02:09.110

Charges 2009

Per unit incl. 2 persons	€ 15,00 - € 26,70
extra person	€ 3,70 - € 6,40
child (2-9 yrs)	€ 2,75 - € 4,35
electricity (3/8A)	€ 3,30 - € 4,80

Camping Cheques accepted.

FR14150 Sunêlia Port'land

Chemin du Castel, F-14520 Port-en-Bessin (Calvados)

Tel: **02 31 51 07 06**. Email: **campingportland@wanadoo.fr** **www.alanrogers.com/FR14150**

The Gerardin family will make you most welcome at Port'land, now a mature site lying 700 metres to the east of the little resort of Port en Bessin, one of Normandy's busiest fishing ports. The 300 pitches are large and grassy with 202 available for touring units, including 128 with 15A electricity. There is a separate area for tents without electricity. The camping area has been divided into zones, some overlooking small fishing ponds and another radiating out from a central barbecue area. There are ten site-owned mobile homes for rent. A member of the 'Sunelia' group.

Facilities

The two sanitary blocks are modern and well maintained. Special disabled facilities. Heated swimming pool (covered in low season) and paddling pool. Bar, restaurant, takeaway. Large TV and games room. Multisports pitch. Fishing. Play area. WiFi access. Off site: Beach 4 km. 27-hole International golf course adjacent. Fishing 600 m. Bicycle hire and riding 10 km. D-Day beaches. Bayeux.

Open: 29 March - 5 November.

Directions

Site is clearly signed off the D514, 4 km. west of Port en Bessin. GPS: N49:20.829 W00:46.274

Charges guide

Per unit incl. 2 persons and electricity	€ 25,00 - € 37,00
extra person	€ 4,80 - € 7,30
child (2-10 yrs)	€ 2,80 - € 4,20

FR56280 Airotel les Sept Saints

B.P. 14, F-56410 Erdeven (Morbihan)

Tel: **02 97 55 52 65**. Email: **info@septsaints.com** **www.alanrogers.com/FR56280**

One is attracted to this campsite on arrival, with a well-tended shrubbery and reception to the left of the entrance and a landscaped pool complex on the right. The 200 pitches are divided equally between mobile homes and touring pitches, arranged in three separate groups: 60 normal touring pitches with electricity (10A), mobile homes, and an area under the trees across the play area for tents. Touring pitches are separated by manicured hedges and are level grass. The heated swimming pool complex, with its slides, jacuzzi and padding pool, and overlooked by the bar terrace, provides a focal point. In July and August there are separate children's clubs for younger children and teenagers and a variety of entertainment in the evenings. The site offers a complete holiday within itself as well as access to the Brittany coast.

Facilities

Two modern toilet blocks include en-suite facilities for disabled visitors and attractive baby rooms. Two laundry rooms. Bar, takeaway and shop (10/6-9/9). Heated swimming pool with slides, Jacuzzi, and paddling pool with mushroom and baby slide (15/5-15/9). Excellent play areas. Multisport pitch. Boules. Grass area for ball games. Bicycle hire. Games room. TV room. Gas supplies. Internet. Off site: Fishing 1.5 km. Riding 3 km. Golf 3 km. Beach and sailing 3 km.

Open: 15 May - 15 September.

Directions

From N165 at Auray take exit for D768 to Carnac and Quiberon. At roundabout entering Plouharnel turn west on D781, following signs to Erdeven and L'Orient. Continue through Erdeven, turn left where site is signed after 1.5 km. and site is 150 m. on the right. GPS: N47:39.317 W03:10.307

Charges guide

Per person	€ 4,00 - € 7,00
child (under 7 yrs)	€ 3,00 - € 5,50
pitch	€ 10,00 - € 18,00
electricity	€ 5,50

FR50050 Kawan Village le Cormoran

Ravenoville-Plage, F-50480 Sainte Mère-Eglise (Manche)

Tel: **02 33 41 33 94**. Email: **lecormoran@wanadoo.fr** **www.alanrogers.com/FR50050**

This welcoming, family run site, close to Cherbourg (45 km) and Caen (95 km), is situated just across the road from a long sandy beach. It is also close to Utah beach and is ideally located for those wishing to visit the many museums, landing beaches and remembrance gardens of WW2. On flat, quite open ground, the site has 100 good size pitches on level grass, all with 6A electricity. Some extra large pitches are available. The well kept pitches are separated by mature hedges and the site is decorated with flowering shrubs. A covered pool, a sauna and a gym are among improvements for 2009. These facilities, plus a shop, comfortable bar and takeaway are open all season.

Facilities

Four toilet blocks, one heated, are of varying styles and ages but all are maintained to a good standard. Laundry. New kitchen facilities. Shop. Bar and terrace. Snacks and takeaway. Outdoor pool (1/6-15/9, unsupervised). New covered pool, sauna and gym (all season). Play areas. Tennis. Boules. Entertainment, TV and games room. Bicycle and shrimp net hire. Riding (July/Aug). Communal barbecues. Off site: Beach 20 m. Sand yachting. Golf (9 holes) 3 km.

Open: 4 April - 27 September.

Directions

From N13 take Ste Mère-Eglise exit and in centre of town take road to Ravenoville (6 km), then Ravenoville-Plage (3 km). Just before beach turn right and site is 500 m. GPS: N49:27.960 W01:14.104

Charges 2009

Per unit incl. 1 or 2 persons and electricity	€ 20,00 - € 32,00
extra person	€ 4,00 - € 7,50
child (3-10 yrs)	€ 2,00 - € 3,00

Camping Cheques accepted.

FR27070 Camping de l'Ile des Trois Rois

1 rue Gilles Nicolle, F-27700 Andelys (Eure)

Tel: **02 32 54 23 79**. Email: **campingtroisrois@aol.com** **www.alanrogers.com/FR27070**

One hour from Paris and 30 minutes from Rouen, L'Ile des Trois Rois has an attractive setting on the banks of the Seine, with a private fishing lake and is a haven of peace. It is overlooked by the impressive remains of the Château-Gaillard and would be ideal as an overnight stop or for longer. The site has been owned by the Français Family for the past four years and they live on site. Within walking distance of the town and shops, the site has 100 spacious and partly shady grass pitches, all with electricity (long leads may be required for some). Water taps are rather scarce. There are also five mobile homes for rent and 60 pitches occupied by private mobile homes/seasonal units. Medieval Festival in Les Andelys – last weekend in June. Bread and cakes are available from a vending machine 24 hrs.

Facilities

Four small, unheated toilet blocks have British style toilets (no seats), showers and washbasins all in cubicles, dishwashing and laundry sinks. One has facilities for disabled people and another has a laundry facility. Motorcaravan service point. Two heated swimming pools (15/5-15/9). Fishing in the Seine or in the private lake. Fenced play area. Animation. Bar and restaurant, evening entertainment (4/7-30/8). Bicycles and barbecues for hire. Internet access and satellite TV. Off site: Day trips to Paris and Rouen. Cycling and walking trails. Riding 5 km. Golf 9 km.

Open: 15 March - 15 November.

Directions

From the A13 motorway, take exit 17 and join the D316 to Les Andelys. In Les Andelys follow signs to Evreux, and the campsite is located just off the island before passing the bridge over the Seine.
GPS: N49:14.155 E01:24.038

Charges guide

Per unit incl. 2 persons	€ 17,00
extra person	€ 5,00
child (under 3 yrs)	free
dog	€ 2,00

FR50080 Kawan Village Haliotis

Chemin des Soupirs, F-50170 Pontorson (Manche)

Tel: **02 33 68 11 59**. Email: **camping.haliotis@wanadoo.fr** **www.alanrogers.com/FR50080**

The Duchesne family have achieved a remarkable transformation of this former municipal site. Situated on the edge of the little town of Pontorson and next to the river Couesnon, Camping Haliotis is within walking, cycling and canoeing distance of Mont Saint-Michel. The site has 152 pitches, including 118 for touring units. Most pitches have electricity and 34 really large ones also have water and drainage. Private sanitary facilities are now available on some 'luxury' pitches. The large, comfortable reception area has been developed to incorporate a bar and restaurant.

Facilities

Very clean, renovated and well equipped toilet block. Laundry facilities. Bar where breakfast is served. Bread to order. Heated swimming pool (cleaned daily) with jacuzzi, separate paddling pool. Sauna and solarium. Good fenced play area. Trampoline. Pétanque. Archery. Large games room. Tennis court. Bicycle hire. Fishing in the River Couesnon. Japanese garden and animal park. Club for children. Off site: Large supermarket, restaurants and takeaways in Pontorson within walking distance. Riding 3 km. Golf 4 km. Fishing 25 km. Beach 30 km.

Open: 1 April - 5 November.

Directions

Site is 300 m. from the town centre, west of D976, alongside the river, and is well signed from the town.
GPS: N48:33.424 W01:30.670

Charges 2009

Per unit incl. 2 persons and electricity	€ 16,50 - € 22,00
with private sanitary facility	€ 18,50 - € 27,00
extra person	€ 4,50 - € 6,00
child (under 12 yrs)	€ 2,00 - € 3,50

Camping Cheques accepted.

FR50110 Camping Saint-Michel

35 route du Mont Saint-Michel, F-50220 Courtils (Manche)

Tel: **02 33 70 96 90**. Email: **infos@campingsaintmichel.com** **www.alanrogers.com/FR50110**

This delightful site is owned and run by an enthusiastic young couple, the Duchesnes. It is located in a peaceful, rural setting, yet is only 8 km. from the busy tourist attraction of Mont St-Michel. The site has 100 pitches which include 36 for touring units and 25 for mobile homes and chalets to rent. Electricity connections (6A) are available and many trees and shrubs provide shade to the pitches. From the restaurant and its terrace overlooking the pool, the site slopes gently down to a small enclosure of farm animals kept to entertain children and adults alike. It is M. and Mme. Duschesne's intention to maintain a quiet and peaceful site, hence there are no discos or organised clubs.

Facilities

The modern, well maintained toilet block has washbasins in cubicles and showers. Separate laundry. Facilities for disabled visitors in the new reception building. All is of an excellent standard. Motorcaravan service point. Shop. Bar (15/3-15/10). Restaurant and takeaway (4/6-13/9). Heated swimming pool (1/5-30/9). Animal farm. Play area. Games room. Bicycle hire. Off site: Fishing 2 km. Riding 3 km. Beach 30 km.

Open: 6 February - 4 November.

Directions

From St Malo take the N137 south and join the N176 east to Pontorson where it becomes the N175. In 20 km. turn northwest on D43 signed Courtils. Site is through village on the left. GPS: N48:37.657 W01:24.960

Charges guide

Per person	€ 4,00 - € 6,00
child (0-7 yrs)	€ 1,80 - € 2,50
pitch incl. electricity	€ 7,50 - € 9,00

FR60010 Camping Campix

B.P. 37, F-60340 Saint Leu-d'Esserent (Oise)

Tel: **03 44 56 08 48**. Email: **campix@orangel.fr** **www.alanrogers.com/FR60010**

This informal site has been unusually developed in a former sandstone quarry on the outskirts of the small town. The quarry walls provide a sheltered, peaceful environment and trees soften the slopes. Not a neat, manicured site, the 160 pitches are in small groups on the different levels with stone and gravel access roads (some fairly steep and muddy in poor weather). Electricity is available to all the pitches. There are many secluded corners mostly for smaller units and tents. Torches are advised.

Facilities

A large building houses reception and two clean, heated sanitary units - one for tourers, the other (open July/Aug) usually reserved for groups. Two suites for disabled people double as baby rooms. Laundry area. Facilities may be congested at peak times. Motorcaravan services. Daily bread and milk. Pizza and other Italian food delivered in the evenings (July/Aug). Play area. Off site: Fishing 1 or 5 km. Riding and golf 5 km.

Open: 7 March - 30 November.

Directions

St Leu-d'Esserent is 11 km. west of Senlis, 5 km. northwest of Chantilly. From north on A1 autoroute take Senlis exit, from Paris the Chantilly exit. Site north of town off D12 towards Cramoisy, and signed in village. GPS: N49:13.509 E02:25.638

Charges guide

Per person	€ 3,50 - € 5,50
pitch	€ 4,00 - € 5,50
electricity (6A)	€ 2,50 - € 3,50

Camping Cheques accepted.

FR62030 Kawan Village Château du Gandspette

133 rue de Gandspette, F-62910 Eperlecques (Pas-de-Calais)

Tel: **03 21 93 43 93**. Email: **contact@chateau-gandspette.com** **www.alanrogers.com/FR62030**

This spacious family run site, in the grounds of a 19th-century château, conveniently situated for the Channel ports and tunnel, provides overnight accommodation together with a range of facilities for longer stays. There are 100 touring pitches, all with electric hook-ups, intermingled with 50 French-owned mobile homes and caravans, and a further 18 for hire. Pitches are delineated by trees and hedging. Mature trees form the perimeter of the site, and here there is access to woodland walks.

Facilities

Two sanitary blocks with a mixture of open and cubicled washbasins. Good facilities for disabled people and babies. Laundry facilities. Motorcaravan service point. Bar, grill restaurant and takeaway (all 15/5-15/9). Swimming pools (15/5-30/9). Playground and playing field. Tennis. Pétanque. Children's room. Entertainment in season. Off site: Supermarket 1 km. Fishing 3 km. Riding, golf 5 km. Bicycle hire 9 km. Beach 30 km.

Open: 22 March - 30 September.

Directions

From Calais follow N43 (St Omer) for 25 km. Southeast of Nordausques take D221 (east). Follow site signs for 5-6 km. From St Omer follow N43 to roundabout at junction with D600. Turn right on D600 (Dunkirk). After 5 km. turn left on D221. Site is 1.5 km. on right. GPS: N50:49.137 E02:10.740

Charges guide

Per unit incl. 2 persons and electricity	€ 17,00 - € 27,00
extra person (over 6 yrs)	€ 5,00 - € 6,00

Camping Cheques accepted.

FR80060 Camping le Val de Trie

Rue des Sources, Bouillancourt-sous-Miannay, F-80870 Moyenneville (Somme)

Tel: **03 22 31 48 88**. Email: **raphael@camping-levaldetrie.fr** **www.alanrogers.com/FR80060**

Le Val de Trie is a natural countryside site in woodland, near a small village. The 100 numbered, grassy pitches are of a good size, divided by hedges and shrubs with mature trees providing good shade in most areas, and all have electricity (6A) and water. Access roads are gravel (site is possibly not suitable for the largest motorcaravans). It can be very quiet in April, June, September and October. If there is no-one on site, just choose a pitch or call at farm to book in. There are a few Dutch tour operator tents (five). This is maturing into a well managed site with modern facilities and a friendly, relaxed atmosphere. There are good walks around the area and a notice board keeps campers up to date with local market, shopping and activity news. English is spoken. The owners of Le Val de Trie have recently opened a new campsite nearby, Le Clos Cacheleux (FR80210).

Facilities

Two clean sanitary buildings include washbasins in cubicles, units for disabled people, babies and children. Laundry facilities. Motorcaravan services. Shop (from 1/4), bread to order and butcher visits in season. Bar with TV (1/4-15/10), snack bar with takeaway (29/4-10/9). Room above bar for children Off site: Riding 14 km. Golf 10 km. Beach 12 km.

Open: 24 March - 15 October.

Directions

From A28 take exit 2 near Abbeville and D925 to Miannay. Turn left on D86 to Bouillancourt-sous-Miannay: site is signed in village.
GPS: N50:05.038 E01:42.779

Charges guide

Per unit incl. 2 persons	€ 14,60 - € 19,60
incl. electricity	€ 16,70 - € 23,60
extra person	€ 3,10 - € 4,90
child (under 7 yrs)	€ 1,90 - € 2,90
dog	€ 0,80 - € 1,30

Camping Cheques accepted.

Camping le Val de Trie ***
VAL DE TRIE
Cottages to rent
Online reservation
Ideal spot for first or last night or longer stay
Situated at only 1 hour from Calais (A16) 12 km from the coast
Quiet and relaxing Fishing pond Swimming pools Bar
BOUILLANCOURT sous MIANNAY 80870 MOYENNEVILLE
Tel : +33 3 22 31 48 88 Fax : +33 3 22 31 35 33
www.camping-levaldetrie.fr raphael@camping-levaldetrie.fr
Camping le Clos Cacheleux
Route de Bouillancourt
80132 Miannay
tel.: +33 3 22 31 48 88
raphael@camping-lecloscacheleux.com
www.camping-lecloscacheleux.com
Online reservation
New
Ideal spot for first or last night or longer stay
1 hour from Calais (A16) 12 km from the coast

FR80210 Camping le Clos Cacheleux

Route de Bouillancourt, F-80132 Miannay (Somme)

Tel: **03 22 19 17 47**. Email: **raphael@camping-lecloscacheleux.fr** **www.alanrogers.com/FR80210**

Le Clos Cacheleux is a well situated campsite of six hectares bordering woodland in the park of the Château Bouillancourt which dates from the 18th century. First opened in July 2008, it is 11 km. from the Bay of the Somme, regarded as being among the most beautiful bays in France. There are 60 very large, grassy pitches (200 sq.m) and all have electricity hook-ups and water points. The owners aim to make your stay as enjoyable as possible by providing high quality services and activities. Visitors have access to the swimming pool, bar and children's club of the sister site – Le Val de Trie (20 m).

Facilities

The single sanitary block is clean and well maintained. Facilities for disabled visitors. Baby room. Laundry room with washing machine and dryer. Motorcaravan service point. At the sister site: shop, bar with terrace, library and TV room, restaurant and takeaway (26/4-2/9). Play area. Boules. Picnic tables. Freezer for ice packs. Barbecue hire. Bicycle hire. Fishing pond. Caravan storage. Some of the above facilities are on the sister site. Off site: Village 1 km. Hypermarket in Abbéville. Sandy beaches of the Picardy coast 12 km. Golf 7 km. Riding 14 km.

Open: 1 April - 15 October.

Directions

From the A28 at Abbéville take the D925 towards Eu and Le Tréport; do not go towards Moyenville. Turn left in Miannay village on the D86 towards Toeufles. The road to Bouillancourt-sous-Miannay is on the left after 2 km. and site is signed in the village.
GPS: N50:05.011 E01:42.806

Charges guide

Per unit incl. 2 persons and electricity	€ 16,70 - € 23,60
extra person	€ 3,10 - € 4,90
child (under 7 yrs)	€ 1,90 - € 2,90
dog	€ 0,80 - € 1,30

FR80090 Kawan Village Caravaning le Val d'Authie

20 route de Vercourt, F-80120 Villers-sur-Authie (Somme)

Tel: **03 22 29 92 47**. Email: **camping@valdauthie.fr** **www.alanrogers.com/FR80090**

In a village location, this well organised site is fairly close to several beaches, but also has its own excellent pool complex, small restaurant and bar. The owner has carefully controlled the size of the site, leaving space for a leisure area with an indoor pool complex. There are 170 pitches in total, but with many holiday homes and chalets, there are only 60 for touring units. These are on grass, some are divided by small hedges, with 6/10A electric hook-ups, and ten have full services. The site has a fitness trail and running track, mountain bike circuit, and plenty of good paths for evening strolls. Ideas for excursions include the 15/16th century chapel and hospice and the Aviation Museum at Rue, a pottery at nearby Roussent, a flour mill at Maintenay, and the steam railway which runs from Le Crotoy to Cayeux-sur-Mer around the Baie de Somme. A 'Sites et Paysages' member.

Facilities

Good toilet facilities include some shower and washbasin units, washbasins in cubicles, and limited facilities for disabled people and babies. Facilities may be under pressure in high season and cleaning variable. Shop (not October). Bar/restaurant (4/4-12/10; hours vary). Swimming and paddling pools with lifeguards in July/Aug). Playground, club room with TV. Weekend entertainment in season (discos may be noisy until midnight, once weekly). Multicourt, beach volleyball, football, boules and tennis court. Internet room. Fitness room including sauna (charged).

Open: 29 March - 12 October.

Directions

Villers-sur-Authie is about 25 km. NNW of Abbéville. From A16 junction 24 take N1 to Vron, then left on D175 to Villers-sur-Authie. Or use D85 from Rue, or D485 from Nampont St Martin. Site is at southern end of village at road junction.
GPS: N50:18.815 E01:41.729

Charges guide

Per unit incl. 2 persons	€ 19,00 - € 25,00
extra person	€ 6,00
child (2-6 yrs)	€ 3,00
electricity (6/10A)	€ 5,00 - € 8,00

Camping Cheques accepted.

The Travel Service BOOK THIS SITE CALL 01580 214000 ...we'll arrange everything

FR80070 Kawan Village la Ferme des Aulnes

1 rue du Marais, Fresne-sur-Authie, F-80120 Nampont-Saint Martin (Somme)

Tel: **03 22 29 22 69**. Email: **contact@fermedesaulnes.com** **www.alanrogers.com/FR80070**

This peaceful site, with 120 pitches, has been developed on the meadows of a small, 17th-century farm on the edge of Fresne and is lovingly cared for by its enthusiastic owner and his hard-working team. Restored outbuildings house reception and the facilities, around a central courtyard that boasts a fine heated swimming pool. A new development outside, facing the main gate, has 20 large level grass pitches for touring. There is also an area for tents. In the centre, a warden lives above a new facility building. The remaining 22 touring pitches are in the main complex, hedged and fairly level. Activities are organised for children and there are indoor facilities for poor weather. From here you can visit Crécy, Agincourt, St Valéry and Montreuil (where Victor Hugo wrote Les Misérables). The nearby Bay of the Somme has wonderful sandy beaches and many watersports.

Facilities

Both sanitary areas are heated and include washbasins in cubicles with a large cubicle for disabled people. Dishwashing and laundry sinks. Shop. Piano bar and restaurant. Motorcaravan service point. TV room. Swimming pool (16 x 9 m; heated and with cover for cooler weather). Jacuzzi and sauna. Fitness room. Aquagym and balneotherapy. Playground. Boules. Archery. Rooms with Play Stations and videos.
Off site: River fishing 100 m. Golf 1 km. Riding 8 km.

Open: 22 March - 2 November.

Directions

From Calais, take A16 to exit 25 and turn for Arras for 2 km. and then towards Abbeville on N1. At Nampont-St Martin turn west on D485 and site will be found in 2 km. GPS: N50:20.157 E01:42.740

Charges guide

Per person	€ 7,00
child (under 7 yrs)	€ 4,00
pitch	€ 7,00
electricity (6/10A)	€ 6,00 - € 12,00

Camping Cheques accepted.

FR77020 Camping le Chêne Gris

24 place de la Gare de Faremoutiers, F-77515 Pommeuse (Seine-et-Marne)

Tel: **01 64 04 21 80**. Email: **info@lechenegris.com** **www.alanrogers.com/FR77020**

This site is being progressively developed by a Dutch holiday company. A principal building houses reception on the ground floor and also an airy restaurant/bar plus a takeaway. Of the 198 pitches, 65 are for touring, many of which are on aggregate stone, the rest (higher up the hill on which the site is built) being occupied by over 100 mobile homes and 25 tents belonging to a Dutch tour operator. Terraces look out onto the heated leisure pool complex and an adventure-type play area for over-fives, whilst the play area for under-fives is at the side of the bar with picture windows overlooking it. The site is next to a railway station with trains to Paris (45 minutes). Disneyland is 20 km.

Facilities

One toilet block with push button showers, washbasins in cubicles and a dishwashing and laundry area. At busy times these facilities may be under pressure. A second block is to be added. Facilities for disabled visitors. Bar, restaurant and takeaway. Pool complex (all season). Off site: Shops, bars and restaurants within walking distance. Fishing and riding 2 km.

Open: 25 April - 8 November.

Directions

Pommeuse is 55 km. east of Paris. From A4 at exit 16 take N34 towards Coulommiers. In 10 km. turn south for 2 km. on D25 to Pommeuse; site on right after level-crossing. Also signed from south on D402 Guignes - Coulommiers road, taking D25 to Faremoutiers. GPS: N48:48.514 E02:59.530

Charges guide

Per unit incl. 2 persons and electricity	€ 29,00 - € 35,00
extra person	€ 2,00 - € 3,50
child (3-11 yrs)	€ 2,00 - € 3,00

Camping Cheques accepted.

FR77030 Camping International de Jablines

Base de Loisirs, F-77450 Jablines (Seine-et-Marne)

Tel: **01 60 26 09 37**. Email: **welcome@camping-jablines.com** **www.alanrogers.com/FR77030**

Jablines is a modern site which, with the accompanying leisure facilities of the adjacent 'Espace Loisirs', provides an interesting, if a little impersonal alternative to other sites in the region. Man-made lakes provide marvellous water activities. The 'Great Lake' as it is called, is said to have the largest beach on the Ile-de-France! The site itself provides 150 pitches, of which 141 are for touring units. Most are of a good size with gravel hardstanding and grass, accessed by tarmac roads and marked by fencing panels and shrubs. All have 10A electricity, 60 with water and drainage also.

Facilities

Two toilet blocks, heated in cool weather, include pushbutton showers, some washbasins in cubicles. Dishwashing and laundry facilities. Motorcaravan service (charged). Shop. Play area. Bar/restaurant adjacent at leisure centre/lake complex with watersports including 'water cable ski', riding activities, tennis and minigolf. Whilst staying on the campsite, admission to the leisure complex is free. Internet point. Ticket sales for Disneyland and Astérix. Off site: Golf 15 km.

Open: 28 March - 25 October.

Directions

From A4 Paris - Rouen turn north on A104. Take exit 8 on D404 Meaux/Base de Loisirs Jablines. From A1 going south, follow signs for Marne-la-Vallée using A104. Take exit 6A Clay-Souilly on N3 (Meaux). After 6 km. turn south on D404 and follow signs. At park entry keep left for campsite. GPS: N48:54.817 E02:44.051

Charges 2009

Per unit incl. 2 persons and 10A electricity	€ 22,00 - € 25,00
extra person	€ 6,00 - € 7,00

Camping Cheques accepted.

FR77040 Caravaning des 4 Vents

Rue de Beauregard, F-77610 Crèvecoeur-en-Brie (Seine-et-Marne)

Tel: **01 64 07 41 11**. Email: **f.george@free.fr** **www.alanrogers.com/FR77040**

This peaceful, pleasant site has been owned and run by the same family for over 35 years. There are around 200 pitches, with many permanent or seasonal units, however, there are 130 spacious grassy pitches for tourists, well separated by good hedges, all with 6A electricity and a water tap shared between two pitches. The whole site is well landscaped with flowers and trees everywhere. This is a great family site with pool and games facilities at the top end so that campers are not disturbed.

Facilities

Three modern sanitary units (heated in cooler weather) provide British style WCs, washbasins (mainly in cubicles) and push button showers. Facilities for disabled people. Laundry facilities. Motorcaravan service point. In high season a mobile snack bar and pizzeria (16.00-23.00), and a baker (07.30-11.00). Well fenced swimming pool (16 m. diameter; June to Sept). Playground. Games room. Riding (high season). Off site: La Houssaye 1 km.

Open: 1 March - 1 November.

Directions

Crèvecoeur is just off the D231 between A4 exit 13 and Provins. From north, pass obelisk and turn right onto the C3 in 3 km. From south 19 km. after junction with N4, turn left at signs to village. Follow site signs. GPS: N48:45.044 E02:53.775

Charges guide

Per unit incl. 2 persons and electricity	€ 25,00
extra person (over 5 yrs)	€ 5,00

FR78010 Camping Caravaning International

1 rue Johnson, F-78600 Maisons-Laffitte (Yvelines)

Tel: **01 39 12 21 91**. Email: **ci.mlaffitte@wanadoo.fr** **www.alanrogers.com/FR78010**

This site on the banks of the Seine is consistently busy, has multilingual, friendly reception staff and occupies a grassy, tree covered area bordering the river. There are 351 pitches, 57 occupied by mobile homes and 70 used by tour operators, plus two areas dedicated to tents. Most pitches are separated by hedges, are of a good size with some overlooking the Seine (unfenced access), and all 195 touring pitches have electricity hook-ups (6A). The roads leading to the site are a little narrow so large vehicles need to take care. Train noise can be expected.

Facilities

Three sanitary blocks, two insulated for winter use and one more open (only used in July/August). Facilities are clean with constant supervision necessary, due to volume of visitors. Provision for people with disabilities. Laundry and dishwashing areas. Motorcaravan service point. Self-service shop. Restaurant/bar. Takeaway food and pizzeria. TV room, table tennis, football area. Internet point. SNCF rep each morning 15/6-15/8 for travel advice. Off site: Sports complex adjoining. Riding 500 m. Bicycle hire 5 km.

Open: 1 April - 31 October.

Directions

Best approached from A13 or A15 autoroute. From A13 take exit 7 (Poissy). Follow D153 (Poissy), the D308 (Maisons-Laffitte), then site signs before town centre. From A15 exit 7 take D184 (St Germain), after 11 km. turn left on D308 (Maisons-Laffitte). Follow site signs. From A1 take A86, then at exit 2 (Bezons) take D308 (Maisons-Laffitte). Follow signs to site on left. GPS: N48:56.394 E02:08.740

Charges guide

Per unit incl. 2 persons and electricity	€ 24,50 - € 30,00

The Travel Service BOOK THIS SITE CALL 01580 214000 ...we'll arrange everything

FR78040 Huttopia Rambouillet

Route du Château d'Eau, F-78120 Rambouillet (Yvelines)

Tel: **01 30 41 07 34**. Email: **rambouillet@huttopia.com** **www.alanrogers.com/FR78040**

This pleasant site has recently been taken over by the Huttopia group who will be developing it, starting with an outdoor, heated swimming pool. It is in a peaceful forest location beside a lake, with good tarmac access roads, site lighting and 190 touring pitches of varying size and surfaces. Some of the individual pitches are divided by hedges, others are more open and sunny. All have electricity, 83 also have water and drainage, with a few hardstandings. Rambouillet itself is an interesting town.

Facilities

Two heated sanitary buildings include British and Turkish style WCs, washbasins (some in cubicles), dishwashing and laundry sinks, plus basic facilities for baby changing and for disabled persons. Washing machine and dryer. Motorcaravan service point. Café/bar and boutique. Good playground. Swimming pool. Off site: Large supermarket at southern end of the town.

Open: 4 April - 5 November.

Directions

Site is southeast of town: from N10 southbound take Rambouillet/Les Eveuses exit, northbound take Rambouillet centre exit, loop round and rejoin N10 southbound, taking next exit. Follow site signs. GPS: N48:37.623 E01:50.727

Charges 2009

Per unit incl. 2 persons	€ 22,00 - € 36,40

Camping Cheques accepted.

The Travel Service BOOK THIS SITE CALL 01580 214000 ...we'll arrange everything

2015

FR78060 Huttopia Versailles

31 rue Berthelot, F-78000 Versailles (Yvelines)

Tel: **01 39 51 23 61**. Email: **versailles@huttopia.com** **www.alanrogers.com/FR78060**

This Huttopia site is rather different. When the French owners visited Canada and experienced 'back to nature' camping, they were so impressed that they decided to introduce the idea to France. Gone are the formal pitches with neatly trimmed hedges and instead there are 145 places of ample size arranged informally amongst the trees. The terrain is as nature intended with very little grass and much of it steep and rugged (there are plans to introduce some terracing). Long electricity leads are required and be prepared to use blocks and corner steadies on many pitches.

Facilities

Three well designed toilet blocks (wood cabin style) provide basic facilities. Special bivouacs set up for cooking and washing up. Restaurant with takeaway food (30/4-27/9 and weekends). Bar. Games room. Simple swimming and paddling pools (May - Sept). Playground. Bicycle hire. Children's club. Off site: Versailles and its château. Fishing 1 km. Golf 3 km. Riding 5 km.

Open: 19 December - 5 November.

Directions

From the front of the château of Versailles take the Avenue de Paris and the site is signed after 2 km. GPS: N48:47.380 E02:09.380

Charges 2009

Per unit with 2 persons and electricity	€ 27,30 - € 41,80
extra person	€ 6,20 - € 8,50
child (2-7 yrs)	€ 3,00 - € 4,30
dog	€ 4,00

FR52030 Kawan Village Lac de la Liez

Peigney, F-52200 Langres (Haute-Marne)

Tel: **03 25 90 27 79**. Email: **campingliez@free.fr** **www.alanrogers.com/FR52030**

Managed by the enthusiastic Baude family, this newly renovated lakeside site is near the city of Langres. Only 10 minutes from the A5, Camping Lac de la Liez provides an ideal spot for an overnight stop en route to the south of France. There is also a lot on offer for a longer stay. The site provides 131 fully serviced pitches, some with panoramic views of the 250 hectare lake with its sandy beach and small harbour where boats and pedaloes may be hired. Ideal for swimming and watersports; access to the lake is down steps and across quite a fast road (in total 150 m). Amenities on the site include indoor and outdoor swimming pools, a restaurant and bar and a shop. As well as all the activities on the lake, sporting activities on site include a tennis court, archery and bicycle hire. The city of Langres with its old ramparts and ancient city centre is within easy reach – it was elected one of the 50 most historic cities in France – and it is well worth a visit.

Facilities

Two toilet blocks have all facilities in cabins (only one is open in low season). Facilities for disabled people and babies. Laundry facilities. Motorcaravan services. Shop, bar and restaurant (with takeaway food). Indoor pool complex with spa and sauna. Heated outdoor pool (15/6-15/9). Games room. Playground. Extensive games area. Tennis (free in low season). Off site: Lake with beach. Boat and bicycle hire and cycle tracks around lake. Fishing 100 m. Riding 5 km. Golf 40 km.

Open: 1 April - 1 November.

Directions

From Langres take the N19 towards Vesoul. After 3 km. turn right, straight after the large river bridge, then follow site signs. GPS: N47:52.440 E05:22.628

Charges guide

Per person	€ 5,00 - € 7,00
child (2-12 yrs)	€ 3,00 - € 4,50
pitch	€ 6,00 - € 8,00
electricity	€ 3,50 - € 5,00
dog	€ 3,00

Camping Cheques accepted.

BOOK THIS SITE
CALL 01580 214000
...we'll arrange everything
The Travel Service

FR88130 Kawan Village Vanne de Pierre

5 rue du camping, F-88100 Saint Dié-des-Vosges (Vosges)

Tel: **03 29 56 23 56**. Email: **vannedepierre@wanadoo.fr** **www.alanrogers.com/FR88130**

La Vanne de Pierre is a neat and attractive site with 118 pitches, many of which are individual with good well trimmed hedges giving plenty of privacy. There are 13 chalets and mobile homes (for rent) and a few seasonal units, leaving around 101 tourist pitches, all multi-serviced with water, drainage and electricity hook-up (6/10A). The reception building has been recently refitted and provides a well stocked small shop plus a restaurant/bar with a takeaway facility (all year but opening hours may vary). A 'Sites et Paysages' member.

Facilities

Main unit is heated with good facilities including washbasins in cubicles. Three family rooms each with WC, basin, and shower and two similar units fully equipped for disabled campers. Dishwashing and laundry rooms. A second, older unit (opened July/Aug). Shop. Bar/restaurant and takeaway. Swimming pool (1/4-30/9, weather permitting). Internet access. Gas supplies. Bicycle hire. Nordic walking is organised. Off site: Golf, tennis, archery and riding all 1 km. Fishing. Supermarkets.

Open: All year.

Directions

St Dié is southeast of Nancy. Site is east of town on north bank of river Meurthe and south of D82 to Nayemont les Fosses. Site is well signed. GPS: N48:17.160 E06:58.199

Charges guide

Per unit incl. 2 persons	€ 15,00 - € 22,00
extra person	€ 4,00 - € 6,00
child (4-10 yrs)	free - € 4,00
electricity	€ 4,00 - € 5,00

Camping Cheques accepted.

FR88040 Kawan Village Lac de Bouzey

19 rue du Lac, F-88390 Sanchey (Vosges)

Tel: **03 29 82 49 41**. Email: **camping.lac.de.bouzey@wanadoo.fr** **www.alanrogers.com/FR88040**

Camping Lac de Bouzey is eight kilometres west of Epinal, overlooking the lake, at the beginning of the Vosges Massif. The 125 individual 100 sq.m. back-to-back grass pitches are arranged on either side of tarmac roads with electricity (6-10A); 100 are fully serviced. They are on a gentle slope, divided by trees and hedging and some overlook the 130 ha. lake with its sandy beaches. Units can be close when the site is busy. In high season there is lots going on for all ages, especially teenagers. Open all year, the site is much quieter in low season. English is spoken.

Facilities

Sanitary block includes a baby room and one for disabled people (there is up and down hill walking). In winter a small, heated section in main building with toilet, washbasin and shower is used. Laundry facilities. Motorcaravan service point. Shop. Bar and restaurant. Heated pool (1/5-30/9). Fishing, riding, games room, archery and bicycle hire. Internet. Soundproof room for cinema and discos (high season). Off site: Golf 8 km.

Open: All year.

Directions

Site is 8 km. west of Epinal on D460 and is signed from some parts of Epinal. Follow signs for Lac de Bouzey and Sanchey. GPS: N48:10.015 E06:21.594

Charges guide

Per unit incl. 2 persons	€ 15,00 - € 25,00
extra person	€ 5,00 - € 9,00
electricity (6-10A)	€ 5,00 - € 6,00

Camping Cheques accepted.

FR17030 Camping le Bois Roland

82 route Royan - Saujon, F-17600 Médis (Charente-Maritime)

Tel: **05 46 05 47 58**. Email: **bois.roland@wanadoo.fr** **www.alanrogers.com/FR17030**

This campsite is in an urban area on a busy N-road but, nevertheless, has some unique features. Over the past 30 years, M. Dupont, the owner, has planted a very large number of tree varieties to mark and separate the pitches and they provide some shade. The site has 88 pitches for touring units, mainly between 80-90 sq.m. All have electricity (some may need long leads) and access to water close at hand. The family run a bar and provide simple takeaway food in July and August and there is a welcoming swimming pool.

Facilities

Two modernised toilet blocks contain a mixture of Turkish and British style toilets (no seats and no paper). Modern showers. Baby changing room. Special facilities for disabled campers. Laundry facilities. Play area for young children. Off site: Buses pass the gate. Supermarket with ATM 2 km. Beach 5 km. Riding 1 km. Fishing 4 km. Bicycle hire 5 km. Golf 10 km.

Open: 23 April - 30 September.

Directions

Site is clearly signed on the west side of the N150, 600 m. north of the village of Medis (the N150 runs between Saujon and Royan). GPS: N45:38.970 W00:57.470

Charges guide

Per unit incl. 2 persons	€ 14,00 - € 17,50
extra person	€ 4,80
child (0-5 yrs)	€ 2,00 - € 3,50
electricity (5/10A)	€ 4,20 - € 4,90

FR17040 Siblu Camping Bonne Anse Plage

La Palmyre, F-17570 Les Mathes-La Palmyre (Charente-Maritime)

Tel: **05 46 22 40 90**. Email: **bonneanseplage@siblu.fr** **www.alanrogers.com/FR17040**

On the edge of the Forêt de la Coubre, just beyond La Palmyre, Bonne Anse Plage is attractively set amongst pines, just a short stroll from a tidal inlet, and just 600 m. from the mouth of the Gironde estuary. This is a spacious, gently undulating site, and is now owned by the Siblu group. There are 850 level, marked pitches, of which around half are for touring units (all with electricity). Most are well shaded, the ones nearer the sea less so and are rather sandier. The reception, restaurant and bar with a spacious outdoor terrace and an impressive pool complex form the social focus.

Facilities

Seven well maintained toilet blocks include facilities for disabled visitors and babies. Motorcaravan service point. Shopping centre. Restaurant and bar. Takeaway food. Large pool complex with water slides (including a junior chute). Playground. Video games room. TV. Minigolf. Football. Trampolines. Bicycle hire. Climbing wall. Entertainment and activities in high season. Internet access. Gas barbecues only. Off site: Supervised, safe beaches 500 m. Fishing, riding 1 km. Zoo 1 km. Golf 5 km. Watersports and tennis. Fitness track.

Open: 1 May - 19 September.

Directions

Leave A10 autoroute at Saintes. Head for Royan (N150). In Royan take signs for La Palmyre (D25). At La Palmyre roundabout follow signs for Ronce-les-Bains. Site is 1 km. on left.
GPS: N45:41.886 W01:11.986

Charges guide

Per unit incl. 3 persons and electricity	€ 37,60 - € 44,80
extra person (over 1 yr)	€ 7,60 - € 9,20

FR17060 Airotel Oléron

Domaine de Montravail, F-17480 Le Château-d'Oléron (Charente-Maritime)

Tel: **05 46 47 61 82**. Email: **info@camping-airotel-oleron.com** **www.alanrogers.com/FR17060**

This family run site on the outskirts of Le Château-d'Oléron has very good facilities, including a superb equestrian centre, a full range of sporting activites and an attractive heated pool complex. This is a mature site with about 270 pitches of a good size, with varying degrees of shade provided by trees and shrubs. It is well laid out with 133 touring pitches and the remainder for mobile homes of which 30 are for rent. Most touring pitches have electricity (10A) and four have their own water and drainage. A full entertainment programme is provided in high season.

Facilities

Two modern toilet blocks with facilities for disabled visitors and babies. Washing machine and dryer. Motorcaravan service point. Shop. Bar, restaurant and takeaway (15/6-15/9). Heated swimming and paddling pools. Equestrian centre. Playground. Multisport court. Tennis. Minigolf. Fishing. Canoe hire. Bicycle hire. TV and games room. Internet access. WiFi. Off site: Supermarket. Local markets. Zoo. Aquarium.

Open: Easter - 30 September.

Directions

Cross the bridge onto the island and continue on D26. At second roundabout turn right, marked Dolus and Le Château. Proceed 500 m. and take first right, marked Campings. Site is 1 km. on the right.
GPS: N45:52.933 W01:12.392

Charges guide

Per unit incl. 2 persons	€ 13,50 - € 22,00
extra person	€ 4,00 - € 6,50
electricity (8A)	€ 3,90

BOOK THIS SITE
CALL 01580 214000
...we'll arrange everything
The Travel Service

FR17280 Camping la Grainetière

Route de Saint-Martin, F-17630 La Flotte-en-Ré (Charente-Maritime)

Tel: **05 46 09 68 86**. Email: **la-grainetiere@free.fr** **www.alanrogers.com/FR17280**

A truly friendly welcome awaits you from the owners, Isabelle and Eric, at La Grainetière. It is a peaceful campsite set in almost three hectares of pine trees which provide some shade for the 65 touring pitches of various shapes and sizes. There are also 50 well spaced chalets for rent. Some pitches are suitable for units up to seven metres (book in advance). There are no hedges for privacy and the pitches are sandy with some grass. Ample new water points and electricity (10A) hook-ups (Euro plugs) serve the camping area. The site is well lit.

Facilities

The unisex sanitary block is first class, with washbasins in cubicles, showers, British style WCs, facilities for children and people with disabilities. Shop (1/4-30/9). Takeaway (July/Aug). Swimming pool (heated 1/4-30/9). Bicycle hire. Fridge hire. TV room. Charcoal barbecues are not permitted. Off site: Beach and sailing 2 km. Bar and restaurant 2 km. Fishing 2 km. Riding 3 km. Golf 10 km.

Open: 1 April - 30 September.

Directions

Follow camping signs from La Flotte, 1 km. from the village. GPS: N46:11.253 W01:20.696

Charges guide

Per unit incl. 2 persons	€ 14,00 - € 24,00
extra person	€ 3,00 - € 7,00
child (0-7 yrs)	€ 2,00 - € 3,00
electricity (10A)	€ 4,00

FR17010 Camping Bois Soleil

2 avenue de Suzac, F-17110 Saint Georges-de-Didonne (Charente-Maritime)

Tel: **05 46 05 05 94**. Email: **camping.bois.soleil@wanadoo.fr** **www.alanrogers.com/FR17010**

Close to the sea, Bois Soleil is a fairly large site in three parts, with 165 serviced pitches for touring units and a few for tents. All the touring pitches are hedged, and have electricity, with water and drainage between two. The main part, Les Pins, is attractive with trees and shrubs providing shade. Opposite is La Mer with direct access to the beach, some areas with less shade and an area for tents. The third part, La Forêt, is for static holiday homes. It is best to book your preferred area as it can be full mid June - late August. There are a few pitches with lockable gates. The areas are well tended with the named pitches (not numbered) cleared and raked between visitors and with an inclusive charge for electricity and water. This lively site offers something for everyone, whether they like a beach-side spot or a traditional pitch, plenty of activities or the quiet life. The sandy beach here is a wide public one, sheltered from the Atlantic breakers although the sea goes out some way at low tide.

Facilities

Each area has one large sanitary block, and smaller blocks with toilets only. Heated block near reception. Cleaned twice daily, they include washbasins in cubicles, facilities for disabled people and babies. Launderette. Nursery. Supermarket, bakery (July/Aug). Beach shop. Restaurant and bar. Takeaway. Swimming pool (heated 15/6-15/9). Steam room. Tennis. Bicycle hire. Play area. TV room and library. Internet terminal. Charcoal barbecues not permitted. Dogs are not accepted 24/6-2/9.
Off site: Fishing, riding 500 m. Golf 20 km.

Open: 4 April - 2 November.

Directions

From Royan centre take coast road (D25) along the seafront of St Georges-de-Didonne towards Meschers. Site is signed at roundabout at end of the main beach. GPS: N45:35.130 W00:59.128

Charges 2009

Per unit incl. 2 persons, 6A electricity	€ 24,00 - € 39,00
tent incl. 2 persons	€ 18,00 - € 35,00
extra person	€ 3,00 - € 8,00
child (3-7 yrs)	free - € 6,00
dog (not 23/6-25/8)	€ 3,50

Less 20% outside July/Aug.
Camping Cheques accepted.

FR85020 Camping du Jard

123 Mal de Lattre de Tassigny, F-85360 La Tranche-sur-Mer (Vendée)

Tel: **02 51 27 43 79**. Email: **info@campingdujard.fr** **www.alanrogers.com/FR85020**

Camping du Jard is a well maintained site between La Rochelle and Les Sables d'Olonne. First impressions are good, with a friendly welcome from M. Marton or his staff. The 242 touring pitches are level and grassy, hedged on two sides by bushes. The smallest are 100 sq.m. (the majority larger) and most are equipped with electricity, half with water and drainage. It is a comparatively new site, but the large variety of trees are beginning to provide a little shade. An impressive pool complex has a toboggan, paddling pool and an indoor pool with jacuzzi. The site is 700 m. from a sandy beach with many shops and restaurants nearby.

Facilities

Three toilet blocks with facilities for babies and disabled people and most washbasins are in cabins. Laundry facilities. Shop (1/6-10/9), restaurant and bar (25/5-10/9). Heated pool with toboggan and paddling pool, plus heated indoor pool with jacuzzi (no Bermuda-style shorts in pools). Sauna, solarium and fitness room. Tennis. Minigolf. Bicycle hire. Play area, games and TV rooms. Internet access. American motorhomes are not accepted. Pets are not accepted.

Open: 26 April - 15 September.

Directions

Site is east of La Tranche-sur-Mer on D46. From D747 (La Roche-sur-Yon - La Tranche) follow signs (La Faute-sur-Mer) along bypass. Take exit for La Grière and then turn east to site.
GPS: N46:20.901 W01:23.242

Charges guide

Per unit incl. 2 persons and electricity	€ 22,40 - € 31,00
extra person	€ 4,50 - € 5,50
child (under 5 yrs)	€ 3,00 - € 4,00

Bois Soleil

Camping ★★★★
Charente-Maritime

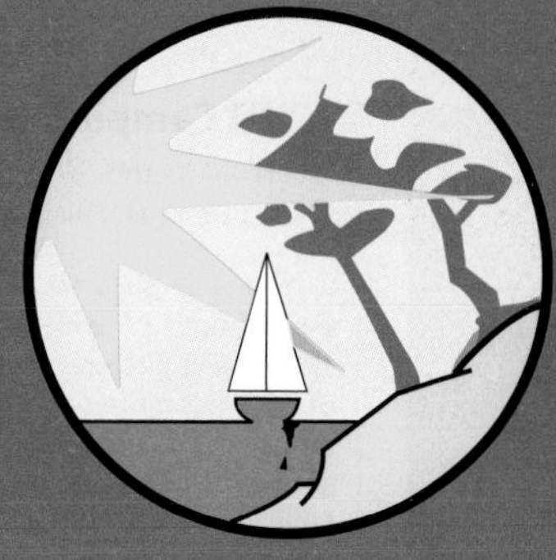

Surrounded by pine trees and a sandy beach on the Atlantic Coast, with one direct access to the beach, Bois Soleil proposes to you many attractions like tennis, tabletennis, children playgrounds and entertainment. Shops, take-away and snack-bar with big TV screen.

Camping Cheque

Spring and Summer

2, avenue de Suzac - 17110 ST GEORGES DE DIDONNE
Tel: 0033 546 05 05 94 - Fax: 0033 546 06 27 43
www.bois-soleil.com / e-mail: camping.bois.soleil@wanadoo.fr

FR85150 Camping la Yole

Chemin des Bosses, Orouet, F-85160 Saint Jean-de-Monts (Vendée)

Tel: **02 51 58 67 17**. Email: **contact@la-yole.com** **www.alanrogers.com/FR85150**

La Yole is an attractive and well run site, two kilometres from a sandy beach. It offers 356 pitches, the majority of which are occupied by tour operators and mobile homes to rent. There are 150 touring pitches, most with shade and separated by bushes and trees. A newer area at the rear of the site is more open. All the pitches are of at least 100 sq.m. and have electricity (10A), water and drainage. The pool complex includes an outdoor pool, a paddling pool, slide and an indoor heated pool with jacuzzi. Entertainment is organised in high season. This is a clean and tidy site, ideal for families with children and you will receive a helpful and friendly welcome.

Facilities

Two toilet blocks include washbasins in cabins and facilities for disabled people and babies. A third block has a baby room. Laundry facilities. Shop. Bar, restaurant and takeaway (1/5-5/9). Outdoor pool and paddling pool. Indoor heated pool with jacuzzi. Play area. Club room. Tennis. Games room. Entertainment in high season. WiFi. Gas barbecues only. Off site: Beach, bus service, bicycle hire 2 km. Riding 3 km. Fishing, golf and watersports 6 km.

Open: 5 April - 26 September.

Directions

Site is signed off the D38, 6 km. south of St Jean-de-Monts in the village of Orouet. Coming from St Jean-de-Monts turn right at l'Oasis restaurant towards Mouette and follow signs to site.
GPS: N46:45.383 W02:00.466

Charges guide

Per unit incl. 2 persons and electricity	€ 16,00 - € 30,00
extra person	€ 3,70 - € 6,50
child (2-9 yrs)	€ 2,15 - € 5,00
baby (0-2 yrs)	free - € 3,50
dog	€ 4,00 - € 5,00

Camping Cheques accepted.

FR85210 Camping les Ecureuils

Route des Goffineaux, F-85520 Jard-sur-Mer (Vendée)

Tel: **02 51 33 42 74**. Email: **camping-ecureuils@wanadoo.fr** **www.alanrogers.com/FR85210**

Les Ecureuils is a wooded site in a quieter part of the southern Vendée. It is undoubtedly one of the prettiest sites on this stretch of coast, with an elegant reception area, attractive vegetation and large pitches separated by low hedges with plenty of shade. Of the 261 pitches, some 128 are for touring units, each with water and drainage, as well as easy access to 10A electricity. This site is popular with tour operators (54 pitches). Jard is rated among the most pleasant and least hectic of Vendée towns. The harbour is home to some fishing boats and rather more pleasure craft. There is a public slipway for those bringing their own boats.

Facilities

Two toilet blocks, well equipped and kept very clean, include baby baths, and laundry rooms. Small shop (bread baked on site). Snack bar and takeaway (1/6-15/9). Bar with snacks and ice creams. Good sized L-shaped swimming pool and separate paddling pool (30/5-15/9). Indoor pool and fitness centre (all season). Two play areas for different age groups. Minigolf. Club for children (5-10 yrs, July/Aug). Bicycle hire. Internet access. Only gas barbecues are allowed. Dogs are not accepted. Off site: Beach, fishing 400 m. Marina and town.

Open: 15 April - late September.

Directions

From Les Sables d'Olonne take the N949 towards Talmont-St Hilaire. Keep right in the centre (D21 towards Jard). From la Roche-sur-Yon follow the D474 and the D49 towards Jard-sur-Mer. From the village follow the signs 'Autre campings' or Camping les Ecureuils. Site is on the left. GPS: N46:24.683 W01:35.382

Charges guide

Per person	€ 5,00 - € 6,90
child (0-9 yrs)	€ 1,50 - € 4,50
pitch incl. electricity, water and drainage	€ 5,00 - € 6,70

FR85280 Camping les Places Dorées

Route de Notre-Dame-de-Monts, F-85160 Saint Jean-de-Monts (Vendée)

Tel: **02 51 59 02 93**. Email: **contact@placesdorees.com** **www.alanrogers.com/FR85280**

Les Places Dorées is owned by the same family as Abri des Pins (FR85090) just across the road. It is a newer site with maturing trees beginning to offer some shade. There are 245 grassy pitches, the quietest being towards the back of the site. Each one is separated, all have 10A electricity and some are also equipped with water and drainage. In low season the site is quiet but it can be noisy in high season with the bar and disco closing late. Recently added are a relaxation area with a heated covered pool, spa facilities (balnéo, hammam and massage), a fitness room and a games room.

Facilities

Three modern toilet blocks include washbasins in cubicles. Facilities for disabled visitors. Laundry facilities. Bread to order. Bar, snack bar and takeaway. Outdoor pool complex with slides, jacuzzi and waterfall (no Bermuda-style shorts). Covered, heated pool, spa facilities, gym. Games room. High season entertainment and children's club at L'Abri des Pins, also activities for adults. Facilities at L'Abri des Pins may be used. Off site: Fishing 500 m. Beach 700 m. Riding 2 km. Golf 5 km.

Open: 1 June - 1 September.

Directions

Site is 4 km. north of St Jean-de-Monts on the D38 St Jean-de-Monts - Notre Dames-de-Monts road on the right hand side, almost opposite L'Abri des Pins. GPS: N46:48.690 W02:06.685

Charges guide

Per pitch incl. 3 persons and electricity	€ 23,00 - € 34,40
extra person	€ 3,70 - € 6,20

No credit cards.

FR85300 Camping la Grand' Métairie

8 rue de la Vineuse en Plaine, F-85440 Saint Hilaire-la-Forêt (Vendée)

Tel: **02 51 33 32 38**. Email: **info@camping-grandmetairie.com** **www.alanrogers.com/FR85300**

Just five kilometres from the super sandy beach at Jard-sur-Mer, La Grand' Métairie offers many of the amenities of its seaside counterparts, but with the important advantage of being on the edge of a delightful, sleepy village otherwise untouched by tourism. It is a busy well run site with a programme of lively entertainment in high season. The site has 180 pitches (50 touring pitches), all with electricity. Some also with water and drainage. The pitches have good shade, are all separated by mature trees and hedges and are reasonable in size.

Facilities

Two modern toilet blocks are very clean and include washbasins mainly in cabins. Units for disabled people. Washing machines and dryers. Fridge hire. Safety deposit boxes. Smart bar/restaurant and takeaway (all 1/5-15/9). Attractive, heated outdoor pool and paddling pool (from 1/5). Indoor pool (all season). Sauna, jacuzzi. Gym. Tennis, minigolf (both free in low season). Visiting hairdressing salon. Internet access. Children's club. Off site: Village shop 100 m. Riding and fishing 5 km. Golf 15 km.

Open: 5 April - 30 September.

Directions

From Les Sables d'Olonne take D949 (La Rochelle) towards Talmont-St Hilaire and Luçon; 7 km. after Talmont turn right on D70 to St Hilaire-la-Forêt. Site is on left before village centre. GPS: N46:26.907 W01:31.580

Charges guide

Per unit incl. 2 persons and electricity	€ 17,00 - € 27,00
extra person	€ 5,00 - € 8,00

Min. stay 7 nights 13/7-17/8.

FR85440 Camping les Brunelles

Le Bouil, F-85560 Longeville-sur-Mer (Vendée)

Tel: **02 51 33 50 75**. Email: **camping@les-brunelles.com** **www.alanrogers.com/FR85440**

This is a well managed site with good facilities and a varied programme of high season entertainment for all the family. In 2007 Les Brunelles was combined with an adjacent campsite to provide 600 pitches. Many of the new pitches have water, electricity and waste, and are in excess of 100 sq.m. to allow easier access for larger units. On the original Les Brunelles site, the touring pitches are all level on sandy grass and separated by hedges, away from most of the mobile homes.

Facilities

Four old, but well maintained and modernised toilet blocks have British and Turkish style toilets and washbasins, both open style and in cabins. Laundry facilities. Shop. Takeaway and large modern, airy bar. Covered pool with jacuzzi (all season). Outdoor pool with slides and paddling pools (1/5-30/9). Tennis. Bicycle hire. Off site: Golf and riding within 15 km. Good supervised sandy beach 900 m. St Vincent-sur-Jard 2 km.

Open: 4 April - 19 September.

Directions

From D21 (Talmont - Longueville), between St Vincent and Longueville, site signed south from main road towards coast. Turn left in Le Bouil (site signed). Site is 800 m. on left. GPS: N46:24.798 W01:31.388

Charges 2009

Per unit incl. 2 persons and electricity	€ 21,00 - € 30,00
extra person	€ 5,00 - € 8,00

Camping Cheques accepted.

FR85480 Camping Caravaning le Chaponnet

Rue du Chaponnet (N16), F-85470 Brem-sur-Mer (Vendée)

Tel: **02 51 90 55 56**. Email: **campingchaponnet@wanadoo.fr** **www.alanrogers.com/FR85480**

This well established family run site is within five minutes' walk of Brem village and 1.5 km. from a sandy beach. The 80 touring pitches are level with varying amounts of grass, some with shade from mature trees. Pitches are separated by tall hedges and serviced by tarmac or gravel roads and have frequent water and electricity points (long leads may be required). Tour operators have mobile homes and tents on 70 pitches and there are 55 privately owned mobile homes and chalets. The pool complex also has a jacuzzi, slides and a paddling pool, together with a sauna and fitness centre. It is overlooked by the spacious bar and snack bar. Entertainment is provided for all ages by day and three or four musical evenings a week provide family fun rather than teenage activities.

Facilities

The five sanitary blocks are well maintained with washbasins in cubicles, some showers and basins have controllable water temperature. Facilities for babies and disabled people. Laundry facilities. Bar, snack bar and takeaway (all 1/6-31/8). No shop but bread and croissants available. Indoor (heated) and outdoor pools. Play area with space for ball games. Tennis. Bicycle hire. Indoor games room. Off site: Shops and restaurants. Beach 1.5 km. Fishing 2 km. Golf 12 km. Riding 10 km.

Open: 1 May - 15 September.

Directions

Brem is on the D38 St Gilles - Les Sables d'Olonne road. Site is clearly signed, just off the one-way system in centre of village.
GPS: N46:36.260 W01:49.946

Charges guide

Per unit incl. 3 persons	€ 19,50 - € 30,00
incl. electricity	€ 23,80 - € 33,90
extra person	€ 4,10 - € 5,50
child (under 5 yrs)	€ 2,60 - € 3,70
dog	€ 3,00

FR85720 Camping Indigo Noirmoutier

23 allée des Sableaux, Bois de la Chaize, F-85330 Noirmoutier-en-l'Ile (Vendée)

Tel: **02 51 39 06 24**. Email: **noirmoutier@camping-indigo.com** **www.alanrogers.com/FR85720**

Located in woodland and on dunes along a two kilometre stretch of sandy beach just east of the attractive little town of Noirmoutier on the island of the same name, this could be paradise for those who enjoy a simple campsite in a natural setting. On land belonging to the ONF (France's forestry commission), this site is operated by Huttopia whose aim is to adapt to the environment rather than take it over. The 500 touring pitches, all with electricity, are situated among the pine trees and accessed along tracks. Those on the sand dunes have fantastic views across the Bay of Bourgneuf.

Facilities

Five sanitary blocks currently provide basic facilities including preset showers and some washbasins in cubicles. The central one is larger and more modern, the others have been refurbished. All have facilities for disabled visitors. Washing machines and dryers. Motorcaravan services point. Playground. Bicycle hire. WiFi (reception, bar, pool). Off site: Riding 4 km. Golf 25 km.

Open: 4 April - 4 October.

Directions

The Ile de Noirmoutier is 70 km. southwest of Nantes. Take D38 road from the mainland, cross bridge to island and continue to Noirmoutier en l'Ile. Go through town past three sets of traffic lights and at roundabout turn right following signs to 'Campings'. GPS: N46:59.815 W02:13.200

Charges 2009

Per unit incl. 2 persons and electricity	€ 16,90 - € 28,50
extra person	€ 3,20 - € 4,60

Camping Cheques accepted.

FR85930 Castel Camping Domaine des Forges

Rue des Forges, F-85440 Avrillé (Vendée)

Tel: **02 51 22 38 85**. Email: **contact@campingdomainedesforges.com** **www.alanrogers.com/FR85930**

Le Domaine des Forges has recently been acquired by Cathy and Thierry Pacteau. They already have experience in owning a caravan site, and it is their intention to create a prestige site with the highest quality of services. Arranged in the beautiful grounds of a 16th-century manor house, the pitches are generous in size (170-300 sq.m) and fully serviced including 32A electricity, internet access and cable TV. At present 140 pitches are ready with a further 155 to be developed over the next few years. The owners' aim is to eventually develop a residential site and there are already mobile homes and chalets on site for viewing. A stylish restaurant has been opened and future plans include an indoor pool, gym, bar and games room. An area of hardstanding pitches for motorcaravans is also planned.

Facilities

Two toilet blocks with facilities for disabled visitors and babies. Laundry facilities. Shop (from 2009). Restaurant. Takeaway (1/7-31/8). Outdoor pool (heated 1/7-31/8). Tennis. Minigolf. Fishing lake. Off site: Village 400 m. Les Sables d'Olonne 25 km. Vendée beaches 8 km.

Open: All year.

Directions

Travel south from La Roche-sur-Yon on the D747 for about 21 km. At the D19, turn right for Avrille (about 6 km). At junction with the D949 turn right and first right again into rue des Forges. Site at the end of the road. GPS: N46:28.565 W01:29.672

Charges 2009

Per unit incl. 2 persons and electricity	€ 16,00 - € 26,00
extra person	€ 2,00 - € 6,00

FR37060 Kawan Village l'Arada Parc

Rue de la Baratière, F-37360 Sonzay (Indre-et-Loire)

Tel: **02 47 24 72 69**. Email: **info@laradaparc.com** **www.alanrogers.com/FR37060**

A good, well maintained site in a quiet location, Camping l'Arada Parc is a popular base from which to visit the numerous châteaux in this beautiful part of France. The 77 grass touring pitches all have electricity and 35 have water and drainage. The clearly marked pitches, some slightly sloping, are separated by trees and shrubs some of which are now providing a degree of shade. An attractive, heated pool is on a pleasant terrace beside the restaurant. Entertainment, themed evenings and activities for children are organised in July/August. This is a new site with modern facilities which is developing well.

Facilities

Two modern toilet blocks provide unisex toilets, showers and washbasins in cubicles. Baby room. Facilities for disabled visitors (wheelchair users may find the gravel access difficult). Laundry facilities. Shop, bar, restaurant and takeaway (all season). Outdoor swimming pool (no Bermuda-style shorts; 1/5-13/9). Heated, covered pool (all season). Play area. Games area. Boules. TV room. Bicycle hire. Internet access. Off site: Tennis 200 m. Fishing 500 m. Golf 12 km. Riding 14 km.

Open: 28 March - 30 October.

Directions

Sonzay is northwest of Tours. From the new A28 north of Tours take the exit to Neuillé-Pont-Pierre which is on the N138 Le Mans - Tours road. Then take D766 towards Château la Vallière and turn southwest to Sonzay. Follow campsite signs. GPS: N47:31.687 E00:27.180

Charges guide

Per unit incl. 2 persons	€ 13,50 - € 17,50
extra person	€ 3,50 - € 4,50
child (2-10 yrs)	€ 2,75 - € 3,50
electricity (10A)	€ 3,50
animal	€ 1,50

Camping Cheques accepted.

FR37030 Camping le Moulin Fort

F-37150 Francueil-Chenonceau (Indre-et-Loire)

Tel: **02 47 23 86 22**. Email: **lemoulinfort@wanadoo.fr** **www.alanrogers.com/FR37030**

Camping Le Moulin Fort is a tranquil, riverside site that has been redeveloped by British owners, John and Sarah Scarratt. The 137 pitches are enhanced by trees and shrubs offering plenty of shade and 110 pitches have electricity (6A). From the snack bar terrace adjacent to the restored mill building a timber walkway over the mill race leads to the unheated swimming pool and paddling pools. The site is ideal for couples and families with young children, although the river is unfenced.

Facilities

Two toilet blocks with all the usual amenities of a good standard, include washbasins in cubicles, baby baths and facilities for disabled visitors. Motorcaravan service point. Shop, bar (limited hours), restaurant and takeaway (all 21/5-19/9). Swimming pool (21/5-19/9). Excellent play area. Minigolf. Games room and TV. Library. Fishing. Bicycle and canoe hire. In high season entertainment for families includes games tournaments and music events. WiFi in bar area. Off site: Riding 12 km. Golf 20 km.

Open: 1 April - 30 September.

Directions

From A85 at exit 11 take D31 towards Bléré and turn east on D976 (Vierzon) for 7 km. then turn north on D80 (Chenonceau) to site. From north bank of Cher (D140/D40) turn south on D80 to cross river between Chenonceau and Chisseaux. Site on left just after bridge. GPS: N47:19.637 E01:05.338

Charges guide

Per unit incl. 2 persons	€ 9,00 - € 22,00
extra person	€ 3,00 - € 5,00
electricity (6A)	€ 4,00

FR37140 Huttopia Rillé

Lac de Rillé, F-37340 Rillé (Indre-et-Loire)

Tel: **02 47 24 62 97**. Email: **rille@huttopia.com** **www.alanrogers.com/FR37140**

This site in a forest by a lake has plenty of potential. It has recently been acquired by the Huttopia group which aims to provide a traffic-free environment. Cars are to be left in a carpark outside the barrier (allowed on site to unload and load). New arrivals must park outside and gain an entry code from reception. There are 146 pitches of which 32 are occupied by rental accommodation and 24 are for motorcaravans in a separate area. The touring pitches are numbered in groups amongst the trees but are not marked; they vary in size and cost.

Facilities

The central toilet block has family rooms (with showers and basins), washbasins in cubicles and facilities for disabled visitors (shower/basin plus separate toilet) but there are no ramps and access for wheelchairs is very difficult. Motorcaravan service point. Heated swimming pool with paddling area (May - Sept). Play area. Fishing. Off site: Riding 6 km. Golf 15 km.

Open: 24 April - 5 November.

Directions

From D766 Angers - Blois road at Château la Vallière take D749 southwest. From N152 Tours - Angers road go northwest at Langeais on D57. In Rillé turn west on D49. Site on right in a short distance. GPS: N47:27.485 E00:13.146

Charges 2009

Per unit incl. 2 persons	€ 19,20 - € 37,00
extra person	€ 5,20 - € 6,80

Camping Cheques accepted.

tel: +33 (0) 4 37 64 22 33 www.huttopia.com

FR45010 Kawan Village les Bois du Bardelet

Route de Bourges, Le Petit Bardelet, F-45500 Gien (Loiret)

Tel: **02 38 67 47 39**. Email: **contact@bardelet.com** **www.alanrogers.com/FR45010**

This attractive, lively family site, in a rural setting, is well situated for exploring the less well known eastern part of the Loire Valley. Two lakes (one for boating, one for fishing) and a pool complex have been attractively landscaped in 12 hectares of former farmland, blending old and new with natural wooded areas and more open field areas with rural views. Bois du Bardelet provides 260 pitches with around 130 for touring units. All are larger than 100 sq.m. and have electrical connections, with some new, luxury pitches of 200 sq.m. with water and waste water.

Facilities

Two sanitary blocks include washbasins in cabins. Facilities for disabled visitors and babies. Washing machines. Shop (1/4-30/9). Bar. Snack bar, takeaway, restaurant (all 1/4-14/9) and pizzeria (8/7-21/8). Outside pool (1/5-31/8). Indoor pool, heated (with purchased card). Aquagym, fitness and jacuzzi room. Games area. Canoeing and fishing. Tennis. Minigolf. Boules. Bicycle hire. Playground. Internet access. Off site: Supermarket 5 km. Riding 7 km.

Open: 1 April - 30 September.

Directions

From Gien take D940 (Bourges). After 5 km. turn right and right again to cross road and follow site signs. From Argent sur Sauldre take D940 (Gien). Site signed to right after 15 km. Entrance is 200 m. GPS: N47:38.491 E02:36.917

Charges 2009

Per unit incl. 2 persons	€ 19,20 - € 32,00
extra person (over 2 yrs)	€ 4,90 - € 6,50

Camping Cheques accepted.

BOOK THIS SITE CALL 01580 214000 ...we'll arrange everything The Travel Service

BOOK THIS SITE CALL 01580 214000 ...we'll arrange everything The Travel Service

FR41070 Kawan Village la Grande Tortue

3 route de Pontlevoy, F-41120 Candé-sur-Beuvron (Loir-et-Cher)
Tel: **02 54 44 15 20**. Email: **grandetortue@wanadoo.fr** **www.alanrogers.com/FR41070**

This is a pleasant, shady site that has been developed in the surroundings of an old forest. It provides 169 touring pitches the majority of which are more than 100 sq.m. 150 have 10A electricity and the remainder are fully serviced. The family owners continue to develop the site with a new multisport court already created. During July and August, they organise a programme of trips including wine/cheese tastings, canoeing and horse riding excursions. Used by tour operators. This site is well placed for visiting the châteaux of the Loire or the cities of Orléans and Tours.

Facilities

Three sanitary blocks offer British style WCs, washbasins in cabins and pushbutton showers. Laundry facilities. Shop selling provisions. Terraced bar and restaurant with reasonably priced food and drink (15/4-15/9). Swimming pool and two shallower pools for children (1/5-30/9). Trampolines, a ball crawl with slide and climbing wall, bouncy inflatable. Multisport court. Off site: Walking and cycling. Bicycle hire 1 km. Fishing 500 m. Golf 10 km. Riding 12 km.

Open: 9 April - 30 September.

Directions

Site is just outside Candé-sur-Beuvron on D751, between Amboise and Blois. From Amboise, turn right just before Candé, then left into site.
GPS: N47:29.389 E01:15.515

Charges guide

Per unit incl. 2 persons	€ 15,00 - € 26,00
incl. electricity	€ 19,50 - € 30,00
extra person	€ 5,00 - € 7,50
child (3-9 yrs)	€ 3,50 - € 5,50
animal	€ 3,70

Camping Cheques accepted.

FR49040 Camping de l'Etang

2007

Route de Saint-Mathurin, F-49320 Brissac (Maine-et-Loire)

Tel: **02 41 91 70 61**. Email: **info@campingetang.com**

www.alanrogers.com/FR49040

At Camping de l'Etang many of the 124 level touring pitches have pleasant views across the countryside. Separated and numbered, some have a little shade and all have electricity with water and drainage nearby. 21 are fully serviced. A small bridge crosses the river Aubance which runs through the site (well fenced) and there are two lakes where fisherman can enjoy free fishing. The site has its own vineyard and the wine produced can be purchased on the campsite. The adjacent Parc de Loisirs is a paradise for young children with many activities (entry is free for campers). These include boating, pedaloes, pony rides, miniature train, water slide, bouncy castle and swings. Originally the farm of the Château de Brissac (yet only 24 km. from the lovely town of Angers), this is an attractive campsite retaining much of its rural charm. A 'Sites et Paysages' member.

Facilities

Three well maintained toilet blocks provide all the usual facilities. Laundry facilities. Baby room. Disabled visitors are well catered for. Motorcaravan service point. Small shop and takeaway snacks when bar is closed. Bar/restaurant serves crêpes, salads, etc. (evenings 15/6-31/8). Swimming pool (heated and covered) and paddling pool. Fishing. Play area. Bicycle hire. Wide variety of evening entertainment in high season. WiFi. No electric barbecues. Off site: Golf and riding 10 km. Sailing 25 km.

Open: 15 May - 15 September.

Directions

Brissac-Quincé is 17 km. southeast of Angers on D748 towards Poitiers. Do not enter the town but turn north on D55 (site signed) in direction of St Mathurin. GPS: N47:21.560 W00:26.065

Charges guide

Per unit incl. 2 persons	€ 15,00 - € 29,00
extra person	€ 5,00 - € 7,00
child (0-10 yrs)	free - € 4,00
electricity	free - € 3,00
dog	€ 3,00 - € 4,00

FR49020 Camping de Chantepie

2008

Saint Hilaire-Saint Florent, F-49400 Saumur (Maine-et-Loire)

Tel: **02 41 67 95 34**. Email: **info@campingchantepie.com**

www.alanrogers.com/FR49020

On arriving at Camping de Chantepie with its colourful, floral entrance, a friendly greeting awaits at reception, set beside a restored farmhouse. The site is owned by a charitable organisation which provides employment for local people with disabilities. Linked by gravel roads (which can be dusty) the 150 grass touring pitches are level and spacious, with some new larger ones (200 sq.m. at extra cost – state preference when booking). All pitches have electricity (6/10A) and are separated by low hedges of flowers and trees which offer some shade. This is a good site for families. The panoramic views over the Loire from the pitches on the terraced perimeter of the meadow are stunning and from here a path leads to the river valley. A 'Sites et Paysages' member.

Facilities

The toilet block is clean and facilities are good with washbasins in cubicles, new showers (men and women separately) and facilities for disabled visitors. Laundry facilities. Baby area. Shop, bar, terraced café and takeaway (all 15/6-31/8). Covered and heated pool, outdoor pool and paddling pool. Play area with apparatus. Terraced minigolf. TV. Video games. Pony rides. Bicycle hire. Internet access. WiFi. Off site: Fishing 500 m. Golf, riding 2 km. Sailing 7 km.

Open: 15 May - 15 September.

Directions

St Hilaire-St Florent is 2 km. west of Saumur. Take D751 (Gennes). Right at roundabout in St Hilaire-St Florent and on until Le Poitrineau and campsite sign, then turn left. Continue for 3 km. then turn right into site road. GPS: N47:17.629 W00:08.571

Charges 2009

Per unit incl. 2 persons	€ 15,00 - € 29,00
extra person	€ 5,00 - € 7,00
child (3-10 yrs)	€ 3,00 - € 4,00
electricity	€ 3,00

BOOK THIS SITE CALL 01580 214000 ...we'll arrange everything The Travel Service

FR86040 Kawan Village le Futuriste

F-86130 Saint Georges-les-Baillargeaux (Vienne)

Tel: **05 49 52 47 52**. Email: **camping-le-futuriste@wanadoo.fr** **www.alanrogers.com/FR86040**

Le Futuriste is a neat, modern site, open all year and close to Futuroscope. With a busy atmosphere, there are early departures and late arrivals. Reception is open 08.00-22.00. There are 118 individual, flat, grassy pitches divided by young trees and shrubs which are beginning to provide some shelter for this elevated and otherwise rather open site (possibly windy). 82 pitches have electricity (6A) and a further 30 have electricity, water, waste water and sewerage connections. All are accessed via neat, level and firmly rolled gravel roads. There are panoramic views over the strikingly modern buildings and night-time bright lights that comprise the popular attraction of Futuroscope. This site is ideal for a short stay to visit the park which is only 1.5 km. away (tickets can be bought at the site) but it is equally good for longer stays to see the region. Details of attractions are available from the enthusiastic young couple who run the site. Note: it is best to see the first evening show at Futuroscope otherwise you will find yourself locked out of the site – the gates are closed at 23.30.

Facilities

Excellent, clean sanitary facilities in two insulated blocks (can be heated). Those in the newest block are unisex. and include some washbasins in cabins and facilities for disabled people. Laundry facilities. Shop (bread to order), bar/restaurant (all 1/5-30/9). Snack bar and takeaway (1/7-31/8). Two heated outdoor pools, one with slide and paddling pool (15/5-15/9). Games room. TV. Boules. Multisport area. Lake fishing. Youth groups not accepted. Off site: Bicycle hire 500 m. Hypermarket 600 m. Golf 5 km. Riding 10 km.

Open: All year.

Directions

From either A10 autoroute or N10, take Futuroscope exit. Site is east of both roads, off D20 (St Georges-les-Baillargeaux). Follow signs to St Georges. Site on hill; turn by water tower and site is on left.
GPS: N46:39.928 E00:23.668

Charges 2009

Per unit incl. 1-3 persons and electricity	€ 18,40 - € 25,00
extra person	€ 2,10 - € 2,90
animal	€ 2,00

Camping Cheques accepted.

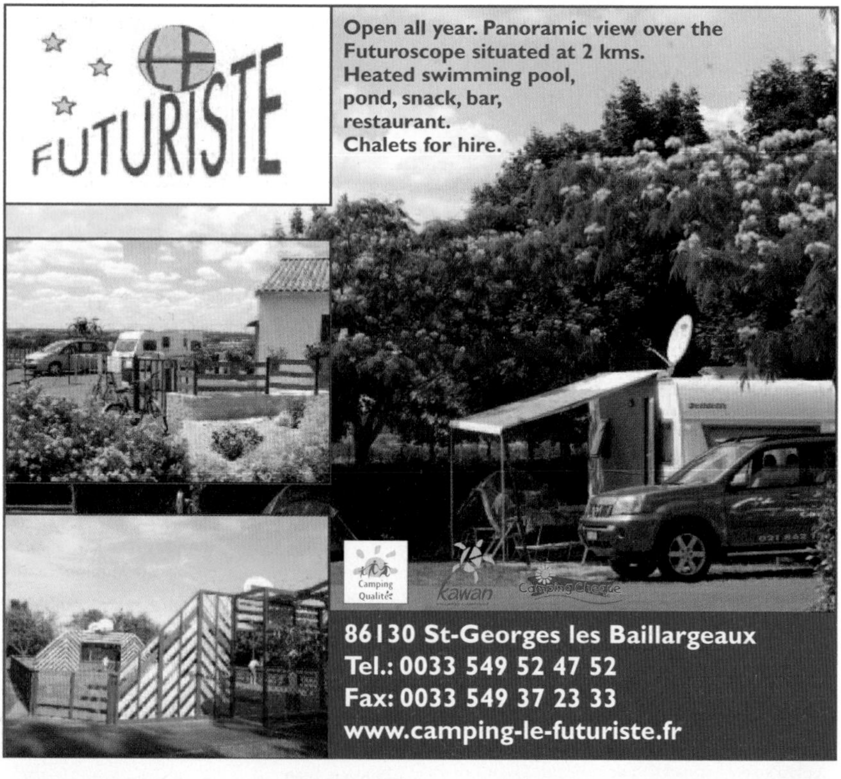

Runner up Alan Rogers Awards 2008

FR71110 Camping du Lac

Le Fourneau, F-71430 Palinges (Saône-et-Loire)

Tel: **03 85 88 14 49**. Email: **camping.palinges@hotmail.fr** **www.alanrogers.com/FR71110**

Camping du Lac is a very special campsite and it is all due to M. Labille, the owner, who thinks of the campsite as his home and every visitor as his guest. The campsite has 50 pitches in total, 16 of which have 10A electricity and 20 are fully serviced. There are six chalets to rent. The site is adjacent to a lake with a beach and safe bathing. Set in the countryside yet within easy reach of many tourist attractions, especially Cluny, the local Château Digoin and Mont St Vincent with distant views of Mont Blanc on a clear day.

Facilities

The central sanitary block provides all necessary facilities including those for campers with disabilities. Washing machine and fridge. Bread and croissants to order. Boules. Play area. TV room. Sports field, lake beach and swimming adjacent. Bicycle and pedalo hire in July/Aug. Motorcaravan services. Off site: Bar/snack bar outside entrance (weekends only outside 1/7-31/8). Riding 200 m. Palinges is within walking distance, cycle and walking routes, museums, cruises and châteaux,

Open: 1 April - 30 October.

Directions

Palinges is midway between Montceau les Mines and Paray le Monial. From Montceau take N70, then turn left onto D92 to Palinges. Follow campsite signs. Site is also well signed from D985 Toulon-sur-Arroux to Charolles road. GPS: N46:33.674 E04:13.528

Charges guide

Per unit incl. 2 persons and electricity	€ 16,80
extra person	€ 2,20
caravan, 2 axle	€ 34,00

No credit cards.

FR25080 Camping les Fuvettes

F-25160 Malbuisson (Doubs)

Tel: **03 81 69 31 50**. Email: **les-fuvettes@wanadoo.fr** **www.alanrogers.com/FR25080**

High in the Jura and close to the Swiss border, Les Fuvettes is a well established family site with a fine, lakeside setting on Lac Saint Point. The lake is large – over 1,000 hectares and a wide range of watersports is possible from the site, including sailing, windsurfing and pedaloes. Most equipment can be hired on site. Pitches here are grassy and of a reasonable size, separated by hedges and small trees. The new swimming pool is impressive with water slides and a separate children's pool. The site's bar/snack bar is housed in an attractive, steep roofed building and offers panoramic views across the lake. Walking and mountain biking are popular pursuits and many trails are available in the surrounding countryside. The Château de Joux is a popular excursion and the nearby Mont d'Or offers fine views towards the Alps. In high season, the site runs an entertainment and excursion programme, including a children's club. Mobile homes and chalets for rent.

Facilities

Three toilet blocks include facilities for babies and disabled people. Shop. Bar and snack bar. Swimming pool with waterslides and jacuzzi. Paddling pool. Play area. Minigolf. Archery. Bicycle hire. Sports pitch. Fishing (permit needed). Boat and pedalo hire. Games room. TV room. Children's club in peak season. Entertainment and excursion programme (July and August). Mobile homes and chalets for rent. Off site: Sailing school. Tennis. Many cycling and walking trails. Many restaurants, cafes and shops in nearby Malbuisson (walking distance).

Open: 1 April - 30 September.

Directions

From Besançon, head south on the N57 and join the D437 beyond Pontarlier signed Lac St Point and Mouthe. This road runs along the easten shores of the lake and passes through Malbuisson. Site is at the end of the village on the right. GPS: N46:47.518 E06:17.600

Charges 2009

Per unit incl. 2 persons and electricity	€ 17,60 - € 26,10
extra person	€ 3,50 - € 5,20
child (under 7 yrs)	€ 1,80 - € 2,90
dog	free - € 1,50

FR71070 Kawan Village Château de l'Epervière

F-71240 Gigny-sur-Saône (Saône-et-Loire)

Tel: **03 85 94 16 90**. Email: **domaine-de-leperviere@wanadoo.fr** **www.alanrogers.com/FR71070**

This site is peacefully situated in the wooded grounds of the 16th-century Château, near the village of Gigny-sur-Saône, and within walking distance of the river where you can watch the river cruise boats on their way to and from Châlon-sur-Saône. There are 160 pitches in total, of which 45 are occupied by tour operators and five units are for rent. The 110 touring pitches, all with 10A electricity (30 fully serviced) are in two distinct areas. The original part, close to the Château and fishing lake, has semi-hedged pitches on level ground with shade from mature trees. The centre of the second area has a more open aspect. Here there are large hedged pitches and mature trees offering shade around the periphery – birdwatchers will love this area. A partly fenced road across the lake connects the two areas. The château's main restaurant serves regional dishes. Gert-Jan, François and their team organise many activities for visitors including wine tasting in the château cellars.

Facilities

Two well equipped toilet blocks include washbasins in cabins, showers, baby rooms, facilities for disabled visitors. Washing machine and dryer. Basic shop (1/5-30/9). Second restaurant with basic menu and takeaway (1/4-30/9). Converted barn housing attractive bar, large TV and games room. Unheated outdoor pool (1/5-30/9). Smaller indoor heated pool, jacuzzi, sauna, paddling pool. Play area. Fishing. Bicycle hire. Off site: Riding 15 km. Golf 20 km. Châlon and Tournus, both 20 km.

Open: 29 March - 30 September.

Directions

From the north, A6 exit Châlon-Sud, or Tournus from the south. Take N6 to Sennecey-le-Grand, turn east on D18 and follow site signs for 6.5 km.
GPS: N46:39.100 E04:56.923

Charges guide

Per unit incl. 2 persons and electricity	€ 23,40 - € 32,20
extra person	€ 5,70 - € 7,70

Camping Cheques accepted.

FR71140 Camping du Pont de Bourgogne

Rue Julien Leneveu, Saint-Marcel, F-71380 Châlon-sur-Saône (Saône-et-Loire)

Tel: **03 85 48 26 86**. Email: **campingchalon71@wanadoo.fr** **www.alanrogers.com/FR71140**

This is a well presented site, useful for an overnight stop or for a few days if exploring the local area and you want a simple site without the frills. It does get crowded in the third week of July during the Châlon street theatre festival. There are 93 fairly small pitches with 6/10A electricity, ten with a gravel surface. The new owners of the site plan to replace or improve the facilities in the near future, but when we visited there was a bar/restaurant serving a good selection of simple meals.

Facilities

Three toilet blocks, two centrally located amongst the pitches and traditional in style and fittings, the third new and modern, alongside the reception building (including facilities for disabled visitors). No shop but essentials kept in the bar (bread to order). Modern bar/restaurant. Simple play area. Bicycle hire arranged. Off site: Municipal swimming pool 300 m. Golf 1 km. Riding 10 km.

Open: 1 April - 30 September.

Directions

From A6 exit 26 (Châlon-Sud) bear right to roundabout and take N80 (Dole) straight on to roundabout at St Marcel. Turn left (fourth exit) and fork right into Les Chavannes. At central traffic lights turn right and under modern river bridge to site entrance. GPS: N46:46.800 E04:52.377

Charges guide

Per person	€ 4,30 - € 5,20
pitch incl. electricity	€ 7,50 - € 9,80

FR71190 Camping de Tournus

Rue des Canes, F-71700 Tournus (Saône-et-Loire)

Tel: **03 85 51 16 58**. Email: **info@camping-tournus.com** **www.alanrogers.com/FR71190**

This very well maintained, pleasant site is just a few minutes from the A6 autoroute, 200 metres from the River Saône and close to the interesting old market town of Tournus. It is ideal for a night halt but deserving of a longer stay. The site has 90 fairly level grassy pitches all for touring, 70 having 6A electricity. A few trees give some pitches varying amounts of shade. The new owners have plans for many improvements including some hardstanding pitches.

Facilities

Two clean toilet blocks near the entrance provide all necessary facilities, including for campers with disabilities. Small café (no alcohol) also stocking some daily necessities and bread to order (all season). Small play area. Internet terminal. Bicycle hire. Off site: Fishing 200 m. Tournus, Saturday market, shops, bars, cafes, banks etc. short walk/bike ride alongside river. Municipal pool next door.

Open: 1 April - 30 September.

Directions

From the A6 take exit 12 for Tournus and the N6 south for just over 1 km. In Tournus (opposite railway station), turn left signed camping and follow signs to site, about 1 km. GPS: N46:34.459 E04:54.571

Charges guide

Per unit incl. 2 persons	€ 14,30 - € 17,70
extra person	€ 3,90 - € 4,90
electricity (6A)	€ 3,50 - € 4,20

FR70020 Camping International du Lac

Avenue des Rives du Lac, F-70000 Vesoul-Vaivre (Haute-Saône)

Tel: **03 84 76 22 86**. Email: **camping_dulac@yahoo.fr** **www.alanrogers.com/FR70020**

This is one of the better examples of a town site and is part of a leisure park around a large lake. The campsite does not have direct access to the lake as it is separated by a security fence, but access is possible at the site entrance. There are 160 good sized, level, grass pitches, all with electricity (10A). Access is from hard roads and pitches are separated by shrubs and bushes. A five kilometre path has been created around the lake for jogging, walking and cycling.

Facilities

Three good quality toilet blocks, one heated, are well spaced around the site and provide a mix of British and Turkish style WCs, washbasins and showers. Baby room. Two superb suites for disabled visitors. Laundry facilities. Motorcaravan service point. Baker calls daily (July/Aug). Play area. Animation (July/Aug). Bicycle hire. TV and games room. Boules. Internet access. Fishing. Off site: Bar and restaurant adjacent. Lake beach 100 m. Sailing 2 km.

Open: 1 March - 31 October.

Directions

On road D457 to west of Vesoul on route to Besançon, well signed around the town.
GPS: N47:37.812 E06:07.700

Charges guide

Per person	€ 3,55
child (under 7 yrs)	€ 1,65
pitch incl. electricity	€ 5,40
vehicle	€ 2,60

FR74070 Camping Caravaning l'Escale

F-74450 Le Grand-Bornand (Haute-Savoie)

Tel: **04 50 02 20 69**. Email: **contact@campinglescale.com** **www.alanrogers.com/FR74070**

You are assured a good welcome in English from the Baur family at this beautifully maintained and picturesque site, situated at the foot of the Aravis mountain range. There are 149 pitches with 122 for touring. Of average size, part grass, part gravel they are separated by trees and shrubs that give a little shade. All pitches have electricity (2-10A) and 86 are fully serviced. Rock pegs are essential. A 200 year old building houses a bar/restaurant offering regional dishes.

Facilities

Good toilet blocks (heated in winter) have all the necessary facilities. Drying room for skis, clothing and boots. Superb pool complex (all season) and outdoor pools (10/6-31/8), jacuzzi and water jets. Cosy bar and restaurant. Play area. Tennis. WiFi. Activities for all.
Off site: Village (5 minutes walk), shops, bars, restaurants, archery, paragliding, golf, minigolf. Bicycle hire 200 m. Riding and golf 3 km. Free bus for cable car.

Open: 5 December - 19 April, 20 May - 27 September.

Directions

From Annecy follow D16 and D909 towards La Clusaz. At St Jean-de-Sixt, turn left at roundabout D4 signed Grand Bornand. Just before village fork right signed Vallée de Bouchet and camping. Site entrance is on right at roundabout in 1.2 km.
GPS: N45:56.412 E06:25.692

Charges guide

Per unit incl. 2 persons	€ 16,00 - € 22,50
electricity (2-10A)	€ 3,80 - € 6,90

FR38080 Kawan Village Au Joyeux Réveil

Le Château, F-38880 Autrans (Isère)

Tel: **04 76 95 33 44**. Email: **camping-au-joyeux-reveil@wanadoo.fr** **www.alanrogers.com/FR38080**

The small town of Autrans is set on a plateau, 1,050 m. high, in the Vercors region. The well organised site is run by a very friendly family (English is spoken). It is on the outskirts of the town, set below a ski jump and short lift. There are 108 pitches with 78 for touring, electricity 2-10A. They are mainly on grass, in a sunny location with fantastic views over the surrounding wooded mountains with small trees giving little shade. The days can be very hot and sunny and the nights quite chilly.

Facilities

The new toilet block is very well appointed, with underfloor heating and all the expected facilities. Another new building houses a bar with terrace, snack bar/takeaway (July and August). New pool area with two pools, toboggan for children, sunbathing area and a separate paddling pool. Small play area. TV room. Internet point. Off site: Autrans with a few shops 500 m. Villard de Lans, supermarket, shops, restaurants, bars, ice rink and many other activities 16 km. Short ski lift is near the site and a shuttle bus runs (in winter) to the longer runs (5 km). Fishing, bicycle hire and riding 300 m. Bus to Villard de Lans and Grenoble.

Open: 1 December - 31 March, 1 May - 30 September.

Directions

From A48, northwest of Grenoble use exit 13 (going south) or 3A (going north). Follow N532 to Sassenage, turn west at roundabout on D531 to Lans en Vercors. At a roundabout turn right on D106 signed Autrans. On entering Autrans turn right at roundabout (site signed) and very shortly right again. This is the only route recommended for caravans and motorcaravans. GPS: N45:10.515 E05:32.870

Charges guide

Per unit incl. 1 or 2 persons	€ 18,50 - € 30,00
extra person	€ 5,00
electricity (2-6A)	€ 2,00 - € 8,00

Winter prices - apply to site.
Camping Cheques accepted.

FR73020 Camping Caravaneige le Versoyen

Route des Arcs, F-73700 Bourg-Saint-Maurice (Savoie)

Tel: **04 79 07 03 45**. Email: **leversoyen@wanadoo.fr** **www.alanrogers.com/FR73020**

Bourg-St-Maurice is on a small, level plain at an altitude of 830 m. on the River Isère, surrounded by mountains. Le Versoyen attracts visitors all year round (except for a short time when they close). The site's 205 unseparated, flat pitches (180 for touring) are marked by numbers on the tarmac roads and all have electrical connections (4/6/10A). Most are on grass but some are on tarmac hardstanding making them ideal for use by motorcaravans or in winter. Trees give shade in some parts, although most pitches have almost none. Duckboards are provided for snow and wet weather.

Facilities

Two acceptable toilet blocks can be heated, although the provision may be hard pressed in high season. British and Turkish style WCs. Laundry. Motorcaravan service facilities. Outdoor and covered pools (July/Aug). Heated rest room with TV. Small bar with takeaway in summer. Free shuttle in high season to funicular railway. Off site: Fishing or bicycle hire 200 m. Tennis and swimming pool 500 m. Riding 1 km. Golf 15 km. Cross-country ski track.

Open: All year (excl. 7 Nov - 14 Dec and 2-25 May).

Directions

Site is 1.5 km. east of Bourg-St-Maurice on the CD119 Les Arcs road.
GPS: N45:37.324 E06:47.010

Charges guide

Per unit incl. 2 persons and electricity	€ 16,10 - € 21,00
extra person	€ 4,00 - € 4,60
child (4-13 yrs)	€ 2,50 - € 4,40
dog	€ 0,50

FR73100 Camping le Reclus

F-73700 Séez (Savoie)

Tel: **04 79 41 01 05**. Email: **contact@campinglerecus.com** **www.alanrogers.com/FR73100**

This small mountain campsite, set in the hills above Bourg-St-Maurice, is enthusiastically run by the Bonato sisters who have great plans to offer the unexpected. The 108 pitches, some gently sloping, are set amongst mature pine trees giving plenty of shade; 90 have electrical connections. The site borders a fast-flowing mountain stream, which is well fenced. The site is undergoing redevelopment, with many new facilities being introduced. A new TV room was just about to open on our visit. The village of Séez is a few minutes' walk away. This site is not recommended for larger units.

Facilities

Two sanitary blocks, the central one more modern, have small shower cubicles with preset hot water; and open style basins. Laundry room with washer/dryer and indoor drying area. Restaurant and takeaway (June - Sept). Small play area. Bread, drinks and ice cream for sale. Bicycle hire. Off site: Shops and bars in the village of Séez. Access to the ski resort of Les Arcs via the funicular railway in Bourg-St-Maurice 2 km. Riding 1 km. Swimming pools 2 km.

Open: All year excl. November.

Directions

From A43 Lyon - Chambéry - Grenoble motorway take A430 to Albertville and RN90 to Moutiers and Bourg St Maurice. Drive through town, at third roundabout follow signs for Tignes and Val d'Isère. Site is 2 km. up the hill on the right on entering village of Séez. GPS: N45:37.555 E06:47.623

Charges guide

Per unit incl. 2 persons	€ 11,20 - € 12,40
extra person	€ 3,60 - € 4,00
electricity (4-10A)	€ 4,00 - € 4,70

The Travel Service BOOK THIS SITE CALL 01580 214000 ...we'll arrange everything

FR33110 Airotel Camping de la Côte d'Argent

F-33990 Hourtin-Plage (Gironde)

Tel: **05 56 09 10 25**. Email: **info@camping-cote-dargent.com** **www.alanrogers.com/FR33110**

Côte d'Argent is a large, well equipped site for leisurely family holidays. It makes an ideal base for walkers and cyclists with over 100 km. of cycle lanes in the area. Hourtin-Plage is a pleasant invigorating resort on the Atlantic coast and a popular location for watersports enthusiasts, The site's top attraction is its pool complex where wooden bridges connect the pools and islands and there are sunbathing and play areas plus an indoor heated pool. The site is spread over 20 hectares of undulating sand-based terrain. The 550 touring pitches, arranged under trees, are not clearly defined and some are on soft sand. Entertainment takes place at the bar near the entrance (until 00.30). There are 48 hardstandings for motorcaravans outside the site, providing a cheap stopover, but with no access to site facilities. The site is well organised and ideal for children.

Facilities

Very clean sanitary blocks include provision for visitors with disabilities. Washing machines. Motorcaravan service points. Large supermarket, restaurant, takeaway, pizzeria bar. Four outdoor pools with slides and flumes. Indoor pool. Massage (Institut de Beauté). Tennis. Play areas. Miniclub, organised entertainment in season. Bicycle hire. Internet. ATM. Charcoal barbecues are not permitted. Hotel (12 rooms). Off site: Path to the beach 300 m. Fishing and riding. Golf 30 km.

Open: 16 May - 13 September.

Directions

Turn off D101 Hourtin-Soulac road 3 km. north of Hourtin. Then join D101E signed Hourtin-Plage. Site is 300 m. from the beach.
GPS: N45:13.381 W01:09.868

Charges guide

Per unit incl. 2 persons and electricity	€ 25,00 - € 44,00
extra person	€ 3,00 - € 7,00
child (2-10 yrs)	€ 2,50 - € 6,00

Camping Cheques accepted.

FR40190 Le Saint-Martin Airotel Camping

Avenue de l'Océan, F-40660 Moliets-Plage (Landes)

Tel: **05 58 48 52 30**. Email: **contact@camping-saint-martin.fr** **www.alanrogers.com/FR40190**

A family site aimed mainly at couples and young families, Airotel St-Martin is a welcome change from most of the sites in this area in that it has only a small number of chalets (85) compared to the number of touring pitches (575). First impressions are of a neat, tidy, well cared for site and the direct access to the beach is an added bonus. The pitches are mainly typically French in style with low hedges separating them plus some shade. Electricity hook ups are 10-15A and a number of pitches also have water and drainage. Entertainment in high season is low key (with the emphasis on quiet nights) – daytime competitions and a miniclub, plus occasional evening entertainment, well away from the pitches and with no discos. With pleasant chalets and mobile homes to rent, and an 18-hole golf course 700 m. away, this would be an ideal destination for a golfing weekend or longer stay.

Facilities

Seven toilet blocks are of a high standard and very well maintained. Baby rooms and facilities for visitors with disabilities. Motorcaravan service point. Washing machines and dryers. Fridge rental. Supermarket. Bars, restaurants and takeaways. Indoor pool (22/3-1/11), jacuzzi and sauna (charged July/Aug). Outdoor pool area (15/6-15/9). Play area. Internet access. Electric barbecues only.
Off site: Bicycle hire 500 m. Golf and tennis 700 m.

Open: 19 March - 11 November.

Directions

From the N10 take D142 to Lèon, then D652 to Moliets-et-Mar. Follow signs to Moliets-Plage, site is well signed. GPS: N43:51.145 W01:23.239

Charges guide

Per unit incl. 1 or 2 adults, 1 child	€ 17,50 - € 43,20
serviced pitch	€ 24,00 - € 48,50
extra person	€ 6,00

Prices are for reserved pitches.

Airotel Camping Caravaning ★★★

Côte d'Argent

POOL COMPLEX OF 3500 M² WITH WATERSLIDES, JACUZZI AND COVERED HEATED SWIMMING POOL

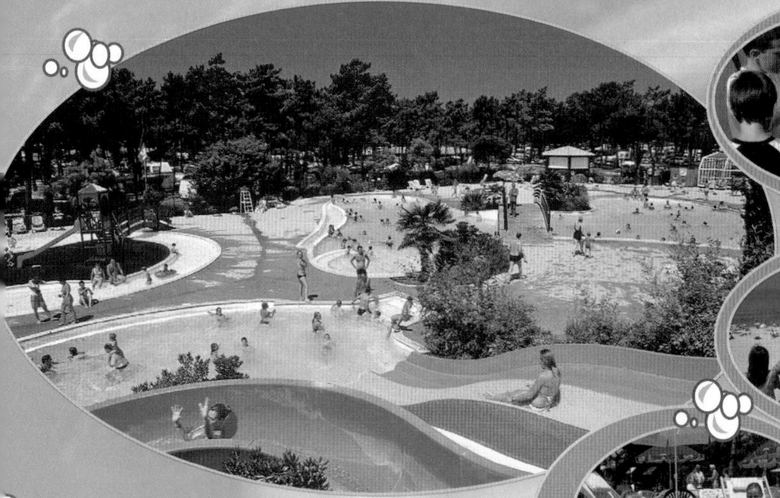

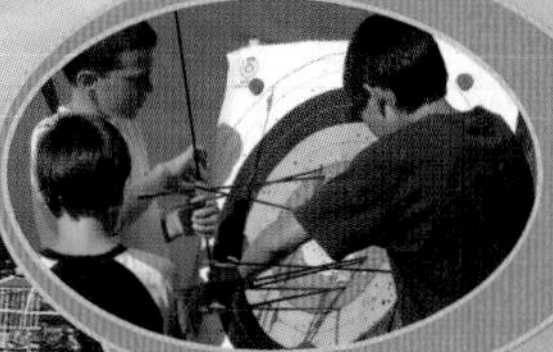

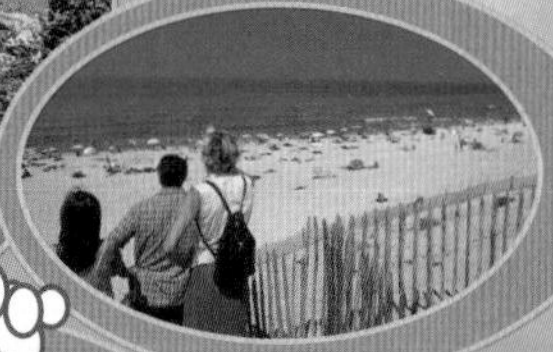

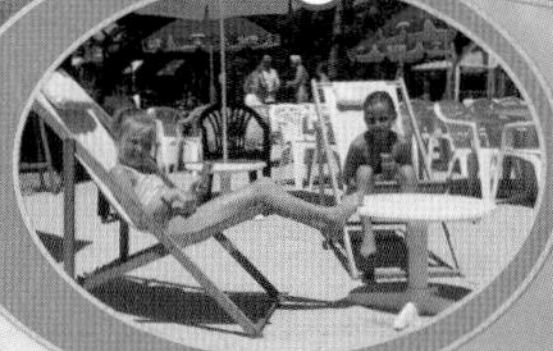

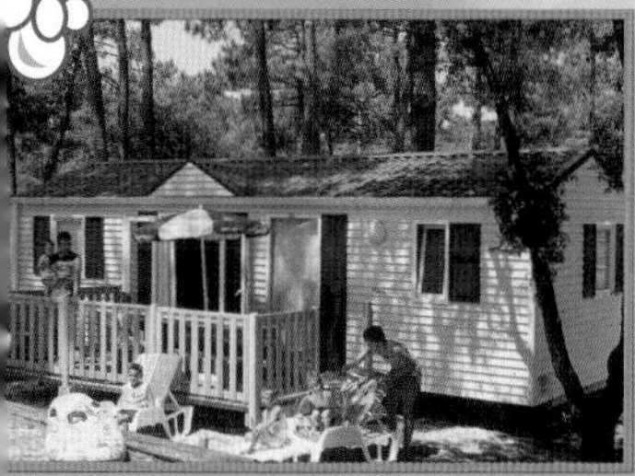

Special low season offers (not in July and August)
14 = 11 and 7 = 6
campsite or accommodations

wifi - hotel - shops - restaurant - bar - provisions - animation (sports) - tennis - horse riding - archery - mini club - games room - sailing (4 km) - surfing (300 m)

Hourtin Plage - Aquitaine - Atlantique Sud

La Côte d'Argent is a beautiful sloping park of 20 ha in the heart of a pine tree forest. At 300 m of a long winding sandy beach at the Atlantic Ocean.
A site in the lee of dunes and the forest, this holiday village enjoys an ideal climate for enjoying relaxing nature holidays.

Sun, Life and fun

Airotel Camping Caravaning de la Côte d'Argent
33990 Hourtin Plage
Tél : 00033 (0)5.56.09.10.25
Fax : 0033 (0)5.56.09.24.96
www.camping-cote-dargent.com - www.cca33.com -
www.campingcoteouest.com

FR33130 Yelloh! Village les Grands Pins

Plage Nord, F-33680 Lacanau-Océan (Gironde)

Tel: **04 66 73 97 39**. Email: **info@yellohvillage-les-grands-pins.com** **www.alanrogers.com/FR33130**

This Atlantic coast holiday site with direct access to a fine sandy beach, is on undulating terrain amongst tall pine trees. A large site with 600 pitches, there are 430 of varying sizes for touring units. One half of the site is a traffic free zone (except for arrival or departure day, caravans are placed on the pitch, with separate areas outside for parking). There is a good number of tent pitches, those in the centre of the site having some of the best views. This popular site has an excellent range of facilities available for the whole season. Especially useful for tent campers are safety deposit and fridge boxes which are available for rent. Mobile homes (2 persons) are for hire. The large sandy beach is a 350 m. stroll from the gate at the back of the site.

Facilities

Four well equipped toilet blocks, one heated, including baby room and facilities for disabled people. Launderette. Motorcaravan services. Supermarket. Bar, restaurant, snack bar, takeaway. Heated swimming pool (lifeguard in July/Aug) with sunbathing surround. Jacuzzi. Free fitness activities. Games room. Fitness suite. Tennis. Two playgrounds. Adventure playground. Bicycle hire. Organised activities. WiFi in the bar (on payment). Only gas barbecues are permitted. Off site: Fishing, golf, riding and bicycle hire 5 km.

Open: 26 April - 20 September.

Directions

From Bordeaux take N125/D6 west to Lacanau-Océan. At second roundabout, take second exit: Plage Nord, follow signs to 'campings'. Les Grand Pins signed to right at the far end of road.
GPS: N45:00.664 W01:11.602

Charges guide

Per unit incl. 2 persons and electricity	€ 14,00 - € 43,00
extra person	€ 5,00 - € 9,00
child (2-12 yrs)	free - € 5,00
dog	€ 4,00

Half-board arrangements available.

tel: +33 466 739 739 www.yellohvillage.com

yelloh! VILLAGE

FR40180 Camping le Vieux Port

Plage Sud, F-40660 Messanges (Landes)

Tel: **01 72 03 91 60**. Email: **contact@levieuxport.com** **www.alanrogers.com/FR40180**

A well established destination appealing particularly to families with teenage children, this lively site has 1,406 pitches of mixed size, most with electricity (6A) and some fully serviced. The camping area is well shaded by pines and pitches are generally of a good size, attractively grouped around the toilet blocks. There are many tour operators here and well over a third of the site is taken up with mobile homes and another 400 pitches are used for tents. The heated pool complex is exceptional boasting five outdoor pools and three large water slides. There is also a heated indoor pool. An enormous 7,000 sq.m. Aquatic Parc is planned for 2009 and all the sanitary facilities are to be renovated. The area to the north of Bayonne is heavily forested and a number of very large campsites are attractively located close to the superb Atlantic beaches. Le Vieux Port is probably the largest and certainly one of the most impressive of these. At the back of the site a path leads across the dunes to a good beach (500 m). A little train also trundles to the beach on a fairly regular basis in high season (small charge). All in all, this is a lively site with a great deal to offer an active family.

Facilities

Nine well appointed, recently renovated toilet blocks with facilities for disabled people. Motorcaravan services. Good supermarket and various smaller shops in high season. Several restaurants, takeaway and three bars (all open all season). Large pool complex (no Bermuda shorts) including new covered pool and Polynesian themed bar. Tennis. Multisport pitch. Minigolf. Bicycle hire. Riding centre. Organised activities in high season including frequent discos and karaoke evenings. Only communal barbecues are allowed. Off site: Fishing 1 km. Golf 8 km.

Open: 1 April - 30 September.

Directions

Leave RN10 at Magescq exit heading for Soustons. Pass through Soustons following signs for Vieux-Boucau. Bypass this town and site is clearly signed to the left at second roundabout.
GPS: N43:47.867 W01:24.067

Charges 2009

Per unit incl. 2 persons	€ 13,00 - € 44,00
extra person	€ 4,00 - € 8,00
child (under 13 yrs)	€ 3,00 - € 5,50
electricity (6/8A)	€ 4,50 - € 8,00
animal	€ 2,50 - € 5,00

Camping Cheques accepted.

FR40250 Camping les Grands Pins

1039 avenue de Losa, F-40460 Sanguinet (Landes)

Tel: **05 58 78 61 74**. Email: **info@campinglesgrandspins.com** **www.alanrogers.com/FR40250**

Approached by a road alongside the lake, this site is set amongst tall pine trees. The gravel pitches are of average size, mostly level and shaded. Hedges divide those available for tourers and these are set amongst the many mobile homes. Large units may find manoeuvring difficult. There may be some aircraft noise at times from a nearby army base. A central pool complex includes a covered heated indoor pool, an outdoor pool, water slide and flume. In early and late season this is a very quiet site with very few facilities open. However, there are plenty of walks, cycle rides and the lake to enjoy. The poolside bar, restaurant and shops are only open in July and August, when the site becomes busy, offering watersports, minigolf, a children's club, boat trips and organised activities. Fishing is also available. The charming small village of Sanguinet is 2 km. away with shops, bars, restaurants and an archaeological museum.

Facilities

Four toilet blocks include washbasins in cabins, showers and British style toilets. Baby bath and provision for disabled visitors. Laundry facilities. Motorcaravan service point. Shop, bar, restaurant and takeaway (1/7-31/8). Indoor pool (all seson). Outdoor pool complex (1/7-31/8). Play area. Games room and TV in bar. Tennis. Bicycle hire (July/Aug). Children's club. Pets not accepted in July/Aug. Barbecues not allowed (dedicated area). Off site: Beach 30 m. Fishing 2 km. Golf and riding 15 km.

Open: 1 April - 31 October.

Directions

Enter Sanguinet from the north on the D46. At one way system turn right. Do not continue on one way system but go straight ahead toward lake (signed) on Rue de Lac. Site is 2 km. on left.
GPS: N44:29.038 W01:05.383

Charges guide

Per unit incl. 2 persons and electricity	€ 16,00 - € 37,00
extra person	€ 4,50 - € 6,50
child (3-7 yrs)	€ 4,00 - € 5,00

FR40060 Camping Club International Eurosol

Route de la Plage, F-40560 Vielle-Saint-Girons (Landes)

Tel: **05 58 47 90 14**. Email: **contact@camping-eurosol.com** **www.alanrogers.com/FR40060**

This attractive and well maintained site is set on undulating ground amongst mature pine trees giving good shade. The 356 pitches for touring are numbered and 209 have electricity with 120 fully serviced. A family site with multilingual entertainers, many games and tournaments are organised and a beach volleyball competition is held each evening in front of the bar. A third covered pool has recently been added to the smart, landscaped pool complex. A sandy beach 700 metres from the site has supervised bathing in high season.

Facilities

Four main toilet blocks and two smaller blocks are comfortable and clean with facilities for babies and disabled visitors. Motorcaravan services. Fridge rental. Well stocked shop and bar. Restaurant, takeaway (from 1/6). Stage for live shows arranged in July/Aug. Outdoor swimming pool complex. Tennis. Multisport court. Bicycle hire. Internet and WiFi. Charcoal barbecues are not permitted. Off site: Riding school opposite. Fishing 700 m.

Open: 9 May - 12 September.

Directions

Turn off D652 at St Girons on D42 towards St Girons-Plage. Site is on left before coming to beach (4.5 km). GPS: N43:57.100 W01:21.087

Charges 2009

Per unit incl.1 or 2 persons and electricity	€ 18,00 - € 33,50
extra person (over 4 yrs)	€ 5,00
dog	€ 2,50

Alan Rogers

This is just a sample of the campsites we have inspected and selected in France. For more campsites and further information, please see the Alan Rogers France guide.

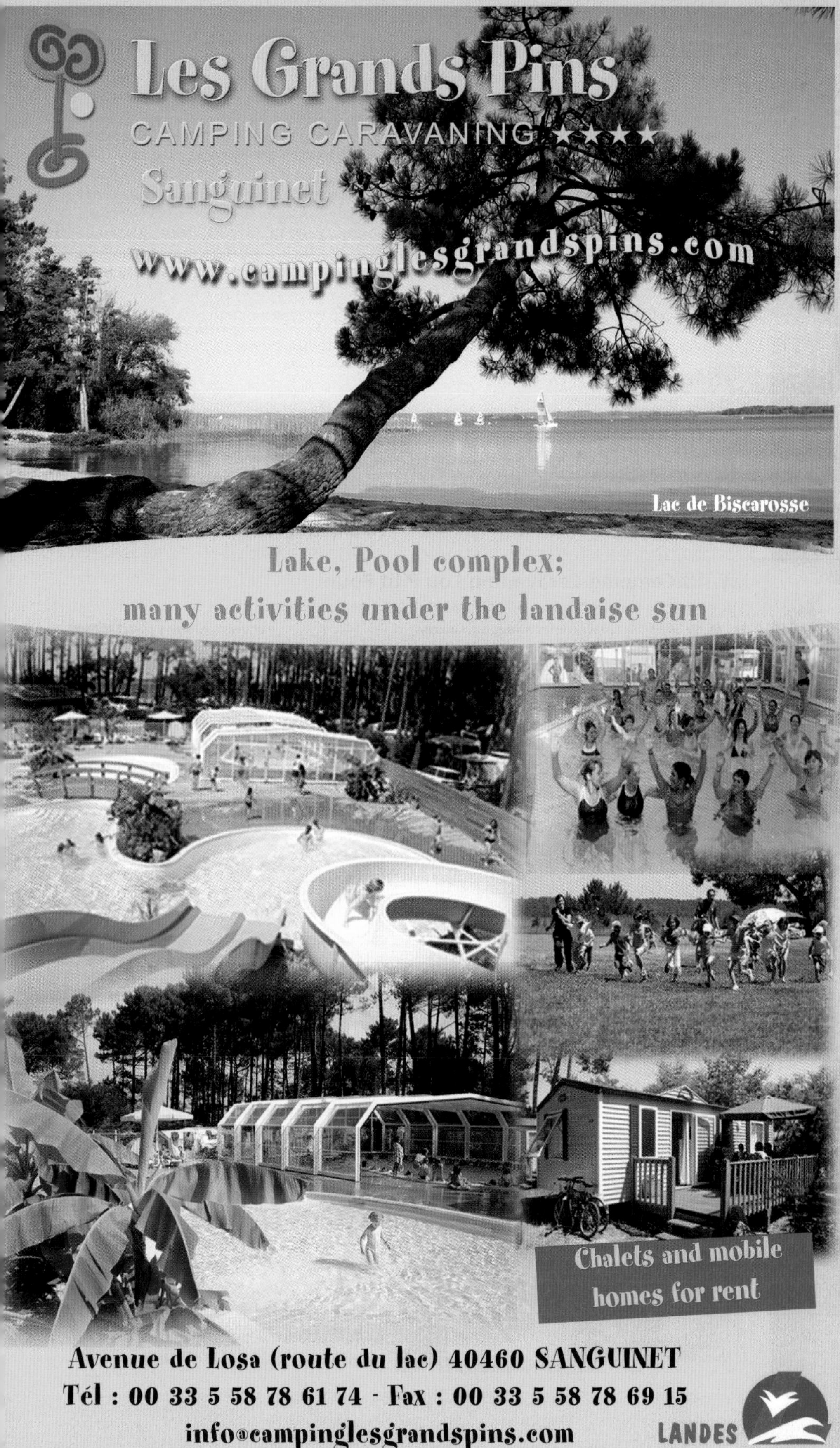
Les Grands Pins
CAMPING CARAVANING ★★★★
Sanguinet
www.campinglesgrandspins.com
Lac de Biscarosse
Lake, Pool complex;
many activities under the landaise sun
Chalets and mobile homes for rent
Avenue de Losa (route du lac) 40460 SANGUINET
Tél : 00 33 5 58 78 61 74 - Fax : 00 33 5 58 78 69 15
info@campinglesgrandspins.com
LANDES

The Travel Service BOOK THIS SITE CALL 01580 214000 ...we'll arrange everything

FR40100 Camping du Domaine de la Rive

Route de Bordeaux, F-40600 Biscarrosse (Landes)

Tel: **05 58 78 12 33**. Email: **info@camping-de-la-rive.fr** **www.alanrogers.com/FR40100**

Surrounded by pine woods, La Rive has a superb beach-side location on Lac de Sanguinet. It provides mostly level, numbered and clearly defined pitches of 100 sq.m. all with electricity connections (6A). The swimming pool complex is wonderful with pools linked by water channels and bridges. There is also a jacuzzi, paddling pool and two large swimming pools all surrounded by sunbathing areas and decorated with palm trees. An indoor pool is heated and open all season. There may be some aircraft noise from a nearby army base. This is a friendly site with a good mix of nationalities. The latest addition is a super children's aquapark with various games. The beach is excellent, shelving gently to provide safe bathing. There are windsurfers and small craft can be launched from the site's slipway.

Facilities

Five good clean toilet blocks have washbasins in cabins and mainly British style toilets. Facilities for disabled visitors. Baby baths. Motorcaravan service point. Shop with gas. Restaurant. Bar serving snacks and takeaway. Swimming pool complex (supervised July/Aug). Games room. Play area. Tennis. Bicycle hire. Boules. Archery. Fishing. Waterskiing. Watersports equipment hire. Tournaments (June-Aug). Skateboard park. Trampolines. Miniclub. No charcoal barbecues on pitches. Off site: Golf 8 km.

Open: 1 April - 30 September.

Directions

Take D652 from Sanguinet to Biscarrosse and site is signed on the right in about 6 km. Turn right and follow tarmac road for 2 km.
GPS: N44:27.607 W01:07.808

Charges guide

Per pitch incl. 2 persons and electricity	€ 20,00 - € 42,00
incl. water and drainage	€ 23,00 - € 45,00
extra person	€ 3,40 - € 7,50
child (3-7 yrs)	€ 2,30 - € 6,00
dog	€ 2,10 - € 5,00

Camping Cheques accepted.

The Travel Service BOOK THIS SITE CALL 01580 214000 ...we'll arrange everything

FR40140 Camping Caravaning Lou P'tit Poun

110 avenue du Quartier Neuf, F-40390 St Martin-de-Seignanx (Landes)

Tel: **05 59 56 55 79**. Email: **contact@louptitpoun.com** **www.alanrogers.com/FR40140**

The manicured grounds surrounding Lou P'tit Poun give it a well kept appearance, a theme carried out throughout this very pleasing site which celebrates its 20th anniversary in 2009. It is only after arriving at the car park that you feel confident it is not a private estate. Beyond this point an abundance of shrubs and trees is revealed. Behind a central sloping flower bed lies the open plan reception area. The avenues around the site are wide and the 168 pitches (142 for touring) are spacious. All have 10A electricity, many also have water and drainage and some are separated by low hedges. The jovial owners make their guests welcome and extend their enthusiasm to organising weekly entertainment for young and old during high season. A 'Sites et Paysages' member.

Facilities

Two unisex sanitary blocks, maintained to a high standard and kept clean, include washbasins in cabins, a baby bath and provision for disabled people. Laundry facilities with washing machine and dryer. Motorcaravan service point. Small shop (1/7-31/8). Café/restaurant (1/7-31/8). Swimming pool (1/6-15/9) Play area. Games room, TV. Half court tennis. Off site: Bayonne 6 km. Fishing and riding 7 km. Golf 10 km. Sandy beaches 10 minutes drive.

Open: 2 June - 12 September.

Directions

Leave A63 at exit 6 and join D817 in the direction of Pau. Site is signed at Leclerc supermarket. Continue for 3.5 km. and site is clearly signed on right.
GPS: N43:31.451 W01:24.730

Charges guide

Per pitch incl. 2 persons and electricity	€ 21,50 - € 32,50
extra person	€ 6,00 - € 7,00
child (under 7 yrs)	€ 4,00 - € 5,00

Check real time availability and at-the-gate prices...
www.alanrogers.com

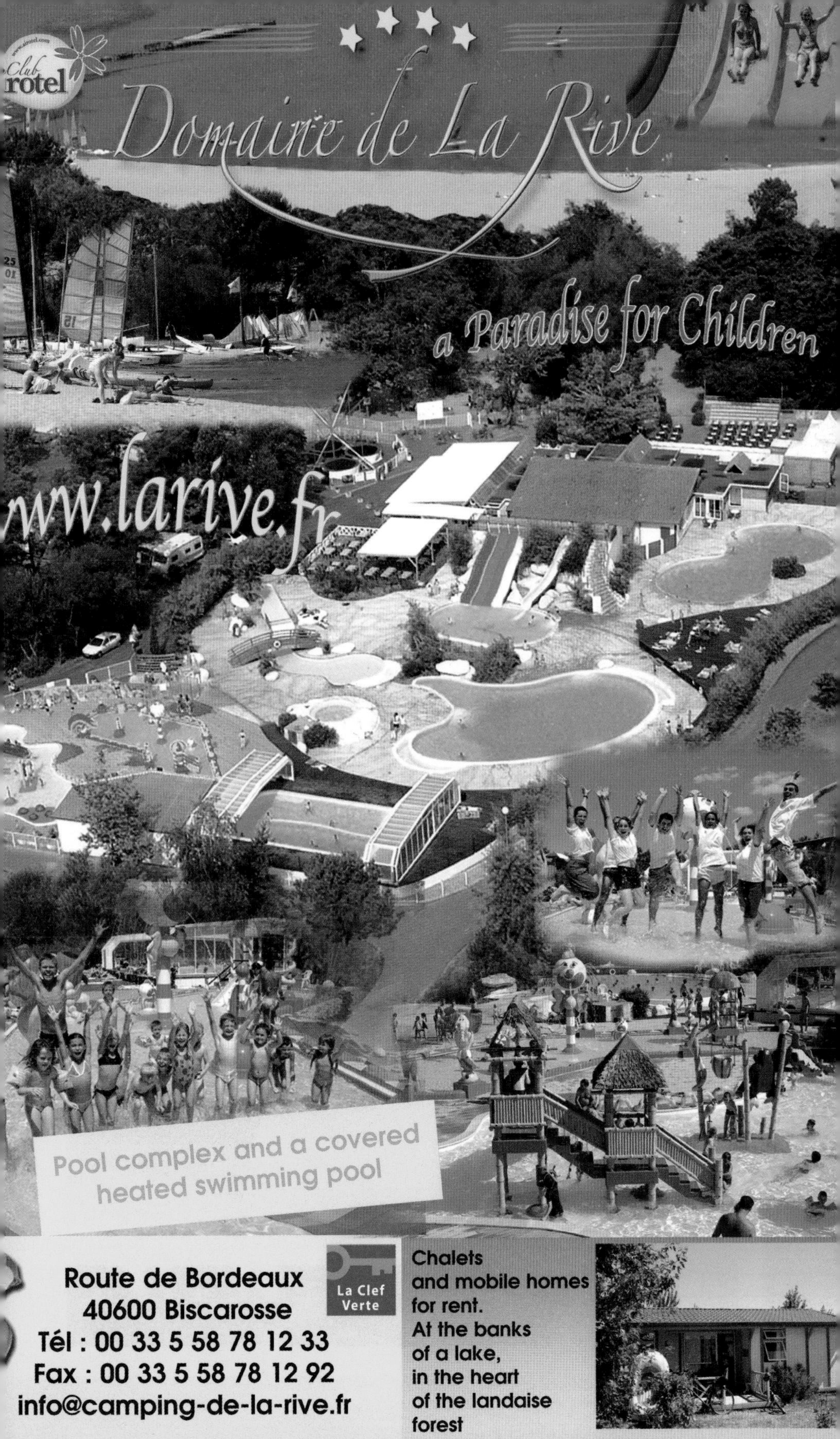

Club rotel
Domaine de La Rive
a Paradise for Children
www.larive.fr
Pool complex and a covered heated swimming pool
Route de Bordeaux
40600 Biscarosse
Tél : 00 33 5 58 78 12 33
Fax : 00 33 5 58 78 12 92
info@camping-de-la-rive.fr
La Clef Verte
Chalets
and mobile homes
for rent.
At the banks
of a lake,
in the heart
of the landaise
forest

FR64110 Sunêlia Col d'Ibardin

F-64122 Urrugne (Pyrénées-Atlantiques)
Tel: **05 59 54 31 21**. Email: **info@col-ibardin.com** **www.alanrogers.com/FR64110**

This family owned site at the foot of the Basque Pyrénées is highly recommended and deserves praise. It is well run with emphasis on personal attention, the friendly family and their staff ensuring that all are made welcome, and is attractively set in the middle of an oak wood with a mountain stream cascading through it. Behind the forecourt, with its brightly coloured shrubs and modern reception area, various roadways lead to the 191 pitches. These are individual, spacious and enjoy the benefit of the shade (if preferred a more open aspect can be found). There are electricity hook-ups (4/10A) and adequate water points. A very attractive chalet 'village' has recently been added. From this site you can enjoy the mountain scenery, be on the beach in 7-10 km. or cross the border into Spain in about 14 km.

Facilities

Two toilet blocks, one rebuilt to a high specification, are kept very clean. WC for disabled people. Dishwashing and laundry facilities. Motorcaravan service point. Shop for basics and bread orders (15/6-15/9). Restaurant, takeaway service and bar (15/6-15/9). Heated swimming pool and paddling pool. Playground and club (adult supervision). Tennis. Boules. Video games. Bicycle hire. Multisport area. Not suitable for American motorhomes.
Off site: Supermarket and shopping centre 5 km. Fishing and golf 7 km. Riding 20 km.

Open: 1 April - 30 September.

Directions

Leave A63 at St Jean-de-Luz sud, exit no. 2 and join RN10 in direction of Urrugne. Turn left at roundabout (Col d'Ibardin) on D4. Site on right after 5 km. Do not turn off to the Col itself, carry on towards Ascain. GPS: N43:20.035 W01:41.077

Charges guide

Per unit incl. 2 persons and electricity	€ 16,50 - € 34,00
extra person	€ 3,00 - € 6,00
child (2-7 yrs)	€ 2,00 - € 3,50
pet	€ 2,50

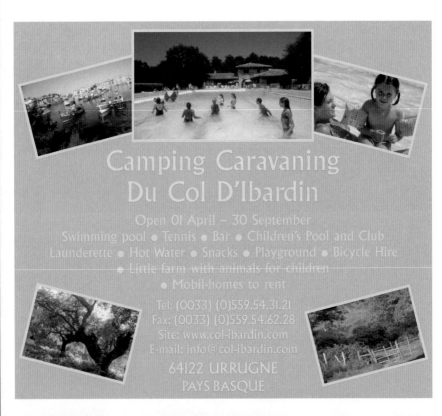

FR24090 Domaine de Soleil Plage

Caudon par Montfort, Vitrac, F-24200 Sarlat-la-Canéda (Dordogne)
Tel: **05 53 28 33 33**. Email: **info@soleilplage.fr** **www.alanrogers.com/FR24090**

This site is in one of the most attractive sections of the Dordogne valley, with a riverside location. The site has 199 pitches, in three sections, with 104 for touring units. The smallest section surrounds the main reception and other facilities. There are 40 mobile homes, 20 chalets and 17 bungalow tents. The site offers river bathing from a sizeable pebble or sand bank. All pitches are bounded by hedges and are of adequate size. Most pitches have some shade and have electricity and many have water and drainage. If you like a holiday with lots going on, you will like this one. Various activities are organised during high season including walks and sports tournaments, and daily canoe hire is available from the site. Once a week in July and August there is a 'soirée' (charged for) usually involving a barbecue or paella, with band and lots of free wine – worth catching! The site is busy and reservation is advisable. Used by a UK tour operators (35 pitches). English is spoken. The site is quite expensive in high season and you also pay more for a riverside pitch, but these have fine river views.

Facilities

Toilet facilities are in three modern unisex blocks. You will need to borrow a plug for the baby bath (€ 5 deposit). Washing machines and dryer. Motorcaravan service point. Well stocked shop. Pleasant bar with TV. Attractive, newly refurbished restaurant with terrace. Very impressive main pool, paddling pool, spa pool and two water slides. Tennis. Minigolf. Playground. Fishing. Canoe and kayak hire. Bicycle hire. Currency exchange. Small library. Off site: Golf 1 km. Riding 5 km.

Open: 1 April - 30 September.

Directions

Site is 6 km. south of Sarlat. From A20 take exit 55 (Souillac) towards Sarlat. Follow the D703 to Carsac and on to Montfort. At Montfort castle turn left for 2 km. down to the river.
GPS: N44:49.500 E01:15.233

Charges guide

Per person	€ 4,50 - € 7,00
child (2-9 yrs)	€ 2,50 - € 4,50
pitch incl. electricity	€ 9,00 - € 15,50
incl. full services	€ 12,00 - € 23,00

Camping Cheques accepted.

FR24130 Camping les Grottes de Roffy

Sainte Nathalène, F-24200 Sarlat-la-Canéda (Dordogne)

Tel: **05 53 59 15 61**. Email: **roffy@perigord.com** **www.alanrogers.com/FR24130**

About five kilometres east of Sarlat, Les Grottes de Roffy is a pleasantly laid out, family site. There are 162 clearly marked pitches, some very large, set on very well kept grass terraces. They have easy access and good views across an attractive valley. Some have plentiful shade, although others are more open, and all have electricity (6A). The reception, bar, restaurant and shop are located within converted farm buildings surrounding a semi-courtyard. The site shop is well stocked with a variety of goods and a tempting epicerie (home made on site) with plenty of ideas for the barbecue and to takeaway. In season there is something for all the family, with evening entertainment (including Jazz and Latin evenings) and daily activities for children. A variety of activities and excursions for all ages includes quad biking, pottery, massage and yoga. Conveniently located for Sarlat and all other Dordogne attractions, this is a good site for families. Used by tour operators.

Facilities

Two toilet blocks with modern facilities are more than adequate. Well stocked shop. Bar and 'gastronomique' restaurant with imaginative and sensibly priced menu. Takeaway (all amenities from 6/5). Good swimming pool complex comprising two deep pools (one heated), a fountain, paddling pool and heated jacuzzi. Tennis. Games room. Play area. Entertainment and activities for all ages. Off site: Fishing 2 km. Bicycle hire 7 km. Riding 10 km. Golf 15 km.

Open: 26 April - 21 September.

Directions

Take D47 east from Sarlat to Ste Nathalène. Just before Ste Nathalène the site is signed on the right hand side of the road. Turn here, and the site is about 800 m. along the lane.
GPS: N44:54.242 E01:16.926

Charges guide

Per person	€ 5,50 - € 7,20
child (2-7 yrs)	€ 4,00 - € 5,50
pitch	€ 7,10 - € 10,30
incl. electricity	€ 9,80 - € 13,10
with full services	€ 11,80 - € 15,10

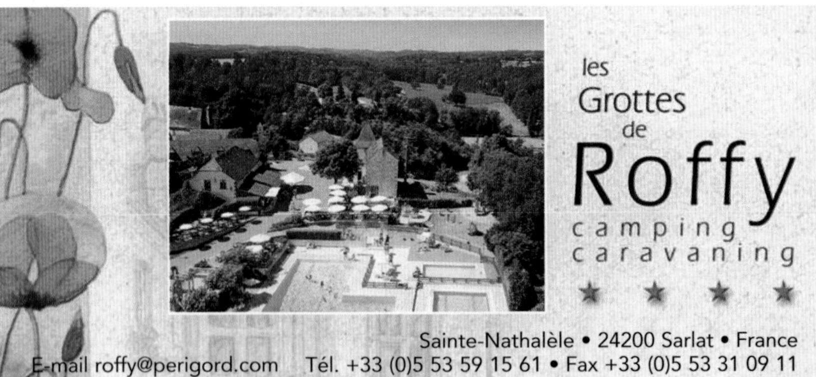

les
Grottes
de
Roffy
camping
caravaning
Sainte-Nathalèle • 24200 Sarlat • France
E-mail roffy@perigord.com Tél. +33 (0)5 53 59 15 61 • Fax +33 (0)5 53 31 09 11

The Travel Service BOOK THIS SITE CALL 01580 214000 ...we'll arrange everything

FR12080 Kawan Village les Genêts

Lac de Pareloup, F-12410 Salles-Curan (Aveyron)

Tel: **05 65 46 35 34**. Email: **contact@camping-les-genets.fr** **www.alanrogers.com/FR12080**

The 163 pitches include 80 grassy, mostly individual pitches for touring units. These are in two areas, one on each side of the entrance lane, and are divided by hedges, shrubs and trees. Most have electricity (6A) and many also have water and waste water drainage. This family run site slopes gently down to the shores of Lac de Pareloup and offers both family holiday and watersports facilities. A full animation and activities programme is organised in high season, and there is much to see and do in this very attractive corner of Aveyron.

Facilities

Two sanitary units with suite for disabled people. The older unit has been refurbished. Baby room. Laundry. Well stocked shop. Bar, restaurant, snacks (main season). Swimming pool, spa pool (from 1/6; unsupervised). Playground. Minigolf. Boules. Bicycle hire. Pedaloes, windsurfers, kayaks. Fishing licences available. WiFi in bar.

Open: 31 May - 11 September.

Directions

From Salles-Curan take D577 for about 4 km. and turn right into a narrow lane immediately after a sharp right hand bend. Site is signed at junction.
GPS: N44:10.670 E02:46.650

Charges guide

Per unit incl. 1 or 2 persons and 6A electricity	€ 13,00 - € 39,00
extra person	€ 4,00 - € 7,00

Camping Cheques accepted.

FR24160 Camping le Grand Dague

Route du Grand Dague, Atur, F-24750 Périgueux (Dordogne)

Tel: **05 53 04 21 01**. Email: **info@legranddague.fr** **www.alanrogers.com/FR24160**

Le Grand Dague is close to Périgueux, in a rural and tranquil setting. Built on a hillside, the site is clean, attractive and very spacious and 68 of the 93 pitches are for touring units. The pitches are only slightly sloping and are divided by tall, mature hedging (electricity 6A). There is a large field suitable for large motorhomes. Those with disabilities might find the roads quite steep. Several large, open grassy areas provide space for youngsters to play. A good range of equipment in the play area helps make this an ideal site for young families.

Facilities

Excellent, part heated sanitary facilities include a baby room and facilities for people with disabilities. Small shop (15/6-15/9). Bar, attractive restaurant with appetising menu and takeaway (both from June). Swimming pool, water slide and paddling pool (from early May). Pétanque. Minigolf. Play area. Fishing. Off site: Paintball outside gate. Riding 5 km. Bicycle hire 8 km. Golf 10 km.

Open: 31 May - 30 September.

Directions

From the Bordeaux - Brive inner ring road in Périgueux take D2 south, signed Atur. Campsite signed. Turn east at roundabout just before entering Atur. Site is in 3 km. GPS: N45:08.880 E00:46.657

Charges guide

Per unit incl. 2 persons and electricity	€ 17,50 - € 27,00
extra person	€ 4,50 - € 6,75
child (0-7 yrs)	€ 3,00 - € 4,50
animal	€ 2,00

FR16060 Camping Marco de Bignac

Lieu-dit Les Sablons, F-16170 Bignac (Charente)

Tel: **05 45 21 78 41**. Email: **info@marcodebignac.com** **www.alanrogers.com/FR16060**

The small village of Bignac is set in peaceful countryside not too far from the N10 road, north of Angoulême. This mature, British owned site is arranged alongside an attractive lake on a level, grassy meadow. The 87 large touring pitches are marked by a trees so there is shade, 80 have electricity (3/6A). There is a hedged swimming pool and plenty of grassy space for ball games. This site is popular with British visitors and is a peaceful, relaxing location for couples or young families. There is no noisy entertainment and all the activities are free of charge.

Facilities

Two traditional style toilet blocks have functional facilities. Washing machine. Bar all year with food high season and weekends. Small shop. Swimming pool (June-September, unsupervised). Football, badminton, tennis, pedaloes, minigolf, boules, fishing, all free. Library. Play area. Pets' corner. Organised activities in high season. A torch may be useful. Off site: Local markets. Riding 5 km. Golf 25 km.

Open: All year.

Directions

From N10 south of Poitiers, 14 km. north of Angoulême, take D11 west to Vars and Basse. Turn right onto D117 to Bignac. Site is signed at several junctions and in village (Camping Bignac). GPS: N45:47.857 E00:03.770

Charges guide

Per pitch incl. 2 persons	€ 15,00 - € 21,00
extra person	€ 3,00 - € 5,00
electricity (3/6A)	€ 2,00 - € 3,00

FR24170 Camping le Port de Limeuil

F-24480 Allés-sur-Dordogne (Dordogne)

Tel: **05 53 63 29 76**. Email: **didierbonvallet@aol.com** **www.alanrogers.com/FR24170**

At the confluence of Dordogne and Vézère rivers, opposite the picturesque village of Limieul, this delightful family site exudes a peaceful and relaxed ambience. There are 65 marked touring pitches on grass, some spacious and all with electricity (5A). The buildings are in traditional Périgourdine style and surrounded by flowers and shrubs. A sports area on a large open grassy space between the river bank and the main camping area adds to the feeling of space and provides an additional recreation and picnic area (there are additional unmarked pitches for tents and camper vans along the bank here).

Facilities

Two clean, modern toilet blocks provide excellent facilities. Bar/restaurant with snacks and takeaway (all 20/5-5/9). Small shop. Swimming pool with jacuzzi, paddling pool and children's slide (1/5-30/9). Badminton, football and boules. Mountain bike hire. Canoe hire, launched from the site's own pebble beach. WiFi in bar area. Off site: The pretty medieval village of Limeuil 200 m. Riding 1 km. Golf 10 km.

Open: 1 May - 30 September.

Directions

Site is 7 km. south of Le Bugue. From D51/D31E Le Buisson to Le Bugue road turn west towards Limeuil. Just before bridge into Limeuil, turn left (site signed), across another bridge. Site shortly on the right. GPS: N44:52.878 E00:53.444

Charges 2009

Per pitch incl. 2 persons	€ 14,00 - € 25,40
extra person	€ 4,50 - € 6,50
electricity (5A)	€ 2,50 - € 3,50

FR24180 Camping Caravaning Saint-Avit Loisirs

Le Bugue, F-24260 Saint Avit-de-Vialard (Dordogne)

Tel: **05 53 02 64 00**. Email: **contact@saint-avit-loisirs.com** **www.alanrogers.com/FR24180**

Although Saint Avit Loisirs is set in the middle of rolling countryside, far from the hustle and bustle of the main tourist areas of the Dordogne the facilities are first class, providing virtually everything you could possibly want without the need to leave the site. This makes it ideal for families with children of all ages. The site is in two sections. One part is dedicated to chalets and mobile homes, whilst the main section of the site contains 199 flat and mainly grassy, good sized pitches, 99 for touring, with electricity (6A), arranged in cul-de-sacs off a main access road.

Facilities

Three modern unisex toilet blocks provide high quality facilities, but could become overstretched (particularly laundry and dishwashing sinks) in high season. Shop, bar, restaurant, cafeteria. Outdoor swimming pool, children's pool, water slide, 'crazy river', heated indoor pool with jacuzzi, fitness room. Soundproofed disco. Minigolf. Boules. BMX track. Tennis. Play area. Canoe trips and other sporting activities. Good walks. Off site: Sarlat and Périgueux for markets and hypermarkets.

Open: 1 April - 27 September.

Directions

Site is 6 km. north of Le Bugue. From D710 Le Bugue - Périgueux road, turn west on narrow and bumpy C201 towards St Avit-de-Vialard. Follow road through St Avit, bearing right and site is 1.5 km. GPS: N44:57.082 E00:50.825

Charges guide

Per person	€ 4,00 - € 9,70
pitch	€ 6,20 - € 14,00
incl. electricity	€ 10,10 - € 19,30
incl. water and drainage	€ 12,90 - € 22,90

FR24310 Camping Caravaning la Bouquerie

F-24590 Saint Geniès-en-Périgord (Dordogne)

Tel: **05 53 28 98 22**. Email: **labouquerie@wanadoo.fr** **www.alanrogers.com/FR24310**

La Bouquerie is a well maintained site, situated within easy reach of the main road network in the Dordogne, but without any associated traffic noise. The main complex is based around some beautifully restored Périgordin buildings. It includes a shop and a bar and restaurant overlooking the pool complex, with a large outdoor terrace for fine weather. The excellent restaurant menu is varied and reasonably priced. Of the 180 pitches, 91 are used for touring units and these are of varying size (80-120 sq.m), flat and grassy, some with shade, and all with electrical connections (10A).

Facilities

Three well maintained toilet blocks with facilities for disabled visitors and baby rooms. Washing machines and covered drying lines. Small shop (15/5-15/9), takeaway food. Bar, restaurant (both 15/5-15/9). Paddling pool, large shallow pool (heated), large deep pool, sunbathing areas with loungers. Carp fishing in lake on site. Bicycle hire. Riding. Off site: Shops and restaurants, etc. in the nearby village of St Geniès.

Open: 19 April - 19 September.

Directions

Site is signed on east side D704 Sarlat - Montignac, about 500 m. north of junction with D64 St Geniès road. Turn off D704 at campsite sign and take first left turn signed La Bouquerie - site is straight ahead. GPS: N44:59.919 E01:14.729

Charges guide

Per pitch incl. 2 persons and electricity	€ 19,00 - € 25,50
extra person	€ 4,60 - € 6,50

FR24350 RCN le Moulin de la Pique

F-24170 Belvès (Dordogne)

Tel: **05 53 29 01 15**. Email: **info@rcn-lemoulindelapique.fr** **www.alanrogers.com/FR24350**

This high quality campsite set in the heart of the Dordogne has fine views looking up to the fortified town of Belvès. It is a splendid rural estate where there is plenty of space and a good mixture of trees and shrubs. Set in the grounds of a former mill, the superb traditional buildings date back to the 18th century. There are 200 level pitches with 154 for touring units, all with 6A electricity, a water point and drainage. The remainder are used for mobile homes to rent. The site is ideally suited for families with young and teenage children as there is so much to do, both on site and in the surrounding area.

Facilities

Three modern sanitary blocks include facilities for people with disabilities. Launderette. Shop. Bar. Restaurant. Snack bar and takeaway. Swimming pools (2 heated). Recreational lake. Playgrounds. Library. Fossil field. Sports field. Tennis. Minigolf. Boules. Satelite TV. Games room. Bicycle hire. Internet facilities. WiFi. Off site: Bars, restaurants and shops in the village of Belvès 2 km. Canoeing 2 km. Riding 5 km. Golf 7 km.

Open: 12 April - 11 October.

Directions

Site is 35 km. southwest of Sarlat on the D710, about 7 km. south of Siorac-en-Périgord. GPS: N44:45.737 E01:00.847

Charges guide

Per pitch incl. 2 persons, electricity and water	€ 18,00 - € 45,50
extra person (over 6 yrs)	€ 5,50

FR24560 Domaine le Cro Magnon

Le Raisse, Allas-les-Mines, F-24220 Saint Cyprien (Dordogne)

Tel: **05 53 29 13 70**. Email: **contact@domaine-cro-magnon.com** **www.alanrogers.com/FR24560**

Le Cro Magnon is pleasantly situated in the heart of the Dordogne valley in the Périgord Noir. The 160 spacious, mostly shady pitches are divided in two different types: tent pitches without electricity and serviced pitches (6A electricity hook up, water and waste water drainage). The site also offers various accommodation for rent. The swimming complex includes two pools (one outdoor, one indoor), one heated, water slides, a jacuzzi and a sauna. Near the entrance of the site are a snack bar, pizzeria, bar, a well stocked shop and the reception. From a viewpoint on the site there are incredible views over the Dordogne valley.

Facilities

Two toilet blocks provide the usual facilities including facilities for disabled visitors. Washing machines. Motorcaravan services. Shop. Bar with TV. Snack bar and takeaway. Swimming pools with slides, jacuzzi and sauna. Multisport court. Boules. Play area. Off site: Canoeing, walking and cycling. Fishing.

Open: 11 May - 30 September.

Directions

From the A20 (Limoges - Brive) take exit 55 for Souillac and Sarlat. In Sarlat take D57 to Vézac, then D703 to St Cyprien. In St Cyprien follow D703, then D50 (left) to Berbiguières and follow signs for site. GPS: N44:50.165 E01:03.754

Charges guide

Per person (over 4 yrs)	€ 3,40 - € 7,00
pitch	€ 5,00 - € 10,40
incl. services	€ 8,10 - € 17,10

FR46240 Camping Quercy Vacances

Mas de la Combe, F-46090 Sainte Pierre-Lafeuille (Lot)

Tel: **05 65 36 87 15**. Email: **quercy-vacances@wanadoo.fr** **www.alanrogers.com/FR46240**

This clean and well run site is owned by a young, English speaking, French couple who are determined to improve the facilities and ambiance. It is only 4.5 km. from the A20 and is an ideal stopover site for holidaymakers travelling to and from Spain. However, it is better than just a stopover site and is worth staying a few extra days. It has 70 large unmarked touring pitches most of which have 6/10A hook-ups. The site facilities include a rustic bar and restaurant.

Facilities

Clean, modern toilet block, recently refurbished. Facilities for campers with disabilities are located in a separate building adjacent to the camping area. Small basic shop. Bar and takeaway. Restaurant serving specials like paella and couscous once a week. Large round swimming pool (20/6-15/9), unsuitable for young children, minimum depth 1.2 m. Live music, dancing (July/Aug). Small play area. Off site: Riding 5 km. Bicycle hire, fishing 10 km.

Open: 1 April - 31 October.

Directions

Leave A20 exit 57 (Cahors). Shortly turn left on N20 and then turn right on small un-named road (site signed) before reaching St Pierre Lafeuille (about 4.5 km. from the A20). Site on right in about 600 m. GPS: N44:31.889 E01:27.585

Charges guide

Per person	€ 3,80 - € 5,00
pitch	€ 5,00 - € 8,80
electricity (6/10A)	€ 3,30 - € 5,50

FR46010 Castel Camping le Domaine de la Paille Basse

F-46200 Souillac-sur-Dordogne (Lot)
Tel: **05 65 37 85 48**. Email: **paille.basse@wanadoo.fr** **www.alanrogers.com/FR46010**

Set in a rural location some 8 km. from Souillac, this family owned site is easily accessible from the N20 and well placed to take advantage of excursions into the Dordogne. It is part of a large domain of 80 hectares, all available to campers for walks and recreation. The site is quite high up and there are excellent views over the surrounding countryside. The 262 pitches are in two main areas – one is level in cleared woodland with good shade, and the other on grass without shade. Numbered and marked, the pitches are a minimum 100 sq.m. and often considerably more. All have electricity (3/6A) with about 80 fully serviced. The site is well placed to take advantage of excursions into the Dordogne. A wide range of activities and entertainment are organised in high season. The site can get very busy in high season and is popular with three tour operators. If you like a livelier type of site, you will enjoy La Paille Basse.

Facilities

Three main toilet blocks all have modern equipment and are kept very clean. Laundry. Small shop with a large selection of wine. Restaurant, bar (open until 02.00 in high season), terrace, pizza takeaway. Crêperie. main swimming pool, a smaller one, paddling pool (unheated), water slides. Sun terrace. Sound-proofed disco (three times weekly in season). TV (with satellite). Cinema below the pool area. Tennis. Play area. Library. Off site: Golf 4 km.

Open: 15 May - 15 September.

Directions

From Souillac take D15 and then D62 roads leading northwest towards Salignac-Eyvignes and after 6 km. turn right at site sign and follow steep and narrow approach road for 2 km.
GPS: N44:56.836 E01:26.354

Charges guide

Per person	€ 5,40 - € 7,00
child (under 7 yrs)	€ 3,80 - € 5,00
pitch	€ 7,80 - € 10,80
incl. water and drainage	€ 9,80 - € 13,00
dog	€ 4,00

Camping Cheques accepted.

Le Domaine de la Paille Basse, half way between Rocamadour and the caves of Lascaux, is an excellent base for excursions enabling you to visit the highlights of two régions. Situated at the top of a hill, La Paille Basse is a restored medieval village in the heart of 200 acres of wooded land. La Paille Basse has carefully combined architectural beauty and modernity, fitting its facilities within the original buildings.
Castel Camping La Paille Basse
★★★★
46200 Souillac
Tel: 0033 565 37 85 48
Fax: 0033 565 37 09 58
LES CASTELS
Camping Cheque

FR46320 Camping les Rives du Célé

Domaine du Surgié, F-46100 Figeac (Lot)

Tel: **05 61 64 88 54**. Email: **contact@marc-montmija.com** **www.alanrogers.com/FR46320**

Very conveniently placed, 2 km. from the town centre of Figeac, this site has a rural location. It is a campsite where activities on site and in the surrounding areas are numerous and it would therefore suit an active family including teenagers. Navigation around the park is easy for larger units due to good design. There are 163 pitches, 103 for touring units, the remaining 60 for mobile homes and gites, all of which are for rent. The pitches are level, with a mixture of shade and sun and all have 10A electricity. The site is split into different areas with the aquatic centre next to the camping area. The restaurant is on the other side of the aquatic centre with further leisure activities on the other side of the restaurant. This works very well as it tends to keep the camping area quieter. The site is very well cared for and with the generous pitches, there is a sense of spaciousness, tranquillity and calm. The restaurant and the aquatic centre look to be fairly new and are high quality facilities. There is a varied programme of organised activities and entertainment laid on, together with a daily children's club. There are many places of interest to visit in this area, most noticeably the vineyards which offer many different types of fine wine local to the area.

Facilities

Three fully equipped, modern sanitary blocks include facilities for babies and disabled people. Laundry. Shop, bar, restaurant and takeaway (all from 30/4). Swimming pool complex. Sports competitions and party nights with themed dining. Children's clubs. Canoeing. Fishing. Minigolf. Boules. Bicycle hire. Off site: Riding 2 km.

Open: 30 April - 30 September.

Directions

From Cahors, take the D653 to Figeac from where the site is well signed. GPS: N44:36.593 E02:03.009

Charges guide

Per unit incl. 2 persons and electricity	€ 12,00 - € 39,00
extra person	€ 3,50 - € 6,00
child (3-12 yrs)	€ 2,00 - € 3,00

FR47110 Le Cabri Holiday Village

Route de Savignac, F-47120 Duras (Lot-et-Garonne)

Tel: **05 53 83 81 03**. Email: **holidays@lecabri.eu.com** **www.alanrogers.com/FR47110**

This is a good quality site set in 14 acres of beautiful countryside, on the border of the Dordogne and the Lot-et-Garonne, between the two rivers of the same name. The views are superb. Le Cabri Holiday Village is an English owned and run, small holiday complex. The new owners, Peter and Eileen Marston who are keen caravanners themselves, have developed 24 new spacious pitches (generally 150 sq.m), all with electricity (4/16A) and water. The open, level pitches are all on hardstandings surrounded by grass and separated by shrubs. Open all year round, the site has excellent facilities including a swimming pool, a fishing pond and other leisure facilities.

Facilities

A recently refurbished sanitary block is centrally located, heated in low season and includes three new private cabins. Separate cabin for disabled visitors. Washing machines, dryers and ironing board. Shop (all year). Restaurant (15/3-20/1) with occasional entertainment year round. Internet access. Swimming pool. Large play area. Boules. Well stocked fishing pond. Off site: Riding 1 km. Golf (international course) 10 km. Tennis 1 km. Watersports 7 km. Canoeing 8 km.

Open: All year.

Directions

In Duras, look for the D203 and follow signs for site. It is less than 1 km. away.
GPS: N44:40.978 E00:11.169

Charges guide

Per person	€ 4,00 - € 5,00
child (under 11 yrs)	€ 2,00 - € 3,00
pitch	€ 5,00 - € 7,00
electricity (4/10A)	€ 3,00 - € 5,00

Special offer (not July/Aug): stay 6 nights, pay for only 5.

FR47010 Kawan Village Moulin du Périé

F-47500 Sauveterre-la-Lemance (Lot-et-Garonne)

Tel: **05 53 40 67 26**. Email: **moulinduperie@wanadoo.fr** **www.alanrogers.com/FR47010**

Set in a quiet area and surrounded by woodlands this peaceful little site is well away from much of the tourist bustle. It has 125 reasonably sized, grassy pitches, all with 6A electricity, divided by mixed trees and bushes with most having good shade. All are extremely well kept, as indeed is the entire site. The attractive front courtyard is complemented by an equally pleasant terrace at the rear. Two small, clean swimming pools overlook a shallow, spring water lake, ideal for inflatable boats and paddling and bordering the lake, a large grass field is popular for games. The picturesque old mill buildings, adorned with flowers and creepers, now house the bar and restaurant. The food is to be recommended here, as is the owner's extensive knowledge of wine that he is pleased to share with visitors. A quiet, friendly site with regular visitors – reservation is advised for July/Aug. Bergerac Airport is an hour away so it may suit those choosing a mobile home or bungalow tent and wanting to travel light.

Facilities

Two clean, modern and well maintained toilet blocks include facilities for disabled visitors. Motorcaravan services. Fridge, barbecue, chemical toilet hire (book in advance). Basic shop. Bar/reception, restaurant and takeaway. Two small swimming pools (no Bermuda-style shorts). Boules. Outdoor chess. Playground. trampoline. Small indoor play area. Bicycle hire. Organised activities in high season; including canoeing, riding, wine tasting visits, sightseeing trips, barbecues, gastronomic meals. Winter caravan storage. Off site: Fishing 1 km. Small supermarket in village and larger stores in Fumel.

Open: 15 May - 18 September.

Directions

From D710, Fumel - Périgueux, turn southeast into Sauveterre-le-Lemance. Turn left (northeast) at far end on C201 signed Château Sauveterre and Loubejec (site also signed). Site is 3 km. on right. GPS: N44:35.410 E01:02.857

Charges guide

Per unit incl. 2 persons	€ 13,05 - € 21,85
incl. electricity	€ 16,95 - € 25,75
extra person	€ 4,20 - € 6,50
child (under 7 yrs)	€ 1,80 - € 3,45
animal	€ 2,15 - € 4,10

Camping Cheques accepted.

FR23010 Castel Camping Château de Poinsouze

Route de la Châtre, B.P. 12, F-23600 Boussac-Bourg (Creuse)

Tel: **05 55 65 02 21**. Email: **info.camping-de.poinsouze@orange.fr** **www.alanrogers.com/FR23010**

Le Château de Poinsouze is a well established site with pitches arranged on the open, gently sloping, grassy park to one side of the Château's main drive – a beautiful plane tree avenue. It is a well designed, high quality site. The 145 touring pitches, some with lake frontage, all have electricity (6-25A), water, drainage and 66 have sewerage connections. The site has a friendly family atmosphere, there are organised activities in main season including dances, children's games and crafts, family triathlons and there are marked walks around the park and woods. All facilities are open all season. This is a top class site with a formula which should ensure a stress-free, enjoyable family holiday. Boussac (2.5 km) has a market every Thursday morning. The massive 12-15th-century fortress, Château de Boussac, is open daily all year. The Château (not open to the public) lies across the lake from the site. Exceptionally well restored outbuildings on the opposite side of the drive house a new restaurant serving superb cuisine, other facilities and the pool area.

Facilities

High quality, sanitary unit, washing machines, dryer, ironing, suites for disabled people. Motorcaravan services. Well stocked shop. Takeaway. Bar, internet, two satellite TVs, library. Restaurant with new mini-bar for low season. Heated swimming pool, slide, children's pool. Fenced playground. Pétanque. Bicycle hire. Free fishing in the lake, boats and lifejackets can be hired. Sports facilities. Dogs are only allowed for one overnight stay between 5/7-16/8.

Open: 8 May - 13 September.

Directions

Site entrance is 2.5 km. north of Boussac on D917 (towards La Châtre). GPS: N46:22.356 E02:12.157

Charges 2009

Per unit incl. 2 persons	€ 13,00 - € 22,00
incl. electricity (6A) water, waste water	€ 16,00 - € 25,00
extra person	€ 3,00 - € 6,00
child (2-7 yrs)	€ 2,00 - € 5,00
dog	€ 3,00

Camping Cheques accepted.

FR23030 Creuse Nature Naturisme

Route de Bétête (D15), F-23600 Boussac (Creuse)

Tel: **05 55 65 18 01**. Email: **creuse.nature@wanadoo.fr** **www.alanrogers.com/FR23030**

This is a very spacious and well maintained naturist site set in the beautiful Limousin region in the centre of France. The 100 large grassy pitches, some slightly sloping, are laid out in an open wooded parkland setting. The 80 touring pitches are mainly positioned around the perimeter of the site or the small fishing lake. A central feature is the pool, bar and restaurant complex. Various activities are organised for all the family and there are many footpaths to enjoy around the borders of the site.

Facilities

Four modern, very clean toilet blocks with the usual facilities (open plan, so little privacy). Facilities for visitors with disabilities. Dishwashing and laundry facilities. Small shop (baker calls). Indoor (heated) and outdoor pools. Paddling pool. Sauna. Bar (all season). Restaurant (July/Aug). Archery (high season). Boules. Bicycle hire. Lake fishing. Internet access. Gas barbecues only on pitches. Off site: Small market town of Boussac 5 km.

Open: 15 April - 31 October.

Directions

Boussac lies 35 km. west of Montluçon, midway between the A20 and A71 autoroutes. In Boussac, site is well signed. Take D15 west for about 3 km. Site is on right. GPS: N46:21.060 E02:10.660

Charges guide

Per person	€ 3,50 - € 6,50
child (under 3 yrs)	free - € 2,00
child (3-11 yrs)	€ 2,50 - € 4,00
pitch with electricity	€ 13,50 - € 15,50

FR01050 Camping des Gorges de l'Oignin

Rue du Lac, F-01580 Matafelon-Granges (Ain)

Tel: **04 74 76 80 97**. Email: **camping.lesgorgesdeloignin@wanadoo.fr** **www.alanrogers.com/FR01050**

This family run, terraced site (English spoken) offers lovely views across the lake to the hills beyond. There are 132 good sized pitches, 70 for touring, separated by young trees and flowering shrubs and with a choice of grass or hardstanding. About half have their own water point and all have 10A electricity. Twin axle caravans are not accepted. The reception, bar/restaurant and pool complex are at the top of the site with a steep road down to the terraces and the rest of the campsite. At the bottom of the site is a large grassy area next to the lake for sunbathing and activities.

Facilities

Two modern, well equipped and clean toilet blocks with all the usual facilities except facilities for disabled people. Bar/restaurant, takeaway and TV room (July/Aug). Swimming pool, paddling pool and new 'lazy river' (1/6-30/9). Playground and sports area. Swimming, fishing and boating on the lake (no motorboats). Off site: Golf 2 km. Riding 2 km. Matafelon 800 m. Thoirette 6 km. Oyonnax with range of shops, market, bar/restaurants 10 km.

Open: 1 April - 30 September.

Directions

Matafelon is 40 km. east of Bourg-en-Bresse. Leave autoroute A404 at Oyonnax, exit 11 and head west on D13 to Matafelon (10 km). On entering village and opposite the Mairie turn left, signed camping, and descend to site (800 m). GPS: N46:15.321 E5:33.430

Charges guide

Per unit incl. 2 persons and electricity	€ 15,20 - € 23,00
extra person	€ 3,40 - € 4,80
child (3-10 yrs)	€ 2,20 - € 3,60

FR07030 Yelloh! Village Soleil Vivarais

Soleil Vivarais, F-07120 Sampzon (Ardèche)

Tel: **04 66 73 97 39**. Email: **info@yellohvillage-soleil-vivarais.com** **www.alanrogers.com/FR07030**

A large, lively, high quality site bordering the River Ardèche, complete with beach, Soleil Vivarais offers much to visitors, particularly families with children. Of the 350 pitches, 110 generously sized, shady and level pitches are for tourers, all with 10A electricity. Rock pegs are advised. During the day the proximity of the swimming pools to the terraces of the bar and restaurant make it a pleasantly social area. In the evening the purpose built stage, with professional lighting and sound system, provides an ideal platform for the regular family entertainment programmes.

Facilities

Modern, clean, well equipped toilet blocks, facilities for people with disabilities. Washing machines, dryers. Motorcaravan services. Small supermarket. Bar/restaurant, takeaways and pizzas. Heated pool. Fishing. Boules. Archery. Bicycle hire. River bathing. Extensive animation programme June - Aug. Off site: Riding 800 m.

Open: 5 April - 14 September.

Directions

On D579, 2 km. south of Ruoms, turn left at roundabout, signed Vallon-Pont-d'Arc. Shortly turn right over river bridge, site on right. GPS: N44:25.774 E04:21.317

Charges 2009

Per unit incl. 2 persons	€ 15,00 - € 43,00
extra person	€ 5,00 - € 7,00

tel: +33 466 739 739 www.yellohvillage.com

Winner Alan Rogers Awards 2008

FR07120 Camping Nature Parc l'Ardéchois

Route touristique des Gorges, F-07150 Vallon-Pont-d'Arc (Ardèche)

Tel: **04 75 88 06 63**. Email: **ardecamp@bigfoot.com** **www.alanrogers.com/FR07120**

This very high quality, family run site is within walking distance of Vallon-Pont-d'Arc. It borders the River Ardèche and canoe trips are run, professionally, direct from the site. This campsite is ideal for families with younger children seeking an active holiday. The facilities are comprehensive and of an extremely high standard, particularly the central toilet block. Of the 244 pitches, there are 225 for tourers, separated by trees and individual shrubs. All have electrical connections (6/10A) and 125 have full services. Forming a focal point are the bar and restaurant (good menus), with a terrace and stage overlooking the attractive heated pool. There is also a large paddling pool and sunbathing terrace. For children, there is a well thought out play area plus plenty of other space for youngsters to play, both on the site and along the river. Activities are organised throughout the season; these are family based – no discos. Patrols at night ensure a good night's sleep. Access to the site is easy and suitable for large outfits. Member of 'Leading Campings Group'.

Facilities

Two well equipped toilet blocks, one superb with everything working automatically. Facilities are of the highest standard, very clean and include good facilities for babies, those with disabilities, washing up and laundry. Four private bathrooms to hire. Washing machines. Well stocked shop. Swimming pool and paddling pool (no Bermuda shorts). Tennis. Very good play area. Internet access. Organised activities, canoe trips. Only gas barbecues are permitted. Communal barbecue area.
Off site: Canoeing, rafting, walking, riding, mountain biking, golf, rock climbing, bowling, wine tasting and dining. Vallon-Pont-d'Arc 800 m. Explore the real Ardèche on the minor roads and visit Labaume, Bazakuc and Largentière (market Tuesday).

Open: 1 April - 30 September.

Directions

From Vallon-Pont-d'Arc (western end of the Ardèche Gorge) at a roundabout go east on the D290. Site entrance is shortly on the right.
GPS: N44:23.873 E04:23.929

Charges guide

Per pitch incl. 2 persons and electricity € 42,00

France

FR07140 Camping les Lavandes

Le Village, F-07170 Darbres (Ardèche)

Tel: **04 75 94 20 65**. Email: **sarl.leslavandes@online.fr** **www.alanrogers.com/FR07140**

Situated to the northeast of Aubenas, in a quieter part of this region, Les Lavandes is surrounded by magnificent countryside, vineyards and orchards. The enthusiastic French owners, who speak good English, run a site that appeals to all nationalities. The 70 pitches (58 for touring) are arranged on low terraces separated by a variety of trees and shrubs that give welcome shade in summer. Electricity 6/10A is available to all. Visit at the end of May to see the campsite trees laden with luscious cherries. Organised activities include wine tasting, shows, musical evenings and children's games. A ride along the panoramic road to Mirabel is a must. Although slightly less sophisticated than some others in the region, this site should appeal to those seeking the real France for a pleasant family holiday. Traditional buildings house the reception (full of tourist information including a touch screen), shop, restaurant, takeaway and cosy bar offering excellent views over the swimming pool to the village (just a stroll away) and hillside beyond.

Facilities

Comprehensive and well maintained facilities, baby room and excellent facilities for disabled people. Washing machine. Small shop (1/7-31/8). Bar, terrace (1/6-31/8). Restaurant (15/6-31/8). Takeaway (15/4-31/8). Swimming pool, paddling pool and sunbathing areas. Two small play areas. Games room. Outdoor chess. Electric barbecues are not permitted. Off site: Fishing 1 km. Riding 3 km. Tennis 5 km. Bicycle hire 15 km. Canoeing, walking, cycling, riding, carting nearby. Climbing. Wonderful area for birds.

Open: 15 April - 30 September.

Directions

Site is best approached from the south. From Montélimar take N102 towards Aubenas. After Villeneuve, in Lavilledieu, turn right at traffic lights on D224 to Darbres (10 km). In Darbres turn sharp left by post office (care needed) and follow site signs. GPS: N44:38.873 E04:30.203

Charges guide

Per unit incl. 2 persons	€ 12,50 - € 18,50
extra person	€ 2,80 - € 3,50
electricity	€ 3,50

FR07150 Camping Domaine de Gil

Route de Vals-les-Bains, Ucel, F-07200 Aubenas (Ardèche)

Tel: **04 75 94 63 63**. Email: **info@domaine-de-gil.com** **www.alanrogers.com/FR07150**

Under new ownership, this very attractive and well organised, smaller site in a less busy part of the Ardèche should appeal to couples and families with younger children. The 80, good sized, level pitches, 43 for touring, are surrounded by a variety of trees offering plenty of shade. All have 10A electricity. The focal point of the site is formed by the beautiful swimming pool, paddling pool and large sunbathing area, with the bar, restaurant and children's play areas all adjacent.

Facilities

Modern well appointed toilet block, washing machine and iron. Motorcaravan services. Basic shop. Bar/restaurant, takeaway (from June). Heated swimming pool, paddling pool. Two play areas. Boules, minigolf, football and tennis. Canoeing, boating and fishing. Organised activities in high season. Only gas and electric barbecues. Off site: Shops at Vals-les-Bain 1.5 km. Aubenas with shops, restaurants, bars 3 km. Canoe trips, canyoning on river Ardèche. Bicycle hire, riding 4 km.

Open: 14 April - 23 September.

Directions

Site north of Aubenas. From southeast (N102), after tunnel, turn right, roundabout (signed Ucel), cross river into Pont d'Ucel (3.5 tonne limit). Bear right and at roundabout, last exit (signed Ucel). Shortly turn left (signed Ucel D218), then right (Ucel D578B). Site is 2 km. GPS: N44:38.558 E04:22.775

Charges guide

Per unit incl. 2 persons	€ 14,00 - € 29,00
extra person	€ 3,50 - € 5,75
electricity	€ 4,00

FR26210 Camping les Bois du Chatelas

Route de Dieulefit, F-26460 Bourdeaux (Drôme)

Tel: **04 75 00 60 80**. Email: **contact@chatelas.com** **www.alanrogers.com/FR26210**

Located at the heart of the the Drôme Provencale, Les Bois du Chatelas is a smart, family run site which has undergone many recent improvements. The site is just 1 km. from the delightful village of Bourdeaux which offers a good range of shops, cafés, etc. There are 120 pitches here of which 69 are occupied by mobile homes. Although situated on a hillside, the pitches are level and of a good size. They all offer electricity, water and drainage. Les Bois du Chatelas is a particularly good choice for those seeking an active holiday. The long distance GR9 footpath passes through the site and there are very many walking and cycle routes close at hand. A popular aquagym is organised in the large outdoor pool in peak season. In the high season, a lively entertainment programme is organized as well as a number of cycling and walking excursions. A 'Sites et Paysages' member.

Facilities

Two heated toilet blocks (on upper and lower levels) with facilities for babies and disabled people (note: the site is hilly and may be unsuitable). Shop. Bar. Restaurant. Indoor swimming pool. Outdoor pool with water slide, waterfall and jacuzzi. Sports pitch. Archery. Play area. Bicycle hire. Entertainment and excursion programme (July/Aug). Mobile homes for rent. Off site: Rafting and canoe trips. Riding 5 km. Fishing 1 km. Very extensive walking and cycle (mountain bike) opportunities. Vercors mountain range.

Open: 7 April - 30 September.

Directions

From the north, leave A7 at exit 16 and join the eastbound D104 to Crest. Upon reaching Crest take D538 south to Bourdeaux and continue towards Dieulefit. Site is on the left 1 km. beyond Bourdeaux and is well signed. GPS: N44:34.737 E05:07.674

Charges guide

Per unit incl. 2 persons	€ 14,00 - € 24,00
extra person	€ 4,20 - € 5,00
child (1-7 yrs)	€ 2,70 - € 2,90
electricity (10A)	€ 4,30 - € 4,50

FR26290 Camping Château de Galaure

F-26330 Châteauneuf-de-Galaure (Drôme)

Tel: **04 75 68 65 22** **www.alanrogers.com/FR26290**

Châteauneuf-de-Galaure is tucked away at the heart of the Drôme département, between Lyon and Valence. This is a spacious site, extending over 11 hectares, with 200 large, grassy pitches (mostly with 10A electrical connections). The river Galaure runs close by and there are three swimming pools on site, including one for children and a large water slide. Châteauneuf is a typically sleepy Provençal village with a couple of good restaurants and surrounded by some very fine countryside. This is excellent walking country and the site's owners will be delighted to recommend routes. Châteauneuf has a fine Franciscan abbey which is currently being restored. A little further afield, Hauterives, is home to the Palais Idéal du Facteur Cheval. This is surely one of Europe's most unexpected tourist sights, an amazing palace built by a postman over a period of 33 years.

Facilities

Two swimming pools with water slides. Children's pool. Play area. Tourist information. Off site: River (fishing) 250 m. Cycle and walking tracks in the surrounding hills. Palais Idéal 8 km.

Open: All year.

Directions

From Lyon head south on the A7 leaving at exit 12 (Chanas) and head east on the D519 as far as Bougé-Chambalud. Head south on the D53 as far as Chateauneuf de Galaure, from where site is clearly signed. GPS: N45:13.413 E04:57.118

Charges guide

Per unit incl. 2 persons and electricity	€ 30,00

FR04120 Camping Indigo Forcalquier

Route de Sigonce, F-04300 Forcalquier (Alpes-de-Haute-Provence)

Tel: **04 92 75 27 94**. Email: **forcalquier@camping-indigo.com** **www.alanrogers.com/FR04120**

Although Camping Indigo is an urban site, there are extensive views over the surrounding country where there are some excellent walks. The pitches are on grass and are of good size, all with electricity, six fully serviced. The site is secure, with an electronic barrier (card deposit required) and there is no entry between 22.30 and 07.00. Local guides lead tours of the historic town and areas. This is an excellent base for visiting Forcalquier, a 15th-century fortified hill town and the Monday market (the best in Haute Provence).

Facilities

Two refurbished toilet blocks with washbasins in cubicles and excellent facilities for disabled visitors. Bar. Snack bar and takeaway (15/6-1/9). Play area. Heated swimming pool. Off site: Shops, banks etc. in town centre 200 m.

Open: 4 April - 18 October.

Directions

From town centre, follow signs for Digne, Sisteron for 400 m, turning sharp left onto Sigonce road after Esso petrol station, then first right and site is 200 m. GPS: N43:57.660 E05:47.226

Charges 2009

Per unit with 2 persons	€ 18,40 - € 27,40
extra person	€ 4,80 - € 5,80

FR69010 Camping Indigo Lyon

Porte de Lyon, F-69570 Dardilly (Rhône)

Tel: **04 78 35 64 55**. Email: **lyon@camping-indigo.com** **www.alanrogers.com/FR69010**

Camping International is a modern overnight site just off the A6 autoroute. Kept busy with overnight trade, reception and the café (in main season) open until quite late. There are 180 separate numbered plots. Many have electricity (10A), water and waste water drainage. Those for caravans are mostly on hardstandings on a slight slope, with another small grassy part, while those for tents are on a flatter area of grass. A very large commercial centre has been developed just outside the site, with eight hotels, restaurants, a supermarket, petrol station, etc. There is some road noise.

Facilities

Three heated sanitary blocks have free hot water (solar heated) and washbasins in cabins. Dishwashing and laundry sinks. Baby changing facilities and washing machines. Motorcaravan service point. Swimming and paddling pools (1/6-15/9, supervised and free). Playground. TV room. Games room. Reading room (books and local information). Boules. Picnic and barbecue area.

Open: All year.

Directions

Travelling south, do not take A46 motorway around Lyon, continue on A6, take exit Limonest, Dardilly, Porte de Lyon. About 8 km. north of Lyon tunnel; turn left for Porte de Lyon (well signed). GPS: N45:49.221 E04:45.624

Charges 2009

Per unit incl. 2 persons	€ 20,40 - € 25,20
extra person	€ 4,10 - € 4,40

Camping Cheques accepted.

FR84020 Domaine Naturiste de Bélézy

F-84410 Bédoin (Vaucluse)

Tel: **04 90 65 60 18**. Email: **info@belezy.com** **www.alanrogers.com/FR84020**

At the foot of Mont Ventoux, surrounded by beautiful scenery, Bélézy is an excellent naturist site with many amenities and activities and the ambience is relaxed and comfortable. The 238 marked pitches are set amongst many varieties of trees and shrubs. Electricity points (12A) are plentiful but long leads are necessary. So far as naturism is concerned, the emphasis is on personal choice, the only stipulation being the requirement for complete nudity in the pools and pool area. An area of natural parkland with an orchard, fishpond and woodland, has a good range of sports facilities.

Facilities

Sanitary blocks differ – newer ones are excellent, with showers and washbasins in cubicles, others have hot showers in the open air, screened by stone dividers. One block has a superb children's section. Shop (22/3-21/9). Excellent restaurant and takeaway. Two swimming pools. Sauna. Tennis. Adventure play area. Activities in low season. Archery. Guided walks. Children's club. Hydrotherapy centre (1/4-30/9). Barbecues are prohibited. Pets are not accepted. Off site: Bédoin 1.5 km.

Open: 23 March - 2 October.

Directions

From A7 autoroute or RN7 at Orange, take D950 southeast to Carpentras, then northeast via D974 to Bédoin. Site is signed in Bédoin, being about 1.5 km. northeast of the village. GPS: N44:08.011 E05:11.247

Charges guide

Per unit incl. 2 persons and electricity	€ 27,00 - € 43,00
extra person	€ 5,00 - € 8,50

Camping Cheques accepted.

FR04010 Sunêlia Hippocampe

Route de Napoléon, F-04290 Volonne (Alpes-de-Haute-Provence)

Tel: **04 92 33 50 00**. Email: **camping@l-hippocampe.com** **www.alanrogers.com/FR04010**

Hippocampe is a friendly family run, 'all action' lakeside site, organised with families in mind and situated in a beautiful area of France. The perfumes of thyme, lavender and wild herbs are everywhere and the higher hills of Haute Provence are not too far away. There are 447 level, numbered pitches (221 for touring units), medium to very large (130 sq.m) in size. All have electricity (10A) and 243 have water and drainage, most are separated by bushes and cherry trees. Some of the best pitches border the lake. The site's restaurant, bar, takeaway and shop have all been completely renewed. Games, aerobics, competitions, entertainment and shows, plus a daily club for younger family members are organised in July/August. A soundproof underground disco is set well away from the pitches and is very popular with teenage customers. Staff tour the site at night ensuring a good night's sleep. The site is, however, much quieter in low season and, with its good discounts, is the time for those who do not want or need entertaining. The Gorges du Verdon is a sight not to be missed and rafting, paragliding or canoe trips can be booked from the site's own tourist information office. Being on the lower slopes of the hills of Haute-Provence, the surrounding area is good for both walking and mountain biking. All in all, this is a very good site for an active or restful holiday and is suitable for outfits of all sizes. English is spoken.

Facilities

Toilet blocks vary from old to modern, all with good clean facilities that include washbasins in cabins. Washing machines. Motorcaravan service point. Bread available (from 26/4). Shop, bar, restaurant and pizzeria (26/4-7/9). Large, pool complex (from 5/4, heated in early and late seasons). Tennis. Fishing. Canoeing. Boules. Several sports facilities (some with free instruction). Charcoal barbecues are not permitted. Off site: Village of Volonne 600 m. Bicycle hire 2 km. Riding 12 km. Various sporting opportunities.

Open: 22 March - 30 September.

Directions

Approaching from the north turn off N85 across river bridge to Volonne, then right to site. From the south right on D4, 1 km. before Château Arnoux.
GPS: N44:06.366 E06:00.933

Charges guide

Per unit incl. 2 persons	€ 13,00 - € 27,00
incl. electricity	€ 16,00 - € 32,00
incl. water/drainage	€ 16,00 - € 39,00
extra person (over 4 yrs)	€ 3,00 - € 6,50

Special low season offers.
Camping Cheques accepted.

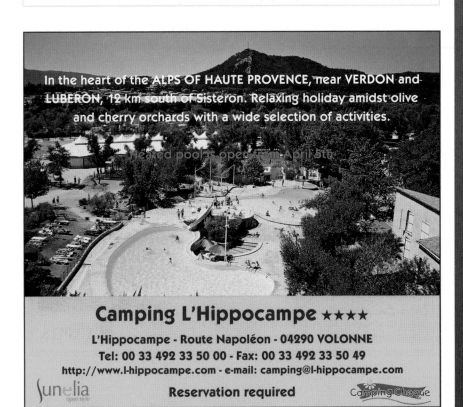

FR04020 Castel Camping le Domaine du Verdon

Domaine du Verdon, F-04120 Castellane (Alpes-de-Haute-Provence)

Tel: **04 92 83 61 29**. Email: **contact@camp-du-verdon.com** **www.alanrogers.com/FR04020**

Close to the 'Route des Alpes' and the Gorges du Verdon. Two heated swimming pools and numerous on-site activities during high season help to keep non-canoeists here. Du Verdon is a large level site, part meadow, part wooded, with 500 partly shaded, rather stony pitches (390 for tourists). Numbered and separated by bushes, they vary in size, have 6A electricity, and 125 also have water and waste water. They are mostly separate from the mobile homes (60) and pitches used by tour operators (110). Some overlook the unfenced river Verdon, so watch the children. This is a very popular holiday area, the gorge, canoeing and rafting being the main attractions, ideal for active families. One can walk to Castellane without using the main road. Dances and discos in July and August suit all age groups – the latest finishing time is around 23.00. (after that time patrols make sure that the site is quiet). The site is popular and very busy in July and August.

Facilities

Refurbished toilet blocks include facilities for disabled visitors. Washing machines. Motorcaravan services. Restaurant, terrace, log fire for cooler evenings. New supermarket. Pizzeria/crêperie. Takeaway. Heated swimming pools, paddling pool with 'mushroom' fountain (all open all season). Organised entertainments (July and August). Play areas. Minigolf. Archery. Organised walks. Bicycle hire. Riding. Small fishing lake. ATM. Room for games and TV. Internet access and WiFi.
Off site: Castellane and the Verdon Gorge 1 km. Riding 2 km. Boat launching 4.5 km. Golf 20 km. Watersports.

Open: 15 May - 15 September.

Directions

From Castellane take D952 westwards towards Gorges du Verdon and Moustiers. Site is 1 km. on left. GPS: N43:50.353 E6:29.638

Charges 2009

Per unit incl. 2 or 3 persons	€ 20,00 - € 33,00
incl. 6A electricity	€ 25,00 - € 41,00
extra person (over 3 yrs)	€ 8,00 - € 13,00
dog	€ 3,00

Camping Cheques accepted.

FR04030 Camping le Moulin de Ventre

Niozelles, F-04300 Forcalquier (Alpes-de-Haute-Provence)

Tel: **04 92 78 63 31**. Email: **moulindeventre@aol.com** **www.alanrogers.com/FR04030**

This is a friendly, family run site in the heart of Haute-Provence, near Forcalquier, a bustling small French market town. Attractively located beside a small lake and 28 acres of wooded, hilly land, which is available for walking. Herbs of Provence can be found growing wild and flowers, birds and butterflies abound – a nature lovers' delight. The 124 level, grassy pitches for tourists are separated by a variety of trees and small shrubs, 114 of them having electricity (6A; long leads may be necessary). Some pitches are particularly attractive, bordering a small stream. The site is well situated to visit Mont Ventoux, the Luberon National Park, the Gorges du Verdon and a wide range of ancient hill villages with their markets and museums etc. English is spoken. A 'Sites et Paysages' member.

Facilities

Refurbished toilet block. Facilities for disabled people. Baby bath. Washing, drying machines. Fridge hire. Bread. Bar/restaurant, takeaway (all season), themed evenings (high season). Pizzeria. Swimming pools (15/5-15/9). New playground. Bouncy castle. Fishing, boules. Some activities organised in high season. No discos. Only electric or gas barbecues. Internet access. Off site: Shops, local market, doctor, tennis 2 km. Supermarket, chemist, riding, bicycle hire 5 km. Golf 20 km. Walking, cycling.

Open: 5 April - 30 September.

Directions

From A51 motorway take exit 19 (Brillanne). Turn right on N96 then turn left on N100 westwards (signed Forcalquier) for about 3 km. Site is signed on left, just after a bridge 3 km. southeast of Niozelles. GPS: N43:56.100 E05:52.520

Charges guide

Per unit incl. 2 persons and electricity	€ 17,20 - € 26,70
extra person (over 4 yrs)	€ 3,50 - € 5,50
child (2-4 yrs)	€ 2,00 - € 3,00
dog	€ 1,50 - € 3,00

No credit cards.

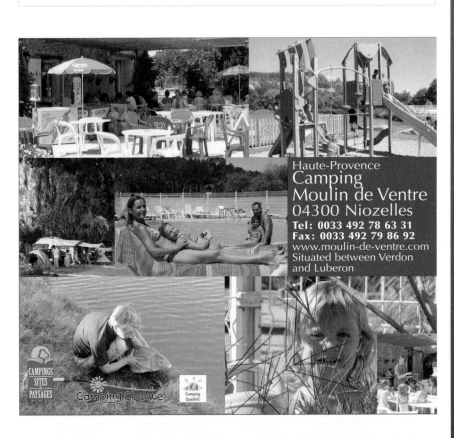

FR32010 Kawan Village le Camp de Florence

Route Astaffort, F-32480 La Romieu (Gers)

Tel: **05 62 28 15 58**. Email: **info@lecampdeflorence.com** **www.alanrogers.com/FR32010**

Camp de Florence is an attractive site on the edge of an historic village in pleasantly undulating Gers countryside. The 183 large, part terraced pitches (95 for tourers) all have electricity, 14 with hardstanding and 25 fully serviced. They are arranged around a large field (full of sunflowers when we visited) with rural views, giving a feeling of spaciousness. The 13th-century village of La Romieu is on the Santiago de Compostela pilgrim route. The Pyrénées are a two hour drive, the Atlantic coast a similar distance. The site has been developed by the friendly Mynsbergen family who are Dutch (although Susan is English). They have sympathetically converted the old farmhouse buildings to provide facilities for the site. The collegiate church, visible from the site, is well worth a visit (the views are magnificent from the top of the tower), as is the local arboretum, the biggest collection of trees in the Midi-Pyrénées.

Facilities

Three toilet blocks provide all the necessary facilities. Washing machines and dryers. Motorcaravan services. Restaurant (1/5-30/9, also open to the public). Takeaway. Bread. Swimming pool area with water slide. Jacuzzi, protected children's pool (open to public in afternoons). Adventure playground, games and pets areas. Bouncy castle, trampoline. Outdoor fitness machines. Games room. Tennis. Pétanque. Bicycle hire. Video shows, discos, picnics, musical evenings. Excursions. Internet and WiFi. Off site: Shop 500 m. in village. Fishing 5 km. Riding 10 km. Walking tours, excursions and wine tasting.

Open: 1 April - 10 October.

Directions

Site signed from D931 Agen - Condom road. Small units turn left at Ligardes (signed), follow D36 for 1 km, turn right turn La Romieu (signed). Otherwise continue until outskirts of Condom and take D41 left to La Romieu, through village to site.
GPS: N43:58.975 E00:30.091

Charges guide

Per unit incl. 2 persons and electricity	€ 16,00 - € 30,90
extra person	€ 3,50 - € 6,90
dog (max. 2)	€ 1,50 - € 2,10

Camping Cheques accepted.

FR09020 Camping l'Arize

Lieu-dit Bourtol, F-09240 La Bastide-de-Sérou (Ariège)

Tel: **05 61 65 81 51**. Email: **camparize@aol.com** **www.alanrogers.com/FR09020**

The site sits in a delightful, tranquil valley among the foothills of the Pyrénées and is just east of the interesting village of La Bastide-de-Sérou beside the River Arize (good trout fishing). The river is fenced for the safety of children on the site, but may be accessed just outside the gate. The 70 large pitches are neatly laid out on level grass within the spacious site. All have 3/6A electricity and are separated into bays by hedges and young trees. An extension to the site gives 24 large, fully serviced pitches and a small toilet block.

Facilities

Toilet block includes facilities for babies and disabled visitors. Laundry room. Motorcaravan services. Small swimming pool and sunbathing area. Entertainment in high season. Weekly barbecues and welcome drinks on Sundays. Fishing, riding and bicycle hire. WiFi. Off site: Restaurants and shops within a few minute's drive. The nearest restaurant is located at the national stud for the famous Merens horses just 200 m. away and will deliver takeaway meals to your pitch. Golf 5 km.

Open: 7 March - 12 November.

Directions

Site is southeast of the village La Bastide-de-Sérou. Take the D15 towards Nescus and site is on right after about 1 km. GPS: N43:00.109 E01:26.723

Charges guide

Per pitch incl. 2 persons and electricity	€ 16,40 - € 31,60
extra person	€ 4,00 - € 5,40
child (0-7 yrs)	€ 3,00 - € 3,60
dog	€ 1,00 - € 1,80

FR31000 Camping le Moulin

F-31220 Martres-Tolosane (Haute-Garonne)

Tel: **05 61 98 86 40**. Email: **info@campinglemoulin.com** **www.alanrogers.com/FR31000**

Set in a 12 hectare estate of woods and fields, Camping Le Moulin is a family run campsite in the foothills of the Pyrénées, close to the interesting medieval village of Martres-Tolosane and situated on the site of an old mill on the bank of the River Garonne. There are 99 pitches (60 for tourers) all with electrical connections. Most pitches are level and grassy, of a good size and with shade from mature trees. A number of very large (150-200 sq.m) 'super' pitches are also available.

Facilities

Large modern sanitary block with separate ladies and gents WCs. Communal area with showers and washbasins in cubicles. Separate heated area for visitors with disabilities. Baby bath. Laundry facilities. Motorcaravan services. Outdoor bar with WiFi. Snack bar and takeaway (July/August). Daily baker's van (except Monday). Heated swimming pool (July/Aug). Tennis. Canoeing. Archery. BMX track. Playground. Games room. Entertainment programme and children's club (high season). Off site: Martres-Tolosane 1.5 km.

Open: 22 March - 30 September.

Directions

From the A64 motorway (Toulouse-Tarbes) take exit 21 (Boussens) or exit 22 (Martres-Tolosane) and follow signs to Martres-Tolosane. Site is well signed from village. GPS: N43:11.429 E01:01.073

Charges guide

Per person	€ 4,20 - € 6,00
child (2-7 yrs)	€ 2,10 - € 3,00
pitch incl. electricity	€ 8,40 - € 18,00

Less 20% outside July/Aug.

FR65060 Castel Camping Pyrénées Natura

Route du Lac, F-65400 Estaing (Hautes-Pyrénées)

Tel: **05 62 97 45 44**. Email: **info@camping-pyrenees-natura.com** **www.alanrogers.com/FR65060**

Pyrénées Natura, at an altitude of 1,000 m, on the edge of the National Park is the perfect site for nature lovers. The 60 pitches (46 for touring), all with electricity, are in a large, level, open and sunny field. Around 75 varieties of trees and shrubs have been planted – but they do not spoil the fantastic views. The reception and bar are in a traditional stone building with an open staircase. A small shop in the old water mill stocks a variety of produce and is unmanned and open all day – pay at reception.

Facilities

First class toilet blocks include facilities for disabled visitors and babies. Washing machine and airers (no lines allowed). Motorcaravan services. Small shop, takeaway (15/5-15/9). Small bar (15/5-15/9). Lounge, library, TV (mainly used for videos of the National Park). Sauna, solarium (free between 12.00-17.00). Music room. Play area for the very young. Small 'beach' beside river. Boules. Giant chess. Weekly evening meal in May, June and Sept. Internet. Off site: Village with two restaurants.

Open: 1 May - 20 September.

Directions

From Lourdes take N21 towards Argelès-Gazost, then exit 2, N2021/D21, into Argelès. Approaching town turn onto D918 towards Aucun. After 8 km, turn left on D13 to Bun, cross the river, then right on D103 to site (5.5 km). Narrow road, few passing places. GPS: N42:56.451 W00:10.631

Charges guide

Per unit incl. 2 persons and electricity (3A)	€ 15,50 - € 24,50
extra person	€ 5,25

FR65080 Kawan Village du Lavedan

Lau-Balagnas, F-65400 Argelès-Gazost (Hautes-Pyrénées)

Tel: **05 62 97 18 84**. Email: **contact@lavedan.com** **www.alanrogers.com/FR65080**

Camping du Lavedan is an old established and very French site set in the Argelès-Gazost valley south of the Lourdes. It is beside the main road so there is some daytime road noise. The 105 touring pitches are set very close together on grass with some shade and all have electricity (2-10A). The area is fine for walking, biking, rafting and of course, in winter, skiing. There is a pool which can be covered in inclement weather and a twice weekly event is organised in July/Aug, weekly in June.

Facilities

Acceptable toilet block. Baby room. Facilities for disabled visitors. Washing machines and dryer in separate block heated in winter. Restaurant with takeaway and terrace (1/5-15/9). Bar, TV (all year). No shop, bread delivery (1/5-15/9). Swimming pool (with cover), paddling pool. Excellent play area. Internet (July/Aug). Boules, table tennis. Off site: Fishing or bicycle hire 1 km. Supermarket or rafting 2 km. Riding 5 km. Golf 15 km.

Open: All year.

Directions

From Lourdes take the N21 (Voie rapide) south, exit 3 (Argelès-Gazost). Take N2021, D921 or D21 towards Luz-St-Sauveur for 2 km. to Lau-Balagnas. Site on right, southern edge of town. GPS: N42:59.293 W00:05.340

Charges guide

Per unit incl. 2 persons	€ 15,00 - € 23,00
electricity (10A max)	€ 1,00
extra person	€ 4,50 - € 6,50

Camping Cheques accepted.

BOOK THIS SITE CALL 01580 214000 ...we'll arrange everything The Travel Service

BOOK THIS SITE CALL 01580 214000 ...we'll arrange everything The Travel Service

FR11050 Camping Rives des Corbières

Avenue du Languedoc, F-11370 Port Leucate (Aude)

Tel: **04 68 40 90 31**. Email: **rivescamping@wanadoo.fr** **www.alanrogers.com/FR11050**

Port Leucate is part of the major Languedoc development which took place during the sixties and seventies and it is now a thriving resort. The campsite is situated on the old coast road into Port Leucate between the Etang de Salas and the beach, 800 m. from the centre of the town and port and only 150 m. from the beach. A mixture of tall poplars and pine trees provide reasonable shade for the 305 pitches. On good-sized sandy plots, all have 6A electricity connections. About 90 are used for mobile homes. With no tour operators this is a good value site, essentially French. A pleasant pool area with a jacuzzi is open when the site is open with other facilities only in high season (July and August) when family entertainment is arranged. This is a good base from which to enjoy this unusual stretch of coast with its various 'étangs' which are very popular for watersports, particularly windsurfing.

Facilities

Four toilet blocks opened as required. Two have mainly Turkish toilets. Facilities for disabled people. Laundry room. Small supermarket, bar and takeaway (July/Aug). Swimming pools. Play area. Daytime games and tournaments and in the evening, live music, karaoke and dancing. Off site: Beach 150 m. (lifeguards July/Aug). Port 800 m. Watersports, tennis, riding and water park. African wildlife reserve at Sigean Fort at Salses.

Open: 1 April - 30 September.

Directions

From the A9 exit 40 follow signs for Port Leucate on D627 (passing Leucate village) for 14 km. Exit the D627 into Port Leucate village. Go right at roundabout into Ave du Languedoc and site is on right after 800 m. GPS: N42:50.009 E03:02.004

Charges guide

Per unit incl. 2 persons and electricity	€ 17,00 - € 21,00
extra person	€ 3,70 - € 4,70

FR11040 Camping le Martinet Rouge Birdie

F-11390 Brousses-et-Villaret (Aude)

Tel: **04 68 26 51 98**. Email: **campinglemartinetrouge@orange.fr** **www.alanrogers.com/FR11040**

Le Martinet Rouge provides a peaceful retreat in the Aude countryside to the north of Carcassonne. It is a small site where the owners have been working hard to improve the facilities. The most striking features of the site are the massive granite boulders (outcrops of smooth rock from the last ice age). The site offers 63 pitches for touring units, all with electricity (3/10A), in two contrasting areas – one is well secluded with irregularly shaped, fairly level, large pitches amongst a variety of trees and shrubs, while the other is on a landscaped gentle hill with mature trees.

Facilities

Four sanitary blocks of various ages, including facilities for disabled visitors, baby bathroom. Laundry facilities. Swimming pool and water slide (15/6-15/9). Small shop (no others locally). Bar, terrace, TV (1/7-15/9). Snack bar (1/7-31/8). Barbecue area. Fitness room. Croquet. Half court tennis. Multisport court. Small play area. Internet access. Off site: Tennis, riding and fishing quite close.

Open: March - November.

Directions

Site is best approached via D118, Carcassonne - Mazamet road. Turn onto D103 15 km. north of Carcassonne to Brousses-et-Villaret. Western outskirts of village turn south to site (signed) in 50 m. GPS: N43:20.350 E02:15.127

Charges guide

Per unit incl. 2 persons	€ 12,50 - € 18,00
extra person	€ 4,50 - € 5,50

No credit cards.

FR11070 Kawan Village les Mimosas

Chaussée de Mandirac, F-11100 Narbonne (Aude)

Tel: **04 68 49 03 72**. Email: **info@lesmimosas.com** **www.alanrogers.com/FR11070**

Six kilometres inland from the beaches of Narbonne and Gruissan, this site benefits from a less hectic situation than others by the sea. The site is lively with plenty to amuse and entertain the younger generation whilst offering facilities for the whole family. A free club card is available in July/Aug to use the children's club, gym, sauna, tennis, minigolf, billiards etc. There are 250 pitches, 150 for touring, many in a circular layout of very good size, most with electricity (6A). There are a few 'grand confort', with reasonable shade, mostly from two metre high hedges. There is also a number of mobile homes and chalets to rent. This could be a very useful site offering many possibilities to meet a variety of needs, on-site entertainment (including an evening on Cathar history), and easy access to popular beaches. Nearby Gruissan is a fascinating village with its wooden houses on stilts, beaches, ruined castle, port and salt beds. Narbonne has Roman remains and inland Cathar castles are to be found perched on rugged hill tops.

Facilities

Sanitary buildings refurbished to a high standard. Washing machines. Shop and 'Auberge' restaurant (open all season). Takeaway. Bar. Small lounge, amusements (July and Aug). Landscaped heated pool with slides and islands (open 1 May), plus the original pool and children's pool (high season). New play area. Minigolf. Mountain bike hire. Tennis. Sauna, gym. Children's activities, sports, entertainment (high season). Bicycle hire. Multisports ground. Off site: Riding. Windsurfing/sailing school 300 m. Gruissan's beach 10 minutes. Lagoon, boating fishing via footpath (200 m).

Open: 21 March - 1 November.

Directions

From A9 exit 38 (Narbonne Sud) take last exit on roundabout, back over the autoroute (site signed from here). Follow signs La Nautique and then Mandirac and site (6 km. from autoroute). Also signed from Narbonne centre.
GPS: N43:08.197 E03:01.537

Charges guide

Per unit incl. 1 or 2 persons	€ 14,00 - € 23,30
incl. electricity	€ 17,50 - € 30,00
incl. water and waste water	€ 21,70 - € 34,00
extra person	€ 4,10 - € 6,50

Camping Cheques accepted.

FR11080 Camping la Nautique

La Nautique, F-11100 Narbonne (Aude)

Tel: 04 68 90 48 19. Email: info@campinglanautique.com www.alanrogers.com/FR11080

Owned and run by a very welcoming Dutch family, this well established site has pitches each with individual sanitary units. It is an extremely spacious site situated on the Etang de Bages, where flat water combined with strong winds make it one of the best windsurfing areas in France. La Nautique has 390 huge, level pitches, 270 for touring, all with 10A electricity and water. Six or seven overnight pitches with electricity are in a separate area. The flowering shrubs and trees give a pleasant feel. Each pitch is separated by hedges making some quite private and providing shade. Entertainment is organised for adults and children from Easter to September (increasing in high season), plus a sports club for supervised surfing, sailing, rafting, walking and canoeing (some activities are charged for). The unspoilt surrounding countryside is excellent for walking or cycling and locally there is horse riding and fishing. English is spoken in reception by the very welcoming Schutjes family. This site caters for families with children including teenagers and is fenced off from the water for safety. Windsurfers can have a key for the gate (with deposit) that leads to launching points on the lake.

Facilities

Each pitch has its own fully equipped sanitary unit. Special facilities for disabled visitors. Laundry. Shop. Bar and restaurant, terrace, TV. Takeaway. All 1/5-30/9. Snack bar 1/7-31/8. Swimming pools, water slide, paddling pool. Play areas. Tennis. Minigolf. Miniclub (high season). Games room. Internet. Only electric barbecues are permitted. Off site: Large sandy beaches at Gruissan (12 km) and Narbonne Plage (20 km). Narbonne 4 km.

Open: 15 February - 15 November.

Directions

From A9 take exit 38 (Narbonne Sud). Go round roundabout to last exit and follow signs for La Nautique and site, then further site signs to site on right in 2.5 km. GPS: N43:08.500 E03:00.140

Charges guide

Per person	€ 5,00 - € 7,50
child (1-7 yrs)	€ 3,00 - € 5,50
pitch incl. electricity, water and sanitary unit	€ 9,50 - € 22,00

FR30080 Kawan Village le Mas de Reilhe

F-30260 Crespian (Gard)

Tel: 04 66 77 82 12. Email: info@camping-mas-de-reilhe.fr www.alanrogers.com/FR30080

This is a comfortable family site nestling in a valley with 95 pitches (76 for touring), most have electricity (6/10A), some also have water and waste water and some of the upper ones may require long leads. The large lower pitches are separated by tall poplar trees and hedges, close to the main facilities but may experience some road noise. The large terraced pitches on the hillside are scattered under mature pine trees, some with good views, more suited to tents and trailer tents but with their own modern sanitary facilities. The heated pool is in a sunny position overlooked by the attractive bar/restaurant. There are no shops in the village, the nearest being at the medieval city of Sommières 10 km. away (and well worth a visit).

Facilities

Good toilet facilities with washbasins in cabins and pre-set showers. Washing machine. Reception with limited shop (bread can be ordered). Bar (6/4-23/9), takeaway and restaurant (1/6-15/9). Small play area. Pentaque. Heated swimming pool (all season). Internet access. Motorcaravan services. Off site: Tennis 500 m. Fishing 3 km. Riding 5 km. Bicycle hire 10 km.

Open: 4 April - 20 September.

Directions

From the A9 take exit Nîmes-ouest signed Alès, then the D999 towards Le Vigan. Site is on the N110 just north of the junction with the D999 at the southern end of the village. GPS: N43:52.759 E04:05.783

Charges guide

Per unit incl. 2 persons	€ 14,00 - € 20,00
electricity (6/10A)	€ 3,30 - € 4,30

Camping Cheques accepted.

FR66070 Yelloh! Village le Brasilia

B.P. 204, F-66141 Canet-en-Roussillon (Pyrénées-Orientales)

Tel: **04 66 73 97 39**. Email: **info@yellohvillage-brasilia.com** **www.alanrogers.com/FR66070**

An impressive family site beside the beach and well managed, Le Brasilia is pretty, neat and well kept with an amazingly wide range of facilities. There are 475 neatly hedged touring pitches all with electricity and many with water and drainage, varying in size from 80 to 120 sq.m. Some of the longer pitches are suitable for two families together. With a range of shade from pines and flowering shrubs, less on pitches near the beach, there are neat access roads (sometimes narrow for large units). There are also over 100 pitches with mobile homes or chalets to rent. The sandy beach here is busy, with a beach club (you can hire windsurfing boards) and a naturist section is on the beach to the west of the site. There is a large California type pool, with sunbathing areas bounded by an attractive mosaic wall and bar. The village area of the site provides bars, a busy restaurant, entertainment (including a night club) and a range of shops. In fact you do not need to stir from the site which is almost a resort in itself also providing a cash dispenser, exchange facilities, telephone, post office, gas supplies and even weather forecasts. It does have a nice, lively atmosphere but is orderly and well run – very good for a site with beach access. Although it is a large site it does not seem so. They seem to have thought of everything, including an escort to your pitch and advice on the best way to site your unit. A 'Yelloh Village' member. A member of 'Leading Campings Group'.

Facilities

Ten modern sanitary blocks are very well equipped and maintained, with British style WCs (some Turkish) and washbasins in cabins. Good facilities for children and for disabled people. Laundry room. Hairdresser. Bars and restaurant. Swimming pool (heated). Play areas. Tennis. Sporting activities. Internet café. Entertainment. Bicycle hire. Fishing. Off site: Riding 5 km. Golf 12 km.

Open: 26 April - 27 September.

Directions

From A9 exit 41 (Perpignan Centre/Rivesaltes) follow signs for Le Barcarès/Canet on D83 for 10 km, then for Canet (D81). At first Canet roundabout, turn fully back on yourself (direction Sainte-Marie) and watch for Brasilia sign almost immediately on right.
GPS: N42:42.280 E03:02.090

Charges guide

Per unit incl. 2 persons and electricity (6A) € 17,00 - € 44,00

yelloh! VILLAGE www.yellohvillage.com tel: +33 466 739 739

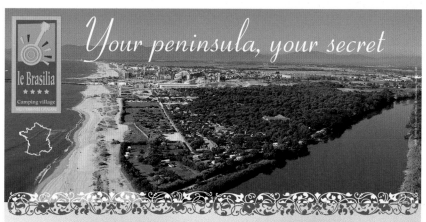

BOOK THIS SITE CALL 01580 214000 ...we'll arrange everything

The Travel Service

FR34070 Yelloh! Village le Sérignan Plage

Le Sérignan Plage, F-34410 Sérignan (Hérault)

Tel: **04 66 73 97 39**. Email: **info@yellohvillage-serignan-plage.com** **www.alanrogers.com/FR34070**

With direct access onto a superb 600 m. sandy beach (including a naturist section) and with three swimming pools and another planned for next year, this is a must for a Mediterranean holiday. It is a friendly, family orientated site with perhaps the most comprehensive range of amenities we have come across. The enthusiastic owners, Jean-Guy and Catherine continually surprise us with their unique style and new developments. A collection of spa pools (balnéo) built in Romanesque style with colourful terracing and columns, overlooked by a very smart restaurant 'Le Villa' is the 'piece de resistance'. The balnéo spa is shared with the adjoining naturist site (under the same ownership). Having recently acquired an adjacent site, there are now over 1,000 pitches with 400 available for touring units and this is now a pretty large campsite. The touring pitches vary in size and in terms of shade and are mainly on sandy soil, all with electricity. There are over 300 mobile homes and chalets to let, plus some 400 privately owned units. The heart of the site developed in the local Catalonian style is some distance from reception and is a busy and informal area with shops, another good restaurant, the Au Pas d'Oc, an indoor pool and a super roof-top bar. A range of entertainment is provided for adults and children in the evenings.

Facilities

Several modern blocks of individual design with good facilities including showers with washbasin and WC. Facilities for disabled people. Baby bathroom. Launderette. Motorcaravan services. Supermarket, bakery and newsagent (all season). Other shops (1/6-15/9). ATM. Restaurants, bar and takeaway. Hairdresser. Balnéo spa. Gym. Heated indoor pool. Outdoor pools (24/4-21/9). Children's clubs. Evening entertainment. Sporting activities. Bicycle hire. Bus to Sérignan village July/Aug. Beach (lifeguards 1/6-15/9). Off site: Riding 2 km. Golf 10 km. Sailing and windsurfing school on beach.

Open: 23 April - 27 September.

Directions

From A9 exit 35 (Béziers Est) follow signs for Sérignan, D64 (9 km). Before Sérignan, turn left, Sérignan Plage (4 km). At small sign (blue) turn right. At T-junction turn left over small road bridge and after left hand bend. Site is 100 m. GPS: N43:15.838 E03:19.260

Charges guide

Per unit incl. 1 or 2 persons and 6A electricity	€ 14,00 - € 44,00
extra person	€ 5,00 - € 8,00
pet	€ 3,00 - € 4,00

Low season offers.

FR66130 Hotel de Plein Air l'Eau Vive

Chemin de Saint-Saturnin, F-66820 Vernet-les-Bains (Pyrénées-Orientales)

Tel: **04 68 05 54 14**. Email: **info@leauvive.com** **www.alanrogers.com/FR66130**

Enjoying dramatic views of the Pic du Canigou (3,000 m), this small site is 1.5 km. from the centre of Vernet-les-Bains in the Pyrénées. It is approached via a twisting road through a residential area. The 70 tourist pitches, with electricity (4/10A) and 45 fully serviced, are on a slight slope, part hedged and some terraced, with a separate tent field. Most pitches have some shade. The site has an attractive, natural pool with water pumped from the nearby stream, with a small beach. There is a central floating safety line across the pool but parents should keep an eye on children.

Facilities

First class toilet facilities and provision for disabled people. Washing machine. Bread, main season. Bar/reception, pool table, library. Snack bar, takeaway (15/5-15/9). A 'meal of the day' can be ordered. Play area. Natural pool for children. Sports field. Bicycle hire. Off site: Fishing 200 m. Swimming pool, thermal centre in village 1 km. Organised rafting, canoeing, hydrospeed trips.

Open: 16 December - 25 October.

Directions

Following N116 towards Andorra. At Ville Franche, turn south, D116, for Vernet-les-Bains. After 5 km, keep right avoiding town. Turn right over bridge towards Sahorre. Immediately turn right (ave de Saturnin) for 1 km. GPS: N42:33.304 E02:22.667

Charges guide

Per unit incl. 2 persons	€ 12,50 - € 21,50
incl. electricity	€ 15,00 - € 25,00
extra person (over 4 yrs)	€ 1,50 - € 2,50

Credit cards accepted 1/6-31/8 only.

Alan Rogers

This is just a sample of the campsites we have inspected and selected in France. For more campsites and further information, please see the Alan Rogers France guide.

The magic of
the Mediterranean

Passerelles RC 67 B 302

Imagine – hot sunshine, blue sea, vineyards, olive and eucalyptus trees, alongside a sandy beach – what a setting for a campsite – not just any campsite either !

With three pool areas, one with four toboggans surrounded by sun bathing areas, an indoor pool for baby swimmers plus a magnificent landscaped, Romanesque spa-complex with half Olympic size pool and a superb range of hydro-massage baths to let you unwind and re-charge after the stresses of work.

And that's not all – two attractive restaurants, including the atmospheric "Villa" in its romantic Roman setting beside the spa, three bars, a mini-club and entertainment for all ages, all add up to a fantastic opportunity to enjoy a genuinely unique holiday experience.

Le Sérignan-Plage - F-34410 SERIGNAN
Tel: 00 33 467 32 35 33 - Fax: 00 33 467 32 26 36
info@leserignanplage.com - www.leserignanplage.com

CAMPING VILLAGES yelloh! VILLAGE

The Travel Service BOOK THIS SITE CALL 01580 214000 ...we'll arrange everything

FR66020 Kawan Village Caravaning Ma Prairie

Route de Saint-Nazaire, F-66140 Canet-en-Roussillon (Pyrénées-Orientales)

Tel: **04 68 73 26 17**. Email: **ma.prairie@wanadoo.fr** **www.alanrogers.com/FR66020**

Ma Prairie is an excellent site and its place in this guide goes back over 30 years. Then it was simply a field surrounded by vineyards. The trees planted then have now matured, more have been planted, along with colourful shrubs providing a comfortable, park-like setting with some 260 pitches, all with electricity and 35 with water and drainage. It is a peaceful haven some 3 km. back from the sea but within walking distance of Canet village itself. The Gil family still provide a warm welcome.

Facilities

Fully equipped toilet blocks, baby bath. Washing machines and dryers. No shop but bread can be ordered. Covered snack bar and takeaway. Air-conditioned bar and restaurant. Large adult pool, splendid children's pool. Play area. Tennis. Bicycle hire. TV. Amusement machines. Dancing three times weekly, busy daily activity programme in season. Caravan storage. Off site: Supermarket 400 m. Riding 600 m. Golf 6 km. Canet Village within walking distance with all amenities. Bus/tram to Canet Plage.

Open: 5 May - 25 September.

Directions

Leave autoroute A9 at Perpignan North towards Barcarès. Site access is from the D11 Perpignan road (exit 5), close to the junction with D617 in Canet-Village. Go under bridge, right at roundabout the left to site. GPS: N42:42.081 E02:59.981

Charges guide

Per unit incl. 2 persons	€ 17,00 - € 30,00
extra person	€ 4,00 - € 7,00
electricity (10A)	€ 4,00 - € 5,00

Camping Cheques accepted.

The Travel Service BOOK THIS SITE CALL 01580 214000 ...we'll arrange everything

FR66250 Huttopia Font-Romeu

Route de Mont-Louis, F-66120 Font-Romeu (Pyrénées-Orientales)

Tel: **04 68 30 09 32**. Email: **font-romeu@huttopia.com** **www.alanrogers.com/FR66250**

This is a large, open site of some seven hectares, nestling on the side of the mountain at the entrance to Font-Romeu. This part of the Pyrénées offer some staggering views and the famous Mont Louis is close by. An ideal base for climbing, hiking or cycling, it would also provide a good stopover for a night or so whilst traveling between Spain and France or to or from Andorra into France. The terraced pitches are easily accessed, with those dedicated to caravans and motorcaravans at the top of the site, whilst tents go on the lower slopes.

Facilities

Two toilet blocks, one behind reception, the other in the centre of the tent pitches. Traditional in style, they are bright and clean with modern fittings. Toilet for children and excellent facilities for visitors with disabilities. Washing machines and dryers at each block. large games hall. Only gas barbecues are permitted. Off site: Opportunities for walking and climbing are close by as are golf, riding, fishing, cycling and tennis. The small town of Font-Romeu is very near with all the usual shops and banking facilities.

Open: 24 May - 27 September, 5 December - 12 April.

Directions

Font-Romeu is on the D118, some 12 km. after it branches off the N116 heading west, just after Mont Louis. This is an interesting road with magnificent views and well worth the climb. Site is just before the town, on the left and accessed off the car park. GPS: N42:30.907 E02:03.110

Charges 2009

Per unit with 2 persons	€ 18,80 - € 34,20
extra person	€ 5,00 - € 6,20

Camping Cheques accepted.

tel: +33 (0) 4 37 64 22 33 www.huttopia.com HUTTOPIA

FR66560 Camping la Sirène

Route de Taxo à la Mer, F-66702 Argelès-sur-Mer (Pyrénées-Orientales)

Tel: **04 68 81 04 61**. Email: **contact@camping-lasirene.fr** **www.alanrogers.com/FR66560**

From the moment you step into the hotel-like reception area you realise that this large site offers the holiday maker everything they could want in a well managed and convenient location close to Argelès-sur-Mer and the beaches. The 740 mobile homes and chalets vary in standard but all are less than five years old, very clean, comfortable and located on neat tidy pitches. There are also some touring pitches. In the summer there are 170 staff on duty to ensure your stay is enjoyable.

Facilities

Restaurant, bar and takeaway. Large shop (all season). Large aqua park, paddling pools, slides, jacuzzi. Games room. Multisports field, tennis, archery, minigolf, football. Theatre, evening entertainment, discos, show time spectacular. Off site: Resort of Argelès sur Mer and its beaches 2 km, as is karting, 10-pin bowling, amusement park and the site's private beach club, Emeraude. Interesting old town of Collioure close by.

Open: 7 April - 28 September.

Directions

Leave A9 motorway, junction 42, take D114, towards Argelès. Leave D114, junction 10 and follow signs for Plage Nord. Site signed after first roundabout. Site on right 2 km. after last roundabout. GPS: N42:34.256 E03:01.744

Charges 2009

Per unit incl. 1-3 persons and electricity	€ 26,00 - € 43,00
extra person	€ 6,00 - € 9,00

FR66570 Camping l'Hippocampe

Route de Taxo à la Mer, F-66702 Argelès-sur-Mer (Pyrénées-Orientales)

Tel: **04 68 81 04 61**. Email: **contact@camping-lasirene.fr** **www.alanrogers.com/FR66570**

A sister site to La Sirène just opposite, this site has some touring pitches along with 170 mobile home and chalet pitches and is aimed at families with young children and adults looking for a quieter site. The mobile homes and chalets are all modern, well maintained and have space around them to provide privacy. The pool on site is dedicated to the smaller children and is a great place for them to gain confidence in the water whilst still being able to play. Entertainment, shops, bars and the full range of activities offered by La Sirène, just across the road. Visitors here also have free access to the beach club Emeraude which offers free transport to Plage Nord where the club is situated complete with bar and snacks.

Facilities

Pool and laundry. Shop, small bar (all season). All other facilities are at La Sirène just across the road. Off site: Beach, Argelès sur Mer within 2 km. Karting, 10-pin bowling, amusement park and riding within 1 km.

Open: 6 April - 28 September.

Directions

Leave A9 junction 42. Take D114, Argelès road. Leave D114 junction 10, follow signs for Plage Nord. Site signed after the first roundabout, on left 2 km. after last roundabout. GPS: N42:34.230 E03:01.839

Charges 2009

Per unit incl. 1-3 persons and electricity	€ 26,00 - € 43,00
extra person	€ 6,00 - € 9,00
child (under 5 yrs)	€ 4,00 - € 6,00

FR66590 Camping le Bois du Valmarie

F-66702 Argelès-sur-Mer (Pyrénées-Orientales)

Tel: **04 68 81 04 61**. Email: **contact@camping-lasirene.fr** **www.alanrogers.com/FR66590**

Pitches here are exclusively for mobile home and chalet accommodation. Le Bois de Valmarie is a member of the same group of sites as La Sirène (FR66560) and L'Hippocampe (FR66570). The site has 181 pitches, the majority of which are available for booking (none available for touring) and is located south of the port beside Racou beach. The site has a pleasant woodland location and a range of amenities including a large swimming pool complex with waterslides. The sea is 50 m. from the site entrance with a sandy beach and within easy walking distance. The site has its own bar and a restaurant but visitors are welcome at La Sirene to enjoy the entertainment and activities on offer.

Facilities

Supermarket. Restaurant. Bar. Beach shop. Takeaway food. Swimming pool with waterslides and separate children's pool. Play area. Mobile homes for rent. Off site: Argelès town centre 3 km.'Blue Bear' activity club. Diving club. Emeraude Beach Club.

Open: 7 April - 28 September.

Directions

Leave autoroute at Perpignan Sud exit and join the N114 southbound toward Argelès. Take exit 13 and follow signs to Le Racou. Site is well signed from here. GPS: N42:32.270 E3:03.267

Charges 2009

Contact the campsite.

FR13060 Camping les Micocouliers

445 route de Cassoulen, F-13690 Graveson-en-Provence (Bouches du Rhône)

Tel: **04 90 95 81 49**. Email: **micocou@free.fr** **www.alanrogers.com/FR13060**

M. et Mme. Riehl started work on Les Micocouliers in 1997 and they have developed a comfortable site. On the outskirts of the town it is only some 10 km. from St Rémy and Avignon. A purpose built, terracotta 'house' in a raised position provides all the facilities. The 65 pitches radiate out from here with the pool and entrance to one side. The pitches are on level grass, separated by small bushes, and shade is developing. Electricity connections are possible (4-13A). There are also a few mobile homes. The popular swimming pool is a welcome addition.

Facilities

Unisex facilities in one unit provide toilets and facilities for disabled visitors (by key), another showers and washbasins in cabins and another dishwashing and laundry facilities. Reception and limited shop (July/Aug) are in another. Swimming pool (12 x 8 m; 5/5-15/9). Paddling pool (1/7-31/8). Play area. Off site: Fishing 5 km. Bicycle hire 1 km. Riding next door. Golf 5 km. Beach 60 km. at Ste Marie de la Mer.

Open: 15 March - 15 October.

Directions

Site is southeast of Graveson. From the N570 at new roundabout take D5 towards St Rémy and Maillane and site is 500 m. on the left. GPS: N43:50.638 E04:46.879

Charges guide

Per unit incl. 2 persons	€ 14,00 - € 18,10
extra person	€ 4,70 - € 6,00
child (2-12 yrs)	€ 3,70 - € 4,70
electricity	€ 3,70 - € 6,60

Camping Cheques accepted.

FR06080 Camping Caravaning les Cigales

505 avenue de la Mer, F-06210 Mandelieu-la-Napoule (Alpes-Maritimes)

Tel: **04 93 49 23 53**. Email: **campingcigales@wanadoo.fr** **www.alanrogers.com/FR06080**

It is hard to imagine that such a quiet, peaceful site could be in the middle of such a busy town and so near Cannes. The entrance (easily missed) has large electronic gates that ensure that the site is very secure. There are only 115 pitches (40 mobile homes) so this is quite a small, personal site. There are three pitch sizes, from small ones for tents to pitches for larger units and all have electricity (6A), some fully serviced. All are level with much needed shade in summer, although the sun will get through in winter when it is needed. The site is alongside the Canal de Siagne and for a fee, small boats can be launched at La Napoule, then moored outside the campsite's side gate. Les Cigales is open all year so it is useful for the Monte Carlo Rally, the Cannes Film Festival and the Mimosa Festival, all held out of the main season. English is spoken.

Facilities

Well appointed, clean, heated toilet blocks. Facilities for babies and disabled visitors. Washing machine. Motorcaravan services. Restaurant and takeaway (May - Oct). Heated swimming pool and large sunbathing area (April - Oct). Small play area. Two games machines. Canal fishing. Off site: Beach 800 m. The town is an easy walk. Two golf courses within 1 km. Railway station 1 km. for trains to Cannes, Nice, Antibes, Monte Carlo. Hypermarket 2 km. Bus stop 10 minutes.

Open: All year.

Directions

From A8, exit 40, bear right. Remain in right hand lane, continue right signed Plages-Ports, Creche-Campings. Casino supermarket on right. Continue under motorway to T-junction. Turn left, site is 60 m. on left opposite Chinese restaurant. GPS: N43:32.348 E06:56.564

Charges 2009

Per unit incl. 2 persons and electricity	€ 37,00 - € 49,50
extra person	€ 7,00
child	€ 3,50

Les Cigales ★★★★
Open all year
800m from the beaches and golf
Camping
Caravaning
Accommodation
Swimming pool
Lagoon for kids
Solarium
Private pontoon
LES CIGALES
505 avenue de la Mer
06210 MANDELIEU LA NAPOULE
Tél. : + 33 493 49 23 53
Fax. : + 33 493 49 30 45
www.lescigales.com
Mail : campingcigales@wanadoo.fr

FR83010 Camping Caravaning les Pins Parasols

3360 rue des Combattants d'Afrique du Nord, F-83600 Fréjus (Var)

Tel: **04 94 40 88 43**. Email: **lespinsparasols@wanadoo.fr** **www.alanrogers.com/FR83010**

Not everyone likes very big sites and Les Pins Parasols with its 189 pitches is of a comfortable size which is quite easy to walk around. It is family owned and run. Although on very slightly undulating ground, virtually all the pitches (all have electricity) are levelled or terraced and separated by hedges or bushes with pine trees for shade. There are 48 pitches equipped with their own fully enclosed, sanitary unit, with WC, washbasin, hot shower and dishwashing sink. These pitches naturally cost more but may well be of interest to those seeking a little bit of extra comfort.

Facilities

Average quality toilet blocks (one heated) providing facilities for disabled people. Small shop with reasonable stocks, restaurant, takeaway (both 15/4-30/9). General room, TV. Swimming pool, attractive rock backdrop, separate long slide with landing pool, small paddling pool (heated). Half-court tennis. Off site: Bicycle hire or riding 2 km. Fishing 6 km. Golf 10 km. Bus from the gate into Fréjus 5 km. Beach 6 km.

Open: 5 April - 27 September.

Directions

From A8 take exit 38 for Fréjus Est. Turn right immediately on leaving pay booths on a small road which leads across to D4, then right again and under 1 km. to site. GPS: N43:27.774 E06:43.542

Charges guide

Per unit incl. 2 persons and electricity	€ 18,00 - € 27,30
pitch with sanitary unit	€ 22,70 - € 34,00
extra person	€ 4,50 - € 6,35
child (under 7 yrs)	€ 3,00 - € 3,85
dog	€ 1,85 - € 2,80

FR83030 Camping Caravaning Leï Suves

Quartier du Blavet, F-83520 Roquebrune-sur-Argens (Var)
Tel: **04 94 45 43 95**. Email: **camping.lei.suves@wanadoo.fr** **www.alanrogers.com/FR83030**

This quiet, pretty site is a few kilometres inland from the coast, two kilometres north of the N7. Close to the unusual Roquebrune rock, it is within easy reach of St Tropez, Ste Maxime, St Raphaël and Cannes. The site entrance is appealing – wide and spacious, with a large bank of well tended flowers. Mainly on a gently sloping hillside, the 310 pitches are terraced with shade provided by the many cork trees which give the site its name. All pitches have electricity and access to water. A pleasant pool area is beside the bar/restaurant and entertainment area. It is possible to walk in the surrounding woods as long as there is no fire alert. Many of the pitches are used for mobile homes.

Facilities

Modern, well kept toilet blocks include washing machines, facilities for disabled visitors. Shop. Good sized swimming pool, paddling pool. Bar, terrace, snack bar, takeaway (all 1/4-30/9). Outdoor stage near the bar for evening entertainment, high season. Excellent play area. Table tennis, tennis, sports area. Internet terminal. Only gas barbecues. Off site: Bus stop at site entrance. Riding 1 km. Fishing 3 km. Bicycle hire 5 km. Golf 7 km. Beach at St Aygulf 15 km.

Open: 1 April - 15 October.

Directions

Leave autoroute at Le Muy and take N7 towards St Raphaël. Turn left at roundabout onto D7 heading north signed La Boverie (site also signed). Site on right in 2 km. GPS: N43:28.677 E06:38.324

Charges guide

Per unit incl. 2 persons	€ 19,00 - € 34,50
incl. 3 persons	€ 21,00 - € 37,00
extra person	€ 4,50 - € 7,50
electricity	€ 4,50

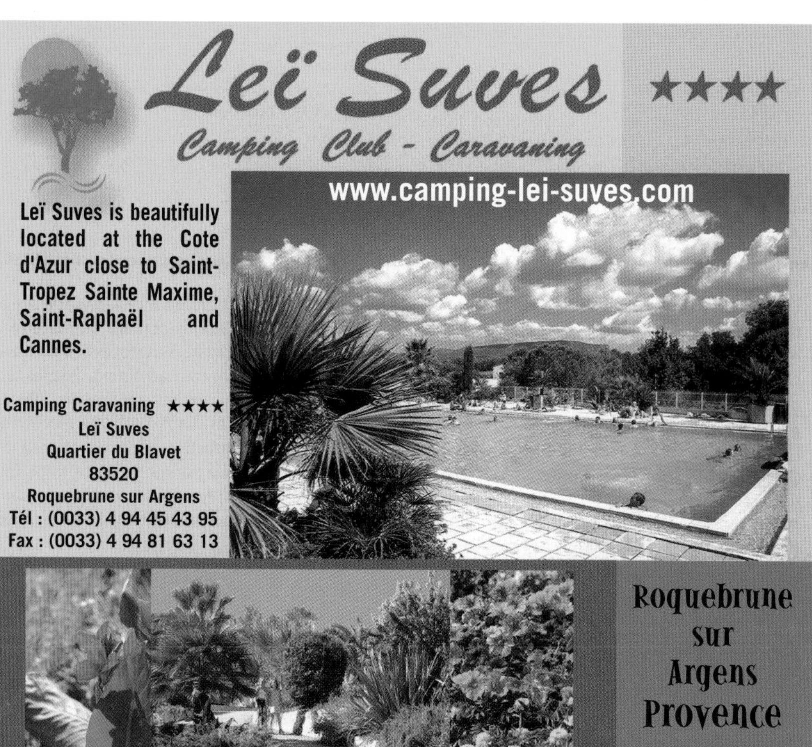

Leï Suves ★★★★
Camping Club - Caravaning
www.camping-lei-suves.com
Leï Suves is beautifully located at the Cote d'Azur close to Saint-Tropez Sainte Maxime, Saint-Raphaël and Cannes.
Camping Caravaning ★★★★
Leï Suves
Quartier du Blavet
83520
Roquebrune sur Argens
Tél : (0033) 4 94 45 43 95
Fax : (0033) 4 94 81 63 13
Roquebrune sur Argens Provence

FR83060 Camping Resort la Baume – la Palmeraie

Route de Bagnols, F-83618 Fréjus (Var)

Tel: **04 94 19 88 88**. Email: **reception@labaume-lapalmeraie.com** **www.alanrogers.com/FR83060**

La Baume is large, busy site about five and a half kilometres from the long sandy beach of Fréjus-Plage, although with its fine and varied selection of swimming pools many people do not bother to make the trip. The pools with their palm trees are remarkable for their size and variety (water slides, etc.) – the very large 'feature' pool a highlight. Recent additions are an aquatic play area and two indoor pools with a slide and a spa area. The site has nearly 250 adequately sized, fully serviced pitches, with some separators and most have shade. Although tents are accepted, the site concentrates mainly on caravanning. It becomes full in season. Adjoining La Baume is its sister site La Palmeraie, providing self-catering accommodation, its own landscaped pool and offering some entertainment to supplement that at La Baume. There are 500 large pitches with mains sewerage for mobile homes. La Baume's convenient location has its 'downside' as there is some traffic noise on a few pitches from the nearby autoroute – somewhat obtrusive at first but we soon failed to notice it. It is a popular site with tour operators.

Facilities

Seven refurbished toilet blocks. Supermarket, several shops. Two bars, terrace overlooking pools, TV. Restaurant, takeaway. Six swimming pools (heated all season, two covered, plus steam room and jacuzzi). Fitness centre. Tennis. Archery (July/Aug). Skateboard park. Organised events, daytime and evening entertainment, some English. Amphitheatre. Discos all season. Children's club (all season). Off site: Bus to Fréjus passes gate. Riding 2 km. Fishing 3 km. Golf 5 km. Beach 5 km.

Open: 4 April - 26 September, with full services.

Directions

From west, A8, exit Fréjus, take N7 southwest (Fréjus). After 4 km, turn left on D4 and site is 3 km. From east, A8, exit 38 Fréjus and follow signs for Cais. Site is signed. GPS: N43:27.599 E06:43.229

Charges 2009

Per unit incl. 2 persons, electricity, water and drainage	€ 19,00 - € 43,00
extra person	€ 5,00 - € 12,00
child (under 7 yrs)	free - € 7,00
dog	€ 4,00 - € 5,00

Min. stay for motorhomes 2 nights.
Large units should book.

FR83020 Castel Camping Caravaning Esterel

Avenue des Golf, Agay, F-83530 Saint Raphaël (Var)

Tel: **04 94 82 03 28**. Email: **contact@esterel-caravaning.fr** **www.alanrogers.com/FR83020**

Esterel is a quality caravan site east of St Raphaël, set among the hills at the back of Agay. The site is three and a half kilometres from the sandy beach at Agay where parking is perhaps a little easier than at most places on this coast. It has 230 pitches for tourers, for caravans but not tents, all have electricity and water tap, 18 special ones have their own en-suite washroom adjoining. Pitches are on shallow terraces, attractively landscaped with good shade and a variety of flowers, giving a feeling of spaciousness. Some 'maxi-pitches' from 110 to 160 sq.m. are available with 10A electricity. Developed by the Laroche family for over 30 years, the site has an attractive, quiet situation with good views of the Esterel mountains. Wild boar occasionally come to the perimeter fence to be fed by visitors. This is a very good site, well run and organised in a deservedly popular area. A pleasant courtyard area contains the shop and bar, with a terrace overlooking the attractively landscaped (floodlit at night) pool complex. A member of 'Les Castels' group.

Facilities

Excellent refurbished, heated toilet blocks. Individual toilet units on 18 pitches. Facilities for disabled people. Laundry room. Motorcaravan services. Shop. Gift shop. Takeaway. Bar/restaurant. Five circular swimming pools (two heated), one for adults, one for children, three arranged as a waterfall (1/4-30/9). Disco. Archery. Minigolf. Tennis. Pony rides. Pétanque. Squash. Playground. Nursery. Bicycle hire. Internet access. Organised events in season. No barbecues. Off site: Golf nearby. Trekking by foot, bicycle or by pony in L'Esterel forest park. Fishing, beach 3 km.

Open: 1 April - 6 October.

Directions

From A8, exit Fréjus, follow signs for Valescure, then for Agay, site on left. The road from Agay is the easiest to follow but it is possible to approach from St Raphaël via Valescure.
GPS: N43:27.253 E06:49.945

Charges guide

Per unit incl. 2 persons, standard pitch	€ 23,00 - € 38,00
'maxi' pitch	€ 28,00 - € 47,00
deluxe pitch	€ 32,00 - € 51,00
extra person	€ 8,50
child (1-7 yrs)	€ 6,50

FR83200 Kawan Village les Pêcheurs

F-83520 Roquebrune-sur-Argens (Var)

Tel: **04 94 45 71 25**. Email: **info@camping-les-pecheurs.com** **www.alanrogers.com/FR83200**

Les Pêcheurs will appeal to families who appreciate natural surroundings together with many activities, cultural and sporting. Interspersed with mobile homes, the 150 good sized touring pitches (electricity 6/10A) are separated by trees or flowering bushes. The Provençal-style buildings are delightful, especially the bar, restaurant and games room, with its terrace down to the river and the site's own canoe station (locked gate). Across the road is a lake used exclusively for water skiing with a sandy beach, a restaurant and minigolf. This popular Riviera site has some new spa facilities including steam pool and sauna. Developed over three generations by the Simoncini family, this peaceful, friendly site is set in more than four hectares of mature, well shaded countryside at the foot of the Roquebrune Rock. Activities include climbing the 'Rock' with a guide. We became more and more intrigued with stories about the Rock and the Holy Hole, the Three Crosses and the Hermit all call for further exploration which reception staff are happy to arrange, likewise trips to Monte Carlo, Ventimigua (Italy) and the Gorges du Verdon, etc. The medieval village of Roquebrune is within walking distance.

Facilities

Modern, refurbished, well designed toilet blocks, baby baths, facilities for disabled visitors. Washing machines. Shop. Bar and restaurant (all open all season). Heated outdoor swimming pool (all season), separate paddling pool (lifeguard in high season), ice cream bar. Games room. Spa facilities. Playing field. Fishing. Canoeing. Waterskiing. Rafting and diving schools. Activities for children and adults (high season), visits to local wine caves. Only gas or electric barbecues. WiFi in reception, bar/restaurant and pool area. Off site: Bicycle hire 1 km. Riding 5 km. Golf 5 km. (reduced fees).

Open: 1 April - 30 September.

Directions

From A8 take Le Muy exit, follow N7 towards Fréjus for 13 km. bypassing Le Muy. After crossing A8, turn right at roundabout towards Roquebrune-sur-Argens. Site is on left after 1 km. just before bridge over river. GPS: N43:27.047 E06:38.010

Charges 2009

Per unit incl. 2 persons and electricity	€ 23,00 - € 41,70
incl. 3 persons	€ 25,50 - € 44,50
extra person	€ 4,00 - € 7,50
child (5-10 yrs)	€ 3,20 - € 6,00
dog (max. 1)	€ 3,10

Camping Cheques accepted.

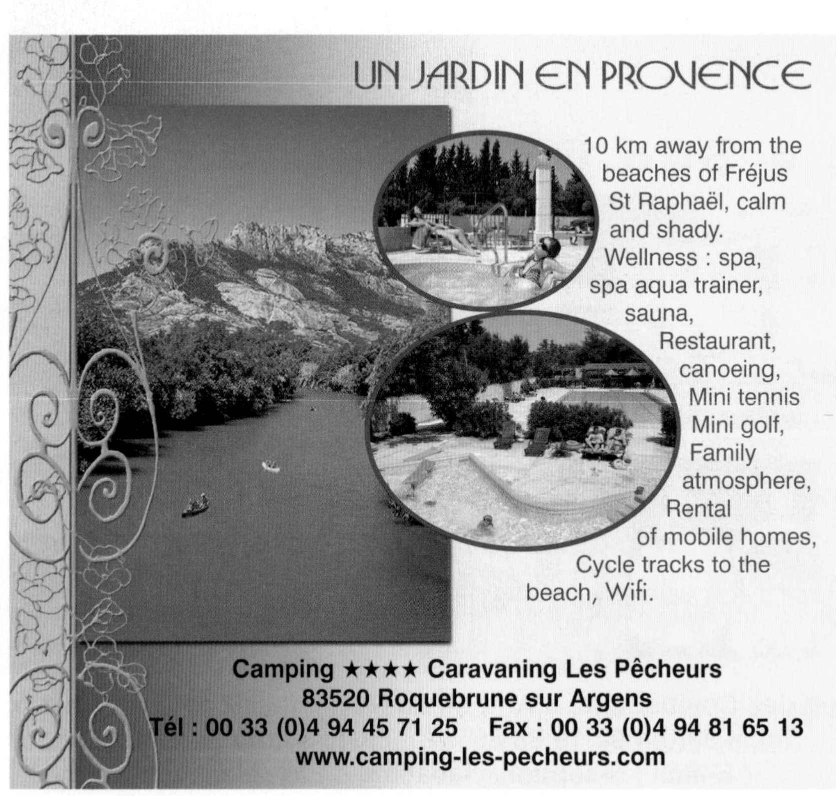

FR83220 Kawan Village Cros de Mouton

B.P. 116, F-83240 Cavalaire-sur-Mer (Var)

Tel: **04 94 64 10 87**. Email: **campingcrosdemouton@wanadoo.fr** **www.alanrogers.com/FR83220**

Cros de Mouton is a reasonably priced campsite in a popular area. High on a steep hillside, about two kilometres from Cavalaire and its popular beaches, the site is a calm oasis away from the coast. There are stunning views of the bay but, due to the nature of the terrain, some of the site roads are very steep – the higher pitches with the best views are especially so. There are 199 large, terraced pitches (electricity 10A) under cork trees with 73 suitable only for tents with parking close by, and 80 for touring caravans. English is spoken by the welcoming and helpful owners. The terrace of the restaurant and the pool area share the wonderful view of Cavalaire and the bay. Olivier and Andre are happy to take your caravan up with their 4 x 4 Jeep if you are worried.

Facilities

Clean, well maintained toilet blocks have all the usual facilities including those for disabled customers (although site is perhaps a little steep in places for wheelchairs). Washing machine. Shop. Bar/restaurant with reasonably priced meals and takeaway. Swimming and paddling pools with many sunbeds on the terrace and small bar for snacks and cold drinks. Small play area. Games room. Off site: Beach 1.5 km. Bicycle hire 1.5 km. Riding 3 km. Golf 15 km.

Open: 15 March - 9 November.

Directions

Take the D559 to Cavalaire-sur-Mer (not Cavalière 4 km. away). Site is about 1.5 km. north of the town, very well signed from the centre.
GPS: N43:10.933 E06:30.966

Charges 2009

Per person	€ 6,30 - € 7,90
child (under 7 yrs)	€ 4,10 - € 4,50
pitch	€ 6,30 - € 7,90
electricity (10A)	€ 4,10 - € 4,50
dog	free - € 2,00

Camping Cheques accepted.

FR83170 Camping Domaine de la Bergerie

Vallée du Fournel, route du Col-du-Bougnon, F-83520 Roquebrune-sur-Argens (Var)

Tel: **04 98 11 45 45**. Email: **info@domainelabergerie.com** **www.alanrogers.com/FR83170**

This excellent site near the Côte d'Azur will take you away from all the bustle of the Mediterranean to total relaxation amongst the cork, oak, pine and mimosa in its woodland setting. The 60 hectare site is quite spread out with semi-landscaped areas for mobile homes and, grassy avenues of 200 separated pitches for touring caravans and tents. All pitches average over 80 sq.m. and have electricity, with those in one area also having water and drainage. The restaurant/bar, a converted farm building, is surrounded by shady patios, whilst inside it oozes character.

Facilities

Four toilet blocks (all refurbished in 2007) are kept clean and include washbasins in cubicles, facilities for people with disabilities, and babies. Supermarket. Bar/restaurant. Takeaway. Pool complex (5/4-30/9) with indoor pool and fitness centre (body building, sauna, gym, etc). Tennis courts. Archery. Roller skating. Minigolf. English speaking children's club. Mini-farm for children. Fishing. Only gas barbecues are permitted. Off site: Riding or golf 2 km. Bicycle hire 7 km. Beach, St Aygulf or Ste Maxime 7 km.

Open: 25 April - 30 September (mobile homes 15 February - 15 November).

Directions

Leave A8 at Le Muy exit on N7 towards Fréjus. Proceed for 9 km. then right onto D7 signed St Aygulf. Continue for 8 km. and then right at roundabout on D8; site is on the right. GPS: N43:24.547 E06:40.481

Charges guide

Per unit incl. 2 persons and electricity (6A)	€ 18,50 - € 40,00
incl. water and drainage	€ 24,00 - € 45,00
extra person	€ 5,00 - € 9,00
child (under 7 yrs)	€ 3,60 - € 6,50

FR83240 Camping Caravaning Moulin des Iscles

Quartier la Valette, F-83520 Roquebrune-sur-Argens (Var)

Tel: **04 94 45 70 74**. Email: **moulin.iscles@wanadoo.fr** **www.alanrogers.com/FR83240**

Moulin des Iscles is a small, pretty site beside the river Argens with access to the river in places for fishing, canoeing and swimming, with some sought after pitches overlooking the river. The 90 grassy, level pitches have water and electricity (6A). A nice mixture of deciduous trees provides natural shade and colour and the old mill house is near the entrance, which has the security barrier closed at night. This is a quiet site with little on-site entertainment. Disabled visitors are made very welcome.

Facilities

Fully equipped toilet block, plus small block near entrance, ramped access for disabled visitors. Some Turkish style toilets. Washbasins have cold water. Baby bath and changing facilities. Washing machine. Restaurant, home cooked dish-of-the-day. Well stocked shop. Library with some English books. TV, pool table, table tennis. Play area, minigolf, boules all outside the barrier. Internet terminal. Canoeing possible. Off site: Bicycle hire 1 km. (cycle way to St Aygulf). Riding and golf 4 km. Beach 9 km.

Open: 1 April - 30 September.

Directions

From A8, exit Le Muy, follow N7 towards Fréjus for 13 km. Cross over A8 and turn right at roundabout through Roquebrune sur Argens towards St Aygulf for 1 km. Site signed on left. Follow private unmade road for 500 m. GPS: N43:26.708 E06:39.470

Charges guide

Per unit incl. 2 or 3 persons	€ 20,00
extra person	€ 3,30

Prices are lower out of high season. Camping Cheques accepted.

FR20040 Riva Bella Nature Resort & Spa

B.P. 21, F-20270 Alèria (Haute-Corse)

Tel: **04 95 38 81 10**. Email: **riva-bella@wanadoo.fr** **www.alanrogers.com/FR20040**

This is a relaxed, informal, spacious site alongside an extremely long and beautiful beach. Riva Bella is naturist from 15 May to 20 September only. It offers a variety of pitches, situated in beautiful countryside and seaside. The site is divided into several areas with 200 pitches and bungalows, some alongside the sandy beach with little shade, others in a wooded glade with ample shade. The huge fish-laden lakes are a fine feature of this site. Although electricity is available in most parts, a long cable may be needed. The ground is fairly flat with terracing for tents.

Facilities

High standard toilet facilities. Provision for disabled people, children and babies. Laundry. Large shop (15/5-15/10). Fridge hire. Restaurant with lake views (all season) with reasonable prices. Excellent beach/snack bar. Bar. Watersports, sailing school, fishing, sub-aqua. Balnéotherapy centre. Sauna. Aerobics. Giant draughts. Archery. Fishing. Riding. Mountain bike hire. Half-court tennis. Walk with llamas. Internet. WiFi. Entertainment.

Open: 30 March - 2 November.

Directions

Site is 12 km. north of Aleria on N198 (Bastia) road. Watch for large signs and unmade road to site and follow for 4 km. GPS: N42:09.691 E09:33.161

Charges 2009

Per unit incl. 2 persons and electricity	€ 15,00 - € 38,00
extra person	€ 5,00 - € 9,00
child (3-8 yrs)	€ 2,00 - € 6,00

Camping Cheques accepted.

With its wealth of scenic and cultural interests, Germany is a land of contrasts. From the flat lands of the north to the mountains in the south, with forests in the east and west, regional characteristics are a strong feature of German life and present a rich variety of folklore and customs.

CAPITAL: BERLIN

Tourist Office

German National Tourist Office
PO Box 2695, London W1A 3TN
Tel: 020 7317 0908
Fax: 020 7317 0917
Email: gntolon@d-z-t.com
Internet: www.germany-tourism.co.uk

Each region in Germany differs greatly to the next. Home of lederhosen, beer and sausages is Bavaria in the south, full of charming forest villages, beautiful lakes, and towering mountains dotted with castles. In the southwest, Baden Württemberg is famous for its ancient Black Forest, with dense woodlands, medieval towns and scenic lakes, this region is a walker's paradise. Further west is the stunningly beautiful, Rhine Valley full of romantic castles, wine villages, woodland walks and river trails. Eastern Germany is studded with lakes and rivers, undulating lowlands that give way to mountains. The north has its lively ports such as Bremen and Hamburg and picturesque coastal towns, where watersports are a popular pastime in the North Sea. The capital city of Berlin, situated in the northeast of the county, is an increasingly popular tourist destination, with its blend of old and modern architecture and huge variety of entertainment on offer.

Population

83.2 million

Climate

Temperate climate. In general winters are a little colder and summers a little warmer than in the UK.

Language

German

Telephone

The country code is 00 49.

Money

Currency: The Euro
Banks: Mon-Fri 08.30-12.30 and 14.00-16.00. Late opening on Thurs until 18.00.

Shops

Mon-Fri 08.30/09.00 to 18.00/18.30.

Public Holidays

New Year's Day; Good Fri; Easter Mon; Labour Day; Ascension; Whit Mon; Unification Day 3 Oct; Christmas, 25, 26 Dec. In some areas: Epiphany 6 Jan; Corpus Christi 22 Jun; Assumption 15 Aug; Reformation 31 Oct; All Saints 1 Nov (plus other regional days).

Motoring

An excellent network of (toll-free) motorways (autobahns) exists in the `West' and the traffic moves fast. Remember in the `East' a lot of road building is going on amongst other works so allow plenty of time when travelling and be prepared for poor road surfaces.

DE3005 Camping Schnelsen Nord

Wunderbrunnen 2, D-22457 Hamburg (Hamburg)

Tel: **040 559 4225**. Email: **service@campingplatz-hamburg.de** **www.alanrogers.com/DE3005**

Situated some 15 km. from the centre of Hamburg on the northern edge of the town, Schnelsen Nord is a suitable base either for visiting this famous German city, or as a night stop before catching the Harwich ferry or travelling to Denmark. There is some traffic noise because the autobahn runs alongside and also some aircraft noise. However, the proximity of the A7 (E45) does make it easy to find. The 145 pitches for short-term touring are of about 100 sq.m, on grass with access from gravel roads. All have 6A electricity and are marked out with small trees and hedges.

Facilities

A deposit is required for the key to the single sanitary block, a well constructed modern building with good quality facilities and heated in cool weather. Good facilities for disabled visitors, with special pitches close to the block. Washing machines and dryers. Motorcaravan service point (for site guests only). Shop (basics only). Playground. Dogs are not accepted. Off site: Bus service, restaurants and shops 10 minutes walk. Swimming pool, tennis courts, golf and fishing nearby.

Open: 1 April - 31 October.

Directions

From A7 autobahn take Schnelsen Nord exit. Stay in outside lane as you will soon need to turn back left; follow signs for Ikea store and site signs.
GPS: N53:38.998 E09:55.736

Charges guide

Per person	€ 6,00
child (3-13 yrs)	€ 3,50
pitch	€ 7,20 - € 11,50
electricity (6A)	€ 2,50

DE3010 Kur & Feriencamping Röders Park

Ebsmoor 8, D-29614 Soltau (Lower Saxony)

Tel: **051 912 141**. Email: **info@roeders-park.de** **www.alanrogers.com/DE3010**

Although near Soltau centre (1.5 km), Ebsmoor is a peaceful location, ideal for visits to the famous Luneburg Heath or as a stop on the route to Denmark. The site is run by the third generation of the Röders family who make their visitors most welcome (each guest receives a local information pack) and speak excellent English. There are 120 pitches (90 touring), all with 6A electricity and 85 with water and drainage. Some 40 pitches have satellite TV connections. Most have hardstanding and there is reasonable privacy between pitches. The central feature of the wooded site is a small lake.

Facilities

Two modern, very clean sanitary blocks (one with under-floor heating) contain all necessary facilities. Excellent, separate unit (including shower) for wheelchair users. Private bathrooms for rent. Laundry room. Motorcaravan services. Gas supplies. Simple shop. Restaurant and takeaway (all Easter - Oct). Play area. Bicycle hire. Internet (free), WiFi (on payment). Off site: Thermal swimming pool 1 km. Fishing and riding 1.5 km. Golf 3 km. 999 km. of cycle paths in the surrounding area. Bus service 100 m.

Open: All year.

Directions

From Soltau take B3 road north and turning to site is on left after 1.5 km. (opposite DCC camping sign) at yellow town boundary sign.
GPS: N53:00.133 E09:50.317

Charges 2009

Per person	€ 6,00
child (4-13 yrs)	€ 4,00
pitch	€ 11,50
electricity (6A) plus meter	€ 1,00
dog	€ 2,00

DE3021 Camping am Stadtwaldsee

Hochschulring 1, D-28359 Bremen (Bremen)

Tel: **042 184 10748**. Email: **contact@camping-stadtwaldsee.de** **www.alanrogers.com/DE3021**

This well designed and purpose built campsite overlooking a lake was opened in October 2005 and is ideally placed for those travelling to northern Europe and for people wishing to visit Bremen and places within the region. There is a bus stop outside the site. Of the 220 level pitches 168 are for touring units, standing on grass with openwork reinforcements at the entrances. All have electricity (16A), water and drainage. The pitches are positioned around the grass roofed sanitary block and are laid out in areas separated by young trees and hedges.

Facilities

Modern sanitary block with free hot showers, facilities for disabled people, five private bathrooms for rental. Washing machines and dryers. Kitchen. Supermarket. Lakeside café/restaurant. Health centre with fitness courses. Play room. Play area. Lake swimming, Naturist beach three minutes walk away. Windsurfing, fishing and scuba diving. Tents for hire. WiFi. Bicycle hire. Off site: Riding 8 km. Golf 10 km.

Open: All year.

Directions

From A27 northeast of Bremen take exit 19 for 'Universitat' and follow signs for University and camping. Site is on the left, 1 km. after leaving the university area. GPS: N53:06.890 E08:49.948

Charges 2009

Per person	€ 8,00 - € 9,00
caravan or motorcaravan incl. electricity (plus per kWh)	€ 10,00 - € 11,00
tent and car	€ 6,50 - € 7,00

DE3055 Camping Prahljust

Lange Brüche 4, D-38678 Clausthal-Zellerfeld (Lower Saxony)

Tel: **053 231 300**. Email: **camping@prahljust.de** **www.alanrogers.com/DE3055**

In a woodland setting, 600 metres high and well away from main roads Camping Prahljust is a quiet site providing plenty of fresh air in an attractive location. The site slopes gently down to a lake which is used for swimming, boating, windsurfing and fishing or in winter ice skating. Of the 800 plus pitches 500 are reserved for tourists. These are arranged in larger open, grass areas separated by hedges with plenty of tree cover and all have electrical connections. The Oberharz is a winter sports region and January and February are the busiest months, with cross-country skiing from the site. During the rest of the year this attractive region has much to offer; rambling, mountain-biking and rock climbing are all popular and the list of interesting places to visit is almost unending. Early mining activity brought wealth to the region resulting in the development of many beautiful medieval towns with their half-timbered houses and impressive public buildings. The reception has a good selection of brochures on display; however the best tourist advice comes from the campsite owner, Rheinhardt Struve, who speaks excellent English.

Facilities

Three modern, heated toilet blocks are well maintained and hold all the usual facilities. Showers are free. Facilities for disabled people. Baby room. Washing machines, dryers, drying room and kitchen. Motorcaravan service point. Shop, restaurant and bar (closed Nov). Indoor, heated swimming pool (12 x 9 m; no shallow end). Sauna and solarium. Massage. Internet access. Fishing. Bicycle hire. Off site: Bus service 1.5 km. Riding 5 km.

Open: All year.

Directions

Leave Clausthal-Zellerfeld on the B242 towards Braunlage. After 1 km. site is signed. Turn south and site is a further 1.5 km.
GPS: N51:47.066 E10:20.985

Charges guide

Per person	€ 4,70
child	€ 4,20
pitch	€ 4,80
electricity per kWh	€ 0,55

Winter charges higher. Camping Cheques accepted.

DE3025 Alfsee Ferien- & Erholungspark

Am Campingpark 10, D-49597 Rieste (Lower Saxony)

Tel: **054 649 2120**. Email: **info@alfsee.com** **www.alanrogers.com/DE3025**

Alfsee has plenty to offer for the active family and children of all ages. It is a really good base for enjoying the many watersports activities available here on the two lakes. Improvements to this already well-equipped site continue. There are now over 800 pitches (many long stay but with 400 for tourers) on flat grass, 85 with 16A electricity, with some shade for those in the original area. A new camping area provides 290 large, serviced pitches. Member of 'Leading Campings Group'.

Facilities

Three excellent sanitary blocks serve the original area with two new first class, heated buildings with family bathrooms (to rent), baby rooms and laundry facilities. Cooking facilities. Motorcaravan services. Gas supplies. Shop, restaurants and takeaway (high season). Pub with internet point. Watersports. Playground, new indoor play centre and entertainment for children. Entertainment hall. Tennis. Trampoline. Minigolf. Go-kart track. Games room. Fishing. Bicycle hire. Riding. Off site: Golf 10 km.

Open: All year.

Directions

From A1 autobahn north of Osnabrück take exit 67 for Neuenkirchen and follow signs for Rieste, Alfsee and site. GPS: N52:29.158 E07:59.529

Charges guide

Per person	€ 3,20 - € 6,20
child or student	€ 2,90 - € 4,20
pitch	€ 8,10 - € 12,50
electricity (once only plus meter)	€ 1,00

DE3065 Camping am Bärenbache

Bärenbachweg 10, Hohegeiss, D-38700 Braunlage (Lower Saxony)

Tel: **055 831 306**. Email: **info@campingplatz-hohegeiss.de** **www.alanrogers.com/DE3065**

Pleasantly situated and over 600 metres high in the Harz, Campingplatz Bärenbache is a quiet, attractive, well run family site having direct access to the forests that surround it. This terraced site on a south facing slope reaps the maximum benefit from the sun throughout the year and offers views of the surrounding hills in an area known for its fresh air. Of the 140 pitches 90 are reserved for tourists all having 10A electrical connections. The level pitches are separated by hedges and are of various sizes, some suitable for one, others for several units.

Facilities

As can be expected in a site that also has a winter season, all facilities are housed internally in the modern, well maintained and heated toilet block. Showers are free. Baby room. Washing machines, dryers and iron, drying room. Small kitchen with cooking rings. Bread to order. Bar/restaurant (all year) beside the pool. Large outdoor heated pool with two separate pools for children. Small playground. Bicycle hire. Off site: Village centre is only a few minutes walk. Riding 3 km. Fishing 10 km.

Open: All year.

Directions

The village of Hohegeiß is 10 km. southeast of Braunlage on the B4 road. Leaving Hohegeiß in the direction of Zorge, site is signed. Turn left before leaving village, 250 m. from the main road.
GPS: N51:39.220 E10:40.080

Charges guide

Per person	€ 4,30 - € 5,00
child (3-14 yrs)	€ 3,10 - € 3,50
pitch	€ 4,90
electricity per kWh	€ 0,53

DE3070 Südsee-Camp

Südsee-Camp 104, D-29649 Wietzendorf (Lower Saxony)

Tel: **051 969 80116**. Email: **forst104@suedseecamp.de** **www.alanrogers.com/DE3070**

Südsee-Camp in the Lüneburger Heide is a large well organised holiday centre where children are especially well catered for. Südsee has its own brochures that include walking, cycling and car tours. There are 1,100 touring pitches of varying types and sizes, all with electricity and most with fresh water, drainage and TV connection. Modern sanitary blocks are well maintained and contain all necessary facilities. Although centred around a large sandy shored lake, the main swimming attraction is the South See Tropical swimming pool. Member of 'Leading Campings Group'.

Facilities

Thirteen, modern well maintained sanitary blocks with all the expected facilities, including facilities for disabled people and private bathrooms to rent. Hot showers need a token. Special areas for children ('Kinderland'), facilities for babies. Laundry rooms. Kitchens. Bars, restaurants and snack bars. Pool complex (on payment). Soundproof disco. Fitness room. Bicycle hire. Games room. Internet. Off site: Riding adjacent. Fishing 2 km. Golf 12 km.

Open: All year.

Directions

From A7 autobahn take exit 45 towards Bergen and Celle on the B3 (campsite is signed). After 6 km. turn left (site again signed). GPS: N52:55.540 E09:57.550

Charges guide

Per unit incl. 2 persons and electricity	€ 18,20 - € 38,00
extra person	€ 3,50 - € 4,50
child (2-18 yrs)	€ 2,00 - € 3,50
dog	€ 2,00 - € 3,00

DE3080 Campingplatz am Hardausee

D-29556 Suderburg-Hosseringen (Lower Saxony)

Tel: **058 267 676**. Email: **info@camping-hardausee.de** **www.alanrogers.com/DE3080**

The Hardausee site is evolving from a 'seasonal only' site into a site for touring units. When we visited, there were 80 touring pitches and 270 seasonal units, but as soon as a seasonal guest leaves, the pitch will be reallocated for touring. Hardausee is on sloping ground although the grassy, marked pitches are mostly level. Some pitches are numbered and most are 100 sq.m. or larger. The newer pitches have hardly any shade, but mature trees surround the older field. There are 45 serviced pitches with 16A electricity, water and drainage.

Facilities

Three heated toilet blocks provide washbasins in cabins and free, controllable hot showers. Washing machines and dryer. Motorcaravan services. Shop (for basics). Bar, restaurant and takeaway (April - Oct, closed Mondays). Large adventure playground. Cycling tours and excursions in the woods. Fishing. Lakeside beach. Off site: Bus service 200 m. Riding 1 km. Bicycle hire 300 m.

Open: All year.

Directions

From Uelzen, follow 4/191 road south towards Braunschweig. Take exit for Suderburg and follow signs for Hösseringen. Site is signed on the right 2 km. before Hösseringen.
GPS: N52:52.475 E10:28.475

Charges guide

Per person	€ 5,00
pitch	€ 5,00 - € 6,00
electricity	€ 2,00

No credit cards.

DE3030 Regenbogen-Camp Tecklenburg

Grafenstrasse 31, D-49545 Tecklenburg-Leeden (North Rhine-Westphalia)

Tel: **054 051 007**. Email: **tecklenburg@regenbogen-camp.de** **www.alanrogers.com/DE3030**

This is a well designed and attractive countryside site with lots of trees and hedges where modern buildings have been built in keeping with the traditional, half timbered style of the region. There are 500 grass touring pitches arranged on large, open areas divided by tall hedges. Trees provide good shade and all pitches have electrical connections. Access from the A30 autobahn is convenient, although this is offset by the fact that some noise from the autobahn is evident in the touring pitch area. Facilities on this site are really good and include a modern pool complex.

Facilities

Four modern, heated toilet blocks have free showers and provision for disabled visitors. Washing machines and dryer. Cooking facilities. Motorcaravan service point. Shop. Large traditional, timbered bar and restaurant (Easter - end Oct and Christmas). Excellent heated pool complex with indoor and outdoor pools, slide and paddling pool. Large play area. Minigolf. Off site: Riding 3 km. Golf 5 km. Fishing 6 km.

Open: All year.

Directions

Leave A30/E30 autobahn at exit 13 towards Tecklenburg. Between the autobahn exit and Tecklenburg, the site is signed at a roundabout. Leeden is a village to the east of Tecklenburg, site is 2 km. from the village. GPS: N52:13.768 E07:53.411

Charges guide

Per person	€ 6,30 - € 7,95
pitch	€ 7,90 - € 13,60
electricity	€ 2,90

DE3180 Camping Sonnenwiese

Borlefzen 1, D-32602 Vlotho (North Rhine-Westphalia)

Tel: **057 338 217**. Email: **info@sonnenwiese.com** **www.alanrogers.com/DE3180**

Sonnenwiese is a first class, family run campsite where care has been taken to make everyone feel at home – there is even an insect hotel! Situated between wooded hills to the north and bordering the Weser river to the south, this 400 pitch site offers 100 touring pitches, all with electricity and most also having water and drainage. In addition, there are special pitches with a private shower, toilet and washbasin unit. The site is particularly orientated towards families with children.

Facilities

The toilet block is modern and maintained to the highest standard. Showers are token operated. Baby room. Washing machines, dryer and ironing board. Cooking facilities. Supermarket. Panorama restaurant with good choice of dishes. Snack bar. Sauna, solarium and fitness room. Club room and room used for children's entertainment. Large adventure play area. Grass bordered lake for swimming. Fishing. Bicycle hire. Off site: Bus service from gate. Golf 4 km. Riding 5 km.

Open: All year.

Directions

Leave A2 autobahn at exit 31, 32 or 33 and head for Vlotho. In Vlotho, cross the Weser river and after 3 km. on the right are the entrances to two campsites. Sonnenwiese is on the left hand side at the end of the entrance road.
GPS: N52:10.250 E08:54.240

Charges 2009

Per person	€ 4,80
pitch	€ 8,00
electricity (plus € 0.40 kWh)	€ 0,50

No credit cards.

DE3182 Ferienpark Teutoburger Wald

Badeanstaltsweg 4, D-32683 Barntrup (North Rhine-Westphalia)

Tel: **052 632 221**. Email: **info@ferienparkteutoburgerwald.de** **www.alanrogers.com/DE3182**

Under Dutch ownership, this site has 135 touring pitches, all with 16A electricity. Just outside the main gate there are nine fully serviced hardstanding pitches designed with motorcaravans in mind. Although the site is sloping, the pitches of about 100 sq.m. are on mainly level grassy areas with some shade. Energy saving equipment has been installed in the toilet block for the production of hot water and use of electricity and gas and the site is actively promoting good environmental practices in order to achieve this.

Facilities

Excellent toilet block with underfloor heating and Roman baths theme inside. Roomy showers and open washbasins. Colourful children's section. Family showers. Dog shower. Laundry facilities. Key system for use of hot water. Motorcaravan service point. Games room with TV. Free WiFi. Play area. Off site: Walking in the adjacent woods. Outdoor pool next door. Spa town of Bad Pyrmont 12 km. Famous fairytale town of Hameln 20 km.

Open: 20 March - 30 September.

Directions

From Hanover, take the A2 west towards Osnabrück. At exit 35 continue on B83 road towards Hameln. In Hameln take the B1 road south towards Barntrup and follow signs. GPS: N51:59.209 E09:06.508

Charges 2009

Per pitch incl. 2 persons and electricity	€ 19,00 - € 26,00
with private sanitary facilities	€ 27,00 - € 36,00
extra person	€ 3,00 - € 5,25

DE3185 Campingplatz Münster

Laerer Werseufer 7, (Wolbecker Strasse), D-48157 Münster (North Rhine-Westphalia)

Tel: **025 131 1982**. Email: **campingplatz-muenster@t-online.de** **www.alanrogers.com/DE3185**

This is a first class site on the outskirts of Münster. Of a total of 570 pitches, 120 are touring units, each with electricity, water, drainage and TV socket. The pitches are level, most with partial hardstanding and others are separated into groups by mature hedges and a number of trees provide shade. The university city of Münster with its many historical buildings and over 500 bars and restaurants, many offering local traditional dishes, is only 5 km. from the site. The city is the main attraction in this region and well worth visiting, especially on market days. Next to the reception desk is a small shop and adjacent is a comfortable bar/restaurant with a terrace. Bicycles are available for hire and there are cycle tour maps for the area. Just outside the campsite there is a bus stop. For those who wish to avoid the stress of driving in busy foreign cities and the even worse problem of finding a parking place, public transport offers a good solution.

Facilities

The two toilet blocks are well designed, modern and maintained to the highest standards. Controllable showers are token operated. Two units for disabled guests. Baby room. Cooking facilities. Washing machine, dryer and ironing facilities. Sauna and solarium. Hairdressing salon. Motorcaravan service point. Shop. Bar/restaurant. Minigolf. Play area. Chess. Tennis. Playroom for children under 8 yrs. Bicycle hire. Security barrier card deposit € 10. Off site: Public open air swimming pool adjacent. Canoeing and fishing. Bus stop 100 m.

Open: All year.

Directions

Site is 5 km. southeast of Münster city centre. Leave A1 autobahn at exit 78 (Münster Süd) and take B51 towards Münster. After 2 km. stay on the B51 in the direction of Bielefeld/Warendorf. After 5 km. turn south (right) towards Wolbeck. Follow site signs. GPS: N51:56.784 E07:41.467

Charges 2009

Per unit incl. 2 persons and electricity	€ 24,00 - € 24,50
extra person	€ 6,00
child (4-11 yrs)	€ 4,00

Various out of season reduction from 10%-20%

DE3202 Erholungszentrum Grav-Insel

Gravinsel 1, D-46487 Wesel (North Rhine-Westphalia)

Tel: **028 197 2830**. Email: **info@grav-insel.com** **www.alanrogers.com/DE3202**

Grav-Insel claims to be the largest family camping site in Germany, providing entertainment and activities to match, with over 2,000 permanent units. A section for 500 touring units runs beside the water to the left of the entrance and this area has been completely renewed. These pitches, all with 10A electricity, are flat, grassy, mostly without shade and of about 100 sq.m. A walk through the site takes you past a nature reserve and to the Rhine where you can watch the barges. Despite its size, this site is very well maintained, calm, clean and spacious and this is down to the family which started it 40 years ago. This site, on the border with Holland, is an excellent stop over for the north and east of Germany. However, once here, you may decide to stay longer to take advantage of the excellent restaurant (special evenings each week), bird watching on the private reserve or to visit Xanten with its Roman amphitheatre in the archaeological park.

Facilities

Excellent sanitary facilities are all housed in a modern building above which is the bar/restaurant (open all year). Touring area augmented by portacabin units to be renewed. Facilities for disabled visitors. Baby room. Launderette. Motorcaravan service point. Large supermarket. Entertainment area with satellite TV. WiFi. Solarium. Large play area on sand plus wet weather indoor area. Boat park. Sailing. Fishing. Swimming. Football (international coaching in high season). Animation in high season. Off site: Bus service 500 m. Attractive town of Xanten 23 km. Nord Park Duisburg, where an old steelworks has been turned into a leisure complex 25 km. Kleve (Cleves), the birthplace of Anne of Cleves 30 km. Warner Bros Movie Park, Bottrop 30 km.

Open: All year.

Directions

Site is 5 km. northwest of Wesel. From the A3 take exit 6 and B58 towards Wesel, then right towards Rees. Turn left at sign for Flüren, through Flüren and left to site after 1.5 km. If approaching Wesel from the west (B58), cross the Rhine, turn left at first traffic lights and follow signs Grav Insel and Flüren. GPS: N51:40.237 E06:33.360

Charges guide

Per person	€ 2,00 - € 3,00
child (under 12 yrs)	€ 1,00 - € 1,50
pitch	€ 3,00 - € 6,50
electricity	€ 3,00
dog	€ 0,50 - € 1,00

DE3205 Campingplatz der Stadt Köln

Weidenweg 35, D-51105 Köln-Poll (North Rhine-Westphalia)

Tel: **022 183 1966**. Email: **die-eckardts@netcologne.de** **www.alanrogers.com/DE3205**

The ancient city of Cologne offers much for the visitor. This wooded park is pleasantly situated along the river bank, with wide grass areas (the manager takes great pains to keep it well) on either side of narrow tarmac access roads with low metal barriers separating it from the public park and riverside walks. Of 140 unmarked, level or slightly undulating touring pitches, 50 have 10A electricity and there is shade for some from various mature trees. Tents have their own large area. Because of its position close to the autobahn bridge over the Rhine, there is road and river noise.

Facilities

The small toilet block has fairly basic facilities, but is heated with free hot water (06.00-12.00, 17.00-23.00) in the washing troughs (to be replaced by washbasins in 2009) and by token in the showers. New facilities for disabled visitors. Open-fronted room for cooking and eating. Washing machine and dryer. Small shop for bread and basic supplies (mid May - Sept). Microwave evening snacks (March - Oct). Fishing. Bicycle hire. Drinks machine. Off site: Bar/café by entrance. Trams and buses to city centre 1 km. across the bridge. Golf 5 km. Riding 15 km.

Open: Easter - 12 October.

Directions

Leave A4 at exit 13 for Köln-Poll (just to west off intersection of A3 and A4). Turn left at first traffic lights and follow international site signs through a sometimes fairly narrow one-way system to the riverside, back towards the motorway bridge. GPS: N50:54.163 E06:59.440

Charges guide

Per person	€ 5,50
child (4-12 yrs)	€ 3,00
pitch incl. car	€ 5,00 - € 7,00
electricity	€ 1,50

DE3210 Feriencamp Biggesee - Vier Jarheszeiten

Am Sonderner Kopf 3, D-57462 Olpe-Sondern (North Rhine-Westphalia)

Tel: **027 619 44111**. Email: **info@biggesee-sondern.com** **www.alanrogers.com/DE3210**

Situated on a gentle, south facing, slope that leads down to the waters edge of the Biggesee, Feriencamp Biggesee blends in well with its wooded surroundings. The 250 touring pitches, all with electricity, are arranged in circles at the top part of the site and on a series of wide terraces lower down. They are grassy with some hardstanding. From the lower part of the site there is access to a large open meadow that ends at the water's edge where swimming is permitted. The attractive Biggesee, with arms branching out into the surrounding hills, is a watersports paradise.

Facilities

Excellent heated sanitary facilities are in two areas. Many washbasins in cabins and special showers for children. Facilities for babies and people with disabilities. Laundry. Motorcaravan services. Cooking facilities. Shop. Restaurant. Bistro (including breakfast). Playroom and playground for smaller children. Grill hut. Fishing. Bicycle hire. Solarium and sauna. Entertainment and excursions. Off site: Train service 1 km. Tennis near. Riding 8 km. Golf 12 km. Restaurant and snacks 300 m. (Easter - 31/10).

Open: All year.

Directions

From A45 (Siegen - Hagen) autobahn, take exit 18 to Olpe (N), and turn towards Attendorn. After 6 km. turn right signed 'Erholungsanlage', then after 100 m. turn right and follow site signs. GPS: N51:04.438 E07:51.390

Charges guide

Per person	€ 4,05 - € 4,65
pitch incl. electricity	€ 12,40 - € 14,45

No credit cards.

DE3002 Camping Park Schlei-Karschau

Karschau 56, D-24407 Rabenkirchen-Faulück (Schleswig-Holstein)

Tel: **04642 920 820**. Email: **info@campingpark-schlei.de** **www.alanrogers.com/DE3002**

Schlei-Karschau is a pleasant, quiet site on the only Baltic Sea fjord in Germany. All you will hear is the wind from the sea and the calls of the birds. This site is ideal if you enjoy fishing or sailing, or you could visit one of the beaches on this coast, just 10 km. further on. The site has 160 open pitches, 100 for touring units, all with at least 6A electricity. There is no shop as yet, but bread can be ordered from a kiosk and a restaurant, with a bar and takeaway, is open in high season.

Facilities

The single sanitary block includes controllable hot showers in cabins with washbasin, child size toilets and washbasins and facilities for disabled visitors. Laundry facilities. Campers' kitchen. Motorcaravan services. Restaurant and bar (daily in high season). New playground. Sports field. Children's activity programme in high season. River fishing (permits from reception). Bicycle hire. Motor boat hire. Off site: Golf 4 km. Riding 6 km. Beach 10 km.

Open: All year.

Directions

Follow the A7 from Hamburg north to Flensburg and take exit Schleswig - Schuby. Take the B201 road towards Kappeln. Drive through Süderbrarup and turn right 5 km. after village to Faulück. Follow signs to site. GPS: N54:37.176 E09:53.049

Charges guide

Per person	€ 4,00 - € 5,00
pitch	€ 7,00 - € 9,00

Camping Cheques accepted.

DE3007 Strandcamping Wallnau

Wallnau 1, D-23769 Fehmarn (Schleswig-Holstein)
Tel: **043 729 456**. Email: **wallnau@strandcamping.de** **www.alanrogers.com/DE3007**

With direct beach access and protected from the wind by a dyke, this family site is on Germany's second largest island (since 1963 joined to the Baltic sea coast by a bridge). This is a quiet location on the western part of Fehmarn island in close proximity to a large bird sanctuary. Of the 800 pitches 400 are for touring, all with electricity and on level grass areas arranged in alleys and separated by hedges. The island is low lying, ideal for leisurely walking or cycle riding especially along the track that runs along the top of the dyke. The beach is a mixture of sand and pebbles and in summer lifeguards are on duty. The southern part is a naturist area. For those with an ornithological interest the bird sanctuary with over 80 species is worth visiting. Swimming, sailing and diving are possible in the sea and there is a windsurfing school. For those who prefer dry land there is pony riding for children and a riding school. During summer there are entertainment programmes for children and courses for adults; twice a week there are film shows and a disco.

Facilities

Heated sanitary blocks (cleaning variable) provide free showers. Child size toilets and showers. Baby rooms. Facilities for disabled guests. Laundry facilities. Motorcaravan service points. Shop. Bar, restaurant and snack bar. Open air stage and soundproof disco. Health/cure centre, solarium and sauna. Archery. Watersports. Minigolf. Internet café. WiFi. Beach fishing. Off site: Boat launching 6 km. Golf 15 km.

Open: 27 March - 25 October.

Directions

Cross the bridge and follow road to Landkirchen and Petersdorf where site is signed. It is 4 km. northwest of the town. GPS: N54:29.257 E11:01.116

Charges 2009

Per person	€ 4,00 - € 7,20
child (under 17 yrs)	€ 2,00 - € 6,30
pitch	€ 6,50 - € 17,00
electricity	€ 2,40

No credit cards. Camping Cheques accepted.

DE3008 Klüthseecamp Seeblick

Klüthseehof 2, D-23795 Klein Rönnau (Schleswig-Holstein)
Tel: **045 518 2368**. Email: **info@kluethseecamp.de** **www.alanrogers.com/DE3008**

Klüthseecamp Seeblick is a modern, family run site situated on a small hill between two lakes. For those travelling on the A1 to Denmark it is a convenient overnight site, but additionally it is a useful base to explore the region. The large, open grass, touring part of the site is divided into smaller areas by some low hedges and young trees. There are 120 pitches on fairly level ground, all with electricity (10/16A) and 70 with water and drainage. The site has two other parts, one accommodating permanent campers, the other for those who prefer camping in natural surroundings.

Facilities

Two cheerful, modern, heated sanitary blocks have washbasins (open or in cabins), six bathrooms to rent and free controllable showers. Facilities for disabled visitors. Attractive baby room. Gas supplies. Laundry room. Sauna, steam bath, massage. TV room. Play room. Bicycle hire. Minigolf. Wellness. Off site: Golf 6 km. Beach 25 km.

Open: All year.

Directions

Site is 26 km. west-northwest of Lübeck. Leave the A1 at exit 27 and travel north towards Kiel on the A21 to exit 13 (Bad Segeberg Sud). Follow the B432 (Hamburger Strasse) into Bad Segeberg and at T-junction with Ziegelstrasse turn left (north) and continue on B432. 300 m. after Klein Rönnau turn right into Stripsdorferweg. Site is signed. GPS: N53:57.661 E10:20.289

Charges guide

Per person	€ 7,50
pitch	€ 3,50 - € 7,80

Camping Cheques accepted.

DE3003 Camping Wulfener Hals

Wulfener Hals Weg 16, D-23769 Wulfen auf Fehmarn (Schleswig-Holstein)

Tel: **043 718 6280**. Email: **camping@wulfenerhals.de** **www.alanrogers.com/DE3003**

If you are travelling to Denmark or on to Sweden, taking the E47/A1 then B207 from Hamburg, and the ferry from Puttgarden to Rødbyhavn, this is a top class, all year round site, either to rest overnight or as a base for a longer stay. Attractively situated by the sea, it is a large, mature site (34 hectares) and is well maintained. It has over 800 individual pitches of up to 160 sq.m. (half for touring) in glades and some separated by bushes, with shade in the older parts, less in the newer areas nearer the sea. There are many hardstandings and 552 pitches have electricity, water and drainage. A separate area has been developed for motorcaravans. It provides 60 extra large pitches, all with electricity, water and drainage, and some with TV aerial points, together with a new toilet block. There is much to do for old and young alike at Wolfener Hals, with a new heated outdoor pool and paddling pool (unsupervised), although the sea is naturally popular as well. The site also has many sporting facilities including its own golf courses and schools for watersports. Member of 'Leading Campings Group'.

Facilities

Five heated sanitary buildings have first class facilities including showers and both open washbasins and private cabins. Family bathrooms for rent. Facilities for disabled people. Laundry. Motorcaravan services. Shop, bar, restaurants and takeaway (April-Oct). Swimming pool (May - Oct). Sauna. Solarium. Jacuzzi. Sailing, windsurfing and diving schools. Boat slipway. Golf courses (18 hole, par 72 and 9 hole, par 27). Riding. Fishing. Archery. Good play equipment for younger children. Bicycle hire. Catamaran hire. Off site: Naturist beach 500 m. Village mini-market 2 km.

Open: All year.

Directions

From Hamburg take A1/E47 north to Puttgarden, cross the bridge onto the island of Fehmarn and turn right twice to Avendorf and follow the signs for Wulfen and the site. GPS: N54:24.783 E11:10.424

Charges guide

Per unit incl. 2 persons and electricity	€ 17,30 - € 40,60
extra person	€ 3,80 - € 8,10
child (2-13 yrs)	€ 2,20 - € 5,40
child (14-18 yrs)	€ 3,30 - € 7,00
water and waste water	€ 2,50

Plus surcharges for larger pitches.
Many discounts available and special family prices.

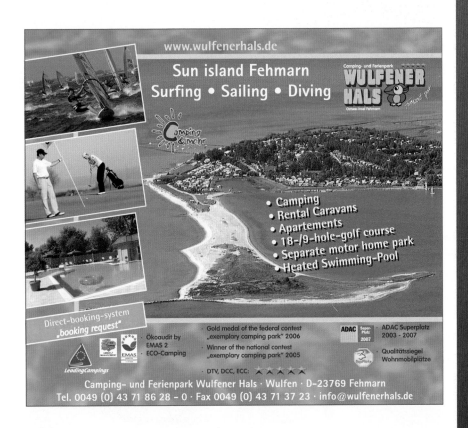

DE3820 Camping Park Havelberge am Woblitzsee

D-17237 Groß Quassow (Mecklenburg-West Pomerania)

Tel: **039 812 4790**. Email: **info@haveltourist.de** **www.alanrogers.com/DE3820**

The Müritz National Park is a very large area of lakes and marshes, popular for birdwatching as well as watersports, and Havelberge is a large, well equipped site to use as a base for enjoying the area. It is quite steep in places here with many terraces, most with shade, less in newer areas, with views over the lake. There are 400 pitches in total with 330 good sized, numbered touring pitches most with 16A electrical connections and 230 pitches on a newly developed area to the rear of the site with water and drainage. Pitches on the new field are level and separated by low hedges and bushes but have no shade. Over 170 seasonal pitches with a number of attractive chalets and an equal number of mobile homes in a separate areas. In the high season this is a busy park with lots going on to entertain families of all ages, whilst in the low seasons this is a peaceful base for exploring an unspoilt area of nature. Member of 'Leading Campings Group'.

Facilities

Four sanitary buildings (one new and of a very high standard) provide very good facilities, with private cabins, showers on payment and large section for children. Fully equipped kitchen and laundry. Motorcaravan service point. Small shop and modern restaurant (April - Oct). The lake provides fishing, swimming from a small beach and non-powered boats can be launched – canoes, rowing boats, windsurfers and bikes can be hired. Play areas and entertainment in high season. Internet access. Off site: Riding 3.5 km.

Open: All year.

Directions

From A19 Rostock - Berlin road take exit 18 and follow B198 to Wesenberg and go left to Klein Quassow and follow site signs.
GPS: N53:18.310 E13:00.080

Charges guide

Per unit incl. motorcaravan, 2 persons and electricity	€ 13,50 - € 22,90
with caravan and car	€ 14,50 - € 25,30
extra person	€ 3,40 - € 6,30
child (2-14 yrs)	€ 1,20 - € 4,20
dog	€ 1,00 - € 4,20

DE3812 Seecamping Flessenow

Am Schweriner See 1A, D-19067 Flessenow (Mecklenburg-West Pomerania)

Tel: **038 668 1491**. Email: **info@seecamping.de** **www.alanrogers.com/DE3812**

Seecamping Flessenow is owned and run by an enthusiastic young Dutch couple. It is on the banks of the Schwerinner See and makes an ideal base for a beach holiday or for an active holiday on the water. There are 250 pitches (170 for touring units), arranged on two rectangular fields to one side of a hardcore access lane (which can become muddy with heavy rain) and on a newer field to the rear of the site. Some pitches have views over the lake and these have some shade from mature trees. All have 10A electricity, 45 with electricity, water and drainage.

Facilities

Three toilet blocks (one older style) with open washbasins and controllable hot showers (token from reception). Baby room with shower. Washing machine and dryer. Motorcaravan services. Kiosk and takeaway (April - Oct; bread to order). Playground. TV room. Lake with beach. Fishing. Watersports. Riding. Bicycle hire. Boat launching. Sailing. Off site: Golf 20 km.

Open: April - October.

Directions

From Schwerin, take the A14 road north along the east side of the lake. At Schwerin Nord turn west towards Rampe and then north on a minor road towards Flessenow. Site is signed from there.
GPS: N53:45.110 E11:19.780

Charges guide

Per unit incl. 2 persons	€ 14,00 - € 22,00
extra person	€ 3,50
child (4-13 yrs)	€ 2,00
electricity	€ 2,00
dog	free

DE3833 Camping & Freizeitpark LuxOase

Arnsdorfer Strasse 1, Kleinröhrsdorf, D-01900 Dresden (Saxony)

Tel: **035 952 56666**. Email: **info@luxoase.de** **www.alanrogers.com/DE3833**

This is a pleasantly situated new park about half an hour from the centre of Dresden, in a very peaceful location with good facilities. It is owned and run by a progressive young family. On open grassland with views across the lake (access to which is through a gate in the site fence) to the woods and low hills beyond, this is a sun-trap with little shade at present. There are 138 large touring pitches (plus 50 seasonal in a separate area), marked by bushes or posts on generally flat or slightly sloping grass. All have 10/16A electricity and 100 have water and drainage. At the entrance is an area of hardstanding (with electricity) for late arrivals. The main entrance building houses the amenities and in front of the building is some very modern play equipment on bark. You may swim, fish or use inflatables in the lake. A wide animation program is organised for children in high season. There are many interesting places to visit apart from Dresden and Meissen, with the fascinating National Park Sächsische Schweiz (Saxon Switzerland) on the border with the Czech Republic offering some spectacular scenery. Boat trips on the Danube can be taken from the tourist centres of Königstein and Bad Schandau and Saxony is also famous for its many old castles, for which an English language guide is available. Bus trips are organised to Prague (Saturday) and Dresden (Tuesday). Member of 'Leading Campings Group'.

Facilities

A well equipped building provides modern, heated facilities with private cabins, a family room, baby room, units for disabled visitors and two units for hire. Jacuzzi. Kitchen. Gas supplies. Motorcaravan services. Shop. Bar and restaurant (Mar - Nov). Bicycle hire. Lake swimming. Sports field. Fishing. Play area. Sauna. Train, bus and theatre tickets from reception. Internet point. WiFi. Minigolf. Fitness room. Regular guided bus trips to Dresden, Prague etc. Off site: Riding next door (lessons available). Public transport to Dresden 1 km. Golf 7.5 km. Nearby Dinosaur park, zoo and indoor karting etc.

Open: 1 March - 7 November (phone in winter).

Directions

From A4 (Dresden - Görlitz) take exit 85 towards Radeberg, soon following signs to site via Leppersdorf and Kleinröhrsdorf.
GPS: N51:07.224 E13:58.806

Charges guide

Per person	€ 5,00 - € 7,00
child (3-15 yrs)	€ 2,50 - € 4,50
motorcaravan or caravan/car	€ 7,50 - € 8,00
tent	€ 7,00 - € 7,50
electricity	€ 2,00

Various special offers in low season.

DE3836 Waldcamping Erzgebirgsblick

An der Dittersdorfer Höhe, D-09439 Amtsberg (Saxony)

Tel: **037 177 50833**. Email: **info@waldcamping-erzgebirge.de** **www.alanrogers.com/DE3836**

The Scheibner family first thought of opening a campsite when touring Canada in 1998, so it is not surprising to find reminders of their trip appearing in the site's buildings with pictures and Canadian names. They found their spot on land once belonging to the Stasi, the East German secret police, and turned it into a well kept and welcoming campsite. It has 90 touring pitches. either under mature pine trees in the woods or on open ground, partly separated by low bushes and shrubs, in front of reception and the sanitary block. All have 16A electricity and there are 12 with electricity, water, drainage and hardstanding.

Facilities

Excellent sanitary facilities with British style toilets, free, controllable hot showers and washbasins (1 cabin each for men and women). Washbasin and toilet for children. Baby room. Bathroom for rent. Washing machines, dryers, iron and board. Fully equipped kitchen, including fridge and dishwasher. Small shop in reception (bread to order). Lounge with dining table, TV and library. Playground. Bicycle hire. Small outdoor paddling pool. Off site: Fishing 5 km. Golf 5 km. Riding 2 km.

Open: All year.

Directions

From Chemnitz, take the B174 southeast towards Gronau. Site is well signed in Amtsberg, off the B174. Take care on the steep roads and the bumpy access road (which is only 100 m).
GPS: N50:45.960 E13:00.869

Charges 2009

Per person	€ 5,00
pitch	€ 7,00
electricity (per kWh)	€ 0,60

No credit cards.

DE3847 Campingplatz Auensee

Gustav-Esche Strasse 5, D-04159 Leipzig (Saxony)

Tel: **034 146 51600**. Email: **info@camping-auensee.de** **www.alanrogers.com/DE3847**

It is unusual to find a good site in a city, but this large, neat and tidy site is one. It is far enough away from roads and the airport to be reasonably peaceful during the day and very quiet overnight and has 168 pitches, all for short-term tourers. It is set in a mainly open area with tall trees and attractive flower beds, with some chalets and 'trekker' huts for rent in the adjoining woodland, home to shoe-stealing foxes. The individual, numbered, flat grassy pitches are large (at least 100 sq.m), all with 16A electricity and five on hardstanding, arranged in several sections.

Facilities

Five central sanitary buildings with WCs, washbasins in cabins and showers. Well equipped rooms for babies and disabled visitors (key access). Kitchen and laundry rooms. Motorcaravan service point. Bar/restaurant and snack bar (all year). Entertainment rooms. Multisport court. Several play areas. Barbecue area. English usually spoken. Off site: Public transport to the city centre every 15 minutes from just outside the site (tickets from reception).Supermarkets 15-20 minutes walk.

Open: All year.

Directions

Site (not well signed) is in an area called Wahren. Best approached from A9 exit 17, turning towards Leipzig on B181 Merseberger Str. After 8 km. turn left on Ludwig Hupfeld. At T-junction, turn left across a railway and immediately right. After crossing two canals, site is on left in 100 m.
GPS: N51:22.185 E12:18.840

Charges guide

Per person	€ 5,00 - € 6,00
pitch incl. electricity	€ 5,00 - € 11,00

DE3855 Oberhof Camping

Am Stausee 09, D-99330 Frankenhain (Thuringia)

Tel: **036 205 76518**. Email: **info@oberhofcamping.de** **www.alanrogers.com/DE3855**

Beside a lake, at an altitude of 700 metres and quietly hidden in the middle of the Thüringer forest, Camping Oberhof has seen many changes since the departure of its former owners, the East German secret police. There are 150 touring pitches, all have 16A electricity and 100 with water and drainage. Access is now via a tarmac road replacing the former steeply descending forest track. From this fairly open site there are views of the surrounding forests and of the lake which is bordered by wide grass areas ideal for a picnic or for just lazing around and enjoying the view.

Facilities

New heated sanitary block with all usual facilities including free hot water, plus 15 bathrooms to rent. Facilities for disabled people. Baby room. Laundry. Motorcaravan services. Gas sales. Modern reception building with shop and attractive restaurant serving traditional dishes. Shop. TV room. Children's club room. Play area. Off site: Bus service 1.5 km. Riding 5 km.

Open: All year.

Directions

From the A4 between Eisenach and Dresden take exit 42 (Gotha). Travel south on the B247 to Ohrdruf then the B88 to Crawinkel, then to Frankenhain. In Frankenhain follow Lütsche Stausee and camping signs. GPS: N50:44.020 E10:45.400

Charges guide

Per unit incl. 2 persons	€ 19,00 - € 21,00

Camping Cheques accepted.

DE3850 Camping Strandbad Aga

Reichenbacherstrasse 14, D-07554 Gera-Aga (Thuringia)

Tel: **036 695 20209**. Email: **info@campingplatz-strandbad-aga.de** **www.alanrogers.com/DE3850**

Strandbad Aga is a useful night stop near the A4/A9 and is within reach of Dresden, Leipzig and Meissen. It is situated in open countryside on the edge of a small lake, with 200 individual, fenced pitches, mostly fairly level, without shade. The 70 touring pitches all have 16A electricity – for stays of more than a couple of days, over-nighters being placed on an open area. The lake is used for swimming, boating and fishing and there is a small playground on one side (close to a deep part).

Facilities

The sanitary building, which has been completely renovated and now includes some family rooms, is at one side, with some washbasins in cabins and hot showers on payment. Large room for wheelchair users. Laundry facilities. Motorcaravan services. Restaurant/bar. Kiosk for drinks, ice creams (high season). Playground. Small lake. Entertainment (high season). Off site: Football 200 m. Shop in village (200 m). Riding and tennis 1 km.

Open: 1 April - 31 October.

Directions

From A4/E40 Chemnitz - Erfurt autobahn take Gera exit (no. 58) then the B2 towards Zeitz, following Bad Köstritz signs at first then site signs.
GPS: N50:57.232 E12:05.210

Charges 2009

Per person	€ 4,00
pitch and car	€ 5,50 - € 6,00
electricity	€ 2,00

No credit cards.

DE3605 Camping Rangau

Campingstrasse 44, D-91056 Erlangen-Dechsendorf (Bavaria (N))

Tel: **091 358 866**. Email: **infos@camping-rangau.de** **www.alanrogers.com/DE3605**

Run by the same family for many years now, this site makes a convenient stopover, quickly and easily reached from the A3 Würzburg - Nürnberg and A73 Bamberg - Nürnberg autobahns and is pleasant enough to stay a bit longer. It has 110 pitches which are mainly for tourists on flat ground, under trees, numbered and partly marked but only about 60-80 sq.m. so it can look cramped when busy. There are also 60 permanent units. There is usually space and, in peak season, overnight visitors can often be put on the adjacent football pitch.

Facilities

A satisfactory sanitary block, heated when cold, has well spaced washbasins (some cabins for ladies) and showers. Good facilities for disabled visitors. A new facility provides washbasins in cabins and WCs. Laundry facilities. Motorcaravan services. Restaurant with terrace. Order bread from reception. Playground. Club/TV room. Off site: Swimming 200 m. Erlangen centre 5 km.

Open: 1 April - 30 September.

Directions

Take exit for Erlangen-West from A3 autobahn, turn towards Erlangen but after less than 1 km. at Dechsendorf turn left and follow to site (site signed).
GPS: N49:37.614 E10:56.460

Charges 2009

Per unit incl. 2 persons and electricity	€ 19,00
extra person	€ 5,50
child (6-12 yrs)	€ 3,50

DE3610 Knaus Campingpark Nürnberg

Hans Kalb Strasse 56, D-90471 Nürnberg (Bavaria (N))

Tel: **091 198 12717**. Email: **nuernberg@knauscamp.de** **www.alanrogers.com/DE3610**

This Knaus site is ideal for visiting the fascinating and historically important city of Nürnberg (Nuremberg). There are 160 shaded pitches, 118 with 10A electrical connections and with water taps in groups. On mainly flat grass among the tall trees, some pitches are marked out with 'ranch' style boards, others still attractively 'wild', some others with hardstanding. When there is an event at the Stadion there is a lot of noise and road diversions are in place. It is well worth checking before planning an arrival.

Facilities

A brand new heated sanitary building offers first class facilities including free showers. Washing machines and dryers. Cooking facilities. Unit for disabled visitors. Gas supplies. Motorcaravan services. Shop. Bar/bistro area with terrace and light meals served. Play area in woodland. Tennis. Large screen TV. Off site: Swimming pool (free entry for campers) and football stadium 200 m. Boat launching 2 km. City centre 4 km. (a 20 minute walk following signs takes you to the underground station).

Open: All year.

Directions

From the A9 (München - Bayreuth) east of Nürnberg, take Nürnberg-Fischbach exit. Proceed 3 km. on dual carriageway towards city then left at first traffic lights (site signed). From city follow 'Stadion-Messe' signs and site is well signed. The entrance road is not obvious. It is opposite a large office block and the sign 'Knaus Campingpark Zufahrt' is quite close to the ground. GPS: N49:25.391 E11:07.292

Charges guide

Per person	€ 6,00
pitch	€ 12,00
electricity	€ 0,50 - € 2,00

No credit cards.

DE3625 Knaus Campingpark Frickenhausen

Ochsenfurter Strasse 49, D-97252 Frickenhausen (Bavaria (N))

Tel: **093 313 171**. Email: **frickenhausen@knauscamp.de** **www.alanrogers.com/DE3625**

This is a pleasant riverside site with good facilities just south of Würzburg, situated towards the northern end of the Romantische Strasse and not far from the A3 Frankfurt to Nürnberg. There are 115 fair sized, numbered touring pitches on generally flat grass, arranged in sections leading from tarmac access roads with flowers around. Most have 6-16A electricity connections. About 80 long stay places are mostly separate nearer the river. All the amenities are in a long block opposite reception.

Facilities

Modernised, heated, sanitary facilities have washbasins (some private cabins), and dishwashing sinks. Soap and paper towels are provided for the toilets. Washing machine and dryer. Cooking facilities. Gas supplies. Restaurant, café/wine bar and shop (1/12-31/10, weekends only in low season). Bread to order. Club room. Large screen TV. Small, free swimming pool (1/5-31/10). Play area on river island. Open air theatre. Bicycle hire. Fishing. Boat marina. Off site: Public swimming pool 300 m. Riding 1 km. Golf and boat launching 15 km.

Open: All year excl. November.

Directions

From the A3 at Würzburg, take exit 71 (Ochsenfurt) and continue on the B13 towards Ochsenfurt and Ansbach. Do not cross the Main into town but follow signs for Frickenhausen and site which is shortly on the right. GPS: N49:40.148 E10:04.480

Charges guide

Per person	€ 6,00
child (4-14 yrs)	€ 3,00
pitch incl. electricity	€ 8,00 - € 17,00
dog	€ 3,00

No credit cards.

DE3632 Azur Camping Altmühltal

Campingstr. 1, D-85110 Kipfenberg (Bavaria (N))

Tel: **084 659 05167**. Email: **kipfenberg@azur-camping.de** **www.alanrogers.com/DE3632**

In the beautiful Altmühltal river valley, this Azur site is in pretty woodland, with lots of shade for much of it. On flat grassland with direct access to the river, one looks from the entrance across to the old Schloss on the hill. Outside the main entrance is a large, flat, grass/gravel field for 60 overnight tourers (with electricity). The main site has 277 pitches, of which 178 are for touring, plus two small areas for tents and one large one (at the end in an open area). Ranging in size up to 90 sq.m. they are generally in small groups marked by trees or bushes.

Facilities

The main sanitary facilities are good, with free hot water (no private cabins), baby room, unit for disabled visitors. Launderette. Kitchen with ovens and cooking rings. These facilities are mostly duplicated portacabin style at the other end of the site (toilets only in low season). Motorcaravan services. Shop combined with reception. Beer garden with campfire and serving snacks in July/Aug. Play area. Fishing. Off site: Supermarket 100 m. Two restaurants within 300 m. Outdoor pool 200 m. Bicycle and canoe hire in town.

Open: 1 April - 31 October.

Directions

From the A9/E45 (Munich - Nürnberg), take exit 59 Denkendorf or 58 Eichstätt and follow the signs to Kipfenberg. GPS: N48:56.904 E11:23.360

Charges guide

Per unit incl. 2 persons and electricity	€ 18,80 - € 25,80
extra person	€ 5,50 - € 7,50
child (2-12 yrs)	€ 3,00 - € 4,50
dog	€ 2,80

DE3710 Azur Ferienpark Bayerischer Wald

Waldesruhweg 34, D-94227 Zwiesel (Bavaria (N))

Tel: **099 228 02595**. Email: **zwiesel@azur-camping.de** **www.alanrogers.com/DE3710**

Bayerischerwald is a large site on the edge of town with views to the hills and a stream running through it. Pleasantly situated nearly 2,000 feet up (it can be cool at night) on a slight slope, there are around 500 pitches, just under 400 of which are individual numbered ones for tourers, but there is not much shade. There are various areas, with motorcaravans taken on a flat open, grassy section, whilst for caravans there are some flat and many sloping or undulating pitches, all with electricity (some 10A Euro, most 16A German) and water points along the central roadway.

Facilities

The two tiled sanitary blocks (one partly modernised) have some private cabins. Facilities for disabled visitors. Baby room. Laundry facilities. Bread orders at reception. Pleasant restaurant/bar (closed November). Off site: Indoor and outdoor pools adjacent. Ski lifts nearby.

Open: All year.

Directions

Site is on north side of Zwiesel. From autobahn A3 Regensburg-Passau, take Deggendorf exit and then B11 to Zwiesel. Take Zwiesel Nord exit and follow Azur signs. GPS: N49:01.530 E13:13.240

Charges guide

Per person	€ 5,25 - € 6,75
pitch with electricity	€ 8,20 - € 9,70

No credit cards.

DE3735 Spessart-Camping Schönrain

Schönrainstrasse 4-18, D-97737 Gemünden-Hofstetten (Bavaria (N))

Tel: **093 518 645**. Email: **info@spessart-camping.de** **www.alanrogers.com/DE3735**

Situated a short distance from the town of Gemünden, with views of forested hills beside the Main river, this is a very friendly, family run site, with excellent facilities. Frau Endres welcomes British guests and speaks a little English. There are 200 pitches, half of which are for touring. They vary in size from 70-150 sq.m. and most have 10A electricity, 20 also with water. Another area has been developed for tents. The site has an outdoor pool open from Whitsun to the end of September. A pleasant small restaurant and bar and a shop are on site with the local full-bodied Franconian wine and schnapps for sale. There are opportunities for walking and riding in the adjacent woods, excursions are organised in the main season and it is possible to hire a bicycle, ride to Würzburg and catch the pleasure boat back, or take a combined bus and cycle ride. Fishing and boating are both very popular in the locality.

Facilities

A superb new sanitary building has card operated entry – the card is prepaid and operates the showers, washing machines and dryers, coffee machine, gas cooker, baby bathroom, jacuzzi etc. Two private bathrooms (complete with wine and balcony!) for rent. Motorcaravan services. General room with sections for very young children, a pool table and arcade games and a TV. Upstairs is a library and internet café, fitness room and solarium. Bar/restaurant (closed Tuesdays). Shop. Swimming pool. Playground. Bicycle hire. Excursions. New 'beauty and wellness' programme. Off site: Bus service 200 m. Menus for local restaurants held in reception with booking service and transport provided. Fishing 400 m. Canoeing, cycling and walking. Drop off/pick up service for cyclists.

Open: 1 April - 30 September.

Directions

From Frankfurt - Würzburg autobahn, take Weibersbrunn-Lohr exit and then B26 to Gemünden. Turn over Main river bridge to Hofstetten. From Kassel - Wurzburg autobahn, leave at Hammelburg and take B27 to Gemünden, and as above. GPS: N50:03.086 E09:39.410

Charges guide

Per person	€ 6,10
child (under 14 yrs)	€ 3,80
pitch	€ 4,50 - € 10,30

Less 10% for stays over 14 days in mid and low seasons.

DE3739 Camping Katzenkopf

Am See, D-97334 Sommerach am Main (Bavaria (N))

Tel: **093 819 215** **www.alanrogers.com/DE3739**

This is an excellent family run site, on the banks of the Main to the east of Wurzburg. For peace and quiet this site is likely to be at the top of the list. There are 250 pitches with some 150 for touring units. All pitches have electricity (6-16A) and 13 provide electricity, water, and drainage. Reception also houses a shop and good tourist information. Wurzburg is an important commercial and cultural centre that was substantially destroyed by bombing and has risen again from the ashes. The town is the home of the excellent Franconian wine. The village of Sommerach, a few minutes walk from the site, is surrounded by vineyards which produce a special local vintage.

Facilities

Excellent, modern toilet blocks include private cabins, free showers and facilities for disabled people and children. Laundry facilities. Motorcaravan service point. Shop, restaurant, bar and takeaway (all open all season). Fishing. Boat launching. Sailing courses. Dogs accepted in part of the site only. Off site: Sailing. Shops and vineyards.

Open: 1 April - 25 October.

Directions

From the A3 take Kitzingen exit and turn towards Schwarzach. After 4 km. turn right towards Sommerach. Just before the village turn left and site is well signed. GPS: N49:49.551 E10:12.334

Charges guide

Per person	€ 5,70 - € 5,90
child (2-14 yrs)	€ 3,00 - € 3,30
pitch	€ 5,40 - € 6,40
electricity	€ 2,50
dog	€ 2,00

No credit cards.

DE3750 Camping Schloss Issigau

Schloss Issigau, D-95188 Issigau (Bavaria (N))

Tel: **092 937 173**. Email: **info@schloss-issigau.de** **www.alanrogers.com/DE3750**

This is an attractive, small family run site with very good facilities and of a type not often found in Germany with less than 50 pitches, all for tourers. Entering a large grass courtyard there are several sections, part terraced and with some old trees giving a little shade in places. As you go through the site it opens up to a largish, sloping tent area beside the small ponds, beyond which is a new play area. There are 45 pitches, around half individual ones ranging in size (up to 120 sq.m). All have 16A electricity, three also with water and drainage.

Facilities

Satisfactory heated sanitary facilities are in an old building with some modern fittings and some washbasins in cabins. Laundry facilities. Baby room. Delightful café/bar and restaurant (daily 12.00-22.00). Games room. Hotel accommodation. Off site: Bus service and small supermarket 300 m. Riding 1.5 km. Fishing 6 km. Golf 10 km. The Naturpark Frankenwald is on the doorstep to the southwest.

Open: 15 March - 31 October, 18 December - 9 January.

Directions

The village of Issigau is between Holle and Berg. From A9 (Berlin - Nuremberg) take exit 31 Berg/Bad Steben. Turn left and follow signs for Berg and then continue straight on towards Holle. Site is signed in Issigau. Go down a small slope and to the right (narrow in places). GPS: N50:22.451 E11:43.273

Charges 2009

Per unit incl. 2 persons	€ 15,00 - € 16,00
extra person	€ 4,50
child (4-14 yrs)	€ 2,50
electricity (plus meter)	€ 1,00
dog	€ 1,50

DE3630 Camping Donau-Lech

Campingweg 1, D-86698 Eggelstetten (Bavaria (S))

Tel: **090 904 046**. Email: **info@donau-lech-camping.de** **www.alanrogers.com/DE3630**

The Haas family have developed this friendly site just off the attractive 'Romantische Strasse' well and run it very much as a family site, providing a useful information sheet in English for their guests. The lake provides swimming and wildlife for children and adults to enjoy. Alongside it are 50 marked touring pitches with 16A electrical connections, on flat grass arranged in rows either side of a tarmac access road. With an average of 120 sq.m. per unit, it is a comfortable site with an open feeling and developing shade. There are three pleasant, flat, grass areas near the entrance for people with tents with unmarked pitches.

Facilities

All amenities are housed in the main building at the entrance with reception. Sanitary facilities are downstairs with free showers and washbasins (no cabins), all of a good standard. Sauna. Washing machine and dryer. Motorcaravan services. Large bar area with terrace. Small shop for basics, bread to order (1/4-31/10). General room. Youth room. Play area. Health studio with massage, manicure and pedicure. Lake for swimming (own risk). Off site: Larger lake used for sailboarding 400 m. Golf course and driving range 1 km. Fishing 3 km. Restaurants and other amenities a short drive.

Open: All year excl. November.

Directions

Turn off main B2 road about 5 km. south of Donauwörth (site signed) at signs for Asbach, Bäumenheim Nord towards Eggelstetten, then follow signs for over 1 km. to site. GPS: N48:40.554 E10:50.450

Charges guide

Per person	€ 5,00
child (2-15 yrs)	€ 2,50
pitch	€ 5,00 - € 7,80
electricity (plus meter)	€ 2,00
dog	€ 2,00

DE3650 Camping Gitzenweiler Hof

Gitzenweiler 88, D-88131 Lindau-Oberreitnau (Bavaria (S))

Tel: **083 829 4940**. Email: **info@gitzenweiler-hof.de** **www.alanrogers.com/DE3650**

Gitzenweiler Hof has been developed into a really well-equipped, first-class site for a family holiday. In a country setting it has about 380 permanent caravans as well as about 450 places for touring units (it is advisable to book for July/Aug). In the touring section many pitches are without markings with siting left to campers, the others in rows between access roads. There are 450 electricity connections (6/16A) and 56 pitches for caravans and motorcaravans with water, drainage and TV connections. A large outdoor swimming pool has attractive surrounds with seats (free for campers). Lindau is an interesting town, especially by the harbour, and possible excursions include the whole of the Bodensee (Lake Constance), the German Alpine Road, the Austrian Vorarlberg and Switzerland. This is a pleasant, friendly, well run site. Member of 'Leading Campings Group'.

Facilities

The toilet blocks have been beautifully renovated and include some washbasins in cabins, a children's bathroom and baby bath. Washing machines, dryers and dishwasher. Motorcaravan services. Shop (limited hours in low season). Two restaurants with takeaway. Large swimming pool in summer (33 x 25 m). Two playgrounds and play room with entertainment in summer. Organised activities. Small animals and ponies for children. Free fishing in lake. Minigolf. Cinema. Club room with arcade games, library and internet points. American motorhomes accepted up to 10 tons. Overnight parking for motorcaravans outside when site is closed in winter.

Open: 27 March - 8 November.

Directions

Site is signed from the B12 4 km. north of Lindau. Also from A96 exit 3 (Weißensberg), and from in and around Lindau. GPS: N47:35.120 E09:42.385

Charges guide

Per person	€ 6,30 - € 7,00
child (3-9 yrs)	€ 2,25 - € 2,50
child (10-15 yrs)	€ 4,05 - € 4,50
pitch	€ 4,50 - € 9,00
serviced pitch	€ 7,50 - € 15,00

Discounts for stays over 14 days and in low season. Overnight hardstanding with electricity outside barrier € 12.

DE3640 Camping Municipal München-Thalkirchen

Zentralländstraße 49, D-81379 München (Bavaria (S))

Tel: **089 723 1707**. Email: **munichtouristoffice@compuserve.com** **www.alanrogers.com/DE3640**

This well cared for municipal site is pleasantly and quietly situated on the southern side of Munich in parkland formed by the River Isar conservation area, 4 km. from the city centre (there are subway and bus links) and tall trees offer shade in parts. The large city of Munich has much to offer and the Thalkirchen site becomes quite crowded during the season. There are 550 touring pitches, all with 10A electricity and shared water and waste water. The pitches are of various sizes (some quite small), marked by metal or wooden posts and rails.

Facilities

There are five refurbished toilet blocks, two of which can be heated, with seatless toilets, washbasins with shelf, mirror and cold water. Hot water for showers and sinks is on payment. Facilities for disabled people. Washing machines and dryers. Shop. Snack bar. Drinks machine (incl. beer). General room with TV pool and games. Good small playground. Bicycle hire. Dormitory accommodation for groups. Maximum stay 14 days. Off site: Restaurant 200 m. Adjacent parkland and Munich zoo.

Open: 15 March - end October.

Directions

From autobahns follow 'Mittel' ring road to southeast of the city centre where site is signed; also follow signs for Thalkirchen or the Zoo and site is close. Well signed now from all over the City. GPS: N48:05.471 E11:32.690

Charges guide

Per person	€ 4,40 - € 8,10
pitch	€ 5,50 - € 10,00
electricity	€ 1,80

Credit cards only accepted for souvenirs.

Germany

DE3635 Camping München-Obermenzing

Lochhausenerstraße 59, D-81247 München (Bavaria (S))

Tel: **089 811 2235**. Email: **campingplatz-obermenzing@t-online.de** **www.alanrogers.com/DE3635**

On the northwest edge of Munich, this site makes a good stopover for those wishing to see the city or spend the night. The flat terrain is mostly covered by mature trees, giving shade to most pitches. Caravan owners are well off here as they have a special section of 130 individual drive-through pitches, mainly separated from each other by high hedges and opening off the hard site roads with easy access. These have 10A electricity connections and about 30 have water and drainage also. About 200 tents and motorcaravans are taken on quite large, level grass areas, with an overflow section, so space is usually available. There is a shop and rest room with TV and a drinks machine (including beer). There is some road noise, but we spent another reasonably undisturbed night here, helped by the new earth bank, and it is a very convenient site.

Facilities

The central sanitary block is large, having been extended, and together with a new portacabin style unit, the provision should now be adequate. Cleaning is satisfactory and there is heating in the low season. Hot showers require tokens, as do some washbasins. Cooking facilities on payment. Washing machine and dryers. Gas supplies. Motorcaravan services. Shop (from May). Bar (from July). TV room. Charcoal barbecues not permitted. Off site: Baker and café nearby. Riding or golf 5 km. Bicycle hire 8 km. Public transport services to the city from very close by. By car the journey might take 20-30 minutes depending on the density of traffic.

Open: 15 March - 31 October.

Directions

Site is in the northwest of the city. From Stuttgart, Nürnberg, Deggendorf or Salzburg, leave A99 at Kreiss-West for München-Lochhausen and turn left into Lochhausener Strasse. The site is a further 1.5 km. GPS: N48:10.489 E11:26.780

Charges guide

Per person	€ 4,70
child (2-14 yrs)	€ 2,00
caravan and car	€ 10,50
motorcaravan	€ 7,50
electricity (plus meter)	€ 0,50

No credit cards.

DE3642 Lech Camping

Seeweg 6, D-86444 Affing-Mühlhausen bei Augsburg (Bavaria (S))

Tel: **082 072 200**. Email: **info@lech-camping.de** **www.alanrogers.com/DE3642**

Situated just north of Ausgburg, this beautifully run site is a pleasure to stay on. Gabi Ryssel, the owner, spends her long days working very hard to cater to every wish of her guests – from the moment you arrive and are given the key to one of the cleanest toilet blocks we have seen, and plenty of tourist information, you are in very capable hands. The 40 level, grass and gravel pitches are roomy and have shade from pine trees. Electricity connections are available (10/16A). This is an immaculate site with a separate area for disabled people to park near the special facilities provided. The site has a very comprehensive camping shop (only a few basic foods as there is a supermarket over the road) and an excellent restaurant overlooking a small lake. A paddling pool (part of the lake cordoned off) is provided for children with a safe little sandy area (toys also thoughtfully supplied) along with sun beds to enjoy the view over the lake. Although this is a rural site, there is easy access by bus (a stop just over the road) to Ausburg, a beautiful German town, which has a brilliant beer festival in April (definitely a must!)

Facilities

The new toilet block (cleaned several times daily) provides British style WCs and good showers with seating area and non slip flooring. Baby room. Separate family bathroom for rent. Five star facilities for disabled visitors. Separate room with washing machine and laundry sinks. Motorcaravan service point. Small shop. Restaurant. Small playground (partially fenced). Bicycle hire. WiFi. Trampolines. Pedal boats and rowing boats (free). Off site: Football field 300 m. Bus service to city. Legoland 25 minute drive. Fishing 4 km. Golf 10 km. Riding 15 km.

Open: 1 April - 4 October.

Directions

Site is northeast of Augsburg at the border of Muhlhausen. Leave E52/A8 (Munich - Stuttgart) at exit 73 and follow signs to Neuburg/Pöttmes. After 3 km. (pass airport on right) on U49 you will see the Muhlhausen sign. Lech Camping is on right. GPS: N48:26.255 E10:55.762

Charges guide

Per unit incl. 2 persons and electricity	€ 23,80 - € 25,50
extra person	€ 5,50 - € 6,00
child (2-15 yrs)	€ 2,50 - € 3,00
dog	€ 2,50

DE3670 Camping Hopfensee

Fischerbichl 17, D-87629 Füssen im Allgäu (Bavaria (S))

Tel: **083 629 17710**. Email: **info@camping-hopfensee.com** **www.alanrogers.com/DE3670**

Hopfensee is a high class site with excellent facilities, catering for discerning visitors, by a lake. It is well placed to explore the very attractive Bavarian Alpine region which, along with the architecture and historical interest of the Royal Castles at Hohenschwangau and the Baroque church at Wies, makes it a very popular holiday area. The 378 tourist pitches for caravans and motorhomes, most with shade, each have 16A electricity, water, drain and cable TV connections. They are marked, numbered and of a good size. Tents are not accepted. At the centre of the site is a large building with an open village-like square in the middle, adorned with cascading flowers. It houses the exceptional sanitary facilities and, on the upper floors, a swimming pool, treatment suites and physiotherapy suites, a full spa centre, fitness centre, cinema and children's play room. There is direct access to the lake for sailing, canoeing etc. and a place for parking boats. Charges are high, but include the pool, super sports building, cinema, etc. Member of 'Leading Campings Group'.

Facilities

The exceptionally good, heated sanitary facilities provide free hot water in washbasins (some in cabins) and large showers. Baby and children's wash rooms. Some private units for rent. Motorcaravan services. Restaurant with terrace overlooks the lake. Bar. Takeaway. Shop. Indoor pool and spa centre. Supervised courses of water treatments, massage, etc. Sauna, solarium and steam bath. Playground and kindergarten. Large games room. Bicycle hire. Tennis. Fishing. Ski school in winter. Small golf academy and discounts for two local courses. No tents taken. Off site: Riding and boat launching 1 km.

Open: 13 December - 8 November.

Directions

Site is 4 km. north of Füssen. Turn off B16 to Hopfen and site is on the left through a car park. If approaching from the west on B310, turn towards Füssen at T-junction with the B16 and immediately right again for the road to Hopfen.
GPS: N47:36.167 E10:41.030

Charges 2009

Per person	€ 8,70 - € 9,90
child (2-12 yrs)	€ 5,30 - € 6,20
child (12-18 yrs)	€ 6,80 - € 9,35
pitch incl. cable TV, electricity	€ 12,65 - € 14,00

No credit cards.

DE3680 Alpen-Caravanpark Tennsee

D-82494 Krün-Obb (Bavaria (S))

Tel: **088 251 70**. Email: **info@camping-tennsee.de** **www.alanrogers.com/DE3680**

Tennsee is an excellent site in truly beautiful surroundings high up (1,000 m) in the Karwendel Alps with super mountain views, and close to many famous places of which Innsbruck (44 km) and Oberammergau (26 km) are two. Mountain walks are plentiful, with several lifts close by. It is an attractive site with good facilities including 120 serviced pitches with individual connections for electricity (up to 16A and two connections), gas, TV, radio, telephone, water and waste water. The other 80 pitches all have electricity and some of these are available for overnight guests at a reduced rate. Reception and restaurants, bar, cellar youth room and a well stocked shop are all housed in attractive buildings. Many activities and excursions are organised to local attractions by the Zick family, who run the site in a very friendly, helpful and efficient manner.

Facilities

The first class toilet block has underfloor heating, washbasins in cabins and private units with WC, shower, basin and bidet for rent. Unit for disabled people with the latest facilities. Baby bath, dog bathroom and a heated room for ski equipment (with lockers). Washing machines, free dryers and irons. Gas supplies. Motorcaravan services. Cooking facilities. Shop. Restaurants with takeaway (waiter, self service and takeaway). Bar. Youth room. Solarium. Bicycle hire. Playground. WiFi. Organised activities and excursions. Bus service to ski slopes in winter. Off site: Fishing 400 m. Riding or golf 3 km.

Open: All year excl. 4 November - 15 December.

Directions

Site is just off main Garmisch-Partenkirchen - Innsbruck road no. 2 between Klais and Krün, 15 km. from Garmisch watch for small sign 'Tennsee + Barmersee' and turn right there for site.
GPS: N47:29.440 E11:15.238

Charges 2009

Per person	€ 7,50 - € 8,00
1-3 children (3-15 yrs)	€ 4,00 - € 6,00
pitch	€ 8,50 - € 12,00

Senior citizens' special rates (not winter).

DE3672 Camping Elbsee

Am Elbsee 3, D-87648 Aitrang (Bavaria (S))

Tel: **083 432 48**. Email: **camping@elbsee.de** **www.alanrogers.com/DE3672**

This attractive site, with its associated hotel and restaurant about 400 m. away, lies on land sloping down to the lake. This is not an area well known to tourists, although the towns of Marktoberdorf, Kaufbeuren and Kempten merit a visit. With this in mind, the owners have set about providing good facilities and a program of activities. All 120 touring pitches have access to electricity (16A) and 78 also have water and drainage. Some of the pitches (those restricted to tents) slope slightly.

Facilities

Two clean, well appointed heated sanitary blocks include free showers, washbasins all in cabins, a children's bathroom and family bathrooms to rent. Facilities for disabled visitors. Dog shower. Motorcaravan service point. Shop (order bread for following day). New playground, indoor play area and activity rooms. TV, games and meeting rooms. Sports field. Fishing. Bicycle hire. Riding. Boat launching. Activity programme (20/7-31/8).
Off site: At hotel, very good restaurant, takeaway and bar. Shop and ATM point 2 km. Golf 12 km.

Open: 15 December - 5 November.

Directions

From centre of Marktoberdorf, take minor road northwest to Ruderatshofen and from there take minor road west towards Aitrang. Just south of Aitrang, site is signed to south of the road. The road to the site (2 km.) is winding and narrow. Caravans can just about pass. GPS: N47:48.166 E10:33.206

Charges 2009

Per unit incl. 2 persons (electricity per kWh)	€ 21,90 - € 24,00
extra person	€ 6,20

Camping Cheques accepted.

DE3685 Camping Allweglehen

D-83471 Berchtesgaden (Bavaria (S))

Tel: **086 522 396**. Email: **campingplatz.allweglehen@t-online.de** **www.alanrogers.com/DE3685**

This all year site occupies a hillside position, with spectacular mountain views. The site access road is steep (14%), particularly at the entrance, but the proprietor will use his tractor to tow caravans if requested. There are 180 pitches (160 for touring), arranged on a series of gravel terraces, separated by hedges or fir trees and all with good views and electrical connections (16A). There is a separate area on a sloping meadow for tents. This is a useful base for sightseeing or relaxing.

Facilities

Two adjacent older style toilet blocks near the restaurant can be heated. A further tiny unit serves the lowest terrace. Bathroom. Baby room. Cleaning and maintenance can be variable. Washing machines, dryers and iron. Motorcaravan services. Gas supplies. Restaurant. Kiosk for essentials (all year). Play area. Small heated pool (small charge, 15/5-15/10). Solarium. Minigolf. Fishing. Excursions. Internet access. Off site: Winter sports nearby. Walks. Riding 2 km. Bicycle hire 3 km. Golf 5 km.

Open: All year.

Directions

Easiest access is via the Austrian autobahn A10 (vignette necessary), Salzburg Sud exit and follow the B305 towards Berchtesgaden. Alternatively take the B305 from Ruhpolding (the pretty Alpenstrasse - winding and with 4 m. height limit), or the B20 from Bad Reichenhall. Site is 4 km. northeast of Berchtesgaden.
GPS: N47:38.833 E13:02.387

Charges guide

Per person	€ 5,40
pitch	€ 7,50 - € 8,50
electricity (per kWh)	€ 0,50

DE3688 Panorama Camping Harras

Harrasser Strasse 135, D-83209 Prien am Chiemsee (Bavaria (S))

Tel: **080 519 04613**. Email: **info@camping-harras.de** **www.alanrogers.com/DE3688**

Panorama Harras is a popular, friendly site on a small, wooded peninsula by the Chiemsee, with good views to the mountains across the lake. With some near the lake, the pitches vary in size (60-100 sq.m) and most have electricity (6A). There are 80 numbered pitches marked by trees, but with no hedges, the site can look and feel crowded at busy times. A separate, all numbered section of gravel hardstanding is provided for motorhomes and an area for tents on grass and gravel.

Facilities

Toilet facilities include family shower rooms with washbasin and toilet (no paper). Pushbutton showers need a token. Baby room. Launderette. Good unit for disabled people. Well stocked shop. Restaurant with bar and takeaway (all open for the whole season). Bicycle hire. Off site: Bus services 1 km. in town. Boat trips on the lake. Golf and riding 5 km. Automobile museum 20 km.

Open: 6 April - 20 October.

Directions

The Chiemsee is north of the A8 (E52, E60) between Munich and Salzburg. Take exit 106 (Bernau) then north towards Prien. After 3 km, at the roundabout, turn east towards Harras (and Kreiskrankenhaus) following site signs. GPS: N47:50.450 E12:22.290

Charges guide

Per person	€ 5,50 - € 6,60
pitch incl. car	€ 5,40 - € 7,40
electricity	€ 1,90

Camping Cheques accepted.

DE3695 Dreiflüsse Camping

Am Sonnenhang 8, Donautat, D-94113 Irring bei Passau (Bavaria (S))

Tel: **085 466 33**. Email: **dreifluessecamping@t-online.de** **www.alanrogers.com/DE3695**

Although the site overlooks the Danube, it is in fact some 9 km. from the confluence of the Danube, Inn and Ilz. Dreiflüsse Camping occupies a hillside position, well above high water level, to the west of Passau with pitches, flat or with a little slope on several rows of terraces. The 180 places for touring units are not all numbered or marked, although 16A electricity connection boxes determine where units pitch, and half have water and drainage. Trees and low banks separate the terraces which are of gravel with a thin covering of grass. There is some road and rail noise (24 hrs). The energetic and very jolly owner, Herr Pitscheneder, is most popular with his guests and gives the site a very friendly air. This is a useful en-route stop or for a longer stay to explore the delights of Passau and the southern part of the Bavarian forest, and is popular with cyclists. The Danube cycle track passes below the site, but although it starts out by following the quiet river bank, it is soon joined by busy roads when cycling towards Passau and in this direction is not recommended.

Facilities

The sanitary facilities are acceptable, if a little old, with two private cabins for women, one for men. Laundry. Motorcaravan services. Gas supplies. Shop (all season). Pleasant, modern Gasthof restaurant with terrace at site entrance, where the reception, shop and sanitary buildings are also located. Small heated indoor swimming pool (1/5-15/9 on payment). Play area. Bicycle hire. New 'Aquakur' Wellness centre added in 2008. Off site: Passau 9 km. Bus service for Passau (4 daily) from outside site, or from Schalding 1.5 km. Riding 3 km. Golf 10 km.

Open: 1 April - 31 October.

Directions

From autobahn A3, take exit 115 (Passau-Nord) from where site is signed. Follow signs from Passau on road to west of city and north bank of Danube towards Windorf and Irring.
GPS: N48:36.389 E13:20.762

Charges guide

Per person	€ 4,50
child (4-14 yrs)	€ 3,50
pitch	€ 5,50 - € 9,50
electricity	€ 3,00
dog	€ 1,50

No credit cards.

DE3686 Strandcamping Waging am See

Am See 1, D-83329 Waging am See (Bavaria (S))

Tel: **086 815 52**. Email: **info@strandcamp.de** **www.alanrogers.com/DE3686**

This is an exceptionally big site on the banks of a large lake fed by clear alpine streams. There are some 700 pitches for touring units out of a total of over 1,200. All the grass, level touring pitches have electricity (16A) with 86 also providing water and drainage. As you would expect with a site of this kind, there is a considerable range of sports facilities and an extensive games and entertainment programme during July and August. A small sandy beach offers facilities for swimming in the lake (lifeguards are in attendance in the high season). An adjoining windsurfing school is available to campers. The site has an large restaurant and beer garden on the banks of the lake and rooms and caravans available to rent. A helicopter pad is next to the well staffed reception! Member of 'Leading Campings Group'.

Facilities

Good sanitary facilities include private cabins and free showers. Facilities for disabled people and children in the four modern blocks. 11 private bathrooms for rent. Laundry facilities. Motorcaravan service point. Shop and internet access at reception. Restaurant and bar. Lake beach. Windsurfing. Tennis. Archery. Minigolf. Fishing. Bicycle hire. WiFi. Dogs are not accepted 20/6-22/8. Off site: Golf 1 km.

Open: 1 April - 31 October.

Directions

From A8 take exit 112 and head towards Traunstein. Turn right on road no. 304 then left towards Waging. Just before bridge turn right and then right towards site. GPS: N47:56.604 E12:44.852

Charges guide

Per person	€ 5,50 - € 6,90
child (3-15 yrs)	€ 2,50 - € 5,10
pitch	€ 6,20 - € 8,20
incl. services	€ 10,60 - € 11,60
dog	€ 2,90

DE3697 Kur & Feriencamping Dreiquellenbad

Singham 40, D-94086 Bad Griesbach (Bavaria (S))

Tel: **085 329 6130**. Email: **info@camping-bad-griesbach.de** **www.alanrogers.com/DE3697**

This site is to the southwest of Passau, a town which dates back to Roman times and lies on a peninsula between the rivers Danube and Inn. Dreiquellenbad is an exceptional site in a quiet, rural area, with 200 pitches, all of which are used for touring units. All pitches have electricity, water, waste water and TV points. English is spoken at reception which also houses a shop and good tourist information. A luxury leisure complex includes indoor and outdoor thermal pools, a sauna, Turkish bath and jacuzzi (the use of which is free to campers). An adjoining building provides various beauty and complementary health treatments. Member of 'Leading Campings Group'.

Facilities

Excellent sanitary facilities include private cabins and free showers, facilities for disabled visitors, special child facilities and a dog shower. Two private bathrooms for rent. Laundry facilities. Bar/restaurant. Motorcaravan services. Shop. Gym. Luxury leisure complex. Play area. Bicycle hire. Fishing. Internet. WiFi. The purchase of more land in 2008 will enable extra Motorcaravan pitches and car parking space by the Spring of 2009. Off site: Golf 2 km. Spa facilities of Bad Griesbach within walking distance.

Open: All year.

Directions

Site is 15 km. from the A3. Take exit 118 and follow signs for Pocking. After 2 km. turn right on B388. Site is in the hamlet of Singham - turn right into Karpfhan then left towards site. GPS: N48:25.204 E13:11.532

Charges 2009

Per person	€ 6,90
child (0-14 yrs)	€ 4,30
pitch	€ 9,90 - € 10,40
electricity (plus meter)	€ 1,00
dog	€ 2,30

DE3720 Internationaler Campingplatz Naabtal

Distelhausen 2, D-93188 Pielenhofen (Bavaria (S))

Tel: **094 093 73**. Email: **camping.pielenhofen@t-online.de** **www.alanrogers.com/DE3720**

International Camping Naabtal is an attractive riverside site in a beautiful tree-covered valley and makes an excellent base for exploring the ancient city of Regensburg on the Danube and other areas of this interesting part of Germany. It is also a good overnight site for those wishing to visit or pass through Austria or the Czech Republic. The best 130 of the 340 pitches are reserved for tourists and they are mainly located on the banks of the river on flat or gently sloping ground under willow and other trees. This is good walking and mountain biking country with many marked trails.

Facilities

Two original, heated toilet blocks are part of larger buildings and there is a newer block for the tent area. Some washbasins are in cabins, showers are on payment. First class unit for disabled people. Washing machines and dryers. Gas supplies. Motorcaravan services. Sauna and solarium. Bar/restaurant (1/4-31/10 plus Xmas/New Year). Small shop (Easter - end Sept). Playground with imaginative apparatus. Large meeting room. Tennis. Bicycle hire. Fishing (permit required). Small boats on river. Off site: Shop and bus service in the village 1.5 km. Golf 15 km.

Open: All year.

Directions

From A3 (Nürnberg - Regensburg) take exit 97 (Nittendorf). Follow road to Pielenhofen and pass under the arch (Camping Naabtal is signed from exit). Cross river and turn right to site. Site is about 11 km. from autobahn exit. From A93 exit 39 onto B8 towards Nittendorf, then at Etterzhausen turn towards Pielenhofen. GPS: N49:03.547 E11:57.610

Charges 2009

Per person	€ 5,35
child	€ 3,35
pitch	€ 6,40
electricity (plus meter)	€ 0,60

No credit cards.

DE3415 Camping Adam

Campingstrasse 1, D-77815 Bühl (Baden-Württemberg)

Tel: **072 232 3194**. Email: **webmaster@campingplatz-adam.de** **www.alanrogers.com/DE3415**

This very convenient lakeside site is by the A5 Karlsruhe - Basel autobahn near Baden-Baden, easily accessed from exit 52 Bühl (also from the French autoroute A35 just northeast of Strasbourg). It is also a useful base for the Black Forest. Most of the touring pitches (180 from 490 total) have electricity connections (10A), many with waste water outlets too. Tents are positioned along the outer area of the lake. At very busy times, units staying overnight only may be placed close together on a lakeside area of hardstanding. The site has a well tended look and good English is spoken. The lake is divided into separate areas for bathing or boating and windsurfing, with a long slide. The public are admitted to this on payment and it attracts many people on fine weekends. The shop and restaurant/bar remain open virtually all year (not Monday or Tuesday in low season), so this is a useful site to use out of season.

Facilities

Two heated sanitary buildings have mostly private cabins in the new block, hot showers on payment, facilities for babies and disabled people. Washing machine and dryer. Gas supplies. Motorcaravan services. Shop (1/4-31/10). Restaurant (1/3-30/10). Takeaway (1/5-31/8). Playground. Bicycle hire. Fishing. Off site: Riding or golf 5 km.

Open: All year (mobile homes 1/4-31/9 only).

Directions

Take A5/E35-52, exit 52 (Bühl), turn towards Lichtenau, go through Oberbruch and left to site. From French autoroute A35 take exits 52 or 56 onto D2 and D4 respectively then turn onto A5 as above. GPS: N48:43.590 E08:05.100

Charges guide

Per person	€ 4,80 - € 7,00
child (3-16 yrs)	€ 2,50 - € 4,00
pitch with services	€ 4,80 - € 8,50
electricity	€ 2,20

CAMPINGPLATZ
ADAM
On the edge of the Black Forest, by a clean swimming and surfing lake. Exemplary sanitary facilities, for handicapped also, each pitch with electricity and waste water. Restaurant with cosy atmosphere and spacious sun terrace. Self-service shop with extensive choice. Children's playground. Beach volleyball. Football. Boccia. Giant waterslide. Bicycle hire. First class spacious mobile homes with 2 bedrooms, fully fitted kitchen, bathroom, separate W.C. heating, hot water and sat.-TV. Open all year.
Directions: Autobahn A5 Karlsruhe-Basel, exit Bühl, towards Oberbruch-Moos.
Tel. 07223-23194 • Fax 07223-8982 • info@campingplatz-adam.de • www.campingplatz-adam.de

DE3420 Freizeitcenter Oberrhein

D-77836 Rheinmunster (Baden-Württemberg)

Tel: **072 272 500**. Email: **info@freizeitcenter-oberrhein.de** **www.alanrogers.com/DE3420**

This large, well equipped holiday site provides much to do and is also a good base for visiting the Black Forest. To the left of reception are a touring area and a section of hardstanding for motorcaravans. The 285 touring pitches (out of 700 overall) all have electricity connections (mostly 16A, 3 pins, a few with 2 pins), and include 180 with water and drainage, but little shade. Two of the site's lakes are used for swimming, with roped-off areas for toddlers, and non-powered boating (the water was very clean when we visited), the third small one is for fishing.

Facilities

Seven top quality, heated toilet buildings have free hot water and very smart fittings. Some have special rooms for children, babies and families. Excellent dog shower! Family wash cabins to rent. Motorcaravan services. Gas supplies. Shop (1/4-31/10). Lakeside restaurant; snack bar (both 1/4-31/10). Modern play areas on sand. Small zoo. Tennis. Bicycle hire. Minigolf. Windsurf school. Swimming and boating lakes. Fishing (charged). Off site: Supermarket 3 km. Riding 4 km. Golf 5 km.

Open: All year.

Directions

Leave A5/E35-52 at exit 51 and travel west in direction of Iffezheim. Turn south onto B36 passing through Hügelsheim to Stollhoffen where at the roundabout site is signed. GPS: N48:46.346 E08:02.490

Charges guide

Per person	€ 5,00 - € 8,50
child (6-16 yrs)	€ 3,00 - € 6,00
child (under 6 yrs)	€ 2,50 - € 4,50
pitch incl. car and electricity	€ 7,50 - € 10,50
dog	€ 2,50 - € 4,50

DE3406 Camping Kleinenzhof

D-75323 Bad Wildbad (Baden-Württemberg)

Tel: **070 813 435**. Email: **info@kleinenzhof.de** **www.alanrogers.com/DE3406**

In the northern Black Forest, a very good area for walking and cross-country skiing, this site runs along the sloping bank of a stream big enough to play in but small enough not to be dangerous. There are excellent facilities, which the owner is still working on improving. The land is terraced and accommodates around 200 seasonal pitches, and 100 touring pitches. All have 16A electricity and all but five have water and drainage. At the far end of the site is a hotel offering free use of the pools.

Facilities

Four sanitary blocks, all heated, are clean with many washbasins in cabins and showers. Facilities for disabled visitors. Baby changing. Children's bathroom. 12 free family bathrooms (many for rent). Dog shower. Laundry facilities. Motorcaravan service point. Gas. Shop. Bar and restaurant (at hotel). Indoor pool. Outdoor pool (May - Sept) and paddling pool. Playground. TV and games room. Internet. Bicycle hire. Off site: Fishing 3 km. Riding 8 km. Golf 25 km.

Open: All year.

Directions

From Pforzheim take B294 south through Birkenfeld and Neuenbürg to Calmbach (20 km.) From here do not go to Bad Wildbad. Continue on B294 to Kleinenzhof (about another 3 km).
GPS: N48:44.284 E08:34.626

Charges guide

Per person	€ 6,60 - € 6,80
child (1-12 yrs)	€ 4,10 - € 4,30
pitch	€ 8,30 - € 8,60
electricity (per kWh)	€ 0,59

DE3432 Schwarzwald Camp

Schiltacher strasse 80, D-77709 Wolfach-Halbmeil (Baden-Württemberg)

Tel: **078 348 59309**. Email: **info@schwarzwald-camp.com** **www.alanrogers.com/DE3432**

This site is set in a quiet position on the side of an attractive valley in the Black Forest. If you would like to dine or wake up to beautiful views across an alpine valley and watch herds of wild deer graze in the meadows opposite, then this is the site for you. Terraced but with little shade as yet, the site has fairly level pitches, many with electricity (16A), water and drainage, and an area which is used for tents. In front of the main building is an area of hardstanding for overnight visitors, also with electricity connections.

Facilities

First class sanitary facilities include private cabins, large free showers including one multi-head, family bathrooms for hire, laundry and a kitchen, in the main building close to the entrance. It also houses reception with a small shop and the restaurant open daily all year. Off site: Wolfach 2 km. Outdoor swimming pool 5 km. Golf 20 km.

Open: All year.

Directions

From A5 Karlsruhe - Freiburg, take exit 55 Offenburg on B33/E531 to Haslach, then on 33/294 through Hausach and soon after left on 294 to Wolfach. Go through tunnel, stay on 294 for 3 km. to Halbmeil. Site on left at end of village.
GPS: N48:17.467 E08:16.690

Charges 2009

Per person	€ 6,50
pitch and car	€ 6,50
electricity (plus € 0.50 kWh)	€ 1,00

DE3437 Camping Hochschwarzwald

Oberhäuserstrasse 6, D-79674 Todtnau-Muggenbrunn (Baden-Württemberg)

Tel: **076 711 288**. Email: **camping.hochschwarzwald@web.de** **www.alanrogers.com/DE3437**

Hochschwarzwald is a small, peaceful, quality site in an attractive wooded valley high up in the Black Forest. Of 85 marked pitches (some with shade), 50 are for tourers (all with 10A electricity) on level terraces of grass and gravel. There is an area at the entrance for overnight stays in high season.This is an extremely popular area, with many summer visitors enjoying walking and cycling, but it is also ideal for winter stays, with skiing from the site. At the back of the site, as well as being able to walk in the woods, you can paddle in a flat area of the stream which tumbles down the hill.

Facilities

Two modern, heated sanitary buildings have good facilities with a few private cabins, a family room and a unit for disabled people. Washing machine and dryer. Small shop for essentials. Restaurant/bar (closed Mondays). Off site: Bus to Freiburg 50 m. Bicycle hire 5 km. Fishing 6 km. Riding 12 km. Golf 14 km. Walking and skiing directly from the site. Heated indoor pool, tennis court and ski school in Muggenbrunn. Todtnau waterfalls 3 km. Freiburg and Titisee both 25 km.

Open: All year.

Directions

Site is about 1 km. beyond Muggenbrunn on the road from Todtnau towards Freiburg.
GPS: N47:51.934 E07:54.970

Charges 2009

Per person	€ 5,30 - € 5,80
child (3-12 yrs)	€ 3,20 - € 3,70
pitch	€ 5,50 - € 6,90
electricity per kWh	€ 0,50
dog	€ 1,80

No credit cards.

DE3440 Camping Kirchzarten

Dietenbacher Straße 17, D-79199 Kirchzarten (Baden-Württemberg)

Tel: **076 619 040910**. Email: **info@camping-kirchzarten.de** **www.alanrogers.com/DE3440**

There are pleasant views of the Black Forest from this municipal site which is within easy reach by car of Titisee, Feldberg and Todtnau, and 8 km. from the large town of Freiburg in Breisgau. It is divided into 496 numbered pitches with electricity, 380 of which are for tourists (some used by tour operators). Most pitches, which are side by side on level ground, are of quite reasonable size and marked out at the corners, though there is nothing to separate them and there are some hardstanding motorcaravan pitches. From about late June to mid-August it does become full. The fine swimming pool complex adjoining the site is free to campers and is a main attraction, with pools for diving, fun, swimming and children, surrounded by spacious grassy sunbathing areas and a play area on sand. It is only a short stroll from the site to the village centre, which has supermarkets, restaurants, etc.

Facilities

The new sanitary building is a splendid addition and includes a large, central section for children, private cabins (some for hire) and a laundry room. Cooking stoves. Washing machines, dryers, irons, sewing machines (all on payment by meter) are available among the other buildings. Restaurant/bar. Shop (May - Sept). Swimming pool complex (15/5-15/9). TV room, play room and youth room. Large playground. Off site: Tennis (covered court, can be booked from site). Adventure playground, fitness track, tennis and minigolf near. Riding 2 km. Golf 4 km.

Open: All year.

Directions

From Freiburg take B31 road signed Donaueschingen to Kirchzarten where site is signed (it is south of the village). GPS: N47:57.625 E07:57.050

Charges 2009

Per person	€ 9,90
child (4-16 yrs)	€ 5,00
pitch	€ 8,00

Every 15th day free.

DE3442 Terrassen Campingplatz Herbolzheim

Im Laue, D-79336 Herbolzheim (Baden-Württemberg)

Tel: **076 431 460**. Email: **s.hugoschmidt@t-online.de** **www.alanrogers.com/DE3442**

This well equipped campsite is in a quiet location on a wooded slope to the north of Freiburg. There are 70 touring pitches, all with electricity (16A) and grass surfaces, on terraces linked by hard access roads with a little shade for some. A separate meadow for tents is at the top of the site (with three cabin toilets) and some pitches are used by a tour operator. This is good walking country and with only occasional entertainment, this is a very pleasant place in which to relax between daily activities.

Facilities

The main toilet facilities are modern, with new facilities for babies and disabled visitors. Laundry facilities. Motorcaravan services. Bar/restaurant (Easter - Sept). Play area. Dogs are not accepted 15/7-15/8. Off site: Large open-air heated municipal swimming pool complex adjacent (1/5-15/9). Restaurants and shops in the village 3 km. Riding, bicycle hire 5 km. Local market on Friday mornings.

Open: 5 April - 3 October.

Directions

From A5 Frankfurt - Basel autobahn take exit 57, 58 or 59 and follow signs to Herbolzheim. Site is signed on south side of town near swimming pool. Go through pool car park and about 350 m. past the pool entrance. GPS: N48:12.966 E07:47.314

Charges 2009

Per unit incl. 2 persons and electricity	€ 8,00 - € 11,00
extra person	€ 7,00
child (0-15 yrs)	€ 3,00
dog	€ 2,00

10% discount after 14 days.

DE3454 Kur & Feriencamping Badenweiler

Weilertalstrasse 73, D-79410 Badenweiler (Baden-Württemberg)

Tel: **076 321 550**. Email: **info@camping-badenweiler.de** **www.alanrogers.com/DE3454**

Badenweiler is an attractive spa centre on the edge of the southern Black Forest, and is the site of the largest Roman baths north of the Alps. It is easily accessed from the A5 or B3, but far enough from them to be peaceful. This well kept, family run campsite with pleasant open views is on a hillside close to Badenweiler and the cure facilities. There are four terraces with 100 large, individual grass pitches, 96 for touring and all with electricity (16A), water and drainage. Reception is part of a building which also houses a bar/café with takeaway snacks in the evenings in high season. Here too is a small shop and a children's room downstairs.

Facilities

Top quality sanitary facilities are contained in two fully tiled buildings, one with toilets and the other with free, controllable hot showers with full glass dividers and washbasins (cabins and vanity style). Family washrooms, facilities for babies and disabled visitors. Washing machines and dryers. Motorcaravan services. Gas supplies. Shop for basics. Play area and play room. Games room. Internet point and WiFi access throughout site. Off site: Municipal outdoor, heated swimming pool, free entry for campers at 200 m. Restaurants 200 m. Shop 300 m. Golf 12 km.

Open: All year excl. 16 January - 14 December.

Directions

From the A5 about midway between Freiburg and Basel take exit 65 onto the B378 to Müllheim, then the L131 signed to Badenweiler-Ost from where site is well signed. GPS: N47:48.592 E07:41.786

Charges 2009

Per unit incl. 2 persons	€ 25,70 - € 29,10
extra person	€ 7,00 - € 8,20
child (2-15 yrs)	€ 3,50 - € 5,25
electricity (per kWh)	€ 0,50
dog	€ 3,00

No credit cards.

DE3428 Terrassen-Camping Oase

Mühlenweg 34, D-77955 Ettenheim (Baden-Württemberg)

Tel: **078 224 45918**. Email: **info@campingpark-oase.de** **www.alanrogers.com/DE3428**

This pleasant well run site lies on wooded land on the western edge of the Black Forest, a very good region for walking and cycling. The level area near the entrance holds the main facilities and 200 touring pitches, all with 6A electricity. Pitches for tents are on grass and there is grass or hardstanding for caravans and motorcaravans. On sloping land further away are 85 terraced seasonal pitches. Just outside the entrance is the family hotel/restaurant, which also has a playground, all open to campers. Europa Park is 7 km. away, and the city of Freiburg is 40 km. to the south. The site is only 5 km. from the A5/E35 autobahn, which makes it an ideal overnight stop on the way to Basel and Switzerland.

Facilities

Two sanitary blocks are heated, clean and well maintained. Many washbasins are in cabins. Showers are coin-operated. Facilities for wheelchair users. Baby room, children's bathroom. Motorcaravan services. Gas supplies. Shop. Restaurant and takeaway (at hotel). TV and club room. Off site: Leisure area. Tennis, riding and bicycle hire within 1 km. Fishing 2 km. Golf 5 km.

Open: Week before Easter - 4 October.

Directions

From A5/E35, exit 57A (Ettenheim), follow L103 road southeast to Ettenheim (about 2.5 km). From here site is signed, and is a further 1 km. along the same road. GPS: N48:14.862 E07:49.652

Charges guide

Per person	€ 6,50
child (1-15 yrs)	€ 3,50
pitch	€ 6,00 - € 9,00
electricity	€ 2,00
dog	€ 1,50 - € 3,00

DE3427 Ferienparadies Schwarzwälder Hof

Tretenhofstr. 76, D-77960 Seelbach (Baden-Württemberg)
Tel: **078 239 60950**. Email: **camping-rezeption@seelbach.org** **www.alanrogers.com/DE3427**

This site lies in a wooded valley, just south of the pleasant village of Seelbach in the Black Forest. The old buildings have been replaced by very attractive ones built in the old traditional style, but containing very modern facilities. There are 160 well drained touring pitches, either grass or hardstanding, all with electricity (10A), water supply and waste water outlet. There is also space for groups in tents. Just at the entrance is the family hotel with a restaurant. Besides a comprehensive general menu, there are also menus for children and older people with smaller appetites. A short walk from the site is a well equipped municipal swimming pool and surrounding grass area. In July/August a good range of activities is organised for all ages, including a children's club. Fishing is possible in the stream which runs along the bottom of the site. The surrounding countryside is good for walking and cycling, and Europa Park is 30 km.

Facilities

Three sanitary blocks, all heated, clean and well maintained, include many washbasins in cabins and free showers. Facilities for wheelchair users. Family rooms (free). Baby room, superb children's bathroom, child size toilets and washbasins. Laundry facilities. Motorcaravan services. Gas supplies. Small shop. Restaurant, snacks and takeaway. TV and club room. Playground. Sauna (free after two night stay). Off site: Swimming 150 m. Bicycle hire 1 km. ATM in Seelbach 1 km. Riding 2 km. Golf 5 km.

Open: All year.

Directions

From A5/E35 autobahn, leave at exit 56 (Lahr). Follow road east through Lahr, until turn south to Seelbach. Go through Seelbach and the site is about 1 km. south. GPS: N48:17.983 E07:56.653

Charges guide

Per person	€ 9,40
child (3-14 yrs)	€ 6,90
pitch with electricity	€ 11,10 - € 12,60
dog	€ 3,00

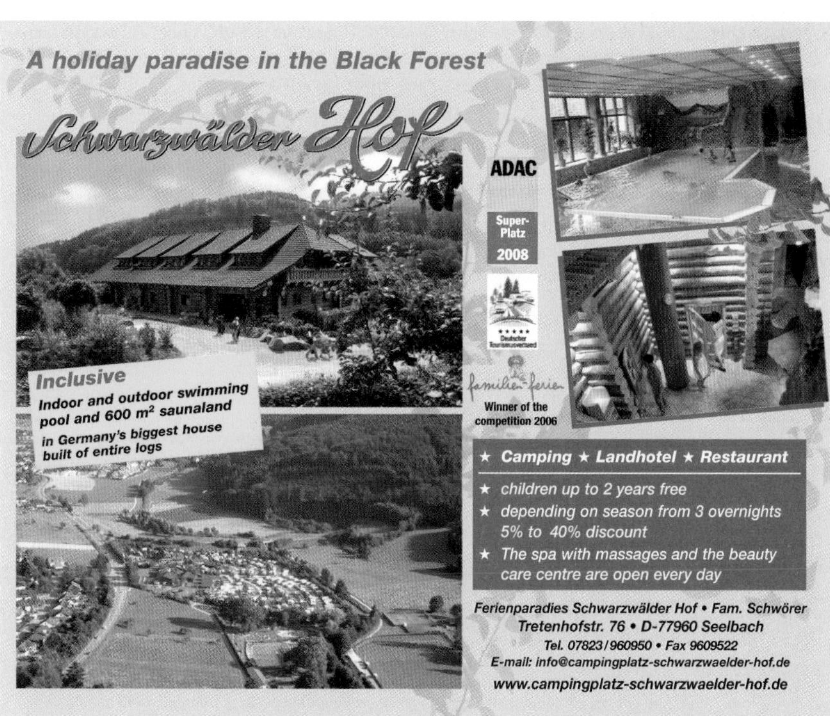

A holiday paradise in the Black Forest
Schwarzwälder Hof
ADAC
Super-Platz 2008
Winner of the competition 2006
Inclusive
Indoor and outdoor swimming pool and 600 m² saunaland
in Germany's biggest house built of entire logs
★ Camping ★ Landhotel ★ Restaurant
★ children up to 2 years free
★ depending on season from 3 overnights 5% to 40% discount
★ The spa with massages and the beauty care centre are open every day
Ferienparadies Schwarzwälder Hof • Fam. Schwörer
Tretenhofstr. 76 • D-77960 Seelbach
Tel. 07823/960950 • Fax 9609522
E-mail: info@campingplatz-schwarzwaelder-hof.de
www.campingplatz-schwarzwaelder-hof.de

198 KM

Hirzberg Camping Freiburg

...sse 99, D-79104 Freiburg (Baden-Württemberg)

...4. Email: **hirzberg@freiburg-camping.de** **www.alanrogers.com/DE3439**

...camping is a quiet city site backing onto meadows and wooded hills, yet within easy reach ...reiburg's old town quarter. To the right of the entrance is reception, a shop, the sanitary facilities and a children's room with a play area outside. Just opposite is a large convenient overnight parking area. The main part of the site is reached by a short climb passing a small reading room and flower decked sitting area. The upper part has 76 pitches, 60 for tourists almost all with 10A electricity connections. Hardcore roads lead to open grass pitches, many under mature trees.

Facilities

Modern heated, well maintained sanitary block provides free hot water, roomy adjustable showers and some washbasins in cabins. Washing machines and dryer. Kitchen with cooking rings on payment. Small shop with essential supplies. Play room and play area. Reading room. Bicycle hire. WiFi over whole site. Off site: Bus service at entrance, tram 300 m. Golf 6 km. Riding 8 km.

Open: All year.

Directions

Site is in the eastern part of the city. To reach it without having to drive through the city, from the B31 take exit Freiberg Kappel (F. Kappel) which is well to the east of the city and follow camping signs. GPS: N47:59.514 E07:52.410

Charges guide

Per person	€ 6,00
pitch incl. electricity	€ 4,50 - € 6,50

DE3436 Campingplatz Bankenhof

Bruderhalde 31, D-79822 Titisee (Baden-Württemberg)

Tel: **076 521 351**. Email: **info@bankenhof.de** **www.alanrogers.com/DE3436**

This peacefully located, fairly informal woodland site, with a friendly atmosphere, is situated just beyond the western end of Lake Titisee. The 190 pitches are on sparse grass and gravel, with some shade from a variety of trees, and 30 are occupied by seasonal units. The site is generally level, although there is a separate grassy area for tents which does have a slight slope. All pitches have electric hook-ups (16A), with gravel roads, and water taps for each area. Although there is some site lighting a torch might be useful for the darker areas under the trees.

Facilities

Two sets of quality sanitary facilities plus three family bath/shower rooms for rent. Well equipped and heated, they include controllable hot showers and some washbasins in cubicles. Facilities for disabled campers, and a unit for children. Kitchen. Laundry. Motorcaravan service point. Shop. Restaurant (closed Nov). Fitness room. TV and cinema room. Adventure play area. Youth room. Bicycle, go-kart and buggy hire. WiFi. Off site: Fishing 500 m. Golf, riding and boat launching within 3 km.

Open: All year.

Directions

From Freiburg take road B31 east to Titisee. Pass through the town centre and continue for 2.5 km. following camping signs. The entrance to Bankenhof is on the left. GPS: N47:53.159 E08:07.842

Charges 2009

Per person	€ 5,40 - € 6,60
child (3-15 yrs)	€ 2,60 - € 2,90
pitch	€ 5,90 - € 7,90
electricity per kWh	€ 0,50

DE3452 Terrassen-Camping Alte Sägemühle

Badstrasse 57, D-79295 Sulzburg (Baden-Württemberg)

Tel: **076 345 51181**. Email: **info@camping-alte-saegemuehle.de** **www.alanrogers.com/DE3452**

This delightful site celebrated its 50th anniversary in 2005 and has erected a stone weighing several tons to commemorate the event. Situated beside a peaceful road, the site lies just beyond the picturesque old town of Sulzburg with its narrow streets. Set in a tree-covered valley with a stream running through the centre, the site has been kept as natural as possible. It is divided into terraced areas, each surrounded by high hedges and trees. Electrical connections (16A) are available on 42 of the 45 large touring pitches, although long leads may be needed.

Facilities

In the main building, facilities are of good quality with two private cabins, separate toilets, dishwashing, washing machine and dryer. Motorcaravan service point. Small shop for basics, beer and local wines (all year). Natural, unheated swimming pool adjacent (June-Aug) with discount to campers. Torch may be useful. New room for tent guests. Off site: Public transport, restaurants and other shops in Sulzburg 1.5 km. Bicycle hire in Sulzburg. Riding 2 km. Fishing 8 km. Europa Park is less than an hour away.

Open: All year.

Directions

Site is easily reached (25 minutes) from autobahn A5/E35. Take exit 64 for Bad Krozingen just south of Freiburg onto the B3 south to Heitersheim, then on and up through Sulzburg, or if coming from the south, exit 65 through Müllheim, Heitersheim and Sulzburg. Reception is to the left of the road. GPS: N47:50.129 E07:43.402

Charges 2009

Per unit incl. 2 persons	€ 18,00 - € 20,50
extra person	€ 6,50
electricity (plus meter)	€ 0,50

DE3450 Ferien-Campingplatz Münstertal

Dietzelbachstr. 6, D-79244 Münstertal (Baden-Württemberg)

Tel: **076 367 080**. Email: **info@camping-muenstertal.de** **www.alanrogers.com/DE3450**

Münstertal is an impressive site pleasantly situated in a valley on the western edge of the Black Forest. It has been one of the top graded sites in Germany for 20 years, and first time visitors will soon realise why when they see the standard of the facilities here. There are 305 individual pitches in two areas, either side of the entrance road on flat gravel, their size varying from 70-100 sq.m. All have electricity (16A) and 200 have drainage, many also with water, TV and radio connections. The large indoor pool with sauna and solarium, and the outdoor pool, are both heated and free. There is a large, grass sunbathing area. The health and fitness centre provides a range of treatments, massages, etc. Children are very well catered for here with a play area and play equipment, tennis courts, minigolf, a games room with table tennis, table football and pool table and fishing. Riding is popular and the site has its own stables. The latest addition is an ice rink for skating and ice hockey in winter. There are 250 km. of walks, with some guided ones organised, and winter sports with cross-country skiing directly from the site (courses in winter – for children or adults and ski hire). The site becomes full in season and reservations, especially in July, are necessary. Member of 'Leading Campings Group'.

Facilities

Three toilet blocks are of truly first class quality, with washbasins, all in cabins, showers with full glass dividers, baby bath, a unit for disabled visitors and individual bathrooms, some for hire. Dishwashers in two blocks. Laundry. Drying room. Motorcaravan services. Well stocked shop (all year). Restaurant, particularly good (closed Nov). Heated swimming pools, indoor all year, outdoor (with children's area) May-Oct. New health and fitness centre. Sauna and solarium. Games room. Bicycle hire. Tennis courses in summer Off site: Village amenities and train station near. Golf 15 km. Freiburg and Basel easy driving distances for day trips.

Open: All year.

Directions

Münstertal is south of Freiburg. From A5 autobahn take exit 64, turn southeast via Bad Krozingen and Staufen and continue 5 km. to the start of Münstertal, where site is signed from the main road on the left. GPS: N47:51.584 E07:45.825

Charges guide

Per person	€ 6,80 - € 7,80
child (2-10 yrs)	€ 4,50 - € 4,95
pitch incl. services	€ 10,70 - € 13,70
dog	€ 3,30

Maestro cards accepted.

DE3445 Camping Belchenblick

Münstertäler strasse 43, D-79219 Staufen (Baden-Württemberg)

Tel: **076 337 045**. Email: **info@camping-belchenblick.de** **www.alanrogers.com/DE3445**

This site stands at the gateway, so to speak, to the Black Forest. Not very high up itself, it is just at the start of the long road climb which leads to the top of Belchen, one of the highest summits of the forest. The site has 200 pitches (180 for touring units), all with electrical connections (10/16A), and 100 with TV and water. On site is a small heated indoor swimming pool and adjacent is a municipal sports complex, including an outdoor pool and tennis courts. Reservation is necessary from early June to late August at this popular site. Charges include free hot water and the indoor pool. A little tractor will site your caravan if required. It is well situated for excursions by car to the best areas of the forest, for example the Feldberg-Titisee-Höllental circuit, and many excellent walks are possible nearby. Staufen is a pleasant little place with character.

Facilities

Three sanitary blocks are heated and have free hot water, individual washbasins (6 in private cabins), plus 21 family cabins with WC, basin and shower (some on payment per night for exclusive use). Washing machine. Gas supplies. Motorcaravan services. Shop (1/3-31/10). Bar (all year). Snacks and takeaway (1/3-31/10). Indoor and outdoor pools. Sauna and solarium. Tennis. Playground with barbecue area. Bicycle hire. Off site: Restaurant near. Fishing 20 Km. Riding 2 km.

Open: All year.

Directions

Take autobahn exit for Bad Krozingen, south of Freiburg, and continue to Staufen. Site is southeast of the town and signed, across an unmanned local railway crossing near the entrance.
GPS: N47:52.307 E07:44.200

Charges 2009

Per unit incl. 2 persons	€ 21,00 - € 24,00
extra person	€ 6,00 - € 7,50
child (2-12 yrs)	€ 4,00
electricity (per kWh)	€ 0,60
dog	€ 2,50

No credit cards.

DE3465 Camping Wirthshof

Steibensteg 12, D-88677 Markdorf (Baden-Württemberg)

Tel: **075 449 627-0**. Email: **info@wirthshof.de** **www.alanrogers.com/DE3465**

Lying 7 km. back from the Bodensee, 12 km. from Friedrichshafen, this friendly site with good facilities could well be of interest to Britons with young children. The 320 individual touring pitches have electrical connections (6-16A) and are of about 80 sq.m. on well tended flat grass, adjoining access roads. There are 100 larger pitches with water, waste water and electricity. No dogs are accepted in July/Aug. and there is a special section for campers with dogs at other times. Many activities are organised for children and adults over a long season.

Facilities

The three heated toilet blocks provide washbasins in cubicles, a unit for disabled people and a children's bathroom. Cosmetic studio. New beauty spa. Laundry facilities. Motorcaravan services. Shop. Restaurant/bar with takeaway. Swimming pool (25 x 12.5 m; 10/5-10/9). Sports field. Adventure playgrounds. Bicycle hire. Normal minigolf; also 'pit-pat', played at table height with billiard cues. Activity programme. Off site: Tennis near. Riding 8 km. Golf and fishing 10 km.

Open: 15 March - 30 October.

Directions

Site is on eastern edge of Markdorf, turn south off B33 Ravensburg road. The site is signed (but not named) from Markdorf.
GPS: N47:42.869 E09:24.558

Charges guide

Per unit inc. 2 persons and electricity	€ 24,50 - € 32,70
extra person	€ 6,50 - € 7,60
child (1-14 yrs)	€ 3,80 - € 4,80

No credit cards.

DE3455 Gugel's Dreiländer Camping

Oberer Wald 3, D-79395 Neuenburg (am Rhein) (Baden-Württemberg)

Tel: **076 317 719**. Email: **info@camping-gugel.de** **www.alanrogers.com/DE3455**

Set in natural heath and woodland, Gugel's is an attractive site with 220 touring pitches either in small clearings in the trees, in open areas or on a hardstanding section used for single night stays. All have electricity (16A), and some also have water, waste water and satellite TV connections. Opposite is a meadow where late arrivals and early departures may spend the night. There may be some road noise near the entrance. The site may become very busy in high season and at Bank Holidays but you should always find room. There is a good atmosphere and it can be recommended for both short and long stays. There is a social room with satellite TV where guests are welcomed with a glass of wine and a slide presentation of the attractions of the area. The Rhine is within walking distance. Neuenburg is ideally placed not only for enjoying and exploring the south of the Black Forest, but also for night stops when travelling from Frankfurt to Basel on the A5 autobahn. The site is winner of a prestigious environmental award. The permanent caravans set away from the tourist area, with their well-tended gardens, enhance rather than detract from the natural beauty.

Facilities

Three good quality heated sanitary blocks include some washbasins in cabins. Baby room. Facilities for disabled visitors. Laundry facilities. Motorcaravan services. Shop. Excellent restaurant. Takeaway (weekends and daily in high season). Wellness centre. Indoor pool. Boules. Tennis. Fishing. Minigolf. Barbecue. Beach bar. Bicycle hire. Community room with TV. Activity programme (high season). Play areas. Off site: Riding 1.5 km. Golf 5 km. Neuenburg, Breisach, Freiburg, Basel and the Black Forest.

Open: All year.

Directions

From autobahn A5 take Neuenburg exit, turn left, then almost immediately left at traffic lights, left at next junction and follow signs for 2 km. to site (called 'Neuenburg' on most signs).
GPS: N47:47.816 E07:33.000

Charges guide

Per unit incl. 2 persons and electricity	€ 24,60
extra person	€ 6,40
child (2-15 yrs)	€ 3,00
dog	€ 3,00

Discount every 10th night, persons free.

Germany

DE3602 Kawan Village Romantische Straße

Munster 67, D-97993 Creglingen-Münster (Baden-Württemberg)

Tel: **079 332 0289**. Email: **camping.hausotter@web.de** **www.alanrogers.com/DE3602**

This poplar tourist area can become very busy during the summer when this site would be much appreciated for its peaceful situation in a wooded valley just outside the small village of Münster. There are 100 grass touring pitches (out of 140), many level, others with a small degree of slope. They are not hedged or fenced, to keep the natural appearance of the woodland. All the pitches have electricity (6A), some shade, and are situated either side of a stream (fenced off from a weir at the top of the site). Good English is spoken by the friendly owners, who also own the restaurant.

Facilities

The main sanitary facilities are of good quality with free hot water. A small unit further into the site is not of the same quality. Launderette. Motorcaravan services. Small shop. Gas. Large, pleasant bar/restaurant (18/3-9/11, closed Mondays). Barbecue area. Heated indoor pool (caps required) and sauna. Minigolf. Play area. Bicycle hire. Rooms to let. Off site: Bus service 200 m. Large lakes for swimming 100 m. and fishing 0.5 km. Riding 3.5 km.

Open: 15 March - 15 November.

Directions

From the Romantische Strasse between Rothenburg and Bad Mergentheim, exit at Creglingen to Münster (3 km). Site is just beyond this village.
GPS: N49:26.357 E10:02.520

Charges 2009

Per person	€ 5,10 - € 6,20
child (3-14 yrs)	€ 3,90 - € 4,00
pitch incl. electricity	€ 8,50 - € 9,50

No credit cards. Camping Cheques accepted.

DE3280 Camping & Ferienpark Teichmann

An der B252, D-34516 Vöhl-Herzhausen (Hesse)

Tel: **056 352 45**. Email: **camping-teichmann@t-online.de** **www.alanrogers.com/DE3280**

Situated near the eastern end of the 27 km. long Edersee and the National Park Kellerwald-Edersee, this attractively set site is surrounded by wooded hills and encircles a six hectare lake which has separate areas for swimming, fishing and boating. Of the 460 pitches 250 are touring, all with 10A electricity and 50 with fresh and waste water connections. The pitches are on level grass, some having an area of hardstanding, and are separated by hedges and mature trees. At the far side of the lake from the entrance is a separate area for tents with its own sanitary block. The adjoining national park, a popular leisure region, offers a wealth of holiday and sporting activities including walking, cycling, (there are two passenger ferries that take cycles) boat trips, cable car and much more, full details are available at the friendly reception. For winter sport lovers the ski centre at Winterberg is only 30 km. away from this all the year round site. With a wide range of facilities for children this is an ideal family site as well as being suited to country lovers who can enjoy the endless forest and lakeside walks/cycle tracks in the park.

Facilities

Three good quality sanitary blocks can be heated and have free showers, washbasins (open and in cabins), baby rooms and facilities for wheelchair users. Laundry. Motorcaravan services. Café and shop (both summer only). Restaurant (closed Feb). Watersports. Boat and bicycle hire. Lake swimming. Fishing. Minigolf. Tennis. Playground. Sauna. Solarium. Disco (high season). Internet access. Off site: New National Park opposite site entrance. Riding 500 m. Cable car (you can take bikes). Aquapark.

Open: All year.

Directions

Site is 45 km. from Kassel. From A44 Oberhausen - Kassel autobahn, take exit 64 for Diemelstadt and head south for Korbach. Site is between Korbach and Frankenberg on the B252 road, 1 km. to the south of Herzhausen at the pedestrian traffic lights.
GPS: N51:10.530 E08:53.440

Charges guide

Per person	€ 5,50 - € 6,90
pitch	€ 10,70 - € 15,90
electricity (10A)	€ 2,40

DE3467 Isnycamping

Lohbauerstr. 59-69, D-88316 Isny (Baden-Württemberg)

Tel: **07562 2389**. Email: **info@isny-camping.de** **www.alanrogers.com/DE3467**

Isny is a delightful spot for families and for others looking for a peaceful stay in a very well managed environment. The site has been developed to a high standard and lies just south of the village in a wood by a lake. In an open area there are 50 individual 100 sq.m. hardstanding pitches with a circular access road. A further area is on a terrace just above. A café with terrace overlooking the lake, serves light snacks during the week and meals at the weekends.

Facilities

The main sanitary unit is first class and has automatic toilet seat cleaning. There are cabins as well as vanity style washbasins, large controllable showers, with full curtain, token operated. Further facilities house showers, WCs, washbasins, and a good unit for disabled visitors. Laundry. Basic motorcaravan services. Café/bar. Reception keeps a few basic supplies. Bicycles to borrow. Off site: Tennis club. Play areas. Restaurant and supermarket 1.5 km.

Open: 1 January - 30 October.

Directions

From the B12 between Lindau and Kempten, turn south at sign in Isny at traffic lights and follow signs up into the woods. GPS: N47:40.697 E10:01.821

Charges 2009

Per person	€ 6,50
child per year of age	€ 0,40
pitch	€ 9,50
electricity per kWh	€ 0,50

Special rates for senior citizens (low season).

DE3490 Hegau Familien Camping

An der Sonnenhalde 1, D-78250 Tengen (Baden-Württemberg)

Tel: **077 369 2470**. Email: **info@hegau-camping.de** **www.alanrogers.com/DE3490**

Located in the sunny southwest corner of Germany, this site, new in 2003, must be one of the best we have seen. It is ultra modern in design and exceptionally high standards are maintained. Located in meadowland in a quiet rural valley close to the Swiss border, it provides excellent opportunities for walking, cycling and sightseeing. All 170 touring pitches (out of a total of 200) have electricity (16A), water and drainage, although water points are shared. The pitches are grassy and level and of a good size. At the bottom of the site is an excellent heated swimming pool.

Facilities

New heated sanitary facilities include private cabins, showers, facilities for disabled visitors and for children. Three family shower rooms for rent (2 also have a bath). Laundry facilities. Motorcaravan service point. Restaurant, small shop and bar opposite reception. Swimming pool, sauna and Turkish bath (charged). Off site: Golf 20 km. Skiing for children possible in the adjoining meadows. Supermarket less than 1 km.

Open: All year.

Directions

From A81 take exit 42 on to B314. At roundabout in Tengen follow international camping signs. Turn right at supermarket on edge of village. From Kommingen follow camp signs turning left towards site at supermarket on edge of village.
GPS: N47:49.036 E08:39.586

Charges guide

Per unit incl. 2 persons	€ 23,00 - € 30,00
extra person	€ 6,00
electricity (per kWh)	€ 0,60

DE3225 Naturpark Camping Suleika 1986

Im Bodental 2, D-65391 Lorch am Rhine (Hesse)

Tel: **067 269 464**. Email: **suleika-camping@t-online.de** **www.alanrogers.com/DE3225**

On a steep hillside in the Rhine-Taunus Nature Park and approached by a narrow and steep system of lanes through the vineyards, this site is steeply arranged on small terraces up the side of the wooded hill with a stream flowing through – the water supply is direct from springs. The surroundings are most attractive, with views over the vineyards to the river below. Of the 100 pitches, 50 are available for touring units. These are mostly on the lower terraces, in groups of up to four units. All have electricity and there are water points. Cars are parked away from the pitches.

Facilities

The excellent toilet block is heated in cool weather and provides some washbasins in cabins for each sex and a nicely furnished baby washroom, with WC, shower and bath. Laundry service. Motorcaravan services. Gas supplies. Restaurant (closed Mon. and Thurs). Small shop (bread to order). Playground. Some entertainment in season. Off site: Bicycle hire. Fishing 300 m. Riding 4 km. The Rheinsteig footpath passes above the site.

Open: 15 March - 31 October.

Directions

Direct entrance road from B42 (cars only), between Rudesheim and Lorch, with height limit of 2.25 m. under railway bridge. Higher vehicles will find the site signed on the south side of Lorch. Site reached via a one-way system of lanes; follow signs.
GPS: N50:01.047 E07:51.206

Charges 2009

Per person	€ 5,00
pitch	€ 3,00 - € 7,00
electricity (plus meter)	€ 0,50 - € 1,00

No credit cards.

DE3265 Lahn Camping

Schleusenweg 16, D-65549 Limburg an der Lahn (Hesse)

Tel: **06431 22610**. Email: **lahncamping@limburg-net.de** **www.alanrogers.com/DE3265**

Pleasantly situated on the bank of the river Lahn (with direct access to it) between the autobahn and the town – both the autobahn viaduct and the cathedral are visible – this is a useful overnight stop for travellers along the Köln-Frankfurt stretch of the A3. The site is on level grass with 200 touring pitches (250 altogether) and 140 have 6A electricity (may need long cables). There are some trees but it is mainly open. It is very popular with many nationalities and can become crowded at peak times, so arrive early. There is road and rail noise.

Facilities

The main sanitary block near reception is old and facilities are poor (showers need a token). A better quality, heated block at the other end of the site is a welcome addition. Laundry facilities. Cookers. Motorcaravan services. Bar/restaurant (evenings and Sundays) and takeaway. Small shop (not Sunday p.m). Fishing (permit on payment). Play area. Bicycle and motorcycle hire.
Off site: Swimming pool opposite. Riding 5 km. Pleasure cruises. Supermarkets, shops and restaurants in town.

Open: 9 April - 25 October.

Directions

Leave A3 autobahn at Limburg-Nord exit and follow road towards town and then signs for 'Camping-Swimming'. GPS: N50:23.338 E08:04.433

Charges guide

Per person	€ 4,50
child (3-14 yrs)	€ 2,40
pitch	€ 8,00
electricity	€ 2,40

No credit cards.

DE3220 Camping Burg Lahneck

Ortsteil Oberlahnstein, D-56112 Lahnstein (Rhineland Palatinate)

Tel: **026 212 765** **www.alanrogers.com/DE3220**

The location of this site is splendid, high up overlooking the Rhine valley and the town of Lahnstein – many of the pitches have their own super views. It consists partly of terraces and partly of open grassy areas, has a cared for look and all is very neat and clean. One can usually find a space here, though from early July to mid-August it can become full. There are 100 individual touring pitches marked but not separated and mostly level, all with electricity (16A). Campers are sited by the management. Reception staff at the site are friendly and charges reasonable.

Facilities

The single central, heated toilet block is of a good standard, and well maintained and cleaned. There are some cabins for both sexes. Showers are on payment. Laundry facilities. Motorcaravan services. Small shop. Playground. Off site: Cafe/restaurant adjoining site; meals also in Burg Lahneck restaurant. Town swimming pool (15/5-31/8, reduced charges for campers). Tennis nearby. Riding 500 m. Fishing 3 km. Bicycle hire 2 km.

Open: Easter/1 April - 31 October.

Directions

From B42 road bypassing the town, take Oberlahnstein exit and follow signs 'Kurcentrum' and Burg Lahneck. GPS: N50:18.200 E07:36.460

Charges guide

Per person	€ 6,00
caravan	€ 6,00
motorcaravan	€ 7,50 - € 8,50
electricity (plus meter)	€ 0,50

No credit cards.

DE3222 Camping Gülser Moselbogen

Am Gülser Moselbogen 20, Güls, D-56072 Koblenz (Rhineland Palatinate)

Tel: **026 144 474**. Email: **info@moselbogen.de** **www.alanrogers.com/DE3222**

This site is set well above the river and has a pleasant outlook to the forested valley slopes. A large proportion of the 16 acre site is taken up by privately owned bungalows, but the touring section of 125 large individual pitches is self contained and accessed by gravel paths leading off the main tiled roads. The flat pitches have little shade as yet, but all have connections for TV and 11/16A electricity and there are water points in each section. A new area of gravel hardstanding has been developed and RVs are accepted.

Facilities

Entry to the excellent, heated sanitary building is by a coded card that also operates the hot water to the showers (free to the washbasins, many of which are in cabins). Unit for disabled visitors. Baby room. Cooking rings (charged). Laundry. Gas supplies. Motorcaravan services. Shop. Café and bistro. Play area. Bicycle hire. Off site: Fishing 200 m. Special area for swimming in the Mosel 200 m. Restaurant 500 m. Güls village 1.5 km. Riding 3 km.

Open: All year.

Directions

Site is 1.5 km. west of village of Güls but easiest access is from the A61. Take exit 38 (Koblenz - Metternich). After 2 km. turn right at roundabout (Winningen). Keep on main road to Winningen until the B416 where you turn left towards Koblenz. Site on right in 3.5 km. GPS: N50:19.954 E07:33.185

Charges 2009

Per person	€ 5,00
pitch	€ 5,00 - € 8,00
electricity (plus € 1.00 connection)	€ 1,50

DE3215 Camping Goldene Meile

Simrockweg 9-13, D-53424 Remagen (Rhineland Palatinate)

Tel: **026 422 2222**. Email: **info@camping-goldene-meile.de** **www.alanrogers.com/DE3215**

This site is on the banks of the Rhine between Bonn and Koblenz. Although there is an emphasis on permanent caravans, there are about 300 pitches for tourists (out of 500), most with 6A electricity and 100 with water and drainage. They are either in the central, more mature area or in a newer area where the numbered pitches of 80-100 sq.m. are arranged around an attractively landscaped, small fishing lake. Just five are by the busy river and there may be some noise from the trains that run on the other side. Access to the river bank is through a locked gate. Adjacent to the site is a large complex of open-air public swimming pools (campers pay the normal entrance fee). They claim always to find space for odd nights, except perhaps at Bank Holidays. This site is in a popular area and, although busy at weekends and in high season, appears to be well run.

Facilities

The main toilet block is heated and clean, with some washbasins in cabins, showers and facilities for wheelchair users. A smaller block serves the newer pitches (no showers). Laundry and cooking facilities. Motorcaravan services. Gas. Shop, bar, restaurant and takeaway (all 1/4-30/10 and some weekends). Play areas. Entertainment for children (July/Aug). Bicycle hire. Main gate locked at 22.00 (also 13.00 - 15.00). Off site: Swimming pool complex adjacent (May-Sept).

Open: All year.

Directions

Remagen is 23 km. south of Bonn on N9 road towards Koblenz. Site is on road close to the Rhine from Remagen to Kripp, signed from N9 south of Remagen. From A61 autobahn take Sinzig exit. GPS: N50:34.457 E07:15.113

Charges 2009

Per person	€ 6,00
child (6-16 yrs)	€ 5,00
pitch incl. electricity	€ 10,70 - € 12,30
dog	€ 1,70

Eurocards accepted.

DE3212 Landal Wirfttal

Wirftstraße, D-54589 Stadtkyll (Rhineland Palatinate)

Tel: **065 979 2920**. Email: **info@landal.de** **www.alanrogers.com/DE3212**

Peacefully set in a small valley in the heath and forest of the hills of the northern Eifel near the Belgian border, Wirfttal has 250 numbered pitches of which 150 are for tourers. They mostly back onto fences, hedges etc. on fairly flat ground of different levels (steel pegs are required for tents and awnings). The pitches (many on gravel) are 80 sq.m. or more, and all have electricity (8A) and TV aerial points with water points around. Five individual pitches have their own water and waste water points. Also part of the site, but separate from the camping, is a large holiday bungalow complex.

Facilities

One main toilet block, and two small units, all heated. All ladies' washbasins and one for men in main block are in cabins. New shop. Restaurant and snacks. Swimming pool complex (discount for campers). Indoor pool (free) and sauna and solarium (on payment) Tennis. Riding. Fishing. Bicycle hire. Sports centre adjacent with squash hall. Play equipment. Adventure playground. Winter sports. Bicycle and sledge hire. Animation in season.

Open: All year.

Directions

Site is 1.5 km. south of Stadtkyll on road towards Schüller. Follow signs in Stadtkyll for Haus an der See). GPS: N50:20.326 E06:32.252

Charges guide

Per unit incl. 2 persons and electricity	€ 14,00 - € 31,00
extra person	€ 3,00
dog	€ 3,00

Less in low season. Special 5, 8 or 10 day rates.

DE3233 Campingplatz Holländischer Hof

D-56820 Senheim (Rhineland Palatinate)

Tel: **026 734 660**. Email: **holl.hof@t-online.de** **www.alanrogers.com/DE3233**

This campsite lies along a bend of the river Moselle, surrounded on three sides by hills, and on the other by the river. An arm of the river intrudes here and a harbour for small boats has been made. A road bridge passes over the very last pitches at one end of the site, but this did not seem to generate any noise nuisance. There are some seasonal pitches, but the site caters mostly for tourists. All 150 pitches have electricity points (6/10A). Dogs are not allowed on the site, but there are a dozen pitches outside the barrier for those who have dogs with them.

Facilities

The main sanitary block includes washbasins (some in cubicles) and showers (by token). Unit for disabled visitors. Laundry facilities. Other toilet facilities in a portacabin unit. Motorcaravan service point. Shop. Gas. Restaurant, snack bar, pizzeria and takeaway (with children's menu) and terrace. Playground. TV room. Games room. Sports field. River fishing. Dogs are not accepted. Off site: Tennis 300 m. Bicycle hire 2 km. ATM point 2 km. Golf 4 km.

Open: Easter - 1 November.

Directions

From Cochem (on the west bank) take B49 upstream (south). At Nehren, cross bridge towards Senheim. From the bridge the site is below on the left. If coming from upstream, take the B49 north from Alf. GPS: N50:04.931 E07:12.521

Charges guide

Per person	€ 4,10
pitch	€ 7,15

No credit cards.

DE3237 Camping In der Enz

In der Enz 25, D-54673 Neuerburg (Rhineland Palatinate)

Tel: **065 642 660**. Email: **camping@basse.de** **www.alanrogers.com/DE3237**

This site is just outside the town, next to the municipal swimming pool complex, and the enthusiastic owners give a very warm welcome which makes this a very pleasant place to stay. The site is bisected by the unfenced River Enz which is little more than a stream at this point. The section nearest the road is occupied by 50 long stay units. The other half, on the other side of the river with its own access road, is solely for tourists. This has 50 very large, open grass pitches, all with electricity (16A), of which 32 are multi-service with water and drainage.

Facilities

New sanitary block of very high quality with the usual facilities and provision for disabled visitors. Baby room. Kitchen and laundry. Family sauna room (extra charge). Play area. Bicycle hire. Internet point. Site is not suitable for American RVs. Off site: Swimming pool complex (May-Sept) and all year restaurant and bar (both adjacent). Fishing, riding and tennis within walking distance. Golf 13 km.

Open: Easter - 31 October.

Directions

Neuerburg is about 50 km. northwest of Trier. From A60 (E29) take exit 6 and head south to Bitburg, then take road 50 west to Sinspelt. Finally turn north for 6 km. to Neuerburg, pass through town and site is 1.5 km. north of the town. GPS: N50:01.668 E06:16.613

Charges guide

Per person	€ 3,00
pitch incl. car	€ 7,00 - € 9,00
electricity (per kWh)	€ 0,50

DE3242 Country Camping Schinderhannes

D-56291 Hausbay-Pfalzfeld (Rhineland Palatinate)

Tel: **06746 80280**. Email: **info@countrycamping.de** **www.alanrogers.com/DE3242**

About 30 km. south of Koblenz, west of the Rhine and south of the Mosel, this site is set in a 'bowl' of land which catches the sun all day. With trees and parkland all around, it is a peaceful and picturesque setting. There are 150 permanent caravans in a separate area from 90 short stay touring pitches on hardstanding. For longer stays, an area around the lake has a further 160 numbered pitches. These are of over 80 sq.m. on grass, some with hardstanding and all with 8A electricity. You can position yourself for shade or sun. The lake is used for swimming, inflatable boats and fishing.

Facilities

The sanitary buildings, which can be heated, are of a high standard with one section, in the reception/shop building, for the overnight pitches and the remainder close to the longer stay places. Facilities for disabled people. Laundry. Bar. Restaurant with takeaway. TV area. Skittle alley. Shop (all amenities 1/3-31/10 and Xmas). Tennis. Fishing. Play area. Rallies welcome. Torches useful. Barrier closed 22.00-07.00.

Open: All year.

Directions

From A61 Koblenz - Ludwigshafen road, take exit 43 Pfalzfeld (30 km. south of Koblenz) and on to Hausbay where site is signed. GPS: N50:06.358 E07:34.093

Charges 2009

Per person	€ 6,50
child (under 14 yrs)	€ 3,00
pitch incl. electricity	€ 8,00

Camping Cheques accepted.

DE3232 Family Camping

Wiesenweg 25, D-56820 Mesenich bei Cochem (Rhineland Palatinate)

Tel: **026 734 556**. Email: **info@familycamping.de** **www.alanrogers.com/DE3232**

Situated beside the River Mosel with views of forest and vineyard, this attractive family run site is on a stretch of the river that is well away from the railway. The 94 touring pitches are among the vines, mainly level, with electricity hook-ups (6/10A), separated by bushes and some with shade. There are 25 pitches with their own water tap and 35 tents available for rent. The site roads are relatively narrow and are not suitable for larger units especially American RVs or twin axle caravans.

Facilities

Well equipped, heated toilet facilities provide good sized showers (on payment), washbasins mainly in cubicles or curtained. Good baby room. Laundry with washing machines and dryer. Shop, bar and restaurant (1/5-8/9). Takeaway (1/5-15/9). Swimming pools (1/6-15/9, weather dependant). Play area. Disco evenings and wine tours in July/Aug. River fishing (with permit). Dogs are not accepted in July/Aug. Off site: Bicycle hire 300 m. Golf 7 km. Riding 10 km. Wine museum. Cochem with its castle and leisure centre 15 km.

Open: 8 April - 8 October.

Directions

From the B49 at Senheim, cross river and follow signs (Mesenich). Site in village on left. Or cross river at Cochem and follow L98 riverside road south to Mesenich. Can also be reached from scenic B421 Kirchberg to Zell road, turning to Senheim 15 km. after Kirchberg (rather winding, steep road at the end). GPS: N50:06.093 E07:11.628

Charges guide

Per unit incl. 2 persons	€ 10,00 - € 14,00
extra person	€ 4,00

No credit cards.

DE3245 Landal Sonnenberg

D-54340 Leiwen (Rhineland Palatinate)

Tel: **065 079 3690**. Email: **info@landal.de** **www.alanrogers.com/DE3245**

With attractive views over the Mosel as you climb the approach road, 4 km. from the wine village of Leiwen and the river, this pleasant site is on top of a hill. It has a splendid free leisure centre incorporating an indoor activity pool with a paddling pool, whirlpool, cascade and slides. Also in this building are tenpin bowling, a sauna, solarium and fitness room, tennis and badminton, plus a snack bar. Combining a bungalow complex (separate) with camping, the site has 150 large, individual and numbered grass/gravel pitches on terraces with electricity (6A) and TV connections.

Facilities

The single toilet block has underfloor heating, washbasins in cabins (all for women, a couple for men). It is stretched in busy times. Separate suite for disabled visitors. Large laundry. Motorcaravan services. Shop. Restaurant, bistro, bar and snacks. Indoor leisure centre with activity pool, climbing wall, 10-pin bowling, tennis and badminton. Minigolf. Playground. Bicycle hire (high season). Disco, entertainment and excursions. Deer park. Off site: Fishing 5 km. Riding or golf 12 km.

Open: 23 March - 3 November.

Directions

From A48/A1 (Trier - Koblenz) take new exit 128 for Bekond, Föhren, Hetzerath and Leiwen. Follow signs for Leiwen and in town follow signs for Ferienpark, Sonnenberg or Freibad on very winding road up hill 4 km. to site. GPS: N49:48.227 E06:53.554

Charges guide

Per unit incl. 2 persons and electricity	€ 22,00 - € 33,00
extra person	€ 3,00
dog	€ 3,00

DE3250 Landal Warsberg

In den Urlaub 1, D-54439 Saarburg (Rhineland Palatinate)

Tel: **065 819 1460**. Email: **info@landal.de** **www.alanrogers.com/DE3250**

On top of a steep hill in an attractive location, this site and the long winding approach road both offer pleasant views over the town and surrounding area. A large, well organised site, there are 461 numbered touring pitches of quite reasonable size on flat or slightly sloping ground, separated in small groups by trees and shrubs, with electrical connections (16A) available in most places. There are some tour operator pitches and a separate area with holiday bungalows to rent. This is a site with friendly staff, which should appeal to all age groups. July and August are very busy.

Facilities

Three toilet blocks of very good quality provide washbasins (many in private cabins) and a unit for disabled visitors. Large launderette. Motorcaravan services. Gas supplies. Shop. Restaurant and takeaway, games rooms adjacent. Swimming pool (all year). Tennis. Minigolf. Bicycle hire. Large playground. Entertainment in season for all ages. 530 metre long 'Rodelbahn' toboggan (small fee). Off site: Riding and fishing 5 km.

Open: 31 March - 30 October.

Directions

From Trier on road 51 site is well signed in the northwest outskirts of Saarburg off the Trierstrasse (signs also for 'Ferienzentrum') and from all round town. Follow signs up hill for 3 km. GPS: N49:37.195 E06:32.609

Charges guide

Per unit incl. 2 persons and electricity	€ 23,00 - € 31,00
extra person	€ 3,50

DE3255 Azur Campingpark am Königsberg

Am Schwimmbad 1, D-67752 Wolfstein (Rhineland Palatinate)

Tel: **063 044 143**. Email: **benspruijt@gmx.de** **www.alanrogers.com/DE3255**

Situated in an area between the Rhine and Mosel rivers in a nature area at the foot of the Königsberg, this is a small attractive, well maintained site with plenty of facilities. Of the 100 pitches, 70 are reserved for tourists and most have electricity, fresh and waste water connections. The level, grass, mainly open pitches are easily reached by tarmac site roads. A large separate meadow is for tents and has a communal grill and covered eating area. Trees and hedges provide some shade and division of the site. A local railway with one train an hour, passes close to the site.

Facilities

Modern comfortable, heated sanitary block with all usual facilities including showers, free hot water and private cabins. Facilities for disabled people. Laundry room. Fridge rental. Shop. Bar/restaurant (all year). Takeaway. Play cabin, play area and games room for children with entertainment daily in summer. Minigolf. Bicycle hire. Fishing. Off site: Large swimming pool complex next to site, free to campers. Shops and other facilities in the village 300 m. Riding 2 km.

Open: All year.

Directions

Wolfstein is 20 km. northwest of Kaiserslautern on the B270. From A6 (Ludwigshafen - Saarbrücken) take exit 15 for Kaiserslauten West and head north towards Lauterecken. In Erfenbach left on B270 towards Lauterecken and Idar-Oberstein. Stay on the B270. Site is signed 300 m. south of the village of Wolfstein. GPS: N49:34.820 E7:37.130

Charges 2009

Per person	€ 5,50 - € 7,00
child (2-12 yrs)	€ 4,25 - € 5,50

DE3256 Azur Camping Hunsrück

Parkstrasse, D-54421 Reinsfeld (Rhineland Palatinate)

Tel: **065 039 5123**. Email: **reinsfeld@azur-camping.de** **www.alanrogers.com/DE3256**

This quiet countryside site, spread over 20 hectares, is situated close to the French and Luxembourg borders. With 980 pitches (600 for touring units), the site is constructed with 29 circular grassed areas, each surrounded by trees, and containing no more than 25 pitches. This creates the impression that you are staying on a small site, although you do have the facilities provided by a larger one. A spacious central meadow opposite a lake is used for caravans and tents and is separated from a playing field by a tree lined stream. This is a quiet and relatively unknown comer of Germany.

Facilities

Six heated sanitary buildings with free hot showers, washbasins in cabins and family bathrooms to rent. Baby rooms. Facilities for disabled people. Laundry facilities. Motorcaravan service point. Gas supplies. Supermarket. Comfortable restaurant/bar with takeaway. Swimming pool. Tennis. Large play area and children's activities.

Open: All year.

Directions

Site is 20 km. southeast of Trier. Leave the A1 at exit 132 (Reinsfeld) and follow sign for Reinsfeld. Continue through village and site is signed to the left just before leaving village.
GPS: N49:68.612 E06:86.780

Charges guide

Per person	€ 5,00 - € 7,00
child (2-12 yrs)	€ 3,00 - € 3,50
pitch incl. electricity	€ 8,70 - € 10,70

DE3260 Knaus Campingpark Bad Dürkheim

In den Almen 3, D-67098 Bad Dürkheim (Rhineland Palatinate)

Tel: **063 226 1356**. Email: **badduerkheim@knauscamp.de** **www.alanrogers.com/DE3260**

This large site is comfortable and has some 550 pitches (about half occupied by permanent caravans) but, being the best site at this well known wine town, it is very busy in main season. However, with some emergency areas they can usually find space for everyone. The site is long with individual pitches of fair size arranged on each side of the central road, which is decorated with arches of growing vines. Growing trees provide some shade and electrical connections are available throughout (16A). There is some noise from light aircraft, especially at weekends.

Facilities

Three large sanitary blocks are spaced out along the central avenue. They are of a high standard (private cabins, automatic taps, etc) and are heated in cool weather. Laundry facilities. Gas supplies. Motorcaravan services. Cooking facilities. Shop. Restaurant. Sports programme. Tennis. Playground. Sauna and solarium. Swimming and non-powered boats on lake. Activity programme (guided tours, biking, canoeing and climbing). Dogs are not accepted.

Open: All year (reduced facilities in November).

Directions

Bad Dürkheim is on the no. 37 road west of Ludwigshafen. Site is on the eastern outskirts, signed from the Ludwigshafen road at traffic lights.
GPS: N49:28.428 E08:11.502

Charges guide

Per person	€ 6,00
child (4-14 yrs)	€ 3,00
pitch incl. electricity (plus meter)	€ 11,20 - € 18,20
dog	€ 2,00

No credit cards.

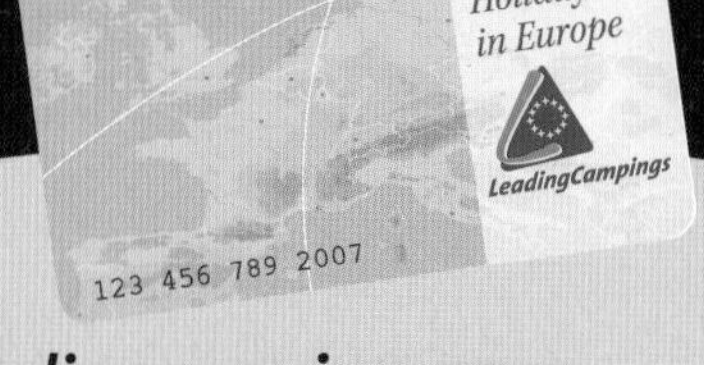

DE3258 Kawan Village Sägmühle

D-67705 Trippstadt (Rhineland Palatinate)
Tel: **063 069 2190**. Email: **info@saegmuehle.de** **www.alanrogers.com/DE3258**

Camping Sägmühle has been in the same family for over 50 years, during which time it has undergone several major developments which have turned it into a first class site. It is peacefully situated beside a lake, in a wooded valley in the heart of the Palatinate Nature Park, and there are many kilometres of walks to enjoy, as well as castles to explore. The 200 touring pitches (half the total) are at least 80 sq.m. or more on flat grass, each with electricity (4A or more) and TV connections, with plenty of water points around. There are three separate areas of pitches. One area is close to the lake and it is a pleasant change to find a site that keeps the lakeside pitches for touring units. A first class restaurant offers you fine local wines, and there is plenty for younger children to enjoy with fishing, swimming and boating in the lake (pedaloes for hire), a fort, minigolf and tennis.

Facilities

Each area has its own sanitary facilities, those beside the lake and the back being first class, while those at the side have been renovated. Private cabins, baby bathroom, facilities for disabled people, launderette. Motorcaravan services. Restaurant serving local specialties and takeaway (lunchtime and evening). Bread available in high season. Solarium. Tennis. Play areas. Mountain bike hire. Boules. Minigolf. Lake fishing. Entertainment daily in high season. Off site: Shops and bus service 10 minutes walk in Trippstadt. Riding 4 km. Golf 25 km. Wilenstein Castle (12th-century ruin) and the famous romantic Karls Valley Gorge are nearby.

Open: All year excl. 1 November - 17 December.

Directions

At Kaiserslautern on A6, take exit 15 (Kaiserslautern West) onto B270 towards Pirmasens. Turn left after 8 km. towards Karlstal/Trippstadt and follow site signs. From the A65 between Karlsruhe and Neustadt take exit 15 or 17 towards Annweiler on the B10. After Annweiler right on B48 to Rinnthal and on towards Kaiserslautern, Johanniskreuz. After 20 km. left to Kaiserslautern, Trippstadt and the next left to Trippstadt. Follow site signs into the valley. GPS: N49:21.104 E07:46.840

Charges 2009

Per person	€ 6,50 - € 7,50
child (under 14 yrs)	€ 2,70 - € 3,40
pitch incl. electricity (4A)	€ 7,70 - € 9,70

Camping Cheques accepted.

DE3254 Camping Harfenmühle

An der Deutschen Edelsteinstrasse, D-55758 Asbacherhütte (Rhineland Palatinate)
Tel: **067 867 076**. Email: **mail@harfenmuehle.de** **www.alanrogers.com/DE3254**

Harfenmühle is quietly situated in a wooded valley in the Naturpark Saar-Hunsrück, an attractive area of Germany just below the Mosel. The site has its own gourmet restaurant and wine cellar. It is a family run, friendly, relaxed partly terraced site, with 100 mostly individual touring pitches. They range in size up to 150 sq.m. with 16A electrical connections and 20 pitches also have water and drainage. With a new, larger meadow for tents, there are also 60 seasonal units and seven chalets.

Facilities

A new toilet block near the site entrance includes good shower cubicles (on payment), facilities for babies and disabled visitors. Launderette. Kiosk with fresh bread daily. Takeaway. Wine cellar/bar. Restaurant with terrace open Wed-Sun. Sauna and solarium. Swimming lake. Water play area (max 30 cm). Off site: Naturpark Saar-Hunsrück. Riding 3 km. and 4.5 km. Bicycle hire 5 km. Golf 10 km. Indoor pool 12 km. Nordic walking park.

Open: All year.

Directions

From the B41 Saarbrücken - Bad Kreuznach, exit north at Fischbach signed towards Herrstein and then on through Morschied to Asbacherhütte, with site entrance on right. GPS: N49:48.217 E07:16.167

Charges 2009

Per person	€ 5,00
pitch	€ 9,00
electricity per kWh	€ 0,50

No credit cards.

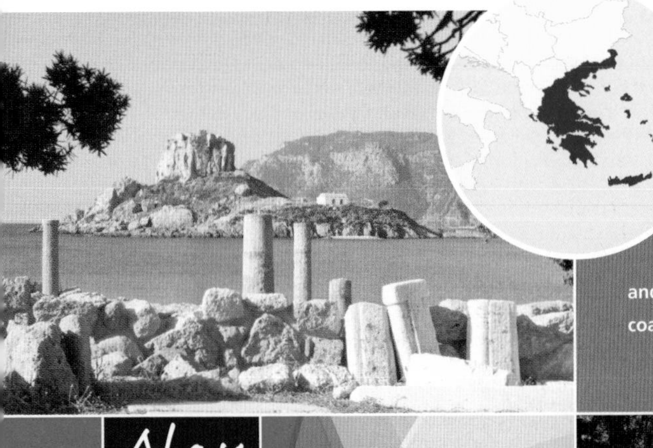

The country's coastline offers huge variety – sheltered bays and coves, golden stretches of sand with dunes, pebbly beaches, coastal caves with steep rocks and volcanic black sand and coastal wetlands.

CAPITAL: ATHENS

Tourist Office

Greek National Tourism Organisation
4 Conduit Street, London W1S 2DJ
Tel: 020 7495 9300
Fax: 020 7287 1369
Email: info@gnto.co.uk
Internet: www.gnto.co.uk

Stretching from the Balkans in the north to the south Aegean, Greece shares borders with Albania, Macedonia, Bulgaria and Turkey.

It is above all a mountainous country – the Pindus range forms the backbone of mainland Greece, extending through central Greece into the Peloponnese and Crete. The majority of islands throughout the Aegean are in fact the mountain peaks of the now submerged landmass of Aegeis, which was once the link between mainland Greece and Asia Minor. Mount Olympus in the north of the country, known from Greek mythology as the abode of the gods, is the highest mountain (2,917 m).

Six thousand islands are scattered in the Aegean and Ionian Seas, a unique phenomenon on the continent of Europe; of these islands, only 227 are inhabited.

Population

10.9 million

Climate

Greece has a Mediterranean climate with plenty of sunshine, mild temperatures and a limited amount of rainfall.

Language

Greek, but most of the people connected to tourism and the younger generations currently practise English and sometimes German, Italian or French.

Telephone

The country code for Greece is 00 30.

Currency

The Euro

Time

GMT + 2 (GMT + 3 from last Sunday in March to last Sunday in October).

Public Holidays

New Year's Day 1 Jan; Epiphany 6 Jan; Shrove Monday Orth. Easter; Independence Day 25 Mar; Easter: Good Friday, Easter Sunday and Easter Monday (Orthodox); Labour Day 1 May; Whit Sunday and Monday (Orthodox); Assumption Day 15 Aug; Ochi Day (National Fest) 28 Oct; Christmas 25/26 Dec.

Motoring

Speed limits are 100-120 km/h on highways unless otherwise posted; 50 km/h in residential areas unless otherwise marked. An international driver's licence is required. Road signs are written in Greek and repeated phonetically in English. Road tolls exist on two highways in Greece, one leading to Northern Greece and the other to the Peloponnese.

GR8000 Camping Batis

40 Klm Kavala, Thessalonika Old Road, GR-65500 Kavala (E.Macedonia & Thrace)

Tel: **251 024 3975**. Email: **info@batis-sa.gr** **www.alanrogers.com/GR8000**

This site is ideally suited, both for those travelling to and from the Turkish border at Ipsala/Kipi and also for those wishing to explore the north of Greece. This refurbished, modern site also offers good low season camping opportunities. It is likely to be very busy with families in the high season. The pitches are small and they are well shaded by tall trees. Istanbul is an easy day's drive away, even allowing for the border formalities. Visas for entry into Turkey are swiftly obtained for €15 (they will not accept Turkish Lira or Sterling).

Facilities

Two excellent toilet blocks (refurbished in 2006) include good showers, WCs and washbasins. Sinks for dishwashing and laundry. Chemical disposal. Restaurant with terrace. Bar. Managed beach. Paddling pool (1/6-1/9). Play area. English is spoken. Off site: Kavala and the Northern Greek coast.

Open: All year.

Directions

From Central Greece leave the motorway at first exit for Kavala. Drive towards the town and site is on the right on an incline after a right hand bend. Driving from the Turkish border exit motorway at first Kavala exit and follow the old road into the town centre. Then follow the promenade out of town to site on the left after 4 km. GPS: N40:54.550 E24:22.400

Charges guide

Per unit incl. 2 persons	€ 12,50 - € 20,50

No credit cards.

GR8120 Camping Poseidon Beach

Platamon-Pieria, GR-60065 Neos Panteleimonas (Central Macedonia)

Tel: **235 204 1654** **www.alanrogers.com/GR8120**

This site is located in a rural area at the foot of Mount Olympus, just off the motorway which follows the coast from Thessalonica to Athens. The area is known for its golden beaches and, as its name suggests, this campsite enjoys direct access. The 250 pitches are on level ground shaded by mature trees and a variety of shrubs and all have 16A electricity. There is a good restaurant, which is open for most of the season. The site is also close to the 10th-century castle of Platamon, which is the principal attraction of the area. There may be some noise from the nearby railway and motorway.

Facilities

Two modern and one refurbished sanitary blocks with mainly British style WCs (one Turkish toilet per block), open washbasins and controllable showers. Chemical disposal. Laundry sinks, washing machines and dryers. Covered dishwashing area. Shop, bar and restaurant (all May - Sept). Fishing.

Open: 1 March - 31 October.

Directions

From E75 Thessaloniki - Athens motorway (toll road) turn left signed Neos Panteleimonas. Cross over railway bridge and turn left onto coastal road. In 500 m. turn right at site sign next to Camping Heraklia. Site is on right in 300 m.
GPS: N40:00.778 E22:35.430

Charges guide

Per person	€ 4,40 - € 5,00
child (2-9 yrs)	€ 2,35 - € 3,00
pitch incl. car	€ 5,90 - € 7,70
electricity	€ 3,40

GR8130 Camping Delphini

GR-63075 Lerissos (Central Macedonia)

Tel: **237 702 2208**. Email: **info@campingdelphini.gr** **www.alanrogers.com/GR8130**

Just 27 km. south of the birthplace of Aristotle is the small town of Lerissos, on the peninsula of Agio Oros, famous for Mount Athos and the Byzantine monasteries. Camping Delphini offers a simple, quiet campsite with 70 pitches which are all for touring units, in a neat, wooded area. The dense trees provide ample shade, so there are none of those horizontal screens found on many Greek campsites. The restaurant and bar provide simple Greek meals and a place to chat to the locals in the cool shade of the terrace or under a parasol. This is a place to visit if you are looking for a restful break and not seeking all the facilities of the bigger beach-front sites.

Facilities

The toilet block includes showers, WCs (some Turkish) and washbasins. Kitchen with sinks, electric hobs and fridges. Laundry with washing machines. Chemical disposal. Bar and simple restaurant. Off site: Agio Oros, Beach 200 m. Boat trips, watersports and parachute jumps.

Open: 1 May - 30 September.

Directions

Camping Delphini is just 2 km. south of Lerissos on the main Agio Oros coast road.
GPS: N40:23.385 E23:53.590

Charges guide

Per person	€ 3,54
pitch	€ 4,16 - € 5,20
electricity	€ 1,00

GR8145 Camping Areti

GR-63081 Neos Marmaras (Central Macedonia)

Tel: **237 507 1430**. Email: **info@camping-areti.gr** **www.alanrogers.com/GR8145**

If you imagine a typical Greek campsite as being set immediately behind a small sandy beach in a quiet cove with pitches amongst pine and olive trees which stretch along way back to the small coast road, then you have found your ideal site. Camping Areti is conveniently located just off the beaten track on the peninsula of Sithonia. It has 130 pitches for touring units. The olive groves at the rear provide hidden parking spaces for caravans and boats that can be brought to the site when the owner is present. The Charalambidi family have clear standards for the site which they meticulously maintain and visitors will not be disappointed.

Facilities

Three excellent toilet blocks include showers, WCs and washbasins. Kitchen with sinks, electric hobs and fridges. Laundry with washing machines. Chemical disposal. Small shop and restaurant. Sandy beach. Bungalows to rent. Fishing, sailing and swimming. Barbecues are not permitted. Off site: Riding, golf and bicycle hire 10 km. Sithonia, Mount Athos and the nearby Spalathronissia islands.

Open: 1 May - 31 October.

Directions

Although the postal address is Neos Marmaras the site is 12 km. south. So stay on the main coast road, past the casino resort at Porto Carras and 5 km. further on turn right towards the site (signed). Then turn right again down to the coast and turn left and on for 1.5 km. Turn right into site access road. Reception is 700 m. GPS: N40:01.451 E23:48.957

Charges guide

Per person	€ 8,10 - € 9,00
pitch	€ 9,90 - € 11,00

No credit cards.

GR8220 Camping Valtos

Valtos Beach, GR-48060 Parga (Epirus)

Tel: **268 403 1287**. Email: **info@campingvaltos.gr** **www.alanrogers.com/GR8220**

Valtos Camping lies two kilometres from the picturesque village of Parga and just 100 m. from the lively sandy beach at Valtos. This is a friendly, unpretentious site with a good range of amenities, including a shop, bar and restaurant. The 92 touring pitches here are of various sizes, all with electrical connections (16A). There is little grass but adequate shade is supplied by a variety of trees. Access to the site is quite narrow and owners of larger motorhomes will need to be careful.

Facilities

Two toilet blocks - one modern and one refurbished. Washing machine. Motorcaravan service point. Shop, bar, takeaway food and restaurant (all May - Sept). Caravans for rent. Off site: Beach 60 m. Water taxi to Parga beach. Bicycle hire 2 km. Sailing, fishing and boat launching 60 m. Boat trips to the Ionian islands. Walking trails.

Open: 1 May - 30 September.

Directions

From Igoumenitsa head south towards Preveza (E55). Turn right to Parga and continue on the coastal road towards Anthousa. Site is signed to the right at the end of Valtos beach road. GPS: N39:17.133 E20:23.390

Charges guide

Per person	€ 4,50 - € 5,00
pitch incl. car	€ 6,50 - € 8,50
electricity	€ 3,00

GR8225 Camping Enjoy-Lichnos

Lichnos, GR-48060 Parga (Epirus)

Tel: **268 403 1171**. Email: **holidays@enjoy-lichnos.net** **www.alanrogers.com/GR8225**

This is a quiet campsite located at the base of a steep and winding road with attractive views of the Ionian Sea and the coastlines towards Preveza and Parga. The site has been created on a steep incline with terraced pitches which tend to be on the small side. The ground levels out in front of the beach and pitches here have sea views. In all there are electricity connections for around 100 pitches and further space for about 300 tents under the shade of the 500 year old olive trees. The sandy beach is the site's main attraction and various water-based activities are available.

Facilities

Unisex toilet blocks in portacabin style units are situated on each terrace with washbasins (cold water only) and showers. Two further sanitary blocks one of which has wheelchair access. Washing machine and ironing. Chemical disposal. Shop. Bar and beach bar. Restaurant with discount for campsite visitors and children's menu. English is spoken. Off site: Parga, ruins of Nekromanteio, island of Lefkada.

Open: 1 May - 31 October.

Directions

From Igoumenitsa head south (E55) towards Preveza. At sign for Parga turn right and follow road for 7 km. At Lichnos village turn left at Lichnos Camping and Apartments. Campsite entrance is 500 m. down steep slope (use low gears). GPS: N39:16.903 E20:26.037

Charges guide

Per person	€ 5,20 - € 5,50
pitch incl. car	€ 7,20 - € 10,30
electricity	€ 4,00

GR8235 Camping Kalami Beach

Plataria, GR-46100 Igoumenitsa (Epirus)

Tel: **266 507 1211**. Email: **info@campingkalamibeach.gr** **www.alanrogers.com/GR8235**

A warm welcome awaits you on your arrival at Camping Kalami Beach. This family run site is ideally situated 8 km. from the ferry port of Igoumenitsa, where it is possible to take cruises to several islands and to Italy. The site is very well cared for with an attractive floral display around the reception building. There are 75 pitches of varying sizes with 10A electricity. Although the site is quite steep in places, the pitches themselves are level and well drained and those at the front of the site above the beach have panoramic views across the sea and to the mountains of Corfu.

Facilities

One sanitary block with British style WCs, washbasins and showers. Second block has showers and washbasins in cabins. Chemical disposal. Laundry room with sinks and washing machines and dryer (token operated). Shop. Bar and restaurant, takeaway. Beach.

Open: 1 March - 31 October.

Directions

From Igoumenitsa head south on the E55 towards Preveza. In 8 km. site is on right, well signed. Entrance is 300 m. down a steep narrow lane. GPS: N39:28.427 E20:14.449

Charges guide

Per person	€ 5,50
pitch incl. car	€ 6,50 - € 9,50
electricity	€ 3,80

No credit cards.

GR8280 Camping Sikia

GR-38500 Kato Gatzea (Thessaly)

Tel: **242 302 2279**. Email: **info@camping-sikia.gr** **www.alanrogers.com/GR8280**

Camping Sikia is an attractive, well maintained site enthusiastically run by the Pandelfi family. The site offers 80 pitches of varying sizes all with 16A electricity. They are arranged on terraces and may become quite dusty during the dry season, but most are well shaded by olive trees. There are superb views from many pitches – the sea to the south and the mountains to the north. There are also 17 apartments to rent. The calm sea and golden beaches of the Pagasitikos Gulf make this a perfect spot for family holidays. The site is just 100 m. from a sand and shingle beach.

Facilities

Two modern and one refurbished sanitary blocks with British style WCs, open washbasins and preset showers. Facilities for disabled visitors are planned. Chemical disposal. Laundry area with sinks, washing machines and ironing facilities. Shop. Bar. TV room. Internet corner. Restaurant. Communal barbecue areas. Fishing. Dogs are not allowed on the beach. Off site: Bicycle hire 1 km. Riding 2 km. Sailing 2 km. Pelion steam railway, boat trips to Skiathos.

Open: 1 April - 31 October.

Directions

Follow E75 south towards Lamia, turn left at sign for Volos onto E92. Follow coastal road towards Argalasti for 18 km. Site is off the coastal road on the right at Kato Gatzea immediately past Camping Hellas. GPS: N39:18.616 E23:06.587

Charges 2009

Per person	€ 5,50 - € 6,80
child (4-16 yrs)	€ 3,00 - € 5,50
pitch incl. car	€ 7,90 - € 8,50
electricity	€ 4,00

GR8285 Camping Hellas International

GR-38500 Kato Gatzea (Thessaly)

Tel: **242 302 2267**. Email: **camping-hellas@argo.net.gr** **www.alanrogers.com/GR8285**

There is a warm welcome from the English speaking brother and sister team who own and run Camping Hellas. The campsite has been in the family since the sixties, when tourists first asked if they could camp overnight and use the facilities of the taverna. It is in a beautiful setting in a 500 year old olive grove, right next to the beach and the calm blue waters of the Pagasitikos gulf. There are around 100 pitches all with 16A electricity. Pitch sizes vary and some parts are more level than others, but shade is plentiful thanks to the olive trees.

Facilities

One modern and one old sanitary block, both very clean with British style toilets and open washbasins. Very good facilities for disabled visitors. Laundry room with sinks and washing machines, ironing facilities. Shop has essentials from 15/4, fully stocked from 1/5. Bar. TV room. Restaurant (from April). Boat launching. Dogs are not allowed on the beach. Off site: Fishing 5 km. Sailing 5 km. Riding 18 km. Bicycle hire 18 km. Pelion steam railway, boat trips to Skiathos.

Open: 15 March - 31 October.

Directions

From the north follow the E75 towards Lamia. Turn left at sign for Volos onto E92. Follow coastal road south towards Argalasti for 18 km. Site is off coastal road on right at Kato Gatzea. GPS: N39:18.650 E23:06.546

Charges guide

Per adult	€ 5,00 - € 6,00
child (4-16 yrs)	€ 3,00 - € 5,00
pitch incl. car	€ 6,30 - € 8,30
electricity	€ 3,60

GR8300 Camping Dounis Beach

GR-30020 Antirrio (Western Greece)

Tel: **263 403 1565**. Email: **campdounis@vahoo.gr** **www.alanrogers.com/GR8300**

At Antirrio the coast comes closest to the Peloponnese. A regular car ferry operated here – it still does today but most of the traffic uses the modern toll bridge to Rio, across the 'little Dardanelles' on the southern shore. There is little more to Antirrio than the bridge and ferry, although beside the harbour, guarding the Gulf of Corinth, stands the originally Frankish and Venetian Kastro Roumelis. Camping Dounis Beach is 1.5 km. away and offers 90 grass pitches all with electricity. A family run site, it is very popular with Greek families who come here every July and August for the beach and the fishing.

Facilities

Two toilet blocks include showers, WCs and washbasins. Sinks for dishwashing and laundry. Chemical disposal. Small shop. Small restaurant (1/7-15/8). Barbecues are not permitted. Off site: Nafpactos and further afield, Patras.

Open: 1 May - 30 November.

Directions

From the Rio - Antirrio toll bridge, site is 1.5 km. from the slip road towards Nafpactos. It is on the right on a left hand bend. Coming from Nafpactos, site is 1.5 km. before Antirrio village and the bridge. GPS: N38:20.508 E21:46.240

Charges guide

Per person	€ 10,00
pitch incl. electricity	€ 11,00

No credit cards.

GR8325 Camping Fournia Beach

Kastro, GR-27050 Killinis (Western Greece)

Tel: **262 309 5095**. Email: **fournia-beach@acn.gr** **www.alanrogers.com/GR8325**

The village of Kastros and the Chlemoutsi castle that towers above it can be seen for miles across the flat landscape towards the coast. Camping Fournia Beach is owned by the four Lefkaditis brothers and their wives have ensured that this new site is awash with flowering shrubs. The site offers 90 first class pitches and modern facilities, and the bar and restaurant sit in a landscaped area high above the beach with spectacular views across the sea to Zakinthos. Steps to the beach provide private access to the sandy cove below. The brothers plan to install a swimming pool.

Facilities

Two modern toilet blocks include showers, WCs and washbasins and good facilities for disabled visitors. Laundry with washing machines, sinks and hot water. Kitchen with hobs, fridge and freezer. Shop. Restaurant and bar overlooking the sea and the island of Zakinthos. Accommodation for rent. Off site: Chlemoutsi castle.

Open: 1 April - 30 October.

Directions

Travel 61 km. south of Patras on the main road to Pyrgos. At traffic lights, turn west signed Killinis and Zakinthos. Site is well signed from here, 15 km. and past village of Kastros. Descend towards the thermal springs and go straight ahead on a left hand hairpin bend towards the beach.
GPS: N37:53.952 E21:06.989

Charges guide

Per unit incl. 2 persons and electricity	€ 16,50 - € 19,85

GR8330 Camping Ionion Beach

Glifa, GR-27050 Vartholomino Ilias (Western Greece)

Tel: **262 309 6395**. Email: **ioniongr@otenet.gr** **www.alanrogers.com/GR8330**

This is a well kept site in a beautiful location by the Ionian Sea, created from former farmland by the Fligos family. Much has changed since they welcomed their first guests in 1982, when they still left plenty of space for growing potatoes. Now it is a modern site with a large pool and a paddling pool and two blocks of apartments to rent. Separated by a variety of trees and oleander bushes, there are 235 pitches with 16A electricity and of between 80 and 100 sq.m. Those at the front of the site have a view over the sea and the island of Zakynthos.

Facilities

Two modern sanitary blocks with British style WCs and showers with washbasins in cabins. Motorcaravan service point. Turkish style chemical disposal point. Laundry room. Shop, bar, restaurant (15/4-15/11). Internet access in bar. Swimming pool (no depth markings) and paddling pool (15/4-15/11). Play area. Off site: Ferries to Zakynthos from Kilini, ancient city of Olympia, Frankish fortress of Chlemoutsi.

Open: All year.

Directions

From Patra head south on E55 towards Pyrgos. At sign for Vartholomio, turn right in town centre, then right at sign for Glyfa and Ionion Beach. In 15 km. campsite sign is on right. Coming from the north of Greece, there is a toll for the Korinthian Gulf bridge.
GPS: N37:50.197 E21:08.028

Charges guide

Per person	€ 5,50 - € 6,00
pitch incl. electricity	€ 10,50 - € 17,00

GR8340 Camping Alphios

GR-27065 Olympia (Western Greece)

Tel: **262 402 2951**. Email: **alphios@otenet.gr** **www.alanrogers.com/GR8340**

High above ancient and modern Olympia, this site enjoys spectacular views, both across the adjoining countryside and to the coast at Pyrgos. It provides 97 pitches of which 40 are for touring units. They all have 16A electricity and many have high reed screens that provide shade. Olympia is a popular tourist destination with dozens of coaches each day bringing tourists from around the world to this small town and the adjoining archaeological sites. However, the area also offers opportunities for walking and cycling amidst some wonderful scenery and this site provides a good base for excursions to the surrounding northern Peloponnese countryside.

Facilities

Two toilet blocks include showers, WCs and washbasins. Two kitchens with sinks for dishwashing, electric hobs and fridges. Laundry with washing machines. Small shop. Bar and restaurant. Swimming pool. Off site: Ancient Olympia. Town centre within walking distance.

Open: 1 April - 15 October.

Directions

Site is at a height of 400 m. to the west of the town, about 1.5 km. from the centre. Go through the town and past the station. Turn right, then at back of the town follow signs up the hill to the site.
GPS: N37:38.590 E21:37.185

Charges guide

Per person	€ 6,00
pitch	€ 6,30 - € 6,80
electricity	€ 3,30

GR8520 Camping Delphi

Delphi-Itea km 4, GR-33054 Delphi (Central Greece)

Tel: **226 508 2209**. Email: **info@delphicamping.com** **www.alanrogers.com/GR8520**

Delphi Camping enjoys a stunning location in a conservation area on the slopes of Mount Parnassus, just 4 km. from ancient Delphi. There are some truly outstanding views over valleys of olive groves across to the Gulf of Corinth. The site's 80 pitches all offer electrical connections (6A) and some benefit from the great views. This is a well managed and well equipped site with an attractive pool and a friendly bar featuring an exhibition of paintings by Avyeris Kanatas, a former owner of the site. The prevailing ambience here is geared towards a peaceful, relaxing stay.

Facilities

Two toilet blocks, one modern and one refurbished. Facilities for disabled visitors. Washing machine. Motorcaravan service point. Shop, bar, takeaway food and restaurant (all April - Oct). Swimming pool. Tennis. Play area. Off site: Bus stop opposite site entrance with regular service to Delphi, Athens and other places of interest. Beach 13 km. Walking trails (for example to Chrisso 3 km).

Open: 1 April - 20 October.

Directions

From Delphi take the road towards Itea. Just after a bridge, 4 km. from Delphi, turn right towards Chrisso. Site is 500 m. on the right.
GPS: N38:28.712 E22:28.484

Charges guide

Per person	€ 6,50
child (4-10 yrs)	€ 4,40
pitch incl. car	€ 7,90 - € 10,00
electricity	€ 3,90

GR8525 Chrissa Camping

Chrisso, GR-33054 Delphi (Central Greece)

Tel: **226 508 2050**. Email: **info@chrissacamping.gr** **www.alanrogers.com/GR8525**

This well kept site is located close to Delphi which was once sacred to the god Apollo and is now the setting for some of the most important monuments of ancient Greek civilisation. The site's situation on a hill ensures stunning views across a vast olive grove to the Gulf of Corinth beyond. There are 60 pitches with electricity connections (16A). They are mainly arranged on terraces as the site is quite steep, which means that everyone can enjoy the views. As the site is in a conservation area, mobile homes are not permitted but there are some round wooden cabins to rent.

Facilities

Modern toilet block with British style WCs, open washbasins and controllable showers. Plastic seats in showers. Motorcaravan service point. Chemical disposal. Laundry room with sinks, washing machine and dryer. Dishwashing room. Shop (1/4-30/10). Bar, restaurant and takeaway (weekends only in winter). Outdoor pool and paddling pool. Barbecues are not allowed. Internet point. Off site: Beach 10 km. Skiing 18 km. Delphi.

Open: All year.

Directions

From Patra head west on E65 (48) towards Itea. Continue towards Delphi and 6 km. from Delphi, Chrisso is signed on the right. Site is directly opposite, clearly signed and entrance is 300 m. down a narrow lane. GPS: N38:28.346 E22:27.549

Charges guide

Per person	€ 5,50 - € 6,50
pitch incl. car	€ 8,00 - € 9,00
electricity	€ 4,00

GR8590 Camping Athens

198-200 Leoforos Athinon, GR-12136 Athens- Peristeri (Attica)

Tel: **210 581 4114**. Email: **info@campingathens.com.gr** **www.alanrogers.com/GR8590**

Camping Athens is an 'all year' site, located to the west of the city and convenient for visiting Athens. The site prides itself on friendly Greek hospitality and offers 66 touring pitches most of which have 16A electricity connections. The pitches are of a reasonable size and are generally well shaded. Smaller pitches are available for tents. The two toilet blocks are of modern design and seemed well maintained when we visited. There is a bus stop opposite the site entrance with a frequent service to the city centre, 7 km. away (tickets are for sale in reception). There are no mobile homes here.

Facilities

Two modern toilet blocks. Washing machines. Shop. Bar. Takeaway food and restaurant. All amenities are available late April - late Oct. WiFi. Excursions can be arranged. Barbecues and open fires are forbidden. Off site: Bus stop opposite site entrance with frequent service to city centre or metro station. Bicycle hire 7 km.

Open: All year.

Directions

From the north (Thessaloniki) take E75 signed Athina Pireas, then the E94 west (towards Korinthos, second exit). Site is on the right after 2 km. and is well signed. From the south (Peloponissos) take E94 towards Athina - Pirea. Continue towards Athens. Site is 4 km. after Dafni monastery. Keep to the right hand lane and make a U-turn in about 800 m.
GPS: N38:00.533 E23:40.326

Charges guide

Per person	€ 8,00
child	€ 4,00
pitch incl. car	€ 9,00 - € 12,00
electricity	€ 4,00

GR8560 Camping Ramnous

174 Poseidon Avenue, GR-19007 Marathonas (Attica)

Tel: **294 552 44**. Email: **ramnous@otenet.gr** **www.alanrogers.com/GR8560**

Famous for the battle that created a world famous race, Marathon needs little introduction. The regular bus service to Athens takes 90 minutes which is not much faster than today's Olympic athletes. However, this site with its 110 pitches is alongside a great sandy beach and is about 6 km. from the village, near the large new town of Nea Makri. Whilst there are sites nearer to Athens, Camping Ramnous has the benefit of its beach location and peace and quiet that is difficult to find near the bustling Greek capital. The bus stops right outside the campsite entrance.

Facilities

Two toilet blocks include showers, WCs and washbasins. Sinks for dishwashing and hobs for cooking. Chemical disposal. Shop, bar and restaurant (1/6-1/9). Water playground for children. Sandy beach with water slide. Off site: Athens 41 km.

Open: All year.

Directions

Heading north out of Nea Makri, site is well signed but turn right towards Schinos and then right again at traffic lights. Just past the Olympic rowing centre turn right towards the site which is on the left.
GPS: N38:07.892 E24:00.419

Charges guide

Per person	€ 6,00 - € 6,50
child	€ 4,50
pitch	€ 9,00 - € 13,00
electricity	€ 3,00

GR8595 Camping Nea Kifissia

Potamou 60 & Dimitsanas str., Adames, GR-14564 Nea Kifissia (Attica)

Tel: **210 620 5646**

www.alanrogers.com/GR8595

Many visitors to Greece will want to spend some time in Athens, the capital. Camping Nea Kifissia offers one of the best opportunities to do that, being in a quiet location with easy access. A small site, run personally by the Komianidou family, there are 66 level pitches, some with shade, in well kept grounds. A regular bus service runs to the Kifissia metro station for fast and regular transport to all the sights. The Acropolis, Parthenon and the Porch of Caryatids are essential viewing.

Facilities

A centrally positioned toilet block includes showers, WCs and washbasins. Chemical disposal. Washing machine. Bar and coffee shop (1/6-20/9). Swimming pool (1/6-20/9). Communal barbecue area. English spoken in reception. Off site: Athens 16 km. (45 minutes by bus/metro).

Open: All year.

Directions

From Athens - Thessaloniki motorway take New Kiffisia exit. Coming from Athens, turn sharp left down Ermionis and turn right into Dimitsanas straight to the site. From the north take the same exit and then almost a U-turn along the small road that runs parallel to the motorway. Site is well signed but turn left down Aigiou to site.
GPS: N38:06.002 E23:47.500

Charges guide

Per person	€ 7,00
pitch	€ 8,00 - € 11,00
electricity	€ 4,00

GR8625 Camping Bekas

Gialasi, GR-21052 Ancient Epidavros (Peloponnese)

Tel: **275 309 9930**. Email: **info@bekas.gr**

www.alanrogers.com/GR8625

Just 60 kilometres south of Corinth you will find the town of Ancient Epidavros, and just south of that is Camping Bekas. With 150 pitches (120 for touring) set amongst the trees you will find shade and a quiet atmosphere. Arranged along a small sand and shingle beach, the site offers opportunities for swimming, sailing and fishing. The Argolid region of the Peloponnese has much to offer the inquisitive tourist. About 12 km. south is the sanctuary of Asclepios. On a hillside lies the theatre, the most famous and best preserved of all the ancient theatres in Greece.

Facilities

Three toilet blocks include the usual facilities including two shower rooms for disabled visitors. Laundry with washing machine. Shop. Bar. Restaurant (15/5-15/9). Internet access. TV room. Sand and shingle beach. Apartments to rent. Off site: Theatre of Epidavros 12 km.

Open: 1 April - 20 October.

Directions

To avoid driving right through the town of Ancient Epidavros take the southern exit towards the town. Turn inland here down a slip road, then turn under the main road above towards the town. On entering the town turn right towards Gialasi and site is 1.6 km. on the left. GPS: N37:37.076 E23:09.475

Charges guide

Per person	€ 5,00 - € 5,50
pitch incl. electricity	€ 10,00 - € 15,00

GR8635 Camping New Triton

Plaka Drepano, GR-21060 Nafplio (Peloponnese)

Tel: **275 209 2128**

www.alanrogers.com/GR8635

What do we look for in a good campsite in Greece? Given the excellent Greek weather, the answer is probably a good, flat pitch with some shade, excellent toilets and showers that are spotlessly clean, a small shop and proximity to a beach and local tavernas. Well, here you have it all! Under the control of the owners, Mr and Mrs George Christopoulous, this is an exceptional site with 40 good size touring pitches under high screens, just across the road from Drepano beach. Local tavernas are within strolling distance and the town's shops are about a mile away.

Facilities

Excellent refurbished toilet blocks include showers, WCs and washbasins. Baby bath. Facilities for disabled visitors. Chemical disposal. Laundry with washing machines and ironing board. Electric hobs for cooking. Fridge and freezer. Small shop (1/6-30/9). Off site: Drepano beach, local tavernas and bars. Assini.

Open: 1 April - 30 October.

Directions

From Nafplio follow the main road west and then turn right towards Drepano. In the town follow the signs Plaka Drepano and turn left towards the coast. At the beach turn right and site is just ahead.
GPS: N37:31.921 E22:53.499

Charges guide

Per person	€ 6,00 - € 7,00
pitch incl. car	€ 6,00 - € 8,00
electricity	€ 3,00

GR8685 Camping Gythion Bay

GR-23200 Gythion (Peloponnese)

Tel: **273 302 2522**. Email: **info@gythiocamping.gr** **www.alanrogers.com/GR8685**

Camping Gythion Bay has 71 unmarked pitches set amongst orange, fig, olive and pine trees and all with electricity. Some trees limit access but the owner Mr Zafirakos is dealing with this to improve the site. Indeed he has also been busy refurbishing the toilets, showers and other facilities. With a good beach alongside the site, there are good opportunities for windsurfing and storage for boards is available. This is a good starting point for excursions to the Caves of Diros and for wider exploration of Lakonia and especially Inner and Outer Mani and Sparta.

Facilities

Four toilet blocks include the usual facilities and facilities for disabled visitors. Sinks for dishwashing. Laundry with washing machines. Chemical disposal. Small shop (1/5-30/9). Bar (1/5-30/9). Restaurant (10/6-17/9). Play area. Windsurfing and limited boat launching. Small beach. Off site: Gythio 4 km.

Open: All year.

Directions

Site is about 4 km. south of the fishing port of Gythio on the road to Aeropoli. It is between two petrol stations on the left and has a wide entrance. GPS: N36:43.725 E22:32.746

Charges guide

Per person	€ 5,00 - € 5,50
pitch incl. car	€ 7,10 - € 11,30
electricity	€ 3,60

GR8690 Camping Anemomilos

GR-24006 Finikounda (Peloponnese)

Tel: **272 307 1120** **www.alanrogers.com/GR8690**

Having found this exceptional site, we are not sure we really want to encourage too many people to come here. We came to stay one night to inspect the site and stayed much longer enjoying the beautiful sandy beach, turquoise sea and the quayside fish restaurants in the nearby village. Many German campers come here for the windsurfing, sailing and beach life generally. The site offers 80 level pitches with good shade and great views. The small picturesque village, just a few minutes walk away, is at the back of the bay. Caiques and fishing boats are drawn up all along the sandy shore, while tavernas serve their fresh catch along the water's edge.

Facilities

Two excellent toilet blocks include showers, WCs and washbasins. Facilities for disabled visitors. Chemical disposal. Laundry with washing machines and ironing boards. Two kitchens with sinks, electric hobs for cooking, fridges and ice machines. Bar and small shop (1/5-31/10). Beach. Off site: Restaurant opposite. Riding. Finikounda and the Inouse Islands. Tractor rides around the local villages!

Open: 1 March - 31 November.

Directions

Site is just 5 minutes walk from the centre of Finikounda. From the village head west and turn left at the end of the wide pavement. The site is 300 m. ahead. GPS: N36:48.324 E21:48.108

Charges guide

Per person	€ 4,50 - € 5,00
child (5-12 yrs)	€ 2,50 - € 3,00
pitch	€ 5,50 - € 7,00
electricity	€ 3,00

GR8695 Camping Finikes

GR-24006 Finikounda (Peloponnese)

Tel: **272 302 8524**. Email: **camping-finikes@otenet.gr** **www.alanrogers.com/GR8695**

This brand new site offers 80 level pitches with good shade and great views. It also has 12 bungalows to rent. Some pitches have high reed screens that give good protection from the blazing Greek sun, and the turquoise sea is great for swimming, windsurfing and sailing. The site is at the western corner of Finikounda Bay and has direct access to the sandy beach. As you would expect from a new site, the facilities are excellent and in low season, when there are 18 or less campers, each is given the keys to a WC and shower for their own personal use.

Facilities

The excellent toilet block includes showers, WCs and washbasins. Facilities for disabled visitors. Kitchen includes sinks, electric hobs and fridges. Laundry. Chemical disposal. Bar, small shop and restaurant. Accommodation to rent. Off site: Finikounda and the Inouse Islands.

Open: All year.

Directions

Site is 2 km. from the centre of Finikounda. From the village head west and turn left into the site. GPS: N36:48.169 E21:46.863

Charges guide

Per person	€ 4,50 - € 5,00
child (4-12 yrs)	€ 3,00 - € 3,50
pitch incl. car	€ 5,50 - € 8,10
electricity	€ 3,00

No credit cards.

MAP 6

Centrally located in Europe, Hungary comprises mountain ranges, hilly regions and flat plains, with the River Danube running through its length. The country also has over one thousan lakes, an abundance of thermal baths, Europe's largest cave system and several notable wine regions.

CAPITAL: BUDAPEST

Tourist Office

Hungarian National Tourist Office
46 Eaton Place, London SW1X 8AL
Tel: 00 800 36 000 000
Fax: 020 7823 1459
Email: info@gotohungary.co.uk
Internet: www.gotohungary.co.uk

An increasingly popular destination, Budapest is divided into two parts by the Danube, the hilly side of Buda on the western bank and the flat plain of Pest on the eastern bank. A cruise along the river will enable you to appreciate this picturesque city with its grand buildings, romantic bridges, museums and art galleries. It also has plenty of spas to tempt you. North of the city, the Danube Bend is one of the grandest stretches of the river, along the banks of which you'll find historic towns and ruins. Further afield in the north-eastern hills, the caves at Aggtelek are another firm favourite.

One of the largest in Europe, Lake Balaton covers an area of nearly 600 square miles and is great for swimming, sailing, windsurfing and waterskiing. It has two distinct shores, the bustling south with its string of hotels, restaurants and beaches, and the north offering a quieter pace with beautiful scenery and sights.

Population

10.2 million

Climate

There are four fairly distinct seasons – hot in summer, mild spring and autumn, very cold winter with snow.

Language

The official language is Magyar, but German is widely spoken.

Telephone

The country code is 00 36.

Money

Currency: Hungarian forints
Banks: Mon-Fri 09.00-14.00, Sat 09.00-12.00.

Shops

Mon-Fri 10.00-18.00, Sat 10.00-14.00. Food shops open Mon-Fri 07.00-19.00, Sat 07.00-14.00.

Public Holidays

New Year; Revolution Day 15 March; Easter Mon; Labour Day; Whitsun; Constitution Day 20 Aug; Republic Day 23 Oct; All Saints Day 1 Nov; Christmas 25, 26 Dec.

Motoring

Dipped headlights are compulsory at all times but main beams should not be used in towns. Motorway stickers must be purchased for the M1 to Budapest, the M7 from Budapest to Lake Balaton and also on the M3 eastward. Also the full length of the M5 (Budapest - Kiskunfelegyhaza). Give way to trams and buses at junctions. Carrying spare fuel in a can is not permitted.

HU5090 Balatontourist Camping Füred

Szechenyi u. 24, H-8230 Balatonfüred (Veszprem County)

Tel: **87 580 241**. Email: **fured@balatontourist.hu** **www.alanrogers.com/HU5090**

This is a large international holiday village rather than just a campsite. Pleasantly decorated with flowers and shrubs, it offers a very wide range of facilities and sporting activities. All that one could want for a family holiday can be found here. The 909 individual pitches (60-120 sq.m), all with electricity (4-10A), are on either side of hard access roads on which pitch numbers are painted. Many bungalows are for rent. Mature trees cover about two-thirds of the site giving shade, with the remaining area being in the open. Directly on the lake with 800 m. of access for boats and bathing, there is a large, grassy area for relaxation, a small beach area for children and a variety of watersports. A water ski drag lift is most spectacular with its four towers erected in the lake to pull skiers around the circuit. There is a swimming pool on site with lifeguards. Along the main road that runs through the site are shops and kiosks, with the main bar/restaurant and terrace overlooking the lake. Other bars and restaurants are around the site. Coach trips and pleasure cruises are organised. The site is part of the Balatontourist organisation, and although public access is allowed for the amenities, security is good. Some tour operators – Danish and German.

Facilities

Six fully equipped toilet blocks around the site include hot water for dishwashing and laundry. Private cabins for rent. Laundry service. Gas supplies. Numerous bars, restaurants, cafés, food bars and supermarket (all 15/4-15/10). Stalls and kiosks with wide range of goods and souvenirs. Excellent swimming pool (20/6-25/9). Sauna. Fishing. Water ski lift. Windsurf school. Sailing. Pedaloes. Play area. Bicycle hire. Tennis. Minigolf. Video games. Internet point. Dogs are not accepted. Off site: Riding 5 km. Close by a street of fast food bars, about 10 in all, offering a variety of Hungarian and international dishes with attractive outdoor terraces under trees.

Open: 10 April - 4 October.

Directions

Site is just south of Balatonfüred, on Balatonfüred - Tihany road and is well signed. Gates closed 13.00-15.00 except at weekends.
GPS: N46:56.735 E17:52.626

Charges 2009

Per unit incl. 2 persons and electricity	HUF 3600 - 9200
extra person	HUF 800 - 1600
child (2-14 yrs)	HUF 600 - 1200

Camping Cheques accepted.

HU5000 Balatontourist Camping Vadvirág

Arany j.u., H-8636 Balatonszemes (Somogy County)

Tel: **843 601 14**. Email: **vadvirag@balatontourist.hu** **www.alanrogers.com/HU5000**

This large Balatontourist site (7 hectares) on the southern shore of Lake Balaton has a beach almost 600 metres long, which is also used by day visitors. On flat grass, just over half the 600 touring pitches are individual ones with electricity connections (16A) for 600. There are 110 pitches for tents. Some shade is provided by a variety of trees. Windsurfing and excellent swimming are possible in the lake and there are pedaloes for hire. A train line runs along the back of the site.

Facilities

Two standard sanitary blocks include some washbasins in cabins, a few private bathrooms for hire and facilities for disabled visitors. Launderette. Motorcaravan services. Shop. Snack bars. Lake swimming with water slide. Three tennis courts. Minigolf. Bicycle hire. Massage and pedicures. Entertainment for children. Off site: Restaurants and gift shop nearby. Riding 2 km.

Open: 17 April - 13 September.

Directions

Balatonszemes is about halfway round the southern side of Lake Balaton and the site is accessed from road 7/E71 turning towards the lake at km. 132, over the railway. GPS: N46:47.850 E17:43.715

Charges 2009

Per unit incl. 2 persons and electricity	HUF 2900 - 5900
extra person	HUF 700 - 1100

Electricity and car included.
No credit cards.

HU5025 Zalatour Thermal Camping

Gyogyfurdo 6, H-8749 Zalakaros (Zala County)

Tel: **933 401 05**. Email: **thermal@zalatour.hu** **www.alanrogers.com/HU5025**

Zalatour Thermál Camping in Zalakaros has 280 attractively laid out, level pitches, all with 10A electricity and varying in size from 30-100 sq.m. (the larger pitches need to be reserved). There are 250 for touring units on grass and gravel (firm tent pegs may be needed) and around 10 hardstandings for larger units and motorcaravans. Mature trees provide useful shade and access roads are gravel. Zalatour attracts many elderly people who spend their day at the thermal spa 200 m. down the road – the waters are reputedly good for rheumatism and other joint problems.

Facilities

Modern and comfortable toilet facilities with British style toilets, open washbasins and controllable, hot showers (free). Facilities for disabled visitors. Full-service laundry including ironing. Campers' kitchen. Motorcaravan service point and car wash. Shop. Bar/restaurant. Massage, acupuncture and pedicure. Sauna. Bicycle hire.
Off site: Fishing, beach 3 km. Golf 500 m. Riding 2 km.

Open: 1 April - 30 September.

Directions

On E71 travelling northeast from Nagykanisza, take exit for Zalakaros. Follow good site signs.
GPS: N46:33.136 E17:07.556

Charges guide

Per person	HUF 1000 - 1200
child (2-14 yrs)	HUF 500 - 600
pitch incl. electricity	HUF 1200 - 1650
tent	HUF 750 - 900

HU5035 Castrum Camping Keszthely

Mora Ferenc utca 48, H-8360 Keszthely (Zala County)

Tel: **833 121 20**. Email: **info@castrum-group.hu** **www.alanrogers.com/HU5035**

Castrum Keszthely is a large site on the southwest corner of Lake Balaton. Although it is next to the main road and a railway and there is a disco nearby, we found it surprisingly quiet at night. It is a real family site with 352 pitches, all for tourers and with electricity (6/12A). The level pitches of up to 90 sq.m. are numbered on a grass and gravel surface (firm tent pegs necessary) and are separated by hedges with shade from a variety of mature trees. It is on the wrong side of the railway that runs along the north side of Lake Balaton and therefore has no direct access to the lake or the beach. However, this is compensated for by a large, well kept outdoor pool.

Facilities

Traditional toilet blocks with British style toilets, open washbasins and pre-set, hot showers (free, hot water variable). Washing machine and spin dryer. Small shop for basics. Bar/restaurant. Swimming pool (25 x 10 m) with oval paddling pool (daily charge). Tennis. Minigolf. Daily activity programme for children in high season. Bus service to Thermal Spa. Bicycle hire. Off site: Fishing and Lake Balaton 1 km.

Open: 1 April - 31 October.

Directions

Follow no. 71 road along Lake Balaton into Keszthely and then follow signs 'Castrum 2900 metres'. Continue straight on for exactly 2,900 metres and turn right towards site.
GPS: N46:46.087 E17:15.573

Charges 2009

Per unit incl. 2 persons and electricity	HUF 3800 - 6000
extra person	HUF 900 - 1200
child (2-10 yrs)	HUF 700 - 900

HU5370 Balatontourist Camping Napfény

Halasz u. 5, H-8253 Révfülöp (Veszprem County)

Tel: **875 630 31**. Email: **napfeny@balatontourist.hu** **www.alanrogers.com/HU5370**

Camping Napfény, an exceptionally good site, is designed for families with children of all ages looking for an active holiday, and has a 200 m. frontage on Lake Balaton. The site's 306 pitches vary in size (60-110 sq.m) and almost all have shade – very welcome during the hot Hungarian summers – and 6-10A electricity. As with most of the sites on Lake Balaton, a train line runs just outside the site boundary. There are steps to get into the lake and canoes, boats and pedaloes for hire. An extensive entertainment programme is designed for all ages and there are several bars and restaurants of various styles. There are souvenir shops and a supermarket. In fact, you need not leave the site at all during your holiday, although there are several excursions on offer, including to Budapest or to one of the many Hungarian spas, a trip over Lake Balaton or a traditional wine tour.

Facilities

The three sanitary blocks have toilets, washbasins (open style and in cabins) with hot and cold water, spacious showers (both preset and controllable), child size toilets and basins, and two bathrooms (hourly charge). Heated baby room. Facilities for disabled people. Launderette. Dog shower. Motorcaravan services. Supermarket. Several bars, restaurants and souvenir shops. Sports field, Tennis. Minigolf. Fishing. Bicycle hire. Canoe, rowing boats and pedalo hire. Extensive entertainment programme for all ages. Off site: Riding 3 km.

Open: 1 May - 30 September.

Directions

Follow road 71 from Veszprém southeast to Keszthely. Site is in Révfülöp.
GPS: N46:49.450 E17:38.240

Charges 2009

Per unit incl. 2 persons and electricity	HUF 3400 - 7150
extra person	HUF 800 - 1200
child (2-14 yrs)	HUF 550 - 900
dog	HUF 550 - 900

Camping Cheques accepted.

HU5380 Balatontourist Camping Venus

H-8252 Balatonszepezd (Veszprem County)

Tel: **875 680 61**. Email: **venus@balatontourist.hu** **www.alanrogers.com/HU5380**

For those who want to be directly beside Lake Balaton and would like a reasonably quiet location, Camping Venus would be a good choice and it is also possibly the best site in Hungary. Apart from the rather noisy train that regularly passes the site, this is a quiet setting with views of the lake from almost all the pitches. From the front row of pitches you could almost dangle your feet from your caravan in the warm water of the lake. There are 88 flat pitches all with at least 4/10A electricity. Varying in size (70-100 sq.m), almost all have shade. Given the small size of the site, Mária Ékes, the manager, gets to know every guest in person and she will make you very welcome. This is a well managed site with modern, well kept sanitary blocks and 24 hour security at the gate. Lake Balaton with its water temperature of about 25° Celsius in summer, is obviously the main attraction here, but you can also make several excursions, for example a trip to Budapest or a gipsy night in Riza.

Facilities

Two good sanitary blocks provide toilets, washbasins (open style and in cabins) with hot and cold water and preset showers. Facilities for disabled people. Child size toilets and basins. Launderette. Motorcaravan services. Shop for basics. Bar. Restaurant. Snack bar. Playground. Daily activity programme with pottery, fairy tale reading, horse shows, tournaments in Sümeg, trips over the lake and to Budapest. Canoe, pedalo, rowing boats and bicycle hire. Off site: Riding 3 km.

Open: 15 May - 6 September.

Directions

On the 71 road between Balatonfüred and Keszthely, site is in Balatonszepezd on the lake side of the road.
GPS: N46:51.648 E17:40.417

Charges 2009

Per unit incl. 2 persons and electricity	HUF 2730 - 5420
extra person	HUF 700 - 960
child (2-14 yrs)	HUF 580 - 750
dog	HUF 580 - 750

HU5040 Balatontourist Camping Autós

Szent István út, H-8621 Zamardi (Somogy County)

Tel: **843 488 63**. Email: **bookings@balatontourists.hu** **www.alanrogers.com/HU5040**

If you have young children or non-swimmers in your party, then the southern shores of the lake where this Balatontourist site is situated are ideal as you can walk out for nearly a kilometre before the water rises to more than a metre in depth. It is a large site with its own direct access to the lake offering 480 pitches, 450 with 16A electricity, but there might be the possibility of noise in high season, although it was peaceful during our visit in early June. There are many tall trees and the more attractive pitches are near the lakeside, including some unshaded ones alongside the water.

Facilities

Three modern, tiled sanitary buildings. Three en-suite private bathrooms can be rented including bath and shower. Warm water to washbasins with single tap. Showers. Facilities for disabled visitors. Laundry facilities (key from reception). Restaurant with excellent menu. Snack bar with terrace (from June). Lake swimming. Fishing. Play equipment by the lake. Off site: Adjacent large water slide area and boats for hire. Shop 50 m.

Open: 13 May - 4 September.

Directions

Exit road no. 7/E71 between Balatonföldvár and Siófok towards Tihany, and the site is well signed. GPS: N46:52.841 E17:54.964

Charges guide

Per person	HUF 670 - 920
child (2-14 yrs)	HUF 510 - 720
caravan	HUF 1000 - 1600
tent	HUF 600 - 900

Electricity and car included.

HU5060 Balatontourist Camping Aranypart

Szent László u.183-185, H-8600 Siófok (Somogy County)

Tel: **84 353 399**. Email: **aranypart@balatontourist.hu** **www.alanrogers.com/HU5060**

Situated right by the famous lake, and near the main tourist town, this very well run site has 682 flat, grassy numbered pitches – 242 for caravans and 437 for tents, just over half being fairly small individual ones. There are 440 electrical connections (10/16A). At the far end of the site is a fenced area where there are 70 excellent bungalows for rent. Groups of younger guests are placed separately from other campers (mainly on the left wing of the site from the entrance). A superb restaurant offers a good menu and there are many sports and entertainment facilities making it very popular with younger visitors.

Facilities

Five toilet blocks of marginal quality and one good block are spread throughout this long site. Laundry facilities at either end with free hot water. Washing machines. Fourteen two-burner cookers in the middle of the site. Supermarket and shops. Snack bars and bars. Pizzeria and restaurant. Two play areas. Moped, bicycle, quadbikes for children. Canoe and pedalo hire. Lake swimming. Off site: Riding 500 m.

Open: 24 April - 13 September.

Directions

Site is 3 km. north of Siófok. From road no. 70, exit at km. 108, cross railway and site is 200 m. well signed. GPS: N46:55.664 E18:06.201

Charges 2009

Per unit incl. 2 persons and electricity	HUF 2650 - 5700
extra person	HUF 850 - 1200
child (2-14 yrs)	HUF 650 - 950

Camping Cheques accepted.

HU5385 Balatontourist Camping Levendula Naturist/FKK

H-8243 Balatonakali (Veszprem County)

Tel: **875 440 11**. Email: **clevendula@balatontourist.hu** **www.alanrogers.com/HU5385**

Levendula is a naturist site and is the latest addition to the Balatontourist chain of sites on the north side of Lake Balaton. It has 123 level unmarked pitches, varying in size from 60-110 sq.m. and separated by low hedges. Almost all have views of the lake and all have electricity (4/10A). The site is attractively landscaped with shrubs and flowers and there is direct access to the lake. As part of the Balatontourist organisation, Levendula has similar amenities to the other sites, including a full entertainment program for children in high season, but without the noise of its larger brothers.

Facilities

Two toilet blocks with modern fittings, including one washbasin in a cabin for men and women. Facilities for disabled people. Heated baby room. Laundry. Campers' kitchen with cooking rings on request. Fish cleaning area. Dog shower. Bar/restaurant with terrace. Shop. Playground with colourful equipment. Watersports. Games room. Animation programme. Excursions. Off site: Riding 1.5 km.

Open: 12 May - 10 September.

Directions

Follow no. 71 road towards Keszthely and site is signed in Balatonakali. GPS: N46:52.760 E17:44.535

Charges guide

Per person	HUF 800 - 1200
child (2-14 yrs)	HUF 600 - 900
pitch incl. electricity	HUF 2600 - 5500

Camping Cheques accepted.

HU5095 Vulkán Resort Camping

Szabadság u. 032/2 hrsz., H-9553 Kemeneskápolna (Vas)

Tel: **95 466 070**. Email: **info@vulkanresort.com**

www.alanrogers.com/HU5095

Vulkán Resort has been recently developed as Hungary's first campsite built according to the five feng shui principles. The theme here is therefore one of relaxation and the site boasts an indoor swimming pool and wellness centre with three different kinds of sauna. The surrounding Sarberg National Park lying at the western end of the Kette Zeugenberger mountain range is a popular environment for hiking and cycling. There are 50 pitches here, all equipped with electricity and water, and a number also with drainage and TV and internet connections.

Facilities

Modern and well maintained sanitary facilities. Indoor swimming pool. Wellness centre with saunas. Play area. Stables and riding. Mobile homes for rent. Free shuttle service for motorcaravanners. Off site: Village centre (shops and restaurants). Sarvar health resort 11 km. Lake Balaton 50 km.

Open: All year.

Directions

Heading south from Sopron on road 84 continue to Sarvar. Shortly beyond here follow signs to Gercé and Vásárosmiske and finally Kemeneskápolna from where the site is well signed.
GPS: N47:12.880 E17:06.026

Charges guide

Per serviced pitch with 2 persons and electricity	€ 18,50
extra person	€ 4,00

HU5110 Dömös Camping

Duna-Part, H-2027 Dömös (Komarom-Esztergom County)

Tel: **334 823 19**. Email: **info@domoscamping.hu**

www.alanrogers.com/HU5110

The area of the Danube Bend is a major tourist attraction and here at Dömös is a lovely modern, well maintained and presented, friendly, peaceful site with large pitches and easy access. There are 107 quite large pitches, of which 80 have 6A electricity, in sections on flat grass, numbered and divided by small plants and some with little shade. At the top of the site is an inviting open air swimming pool and tiny children's pool with a large bar alongside. Sightseeing tours to Budapest, Esztergom and Szentendre are arranged. The Danube is just over 50 m. away and quite fast flowing.

Facilities

The modern, long, brick built sanitary building is tiled with sliding doors and includes large, pre-set hot showers with individual changing, and good facilities for children and disabled visitors. Cooking area. Laundry with washing machines and dryer. Motorcaravan services. Bar. Restaurant. Small café with terrace. Swimming pool (20 x 10 m, all season). Small play area. Off site: Fishing 50 m. Village facilities 300 m. Tennis, minigolf and football field adjacent. Riding 2 km. Bicycle hire 8 km.

Open: 1 May - 15 September.

Directions

Site is between the village and the Danube, off road 11 Esztergom - Visegrad - Szentendre.
GPS: N47:45.927 E18:54.864

Charges guide

Per unit incl. 2 persons and electricity	HUF 3440 - 3770
extra person	HUF 880 - 990
child (2-14 yrs)	HUF 700 - 800
dog	HUF 400

No credit cards (cash only).

HU5120 Gasthof Camping Pihenö

I-es föút, H-9011 Györszentivan-Kertváros (Gyor-Moson-Sopron County)

Tel: **965 230 08**. Email: **piheno@piheno.hu**

www.alanrogers.com/HU5120

This privately owned site makes an excellent night stop when travelling to and from Hungary as it lies beside the main no. 1 road, near the end of the motorway to the east of Györ. It is set amidst pine trees with pitches which are not numbered, but marked out by small shrubs, in a small clearing or between the trees. With space for about 40 touring units, all with electrical connections (6A), and eight simple, one roomed bungalows and four en-suite rooms. On one side of the site, fronting the road, is the reception, bar and pleasant restaurant with terrace (menu in English).

Facilities

A single, small, basic toilet block has just two showers for each sex (on payment) and curtained, communal dressing space. Baby room. Room for washing clothes and dishes with small cooking facility. Washing machine. Order bread at reception the previous evening. Bar. Restaurant with good menu and reasonable prices. Solar heated swimming pool and children's pool (10 x 5 m, June - Sept). Off site: Györ with shops and swimming pool.

Open: 1 April - 30 October.

Directions

Coming from Austria, continue through Györ following signs for Budapest. Continue on road 1 past start of motorway for 3 km. and site is on left. From Budapest, turn right onto road 10 at end of motorway, then as above.
GPS: N47:43.528 E17:42.883

Charges guide

Per person	€ 4,40
pitch	€ 3,40
electricity	€ 1,50

HU5150 Fortuna Camping

Dózsa György út 164, H-2045 Törökbálint (Pest County)

Tel: **233 353 64**. Email: **fortunacamping@axelero.hu** **www.alanrogers.com/HU5150**

This good site lies at the foot of a hill with views of the vineyards, but Budapest is only 25 minutes away by bus. Concrete and gravel access roads lead to terraces where there are 170 individual pitches most bordered with hedges, all with electricity (up to 16A, long leads needed), and 14 with water, on slightly sloping ground. The site is surrounded by mature trees and Mr Szücs, the owner, will proudly name the 150 varieties of bushes and shrubs that edge the pitches. The site has a small restaurant with reasonable prices. An open air swimming pool with flume will help you to cool off in summer with an indoor pool for cooler weather.

Facilities

One fully equipped sanitary blocks and two smaller blocks. Good facilities for disabled people. Six cookers in sheltered area. Laundry facilities. Gas supplies. Motorcaravan services. Bar. Restaurant (18.00-21.00). Snack bar. Essentials from reception (order bread previous day). Outdoor swimming pool with slide (15/5-15/9). Indoor pool. Small play area. Excursions organised. English spoken. Off site: Close to bus terminal for city centre 1 km. Riding 3 km. Fishing 4 km.

Open: All year.

Directions

From M1 (Gyor - Budapest) take exit for Törökbálint following signs for town and then site. Also accessible from M7 Budapest - Balaton road. GPS: N47:25.922 E18:54.066

Charges guide

Per person	€ 6,00
child (4-14 yrs)	€ 4,00
pitch	€ 5,00
electricity	€ 2,00

No credit cards.

HU5165 Zugligeti Niche Camping

Zugligeti ut 101, H-1121 Budapest (Budapest City)

Tel: **129 983 46**. Email: **camping.niche@t-online.hu** **www.alanrogers.com/HU5165**

Zugligeti Niche is in the Buda Hills on steeply sloping ground. There are 200 pitches, all for tourers, on both sides of a steep and winding access road. Pitches on the first half of the site are mostly hardstandings for motorcaravans, off a tarmac and gravel access road. After a sharp right turn, a sandy road takes you further uphill where there are pitches mostly for tents, varying in size from 20-40 sq.m. To the front of the site are two old tram carriages; one functions as reception and there are plans for the other to become a small shop.

Facilities

Scattered around the site are several toilet blocks, renewed in 2007. They include British style toilets, open washbasins and controllable showers (free). Basic shower for disabled visitors. Laundry with sinks and washing machine. Campers' kitchen. Bar/restaurant with good value meals. Torch useful. Free breakfast and free WiFi. Off site: Budapest city centre 30 minutes by public transport.

Open: All year.

Directions

Site is in the Budapest district 3. Coming from the north follow signs for M1 and M7 motorway. Site is well signed from Moszkva Tér. GPS: N47:30.916 E18:58.333

Charges guide

Per person	HUF 1400
child	HUF 700
pitch	HUF 990 - 2550
electricity	HUF 1200

No credit cards.

HU5175 Kek Duna Autoscamping

Föut 70, H-2025 Visegrad (Pest County)

Tel: **263 981 20**. Email: **hotelhon@t-online.hu** **www.alanrogers.com/HU5175**

Just opposite a road that runs alongside the beautiful Danube river, this small site has only 40 pitches (all for tourers and with 4A electricity) and two static units. It is owned by the Honti Hotel 50 m. down the road and this is where reception is located. It is attractively landscaped with low trees, shrubs and flowers. The good size pitches are arranged on well kept, grassy lawns, separated by hedges in the middle field. From some there are good views of Visegrád Castle, once the home of King Mátyás Corvinus. Some road noise can be heard from the main road that runs to Budapest.

Facilities

Adequate portacabin style toilet block and a good shower block with British style toilets, open washbasins and controllable showers (free). Basic kitchen with electric cookers and fridge. Bar with small buffet. Fishing. Canoe hire. Off site: Riding 6 km. Golf 7 km. Restaurants close.

Open: 1 May - 30 September.

Directions

Site is on the right of the no. 11 road running to Budapest at km. 43. GPS: N47:46.985 E18:50.034

Charges guide

Per person	HUF 900
pitch incl. car	HUF 600 - 1200
electricity	HUF 650

No credit cards.

HU5156 Camping Haller

Haller Utca 27, H-1096 Budapest (Budapest City)

Tel: **1 476 3418**. Email: **info@hallercamping.hu** **www.alanrogers.com/HU5156**

Camping Haller is very much a city site, set in the centre of Budapest. It has just 30 pitches, some with hardstanding and some in the shade of trees, most without electricity. The site was previously an old theatre hall and it is close to buses, the metro and trams for visiting the beautiful city of Budapest. From the site it is a few hundred metres walk to the banks of the Danube where you can enjoy an evening stroll after a day visiting the town. Since the site is close to a main road, road noise can be heard. This site is not suitable for campers with tents. Budapest is the bustling capital of Hungary with over 200 museums, more than 80 thermal spas and many large, new shopping malls. The castle area with the Royal palace and the Mátyás church are worth a visit, as are Hero's Square and the park behind it. Relaxation can be enjoyed on Margit island in the Danube. Eating and drinking are important in Hungary. Look carefully and find a good place to enjoy a real Hungarian 'gulyás soup'.

Facilities

Toilet facilities in the main building with WCs and showers. Off site: Budapest city centre with restaurants, pools, museums.

Open: 10 May - 6 October.

Directions

Site is in Pest on the east bank of the Danube. Coming from Vienna via the M1, follow signs for Lagymanyósi Híd. Cross the bridge and continue until you cross the Ülloi út/4. Turn left and then take the second left again into the Haller utca. Site is on the left. GPS: N47:28.564 E19:04.968

Charges guide

Per unit incl. 2 persons and electricity	HUF 6000
extra person	HUF 1200
child (under 14 yrs)	HUF 600
dog	free

No credit cards.

HU5155 Római Camping

Szentendrei ut 189, H-1031 Budapest (Budapest City)

Tel: **138 871 67**. Email: **romaicamping@message.hu** **www.alanrogers.com/HU5155**

Római Camping is a large site with 2,000 pitches within the boundaries of Budapest, next to the Római Fürdo Aqualand centre. There are about 500 touring pitches on level, grassy fields, 180 with 4A electricity. Pitches are under mature trees that provide useful shade with access off tarmac roads. The site is an easy half hour by public transport (first stop ten minutes' walk) to the bustling and interesting city centre of Budapest.

Facilities

Basic toilet facilities (partly refurbished and cleaned twice daily) provide British and Turkish style toilets, open washbasins and controllable, hot showers (free). Laundry with sinks, washing machine and dryer. Motorcaravan service point. Playground. Buffet and bar. Restaurant. Torch useful. Internet access. Off site: Római open-air pool 100 m. Budapest centre 30 minutes by public transport.

Open: All year.

Directions

Coming into town from the north via main road 11, turn left at OMV petrol station. Keep right at the end and continue to keep right until Csalina utca. Turn left at crossing and take first right. Go past swimming pool and turn right again. Coming out of town, take sharp right bend 100 m. after camping sign. GPS: N47:34.480 E19:03.103

Charges guide

Per person	€ 4,10
pitch incl. car	€ 11,00 - € 17,00

No credit cards.

HU5180 Jumbo Camping

Budakalászi út 23-25, H-2096 Üröm (Pest County)

Tel: **263 512 51** www.alanrogers.com/HU5180

Jumbo Camping is a modern, thoughtfully developed site in the northern outskirts of Budapest. The concrete and gravel access roads lead to 55 terraced pitches of varying size, a little on the small size for large units, and some slightly sloping. Hardstanding for cars and caravan wheels, as well as large hardstandings for motorhomes. There is a steep incline to some pitches and use of the site's 4 x 4 may be required. All pitches have 6A electricity (may require long leads) and there are 8 caravan pitches with water and drainage. They are mostly divided by small hedges and the whole area is fenced.

Facilities

Sanitary facilities are excellent, with large showers (communal changing). Dishwashing under cover. Washing machine, iron and cooking facilities on payment. Motorcaravan services. Café (where bread orders taken), milk and butter available. Small, attractive swimming pool (10/6-10/9). Playground with covered area for wet weather. Barbecue area. English spoken and information sheet provided in English. Off site: Shop and restaurant 500 m. The 'Old Swabian Wine-Cellar' said to serve extremely good food. Bus to city 500 m. every 30 minutes. Fishing 8 km.

Open: 1 April - 31 October.

Directions

Site signed on roads to Budapest - 11 from Szentendre and 10 from Komarom. If approaching from Budapest use 11 (site sign appears very quickly after sharp right bend; signs and entry are clearer if using road 10). Can also approach via Gyor on M1/E60 and Lake Balaton on M7/E71. Turn into site is quite acute and uphill.
GPS: N47:36.093 E19:01.200

Charges guide

Per unit incl. 2 persons and electricity	€ 15,10 - € 18,90
extra person	€ 5,00

No credit cards (cash only).

HU5197 Termál Camping

Szederkényi út 53, H-3580 Tiszaújváros (Borsod-Abauj-Zemplen)

Tel: **495 422 10**. Email: **camping@tujvaros.hu** www.alanrogers.com/HU5197

Termál Camping was opened in 2004 and is on the outskirts of Tiszaújváros (the former 'Lenin City') and not far from the River Tisza in eastern Hungary. The site has some 166 grass pitches (all for touring units), of which 16 have 25A electricity. To one end of the site are 8 holiday homes and centrally located is a well equipped toilet block. Since this is a new site, the trees and bushes have not yet fully developed and the site can become hot in the Hungarian summer. The site is next to a tributary of the River Tisza, and there are opportunities for walking, cycling, boating and fishing.

Facilities

One central, modern toilet block with toilets, preset hot showers, and facilities for disabled people. Laundry with washing machines. Kitchen with cooking rings, oven and fridge. Communal barbecue areas. Small buffet/bar. Fishing. Bicycle hire. Torch useful. Some English is spoken. Off site: Thermal spa. Supermarket and swimming pool 300 m.

Open: 15 April - 15 October.

Directions

From M3 motorway from Budapest to the east, take exit for Debrecen and then to Tiszaújváros. On entering town follow the signs to the Thermal Spa bath and the site. GPS: N47:53.900 E21:03.900

Charges guide

Per unit incl. 2 persons	HUF 5000
tent	HUF 4600
dog	HUF 500

HU5205 Oko-Park Camping

Borsod utca 9, H-3323 Eger-Szarvaskö (Heves County)

Tel: **363 522 01**. Email: **info@oko-park.hu** www.alanrogers.com/HU5205

Oko-Park Camping is close to the Baroque style town of Eger, on the edge of the protected Bükk National Park. Buildings on the site are all made of natural materials and there is a well used for watering the plants. Oko-Park has 45 pitches off a single gravel access lane that runs to the back of the site. The grass pitches are level, marked and numbered. All have 16A electricity and are in the shade of mature trees. The disadvantages are a road running alongside, a railway to the back and pitches which may be small for larger units.

Facilities

One toilet block to the front provides toilets, open style washbasins and preset hot showers. Baby bath and changing mat. Basic facilities for disabled people. Laundry facilities. Campers' kitchen. Restaurant with bar for breakfast and dinner (April - Oct). Climbing wall. Playground. Eco tours, walks and wine cave visits. Off site: Eger 9 km. Fishing 7 km. Riding 9 km.

Open: 1 April - 31 October.

Directions

From Budapest, follow M3 motorway east and take exit for Eger. Follow to Eger and, from there, the 25 road north towards Szarvaske. It is the second site on the right. GPS: N47:59.297 E20:19.861

Charges guide

Per person	€ 3,90
pitch	€ 4,90 - € 8,80

HU5210 Diófaház Accommodations

Ady Endre út 12, H-3348 Szilvásvárad (Heves County)

Tel: **363 555 95**. Email: **info@diofahaz.hu** **www.alanrogers.com/HU5210**

Diófaház is an ideal base in northeast Hungary for exploring this wooded part of the country, to visit the stud farm of the famous Lipizzaner horses (one of only five in the world) or to visit the town of Eger, world famous for its culture and red wine. The site is in private grounds on the edge of the village and provides a maximum of six pitches, all with electricity, which makes it quiet and peaceful. Gyöngyi Pap, the owner provides a warm welcome and if you're lucky you may arrive for the weekly barbecue or the home made Hungarian goulash soup.

Facilities

The single, freshly painted toilet block includes washbasins in cabins with hot and cold water, controllable hot showers and sinks with free hot water. Fresh rolls to order every day with home made jam but no shop. Internet access. Discounts at four restaurants in the village if you show your campers card. Off site: Riding 200 m. Bicycle hire 500 m. Fishing 6 km.

Open: All year.

Directions

Take the no. 25 road from Eger north to Szilvásvárad. Site is signed when entering the village. GPS: N48:05.890 E20:23.040

Charges 2009

Per unit incl. 2 persons	€ 10,00
extra person	€ 4,00
electricity per kWh	€ 0,18

HU5245 Camping Füzes

Strand utca 2, H-5241 Abádszálok (Jász-Nagkyun-Szolnok County)

Tel: **059 535 345**. Email: **info@fuzescamping.hu** **www.alanrogers.com/HU5245**

Füzes Camping is beside the beaches of one of the most popular holiday resorts in Eastern Hungary. The site is arranged with grass pitches in the shade of mature 'Füz' trees which provide a cooler environment in the heat of the Hungarian summer. There are around 200 pitches (all for touring units) on both sides of a long tarmac access lane, including 40 with 16A electricity. The popular beaches of Abádszalók are only 200 m. away and here there are many possibilities for water sport, plus restaurants and bars to enjoy the Hungarian lifestyle.

Facilities

One basic toilet block with toilets, controllable hot showers and open style washbasins. Bar and restaurant (all season). Tisza lake with sandy beaches. Fishing. Watersports. Torch useful. German is spoken. Off site: Fishing and beach 200 m. Boat launching 20 km.

Open: May - September.

Directions

From the M3 motorway from Budapest to the east, take the exit for Tiszafüred and continue south after passing Tiszafüred towards Abádszalók. On entering town, turn right towards the beaches and the site. GPS: N47:28.770 E20:35.409

Charges guide

Per person	HUF 1400
child (under 14 yrs)	HUF 1100
caravan or motorcaravan incl. electricity	HUF 1400

HU5255 Martfü Health & Recreation Centre

Tüzép utca, H-5435 Martfü (Jász-Nagkyun-Szolnok County)

Tel: **56 580531**. Email: **martfu@camping.hu** **www.alanrogers.com/HU5255**

The Martfu campsite is new and modern with 61 tourist pitches on newly developed, grassy terrain with rubber hardstandings. Each of around 90 sq.m. and separated by young bushes and trees, all have electricity (16/25A), waste water drainage, cable and satellite TV. There is a water tap per two pitches. There is no shade as yet, which may cause the site to become a real suntrap in summer, when temperatures may rise up to 34 degrees. A small lake and its beach on the site will cool you off. The main attraction at this site is the thermal spa (still under construction when we visited) which is said to aid people with dermal and rheumatic problems.

Facilities

Two modern, heated toilet blocks with British style toilets, open style washbasins, and free, controllable hot showers. Children's toilet and shower. Heated baby room. En-suite facilities for disabled visitors. Motorcaravan services. Laundry. Kitchen. Shop for basics. Takeaway for bread and drinks. Bar with satellite TV and internet. Bowling. Library. Sauna. Jacuzzi. Playing field. Tennis. Minigolf. Fishing. Bicycle hire. Watersports. Off site: Fishing 50 m. Riding 5 km. Boat launching 1,5 km.

Open: All year.

Directions

Driving into Martfu from the north on the 442 road, take the first exit at the roundabout (site is signed). Continue for about 800 m. and site is signed on the right. GPS: N47:01.196 E20:16.111

Charges guide

Per person	HUF 1200
pitch	HUF 900 - 1200
electricity	HUF 250

No credit cards.

HU5260 Jonathermál Motel-Camping

Kökút 26, H-6120 Kiskunmajsa (Bacs-Kiskun County)

Tel: **774 818 55**. Email: **jonathermal@mail.datanet.hu** **www.alanrogers.com/HU5260**

Situated three kilometres to the north of the town of Kiskunmajsa, a few kilometres west of road 5 (E75) from Budapest (140 km.) to Szeged (35 km.) this is one of the best Hungarian campsites. The camping area is large, reached by tarmac access roads, with 250 unmarked pitches in several areas around the motel and sanitary buildings. Some shade is available and more trees are growing. All the 120 large pitches have electricity (6A) and are set on flat grass where you place the pitch number allocated to you. Entrance to the impressive pool complex is charged.

Facilities

A heated sanitary block provides first class facilities including washbasins in cabins and a unit for disabled visitors. Launderette. Kiosk for bread and basics. etc. Smart bar and rest room. Restaurant by pool complex. Large swimming and thermal complex. (1/5-1/10). Massage (on payment). Play area. Tennis. Minigolf. Fishing lake (day permits). Bicycle hire. Riding. German spoken. Accommodation to rent. Off site: Shop opposite entrance, 120 m. Restaurants near. Riding 100 m.

Open: All year.

Directions

From no. 5 (E75) Budapest - Szeged road take Kiskunmajsa exit and site is well signed 3 km. north of the town on road 5402.
GPS: N46:31.280 E19:44.812

Charges guide

Per person	HUF 660 - 840
pitch incl. car	HUF 600 - 840
electricity	HUF 780

Less 5-10% for longer stays. No credit cards.

HU5290 Kemping Nap a Szivemben

Petofi Sándor u. 38-D, H-7081 Simontornya (Tolna County)

Tel: **745 860 60** **www.alanrogers.com/HU5290**

This small, immaculate looking site is under Dutch ownership and was newly opened in 2004. It only has 15 pitches on well kept, grassy lawns, all with 18/22A electricity. The toilet block is amongst the best we have seen in Central Europe. The site is on the main road but it did not appear to be too disturbing. The owner, Mrs Van Rijn, organises Hungarian breakfasts with visits to the Castle (where a Dutch noble family once lived) and wine tastings in their own vineyard. A cycle route has been set out in the local area. Nap a Szivemben is about 35 km. from Lake Balaton.

Facilities

One immaculate, modern toilet block has British style toilets, open washbasins and controllable, free showers. Facilities for disabled visitors. Laundry service at the owner's house. Bar. Outdoor pool (10 x 5 m). Excursions and activities organised. Off site: Fishing and riding 2 km.

Open: Easter - 15 October.

Directions

Site is on the main 61 road running through town. Take exit just before the petrol station on the right on leaving Simontornya.
GPS: N46:45.454 E18:32.698

Charges guide

Per unit incl. 2 persons and electricity	€ 20,00

No credit cards.

HU5300 Kek-Duna Camping

Hösök Tere 23, H-7020 Dunafoldvar (Tolna County)

Tel: **755 411 07**. Email: **postmaster@camping_gyogyfurdo.axelero.net** **www.alanrogers.com/HU5300**

Dunafoldvár is a most attractive town of 10,000 people and you are in the heart of it in just two or three minutes by foot from this site, easily reached via the wide towpath on the west bank of the Danube. For a town site, Kek-Duna is remarkably peaceful. This is a pleasant small site on the banks of the Danube, fenced all round and locked at night, with flat concrete access roads to 50 pitches. All have electricity (16A), the first half being open, the remainder well shaded. Apart from the obvious attractions of the river, the ancient town has a most interesting museum.

Facilities

Modern, tiled sanitary building with nicely decorated ladies' section offers curtained showers with communal changing. The rest of the facilities are of above average standard. Dishwashing outside with cold water. Washing machine. Shop and café (from mid June), town shops close. Bicycle hire. Excursion information. Off site: Tennis 50 m. Thermal swimming pool 200 m. (under the same ownership). Riding 5 km.

Open: All year.

Directions

From the roundabout south of Dunafoldvar turn towards the town centre. At the traffic lights turn right and go down as far as the Danube then turn left, under the green bridge and follow the towpath about 300 m. to the site.
GPS: N46:48.720 E18:55.620

Charges -guide

Per person	HUF 250 - 500
caravan, car incl. electricity	HUF 1200
motorcaravan incl. electricity	HUF 1100
tent and car	HUF 550

HU5320 Máré Vára Camping

Várvölgyi utca 2, H-7332 Magyaregregy (Baranya)

Tel: **724 20126**. Email: **info@camping-marevara.com** **www.alanrogers.com/HU5320**

Máré Vára takes its name from an ancient castle situated a few hundred metres down the road where the German noble family of Mariën once lived. The site is on archaeological ground: where now the main house stands, there used to be a monastery and centuries before that there was an ancient Roman settlement. The Dutch Annevelink family opened this campsite in 2002. When we visited there were just 50 pitches (35 with 10A electricity) but there are plans to extend the site further. The pitches are on slightly sloping, well kept fields and are separated by young trees and attractive lamp posts (a gift from the local brewery). Modern toilet facilities are in an old barn and here in the walls one can see remains of the former monastery. All the facilities were clean and tidy when we were there. Máré Vára is a good base from which to explore this relatively unknown part of Hungary and is only 20 minutes by bus from the interesting historic town of Pécs.

Facilities

Modern and clean toilet facilities (in a former barn) with British style toilets, open washbasins and controllable showers (free, hot water variable). Washing machine. No shop, but bread to order. Buffet with terrace for drinks and ice cream. Swimming pool (7 x 3 m). Playground. Social events organised. TV room with satellite, DVD and video. Off site: Máré Vára Castle 500 m. Fishing 10 km. Riding 3 km.

Open: 30 April - 30 September.

Directions

Magyaregregy is northeast of Pécs. Site is just outside Magyaregregy on the left and well signed. GPS: N46:14.032 E18:18.490

Charges guide

Per unit incl. 2 persons	€ 15,00
extra person	€ 2,40
child (4-12 yrs)	€ 2,00
electricity	€ 2,00
dog	€ 1,00

No credit cards.

HU5315 Camping Forras

Bokréta u. 105, H-7394 Magyarhertelend (Baranya)

Tel: **72 521 110**. Email: **egyesulettelehaz@magyarhertelend.hu** **www.alanrogers.com/HU5315**

This well established site is close to the historic city of Pécs, in a part of Hungary with a Mediterranean style climate. Camping Forras, or 'Bij Balázc' as it is called by some Dutch guests, is also close to the Mescék National Park, where there are many marked walking routes. The site has 120 pitches, all for tourers, off gravel and grass access roads. Of these, 80 are marked and have electricity connections. The remaining pitches are used mainly for tents. The whole site looks well cared for with many different varieties of trees giving a pleasant atmosphere and providing useful shade in summer.

Facilities

The traditional toilet block provides acceptable facilities with British style toilets, open washbasins and controllable showers (free). Washing machine and spin dryer. Bar with library. Basic playground. Minigolf. Torch useful. Off site: Fishing 3 km. City of Pécs is close.

Open: 7 May - 30 September.

Directions

From Pécs, take no. 66 road north towards Sásd. Turn left in Magyarszék towards Magyarhertelend and follow signs. Site is just outside the village on the left. GPS: N46:11.453 E18:08.506

Charges guide

Per person	HUF 750
child (2-13 yrs)	HUF 450
pitch incl. car	HUF 900
electricity (6A)	HUF 500
dog	HUF 450

No credit cards.

MAP 7

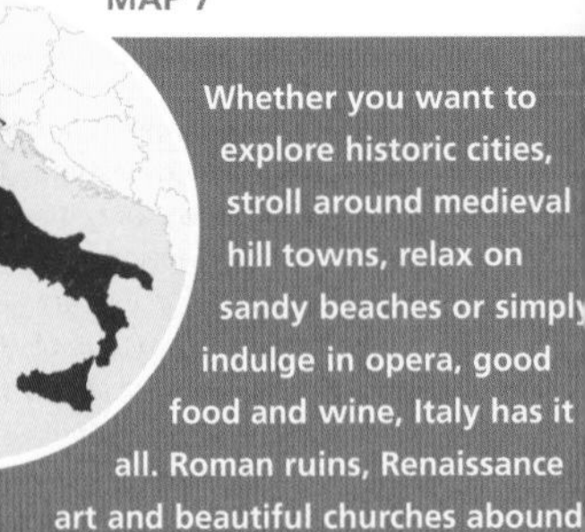

Whether you want to explore historic cities, stroll around medieval hill towns, relax on sandy beaches or simply indulge in opera, good food and wine, Italy has it all. Roman ruins, Renaissance art and beautiful churches abound. The Italian Alps are a haven for winter sports enthusiasts and also offer good hiking trails.

CAPITAL: ROME

Tourist Office

Italian State Tourist Office (ENIT)
1 Princes Street, London W1B 2AY
Tel: 020 7408 1254
Fax: 020 7399 3567
Email: italy@italiantouristboard.co.uk
Internet: www.enit.it

Italy only became a unified state in 1861, hence the regional nature of the country today. With 20 distinct regions, each one has retained its own individualism which is evident in the cuisine and local dialects.

In the north, the vibrant city of Milan is great for shopping and home to the famous opera house, La Scala, as well as Leonardo's Last Supper fresco. It is also a good starting-off point for the Alps; the Italian Lake District, incorporating Lake Garda, Lake Como and Lake Maggiore; the canals of Venice and the lovely town of Verona. Central Italy probably represents the most commonly perceived image of the country and Tuscany, with its classic rolling countryside and the historical towns of Florence, Siena, San Gimignano and Pisa, is one of the most visited areas. Further south is the historic capital of Rome and the city of Naples. Close to some of Italy's ancient sites such as Pompeii, Naples is within easy distance of Sorrento and the Amalfi coast.

Population

57.8 million

Climate

The south enjoys extremely hot summers and mild, dry winters, whilst the mountainous regions of the north are cooler with heavy snowfalls in winter.

Language

Italian. There are several dialect forms and some German is spoken near the Austrian border.

Telephone

The country code is 00 39.

Money

Currency: The Euro. Banks: Mon-Fri 08.30-13.00 and 15.00-16.00.

Shops

Mon-Sat 08.30/09.00-13.00 and 15.30/16.00-19.30/20.00, with some variations in larger cities.

Public Holidays

New Year; Easter Mon; Liberation Day 25 Apr; Labour Day; Republic Day 2 June; Assumption 15 Aug; All Saints 1 Nov; Unity Day 4 Nov; Immaculate Conception 8 Dec; Christmas 25, 26 Dec; plus some special local feast days.

Motoring

Tolls are payable on the autostrada network. If travelling distances, save time by purchasing a 'Viacard' from pay booths or service areas. An overhanging load, e.g. a bicycle rack, must be indicated by a large red/white hatched warning square. Failure to do so will result in a fine.

IT62470 Camping Tranquilla

Via Cave-Oltrefiume 2, I-28831 Baveno (Piedmont)

Tel: **032 392 3452**. Email: **info@tranquilla.com** **www.alanrogers.com/IT62470**

Tranquilla is a family run site on the western slopes above Baveno, close to Lake Maggiore. The site is in two terraced sections, both with electricity connections (6A). The 56 touring pitches are of average size with trees offering plenty of shade. There is a pleasant swimming pool (renovated in 2008) with an attractive new paddling pool. An unusually large restaurant with two terraces is open all season and offers a varied menu at reasonable prices and live entertainment in season. Reception is housed in an attractive old railway carriage from where the Luca family will welcome you. Excellent English is spoken. Tourist information is available and reception will book any of the local activities and facilities including watersports. The lakeside town of Baveno is about 1.5 km. away, down a fairly steep hill. About half way down are bus stops and a there is a weekly market on Mondays. Boat trips to three islands are available from the quay.

Facilities

The southern site has a recent ladies' sanitary block which includes facilities for disabled campers, whilst the male block is older. The northern side has several older, modernised blocks. All are kept very clean. British and Turkish style WCs. Laundry. Motorcaravan services. Bar. Restaurant, pizzeria and takeaway. Swimming pool (10/5-30/9). Aquarium. Play area. Excursions.
Off site: Fishing 800 m. Bus service 800 m. Sailing 1.5 km. Golf, bicycle hire and riding 3 km. Shops nearby.

Open: 20 March - 10 October.

Directions

Baveno is 90 km. northwest of Milan on the western shore of Lake Maggiore, and is on the SS33 road between Arona and Verbania. Site is well signed to the west in the northern part of the town.
GPS: N45:54.711 E08:29.359

Charges guide

Per person	€ 5,00 - € 6,50
pitch incl. electricity	€ 9,20 - € 12,40

Special discounts for Alan Rogers readers.
No credit cards, but travellers cheques and British currency accepted.

IT62463 Camping Holiday

Via 42 Martiri, 28, I-28835 Feriolo di Baveno (Piedmont)

Tel: **0323 28164**. Email: **info@miralago-holiday.com** **www.alanrogers.com/IT62463**

Camping Holiday is located on Lake Maggiore's western shores, close to the resort of Baveno and larger town of Stresa. This is a small site with direct access to a sandy beach. There are just 58 pitches, all of which are equipped with electricity (6A) and satellite TV connections. Premium pitches are available with direct lake access. There are also a number of smaller pitches, suitable for small tents. Although the site is small, there is a bar/restaurant and well stocked shop. A cycle track leads from the site to the village of Feriolo, 600 m. away, and beyond to Baveno. Lake Maggiore is rightly renowned for its lush gardens and magnificent mountain scenery. The Borromean islands are a popular excursion and easily accessible from Stresa. This is also a wonderful area for mountain biking and hiking – the Monte Rosa massif is easily accessible.

Facilities

Bar, restaurant/pizzeria. Shop. Direct access to lake and sandy beach. Play area. Tourist information.
Off site: Feriolo 600 m. Baveno 3 km. Stresa 7 km. Walking and cycle routes. Watersports. Fishing.

Open: 20 March - 21 September.

Directions

Leave the A26 motorway at the Casale exit and join the eastbound S33 as far as Feriolo. Site is clearly signed. GPS: N45:56.161 E08:29.182

Charges guide

Per unit incl. 2 persons and electricity	€ 20,00 - € 29,40
extra person	€ 4,50 - € 6,00

Italy

IT62490 Camping Continental Lido

Via 42 Martiri 156, I-28924 Fondotoce di Verbania (Piedmont)

Tel: **032 349 6300**. Email: **info@campingcontinental.com** **www.alanrogers.com/IT62490**

Continental Lido is a large, bustling site situated on the shore of the charming little Lake Mergozzo, about a kilometre from the better known Lake Maggiore. The 479 average sized touring pitches are back-to-back in regular rows on grass. All have electricity (6A) and there is shade from a variety of trees in some parts. There is a feeling of spaciousness here and the 185 mobile homes are not obtrusive. There is an impressive new pool complex and a small sandy beach slopes gently into the lake where swimming and watersports can also be enjoyed (no powered craft may be used). Pine-clad mountains and a pretty village directly opposite the beach provide a pleasing, scenic background. An unusual feature here is the 9-hole golf course. There is a busy programme of activities from May to September. Under the same ownership as Isolino Camping Village, this site is managed by the son Gian Paolo who speaks good English.

Facilities

Five high standard toilet blocks have free hot water. Facilities for disabled visitors. Washing machines and dryers. Mini-fridges. Well stocked shop and bar/restaurant with terrace and takeaway. Swimming pool complex (26/4-14/9) with slides, rapids and waves, plus free sun loungers and parasols. Snack bars by pool and lake. TV. Tennis. Golf course (9 holes). Playground. Fishing. Windsurfing, pedaloes, canoes, kayaks. Games room. Bicycle hire. Entertainment and activities (mid-June to mid-Sept). Bus on request to Verbania. Off site: Riding 1 km. Sailing 5 km. 18-hole golf 12 km.

Open: 3 April - 21 September.

Directions

Verbania is 100 km. northwest of Milan, on the western shore of Lake Maggiore. Site is off the SS34 road between Fondotoce and Gravellona, 200 m. west of junction with SS33. GPS: N45:56.976 E08:28.835

Charges guide

Per unit incl. 2 persons and electricity	€ 17,70 - € 25,60
extra person	€ 4,30 - € 7,30
child (6-11 yrs)	€ 3,30 - € 5,85

No credit cards.

Camping Cheques accepted.

IT62460 Camping Village Isolino

Via per Feriolo 25, I-28924 Verbania Fondotoce (Piedmont)

Tel: **032 349 6080**. Email: **info@isolino.com** **www.alanrogers.com/IT62460**

Lake Maggiore is one of the most attractive Italian lakes and Isolino is one of the largest sites in the region. Most of the 460 tourist pitches have shade from a variety of trees. Some are of a good size, many in long, angled rows leading to the beach. All have electrical connections (6A) and some have lake views. The bar and restaurant terraces and the very large, lagoon style swimming pool with its island sun deck area have stunning views across the lake to the fir-clad mountains beyond. The social life of the campsite is centred around the large bar which has a stage sometimes used for musical entertainment. A newly constructed amphitheatre provides a home for the programme of activities and entertainment which runs between May and mid-September. The extensive poolside terrace is outside the bar, takeaway and casual eating area. In the restaurant on the floor above some tables share the magnificent views across the lake. The site is well situated for visiting the many attractions of the region which include the famous gardens on the islands in the lake and at the Villa Taranto, Verbania. The Swiss mountains and resort of Locarno are quite near. The site is owned by the friendly Manoni family who also own Camping Continental Lido at nearby Lake Mergozzo. There will be a new fun pool and gym for 2009.

Facilities

Six well built toilet blocks have hot water for showers and washbasins but cold for dishwashing and laundry. Baby room. Laundry facilities. Fridge box hire. Motorcaravan services. Supermarket, bar and takeaway (all season). Swimming pool (25/4-20/9). Amphitheatre. Tennis. Fishing. Watersports. Bicycle hire and guided mountain bike tours. Long beach. Internet access. Good English is spoken. Off site: Golf 2 km. Sailing 5 km. Riding 12 km.

Open: 3 April - 21 September.

Directions

Verbania is 100 km. northwest of Milan on the western shore of Lake Maggiore. From the A26 motorway, leave at exit for Stresa/Baveno, turn left towards Fondotoce. Site is well signed off the SS33 north of Baveno and 300 m. south of the junction with the SS34 at Fondotoce. GPS: N45:56.301 E08:30.005

Charges 2009

Per unit incl. 3 persons and electricity	€ 18,00 - € 47,05
extra person	€ 4,60 - € 7,80
child (3-11 yrs)	free - € 6,40
dog	€ 3,35 - € 7,80

The campsite is situated on the picturesque **Lake Mergozzo**, the cleanest lake of Europe, only 1 km far from **Lake Maggiore**. The sandy beach, long and quiet is ideal for children. Bar, bar on the beach, restaurant, shop, free hot showers, Beachvolleyball, children's playground, football field, basketball and volleyball facilities, two tennis field (free), spinning, table tennis, **animation**, **internet point**. **We rent:** bicycles, canoes and pedalò. Both mobile homes and rooms available for renting. **How to reach us:** from Verbania direction Fondotoce. At the cross road direction Gravellona, straight ahead for 100 mt. 1.200 m² **SWIMMING POOL** for adults and children with NEW SLIDES, wave pool with whirlpool and lazy river, free deckchairs and sunshade parasols.

NEW COVERED ARENA!

CHILDREN GRATIS
0-2 Years all the season.
3-5 Years till 04.07. and from 22.08.09

Special Offer
FROM 5 NIGHTS from 03.04. to 21.05. and from 05.09. to 21.09.09

FROM 7 NIGHTS from 21.05. to 27.06. and from 29.08. to 05.09.09

Lago di Mergozzo
Lago Maggiore

ANIMATION** from **25.04.** to **13.09.09
SWIMMING POOL** from **25.04.** to **13.09.09

Via 42 Martiri, 156
I-28924 FONDOTOCE DI VERBANIA (VB)
Tel. 0039/0323 496300
Fax 0039/0323 496218
info@campingcontinental.com • www.campingcontinental.com

Sandy beach which slightly goes deeper into the water ideal for children. • Bungalows, mobile homes and chalets for rent. • Animation 25.04-12.09.09 swimmingpools 25.04-20.09.09 • New covered arena.

New 2009!
New swimmigpool with watergames and canyon river. • Concrete insideroads. • Fitness and spinning area. • Renewed playground.

Lago Maggiore

CHILDREN GRATIS
0-2 all the season long.
3-5 years till 04.07. and from 22.08.09

Dogs only on reservation from the 27.06 to the 29.08.09

Via Per Feriolo, 25 • I-28924 Fondotoce di Verbania • Tel. 0039/0323496080 • Fax 0039/0323496414
info@isolino.com • www.isolino.it

IT62420 Camping Orta

Via Domodossola 28, I-28016 Orta San Giulio (Piedmont)

Tel: **032 290 267**. Email: **info@campingorta.it** **www.alanrogers.com/IT62420**

Lake Orta is a charming, less visited small lake just west of Lake Maggiore in an area with understated charm. The site is on a considerable slope, and most of the 70 touring pitches (all with 4A electricity) are on the top grass terrace with spectacular views across the lake to the mountains beyond. There are some superb lakeside pitches across the main road (linked by a pedestrian underpass) although there is some traffic noise here. Amenities include a large games and entertainment room and a traditional Italian bar and restaurant serving good value family meals. Some English is spoken by the Guarnori family, who take pride in maintaining their uncomplicated site to a high standard. Book ahead to enjoy the lakeside pitches. If you are anxious about towing a large caravan to the top terraces, the owner will help out with his tractor!

Facilities

Three modern sanitary blocks are clean and well maintained providing mainly British style toilets, coin operated showers and an excellent unit for disabled visitors. Laundry facilities. Motorcaravan services. Excellent shop. Bar and restaurant with basic menu serving good value Italian family meals. Playground. Large games/TV room. WiFi in reception/bar area. Fishing. Bicycle hire. Boat launching. Off site: Riding, golf and sailing all within 10 km.

Open: All year.

Directions

Lake Orta is 85 km. northwest of Milan and just west of Lake Maggiore. Site is on the SR229 between Borgomanero and Omega, 600 m. north of the turn to Orta San Giulio. There is a parking area for arrivals on the lake side of the road, but reception and main entrance are on the opposite side. GPS: N45:48.137 E08:25.216

Charges guide

Per person	€ 5,00 - € 6,50
pitch	€ 8,00 - € 15,00
electricity	€ 2,00

IT62435 Camping Village Lago Maggiore

Via Leonardo da Vinci, 7, I-28040 Dormelletto (Piedmont)

Tel: **0322 497193**. Email: **info@lagomag.com** www.alanrogers.com/IT62435

This site can be found on the southwestern shores of Lake Maggiore, close to the pretty town of Arona. There are 290 pitches here, of which around 90 are available for tourers. Pitches are all equipped with electrical connections and have reasonable shade. A number of brick built chalets and mobile homes are available for rent. The site has direct access to the lake and a sandy beach. On-site amenities include a well stocked shop and a bar/restaurant, which includes a pizzeria, with pizzas cooked on a traditional log stove. A wealth of sports activities is on offer on site, many based around the two pools and sports field. The lake is ideal for watersports – windsurfers and boats can be hired locally. During July and August there is a lively programme of activities and entertainment.

Facilities

Five toilet blocks (a small charge is made for hot water and showers). Private family bathrooms for rent. Motorcaravan services. Bar, restaurant/pizzeria. Shop. Games room. Play area. Swimming pools. Children's pool. Sports field. Entertainment and activity programme (high season) Direct access to lake. Mobile homes and chalets for rent. Off site: Arona 3 km. Walking and cycle routes. Watersports. Fishing.

Open: 1 April - 30 September.

Directions

Leave the A26 motorway at the Sesto Calende exit and join the northbound SS33 as far as Dormelletto. The campsite is clearly signed from the village. GPS: N45:44.000 E08:34.633

Charges 2009

Per unit incl. 2 persons and electricity	€ 22,00 - € 39,00
extra person	€ 5,00 - € 9,00
child (2-6 yrs)	€ 2,50 - € 5,00
dog	€ 4,00 - € 6,00

IT62465 Camping Orchidea

Via 42 Martiri, 2, I-28835 Feriolo di Baveno (Piedmont)

Tel: **0323 282 57**. Email: **camping.orchidea@libero.it** www.alanrogers.com/IT62465

Camping Orchidea can be found on the western bank of Lake Maggiore, 35 km. south of the Swiss border and 5 km. from Stresa. This site has direct access to the lake and a sandy beach. Orchidea has recently been refurbished and has a good range of modern amenities, including a shop, bar and restaurant. Watersports are understandably popular here and pedaloes and kayaks can be rented on site. Pitches are grassy and generally well shaded, all with electricity. Some pitches are available facing the lake (a supplement is charged in peak season). There are caravans and mobile homes available for rent. Stresa, nearby, is an important town with 5,000 inhabitants and has a harbour with regular boat trips to the Borromean islands, and also a cable car to the summit of Monte Mottarone, passing the stunning Giardino Botanico Alpinia, world renowned mountain gardens.

Facilities

Three toilet blocks have been modernised and all have hot and cold water throughout. Shop. Restaurant. Bar. Takeaway. Direct lake access. Pedalo and kayak hire. Fishing. Playground. Children's club. Mobile homes and caravans for rent. Off site: Walking and cycle trails. Stresa 5 km. Tennis. Riding.

Open: 15 March - 5 October.

Directions

Take the Baveno/Stresa exit from the A26 (autostrada dei Trafori) and head north on the Via Sempione. In Feriolo follow signs to the campsite. GPS: N45:56.004 E08:28.872

Charges guide

Per person	€ 4,60 - € 7,50
child (under 12 yrs)	€ 3,20 - € 5,50
pitch	€ 8,50 - € 19,00
electricity (6A)	€ 2,60

IT62464 Camping Miralago

Via 42 Martiri, 34, I-28835 Feriolo di Baveno (Piedmont)

Tel: **0323 28226**. Email: **miralago@miralago-holiday.com** **www.alanrogers.com/IT62464**

Miralago is a sister site of IT62463 (Camping Holiday) and is also located on the western banks of Lake Maggiore, close to the little resort of Feriolo. Unusually, many of the pitches here have direct access to the lake or to the River Toce at the point where it runs into the lake. There are 74 pitches here, all of which are equipped with electricity (6A) and satellite TV connections. Premium pitches are available with direct lake access. On-site amenities include a bar and a play area for children. A cycle track leads from the site to Feriolo, 500 m. away.

Facilities

Bar. Play area. Tourist information. Direct access to lake and sandy beach. Off site: Feriolo 500 m. Baveno 3 km. Stresa 7 km. Walking and cycle routes. Watersports. Fishing.

Open: 20 March - 5 October.

Directions

Leave the A26 motorway at the Casale exit and join the eastbound S33 as far as Feriolo. Site is clearly signed from the village.
GPS: N45:56.033 E08:29.083

Charges guide

Per unit incl. 2 persons and electricity	€ 23,30 - € 31,30
extra person	€ 5,00 - € 6,50
child (2-12 yrs)	€ 4,50 - € 5,50

IT62440 Camping Solcio

Via al Campeggio, I-28040 Solcio di Lesa (Piedmont)

Tel: **032 274 97**. Email: **info@campingsolcio.com** **www.alanrogers.com/IT62440**

Camping Solcio is a family-run site on the lakeside and has lovely views over the lakes and the green hills which surround some of the site. The neat pitches are 60-90 sq.m. with 6A electricity. Mostly shaded by trees, The 105 touring pitches are on flat sand and grass and access is easy. A very pleasant restaurant and a bar back onto a large building alongside the site, and there are some views of the lake from the terraces. You will have a view of the railway halfway up the hills alongside the site, so there is rail noise at times. The lakeside is good for safe swimming and, as the site is next to a large boat repair building plus its moorings, there is no through traffic in terms of fast boats. All manner of watersports are available here and the beach is of coarse sand. An ambitious entertainment programme is arranged for children in high season, and there is adventure sport for the over 10s. This is a pleasant site with modest facilities and it may suit those who do not seek the luxuries of the larger sites. English and Dutch are spoken and the site is very popular with Dutch campers.

Facilities

One main central toilet block is smart and clean. Toilets here are British style. An older block nearer reception has mixed Turkish and British style toilets. Facilities for disabled visitors. Baby room. Washing machine. Restaurant and bar with terrace. Basic shop. Full animation programme in season. Play areas. Bicycle hire. Internet. Torches useful. Off site: Town facilities 1 km. Riding 5 km. Golf 10 km. Public transport 300 m. ATM 2 km.

Open: 7 March - 20 October.

Directions

Site is on the west side of Lake Maggiore. From A4 (Milan - Torino) take the A8 to Castelletto Sticino. Then north on SS33 towards Stresa and look for site sign at km. 57 marker at town of Lesa. Take the narrow access road to the site.
GPS: N45:48.952 E08:32.977

Charges guide

Per person	€ 5,00 - € 7,50
child (3-13 yrs)	€ 3,70 - € 6,00
pitch	€ 8,40 - € 21,50
electricity	€ 2,50 - € 2,60

IT62485 Camping Conca d'Oro

Via 42 Martiri 26, I-28835 Feriolo di Baveno (Piedmont)

Tel: **032 328 116**. Email: **info@concadoro.it**

www.alanrogers.com/IT62485

Conca d'Oro is a delightful site with spectacular views across Lake Maggiore to the distant mountains. The first impression is one of spaciousness and colour. There are just a dozen mobile homes for rent, the rest of the 210 grass plots being good sized touring pitches. All have 6A electrical connections; they are marked by young trees and azalea bushes. The land slopes gently down to a sandy beach. An attractive restaurant serves a varied range of dishes and there is a good bar and pizzeria and a well stocked shop. The young owners Maurizio and Allesandra are sure to give you a warm welcome. The site is close to the lakeside town of Baveno from where boat trips are available to the three small islands on this part of Lake Maggiore. Fishing and boat launching are possible from the beach at the site, and sailing plus other watersports can be enjoyed from various points on the lake. There are nature reserves nearby and drives out into the surrounding mountains provide opportunities for walkers, cyclists and climbers.

Facilities

Three toilet blocks provide all necessary facilities kept in immaculate condition, including controllable showers and open style washbasins; some toilets with washbasins. En-suite unit for disabled visitors. Laundry room. Motorcaravan service point. Bar, restaurant, pizzeria and shop (all season). Swimming, fishing and boat launching from beach. Bicycle hire. Off site: Riding 700 m. Golf 1 km. Sailing 7 km. Shops, bars and restaurants nearby.

Open: 24 March - 23 September.

Directions

Baveno is 90 km. northwest of Milan on the western shore of Lake Maggiore. Site is off the SS33 road between Baveno and Fondotoce di Verbania, 1 km. south of the junction with the SS34 and is well signed. GPS: N45:56.168 E08:29.209

Charges guide

Per unit incl. 2 persons	€ 18,50 - € 28,90
extra person	€ 5,00 - € 7,50
child (2-13 yrs)	€ 3,50 - € 6,50
electricity	€ 2,50

Italy

IT62495 Camping La Quiete

Via Turati 72, I-28040 Fondotoce di Verbania (Piedmont)

Tel: **0323 496 013**. Email: **info@campinglaquiete.it** www.alanrogers.com/IT62495

La Quiete is a small site, attractively located on the shore of Lake Mergozzo, a small lake to the west of the much larger Lake Maggiore. There are 180 pitches here, mostly well shaded and with electrical connections (6A), many of which have fine views across the lake. A number of mobile homes are available for rent. On-site amenities include a shop and bar/restaurant, as well as a sports field and volleyball court. This is excellent mountain biking and walking country and the site owners will be pleased to recommend possible routes. Verbania, nearby, is an elegant resort town on Lake Maggiore, created by the merging of the towns of Pallanza and Intra. Here, the magnificent Giardini Botanici Villa Taranto are well worth a visit. They were created between 1931 and 1940 by Scotsman Neil McEacharn who undertook substantial changes to the landscape and added over eight kilometres of water pipes.

Facilities

Bar/restaurant. Shop. Sports field. Volleyball. Games room. Play area. Direct access to Lake Mergozzo. Off site: Lake Maggiore. Verbania. Walking and cycle routes. Watersports. Fishing.

Open: 6 April - 28 September.

Directions

Leave the A26 motorway at the Casale exit and join the eastbound S34 as far as Fondotoce. Head north here on SP54 and the campsite is clearly signed. GPS: N45:57.212 E08:28.647

Charges guide

Per unit incl. 2 persons and electricity € 22,00

IT64120 Villaggio Camping Valdeiva

Localitá Ronco, I-19013 Deiva Marina (Ligúria)

Tel: **018 782 4174**. Email: **camping@valdeiva.it** www.alanrogers.com/IT64120

A mature site three kilometres from the sea between the famous Cinque Terre and Portofino, Valdeiva is open all year. It is situated in a valley amongst dense pines so views are restricted. On flat ground and separated, most of the 140 pitches are used for permanent Italian units. There are 40 pitches for tents and touring units but in high season tourers can expect to be put onto a sloping overflow area by the road with no shade. The main touring pitches are in a square at the bottom of the site, some with shade, all with electricity (3A). Cars may be required to park in a separate area depending on the season. There was late night noise from residents when we stayed in high season. We see this as a transit site rather than for extended stays. The site does have a small pool, which is very welcome. The beach is pleasant and the surrounding village has several bars and restaurants. There are very pleasant walks and treks in the unspoilt woods of Liguria or the most interesting option is a visit to Cinque Terre, five villages, some of which can only be reached by rail, boat or by cliff footpath. Their history is one of fishing but now they also specialise in wines. Some of the vineyards can only be reached by boat.

Facilities

The toilet block nearest the touring pitches provides cramped facilities. A new block is in the centre of the site. WCs are mainly Turkish, but there are some of British style. Laundry facilities. Shop, bar/restaurant and takeaway (all 15/6-10/9). Small swimming pool. Play area. Bicycle hire. Internet access. WiFi. Off site: Beach 3 km.

Open: All year excl. 11 January - 9 February and 6 November - 5 December.

Directions

Leave A12 at Deiva Marina exit and follow signs to Deiva Marina. Site signs are clear at the first junction and site is on left 3 km. down this road. GPS: N44:13.482 E09:33.101

Charges guide

Per person (over 6 yrs)	€ 6,00
pitch	€ 10,00 - € 23,00
small tent	€ 7,00 - € 13,00

IT64030 Camping Baciccia

Via Torino 19, I-17023 Ceriale (Ligúria)

Tel: **018 299 0743**. Email: **info@campingbaciccia.it**

www.alanrogers.com/IT64030

This friendly, family run site is a popular holiday destination. Baciccia was the nickname of the present owner's grandfather who grew fruit trees and tomatoes on the site. Tall eucalyptus trees shade the 120 tightly packed pitches which encircle the central facilities block. The pitches are on flat ground and all have electricity. There is always a family member by the gate to greet you, and Vincenzina and Giovanni, along with their adult children Laura and Mauro, work tirelessly to ensure that you enjoy your stay. The restaurant is informal and, as no frozen food is served, the menu is necessarily simple but is traditional Italian food cooked to perfection. The restaurant overlooks a large swimming pool and there are organised water polo and pool games, as well as a half size tennis court and boules. The private beach is a short walk (or free shuttle service) and the town has the usual seaside attractions but it is also worth visiting the tiny traditional villages close by. This site may suit campers looking for a family atmosphere with none of the brashness of large seaside sites. If you have forgotten anything by way of camping equipment just ask and the family will lend it to you. Free shuttle service to Ceriale's beaches.

Facilities

Two clean and modern sanitary blocks near reception have British and Turkish style WCs and hot water throughout. Laundry. Motorcaravan services. Restaurant/bar. Shop. Pizzeria and takeaway. Two swimming pools (20/3-31/10) and private beach. Tennis. Boules. Play area. Bicycle hire. Woodburning stove and barbecue. Internet point. Fishing. Diving. Entertainment for children and adults in high season. Excursions. Off site: Department store 150 m. Aquapark 500 m. Riding and golf 5 km. Parachuting school 10 km. Ancient town (2,000 years old) of Albenga 3 km.

Open: 20 March - 5 November, 1 December - 10 January.

Directions

From the A10 between Imperia and Savona, take Albenga exit. Follow signs Ceriale/Savona and Aquapark Caravelle (which is 500 m. from site) and then site signs. Site is just south of Savona. GPS: N44:04.963 E08:12.964

Charges guide

Per unit incl. up to 3 persons (over 2 yrs)	€ 28,00 - € 47,00
extra person	€ 5,00 - € 9,00
half pitch incl. 2 persons, no car	€ 16,00 - € 32,00
dog	€ 2,00 - € 4,00

Discounts for stays in excess of 7 days.
Discount for readers 10% in low season.

Family Bungalow-Camping, 500 mt from the seaside, placed in a green and quiet area. Bungalows-Chalets and Holiday Homes from 2 to 6 people, with kitchenette, bathroom,1 or 2 bedrooms, air-conditioning, heating, linen. Renting caravans. **2 swimming pools open from 1st April to 31 October.** Internet point, tourist info, tennis, playground, barbeque, animation, bar, restaurant, minimarket, washingmachines, dryer, sanitary facilities with warm water free, camper service. Motorcaravan waste discharge point.
OPEN ALL YEAR. Shuttle service to the best beaches free of charges. Special offers in low season: see our website!

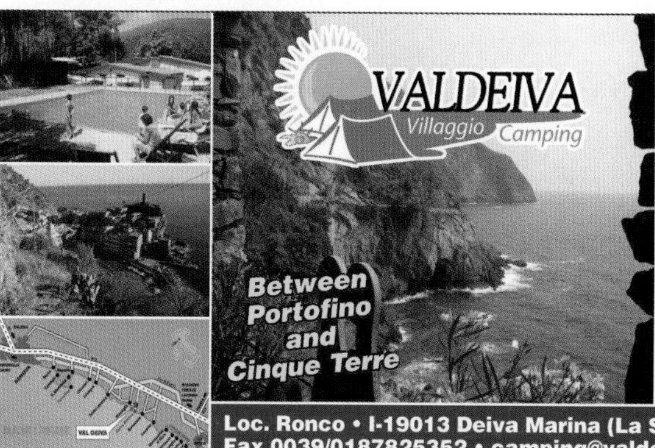

Camping Valdeiva Village is situated in a quiet zone of Ligurian Eastern coast, a few minutes by train from Cinque Terre, Tigullio Golf (Portofino, Santa Margherita, Rapallo) and 60 km from Genova, European Capital City of Culture 2004. It's placed in the inland of Deiva Marina at only 3 km from the town. Grocery store, bar, restaurant, pizza-shop with possibility of take away. Swimmingpool, automatic laundry, games for children, ping-pong, bowling-green, internet point, Wi-Fi, mountainbikes. Our rented bungalows with TV-Sat and caravans are of modern conception, all equipped with kitchen, bathroom with shower and heated. Open all year round. **FREE BUS SERVICE TO TRAIN STATION ALL YEAR ROUND.**

Loc. Ronco • I-19013 Deiva Marina (La Spezia) • Tel. 0039/0187824174
Fax 0039/0187825352 • camping@valdeiva.it • www.valdeiva.it

IT64010 Camping Villaggio dei Fiori

Via Tiro a Volo 3, I-18038 San Remo (Ligúria)

Tel: **018 466 0635**. Email: **info@villaggiodeifiori.it** **www.alanrogers.com/IT64010**

Open all year round, this open and spacious site has high standards and is ideal for exploring the Italian Riviera or for just relaxing by the enjoyable, filtered sea water pools. Unusually all the pitch areas at the site are totally paved and there are some extremely large pitches for large units (ask reception to open another gate for entry). All pitches have electricity (3/6A), 50 also have water and drainage, and there is an outside sink and cold water for every four. There is ample shade from mature trees and shrubs, which are constantly watered and cared for in summer. The 'Gold' pitches and some wonderful tent pitches have pleasant views over the sea. There is a path to a secluded and pleasant beach with sparkling waters, overlooked by a large patio area. The rocky surrounds are excellent for snorkelling and fishing, with ladder access to the water. The friendly management speak excellent English and will supply detailed touring plans. Activities and entertainment are organised in high season for adults and children. Excursions are offered (extra cost) along the Italian Riviera dei Fiori and the French Côte d'Azur, including night excursions to Nice and Monte Carlo. Buses run from outside the site to Monte Carlo, Nice, Cannes, Eze and many other places of interest. This is a very good site for visiting all the attractions in the local area.

Facilities

Three clean and modern toilet blocks have British and Turkish style WCs and hot water throughout. Baby rooms. Facilities for disabled campers. Laundry facilities. Motorcaravan services. Bar sells essential supplies. Large restaurant. Pizzeria and takeaway (all year). Sea water swimming pools (small extra charge in high season) and whirlpool spa (June - Sept). Tennis. Play area. Fishing. Satellite TV. Internet access. Bicycle hire. Dogs are not accepted. Off site: Shop 150 m. Riding and golf 2 km.

Open: All year.

Directions

From SS1 (Ventimiglia - Imperia), site is on right just before San Remo. There is a sharp right turn if approaching from the west. From autostrada A10 take San Remo Ouest exit. Site is well signed. GPS: N43:48.070 E07:44.920

Charges guide

Per unit incl. 4 persons	€ 27,00 - € 56,00
electricity (3A-6A)	€ 2,00 - € 4,00

Some charges due on arrival.
Discounts for stays in excess of 7 days.
Discount for readers 10% in low season.
Camping Cheques accepted.

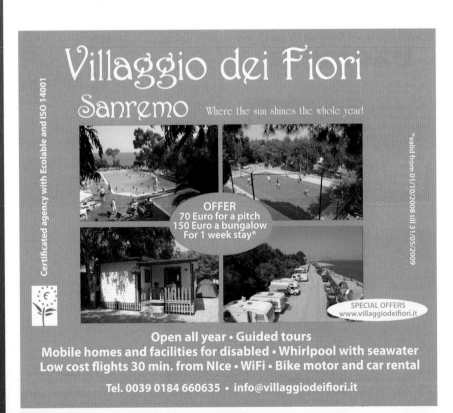

IT64190 Camping River

Localitá Armezzone, I-19031 Ameglia (Ligúria)

Tel: **018 765 920**. Email: **info@campingriver.com** **www.alanrogers.com/IT64190**

Ameglia, near La Spezia, is just south of the A12 autrostada and this site is just 5 km. from the Sarzana exit. Close to Le Cinque Terre and on the banks of the Magna river, this popular site provides 100 touring pitches and about the same number for static caravans. With its own small marina and excellent swimming pools, the site provides a busy location for a short stop or a longer stay to explore Liguria. The narrow access road will stop larger motorhomes from gaining access, but when we visited there were a large number of twin axle caravans on site. The river provides boat launching facilities and good fishing opportunities further up river. The site has direct access to the water and a small marina with docking facilities for visitors. A busy entertainment programme is provided from mid June.

Facilities

Two sanitary blocks provide toilets (some Turkish style), washbasins and unisex showers. Facilities for disabled campers. Motorcaravan service point. Restaurant and bar. Shop. Pizzeria. Swimming pool and sun deck. Boat launching. Fishing. Mobile homes and bungalows to rent. Off site: Tennis 200 m. Archery. Sailing. Scuba diving. Le Spezia. La Cinque Terre.

Open: 1 April - 30 September.

Directions

Take Sarzana exit on the A12 (Genoa - Livorno) and follow the signs initially towards Lerici. After 3 km. follow signs to Bocca di Magra and Ameglia where the site is well signed off to the left. The final access road is narrow and has a tight bend so larger units might experience some difficulty.
GPS: N44:04.552 E09:58.208

Charges guide

Per person	€ 4,50 - € 9,20
child (2-10 yrs)	€ 2,30 - € 7,00
pitch	€ 18,00 - € 45,80
dog	€ 2,00 - € 3,00

IT64110 Camping Miraflores

Via Savagna 10, I-16035 Rapallo (Ligúria)

Tel: **018 526 3000**. Email: **camping.miraflores@libero.it** **www.alanrogers.com/IT64110**

This site has been recommended by our Italian agent and we plan to undertake a full inspection in 2009. Camping Miraflores is located on the Ligurian coast, close to the famous resort of Portofino and the Cinque Terre. Pitches are mostly terraced with separate areas for tents (small pitches) and caravans or motor homes. There are also a number of mobile homes for rent. The site has recently added a small swimming pool. Rapallo is an attractive resort in its own right with an interesting old town centre. The A12 motorway (Rapallo exit) is very close to the site and there may be some road noise.

Facilities

Bar. Shop. Pizzeria and takeaway meals. Games room. Playground. Swimming pool. Mobile homes for rent. Off site: Nearest beach 1.5 km. Tennis, riding, fishing, golf. Rapallo centre 1.5 km.

Open: All year.

Directions

Site is located very close to the Rapallo exit from the A12 motorway. From this point, follow signs to Rapallo and the site is well signed. GPS: N44:21.552 E09:12.545

Charges guide

Per person	€ 6,00 - € 6,50
pitch incl. electricity	€ 11,00 - € 13,50

IT62610 Camping Del Sole

Via per Rovato 26, I-25049 Iseo (Lombardy)

Tel: **030 980 288**. Email: **info@campingdelsole.it** **www.alanrogers.com/IT62610**

Camping Del Sole lies on the southern edge of Lake Iseo, just outside the pretty lakeside town of Iseo. The site has 306 pitches, many taken up with chalets and mobile homes. The 180 touring pitches all have 3A electricity and some have fine views of the surrounding mountains and lake. Pitches are generally flat and of a reasonable size, but cars must park in the carpark. The site has a wide range of excellent leisure amenities, including a large swimming pool. There is a bar and restaurant with a pizzeria near the pool and entertainment area and a second bar by the lake. The site is near the delightful waterfront area of the town where you can enjoy classic Italian architecture, stroll around the shops or enjoy a meal in one of the many restaurants. There is a boat launching facility at the lakeside. There is a lively entertainment programme and excursions around the lake are organised, notably to Lake Iseo's three islands where you can sit at a street café or enjoy a walk while enjoying the magnificent scenery. Excursions are also organised to the wine cellars of Franciacorta.

Facilities

Sanitary facilities are modern and well maintained, including special facilities for disabled visitors. Washing machines and dryers. Bar, restaurant, pizzeria and snack bar. Supermarket. Motorcaravan service point. Bicycle and canoe hire. Swimming pool with children's pool. Bicycle and pedal boat hire. Tennis. Entertainment in high season. Off site: Golf 5 km. Riding 6 km.

Open: 4 April - 27 September.

Directions

From the A4 Milan - Venice autostrada take Rovato exit and at roundabout go north on SPX1 following signs for Lago d'Iseo for 12 km. Site is well signed to left at large roundabout. From Brescia on SS510, turn north before Iseo towards Rovato and turn right to site. GPS: N45:39.425 E10:02.244

Charges guide

Per unit incl. 2 persons	€ 18,30 - € 35,20
extra person	€ 4,70 - € 8,50
child (under 12 yrs)	free - € 6,90

Camping Cheques accepted.

IT62600 Camping Europa Silvella

Via Silvella 10, I-25010 San Felice del Benaco (Lake Garda)
Tel: **036 565 1095**. Email: **info@europasilvella.it** **www.alanrogers.com/IT62600**

This large, modern, lakeside site was formed from the merger of two different sites with the result that the 340 pitches (about 108 for tourers) are spread among a number of different sections of varying type. The marked pitches alongside the lake are in smaller groups and closer together; the main bar, restaurant and shop are located here. The main area is at the top of a steepish hill on slightly sloping or terraced grass and has slightly larger pitches. There is reasonable shade in many parts and all pitches have electricity. A large new swimming pool complex also provides a daytime bar and restaurant serving lunches. There is considerable tour operator presence (160 pitches) and there are 50 bungalows, mobile homes and log cabins to rent. The site has frontage to the lake in two places with a beach, jetty and moorings. The private beach is very pleasant, with all manner of watersports available.

Facilities

Toilet blocks include washbasins in cabins, facilities for disabled visitors and a superb children's room with small showers. Laundry. Shop. Restaurant/Pizzeria. Swimming pools (hats required) with bar. Tennis, volleyball and five-a-side soccer. Playground. Bowling alley. Animation and entertainment (every night in July/August). Disco for children. Tournaments. Fishing and boat launching. First aid room. Off site: Golf 5 km. Riding 12 km.

Open: 25 April - 20 September.

Directions

San Felice is on the western shore of Lake Garda at the southern end. From A4 Milan - Venice autostrada take Desenzano exit and head north on SS572 towards Saló for 14 km, turn right towards San Felice and follow brown tourist signs with site name (about 3 km). GPS: N45:34.471 E10:32.095

Charges guide

Per person	€ 4,50 - € 9,50
child (1-4 yrs)	€ 3,50 - € 8,00
pitch incl. electricity	€ 11,00 - € 21,50
pitch with services	€ 12,50 - € 23,50
dog	€ 4,00 - € 8,50

LAGO
DI
GARDA
è...
Consorzio di Promozione e
Commercializzazione Turistica

REGIONE VENETO

LAGO DI GARDA è...
Consorzio di Promozione e Commercializzazione Turistica

REGIONE VENETO

LAZISE LAKE GARDA

PACENGO - LAKE GARDA

www.campinglazise.net

IT62540 Camping Lido

Via Peschiera 2, I-37017 Pacengo (Lake Garda)

Tel: **045 759 0611**. Email: **info@campinglido.it** **www.alanrogers.com/IT62540**

Camping Lido is one of the largest and amongst the best of the 120 campsites around Lake Garda and is situated at the southeast corner of the lake. There is quite a slope from the entrance down to the lake so many of the 683 grass touring pitches are on terraces which give lovely views across the lake. They are of varying size, separated by hedges, all have electrical connections and 57 are fully serviced. This is a most attractive site with tall, neatly trimmed trees standing like sentinels on either side of the broad avenue which runs from the entrance right down to the lake.

Facilities

Seven modern toilet blocks (three heated) include provision for disabled visitors and three family rooms. Washing machines and dryer. Fridge rental. Restaurant, bars, pizzeria, takeaway and supermarket. Swimming pool, paddling pool and slides. Fitness centre. Playground. Tennis. Bicycle hire. Watersports. Fishing. Activity programme (high season). Shingle beach with landing stage and mooring for boats. Dogs are not accepted in high season (5/7-15/8). Off site: Gardaland theme park.

Open: 20 March - 11 October.

Directions

Leave A4 Milan - Venice motorway at exit for Peschiera. Head north on east side of lake on SS249. Site entrance on left after Gardaland Theme Park. GPS: N45:28.198 E10:43.225

Charges guide

Per person	€ 4,50 - € 7,00
child (3-5 yrs)	€ 3,00 - € 4,10
pitch incl. services	€ 8,60 - € 17,00

See advertisement on pages 268-269

IT62545 Camping Spiaggia d'Oro

Via Sentieri, 2, I-37017 Lazise (Lake Garda)

Tel: **045 7580 007**. Email: **info@campingspiaggiadoro.com** **www.alanrogers.com/IT62545**

Spiaggia d'Oro is a well equipped family site near Lazise on Lake Garda's eastern bank. This is a large site with grassy pitches and a selection of chalets and mobile homes for rent. The site has its own sandy beach with a beach volleyball court. A fitness centre is a recent addition and it has been developed with a good range of high specification equipment. The swimming pool complex is impressive with three pools, one for children with a slide and water games. This is a lively site in high season with a varied activity programme and a club for children.

Facilities

Supermarket. Bar. Snack bar. Swimming pools with waterslide. Separate children's pool. Fitness centre. Tennis. Playground. Children's club and entertainment programme. Direct access to beach. Mobile homes and chalets for rent. Off site: Shops, cafés and restaurants in Lazise and Peschiera. Verona 35 km.

Open: 14 March -15 October.

Directions

Leave the A4 autostrada at exit for Castelnuovo del Garda. Head north on the SR450. Leave at Ca Isidoro and join the westbound SP5 to Lazise. Site is clearly signed from here. GPS: N45:29.830 E10:44.284

Charges guide

Per unit incl. 2 persons	€ 20,00 - € 39,40

No credit cards.

See advertisement on pages 268-269

IT62535 Camping du Parc

I-37017 Lazise sul Garda (Lake Garda)

Tel: **045 758 0127**. Email: **duparc@camping.it** **www.alanrogers.com/IT62535**

Camping du Parc is a very pleasant, family owned site which resembles a Tardis, in that it extends and extends as you progress further through the site. Olive groves are interspersed with the pitch areas which gives an open and green feel. The site is set on a slope which goes down to the lakeside beach of soft sand. The 150 pitches are terraced, which takes out much of the slope, and all have 6A electricity and water. Units above 10 m. long will be challenged by some of the corners here. Pitches are separated by trimmed hedges and some have shade, others views of the lake.

Facilities

Four modern sanitary blocks are well placed and have free hot water throughout. Three blocks have facilities for disabled campers, one for children and babies. Washing machines and dryers. Motorcaravan services. Well stocked small supermarket. Restaurant with lake views. Pizzeria with terrace and views. Takeaway. Beach bar. Pool bar. Swimming pool. Large paddling pool with slides. Children's entertainment programme. Play area. Tennis. Multisport court. Fishing. Internet and WiFi. Off site: Golf 10 km. Bicycle hire 500 m. Riding 1 km. Gardaland.

Open: 10 March - 30 September.

Directions

Leave A4 Venice - Milan autostrada by taking the Brennero exit to Lake Garda and then on to Lazise. At the lakeside in town turn left and follow signs for site. GPS: N45:29.917 E10:44.248

Charges guide

Per person	€ 5,60 - € 8,70
child (1-5 yrs)	€ 1,50 - € 5,10
pitch	€ 11,30 - € 19,50
dog	€ 1,50 - € 5,10

See advertisement on pages 268-269

IT62520 Camping San Francesco

Strada Vicinale, I-25015 Rivoltella (Lake Garda)

Tel: **030 911 0245**. Email: **moreinfo@campingsanfrancesco.com** **www.alanrogers.com/IT62520**

San Francesco is a large, very well organised site situated to the west of the Simione peninsula on the south east shores of Lake Garda. The pitches are generally on flat gravel and sand and enjoy shade from mature trees. There are three choices of pitch of different sizes with either 3A or 6A electricity; 35 are fully serviced. They are marked by stones but there is no division between them. A wooded beach area of about 400 m. on the lake is used for watersports and there is a jetty for boating. There are delightful lake views from the restaurant and terrace. There is also a new shopping centre with a games area, bazaar and takeaway. The sports centre, pools and entertainment area are all located across a busy road away from the pitches and safely accessed by a tunnel. As with most sites in Italy, reception closes for siesta, but there is a waiting area with electricity. This is a good quality site which is great for families.

Facilities

Sanitary facilities are in two large, modern, centrally located buildings. Very clean and well equipped. Excellent facilities for disabled campers. Shop. Restaurant. Bar. Pizzeria. Takeaway and snacks. In a separate area across the road: swimming pools (15/4-20/9) and jacuzzi, sports centre and tennis. Playground. Entertainment programme, organised activities and excursions. Bicycle hire arranged. Torches required in some areas. Internet access. Off site: Riding 5 km. Golf 10 km.

Open: 1 April - 30 September.

Directions

From autostrada A4, between Brescia and Verona, exit towards Simione and follow signs to Simione and site. GPS: N45:27.921 E10:35.681

Charges guide

Per person	€ 6,00 - € 10,00
child (under 6 yrs)	free - € 8,00
pitch incl. electricity	€ 12,00 - € 22,00
superior pitch	€ 16,00 - € 30,90

Camping Cheques accepted.

IT62530 Camping Piani di Clodia

Localitá Bagatta, I-37017 Lazise (Lake Garda)

Tel: **045 759 0456**. Email: **info@pianidiclodia.it** **www.alanrogers.com/IT62530**

Piani di Clodia is one of the best large sites on Lake Garda and it has a positive impression of space and cleanliness. It is located on a slope between Lazise and Peschiera in the southeast corner of the lake, with lovely views across the water to Simione's peninsula and the mountains beyond. The site slopes down to the water's edge and has over 950 pitches, all with electricity (6A), 250 with electricity, water and drainage, terraced where necessary and back to back from hard access roads. There is some shade from mature and young trees.

Facilities

Seven modern, immaculate sanitary blocks, well spaced around the site. British and Turkish style WCs. All have facilities for disabled visitors and one has a baby room. Washing machines, dryers and laundry service. Motorcaravan services. Shopping complex with supermarket and general shops. Two bars. Self-service restaurant with takeaway. Pizzeria. Ice cream parlour. Swimming pools. Tennis. Gymnastics. Fishing. Bicycle hire. Large playground. Outdoor theatre with animation programme. Off site: Riding 6 km. Golf 12 km. Theme parks nearby.

Open: 20 March - 15 October.

Directions

Lazise is on the southeast side of Lake Garda about 30 km. west of Verona. From north on Trento - Verona A22 autostrada take Affi exit then follow signs for Lazise and site. From south on A4 Brescia - Venice motorway take Peschiera exit and site is 6 km. towards Lazise and Garda on SS249.
GPS: N45:28.963 E10:43.759

Charges guide

Per person	€ 4,80 - € 10,30
child (1-9 yrs)	€ 3,10 - € 6,70
pitch incl. electricity	€ 9,80 - € 29,00

See advertisement on pages 268-269

IT62550 Camping La Quercia

I-37017 Lazise sul Garda (Lake Garda)

Tel: **045 647 0577**. Email: **laquercia@laquercia.it** **www.alanrogers.com/IT62550**

Celebrating its 50th anniversay in 2008, La Quercia is a spacious, popular site on a slight slope leading down to Lake Garda and is decorated by palm trees and elegantly trimmed hedges. Accommodating up to 950 touring units, pitches are mostly in regular double rows between access roads, all with electricity (6A). Most are shaded by mature trees, although those furthest from the lake are more open to the sun. Much of the activity centres around the impressive pool complex with its fantastic slides and the terrace bar, restaurant and pizzeria which overlook the entertainment stage. The daytime activities and evening entertainment are very professional with the young team working hard to involve everyone (some courses require enrolment on a Sunday). La Quercia has a fine sandy beach on the lake, with diving jetties and a roped off section for launching boats or windsurfing (high season). Another restaurant serving traditional Italian food is located closer to the beach. The site is a short distance from the delightful lakeside towns of Lazise and Peschiera, which have a wide choice of restaurants, and is a short drive from Verona, one of Italy's finest cultural centres.

Facilities

Six toilet blocks are perfectly sufficient and are of a very high standard. Laundry. Supermarket. General shop. Bar, restaurant, self-service restaurant and pizzeria. Swimming pools (small charge). Tennis. Riding. Aerobics, judo and yoga. Scuba club. Playground with water play. Organised events (sports competitions, games, etc.) and free courses (e.g. swimming, surfboarding). Canoeing. Roller-blading. Archery. Minigolf. Evening entertainment or dancing. Baby sitting service. Internet. ATM. Free weekly excursion. Off site: Bicycle hire 300 m. Golf 10 km. Gardaland, Movieland and Caneva Aqua Park nearby.

Open: 10 days before Easter - 30 September.

Directions

Lazise is on the southeast side of Lake Garda about 30 km. west of Verona. From north on Trento - Verona A22 autostrada take Affi exit then follow signs for Lazise and site. From south on A4 Brescia - Venice motorway, take Peschiera exit and site is 7 km. towards Lazise and Garda on SS249.
GPS: N45:29.606 E10:43.969

Charges guide

Per person	€ 5,30 - € 10,90
child (5-7 yrs)	free - € 7,20
pitch	€ 10,30 - € 29,10

Low season discount for pensioners.

IT63580 Camping Park Delle Rose

Strada San Gaetano 20, I-37017 Lazise (Lake Garda)

Tel: **045 647 1181**. Email: **info@campingparkdellerose.it** **www.alanrogers.com/IT63580**

An orderly, well designed site with a feeling of spaciousness, Delle Rose is on the east side of Lake Garda, three kilometers from the attractive waterside village of Peschiera. The 396 pitches are of average size, most with grass and shade and laid out in 30 short, terraced avenues. The ratio of recreational area to pitches is unusually high, particularly for sites at Lake Garda. Unusually, reception is located one third of the way into the site. On approach one sees the attractive restaurant, gardens and comprehensive sporting facilities including the pool complex with its stylish terraced bar and animation area close by. There is a large car park at the modern reception centre where many languages including English and Dutch are spoken. The well stocked grocery market, general store selling fresh vegetables, and the medical centre are centrally located. At the lake a small, curved sandy beach is contained by a low wall. The water's edge is pebbled and shallow, but a long jetty extends into the water with a ladder giving easy access to deeper water. Boat launching is at the narrow end of the beach where there is a small beach bar. Ample boat and trailer parking is available behind the supermarket. Ideally designed for families, with sporting and recreational areas totally separate, leaving the pitch area as a peaceful zone.

Facilities

Five very clean, modern sanitary blocks with hot water. Private bathrooms for hire. Baby rooms. Facilities for disabled visitors. Washing machines. Motorcaravan service point. Bar/restaurant, takeaway and pool bar. Shops. New pool with flumes. Tennis. Archery. Minigolf. Play area and miniclub. Fishing (with permit). Beach. Entertainment (high season). Excursions. Dogs and motorbikes are not accepted. Off site: Peschiera 2 km. Golf 6 km.

Open: 4 April - 30 September.

Directions

From A4 Milan - Venice take exit for Perschiera, west of Verona. Travel north towards Lazise. Site is on the southeastern lakeside 2.5 km. north of Peschiera and well signed. GPS: N45:28.980 E10:43.910

Charges guide

Per person	€ 4,50 - € 8,50
pitch	€ 8,50 - € 16,00

See advertisement on pages 268-269

COMPANY WITH ENVIRONMENTAL MANAGEMENT SYSTEM CERTIFIED BY DNV
ISO 14001
COMPANY WITH QUALITY SYSTEM CERTIFIED BY DNV
ISO 9002
The Camping No. of Lake Garda!
Your front line seat on Lake Garda!
CAMPING LA QUERCIA, YOUR HOLIDAY FILM
Shady emplacements – Heated toilet bloks for both grown-up's and children – 24 hours Warm water – Restaurant – Pizzeria – Cocktail Bar – Funny Bar on the beach – Swimmingpools with slides – Whirlpool – Full-comfort maxicaravans and bungalows for 4-5 persons with sight on the lake – The widest sand beach on the lake – Theatre – Supermarket – Butcher's shop – Pastry- and bakers shop – Typical products of the lake – Fresh fruit and vegetables every days – Tobacconist's shop – International newspaper kiosk – Rent a car service – Fax service – Professional animators – Animation for children and teenagers – Tennis – Canoe – Archery – Surfing – Judo – Football – Fitness gym – Spinning – Horse-riding.
6500 SQUARE METRES OF CLEAN AND SAFE PRIVATE BEACH, JUST A FEW METRES AWAY FROM ALL THE AMENITIES.
900 SHADY SPOTS IN BEAUTIFULLY-TENDED GROUNDS.
18 AREAS WITH FACILITIES FOR SPORTS AND LEISURE ACTIVITIES.
CAMPING ★★★★ LA QUERCIA
... more than a camping!
Information and booking:
+ 39.045.6470577
laquercia@laquercia.it
www.laquercia.it
LAZISE SUL GARDA • VERONA • ITALY

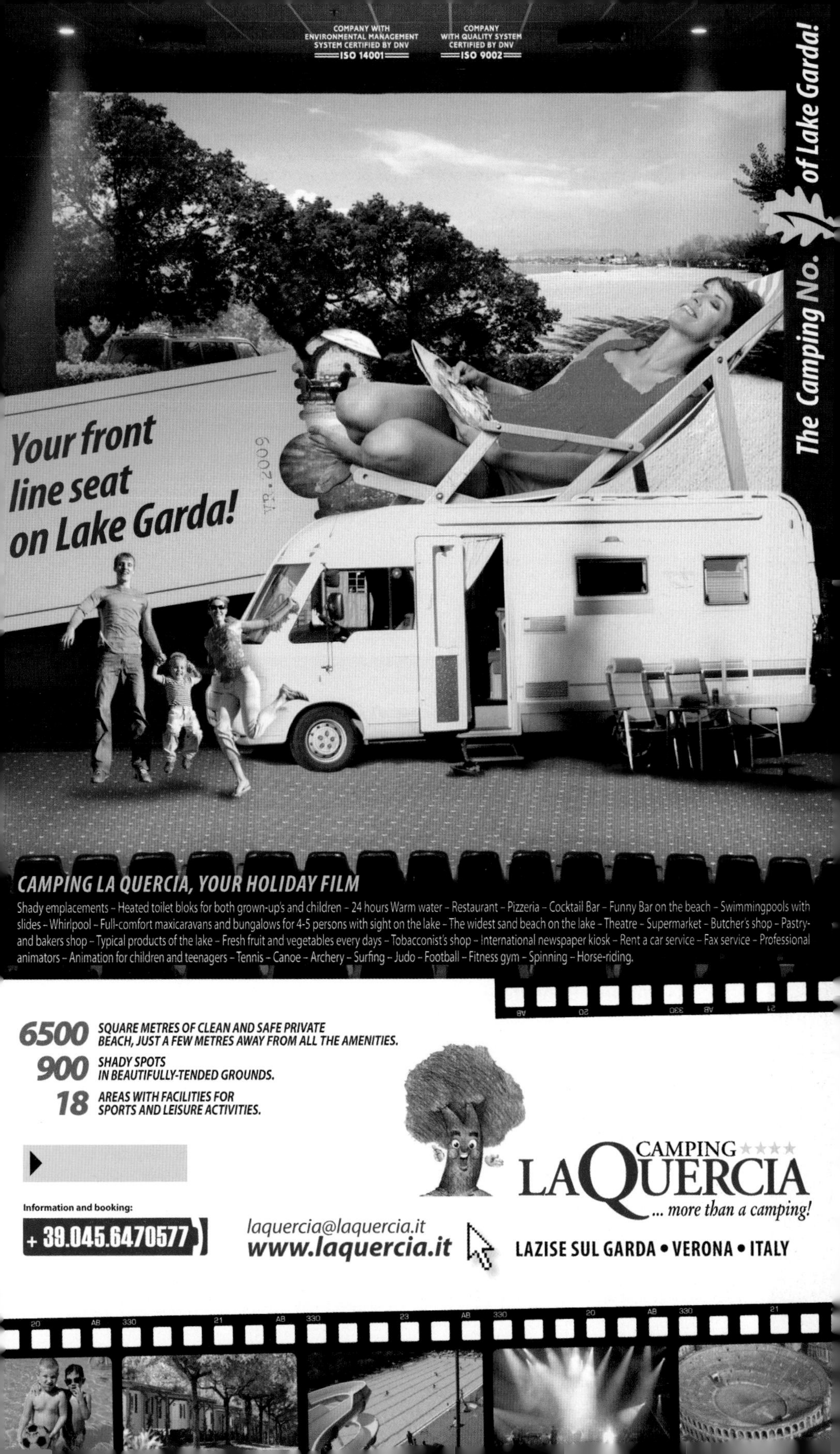

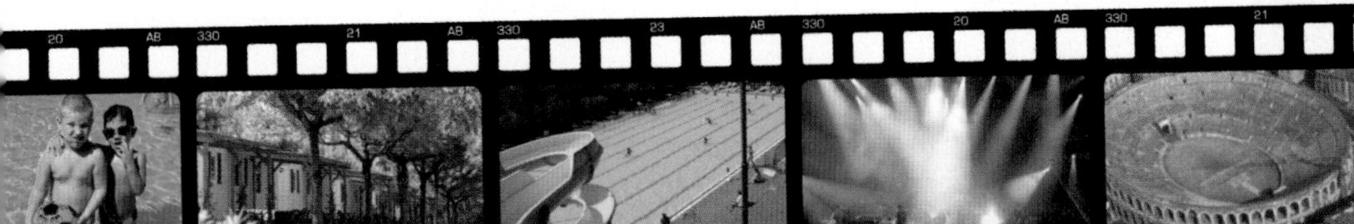

IT63600 La Rocca Camp

Localitá San Pietro, I-37011 Bardolino (Lake Garda)

Tel: **045 721 1111**. Email: **info@campinglarocca.com** **www.alanrogers.com/IT63600**

This site was one of the first to operate on the Lake and the family has a background of wine and olive oil production. La Rocca is in two areas, each side of the busy A249, the upper part being used mostly for bungalows, although some touring pitches are here and these have great lake views. The remaining touring pitches are on the lower part of the site, along with the main facilities. There is access between the two parts via a tunnel. The 450 pitches are mostly on terraces with shade, 6A electricity and access from narrow tarmac roads. The site is very popular with Dutch campers and all the guests seemed happy when we visited. It is a family site and, with the pools and direct access to the lake, provides a choice of watersports. The huge Gardaland theme park is close by (a free bus runs from the site gate). Many of the facilities have been renewed here and the owners are keen to please their guests. This site is not ideal for campers with mobility problems as there are large distances to cover to get to some facilities and the only access to the pool is by over 30 steps, but otherwise it is a pleasant place to spend time relaxing.

Facilities

Four toilet blocks with two on each side of the site. WCs are mixed British and Turkish style and showers are controllable. Facilities for disabled visitors but many steps to pool. Children's facilities and baby baths. Washing machines. New motorcaravan services. Shop and bakery. Restaurant, bar and takeaway with large terrace. Swimming and paddling pools (lifeguard). Sun terrace. Pool bar. Play area. Animation programme in season. Miniclub. Internet point. Bicycle hire. Games room. Watersports. Torches useful. Off site: Public transport at gate. Boat launching 200 m. Riding 8 km. ATM 1.5 km.

Open: 3 April - 5 October.

Directions

Site is on the east side of Lake Garda, on the lake ring road 249. From the A4 take Pescheria exit and the 249 north for Garda (there are many signs for Gardaland). Site is well signed approaching village of Bardolino. GPS: N45:33.830 E10:42.856

Charges guide

Per person	€ 4,90 - € 8,50
child (2-11 yrs)	free - € 6,50
pitch	€ 8,90 - € 18,80
dog	€ 2,60 - € 5,20

LA ROCCA CAMP
DIRECTLY ON THE LAKE
APARTMENTS
• DELUXE MAXICARAVANS
• SPORT AND ACTIVITIES FOR CHILDREN AND ADULTS
• INTERNET POINT
• KAYAK TOUR
I-37011 Bardolino (VR) - Tel. +39 045 7211111 - Fax +39 045 7211300
www.campinglarocca.com - info@campinglarocca.com

IT62555 Camping Belvedere

Via Belvedere, 9, I-37017 Lazise (Lake Garda)

Tel: **045 759 0228**. Email: **info@campingbelvedere.com** **www.alanrogers.com/IT62555**

Belvedere is a pleasant, family site located between Pacengo and Lazise at the south eastern corner of Lake Garda. There's a good selection of amenities here including a restaurant with an attractive terrace overlooking the lake. Other facilities include a swimming pool, supermarket and renovated toilet blocks. Pitches are of varying sizes and are grassy, with reasonable shade. This is a popular corner of the lake and Belvedere is just 200 m. from the Caneva water park, and also very close to Gardaland. A lively entertainment and activities programme is run during July and August.

Facilities

Bar. Restaurant. Snack bar. Supermarket. Swimming pool. Children's pool. Volleyball. Tennis. Play area. Direct access to lake and sandy beach. Mobile homes and chalets for rent. Entertainment and activity programme. Off site: Lazise with bars, shops and restaurants. Caneva water park 200 m. Gardaland theme park 3 km.

Open: 15 March - 5 October.

Directions

Leave the A4 (Milan - Venice) at the Castelnuovo del Garda exit. Head north on the SR450. Leave at Ca Isidoro and join the westbound SP5 to Lazise. Site is clearly signed. GPS: N45:28.771 E10:43.367

Charges guide

Per unit incl. 2 persons	€ 18,00 - € 31,50

See advertisement on pages 268-269

IT63570 Campings Cisano & San Vito

Via Peschiera 48, I-37010 Cisano di Bardolino (Lake Garda)

Tel: **045 622 9098**. Email: **cisano@camping-cisano.it** **www.alanrogers.com/IT63570**

This is a combination of two sites and some of the 700 pitches have superb locations along the 1 km. of shaded lakeside contained in Cisano. Some are on sloping ground and most are shaded but the San Vito pitches have no lake views. Both sites have a family orientation and considerable effort has been taken in the landscaping to provide maximum comfort even for the largest units. San Vito is the smaller and more peaceful location with no lakeside pitches and shares many of the facilities of Cisano which is a short walk across the road. Each site has its own reception. A reader reports that a 2 m. fence separating the pitches from the beach and lake has been constructed at Cisano, with several gates, but only two that open at the moment, at the extreme ends of the beach. The support facilities are constantly upgraded, although visitors with disabilities should select their pitch carefully (there are some slopes in Cisano). On the San Vito site there is a pleasant family style restaurant (some road noise) which also sells takeaway food. San Vito is accessed through a tunnel under the road. Excellent pools and play equipment, along with a children's club and entertainment in high season are all here. The friendly efficient staff speak English.

Facilities

Plentiful, good quality sanitary facilities are provided in both sites (9 blocks at Cisano and 2 at San Vito). Facilities for disabled visitors. Fridge hire. Shop. Bar. Restaurant. Swimming pool. Play area. Fishing and sailing. Free windsurfing and canoeing. Boat launching. Internet access. Dogs are not accepted (cats are). Motorcycles not allowed on site (parking provided). Off site: Indoor pool, bicycle hire and tennis 2 km. Riding 15 km. Golf 20 km.

Open: 1 April - 1 October.

Directions

Leave A4 autoroute at Pescheria exit and head north towards Garda on lakeside road. Pass Lazise and site is signed (small sign) on left halfway to Bardolina. Site is 12 km. beyond the Gardaland theme park. GPS: N45:31.374 E10:43.656

Charges guide

Per person	€ 4,00 - € 10,50
child	free - € 4,00
pitch	€ 9,00 - € 19,00

Camping Cheques accepted.

IT63010 Eurocamping Pacengo

Via Porto 13, I-37010 Pacengo di Lazise (Lake Garda)

Tel: **045 759 0012**. Email: **info@eurocampingpacengo.it** **www.alanrogers.com/IT63010**

Eurocamping is a large site at the southeast corner of Lake Garda, with direct lake access and with a pleasant beach. It is good site for launching boats as there is a little harbour/marina area adjoining the site. Expanded recently, it now includes an area of mobile homes. Most pitches, although quite small, are attractive with very good shade and all have electricity (4A). The new pool is popular and incorporates a jacuzzi. Although not the most manicured of sites, Eurocamping is a friendly, typically Italian site. It is equipped to a good standard, although there are some older bungalows on the site.

Facilities

The sanitary blocks, although quite old, have been refurbished and are kept clean. Well stocked supermarket. Bar, restaurant and pizzeria (closed Tuesday in low season). Swimming pools (15/5-22/9). Second bar at the poolside. Large play area. Tennis. Fishing. Boat launching. Organised entertainment (July/Aug). Off site: Theme parks within 1.5 km. Riding 2 km. Bicycle hire 5 km. Golf 7 km.

Open: 20 March - 22 September.

Directions

From north on A22 autostrada take Affi exit then follow signs for Lazise and site. From south on A4 (Brescia - Venice) take Peschiera exit and follow signs for Lazise. At traffic lights in Pacengo, turn towards lake for 500 m. GPS: N45:28.029 E10:42.980

Charges guide

Per unit incl. 2 persons	€ 14,80 - € 24,30

See advertisement on pages 268-269

IT62630 Camping Bella Italia

Via Bella Italia 2, I-37019 Peschiera del Garda (Lake Garda)

Tel: **045 640 0688**. Email: **bellaitalia@camping-bellaitalia.it** **www.alanrogers.com/IT62630**

Peschiera is a picturesque village on the southern shore of Lake Garda and Camping Bella Italia is an attractive, large, well organised and very busy site in the grounds of a former farm, just west from the centre of the village. Although over half of the 1,200 pitches are occupied by the site's own mobile homes and chalets and by tour operators, there are some 400 tourist pitches, most towards the lakeside and reasonably level on grass under trees. All have electricity (6A) and are separated by shrubs. There are some fine views across the lake to the mountains beyond. The pitches are grouped in regular rows on either side of hard access roads (which are named after European cities) and the wide central road which leads to the shops and pleasant restaurants. The site slopes gently down to the lake with access to the water for swimming and boating and to the lakeside public path. A feature of the site is the group of pools of varying shapes and sizes with an entertainment area and varied sports provision nearby. A range of supervised activities is organised. Regulations are in place to ensure a peaceful site particularly during the afternoon siesta and during the hours of darkness. English is spoken by the friendly management.

Facilities

Six modern toilet blocks have British style toilets, washbasins and showers. Baby rooms and facilities for disabled visitors. Washing machines. Motorcaravan services. Shops. Bars. Waiter service restaurant and terrace and two other restaurants (one in the old farm building). Swimming pools. Tennis. Archery. Playgrounds (small). Games room. Watersports. Bicycle hire. Organised activities. Internet access. Dogs are not accepted.
Off site: Fishing 1 km. Golf and riding 5 km. Gardaland, Italy's most popular theme park is about 2 km. east of Peschiera.

Open: 28 March - 11 October.

Directions

Peschiera is 32 km. west of Verona. From A4 take exit for Peschiera del Garda and follow SS11 towards Brescia. Site is at the large junction at the western entrance to the village. GPS: N45:26.499 E10:40.752

Charges 2009

Per person	€ 6,00 - € 12,50
child (3-5 yrs)	free - € 5,00
pitch	€ 13,00 - € 23,00

Four charging seasons.
No credit or debit cards.

Camping Cheques accepted.

IT62660 Camping Gasparina

Via Gasparina 13, I-37010 Cavalcaselle (Lake Garda)

Tel: **045 755 0775**. Email: **info@gasparina.com** **www.alanrogers.com/IT62660**

Gasparina is of average size for this area and of reasonable quality, but a little away from the towns around the lake. It is in a peaceful location and has the feeling of being in the countryside. As the site slopes gently towards the lake, levellers are needed in some parts. There are 363 grass touring pitches in back-to-back rows separated by gravel roads. Many trees and flowers adorn the site, with shade in most parts. The pleasant swimming pools are separated from the restaurant terraces by a neat, well clipped hedge. Just beyond the site fence is a beach and pleasant promenade. Boats can be launched here. Near reception are the supermarket and a bar/restaurant with three terraces and, when we visited, good prices.

Facilities

Two refurbished and one new toilet block have the usual facilities with warm water in two blocks. Facilities for disabled visitors. Washing machines and dryer. Shop. Bar/restaurant with terrace. Swimming pool. Playground. Tennis courts. Watersports. Entertainment in high season. Dogs and other pets are not accepted. Off site: Bicycle hire 2 km. Riding 3 km.

Open: 1 April - 1 September.

Directions

Leave A4 Milan - Venice motorway at exit for Peschiera, go north on east side of lake on SS249 towards Lazise for entrance road on your left. GPS: N45:27.323 E10:42.102

Charges guide

Per unit incl. 4 persons	€ 21,00 - € 39,00
extra person	€ 4,00 - € 6,00
boat trailer	€ 10,00 - € 18,00

IT62840 Camping Belvedere

Via Cavalle 5, I-25080 Manerba del Garda (Lake Garda)

Tel: **036 555 1175**. Email: **info@camping-belvedere.it** **www.alanrogers.com/IT62840**

Situated along a promontory reaching into Lake Garda, this friendly, traditional campsite has been landscaped with terracing to give many of the 85 touring pitches a good vantage point to enjoy the wonderful views. They are mainly on hardstanding and all have 6A electricity. From the top of the terrace a long ramp (or 56 steps) takes you to the lakeside area with access to the long pebbly beach for a relaxing swim and for boat launching. The delightful restaurant and bar with pretty flowers is under shady trees at the water's edge. The site has grass areas and attractive trees give many pitches a cool canopy. Italian villages with lots of atmosphere are close by as are the huge theme parks the area is known for. The landscaping and atmosphere are delightfully Mediterranean with charming Italian vistas. There are no facilities for disabled campers and really young children would require supervision as the terracing is unguarded in places.

Facilities

Five traditional sanitary blocks are well maintained and kept clean. Washing machine. Motorcaravan service point. Shop selling basics. Restaurant, bar and takeaway are all open most of the season. Play area. Tennis. Music and TV in bar. Fishing. Torches useful. Mobile homes to rent. Off site: Golf and bicycle hire 2 km. Riding 4 km. Watersports nearby. Bars and restaurant a short walk away. Theme parks.

Open: 4 April - 4 October.

Directions

Manerba is on western shore of Lake Garda at the southern end. From A4 Milan - Venice autostrada take Desenzano exit and head north on SS572 towards Salo for about 11 km. and look for site signs. Turn right off main road, then right again along Via Belvedere. GPS: N45:33.724 E10:33.789

Charges guide

Per unit incl. 2 persons and electricity	€ 15,50 - € 28,50
extra person	€ 3,75 - € 6,75
child (3-11 yrs)	€ 3,00 - € 5,40
dog	€ 2,00 - € 4,00

IT62860 Camping Baia Verde

Via del Edera 19, I-25080 Manerba del Garda (Lake Garda)
Tel: **036 565 1753**. Email: **info@campingbaiaverde.com** **www.alanrogers.com/IT62860**

Baia Verde is a new campsite located in the southwestern corner of Lake Garda. When we visited in late May 2007, construction was nearing completion and both the potential and the drawbacks were evident. The 69 touring pitches are in regular rows on flat, open ground where rough grass has been planted and young trees mark the corners of pitches; until these have grown there will be no shade. On the other hand, everything is being built to a very high standard and the restaurant block and the building housing all other facilities are in traditional style. All pitches are fully serviced and there are 12 'super' pitches with private facilities. Heated swimming and paddling pools are attractively designed and nearby is a play area and sports pitch. The bar and restaurant will be open all season, as will the pool complex. The lake is just two minutes' walk away; this is the quieter, less commercialised side of Lake Garda, but popular attractions such as the Gardaland theme park and Caneva water park are an easy drive away.

Facilities

Full range of high quality sanitary facilities in an impressive three storey building in the style of an Italian villa. Baby and children's rooms. Facilities for disabled visitors. Washing machines and dryers. Above will be a large TV lounge and on the roof is a sunbathing area with jacuzzi. An entertainment and activity programme in high season is planned. Bicycle hire. Off site: Manerba del Garda 1 km. Beach with fishing, swimming and boat launching 400 m. Golf and riding 2 km. Cycle and walking trails.

Open: 26 May - 15 September.

Directions

Manerba is on western shore of Lake Garda at the southern end. From A4 Milan - Venice autostrada take Desenzano exit and head north on SS572 towards Saló for about 12 km; then turn right following signs to site. GPS: N45:33.680 E10:33.208

Charges guide

Per unit incl. 2 persons and electricity	€ 22,00 - € 40,00
extra person	€ 4,50 - € 9,00
child (3-11 yrs)	€ 3,00 - € 7,50

OK. !

IT62800 Camping Villaggio Weekend

Via Vallone della Selva 2, I-25010 San Felice del Benaco (Lake Garda)

Tel: **036 543 712**. Email: **info@weekend.it** **www.alanrogers.com/IT62800**

Created among the olive groves and terraced vineyards of the Chateau Villa Louisa, which overlooks it, this modern well equipped site enjoys some superb views over the small bay which forms this part of Lake Garda. There are 230 pitches, all with electricity, of which about 30% are taken by tour operators and statics. The touring pitches are in several different areas, and many enjoy superb views. Some pitches for larger units are set in the upper terraces on steep slopes, manoeuvring can be challenging and low olive branches may cause problems for long or high units.

Facilities

Three sanitary blocks, one below the restaurant/shop, are modern and well maintained. Mainly British style WCs, a few washbasins in cabins and facilities for disabled people in one. Baby room. Laundry. Bar/restaurant (waiter service). Takeaway. Shop. Supervised swimming pool and paddling pool. Entertainment programme all season. TV. Barbecues. All facilities are open throughout the season. Two playgrounds. English spoken. Internet points. Off site: Fishing 2 km. Golf 6 km. Riding 8 km. Windsurfing, water skiing and tennis near.

Open: 19 April - 21 September.

Directions

Approach from Saló (easier when towing) and follow site signs. From Milano - Venezia autostrada take Desenzano exit towards Saló and Localita Cisano - San Felice. Watch for narrow right fork after Cunettone roundabout. Pass petrol station on left, then turn right towards San Felice for 1 km. Site is next left. GPS: N45:35.591 E10:31.853

Charges guide

Per person	€ 5,75 - € 9,50
pitch incl. electricity	€ 15,00 - € 31,00

Camping Cheques accepted.

IT63590 Camping Serenella

Localitá Mezzariva 19, I-37011 Bardolino (Lake Garda)

Tel: **045 721 1333**. Email: **serenella@camping-serenella.it** **www.alanrogers.com/IT63590**

Situated alongside Lake Garda, Serenella has 300 average size pitches, some with good lake views. Movement around the site may prove difficult for large units (look for the wider roads). The pitches are shaded and have 3A electricity. A long promenade with brilliant views of the mountains and lake runs the length of the campsite. It is dotted with grassy relaxation areas and beach bars where snacks are served and the atmosphere is charming. The pleasant pool complex is near an older style 'taverna' where delicious, sensibly priced food is served. There is some road noise at some of the amenities and the pool. There is an entertainment programme from May to September, a small market and a variety of tiny bungalows throughout the site. Serenella is popular with Italians and international guests.

Facilities

Five clean, well equipped sanitary blocks, include three that are more modern with laundry facilities. British style toilets, free hot water throughout. Facilities for disabled visitors. Laundry facilities. Freezer. Bar/restaurant, takeaway and shop. Watersports. Entertainment programme for all in high season. Play area. Bicycle hire. Boat launching. Minigolf. Tennis. Satellite TV. Internet and WiFi. Dogs are not accepted. Motorcyles are not allowed. Off site: Beach with fishing and watersports. Golf 3 km. Riding 3.5 km. Town 3 km. Gardaland. Verona 35 km.

Open: 28 March - 18 October.

Directions

From E70 Milan - Venice autostrada take Pescheria exit and follow signs to Bardolino. Site is on lakeside between Bardolino and Garda, about 4 km. south of Garda. GPS: N45:33.563 E10:42.994

Charges guide

Per person	€ 4,00 - € 9,00
child (4-10 yrs)	free - € 4,00
pitch	€ 9,50 - € 17,00

IT60050 Villaggio Turistico Camping Europa

Via Monfalcone 12, I-34073 Grado (Friuli - Venézia Giúlia)

Tel: **043 180 877**. Email: **info@villaggioeuropa.com** **www.alanrogers.com/IT60050**

This large flat, good quality site is beside the sea and has 500 pitches, with 400 for touring units. They are all neat, clean and marked, most with shade and 6/10A electricity, 180 are fully serviced. The terrain is undulating and sandy in the areas nearer the sea, where cars have to be left in parking places. An impressive, large new Aquatic Park covers 1,500 sq.m. with two slides (100 m. and 60 m. long and many other features. With many shallow areas it is very popular with children and there are lifeguards. A new pool bar is an attractive feature. There is direct access to the beach. The water recedes up to 200 m. from the beach, but leaves a natural paddling pool which is enjoyed by children when it is hot. A narrow wooden jetty gives access to deeper water. This is a neat, well managed site which is probably the best in the area.

Facilities

Five excellent, refurbished toilet blocks are well designed and very clean. Free hot water in all facilities, mostly British style WCs and excellent facilities for disabled people. Baby showers and baths. Washing machines. Motorcaravan services. Large supermarket, small general shop (all season). Large bar and restaurant with takeaway (all season). Swimming pools (1/5-20/9). Tennis. Fishing. Bicycle hire. Playground. Full entertainment programme in season. Internet access. Off site: Golf 500 m. Riding 10 km.

Open: 25 April - 27 September.

Directions

Site is 4 km. east of Grado on road to Monfalcone. Take the 35L road to Grado from west, continue through town to Grado Pineta on the beach road. Site is 2 km. GPS: N45:41.789 E13:27.357

Charges 2009

Per unit incl. 2 persons and electricity	€ 19,00 - € 42,00
extra person	€ 5,50 - € 10,50
child (12-16 yrs)	€ 3,50 - € 9,50
child (3-11 yrs)	€ 3,00 - € 7,00
dog	€ 3,00 - € 6,00

Less 10% for longer stays out of season.

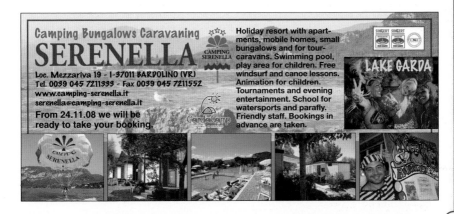

IT60080 Camping Sabbiadoro

Via Sabbiadoro 8, I-33054 Lignano Sabbiadoro (Friuli - Venézia Giúlia)

Tel: **043 171 455**. Email: **campsab@lignano.it** **www.alanrogers.com/IT60080**

Sabbiadoro is a large, good quality site in two parts with separate entrances and efficient receptions. It has 1,215 pitches and is ideal for families who like all their amenities to be close by. This does mean that the site is busy and noisy with people having fun. Quite tightly packed, the pitches vary in size, are shaded by attractive trees and have electricity, TV and internet connections. You may wish to cover your car and unit to prevent sap covering it over time. The facilities are all in excellent condition and well thought out, especially the pool complex, and everything here is very modern, safe and clean. Open in high season, the smaller and quieter part of the site with entrance from Viale Central, is only a few metres away from the main site entrance in Via Sabbiadoro. This has four new sanitary blocks, 41 fixed pitches for touring units, an area for tents and a section of mobile homes to rent. The site's private beach (with 24 hour guard) is only 250 m. away. Shopping and nightlife can be found in the town of Sabbiadoro itself, more so in Pineta about 1.5 km. away.

Facilities

Well equipped sanitary facilities with free showers includes superb facilities for disabled visitors. Washing machines and dryers. Motorcaravan service point. Huge supermarket (all season). Bazaar. Good restaurant, snack bar and takeaway (15/5-28/9). Heated outdoor pool complex with separate fun pool area, slides and fountains (all season). Heated indoor children's pool. Disco. TV room. Internet. Play areas. Tennis. Fitness centre. Boat launching. Entertainment in the main season.

Open: 15 March - 28 September.

Directions

Leave A4 at Latisana exit, west of Trieste. From Latisana follow road to Lignano, then Sabbiadoro. Site is well signed as you approach the town. GPS: N45:40.919 E13:07.546

Charges guide

Per person	€ 4,80 - € 9,00
child (3-12 yrs)	€ 3,00 - € 5,00
pitch	€ 7,20 - € 14,50
incl. electricity	€ 8,20 - € 15,50

IT60020 Camping Aquileia

Via Gemina,10, I-33051 Aquileia (Friuli - Venézia Giúlia)

Tel: **043 191 042**. Email: **info@campingaquileia.it** **www.alanrogers.com/IT60020**

Situated in former parkland under mature trees, Camping Aquileia, with 121 level and grass touring pitches, is a quiet site 10 km. away from the bustling coastal beaches. The pitches all with 4/6A electricity are separated from the entrance, pool and play areas by tall hedges and the more peaceful part of the site with the newer sanitary block is at the rear of the site. The now small town of Aquileia, founded in 181 BC, became one of the most important Roman military and trading posts and is now a UNESCO world heritage site. In the basilica, only a short walk from the campsite, along the former harbour, lays one of the world's most magnificent mosaics. From reception tours can be organised with the town's tourist office to the regions archaeological sites.

Facilities

Two sanitary blocks with free hot water, controllable showers and washbasins in cabins. Facilities for disabled people. Laundry facilities. Motorcaravan service point. Restaurant, bar and automat for drinks and ice cream. Large playing field with playground. Swimming and paddling pools. Bicycle hire. Mobile homes and chalets for rent. Off site: Supermarket. Riding 12 km. The historic towns of Trieste, Gorizia and the beach resort of Grado.

Open: 25 April - 15 September.

Directions

From the A4 (Venice - Trieste) take exit for Palmanova and travel south for 20 km. towards Grado. Just after entering Aquileia turn left at traffic lights, signed Trieste and Goriza and site is 400 m. on the right. GPS: N45:46.551 E13:22.250

Charges guide

Per person	€ 5,00 - € 7,00
child (3-12 yrs)	€ 3,00 - € 4,70
pitch incl. electricity	€ 8,00 - € 21,00

IT61990 Camping Corones

I-39030 Rasen (Trentino - Alto Adige)

Tel: **047 449 6490**. Email: **info@corones.com** **www.alanrogers.com/IT61990**

Situated in a pine forest clearing at the foot of the attractive Antholz valley in the heart of German-speaking Südtirol, Corones is ideally situated both for winter sports enthusiasts and for walkers, cyclists, mountain bikers and those who prefer to explore the valleys and mountain roads of the Dolomites by car. There are 135 level pitches, all with electricity (16A) and many also with water and drainage and satellite TV. The Residence offers luxury appartments and there are authentic Canadian log cabins for hire. The bar/restaurant and small shop are open all season. From the site you can see slopes which in winter become highly rated ski pistes. A short drive up the broad Antholz/Anterselva valley takes you to an internationally important Biathlon Centre. A not-so-young British couple who were on site when we visited had just driven up the valley and over the pass into Austria and then back via another pass. Back on site, a small pool and paddling pool could be very welcome. There is a regular programme of free excursions and occasional evening events are organised. Children's entertainment is provided in July and August.

Facilities

The central toilet block is traditional but well maintained and clean. Additional facilities below the Residence are of the highest quality including individual shower rooms with washbasins, washbasins with all WCs, a delightful children's unit and an excellent facility for disabled visitors. Fully equipped private shower rooms for hire. Luxurious Wellness Centre with saunas, solarium, jacuzzis, massage, therapy pools and heat benches. Heated outdoor swimming and paddling pools (4/5-20/10). Play area. Internet facilities. Off site: Tennis 800 m. Bicycle hire 1 km. Riding and fishing 3 km. Golf (9 holes) 10 km. Canoeing/kayaking 15 km.

Open: 6 December - 30 March, 4 May - 31 October.

Directions

Rasen/Rasun is 85 km. northeast of Bolzano. From Bressanone/Brixen exit on A22 Brenner - Modena motorway, go east on SS49 for 50 km. then turn north (signed Razen/Antholz). Turn immediately west at roundabout in Niederrasen/Rasun di Sotto to site on left in 100 m. GPS: N46:46.551 E12:02.231

Charges guide

Per unit incl. 2 persons and electricity	€ 18,50 - € 26,70
extra person	€ 4,50 - € 7,30
child (3-15 yrs)	€ 3,00 - € 5,90

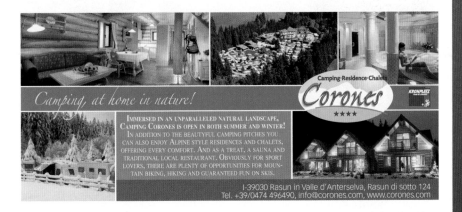

IT60065 Camping Tenuta Primero

Via Monfalcone, 14, I-34073 Grado (Friuli - Venézia Giúlia)
Tel: **043 189 6901**. Email: **info@tenuta-primero.com** **www.alanrogers.com/IT60065**

Tenuta Primero was established in 1962 and has been a popular family site ever since. The third generation of the Marzola family continue to run the site and have made many improvements over the years. This is a large site with its own private beach and 800 pitches of varying sizes, including some new, large 'executive' pitches, with beach front locations, 10A electricity and a private water supply. Nine toilet blocks are dispersed around the site, some equipped with facilities for disabled visitors. There are no fewer than three restaurants here (including a pizzeria and a fish restaurant) and two bars, as well as a separate disco. Alongside the campsite is a large private marina with moorings for over 200 boats and a maintenance area. Tenuta Primero also comprises an 18-hole championship golf course and a 9-hole executive course. Special rates are available for campers. Grado is a fascinating resort 5 km. distant. The old town predates Venice and has a similar appeal.

Facilities

Supermarket. Bars and restaurants. Pizzeria. Swimming and paddling pools. Disco. Beauty salon. Aerobics and aquagym. Windsurfing and sailing lessons. Play area. Sports pitches. Bicycle hire. Entertainment and activity programme. Children's activities. Direct access to beach. Mobile homes and chalets for rent. Off site: Campsite harbour. Two golf courses. Cycle track to Grado. Shops, restaurants and bars in Grado. Riding 2 km.

Open: 1 April - 4 October.

Directions

Take the Palmanova exit from the A4 autostrada and drive to Grado on the SS352 passing through Aquileia and Cervignano. Continue towards Monfalcone on the SP19 and the site can be found on the right after 5 km.
GPS: N45:42.306 E13:27.845

Charges guide

Per person	€ 5,00 - € 11,00
child (3-11 yrs)	free - € 7,00
child (12-15 yrs)	€ 4,00 - € 9,00
pitch incl. electricity	€ 9,00 - € 24,00

IT62070 Camping Residence Sägemühle

Dornweg 12, I-39026 Prad am Stilfserjoch (Trentino - Alto Adige)

Tel: **047 361 6078**. Email: **info@campingsaegemuehle.com** **www.alanrogers.com/IT62070**

This small site in the countryside is alongside a little village and has attractive views of the surrounding mountains where skiing is popular in the winter. The grass pitches are neat and level, some have shade and most have water, electricity, drainage and pretty views. For a tiny campsite there is a lot on offer here. The indoor pool area is welcoming to cool oneself in the summer and relax in warm water after skiing in winter. Cleverly placed under the pool, the amenities include a tiny gymnasium, sauna and a TV/games room. The steps may prove difficult for those with mobility problems, although the facilities for disabled visitors are on ground level. Animation is provided in July and August and shared with a sister site. We visited in high summer season but the area is a renowned winter sports area. The friendly owners speak some English and Dutch.

Facilities

The main modern toilet block is under the pool complex. All WCs are British style and the showers are of high quality. A new sanitaire building has 24 private cabins for hire. Facilities for disabled visitors. Children's facilities and baby baths, plus a new second play area. Washing machines. Restaurant and bar. Indoor swimming pool. Spa and sauna. Entertainment programme in season. Miniclub. Play area. Internet. Torches useful. Off site: Town facilities. Natural spring for paddling close by. Bicycle hire 300 m. Riding 800 m. Golf 30 km.

Open: All year excl. 7 November - 19 December.

Directions

Site is west of Bolzano. From A38/S40 west of Bolzano, take exit for Pso dello Stelvio/Stilfserjoch (also marked S38) and village of Prad am Stilfserioch. Site is well signed from here.
GPS: N46:37.016 E10:35.467

Charges guide

Per person	€ 8,50 - € 9,50
child (11-15 yrs)	€ 6,20 - € 7,50
child (2-10 yrs)	€ 5,20 - € 5,90
pitch	€ 10,50 - € 12,00
electricity	€ 2,50

IT62090 Camping Vidor – Family & Wellness Resort

Strada de Ruf de Ruacia 19, I-38036 Pozza di Fassa (Trentino - Alto Adige)

Tel: **0462 760022**. Email: **info@campingvidor.it** **www.alanrogers.com/IT62090**

This family run site is in a natural setting 2 km. from the town of Pozza. Vidor has had some major upgrading in 2008 with a new building housing reception, a camping shop, restaurant and pizzeria, café with terrace and lounge, indoor heated swimming pool, beauty and wellness centres, fitness room, baby club, indoor playrooms, cinema and conference room, TV room and internet corner. Pitches are of average size with 1-6A electricity for standard pitches (all with water and waste water) and up to 16A for fully serviced pitches (with hardstanding). Chocks are advisable. The local area is excellent for hiking in summer and skiing in winter. This augments the existing excellent sanitary facilities. A hundred metres from the site a large restaurant serves local cuisine.

Facilities

Two excellent hotel standard sanitary blocks provide hot water throughout and good showers with private bathrooms for hire. British style toilets. Facilities for disabled visitors. Washing machines, drying room and dryer. Bar/restaurant, takeaway and shop, wellness, heated indoor pool (with whirlpool etc). WiFi over whole site. Animation programme. Off site: Town 2 km. with usual facilities. Fishing 500 m. Ski lift 1 km. Golf 8 km.

Open: All year except November.

Directions

From A22 Trento - Bolzano road take S48 to Pozza di Fassa. Take the road south to Meida and Valle S Nicola. Cross the bridge and site is well signed in 2 km. GPS: N46:25.230 E11:42.480

Charges guide

Per person	€ 6,50 - € 8,50
pitch	€ 7,50 - € 15,00

Camping Cheques accepted.

IT62080 Camping Gamp

Via Gries 10, I-39043 Chiusa (Trentino - Alto Adige)

Tel: **047 284 7425**. Email: **info@camping-gamp.com** **www.alanrogers.com/IT62080**

This is a little gem of a site in every respect but one. It is situated in the picturesque Isarco valley in the mountainous, Südtirol region of northern Italy. Across the valley from the site is a tree clad hill rising to a cliff, topped by a picturesque convent. There are 80 fully serviced pitches including TV and internet connections. It is ideally located for a stopover on the A22 Brenner - Modena motorway, and therein lies its one drawback: the motorway passes above the site on a viaduct and there is inevitably a steady rumble of noise; more noticeable is the rattle of trains passing below the site. This aside, it is an ideal base from which to explore the mountains and valleys of this atttractive region. There are numerous way-marked tracks to delight walkers and mountainbikers. Back on site the amenities are modern and equipped to a high standard. Above the pitches is an associated Gasthof with a pleasant bar and terrace plus a restaurant with an interesting menu. Here also is a small, but unfenced pool and adjacent children's play area. Camping Gamp is open all year and is well located for winter sports holidays.

Facilities

Modern toilet block with excellent facilities, including controllable showers, baby room, and special children's washbasins. Hot water to dishwashing and laundry sinks. Motorcaravan overnight area with service point. Restaurant with takeaway, shop (April - Oct). Bar (closed Jan/Feb). Music and dancing. Off site: Bicycle hire 300 m. Fishing 1 km. Riding 5 km. Golf and skiing 12 km.

Open: All year.

Directions

Klausen/Chiusa is 40 km. northeast of Bolzano. Camping Gamp is only 800 m. away from the A22 motorway (Brenner - Verona). Take exit for Klausen/Grödental, turn left and then right in 700 m. Site is well signed. GPS: N46:38.478 E11:34.406

Charges guide

Per person	€ 5,50 - € 7,00
child (10-14 yrs)	€ 4,30 - € 4,90
child ((3-9 yrs)	€ 2,70 - € 3,90
pitch	€ 10,50 - € 14,00

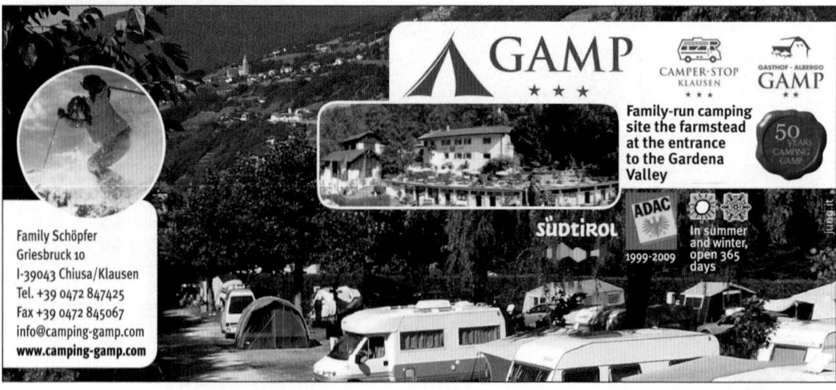

IT62100 Camping Steiner

Kennedy Straße 32, I-39055 Laives (Bolzano) (Trentino - Alto Adige)

Tel: **047 195 0105**. Email: **info@campingsteiner.com** **www.alanrogers.com/IT62100**

Camping Steiner is very central for touring with the whole of the Dolomite region within easy reach. It has its share of overnight trade but, with much on-site activity, one could spend an enjoyable holiday here, especially now the SS12 by which it stands has a motorway alternative. The 200 individual touring pitches, mostly with good shade and hardstanding, are in rows with easy access and all have electricity (6A). There are also 30 chalets available to rent. There is a family style pizzeria/restaurant, and indoor and outdoor pools. This friendly, family run site has a long tradition of providing a happy camping experience in the more traditional style – the owner remembers Alan Rogers who stayed here on many occasions. We met a British couple during our visit who had only intended to stay for one night but decided to stay for one week as it is so easy to get to different parts of the Dolomites and ideal for walking.

Facilities

The two sanitary blocks are equipped to a high standard, one having been completely refurbished. They can be heated in cool weather. Shop. Bar/pizzeria/restaurant with takeaway service, (April - Oct). Cellar bar with taped music, dancing at times. Outdoor pool (April - Oct, heated in spring), with paddling pool, and a smaller covered heated pool (all season, except July/Aug). Playground. Bicycle hire. Dogs are not accepted in July/Aug. Off site: Fishing 2 km. Riding 12 km. Golf 28 km.

Open: 1 April - 8 November.

Directions

Site is by the SS12 on northern edge of Leifers, 8 km. south of Bolzano. If approaching from north, at the Bolzano-Süd exit from A22 Brenner - Modena motorway follow Trento signs for 7 km. From the south on motorway take Ora exit, then north on SS12 towards Bolzano for 14 km. GPS: N46:25.773 E11:20.628

Charges guide

Per person	€ 5,00 - € 7,00
child (0-9 yrs)	€ 3,00 - € 5,00
pitch incl. 6A electricity	€ 12,00 - € 14,00

IT62085 Camping Sass Dlacia

Localitá Sciarè 11, I-39055 Saint Kassian (Trentino - Alto Adige)

Tel: **0471 849 527**. Email: **info@campingsassdlacia.it** **www.alanrogers.com/IT62085**

Sass Dlacia is located amid the beautiful mountain scenery of the northern Dolomites, west of Cortina. Pitches here are grassy and of a reasonable size with superb mountain views on all sides. All have electrical connections (6/10A). A number of apartments are available for rent. The site is open all year and is popular for both summer and winter holidays, offering a ski hire service to guests in the winter. On site amenities include a well stocked shop and a smart bar/restaurant specializing in local cuisine and incorporating a pizzeria, with pizzas cooked on a traditional log stove. A wealth of activities is on offer in the area, including mountain biking, hiking and rock climbing. The site's friendly owners will be pleased to recommend routes and activity ideas. Cortina d'Ampezzo is around 30 km. distant and is well known for its designer shops and elegant hotels.

Facilities

Bar and restaurant/pizzeria. Shop. Play area. Tourist information. Appartments for rent. Off site: Nearby resort of San Cassiano. Walking and cycle routes. Rock climbing. Fishing. Cortina d'Ampezzo resort 27 km.

Open: All year.

Directions

Leave A22 at Bressanone exit and head east on the SS49 to Casteldarne and then south on SS244 and SP37 to San Cassiano, via San Martino, Badia and La Villa. Site is signed. GPS: N46:33.255 E11:58.195

Charges 2009

Per unit incl. 2 persons	€ 17,50 - € 36,00
extra person	€ 5,00 - € 7,00

IT62040 Camping Seiser Alm

Saint Konstantin 16, I-39050 Völs am Schlern (Trentino - Alto Adige)

Tel: **047 170 6459**. Email: **info@camping-seiseralm.com** **www.alanrogers.com/IT62040**

What an amazing experience awaits you at Seiser Alm! Elisabeth and Erhard Mahlknecht have created a superb site in the magnificent Sudtirol region of the Dolomite mountains. Catering for families and delightfully peaceful, towering peaks provide a magnificent backdrop when you dine in the charming, traditional style restaurant on the upper terrace. The 150 touring pitches are of a very high standard with 16A electricity supply, 120 with gas, water, drainage and TV connections. Guests were delighted with the site when we visited, many coming to walk or cycle, some just to enjoy the surroundings. There are countless things to see and do here. Enjoy the grand 18-hole golf course alongside the site or join the plethora of excursions and activities. Buses and cable cars provide an excellent service for summer visitors and skiers alike. In keeping with the natural setting, the majority of the luxury facilities are set into the hillside. Elisabeth's designs incorporating Grimm fairy tales are tastefully developed in the superb children's bathrooms that are in a magic forest setting. For quiet, quality camping in a crystal clean environment, visit this immaculate site.

Facilities

One luxury underground block is in the centre of the site. 16 private units are available. Excellent facilities for disabled visitors. Fairy tale facilities for children. Infra red sensors, underfloor heating and gently curved floors to prevent slippery surfaces. Constant fresh air ventilation. Washing machines and large drying room. Sauna. Supermarket. Quality restaurant and bar with terrace. Entertainment. Miniclub. Children's adventure park and play room. Rooms for ski equipment. Torches useful. Off site: Riding alongside site. Golf 18-hole course (discounts) 1 km. Fishing 1 km. Bicycle hire 2 km. Lake swimming 2 km. ATM 3 km. Walks. Skiing in winter.

Open: All year excl. 5 November - 20 December.

Directions

From A22-E45 take Bolzano Nord exit. Take road for Prato Isarco/Blumau, then road for Fie/Vols. Take care as the split in the road is sudden and if you miss the left fork as you enter a tunnel (Altopiano dello Sciliar/Schlerngebiet) you will pay a heavy price in extra kilometres. Enjoy the climb to Vols am Schlern and site is well signed. GPS: N46:32.006 E11:32.001

Charges 2009

Per person	€ 6,00 - € 8,50
child (2-15 yrs)	€ 3,40 - € 6,80
pitch	€ 3,00 - € 11,00
electricity (per kWh)	€ 0,60

Camping Cheques accepted.

CAMPING
Seiser Alm
DOLOMITEN
The flair of the Dolomites all year round!
www.berge.at
ADAC Auszeichnung
CAMPING SEISER ALM
I-39050 VÖLS am Schlern, St. Konstantin 16 (BZ)
Tel. 0039 0471 706459 · Fax 0039 0471 707382
info@camping-seiseralm.com · www.camping-seiseralm.com

IT62120 Camping Latsch an der Etsch

Reichstraße 4, I-39021 Laces-Latsch (Trentino - Alto Adige)

Tel: **047 362 3217**. Email: **info@camping-latsch.com** **www.alanrogers.com/IT62120**

Gasthof Camping Latsch is 640 m. above sea level between main road and the river, with splendid views across to the surrounding mountains. About 20 of the 100 touring pitches are on a terrace by reception with the remainder on a lower terrace alongside the river. They are in regular rows which are separated by hedges with thin grass on gravel. All have electricity and 47 also have water, drainage and TV points. Trees provide shade to some parts. A large underground car park protects vehicles from winter snow and summer sun and, if used, gives a reduction in pitch charges. Another interesting feature is a water wheel which provides 3 kW. of power and this is supplemented by solar heating. Although right by a main road, the Gasthof and terracing screen out most of the road noise. Mountain walkers will be in their element and chairlifts give access to higher slopes. Interesting drives can be made over nearby passes with Merano, Bolzano, the Dolomites and the duty-free town of Livigno within range. Friendly staff speak excellent English.

Facilities

The traditional but well maintained sanitary block is on two floors, has all the usual facilities and is heated in cool weather. Excellent private bathrooms for hire. No facilities for disabled visitors. Washing machine and dryer. Motorcaravan service point. Shop, bar and pleasant restaurant. Small heated indoor pool, sauna, solarium and fitness room. Larger outdoor pool. Playground. Off site: Bicycle hire 1 km. Riding 7 km. Skiing 6 km.

Open: 6 December - 9 November.

Directions

Latsch/Laces is 28 km. west of Merano on the SS38 Bolzano - Silandro road. Site entrance is by the Hotel Vermoi (keep on main road, don't turn off to the village). GPS: N46:37.337 E10:51.870

Charges guide

Per person	€ 6,60 - € 7,60
child (3-12 yrs)	€ 5,60 - € 6,60
pitch incl. electricity	€ 13,70 - € 16,30

Reduction on pitch fee if underground car park used.

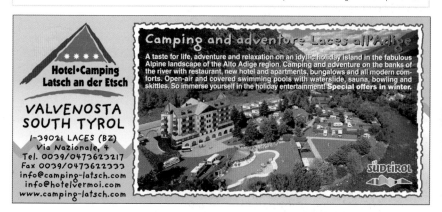

IT62260 Camping Punta Lago

Via Lungo Lago 42, I-38050 Calceranica al Lago (Trentino - Alto Adige)

Tel: **046 172 3229**. Email: **info@campingpuntalago.com** **www.alanrogers.com/IT62260**

There is something quite delightful about the smaller Italian lakes. Lago di Caldonazzo is in a beautiful setting about 2 km. from the historic village of Calceranica which has summer markets. This well designed site has 140 level, shaded pitches on grass. Of a good size, all have electricity and 50 are serviced with water and drainage. A small road separates the site from the grass banks of the lake where all kinds of non-motorised watersports can be enjoyed. There are excellent restaurants within 50 m. of the gate. The site itself has a large snack bar with wonderful views of the lake and the most amazing ice cream and fruit concoctions. The campsite first opened 45 years ago and brothers Gino and Mauro continue the friendly family tradition of ensuring you enjoy your holiday.

Facilities

One central sanitary block has superb facilities with hot water throughout. Well designed washbasin area. Excellent facilities for disabled campers and babies. Private units for rent, some with massage baths. Washing machines and dryer. Freezer. Shop. Bar/snack bar. Fishing (with permit). Modern comprehensive play area. Internet access. Cinema. TV. Off site: Town 1 km. and ATM. Watersports. Bicycle hire 1 km. Riding 3 km. Golf 20 km.

Open: 1 May - 15 September.

Directions

From A22 Bolzano - Trento autostrada take the SS47 towards Padova and then turn for Lago di Caldonazzo. Approaching town from the west continue along Via Donegani, turn left into Via al Lago and right at lake into Via Lungolago. Site is on the right. GPS: N46:00.138 E11:15.270

Charges guide

Per person	€ 6,50 - € 9,00
pitch incl. electricity	€ 10,00 - € 16,00

IT62320 Camping Al Sole

Via Maffei 127, I-38060 Molina di Ledro (Trentino - Alto Adige)

Tel: **046 450 8496**. Email: **info@campingalsole.it** **www.alanrogers.com/IT62320**

Lake Ledro is only 9 km. from Lake Garda, its sparkling waters and breathtaking scenery offering a low key alternative for those who enjoy a natural setting. The drive from Lake Garda is a real pleasure and prepares you for the treat ahead. This site has been owned by the same friendly family for over 40 years and their experience shows in the layout of the site with its mature trees and the array of facilities provided. Situated on the lake with its own sandy beach, pool and play area, the facilities include an outstanding 'wellness' centre. The 'Chiva Som' provides a whirlpool, solarium, beauty therapies, aromatic showers and massage room. The sauna has panoramic views over the lake and mountains and there is a heated outdoor spa pool where one can relax under the stars at night. We are told this is a brilliant experience in the summer and even more spectacular when there is snow! Fully serviced pitches were also added. This is a very pleasant, peaceful site for extended stays or sightseeing. The local community welcomes tourists and offers free hiking programmes beginning with a Monday evening information night so that you can choose appropriate guided walks.

Facilities

Superb toilet block with well appointed facilities. Five private bathrooms. Excellent facilities for disabled people. Baby room. Laundry facilities. Freezer. Motorcaravan services. Small supermarket. Restaurant and pizzeria. Bar and takeaway. Sun decks and snack bar at the lake. 'Chiva Som' wellness centre. Swimming pool. Play area. Bicycle hire. Entertainment in July/Aug. Children's club.

Open: Easter - 8 October.

Directions

From autostrada A22 exit for Lake Garda North to Riba del Garda. In Riva follow sign for Ledro valley. Site is well signed as you approach Lago di Ledra. GPS: N45:52.683 E10:46.064

Charges guide

Per person	€ 6,00 - € 9,00
child (2-11 yrs)	€ 4,50 - € 6,00
pitch incl. electricity	€ 8,00 - € 16,50

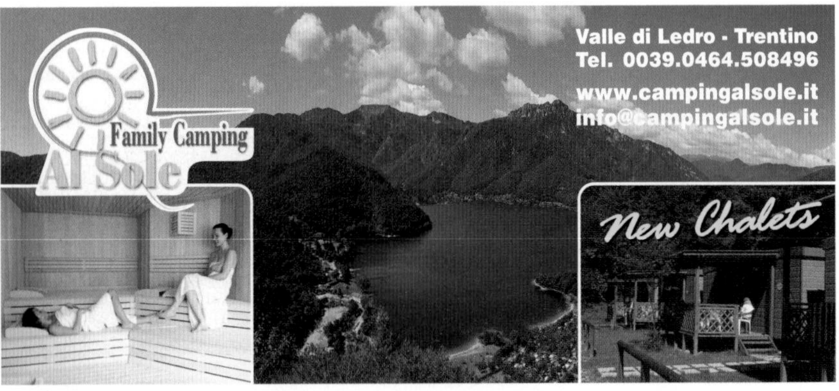

Family Camping
Al Sole
Valle di Ledro - Trentino
Tel. 0039.0464.508496
www.campingalsole.it
info@campingalsole.it
New Chalets

IT62290 Camping Lévico

Localitá Pleina 5, I-38056 Lévico Terme (Trentino - Alto Adige)

Tel: **046 170 6491**. Email: **mail@campinglevico.com** **www.alanrogers.com/IT62290**

Sister site to Camping Jolly, Camping Levico is in a natural setting on the small, very pretty Italian lake also called Levico which is surrounded by towering mountains. The sites are owned by two brothers – Andrea, who manages Levico, and Gino, based at Jolly. Both campsites are charming. Levico has some pitches along the lake edge and a quiet atmosphere. There is a shaded terrace for enjoying pizza and drinks in the evening. Pitches are of a good size, most grassed and well shaded with 6A electricity. The beautiful grass shores of the lake are ideal for sunbathing and the crystal clear water is ideal for enjoying (non-motorised) water activities. This is a site where the natural beauty of an Italian lake can be enjoyed without being overwhelmed by commercial tourism. All the amenities at Camping Jolly can be enjoyed by traversing a very pretty walkway along a stream.

Facilities

Four modern sanitary blocks. Mostly British style toilets. Single locked unit for disabled visitors. Washing machines and dryer. Ironing. Motorcaravan services. Bar/restaurant, takeaway and good shop. Play area. Miniclub and animation (high season). Fishing. Internet. Kayak hire. Tennis. Torches useful. Off site: Town 2 km. Bicycle hire 1.5 km. Boat launching 500 m. Riding 3 km. Golf 7 km.

Open: 1 April - 11 October.

Directions

From A22 Verona - Bolzano road take turn for Trento on S47 to Levico Terme where campsite is very well signed. GPS: N46:00.479 E11:17.000

Charges guide

Per person	€ 5,00 - € 9,50
child (3-11 yrs)	€ 4,00 - € 6,00
pitch incl. electricity (6A)	€ 7,50 - € 18,00

IT62000 Camping Olympia

Camping 1, I-39034 Toblach (Trentino - Alto Adige)

Tel: **047 497 2147**. Email: **info@camping-olympia.com** **www.alanrogers.com/IT62000**

In the Dolomite mountains, Camping Olympia maintains its high standards and is constantly being upgraded. The 300 pitches have been relaid in a regular pattern and tall pine trees and newly planted shrubs and hedges make this a very pleasant and attractive site. There are tree-clad hills on either side and craggy mountains beyond. The 238 touring pitches all have electricity and a TV point. There are 20 fully serviced pitches with water, waste water, gas, telephone and satellite TV points. Some accommodation is available for rent, and there are 62 seasonal caravans which are mainly grouped at one end of the site. A little fish pond with a fountain and surrounded by flowers makes an attractive central feature, whilst on the far side of the site, a gate leads out into the woods where there is a little play area and a few animals. The site is an ideal base from which to explore this part of German-speaking Südtirol on foot, by bicycle or by car – and Austria is just up the road!

Facilities

The main toilet block has been refurbished to a high standard. Rooms with WC, washbasin and shower to rent. Baby room. Facilities for disabled visitors. Two small blocks provide further WCs and showers. Motorcaravan service point. Shop. Attractive bar, restaurant and pizzeria (all year). Second bar with grill and terrace by pool (10/6-30/9; 20/12-Easter). Heated swimming pool (20/5-15/9). Sauna, solarium, steam bath and whirlpools. Fishing. Bicycle hire. Play area. WiFi. Programme of activities and excursions. Entertainment in high season. Off site: Tennis and minigolf nearby. Riding and golf 3 km.

Open: All year.

Directions

Toblach/Dobbiaco is about 100 km. northeast of Bolzano. Site is west of the town. From the A22 Innsbruck - Bolzano autostrada, take exit for Bressanone/Brixen and travel east on SS49 for 60 km. Site signed to left just after a short tunnel. From Cortina take SS48 and SS51 northwards then turn west on SS49 for 1.5 km.

GPS: N46:44.086 E12:11.638

Charges guide

Per person	€ 8,00 - € 10,00
child (3-12 yrs)	€ 4,50 - € 8,00
pitch	€ 8,00 - € 12,50
dog	free - € 4,50

Supplement for serviced pitch (14/7-19/8).

IT62030 Caravan Park Sexten

Saint Josef Strasse 54, I-39030 Sexten (Trentino - Alto Adige)

Tel: **047 471 0444**. Email: **info@parksexten.com** **www.alanrogers.com/IT62030**

Caravan Park Sexten is 1,520 metres above sea level and has 268 pitches, some very large and all with electricity (16A) and TV connections, and with water and drainage in summer and winter (underground heating stops pipes freezing). Some pitches are in the open to catch the sun, others are tucked in forest clearings by the river. They are mostly gravelled to provide an ideal all-year surface. It is the facilities that make this a truly remarkable site; no expense or effort have been spared to create a luxurious environment that matches that of any top class hotel. The brand new health spa has every type of sauna, Turkish and Roman baths, whirlpools, sunbeds, herbal and hay baths, hairdressing and beauty treatment salons, relaxation and massage rooms and a remarkable indoor pool with children's pool, Kneipp therapy pool and whirlpools. The timber of the buildings is from 400 year old farmhouses and is blended with top quality modern materials to create amazing interiors and (mainly) authentically Tyrolean exteriors. The restaurant, bars and taverna are of equally high quality. Sexten is in the Dolomites, in the German-speaking Südtirol, where the scenery is often spectacular and there is a wide variety of leisure activities on offer from gentle walking to extreme summer and winter sports. Member 'Leading Campings Group'.

Facilities

The three main toilet blocks are remarkable in design, fixtures and fittings. Heated floors. Controllable showers. Hairdryers. Luxurious private facilities to rent. Children and baby rooms. En-suite facilities for disabled visitors. Laundry and drying room. Motorcaravan services. Shop. Bars and restaurants with entertainment 2-3 nights a week. Indoor pool. Heated outdoor pool (1/6-30/9). High quality health spa. New outdoor play area for children. Good range of activities for all. Tennis. Bicycle hire. Climbing wall. Fishing. Adventure activity packages. Internet access and WiFi (whole site). Off site: Skiing 900m. (free bus to 2 ski lifts within 5 km). Walking, cycling and climbing. Fishing. Riding, golf and villages nearby.

Open: All year.

Directions

Sexten/Sesto is 110 km. northeast of Bolzano. From Bressanone/Brixen exit on A22 Brenner - Modena motorway follow the SS49 east for about 60 km. Turn south on SS52 at Innichen/San Candido and follow signs to Sexten. Site is 5 km. past village (signed). GPS: N46:40.059 E12:23.950

Charges 2009

Per person	€ 7,00 - € 12,50
child	€ 1,00 - € 10,50
pitch (80-280 sq.m)	€ 5,00 - € 22,00
electricity per kWh (16A)	€ 0,70
dog	€ 2,00 - € 6,00

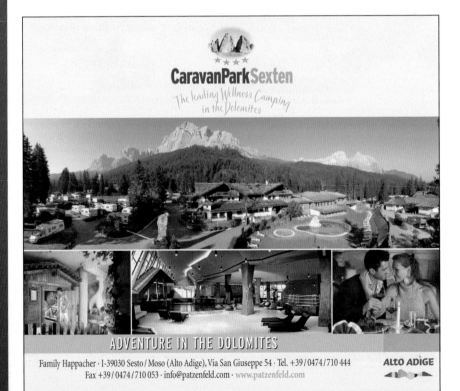

IT60400 Camping Village Garden Paradiso

Via Baracca 55, I-30013 Cavallino-Treporti (Veneto)

Tel: **041 968 075**. Email: **info@gardenparadiso.it**

www.alanrogers.com/IT60400

There are many sites in this area and there is much competition in providing a range of facilities. Garden Paradiso is a good seaside site which also provides three excellent, centrally situated pools, a fitness centre, minigolf, a train to the market and other activities for children. Compared with other sites here, this one is of medium size with 776 pitches. All have electricity (4/6A), water and drainage points and all are marked and numbered with hard access roads, under a good cover of trees. Flowers and shrubs give a pleasant and peaceful appearance. The restaurant, with self-service at lunch time and waiter service at night, is near the beach with a bar/snack bar in the centre of the site. The site is directly on the sea with a beach of fine sand. Used by tour operators (35 pitches).

Facilities

Four brick, tiled toilet blocks are fully equipped with a mix of British and Turkish style toilets. Facilities for babies. Dishwashing and laundry sinks. Washing machines and dryers. Motorcaravan services. Shopping complex. Restaurant (23/4-30/9). Snack bar and takeaway. Swimming pools. Fitness centre. Tennis. Minigolf. Play area. Organised entertainment and excursions (high season). Bicycle hire. Dogs are not accepted. Off site: Riding 2 km. Fishing 2.5 km.

Open: 23 April - 30 September.

Directions

Leave Venice - Trieste autostrada either by taking airport or Quarto d'Altino exits; follow signs to Jésolo and Punta Sabbioni. Take first road left after Cavallino and site is a little way on the right. GPS: N45:28.738 E12:33.815

Charges guide

Per unit incl. 2 persons, electricity, water and drainage	€ 19,30 - € 41,20
extra person	€ 4,65 - € 9,10
junior (6-12 yrs) or senior (over 60 yrs)	€ 3,10 - € 7,00
child (3-5 yrs)	free - € 5,90

Less 10% for stays over 30 days (early), or 20 days (late) season.

Runner up Alan Rogers Awards 2008

IT60030 Centro Vacanze Pra' Delle Torri

P.O. Box 176, I-30021 Caorle (Veneto)
Tel: **042 129 9063**. Email: **info@pradelletorri.it**

www.alanrogers.com/IT60030

Pra' Delle Torri is another Italian Adriatic site which has just about everything! Pitches for camping, hotel, accommodation to rent, one of the largest and best equipped pool complexes in the country and a golf course where lessons for beginners are also available. Many of the 1,300 grass pitches (with electricity) have shade and they are arranged in zones. When you book in at reception you are taken by electric golf buggy to select your pitch. There are two good restaurants, bars and a range of shops arranged around an attractive square. Recent additions include a crèche and a supervised play area for young children. The pool complex is the crowning glory with indoor (Olympic size) and outdoor pools with slides and many other features. Other super amenities include a large grass area for ball games, a good playground, a babies' car track, and a whole range of sports, fitness and entertainment programmes, along with a medical centre, skincare and other therapies. The site has its own sandy beach and Porto Santa, Margherita and Caorle are nearby. One could quite happily spend a whole holiday here without leaving the site but the attractions of Venice, Verona, etc. might well tempt one to explore the area.

Facilities

Sixteen excellent, high quality toilet blocks with the usual facilities including very attractive 'Junior Stations'. Units for disabled visitors. Motorcaravan service point. Large supermarket and wide range of shops, restaurants, bars and takeaways. Indoor and outdoor pools. Tennis. Minigolf. Fishing. Watersports. Archery. Diving. Fitness programmes and keep fit track. Crèche and supervised play area. Bowls. Mountain bike track. Wide range of organised sports and entertainment. Dogs are not accepted. Off site: Riding 3 km.

Open: 4 April - 27 September.

Directions

From A4 Venice - Trieste motorway leave at exit for Sto Stino di Livenze and follow signs to Caorle then Sta Margherita and signs to site.
GPS: N45:34.387 E12:48.749

Charges guide

Per person	€ 3,90 - € 9,00
child (2-5 yrs)	free - € 6,50
senior (over 60 yrs)	€ 2,95 - € 7,95
pitch incl. electricity	€ 7,30 - € 40,00
tent pitch	€ 5,10 - € 16,00

Min. stay 2 nights.

IT60100 Camping Capalonga

Via della Laguna 16, I-30020 Bibione-Pineda (Veneto)
Tel: **043 143 8351**. Email: **capalonga@bibionemare.com** **www.alanrogers.com/IT60100**

A quality site right beside the sea, Capalonga is a large site with 1,350 pitches of variable size (70-90 sq.m). Nearly all marked out, all have electrical connections, some have water and drainage, and there is good shade almost everywhere. The site is pleasantly laid out – roads run in arcs which avoids the square box effect. Some pitches where trees define the pitch area may be tricky for large units. The very wide, sandy beach, which is cleaned by the site, shelves extremely gently so is very safe for children and it never becomes too crowded. A concrete path leads out towards the sea to avoid too much sand-walking and the water is much cleaner here than at most places along this coast. A large lagoon runs along the other side of the site where boating (motor or sail) can be practised and a landing stage and moorings are provided. There is also a swimming pool on site. Capalonga is an excellent site, with comprehensive facilities.

Facilities

Seven toilet blocks are well and frequently cleaned. Two newer blocks built side by side have facilities for disabled people and very fine children's rooms. British and some Turkish style toilets, some washbasins in private cabins. Launderette. Motorcaravan services. Large supermarket. General shop. Self-service restaurant and separate bar. Swimming pool (25 x 12.5 m; 19/5-15/9). Boating. Fishing. Playground. Free animation programme. Dogs are not accepted.

Open: 28 April - 30 September.

Directions

Bibione is about 80 km. east of Venice, well signed from afar on approach roads. 1 km. before Bibione turn right towards Bibione Pineda and follow site signs. GPS: N45:37.830 E12:59.615

Charges guide

Per person	€ 5,70 - € 10,50
child (1-4 yrs)	free - € 5,00
child (5-10 yrs)	free - € 8,00
pitch	€ 10,50 - € 24,00

IT60150 Camping Residence Il Tridente

Via Baseleghe 12, I-30020 Bibione-Pineda (Veneto)
Tel: **043 143 9600**. Email: **tridente@bibionemare.com** **www.alanrogers.com/IT60150**

This is an unusual site in that only half the area is used for camping. Formerly a holiday centre for deprived children, it occupies a large area of woodland stretching from the main road to the sea. It is divided into two parts by the Residence, an apartment block of first class rooms which are for rent. The 226 tourist pitches (483 in total) are located amongst tall pines in the area between the entrance and the Residence. Pitch size varies according to the positions of the trees (70-100 sq.m) and all have electricity connections (6/10A). Between the Residence and the sea is a pleasant open area used for sports facilities and the two excellent pools. The ground slopes gently from the main building to the beach of fine sand and this is used as the recreation area with two swimming pools – one 25 x 12.5 m. and a smaller children's pool – tennis courts, table tennis and sitting and play places. With thick woodland on both sides, Il Tridente is a quiet, restful site with excellent facilities.

Facilities

Three sanitary blocks are of excellent quality. Mixed British and Turkish style WCs in cabins with washbasins. Facilities for disabled people. Laundry. The Residence includes a restaurant and bar. Motorcaravan services. Supermarket. Swimming pools. Playground. Tennis. Gym. Fishing. Internet. Animation (high season). Dogs are not accepted. Off site: Bicycle hire 1 km. Riding 2 km. Golf 10 km.

Open: 12 April - 17 September.

Directions

From A4 Venice - Trieste autostrada, take Latisana exit and follow signs to Bibione and then Bibione Pineda and site signs. GPS: N45:37.998 E13:04.000

Charges guide

Per person	€ 5,70 - € 10,00
child (1-4 yrs)	free - € 4,50
child (5-10 yrs)	free - € 6,50
pitch incl. electricity	€ 10,50 - € 19,00

IT60220 Camping Village Portofelice

Viale dei Fiori 15, I-30020 Eraclea Mare (Veneto)

Tel: **042 166 411**. Email: **info@portofelice.it** **www.alanrogers.com/IT60220**

Portofelice is an efficient and attractive coastal site with a sandy beach and plenty of well organised activity. There were many happy customers when we visited. It is unusual in being separated from the sea by a protected pine wood with a gravel path between the two. It is of medium size for this part of Italy with 532 touring pitches and 200 occupied by static caravans, bungalows and tour operators' accommodation. The pitches are arranged in rectangular blocks or zones in regular rows, separated by hedges from hard access roads and with either natural or artificial shade. Cars are parked separately. All pitches have electricity and 208 also have water, drainage and TV sockets. The social life of the site is centred around the stunning pool complex where the shops, pizzeria, bar, café and restaurant are also located. A wide range of entertainment and activities are organised for adults and children. If you can drag yourself away from the holiday village, you can explore the region by car with Venice, the Dolomites and the Italian Lakes within easy reach.

Facilities

Two modern sanitary blocks have the usual facilities with slightly more Turkish style toilets than British. Baby room and special children's block (0-12 yrs). Facilities for disabled people. Supermarket/bazaar. Pizzeria and takeaway. Restaurant with waiter service. Three superb pools with waterfalls, slides and area for disabled guests, hydro-massage. Playgrounds. Go-kart track. Pedaloes. Tennis. Sandy beach. Bicycle hire. ATM. Organised activity and entertainment programmes. WiFi. Dogs are not accepted. Off site: Riding 200 m. Golf 6 km.

Open: 9 May - 16 September.

Directions

From A4 Venice - Trieste motorway take exit 'S Dona/Noventa' and go south through S Dona di Piave and Eraclea to Eraclea Mare where site is signed. GPS: N45:33.214 E12:46.051

Charges 2009

Per person	€ 3,60 - € 9,90
senior (over 60 yrs)	€ 3,00 - € 8,30
child (2-5 yrs)	free - € 7,20
pitch depending on type	€ 7,80 - € 22,50

IT62050 Camping International Dolomiti

Via Campo di Sotto, I-32043 Cortina d'Ampezzo (Veneto)

Tel: **043 624 85**. Email: **campeggiodolomiti@tin.it** **www.alanrogers.com/IT62050**

Cortina is a pleasant provincial town with many interesting shops and restaurants. A bus runs from the campsite gate to the town centre. The strength of this site is its beautiful mountain scenery and quiet location in a grassy meadow beside a fast flowing river (with a steep embankment but no fences). The site is dedicated to tourers with 390 good sized pitches, all with electricity (2A) and about half with shade. The site does not take reservations so arrive early in the day in the first three weeks of August to improve your chance of obtaining a pitch.

Facilities

The large central toilet block (only open in high season) is quite old but should now be refurbished. Washbasins have hot water sprinkler taps. A smaller heated block is open all season and is well equipped and kept very clean. Facilities for disabled visitors. Washing machines. Gas supplies. Coffee and drinks bar and shop (restricted hours in low season). Heated pool (5/7-25/8). Playground (hard base). Off site: Restaurant 600 m. Supermarket 1 km. Fishing 1 km. Golf 2 km. Bicycle hire and riding 3 km.

Open: 1 June - 20 September.

Directions

Cortina is 60 km. north of Belluno. Site is 3 km. south of town off the SS51 from Toblach/Dobbiaco to Belluno and Veneto. Follow signs to site, turning right towards Campo from north or left in Zuel from south. GPS: N46:30.974 E12:08.160

Charges guide

Per person	€ 7,00 - € 9,30
child (under 6 yrs)	€ 5,00 - € 7,00
pitch incl. electricity	€ 9,00 - € 13,50

IT60560 Camping Miramare

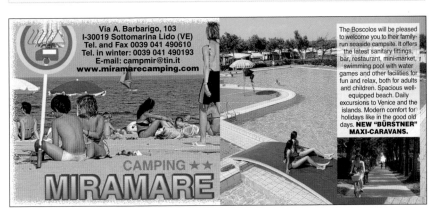

Via Barbarigo 103, I-30019 Sottomarina di Chioggia (Veneto)
Tel: **041 490 610**. Email: **camping@tin.it** **www.alanrogers.com/IT60560**

Camping Miramare sits on both sides of the road leading to it. Reception is on the beach side, along with most of the amenities, the other side is very peaceful with just sports amenities and a sanitary block. The touring pitches are separated from the permanent units. All have 6A electricity, some have water and drainage, Some have land views and others have shade. The beach is of soft sand with very safe bathing and a lifeguard. You can hire sunshades and loungers. The restaurant offers traditional food and a plethora of pizzas which can be enjoyed on the terraces. Some of these overlook the large safe paddling pool. Children have several play areas and there is entertainment all season. The separated swimming pool is excellent, with two diving boards and a lifeguard. The site lies close to the ancient city of Chioggia, famous for its fishing and Venice-like construction. It is well worth a visit on a bicycle as it has an amazing history. An excursion to Venice naturally holds a strong appeal, but other stunning cities are also close at hand, notably Padova, Vicenza, Treviso and, a little further afield, Verona. This is a pleasant, family oriented site which has a distinct Italian feel. English is spoken.

Facilities

Three identical, modern, clean blocks, one of which is in the area of the permanent campers. Push button hot showers and primarily Turkish style toilets. Facilities for disabled guests. Baby room. Laundry. Motorcaravan service point. Pleasant bar. Restaurant. Pizzeria and takeaway. Shop. Excellent swimming pool and paddling pool. Several play areas. Multisport court. Entertainment and children's activities in high season. Mobile homes to rent. Dogs are not accepted. Off site: Bicycle hire 1 km. Fishing 1 km. Sailing 1 km. Riding 6 km. Golf 20 km.

Open: 5 April - 20 September.

Directions

Site is off the S309 south of Chioggia. Follow signs to Sottomaria, crossing the Laguna del Lusenzo, then look for site signs. Site is off Viale Mediterranneo road to the right. Site is the second of many along this narrow road. GPS: N45:11.417 E12:18.217

Charges guide

Per person	€ 4,50 - € 7,50
child (under 6 yrs)	€ 2,25 - € 3,80
pitch	€ 9,50 - € 16,50

IT60500 Camping Della Serenissima

Via Padana 334/a, I-30034 Oriago (Veneto)
Tel: **041 921 850**. Email: **camping.serenissima@shineline.it** **www.alanrogers.com/IT60500**

This is a delightful little site of some 155 pitches (all with 16A electricity) where one could stay for a number of days whilst visiting Venice (12 km), Padova (24 km), Lake Garda (135 km) or the Dolomites. There is a good service by bus to Venice and the site is situated on the Riviera del Brenta, a section of a river with some very large old villas. A long, narrow and flat site, numbered pitches are on each side of a central road. There is good shade in most parts with many trees, plants and grass.

Facilities

Sanitary facilities are of a good standard with all facilities in private cabins. Facilities for disabled visitors. Motorcaravan services. Gas supplies. Shop (all season). Bar. Restaurant and takeaway (1/6-31/10). Play area. Fishing. Bicycle hire. Reduced price bus ticket to Venice if staying for 3 days. No entertainment but local markets, etc. all well publicised. Off site: Golf or riding 3 km.

Open: Easter - 10 November.

Directions

From the A4 take exit for Oriago-Mira then signs for Ravenna, Padova (SS11) to Oriago. On A27 or SS309 take exit for Venezia-Mestre then signs for Ravenna, Padova and Milano. After Padova-Riviera del Brenta follow signs to Oriago. GPS: N45:27.234 E12:10.333

Charges guide

Per person	€ 7,00 - € 8,00
pitch	€ 12,00 - € 13,00

Winner Alan Rogers Awards 2008

IT60200 Camping Union Lido Vacanze

Via Fausta 258, I-30013 Cavallino-Treporti (Veneto)

Tel: **041 257 5111**. Email: **info@unionlido.com** **www.alanrogers.com/IT60200**

This amazing site is very large, offering everything a camper could wish for, is extremely well organised and it has been said to set the standard that others follow. It lies right beside the sea with direct access to a long, broad sandy beach which shelves very gradually and provides very safe bathing (there are lifeguards). The site itself is regularly laid out with parallel access roads under a covering of poplars, pine and other trees providing good shade. There are 2,600 pitches for touring units), all with 6A electricity and 1,684 also have water and drainage. Because of the size of the site there is an internal road train and amenities are repeated through the site. You really would not need to leave this site – everything is here, including a sophisticated 'wellness' centre. Overnight parking is provided outside the gate with electricity, toilets and showers for those arriving after 21.00 hrs. There are two aqua parks, one with fine sand beaches (a first in Europe) and both with swimming pools, lagoon pools for children, a heated whirlpool and a slow flowing 160 m. 'river'. A heated pool for hotel and apartment guests is open to others on payment. A huge selection of sports is offered, along with luxury amenities too numerous to list. Entertainment and fitness programmes are offered in season. A golf academy (with a professional) has a driving range, pitching and putting greens and practice bunker, and a diving centre offers lessons and open water diving. Union Lido is above all an orderly and clean site, achieved by reasonable regulations to ensure quiet, comfortable camping and by good management. Member of 'Leading Campings Group'.

Facilities

Fifteen well kept, fully equipped toilet blocks which open and close progressively during the season. Eleven blocks have facilities for disabled people. Launderette. Motorcaravan service points. Gas supplies. Comprehensive shopping areas set around a pleasant piazza (all open until late). Eight restaurants each with a different style. Nine pleasant and lively bars. Impressive aquaparks (from 15/5). Tennis. Riding. Minigolf. Skating. Bicycle hire. Archery. Two fitness tracks in 4 ha. natural park with play area and supervised play for children. Golf academy. Diving centre and school. Windsurfing school in season. Boat excursions. Recreational events. Church service in English in July/Aug. Hairdressers. Internet cafés. ATM. Dogs are not accepted. Off site: Boat launching 3.5 km. Aqualandia (special rates).

Open: 1 May - 30 September, with all services.

Directions

From Venice - Trieste autostrada leave at exit for airport or Quarto d'Altino and follow signs first for Jesolo and then Punta Sabbioni, and site will be seen just after Cavallino on the left.
GPS: N45:28.073 E12:31.822

Charges guide

Per person	€ 6,50 - € 10,00
child (1-5)	€ 3,70 - € 6,90
child (6-11yrs)	€ 5,20 - € 8,50
pitch incl. electricity	€ 15,60 - € 26,20
pitch with water and drainage	€ 15,60 - € 50,00

Three different seasons:
(i) high season 29/6-31/8;
(ii) mid-season 18/5-29/6 and 31/8-14/9, and
(iii) off-season, outside these dates.

IT60210 Italy Camping Village

Via Fausta 272, I-30013 Cavallino-Treporti (Veneto)

Tel: **041 968 090**. Email: **info@campingitaly.it** **www.alanrogers.com/IT60210**

Italy Camping Village, under the same ownership as the better known Union Lido which it adjoins, is suggested for those who prefer a smaller site where less activities are available (although those at Union Lido may be used by guests here, charges applying). The 180 touring pitches are on either side of sand tracts off hard access roads under a cover of trees. All have 6A electricity connections and 70 are fully serviced. Being small (60-70 sq.m), they are impossible for large units, particularly in high season when cars are parked everywhere. There is direct access to a gently sloping sandy beach. A pleasant, heated, swimming pool has slides and a whirlpool at one end. Strict regulations regarding undue noise here make this a peaceful site and with lower charges than some in the area, this would be a good choice for families with young children where it is possible to book in advance.

Facilities

Two good quality, fully equipped sanitary blocks include facilities for disabled visitors. Washing machines. Shop. Restaurant. Bar beside beach. Heated swimming pool (17 x 7 m). Small playground, miniclub and children's disco. Weekly dance for adults. Bicycle hire. Barbecues are only permitted in a designated area. Dogs are not accepted. Off site: Use of facilites at IT60200 Union Lido. Sports centre 500 m. Golf or riding 500 m.

Open: 21 April - 22 September.

Directions

From Venice - Trieste A4 autostrada leave at exit for airport or Quarto d'Altino and follow signs for Jesolo and Punta Sabbioni. Site on left after Cavallino.
GPS: N45:28.102 E12:32.003

Charges guide

Per person	€ 4,80 - € 7,90
child (1-6 yrs)	free - € 6,10
pitch incl. electricity	€ 8,70 - € 19,30
pitch incl. electricity and water	€ 8,20 - € 20,80

Three charging seasons.

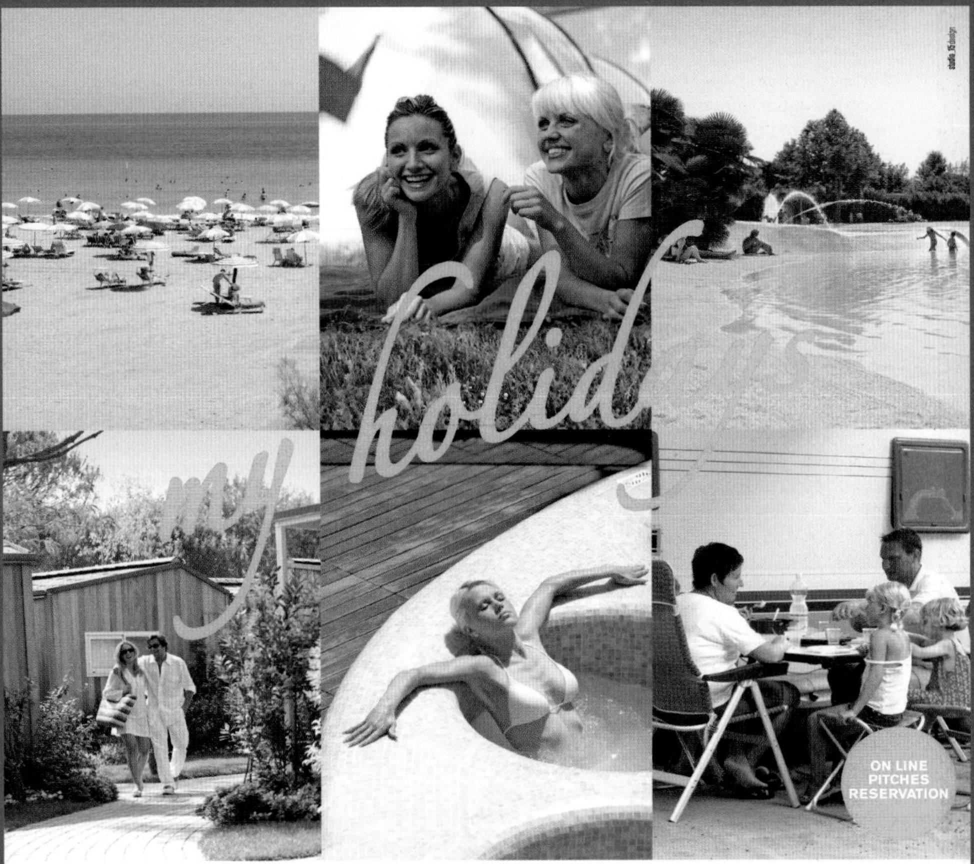

my holidays

ON LINE PITCHES RESERVATION

PARK & RESORT
CAMPING
LODGING
HOTEL
★ ★ ★ ★ www.unionlido.com

Union Lido Vacanze is situated on the green Cavallino Riviera, between the splendid Venetian lagoon and the Adriatic Sea.

Open from 23rd April to 27th September.

- **Venice** and it's magnificent islands can be reached across water very easily.
- Spacious and well maintained pitches.
- Modern washrooms with disabled facilities. Also baby changing room and showers for the smaller guests.

BUNGALOWS, CAMPING HOMES, MOBILE HOMES, MAXI CARAVANS PROVIDED WITH EVERY COMFORT.

- Rooms, villas and apartments at the high quality Art&Park Hotel, the only 4 star hotel in the area, with it's own heated swimming pool, Jacuzzi and children's mini pool.
- The Gourmet Club Union Lido boasts 8 restaurants and 11 bars on site.
- 2 supermarkets and over 20 shops of various types.
- Fine sandy beach 1 km in length, safe for children playing.
- 2 Aqua Parks with pools for a total of 11.000 m^2; entrance to the parks is included in the price.
- The Marino Club health Spa with sea view, salt water oasis with exclusive treatments.
- Entertainment and sport for both children and adults.
  Diving school, surf school, golf academy, horse-riding, archery, multi-use sportground.
  Excursions and trips to unforgettable destinations.

Visit our website **www.unionlido.com** for more information on our packages and super offers, check out the last minute offers too.....for unrepeatable opportunities.

NEWS 2009
- Garden suite hotel
- Camping suite
- Pitches MV Collection
- Extension of the Wi-Fi connection
- Completion of renewal programme for hotel rooms on the 1st and 4th floor
- Completion of renewal programme for apartments Murano\Torcello
- Light Design exterior Murano\Torcello

30013 CAVALLINO
VENEZIA - ITALIA
Camping Park & Resort
Tel. Camping +39 041 25 75 111
Tel. Art&Park Hotel +39 041 96 80 43
Telefax +39 041 53 70 355
info@unionlido.com
booking@unionlido.com

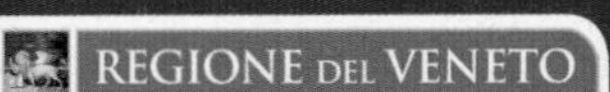

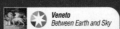

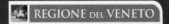

IT60450 Camping Marina di Venezia

Via Montello 6, I-30013 Punta Sabbioni (Veneto)

Tel: **041 530 2511**. Email: **camping@marinadivenezia.it** **www.alanrogers.com/IT60450**

This is a very large site (2,862 pitches) with much the same atmosphere as many other large sites along this appealing stretch of coastline. Marina di Venezia, however, has the advantage of being within walking distance of the ferry to Venice. It will appeal particularly to those who enjoy an extensive range of entertainment and activities, and a lively atmosphere. Individual pitches are marked out on sandy ground, most separated by trees or hedges. They are of an average size for the region (around 80 sq.m) and all are equipped with electricity and water. The site's excellent sandy beach is one of the widest along this stretch of coast and has a pleasant beach bar. The main pool is Olympic sized and there is also a very large children's pool adjacent. This is a well run site with committed management and staff. A magnificent Aqua Marina Park swimming-pool complex has been added.

Facilities

Ten modern toilet blocks are maintained to a high standard with good hot showers and a reasonable proportion of British-style toilets. Good provision for disabled visitors. Washing machines and dryers. Range of shops. Several bars, restaurants and takeaways. Swimming pools (no slides). Several play areas. Tennis. Windsurf and catamaran hire. Kite hire. Wide range of organised entertainment. WiFi internet access in all bars and cafés. Church.

Open: 25 April - 30 September.

Directions

From A4 motorway, take Jesolo exit. After Jesolo continue towards Punta Sabbioni. Site is clearly signed to the left towards the end of this road, close to the Venice ferries. GPS: N45:26.250 E12:26.283

Charges guide

Per person	€ 4,25 - € 8,50
child or senior (under 5, over 60)	€ 3,60 - € 6,90
pitch incl. electricity and water	€ 10,75 - € 20,65
dog	€ 1,05 - € 2,70

IT60460 Camping Miramare

Punta Sabbioni, I-30010 Cavallino-Treporti (Veneto)

Tel: **041 966 150**. Email: **info@camping-miramare.it** **www.alanrogers.com/IT60460**

This family owned site is well located, being one of the closest sites to the Punta Sabbione ferry and offering a free bus service to the ferry and the local beach. It has an unusually long season compared with others in the area. Miramare is ideally located for exploring Venice and its islands, as well as the Lido di Venezia. There are 130 level pitches here, all with 6A electricity. They intend to increase the numbers by 50% this year. The shop is superb for a small site and the restaurant, 50 m. outside of the gate, is renowned for its excellent regional meals. An internet terminal is also here. Unusually, the site runs a free cycle loan scheme. The site is kept clean and most pitches have shade from mature trees and are level. Ask about the campsite logo – the 'Venetian iron'- very interesting, and the secret of the local flamingoes!

Facilities

Two toilet blocks (one heated in low season) with facilities for disabled people and babies. Motorcaravan service point. Excellent supermarket/shop. Bar, restaurant and pizzas from the oven in the restaurant. Takeaway. Play area. Internet point. Free bicycle hire. Dogs are not accepted. Free shuttle bus to Punta Sabbioni square (departure point for trips to Venice and the islands) and to the nearest beach on the Adriatic Coast. Off site: Fishing 2 km. Boat launching 1.5 km. Beach 1.8 km. Golf 8 km. Riding 8 km.

Open: Easter - early November.

Directions

Leave the A4 autostrada at exit for Venezia Mestre and follow signs to Noventa/San Dona GPS: N45:26.421 E12:25.266

Charges guide

Per person	€ 4,70 - € 7,20
child (1-10 yrs)	€ 3,10 - € 5,40
pitch	€ 10,10 - € 17,00

TOURIST ENVIRONMENTAL MANIFESTO VENETO - CAVALLINO QUALITY CAMPING 2009

Parco Turistico di Cavallino Treporti

Veneto *Between Earth and Sky*

REGIONE DEL VENETO

LR. 33/02

IT60370 Camping Jesolo International

Viale A. da Giussano, I-30016 Lido di Jesolo (Veneto)

Tel: **042 197 1826**. Email: **info@jesolointernational.it** **www.alanrogers.com/IT60370**

At this brilliant family resort style site with a focus on sporting activities, you can plan the cost of your holiday with confidence. The amazing array of on-site activities is free and there are large discounts for some off-site attractions. Jesolo International is located on a beautiful promontory with 700 metres of uncrowded white sandy beach and slowly shelving waters for safe swimming. As the site is narrow, all the pitches are close to the sea. There is a choice of three types of pitch, all flat, well shaded and with 10-20A electricity, water and drainage. Most also have a satellite TV connection supplying 26 free channels. The superb pool complex, where an excellent animation programme is presented each night, is centrally located and very spacious. The pool is open one night a week for a supervised pool party. The dynamic director Sergio Comino works long hours to maintain and improve this high quality family orientated site, to combine a unique holiday experience for guests, with real value for money. As the site is community owned, profits are returned to the guests in the form of facilities, sporting opportunities and entertainment. Cleanliness and security are high priorities. Electronic tags are given to guests to gain entrance and exit to the beach gates and this, combined with video surveillance of these key locations, allows guests to feel secure. Children's passes exclude them from accessing the beach or the hydro massage whirlpools reserved for adults alone. A ferry service to Venice leaves from the marina adjoining the campsite and takes just 40 minutes to reach St Mark's Square in the heart of the city.

Facilities

Sanitary facilities include 72 modern, continually cleaned bathroom units (shower, toilet and basin), private bathrooms (extra cost) and baby rooms. Washing machines and dryers. Fridge boxes. Motorcaravan service point. Supermarket. Family style restaurant. Beach bar with snacks. Pool bar serving light lunches. Sports centre. Children's club and inflatable fun park on the beach. Indoor gym. Tennis courts and lessons (equipment provided). Golf (lessons, equipment and fees all free). Sailing with tuition and canoe courses. Introductory scuba dive lesson. Pedal boats. Language courses. Large grassy play area with adventure style equipment. Free internet. Dogs are not accepted. Off site: Golf 2 km. (free lesson and use of 18-hole course with equipment). Aqualandia 1.5 km. (30% discount). Ferry to Venice and Murano 200 m. Jesolo promenade with shops, restaurants and bars 500 m.

Open: 24 April - 30 September.

Directions

From A4 Venice - Trieste autostrada take Dona di Piave exit and follow signs to Jesolo then Punta Sabbioni. Turn off to Lido di Jesolo just before the Cavallino bridge where the site is well signed. GPS: N45:29.061 E12:35.319

Charges guide

Per person (over 5 yrs)	€ 5,50 - € 11,00
child (1-5 yrs)	free - € 4,00
serviced pitch	€ 13,00 - € 25,50

IT60320 Camping Village Cavallino

Via delle Batterie 164, I-30013 Cavallino-Treporti (Veneto)

Tel: **041 966 133**. Email: **info@campingcavallino.com** **www.alanrogers.com/IT60320**

This large, well ordered site is run by a friendly, experienced family who have other sites in this guide and offer tours between their sites. It lies beside the sea with direct access to a superb beach of fine sand, which is very safe and has lifeguards. The site is thoughtfully laid out with a large number of unusually large pitches shaded by olives and pines. All 445 touring pitches have 6A electricity and there is a 10% tour operator presence. The site has mobile homes to rent, most with air conditioning. For visiting Venice, there is a bus to the ferry at Punta Sabbioni which is 20 minutes away. The charming ferry journey takes 40 mins. and drops you directly at Saint Marco Square after negotiating its way around the gondolas.

Facilities

The clean, modern toilet blocks are well spaced and can be heated. They provide a mixture of Turkish and British style WCs with facilities for disabled campers. Launderette. Motorcaravan services. Supermarket. Two restaurants. Takeaway. Pizzeria. Swimming pools and whirlpool (May - Sept). Minigolf. Play area. Bicycle hire. Fishing. Animation mostly for younger guests. WiFi area. Dogs accepted in certain areas. Mobile homes to rent. Off site: Golf 1 km. Riding 2 km. Bus at gate.

Open: 15 March - 20 October.

Directions

From Venice - Trieste autostrada leave at exit for airport or Quarto and Altino. Follow signs, first for Jesolo, then Punta Sabbioni. Site signs just after Cavallino on the left. GPS: N45:27.400 E12:30.033

Charges guide

Per unit incl. 2 persons water and electricity	€ 16,00 - € 40,00
extra person (10-59 yrs)	€ 2,00 - € 10,00
child (3-9 yrs)	free - € 8,00

Min. stay in high season one week.

barkation point, parking places on average just 60 metres from the beach. Its large number of inclusive services make it unbeatable value for money: wi-fi, banana boat, beach loungers and umbrellas on the beach and at the pool, use of Aqualandia, the best Italian waterpark (as often as you like, 2 Km), entrance to „Adventure Minigolf", golf on the Jesolo eighteen-hole course of Jesolo (3 Km), diving, padalos, canoes, catamarans, pony riding, heated jacuzzis, tennis, pirate ships, kart racing on the Jesolo race track (4 Km), outstanding fitness centre, a centre for the kids, animation. Great conditions in the Jesolo exclusive beauty and wellness club.
Unique monitoring system.
Charge-free booking.
Exceptionally appointed luxury mobile homes owned by the campsite and outstanding service.
Alan Rogers
Unique Site Campsite
ECO CAMPING
JESOLO INTERNATIONAL CLUB ★★★★ CAMPING

IT60410 Camping Village Europa

Via Fausta 332, I-30013 Cavallino-Treporti (Veneto)

Tel: **041 968 069**. Email: **info@campingeuropa.com** **www.alanrogers.com/IT60410**

Europa has a great position with direct access to a fine sandy beach with lifeguards. There are 411 touring pitches, all with 8A electricity, some with water, drainage and satellite TV connections. There is a separate area for campers with dogs and some smaller pitches are available for those with tents. The site is kept beautifully clean and neat and there is an impressive array of restaurants, bars, shops and leisure amenities which are cleverly laid out along an avenue. They include a jewellers, a doctor's surgery, internet services and much more. Leisure facilities are arranged around the site. A professional team provides entertainment and regular themed 'summer parties'. Some restaurant tables have pleasant sea views. Venice is easily accessible by bus and then ferry from Punta Sabbioni.

Facilities

Three superb toilet blocks are kept pristine and have hot water throughout. Facilities for disabled visitors. Washing machines. Large supermarket and shopping centre. Bars, restaurants, cafés and pizzeria. New 'aqua park'. Spa centre planned. Tennis. Games room. Children's clubs. Playground. Entertainment. Internet access. Direct access to the beach. Windsurf and pedalo hire. Off site: Riding 1 km. Golf and fishing 2 km. ATM 500 m.

Open: 4 April - 30 September.

Directions

From A4 autostrada (approaching from Milan) take Mestre exit and follow signs initially for Venice airport and then Jesolo. From Jesolo, follow signs to Cavallino from where site is well signed.
GPS: N45:28.428 E12:32.942

Charges guide

Per person	€ 4,00 - € 7,90
child (2-5 yrs)	€ 3,00 - € 6,90
pitch	€ 8,20 - € 20,50

IT60470 Camping Scarpiland

I-30010 Treporti (Veneto)

Tel: **041 966 488**. Email: **info@scarpiland.com** **www.alanrogers.com/IT60470**

Scarpiland faces the Adriatic and has a fine sandy beach. This campsite is a most peculiar shape in that it is dissected by rows of accommodation to rent belonging to the site with long separating fences. This forces campers in the touring area to have long walks to the single beach access. It is a large site with the informal touring pitches under the shade of mature pines. Pitches vary in size (70-90 sq.m) with 6A electricity. The irregular tree placing will challenge some units. The site has an attractive woodland setting but there is a very long walk to the two sanitary blocks. The first very small block is unisex and has all Turkish toilets, we envisage problems here at peak periods. The larger block is even further away but has British style toilets and hot showers. The only chemical disposal site is in this block. Few activities are on offer but much is available outside the site. The site's entertainment team organise activities for the children in a small staged area. All other amenities are worryingly situated on the main road which serves the site. All are open fronted and the games area and some shops are across the road so children must be carefully supervised. There is a selection of shops plus a bar and restaurant all open to the public.

Facilities

Two sanitary blocks one large one very small with Turkish style toilets only. Dated facilities for babies in the large block and one unit for disabled visitors. Restaurant/pizzeria. Ice cream parlour. Newsagent. Supermarket. Butcher. Souvenir shop. Greengrocer and local produce (all on the main road). Bicycle hire. Internet. Off site: Golf 3.4 km. Riding 3.4 km. Boat launching 5 km.

Open: 24 April - 22 September.

Directions

From Milan, take A4 autostrada to Venice and then continue towards Trieste as far as the A27 intersection, then follow signs to the airport. At the end of the bypass, follow signs to San Doná and Jesolo. When you reach Jesolo, follow directions to Lido del Cavallino and Punta Sabbioni. From here the site is clearly signed. GPS: N45:27.304 E12:29.324

Charges guide

Per unit incl. 2 persons	€ 15,20 - € 30,70
extra person	€ 4,00 - € 7,50

www.cavallinoqualitycamping.com

MANIFESTO TURISTICO AMBIENTALE VENETO
CAVALLINO QUALITY CAMPING 2009

The sensitivity of operators in the tourism sector towards the unique and precious environment in their Region has led to the development of the "Veneto Environmental Tourism Manifesto", which is today the most concrete example of eco-compatible tourism in Europe.

IT60330 Villaggio Turistico Malibu Beach

Viale Oriente 78, I-30016 Lido di Jesolo (Veneto)

Tel: **042 136 2212**. Email: **info@campingmalibubeach.com** **www.alanrogers.com/IT60330**

This is a family site, twinned with Camping Waikiki (IT60340) nearby which has direct access to a beach. Malibu Beach has 407 pitches with 150 for touring units, all with 6A electricity. The touring pitches are set back from the beach, with the pitches in between being used for mobile homes and chalets. All are well shaded by pine trees and there are some fully serviced pitches with electricity and water. The beach is of soft sand, shelves gently and has lifeguards and the usual Italian sunshades and loungers for hire.

Facilities

Three clean blocks provide good facilities, including for disabled visitors and children. Bar, restaurant and pizzeria. Shop. Games room. Fitness centre. Hairdresser. Massage. Swimming pool and paddling pool (hats compulsory). Playground. Children's club. Entertainment programme. Direct access to the beach. Fridge box hire. WiFi (at restaurant). Dogs are not accepted. Mobile homes and chalets for rent. Off site: Lido de Jesolo, excursions to Venice. Riding. Golf. Walking and cycling trails.

Open: 15 May - 13 September.

Directions

From A4 autostrada (from Milan) take Mestre exit and follow signs initially for Venice airport and then Jesolo. From Jesolo, follow signs to Jesolo Pineta and site is well signed. GPS: N45:31.431 E12:42.009

Charges guide

Per person	€ 4,95 - € 8,10
child (2-7 yrs) and seniors over 65	€ 3,50 - € 6,55
pitch incl. electricity	€ 8,60 - € 22,00

No credit cards. Minimum stay 2 nights.

IT60530 Camping Fusina

Via Moranzani 79, I-30030 Fusina (Veneto)

Tel: **041 547 0055**. Email: **info@camping-fusina.com** **www.alanrogers.com/IT60530**

This is one of those sites that take one by surprise. This is old fashioned camping, but what fun, and we met English speaking people who have been coming here for 30 years. Choose from 500 well shaded, flat and grassy informal pitches or a position with views over the lagoon to the towers in Saint Mark's Square. With water on three sides there are welcoming cool breezes and fortunately many trees hide the industrial area close by. Those who don't wish to be disturbed by the lively bar can choose from the many superb informal waterside pitches on the far end of the site. The site owns a large ferry car park and a 700-boat marina which accepts and launches all manner of craft. A deep water channel carries huge ships close by and the water views are never boring. Fusina offers a very easy and comfortable, 20 minute ferry connection to the cultural heart of Venice, Accademia. Many of the staff are Australian/New Zealand people and English is used everywhere. We recommend a visit to coincide with one of the many festivals which culminate in vibrant firework displays.

Facilities

Modern, well equipped facilities include units for disabled visitors, along with some older units. Laundry facilities. Motorcaravan services. Shop (15/3-31/10). Charming restaurant (no credit cards). Pizzeria and beer garden. Lively bar. Satellite TV. Playground. Boat hire. Marina with maintenance facilities. Air conditioned London Cyber bus (really!) and 'Info bus' for information and tickets. ATM. Torches useful. Off site: Excellent public transport and ferry connections to Venice.

Open: All year.

Directions

From SSII Padua - Venice road follow site signs on road east of Mira, turning right as signed. Site is in Fusina at end of peninsula and is well signed (also as 'Fusina parking'). GPS: N45:25.150 E12:15.416

Charges guide

Per person	€ 8,00 - € 9,00
child (5-12 yrs)	€ 4,50
caravan	€ 9,00
motorcaravan	€ 14,00
tent	€ 8,50 - € 9,00

IT60340 Camping Waikiki

Viale Oriente 144, I-30016 Lido di Jesolo (Veneto)

Tel: **042 198 0186**. Email: **info@campingwaikiki.com**

www.alanrogers.com/IT60340

Waikiki is twinned with IT60330 Malibu Beach which is close by. This site also has direct access to a broad, soft sandy beach across a 300 m. grass area which has a boarded walkway. The beach shelves slowly so swimming is safe for children, there are sunshades and loungers to hire and lifeguards on the beach. The touring pitches here are shaded by pines and other trees, some close to the beach fence, but others with sea views. Relatively flat, all have 6A electricity and some have water. On site amenities include an attractive swimming pool and paddling pool, both with lifeguards. An attractive restaurant/pizzeria with a very large terrace offers a good choice of reasonably priced food and there is a well stocked supermarket. Entertainment is provided daily. A regular bus service runs from the campsite to Jesolo, where there is an excellent selection of shops, bars and restaurants.

Facilities

Three good toilet blocks are smart and clean. Facilities for disabled visitors and children. Shop and bazaar. Bar. Restaurant/pizzeria. Swimming and paddling pools (hats compulsory). Games room. Fitness centre. Playground. Children's club. Entertainment programme. Direct access to the beach. Dogs are not accepted. Mobile homes and chalets for rent. Off site: Lido de Jesolo, excursions to Venice, Vicenza and Padova. Riding. Golf.

Open: 12 May - 11 September.

Directions

From A4 autostrada (approaching from Milan) take Mestre exit and follow signs initially for Venice airport and then Jesolo. From Jesolo, follow signs to Jesolo Pineta and site is well signed.
GPS: N45:31.875 E12:43.328

Charges guide

Per person	€ 3,75 - € 7,00
child (2-7 yrs) or senior (over 65)	€ 2,90 - € 4,90
pitch incl. electricity	€ 7,10 - € 18,85

No credit cards. Minimum stay 2 nights.

IT60140 Villaggio Turistico Internazionale

Via Colonie 2, I-30020 Bibione (Veneto)

Tel: **043 144 2611**. Email: **info@vti.it** **www.alanrogers.com/IT60140**

This is a large, professionally run tourist village which offers all a holidaymaker could want. The Granzotto family have owned the site since the sixties and the results of their continuous improvements are impressive. There are 350 clean pitches, many fully serviced, shaded by mature trees and mostly on flat ground. The site's large sandy beach is excellent (umbrellas and loungers available for a small charge), as are all the facilities within the campsite where English speaking, uniformed assistants will help when you arrive. The tourist village is split by a main road with the main restaurant, cinema and children's club on the very smart chalet side.

Facilities

Renovated apartments. Four modern toilet blocks house excellent facilities with mainly British style toilets. Excellent provision for children and disabled campers. Air conditioning in all accomodation. Washing machines and dryers. Motorcaravan service point. Supermarket. Bazaar. Good restaurant. Snack bar. New pool complex. Fitness centre. Disco. TV. Cinema and theatre. Internet. Play areas. Tennis. Electronic games. Off site: Bicycle hire 1 km. Riding 3 km. Golf 6 km. Fishing.

Open: 9 April - 27 September.

Directions

Leave A4 east of Venice at Latisana exit on Latisana road. Then take road 354 towards Ligmano, after 12 km. turn right to Beuazzana and then left to Bibione. Site is well signed on entering town. GPS: N45:38.600 E13:02.140

Charges 2009

Per person	€ 5,00 - € 9,70
child (under 5 yrs)	free - € 5,00
pitch incl. electricity	€ 9,00 - € 21,00
incl. water	€ 12,00 - € 27,00

IT60280 Camping Vela Blu

Via Radaelli 10, I-30013 Cavallino-Treporti (Veneto)

Tel: **041 968 068**. Email: **info@velablu.it** **www.alanrogers.com/IT60280**

Thoughtfully landscaped within a natural wooded coastal environment, the tall pines here give shade while attractive flowers enhance the setting while and paved roads give easy access to the pitches. The 280 pitches vary in size (55-100 sq.m) and shape, but all have electricity (4/6A) and 80 have drainage. A sister site to nos. IT60360 and IT60140, Vela Blu is a relatively new, small, family style site and a pleasant alternative to the other massive sites on Cavallino. The clean, fine sand beach runs the length of one side of the site with large stone breakwaters for fun and fishing.

Facilities

Two excellent modern toilet blocks include baby rooms and good facilities for disabled visitors. An attendant is on hand to maintain high standards. Laundry facilities. Motorcaravan service point. Medical room. Shop. Bar. Gelateria. Restaurant and takeaway. Games room. Satellite TV room. Pedalos. Windsurfing. Fishing. Bicycle hire. Entertainment. Off site: Bars, restaurants and shops. Ferry to Venice. Theme parks.

Open: 4 April - 15 September.

Directions

Leave A4 Venice - Trieste motorway at exit for 'Aeroporto' and follow signs for Jesolo and Punta Sabbioni. Site is signed after village of Cavallino. GPS: N45:27.409 E12:30.432

Charges guide

Per person	€ 3,90 - € 7,70
pitch incl. all services	€ 8,40 - € 16,50

Camping Cheques accepted.

IT60420 Camping Alba d'Oro

Via Triestina SS 14 km 10, Ca'Noghera, I-30030 Mestre (Veneto)

Tel: **041 541 5102**. Email: **albadoro@tin.it** **www.alanrogers.com/IT60420**

This well managed site is ideal for visiting Venice and the site's bus service takes you directly to the bus station on the west side of the city. There is always room here and on arrival you can select your own pitch. There is a separate area for backpackers and yet another for families. The 140 pitches, all with electricity, are of reasonable size and separated. The good sized pool is especially welcome after a hot day spent visiting Venice. The site is close to the airport and loud aircraft noise will be heard on some pitches especially to the east, although no night flying is permitted.

Facilities

The four modern sanitary blocks are kept very clean. One block has facilities for disabled campers. Launderette. Motorcaravan services. Supermarket. Restaurant with terrace overlooking the pool and serving good food at reasonable prices. Part of the same complex, is a lively bar with entertainment in season. Pizzerias. Bicycle hire. Marina. Bus service April - Oct. Shuttle bus to Verona.

Open: All year.

Directions

From Venice - Trieste autostrada leave at exit for airport and follow signs for Jesolo on the SS14. Site is on right at 10 km. marker. GPS: N45:30.996 E12:21.282

Charges guide

Per person	€ 7,00 - € 8,20
child (3-10 yrs)	€ 4,50 - € 5,60
pitch incl. car	€ 13,00 - € 14,40

IT60550 Villaggio Turistico Isamar

Isolaverde, via Isamar 9, I-30010 Sa Anna di Chioggia (Veneto)
Tel: **041 553 5811**. Email: **info@villaggioisamar.com** **www.alanrogers.com/IT60550**

Many improvements have been made here over the years and these continue at this busy, well managed site. The largest camping area, which may be cramped at times, is under pines and grouped around the swimming pool; the large modern sanitary block, and shops, etc. are near reception. A smaller camping area is situated under artificial shade near the beach with an Olympic size, salt water swimming pool, paddling pool and four new pools, a covered entertainment section, pizzeria, bar/restaurant and a small toilet block. Between these sections are well constructed holiday bungalows. A third camping area has been developed mainly for the site's own accommodation. The pitches, on either side of hard access roads, vary in size and all have electrical connections. Although directly by the sea, with its own sandy beach, it is a fair way from the entrance to the sea. The site has a much higher proportion of Italian holidaymakers than many other sites. It is also popular with Germans and Dutch and may become crowded in high season.

Facilities

The main toilet blocks are fully equipped and of good quality with British style WCs (small block has only Turkish style). Laundry. Motorcaravan services. Gas supplies. Fridge hire. Hairdresser. Supermarket and general shopping centre. Large bar/pizzeria and self-service restaurant. Swimming pools. Tennis. Playground. Disco. Games room. Riding. Bicycle hire. Extensive entertainment and fitness programme. Supervised play for children over 4 yrs old. Dogs are not accepted. Off site: Fishing 500 m.

Open: 13 May - 16 September.

Directions

Turn off main 309 road towards sea just south of Adige river about 10 km. south of Chioggia, and proceed 5 km. to site. GPS: N45:09.910 E12:19.195

Charges guide

Per person	€ 3,50 - € 9,80
child (2-5 yrs)	€ 2,50 - € 8,30
pitch incl. full facilities	€ 6,90 - € 23,00

Less 10% for stays in low season for over 2 weeks.

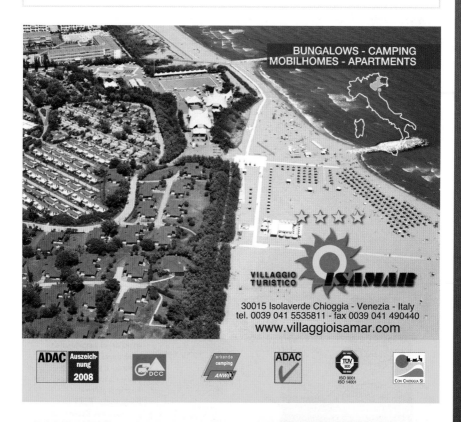

IT60900 Camping Arizona

Via Tabiano 42/A, I-43039 Tabiano di Salsomaggiore Terme (Emília-Romagna)

Tel: **052 456 5648**. Email: **info@camping-arizona.it** **www.alanrogers.com/IT60900**

Tabiano and Salsomaggiore Terme are thermal springs dating back to the Roman era and the beneficial waters have given rise to attractive inland resort towns. The focus on water is developed within this family-run site. The complex of four large pools, long water slides, jacuzzi and play area are set in open landscaped grounds with good views and are also open to the public. Camping Arizona is a simple site set on steep slopes and is 500 m. from the town of Tabiano. Access is easy to the lower pitches for even the largest of units. The 350 level pitches vary from 50-90 sq.m. Those on terraces enjoy shade from mature trees, others have no shade. All have access to electricity (3A) and water points are within 30 m. On site traffic is kept to a minimum during the high season – with the exception of loading and unloading, vehicles must be parked in the large adjacent car park and golf trolleys are provided for use during your stay. Sporting facilities include the water park area, tennis, volleyball and basketball and a five-a-side football pitch on synthetic grass. Younger children will be entertained by the large, supervised play centre with bouncy castle, ball pool and other games.

Facilities

Sanitary facilities in four dated blocks are rather tired but kept clean. Two new blocks are planned for 2009. Mostly Turkish style WCs, open style washbasins and hot water throughout. Facilities for disabled visitors. Washing machines and dryers. Small well stocked shop (all facilities from 1/4). Restaurant/bar with patio. Swimming pools, slides and jacuzzi (18/5-15/9, also open to the public but free for campers). Tennis. Boules. Play centre. Bicycle hire. Off site: Pub outside gate. Fidenza shopping village with designer outlets 8 km. Fishing 4 km. Golf 6 km.

Open: 20 March - 15 October.

Directions

From autostrada A1 take exit for Fidenza and follow signs for Tabiano. The site is on left 500 m. after Tabiano town centre. GPS: N44:48.400 E10:00.610

Charges guide

Per person	€ 6,00 - € 8,50
child (2-9 yrs)	€ 4,00 - € 6,50
pitch	€ 8,00 - € 13,50
dog	€ 2,00 - € 2,50

No credit cards.

IT60650 Camping Bungalow Park Tahiti Village

Viale Libia 133, I-44020 Lido delle Nazioni (Emília-Romagna)

Tel: **053 337 9500**. Email: **info@campingtahiti.com** **www.alanrogers.com/IT60650**

Tahiti is an excellent, extremely well run site, thoughtfully laid out less than 1 km. from the sea (a continuous, small, fun, road-train link is provided). Flowers, shrubs, ponds and attractive wooded structures enhance its appearance and, unlike many campsites of this size, it is family owned and run. The 469 pitches are of varying size, back to back from hard roads and defined by trees with shade in most areas. There are 30 pitches with a private unit containing a WC and washbasin. Electricity is available throughout and 100 pitches also have water and drainage. English is spoken. The British have not yet really discovered this site but it is popular with other European campers. The site is very busy in season with much coming and going, but all is always under control – it is superb, especially for families with children. It is also keen on recycling and even has a facility for exhausted batteries. They have thought of everything here and the manager Stefano is a dynamo who seems to be everywhere, ensuring the impressive standards are maintained. The staff are smart and attentive. As well as the 25 x 12 m. swimming pool, there is 'Atoll Beach', a Caribbean style water-play fun area with palms, plus a jacuzzi, bar and terrace (small extra charge for 'wet' activities). A new 'Thermal Oasis' offers health and beauty treatments.

Facilities

All toilet blocks are of a very high standard. British and Turkish style WCs. Baby room. Large supermarket. Two waiter service restaurants. Bar. Pizzeria. Takeaway. Swimming pools. Fitness and beauty centre. Several playgrounds and miniclub. Gym. Tennis. Floodlit sports area. Minigolf. Bicycle hire. Entertainment and excursions (high season). 'Disco-pub'. ATM. Internet. Free transport to the beach. Torches needed in some areas. Dogs are not accepted. Off site: Fishing 300 m. Riding 500 m.

Open: 6 April - 20 September.

Directions

Turn off SS309 35 km. north of Ravenna to Lido delle Nazioni (north of Lido di Pomposa) and follow site signs. GPS: N44:43.907 E12:13.631

Charges guide

Per person	€ 4,60 - € 9,40
child (under 8 yrs)	free - € 7,10
pitch acc. to season and type and facilities	€ 8,90 - € 28,90
pitch incl. sanitary facility	€ 17,90 - € 54,90

IT60750 Kawan Village Florenz

Viale Alpi Centrali 199, I-44020 Lido degli Scacchi (Emília-Romagna)

Tel: **053 338 0193**. Email: **info@campingflorenz.com** **www.alanrogers.com/IT60750**

Popular with Italian families for over 30 years, Camping Florenz has many loyal campers who stay for the whole season. The area which is most sought after by tourers is over the sand dunes along the seafront where there are good sized, shaded and level pitches with views of the water. The gently shelving beach has fine grey sand and lots of chairs and umbrellas. Away from the beach area there is heavy shade cover from pine trees. The pitches are mostly a mixture of sand and grass, of a good size and level, all with electricity (3A).

Facilities

Six mixed mostly old sanitary blocks with half British, half Turkish style toilets and preset showers. Some unisex showers at beach. Good facilities for disabled people. Motorcaravan service point. Good supermarket. Restaurant and bar with TV. Large outdoor pool. Activities and children's club in season. Play area. Excellent beach for swimming and boat launching. Beach bar. Bicycle hire. WiFi. Off site: Restaurants and shops 1 km.

Open: 4 April - 27 September.

Directions

Site is at Lido degli Scacchi just off the S309 running between Chioggia and Ravenna. Both Lido degli Scacchi and site are well signed from the S309. GPS: N44:42.084 E12:14.324

Charges guide

Per person	€ 4,40 - € 9,00
child (3-10 yrs)	free - € 5,60
pitch	€ 10,00 - € 25,60

Camping Cheques accepted.

IT66190 Numana Blu Camping Village

Via Costaverde 37, I-60026 Numana (Marche)

Tel: **071 739 0993**. Email: **info@numanablu.it** **www.alanrogers.com/IT66190**

Numana Blu lies on the Conero Riviera, south of Ancona, just 300 metres from the sea, and close to the town of Marcelli. Beneath the site's 12,000 trees there are 380 shady pitches, most offering electrical connections. Separate areas have a range of rentable accommodation, including chalets and bungalows. There's plenty to do here but the site retains a relaxed atmosphere. In peak season there are several children's clubs catering for different ages. The site also boasts an impressive array of leisure amenities including a large swimming pool, a restaurant/pizzeria and supermarket. This is a friendly site with multilingual reception staff. The beach is a short walk and offers private facilities. Numana is less than a kilometre away and has all the amenities of a typical Italian resort. The Sirolo National Park is very close and well worth a visit.

Facilities

Supermarket. Bar, restaurant/pizzeria and takeaway meals. Swimming pool and children's pool. Playground. Bicycle hire. Football pitch. Tennis. Children's clubs. Entertainment programme in high season. Off site: Beach 300 m. Conero Riviera, Monte Conero (at 572 m. the highest peak in the area) and Ancona. Riding. Cycle and walking trails. Golf.

Open: 1 May - 10 September.

Directions

Take the Loreto Porto Recanati exit from the A14 autostrada and follow signs to Numana. Site is south of Numana, 1.5 km. from the small town of Marcelli. GPS: N43:28.517 E13:37.751

Charges guide

Per person	€ 4,50 - € 9,50
child (under 6 yrs)	€ 2,80 - € 6,90
pitch	€ 11,00 - € 23,50
tent pitch	€ 6,90 - € 15,30
electricity	€ 3,00

IT66170 Camping Perticara

Via Serra Masini 10/d, Perticara, I-61017 Novafeltria (Marche)

Tel: **054 192 7602**. Email: **info@campingperticara.com** **www.alanrogers.com/IT66170**

High in the Marche hills, not far from San Marino, Ravenna and Rimini, is Camping Perticara, a brand new, purpose built camping site with glorious views across a valley to the mountains and the nearby traditional village of Perticara. Its 80 pitches have water and drainage and are very large, all arranged on terraces to take advantage of the fabulous scenery. Good sized trees have been planted to provide shade in the future. The shop, bar and restaurant area is attractively presented.

Facilities

Two immaculate modern units provide really excellent facilities with all the extras. Facilities are all in large luxury cabins with shower, toilet and basin. Units for disabled campers are of the same standard. Washing machine and dryers. Gas. Small shop. Restaurant (limited menu but good value). Snack bar. Swimming and paddling pools. Small play areas. Animation (miniclub) in high season. Torches useful. Off site: Bicycle hire 500 m. Fishing 10 km. Golf 25 km.

Open: 24 April - 20 September.

Directions

After Bologna on the A1 take A14 towards Ancona and exit for Rimini Nord. After 200 m. turn right (San Leo), over five roundabouts (San Leo, Montefeltro). At traffic lights turn right to Novafeltria (32 km). At Novafeltria, 400 m. after lights, turn right towards Perticara. Climb for 7 km. (under 12%) and at top turn left towards Santa Agata Feltria. After 400 m. turn right to site.
GPS: N43:53.010 E12:17.004

Charges 2009

Per person	€ 5,50 - € 8,50
pitch	€ 11,00 - € 15,00

IT65070 Camping Panorama

Strand Panorama, I-61010 Fiorenzuola di Focara (Marche)

Tel: **072 120 8145**. Email: **info@campingpanorama.it** **www.alanrogers.com/IT65070**

Camping Panorama is a peaceful site located on a scenic coastal drive within a small national park (Parco del San Bartolo) and quite close to the delightful town of Pesaro. The site lies 100 metres above the sea and a pleasant path leads to the beach below. There are 150 pitches ranging in size from 45-100 sq.m. Most have electrical connections and all are well shaded. This is a largely undeveloped area and has many opportunities for walking and mountain biking.

Facilities

Centrally located toilet block. Swimming pool and children's pool. Bar, pizzeria. TV room. Play area. Sports court. Tourist information. Off site: Riding. Golf. Nearest village is Fiorenzuola di Focara 2 km, a pretty village perched over the sea with bars, shops and restaurants. Pesaro 6 km. San Marino 42 km. Urbino 50 km. Mountain biking and walking.

Open: 21 April - 30 September.

Directions

From A14 (Bologna - Taranto) take Cattolica exit and join SS16 southbound towards Siligata. Here join the coast road (Strad Panoramico) towards Fionenzuola. Site is beyond this town and Fiorenzuola di Focara and before reaching Pesaro.
GPS: N43:56.501 E12:50.751

Charges guide

Per person	€ 6,00 - € 9,00
pitch	€ 9,50 - € 13,00
electricity	€ 2,50

No credit cards.

IT66270 Camping Boschetto di Piemma

Loc Santa Lucia 38/C, I-53037 San Gimignano (Tuscany)

Tel: **0577 940352**. Email: **info@boschettodipiemma.it** **www.alanrogers.com/IT66270**

The medieval Manhattan of San Gimignano is one of Tuscany's most popular sites. This new campsite lies just 2 km. from the town and there are 100 small pitches here, all with electricity (10A). The site is in a wood surrounded by olive groves and vineyards and has been developed with much care for the environment, using rain water for irrigation, for example. San Gimignano has been classified by UNESCO as a world heritage site and is best known for its towers dating back to the 11th century.

Facilities

Excellent sanitary block and facilities for disabled visitors. Restaurant/pizzeria and bar. Shop (specialising in local produce). Swimming pool (15/5-15/9, small charge). Tennis (lessons available). Sports pitch. Playground. Entertainment and activity programme in high season. Apartments for rent. Off site: San Gimignano 2 km. Cycle and walking trails, riding, golf.

Open: 1 April - 30 October.

Directions

Take the Poggibonsi Nord exit from the Florence - Siena superstrada. Then follow signs to San Gimignano. At first roundabout follow signs to Volterra and then take first road to the left, signed Santa Lucia. Site is located close to the sports area.
GPS: N43:27.196 E11:03.215

Charges guide

Per person	€ 6,50 - € 9,40
pitch	€ 5,00 - € 13,00

IT66080 Camping Torre Pendente

Viale delle Cascine 86, I-56122 Pisa (Tuscany)

Tel: **050 561 704**. Email: **info@campingtorrependente.it** **www.alanrogers.com/IT66080**

Torre Pendente is a most friendly site, well run by the Signorini family who speak good English and make everyone feel welcome. It is amazingly close to the famous leaning tower of Pisa and obviously its position means it is busy throughout the main season. It is a medium sized site, on level, grassy ground with some shade from trees and lots of artificial shade. There are 220 touring pitches, all with electricity. All site facilities are near the entrance including a pleasant swimming pool complex with pool bar and a large terrace. Here you can relax and enjoy drinks and snacks or find more formal fare in the restaurant with an à la carte menu. This is a very busy site in high season with many nationalities discovering the delights of Pisa. It is ideal for exploring the tower and other attractions.

Facilities

Three new toilet blocks are clean and smart with British style toilets and good facilities for disabled campers. Private cabins for hire. Hot water at sinks. Washing machines. Motorcaravan services. New supermarket. New restaurant, bar and takeaway. Swimming pool with pool bar, paddling pool and spa. Playground. Boules. Animation in high season. Internet access. Off site: Bicycle hire. Riding 3 km. Fishing 10 km.

Open: 1 April - 15 October.

Directions

From A12, exit at Pisa Nord and follow for 5 km. to Pisa. Do not take first sign to town centre. Site is well signed at a later left turn (Viale delle Cascine). GPS: N43:43.270 E10:22.590

Charges guide

Per person	€ 8,00 - € 9,00
child (3-10 yrs)	€ 4,50 - € 5,00
pitch	€ 6,00 - € 15,00
dog	€ 1,60

IT66060 Camping Europa

Viale dei Tigli, casella postale 115, I-55043 Torre del Lago Puccini (Tuscany)

Tel: **058 435 0707**. Email: **info@europacamp.it** **www.alanrogers.com/IT66060**

Europa is a large, flat, rectangular site with roads on all four sides of the site. There are 400 pitches in 17 rows, several with well established permanent pitches, three with bungalows to rent. The site's facilities including a bar, shop and air conditioned restaurant, are in rows 5 and 6. The touring pitches in rows 12-17 are flat, very sandy and close together (55-70 sq.m). Some have shade from small trees or artificial cover and electricity is available. The site has been owned by the Morescalchi family since 1967 and they are very keen that you have an enjoyable stay. The pool and its separate paddling pool are pleasant (charged). A bicycle is a possibility for the beach 1 km. away or a brisk 20 minute walk through towering trees on a forest trail. However, there is a minibus and once there the sand is soft and the beach shelves gently. Europa is well situated for visiting many interesting places around such as Lucca, Pisa, Florence and the wealth of Puccini related historical items.

Facilities

Two sanitary blocks provide hot and cold showers (€ 0.40 token from reception). Toilets are mixed Turkish and British style. Facilities for disabled visitors. Laundry facilities. Cleaning goes on non-stop here. Motorcaravan service point outside gate. Bar/restaurant (air conditioned). Small shop. Good swimming pool (caps required). Large play area. Entertainment. Miniclub. Bicycle hire. Internet access. Dogs are not accepted 3/7-24/8. Torches useful. Off site: Beach 1 km. Fishing. Golf 17 km. Riding 2 km.

Open: -- April - 10 October.

Directions

From A11-12 to Pisa Nord take Viareggio exit. Turn south on Via Aurelia towards Pisa and then towards the sea for Marina di Torre Lago Puccini. Follow clear signs for site. GPS: N43:49.850 E10:16.233

Charges 2009

Per person	€ 4,00 - € 8,50
child (2-10 yrs)	€ 2,50 - € 4,50
pitch	€ 8,50 - € 17,00
car	€ 4,00 - € 8,00
dog	€ 2,00

IT66245 Camping Colleverde

Via Scacciapensieri 47, I-53100 Siena (Tuscany)

Tel: **0577 332 545**. Email: **info@campingcolleverde.com** **www.alanrogers.com/IT66245**

Camping Colleverde enjoys a panoramic setting overlooking the beautiful Tuscan city of Siena and the surrounding Chianti hills. The site is open for a long season and is a good base for visiting the city with good public transport connections. A bus stop is just 200 m. away and the railway station is 1.5 km. There are 220 pitches (around 80 sq.m. each), most of which are equipped with electricity. There are 25 which are occupied by mobile homes (which can be reserved for short stays). On site facilities include a swimming pool, a pizzeria/restaurant and a shop. Siena needs little introduction and is undeniably one of Tuscany's finest medieval cities, famous for its Palio horse race and its fine cathedral. Colleverde is however also a good base for exploring other gems such as San Gimignano and other small towns such as Montepulciano and Montalcino. This is good country to explore on foot or by bike, and bicycle hire is available on site.

Facilities

Shop. Bar. Restaurant/pizzeria. Swimming and paddling pools. Play area. Bicycle rental. Mobile homes for rent. Off site: City centre 2 km. Railway station 1.5 km. Chianti countryside. Cycle and walking tracks.

Open: 1 March - 31 December.

Directions

Site is north of the city. From the north, leave RA3 superstrada (Florence - Siena) at Siena Nord exit. Follow SR222 to Belverde and then turn right into the Toscana, then left into Via Nazareno Orlandi. Site is well signed. GPS: N43:20.263 E11:19.829

Charges guide

Per unit incl. 2 persons	€ 23,50 - € 30,10
extra person	€ 9,00

IT66110 Camping Il Poggetto

Via Il Poggetto 143, I-50067 Troghi - Firenze (Tuscany)

Tel: **055 830 7323**. Email: **info@campingilpoggetto.com** **www.alanrogers.com/IT66110**

This superb site has a lot to offer. It benefits from a wonderful panorama of the Colli Fiorentini hills with acres of the Zecchi family vineyards to the east adding to its appeal and is just 15 km. from Florence. The charming and hard working owners Marcello and Daniella have a wine producing background and you can purchase their fine wines at the site's shop. Their aim is to provide an enjoyable and peaceful atmosphere for families. All 106 pitches are of a good size and have electricity and larger units are welcome. On arrival you are escorted to view available pitches then assisted in taking up your chosen pitch. The restaurant offers excellent Tuscan fare including pizzas, pastas and delicate 'cucina casalinga' (home cooking). The locals also come here to eat. An attractive flower-bedecked terrace overlooks the two pools. Enjoy the typically Tuscan views and revel in the choice of Chianti from the region. A regular bus service runs directly from the site to the city. English is spoken at this delightful family site.

Facilities

Two spotless sanitary blocks with a mix of British and Turkish style WCs are a pleasure to use. Three private sanitary units for hire. Five very well equipped units for disabled campers. Separate facilities for children and baby room. Laundry facilities. Motorcaravan services. Gas supplies. Shop. Bar. Restaurant. Takeaway. Swimming pools and jacuzzi (1/5-30/9). Fitness room. Bicycle and scooter hire. Playground and entertainment for children all season. Excursions and organised trekking. Internet point. Off site: Tennis 100 m. Fishing 2 km. Golf 12 km. Bus service to the centre of Florence.

Open: 1 April - 15 October.

Directions

Exit A1 at Incisa southeast of Florence and turn right onto the SS69. After about 4 km. turn left following 'Pian dell Isola'. At next crossing turn right towards Firenze and follow the site signs. Do not use your satellite navigation here as you may be taken into the steep and narrow streets of the nearby village. GPS: N43:42.083 E11:24.316

Charges guide

Per person	€ 7,50 - € 9,00
child (0-10 yrs)	€ 5,00 - € 6,00
pitch	€ 13,50 - € 18,00

IT66310 Camping Mareblu

Localitá Mazzanta, I-57023 Cecina Mare (Tuscany)

Tel: **058 662 9191**. Email: **info@campingmareblu.com** **www.alanrogers.com/IT66310**

Mareblu is a well equipped family site with an impressive range of amenities, including a large swimming pool with an attractive terraced surround, and shopping complex incorporating a greengrocer, hair salon, newsagent and internet centre. There is also a sandy beach 300 m. away, accessed through a pinewood. The pitches at Mareblu are well shaded and are all equipped with electrical connections (6A). Parking for all cars is in a dedicated area at the front of the site which ensures a pleasant traffic free ambience within the site. The site is close to Cecina Mare, a popular resort with easy access to some of Tuscany's great cities, and the island of Elba.

Facilities

Five modern toilet blocks include facilities for disabled visitors. Shopping centre. Bar, restaurant and self-service cafeteria, pizzeria and takeaway. Swimming and paddling pools. Play area. Games field. Boules. Bicycle hire. Entertainment. Miniclub. Internet access. Direct access to beach. Off site: Tennis. Riding. Watersports and diving. Excursions.

Open: 20 March - 16 October.

Directions

Site is south of Livorno. From north, take A12 to Rosignano and then join the E80 to Vada, then to La Mazzanta. From here site is well signed. GPS: N43:19.105 E10:28.411

Charges guide

Per person	€ 4,30 - € 8,10
child (0-10 yrs)	€ 3,20 - € 6,50
pitch incl. electricity	€ 5,50 - € 12,50
car	€ 1,70 - € 3,80

Camping Cheques accepted.

IT66000 Camping Barco Reale

Via Nardini 11, I-51035 San Baronto di Lamporecchio (Tuscany)

Tel: **057 388 332**. Email: **info@barcoreale.com** **www.alanrogers.com/IT66000**

Just forty minutes from Florence and an hour from Pisa, this site is beautifully situated high in the Tuscan hills close to the fascinating town of Pistoia. Part of an old walled estate, there are impressive views of the surrounding countryside. It is a quiet site of 15 hectares with 250 pitches with good shade from mature pines and oaks. Some pitches are huge with great views and others are very private. Most are for tourers, but some have difficult access (site provides tractor assistance). All 187 touring pitches have electricity and 40 have water and drainage. The site has an attractive bar, a smart restaurant with terraces (try the traditional dishes) and a leased shop. The pools have stunning views to the west (on a clear day you may see the island of Capraia). This is a most attractive and popular site, which will appeal to those who prefer a quiet site but with plenty to do for all age groups. In high season an information kiosk supplies tourist information, makes bookings and help in general. Used by tour operators. Member of 'Leading Campings Group'.

Facilities

Three modern sanitary blocks are well positioned and kept very clean. Good facilities for disabled people (dedicated pitches close by). Baby room. Laundry facilities. Motorcaravan services. Dog shower. Shop. Restaurant. Bar. Supervised pool (caps required; 1/5-30/9). Playgrounds. Bowls. Bicycle hire. Internet. Disco. Entertainment. Excursions. Off site: Village 1 km. Fishing 8 km. Golf 15 km.

Open: 1 April - 30 September.

Directions

From Pistoia take Vinci - Empoli - Lamporecchio signs to San Baronto. From Empoli signs to Vinci and San Baronto. Final approach involves a sharp bend and a steep slope. GPS: N43:50.514 E10:54.678

Charges guide

Per person	€ 7,10 - € 9,90
child (3-11 yrs)	€ 3,80 - € 6,20
pitch	€ 10,00 - € 15,50

Discounts for longer stays except in high season.

IT66290 Camping Tripesce

Via Cavalleggeri 88, I-57018 Vada (Tuscany)

Tel: **058 678 8167**. Email: **info@campingtripesce.com** **www.alanrogers.com/IT66290**

Neat and tidy, this family owned and run site has the great advantage of direct beach access through three gates (CCTV). The beach is of fine sand with a very gentle shelving – super for children, with watersports and a lifeguard, in season. This great beach makes up for the lack of a pool on the site and the fairly small size of the 230 pitches. All have 4A electricity and 60 are serviced with water and drainage with some shade provided by young trees and artificial shade. The site is contained within a rectangle and bungalows for rent are discreetly placed near reception. A pleasant bar with a terrace is alongside the small restaurant, and just across the road is a well stocked shop. The play area is modern and pleasant but slides end on gravel or concrete so children will need supervision. There is a small range of activities and a miniclub. Everything is kept spotlessly clean. The site has many German guests as demonstrated in the German language notices around the site. If you are a beach enthusiast this could be for you, especially the beach side pitches. This is a relaxing site without the razzmatazz of the larger sites along the coast and principally car-free.

Facilities

Three clean, fresh toilet blocks provide hot and cold showers (water is solar heated and free). British and Turkish style toilets. Facility for disabled visitors. Washing machines. Motorcaravan service points. Bar/restaurant and takeaway. Shop. Excellent beach. Aquarobics and aerobics (high season). Play area (supervision required). Miniclub (high season). Internet and WiFi. Fishing. Dogs are not accepted May - Sept. Off site: Bus service 300 m. Seaside town 1 km. Riding 5 km. ATM 1 km.

Open: Week before Easter - 20 October.

Directions

From S1 autostrada (free) between Livorno and Grosetto head south and take Vada exit. Site is well signed along with lots of others as you approach the town. GPS: N43:20.581 E10:27.495

Charges guide

Per person	€ 5,00 - € 8,00
child (0-7 yrs)	€ 3,00 - € 5,00
pitch incl. car and electricity	€ 10,00 - € 20,00

No credit cards.

IT66450 Parco Delle Piscine

Via del Bagno Santo 29, I-53047 Sarteano (Tuscany)

Tel: **057 826 971**. Email: **info@parcodellepiscine.it** **www.alanrogers.com/IT66450**

On the spur of Monte Cetona, Sarteano is a spa, and this large, smart site utilises that spa in its very open environs. The site is well run with an excellent infrastructure and there is a friendly welcome from the English speaking staff. The 509 individual, flat pitches, are all of a good size and fully marked with high neat hedges giving real privacy. The novel feature here is the three unique swimming pools fed by the natural thermo-mineral springs. These springs have been known since antiquity as 'del Bagno Santo' which flows at a constant temperature of about 24°C.

Facilities

Two heated toilet blocks are of high quality with mainly British style WCs, many cubicles also with bidet and numerous sinks for laundry and dishwashing (with hot water). Gas supplies. Motorcaravan services. Restaurant/pizzeria with bar. Takeaway. Coffee bar. Swimming pools. Satellite TV room and mini-cinema with 100 seats and very large screen. Tennis. Exchange facilities. Free guided cultural tours. Internet. Dogs are not accepted. Off site: Bicycle hire 100 m. Riding 3 km.

Open: 1 April - 30 September.

Directions

From autostrada A1 take Chiusi/Chianciano exit, from where Sarteano is well signed (6 km). In Sarteano follow camping/piscine signs to site (entrance sign reads Piscine di Sarteano). GPS: N42:59.249 E11:51.898

Charges guide

Per person	€ 10,50 - € 14,50
child (3-10 yrs)	€ 6,50 - € 8,50
pitch	€ 10,50 - € 21,50
electricity	€ 5,00

IT66380 Campéole Park Albatros

Pineta di Torre Nuova, I-57027 San Vincenzo (Tuscany)

Tel: **056 570 1018**. Email: **nadine.ferran@atciat.com** **www.alanrogers.com/IT66380**

Camping Albatros is another venture for the Cardini/Vanucchi families and is situated on the historic Costa Degli Etruschi where natural parks abound. A group of conical buildings form the hub of the original, somewhat dated, infrastructure of Albatros. This theme of circles is continued through the peaceful new development in the form of round buildings and the placing of mobile homes in curves. The 300 new touring pitches are in a separate area on flat ground of 110 sq.m. All have water, drainage, 10A electricity and some shade from newly planted trees. The restaurant, bar and shopping complex are under natural pines at the hub. They provide a quality range of goods and services. There is also a vast new, air-conditioned supermarket and a new lagoon pool, bar and entertainment area. The new, architect designed, circular, bamboo covered toilet block on the touring side is amazing with brilliant children's rooms. Albatros aims to provide a wide range of services; your visits to the local beach some 800 m. away will be assisted by site transport. There is much to see and explore in the area and a wide range of excursions and walks can be organised.

Facilities

Two toilet blocks are on site. The new circular block is superb! All WCs are British style and the showers are really good, as are facilities for disabled visitors and children. Washing machines. Central area includes bar, restaurant and pizzeria with large terrace. Entertainment programme in season. Miniclub (4-12 yrs). Play areas. Lagoon pool complex. Bicycle hire. No barbecues allowed. Internet. Torches very useful. Off site: Beach 800 m. Riding 1 km. Buses from the gate in high season.

Open: 24 April - 15 October.

Directions

Site is northwest of Grosseto and south of Livorno on the coast. From the SS1 take San Vincenzo exit. Site is well signed as you approach the village. GPS: N43:02.983 E10:33.516

Charges guide

Per person	€ 6,00 - € 12,00
child (2-12 yrs)	€ 4,00 - € 9,00
pitch	€ 8,50 - € 17,00
dog	€ 1,50 - € 3,50

IT66600 Camping Maremma Sans Souci

I-58043 Castiglione della Pescaia (Tuscany)

Tel: **056 493 3765**. Email: **info@maremmasanssouci.it** **www.alanrogers.com/IT66600**

This delightful seaside site is owned and run by the Perduca family and sits in natural woodland on the coast road between Follonica and Grosseto. The minimum amount of undergrowth has been cleared to provide 370 individually marked and hedged, flat pitches for camping. Cars are parked in a secure car park near the entrance. There is a wide road for motorcaravans but other roads are mostly narrow and bordered by trees. Access to some parts is difficult so each pitch is earmarked either for caravans or for tents. All caravan and motorhome pitches have electrical connections.

Facilities

Five small, very clean, mature toilet blocks are well situated around the site. Free showers, plus lots of little extras such as hair dryers and soap dispensers, etc. Three blocks have private cabins each with WC, basin and shower. Separate facilities for disabled campers. Motorcaravan services. Laundry. Shop. Excellent restaurant. Bar with snacks. Sailing school. Torches required in some areas. Dogs are not accepted 16/6-31/8. Off site: Excursions organised to Elba and Rome.

Open: 1 April - 31 October.

Directions

Site is 2.5 km. northwest of Castiglione on road to Follonica on the S322. GPS: N42:46.406 E10:50.635

Charges guide

Per person	€ 7,00 - € 11,00
child (2-6 yrs)	€ 5,00 - € 8,00
pitch and car	€ 9,00 - € 15,00

IT66750 Camping Cieloverde

Via della Trappola 180, I-58100 Marina di Grosseto (Tuscany)

Tel: **056 432 1611**. Email: **info@cieloverde.it** **www.alanrogers.com/IT66750**

Cieloverde Camping Village lies in the heart of the Tuscan Maremma, between Marina di Grosseto and Principina, bordering the Maremma Natural Park. The huge site lies deep in a long established pinewood, looking out onto the Costa d'Argento where a sandy beach slopes gently down to the sea. The 1000 touring pitches (all around 100 sq.m.) are in circular zones around sanitary blocks and all have 3A electricity and offer telephone connections. Parking is in designated areas away from the camping area. A wide range of entertainment is organised , including shows, dance events, open air cinema and games. The site also offers a 2.8 km. 'Percorso Verde' (Green Route) with 16 exercise areas. There is also a new adventure park, Tarzaland, where it is possible to explore the treetops via a network of aerial walkways, ropes and swings. Surrounding the site is a large natural park where fallow deer, red deer, moufflon sheep and other animals roam free. The site restaurant, takeaway and bars are central and you will find typical Maremma recipes, grills and freshly caught fish dishes.

Facilities

Modern toilet blocks. Shops, restaurant and takeaway. Pizzeria. Bars. Hairdresser. Play area. Games room. Archery. Cinema. Chapel. 'Tarzaland' adventure park. Transport to the beach. Dogs are not accepted in high season. Off site: Watersports. Fishing (with licence). Marina di Grossetto. Riding 5 km. Golf 30 km.

Open: 9 May - 23 September.

Directions

Site is west of Grosseto on the coast. Take care here as Grosseto has only one way of crossing the railway for anything other than cars. Follow Grosseto signs from S1 (the Aurelia) and cross town following road to Castiglione della Pescaia until you connect with signs for Marina di Grosseto. Site signed. We stress this is the only way across town.
GPS: N42:42.785 E11:00.446

Charges guide

Per person	€ 5,50 - € 14,00
child (2-5 yrs)	€ 3,90 - € 9,00
pitch	€ 5,90 - € 19,00

Camping Cheques accepted.

IT66810 Camping Capalbio

Strada Litoranea del Chiarone, Localitá Graticciaia, I-58010 Chiarone Scalo bei Capálbio (Tuscany)
Tel: **056 489 0101**. Email: **mauro.ricci@ilcampeggiodicapalbio.it** **www.alanrogers.com/IT66810**

This site has been recommended by our Italian agent and we plan to undertake a full inspection in 2009. Camping di Capalbio is a coastal site in southern Tuscany. The site is next to a wide sandy beach and has a good range of amenities, including a bar, restaurant and supermarket. There are 175 shady pitches here including a number of mobile homes. Various activities are organised on the beach including volleyball and a number of games and competitions. This is a lively site in peak season with evening entertainment based around the beachside bar and restaurant. This part of southern Tuscany is sometimes overlooked given the wealth of places of interest further north. However, the ancient village of Capalbio and the beautiful Lago di Burano are both well worth discovering.

Facilities

Supermarket. Bar. Restaurant. Beach bar. Takeaway food. Motorcaravan services. Entertainment and activities in peak season. Direct access to beach. Play area. Mobile homes and chalets for rent. Dogs are not accepted.
Off site: Capalbio 12 km. Lago di Burano Nature Reserve 4 km. Saturnia hot springs and thermal spa 30 km. Walking and cycle trails.

Open: 30 March - 23 September.

Directions

Head south from Livorno and Pisa on the SS1 (Via Aurelia). Shortly after passing the Lago di Burano, ignore sign to Capalbio to the left, but take the next road to the right (signed Chiarone Scalo). Site is well signed from here. GPS: N42:22.837 E11:26.840

Charges guide

Per person	€ 6,00 - € 13,00
child (4-8 yrs)	€ 4,00 - € 8,00
pitch incl. electricity	€ 6,00 - € 15,00

Camping Cheques accepted.

IT66760 Camping Village Rocchette

Localitá Le Rocchette 62, I-58043 Castiglione della Pescaia (Tuscany)
Tel: **0564 941 123**. Email: **booking@rocchette.com** **www.alanrogers.com/IT66760**

Camping Village Rocchette can be found at the heart of the Maremma woods, 6 km. to the north of Castiglione della Pescaia. The site extends over 70,000 sq.m. of pinewood with a path leading to the sandy beach, just 300 m. away. Pitches are well shaded and of varying sizes, many with electrical connections. Village Rocchette also offers 75 well equipped brick bungalows for rent. On site amenities include a new, large swimming pool with spa baths and two pools for children, as well as a tennis court and sports field. This is a popular site in high season and bookings at this time must be for a minimum of 15 days. Castiglione is a delightful seaside town, best known for its beaches.

Facilities

Bar. Restaurant. Swimming pool with spa baths. Two children's pools. Tennis. Sports field. Supermarket and other shops. Play area. Entertainment and activity programme. Direct access to beach 300 m. Bungalows for rent. Off site: Shops, restaurants and bars in Castiglione 6 km. Riding 2 km. Golf 12 km.

Open: 21 March - 25 October.

Directions

Approaching from the north, take the Follonica Nord exit from the E80/S1 superstrada and head south to Castiglione on the S322. Before reaching Castiglione, turn right onto towards Roccamare and Rocchette. Site well signed. GPS: N42:46.756 E10:48.074

Charges 2009

Per unit incl. 2 persons and electricity	€ 20,00 - € 39,00
extra person	€ 6,00 - € 12,00
child (1-5 yrs)	€ 4,00 - € 8,00
dog	€ 6,00 - € 12,00

IT66710 Camping International Argentario

Localitá Torre Saline, I-58010 Albinia (Tuscany)
Tel: **056 487 0302**. Email: **info@argentariocampingvillage.com** **www.alanrogers.com/IT66710**

Argentario is really two separate campsites with a large holiday villa complex, all sharing the common facilities. The pools, entertainment area and bar area, like the villa complex are new and elegantly designed. The large irregularly shaped pool and smaller circular paddling pool are very inviting. Entertainment is organised daily by the team where there is something for everyone, young and old. The 806 pitches with 300 for tourers are small but mostly flat and on a surface of dark sand and pine needles, all are shaded by tall pines. The area is quite dusty and many of the pitches are a very long way from the amenities. Motorcaravans are parked in a large separate open square. Some campers may find the long walks trying, especially as the older style facilities are tired and stressed during peak periods. A basic restaurant and pizzeria is remote from the touring section and has no views. The beach of dark sand has attractive views across to the mountains. We see this site more for short stays than extended holidays and as unsuitable for disabled campers.

Facilities

Three mature blocks have mostly Turkish style toilets, a few cramped showers with hot water and cold water at the sinks (showers are very busy at peak periods). Facilities for disabled campers but the sand surface and remoteness of some facilities are unsuitable. Washing machines. Motorcaravan service point. Shop. Restaurant, bar and takeaway. Swimming pools. Tennis. Boat hire. Minigolf. ATM. Cars are parked in a separate car park in high season. Torches very useful. Dogs are not accepted. Off site: Bar and restaurant on the beach. Boat launching and riding 1 km. Golf 20 km.

Open: Easter/1 April - 30 September.

Directions

Site is south of Grosseto, off the SS1 at the 150 km. mark, signed Porto S. Stefano. Ignore the first 'combined' campsite sign and proceed 300 m. to the main entrance. GPS: N42:29.774 E11:11.648

Charges guide

Per person	€ 7,00 - € 11,50
child (1-6 yrs)	€ 4,00 - € 7,00
pitch	€ 7,00 - € 11,50

IT66670 Camping La Finoria

Via Monticello 66, I-58023 Gavorrano (Tuscany)
Tel: **056 684 4381**. Email: **info@campeggiolafinoria.it** **www.alanrogers.com/IT66670**

An unusual site, primarily for tents, La Finoria is set high in the mountains with incredible views. It is a rugged site with a focus on nature. Italian school children attend education programmes here. The three motorcaravan pitches are at the top of the site for those who enjoy a challenge, with a dozen caravan pitches on lower terraces accessed by a steep gravel track. Under huge chestnut trees there is a very pretty terraced area for tents. These have a private natural feel which some might say is what camping is all about. Electricity (3A) is available to all pitches, although long leads may be needed. If you visit in November you can help collect the olives and make olive oil or in October gather chestnuts for purée, wild berries in May and make jam. Campers are invited to take part in the educational programmes in the 'LEA' building (Laboratario di Educazione Ambientale). The restaurant reflects the owner's attention to detail – the food here is wonderful and all the pasta is homemade. The views of Elba and the Gulf of Follonica from the terrace by day and night are stunning. After an exhausting day communing with nature, or exploring the area, there is a large pool for a refreshing swim before enjoying the night views.

Facilities

Two blocks provide British and Turkish style toilets, hot showers and cold water at washbasins and sinks. Facilities for disabled campers. Washing machines and dryer. Quaint, small shop (closed Jan/Feb). Good restaurant and bar (closed Jan/Feb). Swimming pool (May - Sept). Tennis. Lessons on the environment. Excursions. Torches essential. Off site: Riding 2 km. Village 3 km. Bicycle hire 6 km. Golf 8 km. Site's private beach and fishing 12 km.

Open: All year.

Directions

From SS1 (Follonica - Grosseto) take Gavorrano exit, then Finoria road. This is a steady, steep climb for some 10 minutes. Start to descend and at junction (the only one), look left (difficult turn) downhill for a large white sign to site. Access to site only possible for small units. GPS: N42:55.350 E10:54.740

Charges guide

Per person	€ 3,00 - € 10,00
pitch	€ 4,00 - € 13,00

IT66100 Camping Panoramico Fiesole

Via Peramonda 1, I-50014 Fiesole (Tuscany)

Tel: **055 599 069**. Email: **panoramico@florencecamping.com** **www.alanrogers.com/IT66100**

This is a mature but pleasant site in a fine hilltop situation offering wonderful views over Florence in the distance – on some evenings you can hear music from the nearby Roman amphitheatre famous for its classical entertainment in summer. It can become crowded in the main season and a very steep final access can be very difficult for larger units although the site will assist with a jeep. The 120 pitches, all with electricity (5A), are on terraces and steep walks to and from the various facilities could cause problems for people with mobility problems. There is shade in many parts. Pitches are separated, motorcaravans and caravans in the upper area and tents on the lower terraces. The last approach to the site takes you through the charming village of Fiesole but there are some challenging turns and tight squeezes (look for the helpful wall mounted mirrors). Fiesole itself is interesting, its history predating that of Florence. It was founded in the 7th century BC when the Estruscan colony here was a powerful force in Italy. The site is appreciably fresher and quieter than nearer the very busy city. A shuttle bus service operates one way from the site to the centre of town (08.30-11.45) to connect with the service to Florence (tickets from site office). However, it is an extremely long uphill walk back to the campsite from the town and thus the local bus (to within 300 m. of the site) or a taxi may be essential.

Facilities

Two tastefully refurbished toilet blocks have mainly British style WCs, free hot water in washbasins and good showers. Washing machines and dryers. Fridges, irons and little cookers for campers' use. Shop (1/4-31/10). Bar and restaurant (1/4-31/10). Swimming pool (1/6-30/9). Play area. Nursery. Torches required in some parts. English is spoken. Free shuttle service to Fiesole.

Open: All year.

Directions

From A1 take Firenze-Sud exit and follow signs to Fiesole (NNE of central Firenze). From Fiesole centre follow SP54 and camping signs out of town for 1 km; the roads are very narrow both through the town and the final steep access is difficult. Site is signed on the right from Fiesole. Do not try to enter from the north as the left turn is extremely difficult. GPS: N43:48.409 E11:18.370

Charges guide

Per person	€ 10,80 - € 11,00
child (3-12 yrs)	€ 7,40 - € 7,70
pitch incl. electricity	€ 16,00 - € 16,80

IT66050 Camping Mugello Verde

Via Massorondinaio 39, I-50037 San Piero a Sieve (Tuscany)

Tel: **055 848 511**. Email: **mugelloverde@florencecamping.com** **www.alanrogers.com/IT66050**

Mugello Verde is a country hillside site with long curving terraces and one tarmac access road. Some pitches offer good views. English is spoken at reception where much tourist information is available – ask for the limited dates of the Ferrari team practices and the racing on the nearby International Mugello racing track! There are 200 good sized pitches for motorcaravans and caravans with smaller areas for tents. All pitches have electricity (6A) and mature trees provide shade. We met British campers who liked the site's charm and loved the proximity to the Ferrari race track, but found the facilities a little rustic and the pitches somewhat unkempt.

Facilities

Two toilet blocks on the terraces have been refurbished to a good standard and facilities are clean and relatively modern with mixed British and Turkish style WCs. Most washbasins have hot water. Comprehensive facilities for disabled campers. Laundry facilities. Shop. Restaurant/bar and pizzeria (all season). Swimming pool (15/6-15/9; no paddling pool). Play area. Tennis. Off site: Riding, golf, bicycle hire and fishing, all within 5 km.

Open: All year.

Directions

From A1 autostrada take Barberino del Mugello exit and follow SS65 towards San Piero a Sieve and before town, turn left and just past Tamoil garage turn right to site. GPS: N43:57.689 E11:18.618

Charges guide

Per person	€ 7,00 - € 8,00
child (3-12 yrs)	€ 3,00 - € 5,00
pitch	€ 11,00 - € 13,50

Camping Cheques accepted.

IT66090 Camping Internazionale

Via San Cristofano 2, Bottai, I-50029 Firenze (Tuscany)

Tel: **055 237 4704**. Email: **internazionale@florencecamping.com** **www.alanrogers.com/IT66090**

Camping Internazionale is set in the hills about 5 km. south of Florence, and 8 km. from the Duomo with its wonderful dome by Brunelleschi. There is a 800 m. walk to a bus stop which will take you into Florence. This is a well shaded, terraced site with 240 touring pitches set around the top of a hill. These all have electricity with water obtained from the laundry and kitchen areas or the motorcaravan service point only. The site is often lively at night with young people from tour groups enjoying themselves, however this area is located well away from the touring pitches. Although it is a very green site, the camping area is somewhat more open with two electricity pylons at the top of the hill and some noise from the busy motorway which is below and next to the site. The two toilet blocks are clean and well equipped with many washing machines and dryers. Although showers are a little small they are fully adjustable with free hot water. There is a kitchen area stocked with pots, pans etc, gas hobs and free use of refrigerators. Two good sized pools, one for children, are fenced with a nice playground adjacent. The inviting restaurant with its open bar area has a good menu. This site offers an easily accessible location to explore Florence and of the city sites, is probably the most family friendly.

Facilities

Two toilet blocks include free hot showers. Laundry. Kitchen facilities. Motorcaravan service point. Shop. New bar and restaurant at the lower level. Evening entertainment. Two swimming pools. Playground. Off site: Florence 5 km.

Open: 1 April - 31 October.

Directions

From A1 take Firenza Certosa exit towards Florence. The turn to the site is just outside Bottai – turn left if coming from this direction (if you reach Galluzzo you have gone too far). From Florence take Via Senese (S2) through Galluzzo, turn right at site sign just before entering Bottai. Continue 500 m. to site. GPS: N43:43.425 E11:13.179

Charges guide

Per person	€ 9,50 - € 10,00
child (3-12 yrs)	€ 6,50 - € 6,80
caravan and car, or motorcaravan	€ 15,00 - € 16,80

IT66430 Camping Village Europa

Localitá San Donato 8, I-06065 Passignano sul Trasimeno (Umbria)

Tel: **075 827405**. Email: **info@camping-europa.it** **www.alanrogers.com/IT66430**

The shores of Lake Trasimeno are dotted with a large number of campsites but we feel that Camping Village Europa has something different to offer. This is a high quality friendly site which, with just 100 pitches, is relatively small but which still manages to offer a wide range of amenities. The pitches are separated into four groups by clusters of mature trees, although shade on the pitches is quite limited. All the pitches offer 6A electrical connections. A regular bus service links the site with the nearby town of Passignano and its railway station. The site has its own private beach on Lake Trasimeno with a wide range of watersports available and beach parties in peak season.

Facilities

Three toilet blocks are maintained to a high standard with facilities for disabled users. Washing machines and dryers. Shop. Bar, restaurant, pizzeria and takeaway. Swimming pool. Play area. Children's club. Evening entertainment. Sports pitch. Direct access to lake and beach. Off site: Passignano 2 km. Perugia 30 km. Assisi 45 km. Riding, tennis, watersports.

Open: Easter - 10 October.

Directions

From Passignano take the road towards Perugia. Turn off this road after 1 km. and the site is clearly signed. GPS: N43:10.933 E12:09.900

Charges 2009

Per person	€ 5,50 - € 6,50
child (3-10 yrs)	€ 4,50 - € 5,60
caravan or motorcaravan	€ 6,00 - € 7,50
tent	€ 5,30 - € 6,30

IT66530 Camping Listro

Via Lungolago, I-06061 Castiglione del Lago (Umbria)

Tel: **075 951 193**. Email: **listro@listro.it** **www.alanrogers.com/IT66530**

This is a simple, pleasant, flat site with the best beach on Lake Trasimeno. Listro provides 110 pitches all with electricity with 70% of the pitches enjoying the shade of mature trees. Younger campers are in a separate area of the site, ensuring no noise disturbance and some motorcaravan pitches are right on the lakeside giving stunning views out of your windows. Facilities are fairly limited with a small shop, bar and snack bar, and there is no organised entertainment. English is spoken and British guests are particularly welcome. If you enjoy the simple life and peace and quiet in camping terms then this site is for you. The campsite's beach is private and the lake has very gradually sloping beaches making it very safe for children to play and swim. This also results in very warm water, which is kept clean as fishing and tourism are the major industries hereabouts. Camping Listro is a few hundred yards north of the historic town of Castiglione and the attractive town can be seen rising up the hillside from the site.

Facilities

Two screened sanitary facilities are very clean with British and Turkish style WCs. Facilities for disabled visitors. Washing machine. Motorcaravan services. Bar. Shop. Snack bar. Play area. Fishing. Bicycle hire. Private beach. Off site: Town 800 m. Bars and restaurants nearby. Good swimming pool and tennis courts (discounts using the campsite card).

Open: 1 April - 30 September.

Directions

From A1/E35 Florence-Rome autostrada take Val di Chiana exit and join the Perugia (75 bis) superstrada. After 24 km. take Castiglione exit and follow town signs. Site is clearly signed just before the town. GPS: N43:08.000 E12:02.390

Charges 2009

Per person (over 3 yrs)	€ 4,10 - € 4,90
pitch	€ 4,10 - € 4,90
car	€ 1,50 - € 2,00
motorcycle	€ 1,10 - € 1,50

Less 10% for stays over 8 days in low season.

IT66520 Camping Villaggio Italgest

Via Martiri di Cefalonia, I-06063 Sant Arcangelo Magione (Umbria)

Tel: **075 848 238**. Email: **camping@italgest.com** **www.alanrogers.com/IT66520**

Directly on the shore on the south side of Lake Trasimeno, which is almost midway between the Mediterranean and the Adriatic, Sant Arcangelo is ideally placed for exploring Umbria and Tuscany. The area around the lake is fairly flat but has views of the distant hills and can become very hot during summer. Villaggio Italgest is a pleasant site with 208 touting pitches on level grass and, except for the area next to the lake, under a cover of tall trees. All pitches have electrical connections and cars are parked away from the pitches. The site offers a wide variety of activities and tours are organised daily. There is entertainment for children and adults in high season, including Italian language and civilisation courses. The bar/disco remains open until 02.00 hrs. There is a good sized swimming pool area, one pool with slides, a smaller paddling pool and a whirlpool. The site has a marina for boats with a crane. Whether you wish to use this site as a base for exploration or as a place to relax, you will find this a most pleasant place to stay. English is spoken.

Facilities

The one large and two smaller sanitary blocks have mainly British style WCs and free hot water in the washbasins and showers. Facilities for disabled people. Motorcaravan services. Washing machines and dryers. Kitchen. Bar, restaurant, pizzeria and takeaway (all season). Shop. Recently enlarged Swimming pool. Tennis. Play area. TV (satellite) and games rooms. Disco. Films. Watersports, motorboat hire and lake swimming. Fishing. Mountain bike and scooter hire. Internet point. Wide range of activities, entertainment and excursions. Off site: Golf, parachuting, riding, canoeing and sailing close.

Open: 1 April - 30 September.

Directions

Site is on the southern shore of Lake Trasimeno. Take Magione exit from the Perugia spur of the Florence - Rome autostrada, proceed southwest round the lake to S. Arcangelo where site is signed. GPS: N43:05.180 E12:09.230

Charges 2009

Per person	€ 6,00 - € 8,50
child (3-9 yrs)	€ 4,00 - € 6,50
pitch	€ 6,00 - € 11,50
small tent pitch	€ 5,00 - € 7,00
car	€ 2,00 - € 2,50

Camping Cheques accepted.

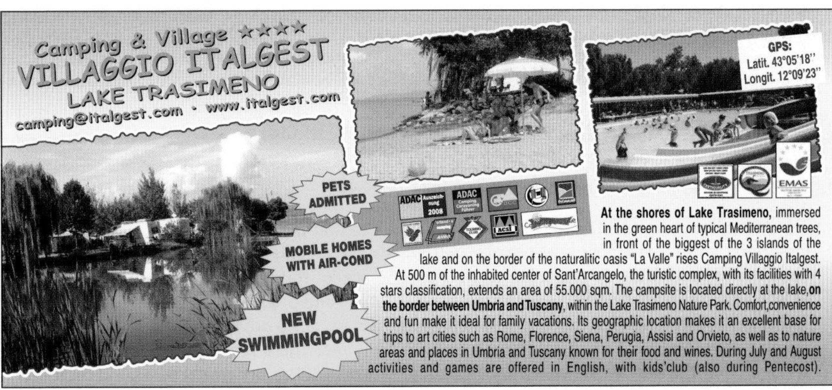

IT66490 Camping Punta Navaccia

I-06069 Tuoro sul Trasimeno (Umbria)

Tel: **075 826 357**. Email: **navaccia@camping.it** **www.alanrogers.com/IT66490**

Situated on the north side of Lake Trasimeno and run by friendly and welcoming owners, this is a large site with over 70,000 sq.m. and 400 touring pitches (200 with 4A electricity) and all with shade. The campsite has a long (stony) beach with facilities for mooring and launching your boat. There are 60 mobile homes with air conditioning for rent. The site is ideally located for exploring Umbria and its famous cities, such as Assisi and Perugia. Tuscany and its cities of Siena and Florence are also within easy reach and it is even possible to visit Rome for a day trip.

Facilities

Sanitary block with British style WCs, showers and some private cabins. Washing machine and dryer. Motorcaravan service point. Heated swimming and paddling pools. Shop. Restaurant and takeaway (April - Oct). Play area. Tennis. Large covered amphitheatre. Disco. Cinema screen. Miniclub. Entertainment is organised in high season. Daily boat trip around island (free). Off site: Sandy beach 200 m. Windsurfing, sailing and canoeing 200 m.

Open: 15 March - 31 October.

Directions

Going south on the A1 (Florence/Firenze - Rome), take exit for Val di Chiana to Perugia near Bettolle. After 15 km. take Tuoro sul Trasimeno exit. Site is well signed. GPS: N43:11.515 E12:04.599

Charges guide

Per unit incl. 2 persons	€ 18,00 - € 25,00
extra person	€ 6,00 - € 8,50
child (2-9 yrs)	€ 4,00 - € 6,00

BOOK THIS SITE CALL 01580 214000 ...we'll arrange everything The Travel Service

BOOK THIS SITE CALL 01580 214000 ...we'll arrange everything The Travel Service

IT66460 Camping La Spiaggia

Via Europa 22, I-06065 Passignano sul Trasimeno (Umbria)

Tel: **075 827 246**. Email: **info@campinglaspiaggia.it** **www.alanrogers.com/IT66460**

This recently opened site has its own beach and is pleasantly covered with pine and oak trees to provide lots of shade. The 50 spacious pitches are clearly defined and separated by dwarf hedges with 6A electricity available. This is an attractive, compact site which is well managed and cared for. A small café/restaurant has a terrace overlooking the lake and a small shop provides fresh bread to order. All sorts of activities are possible on the lake including canoeing, sailing and windsurfing and there are numerous possibilities for hiking or mountain biking in the surrounding hills. The relaxed atmosphere and easy going manner of the site make this a very restful place to visit. The town of Passignano sul Trasimeno is very close with lively bars and restaurants and a docking point for the lake steamer.

Facilities

The new toilet block is very clean and modern with free hot water, It includes facilities for disabled visitors and a baby room. Separate laundry room. Small shop. Bar/restaurant with terrace. Lake swimming. Play area. Bicycle hire. Off site: Restaurant in front of camping. New swimming pool 100 metres with discount for campers.

Open: 22 March - 11 October.

Directions

From A1 (Firenze - Roma) take Beltolle exit towards Perugia (S326). Follow this to Passignano exit (30 km. from the A1). Take the exit and go towards town (site signed). GPS: N43:11.333 E12:08.983

Charges 2009

Per person	€ 6,00 - € 7,00
child (3-10 yrs)	€ 4,00 - € 5,50
pitch	€ 6,00 - € 9,00
car	€ 2,50

IT67850 Camping Internazionale Lago di Bracciano

Via del Pianoro 4, I-00069 Trevignano Romano (Lazio)

Tel: **069 985 032**. Email: **info@camping-inter-lagodibracciano.com** **www.alanrogers.com/IT67850**

Lago di Bracciano, just 45 km. north of Rome, is of a size that provides excellent opportunities for watersports and is inevitably very popular with windsurfers. With some pitches alongside a little beach, the site provides 110 pitches of which about 50 are for tourers. Our pitch had a full view of the lake and the gentle breeze made the temperature at the end of June quite bearable. Some shade is provided by large trees. A bar and restaurant near the entrance are behind the site's small pool and play area. The local bus has a regular service to Rome. There are various opportunities for excursions that the site owners will be pleased to tell you about. This site would be a good choice for long or short stays, especially in low season.

Facilities

The single toilet block is well equipped. Facilities for disabled visitors. Washing machine. Motorcaravan service point. Small shop. Bar and restaurant/pizzeria. Small swimming pool (15/5-15/9). Play area. Barbecue area (not allowed on pitches). Internet access. Mobile homes and bungalows to rent. Off site: Lago di Bracciano.

Open: 1 April - 30 September.

Directions

From the Rome GRA take exit 5 on SS2 towards Cassia. Turn left at Trevignano exit (km. 35) and follow SP4a towards the lake where you will find the site on the left. The access road and gate are max. 2.6 m. wide. GPS: N42:08.683 E12:16.119

Charges guide

Per person	€ 6,00 - € 7,00
child (3-10 yrs)	€ 4,50 - € 5,50
pitch incl. car and electricity	€ 11,00 - € 14,00
dog	€ 3,20 - € 3,70

IT68090 Camping Tiber

Via Tiberina km 1,400, I-00188 Roma (Lazio)

Tel: **063 361 0733**. Email: **info@campingtiber.com**

www.alanrogers.com/IT68090

An excellent city site with sound facilities and a dynamic approach to hosting visitors during their stay, Camping Tiber is also remarkably peaceful. It is ideally located for visiting Rome with an easy train service (20 minutes to Rome) a free shuttle bus every 30 minutes and trams for later at night. The 350 tourist pitches (with electricity) are mostly shaded under very tall trees and many have very pleasant views over the river Tiber. This mighty river winds around two sides of the site boundary (safely fenced) providing a cooling effect for campers. There is a new section with some shade, and bungalows to rent are in a separate area. A small but pleasant outdoor pool with a bar awaits after a busy day in the city. The excellent main bar, beer garden and restaurant all have terraces and, along with the takeaway, give good value. The site is extremely well run and especially good for campers with disabilities. Visiting the delights of Rome is easy from here.

Facilities

Fully equipped, very smart sanitary facilities include hot water everywhere, private cabins, a baby room and very good facilities for disabled campers. Laundry facilities. Motorcaravan service point. Shop. Bar, restaurant, pizzeria and takeaway. Swimming pool (hat required) and bar. Play area. Fishing. Internet access. Free shuttle bus to the underground station every 15 or 30 minutes according to season. Torches useful. WiFi. Off site: Local bars, restaurants and shops. Golf or riding 20 km.

Open: 15 March - 31 October.

Directions

From Florence, exit at Rome Nord Fiano on A1 and turn south onto Via Tiberina and site is signed. From other directions on Rome ring road (GRA) take exit 6 northbound on S3 Via Flaminia following signs to Tiberina. GPS: N42:00.570 E12:30.140

Charges guide

Per person	€ 9,30 - € 10,50
child (3-12 yrs)	€ 6,40 - € 7,50
motorcaravan	€ 10,40 - € 12,20
caravan and car	€ 11,50 - € 13,40

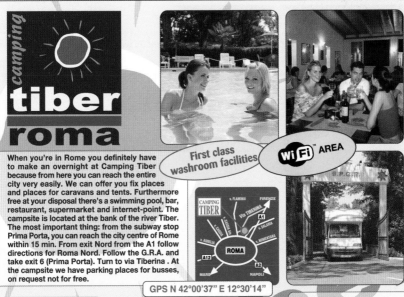

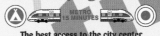

IT68110 I Pini Camping

Via delle Sassete 1/A, Fiano Romano, I-00065 Roma (Lazio)

Tel: **076 545 3349**. Email: **ipini@ecvacanze.it**

www.alanrogers.com/IT68110

The many years Roberto and his Australian born wife Judy have spent in the camping industry are reflected in this site, built only a few years ago. The 117 pitches are set on shaded grassy terraces with views of the nearby hills, access is easy for all units via tarmac roads, and everything is here, including a well stocked and reasonable supermarket. The beautifully designed restaurant with its high ceilings and wooden beams are typical of the thought that has gone into making I Pini a place where you can relax between exciting visits discovering the wonders of Rome or other nearby attractions. What could be more wonderful after several days or nights in Rome (travelling to and from I Pini by air conditioned bus) exploring all the amazing sights before returning to the cool breezes of this hillside site. Simone, Roberto's daughter is responsible for the restaurant and we recommend sampling the excellent menu while admiring the views on the large terrace with entertainment in high season. This is a family business with son Robbie also sharing in the task of making your stay enjoyable. Thought has gone into the location of the bungalow village which is separate from the camping. This very friendly and well ordered site is great for families.

Facilities

The single excellent sanitary block is spotless and hot water is free. Two well equipped units for disabled visitors. Washing machines and dryers. Motorcaravan services. Bar. Restaurant. Snack bar and pizza oven. Pleasant market. Swimming pool (with lifeguard). Tennis. Play area. Entertainment (1/6-30/8). Internet access. Torches required in some areas. Air conditioned buses to Rome daily.
Off site: Fishing 3 km. Golf and riding 20 km.

Open: 30 March - 2 November.

Directions

From Rome ring road (GRA) take A1 exit to Fiano Romano. As you enter the town turn right along via Belvedere opposite an IP petrol station and follow camping signs (there is only the one site).
GPS: N42:09.360 E12:34.370

Charges 2009

Per person	€ 9,00 - € 10,80
child (2-12 yrs)	€ 5,80 - € 7,10
pitch incl. electricity	€ 10,50 - € 12,30

IT68120 Kawan Village Roma Flash

Via Settevene Palo km 19,800, I-00062 Bracciano (Lazio)

Tel: **069 980 5458**. Email: **info@romaflash.it**

www.alanrogers.com/IT68120

This excellent site is in a superb location with magnificent views over Lake Bracciano, the source of Rome's drinking water. When we visited, although it was busy, it was still peaceful and relaxing. There are 275 pitches in total and facilities include a restaurant with a large terrace and small indoor area both overlooking the lake where you can enjoy a good menu and pizzas. The owners Elide and Eduardo speak excellent English and go out of their way to ensure guests enjoy their holiday.

Facilities

Two new large toilet blocks are very well appointed. Free hot water throughout and fully adjustable showers. Facilities for disabled visitors and children. Laundry facilities. Gas supplies. Bar/pizzeria. Small shop. Swimming pool (caps compulsory). Play area. Watersports. Games room. Animation for children in high season. Excursions.
Off site: Rome (40 minutes).

Open: 1 April - 30 September.

Directions

From E35/E45 north of Rome, take Settebagni exit. Follow GRA orbital road west to Cassia exit. Follow sign for Lago Bracciano to town of Bracciano. Site is well signed southeast of town on the SP4A.
GPS: N42:07.896 E12:10.423

Charges guide

Per person	€ 5,00 - € 7,50
pitch	€ 4,00 - € 11,00

Camping Cheques accepted.

IT68190 Camping Villaggio Settebello

Via Flacca km 3,6, I-04020 Salto di Fondi (Lazio)

Tel: **077 159 9132**. Email: **settebello@settebellocamping.com** **www.alanrogers.com/IT68190**

The SS213 hugs this beautiful coast line for many miles, running between small towns and villages and alongside the pine forests that are directly behind the beach. Camping Settebello, an attractive and well managed site, is in a rural area but unfortunately the site straddles this busy road and inevitably there is traffic noise. The touring pitches are all on the beach side of the site in a wooded area. The ground rises before the beach and this is where many of the bungalows for rent have been built. With a total of 600 pitches about 260 are available for touring units. The remainder are used for seasonal caravans (225), mobile homes (16) and bungalows (101). Given the site's popularity, it naturally provides many sporting and social activities. Being midway between Rome and Naples, it is a good point to break a journey when travelling, or perhaps for a longer stay in the low season. Most of the sporting activities are on the other side of the road but these can be accessed by a subway.

Facilities

Five toilet blocks include showers, WCs (Turkish and British style) and washbasins. Facilities for disabled visitors. Motorcaravan service point. Small shop. Bar and restaurant (1/6-10/9). Swimming pool and children's pool (1/6-30/8). Skating. Tennis. Minigolf. Entertainment and children's club. Disco. Amphitheatre and cinema. Dogs (or cats) are not accepted. Bungalows and mobile homes to rent. Bicycle hire. Off site: Narrow public beach. Fondi 10 km. Riding 20 km. Watersports.

Open: 1 April - 30 September.

Directions

The Via Flacca is a comparatively short stretch of the SS213 between Sperlonga and Terracina. The site straddles this road at km. 3.6 which is close to Terracina. Turn towards the beach to find reception. GPS: N41:17.689 E13:19.190

Charges guide

Per unit incl. 2 persons	€ 20,00 - € 62,00
extra person	€ 7,00 - € 15,00
child (3-12 yrs) or senior (over 65 yrs)	€ 6,00 - € 12,00

Camping Cheques accepted.

IT68130 Camping Porticciolo

Via Porticciolo, I-00062 Bracciano (Lazio)

Tel: **069 980 3060**. Email: **info@porticciolo.it** **www.alanrogers.com/IT68130**

This small family run site, useful for visiting Rome, has its own private beach on the southwest side of Lake Bracciano. A pleasant feature is that the site is overlooked by the impressive castle in the village of Bracciano. There are 170 pitches (160 for tourers) split into two sections, some with lake views and 120 having electricity. Pitches are average-sized and shaded by very green trees that are continuously watered in summer by a neat overhead watering system.

Facilities

Three somewhat rustic, but clean, sanitary units with children's toilet and showers. Hot showers (by token). Laundry facilities. Motorcaravan services. Gas supplies. Shop (basics). Bar. Trattoria/pizzeria (15/5-5/9). Tennis. Play area. Bicycle hire. Fishing. Internet point and free WiFi. Torches required in some areas. Excursions 'Rome By Night' and nearby nature parks. Off site: Bus service from outside the gate runs to central Rome. Air conditioned train service from Bracciano (1.5 km) into the city - the site runs a connecting bus (09.00 daily). Riding 2 km.

Open: 1 April - 30 September.

Directions

From Rome ring road (GRA) northwest side take Cassia exit to Bracciano S493 (not Cassia bis which is further northeast). 2 km. before Bracciano village, just after going under a bridge follow site signs and turn along the lake away from Anguillara. Site is 1 km.on the SP1f and has a steep entrance. GPS: N42:06.335 E12:11.167

Charges guide

Per person	€ 5,00 - € 7,00
tent, caravan or motorcaravan and electricity	€ 5,00 - € 8,00

IT68100 Camping Seven Hills

Via Cassia 1216, I-00189 Roma (Lazio)

Tel: **063 031 0826**. Email: **info@sevenhills.it**

www.alanrogers.com/IT68100

Close to Rome, this site provides a quieter, garden setting in some areas, but has a very lively, busy atmosphere in others. It is situated in a delightful valley, flanked by two of the seven hills of Rome and is just off the autostrada ring road (GRA) to the north of the city. The site runs a bus shuttle service every 30 minutes in the mornings to the local station and one return bus to Rome each day (09.00, returning at 18.00). The 80 pitches for touring units (3A electricity to some) are not marked, but the management supervise in busy periods. Arranged in two sections, the top half, near the entrance, restaurant and shop consists of small, flat, grass terraces with two to four pitches on each, with smaller terraces for tents. Access to some pitches may be tricky. The flat section at the lower part of the site is reserved mainly for ready erected tents and cabins used by international tour operators who bring guests by coach. These tend to be younger people and the site, along with its often busy pool, has a distinctly youthful feel. Consequently there may be a little extra noise, so choose your pitch carefully. The site is a profusion of colour with flowering trees and shrubs and a good covering of trees provides shade. English is spoken and many notices are in English. All cash transactions on the site are made with a card from reception. This is an extremely busy site with up to 15 touring buses with their occupants on the site during high season, in addition to a very busy camping routine.

Facilities

Three soundly constructed sanitary blocks are well situated around the site, with open plan washbasins, and hot water in the average sized showers. Facilities for disabled campers. Well stocked shop. Bar/restaurant and terrace. Money exchange. Swimming pool at the bottom of the site with bar/snack bar and a room where the younger element tends to congregate (separate pool charge). Disco. Excursions. Bungalows to rent.
Off site: Golf 4 km.

Open: 15 March - 1 November.

Directions

From ring road exit 3 take Via Cassia (SS2 Viterbo, NOT Via Cassia Bis) and look for site signs. Turn right after 1 km. and follow small road, Via Italo Piccagli for 1 km. to site. This narrow twisting road is heavily parked on during the day so access can be interesting. GPS: N41:59.580 E12:25.011

Charges guide

Per person (over 4 yrs)	€ 6,50 - € 9,50
pitch incl. car	€ 6,50 - € 5,00

No credit cards.

IT67915 Camping Le Foci

Via Fonte dei Cementi, I-67030 Opi (Abruzzo)

Tel: **086 391 2233**. Email: **lefoci@tin.it**

www.alanrogers.com/IT67915

This site has been recommended by our Italian agent and we plan to conduct an inspection this year. Camping Le Foci has a fine setting high in the Abruzzo National Park. There are 210 pitches here, of which 80 are reserved for tents and the rest for caravans or motorcaravans. All pitches are equipped with electrical connections (5A). This is dramatic mountain country and the tranquillity is disturbed only by cow bells. The delightful mountain village of Opi is close and from here the views are amongst the finest in the National Park. The site was created in 1980 by the Ferrazza family with a strong desire to create a holiday centre in harmony with its beautiful environment. Since then, all development has been guided by the same principles. A new, low intensity lighting scheme is a good example of this. This is also a very rich area for walking and mountain biking. The site management will be pleased to recommend possible itineraries.

Facilities

Centrally located toilet block with token operated showers. Shop. Bar. Restaurant. TV room. Play area. Caravans for rent. Off site: Nearest town is Opi with bars, shops and restaurants 2 km. Riding 2 km. Covered swimming pool and tennis 6 km. Chair lift 6 km.

Open: All year.

Directions

From the A24 autostrada (Rome - Pescara) take Pescina exit. Join the SS83 following signs to the Abruzzo National Park. Pass through Pescasseroli and contune to Opi, from where the site is well signed. GPS: N41:47.124 E13:05.003

Charges guide

Per person	€ 5,00 - € 7,00
child (3-7 yrs)	€ 3,00 - € 5,00
pitch	€ 8,00 - € 10,00

IT68040 Camping Village Eurcamping

Lungomare Trieste Sud, I-64026 Roseto degli Abruzzi (Abruzzo)

Tel: **085 899 3179**. Email: **eurcamping@camping.it** **www.alanrogers.com/IT68040**

Eurcamping is about 2 km. south of the small town of Roseto degli Abruzzi, on the small coastal road which runs parallel to the SS16. This is a quiet site, situated beside the sea, with a total of 265 small pitches (many under green screens) and all with electicity (3/6A). Accessing the site may be difficult for higher units as you have to pass under the coastal railway line and many of the bridges offer less than 2 m. headroom. There is some road noise but little noise from the railway. There are good facilities and some entertainment is provided for children in high season. There is a small harbour and yacht club nearby and a small sandy section of the beach, 75 m. away is belongs to the site.

Facilities

Three sanitary blocks with free hot showers. Facilities for disabled people. Motorcaravan services. Laundry. Bar. Restaurant. Takeaway. Pizzeria. Shop. Swimming pools (hats must be worn) with solarium terrace. Play area and sports ground. Tennis. Bowling. Internet point. Bicycle hire. Enterainment in high season. Clubs for children and teenagers. Pets are allowed only on assigned pitches. Off site: Beach. Canoe and pedalo hire.

Open: 1 April - 31 October.

Directions

From north or south on A14 motorway, take exit for Roseto degli Abruzzi. Turn on SS150 to Roseto degli Abruzzi. From Rome and L'Aquila on A24 motorway take exit for Villa Vomano-Teramo, onto SS150 (Roseto degli Abruzzi). GPS: N42:39.466 E14:02.116

Charges guide

Per person	€ 4,00 - € 10,00
pitch	€ 8,00 - € 17,00

Camping Cheques accepted.

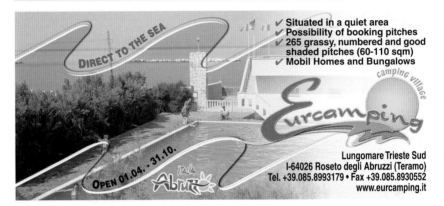

IT68000 Camping Europe Garden

Via Belvedere 11, I-64028 Silvi (Abruzzo)

Tel: **085 930 137**. Email: **info@europegarden.it** **www.alanrogers.com/IT68000**

This site is 13 km. northwest of Pescara and, lying just back from the coast (2 km.) up a very steep hill, it has pleasant views over the sea. The 204 pitches (40 for touring), all with electricity, are mainly on good terraces – access may be difficult on some pitches. However, if installation of caravans is a problem a tractor is available to help. When we visited the site was dry but we suspect life might become difficult on some pitches after heavy rain. Most pitches are shaded.

Facilities

Two good toilet blocks are well cleaned and provide mixed British and Turkish style WCs. Washing machines. Restaurant. Bar. Swimming pool, small paddling pool and jacuzzi. Tennis. Playground. Entertainment. Free weekly excursions (15/6-8/9). Free bus service (18/5-7/9) to beach. Dogs are not accepted.

Open: 27 April - 20 September.

Directions

Turn inland off S16 coast road at km. 433 for Silvi Alta and follow site signs. From autostrada A14 take Pineto exit from north or Pescara Nord exit from the south. GPS: N42:34.043 E14:05.548

Charges guide

Per person	€ 5,00 - € 10,00
pitch incl. electricity	€ 8,50 - € 19,00

IT68200 Baia Domizia Villaggio Camping

I-81030 Baia Domizia (Campania)

Tel: **082 393 0164**. Email: **info@baiadomizia.it** **www.alanrogers.com/IT68200**

This large, beautifully maintained seaside site is about 70 kilometres northwest of Naples, and is within a pinewood, cleverly left in its natural state. Although it does not feel like it, there are 750 touring pitches in clearings, either of grass and sand or on hardstanding, all with electricity. Finding a pitch may take time as there are so many good ones to choose from, but staff will help in season. Most pitches are well shaded, however there are some in the sun for cooler periods. The central complex is superb with well designed buildings providing for all needs (the site is some distance from the town). Restaurants, bars and a 'gelaterie' enjoy live entertainment and attractive water lily ponds surround the area. The entire site is attractive, with shrubs, flowers and huge green areas. Near the entrance is a new swimming pool complex complete with hydromassage points and a large sunbathing area. The supervised beach is 1.5 km. of soft sand and a great attraction. A large grassy field overlooking the sea is ideal for picnics and sunbathing. A wide range of sports and other amenities are provided. The site is very well organised with particular regulations (e.g. no dogs or loud noise), so the general atmosphere is relaxing and peaceful. Although the site is big, there is never very far to walk to the beach, and although it may be some 300 m. to the central shops and restaurant from the site boundaries, there is always a nearby toilet block. It is the ideal place to recover from the rigours of touring or to relax and allow the professionals to organise tours for you to Rome, Pompeii, Sorrento etc. Charges are undeniably high, but this site is well above average and most suitable for families with children. Member of 'Leading Campings Group'.

Facilities

Seven new toilet blocks have hot water in washbasins (many cabins) and showers. Good access and facilities for disabled people. Washing machines, spin dryers. Motorcaravan services. Gas supplies. Supermarket and general shop. Large bar. Restaurants, pizzeria and takeaway. Ice cream parlour. Swimming pool complex. Playground. Tennis. Bicycle hire. Windsurfing hire and school. Disco. Excursions. Torches required in some areas. Dogs are not accepted. Off site: Fishing and riding 3 km.

Open: 30 April - 20 September.

Directions

The turn to Baia Domizia leads off the Formia - Naples road 23 km. from Formia. From Rome - Naples autostrada, take Cassino exit to Formia. Site is to the north of Baia Domizia and well signed. Site is off the coastal road that runs parallel to the SS7 qtr. GPS: N41:12.432 E13:47.481

Charges guide

Per person	€ 5,10 - € 10,80
child (1-5 yrs)	free - € 8,50
pitch incl. electricity (3A)	€ 11,10 - € 22,40

IT68380 Camping Nettuno

Via A. Vespucci 39, Marina del Cantone, I-80061 Massa Lubrense (Campania)

Tel: **081 808 1051**. Email: **info@villaggionettuno.it** **www.alanrogers.com/IT68380**

Situated in a protected area called the 'Punta Campanella', away from the busiest tourist areas of the Amalfi Coast, but not the appalling roads, this tiny campsite of only 42 pitches (4A) is a delight. Owned and run by the friendly Mauro family, who speak excellent English, it is nestled in the bay of Marina del Cantone between Positano and Capri. Pitches are informally arranged some with fabulous sea views (extra charge) and almost all with shade. There are also about 50 mobile homes. The single small sanitary block is centrally located and newly refurbished with good quality finishes. The site has two pathways to the nearby beach that, unusually for the area, involves little walking or steps. With their own diving centre, a designated BIZAC dive site, this is a popular site for all divers. Excursions are arranged to the Isle of Capri and Amalfi Coast on alternate days, there are also diving or snorkelling trips and excursions into the natural park area only accessible by boat.

Facilities

One clean and newly refurbished sanitary block with excellent facilities for disabled people (and access via a ramp to the beach). Washing machine. Motorcaravan service point. Gas supplies. Small, well stocked shop. Delightful restaurant with sea views. Bar (lively at night). Dive centre. Excursions. TV in bar area. Small play area. Free tennis arranged at court next door. Off site: Small beach (pebbles) 5 m. from bottom of site. Excellent restaurants 100 m. Amalfi Coast, Capri, nature parks, walking etc.

Open: 1 March - 2 November.

Directions

From A3 (Naples - Salerno), take Castellamare di Stabia exit onto S145. Pass Castellamare, follow signs to Meta di Sorrento through Vico Equense bypass tunnel and turn off towards Positano in Meta. After 5 km. turn to S. Agata dei due Golfi (6.5 km) then follow signs to Nerano and finally Marina del Cantone. Site entrance is 50 m. past the reception and dive centre. You will need to go on for 100 m. to turn round in order to enter site with its steep and narrow entrance. GPS: N40:34.996 E14:21.197

Charges guide

Per person	€ 6,50 - € 9,00
pitch incl. electricity	€ 10,00 - € 16,50

Camping Cheques accepted.

IT68890 Villaggio Camping Costa Verde

Capo Vaticano di Ricadi, I-89865 San Nicolo di Ricadi (Calabria)
Tel: **096 366 3090**. Email: **tropea@costaverde.org** **www.alanrogers.com/IT68890**

The coast near Capo Vaticano is listed as one of the best 100 in the world and one of the top three in Italy. From our pitch the sandy beach was just five metres below, down a flight of steps, and we had an unobstructed view of the turquoise sea, the beach and beyond; what more can you ask for? Camping Costa Verde nestles in a small bay, almost hidden from the surrounding area. With its 80 shaded pitches, it offers all year round camping in a beautiful location.

Facilities

The toilet block includes showers, WCs and washbasins. Washing machine. Small shop (1/5-30/10). Bar/coffee shop and restaurant (1/5-30/10). Good sandy beach. Excursions arranged. Children's club in high season. Disco. Apartments to rent. Dogs are not accepted in July/Aug. Barbecues not permitted. Off site: Tropea and Capo Vaticano.

Open: All year.

Directions

From the A3 take Rosarno exit and go through the town. Follow signs for Nicotera then Tropea. Before Tropea look for signs for Ricadi and at a junction, amongst others, for Costa Verde (if you reach the railway viaduct you have gone too far). Turn left here, then right for site. The last 400 m. is a narrow, steep, winding road. GPS: N38:38.344 E15:50.056

Charges guide

Per person	€ 5,50 - € 11,00
pitch incl. car	€ 8,80 - € 16,50

IT68650 Camping Riva di Ugento

Litoranea Gallipoli, Santa Maria di Leuca, I-73059 Ugento (Puglia)
Tel: **083 393 3600**. Email: **info@rivadiugento.it** **www.alanrogers.com/IT68650**

There are some campsites where you can be comfortable, have all the amenities at hand and still feel you are connecting with nature. Under the pine and eucalyptus trees of the Bay of Taranto foreshore is Camping Riva di Ugento. Its 900 pitches are nestled in and around the sand dunes and the foreshore area. They have space and trees around them and the sizes differ as the environment dictates the shape of most. The sea is only a short walk from most pitches and some are at the water's edge. The site buildings resemble huge wooden umbrellas and are in sympathy with the environment. There are swimming and paddling pools, although these are expensive to use in high season. A cinema also shows special events via satellite TV near the main bar and restaurant area. The area is sandy but well shaded, and the sea breezes, scented with pine give the site a cool fresh feel. This site has an isolated, natural feel that defies its size. Cycling along the kilometre of beach, we enjoyed the tranquillity of the amazing pitches – shaded, private and inviting. We were sorry to leave the site which was by far the best we found in the area.

Facilities

Twenty toilet blocks all with WCs, showers and washbasins. New bathrooms. Bar. Restaurant and takeaway. Swimming and paddling pools. Tennis. Bicycle hire. Watersports incl. windsurfing school. Cinema. TV in bar. WiFi. Entertainment for children. Dogs are not accepted. A new play area for children has been added. Beach volleyball. Off site: Fishing. Riding 500 m. Boat launching 4 km. Golf 40 km.

Open: 15 May - 30 September.

Directions

From Bari take the Brindisi road to Lecce, then SS101 to Gallipoli, followed by the SR274 towards S. Maria di Leuca, and exit at Ugento. Site well signed and turn right at traffic lights on SS19. Bumpy approach road. GPS: N39:52.485 E18:08.467

Charges guide

Per pitch incl. 2 persons and 1 child	€ 19,00 - € 41,00
extra person (over 2 yrs)	€ 5,00 - € 9,00

Camping Cheques accepted.

IT68705 Camping Porto Cesareo

Via Torre Lapillo, Torre Columena, I-73010 Porto Cesareo (Puglia)

Tel: **0833 565312**. Email: **info@portocesareocamping.it** **www.alanrogers.com/IT68705**

Porto Cesareo is a new site, attractively located in the Salento region of Puglia, to the north of Gallipoli. The site forms a part of Terrestre Palude park and is a short walk from the white sandy beaches of Torre Lapilolo bay. The site is well equipped with a swimming pool, self service restaurant and sports field. There are 200 pitches here, some of which are occupied by mobile homes (available for rent). There is little natural shade yet and pitches are therefore equipped with artificial shade and vary in size from 60-90 sq.m. The city of Lecce is close and is well worth a visit. Lecce is the most important town of the Salentine peninsula (Italy's heel) and is often known as the Florence of the south, thanks to its cultural riches, many of which date back to ancient Greek and Roman times. Porto Cesareo is an attractive resort with excellent opportunities for subaqua diving.

Facilities

Bar/restaurant. Shop. Swimming pool. Sports field. Volleyball. Games room. Play area. Tourist information. Mobile homes for rent. Off site: Porto Cesareo. Lecce. Gallipoli. Watersports. Fishing.

Open: 7 June - 7 September.

Directions

Approaching from the north (Taranto) head southeast on S7 as far as Manduria, and then continue on S174 to Porto Cesareo. Site is clearly signed from here. GPS: N40:17.398 E17:49.632

Charges 2009

Per unit incl. 2 persons and electricity	€ 22,10 - € 39,50
extra person	€ 5,40 - € 10,90
child (under 5 yrs)	€ 2,90 - € 5,90

IT69190 Camping Scarabeo

I-97017 San Croce Camerina (Sicily)

Tel: **093 291 8096**. Email: **info@scarabeocamping.it** **www.alanrogers.com/IT69190**

Camping Scarabeo is a beautiful site located in Punta Braccetto, a little fishing port in Sicily's southeastern corner. It is a perfect location with exceptional facilities to match. Split into two separate sites (just 50 m. apart) with a total of 80 pitches, it is being constantly improved with care by Angela di Modica. All pitches are well shaded, some naturally and others with an artificial cane roof and have 3 or 6A electricity. Scarabeo lies adjacent to a sandy beach and the little village is close by. The site layout resembles a Sicilian farm courtyard and is divided into four principal areas. The ancient Greek ruins of Kamerina and Caucana are just a few kilometres from the site and their ruins can be reached by bike. The Riserva Naturale at the mouth of the River Irminio is also a popular excursion.

Facilities

Exceptional sanitary blocks provide personal WC compartments (personal key access). Ample hot showers (free low season). Facilities for disabled visitors. Washing machine. Direct access to beach. Playground. Entertainment programme in high season. Mobile homes for rent. Off site: Supermarket 4 km. Restaurant/café 500 m. Cycling and walking trails.

Open: All year.

Directions

Site is 20 km. southwest of Ragusa. From Catania, take S194 towards Ragusa and, at Comiso, follow signs to San Croce Camerina, then Punta Braccetto, from where site is well signed. Use second entrance for reception. GPS: N36:48.985 E14:27.962

Charges guide

Per person	€ 4,00 - € 8,50
child (3-6 yrs)	€ 2,00 - € 5,00
pitch	€ 4,00 - € 11,00

Excellent long term discounts in low season.

IT69250 Camping Il Peloritano

Ctra Tarantonio SS113 dir, Rodia, I-98161 Messina (Sicily)

Tel: **090 348 496**. Email: **il_peloritano@yahoo.it** **www.alanrogers.com/IT69250**

Set in a 100-year-old olive grove which provides shade for the 50 informally arranged pitches, Camping Il Peloritano is a quiet uncomplicated site, off the coast road, with excellent clean facilities. It is a 200 m. walk to the sandy beach and about 2 km. to the nearby village. The friendly owners, Patrizia Mowdello and Carlo Oteri, provide help and assistance to arrange excursions to the Aeolian Islands, Taormina and Mount Etna and will do everything to make your stay a pleasant one.

Facilities

Single refurbished toilet block provides hot showers (by token). Good facilities for disabled visitors. Washing machine. Motorcaravan service point. Small shop and bar. Meals can be ordered in from local restaurants. Excursions arranged. Sub-aqua school and diving with guide. Bowls. Bicycle hire. Off site: Sandy beach 200 m. Small seaside village 2 km. Riding 2 km.

Open: 1 March - 31 October.

Directions

From Messina on the A20 motorway take Villafranca exit then follow 'Messina dir' and Tarantonio for 2 km. From Palermo on the A20, take exit for Rometta and signs for Messina and Tarantonio for about 5 km. GPS: N38:15.559 E15:28.069

Charges guide

Per person	€ 5,00 - € 8,00
child (3-7 yrs)	€ 3,00 - € 5,00
pitch incl. electricity	€ 9,50 - € 15,50

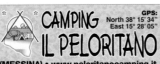

The Travel Service
BOOK THIS SITE
CALL 01580 214000
...we'll arrange everything

IT69350 Camping Rais Gerbi

Ctra Rais Gerbi, SS113, km 172.9, I-90010 Finale di Pollina (Sicily)

Tel: **092 142 6570**. Email: **camping@raisgerbi.it** **www.alanrogers.com/IT69350**

Rais Gerbi provides very good quality camping with excellent facilities on the beautiful Tyrrhenian coast not far from Cefalu. This attractive terraced campsite is shaded by well established trees and the good size pitches vary from informal areas under the trees near the sea to gravel terraces and hardstandings. Most have stunning views, many with their own sinks and with some artificial shade to supplement the trees. From the mobile homes to the unusual white igloos, everything here is being established to a high quality. The large pool with its entertainment area and the restaurant, like so much of the site, overlook the beautiful rocky coastline and aquamarine sea. Vincenzo Cerrito who speaks excellent English has been developing the site for many years and is continually improving the resort style facilities. A frequently used rail line in a cutting, then a tunnel, divides part of the site. The cutting is well fenced and lined with trees but has some impact and one is unaware of the tunnel under the site. Budget airlines fly into a nearby airport and it is possible to rent tents or accommodation at the site. Packages are available to tour the island and use other campsites near major attractions in Sicily (reception staff will advise). Try to visit in spring and autumn when the weather is usually perfect and the site is less busy.

Facilities

Excellent new sanitary blocks with British style toilets, free hot showers in generous cubicles. Small shop. Casual summer terrace and indoor (winter) restaurant. Entertainment area and pool near the sea. Tennis. High quality accommodation and tents for rent. Rocky beach at site. Off site: Small village of Finale 500 m. Larger historic town of Cefalu 12 km.

Open: All year.

Directions

Site is on the SS113 running along the east - north coast of the island, km. 172.9 just west of the village of Finale. It is 12 km. east of Cefalu and 11 km. north of Pollina. GPS: N38:01.397 E14:09.238

Charges guide

Per person	€ 5,00 - € 10,00
pitch incl. electricity	€ 12,00 - € 26,00

IT69230 Camping Jonio

Via Villini a Mare 2, Ognina, I-95126 Catania (Sicily)

Tel: **095 491 139**. Email: **info@campingjonio.com** **www.alanrogers.com/IT69230**

This is a small, uncomplicated and tranquil city site with the advantage of being on top of the cliff at the waters edge. The 70 level touring pitches are on gravel with shade from some tall trees and artificial bamboo screens. There are some clean high quality sanitary facilities (also some private facilities for hire). There is no pool but the views of the water compensate and there are delightful rock pools in the sea just a few steps from the campsite. A new attractive restaurant offers food in the summer high season. Camping Jonio is ideal for a short stay to unwind.

Facilities

Sanitary facilities are modern and clean in two blocks, one small block for men and another for women. Laundry with roof top drying area. Motorcaravan services. Shop. Bar and restaurant. Basic old style playground (supervision recommended). Entertainment (high season). Diving school. Access to small gravel beach. Excursions. Dogs are not accepted in July/Aug. Off site: Large town of Catania, many historical sites and Mount Etna.

Open: All year.

Directions

From A18 Catania exit follow signs to the SS114 coast road in the direction of Ognina. Site is off the SS114 (signed) on the northeast outskirts of town. Access to site is off the small one way system and via the site's separate car park. GPS: N37:31.939 E15:07.204

Charges guide

Per person	€ 7,00 - € 10,00
pitch incl. car	€ 11,00 - € 20,00
electricity	€ 3,00

IT69300 Camping Villaggio Marinello

Via del Sol 17, I-98060 Oliveri (Sicily)

Tel: **094 131 3000**. Email: **marinello@camping.it** **www.alanrogers.com/IT6930**

Camping Marinello is located alongside the sea with direct access to a lovely uncrowded sandy beach with an informal marina at one end and a spot of sand and natural pool areas at the other. The 220 gravel touring pitches here are shaded by tall trees. We enjoyed a delicious traditional meal in the excellent terraced restaurant with its lovely sea views. The Greco family have been here for over 30 years and work hard to ensure that their guests enjoy a pleasant stay. There is some noise from the coastal rail line which runs along the length of the site. Tours are arranged to major sightseeing destinations such as Mount Etna, Taormina and the nearby Aeolian Islands. The nearby resort area town has lots of attractions for the tourist and the site is easily accessible from the ferry at Messina.

Facilities

Two sanitary blocks with free hot showers, one is not currently used and is awaiting a much needed refurbishment and heating. Washing machines. Bazaar, market and supermarket. Bar with sea views. Restaurant and terraced eating area also with views. Electronic games. Piano bar in high season. Dogs are not accepted in July and August. Off site: Seaside resort style town of Oliveri.

Open: All year.

Directions

From A20 motorway take Falcone exit and follow signs to Oliveri. At the town turn north towards the beach (site sign), then turn west along the beach and continue 1 km. to site. You will need to make a right turn immediately before a small narrow bridge (2.2 m. high and 2.5 m. wide). GPS: N38:07.937 E15:03.263

Charges guide

Per person (over 3 yrs)	€ 4,50 - € 9,00
pitch incl. electricity	€ 13,00 - € 21,00
car	€ 3,00 - € 5,00

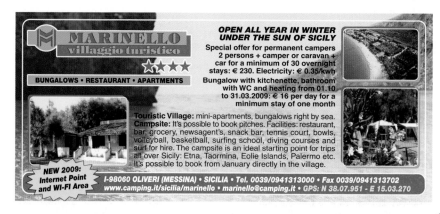

IT69160 Sporting Club Village & Camping

Ctra Bocca Arena, I-91026 Mazara del Vallo (Sicily)

Tel: **0923 947 230**. Email: **info@sportingclubvillage.com** **www.alanrogers.com/IT69160**

Sporting Club Village has been recommended by our Italian agent and we plan to undertake a full inspection this year. Mazara del Vallo can be found on Sicily's southwestern coast. As the crow flies, Tunisia is not far, and the town has a distinct Arabic influence in its winding streets. The site is 2.5 km. from Mazara and boasts some good amenities including a large swimming pool, surrounded by tall palm trees. Pitches here are grassy and generally well shaded. This is a lively site in high season with a wide range of activities and a regular entertainment programme. The nearest beach is 350 m. away and the site is also adjacent to a nature reserve. Sporting Club's focal point, however, is its restaurant with typical Sicilian dishes on offer, notably locally caught fish.

Facilities

Good sports club with swimming pool, gymnasium, floodlit football pitches, tennis and volleyball. Restaurant, bar and large reception/function room. Off site: Beach 350 m. Mazara 2.5 km. Various excursions organised by the site, for example to the acropolis at Selinunte (25 km) or the island of Mozia.

Open: 15 March - 15 October.

Directions

From the A29 take the Mazara del Vallo exit and head towards the town. Go straight over the first roundabout and after about 1.5 km. turn right at the traffic lights toward the beach. At the roundabout exit left and go straight ahead to the site, not over the bridge.
GPS: N37:38.188 E12:36.979

Charges guide

Per person	€ 4,50 - € 7,00
child (4-10 yrs)	€ 3,00 - € 4,50
pitch incl. car	€ 10,50 - € 21,00

IT69550 Camping Baia Blu La Tortuga

Pineta di Vignola Mare, I-07020 Aglientu (Sardinia)

Tel: **079 602 200**. Email: **info@baiablu.com** **www.alanrogers.com/IT69550**

In the northeast of Sardinia and well situated for the Corsica ferry, Baia Blu is a large, professionally run campsite. The beach with its golden sand, brilliant blue sea and pretty rocky outcrops is warm and inviting. The site's 350 touring pitches, and almost as many mobile homes (most with air conditioning), are of fine sand and shaded by tall pines with banks of colourful oleanders and wide boulevards providing good access for units. Four exceptionally good toilet blocks provide a good ratio of excellent facilities to pitches including some combined private shower/washbasin cabins for rent. This is a busy bustling site with lots to do and attractive restaurants.

Facilities

Four excellent blocks (two with solar panels for hot water) with free hot showers, WCs, bidets and washbasins. Facilities for disabled people. Washing machines and dryers. Motorcaravan services. Supermarket. Gas. Bazaar. New bar and restaurant. Beachside restaurant and bar. Self-service restaurant. Snack bar and takeaway. Gym. Playground. Tennis. Games and TV rooms. Windsurfing and diving schools. Internet point and WiFi area. Massage centre. Entertainment and sports activities (mid May - Sept). Excursions. Barbecue area (not permitted on pitches). Off site: Disco 50 m. Riding 18 km.

Open: 15 March - 20 October.

Directions

Site is on the north coast between towns of Costa Paradiso and S. Teresa di Gallura (18 km) at Pineta di Vignola Mare and is well signed.
GPS: N41:07.567 E09:04.033

Charges guide

Per unit incl. 2 persons, water and electricity	€ 17,00 - € 47,00
tent pitch incl. electricity	€ 13,00 - € 37,00
extra person (10-59 yrs)	€ 2,00 - € 11,00
junior (3-9 yrs)	€ 2,00 - € 9,00
dog	€ 3,50 - € 8,00

IT69960 Camping Mariposa

Via Lido 22, I-07041 Alghero (Sardinia)

Tel: **079 950 360**. Email: **info@lamariposa.it** **www.alanrogers.com/IT69960**

Mariposa is situated right by the sea with its own beach and the range of sports available here probably makes it best suited for active young visitors. Kite surfing, diving, windsurfing, sailing, surfing and paragliding courses are all available here on payment, whilst evening entertainment is provided free. Pitches range in size from 50-80 sq.m. so they are also better suited for tents, although they do all have 6A electrical connections and caravans and motorcaravans are welcome. However, there are few marked pitches and the land is undulating and may be unsuitable for units which tend to park beside roads. Cars must be parked away from the pitches. Alghero (1.5 km.) still has a strong Catalan flavour from its 400 year occupation by the Spanish. There are many small coves and the Neptune caves are well worth a visit.

Facilities

The sanitary facilities are fairly basic, open plan, with cold washbasins and troughs, dishwashing and laundry sinks and an equal amount of warm (token needed) and cold showers. Washing machines and dryer. Motorcaravan service point. Shop, self-service restaurant and bar (all 10/6-30/9). Bicycle hire. Dogs are not accepted in July/Aug.

Open: 1 April - 31 October.

Directions

Alghero is on the northwest coast, about 35 km. southwest of Sassari. Mariposa is at the north of the town. Turn left at the main traffic lights towards the Lido and then left again at the T-junction, the site is immediately on the right.
GPS: N40:34.731 E08:18.752

Charges guide

Per person	€ 8,00 - € 11,00
child (3-12 yrs)	€ 4,00 - € 8,50
pitch	free - € 14,00
car	free - € 4,00
electricity	€ 2,50

IT69720 Camping L'Ultima Spiaggia

Localitá Planargia, I-08042 Bari Sardo (Sardinia)

Tel: **078 229 363**. Email: **info@campingultimaspiaggia.it** **www.alanrogers.com/IT69720**

A great name for this campsite 'the ultimate beach' and the beach really is extremely good, along with the bright colourful decor and amenities. We think you will enjoy this clean and pleasant site, although little English is spoken. The 250 pitches are terraced on sand, some enjoy sea views and are located at the end of the site. New mobile homes occupy the top of the site which slopes towards the sea. The good entertainment programme can be enjoyed from the terrace of the friendly restaurant which offers a reasonably priced menu which includes the local seafood specialities. Access to the fine beach (with lifeguard) and watersports is gained through a security gate. Sub-aqua diving is extremely good hereabouts.

Facilities

Two toilet units include mainly Turkish style toilets and good facilities for disabled campers. Washing machines. Motorcaravan service point. Small supermarket. Restaurant and snack bar. Play areas. Windsurfing. Aerobics. Riding. Tennis. Minigolf. Canoeing. Bicycle hire. Miniclub. Entertainment. Excursions. Torches useful. Off site: Restaurants, bars and shops. Fishing. Boat launching.

Open: 20 April - 30 September.

Directions

Site is on east coast of Sardinia, well signed from SS125 in village of Bari Sardo. Note that the roads are very winding from the north - allow lots of time.
GPS: N39:49.146 E09:40.206

Charges guide

Per person	€ 6,50 - € 13,50
child (1-6 yrs)	€ 3,50 - € 6,50
pitch	€ 6,00 - € 14,50
electricity	€ 3,00

The independent Principality of Liechtenstein is the fourth smallest country in the world. Nestled between Switzerland and Austria, it has a total area of 157 square kilometres (61 square miles).

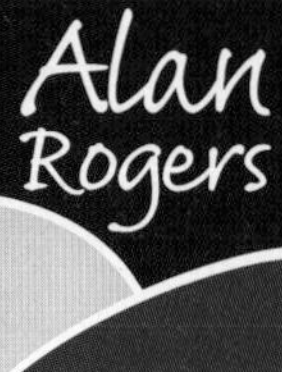

If you like clean mountain air and peaceful surroundings, then a visit to Liechtenstein would be worthwhile. The little town of Vaduz (the Capital) is where you will find most points of interest, including the world famous art collection (Kunstmuseum), which holds paintings by Rembrandt and other world famous artists. Above the town of Vaduz is the restored twelfth-century castle, now owned by the prince of Liechtenstein (not open to the public). Take a walk up to the top of the hill, you can view Vaduz and the mountains stretched out below. Situated on a terrace above Vaduz is Triesenberg village, blessed with panoramic views over the Rhine Valley, a pretty village with vineyards and ancient chapels. Malbun is Liechtenstein's premier mountain resort, popular in both winter and summer, for either skiing or walking.

FL7580 Camping Mittagspitze

Sägastrasse 29, FL 9495 Triesen

Tel: **392 3677**. Email: **info@campingtriesen.li**

www.alanrogers.com/FL7580

Camping Mittagspitze is attractively and quietly situated for visiting the Principality. Probably the best site in the region, it is on a hillside and has all the scenic views that one could wish for. Extensive broad, level terraces on the steep slope provide unmarked pitches (a reader tells us that spacing causes problems in high season) and electricity connections are available. There is little shade. Of the 240 spaces, 120 are used by seasonal caravans. Liechtenstein's capital, Vaduz, is 7 km, Austria is 20 km. and Switzerland 3 km.

Facilities

Two good quality sanitary blocks (the one near reception is new) provide all the usual facilities. Washing machine, dryer and ironing. Room where one can sit or eat with cooking facilities. Shop (1/6-31/8). Restaurant (all year). Small swimming pool (15/6-15/8), not heated but very popular in summer. Playground. Fishing. New TV room. Off site: Tennis and indoor pool nearby. Riding and bicycle hire 5 km.

Open: All year.

Directions

From A3 take Trübbach exit 10 and follow road towards Balziers. Then head towards Vaduz and site is 2 km. south of Triesen on the right. Site is signed. GPS: N47:05.142 E09:31.554

Charges guide

Per person	€ 8,50
child (3-14 yrs)	€ 4,00
pitch	€ 8,00 - € 10,00
electricity (6A)	€ 5,00

MAP 2

The Grand Duchy of Luxembourg is a sovereign state, lying between Belgium, France and Germany. Divided into two areas: the spectacular Ardennes region in the north and the rolling farmlands and woodland in the south, bordered on the east by the wine growing area of the Moselle Valley.

CAPITAL: LUXEMBOURG CITY

Tourist Office

Luxembourg Tourist Office
122 Regent Street, London W1B 5SA
Tel: 020 7434 2800
Fax: 020 7734 1205
Email: tourism@luxembourg.co.uk
Internet: www.luxembourg.co.uk

From wherever you are in Luxembourg you are always within easy reach of the capital, Luxembourg-Ville, home to about one fifth of the population. The city was built upon a rocky outcrop, and has superb views of the Alzette and Petrusse Valleys. Those who love the great outdoors must make a visit to the Ardennes, with its hiking trails, footpaths and cycle routes that take you through beautiful winding valleys and across deep rivers, a very popular region for visitors. If wine tasting takes your fancy, then head for the Moselle Valley, particularly if you like sweet, fruity wines. From late spring to early autumn, wine tasting tours take place in cellars and caves. The Mullerthal region, known as the 'Little Switzerland', lies on the banks of the river Sûre. The earth is mostly made up of soft sandstone, so through the ages many fascinating gorges, caves and formations have emerged.

Population

483,800

Climate

A temperate climate prevails, the summer often extending from May to late October.

Language

Letzeburgesch is the national language, with French and German also being official languages.

Telephone

The country code is 00 352.

Money

Currency: The Euro
Banks: Mon-Fri 08.30/09.00-12.00 and 13.30-16.30.

Shops

Mon 14.00-18.30. Tues to Sat 08.30-12.00 and 14.00-18.30 (grocers and butchers at 15.00 on Sat).

Public Holidays

New Year; Carnival Day mid-Feb; Easter Mon; May Day; Ascension; Whit Mon; National Day 23 June; Assumption 15 Aug; Kermesse 1 Sept; All Saints; All Souls; Christmas 25, 26 Dec.

Motoring

Many holidaymakers travel through Luxembourg to take advantage of the lower fuel prices, thus creating traffic congestion at petrol stations, especially in summer.
A Blue Zone area exists in Luxembourg City and various parts of the country (discs from tourist offices) but meters are also used.

LU7620 Europacamping Nommerlayen

L-7465 Nommern

Tel: **878 078**. Email: **nommerlayen@vo.lu**

www.alanrogers.com/LU7620

This is a top quality site in central Luxembourg with fees to match, but it has everything! A large, central building housing most of the services and amenities opens onto a terrace around an excellent swimming pool complex with two main pools and an imaginative watery playground. The 367 individual pitches (100 sq.m) are on grassy terraces, all have access to electricity (2/16A) and water taps. Interestingly enough the superb new sanitary block is called 'Badtemple' (its architecture suggesting this title as the entrance with colonnades supporting a canopy is reminiscent of a Greek temple). To gain entry to the sauna and to obtain hot water for washbasins, showers and sinks, one pays to have a cash equivalent charged into a triangular shaped plastic block which is then inserted into a slot. Member of 'Leading Campings Group'.

Facilities

A large, high quality, modern sanitary unit provides some washbasins in cubicles, facilities for disabled people, and family and baby washrooms. The new block also includes special rooms for children and disabled visitors, plus a sauna. Twelve private bathrooms for hire. Laundry. Motorcaravan service point. Supermarket. Restaurant. Snack bar. Bar (all 4/4-8/11). Heated swimming pools (1/5-15/9). Solarium. Fitness programmes. Bowling. Playground. Large screen TV. Entertainment in season. Bicycle hire. Off site: Riding 1 km. Fishing and golf 5 km.

Open: 1 February - 1 December.

Directions

Take the 118 road between Mersch and Larochette. Site is signed 3 km. north of Larochette towards the village of Nommern on the 346 road.
GPS: N49:47.097 E06:09.920

Charges 2009

Per unit incl. 2 persons and 2A electricity, acc. to pitch and facilities	€ 20,00 - € 37,00
extra adult	€ 5,50
child (under 18 yrs)	€ 3,50
dog	€ 2,85
electricity (16A) plus	€ 3,75

No credit cards.

LU7660 Camping Kockelscheuer

22 route de Bettembourg, L-1899 Luxembourg

Tel: **471 815**. Email: **caravani@pt.lu** **www.alanrogers.com/LU7660**

Camping Kockelscheuer is 4 km. from the centre of Luxembourg city and quietly situated (although there can be some aircraft noise at times). On a slight slope, there are 161 individual pitches of good size, either on flat ground at the bottom or on wide flat terraces with easy access, all with 16A electricity. There is also a special area for tents, with picnic tables and, in the reception building, a campers' lounge. For children there is a large area with modern play equipment on safety tiles and next door to the site is a sports centre. Charges are very reasonable. There is a friendly welcome although little English is spoken. Visit Luxembourg City by bus. Here, there are shops, museums and the Grand Duke's Palace. Explore some of the 23 km. of defensive tunnels built in the Middle Ages under the City. The area south of the campsite has several old mining towns, many of which have excellent museums and walks to discover the old workings. Nearby there are two very large parks – the one at Bettembourg is a fairy tale park.

Facilities

Two fully equipped, identical sanitary buildings, both very clean. Washing machines. Motorcaravan services. Shop (order bread the previous day). Snack bar. Restaurant in adjacent sports centre also with minigolf, tennis, squash, etc. Rest room. No entry or exit for vehicles (reception closed) 12.00-14.00. Off site: Bus 200 m. every 15 minutes to Luxembourg. Swimming pool 5 km.

Open: 1 week before Easter - 31 October.

Directions

Site is SSW of Luxembourg city on the N13 to Bettembourg (road is also known locally as the 186). From the south, exit A4 at junction signed Kockelscheuer onto N4. In 2 km. turn right (Kockelscheuer and campsite) and continue to follow the signs. GPS: N49:34.308 E06:06.540

Charges guide

Per person	€ 3,75
child (3-14 yrs)	€ 2,00
pitch	€ 4,50
electricity (1 or 2 days)	€ 0,40 - € 2,20

No credit cards.

LU7650 Camping de la Sûre

Abca. 491.

23 route de la Sûre, L-9390 Reisdorf

Tel: **836 246**. Email: **ren2@pt.lu** **www.alanrogers.com/LU7650**

Camping de la Sûre is on the banks of the river that separates Luxembourg and Germany. It is a pleasant site close to Reisdorf with 180 numbered pitches (120 with 10A electricity). These are not separated but are marked with trees that provide some shade. There are caravan holiday homes in a fenced area towards the back of the site, leaving the prime pitches for touring units. Ongoing redevelopment is almost complete with new roads and a new toilet block.

Facilities

Modern, clean sanitary facilities recently refitted and extended, including some washbasins in cubicles. Laundry. Small shop. Café/bar. Takeaway. Playground. Minigolf. Sports field. Canoeing. Fishing Off site: Town centre within easy walking distance. Cycle ways abound. Bicycle hire 200 m. Golf 8 km.

Open: 1 April - 30 October.

Directions

From the river bridge in Reisdorf, take the road to Echternach, de la Sûre is the second campsite on the left. GPS: N49:52.202 E06:16.050

Charges guide

Per person	€ 5,00
pitch	€ 5,50
electricity	€ 2,50
dog	€ 2,50

25% reduction in low season. No credit cards.

LU7610 Camping Birkelt

1 rue de la Piscine, L-7601 Larochette

Tel: **879 040**. Email: **info@camping-birkelt.lu** **www.alanrogers.com/LU7610**

This is very much a family site, the price representing the range of facilities provided. It is well organised and well laid out, set in an elevated position in attractive, undulating countryside. A tarmac road runs around the site with 424 large grass pitches, some slightly sloping, many with a fair amount of shade, on either side of gravel access roads in straight rows or circles. All pitches have 6A electricity. An all weather swimming pool complex is just outside the site entrance (free for campers) and entertainment for children is arranged in high season. The site is very popular with tour operators (140 pitches).

Facilities

Three modern sanitary buildings well situated around the site include mostly open washbasins (6 cabins in one block). Baby baths. Facilities for wheelchair users. Laundry facilities. Dishwashers. Motorcaravan service point. Shop. Coffee bar. Restaurant with terrace. Swimming pool. Outdoor pool for toddlers. Massage. Play areas. Minigolf. Tennis. Bicycle hire. Riding. Balloon flights. Internet points. WiFi. Off site: Golf and bicycle hire 5 km. Fishing and kayaking 10 km.

Open: 28 March - 8 November.

Directions

From N7 (Diekirch - Luxembourg City), turn onto N8 at Berschblach (just past Mersch) towards Larochette. Site is signed on the right 1.5 km. from Larochette. Approach road is fairly steep and narrow. GPS: N49:47.105 E06:12.620

Charges guide

Per unit incl. 2 persons and electricity	€ 18,50 - € 33,50
extra person	€ 4,00

Less 25% in low season.
Camping Cheques accepted.

LU7640 Camping Auf Kengert

L-7633 Larochette-Medernach

Tel: **837186**. Email: **info@kengert.lu** **www.alanrogers.com/LU7640**

A friendly welcome awaits you at this peacefully situated, family run site, 2 km. from Larochette. It lies 24 km. northeast of Luxembourg city and provides 180 individual pitches, all with electricity. Some are in a very shaded woodland setting, on a slight slope with fairly narrow access roads. There are also eight hardened pitches for motorcaravans on a flat area of grass, complete with motorcaravan service facilities. Further pitches are in an adjacent and more open meadow area. There are also site owned chalets and caravans. This site is popular in season, so early arrival is advisable, or you can reserve.

Facilities

The well maintained sanitary block in two parts includes a modern, heated unit with some washbasins in cubicles, and excellent, fully equipped cubicles for disabled visitors. The showers, facilities for babies, additional WCs and washbasins, plus laundry room are located below the central building which houses the shop, bar and restaurant. Motorcaravan services. Gas supplies. Indoor and outdoor play areas. Solar heated swimming pool (Easter - 30/9). Paddling pool. Off site: Bicycle hire. Golf, fishing and riding 8 km.

Open: 1 March - 8 November.

Directions

From Larochette take the CR118/N8 (towards Mersch) and just outside town turn right on CR119 towards Schrondweiler, site is 2 km. on right. GPS: N49:47.995 E06:11.890

Charges 2009

Per unit incl. 2 persons and electricity	€ 20,00 - € 32,00
extra person	€ 9,00 - € 15,00
child (4-17 yrs)	€ 5,00 - € 7,00
dog	€ 1,25

20% reduction for students, walkers and cyclists.

LU7670 Camping des Ardennes

10 op der Héi, L-9809 Hosingen

Tel: **921 911** www.alanrogers.com/LU7670

A good value, small municipal site, Camping Ardennes is located on the edge of this attractive small town with an easy level walk to all amenities and parks and some floral arrangements to admire during the summer season. The 48 touring pitches are level, open and grassy. All have electricity (10A) and are arranged on either side of surfaced roads, with a few trees providing a little shade in places. Adjacent sports complex with tennis and football, etc. This site is useful as a stopover if travelling along the N7.

Facilities

The single well appointed, modern, clean sanitary block can be heated in winter and includes separate men's and women's facilities. Laundry facilities. Café/bar (opening variable). Barbecue. Playground. Skis and winter sports equipment for hire. Rooms for rent (B&B). English spoken.

Open: All year.

Directions

Hosingen is on the N7 21 km. north of Diekirch. Site and sports complex are signed in the village. 20 m. after leaving the main road turn right. Site is 100 m. on the left. GPS: N50:00.463 E06:05.410

Charges guide

Per person	€ 4,50
pitch incl. electricity	€ 6,75

LU7680 Camping Kohnenhof

Maison 1, L-9838 Obereisenbach

Tel: **929 464**. Email: **kohnenhof@pt.lu** www.alanrogers.com/LU7680

Nestling in a valley with the River Our running through it, Camping Kohnenhof offers a very agreeable location for a relaxing family holiday. From the minute you stop at the reception you are assured of a warm and friendly welcome. Numerous paths cross through the wooded hillside so this could be a haven for walkers. A little wooden ferry crosses the small river across the border to Germany. The river is shallow and safe for children (parental supervision essential). During the high season, an entertainment programme is organised for parents and children.

Facilities

Heated sanitary block with showers and washbasins in cabins. Motorcaravan service point. Laundry. Bar, restaurant, takeaway. Games and TV room. Baker calls daily. Sports field with play equipment. Boules. Bicycle hire. Golf weeks. Discounts on six local 18-hole golf courses. WiFi. Off site: Bus to Clervaux (with monastery) and Vianden (with castle) stops (4 times daily) outside site entrance. Riding 5 km. Golf 15 km.

Open: 15 March - 10 November.

Directions

Take N7 north from Diekirch. At Hosingen, turn right onto the narrow and winding CR324 signed Eisenbach. Follow site signs from Eisenbach or Obereisenbach. GPS: N50:00.961 E06:08.160

Charges 2009

Per unit incl. 2 persons and electricity	€ 19,90 - € 28,00
extra person	€ 4,00

Camping Cheques accepted.

LU7770 Camping Val d'Or

Um Gaertchen 2, L-9747 Enscherange

Tel: **920 691**. Email: **valdor@pt.lu** www.alanrogers.com/LU7770

Camping Val d'Or is one of those small family-run countryside sites where you easily find yourself staying longer that planned. Set on lush meadowland under a scattering of trees, the site is divided into two by the tree lined Clerve river as it winds its way slowly through the site. Two footbridges go some way to joining the site together and there are two entrances for vehicles. There are 76 level grass touring pitches, all with electricity (4A). and with some tree shade. There are open views of the surrounding countryside with its wooded hills. The site's Dutch owners speak good English.

Facilities

Next to the reception is a heated sanitary block where some facilities are found, others including some showers are located, under cover, outside. Showers are token operated, washbasins open style. Laundry room. Gas supplies. Bar. Swimming or paddling in river. Three play areas. Bicycle hire. Off site: Fishing and golf 10 km.

Open: All year.

Directions

From A26/E25 (Liège - Luxembourg) exit 54 travel to Bastogne. From Bastogne take N84/N15 towards Diekirch for 15 km. At crossroads turn left (northeast) towards Wiltz following signs for Clervaux. Pass though Wiltz and entering Weidingen there is a VW garage on the right; 500 m. after the garage turn right on the Wilderwiltz road. In Wilderwiltz follow signs for village of Enscherange where site is signed. GPS: N50:00.012 E05:59.450

Charges 2009

Per unit incl. 2 persons and electricity	€ 21,00
extra person	€ 5,00

No credit cards.

Luxembourg

E.16 Asci. 485

LU7850 Camping Fuussekaul

4 Fuussekaul, L-9156 Heiderscheid

Tel: **268 8881**. Email: **info@fuussekaul.lu**

www.alanrogers.com/LU7850

Children who visit Fuussekaul (the name means fox hole) won't want to leave as there is so much for them to do. Apart from a fun pool, exciting play areas, and an entertainment programme, children and parents can bake their own pizzas in the open-air oven. Of the 370 pitches, 220 of varying sizes are for touring units, all with a 6A electricity connection. The touring area (separate from the chalets and seasonal pitches) is well endowed with modern facilities, although there is no provision for visitors with disabilities. An entertainment programme continues throughout the main holiday season. This includes little shows and theatre productions, and various sporting activities. On the opposite side of the road (pedestrian access via an under-road passage) is a service and parking area for six motorcaravans. Each pitch has a hook-up, fresh water tap and waste water disposal point. There is also a drive-over service point.

Facilities

Four excellent sanitary blocks provide showers (token € 0.50), washbasins (in cabins and communal) and children and baby rooms with small toilets, washbasins and showers. Laundry. Parking and service area for motorcaravans. Well stocked shop. Bar. Restaurant and takeaway. Swimming pools. Suite with sauna and sunbeds. Beauty salon. Playgrounds. Cross-country skiing when snow permits. Bicycle hire. Children's club. Bowling centre. Off site: Castles, museums and walks all within a reasonable distance. Bus stops outside site entrance. Riding 500 m. Fishing 3 km. Supermarket and shops in Ettelbruckt 7 km.

Open: All year.

Directions

Take N15 from Diekirch to Heiderscheid. Site is on left at top of hill just before reaching the village. Motorhome service area is signed on the right. GPS: N49:52.650 E05:59.570

Charges guide

Per unit incl. 2 persons	€ 18,50 - € 32,00
extra person	€ 2,50
electricity	€ 0,40
dog	€ 2,00

LU7780 Camping Woltzdal

Maison 12, L-9974 Maulusmühle

Tel: **998 938**. Email: **info@woltzdal-camping.lu**

www.alanrogers.com/LU7780

Set by a stream in a valley, Camping Woltzdal is one of the many delightful sites in the Ardennes, a region of wooded hills and river valleys that crosses the borders of Belgium, France and Luxembourg. The site has 83 touring pitches, set on grass amongst fir trees; all with 4A electricity. They are fairly open with views of the surrounding hills. A railway passes the site but there are only trains during the day and they are not disturbing. This is a family-run site where in the bar/restaurant, one brother cooks, the other serves the guests and their father runs the bar.

Facilities

The heated sanitary block contains the usual facilities; showers are coin operated, washbasins open. Laundry room. Service points for motorcaravans. Reception and small shop. Bar and a restaurant/snack bar. Children's library/activity room. WiFi. Play area. Boules. Mountain bike hire. Entertainment programme for children in high season. Off site: Fishing and golf 6 km. Riding 20 km.

Open: 15 March - 1 November.

Directions

Site is 6 km. north of Clervaux on the CR335 road. Leave Clervaux in the direction of Troisvierge and site is signed in the 12 house village of Maulusmühle. GPS: N50:05.477 E06:01.670

Charges guide

Per unit incl. 2 persons and electricity	€ 18,90 - € 19,60
extra person	€ 5,90

LU7880 Camping Trois Frontières

Hauptstrooss 12, L-9972 Lieler

Tel: **998 608**. Email: **camp.3front@cmdnet.lu** **www.alanrogers.com/LU7880**

On a clear day, it is possible to see Belgium, Germany and Luxembourg from the campsite swimming pool, hence its name: Les Trois Frontières. Martin and Esther Van Aalst own and manage the site themselves and all visitors receive a personal welcome and immediately become part of a large happy family. Most of the facilities are close to the entrance, leaving the camping area quiet, except for the play area. The restaurant/takeaway provides good quality food at reasonable prices, served either inside or on the pleasant terrace with flower borders and overlooking the pool which is now covered and heated.

Facilities

Unisex facilities include excellent showers, washbasins in cabins, British style WCs, suite for visitors with disabilities, plus baby bath and changing station. More WCs in second building (down some steps). Laundry. Swimming pool (1/4-31/10). Play area. Boules. Games room. Bicycle hire. Off site: Shops 2.3 km. Golf and riding 12 km. Clervaux 12 km.

Open: All year.

Directions

Take N7 northward from Diekirch. 3 km. south of Weiswampach turn right onto CR338 to Lieler (site signed here). Site is on right as you enter the village. GPS: N50:07.404 E06:06.310

Charges guide

Per pitch incl. 2 persons	€ 16,00 - € 21,00
extra person	€ 6,50 - € 7,00
child (under 12 yrs)	€ 3,50 - € 3,90
electricity (4A)	€ 2,50
pet	€ 2,00

Reduction during low season for visitors over 55 yrs.

LU7890 Camping Haute Sûre

34 rue J. de Busleyden, L-9639 Boulaide

Tel: **993 061**. Email: **info@campinghautesure.com** **www.alanrogers.com/LU7890**

Located in a small village in a fairly remote area of the Grand Duchy, this site is very peaceful with some outstanding views over the Sûre valley. There are 87 pitches, 12 used by a Dutch tour operator, tents and two chalets for rent. The 73 large pitches for tourists are on well kept grass, generally with a slight slope, all have electricity hook-ups (6A) with a water tap serving four pitches. The emphasis at Haute Sûre is very much geared towards families, especially those with younger children, with an excellent adventure style playground. There is a small, well fenced outdoor swimming pool with a completely separate, fenced paddling pool.

Facilities

A modern building with underfloor heating provides good facilities including spacious showers (a water saving feature means that the preset showers are timed, giving 5 minutes use, then 5 minutes down time before being available for re-use). Children's washbasins. Separate unisex baby room. Excellent suite for disabled campers, with its own baby facilities. Laundry. Shop. Restaurant, bar and takeaway (all 15/4-15/9). Swimming and paddling pools (15/4-15/9). Small games room. Adventure playground. Children's entertainment. Off site: Internet cafe 6 km. Fishing 3 km. Golf 30 km. Riding in village.

Open: 15 April - 15 September.

Directions

Boulaide is 15 km. northeast of Martelange on the Belgium border. From Bastogne take N4 south for 22 km. to Martelange. From Martelange take N23 east and after about 4 km. turn north on minor road CR309, through Bigonville to Boulaide. Site is towards the northern end of village. GPS: N49:53.362 E05:48.899

Charges guide

Per unit incl. 2 persons	€ 25,00
incl. 3 persons	€ 27,50
incl. 4 persons	€ 30,00

With vast areas of the Netherlands reclaimed from the sea, nearly half of the country lies at or below sea level. The result is a flat, fertile landscape, criss-crossed with rivers and canals. Famous for its windmills and bulb fields, it also boasts some of the most impressive coastal dunes in Europe.

CAPITAL: AMSTERDAM

Tourist Office

Netherlands Board of Tourism
PO Box 30783, London WC2B 6DH
Tel: 020 7539 7958
Fax: 020 7539 7953
Email: info-uk@holland.com
Internet: www.holland.com/uk

There is more to the Netherlands than Amsterdam and the bulb fields. Granted, both are top attractions and no visitor should miss the city of Amsterdam with its delight of bridges, canals, museums and listed buildings or miss seeing the spring-time riot of colour that adorns the fields and gardens of South Holland. This is a country with a variety of holiday venues ranging from lively seaside resorts to picturesque villages, idyllic old fishing ports and areas where nature rules. The Vecht valley is an area of natural beauty which centres around the town of Ommen. Giethoorn is justly dubbed the 'Venice of the North'. The Alblasserwaard polder offers time to discover the famed windmills of Kinderdijk, cheese farms and a stork village. The islands of Zeeland are joined by amazing feats of engineering, particularly the Oosterschelde storm surge barrier. Island hopping introduces lovely old towns such as Middelburg, the provincial capital Zierikzee with its old harbour or the quaint old town of Veere.

Population

15.9 million

Climate

Temperature with mild winters and warm summers.

Language

Dutch. English is very widely spoken, so is German and to some extent French. In Friesland a Germanic language, Frisian is spoken.

Telephone

The country code is 00 31.

Money

Currency: The Euro
Banks: Mon-Fri 09.00-16.00/1700.

Shops

Mon-Fri 09.00/09.30-17.30/18.00.
Sat to 16.00/17.00. Later closing hours in larger cities.

Public Holidays

New Year; April Fools Day 1 April; Good Fri; Easter Mon; Queen's Birthday 30 April; Labour Day; Remembrance Day 4 May; Liberation Day 5 May; Ascension; Whit Mon; SinterKlaas 5 Dec; Kingdom Day 15 Dec; Christmas 25, 26 Dec.

Motoring

There is a comprehensive motorway system but, due to the high density of population, all main roads can become very busy, particularly in the morning and evening rush hours. There are many bridges which can cause congestion. There are no toll roads but there are a few toll bridges and tunnels notably the Zeeland Bridge, Europe's longest across the Oosterschelde.

NL5510 Camping Groede

Zeeweg 1, NL-4503 PA Groede (Zeeland)

Tel: **0117 371 384**. Email: **info@campinggroede.nl** **www.alanrogers.com/NL5510**

Camping Groede is a friendly, fair-sized site by the same stretch of sandy beach as no. NL5500. Family run, it aims to cater for the individual needs of visitors and to provide a good all-round holiday. Campers are sited as far as possible according to taste – in family areas, in larger groups or on more private pitches for those who prefer peace and quiet. In total, there are 500 pitches for tourists (plus 380 seasonal units), all with electrical connections (4-10A) and 300 with water and drainage connections. A new field has been added with 63 fully serviced large pitches. Camping Groede is ideally sited for ferry stopovers (Breskens) and short stay visitors including hikers are very welcome, as well as long stay holiday makers. Access to the beach is good for wheelchairs and baby buggies. A nature reserve is being constructed adjacent to the site. Run by the family van Damme, who ask visitors to complete a confidential questionnaire to ensure that their site offers the best possible service and provide you with a comprehensive information booklet.

Facilities

Toilet facilities are excellent with a high standard of cleanliness, including some wash cabins, baby baths, family room and a dedicated unit for persons with disabilities. Motorcaravan services. Gas supplies. Shop, restaurant and snack bar (all weekends only in low seasons). Recreation room. Internet access. Sports area. Several play areas (bark base). Plenty of activities for children in peak season. Bicycle hire. Fishing.
Off site: Riding 1 km. Golf 11 km.

Open: 24 March - 31 December.

Directions

From Breskens take the coast road for 5 km. to site. Alternatively, the site is signed from Groede village on the more inland Breskens - Sluis road.
GPS: N51:23.749 E03:29.263

Charges guide

Per pitch incl. 2 persons € 17,00 - € 30,00
No credit cards.

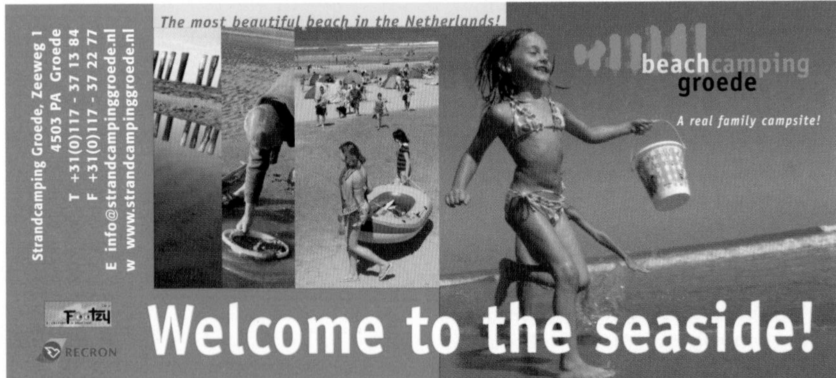

NL5500 Vakantiepark Pannenschuur

Zeedijk 19, NL-4504 PP Nieuwvliet (Zeeland)
Tel: **0117 372 300**. Email: **info@pannenschuur.nl**
www.alanrogers.com/NL5500

This is one of several coastal sites on the narrow strip of the Netherlands between the Belgian frontier near Knokke and the Breskens ferry. Quickly reached from the ports of Ostend, Zeebrugge and Vlissingen, it is useful for overnight stops or for a few days to enjoy the seaside. A short walk across the quiet coast road and steps over the dyke bring you to the open, sandy beach. Quite a large site, most of the 595 pitches are taken by permanent or seasonal holiday caravans but there are also 165 pitches for tourists, mostly in their own areas.

Facilities

Four toilet blocks including two new, heated buildings, provide first class facilities including children's washrooms, baby rooms and some private cabins. Hot water is free. Launderette. Motorcaravan services. Gas supplies. Supermarket. Restaurant, snack bar and takeaway. Swimming pool, sauna and solarium. Large games room with soft drinks bar. Internet access. Playground and play field. Bicycle hire. Organised activities in season. Off site: Fishing 500 m. Riding 2 km. Golf 5 km.

Open: All year (all amenities closed 14/1-31/1).

Directions

At Nieuwvliet, on the Breskens - Sluis minor road, 8 km. southwest of Breskens, turn towards the sea at sign for Nieuwvliet-Bad and follow signs to site GPS: N51:23.013 E03:26.431

Charges guide

Per unit (max. 5 persons)	
incl. electricity	€ 25,00 - € 40,00
extra person	€ 4,00

Rates available for weekly stays.

NL6925 Camping Weltevreden

Melsesweg, NL-4374 NG Zouteland (Zeeland)
Tel: **0118 561 321**. Email: **info@campingweltevreden.nl**
www.alanrogers.com/NL6925

Camping Weltevreden is on Zeeland's 'Riviera', the area of the Dutch coast with the highest recorded annual hours of sunshine. It is a family site with a pleasant ambiance, located just behind the high, grassy dunes between Zoutelande and Westkapelle. This attractively landscaped site is only 100 m. from the sandy North Sea beaches. There are 144 pitches (50 for tourers) on well kept, grassy lawns, connected by narrow tarmac roads. Separated by a variety of low bushes and shrubs, all the touring pitches have 6A electricity, water and drainage.

Facilities

One central, modern toilet block with British style toilets, washbasins (open and in cabins), free hot showers, baby room and special children's section. Laundry facilities. Well stocked shop. Boules. Basketball. Table football. Small play area. Dogs are not accepted. English is spoken. Off site: Beach 100 m. Fishing 100 m. Bicycle hire 1 km. Riding 3 km. Golf 6 km.

Open: April - October.

Directions

From Zoutelande, follow the coastal road towards Westkapelle. Site is on the left just outside Zoutelande. GPS: N51:30.545 E03:25.046

Charges guide

Per unit incl. 2 persons	€ 12,50
incl. electricity	€ 20,00 - € 31,00
extra person	€ 5,00
child (0-5 yrs)	€ 2,75

NL6930 Camping Schoneveld

Schoneveld 1, NL-4511 HR Breskens (Zeeland)
Tel: **0117 383 220**. Email: **schoneveld@zeelandnet.nl**
www.alanrogers.com/NL6930

This site is well situated within walking distance of Breskens and it has direct access to sand dunes. It has around 200 touring pitches and has many static vans, although these are kept apart. The touring pitches are behind reception, laid out in fields which are entered from long avenues that run through the site. There are also twelve car parking bays. One ultra modern and very clean toilet block serves this area. The complex at the site entrance houses reception, a restaurant and a recreation room. Also near the entrance are the indoor pool, tennis courts and a football field.

Facilities

One large sanitary block provides showers, wash cubicles, child size toilets and washbasins, baby room, en-suite unit for disabled visitors. Motorcaravan service point. Restaurant. 'Fun Food Plaza' and takeaway (5/4-31/10). Bowling. Indoor pool. Tennis. Football field. Play area. Organised entertainment in July/Aug. Bicycle hire. WiFi internet access. Off site: Fishing 200 m. Boat launching 3 km. Golf or riding 10 km.

Open: All year.

Directions

From Breskens port follow N58 south for about 1 km. and turn right at camping sign. Site is 500 m. GPS: N51:24.064 E03:32.085

Charges guide

Per unit incl. 2 persons	€ 19,50 - € 33,00
incl. 3 persons	€ 22,50 - € 36,00
incl. 5 persons	€ 28,50 - € 42,00
tent pitch incl. 1 or 2 persons	€ 15,00
extra person	€ 3,00

Camping Cheques accepted.

NL5555 Camping de Oase

Roelandseweg 8, NL-4325 CS Renesse (Zeeland)

Tel: **0111 461 358**. Email: **info@campingdeoase.nl** **www.alanrogers.com/NL5555**

De Oase is situated just south of the lively holiday resort of Renesse at Schouwen-Duiveland, one of the islands in Zeeland. At 1.5 km from the North Sea and its long sandy beaches and connected to the many cycle and walking tracks that are laid out in this typically flat Dutch landscape, this site is ideal for those who like an active holiday. There are some 450 pitches, 146 for touring units. They are grassy and spacious (100-180 sq.m) and all have electricity (6/10A), water, drainage and WiFi; 90 are also equipped with TV connections. There are 30 mobile homes for rent. The many cafés, bars and discos make Renesse's nightlife very popular. Of course, you can also ignore the hustle and bustle and stay near your quiet pitch and just relax. Campers may use the Schouwen-Duiveland pass for free public transport, free entrance to museums and discounts at many other places. A 'park & ride' bus service is near the site entrance.

Facilities

New spacious sanitary facilities are state of the art, including rooms for babies, children and disabled visitors. Family showers. Launderette. Shop with fresh bread. Recreation areas and sports fields. Entertainment for children in high season. Dogs are not accepted.
Off site: Beach 1.5 km. Riding 500 m. Renesse centre 300 m. Dreischor 25 km. Town of Zierikzee 25 km.

Open: 15 March - 1 November.

Directions

Site is just south of Renesse. Follow signs for Renesse Transferium and site is opposite.
GPS: N51:43.703 E03:46.307

Charges 2009

Per unit incl. 2 persons and electricity	€ 19,50 - € 30,00
extra person (over 3 yrs)	€ 4,85

NL5570 Camping De Molenhoek

Molenweg 69a, NL-4493 NC Kamperland (Zeeland)

Tel: **0113 371 202**. Email: **molenhoek@zeelandnet.nl** **www.alanrogers.com/NL5570**

This family-run site makes a pleasant contrast to the livelier coastal sites in this popular holiday area. It is rurally situated 3 km. from the Veerse Meer which is very popular for all sorts of watersports. Catering for 300 permanent or seasonal holiday caravans and 100 touring units, it is neat, tidy and relatively spacious. The marked touring pitches are divided into small groups with surrounding hedges and trees giving privacy and some shade, and electrical connections are available. A large outdoor pool is Molenhoek's latest attraction. Entertainment is organised in season (dance evenings, bingo, etc.) as well as a disco for youngsters. Although the site is quietly situated, there are many excursion possibilities in the area.

Facilities

Sanitary facilities in one fully refurbished and one newer block, include some washbasins in cabins. Toilet and shower facilities for disabled visitors and for babies. Laundry facilities. Motorcaravan services. Simple bar/restaurant with terrace and TV room. Restaurant/bar. Swimming pool (15/5-15/9). Playground. Bicycle hire. Off site: Tennis and watersports close. Riding 1 km. Shop 2 km. Fishing 2.5 km.

Open: 1 April - 28 October.

Directions

Site is west of the village of Kamperland on the 'island' of Noord Beveland. From the N256 Goes - Zierikzee road, exit west onto the N255 Kamperland road. Site is signed south of this road. GPS: N51:34.704 E03:41.785

Charges guide

Per unit incl. 2 or 3 persons and electricity	€ 21,00 - € 33,50
extra person	€ 3,50 - € 4,50
dog	€ 2,50 - € 3,00

No credit cards.

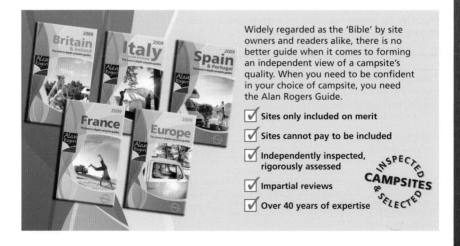

NL6920 Camping 't Veerse Meer

Veerweg 71, NL-4471 NB Wolphaartsdijk (Zeeland)

Tel: **0113 581 423**. Email: **info@campingveersemeer.nl** **www.alanrogers.com/NL6920**

This well cared for, family run site is beside the Veerse Meer on the island of Noord Beveland in Zeeland. Emphasis at this site is on a neat appearance, quality facilities and a friendly reception. The site spreads over both sides of the road. One area provides 15 pitches with individual sanitary facilities (some seasonal), fully serviced hardstanding pitches for motorcaravans and a tent field at the far end. There are 40 generous touring pitches in another area, many fully serviced and separated by hedging. A feature of this campsite is a narrow canal crossed by a bridge. Not only is the site's location idyllic for watersports enthusiasts, it is also an excellent and picturesque setting for cyclists and walkers. The original part of the site is where you will find reception, a bar and the main toilet block (recently renovated to provide water heated by solar panels).

Facilities

The single updated toilet block has showers (token operated), open style wash areas, two wash cabins, child size WC and a baby bath. Laundry. Motorcaravan service point. Bar. WiFi. Play area. Organised events for all in high season. Bicycle hire. Fishing.

Open: 1 April - 31 October.

Directions

From N256 Goes-Zierikzee road take Wolphaartsdijk exit. Follow through village and signs to site. GPS: N51:32.662 E03:48.769

Charges guide

Per unit incl. 2 persons	€ 14,00 - € 21,50
extra person	€ 2,50 - € 3,00

No credit cards.

NL6915 Camping Linda

Oostelijke kanaalweg 4, NL-4424 NC Wemeldinge (Zeeland)

Tel: **0113 621 259**. Email: **info@campinglinda.nl** **www.alanrogers.com/NL6915**

Camping Linda is a welcoming, family run site, situated on the shores of the Oosterachelde, with direct access to a small beach. The area is ideal for watersports enthusiasts and particularly popular with divers. Pitches are a good size, level and grassy, with 100 out of 350 places reserved for touring. Most of these are situated in the quieter part of the site, across a narrow country road and nearest to the beach access. Other pitches are closer to the reception area. All have electricity (6A), water and TV connection. In high season a comprehensive entertainment programme is organised.

Facilities

Three modern, clean sanitary buildings with showers (coin operated) and washbasins (some in cabins). Well equipped children's shower and baby room. No facilities for disabled people. Motorcaravan service point. Laundry facilities. Small shop (w/ends only). Bar. Restaurant. Takeaway. Play areas and play field. Games room. Mobile homes and chalets for rent. Off site: Marina adjoining site. Kapelle 3 km. with indoor and outdoor pools. Golf 6 km.

Open: 1 April - 1 November.

Directions

From the south, take A58 towards Vlissingen. Leave at junction 35 and head north towards Kapelle. Continue on N670 to Wemeldinge. Site is next to Yacht Haven and is well signed. GPS: N51:31.080 E04:00.299

Charges guide

Per unit incl. 2 persons	€ 14,00 - € 19,50
extra person	€ 2,00 - € 4,00
child (3-13 yrs)	€ 3,50

NL5580 Camping De Veerhoeve

Veerweg 48, NL-4471 NC Wolphaartsdijk (Zeeland)

Tel: **0113 581 155**. Email: **info@deveerhoeve.nl** **www.alanrogers.com/NL5580**

This is a family-run site near the shores of the Veerse Meer which is ideal for family holidays. It is situated in a popular area for watersports and is well suited for sailing, windsurfing or fishing enthusiasts, with boat launching 100 m. away. A sandy beach and recreation area ideal for children is only a five minute walk. As with most sites in this area there are many mature static and seasonal pitches. However, part of the friendly, relaxed site is reserved for touring units with 90 marked pitches on grassy ground, all with electrical connections. A member of the 'Holland Tulip Parcs' group.

Facilities

Sanitary facilities in three blocks have been well modernised with full tiling. Hot showers are on payment. Laundry facilities. Motorcaravan services. Supermarket (all season). Restaurant and snack bar. TV room. Tennis. Playground and play field. Games room. Bicycle hire. Fishing. Accommodation for groups. Max. 1 dog per pitch. WiFi. Off site: Slipway for launching boats 100 m. Riding 2 km. Golf 5 km.

Open: 1 April - 30 October.

Directions

From N256 Goes-Zierikzee road take Wolphaartsdijk exit. Follow through village and signs to site (be aware - one of the site signs is obscured by other road signs and could be missed).
GPS: N51:32.807 E03:48.807

Charges guide

Per pitch incl. up to 4 persons	€ 21,50 - € 24,50
incl. electricity (6A), water and drainage	€ 22,50 - € 25,50
incl. TV connection	€ 24,00 - € 27,50

Camping Cheques accepted.

NL5502 Camping Cassandria-Bad

Strengeweg 4, NL-4525 LW Retranchement (Zeeland)

Tel: **0117 392 300**. Email: **cassandria@zeelandnet.nl** **www.alanrogers.com/NL5502**

Cassandria Bad was established in 1992, lying very close to the Belgian border and the resort of Cadzand Bad, just under 2 km. from the nearest North Sea beach. Pitches are grassy and of a reasonable size; some are privately let for the full season. All pitches are equipped with 10A electricity and cable TV connections. Unusually, except for loading and unloading, cars are not allowed in the camping area, and a large parking area is provided at the entrance. On-site amenities include a snack bar, small shop and games room. During the peak season, a variety of activities is organized, including karaoke, bingo and sports tournaments. This part of the Netherlands, south of the Schelde, has strong contacts with Belgium and trips to Bruges and Gent are popular. Retranchement translates as 'bulwarks' and there are still remains of vast earthen sea walls, although now this area is best known as a paradise for nature lovers and walkers.

Facilities

Small shop with daily delivery of fresh bread. Snack bar. Sports field. Games room. Playground. Off site: Nearest beach 1.7 km. Walking and cycle routes. Fishing 5 km.

Open: 15 March - 31 October.

Directions

Approaching from the west and Bruges, use the Belgian N31 and then N376 towards Knokke-Heist and then across the Dutch border to Sluis. Here take the road to Groede and turn left towards Cadzand Bad at the second crossroads. Site is well signed from here. GPS: N51:21.968 E03:23.150

Charges guide

Per unit incl. up to 4 persons	€ 28,50
extra person	€ 3,75

Discounts available in low season.

Netherlands

NL5560 Camping De Wijde Blick

Lagezoom 23, NL-4325 CP Renesse (Zeeland)

Tel: **0111 468 888**. Email: **wijdeblick@ardoer.com** **www.alanrogers.com/NL5560**

The van Oost family run this neat campsite in a pleasant and personal way. It is located on the outskirts of the village of Renesse in a quiet rural spot. Much redevelopment took place during 2005 and De Wijde Blick now has 316 pitches of which 234 are for touring units. These include 203 fully serviced pitches. There are private sanitary facilities and 31 attractively arranged motorcaravan pitches with hardstanding. All the touring pitches have 6/10A electricity and are 90-120 sq.m. in area. There are special 'bike and hike' pitches for those touring without a car. Those with cars must park away from the pitch areas. Children are welcomed by the campsite mascot, Billy Blick and will thoroughly enjoy the large new playground, the indoor activity room or an evening at the theatre wagon. The new toilet block is solar heated, with a special children's section and an interesting schedule of how the technology works. This is a real holiday area and there are restaurants and shops in the village (and a market on Wednesdays). The beach is 2 km. from the site and a free bus service runs to Renesse from May to September.

Facilities

Three modern toilet blocks, all refurbished to very high standard, are first class, heated and with clean facilities including washbasins in cabins, controllable showers, facilities for disabled people, microwave and fridge. Bath (on payment). Laundry (with cartoons for children). Gas supplies. Motorcaravan services. Shop. Restaurant/bar (15/3-31/10). Swimming pool (1/5-15/9). WiFi. Good playground. Bicycle hire. Activities for children. Dogs are not accepted 16/3-23/8. Off site: Tennis and minigolf. Riding and fishing 1.5 km. Golf 10 km. Beach 2 km.

Open: All year.

Directions

Renesse is on the island of Schouwen (connected to the mainland by a bridge and three dams). On the N57 from Middelburg take the Renesse exit. After 2 km. follow road 106 to the left and then site signs. Site is on the east side of the village.
GPS: N51:43.106 E03:46.028

Charges 2009

Per unit incl. 2 persons	€ 17,00 - € 29,50
extra person	€ 4,50

CAMPING
De Wijde Blick
-Groeten uit Renesse-
Ardöer.com
CAMPING DE WIJDE BLICK - Lagezoom 23 - 4325 CP Renesse
T. +31 (0)111 468 888 - F +31 (0)111 468889 - E wijdeblick@ardoer.com - www.ardoer.com/wijdeblick

NL6950 Camping International Renesse

Scharendijkseweg 8, NL-4325 LD Renesse (Zeeland)

Tel: **0111 461 391**. Email: **info@camping-international.net** **www.alanrogers.com/NL6950**

Situated 300 metres from the beach at Renesse in Zeeland, this is a friendly, family run site. Its owners have set high standards, which is demonstrated by the immaculate and tastefully decorated sanitary facilities. There are 200 pitches, all for touring units and with electricity connections 4-16A). These are a generous size and laid out in bays and avenues surrounded by hedging. Around a courtyard area beyond reception is a supermarket and a bar which is attractively decorated. Outside bench seating and umbrellas turns this corner of the camping into a popular meeting place.

Facilities

Two luxury sanitary blocks provide showers, washbasins (some in cabins) and a baby room. Laundry room. Motorcaravan service point. Supermarket. Bar. Games room. TV. Play area. Bicycle hire. Entertainment in high season for all.

Open: 1 March - 31 October.

Directions

From Zierikzee follow N59 to Renesse for about 15 km. and turn right at roundabout (before town) onto local road signed R101. Continue for about 1 km. and turn left, then 1st right to site on right.
GPS: N51:44.388 E03:47.347

Charges guide

Per unit incl. 2 persons and electricity (4A)	€ 23,50
extra person	€ 4,50

NL6952 Camping Julianahoeve

Hoogenboomlaan 42, NL-4325 DM Renesse (Zeeland)

Tel: **0111 461 414**. Email: **julianahoeve@ardoer.com** **www.alanrogers.com/NL6952**

A very large site with 1,400 pitches, Camping Julianahoeve has 383 for touring units. You cannot get much closer to the sea in the Netherlands and the site is right beside the beach via a path through the dunes. The island of Schouwen-Duiveland is said to be the sunniest place in the Netherlands, so you will probably be using the beach quite often. The grass pitches vary in size (80-120 sq.m), all have electricity (6-16A) and 140 are fully serviced. They are arranged in areas that are separated by hedging. The site has many facilities designed to make your stay as pleasant as possible, including a supermarket, cafeteria with terrace, snack bar and several play fields and sports pitches. A new indoor pool complex is due to open in 2009. The popular beach resort of Renesse is only 15 minutes' walk away. Member of the 'Ardoer Group'.

Facilities

Several well appointed toilet blocks serve the site with facilities for younger children, babies and disabled visitors. Launderette. Supermarket. Café with terrace. Snack bar. Indoor pool complex (from 2009). Play areas. Sports pitches. WiFi. Dogs are not accepted. Off site: Fishing 500 m. Golf and riding 1 km. Boat launching 5 km.

Open: 14 March - 26 October.

Directions

From the A5 take exit 12 and follow the N57 through Ouddorp, then follow signs to Renesse. Site is well signed from the town.
GPS: N51:43.850 E3:45.283

Charges guide

Per unit incl. 2 persons and electricity	€ 16,00 - € 30,50
extra person (over 2 yrs)	€ 4,00 - € 5,00

NL5600 Kawan Village Delftse Hout

Korftlaan 5, NL-2616 LJ Delft (Zuid-Holland)

Tel: **0152 130 040**. Email: **info@delftsehout.nl** **www.alanrogers.com/NL5600**

Pleasantly situated in Delft's park and forest area on the eastern edge of the city, this well run, modern site is part of the Koningshof group. It has 200 tourist pitches quite formally arranged in groups of 4 to 6 and surrounded by attractive young trees and hedges. All have sufficient space and electrical connections (10A). Modern buildings near the entrance house the site amenities. A good sized first floor restaurant serves snacks or full meals and has an outdoor terrace overlooking the swimming pool and pitches. Walking and cycling tours are organised and there is a recreation programme in high season.

Facilities

Modern, heated toilet facilities include a spacious family room and children's section. Facilities for disabled visitors. Laundry. Motorcaravan services. Shop for basic food and camping items (1/4-1/11). Restaurant and bar (1/4-1/10). Small outdoor swimming pool (15/5-15/9). Adventure playground. Recreation room. Internet access. Bicycle hire. Gas supplies. Off site: Fishing 1 km. Riding or golf 5 km. Regular bus service to Delft centre.

Open: All year.

Directions

Site is 1 km. east of Delft. From A13 motorway take Delft - Pijnacker (exit 9), turn towards Pijnacker and then right at first traffic lights, following camping signs through suburbs and park to site.
GPS: N52:01.060 E04:22.745

Charges guide

Per unit incl. 2 persons and electricity	€ 22,50 - € 26,00
extra person (3 yrs and older)	€ 2,00
dog (1 per pitch)	€ 3,00

Low season discounts and for senior citizens (over 55). Special packages.
Camping Cheques accepted.

NL5630 Kawan Village Koningshof

Elsgeesterweg 8, NL-2231 NW Rijnsburg (Zuid-Holland)

Tel: **0714 026 051**. Email: **info@koningshofholland.nl** **www.alanrogers.com/NL5630**

This popular site is run in a personal and friendly way. The 200 pitches for touring units (some with hardstandings for larger units) are laid out in groups of four or twelve, divided by hedges and trees and all with electrical connections (10A). Cars are mostly parked in areas around the perimeter and 100 static caravans, confined to one section of the site, are entirely unobtrusive. Reception, a pleasant good quality restaurant, bar and a snack bar are grouped around a courtyard style entrance which is decorated with seasonal flowers. The site has a small outdoor, heated pool (13.5 x 7 m), with a separate paddling pool and imaginative children's play equipment. Recent additions are a recreation hall, an indoor swimming pool and a unique children's play pool with water streams, locks and play materials. The site has a number of regular British visitors from club connections who receive a friendly welcome, with English spoken. Used by tour operators (25 pitches). A very useful local information booklet (in English) is provided for visitors. A member of the 'Holland Tulip Parcs Group'.

Facilities

Three good toilet blocks, two with underfloor heating, with washbasins in cabins and provision for disabled visitors. Laundry facilities. Motorcaravan services. Gas supplies. Shop (1/4-15/10). Bar (1/4-1/11). Restaurant (1/4-10/9). Snacks and takeaway (1/4-1/11). Small outdoor pool (unsupervised; 15/5-15/9). Indoor pool (15/3-15/11). Solarium. Adventure playground and sports area. Tennis. Fishing pond (free). Bicycle hire. Entertainment in high season. Room for shows. One dog per pitch accepted in a limited area of the site. Off site: Sandy beach 5 km. Riding or golf 5 km. Den Haag 15 km. and Amsterdam 30 km.

Open: All year.

Directions

From N44/A44 Den Haag - Amsterdam motorway, take exit 7 for Oegstgeest and Rijnsburg. Turn towards Rijnsburg and follow site signs.
GPS: N52:12.007 E04:27.374

Charges 2009

Per unit incl. 2 persons and electricity	€ 27,00 - € 33,50
extra person (over 3 yrs)	€ 3,75
dog (see text)	€ 3,00

Senior citizen discounts, group rates and special packages. Camping Cheques accepted.

NL6980 Camping De Krabbeplaat

Oude Veerdam 4, NL-3231 NC Brielle (Zuid-Holland)

Tel: **0181 412 363**. Email: **info@krabbeplaat.nl** www.alanrogers.com/NL6980

Camping de Krabbeplaat is a family run site situated near the ferry port in a wooded, recreation area next to the 'Brielse Meer' lake. There are 510 spacious pitches, with 100 for touring units, 68 with electricity (10A) and cable connections and a water supply nearby. A separate field is used for groups of up to 450 guests. A nature conversation plan exists to ensure the site fits into with its natural environment. The lake and its beaches provide the perfect spot for watersports and relaxation and the site has its own harbour where you can moor your own boat. The beach is 7 km. from the site for those who prefer the sea. Plenty of cultural opportunities can be found in the historic towns of the area. Because of the large range of amenities and the tranquil nature of the site, De Krabbeplaat is perfect for families and couples.

Facilities

One large and two smaller heated toilet blocks in traditional style provide separate toilets, showers and washing cabins. High standards of cleanliness, a dedicated unit for disabled persons and provision for babies. Warm water is free of charge. Launderette. Motorcaravan services. Supermarket and snack bar (1/4-1/10). Restaurant (July/Aug). Recreation room. Youth centre. Tennis. Playground and play field. Animal farm. Bicycle and children's pedal hire. Canoe, surf, pedal boat and boat hire. Fishing. WiFi. Two cottages for hikers. No dogs allowed.

Open: 27 March - 25 October.

Directions

From the Amsterdam direction take the A4 (Europoort), then the A15 (Europoort). Take exit for Brielle on N57 and, just before Brielle, site is signed. GPS: N51:54.582 E04:11.121

Charges 2009

Per unit incl. 2 persons and electricity	€ 16,50 - € 22,00
extra person	€ 3,10
child (under 12 yrs)	€ 2,70

NL5640 Vakantiecentrum Kijkduinpark

Machiel Vrijenhoeklaan 450, NL-2555 NW Den Haag (Zuid-Holland)

Tel: **0704 482 100**. Email: **info@kijkduinpark.nl** www.alanrogers.com/NL5640

This is now an ultra-modern, all year round centre and family park, with many huts, villas and bungalows for rent and a large indoor swimming pool complex. The wooded touring area is immediately to the left of the entrance, with 330 pitches in shady glades of bark covered sand. All pitches have electricity 10A, water, waste water and cable TV connections. In a paved central area stands a supermarket, snack bar and restaurant. The main attraction here is the Meeresstrand, 500 m. from the site entrance. This is a long, wide sandy beach with flags to denote suitability for swimming. Windsurfing is popular.

Facilities

There are five modern sanitary blocks (key entry, € 20 deposit). Four private cabins for rent. Launderette. Snack bar. Shop. Restaurant. Supermarket. Indoor pool. Sun beds. Tennis. Bicycle hire. Special golfing breaks. Entertainment and activities organised in summer. Internet. Off site: Beach, golf and fishing 500 m. Riding 5 km.

Open: All year.

Directions

Site is southwest of Den Haag on the coast and Kijkduin is well signed as an area from all round Den Haag. GPS: N52:03.581 E04:12.671

Charges guide

Per unit incl. 5 persons and electricity	€ 19,00 - € 37,00
incl. electricity, water and drainage	€ 20,00 - € 48,25
extra person	€ 4,00

CAMPING ON THE SVR FARMS

(KAMPEREN BIJ DE SVR-BOER)

A great choice of farm sites all over Europe

More and more tourists prefer camping on the farm. Camping or staying the night without all the frills is increasingly popular with families and couples.

The SVR (Stichting Vrije Recreatie, 'Foundation for Free Recreation', Meerkerk, Holland) is the founder of 'Kamperen bij de Boer' and now includes 2000 affiliated small scale farm sites; 1200 in the Netherlands, 800 in the rest of Europe and no less than 350 in France.

Enjoyment for all ages

A farm is an exciting place to be, especially during holidays. There are plenty of great things to do, such as feeding the animals, helping to milk the cows, witnessing the birth of a calf or foal, jumping ditches, helping to pick the fruit, riding on a hay wagon and much more. A holiday on the farm means 'smell, touch, taste'.

For parents, camping on the farm is first of all enjoying country life with the very reasonable prices of the SVR-farmers.

SVR has experienced enormous growth. A couple with a caravan and car, a tent or a camper will only pay € 12 - € 15 all inclusive for one night. However, you do need be a contributor to the SVR, but that is no obstacle. For only € 10 a year you and your family can become contributors!

Are you interested and do you want to enjoy a different holiday?

See our website: www.svr.nl or call and ask for more information: +31 (0)183 35.27.41

Or fill in this form now:

Registration Form

(send in a stamped envelope to SVR - Broekseweg 75 - 4231 VD Meerkerk, NL)

Name: .... Intials: ....

Address:...

....

Town: .... Postcode: ....

Telephone:...

We wish to become contributors to the Stichting Vrije Recreatie, and will pay € .... yearly (minimum € 10) valid for the whole family.

The contribution is included,
or has been paid by Bank Payment using IBAN: NL02 PSTB 0002 1661 00, BIC: PSTBNL21
(delete what is not applicable).

We would like to be informed about sites in the .... region.

Signature: .... Date: ....

NL6970 Camping 't Weergors

Zuiddijk 2, NL-3221 LJ Hellevoetsluis (Zuid-Holland)

Tel: **0181 312 430**. Email: **weergors@pn.nl** **www.alanrogers.com/NL6970**

A rustic style site built around old farm buildings, 't Weergors has a comfortable mature feel. At the front of the site is a well presented farmhouse which houses reception and includes the main site services. Around the courtyard area is one of the three sanitary blocks which is unsophisticated, but clean and functional. There are plans to replace this with a new reception and shop and build a new toilet block elsewhere. There are currently 100 touring pitches (plus seasonal and static places), with another field at the back of the site under development to provide a further 70 or 80 touring places.

Facilities

Three sanitary blocks have showers (by token), washbasins, some in cabins, child size WCs and a baby bath. Laundry facilities. Motorcaravan service point. Small shop (1/4-31/10). Restaurant and bar. Snack bar. Tennis. Recreation room/TV. Internet access. Play area. Paddling pool. Organised entertainment in high season. Fishing. Bicycle hire. Rally field.

Open: 22 March - 31 October.

Directions

From Rotterdam join A15 west to Rozenburg exit 12 and join N57 south for 11 km. Turn left on N497 signed Hellevoetsluis and follow site signs for 4.5 km. to roundabout. Turn right at roundabout to site 1.5 km. on right. GPS: N51:49.766 E04:06.971

Charges 2009

Per unit inc 2 persons and electricity	€ 17,00 - € 19,00
extra person	€ 3,50

Camping Cheques accepted.

NL5680 Camping Noordduinen

Campingweg 1, NL-2221 EW Katwijk (Zuid-Holland)

Tel: **0714 025 295**. Email: **info@noordduinen.nl** **www.alanrogers.com/NL5680**

This is a large, well managed site surrounded by dunes and sheltered partly by trees and shrubbery, which also separate the various camping areas. The 200 touring pitches are marked and numbered but not divided. All have electricity (10A) and 45 are fully serviced with electricity, water, drainage and TV connection. There are also seasonal pitches and mobile homes for rent. Entertainment is organised in high season for various age groups. A new complex with indoor and outdoor pools, restaurant, small theatre and recreation hall provides a good addition to the site's facilities.

Facilities

The three sanitary blocks are modern and clean, with washbasins in cabins, a baby room and provision for people with disabilities. Hot water for showers is on payment. Laundry. Motorcaravan services. Supermarket. Bar. Restaurant. Recreation room. Swimming pool complex. Play area. Only gas barbecues are permitted. Fishing. Dogs are not accepted. Off site: Beach 300 m. Katwijk within walking distance. Riding 150 m.

Open: 31 March - 28 October.

Directions

Leave A44 at exit 8 (Leiden - Katwijk) to join N206 to Katwijk. Take Katwijk Noord exit and follow signs to site. GPS: N52:12.662 E04:24.587

Charges guide

Per pitch incl. 2 persons	€ 15,00 - € 35,00
electricity (10A)	€ 4,50
extra person	€ 4,00

NL5690 Camping De Victorie

Broekseweg 75-77, NL-4231 VD Meerkerk (Zuid-Holland)

Tel: **0183 352 741**. Email: **info@campingdevictorie.nl** **www.alanrogers.com/NL5690**

Within an hour's drive of the port of Rotterdam you can be pitched on this delightful, spacious site in the 'green heart' of the Netherlands. De Victorie, a working farm and a member of a club of small, 'green' sites, offers an alternative to the bustling seaside sites. A modern building houses reception, open plan office and space with tables and chairs, where the friendly owners may well invite you to have a cup of coffee. The 73 grass pitches (100-200 sq.m) are level and have 4A electricity supply. Everything about the site is surprising and contrary to any preconceived ideas.

Facilities

The main sanitary block is kept spotlessly clean, tastefully decorated and fully equipped. Showers are on payment. Laundry room. Additional sanitary facilities are around the site. Farm shop and small bar (once a week). Play area. Trampoline, and play field. Bicycle hire. Fishing. Riding. WiFi. Off site: Golf 15 km.

Open: 15 March - 31 October.

Directions

From Rotterdam follow A15 to junction with A27. Proceed 6 km. north on A27 to Noordeloos exit (no. 25) and join N214. Site is signed about 200 m. after roundabout at Noordeloos.
GPS: N51:56.174 E04:57.449

Charges guide

Per unit incl. 2 persons and electricity	€ 10,00 - € 12,00
extra person	€ 2,50

No credit cards. Large units may be charged extra.

NL5620 Vakantiepark Duinrell

Duinrell 1, NL-2242 JP Wassenaar (Zuid-Holland)

Tel: **0705 155 257**. Email: **info@duinrell.nl** **www.alanrogers.com/NL5620**

A very large site, Duinrell's name means 'well in the dunes' and the water theme is continued in the adjoining amusement park and in the extensive indoor pool complex. The campsite itself is very large with 900 tourist places on several flat grassy areas (80-100 sq.m) and it can become very busy in high season. As part of a continuing improvement programme, 850 marked pitches have electricity, water and drainage connections and some have cable TV. Amenities shared with the park include restaurants, a pizzeria and pancake house, supermarket and a theatre. Entry to the popular pleasure park is free for campers – indeed the camping areas surround and open out from the park.

Facilities

Six heated toilet blocks serve the touring areas. Laundry facilities. Amusement park and Tiki tropical pool complex. Restaurant, cafés, pizzeria and takeaways (weekends only in winter). Supermarket. Entertainment and theatre with shows in high season. 'Rope Challenge' trail and 'Forest Frisbee' trail. Bicycle hire. Minibowling. Diving experience package. All activities have extra charges. Off site: Beach 3.5 km. Riding 5 km. Golf 10 km.

Open: All year.

Directions

Site is signed from the N44/A44 (Den Haag - Amsterdam), but from the south the turning is 5 km. after passing sign for start of Wassenaar town, then follow site signs. GPS: N52:08.785 E04:23.242

Charges 2009

Per person (over 3 yrs)	€ 9,00

Special package offers.
Overnight stays between 17.00 - 10.00 hrs (when amusement park closed) less 25%.

NL5665 Camping Zeeburg

Zuider IJdijk 20, NL-1095 KN Amsterdam (Noord-Holland)

Tel: **020 694 4430**. Email: **info@campingzeeburg.nl** **www.alanrogers.com/NL5665**

Camping Zeeburg is attractively located to the east of Amsterdam on an island in the IJmeer and, unusually, combines a sense of nature with the advantage of being just 20 minutes from the city centre. In a sense Zeeburg reflects the spirit of Amsterdam, claiming to be 'open, friendly and tolerant'. The site offers larger caravan and motorhome pitches and smaller (and cheaper) tent pitches. Most pitches have views over the IJmeer. All caravan and motorhome pitches have a 10A electrical connection. Tent pitches cannot be booked in advance and the maximum duration allowed on site is 14 days. Zeeburg also offers a number of low cost wooden cabins. The city centre is 5 km. away and is easily accessed by cycle (hire available on site). Alternatively, a regular bus service runs close to the site. On-site amenities include a bar/restaurant, a shop including a bakery (which claims to bake Amsterdam's best croissants), a children's farm and a canoe rental service. The wetlands of the IJmeer are well worth exploration, extending to the Diemerpark and new city of IJburg.

Facilities

Shop. Bar/restaurant. Playground. Games room. Bicycle hire. Motorcaravan services. Children's farm. Canoe hire. Cabins to rent. Off site: Swimming pool. Buses and trains to city centre.

Open: All year.

Directions

Site is on the eastern side of Amsterdam. From the A10 (Amsterdam ring road) take exit S114 to Zeeburg. Then follow signs to the city centre and, before reaching the Piet Hein tunnel turn left and then right into the campsite. The site is well signed from the A10. GPS: N52:21.919 E04:57.523

Charges guide

Per unit incl. 2 persons and electricity	€ 15,00 - € 26,00
extra person	€ 3,50 - € 5,50
child (2-12 yrs)	€ 2,50 - € 3,50

Reduced rates for tents.

NL5675 Camping Vliegenbos

Meeuwenlaan 138, NL-1022 AM Amsterdam (Noord-Holland)

Tel: **020 636 8855** **www.alanrogers.com/NL5675**

Vliegenbos enjoys an appealing location in the middle of a large wood, but just 10 minutes from the lively centre of Amsterdam. It also has good access to the Waterland region, best known for its open expanses and picturesque towns such as Marken, Edam and Volendam. The site has recently celebrated its 50th anniversary. It extends over an 8.5 acre site and has a good range of amenities including a restaurant, shop and recently renewed toilet blocks with facilities for disabled visitors. Pitches here are grassy and most have electrical connections. A separate, open field is available for tents (without electricity). Several 'Trekkers cabins' can be reserved in advance. The site reception is open from 09.00 until 21.00 throughout the season and is able to offer advice on sightseeing options, as well as exploration of the Waterland by cycle. There is a bus stop 200 m. from the campsite with a good service to the city centre. Alternatively, a ferry operates from Centraal Station to a terminal 15 minutes walk from the site.

Facilities

Renoveted toilet blocks include facilities for disabled people. Motorcaravan services. Restaurant. Shop. Cabins for rent. Reservations are not accepted for touring pitches. Dogs are not accepted. Off site: Bus stop 200 m. Cycle tracks in the surrounding Waterland. Ferry terminal 15 minutes walk.

Open: 1 April - 30 September.

Directions

Leave the A10 Amsterdam ring road at exit S116 and follow signs to Camping Vliegenbos.
GPS: N52:23.433 E04:55.685

Charges 2009

Per unit incl. 2 persons and electricity	€ 28,50
extra person	€ 8,00
child (2-14 yrs)	€ 5,00

NL6960 Recreatiepark De Klepperstee

Vrijheidsweg 1, NL-3253 ZG Ouddorp (Zuid-Holland)

Tel: **0187 681 511**. Email: **info@klepperstee.com** **www.alanrogers.com/NL6960**

De Klepperstee is a good quality, family site. The site itself is peacefully located in tranquil countryside amid renowned nature reserves and just outside the village of Ouddorp in Zuid Holland. It offers excellent recreation areas that are spread over the centre of the site giving it an attractive open parkland appearance which is enhanced by many shrubs, trees and grass areas. The 338 spacious touring pitches are in named avenues, mostly separated by hedging and spread around the perimeter, together with the seasonal and static caravans. A variety of play equipment ensures hours of non-stop fun for children.

Facilities

One main sanitary block and a number of WC/shower units around the touring area provide free hot showers, washbasins, some in cabins (hot water only), baby bath and shower, child size toilets and a unit for people with disabilities. Laundry. Motorcaravan service point. Supermarket. Restaurant, bar and takeaway. Play areas. Tennis. TV, pool and electronic games. Entertainment. No animals are accepted and no single sex groups. Off site: Beach 600 m. Fishing 500 m. Riding, bicycle hire 4 km. Golf 10 km.

Open: Easter - 31 October.

Directions

From Rotterdam follow A15 west to Rozenburg exit 12 and join N57 south for 22 km. Take exit for Ouddorp and follow signs for 'Stranden'. Site is on the left after about 3 km.
GPS: N51:48.961 E03:53.983

Charges guide

Per unit incl. up to 4 persons	€ 10,00 - € 29,00
incl. 6A electricity	€ 12,50 - € 31,50
incl. 10A electricity	€ 17,50 - € 34,00
extra person	€ 2,75

NL5660 Camping Het Amsterdamse Bos

Kleine Noorddijk 1, NL-1187 NZ Amstelveen (Noord-Holland)

Tel: **0206 416 868**. Email: **info@campingamsterdam.com** www.alanrogers.com/NL5660

Het Amsterdamse Bos is a large park to the southwest of Amsterdam, one corner of which has been specifically laid out as the city's municipal campsite and is now under family ownership. Close to Schiphol Airport (we only noticed a little noise), it is about 12 km. from central Amsterdam. The site is well laid out alongside a canal, with unmarked pitches on separate flat lawns mostly backing onto pleasant hedges and trees, with several areas of paved hardstandings. It takes 400 touring units, with 100 electrical connections (10A) and some with cable TV. An additional area is available for tents and groups. The site has a new reception, the former restaurant is now a cooking and dining area and there are new cabins to rent. An excellent base for visiting Amsterdam; a local bus service to the city is just 300 m. from the site.

Facilities

Three new sanitary blocks are light and airy. Facilities for babies and disabled visitors. Laundry facilities. Motorcaravan services. Gas supplies. Small shop with basics. Fresh bread from reception. Cooking and dining area. Play area. Bicycle hire. Internet. Off site: Fishing, boating, pancake restaurant in the park. Riding 5 km.

Open: 15 March - 15 December.

Directions

Amsterdamse Bos and site are west of Amstelveen. From the A9 motorway take exit 6 and follow N231 to site (2nd traffic light).
GPS: N52:17.614 E04:49.378

Charges guide

Per person	€ 5,00
child (4-12 yrs)	€ 2,50
caravan and car	€ 11,00
electricity (10A)	€ 4,50
dog	€ 2,50

Group reductions.

NL5670 Gaasper Camping Amsterdam

Loosdrechtdreef 7, NL-1108 AZ Amsterdam (Noord-Holland)

Tel: **0206 967 326** **www.alanrogers.com/NL5670**

Amsterdam is probably the most popular destination for visits in the Netherlands, and Gaasper Camping is on the southeast side, a short walk from a Metro station with a direct 20 minute service to the centre. The site is well kept and neatly laid out on flat grass with attractive trees and shrubs. There are 350 touring pitches in two main areas – one more open and grassy, mainly kept for tents (30 pitches with 10A connections), the other more formal with numbered pitches mainly divided by shallow ditches or good hedges. Areas of hardstanding are available and all caravan pitches have electrical connections (10A).

Facilities

Three modern, clean toilet blocks (one unisex) for the tourist sections are an adequate provision. Nine new cabins with basin and shower. Hot water for showers and some dishwashing sinks on payment. Facilities for babies. Washing machine and dryer. Motorcaravan services. Gas supplies. Supermarket (1/4-1/11), café/bar/restaurant plus takeaway (1/5-1/9). Play area on grass. Off site: Riding 200 m. Fishing 1 km. Golf 4 km.

Open: 15 March - 1 November.

Directions

Take exit No.1 for Gaasperplas - Weesp (S113) from the section of A9 motorway which is on the east side of the A2. Note: do not take the Gaasperdam exit (S112) which comes first if approaching from the west. GPS: N52:18.776 E04:59.489

Charges guide

Per person	€ 5,00
pitch incl. car	€ 10,25 - € 11,25
electricity (10A)	€ 3,50

NL5700 Buitencentrum Molengroet

Molengroet 1, NL-1723 PX Noord-Scharwoude (Noord-Holland)

Tel: **0226 393 444**. Email: **info@molengroet.nl** **www.alanrogers.com/NL5700**

Molengroet is a pleasant, modern site, located near a watersports complex and only 40 km. from Amsterdam. It is a good place to stop on the way to the Afsluitdijk (the 32 km. dike across the top of the Ijsselmeer) or as an ideal holiday site for watersports enthusiasts. The pitches are grouped according to services provided, ranging from simple pitches with 6A electricity and TV connections, to fully serviced pitches with 10A electricity, TV, water and drainage. Other pitches have private sanitary facilities, others are used for chalets. Recent developments to the park's facilities include a play area, a heated swimming pool, a sports field and a children's farm.

Facilities

Modern, heated sanitary facilities. Some private facilities for rent. Motorcaravan services. Gas supplies. Shop. Restaurant/bar. Café and takeaway snacks. Swimming pool. Play area. Children's farm. Sports field. Fishing. Bicycle hire. Surfboards and small boats for hire. Entertainment is organised in high season.
Off site: Watersports. Tennis, squash, sauna, and swimming nearby. Riding or golf 5 km.

Open: 1 April - 31 October.

Directions

From Haarlem on A9 to Alkmaar take N245 towards Schagen. Site is southwest of Noord Sharwoude on the N245, signed to west on road to Geestermerambacht GPS: N52:41.673 E04:46.262

Charges guide

Per unit incl. 2 persons and electricity	€ 19,00 - € 26,00

Reductions in low season and for longer stays. Camping Cheques accepted.

See sites NL6870, NL6862 and NL 6872 on the following pages.

NL5720 Camping Jachthaven Uitdam

Zeedijk 2, NL-1154 PP Uitdam (Noord-Holland)

Tel: **0204 031 433**. Email: **info@campinguitdam.nl** **www.alanrogers.com/NL5720**

Situated beside the Markermeer which is used extensively for watersports, this large site has its own private yachting marina (300 yachts and boats). It has 200 seasonal and permanent pitches, many used by watersports enthusiasts, but also offers 260 marked tourist pitches (180 with 4/6A electricity) on open, grassy ground overlooking the water and 24 mobile homes to rent. There is a special area for campers with bicycles. Very much dominated by the marina, this site will appeal to watersports enthusiasts, with opportunities for sailing, windsurfing and swimming, or for fishing, but it is also on a pretty stretch of coast. Much construction was underway when we visited, but this was mainly in the seasonal areas. All the touring pitches have been upgraded with new drainage and there are new cabins for rent. Uitdam is 15 km. northeast of Amsterdam and is close to the ancient, small towns of Marken, Volendam and Monnickendam. The views over the IJsselmeer from both ends of the touring fields are wonderful and this alone makes this site well worth visiting.

Facilities

Two good toilet blocks and one rather basic toilet block with toilets only. Good facilities include hot showers on payment, toilets, washbasins and a baby room. Motorcaravan services. Gas supplies. Shop (1/4-1/10). Bar/restaurant (weekends and high season). TV room. Tennis. Playground and paddling pool. Bicycle hire. Fishing. Yacht marina (with fuel) and slipway. Watersports. Entertainment in high season. Off site: Riding 4 km. Sailing 6 km. Golf 12 km.

Open: 1 March - 1 November.

Directions

From A10, take exit S116 onto the N247 towards Volendam. Then take Monnickendam exit south in direction of Marken on N518, then Uitdam. Site is just outside Uitdam. GPS: N52:25.668 E05:04.408

Charges guide

Per unit incl. 2 persons	€ 22,50
tent incl. 2 persons	€ 15,50 - € 19,00
extra person (over 3 yrs)	€ 3,00
boat on trailer	€ 7,00

NL6870 Kennemer Duincamping De Lakens

Zeeweg 60, NL-2051 EC Bloemendaal aan Zee (Noord-Holland)

Tel: **0235 411 570**. Email: **delakens@kennemerduincampings.nl** **www.alanrogers.com/NL6870**

De Lakens is part of de Kennemer Duincampings group and is beautifully located in the dunes at Bloemendaal aan Zee. This site has 940 reasonably large, flat pitches with a hardstanding of shells. There are 410 for tourers (235 with 16A electricity) and the sunny pitches are separated by low hedging. This site is a true oasis of peace in a part of the Netherlands usually bustling with activity. From this site it is possible to walk straight through the dunes to the North Sea. Although there is no pool, there is the sea. A separate area is provided for groups and youngsters to maintain the quiet atmosphere. It is not far to Amsterdam or Alkmaar and its cheese market. We feel you could have an enjoyable holiday here.

Facilities

The six toilet blocks for tourers (two brand new) include controllable showers, washbasins (open style and in cabins), facilities for disabled people and a baby room. Launderette. Motorcaravan service points. Bar/restaurant and snack bar. Supermarket. Adventure playgrounds. Bicycle hire. Entertainment program in high season. Dogs are not accepted. Off site: Beach and riding 1 km.

Open: 20 March - 1 November.

Directions

From Amsterdam go west to Haarlem and follow the N200 from Haarlem towards Bloemendaal aan Zee. Site is on the N200, on the right hand side. GPS: N52:24.338 E04:35.191

Charges guide

Per pitch incl. 4 persons	€ 14,10 - € 27,45
incl. electricity	€ 18,40 - € 28,70
extra person	€ 4,20

NL5735 Camping Tempelhof

Winner Alan Rogers Awards 2008

Westerweg 2, NL-1759 JD Callantsoog (Noord-Holland)

Tel: **0224 581 522**. Email: **info@tempelhof.nl** www.alanrogers.com/NL5735

This first class site on the Dutch coast has 500 pitches with 250 for touring units, the remainder used by seasonal campers and a number of static units (mostly privately owned). All touring pitches have electricity (10/16A), water, drainage and TV aerial point. The grass pitches are arranged in long rows which are separated by hedges and shrubs, with access from hardcore roads. There is hardly any shade. Tempelhof is close to the North Sea beaches (1 km), but the site has a heated indoor pool with a paddling pool, water slide and new fitness room. There are facilities for football, handball, volleyball and tennis and a climbing wall. In high season a full entertainment programme is arranged for children with water games, sports activities and music. Many of these activities take place in the new recreation hall with its stage. With all these activities, you may not want to leave the site other than to go to the beach. However, the site is close to the ferry port of Den Helder where you can catch a ferry to the largest Dutch Island of Texel. Tempelhof is also close to the cheese market in Alkmaar and only 60 km. or so from Amsterdam. Member of 'Leading Campings Group'.

Facilities

Two recently renovated toilet blocks have modern facilities including washbasins (open style and in cabins) and controllable hot showers (SEP key). Children's section and baby room. Private bathroom. Facilities for disabled visitors. Fully equipped laundry. Motorcaravan services. Shop, restaurant, takeaway and bar (1/4-1/11). Swimming pool with paddling pool. Fitness room. Recreation hall. Trim court. Play area. Extensive animation programme in high season. WiFi. Bicycle hire. Off site: Fishing 500 m. Beach 1 km. Golf 6 km. Riding 4 km.

Open: All year.

Directions

From Alkmaar take N9 road north towards Den Helder. Turn left towards Callantsoog on the N503 road and follow site signs.
GPS: N52:50.497 E04:42.915

Charges 2009

Per unit incl. 2 persons	€ 18,00 - € 36,00
extra person	€ 3,00
electricity per kWh	€ 0,35

Camping Tempelhof
From € 18,- a night including 2 persons
Westerweg 2 • 1759 JD Callantsoog • T: +31 (0)224 581522
F: +31 (0)224 582133 • E: info@tempelhof.nl • W: www.tempelhof.nl
ADAC
ANWB
IT'S ALWAYS GREAT AT CAMPING TEMPELHOF

NL6862 Kennemer Duincamping Geversduin

Beverwijkerstraatweg 205, NL-1901 NH Castricum (Noord-Holland)

Tel: **0251 661 095**. Email: **geversduin@kennemerduincampings.nl** www.alanrogers.com/NL6862

The comfortable, family site of Gerversduin lies in an area of forests and sand dunes. The site offers 614 pitches of which 221 for are for touring units and 14 for accommodation to rent. With good shade and privacy, most of the pitches have 4/16A electricity connections. The pitches without electricity have a unique location and cars must be parked elsewhere. In high season, many activities are organised for youngsters including the unusual opportunity to join a forestry worker for the day.

Facilities

Three sanitary blocks with WCs, open style basins, preset hot showers and family shower rooms including baby room. Facilities for disabled visitors. Laundry with washing machines and dryers. Supermarket. Snack bar and café for meals with large terrace. Recreation area. Sports pitch. Play area. Bicycle hire. Internet. Safes. Only gas barbecues are permitted. Dogs only accepted in designated areas. Off site: Beach 4 km. Riding 6 km. Golf and sailing 9 km.

Open: 20 March - 26 October.

Directions

On the A9 (Amsterdam - Alkmaar) take exit for the N203 and on north towards Castricum. In Castricum follow signs to the station. From there drive south towards Heemskerk via the Beverwijkse straatweg. Site is south of Castricum and signed on the Beverwijkse straatweg. GPS: N52:31.822 E04:38.903

Charges guide

Per unit incl. 4 persons	€ 22,45 - € 32,55
incl. electricity	€ 25,85 - € 38,00
extra person (over 2 yrs)	€ 4,25

NL6872 Kennemer Duincamping Bakkum

Zeeweg 31, NL-1901 NZ Castricum aan Zee (Noord-Holland)

Tel: **0251 661 091**. Email: **bakkum@kennemerduincampings.nl** **www.alanrogers.com/NL6872**

Kennemer Duincamping Bakkum lies in a wooded area in the centre of the protected dune reserve. There are 1,800 pitches of which 400 are used for touring units. These pitches are spacious and equipped with 10A electricity. Mobile homes and seasonal units use the remaining 800 pitches in separate areas of the site. For safety and tranquillity the majority of the site is kept free of cars. The dunes are accessible from the site and offer plenty of opportunities for walking and cycling.

Facilities

Two toilet blocks for tourers with toilets, washbasins in cabins, free, controllable showers and family shower rooms. Facilities for disabled visitors. Laundry area. Excellent supermarket, baker, fish shop and chicken shop. Snack bar and restaurant. Play area. Sports pitch. Tennis. Bicycle hire. Activities for children and teens. Motorbikes are not accepted. Off site: Beach 1 km. Fishing 1 km. Supermarket, bar, restaurant, swimming pool 2 km. Riding 4 km. Golf 7 km.

Open: 20 March - 26 October.

Directions

On the A9 between Alkmaar and Amsterdam take exit west onto the N203. Turn left onto the Zeeweg (N513) and after a few kilometres the site is on the right. GPS: N52:33.684 E04:37.986

Charges guide

Per unit incl. 4 persons	€ 15,10 - € 24,25
extra person (over 2 yrs)	€ 3,15
electricity (10A)	€ 7,60

NL5710 Camping It Soal

Suderséleane 27, NL-8711 GX Workum (Friesland)

Tel: **0515 541 443**. Email: **info@itsoal.nl** **www.alanrogers.com/NL5710**

This is an attractive, child-friendly site with 800 m. of beach, situated directly beside the IJsselmeer with a canal on one side. It is ideal for those who enjoy water sports as there are many activities on the lake, including windsurfing, sailing, swimming and fishing. There are 650 pitches here, of which 400 are good sized, individual, flat and grassy for tourers, with 4/6A electrical connections. A few pitches also have water and drainage. In separate areas, the other pitches are taken by seasonal guests and about 50 static units. Dogs are only allowed in one area and cars must be left in a car park.

Facilities

Sanitary facilities are clean and include toilets, washbasins (open and in private cabins) and free, controllable showers. Facilities for disabled visitors. Baby room. Laundry facilities. Shop, restaurant and takeaway (1/4-1/10). Play areas. Tennis. Video games room. Skate track. Bicycle hire. Fishing. Boat launching. Beach. Surfboards and sailing boats for hire. Entertainment programme. Off site: Riding 10 km. Golf 15 km. Good opportunities for cycling, walking, skating and fishing.

Open: 1 April - 31 October.

Directions

From Groningen on the A7 (via Drachten, Joure and Sneek), exit just before Bolsward onto the N359 towards Workum, then exit Workum. Pass through village, follow sign (IJsselmeer) and then site signs. GPS: N52:58.140 E05:24.863

Charges guide

Per unit incl. 1 or 2 adults and electricity	€ 18,50 - € 27,00
extra person	€ 2,50
dog	€ 5,00

NL5760 Kawan Village De Kuilart

Kuilart 1, NL-8723 CG Koudum (Friesland)

Tel: **0514 522 221**. Email: **info@kuilart.nl** **www.alanrogers.com/NL5760**

De Kuilart is a well run, modern and partly car-free site by Friesland's largest lake. With its own marina and private boating facilities, it attracts many watersports enthusiasts. The 450 pitches here are set in groups of 10 to 16 on areas of grass surrounded by well established hedges. There are 175 for touring units, all with electricity (6-16A), water, waste water, WiFi and TV connections, and 20 new pitches with private sanitary facilities. The restaurant provides good views of the lake.

Facilities

Four modern, heated sanitary blocks well spaced around the site with showers on payment and most washbasins (half in private cabins) have only cold water. Launderette. Motorcaravan services. Gas supplies. Restaurant/bar (4/4-3/11). Supermarket (11/4-7/9). Indoor pool (3 sessions daily, 4/4-3/11). Sauna and solarium. Sports field. Play areas. Tennis. Bicycle hire. Fishing. Animation team (high season). Internet access. Lake swimming area. Marina (600 berth) with windsurfing, boat hire and boat shop. Garage at harbour. Off site: Riding or golf 4 km.

Open: All year.

Directions

Site is southeast of Koudum, on the Fluessen lake. Follow the camping sign off the N359 Bolsward - Lemmer road GPS: N52:54.150 E05:27.972

Charges guide

Per unit incl. 2 persons, electricity	€ 16,80 - € 22,10
serviced pitch	€ 18,30 - € 23,80
'supercomfort' pitch	€ 23,30 - € 34,20
extra person	€ 4,10

Special weekend rates at B.Hs.
Camping Cheques accepted.

NL6080 Camping De Zeehoeve

Westerzeedijk 45, NL-8862 PK Harlingen (Friesland)

Tel: **0517 413 465**. Email: **info@zeehoeve.nl** **www.alanrogers.com/NL6080**

Superbly located, directly behind the sea dyke of the Waddensea and just a kilometre from the harbour of Harlingen, De Zeehoeve is an attractive and spacious site. It has 300 pitches (125 for tourers), all with 10A electricity and 20 with water, drainage and electricity. There are 16 hardstandings for motorcaravans and larger units. Some pitches have views over the Harlingen canal where one can moor small boats. An ideal site for rest and relaxation, for watersports or to visit the attractions of Harlingen and Friesland. After a day of activity, one can wine and dine in the site restaurant or at one of the many pubs in the town. This splendid location allows visitors the opportunity to watch the sun slowly setting from the sea dyke. You can also stroll through Harlingen or take the ferry to Vlieland or Terschelling. It is possible to moor boats at Harlingen, to hire a boat or book an organised sailing or sea fishing trip.

Facilities

Hikers' cabins and boarding houses. Three sanitary blocks include open style washbasins with cold water only, washbasins in cabins with hot and cold water, controllable showers (on payment). Family showers and baby bath. Facilities for disabled people. Cooking hob. Launderette. Sinks with free hot water. Motorcaravan services. Bar/restaurant (1/7-31/8). Internet access. Play area. Bicycle hire. Pedaloe and canoe hire. Fishing. Extensive entertainment programme in July/Aug. Off site: Beach 200 m. Riding 10 km.

Open: 1 April - 15 October.

Directions

From Leeuwarden take A31 southwest to Harlingen, then follow site signs. GPS: N53:09.742 E05:25.013

Charges guide

Per unit incl. 2 persons, electricity	€ 16,10 - € 18,60
extra person	€ 3,80
child (4-11 yrs)	€ 3,30
tent (no car) incl. 2 persons	€ 13,60
pet	€ 3,00

NL6030 Recreatieoord Klein Vaarwater

Klein Vaarwaterweg 114, NL-9163 ME Buren (Friesland)

Tel: **0519 542 156**. Email: **info@kleinvaarwater.nl** **www.alanrogers.com/NL6030**

Recreatieoord Klein Vaarwater is a bustling family holiday park on the interesting island of Ameland. The site is 800 m. from the North Sea beaches and has its own indoor pool, with bars, restaurants, supermarket and party centre. Klein Vaarwater has 190 touring pitches, of which 130 have 10A electricity, water, waste water and cable. Pitching is off hardcore access lanes, close to nature, on fields taking 6-10 units, on a grass and sand underground. There is some shade to the back from trees and bushes and level pitches are numbered and partly separated by young trees.

Facilities

Two older style toilet blocks (maintenance variable) with toilets, open style washbasins, preset hot showers (coin operated) and facilities for disabled people. Washing machines and dryers. Supermarket. Bar. Restaurants. Snack bar. Café. Boutique. Indoor pool (25 x 15 m) with waterslide and fun paddling pool. Full fitness programme. Bicycle hire. Playing field. Boules. Bowling alley. Minigolf. Animation programme for young and old. Off site: Beach 800 m. Village of Buren 500 m.

Open: April - October.

Directions

From Leeuwarden, follow N357 all the way north to Holwerd and take the ferry to Ameland (reservations necessary in high season). On the island, follow the signs for Buren and then site signs.
GPS: N53:27.215 E05:48.268

Charges guide

Per person	€ 3,65
pitch incl. electricity	€ 6,75
car	€ 3,00

Camping Cheques accepted.

NL5750 Camping De Kleine Wielen

Groene Ster 14, NL-8926 XE Leeuwarden (Friesland)

Tel: **0511 431 660**. Email: **info@dekleinewielen.nl** **www.alanrogers.com/NL5750**

Camping De Kleine Wielen (small wheels) is named after a small lake of the same name that lies in the 1,000 ha nature and recreation area of 'De Groene Ster'. The campsite is adjacent to the lake – possible activities include boating in the lake or cycling and walking around this beautiful area of forest, grassland and ponds. The site provides 480 pitches, of which 350 are for touring units. The remaining pitches are used for privately owned mobile homes. All the touring pitches have 4A electricity and many have wonderful views over the water and surrounding countryside. The position of the site next to the water (the lake is not fenced) opens up many opportunities for sailing, rowing, canoeing or windsurfing. You can follow the river leading from the lake by boat or on shore by bicycle or car as it leads through the villages and towns such as Hindeloopen, Stavoren and Dokkum. With its central Friesland location, Camping De Kleine Wielen ideal for a taste of the real 'Friesland' culture and is definitely worth visiting.

Facilities

Four modern sanitary blocks with washbasins in cabins and preset showers (coin operated). Facilities for disabled visitors. Motorcaravan service point. Shop (1/5-30/9). Café/restaurant and snack bar (1/4-30/9). Playground. Sports pitch. Minigolf. Lake. Fishing. Rowing boats. Surf boards. Extensive recreation programme in July and August. Off site: Golf 1 km. Boat launching 2 km. Riding 5 km.

Open: 1 April - 30 September.

Directions

From the N355 turn off east towards Leeuwarden and follow campsite signs.
GPS: N53:12.990 E05:53.222

Charges guide

Per person	€ 3,20 - € 3,65
child (2-12 yrs)	€ 1,90 - € 2,05
pitch incl. car	€ 6,25 - € 6,95
electricity (4A)	€ 2,75

NL6040 Recreatiecentrum Bergumermeer

Solcamastraat 30, NL-9262 ND Sumar (Friesland)

Tel: **0511 461 385**. Email: **info@bergumermeer.nl** **www.alanrogers.com/NL6040**

Recreatiecentrum Bergumermeer's location beside the Bergum lake, makes it ideal for lovers of watersports, with sailing, surfing and canoeing available, as well as swimming from two sandy beaches. There is also a large, heated indoor swimming pool and fun paddling pool. The site provides 300 good sized, flat touring pitches for both caravans and tents, some with attractive views over the Prinses Margrietkanaal and the surrounding countryside, others with views over the lake. All pitches are fully serviced with 10A electricity, water and drainage, and there are 10 large hardstandings.

Facilities

Three sanitary buildings offer private cabins, children's toilets, baby bath and facilities for disabled visitors. Children's section in one block. Launderette. Freezer. Shop. Bar/restaurant. Pancake restaurant. Heated indoor pool. Solarium. Play area. Children's farm. Tennis. Minigolf. Fishing. Sailing dinghies, motorboats and canoes for hire. Animation programme in high season. Club space with disco. Bicycle hire. Boat launching. Beach. Off site: Riding 5 km. Golf 19 km.

Open: 27 March - 31 October.

Directions

Either go north from Amsterdam via the A7/E22 through Leeuwarden towards Drachten, or east from Amsterdam via A6, onto the A7 (Leeuwarden and Groningen), then onto N31 (De Haven, Drachten) and in either case onto the N356 towards Bergum following site signs.
GPS: N53:11.476 E06:07.457

Charges guide

Per unit incl. 2 persons and electricity	€ 18,50 - € 27,50
extra person	€ 4,50

Netherlands

NL6110 Camping 't Plathuis

Bourtangerkanaal Noord 1, NL-9545 VJ Bourtange (Groningen)

Tel: **0599 354 383**. Email: **info@campingplathuis.nl** **www.alanrogers.com/NL6110**

Camping 't Plathuis is beautifully located in the fortified village of Bourtange. This small town dates back to the times of the invasion of the Bishop of Münster in the 1600s. The site has 92 touring pitches, most on well established, grass fields with shade from the mature trees that surround the site. On the newest area at the back of the site there are 22 serviced pitches with 6-16A electricity, water and drainage, including 14 with cable TV. There are plans to further extend the site. To the front of the site is a lake for swimming and fishing with a sandy beach. The southeastern part of Groningen is a beautiful area, ideal for walking and cycling trips. Across the road from the site is a canal for fishing and boating (canoe hire on site). Besides spending some time in Bourtange, there is easy access to Germany for touring or visiting towns such as Leer, or even Bremen. This is a site for those who enjoy peace and quiet, walking, biking, nature and culture.

Facilities

Single older style, but neat and adequate, heated toilet block with toilets, washbasins (open style and in cabins) and coin operated controllable, hot showers. Second portacabin block in the new field. Family shower rooms. Baby room. Facilities for disabled visitors. Laundry facilities. Shopping service for basics. Bread to order. Bar. Snack bar. Lake for swimming and fishing. Canoe hire. Playground. Off site: Village of Bourtange.

Open: 1 April - 31 October.

Directions

From A7 take exit 47 for Winschoten and continue on N367 towards Vlagtwedde. In Vlagtwedde turn on N368 towards Bourtange. Site is on the right 200 m. after entering the village.
GPS: N53:00.587 E07:11.080

Charges guide

Per unit incl. 2 persons	€ 12,00 - € 14,95
incl. water and drainage	€ 14,50 - € 17,45
electricity (6A)	€ 2,50

NL6090 Camping Lauwersoog

Strandweg 5, NL-9976 VS Lauwersoog (Groningen)

Tel: **0519 349 133**. Email: **info@lauwersoog.nl** **www.alanrogers.com/NL6090**

The focus at Camping Lauwersoog is very much on the sea and watersports. One can have sailing lessons or hire canoes and, with a new extension, there is direct access to the beach from the site. There are 450 numbered pitches with 225 for tourers. Electricity (4/6A) is available at 200 pitches and 86 have water, drainage, electricity and cable connections. The pitches are on level, grassy fields (some beside the beach), partly separated by hedges and some with shade from trees. A new building in the marina houses a restaurant, bar, shop and laundry, and also provides beautiful views over the Lauwersmeer.

Facilities

The two toilet blocks for tourers provide washbasins (open style and in cabins), preset showers and child size toilets. Facilities for disabled people. Laundry. Campers' kitchen. Ice pack service. Motorcaravan service. New restaurant, bar, snack bar and shop. Playground. Sailing school. Canoe hire. Surfing lessons (July/Aug). Bicycle and go-kart hire. Boules. Internet access. Extensive entertainment programme for all ages in high season. Torch useful. Off site: Riding 5 km.

Open: All year.

Directions

Follow N361 from Groningen north to Lauwersoog and then follow site signs.
GPS: N53:24.123 E06:13.039

Charges guide

Per unit incl. 2 persons, 6A electrcity	€ 24,50
serviced pitch (125 sq.m)	€ 27,50
extra person	€ 4,00
dog	€ 4,00

Camping Cheques accepted.

NL6120 Kawan Village 't Strandheem

Parkweg 2, NL-9865 VP Opende (Groningen)

Tel: **0594 659 555**. Email: **info@strandheem.nl** **www.alanrogers.com/NL6120**

Camping Strandheem has 330 quite large, numbered pitches (110 sq.m) some with hardstanding and suitable for motorcaravans. All with electricity, there are 180 used for touring units, partly separated by low hedges but without much shade. Of these, 34 pitches have water points, drainage and cable TV connections. The De Bruinewoud family will give you a warm welcome. The new reception building houses an attractive bar, a full restaurant, a disco for teenagers and a shop. The site has a lot to offer, especially for youngsters.

Facilities

Two modern toilet buildings have washbasins (open style and in cabins), controllable showers, child size toilets and basins, a good baby room and fully equipped bathroom. Facilities for disabled people. Launderette. Motorcaravan service. New shop. Restaurant and bar. Café and snack bar. Covered swimming pool (5 x 5 m) with separate paddling pool, slide and sun terrace. Playgrounds. New covered play area with stage. Minigolf. Fishing. Bicycle hire. Boules. Lake with beach (€ 1 p/p per day). Extensive recreation program (July/Aug). Film and card nights. Off site: Lake with beach 100 m. Riding 6 km. Golf 15 km.

Open: 1 April - 1 October.

Directions

Follow A7 west from Groningen towards Heerenveen and take exit 31. Follow campsite signs from there. GPS: N53:09.167 E06:11.483

Charges guide

Per unit incl. 2 persons and electricity	€ 17,00 - € 25,00
extra person	€ 3,75
private sanitary facility	€ 7,50
dog	€ 3,75

Camping Cheques accepted.

NL5770 Camping Stadspark

Campinglaan 6, NL-9727 KH Groningen (Groningen)

Tel: **0505 251 624**. Email: **info@campingstadspark.nl** **www.alanrogers.com/NL5770**

The Stadspark is a large park to the southwest of the city, well signed and with easy access. The campsite is within the park with many trees and surrounded by water. It has 200 pitches with 150 for touring units, of which 75 have 6A electricity and 30 are fully serviced with electricity, water and drainage. The separate tent area is supervised directly by the manager. Buses for the city leave from right outside and timetables and maps are provided by Mrs van der Veer, the helpful, English speaking manager. Groningen is a very lively city with lots to do.

Facilities

Two sanitary blocks, one totally refurbished, provide hot water for showers. Motorcaravan service point. Shop (15/3-15/10). Restaurant, café, bar and takeaway (1/4-15/9). Internet access in reception. Bicycle hire. Some play equipment and small paddling pool. Fishing. Canoeing. Off site: Riding and golf 5 km. Boat launching 6 km.

Open: 15 March - 15 October.

Directions

From Assen on A28 turn left on the A7. Turn on N370 and follow site signs (Stadspark, quite close). GPS: N53:12.054 E06:32.142

Charges guide

Per unit incl. 2 persons	€ 15,00
extra person	€ 1,50 - € 2,50
electricity	€ 2,00

No credit cards.

NL6134 Camping Vorrelveen

Vorrelveen 10, NL-9411 VP Beilen (Drenthe)

Tel: **0593 527 261**. Email: **info@campingvorrelveen.nl** **www.alanrogers.com/NL6134**

In comparison with the larger (and justifiably popular) campsites in Drenthe, Camping Vorrelveen is a small, farm based site which reflects the pleasant countryside. The site is located on a working farm and enjoys beautiful views of the surrounding country. There are just spacious 30 pitches, all with 6A electricity, and the owners do their best to ensure a very personal, tranquil atmosphere. For example, your bread for breakfast will be delivered to your pitch and, in the evening, you can order home made pizzas and other dishes prepared in the farm kitchen!

Facilities

Toilet block including a family shower. The same building houses a large room for meals and socialising. Essential supplies kept at the farmhouse. Play area with cable track and children's fort. Pétanque. Motorcaravan services (with pitches on hardstanding). Bicycle hire. Tents (incl. breakfast) for rent. Off site: Fishing 800 m. The museum villages of Orvelte and Kabouterland (Pixieland).

Open: April - October.

Directions

Take exit 30 from the A28 following signs to Smilde. Turn right at the third bridge towards Hijken and then immediately turn left towards Vorrelveen. After a further 3 km. the site is on the left. GPS: N52:52.800 E06:26.520

Charges guide

Per person	€ 3,50
child (2-12 yrs)	€ 3,00
pitch incl. electricity	€ 7,00

NL5790 Rekreatiepark 't Kuierpadtien

Oranjekanaal NZ 10, NL-7853 TA Wezuperbrug (Drenthe)

Tel: **0591 381 415**. Email: **info@kuierpad.nl** **www.alanrogers.com/NL5790**

Professionally run, this all year round site is suitable as a night stop, or for longer if you wish to participate in all the activities offered in July and August. The site itself is in a woodland setting on the edge of the village. The 525 flat and grassy pitches for touring units (with 653 in total) are of reasonable size. All have 4/6/10A electricity and 32 are fully serviced with electricity, TV aerial point, water and drainage. On-site activities encompass canoeing, windsurfing, water chutes and the dry ski slope, which is also open during the winter so that the locals can practise.

Facilities

Eight quite acceptable sanitary blocks, including a new one, with hot showers (17.30-10.00 in July/Aug). Facilities for disabled visitors. Laundry. Motorcaravan services. Supermarket (1/4-15/9) but bread all year. Restaurant and bar with TV. Takeaway. Indoor pool (all year). Outdoor pool (1/4-15/9). Sauna, solarium and whirlpool. Internet access. Tennis. Dry ski slope. Play areas. Minigolf. Lake with beach. Boat rental. Off site: Fishing 500 m. Riding 1 km. Golf 1.5 km.

Open: All year.

Directions

From N34 Groningen - Emmen road exit near Emmen onto N31 towards Beilen. Turn right into Schoonord where left to Wezuperbrug. Site is at beginning of village on the right.
GPS: N52:50.420 E06:43.620

Charges guide

Per unit incl. 2 persons	€ 22,50 - € 33,50
extra person	€ 5,50
serviced pitch	€ 6,00

No credit cards. Camping Cheques accepted.

NL6140 Camping De Valkenhof

Beilerstraat 13a, NL-9431 GA Westerbork (Drenthe)

Tel: **0593 337 546**. Email: **info@camping-de-valkenhof.nl** **www.alanrogers.com/NL6140**

De Valkenhof is a spacious family site with 142 pitches, partly in the woods and partly on open fields without hedges to separate them. All the pitches are for touring units and have 4A electricity. There are 11 serviced pitches with electricity, water and drainage. Cars are not permitted on the campsite itself and this, together with the large pitches, provides for a really quiet holiday. Other than a recreation room for youngsters, a large outdoor pool (over 1,000 sq.m) and sanitary buildings, the site has few amenities but you'll find all you need in the village.

Facilities

Two modern toilet blocks have washbasins (open style and in cabins, only one block with hot water at the basins), preset showers and toilets. New children's section with baby room. Facilities for disabled visitors. Motorcaravan services. Laundry. Basic provisions and some snacks from reception. Entertainment for children in high season. Giant chess. Boules. Library. Games room. Only gas barbecues are permitted. Off site: Outdoor pool 300 m. Riding 500 m. Bicycle hire 2 km. Fishing 4 km.

Open: 1 April - 1 October.

Directions

Travelling north from Zwolle on the A28, take exit for Beilen - Westerbork. Follow N31 eastwards and take exit for Westerbork. From there follow campsite signs. GPS: N52:51.193 E06:35.704

Charges guide

Per unit incl. 2 persons	€ 18,80 - € 23,50
extra person	€ 4,25
serviced pitch	€ 6,00

No credit cards.
Camping Cheques accepted.

NL6160 Camping Ruinen

Oude Benderseweg 11, NL-7963 PX Ruinen (Drenthe)

Tel: **0522 471 770**. Email: **info@camping-ruinen.nl** **www.alanrogers.com/NL6160**

Camping Ruinen is a large, spacious site with 299 pitches in the woods of Drenthe. All 276 touring pitches have electricity (4/10A) and include 105 serviced pitches with water, drainage, cable TV and electricity connections. The numbered pitches are over 100 sq.m. in size and are on large, grassy fields. They are separated by hedges and in the shade of trees and there are some hardstandings for camper vans. At this comfortable site you can relax by cycling or walking through the woods or over the moors, or join organised trips in groups on a regular basis.

Facilities

Four well-spaced toilet blocks provide washbasins (open style and in cabins), child-size toilets, bathrooms, child-size baths and a baby room. Facilities for disabled visitors. Laundry. Motorcaravan services. Shop. Restaurant. Pancake restaurant. Play areas between pitches. Boules. Minigolf. Bicycle hire. Full entertainment programme in high season. WiFi. Dogs are allowed on certain pitches only. Off site: Riding 400 m. Fishing 3 km. Golf 18 km.

Open: 1 April - 1 October.

Directions

From Zwolle follow A28 north and take Ruinen exit. Follow site signs from there.
GPS: N52:46.495 E06:22.196

Charges guide

Per unit incl. 2 persons and electricity	€ 21,20 - € 26,25
extra person	€ 3,20 - € 4,25
serviced pitch, plus	€ 6,00

No credit cards. Camping Cheques accepted.

NL6153 Vakantiepark Witterzomer

Witterzomer 7, NL-9405 VE Assen (Drenthe)

Tel: **0592 393 535**. Email: **info@witterzomer.nl** **www.alanrogers.com/NL6153**

Attractively located in a century old area of woodland and fields in the province of the 'Hunebedden', this is an attractive, large and well organised site. The Hunebedden are prehistoric monuments, built of enormous granite boulders and older than Stonehenge. The 600 touring pitches at Witterzomer are on grass with a woodland setting, with varying degrees of shade and 4/6A electricity. Most also have also TV connections and some have private sanitary facilities. All the amenities at this site are of excellent quality and are particularly targeted at families. The main building at the entrance houses the reception, a well stocked shop and a bar/restaurant with a good menu and takeaway meals. A terrace overlooks the swimming pool which has three features: a paddling pool, a children's pool and a larger pool for adults.

Facilities

Good heated toilet blocks include separate facilities for babies and disabled persons, as well as family bathrooms. Laundry. Shop. Restaurant/bar and takeaway (all 1/4-31/10). Heated swimming pools. Sports field and games room. Tennis. TV room. Bicycle and mountain bike hire. Minigolf. Pony riding. Fishing (lake). Internet and WiFi. Off site: Golf 6 km. Assen 4 km. Several nature parks. Groningen 30 km.

Open: All year.

Directions

Site is 4 km southwest of Assen. From A28 exit 33 follow N371 (Balkenweg) to Assen. After 200 m. turn right (Europaweg) and again after 200 m. to the right onto Witterhoofdweg. Follow this road for around 2 km. (underneath A28) to the site.
GPS: N52:58.812 E06:30.318

Charges guide

Per unit incl. 2 persons and electricity	€ 16,00 - € 25,50
extra person	€ 3,60
dog	€ 4,00

NL6130 Camping De Vledders

Zeegersweg, NL-9469 PS Schipborg (Drenthe)
Tel: **0504 091 489**. Email: **info@devledders.nl** **www.alanrogers.com/NL6130**

Camping De Vledders is set in the centre of one of the most beautiful nature reserves in Holland, between the Drentsche Hondsrug and the Drentsche AA river. This attractive site is landscaped with many varieties of trees and shrubs. About one third of the site is aimed at tourers with pitching on rectangular, grassy fields, separated by well kept hedges. There is some road noise. The level pitches are around 100 sq.m in size with some shade provided at the back from mature trees and hedges. Static units and seasonal pitches are on separate fields. In one corner of the site there is an attractive lake with sandy beaches.

Facilities

Two toilet blocks with toilets, washbasins (open style and in cabins) and controllable hot showers. Family shower rooms. Baby room. En-suite facilities for disabled people. Shop for basics. Snack bar. TV in reception. Lake with fishing, boating, windsurfing. Football field. Riding. Nordic walking. Playground. Some animation for children in season. Torch useful. Off site: Sub-tropical pool in Zuidlaren. Sprookjeshof theme park in Zuidlaren. City of Groningen.

Open: April - October.

Directions

From the A28 take exit 35 and continue towards Zuidlaren. Just before Zuidlaren follow signs for Schipborg and then site signs.
GPS: N53:04.756 E06:39.937

Charges guide

Per unit incl. 2 persons and electricity	€ 20,25
extra person	€ 2,75
dog	€ 2,75

Allure Parks

Allure Parks are a group of seven well equipped sites, all of which can be found within the Utrechtse Heuvelrug National Park. This is a unique, natural area, relatively little known by visitors from the UK, but with a long and fascinating history, and ideal for exploration by cycle, on horseback or on foot. Aside from its attractive forested setting, there is a great deal to see here – many fascinating churches, museums, gardens, forts, windmills, castles and much more. We are featuring three Allure sites which we feel may be of interest. However, you may also wish to consider their site 't Eekhoornnest (NL6095) near the pretty town of Soest. This site has no touring pitches but offers an attractive range of chalets and apartments for rent, some even fitted out with dishwashers, fireplaces and jacuzzis! 't Eekhoornnest is a good base for visiting Amsterdam, Utrecht and Amersfoort, and the palace of the former Queen of the Netherlands is close by - well worth a visit! (www.eekhoornnest.nl)

NL6824 Allurepark Zeven Linden

Zevenlindenweg 4, NL-3744 BC Baarn (Utrecht)

Tel: **0356 668 330**. Email: **info@dezevenlinden.nl** **www.alanrogers.com/NL6824**

Zeven Linden was created in 1938 and since then has been a popular site for those seeking a peaceful holiday in a natural setting. There are 261 spacious touring pitches here spread over 13 separate fields. Unusually, the whole area is car-free, which goes a long way to ensuring peace and quiet, as well as improving safety for children around the site. The site is located on the northern fringe of the Utrechtse Heuvelrug, a heavily forested area. Within walking distance you can visit Drakensteyn castle, Soestdijk palace and the beautiful village of Lage Vuursche. Pitches are large and grassy, mostly with electrical connections. A unique feature here is the 'hut forest', where you can build your own bivouac or hut.

Facilities

Modern, child friendly and spacious toilet blocks (two heated in low season). Two blocks have special family rooms with family showers and a separate children's area. Special facilities for disabled visitors. Washing machine and dryer. Small shop. Small field with animals. Football pitch. Hut forest. Off site: Recently renovated swimming pool 'Bosbad de Vuursche' 600 m.

Open: 31 March - 17 October.

Directions

Approaching from the west, site is well signed from the N415 Hilversum - Baarn road shortly before reaching the intersection with the N221.
GPS: N52:11.791 E05:14.848

Charges guide

Per unit incl. 2 persons, water and electricity	€ 20,00 - € 29,00

NL6832 Allurepark Laag Kanje

Laan V. Laagkanje 1, NL-3951 KD Maarn (Utrecht)

Tel: **0343 441 348**. Email: **allurepark@laagkanje.nl** **www.alanrogers.com/NL6832**

Originally part of a great estate, Allurecamping Laag Kanje has been developed into a top quality campsite over the last 40 years with the unusual, but attractive feature that cars are not allowed in the camping area. There are also mobile homes and chalets available to rent. This is a spacious site with a relaxed and tranquil atmosphere. The park is located at the heart of the forest, so sandy beaches may be the last thing you would expect here. However, there is a fine sandy beach alongside the site – ideal for swimming.

Facilities

Modern toilet blocks with special facilities for children and disabled people. Three blocks are heated in the low season. Small restaurant and snack bar. Well stocked shop with fresh products available daily. Entertainment and activity programme for adults and children.
Off site: Hiking and cycling. Utrecht, Amersfoort, Zeist, Wijk bij Buurstede museum. Dolfinarium at Hardewijk (dolphin aquarium). Lake swimming. Beach and woods adjacent.

Open: 1 April - 21 September.

Directions

Heading south from Amersfoort on the N227 towards Doorn, site is well signed shortly before arrival at the village of Maarn.
GPS: N52:04.634 E05:22.759

Charges guide

Per unit incl. 2 persons and electricity	€ 19,50 - € 27,00
extra person (over 2 yrs)	€ 2,00 - € 2,95

NL6838 Allurepark De Krakeling

Woudenbergseweg 17, NL-3707 HW Zeist (Utrecht)

Tel: **0306 915 374**. Email: **krakeling@allurepark.nl** **www.alanrogers.com/NL6838**

Allurepark De Krakeling is a spacious (22 ha) campsite with 350 touring pitches, spread over several grassy fields. All pitches are surrounded by hedges and are supplied with 6A electricity and a cable TV connection (additional charge). There is also a number of mobile homes and chalets for rent. The site is attractively located in the middle of the Zeister forest and is a good choice for a family holiday with a wide range of facilities and a lively entertainment programme for young and old. The site enjoys a very pleasant natural setting, with plenty of routes for walking and cycling in the forest.

Facilities

Toilet block with facilities for babies and disabled visitors. Laundry facilities. Motorcaravan services. Supermarket. Snack bar and takeaway. Restaurant/bar. Games room. TV. Play area. Sports area. Animation programme. Hairdresser. Off site: Forest walking and cycling routes. Visits to the Krommerijn and Gelderese valleys. Historic towns of Utrecht (12 km) and Amersfoort (10 km) and nearby town of Zeist with many shops, restaurants and cafés 3 km.

Open: 1 April - 1 October.

Directions

Take Zeist Oost exit from the A28 motorway (heading from Utrecht) and follow signs to Zeist. Site is well signed from the village.
GPS: N52:05.563 E05:16.972

Charges guide

Per unit incl. 2 persons, water and electricity	€ 20,00 - € 24,70
extra person (over 2 yrs)	€ 1,00 - € 2,50

NL6466 Camping De Koeksebelt

Zwolseweg 13, NL-7731 BC Ommen (Overijssel)

Tel: **0529 451 378**. Email: **info@koeksebelt.nl** **www.alanrogers.com/NL6466**

Camping De Koeksebelt is a well maintained, green site with 250 fully serviced, spacious touring pitches. All are equipped with 10A electricity, water, drainage and TV cable connections and are accessed off paved roads. Some hardstandings are available. Many of the pitches are on the banks of the river and are ideal for anglers as they can fish from their pitch. Good play areas will appeal to both children and their parents. The sanitary facilities are modern and very well maintained. The site borders a large wooded area and is near the town of Ommen where the amenities include a swimming pool. The centre of Ommen is a 500 m. walk from the site and in summer this is a bustling town with good shopping and several restaurants. Guests at De Koeksebelt receive free tickets to the open air pool (900 m). Close to the site are the Hellendoorn and Slagharen theme parks. The site offers free fishing boats for use in the Vecht river. Member of the 'Ardoer Group'.

Facilities

Three modern toilet blocks with toilets, washbasins in cabins and controllable hot showers. Free bathroom. Baby room. Toilet for disabled visitors. Laundry with washing machines, dryers, spin dryer, iron and board. Small shop for basics. Canteen for drinks and light meals. Playing field. Tennis. Fishing. Watersports. Boules. Free boats for fishing. Internet access and WiFi. Max. 2 dogs per pitch. Off site: Golf 8 km. Bicycle hire 1.5 km. Riding 25 km.

Open: 31 March - 31 October.

Directions

From the A28 take exit for Ommen and continue east towards Ommen on the N340. In Ommen, go right at traffic lights to cross the Vecht River. After 300 m. turn right at exit r102 and site is on the right after 500 m. GPS: N52:31.001 E06:24.837

Charges guide

Per unit incl. 2 persons and electricity	€ 23,00 - € 30,50
extra person	€ 4,50
dog	€ 3,25

No credit cards.

NL6470 Camping De Papillon

Kanaalweg 30, NL-7591 NH Denekamp (Overijssel)

Tel: **0541 351 670**. Email: **info@depapillon.nl** **www.alanrogers.com/NL6470**

De Papillon is perhaps one of the best campsites in The Netherlands. The site is well thought through with an eye for detail and for nature and the environment. For example, at the toilet blocks, waste water from the showers is used to flush the toilets, all buildings are heated by solar energy and all rubbish is separated for recycling. The 320 touring pitches are spacious, averaging 110-120 sq.m. and all have electricity (4-10A) and an extra 120 'comfort' pitches have been created in 2008. Arranged in small grassy fields surrounded by hedges and trees, each field provides a small play area.

Facilities

Two large sanitary buildings with showers, toilets, washbasins in cabins, facilities for babies and for disabled visitors. This building is designed in the shape of a 'papillon' (butterfly). Laundry room. Spacious reception area with supermarket, restaurant, bar and takeaway. Heated pool with children's pool and sliding roof. Lake swimming with sandy beach. New modern adventure play area and smaller play areas. Pétanque. Bicycle hire. Fishing pond. Tennis. Pets to stroke. Luxury bungalows to rent.

Open: 1 April - 1 October.

Directions

From the A1 take exit 32 (Oldenzaal - Denekamp) and continue to Denekamp. Pass Denekamp and turn right at village of Noord-Deurningen and follow signs to site. GPS: N52:23.520 E07:02.940

Charges 2009

Per unit incl. 2 persons and 4A electricity	€ 25,00
incl. full services, plus	€ 3,25
extra person	€ 4,00

NL5980 Camping De Roos

Beerzerweg 10, NL-7736 PJ Beerze-Ommen (Overijssel)

Tel: **0523 251 234**. Email: **info@campingderoos.nl** **www.alanrogers.com/NL5980**

De Roos is a family run site in an area of outstanding natural beauty, truly a nature lover's campsite, immersed in an atmosphere of tranquillity. It is situated in Overijssel's Vecht Valley, a unique region set in a river dune landscape on the River Vecht. The river and its tributary wind their way around and through this spacious campsite. It is a natural setting that the owners of De Roos have carefully preserved. The 285 pitches and necessary amenities have been blended into the landscape with great care. Pitches, many with electricity hook-up (6A), are naturally sited, some behind blackthorn thickets, in the shadow of an old oak, or in a clearing scattered with wild flowers. For some there are lovely views over the Vecht river. De Roos is a car-free campsite during peak periods – vehicles must be parked at the car park, except on arrival and departure. Swimming, fishing and boating are possible on the river, or from an inlet that runs up into the site, where there is a small beach with an area for swimming and landing stages with steps. The enthusiastic owners have compiled walking and cycling routes (written in English) which follow the ever-changing countryside of the Valley.

Facilities

Four well maintained sanitary blocks are kept fresh and clean. The two larger blocks are heated and include baby bath/shower and wash cabins. Launderette. Motorcaravan services. Gas supplies. Health food shop and tea room (1/5-1/9). Bicycle hire. Boules. Several small playgrounds and field for kite flying. River swimming. Fishing. Dogs are not accepted (and cats must be kept on a lead!). Torch useful. Off site: Riding 6 km. Golf 10 km.

Open: 10 April - 4 October.

Directions

Leave A28 at Ommen exit 21 and join N340 for 19 km. to Ommen. Turn right at traffic lights over bridge and immediately left on local road towards Beerze. Site on left after 7 km. just after Beerze village sign. GPS: N52:30.647 E06:30.922

Charges 2009

Per unit incl. 2 persons and electricity	€ 19,10
extra person (over 3 yrs)	€ 3,50

Discounts in low season and special packages.

NL5990 Camping De Vechtstreek

Grote Beltenweg 17, NL-7794 RA Rheeze-Hardenberg (Overijssel)

Tel: **0523 261 369**. Email: **info@sprookjescamping.nl** **www.alanrogers.com/NL5990**

It would be difficult for any child (or adult) to pass this site and not be curiously drawn to the oversized open story book which marks its entrance. From here young children turn the pages and enter the exciting world of Hannah and Bumpie, two of the nine characters around which this site's fairy tale theme has been created. There are 270 touring pitches mostly laid out in bays which accommodate around 12 units. In the centre of each is a small play area. The area at the back of the site has been upgraded with new hook-ups, a gravel road and attractive lighting.

Facilities

Three modern, well equipped and heated toilet blocks include a baby room, separate child sections and family showers. Excellent laundry room. Sauna, solarium and jacuzzi. Well stocked supermarket. Restaurant, snack bar and takeaway (all season). Play areas. Fairy tale water play park (heated). Daily activity club. Internet access. Football field. Theatre. Access to a fishing, swimming and boating recreation area at rear of site (200 m).

Open: 1 April - 15 September.

Directions

From Ommen take N34 Hardenberg road for 9 km. Turn right on N36 and proceed south for 3.5 km. Turn left at first crossroads and after 200 m. left again on local road towards Rheeze. Site is clearly signed to the left in 2 km. Follow signs for 'Sprookjescamping'. GPS: N52:32.764 E06:34.249

Charges guide

Per unit incl. 2 persons and electricity	€ 29,50 - € 39,00
extra person	€ 5,75

NL5985 Kampeercentrum De Beerze Bulten

Kampweg 1, NL-7736 PK Beerze-Ommen (Overijssel)

Tel: **0523 251 398**. Email: **info@beerzebulten.nl** **www.alanrogers.com/NL5985**

Kampeercentrum De Beerze Bulten is a large holiday park with all the amenities one could think of. Beside reception is a large, partly underground 'Rabbit Hole' providing a large indoor playground for children, a theatre for both indoor and outdoor shows and a buffet. De Beerze Bulten has over 500 pitches, all for touring units. In the shade of mature trees in woodland, all the pitches are level and numbered, all with 6/10A electricity, water, drainage and cable. To the back of the site is large lake area with a sandy beach and adventure play equipment. Centrally located on the site is a full 'wellness' spa centre. As well as heated indoor and outdoor pools, a fun paddling pool, jet stream, several different saunas and a water playground, this also offers full fitness facilities and a special 'salt cave' treatment for those suffering from asthma or skin troubles. De Beerze Bulten will provide a relaxing and active family holiday and if the site doesn't offer enough, there is always the extensive surrounding woodland for walking and cycling.

Facilities

Several toilet blocks, well placed around the site, with toilets, washbasins in cabins and hot showers (key). Laundry. Shop. Bar and restaurant with open air terrace. Snack bar. Heated indoor and outdoor pool complex and spa centre. Multisport court. Bicycle hire. Indoor playground and theatre. Playgrounds. WiFi internet. Full animation team in season and school holidays. Dogs only allowed on some fields.

Open: All year.

Directions

From A28, take exit 21 for Ommen and continue east towards Ommen. From Ommen, follow N34 northeast and turn south on N36 at crossing. Site is signed from there. GPS: N52:30.683 E06:32.770

Charges guide

Per unit incl. 2 persons and full service pitch	€ 25,50 - € 39,50
extra person	€ 3,50 - € 4,50
dog	€ 3,50

NL6000 Vechtdalcamping Het Tolhuis

Het Lageveld 8, NL-7722 HV Dalfsen (Overijssel)

Tel: **0529 458 383**. Email: **tolhuis@gmx.net** **www.alanrogers.com/NL6000**

Vechtdalcamping Het Tolhuis is a pleasant, well established site with 145 pitches. Of these, 70 are for tourers, arranged on well kept, grassy lawns off paved and gravel access roads. All touring pitches have 4/10A electricity, water, waste water, cable and WiFi internet. Some are shaded by mature trees and bushes, others are more in the open. The touring pitches are located apart from static units. To the rear of the site is an open air pool (25 x 8 m. and heated by solar power) with a small paddling pool for toddlers. Along the lane running from reception to the back of the site is a takeaway for drinks and snacks.

Facilities

Two heated toilet blocks, one immaculate new one to the front and an older one to the back, with toilets, washbasins (open style and in cabins) and controllable hot showers (key). Special, attractive children's section. Family shower rooms. Baby room. Laundry. Small shop (bread to order). Café for snacks and drinks. Open air pool with paddling pool. Playing field. Playground and trampoline. Animation team for children in high season. ATM point. Internet. Off site: Restaurant 2 km. Fishing 5 km.

Open: 1 April - 1 October.

Directions

From the A28 take exit 21 and continue east towards Dalfsen. Site is signed in Dalfsen. GPS: N52:30.136 E06:19.344

Charges guide

Per unit incl. 2 persons and electricity	€ 20,00 - € 32,25
extra person	€ 4,00
dog (not high season)	€ 3,00

NL6004 Vakantiepark Het Stoetenslagh

Elfde Wijk 42, NL-7797 HH Rheezerveen-Hardenberg (Overijssel)

Tel: **0523 638 260**. Email: **info@stoetenslagh.nl** **www.alanrogers.com/NL6004**

Arriving at Het Stoetenslagh and passing reception, you reach the pride of the campsite; a large natural lake with several little beaches. Many hours can be spent swimming, canoeing or sailing a dinghy here. Spacious grass pitches (100 sq.m) are divided between several fields, arranged around clean sanitary buildings. Each field also has a small volleyball area and climbing frames. You may choose between 'nature' pitches, standard pitches or serviced pitches with water, drainage, 6/10A electricity and cable connection. There are climbing frames for children, much space for playing, a children's club and, particularly popular with little ones, a small animal farm. Teenagers are also very welcome and the site provides a range of activities, including sports, outdoor camping trips, discos and more, all organized by a special animation team. When the weather takes a turn for the worse, there are indoor activities such as curling, bowling or archery. The site surroundings are good for long walks and bike trips through the woods and moors. Close to Het Stoetenslagh are the museum village of Orvelte, the zoo at Emmen and the theme parks of Slgharen and Hellendoorn.

Facilities

Five toilet blocks include private cabins, baby facilities, family showers and facilities for disabled visitors. Shop. Beach shower. Washing machines and dryers. Motorcaravan service point. Restaurant with bar. Snack bar with takeaway. Disco, bowling, curling and archery (all indoor). New indoor pool (opening planned before May 09). Natural pool with sandy beaches. Canoeing. Play areas. Activities for children and teenagers. Bouncy castle. Off site: Fishing 3 km. Golf 15 km.

Open: 21 March - 21 October.

Directions

On the N34 travel towards Ommen and go through town. At TINQ petrol station a few kilometres outside Ommen follow signs for 'Stoetenslagh' following Het Zwarte Pad. About 3 km. after Rheezerveen, follow site signs right and site is on right after 3 km. GPS: N52:35.216 E06:31.829

Charges guide

Per serviced pitch incl. 2 persons, water, waste water and electricity	€ 19,00 - € 32,00
extra person	€ 3,00

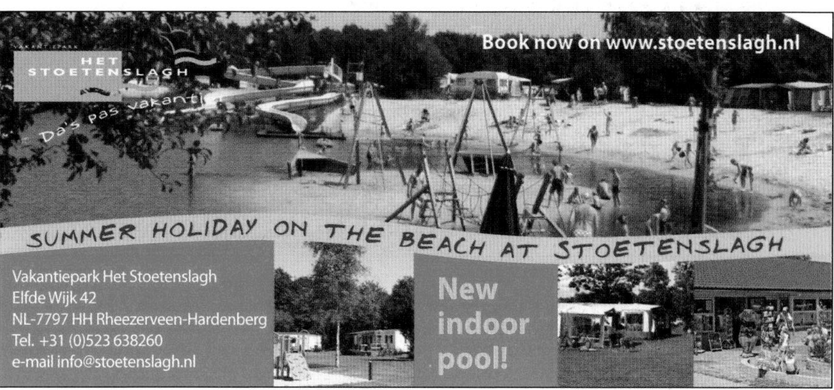

Book now on www.stoetenslagh.nl
HET STOETENSLAGH
Da's pas vakantie
SUMMER HOLIDAY ON THE BEACH AT STOETENSLAGH
Vakantiepark Het Stoetenslagh
Elfde Wijk 42
NL-7797 HH Rheezerveen-Hardenberg
Tel. +31 (0)523 638260
e-mail info@stoetenslagh.nl
New indoor pool!

NL5780 Kawan Village De Zanding

Vijverlaan 1, NL-6731 CK Otterlo (Gelderland)

Tel: **0318 596 111**. Email: **info@zanding.nl** **www.alanrogers.com/NL5780**

De Zanding is a family run, highly rated site that offers almost every recreational facility, either on site or nearby, that active families or couples might seek. After the entrance, a lake is to the left where you can swim, fish, sunbathe or try a two-person canoe. There are many sporting options and organised high season programmes. There are 463 touring pitches spread around the site (all with 4/6/10A electricity), some individual and separated, others in more open spaces shaded by trees. Some serviced pitches are in small groups between long stay units and there is another area for tents.

Facilities

First class sanitary facilities are housed in five modern blocks that are clean, well maintained and well equipped. Good provision for babies and people with disabilities. Laundry. Kitchen. Motorcaravan services. Gas supplies. Supermarket. Restaurant/bar (30/3-28/10). Lake swimming. Fishing. Tennis. Minigolf. Boules. Five play areas. Bicycle hire. Organised activities.

Open: 3 April - 31 October.

Directions

Leave A12 Utrecht - Arnhem motorway at Oosterbeek at exit 25 and join N310 to Otterlo. Then follow camping signs to site, watching carefully for entrance. GPS: N52:05.586 E05:46.654

Charges guide

Per unit incl. 2 persons and electricity	€ 21,00 - € 32,90
extra person	€ 4,70

Camping Cheques accepted.

NL5950 Rekreatiecentrum Heumens Bos

Vosseneindseweg 46, NL-6582 BR Heumen (Gelderland)

Tel: **0243 581 481**. Email: **info@heumensbos.nl** **www.alanrogers.com/NL5950**

The area around Nijmegen, the oldest city in the Netherlands, has large forests for walking or cycling, nature reserves and old towns to explore, as well as being quite close to Arnhem. The site covers 16 ha. and is open over a long season for touring families (no groups of youngsters allowed) and all year for bungalows. It offers 165 level, grass pitches for touring units, all with electricity (6A) and cable TV connections. Numbered but not separated, in glades of 10 and one large field, all have easy access with cars parked elsewhere. One small section for motorcaravans has some hardstandings. The restaurant, which offers a good menu and a new terrace, is close to the comfortable bar and snack bar. An open air swimming pool with a small children's pool is maintained at 28 degrees by a system of heat transfer from the air. Mr Van Velzen and his sons took over this site in 2002 and are planning new buildings and an internet point.

Facilities

The main, high quality sanitary building, plus another new block, are modern and heated, providing showers on payment. Rooms for families and disabled people. Another smaller building has acceptable facilities. Smart launderette. Motorcaravan services. Gas supplies. Shop. Bar, restaurant and snack bar. Heated swimming pool (from 1/5). Bicycle hire. Tennis. Boules. Glade area with play equipment on sand and grass. Activity and excursion programme (high season). Large wet weather room. Off site: Riding 300 m. Fishing 2 km. Golf 10 km.

Open: 1 April - 1 November.

Directions

From A73 (Nijmegen - Venlo) take exit 3 (4 km. south of Nijmegen) and follow site signs.
GPS: N51:46.149 E05:49.230

Charges guide

Per pitch incl. 2 persons, caravan or tent	€ 16,00 - € 25,00
dog (max. 1)	€ 4,00
electricity	€ 2,50

Special low season weekends (incl. restaurant meal) and special deal for over 55 yr olds.

NL5870 Camping De Vergarde

Erichemseweg 84, NL-4117 GL Erichem (Gelderland)

Tel: **0344 572 017**. Email: **info@devergarde.nl** **www.alanrogers.com/NL5870**

Situated north of 's Hertogenbosch and west of Nijmegen and Arnhem, De Vergarde has been developed on a former orchard with a beautiful old farmhouse at its entrance. The site is in two sections on either side of a lake. Static holiday caravans are on the left, with the 225 touring pitches to the right. About a third of these are taken by seasonal units. Arranged in sections, each named after a fruit tree, access is good. The pitches are numbered on flat grass and include electricity (6A), water, drainage and TV connections. There are trees all around the perimeter (but not much shade on the pitches).

Facilities

Good sanitary facilities in three blocks include family showers and baby bathrooms. Most, but not all, hot water is on payment. Washing machines. Motorcaravan services. Heated swimming pool and attractive paddling pool (1/5-1/9). Shop (1/5-1/10). Restaurant (1/5-1/10). Play area and large indoor games room. Pony riding. Pets corner. Minigolf. Bicycle hire. Games room. Two tennis courts. Fishing.

Open: 1 March - 30 October.

Directions

From A15 Dordrecht - Nijmegen road exit at Tiel West (also McDonald's) and follow signs to site.
GPS: N51:53.939 E05:21.646

Charges guide

Per unit incl. 2 persons and electricity	€ 15,00 - € 25,00
extra person (over 2 yrs)	€ 2,50 - € 3,50
dog (max. 1)	€ 2,00 - € 3,00

Special weekly rates. Low season less 20%.

NL6285 Camping De Wildhoeve

Hanendorperweg 102, NL-8166 JJ Emst-Gortel (Gelderland)

Tel: **0578 661 324**. Email: **info@wildhoeve.nl** **www.alanrogers.com/NL6285**

Camping De Wildhoeve is a welcoming, privately owned site with many amenities of the type one would normally find on larger holiday camps. The well maintained site is located in woodland and has 400 pitches with 330 for tourers. Pitching is in several areas, mostly in the shade of mature conifers. Partly separated by trees and bushes, the level pitches are numbered and all have 6/12A electricity, water and drainage. Behind reception is an octagonally shaped sub-tropical pool with a large water slide and fun paddling pool. Next to reception is a water adventure playground. To the front of the site are tennis courts and next to that is an open air pool with a large slide. Here also are a shop, bar/restaurant with TV and games room with electronic games and a snack bar. Many activities are organised for children, including open air theatre, and for adults there are craft workshops. The toilet facilities on this site are excellent and include one block that has a special children's section with an area for children with disabilities.

Facilities

Four well placed, heated blocks with toilets, washbasins (open style and in cabins) and free, preset hot showers. Special children's section with showers, basins and toilets. Baby room. Family shower room. Facilities for disabled children. Laundry facilities. Shop. Bar/restaurant with TV. Snack bar. Indoor and outdoor pools with slides and paddling pool. Water adventure playground. WiFi internet. Bicycle hire. Tennis. Open air theatre. Craft workshops. Dogs are not accepted.

Open: April - October.

Directions

From the A28, take exit 15 (Epe/Nunspeet). Continue east towards Epe and at traffic lights, turn south towards Emst. Continue straight ahead at roundabout in Emst. Turn right at church, into Hanendorperweg. Site is on the right after 3.5 km. GPS: N51:18.821 E05:55.624

Charges guide

Per unit incl. 2 persons	€ 19,00 - € 34,25
3 persons	€ 22,50 - € 38,75
4 persons	€ 26,00 - € 43,25

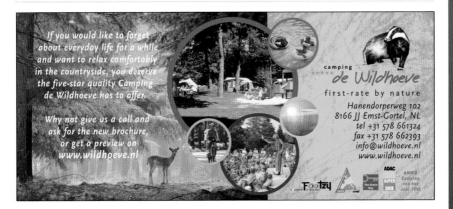

NL6290 Camping Eiland van Maurik

Rijnbandijk 20, NL-4021 GH Maurik (Gelderland)

Tel: **0344 691 502**. Email: **info@eilandvanmaurik.nl** **www.alanrogers.com/NL6290**

Camping Eiland van Maurik is beside a lake in the centre of an extensive nature and recreation park in the Nederrijn area. These surroundings are ideal for all sorts of activities – swimming, windsurfing, waterskiing or para-sailing, relaxing on the beach or fishing. The site has 365 numbered, flat pitches, with 155 for touring units, all with 10A electricity and cable TV connections and 64 also with water and drainage. You could enjoy pancakes in the 'Oudhollandse' restaurant and the views over the water. There is direct access from the site to the lakeside beach.

Facilities

The three toilet blocks for tourers include washbasins (open style and in cabins), controllable showers and a baby room. Launderette with iron and board. Shop. Bar/restaurant (1/4-1/10). Play areas (one indoors). Play field. Tennis. Minigolf. Bicycle hire. Go-karts. Water skiing. Sailing and motorboat hire. Para-sailing. Animal farm. Entertainment in high season (incl. riding). Off site: Shop, restaurant and bar nearby. Golf 9 km.

Open: 1 April - 1 October.

Directions

From the A2 (Utrecht - 's Hertogenbosch) take the Culemborg exit towards Kesteren and follow signs for 'Eiland Maurik'. From the A15 (Rotterdam - Nymegen) take exit 33 Tiel towards Maurik and follow signs as above. GPS: N51:58.593 E05:25.807

Charges guide

Per unit incl. 2 persons, electricity and local tax	€ 17,50 - € 25,00
extra person (under 2 yrs free)	€ 3,50

No credit cards. Camping Cheques accepted.

NL6310 Recreatiepark Arnhem

Kemperbergerweg 771, NL-6816 RW Arnhem (Gelderland)

Tel: **0264 431 600**. Email: **arnhem@holiday.nl** **www.alanrogers.com/NL6310**

Recreatiepark Arnhem is a wooded site in the Veluwe region of the Netherlands, close to the 'Hooge Veluwe' National Park. The 750 pitches are partly in the sun and partly in the shade of tall trees and there are 500 for touring units, some with hardstanding. This is a perfect base for visiting the National Park, the Kroller Muller museum or the outdoor museum. You could also go riding or play golf nearby or experience the silence high up in the air in a glider from Terlet airport. There is also plenty to do on the site including tennis and minigolf.

Facilities

Modern sanitary blocks provide free hot showers, facilities for disabled visitors and a baby room. Fully equipped launderette. Motorcaravan services. Supermarket. Café. Bar. Tennis. Minigolf. Sports field. Boules. Open air theatre. Several playgrounds. Adventure pond. Swimming pool and paddling pool. Entertainment programme in high season. Bicycle hire. Off site: Arnhem for shopping. Burgers Zoo. Kroller Moller museum. Airborne museum. Riding and golf. Gliding. Balloon trips and boat trips.

Open: 1 April - 26 October.

Directions

From the A50 take exit 21 for Schaarsbergen. Go to Schaarsbergen and follow the site signs.
GPS: N52:00.959 E05:52.980

Charges guide

Per unit incl. 2 adults, 2 children and 4A electricity € 12,00 - € 32,00

NL5960 Camping De Wielerbaan

Zoomweg 7-9, NL-6705 DM Wageningen-Hoog (Gelderland)

Tel: **0317 413 964**. Email: **info@wielerbaan.nl** **www.alanrogers.com/NL5960**

This family run park has an interesting history and a natural setting at a point where the Veluwe, the valley of Gelderland and the picturesque area of Betuwe meet. Translated 'Wielerbaan' means 'cycle race track' which still stands in the heart of this site. The present owners have utilised this area to accommodate recreation facilities which include an indoor swimming pool. Touring pitches in a meadow setting are serviced with water, electricity and drainage. Planned cycles routes are available at reception, or maps to choose your own way. It is possible to go by boat to Arnhem.

Facilities

Four toilet blocks of a reasonable standard provide wash cabins, showers and a baby room. Launderette. Gas supplies. Shop. Small restaurant. Snacks and takeaway. Library. Swimming pool. Minigolf. Boules. Ten small play areas. Organised entertainment in high season.
Off site: Golf 500 m. Fishing 5 km. Boat launching.

Open: All year.

Directions

Leave A12 at exit 24 towards Wageningen and continue for 4.5 km. to second roundabout, where site is clearly signed. Follow signs to site, 1.5 km. from the town. GPS: N51:59.199 E05:47.275

Charges guide

Per unit incl. 2 persons and electricity € 10,50 - € 31,00
extra person € 7,00 - € 8,00
dog (max. 2) € 3,00

NL6190 Rekreatiepark Hazevreugd

Vormtweg 9, NL-8321 NC Urk (Flevoland)

Tel: **0527 681 785**. Email: **info@hazevreugd.nl** **www.alanrogers.com/NL6190**

Recreatiepark Hazevreugd, set in the Urkerbos on the former island Urk, is a true family site with lots of sporting facilities. You can hire go-karts and bikes, go surfing from the beaches of the IJsselmeer or go riding in the woods. The site has 220 pitches, 192 for tourers, all with shade and 6A electricity. There are also 63 serviced pitches with water, electricity and drainage and separate pitches for motorcaravans, which will become hardstandings. In high season an entertainment team organises sports competitions, scouting expeditions and entertainment evenings.

Facilities

Two modern toilet blocks have washbasins (open style and in cabins), preset showers, child size toilets, family showers and a baby room. Facilities for disabled visitors. Laundry. Motorcaravan services. Shop (bread to order). Bar/restaurant and snack bar. Outdoor pool (40 sq.m) with paddling pool. Playground. Sports court. Boules. Bicycle and go-kart hire. Recreation hall with games. Satellite TV. Off site: Fishing, boat launching and beach 2 km.

Open: April - September.

Directions

Follow the A6 from Almere to the north and take exit 13 to Urk (N352). Site is next to the Urkerbos and well signed. GPS: N52:40.764 E05:36.492

Charges guide

Per unit incl. 2 persons € 15,00 - € 19,50
extra person € 2,50
No credit cards.

NL6425 Recreatiecentrum De Twee Bruggen

Meenkmolenweg 13, NL-7109-AH Winterswijk (Gelderland)

Tel: **0543 565 366**. Email: **info@detweebruggen.nl** **www.alanrogers.com/NL6425**

De Twee Bruggen is a spacious recreation park set in the countryside. The pitches are divided between several fields of varying sizes. Although the fields are surrounded by tall trees, the ground is open and sunny. Indoor and outdoor swimming pools can be enjoyed by children and adults. At the indoor pool there is a covered terrace and, for relaxation, a sauna and jacuzzi. Adjacent to the pool is a small, open air theatre, where shows are staged in high season. The restaurant at the entrance of the campsite is of high quality and also attracts many outside visitors. A small shopping centre, including a supermarket and more is beside reception. Bread is baked each morning. A variety of mobile homes and chalets is for rent. The German border is within 20 minutes of the site.

Facilities

Three modern, well maintained sanitary buildings include showers and washbasins in private cabins. Facilities for disabled visitors. Washing machines and dryers. Supermarket. Bar and restaurant. Takeaway. Heated swimming pool (30/4-7/9). Heated indoor pool (all year). Paddling pool. Sauna. Jacuzzi. Supermarket. Tennis courts. Bicycles hire. Minigolf. Bowling. Playground. Bouncy castle. Deer field.

Open: All year.

Directions

Take the A18 towards Varsseveld which will turn onto the N18. In Varsseveld follow signs for Aalten (N318). In Aalten follow signs for Winterswijk. Drive through Aalten and site is signed after about 4 km. GPS: N51:56.976 E06:38.862

Charges guide

Per unit incl. 2 persons	€ 16,00 - € 37,00
extra person	€ 1,00 - € 2,00

NL6195 Rivièra Parc

Spijkweg 15, NL-8256 RJ Biddinghuizen (Flevoland)

Tel: **0321 33 13 44**. Email: **info@riviera.nl** **www.alanrogers.com/NL6195**

This Dutch Rivièra at the Veluwe Lake actually comprises two campsites with some shared amenities. Camping Rivièra Beach lies beyond the dykes, close to the water and the beach, while the bigger Rivièra Parc can be found within the dykes, with 1,220 pitches, 600 reserved for touring, all on grass and all with 4/10A electricity. There are also 200 serviced pitches (large with water, drainage and TV connection). The site boasts a very impressive range of facilities, even including a Snow Village with real snow and the opportunity for summer skiing! Other amenities are targeted at families with children up to 14 years, such as the covered play area and indoor swimming pool. In the wooded surroundings, opportunities for walking, cycling and riding are excellent.

Facilities

Good heated toilet blocks with separate facilities for babies and disabled persons. Family rooms. Restaurants. Café. Snack bar. Takeaway food. Supermarket. Swimming pool with slide. Covered play area. Bowling. Bicycle and go-kart hire. Fishing. Amusement arcade. Internet access. Around 75 mobile homes and bungalows for hire.
Off site: Riding. Watersports. Walibi World theme park 2 km. Golf 7 km.

Open: 27 March - 30 November.

Directions

Site is 2 km. southwest of Elburg. From A28 take exit to Elburg (N309). At Elburg follow signs for Dronten. Cross the bridge over the Veluwe Lake and immediately turn left (N306). Site is well signed from here and is on the left after 2 km.
GPS: N52:26.803 E05:47.534

Charges 2009

Per unit incl. up to 4 persons, vehicle and electricity	€ 27,00 - € 42,00

NL6200 Recreatiegebied Erkemederstrand

Erkemederweg 79, NL-3896 LB Zeewolde (Flevoland)

Tel: **0365 228 421**. Email: **info@erkemederstrand.nl** **www.alanrogers.com/NL6200**

The Erkemerderstrand (the beach of Erkemede) is a leisure park at Flevoland, with direct access to the Nuldernauw, a sandy beach, water and a forest. It provides a campsite for families, a marina, an area for youngsters to camp, a camping area for groups and a recreation area for day visitors. The campsite itself is divided into two areas: one before the dyke at the waterfront and one behind the dyke. The pitches are spacious (around 125 sq.m) and all have electricity, water and drainage. The focal point of the site and marina is the beach restaurant 'De Jutter'.

Facilities

Four neat and clean toilet blocks (access by key, exclusively for campers). Washbasins in cabins, showers and family bath rooms (free hot water). Dishwashing and laundry facilities in heated buildings. Shop for basic provisions. Bar, restaurant and takeaway. Several play areas and children's farm. Watersports facilities and lake swimming. Football pitch. Minigolf. Bicycle hire. Extended animation programme.

Open: 20 March - 25 October.

Directions

From the A28 (Utrecht - Zwolle) take exit 9 for Nijkerk and Almere and follow N301 to Zeewolde. Cross the bridge and turn right following signs to site. From Amsterdam/Almere, take exit 5 and follow N27 to Zeewolde; this road changes into the N305. Then take N301 to Nijkerk. For the bridge turn right and follow signs to site.
GPS: N52:16.212 E05:29.322

Charges guide

Per unit incl. 2 persons and electricity	€ 22,50 - € 28,50
extra person	€ 2,50
dog	€ 2,00

NL5538 Camping De Heide

Bemmelenberg 12, NL-4614 PG Bergen op Zoom (Noord-Brabant)

Tel: **0164 235 659**. Email: **info@campingdeheide.nl** **www.alanrogers.com/NL5538**

With a pleasant, rural location in a wooded area, this is a medium sized holiday campsite with facilities of a marginal standard. There are 375 pitches with 100 for touring units, 70 of which have electricity (4A). The remaining 30 are for tents. Arranged in rows, the flat, numbered pitches are separated by hedges and trees. Cars are parked separately. The grass was very wet when we visited. A small unheated swimming pool with a separate pool for children (unattended) provides entertainment on warm days. There is good children's club with all-day activities in season.

Facilities

Two traditional style toilet blocks are quite adequate but have only cold water to the open plan washbasins. Good controllable showers (charged). Facilities for babies and disabled visitors. Laundry room. Small shop in reception with very basic supplies. Play area. Outdoor swimming pool. Off site: Golf 3 km.

Open: Easter - September.

Directions

Site is well signposted from Bergen op Zoom. GPS: N51:30.673 E04:18.991

Charges 2009

Per unit incl. up to 4 persons and electricity	€ 16,50 - € 30,00
extra person	€ 4,00
dog (max. 2)	€ 3,00

NL5540 Camping De Katjeskelder

Katjeskelder 1, NL-4904 SG Oosterhout (Noord-Brabant)

Tel: **0162 453 539**. Email: **kkinfo@katjeskelder.nl** **www.alanrogers.com/NL5540**

This site is to be found in a wooded setting in a delightful area of Noord Brabant. It is well established and offers extensive facilities with a new and impressive ultra-modern reception area. Around the 25 hectare site there are many bungalows and 102 touring pitches, all with electricity and water, plus 13 fully serviced pitches. Motorcaravans are now accepted (on hardstandings near the entrance), as well as tents and caravans. The site has a 'cat' theme, hence the cat names including that of the restaurant, the 'Gelaarsde Kat' (Puss in Boots) which is situated in the 'Tropikat' complex.

Facilities

One modern, heated sanitary block (may be stretched in high season) provides facilities including a family shower room, baby room and provision for disabled people. Laundry. Supermarket. Restaurant, bar, snack bar, pizzeria ('pizzacat') and takeaway (the 'Hapjeskat') Indoor tropical pool. Outdoor swimming pools (all season). Play field. Tennis. Bicycle hire. Minigolf. Several play areas for small children. Large adventure playground. Entertainment for children all season. Off site: Oosterheide nature park and Dorst forest.

Open: All year.

Directions

From A27 Breda - Gorinchem motorway take Oosterhout Zuid exit 17 and follow signs for 7 km. to site GPS: N51:37.799 E04:49.926

Charges guide

Per unit incl. up to 5 persons, electricity, water and TV connections	€ 22,00 - € 39,00
extra person	€ 4,00

NL5910 Vakantiecentrum De Hertenwei

Wellenseind 7-9, NL-5094 EG Lage Mierde (Noord-Brabant)

Tel: **0135 091 295** www.alanrogers.com/NL5910

Set in the southwest corner of the country quite close to the Belgian border, this relaxed site covers a large area. In addition to 100 quite substantial bungalows with their own gardens (some residential, 30 to let and 32 mobile homes), the site has some 335 touring pitches. These are in four different areas on oblong meadows surrounded by hedges and trees, with the numbered pitches around the perimeters. There is a choice of pitch size (100 or 150 sq.m) and all have 6A electrical connections, water and drainage, and even a cable TV connection as well.

Facilities

Four toilet blocks are of slightly differing types, all of quite good quality and well spaced around the site. Virtually all washbasins are in private cabins and the blocks can be heated in cool weather. Units for disabled visitors and baby baths. Launderette. Motorcaravan services. Supermarket (Easter - end Oct). Bar by indoor pool (13 x 6 m, charged). Three outdoor pools, the largest 25 x 10 m. (26/4-31/8). Restaurant, cafeteria with snack bar. Disco. Tennis. Playgrounds and play meadows. Sauna, solarium and jacuzzi. Bicycle hire. Off site: Supermarket 2 km. Bus to Tilburg or Eindhoven. Fishing, riding 4 km.

Open: All year.

Directions

Site is by N269 Tilburg - Reusel road, 2 km. north of Lage Mierde and 16 km. south of Tilburg.
GPS: N51:25.130 E05:08.250

Charges 2009

Per unit incl. 2 persons and electricity	€ 24,00 - € 35,75
extra person	€ 4,00
dog	€ 4,00

Less 25-40% in low seasons.

NL5970 Camping De Paal

Paaldreef 14, NL-5571 TN Bergeyk (Noord-Brabant)

Tel: **0497 571 977**. Email: **info@depaal.nl** www.alanrogers.com/NL5970

A first class campsite, De Paal is especially suitable for families with young children. Situated in 42 hectares of woodland, there are 530 touring pitches, ranging in size up to 150 sq.m. (plus 70 seasonal pitches). The pitches are numbered and separated by trees and all have 6A electricity, TV, water, drainage and a bin. There are 40 pitches with private sanitary facilities which are partly underground. With child safety in mind, there is a play area on each group of pitches.

Facilities

High quality sanitary facilities are ultra modern, including wash cabins, family rooms and baby baths, all with lots of space. Facilities for disabled visitors. Launderette. Motorcaravan services. Underground supermarket. Restaurant (high season), bar and snack bar (all season). Indoor pool (supervised in high season). Outdoor pool (May - Sept). Bicycle hire. Tennis. Play areas. Theatre. WiFi internet access. Off site: Tennis complex (Sept-May). Riding and covered wagons for hire 500 m. Fishing 4 km.

Open: Easter/1 April - 31 October.

Directions

From E34 Antwerpen-Eindhoven road take exit 32 (Eersel) and follow signs for Bergeyk and site (2 km. from town). GPS: N51:20.181 E05:27.302

Charges guide

Per pitch incl. 2 persons and services	€ 26,00 - € 38,00
extra person (over 1 yr)	€ 5,00
cyclist	€ 9,00
dog	€ 5,00

NL5880 Vakantiepark Dierenbos

Vinkeloord 1, NL-5382 JX Vinkeloord (Noord-Brabant)

Tel: **0735 343 536**. Email: **info@libema.nl** www.alanrogers.com/NL5880

Run by the same group as Beekse Bergen (NL5900), Vinkeloord is a large site with motel accommodation and a bungalow park, in addition to its 500 camping pitches. These are divided into several grassy areas, many in an attractive wooded setting. There are 381 for touring units, all with electrical connections (4-10A and some with full services (water and TV connection). A small, landscaped lake has sandy beaches and is overlooked by a large, modern play area.

Facilities

Eight toilet blocks are well situated with a mixture of clean and simple facilities (some unisex) with some warm water for washing and some individual washbasins. Baby room. Supermarket. Bar. Modern restaurant. Snack bar/takeaway (high season). Outdoor heated swimming pools (1/6-1/9). Indoor pool (on payment). 10-pin bowling. Tennis. Minigolf. Boules. Sports field. Bicycle hire. Pedaloes. Fishing. Barbecue area. Play areas on sand. Organised activities in season. Max. 1 dog per pitch.

Open: 21 March - 26 October.

Directions

Site is signed from the N50/A50 road between 's Hertogenbosch and Nijmegen, about 10 km. east of 's Hertogenbosch at Vinkel.
GPS: N51:42.479 E05:25.979

Charges guide

Per unit incl. 2 persons and electricity	€ 13,00 - € 28,00

NL6630 Camping Ter Spegelt

Postelseweg 88, NL-5521 RD Eersel (Noord-Brabant)

Tel: **0497 512 016**. Email: **info@terspegelt.nl** **www.alanrogers.com/NL6630**

Camping Ter Spergelt is a real delight. There are three large lakes, one for swimming, one for boating and the other for fishing and diving. The site has 800 pitches, with 420 for touring units and tents and 30 mobile homes for rent. The remaining pitches are used by seasonal units. All touring pitches have electricity, water and drainage and with a little luck, a view over the lakes. We can recommend this site to people who like to participate in activities (organised with a variety of sports and outdoor activities, campfires and themed dinners) and to families with children. You can try diving with professional equipment and lessons. There is a large covered beach (a greenhouse effect) with white sand, a swimming pool with natural lake water and a slide – ideal if the weather is poor. For relaxing activities, there are facilities for golf and horse riding near the campsite. You can enjoy an evening meal at the beachside restaurant 'De Wijde Blick' and enjoy a drink in the bar, along with plenty of evening entertainment.

Facilities

Six toilet blocks, one heated by solar panels, provide toilets, washbasins (open and in cubicles) and showers. Facilities for disabled visitors. Washbasins for children. Heated baby rooms with changing mat and bath. Laundry. Motorcaravan services. Supermarket. Restaurant. Bar. Snack bar. Swimming pools. Entertainment and activities. Watersports and diving. Minigolf. Bicycle hire. Tennis. Dogs are not accepted. Off site: Riding 2 km. Golf 7 km.

Open: 29 March - 27 October.

Directions

From Utrecht follow the A2 south towards Eindhoven, then Maastricht. Take exit for Antwerpen and follow signs for Eersel. From Eersel follow site signs. GPS: N51:20.174 E05:17.624

Charges guide

Per unit incl. 2 persons € 25,00 - € 30,00

NL5900 Beekse Bergen Camping

Beekse Bergen 1, NL-5081 NJ Hilvarenbeek (Noord-Brabant)

Tel: **0135 491 100**. Email: **info@libema.nl** **www.alanrogers.com/NL5900**

Beekse Bergen is a large impressive leisure park set around a very large, attractive lake near Tilberg. The park offers a range of amusements which should keep the most demanding of families happy! These include not only water based activities, but also a small amusement park and much more. On the far side of the lake, there are two distinct campsites – one on flat meadows near the lake, the other in a more secluded wooded area reached by a tunnel under the nearby main road. The 420 pitches are about 100 sq.m. and all have electricity and cable connections (4/6A). There are 62 with full services.

Facilities

Sanitary facilities are quite adequate in terms of numbers, cleanliness and facilities including some washbasins in private cabins. Launderettes. Restaurants, cafés and takeaway (weekends only in low seasons). Supermarket. Playgrounds. Indoor pool. Beaches and lake swimming. Watersports including rowing boats (free) and canoe hire. Amusements. Tennis. Minigolf. Fishing. Recreation programme. Bicycle hire. Riding. Twin axle caravans not accepted. Bungalows and tents to rent. Off site: Golf 5 km. The award winning Efteling amusement park

Open: 21 March - 26 October.

Directions

From A58/E312 Tilburg - Eindhoven motorway, take exit to Hilvarenbeek on the N269 road. Park and campsite are signed Beekse Bergen.
GPS: N51:28.979 E05:07.680

Charges guide

Per unit incl. 2 persons and electricity € 18,00 - € 32,00

Discounts for weekly stays.
Camping packages available.

NL6790 Camping De Kienehoef

Zwembadweg 35-37, NL-5491 TE Sint-Oedenrode (Noord-Brabant)

Tel: **0413 472 877**. Email: **info@kienehoef.nl** **www.alanrogers.com/NL6790**

Camping de Kienehoef is at Sint Oedenrode in Noord Brabant, which boasts many historical sights, including two castles. This site is well cared for and attractively laid out with reception to the right of the entrance. Behind this area is a heated swimming pool. The generous pitches are mostly laid out in bays and placed between trees and shrubs to the right of a long avenue leading through the site. The touring pitches are on three separate fields amongst pitches used for caravan holiday homes. There are some 40 serviced pitches with electricity, water and drainage.

Facilities

Two modern, clean and well maintained toilet blocks include preset showers and some shower/wash cubicles, also family and baby rooms. Laundry area with iron and board. Motorcaravan services. Shop, restaurant/bar and snacks (all 1/5-15/9). Heated outdoor pool (1/5-15/9). Lake fishing. Bicycle hire. Sports field. Tennis. Dogs and other pets are not accepted. Off site: Golf 1 km. Riding 15 km.

Open: 28 March - 28 October.

Directions

Leave A2 s'Hertogenbosh - Eindhoven motorway at exit 27 and follow signs to Sint Oedenrode. Site is well signed from village.
GPS: N51:34.653 E05:26.809

Charges guide

Per unit incl. 2 persons and electricity € 24,00 - € 29,00

Camping Cheques accepted.

NL6530 Terrassencamping Gulperberg Panorama

Berghem 1, NL-6271 NP Gulpen (Limburg)

Tel: **0434 502 330**. Email: **info@gulperberg.nl** **www.alanrogers.com/NL6530**

Gulperberg Panorama is just three kilometres from the attractive village of Gulpen. Pitches are large and flat on terraces overlooking the village on one side and open countryside on the other. Many have full services. English is spoken in the reception, although all written information is in Dutch (ask if you require a translation). Gulperberg Panorama is a haven for children. During the high season there is a weekly entertainment programme to keep them occupied. The site is not suitable for visitors with disabilities. Dogs are restricted to one section of the campsite.

Facilities

Four modern sanitary blocks have excellent facilities. Family shower room and baby room. Laundry. Shop (27/4-31/8). Bar. Takeaway. New restaurant with terrace. Swimming pool (29/4-15/9). Three play areas. Giant 'air cushion'. TV and games room. Entertainment programme for all. Off site: Golf and bicycle hire 3 km. Fishing 4 km. Riding 5 km. Further afield are caves, museums and Maastricht with shops. Beach 15 km.

Open: Easter - 31 October.

Directions

Gulpen is east of Maastricht. Take N278 Maastricht - Aachen. Site is signed just as you enter Gulpen at the traffic lights. Turn right and follow camping signs for about 3 km. GPS: N50:48.404 E05:53.647

Charges guide

Per unit incl. 2 persons and electricity	€ 17,10 - € 22,85
extra person (over 2 yrs)	€ 2,40 - € 3,50

Camping Cheques accepted.

NL6540 Camping Rozenhof

Camerig 12, NL-6294 NB Vijlen-Vaals (Limburg)

Tel: **0434 551 611**. Email: **info@campingrozenhof.nl** **www.alanrogers.com/NL6540**

Camping Rosenhof is a friendly, family run site and its hillside location offers views over a valley that has won awards for its natural beauty. This partially wooded, hilly region is popular with countryside lovers, ramblers and cyclists. Rosenhof has 101 pitches arranged on a series of small terraced, hedged meadows. There are 82 used for touring units, some with hardstanding and all with electricity, water and drainage. A number of mature trees afford some shade. A rustic restaurant has a large terrace and, as the site's name suggests, roses and plants are much in evidence.

Facilities

To the rear of reception, the heated modern sanitary unit houses all the usual facilities including controllable showers, washbasins open and in cabins. Facilities for disabled people. Baby room and family shower room. Washing machines and dryers. Shop. Restaurant/bar and takeaway. Gas supplies. Playground, play room and pets corner for children. Riding. Bicycle hire. Off site: Fishing 5 km. Golf 9 km.

Open: All year.

Directions

Leave A76/E314 at Knooppunt Bochtolz (not exit for Bocholtz town) and follow N281 southwest towards Vaals for 3 km. to T-junction with N278. Turn left, then first right (Mamelisserweg) to Vijlen. In Vijlen second road to the right (Vijlen Berg) and straight on for 4 km. to T-junction at the other side of the forest. Turn right and continue for 300 m. the site is to the right. GPS: N50:46.189 E05:55.705

Charges guide

Per unit incl. 2 persons and electricity	€ 20,00
extra person (over 3 yrs)	€ 2,50

Runner up Alan Rogers Awards 2008

NL6520 Camping BreeBronne

Lange Heide 9, NL-5993 PB Maasbree (Limburg)

Tel: **0774 652 360**. Email: **info@breebronne.nl** **www.alanrogers.com/NL6520**

One of the top campsites in the Netherlands, BreeBronne is set around a large lake in a forest region. There are 370 pitches, of which 220 are for touring units. These are at least 100 sq.m. in size and all have electricity (10A), water, waste water and cable TV connections. The touring pitches are placed in separate areas from the static units and some pitch areas are kept for people without dogs. The lake provides a sandy beach with a water slide and opportunities for swimming, sailing and windsurfing. Alternatively, you can swim in the heated open air pool or the 'sub-tropical' heated indoor pool with its special children's area. Possible excursions from the site might include a visit to Arcen, beside the Maas river, with its Schloss garden and the nearby naturally heated thermal bath. There are boat trips on the Maas. Shopping in Venlo is good with its Saturday morning market. Member of 'Leading Campings Group'.

Facilities

The sanitary facilities are top class with a special section for children, decorated in fairy tale style, and excellent provision for disabled visitors and seniors. Launderette. Dog shower. Solarium. Private bathrooms for hire. Shop (1/4-31/10). Bar and 'De Bron' restaurant with regional specialities (all year). Takeaway. Outdoor swimming pool (15/5-1/10). Indoor pool with area for children (all year). Play area. Play room. Internet. Tennis. Animation. Fishing. Bicycle hire. Off site: Fishing 2 km. Golf and riding 5 km. Walking in the National Parks.

Open: All year.

Directions

Breebronne is 8 km. west of Venlo. From autobahn A67 towards Eindhoven take exit 38 and head south on the 277 road. After 3 km. fork right for Maasbree, then left (Maasbree) on the 275. At roundabout in Maasbree take third exit (site signed). Go through town and turn right after 2 km. to site 1 km. on left. GPS: N51:21.999 E06:02.499

Charges guide

Per unit incl. 4 persons	€ 27,70 - € 45,40
extra person	€ 4,80
dog	€ 5,30
private bathroom	€ 11,80

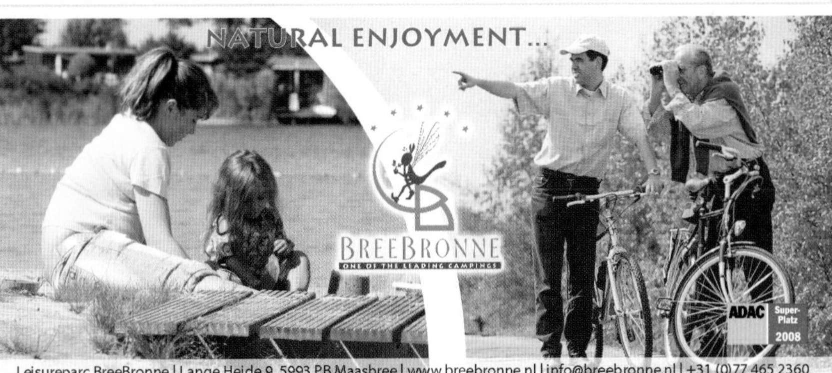

NL6580 Recreatieterrein De Gronselenput

Haasstao 3, NL-6321 PK Wijlre (Limburg)

Tel: **0434 591 645**. Email: **gronselenput@paasheuvelgroep.nl** **www.alanrogers.com/NL6580**

Camping Gronselenput is a small, quiet, countryside site located at the end of a tree lined lane. Family run, it has 60 grassy level pitches 55 of which are for tourists, 40 having 6A electricity. With a peaceful location between a wooded hill and the river Geul, it is popular with visitors with younger children and those seeking a quiet site. Cars are parked separately from the camping area. The site is set out in a series of small hedged meadows with pitches tending to be located around the edges.

Facilities

In the sanitary block hot water for showers is free. Entry to the toilets is directly from outside. Two baby areas. Washing machines and spin dryer. Gas supplies. Shop (excellent English spoken). Bar selling pizzas with a partly covered terrace facing one of the playgrounds. Large room used for organised children's activities. Off site: Fishing possible in the river Geul (with permit). Riding and bicycle hire 15 km. Golf 25 km.

Open: 1 April - 1 November.

Directions

Site is near village of Wijlre, 10 km. northwest of Aachen. Leave A4/E314/A76 at Knooppunt Bocholtz 2 km. northwest of the German border (not exit for Bocholtz town). Follow N281 southwest for 5 km. and at junction turn right (northwest) to Wittem on the N278. In Wittem, at traffic lights turn right on N595 to Wijlre. Just after entering Wijlre site is signed to the left. GPS: N50:50.530 E05:52.649

Charges guide

Per unit incl. 2 persons and electricity	€ 17,75 - € 23,75
extra person	€ 2,60 - € 22,70

Netherlands

NL6510 Kawan Village De Schatberg

Midden Peelweg 5, NL-5975 MZ Sevenum (Limburg)

Tel: **077 4677 777**. Email: **info@schatberg.nl** **www.alanrogers.com/NL6510**

In a woodland setting of 86 hectares, this family run campsite is more reminiscent of a holiday village, with a superb range of activities that makes it an ideal venue for families. Look out for the wallabies and the deer! A large site with 1,100 pitches and many mobile homes and seasonal or weekend visitors, there are 500 touring pitches. All have electricity (6/10A), cable, water and drainage and average 100 sq.m. in size. They are on rough grass terrain, mostly with shade, but not separated. Forty pitches have private sanitary facilities. Road noise can be heard in some areas of this large campsite. The site is well situated for visits to Germany and Belgium, also easily accessible from the port of Zeebrugge. The surrounding countryside offers the opportunity to enjoy nature, either by cycling or walking. For the more 'stay on site' visitor the location is excellent with several lakes for fishing, windsurfing and swimming, plus an extensive range of activities and a heated outdoor swimming pool. A feature at De Schatberg is the attractive restaurant/bar area and the reception and indoor pool, manned by friendly staff.

Facilities

Five modern, fully equipped toilet blocks, supplemented by three small wooden toilet units to save night time walks, receive heavy use in high season and maintenance can be variable. Family shower rooms, baby baths and en-suite units for disabled visitors. Washing machines and dryers. Motorcaravan service point. Supermarket. Restaurant, bar and takeaway. Pizzeria. Pancake restaurant. Indoor and outdoor pools. Tennis. Minigolf. Trampoline. Play areas. Fishing. Watersports. Bicycle hire. Mini train. Games room. Entertainment in high season. Off site: Golf 4 km.

Open: All year.

Directions

Site is 8 km. west-northwest of Venlo. Leave the A67 Eindhoven - Venlo motorway at Helden, exit 38. Travel north on the 277 for 500 m. and site is signed at new roundabout.
GPS: N51:22.922 E05:58.641

Charges 2009

Per unit incl. up to 4 persons and electricity € 19,65 - € 40,20

Camping Cheques accepted.

NL6515 Camping Oolderhuuske

Oolderhuuske 1, NL-6041 TR Roermond (Limburg)

Tel: **0475 588 686**. Email: **info@oolderhuuske.nl** **www.alanrogers.com/NL6515**

When staying on this interesting site, which is part of a resort complex, you know you are on holiday. The site is situated at the end of an island on a low lying spit of land in the River Mass and has 260 pitches, 80 of which are touring. All have electricity, are level, grassed and many are waterside – no pitch lies more than 60 m. from the water. From the campsite beach and jetty there are wide ranging views over large stretches of open water.

Facilities

One floating block, with facilities for disabled people, and two portacabin style sanitary units provide toilets, free showers, washbasins. Motorcaravan service point. Bar, restaurant with terrace, snacks and takeaway. Small indoor pool, gym, sauna, steam bath, solarium. Sport fields. Tennis. Playgrounds. Bicycle hire. Boat launching. High season entertainment. Off site: Floating houses. Visit the towns of Maastricht and Aachen.

Open: 1 April - 31 October.

Directions

Coming from Maastricht on the A2 (Maastricht - Eindhoven) take exit for Roermond and Maasbracht and continue to Roermond (centrum). In Roermond follow signs for Eindhoven and, just after the Muse river bridge turn right to Hatenboer/de Weerd. Follow brown signs. GPS: N51:11.517 E05:56.652

Charges guide

Per unit incl. up to 4 persons and electricity € 24,00 - € 27,00

MAP 8

A land full of contrasts, from magnificent snow capped mountains, dramatic fjords, vast plateaux with wild untamed tracts, to huge lakes and rich green countryside. With nearly one quarter of the land above the Arctic Circle, Norway has the lowest population density in Europe.

CAPITAL: OSLO

Tourist Office

Norwegian Tourist Board
Charles House, 5 Lower Regent Street
London SW1Y 4LR
Tel: 020 7839 2650
Email: infouk@ntr.no
Internet: www.visitnorway.com

Norway is made up of five regions. In the heart of the eastern region and the oldest of the Scandinavian capitals, Oslo is situated among green hills and vast forest areas, rich in Viking folklore and traditions. If your main reason for visiting Norway is to see the fjords then head to the west. They are magnificent, with waterfalls and mountains that plunge straight down into the fjords. Trondheim, the third largest city, is in the heart of central Norway, steeped in history with a mixture of old wooden houses and modern architecture. Southern Norway sees the most sun, a popular holiday destination for the Norwegians, with a coastline ideal for swimming, sailing, scuba diving and fishing. The north is the 'Land of the Midnight Sun', where the sun never sets in summer and in winter it fails to rise. The scenery is diverse with forested valleys, stark mountains and lush valleys, and there are also coastal cities to explore, including Tromsø, which boasts the world's most northerly brewery.

Population

4.7 million

Climate

Weather can be unpredictable, although less extreme on the west coast. Some regions have 24 hours of daylight in summer but none in winter.

Language

Norwegian, but English is widely spoken.

Telephone

The country code is 00 47.

Money

Currency: Norwegian Krone
Banks: Mon-Fri 09.00-15.00.

Shops

Mon-Fri 09.00-16.00/17.00, Thu 09.00-18.00/20.00 and Sat 09.00-13.00 /15.00.

Public Holidays

New Year's Day; King's Birthday 21 Feb; Holy Thursday; Good Friday; Easter Monday; May Day; Liberation Day 8 May; Constituition Day 17 May; Ascension; Whit Monday; Queen's Birthday 4 July; Saint's Day 19 July; Christmas 25, 26 Dec.

Motoring

Roads are generally uncrowded around Oslo and Bergen but be prepared for tunnels and hairpin bends. Certain roads are forbidden to caravans or best avoided (advisory leaflet from the Norwegian Tourist Office). Vehicles must have sufficient road grip and in winter it may be necessary to use winter tyres with or without chains. Vehicles entering Bergen on week-days must pay a toll and other tolls are also levied on certain roads.

NO2315 Ringoy Camping

N-5780 Kinsarvik (Hordaland)

Tel: **53 66 39 17**. Email: **toreivr@kinsarvik.net**

www.alanrogers.com/NO2315

Although the village of Ringoy is quiet and peaceful, it occupies a pivotal position, lying not only midway between two principal ferry ports of Upper Hardangerfjord (Kinsarvik and Brimnes), but also near the junction of two key roads (routes 7 and 13). This site is basically a steeply sloping field running down from the road to the tree-lined fjord with two flat terraces and the shore area for camping. The owners, the Raunsgard family, are particularly proud of the site's remarkable shore-side barbecue facilities. On arrival you find a place as there is no reception – someone will call between 8 and 9 pm.

Facilities

The toilet block is small and simple (with metered showers), but well designed, constructed and maintained. It is possibly inadequate during peak holiday weeks in July. Rowing boat (free). Off site: Supermarket, bank and other facilities in Kinsarvik 10 km.

Open: 15 May - 15 September.

Directions

Site is on route 13, midway between Kinsarvik and Brimnes. GPS: N60:26.467 E06:46.793

Charges guide

Per person	NOK 10
child (0-12 yrs)	NOK 5
pitch incl. electricity (10A)	NOK 120

No credit cards.

NO2320 Odda Camping

Borsto, N-5750 Odda (Hordaland)

Tel: **41 32 16 10**. Email: **post@oppleve.no**

www.alanrogers.com/NO2320

Bordered by the Folgefonna glacier to the west and the Hardangervidda plateau to the east and south, Odda is an industrial town with electro-chemical enterprises based on zinc mining and hydro-electric power. This site has been attractively developed on the town's southern outskirts. It is spread over 2.5 acres of flat, mature woodland, which is divided into small clearings by massive boulders. Access is by well tended tarmac roads which wind their way among the trees and boulders. There are 55 tourist pitches including 36 with electricity. The site fills up in the evenings and can be crowded with facilities stretched from the end of June to early August.

Facilities

A single timber building at the entrance houses the reception office and the simple, but clean sanitary facilities which provide, for each sex, 2 WCs, one hot shower (on payment) and 3 open washbasins. A new building provides additional unisex toilets, showers and laundry facilities. Small kitchen with dishwashing facilities. Mini shop. Off site: Town facilities close.

Open: All year.

Directions

Site is on the southern outskirts of Odda, signed off road to Buar, with a well marked access. GPS: N60:03.192 E06:32.628

Charges guide

Per person	NOK 10
tent and car	NOK 110
caravan or motorcaravan	NOK 130
electricity	NOK 40

No credit cards.

NO2330 Eikhamrane Camping

N-5776 Nå (Hordaland)

Tel: **53 66 22 48**

www.alanrogers.com/NO2330

About halfway along the western shore of Sørfjord is Eikhamrane Camping. Arranged on a well landscaped and partly terraced field which slopes alongside the road to a pebbly lakeside beach, it was formerly part of an orchard which still extends on both sides of the site. There is room for 40 units on unmarked, well kept grass with 20 electrical hook ups (10A). There are attractive trees and good gravel roads, with areas of gravel hardstanding for poor weather. Many pitches overlook the fjord where there are also picnic benches.

Facilities

Two small timber toilet blocks, one for toilets with external access, the other for washbasins (open) and showers (on payment). Both are simple but very well kept. Small kitchen and two laundry sinks outside, under cover. Some supplies kept at reception office in the old farmhouse, home of the owner (bread and milk to order). Watersports (sailing, canoeing and rowing), and fishing in fjord. Off site: Digranes nature reserve (birdwatching) nearby.

Open: 1 June - 31 August.

Directions

Site is on road 550 about 8 km. south of the village of Nå, on the western shore of Sørfjord, 32 km. south of Utne and 16 km. north of Odda. GPS: N60:10.984 E06:33.104

Charges guide

Per person	NOK 10
child (4-12 yrs)	NOK 5
pitch	NOK 100
electricity	NOK 25

No credit cards.

NO2350 Espelandsdalen Camping

N-5736 Granvin (Hordaland)

Tel: **56 52 51 67**. Email: **post@espelandsdalencamping.no** **www.alanrogers.com/NO2350**

If one follows Hardangerfjord on the map and considers the mighty glacier which once scooped away the land along its path, it is easy to imagine that it started life in Espelandsdalen. For generations farmers have struggled to make a living out of the narrow strip of land between water and rock. One of these farmers has converted a narrow, sloping field bisected by the road (572) into a modest lakeside campsite taking about 50 units. The grassy meadow pitches below the road run right down to the lake shore. There are 30 electrical hook ups (10A). Campers come here for the fishing and walking, or just to marvel at the views of the valley and its towering mountain sides. Espelandsdalen runs from Granvin to Ulvik, both of which lie at the heads of their respective arms of Hardangerfjord. A minor road (route 572) links the two small towns with sharp climbs at either end. The valley bed here is occupied by a series of connected lakes, popular with canoeists.

Facilities

A newly refurbished sanitary block consists of a washing trough with hot water, a shower on payment and WCs. Some basic foodstuffs are kept in the office. Swimming, fishing and boating in lake. Boat hire. Off site: Pleasant walk to local waterfall.

Open: 1 May - 31 August.

Directions

The northern loop of the 572 road follows Espelandsdalen and the campsite is on this road, about 6 km. from its junction with route 13 at Granvin. GPS: N60:35.545 E06:48.390

Charges guide

Per person	NOK 15
child (4-12 yrs)	NOK 10
pitch	NOK 90
electricity	NOK 35

No credit cards.

NO2360 Ulvik Fjord Camping

N-5730 Ulvik (Hordaland)

Tel: **91 17 96 70**. Email: **camping@ulvik.org** **www.alanrogers.com/NO2360**

Ulvik was discovered by tourists 150 years ago when the first liners started operating to the head of Hardangerfjord. This pretty little site is 500 m. from the centre of the town and occupies what must once have been a small orchard running down to the fjord beside a small stream. There is room for about 80 units on undulating ground which slopes towards the fjord, with some flat areas and 32 electrical connections and six cabins. Access is by winding roads, either along the side of the fjord or up a steep narrow road behind the town – probably not to be recommended for caravans.

Facilities

New facilities in a small wooden building which houses reception and the well kept sanitary facilities. For each sex there are 2 open washbasins, WCs and 2 modern showers on payment. Kitchen with cooker and dishwashing sink. Washing machine. Bicycle hire. Boat slipway, fishing and swimming in fjord. Jetty with rowing boat (free). Large barbecue area and hot tub. Off site: Hotel opposite, shops and restaurants in town.

Open: 1 May - 15 September.

Directions

Ulvik is reached by road no. 572; the site is on the southern side of the town, opposite the Ulvikfjord Pension. There is a ferry from road no. 7 at Brimnes. Cars and caravans can also connect with road 7 via a tunnel. GPS: N60:33.908 E06:54.487

Charges guide

Per pitch	NOK 130
electricity	NOK 20

NO2375 Lærdal Ferie & Fritidspark

Grandavegens, N-6886 Lærdal (Sogn og Fjordane)

Tel: **57 66 66 95**. Email: **info@laerdalferiepark.com** **www.alanrogers.com/NO2375**

This site is beside the famous Sognefjord, the longest fjord in the world. It is ideally situated if you want to explore the glaciers, fjords and waterfalls of the region. The 100 pitches are level with well trimmed grass. They are connected by tarmac roads and are suitable for tents, caravans and motorcaravans. There are 80 electrical hook-ups. The fully licensed restaurant serves traditional meals as well as snacks and pizzas. The pretty little village of Laerdal, only 400 m. away, is well worth a visit. A walk among the old, small wooden houses is a pleasant and interesting experience. You can hire boats on the site for short trips on the fjord. Guided hiking, cycling and fishing trips are also available. The site also provides cabins, flats and rooms to rent, plus a brand new motel, all very modern and extremely tastefully designed.

Facilities

Two modern and well decorated sanitary blocks with washbasins (some in cubicles), showers on payment, and toilets. Facilities for disabled visitors. Children's room. Washing machine and dryer. Kitchen. Motorcaravan services. Small shop. Bar, restaurant and takeaway (20/5-5/9). TV room. Playground. Motorboats, rowing boats, canoes, bicycles and pedal cars for hire. Bicycle hire. Fishing. Internet (WiFi) at reception. Off site: Cruises on the Sognefjord 400 m. The Norwegian Wild Salmon Centre 400 m. Riding 500 m. Golf 12 km. The Flåm railway 40 km.

Open: All year, by telephone request 1 Nov. - 14 March.

Directions

Site is on road 5 (from the Oslo - Bergen road, E 16) 400 m. north of Laerdal village centre.
GPS: N61:05.986 E07:28.177

Charges guide

Per unit incl. 2 persons	NOK 140
incl. electricity	NOK 175
extra person	NOK 48
child (4-18 yrs)	NOK 24 - 36

Camping Cheques accepted.

NO2370 Botnen Camping

N-5961 Brekke (Sogn og Fjordane)

Tel: **57 78 54 71**. Email: **joker.brekke@ngbutikk.net** **www.alanrogers.com/NO2370**

For those setting forth north on E39 from Bergen there are surprisingly few attractive sites until one reaches the southern shore of mighty Sognefjord. At Brekke is a well known tourist landmark, the remarkable Breekstranda Fjord Hotel, a traditional turf-roofed complex which tourist coaches are unable to resist. A mile or two beyond the hotel, also on the shore of the fjord, is the family run Botnen Camping. This simple site slopes steeply towards the fjord, providing wonderful views to distant mountains from individual, mostly level pitches. It has its own jetty and harbour, with motor boats and canoes for hire.

Facilities

Toilet block with washbasins and showers (on payment). Small kitchen with microwave, hotplate and washing machine. Small shop. Play area. Swimming, fishing and boating in fjord. Boats and canoes for hire. Off site: Hiking, fishing and boating.

Open: 1 June - 31 August.

Directions

Site is on the coast road west of Brekke, 11 km. from E39. GPS: N61:02.000 E05:17.999

Charges guide

Per person	NOK 15
caravan or motorcaravan	NOK 90
tent	NOK 80
electricity	NOK 20

NO2390 Kjørnes Camping

N-6856 Sogndal (Sogn og Fjordane)

Tel: **57 67 45 80**. Email: **camping@kjornes.no** **www.alanrogers.com/NO2390**

Kjørnes Camping is idyllically situated on the Sognefjord, 3 km. from the centre of Sogndal. It occupies a long open meadow which is terraced down to the tree lined waterside. The site has 100 pitches for camping units (90 with electricity), nine cabins and two apartments for rent. Located at the very centre of the 'fjord kingdom' by the main no. 5 road, this site is the ideal base from which to explore the Sognefjord. You are within a short drive (maximum one hour) from all the major attractions including the Jostedal glacier, the Nærøyfjord, the Flåm Railway, the Urnes Stave Church and Sognefjellet. This site is ideal for those who want to enjoy the peace and quiet, lovely scenery or a spot of fishing. Access is via a narrow lane with passing places, which drops down towards the fjord three kilometres from Sogndal.

Facilities

A new, high quality sanitary building was added in 2008. Baby room. Facilities for disabled visitors. A new building provides a kitchen with cooking facilities, dishwasher, a dining area overlooking the fjord, and laundry facilities. Small shop (20/6-20/8). Satellite TV, WiFi and internet. Off site: Hiking, glacier walks, climbing, rafting, walking around Sognefjord. Details from reception.

Open: 1 May - 1 October.

Directions

Site is off the Rv 5, 3 km. east of Sogndal, 8 km. west of Kaupanger. GPS: N61:12.674 E07:07.263

Charges guide

Per person	NOK 30
child (4-12 yrs)	NOK 10
pitch	NOK 100
electricity	NOK 30

NO2380 Tveit Camping

N-6894 Vangsnes (Sogn og Fjordane)

Tel: **57 69 66 00**. Email: **tveit@online.no** **www.alanrogers.com/NO2380**

Located in the district of Vik on the south shore of Sognefjord, 4 km. from the small port of Vangsnes, Tveit Camping is part of a small working farm and it is a charming neat site. Reception and a kiosk open most of the day in high season, with a phone to summon assistance at any time. Three terraces with wonderful views of the fjord provide 35 pitches with 30 electricity connections (10A) and there are also site owned cabins. On the campsite you will find a restored Iron Age burial mound dating from 350-550AD, whilst the statue of 'Fritjov the Intrepid' towers over the landscape at Vangsnes.

Facilities

Modern, heated sanitary facilities provide showers on payment, a unit for disabled visitors, kitchens with facilities for dishwashing and cooking, and laundry facilities (hot water on payment). Motorcaravan services. Kiosk (15/6-15/8). TV rooms. Playground. Harbour for small boats, slipway and boat/canoe hire. Fishing. WiFi is planned. Off site: Shop, café and pub by ferry terminal in Vangsnes 4 km. Riding 15 km.

Open: Mid April - mid October.

Directions

Site is by Rv 13 between Vik and Vangsnes, 4 km. south of Vangsnes. GPS: N61:08.386 E06:37.172

Charges guide

Per person (over 5 yrs)	NOK 15
pitch	NOK 120
electricity	NOK 25

No credit cards.

NO2385 PlusCamp Sandvik

Sandvik Sor, N-6868 Gaupne (Sogn og Fjordane)

Tel: **57 68 11 53**. Email: **sandvik@pluscamp.no** **www.alanrogers.com/NO2385**

Sandvik is a compact, small site on the edge of the town of Gaupne close to the Nigardsbreen Glacier. It provides 60 touring pitches, 48 with electrical connections (8/16A), arranged on fairly level grassy terrain either side of a road. A large supermarket, post office, banks, etc. are all within a level 500 m. stroll. A café in the reception building is open in summer for drinks and meals and the small shop sells groceries, ices, soft drinks, sweets, etc. This is a useful site for those using the spectacular Rv 55 high mountain road from Lom to Sogndal or for visiting the Nigardsbreen Glacier and Jostedalsbreen area of Norway.

Facilities

The single, fully equipped, central sanitary unit includes washbasins with dividers and two hot showers per sex (on payment). Multi-purpose unit for families or disabled visitors with baby changing and a further WC, basin and shower with ramp. Small campers' kitchen. Tables, chairs and TV. Laundry. Playground. Boat hire. Fishing. Bicycle hire. Off site: Nigardsbreen (glacier). Sognefjellet.

Open: All year.

Directions

Signed just off Rv 55 Lom-Sogndal road on eastern outskirts of Gaupne. GPS: N61:24.032 E07:18.029

Charges guide

Per pitch incl. up to 4 persons	NOK 140
electricity	NOK 30

NO2400 PlusCamp Jolstraholmen

Postboks 11, N-6847 Vassenden (Sogn og Fjordane)

Tel: **57 72 89 07**. Email: **jolstraholmen@pluscamp.no** **www.alanrogers.com/NO2400**

This family run site is situated on the E39 between Sognefjord and Nordfjord. It is located between the road and the fast-flowing Jolstra River (renowned for trout fishing), 1.5 kilometres from the lakeside village of Vassenden, behind the Statoil filling station, restaurant and supermarket complex which is also owned by the family. The 35 pitches (some marked) are on grass or gravel hardstanding all with electricity (10A), five also have water and waste points and some have TV connections. A river tributary runs through the site and forms an island on which some pitches are located.

Facilities

The main heated sanitary facilities, fully equipped in rooms below the complex, include showers on payment plus one family bathroom per sex. Small unit located on the island. Two small kitchens provide dishwashing and cooking facilities (free of charge). Laundry. Supermarket and café. Restaurant. Garage. Covered barbecue area. Playground. Water slide (open summer, weather permitting). Rafting. Fishing. Guided walks. Boat hire. Off site: 9-hole golf course 50 m. Ski slopes within 1 km.

Open: All year.

Directions

Site is beside the E39 road, 1.5 km. west of Vassenden, 18 km. east of Førde.
GPS: N61:29.272 E06:05.059

Charges guide

Per unit incl. 1-4 persons	NOK 135 - 175
small tent incl. 2 persons	NOK 80 - 120
electricity	NOK 40

NO2436 Byrkjelo Camping

N-6826 Byrkjelo (Sogn og Fjordane)

Tel: **91 73 65 97**. Email: **byrkjelocamping@sensewave.com** **www.alanrogers.com/NO2436**

This neatly laid out and well equipped small site offers 25 large marked and numbered touring pitches, all with electrical connections (10A) and 15 with gravel hardstandings. It is a good value site in a village location with neatly mown grass, attractive trees and shrubs with a warm welcome from the owners. Fishing is possible in the river adjacent to the site. Reception and a small kiosk selling ices, sweets and soft drinks, are housed in an attractive cabin and there is a bell to summon the owners should they not be on site when you arrive.

Facilities

The good heated sanitary unit includes 5 shower rooms each with washbasin, on payment. Facilities for families with babies and disabled visitors, incorporating a WC, basin and shower with handrails, etc. Campers' kitchen with dining area. Laundry facilities. Motorcaravan services. Kiosk. TV room. Minigolf. Small playground. Fishing. Swimming pool and children's pool (20/6-20/8), both heated (fee charged). Off site: Riding 4 km. Golf 15 km. Ideal base for Nordfjord and Jostedalsbreen. Rafting.

Open: 1 May - 1 October.

Directions

Site is beside the E39 in the village of Byrkjelo, 19 km. east of Sandane.
GPS: N61:43.826 E06:30.507

Charges guide

Per person	NOK 10
child	NOK 5
pitch	NOK 125
electricity	NOK 30

NO2452 Trollveggen Camping

Horgheimseidet, N-6300 Åndalsnes (Møre og Romsdal)

Tel: **71 22 37 00**. Email: **post@trollveggen.no** **www.alanrogers.com/NO2452**

The location of this site provides a unique experience – it is set at the foot of the famous vertical cliff of Trollveggen (the Troll Wall), which is Europe's highest vertical mountain face. The site is pleasantly laid out in terraces with level grass pitches. The facility block, the four cabins and the reception are all very attractively built with grass roofs. Beside the river is an attractive barbecue area where barbecue parties are sometimes arranged. This site is a must for people who love nature. The site is surrounded by the Troll Peaks and the Romsdalshorn Mountains with the rapid river of Rauma flowing by. Here in the beautiful valley of Romsdalen you have the ideal starting point for trips to many outstanding attractions such as 'The Troll Road' to Geiranger or to the Mandalsfossen waterfalls. In the mountains there are nature trails of various lengths and difficulties. The campsite owners are happy to help you with information. The town of Åndalsnes is 10 km. away and has a long tourism tradition as a place to visit. It is situated in the inner part of the beautiful Romsdal fjord and has a range of shops and restaurants.

Facilities

One heated toilet block provides washbasins, some in cubicles, and showers on payment. Family room with baby bath and changing mat, plus facilities for disabled visitors. Communal kitchen with cooking rings, small ovens, fridge and sinks (free hot water). Laundry facilities. Motorcaravan service point. Barbecue area (covered). Playground. Duck pond. Off site: Climbing, glacier walking and hiking. Fjord fishing. Sightseeing trips. The Troll Road. Mardalsfossen (waterfall). Geiranger and Åndalsnes.

Open: 10 May - 20 September.

Directions

Site is located on the E136 road, 10 km. south of Åndalsnes. It is signed. GPS: N62:29.674 E07:45.500

Charges guide

Per unit incl. 2 persons	NOK 130 - 140
electricity	NOK 40

Camping Cheques accepted.

NO2450 Bjolstad Camping

N-6445 Malmefjorden (Møre og Romsdal)

Tel: **71 26 56 56**. Email: **post@bjolstad.no** **www.alanrogers.com/NO2450**

This is delightful small, rural site, which slopes down to Malmefjorden, a sheltered arm of Fraenfjorden. Bjølstad has space for just 55 touring units on grassy, fairly level, terraces either side of the tarmac central access road. A delight for children is a large, old masted boat which provides hours of fun playing at pirates or Vikings. At the foot of the site is a waterside barbecue area, a shallow, sandy, paddling area for children and a jetty. Both rowing and motorboats (with life jackets) can be hired, one can swim or fish in the fjord.

Facilities

The very basic, clean, heated sanitary unit includes two showers per sex (on payment), plus washbasins with dividers. Small campers' kitchen. Laundry service at reception. Playground. Boat hire. Fjord fishing and swimming. Dogs are not accepted in cabins. Off site: Riding 9 km. Golf 12 km.

Open: 1 June - 30 September (maybe before on request).

Directions

Turn off Rv 64 on northern edge of Malmefjorden village towards village of Lindset (lane is oil bound gravel). Site is 1 km. GPS: N62:48.875 E07:13.518

Charges guide

Per pitch	NOK 120 - 150
electricity	NOK 60

NO2460 Prinsen Strandcamping

Gåseid, N-6015 Ålesund (Møre og Romsdal)

Tel: **70 15 21 90**. Email: **post@prinsencamping.no** **www.alanrogers.com/NO2460**

Prinsen is a lively, fjordside site, five kilometres from the attractive small town of Alesund. It is a more attractive option than the more crowded sites closer to town, even so, this is mainly a transit and short-stay site. Divided by trees and shrubs, and sloping gently to a small sandy beach with views down Borgundfjord, the site has 100 grassy pitches, 34 cabins and seven rooms, 110 electricity connections (16A) and 75 cable TV hook-ups. Reception shares space with the kiosk and freshly baked bread can be ordered daily.

Facilities

The main heated sanitary unit in the reception building is fully equipped with mostly open washbasins, showers on payment and a sauna for each sex. Kitchen. Laundry facilities. Additional older facilities mainly serving rooms and cabins, but include multi-purpose bathroom for disabled people, families and baby changing (key from reception). Motorcaravan service point. Kiosk (1/6-1/9). TV room. Barbecue areas. Playground. Slipway and boat hire. Fishing. Off site: Restaurant 800 m. Supermarket 1 km. Aksla and Fjellstua Viewpoint (418 steps to the point).

Open: All year.

Directions

Turn off E136 at roundabout signed to Hatlane and site. Follow signs to site.
GPS: N62:27.509 E06:15.192

Charges guide

Per pitch	NOK 200

NO2490 Skjerneset Brygge Camping

Ekkilsøya, N-6530 Averoy (Møre og Romsdal)

Tel: **71 51 18 94**. Email: **info@skjerneset.com** **www.alanrogers.com/NO2490**

The tiny island of Ekkilsøya lies off the larger island of Averøy and is reached via a side road and bridge from road 64 just south of Bremsnes from where the ferry crosses to Kristiansund. At Skjerneset Camping there is space for 30 caravans or motorcaravans on gravel hardstandings around a rocky bluff and along the harbour's rocky frontage and all have electricity connections. A small grassy area for 5 tents is under pine trees in a hollow on the top of the bluff together with five fully equipped cabins. Note: this is a working harbour with deep unfenced water very close to the pitches.

Facilities

Unisex sanitary facilities are heated, but basic and include washbasins in cubicles. Two new sanitary blocks. Kitchen. Small laundry. Motorcaravan service point. Kiosk for basic packet foods, crisps, ices, sweets, postcards etc. Satellite TV. Motor boat hire. Organised sea fishing or sightseeing trips in the owner's sea-going boat, and for non anglers who want a fish supper, fresh fish are usually available on site.

Open: All year.

Directions

Site is on the little island of Ekkilsøya which is reached via a side road running west from the main Rv 64 road, 1.5 km. south of Bremsnes.
GPS: N63:04.881 E07:35.767

Charges guide

Per person	NOK 150
pitch	NOK 250 - 500
electricity (10/16A)	NOK 25

No credit cards.

NO2415 Kautokeino Fritidssenter & Camping

Suonpatjavri, N-9520 Kautokeino (Finnmark)

Tel: **78 48 57 33** **www.alanrogers.com/NO2415**

This is a friendly, lakeside site, 8 km. south of Kautokeino. The 50 pitches are not marked but are generally on a firm sandy base amongst low growing birch trees, with 20 electric hook-ups (16A) available. There are also cabins and motel rooms for rent. Although the grass is trying to grow, the ground is frozen from September until May so there are mainly hardstandings with some grass areas. The site is 35 km. north of the Finnish Border and is one day's drive from North Cape. During the season, when there are enough guests, the owner arranges an evening campfire around two Sami tents, with 'lectures' about the Sami people.

Facilities

The modern sanitary building is heated and well maintained, with 2 British style WCs, 2 open washbasins and 2 showers (on payment) per sex. Small kitchen. Laundry facilities. Separate bathroom for disabled people, also containing baby facilities. Football. Canoes, boats and pedalos for hire. Free fishing available in lake.
Off site: Kautokeino (Sami Museum), Juhl's Silver Gallery.

Open: 1 June - 30 September.

Directions

Site is 8 km. south of Kautokeino on road Rv 93. GPS: N68:56.841 E23:05.376

Charges guide

Per pitch	NOK 140
electricity	NOK 20

NO2425 Kirkeporten Camping

Box 22, N-9763 Skarsvag (Finnmark)

Tel: **78 47 52 33**. Email: **kipo@kirkeporten.no** **www.alanrogers.com/NO2425**

This is the most northerly mainland campsite in the world (71/06) and considering the climate and the wild unspoilt location it has to be one of the best sites in Scandinavia, and also rivals the best in Europe. The 40 pitches, 22 with electricity are on grass or gravel hardstanding in natural 'tundra' terrain beside a small lake, together with 16 rental cabins and five rooms. We advise you to pack warm clothing, bedding and maybe propane for this location. Note: Overnighting at Nordkapp Centre is permitted but it is on the very exposed gravel car park with no electric hook-ups or showers.

Facilities

Excellent modern sanitary installations in two underfloor heated buildings. They include a sauna, two family bathrooms, baby room, and excellent unit for disabled visitors. Laundry. Kitchen with hot plates, sinks and a dining area. Motorcaravan service point. Reception, restaurant and mini shop at the entrance open daily. Off site: North Cape, Kirkeporten.

Open: 20 May - 1 September.

Directions

On the island of Magerøya, from Honningsvåg take the E69 for 20 km. then fork right signed Skarsvåg. Site is on left after 3 km. just as you approach Skarsvåg. GPS: N71:06.456 E25:48.761

Charges guide

Per person	NOK 20
pitch	NOK 150
electricity (16A)	NOK 20

NO2428 Andenes Camping

Storgata 53, N-8483 Andenes (Nordland)

Tel: **76 14 12 22**. Email: **erna.strom@norlandia.no** **www.alanrogers.com/NO2428**

Many campsites in Norway have simple and basic facilities with little evidence of security. Often, one arrives, finds a pitch and you pay later when reception opens. Andenes Camping is a classic example but this extremely popular exposed site at sea level, is only three kilometres from the base of 'Whalesafari'. An area of uneven ground provides space for an unspecified number of touring units and you park where you like. The ground is mainly of grass with some hardstanding. Twenty units only can access 16A electricity and if you want electricity you are advised to arrive by mid-afternoon.

Facilities

The reception building houses clean sanitary facilities, each providing 2 toilets, 2 showers (charged) and 3 washbasins. In each, one toilet is suitable for disabled people and includes a hand basin. Small kitchen (free). Motorcaravan service point. Picnic tables. Swings for children. Off site: Well stocked supermarket 250 m. On approach to town a garage, caravan dealer and another supermarket. From the nearby village of Bleik (8 km), trips for deep sea fishing and visits to Bleiksøya one of Norway's most famous bird cliffs, home to 80,000 pairs of puffins and 6,000 kittiwakes.

Open: 1 June - 30 September.

Directions

Travelling north on road 82, site is on left 3 km. before Andenes. GPS: N69:17.988 E16:03.072

Charges guide

Per pitch	NOK 120
incl. electricity	NOK 130
tent	NOK 90

NO2432 Harstad Camping

Nesseveien 55, N-9411 Harstad (Troms)

Tel: **77 07 36 62**. Email: **postmaster@harstad-camping.no** **www.alanrogers.com/NO2432**

For those visiting or exiting Lofoten and Vesterålen, this well established, popular site close to Harstad, provides an excellent stopping point on Hinnøya, the largest island in Norway. In a delightful setting with fine views, the campsite has space for 120 units as it slopes down to Vågsfjorden. Pitches are not marked, but by the waters edge a flat area provides most of the 33 electricity hook-ups (16A). This part of the site is sought after and we advise a mid-afternoon arrival for the possibility of a level pitch and/or electricity connection.

Facilities

Good facilities include British style WCs, washbasins and showers (two for each sex, NOK 10 for 4 minutes). Room for disabled visitors. Laundry room (hot water NOK 5). Kitchen, tables and chairs. Reception has a small selection of soft drinks, ices, sweets, crisps, some tinned foods and postcards (no bread or milk). Off site: One of northern Norway's largest shopping centres, including a garage and supermarket at 2 km.

Open: All year.

Directions

Travelling north on road 83, site is on right 3 km. before Harstad. After turning right, turn immediate left and site is 1 km. along firm unmade road (site signed from either direction).
GPS: N68:46.339 E16:34.727

Charges guide

Per pitch	NOK 175
incl. electricity	NOK 200

NO2435 Solvang Camping

Box 1280, N-9505 Alta (Finnmark)

Tel: **78 43 04 77**. Email: **solvangcamp@hotmail.com** **www.alanrogers.com/NO2435**

This is a restful little site with a welcoming atmosphere. It is set well back from the main road, so there is no road noise. The site overlooks the tidal marshes of the Altafjord, which are home to a wide variety of birdlife, providing ornithologists with a grandstand view during the long summer evenings bathed by the Midnight Sun. The 30 pitches are on undulating grass amongst pine trees and shrubs, and are not marked, although there are 16 electric hook-ups (16A). The site is run by a church mission organisation. All facilities are brand new.

Facilities

New block with reception and floor-heated sanitary facilities with wash basins in cubicles, showers and a family room. Facilities for disabled visitors. Sauna. New kitchen with cooker, sinks and dining area. Washing machine and dryer. Large TV room. Football field. Play area. Off site: Alta Museum. Rock carvings.

Open: 1 June - 10 August.

Directions

Site is signed off the E6, 10 km. north of Alta. GPS: N69:58.781 E23:28.085

Charges guide

Per pitch incl. 2 persons and electricity	NOK 150

NO2455 Ballangen Camping

N-8540 Ballangen (Nordland)

Tel: **76 92 76 90**. Email: **ballcamp@c2i.net** **www.alanrogers.com/NO2455**

Ballangen is a pleasant, lively site conveniently located on the edge of a fjord with a small sandy beach, with direct access off the main E6 road. The 150 marked pitches are mostly on sandy grass, with electricity (10/16A) available to all. There are a few hardstandings, also 54 cabins for rent. A TV room has tourist information, a coffee and games machines and there is a heated outdoor pool and waterslide (charged), free fjord fishing, and boat hire. An interesting excursion is to the Martinstollen mine where visitors are guided through the dimly lit Olav Shaft 500 m. into the mountain.

Facilities

Toilet facilities include some washbasins in cubicles. Facilities for disabled visitors, sauna and solarium. Kitchen with dishwashing sinks, 2 cookers and covered seating area. Laundry. Motorcaravan services. Well stocked shop. Café and takeaway (main season). TV/games room. Swimming pool and waterslide (charged). Minigolf. Fishing. Golf. Boat and bicycle hire. Pedal car hire. Mini zoo. Playground. Covered barbecue areas. Off site: Riding 2 km. Ballangen 4 km. has supermarket and other services. Narvik 40 km.

Open: 1 March - 31 December.

Directions

Access is off the E6, 4 km. north of Ballangen, 40 km. south of Narvik. GPS: N68:20.333 E16:51.468

Charges guide

Per pitch	NOK 170
electricity	NOK 40

NO2465 Lyngvær Lofoten Bobilcamping

N-8310 Kabelvag (Nordland)

Tel: **76 07 87 81**. Email: **relorent@c2i.net** **www.alanrogers.com/NO2465**

Some camping sites on Lofoten are very basic with extremely limited facilities but Lyngvaer is in complete contrast. This established site is very popular, with many customers returning. In the centre of Lofoten alongside a tidal fjord with mountains all around, the setting and location is quite idyllic. Large terraces provide fine views for most of the 200 pitches, mainly grass, some with hardstanding, with electricity for 110 (10/16A). Fresh water, waste water and chemical disposal is free for guests (otherwise waste disposal and fresh water NOK 50). Lyngvaer provides a base to absorb the island's scenery and traditions and the general area is good for walking, ornithology and photography.

Facilities

Toilet facilities are spotlessly clean with showers in small cubicles (NOK 10 for 6 minutes). Extra unisex showers and toilets are beside reception. Communal kitchen with cooking, dishwashing and fish freezer (free). Large sitting area with satellite TV. Play areas. Boat hire. Fishing (fish cleaning area). Off site: Within a reasonable distance, manufacturing of metal birds, glass blowing, Viking museum, aquarium and the capital of Lofoten, Svolvaer.

Open: 1 May - 30 September.

Directions

On disembarking the ferry (Skutvik - Svolvaer) turn southwest on E10 signed Lofoten. Site is on left in 18 km. (There is a campsite about 6 km. from Skutvik on the left on approach, details unknown). GPS: N68:13.417 E14:12.966

Charges guide

Per unit incl. 1 person	NOK 100
extra person	NOK 5
electricity	NOK 20

Eighth night free.

NO2475 Saltstraumen Camping

Bok 85, N-8056 Saltstraumen (Nordland)

Tel: **75 58 75 60**. Email: **saltstraumen@pluscamp.no** **www.alanrogers.com/NO2475**

On a coastal route, this extremely popular site, in a very scenic location with a magnificent backdrop, is close to the largest Maelstrom in the world. It is an easy short walk to this outstanding phenomenon. As well as 20 cabins, the site has 60 plain touring pitches mostly on level, gravel hardstandings in rows, each with electricity. A few 'softer' pitches are available for tents. The site is 33 km. from Bodø and 50 km. from Fauske. You are advised to arrive by late afternoon. The fjord close by is renowned for the prolific numbers of coalfish and cod caught from the shore. Many have a go at catching their evening meal!

Facilities

Basic but heated sanitary facilities are clean and fully equipped. Separate shower areas for men and women have dividers, shower curtains and communal changing. Kitchen with two full cookers, fish cleaning area and fish freezer. Laundry facilities. Motorcaravan service point. TV room. Playground. Minigolf. Fishing. Off site: Well stocked mini supermarket and snack bar outside site entrance. Hotel and cafeteria nearby. This area is said to be the fourth best location in the world for diving.

Open: All year.

Directions

Travelling from the south: Before Rognan take Rv 812 signed Saltstraumen. At junction with Rv 17 turn right. Site on left immediately after second bridge. From the north: From Rv 80 (Fauske -Bodø) turn south on Rv 17, site is 12 km. at Saltstraumen on right immediately before bridge.
GPS: N67:14.078 E14:37.309

Charges guide

Per unit incl. 2 persons	NOK 90 - 120
extra person	NOK 15
electricity	NOK 30

NO2485 Krokstrand Camping

Krokstrand, Salt Jellveien 1573, N-8630 Storforshei (Nordland)

Tel: **75 16 60 02** **www.alanrogers.com/NO2485**

This site is a popular resting place for all nationalities on the long trek to Nordkapp and it is only 18 km. from the Arctic Circle with its Visitor Centre. There are 45 unmarked pitches set amongst birch trees with electrical connections (10A) for 28 units. In late spring and early summer the river alongside, headed by rapids is impressive with the possibility of mountains close by still being snow-capped. The small reception kiosk is open 08.00 - 10.00 and 15.00 - 22.00 in high season, otherwise campers are invited to find a pitch and pay later.

Facilities

Well maintained, spotlessly clean, small sanitary unit includes two showers per sex (on payment). Laundry with washing machine and dryer. Small kitchen with double hot plate and dishwashing sink. Motorcaravan services. Brightly painted play area with trampoline, well maintained. Minigolf. Fishing. Off site: Hotel with café/restaurant just outside site entrance (same ownership as the site) with good meals, snacks and very basic provisions. Souvenir shop.

Open: 1 June - 20 September.

Directions

Entrance is off E6 at Krokstrand village opposite hotel, 18 km. south of the Arctic Circle.
GPS: N66:28.072 E15:04.594

Charges guide

Per person	NOK 15
child	NOK 10
pitch	NOK 110
electricity	NOK 30

No credit cards.

NO2495 Vegset Camping

N-7760 Snåsa (Nord-Trøndelag)

Tel: **74 15 29 50**. Email: **mveg@online.no** **www.alanrogers.com/NO2495**

This small, basic but pleasant site is seven kilometres south of Snåsa, directly beside the E6 road on the banks of Lake Snåsavatn. It consists of ten site-owned chalets, a number of static units and a small area for about 20 touring units on slightly sloping ground. There are 10A electricity connections available. For those travelling to or from Northern Norway, Vegset provides a good resting point or night halt. Snåsa is a centre for the South Lapp people who have their own boarding school, museum and information centre there.

Facilities

The satisfactory toilet block provides showers (NOK 10), plus a shower with toilet suitable for disabled people. Kitchen. Kiosk selling emergency groceries doubles as a TV room (end June - mid Aug). Swimming, boat hire and fishing (licence from site).

Open: Easter - 10 October.

Directions

Site is just off the E6 road, 7 km. south of Snåsa.
GPS: N64:15.954 E12:17.204

Charges guide

Per pitch	NOK 110
electricity	NOK 30

NO2500 Tråsåvika Camping

Orkanger, N-7354 Viggja (Sør Trøndelag)

Tel: **72 86 78 22**. Email: **jowiggen@start.no** **www.alanrogers.com/NO2500**

On a headland jutting into the Trondheimfjord some 40 km. from Trondheim, Trasavika commands an attractive position. For many this compensates for the extra distance into town. The 65 pitches (some slightly sloping) are on an open grassy field at the top of the site, or on a series of terraces below, which run down to the small sandy beach, easily accessed via a well designed gravel service road. There are 48 electricity connections (10A). To one side, on a wooded bluff at the top of the site, are 14 cabins (open all year), many in traditional style with grass roofs.

Facilities

The neat, fully equipped, sanitary unit includes two controllable hot showers per sex (on payment). Hot water on payment in kitchen and laundry which have a hot plate, dish and clothes washing sinks, washing machine and dryer. Shop. Café (20/6-30/8). TV/sitting room. Play area. Jetty and boat hire. Free fjord fishing with catches of good sized cod from the shore.

Open: 1 May - 10 September.

Directions

Site is to the west of Viggja with direct access from the E39 between Orkanger and Buvik, 21 km. from the E6 and 40 km. west of Trondheim. There is a new E39 which you now must take off from in Bersa or Orkanger. 6 km. each direction. GPS: N63:20.812 E09:57.740

Charges guide

Per pitch	NOK 170
electricity	NOK 40

NO2505 Magalaupe Camping

Engan, N-7340 Oppdal (Sør Trøndelag)

Tel: **72 42 46 84**. Email: **camp@magalaupe.no** **www.alanrogers.com/NO2505**

This is a rural, good value, riverside site in a sheltered position with easy access from the E6. Fairly simple facilities are offered but there are a host of unusual activities in the surrounding area. The 52 unmarked and grassy touring pitches (42 with 16A electricity) are in natural surroundings amongst birch trees and rocks and served by gravel access roads. There are also eight attractive and fully equipped site owned cabins. As the site rarely fills up, the simple facilities should be adequate at most times. Activities in the area include caving, canyoning, rafting, gold panning, mineral hunting, and musk oxen, reindeer and elk safaris.

Facilities

Small, clean, heated sanitary unit fully equipped and the showers are on payment. Extra WC/washbasin units in reception building. Small kitchen with dishwashing facilities, hot plate, fridge and freezer, plus a combined washing/drying machine. Kiosk for ices, soft drinks, etc. Bar (mid June - Aug). TV lounge. Fishing. Bicycle hire. Off site: Supermarkets and other services in Oppdal 11 km. Riding or golf 12 km. Organised walking, cycling and car tours.

Open: All year.

Directions

Site is signed on E6, 11 km. south of Oppdal. GPS: N62:29.822 E09:35.121

Charges guide

Per pitch	NOK 100
tent	NOK 80
electricity	NOK 20

No credit cards.

NO2510 Håneset Camping

Osloveien, N-7374 Roros (Sør Trøndelag)

Tel: **72 41 06 00** **www.alanrogers.com/NO2510**

At first sight Håneset Camping is neither promising, lying between the main road and the railway, nor is the gritty sloping ground of the site very imaginatively landscaped – for grass, when it grows up here, is rather coarse and lumpy. However, as we soon discovered, it is the best equipped campsite in the town, and ideal to cope with the often cold, wet weather of this bleak 1,000 m. high plateau. The 50 unmarked touring pitches all have access to electricity (10/16A), and most facilities are housed in the main complex building. People flock from all over Europe to visit this remarkably well preserved mining town.

Facilities

Heated sanitary facilities provide three separate rooms for each sex, fully equipped with showers on payment. Washing machine and two clothes washing sinks. Kitchen. Huge sitting/TV room and two well equipped kitchens which the owners, the Moen family, share fully with their guests, plus 9 rooms for rent. Off site: Town 20 minutes walk.

Open: All year.

Directions

Site is on the Rv 30 leading south from Røros to Os, 3 km. from Røros. GPS: N62:34.047 E11:21.118

Charges guide

Per pitch incl. 4 persons	NOK 160
electricity	NOK 30

No credit cards.

NO2515 Gjelten Bru Camping

N-2560 Alvdal (Hedmark)

Tel: **62 48 74 44**

www.alanrogers.com/NO2515

Located a few kilometres west of Alvdal, this peaceful little site, with its traditional turf roof buildings, makes an excellent base from which to explore the area. The 50 touring pitches are on level neatly trimmed grass, served by gravel access roads and with electricity (10A) available to all. Some pitches are in the open and others under tall pine trees spread along the river bank. Across the bridge on the other side of the river and main road, the site owners also operate the local, well stocked market and post office.

Facilities

Heated toilet facilities are housed in two buildings. One unit has been refurbished, the other is of newer construction. There is a mix of conventional washbasins and stainless steel washing troughs, and hot showers on payment. Separate unit with WC, basin, shower and handrails for disabled visitors. Two small kitchens provide dishwashing facilities, hot plates and an oven all free of charge. Laundry facilities. Shop. TV room. Swings. Fishing. Off site: Supermarket and post office nearby. Bicycle hire 5 km.

Open: All year.

Directions

On the road 29 at Gjelten 3.5 km. west of Alvdal. Turn over the river bridge opposite village store and post office, and site is immediately on right. GPS: N62:07.871 E10:34.126

Charges guide

Per pitch	NOK 140
electricity	NOK 20

NO2525 Østre Æra Camping

N-2460 Osen (Hedmark)

Tel: **62 44 49 11**. Email: **info@ostre-aera-camping.com**

www.alanrogers.com/NO2525

This all year site is located on the banks of the Osa river, where you can catch trout and prepare it in the site's barbecue hut for dinner. The site has 90 pitches (including 60 seasonal), all with 10A electricity and on level grass. There are also 20 cabins for rent. A swimming pool is heated during peak season and has a 50 m. slide. Visit in winter for ice fishing in the Osa lake or good ski facilities in Trysil and Reva, cross country as well as downhill. The small town of Rena is 25 km. away, located in the centre of Norway's largest forest and mountain area.

Facilities

Two toilet blocks, one small and unheated. Washbasins with dividers and showers on payment. Facilities for disabled visitors. Laundry. No kitchen. Small shop. TV room next to reception. Heated pool with 50 m. slide. Football field. Playground. Barbecue hut. WiFi. Fishing.

Open: All year.

Directions

Site is on road no. 215, 25 km. northeast of Rena, and is signed. GPS: N61:14.148 E11:39.748

Charges guide

Per unit incl. electricity	NOK 125 - 195

NO2545 Plus Camp Rustberg

N-2636 Oyer (Oppland)

Tel: **61 27 77 30**. Email: **rustberg@online.no**

www.alanrogers.com/NO2545

Conveniently located beside the E6, 23 km. from the centre of Lillehammer, this attractive terraced site provides a comfortable base for exploring the area. Like all sites along this route it does suffer from road and train noise at times, but the site's facilities and nearby attractions more than compensate for this. There are 70 pitches with 30 available for touring units, most reasonably level and with some gravel hardstandings available for motorcaravans. There are 70 electrical connections (16A). A small open air, heated swimming pool has a water slide.

Facilities

Heated, fully equipped sanitary facilities include washbasins in cubicles, showers on payment and free saunas. Two good family bathrooms. Unit for disabled people. Campers' kitchen and dining room with microwave oven and double hob. Laundry. Motorcaravan services. Restaurant. Solarium (on payment). Kiosk for basics. Swimming pool and slide (1/6-31/8, weather permitting). Billiards. Golf. Playground. New reception and café. Off site: Forest walks directly from site. Fishing in the nearby river, day licence from reception. Golf 7 km. Children's farm and pony riding.

Open: All year.

Directions

Site is well signed from the E6, 20 km. north of Lillehammer (North) exit. GPS: N61:16.815 E10:21.657

Charges guide

Per pitch incl. electricity	NOK 175 - 200

NO2615 Olberg Camping

Sandsveien 4, Olberg, N-1860 Trogstad (Østfold)

Tel: **69 82 86 10**. Email: **froesol@online.no** **www.alanrogers.com/NO2615**

Olberg is a newly developed, delightful small farm site, close to lake Øyeren and within 70 km. of Oslo. There are 35 large, level pitches and electricity connections (10-16A) are available for 28 units located on neatly tended grassy meadow with trees and shrubs. The reception building also houses a small gallery with paintings, glasswork and other crafts. A short drive down the adjacent lane takes you to the beach on Lake Øyeren, and there are many woodland walks in the surrounding area. Please bear in mind that this is a working farm.

Facilities

Excellent, heated sanitary facilities are fully equipped and include a ramp for wheelchair access and one bathroom for families or disabled visitors. Laundry facilities. Small kitchenette with full size cooker and food preparation area. Kiosk. Snacks available. Craft gallery. Playground. Off site: Fishing 3 km. Golf, tropical pool and spa 18 km.

Open: 1 May - 1 October, other times by arrangement.

Directions

Site is signed on Rv 22, 20 km. north of Mysen on southern edge of Båstad village.
GPS: N59:41.296 E11:17.575

Charges guide

Per unit incl. 2 persons	NOK 175
tent incl. 2 persons	NOK 175

NO2590 Sandviken Camping

N-3650 Tinn Austbygd (Telemark)

Tel: **35 09 81 73**. Email: **kontakt@sandviken-camping.no** **www.alanrogers.com/NO2590**

Sandviken is a remote, lakeside site, in a scenic location, suitable for exploring Hardangervidda. With its own shingle beach, at the head of Tinnsjo Lake, it provides 150 grassy, mostly level, pitches. In addition to 50 seasonal units and 12 cabins, there are 85 numbered tourist pitches with electricity (10/16A), plus an area for tents, under trees along the waterfront. The office/reception kiosk also sells sweets, soft drinks, ices etc. and a baker calls daily in July. A 1 km. stroll takes you to the tiny village of Tinn Austbygde which has a mini-market, bakery, café, bank, garage and post office.

Facilities

Tidy heated sanitary facilities include some washbasins in cubicles, showers on payment, sauna, solarium and a dual-purpose disabled/family bathroom with ramped access and baby changing mat. Kitchen and laundry rooms (hot water on payment). Motorcaravan services. Kiosk (20/6-1/9). Playground. TV and games room. Minigolf. Fishing and watersports. Boat hire.
Off site: Handicraft exhibition 5 km. Riding 15 km. At Rjukan (27 km) industrial museum, cable car, Gausta peak.

Open: All year.

Directions

Easiest access is via the Rv 37 from Gransherad along the western side of the lake.
GPS: N59:59.352 E08:49.069

Charges guide

Per person	NOK 15
child (4-18 yrs)	NOK 10
caravan or motorcaravan	NOK 110 - 150
tent and car	NOK 95 - 115

NO2600 Rysstad Feriesenter

N-4748 Rysstad (Aust-Agder)

Tel: **37 93 61 30**. Email: **post@rysstadferie.no** **www.alanrogers.com/NO2600**

Setesdal is on the upper reaches of the Otra river which runs north from the southern port of Kristiansand and right up to the southern slopes of Hardangervidda. The small village of Rysstad is named after the family who have developed camping in this area. The site occupies a wide tract of woodland between the road and the river towards which it shelves gently, affording a splendid view of the valley and the towering mountains opposite. The site is in effect divided into two sections; one is divided by trees and hedges into numbered pitches, some occupied by chalets, the other is an adjacent open field and 20 electrical connections are available (six with satellite TV).

Facilities

Sanitary facilities have showers on payment, washbasins in cubicles, dishwashing sinks and a cooker. Laundry facilities. Play area and amusement hut. Sports field. Fishing, swimming and boating (boats for hire). Fitness track. Bicycle hire. Centre includes café, mini shop and restaurant. Handicraft shop. Area on the river's edge for barbecues and entertainment with an arena-type setting. New 5 room motel, open all year. Off site: Village within walking distance. Bank, shop, petrol station.

Open: 1 May - 1 October.

Directions

Site is about 1 km. south of junction between route 9 (from Kristiansand) and the extended route 45 (from Stavanger).
GPS: N59:05.464 E07:32.434

Charges guide

Per person	NOK 20
child (4-12 yrs)	NOK 10
caravan or tent	NOK 130
hiker	NOK 60
electricity	NOK 25

NO2610 Neset Camping

N-4741 Byglandsfjord (Aust-Agder)

Tel: **37 93 42 55**. Email: **post@neset.no** **www.alanrogers.com/NO2610**

On a semi-promontory on the shores of the 40 km. long Byglandsfjord, Neset is a good centre for activities or as a stop en route north from the ferry port of Kristiansand (from England or Denmark). Neset is situated on well kept grassy meadows by the lake shore with the water on three sides and the road on the fourth, and provides 200 unmarked pitches with electricity and cable TV available. The main building houses reception, a small shop and a restaurant with fine views over the water. This is a well run, friendly site where one could spend an active few days. Byglandsfjord offers good fishing (mainly trout) and the area has marked trails for cycling, riding or walking in an area famous for its minerals.

Facilities

Three modern sanitary blocks which can be heated, all with comfortable hot showers (some on payment), washing up facilities (metered hot water) and a kitchen. Restaurant and takeaway (15/6-15/8). Shop (1/5-1/10). Campers' kitchen. Playground. Lake swimming, boating and fishing. Excellent new barbecue area and hot tub. Bicycle, canoe and pedalo hire. Climbing, rafting and canoeing courses arranged (including trips to see beavers and elk). Cross-country skiing possible in winter. Off site: Rock climbing wall. Marked forest trails.

Open: All year.

Directions

Site is on route 9, 2.5 km. north of the town of Byglandsfjord on the eastern shores of the lake. GPS: N58:41.309 E07:48.079

Charges guide

Per person	NOK 10
pitch	NOK 160
child (5-12 yrs)	NOK 5
electricity	NOK 30

Camping Cheques accepted.

NO2660 Preikestolen Camping

Jørssangvegen 265, Preikestolvegen 97, N-4100 Jørpeland (Rogaland)

Tel: **51 74 97 25**. Email: **info@preikestolencamping.com** **www.alanrogers.com/NO2660**

Taking its name from one of Norway's best known attractions, the Preikestolen (Pulpit Rock) cliff formation, Preikestolen Camping is situated in the beautiful region of Rogaland, surrounded by high mountains and deep fjords. This is a site where you could easily stay a few days to explore the beautiful region. The friendly owners are happy to help with maps and guidance. The site is laid out in a relaxed way with an open, level grass area where trees and bushes create pleasant little 'rooms' for your tent, caravan or motorcaravan. There are 100 pitches, 56 with electricity (10/16A), water tap and waste water drainage.

Facilities

The modern heated sanitary block has showers, washbasins in cubicles and facilities for disabled visitors. Room with dishwashing sinks but no cookers. All with free hot water. Washing machines and dryers. Motorcaravan service point. Freezer. Small shop and craft shop (15/5-15/9). Restaurant and takeaway (15/5-15/9). Fishing. Internet (WiFi). Off site: Preikestolen. Stavanger. Lysefjordsentret salmon park in Oanes. Rock carvings at Solbakk. Golf 500 m. Riding 15 km. Helicopter sightseeing and guided nordic walking trips.

Open: 1 March - 1 December.

Directions

Site is on road 13, 3 km. south of Jörpeland. Follow signs to site. GPS: N58:59.933 E06:05.530

Charges guide

Per person	NOK 30
child	NOK 20
pitch	NOK 150
electricity	NOK 30

MAP 9

Portugal is a relatively small country occupying the southwest part of the Iberian peninsula, bordered by Spain in the north and east, with the Atlantic coast in the south and west. In spite of its size, the country offers a tremendous variety in both its way of life and traditions.

CAPITAL: LISBON

Tourist Office

Portuguese National Tourist Office
11 Belgrave Square, London SW1X 8PP
Tel: 0845 355 1212
E-mail: info@visitportugal.com
Internet: www.visitportugal.com

Most visitors looking for a beach type holiday head for the busy Algarve, with its long stretches of sheltered sandy beaches, and warm, clear Atlantic waters, great for bathing and watersports. With its monuments and fertile rolling hills, central Portugal adjoins the beautiful Tagus river that winds its way through the capital city of Lisbon, on its way to the Atlantic Ocean. Lisbon city itself has deep rooted cultural traditions, coming alive at night with buzzing cafés, restaurants and discos. Moving southeast of Lisbon the land becomes rather impoverished, consisting of stretches of vast undulating plains, dominated by cork plantations. Consequently most people head for the walled town of Evora, an area steeped in two thousand years of history. The Portuguese consider the Minho area in the north to be the most beautiful part of their country, with its wooded mountains and wild coastline, a rural and conservative region with picturesque towns.

Population

10.6 million

Climate

The country enjoys a maritime climate with hot summers and mild winters with comparatively low rainfall in the south, heavy rain in the north.

Language

Portuguese

Telephone

The country code is 00 351.

Money

Currency: The Euro
Banks: Mon-Fri 08.30-11.45 and 13.00-14.45. Some large city banks operate a currency exchange 18.30-23.00.

Shops

Mon-Fri 09.00-13.00 and 15.00-19.00.
Sat 09.00-13.00.

Public Holidays

New Year; Carnival (Shrove Tues); Good Fri; Liberty Day 25 Apr; Labour Day; Corpus Christi; National Day 10 June; Saints Days; Assumption 15 Aug; Republic Day 5 Oct; All Saints 1 Nov; Immaculate Conception 8 Dec; Christmas 24-26 Dec.

Motoring

The standard of roads is very variable, even some of the main roads can be very uneven. Tolls are levied on certain motorways (auto-estradas) out of Lisbon, and upon southbound traffic at the Lisbon end of the giant 25th Abril bridge over the Tagus. Parked vehicles must face the same direction as moving traffic.

Winner Alan Rogers Awards 2008

PO8202 Camping Turiscampo

EN125, Espiche, Luz, P-8600 Lagos (Faro)

Tel: **282 789 265**. Email: **info@turiscampo.com** **www.alanrogers.com/PO8202**

This site is being thoughtfully refurbished and updated to include most of the existing infrastructure since it was purchased by the friendly Coll family, who are known to us from their previous Spanish site. Work was still in progress when we visited but the site does show great promise and will become a quality site. The site provides 206 pitches for tourers mainly in rows of terraces, all with electricity and some with shade. They vary in size (70-120 sq.m). The upper areas of the site are being developed and are mostly destined for bungalows (which are generally separate from the touring areas). A new, elevated Californian style pool plus a children's pool have been constructed and the supporting structure is a clever water cascade and surround. There is a large sun lounger area on astroturf. One side of the pool area is open to the road. The restaurant/bar has been tastefully refurbished and Giovanni and staff are delighted to use their excellent English, providing good fare at reasonable prices. The restaurant has two patios one of which is used for live entertainment and discos in season and the other for dining out. The sea is 2 km. and the city of Lagos 4 km. with all the attractions of the Algarve within easy reach. This is a very good site for families and for 'Snowbirds' to over-winter.

Facilities

The two existing toilet blocks have been refurbished and a new block added containing modern facilities for disabled campers. The site reports a further new, heated block. Hot water throughout. Facilities for children. Washing machines. Shop. Gas supplies. Restaurant/bar. Swimming pool (March - Oct) . Bicycle hire. Entertainment in high season. Playground. Adult art workshops, aqua gymnastics and miniclub (5-12 yrs) in season. Pétanque. Archery. Sports field. Internet. WiFi on payment. Bungalows to rent. Off site: Fishing and beach 2 km. Golf 4 km. Sailing 5 km. Boat launching 5 km. Riding 10 km.

Open: All year.

Directions

Take exit 1 from the N125 Lagos - Vila do Bispo road. The impressive entrance is about 3 km. on the right. GPS: N37:06.067 W08:43.967

Charges guide

Per person	€ 3,00 - € 5,80
child (3-10 yrs)	€ 1,60 - € 2,90
pitch incl. electricity	€ 7,90 - € 16,70
dog	€ 1,00 - € 1,50

Camping Cheques accepted.

PO8220 Orbitur Camping Quarteira

Estrada da Fonte Santa, avenida Sá Cameiro, P-8125-618 Quarteira (Faro)

Tel: **289 302 826**. Email: **info@orbitur.pt** **www.alanrogers.com/PO8220**

This is a large, busy attractive site on undulating ground with some terracing, taking 795 units. On the outskirts of the popular Algarve resort of Quarteira, it is 600 m. from a sandy beach which stretches for a kilometre to the town centre. Many of the unmarked pitches have shade from tall trees and there are a few small individual pitches of 50 sq.m. with electricity and water for reservation. There are 680 electrical connections. The site encourages long winter stays.

Facilities

Five toilet blocks provide British and Turkish style toilets, washbasins with cold water, hot showers plus facilities for disabled visitors. Washing machines. Motorcaravan services. Supermarket. Self-service restaurant (closed Nov). Takeaway (from late May). Swimming pools (April - Sept). Tennis. Open air disco (high season). Off site: Bus to Faro. Fishing 1 km. Bicycle hire (summer) 1 km. Golf 4 km.

Open: All year.

Directions

Turn off N125 for village of Almancil. In the village take road south to Quarteira. Site is on the left 1 km. after large, official town welcome sign. GPS: N37:04.000 W08:05.000

Charges guide

Per person	€ 3,10 - € 5,50
caravan and car	€ 6,90 - € 13,00
electricity	€ 2,50 - € 3,10

PO8230 Camping Olhão

Pinheiros de Marim, P-8700 Olhão (Faro)

Tel: **289 700 300**. Email: **parque.campismo@sbsi.pt** **www.alanrogers.com/PO8230**

This site, with around 800 pitches, is open all year. It has many mature trees providing good shade. The pitches are marked, numbered and in rows divided by shrubs, although levelling will be necessary and the trees make access tricky on some. There is electricity for 102 pitches (6A) and a separate area for tents. Permanent and long stay units take 20% of the pitches, the touring pitches filling up quickly in July and August, so arrive early. There is some noise nuisance from an adjacent railway. The site has a relaxed, casual atmosphere. Amenities include very pleasant swimming pools and tennis courts, a reasonable restaurant/bar and a café/bar with TV and games room. All are very popular with the local Portuguese who pay to use the facilities. The large, sandy beaches in this area are on offshore islands reached by ferry and are, as a result, relatively quiet; some are reserved for naturists. This site can get very busy in peak periods and maintenance can be variable. There was a large, low season British contingent when we visited, enjoying the low prices.

Facilities

Eleven sanitary blocks are adequate, clean when seen, and are specifically sited to be a maximum of 50 m. from any pitch. One block has facilities for disabled visitors. Laundry. Excellent supermarket. Kiosk. Restaurant/bar. Café and general room with cable TV. Playgrounds. Swimming pools (April - Sept) and tennis courts (fees for both). Bicycle hire. Internet at reception. Off site: Bus service to the nearest ferry at Olhão 50 m. from site. Riding 1 km. Indoor pool 2 km. Fishing 2 km. Golf 20 km.

Open: All year.

Directions

Just over 1 km. east of Olhão, on EN125, take turn to Pinheiros de Marim. Site is back off the road on the left. Look for very large, white, triangular entry arch as the site name is different on the outside wall. GPS: N37:02.117 W07:49.350

Charges guide

Per person	€ 2,30 - € 4,10
child (5-12 yrs)	€ 1,30 - € 2,30
pitch	€ 1,75 - € 7,60
electricity	€ 2,00

Less for longer winter stays.

Camping
Olhão
★★★
Open All Year
Tennis
Football
Bar
Swimming Pool
Restaurant
Bungalows
Mobile Homes
parque.campismo@sbsi.pt
Algarve - Portugal
www.sbsi.pt/camping
351 289 700 300

PO8430 Orbitur Camping Sagres

Cerro das Moitas, P-8650-998 Sagres (Faro)

Tel: **282 624 371**. Email: **info@orbitur.pt** **www.alanrogers.com/PO8430**

Camping de Sagres is a pleasant site at the western tip of the Algarve, not very far from the lighthouse in the relatively unspoilt southwest corner of Portugal. With 960 pitches for tents and 120 for tourers, the sandy pitches, some terraced, are located amongst pine trees that give good shade. There are some hardstandings for motorhomes and electricity throughout. The fairly bland restaurant, bar and café/grill provide a range of reasonably priced meals. This is a reasonable site for those seeking winter sun, or as a base for exploring this 'Land's End' region of Portugal.

Facilities

Three spacious toilet blocks are showing some signs of wear but provide hot and cold showers and washbasins with cold water. Washing machines. Motorcaravan services. Supermarket. Restaurant/bar and café/grill (all Easter and June - Oct). TV room. Satellite TV in restaurant. Bicycle hire. Barbecue area. Playground. Fishing. Off site: Buses from village 1 km. Beach and fishing 2 km. Boat launching 8 km. Golf 12 km.

Open: All year.

Directions

From Sagres, turn off the N268 road west onto the EN268. After about 2 km. the site is signed off to the right. GPS: N37:01.367 W08:56.750

Charges guide

Per person	€ 2,50 - € 4,50
child (5-10 yrs)	€ 1,30 - € 2,50
caravan and car	€ 5,60 - € 10,20
electricity (6A)	€ 2,50 - € 3,10

PO8210 Parque de Campismo Albufeira

EN125 Ferreiras - Albufeira, P-8200-555 Albufeira (Faro)

Tel: **289 587 629**. Email: **campingalbufeira@mail.telepac.pt** **www.alanrogers.com/PO8210**

The spacious entrance to this site will accommodate the largest of units (watch for severe speed bumps at the barrier). One of the better sites on the Algarve, it has pitches on fairly flat ground with some terracing, trees and shrubs giving reasonable shade in most parts. There are some marked and numbered pitches of 50-80 sq.m. Winter stays are encouraged with many facilities remaining open including a pool. An attractively designed complex of traditional Portuguese style buildings on the hill, with an unusually shaped pool and two more for children, forms the central area of the site. It has large terraces for sunbathing and pleasant views and is surrounded by a variety of flowers, shrubs and well watered lawns, complete with a fountain. The 'à la carte' restaurant, impressive with its international cuisine, and the very pleasant self-service one; both have views across the three pools. A pizzeria, bars and a soundproofed disco are great for younger campers.

Facilities

The toilet blocks include hot showers. Launderette. Very large supermarket. Tabac (English papers). Waiter and self-service restaurants. Pizzeria. Bars. Satellite TV. Soundproof disco. Swimming pools. Tennis. Playground. Internet access. First aid post. Car wash. ATM. Car hire. Off site: Site bus service from gate to Albufeira every 45 minutes (2 km). Theme parks nearby. Beaches.

Open: All year.

Directions

From N125 coast road or N264 (from Lisbon) at new junctions follow N395 to Albufeira. Site is about 2 km. on the left. GPS: N37:06.383 W08:15.217

Charges guide

Per car and caravan with 2 persons	€ 23,10 - € 23,65
motorcaravan with 2 persons	€ 19,60 - € 23,15
tent and car with 2 persons	€ 22,30 - € 22,70
electricity	€ 2,90

PO8200 Orbitur Camping Valverde

Estrada da Praia da Luz, Valverde, P-8600-148 Lagos (Faro)

Tel: **282 789 211**. Email: **info@orbitur.pt** **www.alanrogers.com/PO8200**

A little over a kilometre from the village of Praia da Luz and its beach and about 7 km. from Lagos, this large, well run site is certainly worth considering for your stay in the Algarve. It has 600 numbered pitches, of varying sizes, which are enclosed by hedges. All are on flat ground or broad terraces with good shade in most parts from established trees and shrubs. The site has a swimming pool with a long curling slide and a paddling pool (under 10s free, adults charged). This is an excellent site with well maintained facilities and good security. It attracts a good number of long-term winter visitors and is one of the better Orbitur sites.

Facilities

Six large, clean, toilet blocks have some washbasins and sinks with cold water only, and hot showers. Units for disabled people. Laundry. Motorcaravan services. Supermarket, shops, restaurant and bar complex with both self-service and waiter service in season (closed November). Takeaway. Coffee shop. Swimming pool (April - Sept) with slide and paddling pool (June - Sept). Playground. Tennis. Satellite TV in bar. Disco. Pub. Excursions. Off site: Bus service from site gate. Beach and fishing 1.5 km. Bicycle hire 3 km. Golf 10 km.

Open: All year.

Directions

From Lagos on N125 road, after 7 km. turn south to Praia da Luz. At the town follow Orbitur camping signs. The beach road is narrow and cobbled and is very challenging in a large unit. GPS: N37:05.984 W08:43.046

Charges guide

Per person	€ 2,90 - € 5,40
child (5-10 yrs)	€ 1,50 - € 3,00
caravan and car	€ 6,80 - € 12,00
electricity	€ 2,50 - € 3,10

Off season discounts (up to 70%).

PO8175 Zmar - Eco Camping Resort

Herdade de Mateus EN393/1, San Salvador, P-7630 Odemira (Beja)

Tel: **707 200 626**. Email: **info@zmar.eu** **www.alanrogers.com/PO8175**

Zmar is an exciting new project which will open in 2009. We plan to undertake a full inspection during the coming season. The site is located at Zambujeira do Mar, on the Alentejo coast. This is a highly ambitious initiative to be developed along very strict environmental lines. Renewable resources, for example, such as locally harvested timber and recyclable plastic will be used wherever possible. Solar energy will be used whenever practicable. Pitches will be around 100 sq.m. and will mostly benefit from artificial shade. Caravans and wood clad mobile homes will also be available for rent. The swimming pool complex will feature a large outdoor pool and an indoor pool area with a wellness centre. An innovative children's play park is planned with climbing nets, labyrinths and caves. There will also be a children's farm and a large play house. For adults, many sports amenities will also be available around the resort's 81 hectare park. These will include a sports field, bicycle hire and tennis courts. Zmar's restaurant will be open throughout the season and will focus on local produce and traditional cuisine.

Facilities

Bar. Restaurant. Crêperie. Takeaway food. Supermarket. Swimming pool. Covered pool. Wellness centre. Sports field. Games room. Children's play area and play house. Bicycle hire. Activity and entertainment programme. Mobile homes and caravans for rent. Caravan repair and servicing. Off site: Vicentina coast and the Alentejo natural park. Sines (birthplace of Vasco de Gama). Cycle and walking tracks. Sea fishing.

Open: All year.

Directions

Leave the A2 motorway at exit 12 (Ourique) and head west on IP2 to Ourique. Then continue west on N123 to Garvao. Here take the N369 and N263 to Odemira. Continue on N393 through Boavista to Zambujeira do Mar. GPS: N37:36.253 W8:43.885

Charges 2009

Not set yet. Contact the site.

Alan Rogers

This is just a sample of the campsites we have inspected and selected in Spain & Portugal. For more campsites and further information, please see the Alan Rogers Spain & Portugal guide.

PO8170 Parque de Campismo São Miguel

São Miguel, Odeceixe, P-7630-592 Odemira (Beja)

Tel: **282 947145**. Email: **camping.sao.miguel@mail.telepac.pt** **www.alanrogers.com/PO8170**

Nestled in green hills near two pretty white villages, 4 km. from the beautiful Praia Odeceixe (beach) is the attractive camping park São Miguel. Unusually the site works on a maximum number of 700 campers, you find your own place (there are no defined pitches) under the tall trees, there are ample electrical points, and the land slopes away gently. Wooden chalet style accommodation to rent is in a separate area, but some mobile homes share the two traditional older style sanitary blocks. The main building houses the reception, restaurant, bars and supermarket.

Facilities

Two older style toilet blocks with British style WCs and free hot showers. Washing machines. Toilets and basins for disabled campers but no shower. Shop (June - Sept). Self-service restaurant (March - Oct). Bar, snacks and pizzeria (June - Sept). Satellite TV. Playground. Tennis (charged). Swimming pool (charged). Dogs are not accepted. Torches useful. Off site: Bus from gate. Historic village of Odeceixe 2 km. Beach, fishing and sailing 4 km. Riding 20 km. Site is inside the Alentejo nature park.

Open: All year.

Directions

Between Odemira and Lagos on the N120 just before the village of Odeceixe on the main road well signed. GPS: N37:26.321 W08:45.341

Charges guide

Per person	€ 3,90 - € 6,00
child (5-10 yrs)	€ 2,20 - € 3,30
pitch	€ 3,90 - € 11,00
electricity	€ 3,25

Plus 7% VAT.

PO8130 Orbitur Camping Guincho

EN 247, Lugar da Areia - Guincho, P-2750-053 Cascais (Lisbon)

Tel: **214 870 450**. Email: **info@orbitur.pt** **www.alanrogers.com/PO8130**

Although this is a popular site for permanent Portuguese units with 1,295 pitches, it is nevertheless quite attractively laid out among low pine trees and with the A5 autostrada connection to Lisbon (30 km), it provides a useful alternative to sites nearer the city. This is viewed as an alternative for visiting Lisbon, not a holiday site. There is a choice of pitches (small – mainly about 50 sq.m) mostly with electricity, although siting amongst the trees may be tricky, particularly when the site is full. Located behind sand dunes and a wide, sandy beach, the site offers a wide range of facilities.

Facilities

Three sanitary blocks, one refurbished, are in the older style but are clean and tidy. Washbasins with cold water but hot showers. Facilities for disabled visitors. Washing machines and dryers. Motorcaravan services. Gas. Supermarket. Restaurant, bar and terrace. General room with TV. Tennis. Playground. Entertainment in summer. Chalets to rent. Off site: Bus service from gate. Excursions. Riding 500 m. Beach 800 m. Fishing 1 km. Golf 3 km.

Open: All year.

Directions

Approach from either direction on N247. Turn inland 6.5 km. west of Cascais at site sign. Travelling direct from Lisbon, the site is well signed as you leave the A5 autopista. GPS: N38:43.270 W09:28.000

Charges guide

Per person	€ 2,70 - € 4,80
child (5-10 yrs)	€ 1,40 - € 2,50
caravan and car	€ 6,70 - € 11,30
electricity	€ 2,50 - € 3,10

PO8450 Parque de Campismo Colina do Sol

Serra Dos Mangues, P-2465 São Martinho do Porto (Leiria)

Tel: **262 989 764**. Email: **parque.colina.sol@dix.pt** **www.alanrogers.com/PO8450**

Colina do Sol is a well appointed site with its own swimming pool and near the beach. Only 2 km. from the small town of São Martinho do Porto, it has around 350 pitches marked by fruit and ornamental trees on grassy terraces. Electricity (6A) is available. The attractive entrance with its beds of bright flowers, is wide enough for even the largest of outfits, and the surfaced roads are very pleasant for manoeuvring. There is a warm welcome and good English is spoken. The beach is at the rear of the site, with access via a gate which is locked at night. We are told that swimming in the sea requires great care when there are large waves – there is no lifeguard.

Facilities

Two large, clean and modern toilet blocks provide British style WCs (some with bidets), washbasins, some with hot water. Laundry sinks are outside but covered. Motorcaravan services. Supermarket. Bar and restaurant (1/7-31/8). Satellite TV. Swimming pool (1/7-10/9). Off site: Bus from the gate to nearby towns. Shop, restaurant and bar within 200 m. Beach (no lifeguard).

Open: All year, excl. 25 December.

Directions

Turn from EN 242 (Caldas - Nazaré) road northeast of São Martinho do Porto. Site is clearly signed. GPS: N39:31.370 W09:07.380

Charges guide

Per person	€ 3,65 - € 4,30
child (4-10 yrs)	€ 1,79 - € 2,10
pitch	€ 6,92 - € 9,85
electricity	€ 2,60

PO8110 Orbitur Camping Valado

Rua dos Combatentes do Ultramar 2, Valado, P-2450-148 Nazaré (Leiria)

Tel: **262 561 111**. Email: **info@orbitur.pt** **www.alanrogers.com/PO8110**

This popular site is close to the old, traditional fishing port of Nazaré which has now become something of a holiday resort and popular with coach parties. The large sandy beach in the town (about 2 km. steeply downhill) is sheltered by headlands and provides good swimming. The campsite is on undulating ground under tall pine trees, has 503 pitches and, although some smallish individual pitches with electricity and water can be reserved, the bulk of the site is not marked out and units are close together during July/August. About 375 electrical connections are available.

Facilities

The three toilet blocks have British and Turkish style WCs, washbasins (some cold water) and 17 hot showers, all very clean when inspected. Laundry. Motorcaravan services. Gas supplies. Supermarket. Bar, snack bar and restaurant with terrace (Easter and June - Oct). TV/general room. Playground. Tennis. Off site: Bus service 20 m. Fishing and bicycle hire 2 km.

Open: 1 February - 30 November.

Directions

Site is on the Nazaré - Alcobaca N8-5 road, 2 km. east of Nazaré. GPS: N39:35.604 W09:01.670

Charges guide

Per person	€ 2,30 - € 4,10
child (5-10 yrs)	€ 1,20 - € 2,10
caravan and car	€ 5,10 - € 9,30
electricity	€ 2,50 - € 3,10

PO8480 Orbitur Camping Foz do Arelho

Rua Maldonado Freitas, P-2500-516 Foz do Arelho (Leiria)

Tel: **262 978 683**. Email: **info@orbitur.pt** **www.alanrogers.com/PO8480**

This is a large and roomy ex-municipal site and improvements are still taking place. It is 2 km. from the beach and has a new central complex with a most impressive swimming pool and separated children's pool with lifeguard. Pitches are generally sandy with some hardstandings. They vary in size and are unmarked on two main levels with wide tarmac roads. There is some shade and all touring pitches have electricity (5/15A). The large two storey, brick-faced building contains all the site's leisure facilities but has no ramped access and there are no sanitary facilities for disabled campers. This is a pleasant site with sound facilities but probably not recommended if you have special needs.

Facilities

Four identical modern sanitary buildings (solar heating) with seatless British and Turkish style WCs and free showers. Washing machine in one. No facilities for disabled campers. No chemical disposal point. Supermarket. Bar/snacks and restaurant. (closed November). Children's club. Games room. Small new amphitheatre. Playground – supervision needed. Bus service. Doctor's room. Torches useful. Off site: Bus 500 m. Seaside town 2 km. Fishing 2 km.

Open: All year.

Directions

Site is north of Lisbon and west of Caldos la Rainha. From the A8 take N360 to Foz de Arelho. Site is well signed. GPS: N39:25.840 W09:12.050

Charges guide

Per person	€ 2,70 - € 4,80
child (5-10 yrs)	€ 1,40 - € 2,50
caravan and car	€ 6,70 - € 11,30
electricity	€ 2,50 - € 3,10

PO8100 Orbitur Camping São Pedro de Moel

Rua Volta do Sete, P-2430 São Pedro de Moel (Leiria)

Tel: **244 599 168**. Email: **info@orbitur.pt** **www.alanrogers.com/PO8100**

This quiet and very attractive site is situated under tall pines, on the edge of the rather select small resort of São Pedro de Moel. This is a shady site which can be crowded in July and August. The 525 pitches are in blocks and unmarked (cars may be parked separately) with 404 electrical connections. A few pitches are used for permanent units. Although there are areas of soft sand, there should be no problem in finding a firm place. The large restaurant and bar are modern as is the superb swimming pool, paddling pool and flume (there is a lifeguard).

Facilities

Four clean toilet blocks have mainly British style toilets (some with bidets), some washbasins with hot water. Hot showers are mostly in one block. Laundry. Motorcaravan services. Gas supplies. Supermarket. Large restaurant and bar with terrace (closed in November). Swimming pools (31/3-30/9). Satellite TV. Games room. Playground. Tennis. Off site: Bus service 100 m. Beach 500 m. Fishing 1 km.

Open: All year.

Directions

Site is 9 km. west of Marinha Grande, on the right as you enter São Pedro de Moel. GPS: N39:45.450 W09:01.600

Charges guide

Per person	€ 2,70 - € 4,80
child (5-10 yrs)	€ 1,40 - € 2,50
caravan and car	€ 6,70 - € 11,30
electricity	€ 2,50 - € 3,10

Off season discounts (up to 70%).

PO8460 Camping Caravaning Vale Paraiso

EN242, P-2450-138 Nazaré (Leiria)

Tel: **262 561 800**. Email: **info@valeparaiso.com** **www.alanrogers.com/PO8460**

A pleasant, well managed site, Vale Paraiso improves every year, with the latest additions being new reception buildings and pool areas. The owners are keen to welcome British visitors and English is spoken. The site is by the main N242 road in eight hectares of undulating pine woods. There are 650 shady pitches, many on sandy ground only suitable for tents. For other units there are around 250 individual pitches of varying size on harder ground with electricity available. A large range of sporting and leisure activities includes an excellent outdoor pool and paddling pool.

Facilities

Spotless sanitary facilities have hot water throughout. Nearly all WCs are British style. Facilities for disabled visitors. Baby baths. Laaundry facilities. Motorcaravan services. Supermarket (1/5-30/9). Restaurant (15/5-15/9). Café/bar with satellite TV. Takeaway. Tabac. Swimming and paddling pools (March - Sept; free for under 11s). Pétanque. Leisure games. Amusement hall. Bicycle hire. Safety deposit. E-mail and fax facilities. Apartments and mobile homes to rent. Off site: Bus from gate. Fishing 2 km. Boat launching 2 km. Riding 6 km. Golf 40 km.

Open: 1 January - 18 December and 28 - 31 December.

Directions

Site is 2 km. north of Nazaré on the EN242 Marinha Grande road. GPS: N39:37.131 W09:03.230

Charges 2009

Per person	€ 3,20 - € 4,50
child (3-10 yrs)	€ 1,60 - € 2,30
pitch	€ 6,00 - € 17,80
electricity (4-10A)	€ 2,70

Credit cards accepted for amounts over € 150. Camping Cheques accepted.

PO8050 Orbitur Camping São Jacinto

EN 327 km 20, São Jacinto, P-3800-909 Aveiro (Aveiro)

Tel: **234 838 284**. Email: **info@orbitur.pt** **www.alanrogers.com/PO8050**

This small site is in the Sao Jacinto nature reserve, on a peninsula between the Atlantic and the Barrinha, with views to the mountains beyond. The area is a weekend resort for locals and can be crowded in high season – it may therefore be difficult to find space in July/Aug, particularly for larger units. This is not a large site, taking 169 units on unmarked pitches, but in most places trees provide natural limits and shade. Swimming and fishing are both possible in the adjacent Ria, or the sea, 20 minutes walk from a guarded back gate. A deep bore-hole supplies the site with drinking water.

Facilities

Two toilet blocks, very clean when inspected, contain the usual facilities. Dishwashing and laundry sinks. Washing machine and ironing board in a separate part of the toilet block. Motorcaravan services. Shop. Restaurant, bar and snack bar (Easter and June-Oct). Playground. Five bungalows to rent. Off site: Bus service 20 m. Fishing 200 m. Bicycle hire 10 km.

Open: 1 February - 31 October.

Directions

Turn off N109 at Estarreja to N109-5 to cross bridge over Ria da Gosta Nova and on to Torreira and São Jacinto. From Porto go south N1/09, turn for Ovar on the N327 which leads to São Jacinto. GPS: N40:40.498 W08:43.377

Charges guide

Per person	€ 2,30 - € 4,10
caravan and car	€ 5,10 - € 9,30
electricity	€ 2,50 - € 3,10

PO8400 Campismo O Tamanco

Rua do Louriçal 11, Casas Brancas, P-3105-158 Outeiro do Louriçal (Leiria)

Tel: **236 952 551**. Email: **tamanco@mac.com** **www.alanrogers.com/PO8400**

O Tamanco is a peaceful countryside site, with a homely almost farmstead atmosphere; you will have chickens and ducks wandering around and there is a Burro here. The young Dutch owners, Irene and Hans, are sure to give you a warm welcome at this delightful little site. The 75 good sized pitches are separated by cordons of all manner of fruit trees, ornamental trees and flowering shrubs, on level grassy ground. There is electricity to 72 pitches and five pitches are suitable for large motorhomes. The site is lit and there is nearly always space available.

Facilities

The single toilet block provides very clean and generously sized facilities including washbasins in cabins, with easy access for disabled visitors. As facilities are limited they may be busy in peak periods. Hot water throughout. Washing machine. Bar/restaurant. Roofed patio with fireplace. TV room/lounge (satellite). Internet access. Swimming pool. Off site: Bus service 1 km. Lake 2 km. Beach 11 km. Market in nearby Lourical every Sunday.

Open: All year.

Directions

From the A17 Lisboa - Porto, take exit 10 for Carrico, turn right at the roundabout and O Tamanco is on the left. GPS: N39:59.500 W08:47.310

Charges 2009

Per person	€ 3,90
child (up to 10 yrs)	€ 2,10
pitch with electricity	€ 8,45 - € 10,85

No credit cards.

PO8370 Parque de Campismo de Cerdeira

P-4840 Campo do Gerês (Braga)

Tel: **253 351 005**. Email: **info@parquecerdeira.com** **www.alanrogers.com/PO8370**

Located in the National Park of Peneda Gerês, amidst spectacular mountain scenery, this excellent site offers modern facilities in a truly natural area. The National Park is home to all manner of flora, fauna and wildlife, including the roebuck, wolf and wild boar. The well fenced, professional and peaceful site has some 600 good sized, unmarked, mostly level, grassy pitches in a shady woodland setting. Electricity is available for most pitches, though some long leads may be required. A very large timber complex, tastefully designed with the use of noble materials, granite and wood, provides a superb restaurant with a comprehensive menu. A pool with a separated section for toddlers is a welcome, cooling relief in the height of summer. There are unlimited opportunities in the immediate area for fishing, riding, canoeing, mountain biking and climbing, so take advantage of this quality mountain hospitality.

Facilities

Four very clean sanitary blocks provide mixed style WCs, controllable showers and hot water. Laundry. Gas supplies. Shop. Restaurant/bar (1/4- 6/10, plus weekends and holidays). Playground. Bicycle hire. TV room (satellite). Medical post. Good tennis courts. Minigolf. Car wash. Barbecue area. Torches useful. English spoken. Attractive bungalows to rent. Dogs are not accepted June - August. Off site: Fishing and riding 800 m.

Open: All year.

Directions

From north, N103 (Braga - Chaves), turn left at N205 (7.5 km. north of Braga). Follow N205 to Caldelas Terras de Bouro and Covide where site is clearly marked to Campo do Gerês. An eastern approach from the N103 is for the adventurous but will be rewarded by magnificent views over mountains and lakes. GPS: N41:45.811 W08:11.330

Charges 2009

Per person	€ 3,20 - € 5,00
child (5-11 yrs)	€ 2,00 - € 3,20
pitch	€ 4,30 - € 9,00
electricity (6/10A)	€ 2,50 - € 3,75

PO8030 Orbitur Camping Rio Alto

EN13 km 13 Rio Alto-Est, Estela, P-4570-275 Póvoa de Varzim (Porto)

Tel: **252 615 699**. Email: **info@orbitur.pt** **www.alanrogers.com/PO8030**

This site makes an excellent base for visiting Porto which is some 35 km. south of Estela. It has around 700 pitches on sandy terrain and is next to what is virtually a private beach. There are some hardstandings for caravans and motorcaravans and electrical connections to most pitches (long leads may be required). The area for tents is furthest from the beach and windswept, stunted pines give some shade. There are arrangements for car parking away from camping areas in peak season. There is a quality restaurant, snack bar and a large swimming pool across the road from reception.

Facilities

Four refurbished and well equipped toilet blocks have hot water. Laundry facilities. Facilities for disabled campers. Gas supplies. Shop (1/6-31/10). Restaurant, bar, snack bar (1/5-31/10). Swimming pool (1/6-30/9). Tennis. Playground. Games room. Surfing. TV. Medical post. Car wash. Evening entertainment twice weekly in season. Off site: Fishing. Golf. Bicycle hire. Riding (all within 5 km).

Open: All year.

Directions

From A28 leave at exit 18 signed Fao/Apuila. At roundabout take N13 in direction of Pavoa de Varzim/Porto for 2.5 km. At Hotel Contriz, turn right onto narrow cobbled road. Site well signed in 2 km. GPS: N41:26.702 W08:45.460

Charges guide

Per person	€ 2,90 - € 5,40
caravan and car	€ 6,80 - € 12,00
electricity (5/15A)	€ 2,50 - € 3,10

Slovakia is a small scale country in the heart of Europe, consisting of a narrow strip of land between the spectacular Tatra Mountains and the river Danube. Picturesque, there are historic castles, evergreen forests, rugged mountains, cave formations, and deep lakes and valleys.

CAPITAL: BRATISLAVA

Tourist Office

Czech & Slovak Tourist Centre
16 Frognal Parade,
Finchley Road,
London NW3 5HG
Tel: 020 7794 3263 Fax: 020 7794 3265
E-mail: info@czechtravel.co.uk
Internet: www.slovakiatourism.sk

Slovakia has much to offer the visitor with an abundance of year round natural beauty. Its terrain varies impressively; the Carpathian Arc Mountains take up nearly half the country and include the Tatra Mountains, with their rugged peaks, deciduous forests and lakes. Southern and eastern Slovakia is mainly a lowland region and home to many thermal springs, with several open to the public for bathing. Many Hungarians have moved to this area and there is a strong Hungarian influence.

Slovakia has over four thousand registered caves, twelve are open to the public and vary from drop stone to glacial; each one claims to have healing benefits for respiratory disorders. The capital, Bratislava is situated on the river Danube and directly below the Carpathian Mountains. Although it may not be as glamorous as Prague, it contains many fascinating buildings from nearly every age and is a lively cheerful city.

Population

5.4 million

Climate

Cold winters and mild summers.
Hot summers and some rain in the eastern lowlands.

Language

Slovak

Telephone

The country code is 00 421.

Money

Currency: The Koruna
Banks: Mon-Fri 08.00-13.00 and 14.00-17.00.

Shops

Mon-Fri 09.00-12.00 and 14.00-18.00.
Some remain open at midday.
Sat 09.00-midday.

Public Holidays

New Year; Easter Mon; May Day; Liberation Day 8 May; Saints Day 5 July; Festival Day 5 July; Constitution Day 1 Sept; All Saints 1 Nov; Christmas 24-26 Dec.

Motoring

A full UK driving licence is acceptable.The major route runs from Bratislava via Trencin, Banska, Bystrica, Zilina and Poprad to Presov. A windscreen sticker which is valid for a year must be purchased at the border crossing for use on certain motorways. Vehicles must be parked on the right.

SK4900 Autocamping Trusalová

SK-03853 Turany (Zilina)

Tel: **043 429 2636**. Email: **autocampingtrusalova@zoznam.sk** **www.alanrogers.com/SK4900**

Autocamping Trusalová is situated right on the southern edge of the Malá Fatra National Park, northeast of the historic town of Martin which has much to offer to tourists. The site is in two halves, one on the left of the entrance and the other behind reception on a slight slope. Surrounded by trees with a stream rushing along one side, pitches are grass from a hard road with room for about 150 units and there are some bungalows. We received a most friendly welcome from the German speaking staff. A quiet, orderly and pleasant campsite.

Facilities

Each half has its own old, but clean and acceptable, toilet provision including hot water in basins, sinks and showers. Motorcaravan service point. Each section has a covered barbecue area with raised fire box, chimney, tables and chairs. TV lounge. Playground. Outdoor chess board. Bicycle hire. Off site: Bar just outside site. Restaurants 500 m. or 1 km. Shops in the village 3 km.

Open: 1 June - 15 September.

Directions

Turn north between the Auto Alles car dealer and the Restaurica of the same name on road 18/E50 near the village of Turany to campsite. GPS: N49:08.300 E19:03.000

Charges guide

Per person	SKK 100
pitch	SKK 100 - 170
electricity	SKK 100

No credit cards.

SK4905 Autocamping Stara Hora

Oravska Priehrada, SK-02901 Namestovo (Zilina)

Tel: **043 552 2223**. Email: **camp.s.hora@stonline.sk** **www.alanrogers.com/SK4905**

Stara Hora has a beautiful location on the Orava artificial lake. It is in the northeast of Slovakia in the Tatra Mountains and attracts visitors from all over Europe which creates a happy and sometimes noisy atmosphere. The site has its own pebble beach with a large grass area behind it for sunbathing. Autocamping Stara Hora is on steeply sloping ground with 160 grassy pitches, all for touring units and with 10A electricity. The lower pitches are level and have good views over the lake, pitches at the top are mainly used by tents.

Facilities

The modern toilet block has British style toilets, open washbasins and controllable hot showers (free). It could be pressed in high season and hot water to the showers is only available from 07.00-10.00 and from 19.00-22.00. Shop for basics. Bar and lakeside bar. Small restaurant. Basic playground (new playground planned). Pedalo, canoe and rowing boat hire. Waterskiing. Fishing (with permit). Torch useful. Off site: Slanica Island.

Open: May - September.

Directions

From Ruzomberok take E77 road north towards Trstena. Turn left in Tvrdosin on the 520 road towards Námestovo. Site is on the right. GPS: N49:23.135 E19:31.657

Charges guide

Per person	€ 2,42
child	€ 1,21
pitch incl. car	€ 3,04
electricity	€ 2,73

SK4910 Autocamping Turiec

Kolonia hviezda 92, SK-03608 Martin (Zilina)

Tel: **043 428 4215**. Email: **recepcia@autocampingturiec.sk** **www.alanrogers.com/SK4910**

Turiec is situated in northeast Slovakia, 1.5 km. from the small village of Vrutky, 4 km. north of Martin, at the foot of the Lucanska Mala Fatra mountains and with castles nearby. This good site has views towards the mountains and is quiet and well maintained. Holiday activities include hiking in summer, skiing in winter, both downhill and cross country. There is room for about 30 units on grass inside a circular tarmac road with some shade from tall trees. Electrical connections are available for all places. You will receive a friendly welcome from Viktor Matovcik and his wife Lydia who are constantly improving the site.

Facilities

One acceptable sanitary block to the side of the camping area, but in winter the facilities in the bungalow at the entrance are used. Cooking facilities. Badminton. Rest room with TV. Small games room. Covered barbecue. Off site: Shop outside entrance. Swimming pool 1.5 km.

Open: All year.

Directions

Site is signed from E18 road (Zilina - Martin) in the village of Vrutky, 3 km. northwest of Martin. Turn south on the bend and follow signs to Martinské Hole. GPS: N49:06.708 E18:53.844

Charges guide

Per unit incl. 2 persons, electricity	€ 17,10
person	€ 4,30
child (6-12 yrs)	€ 2,65
dog	€ 1,30

SK4915 Autocamping Liptovsky Trnovec

SK-03222 Liptovsky Trnovec (Zilina)

Tel: **044 559 8458**. Email: **atc.trnovec@atctrnovec.sk** **www.alanrogers.com/SK4915**

This is a good Slovakian site beside the Liptovská Mara reservoir, also close to the Tatra Mountains which are popular for climbing, hiking and mountain biking. The lake can be used for sailing, surfing, boating and pedaloes. Bicycles are also available for hire. There are 250 pitches, all used for touring units and with 14A electricity. With tarmac access roads, the level pitches are on a circular, grassy field and as pitching is rather haphazard, the site can become crowded in high season. Mature trees provide some shade, but in general this is an open site.

Facilities

Two good modern toilet blocks have British style toilets, washbasins in cabins and showers. Facilities for disabled visitors. Washing machines. Campers' kitchen. Bar with covered terrace and takeaway service. Basic playground. Minigolf. Fishing. Bicycle hire. Canoe hire and boat rental. Games room with arcade machines. Beach. Off site: New Tatralandia Aqua Park nearby. Walking in the Lower Tatra Mountains, or climbing in the Higher Tatra Mountains.

Open: 1 May - 15 October.

Directions

From E50 road take exit for Liptovsky Mikulás and turn left towards Liptovsky Trnovec on 584 road. Continue alongside the lake to site on the left. GPS: N49:06.668 E19:37.767

Charges guide

Per person	SKK 70 - 110
child (4-15 yrs)	SKK 25 - 60
pitch incl. car	SKK 105 - 220

SK4940 Autocamping Neresnica

Neresnická cesta, SK-96001 Zvolen (Banská Bystrica)

Tel: **045 533 2651** **www.alanrogers.com/SK4940**

If you are travelling through Slovakia from Hungary to Poland and looking for a night stop or exploring the central Slovak area, Neresnica is well situated, being on the main 66/E77 highway just to the south of the town. The glories of Zvolen lie in the past rather than the present, but this basic but clean site, under private ownership, is surrounded by trees with a rushing steam along one side. The level site has room for 65 units with unmarked pitches of grass from tarmac roads and electrical connections (10A) for about 60%. Apart from Slovak, only German is spoken.

Facilities

Two sanitary blocks, one at either end of the site, are basic rather than luxurious but clean with cold water in cabins for washing and hot water for dishes. A few showers have been installed in former WC compartments, but they are at least 16 inches high and, if you are over 5 ft tall, you might have a problem. Covered areas have barbecue pits with tables and benches. Restaurant (at entrance) sometimes provides music from a violin, cello, zither trio. Off site: Shops 200 m. Swimming pool 200 m.

Open: 1 April - 20 October.

Directions

From Zvolen centre take road 66/E77 towards Sahy. Site is signed as Neresnica and/or Camping Salas at junction with 50/E571 road to Lucenec. The site is on the left just beyond the Slovnaft petrol station. GPS: N48:33.868 E19:08.049

Charges guide

Per person	SKK 100
child (10-18 yrs)	SKK 50
pitch	SKK 90 - 120
electricity	SKK 65

SK4920 Autocamping Trencin

Na Ostrove, P.O. Box 10, SK-91101 Trencin (Trencin)

Tel: **032 743 4013**. Email: **autocamping.tn@mail.pvt.sk** **www.alanrogers.com/SK4920**

Trencin is an interesting town with a long history and dominated by the partly restored castle which towers high above. The small site with room for 30 touring units (all with electricity) and rooms to let, stands on an island about one kilometre from the town centre opposite a large sports complex. Pitches occupy a grass area surrounded by bungalows, although when the site is busy, campers park between and almost on top of the bungalows. The castle is high on one side and woods and hills on the other. There is some rail noise. This is a very neat, tidy and friendly site.

Facilities

Toilet block is old but tiled and clean with hot water in the washbasins (in cabins with curtains) and showers (doors and curtains) under cover but not enclosed. Hot water for washing clothes and dishes. Electric cookers, fridge/freezer, tables and chairs. Little shade. Bar in high season. Boating and fishing in river. Off site: Restaurants 200 m. Shops 300 m. Tennis, indoor and outdoor swimming pools within 400 m.

Open: 1 May - 15 September.

Directions

Initially you need to follow signs for 61 Zilina and having crossed the river, bear left. Turn left at first main traffic lights, under the railway and left again. Then turn right after the stadium. Site is over the canal, on the left. GPS: N48:52.996 E18:02.440

Charges guide

Per person	SKK 170 - 200
pitch	SKK 50 - 150
electricity	SKK 100

No credit cards.

SK4925 Camping Lodenica

Slnava 1, SK-92101 Piestany (Trnava)

Tel: **033 762 6093** **www.alanrogers.com/SK4925**

This site is 1.5 kilometres south of the most important spa in the Slovak Republic and lies in a quiet forest setting on the shores of the Sinava lake, close to the town of Piestany. Lodenica is divided into three main camping areas with 250 pitches (150 with electricity), the first right behind the entrance and a large, circular field with pitching close to the electricity boxes. Pitches on the second field to the back are separated by low hedges and the third field is in the 'Arena' and surrounded by a wooden fence, rather like a fortress. Among the pitches are mature trees which provide shade.

Facilities

One traditional toilet block with toilets, open style washbasins (cold water only) and hot showers. Laundry with 5 sinks. Campers' kitchen with gas hob and oven. Good value bar/restaurant. Playing field. Rowing boats, canoes and surfboards for hire at the lake. Water-skiing. Bicycle hire. Off site: Fishing and beach 200 m. Piestany town with shops, hot food, bars, indoor and outdoor pools 1.5 km. Riding 5 km.

Open: 1 May - 30 September.

Directions

Take motorway form Bratislava towards Trencin and exit at Piestany. At first main junction turn right at traffic lights and go south. Turn left at the hospital towards site. GPS: N48:39.450 E17:49.442

Charges guide

Per person	SKK 90
pitch	SKK 120
electricity	SKK 80

No credit cards.

SK4950 Autocamping Zlaté Piesky

Senecka cesta c 2, SK-82104 Bratislava (Bratislava)

Tel: **024 445 0592**. Email: **kempi@netax.sk** **www.alanrogers.com/SK4950**

Bratislava undoubtedly has charm, being on the Danube and having a number of interesting buildings and churches in its centre. However, industry around the city, particularly en route to the site from the south, presents an ugly picture and gives no hints of the hidden charms. Zlaté Piesky (golden sands) is part of a large, lakeside sports complex which is also used during the day in summer by local residents. The site is on the northeast edge of the city with 200 touring pitches, 120 with electrical connections, on level grass under tall trees. For a night stop or a short stay, this might suit.

Facilities

Four toilet blocks, two for campers and two for day visitors, are good and clean. Two restaurants, one with waiter service, the other self service. Many small snack bars. Shops. Lake for swimming and watersports with large beach area. Minigolf. Play areas. Room with billiards and electronic games. Disco. Off site: Tesco supermarket nearby.

Open: 1 May - 15 October.

Directions

From E75 Bratislava - Trencin motorway exit towards Zlaté Piesky just north of the airport. Head towards Bratislava on the 61/E571 and immediately after the footbridge turn left at the traffic lights. The site is a little way ahead on the left.
GPS: N48:11.295 E17:11.138

Charges guide

Per person	SKK 100
pitch	SKK 110 - 160
electricity	SKK 90

No credit cards.

SK4980 Autocamping Levocská Dolina

Kovásvá vila 2, SK-05401 Levoca (Presov)

Tel: **053 451 2701**. Email: **rzlevoca@pobox.sk** **www.alanrogers.com/SK4980**

According to the owner, Mr Rusnák, this campsite is one of the top ten sites in Slovakia and we agree. The site forms part of a restaurant and pension business and the good value restaurant is welcoming. The entrance is attractively landscaped with varieties of shrubs and colourful flowers and the whole site looks well cared for. There are 60 pitches (all for tourers) and 27 electricity connections. On grassy fields with views of the mountains, there is some terracing. The main road runs steeply uphill and then continues on grass roads. This may cause larger units some difficulty in bad weather.

Facilities

Well renovated toilet block with British style toilets, open washbasins and controllable, hot showers (free). Campers' kitchen. Sauna. Whirlpool. Bar/restaurant. Basic playground. Torch useful. Off site: Lake with pedalo hire 300 m. Dobsinska Ice Caves and Slovakian Paradise. Town of Levoca.

Open: All year.

Directions

From Liptovsky Mikulás, take the E50 road east towards Levoca. In Levoca follow site signs. Site is 3 km. north of the town.
GPS: N49:02.939 E20:35.210

Charges guide

Per person	SKK 85
pitch	SKK 40 - 150
electricity	SKK 110

MAP 1

What Slovenia lacks in size it makes up for in exceptional beauty. Situated between Italy, Austria, Hungary and Croatia, it has a diverse landscape with stunning Alps, rivers, forests and the warm Adriatic coast.

CAPITAL: LJUBLJANA

Tourist Office

Slovenian Tourist Office
South Marlands, Itchingfield,
Horsham RH13 0NN
Tel: 0870 225 5305
E-mail: slovenia.tourism@virgin.net
Internet: www.slovenia.info

With its snow capped Julian Alps and the picturesque Triglav National park that includes the beautiful lakes of Bled and Bohinj, and the peaceful Soca River, it is no wonder that the northwest region of Slovenia is so popular. Stretching from the Alps down to the Adriatic coast is the picturesque Karst region, with pretty olive groves and thousands of spectacular underground caves, including the Postojna and Skocjan caves. Although small, the Adriatic coast has several bustling beach towns such as the Italianised Koper resort and the historic port of Piran, with many opportunities for watersports and sunbathing. The capital Ljubljana is centrally located, with Renaissance, Baroque and Art Nouveau architecture, you will find most points of interest are along the Ljubljana river. Heading eastwards the landscape becomes gently rolling hills, and is largely given over to vines (home of Lutomer Riesling). Savinja with its spectacular Alps is the main area for producing wine.

Population

2 million

Climate

Warm summers, cold winters with snow in the Alps.

Language

Slovene, with German often spoken in the north and Italian in the west.

Telephone

The country code is 386.

Money

Currency: The Euro. Banks: Mon-Fri 08.30-16.30 with a lunch break 12.30-14.00, plus Saturday mornings 08.30-11.30.

Public Holidays

New Year; Culture Day 8 Feb; Easter Monday; Resistance Day 27 Apr; Labour Day 1-2 May; National Day 25 Jun; Peoples' Day 22 July; Assumption; Reformation Day 31 Oct; All Saint's Day; Christmas Day; Independence Day 26 Dec.

Motoring

A small, but expanding network of motorways. A 'vignette' system for motorway travel is in place. The cost is around € 35 (for a six month vignette) and they can be purchased at petrol stations and DARS offices in Slovenia and neighbouring countries near the border. For more information: www.cestnina.si. Winter driving equipment (winter tyres or snow chains) is mandatory between 15 Nov and 15 March. By law, you must have your headlights on **at all times**, while driving in Slovenia. You are also required to carry a reflective jacket, a warning triangle and a first aid kit in the vehicle. Do not drink and drive – any trace of alcohol in your system will lead to prosecution.

SV4150 Camping Kamne

Dovje 9, SLO-4281 Mojstrana
Tel: **045 891 105**. Email: **info@campingkamne.com** **www.alanrogers.com/SV4150**

For visitors proceeding down the 202 road, from Italy or the Wurzen Pass, towards the prime attractions of the twin lakes of Bled and Bohinj, a delightfully informal little site is to be found just outside the village of Mojstrana. For those arriving via the Karavanke Tunnel the diversion along the 202 is very well worth it. Owner Franc Voga opened the site in 1988, on a small terraced orchard. He has steadily developed the facilities, adding a small pool, two tennis courts and improved all other facilities. The little reception doubles as a bar. Locals wander up for a beer and a chat while enjoying the view across the valley of the Julian Alps. The site is popular with walkers as three valleys lead west into the mountains from Mojstrana, including the trail to the ascent of Triglav, at nearly 3,000 m. the highest point of the Julian Alps.

Facilities

The small excellent sanitary block is of a high quality and well maintained. Reception/bar. Small swimming pool. Two tennis courts. TV room. Mountain bike hire. Franc's English is good and his daughter Anna is fluent. Twice weekly excursions to the mountains (free) in July and August. Two new apartments and bungalows now available to rent. Off site: Walking trails.

Open: All year.

Directions

Site is well marked on north side of the 202, 4 km. from Jesenice, just to west of exit for Mojstrana. Site is 4 km. from the Karawanken tunnel.
GPS: N46:27.872 E13:57.472

Charges guide

Per unit incl. 2 persons and electricity	€ 17,50 - € 19,50
child (5-17 yrs)	€ 4,50 - € 5,00
dog	€ 2,00

SV4235 Kamp Klin

Lepena 1, SLO-5232 Soca
Tel: **053 889 513**. Email: **kampklin@volja.net** **www.alanrogers.com/SV4235**

Kamp Klin is next to the confluence of the Soca and Lepenca rivers and is surrounded by mountains. Being next to two rivers, the site is also a suitable base for fishing, kayaking and rafting. The campsite has only 50 pitches, all for tourers and with electricity, on one large, grassy field, connected by a circular, gravel access road. It is attractively landscaped with flowers and young trees, but this also means there is not much shade. Some pitches are right on the bank of the river (unfenced) and there are beautiful views of the river and the mountains. Kamp Klin is privately owned and there is a 'pension' next door, all run by the Zorc family, who serve the local dishes with compe (potatoes), cottage cheese, grilled trout and local salami in the restaurant. The park is close to the Triglav National Park and from here it is only a short drive to the highest point of Slovenia, the Triglav mountain and its beautiful viewpoint with marked walking routes. Like so many Slovenian sites in this area, this is a good holiday base for the active camper.

Facilities

One modern toilet block and a portacabin style unit with toilets and controllable showers. Laundry with sinks. Bar/restaurant. Play field. Fishing (permit required). Torch useful. Off site: Riding 500 m. Bicycle hire 10 km.

Open: All year.

Directions

Site is on the main Kranjska Gora - Bovec road and is well signed in Soca. Access is via a sharp turn from the main road and over a small bridge that may be difficult for larger units.
GPS: N46:19.804 E13:38.640

Charges guide

Per person	€ 5,50 - € 7,20
child (7-12 yrs)	€ 2,80 - € 3,60
electricity	€ 2,40

This is just a sample of the campsites we have inspected and selected in Italy, Croatia & Slovenia. For more campsites and further information, please see the Alan Rogers Italy guide.

Runner up Alan Rogers Awards 2008

SV4210 Camping Sobec

Sobceva cesta 25, SLO-4248 Lesce

Tel: **045 353 700**. Email: **sobec@siol.net**

www.alanrogers.com/SV4210

Sobec is situated in a valley between the Julian Alps and the Karavanke Mountains, in a pine grove between the Sava Dolinka river and a small lake. It is only 3 km. from Bled and 20 km. from the Karavanke Tunnel. There are 500 unmarked pitches on level, grassy fields off tarmac access roads (450 for touring units), all with 16A electricity. Shade is provided by mature pine trees and younger trees separate some pitches. Camping Sobec is surrounded by water – the Sava river borders it on three sides and on the fourth is a small, artificial lake with grassy fields for sunbathing. Some pitches have views over the lake, which has an enclosed area providing safe swimming for children. This site is a good base for an active holiday, since both the Sava Dolinka and the Sava Bohinjka rivers are suitable for canoeing, kayaking, rafting and fishing, whilst the nearby mountains offer challenges for mountain climbing, paragliding and canyoning.

Facilities

Three traditional style toilet blocks (two refurbished, one old) with mainly British style toilets, washbasins in cabins and controllable hot showers. Child size toilets and basins. Well equipped baby room. Facilities for disabled visitors. Laundry facilities. Motorcaravan services. Supermarket, bar/restaurant. Stage for live performances. Playgrounds. Rafting, canyoning and kayaking organised. Miniclub. Tours to Bled and the Narodni National Park organised. Off site: Golf and riding 2 km.

Open: 21 April - 30 September.

Directions

Site is off the main road from Lesce to Bled and well signed just outside Lesce.
GPS: N46:21.364 E14:08.995

Charges guide

Per person	€ 10,20 - € 12,00
child (7-14 yrs)	€ 7,70 - € 9,00
electricity (16A)	€ 3,20
dog	€ 3,20

SV4200 Camping Bled

Kidriceva 10c Sl, SLO-4260 Bled

Tel: **045 752 000**. Email: **info@camping-bled.com** **www.alanrogers.com/SV4200**

On the western tip of Lake Bled is Camping Bled. The waterfront here is a small public beach immediately behind which gently runs a sloping narrow wooded valley. Pitches at the front, used mainly for over-nighters, are now marked, separated by trees and enlarged, bringing the total number down to 280. In areas at the back, visitors are free to pitch where they like. Some visitors might be disturbed by the noise coming from trains as they trundle out of a high tunnel overlooking the campsite on the line from Bled to Bohinj. But this is a small price to pay for the pleasure of being in a pleasant site from which the lake, its famous little island, its castle and its town can be explored on foot or by boat. Unlike at many other Slovenian sites the number of statics (and semi-statics) here appears to be carefully controlled with touring caravans, motorcaravans and tents predominating.

Facilities

Toilet facilities in five blocks are of a high standard (with free hot showers). Two blocks are heated. Solar energy used. Washing machines and dryers. Motorcaravan services. Gas supplies. Fridge hire. Supermarket. Restaurant. Play area and children's zoo. Games hall. Trampolines. Organised activities in July/August including children's club, excursions and sporting activities. Mountain bike tours. Live entertainment. Fishing. Bicycle hire. Internet access and WiFi. Off site: Riding 3 km. Golf 5 km. Within walking distance of waterfront and town. Restaurants nearby.

Open: 20 March - 15 October.

Directions

From the town of Bled drive along south shore of lake to its western extremity (some 2 km) to the site. GPS: N46:21.693 E14:04.845

Charges guide

Per person	€ 8,50 - € 11,50
child (7-13 yrs)	€ 5,95 - € 8,05
electricity	€ 3,00
dog	€ 1,50 - € 2,50

Less 10% for stays over 6 days. Camping Cheques accepted.

SV4250 Camping Danica Bohinj

Triglavska 60, SLO-4265 Bohinjska Bistrica

Tel: **045 747 820**. Email: **info@camp-danica.si** **www.alanrogers.com/SV4250**

For those wanting to visit the famous Bohinj valley, which stretches like a fjord right into the heart of the Julian Alps, an ideal site is Danica Bohinj which lies in the valley 3 km. downstream of the lake. Danica occupies a rural site that stretches from the main road leading into Bohinj from Bled (25 km. away), to the bank of the newly formed Sava river. It is basically flat meadow, broken up by lines of natural woodland. This excellent site has 165 pitches, 145 for touring units, all with 10A electricity and forms an ideal base for the many sporting activities the area has to offer.

Facilities

Two good toilet blocks with open plan washbasins and hot showers. Facilities for disabled visitors. Laundry facilities (expensive). Motorcaravan service point. Small shop. Bar (also used by locals, open until 01.00 and can be noisy). Café. Tennis. Fishing. Bicycle hire. Excursions in the Triglavski National Park. Off site: Riding 6 km. Canoeing, kayaking, rafting and numerous walking and mountain bike trails.

Open: May - September.

Directions

Driving from Bled to Bohinj, the well signed site lies just behind the village of Bohinjska Bistrica on the right hand (north) side of the road. GPS: N46:16.401 E13:56.921

Charges guide

Per person	€ 7,00 - € 10,00
child (7-14 yrs)	€ 5,60 - € 7,50
electricity	€ 2,50
dog	€ 2,00

Less 10% for stays over 7 days.

SV4340 Camping Ljubljana Resort

Dunajska Cesta 270, SLO-1000 Ljubljana

Tel: **015 683 913**. Email: **ljubljana.resort@gpl.si** **www.alanrogers.com/SV4340**

Located only five kilometres north of central Ljubljana on the relatively quiet bank of the river Sava, Ljubljana Resort is an ideal city campsite. This relaxed site is attached to – but effectively separated from – the sparkingly modern Laguna swimming pool complex (open 1/6-15/9). The site has 220 pitches, largely situated between mature trees and all with electricity connections (16A). A modern toilet block is operational in summer while a smaller heated block is opened in winter. The main building and the pool complex provide several bars, restaurants and takeaways to cater for the campsite guests and day visitors. In the far corner of the site an 'adrenaline park' (only under supervision) offers a quick introduction to the Slovenian lifestyle, while a range of more conventional sports (tennis, beach volleyball, indoor badminton and a gym) are here as well.

Facilities

The modern toilet block includes facilities for disabled people, a baby room and children's toilet and shower. Motorcaravan service point. Laundry service. Internet access. Airport transfer service. Bicycle hire. New play area. Animation for children in July and August.
Off site: Ljubljana centre 5 km.

Open: All year.

Directions

From either direction on the northern city ring road, take exit for Ljubljana-Jezica north towards Crnuce for a little over 1 km. (through Dunajska cesta). Site is signed (blue sign) on the right just before railway crossing and bridge over the river.
GPS: N46:05.851 E14:31.122

Charges 2009

Per person	€ 9,00 - € 17,00
child (3-12 yrs)	€ 6,00 - € 13,00
electricity	€ 3,50

Camping Cheques accepted.

LJUBLJANA RESORT
HOTEL & CAMPING
www.ljubljanaresort.si
+386 (0)1 568 39 13
GPS: 46°05'51.61"N 14°31'08.04"E
Dunajska 270 | Ljubljana | Slovenia

SV4265 Lazar Kamp

Gregorciceva, SLO-5222 Kobarid

Tel: **053 885 333**. Email: **edi.lazar@siol.net** **www.alanrogers.com/SV4265**

This new campsite high above the Soca river has a good location. However, the road to the site from the Napoleon Bridge is narrow, twisting and unmade and is not really suitable for most modern motorcaravans or larger caravans, although the owner of the site does insist that it is possible. With a large overhanging cliff face on the left and a low stone wall, or rusting railings on the right (before the 100 foot drop into the river) it is not for the fainthearted. The site is very suitable for tents and those with small outfits and offers 50 pitches (all with electricity) and good facilities.

Facilities

The sanitary block is of a good standard and includes facilities for disabled visitors. Washing machine. Fridge. Bar. Crêperie and grill with terrace area. Internet access. Ranch style clubroom. Excursions and lots of local sporting activities.

Open: 1 April - 31 October.

Directions

Site is on a side road leading east out of Kobarid towards Bosec, just beyond the so-called Napoleon's Bridge. It is not well signed but follow Kamp Koren signs to the bridge then the site is straight on down the narrow unmade road.
GPS: N46:15.308 E13:35.176

Charges guide

Per person	€ 8,00 - € 10,00
child (7-14 yrs)	€ 4,00 - € 5,00
electricity	€ 2,00

SV4270 Kamp Koren Kobarid

Drenzniske Ravne 33, SLO-5222 Kobarid

Tel: **053 891 311**. Email: **info@kamp-koren.si** **www.alanrogers.com/SV4270**

The campsite, run to perfection by Lidija Koren, occupies a flat, tree-lined meadow on a wide ledge which drops down sharply to the Soca river and a new, terraced area behind reception. A small, site with just 60 pitches, it is deservedly very popular with those interested in outdoor sports, including paragliding, canoeing, canyoning, rafting and fishing. Equally, a pleasant atmosphere is generated for those seeking a quiet and relaxing break. The Julian Alps and in particular the Triglav National Park is a wonderful and under-explored part of Slovenia that has much to offer.

Facilities

Two attractive log-built toilet blocks are of a standard worthy of a high class private sports club. Facilities for disabled visitors. Laundry facilities. Motorcaravan services. Shop (March - Nov). Café dispenses light meals, snacks and drinks apparently without much regard to closing hours. Sauna. Play area. Bowling. Fishing. Bicycle hire. Canoe hire. Climbing walls for adults. Off site: Town within walking distance. Riding 5 km. Golf 20 km. Guided tours in the Soca valley and around Slovenia start from the campsite.

Open: 15 March - 1 November.

Directions

Site is on a side road that leads east out of Kobarid towards Bovec, just beyond so-called Napoleon's Bridge, well signed on the left.
GPS: N46:15.045 E13:35.195

Charges guide

Per person	€ 8,50 - € 10,00
child (7-13 yrs)	€ 4,25 - € 5,00
electricity	€ 4,00
dog	€ 1,00

SV4330 Camping Pivka Jama

Veliki Otok 50, SLO-6230 Postojna

Tel: **057 203 993**. Email: **autokamp.pivka.jama@siol.net** **www.alanrogers.com/SV4330**

Postojna is renowned for its extraordinary limestone caves which form one of Slovenia's prime tourist attractions. Pivka Jama is a most convenient site for the visitor, being midway between Ljubljana and Piran and only about an hour's pleasant drive from either. The 300 pitches are not clustered together but nicely segregated under trees and in small clearings, all connected by a neat network of paths and slip roads. Some level, gravel hardstandings are provided. The facilities are both excellent and extensive and run with obvious pride by enthusiastic staff.

Facilities

Two toilet blocks with very good facilities. Washing machines. Motorcaravan service point. Campers' kitchen with hobs. Supermarket. Bar/restaurant. Swimming pool and paddling pool. Tennis. Bicycle hire. Daytrips to Postojna Caves and other excursions organised. Off site: Fishing 5 km. Riding or skiing 10 km. Golf 30 km.

Open: March - October.

Directions

Site is 5 km. from Postojna. Take the road leading east from Postojna and then northwest towards the Postojna Cave. Site is well signed 4 km. further along this road. GPS: N45:48.320 E14:12.274

Charges guide

Per person	€ 9,90
child (7-14 yrs)	€ 7,90
electricity	€ 3,50

SV4405 Camping Menina

Varpolje 105, SLO-3332 Recica ob Savinji

Tel: **035 835 027**. Email: **info@campingmenina.com** **www.alanrogers.com/SV4405**

Menina Camping is in the heart of the 35 km. long Upper Savinja Valley, surrounded by 2,500 m. high mountains and unspoilt nature. It is being improved every year by the young, enthusiastic owner, Jurij Kolenc and has 200 pitches, all for touring units, on grassy fields under mature trees and with access from gravel roads. All have 6-10A electricity. The Savinja river runs along one side of the site, but if its water is too cold for swimming, the site also has a lake which can be used for swimming as well. This site is a perfect base for walking or mountain biking in the mountains.

Facilities

Two toilet blocks (one new) have modern fittings with toilets, open plan washbasins and controllable hot showers. Motorcaravan service point. Bar/restaurant with open air terrace (evenings only) and open air kitchen. Sauna. Playing field. Play area. Fishing. Mountain bike hire. Giant chess. Russian bowling. Excursions (52). Live music and camp fire gatherings. Indian village. Hostel. Skiing in winter. Off site: Fishing 2 km. Recica and other villages with much culture are close. Indian sauna at Coze.

Open: 1 April - 15 November.

Directions

From Ljubljana take A1 towards Celje. Exit at Sentupert and turn north towards Mozirje. Follow signs Recica ob Savinj from there. Continue through Recica to Nizka and follow site signs.
GPS: N46:18.701 E14:54.548

Charges guide

Per person	€ 7,00 - € 8,00
child (5-15 yrs)	€ 4,00 - € 5,00
electricity	€ 2,80 - € 4,20
dog	€ 2,50

SV4440 Camping Terme Ptuj

Pot v toplice 9, SLO-2251 Ptuj

Tel: **027 494 100**. Email: **info@terme-ptuj.si** www.alanrogers.com/SV4440

Camping Terme Ptuj is close to the river, just outside the interesting town of Ptuj. It is a small site with only 100 level pitches, all for tourers and all with 10A electricity. In two areas, the pitches to the left are on part grass and part gravel hardstanding and are mainly used for motorcaravans. The pitches on the right hand side are on grass under mature trees, off a circular, gravel access road. In this area a promising new toilet block was being built when we visited. The main attraction of this site is clearly the adjacent thermal spa and fun pool complex that also attracts many local visitors. It has several slides and fun pools, as well as a sauna, solarium and spa bath. The swimming pools are free for campsite guests. This site would also be a useful stopover en-route to Croatia and the beautiful historic towns of Ptuj and Maribor are well worth a visit.

Facilities

Modern toilet block with British and Turkish style toilets, open washbasins and controllable, hot showers (free). En-suite facilities for disabled visitors with toilet and basin. Two washing machines. Football field. Torch useful. Off site: Large thermal spa 100 m. Bar/restaurant and snack bar 100 m.

Open: All year.

Directions

From Maribor go southeast towards Ptuj and follow the site signs. Site is on the left before you cross the river and not very well signed.
GPS: N46:25.361 E15:51.297

Charges guide

Per person	€ 12,50 - € 15,50
child (4-14 yrs)	€ 6,25 - € 10,85
electricity	€ 3,50

Camping Cheques accepted.

One of the largest countries in Europe with glorious beaches, a fantastic sunshine record, vibrant towns and laid back sleepy villages, plus a diversity of landscape, culture and artistic traditions, Spain has all the ingredients for a great holiday.

CAPITAL: MADRID

Tourist Office

Spanish Tourist Office,
PO Box 4009, London W1A 6NB
Tel: 0845 940 0180
Email: londres@tourspain.es
Internet: www.spain.info

Spain has a huge choice of beach resorts. With charming villages and attractive resorts, the Costa Brava boasts spectacular scenery with towering cliffs and sheltered coves. There are plenty of lively resorts, including Lloret, Tossa and Calella, plus several quieter ones. Further along the east coast, the Costa del Azahar stretches from Vinaròs to Almanzora, with the great port of Valencia in the centre. Orange groves abound. The central section of the coastline the Costa Blanca, has 170 miles or so of silvery-white beaches. Benidorm is the most popular resort. The Costa del Sol lies in the south, home to more beaches and brilliant sunshine, whilst in the north the Costa Verde is largely unspoiled, with clean water, sandy beaches and rocky coves against a backdrop of mountains.

Beaches and sunshine aside, Spain also has plenty of great cities and towns to explore, including Barcelona, Valencia, Seville, Madrid, Toledo and Bilbao, all offering an array of sights, galleries and museums.

Population

39.5 million

Climate

Spain has a very varied climate. The north is temperate with most of the rainfall; dry and very hot in the centre; subtropical along the Mediterranean.

Language

Castilian Spanish is spoken by most people with Catalan (northeast), Basque (north) and Galician (northwest) used in their respective areas.

Telephone

The country code is 00 34.

Money

Currency: The Euro
Banks: Mon-Fri 09.00-14.00.
Sat 09.00-13.00.

Shops

Mon-Sat 09.00-13.00/14.00 and 15.00/16.00-19.30/20.00. Many close later.

Public Holidays

New Year; Epiphany; Saint's Day 19 Mar; Maundy Thurs; Good Fri; Easter Mon; Labour Day; Saint's Day 25 July; Assumption 15 Aug; National Day 12 Oct; All Saints Day 1 Nov; Constitution Day 6 Dec; Immaculate Conception 8 Dec; Christmas Day.

Motoring

The surface of the main roads is on the whole good, although secondary roads in some rural areas can be rough and winding. Tolls are payable on certain roads and for the Cadi Tunnel, Vallvidrera Tunnel and the Tunnel de Garraf on the A16.

ES80200 Camping Internacional de Amberes

Playa de la Rubina, E-17487 Empúriabrava (Girona)

Tel: **972 450 507**. Email: **info@campingamberes.com** **www.alanrogers.com/ES80200**

Situated in the 'Venice of Spain', Empúriabrava is interlaced with inland waterways and canals, where many residents and holidaymakers moor their boats directly outside their homes on the canal banks. Internacional de Amberes is a large friendly site 50 m. from the wide, sandy beach, which is bordered on the east and west by the waterway canals. The site has 700 touring pitches, most enjoying some shade from strategically placed trees. All have electricity and water connections.

Facilities

Toilet facilities are in five fully equipped blocks. Washing machines. Motorcaravan services. New modern supermarket, bakery and shop. Restaurant/bar. Disco bar. Takeaway. Pizzeria. Watersports with windsurfing school. Organised sports activities, children's programmes and entertainment. Swimming pool. New playground. Pétanque. Tennis. Internet café and WiFi. Dog Shower. Apartments. Off site: Beach 200 m. Fishing 300 m. Bicycle hire and boat launching 500 m. Riding 1 km. Golf 3 km.

Open: 1 April - 15 October.

Directions

Empúriabrava is north of Girona and east of Figueras on the coast. From AP7/E15 take exit 3 south or exit 4 north (note there is no exit 3 north), then N11 to the C260 towards Roses. At Empúriabrava follow camping signs to site.
GPS: N42:15.160 E03:07.902

Charges 2009

Per person (over 3 yrs)	€ 3,60 - € 4,00
pitch incl. electricity and water (85 sq.m)	€ 14,50 - € 31,50

No credit cards.

ES80800 Camping El Delfin Verde

Ctra de Torroella de Montgrí, E-17257 Torroella de Montgrí (Girona)

Tel: **972 758 454**. Email: **info@eldelfinverde.com** **www.alanrogers.com/ES80800**

A large, popular and high quality site in a quiet location, El Delfin Verde has its own long beach stretching along its frontage. A prime feature of the site is an attractive large pool in the shape of a dolphin with a total area of 1,800 sq.m. El Delfin Verde is a large site with 1,420 touring pitches and around 6,000 visitors at peak times. It is well managed by friendly staff. Level grass pitches nearer the beach are marked and many are separated by small fences and hedging. All have electricity (5/6A) and access to water points. A stream runs through the centre of the site. There is shade in some of the older parts and a particularly pleasant area of pine trees in the centre provides marked but not separated pitches (sandy and not so level).

Facilities

Six excellent large and refurbished toilet blocks plus a seventh smaller block, all with resident cleaners, have showers using desalinated water and some washbasins in cabins. Laundry facilities. Motorcaravan services. Supermarket and shops. Swimming pools (with lifeguard). Two restaurants, grills and pizzerias. Three bars. 'La Vela' barbecue and party area. Large sports area. 2 km. exercise track. Dancing and entertainment weekly in season. Excursions. Bicycle hire. Minigolf. Playground. Trampolines. Fishing. Hairdresser. Car servicing. Gas supplies. Internet access. Dogs are not accepted in high season (11/7-14/8). Off site: Golf 4 km. (20% discount). Riding 4 km.

Open: 4 April - 27 September.

Directions

Torroella de Montgri is close to the coast east of Girona. From A7/E15 take exit 6 and C66 (Palafrugell). Then the GI 642 east to Parlava and turn north on C31. GPS: N42:00.718 E03:11.284

Charges 2009

Per unit incl. 2 person and electricity	€ 30,50 - € 55,00
extra person	€ 4,75 - € 5,50
child (2-9 yrs)	€ 4,00 - € 5,00
dog (excl 11/7-14/8)	€ 4,00

Special offers on long stays in low season.

ES80350 Kawan Village L'Amfora

Runner up Alan Rogers Awards 2008

2 avenida Josep Tarradellas, E-17470 Sant Pere Pescador (Girona)

Tel: **972 520 540**. Email: **info@campingamfora.com** **www.alanrogers.com/ES80350**

This super, spacious site is family run and friendly. It has a Greek theme which is manifested mainly in the restaurant and pool areas. The site is spotlessly clean and well maintained and the owner operates in an environmentally friendly way. There are 830 level, grass pitches (730 for touring) laid out in a grid system, all with 10A electricity. Attractive trees and shrubs have been planted around each pitch. There is good shade in the more mature areas and these pitches include 64 large pitches (180 sq.m), each with an individual sanitary unit (toilet, shower and washbasin). The newer area is more open with less shade and you can choose which you would prefer. Three excellent sanitary blocks (one heated) are fully equipped and offer free hot water, each with staff on almost permanent duty to ensure very high standards are maintained. There is extra provision near the pool area. Access is good for disabled visitors. At the entrance an inviting terraced bar and two restaurants overlook a smart pool complex that includes pools for children and two water slides. In high season (from July) there is ambitious evening entertainment (pub, disco, shows) and an activity programme for children. Right beside the site, the magnificent sandy beach on the Bay of Roses offers good conditions for children and a choice of high season watersport activities.

Facilities

Three main toilet blocks, one heated, provide washbasins in cabins and roomy free showers. Baby rooms. Laundry facilities. Motorcaravan services. Supermarket. Terraced bar, self-service and waiter service restaurants. Pizzeria/takeaway. Restaurant and bar on the beach with limited menu (high season). Disco bar. Swimming pools (1/5-30/9). Pétanque. Tennis. Bicycle hire. Minigolf. Play area. Entertainment and activities. Windsurfing. Boat launching and sailing. Fishing. Exchange facilities. Games and TV rooms. Internet room and WiFi. Car wash. Torches required in beach areas. Off site: Riding 4 km. Golf 15 km.

Open: 4 April - 30 September.

Directions

From the north on A17/E15 take exit 3 onto the N11 towards Figueres and then shortly onto the C260 towards Roses. At Castello d'Empúries turn right onto the GIV-6216 to Sant Pere. From the south on the A17 use exit 5 (L'Escala) and turn to Sant Pere in Viladamat. Site is well signed in the town. GPS: N42:10.888 E03:06.243

Charges 2009

Per person	€ 3,70 - € 5,00
child (2-9 yrs)	free - € 4,00
pitch incl. electricity	€ 16,00 - € 41,00
incl. sanitary unit	€ 25,00 - € 65,00
dog	€ 2,50 - € 4,80

Senior citizens specials. No credit cards. Camping Cheques accepted.

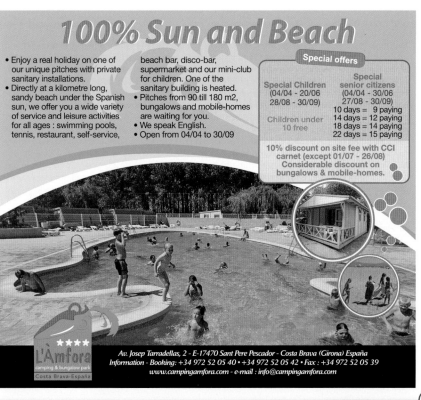

ES80300 Camping Nautic Almata

Ctra Giv 6216, km 11,6, E-17486 Castelló d'Empúries (Girona)

Tel: **972 454 477**. Email: **info@almata.com** **www.alanrogers.com/ES80300**

In the Bay of Roses, south of Empúriabrava and beside the Parc Natural dels Aiguamolls de l'Empordá, this is a site of particular interest for nature lovers (especially bird watchers). Beautifully laid out, it is arranged around the river and waterways, so will suit those who like to be close to water or who enjoy watersports and boating. It is worth visiting because of its unusual aspects and the feeling of being on the canals, as well as being a high quality beachside site. A large site, there are 1,109 well kept, large, numbered pitches, all with electricity and on flat, sandy ground. There are some pitches right on the beach. As you drive through the natural park to the site watch for the warning signs for frogs on the road and enjoy the wild flamingos alongside the road. The name no doubt derives from the fact that boats can be tied up at the small marina within the site and a slipway also gives access to a river and thence to the sea. Throughout the season there is a varied entertainment programme for children and adults. The facilities on this site are impressive. Some tour operators use the site.

Facilities

Toilet blocks of a high standard include some en-suite showers with basins. Good facilities for disabled visitors. Washing machines. Gas supplies. Excellent supermarket. Restaurant and bar. Two separate bars by beach where discos held in main season. Water-ski, diving and windsurfing schools. 300 sq.m. swimming pool. Tennis, squash, volleyball and 'fronton'. Minigolf. Games room. Extensive riding tuition with own stables and stud. Children's play park (near river). Fishing (licence required). Car, motorcycle and bicycle hire. Hairdresser. Torches are useful near beach. Off site: Canal trips 18 km. Aquatic Park 20 km.

Open: 16 May - 20 September, including all facilities.

Directions

Site is signed at 26 km. marker on C252 between Castelló d'Empúries and Vildemat, then 7 km. to site. Alternatively, on Sant Pescador - Castelló d'Empuries road head north and site is signed.
GPS: N42:12.750 E03:05.166

Charges 2009

Per pitch incl. up to 6 persons	€ 22,00 - € 44,00
extra person (over 3 yrs)	€ 2,40 - € 4,75
dog	€ 4,90 - € 6,40
boat or jet ski	€ 8,90 - € 12,00

No credit cards.

ES80400 Camping Las Dunas

Ctra San Marti - Sant Pere, E-17470 Sant Pere Pescador (Girona)

Tel: **972 521 717**. Email: **info@campinglasdunas.com** **www.alanrogers.com/ES80400**

Las Dunas is an extremely large, impressive and well organised site with many on-site activities and an ongoing programme of improvements. It has direct access to a superb sandy beach that stretches along the site for nearly a kilometre with a windsurfing school and beach bar. There is also a much used swimming pool with large double children's pools. Las Dunas is very large, with 1,700 individual hedged pitches (1,479 for tourers) of around 100 sq.m. laid out on flat ground in long, regular parallel rows. All have electrical connections and 180 also have water and drainage. Shade is available in some parts of the site. Pitches are usually available, even in the main season. Much effort has gone into planting palms and new trees here and the results are very attractive. The large restaurant and bar have spacious terraces overlooking the swimming pools and you can enjoy a very pleasant more secluded cavern styled pub. A magnificent disco club is close by in a soundproof building (although people returning from this during the night can be a problem for pitches in the central area of the site). With free quality entertainment of all types in season and positive security arrangements, this is a great site for families with teenagers. Everything is provided on site so you don't need to leave it during your stay. Member of 'Leading Campings Group'.

Facilities

Five excellent large toilet blocks (with resident cleaners 07.00-21.00) have British style toilets, controllable hot showers and washbasins in cabins. Excellent facilities for youngsters, babies and disabled people. Laundry facilities. Motorcaravan services. Extensive supermarket and other shops. Large bar with terrace. Large restaurant. Takeaway. Ice cream parlour. Beach bar in main season. Disco club. Swimming pools. Playgrounds. Tennis. Minigolf. Sailing/windsurfing school and other watersports. Programme of sports, games and entertainment, partly in English (15/6-31/8). Exchange facilities. ATM. Safety deposit. Internet café. WiFi. Dogs taken in one section. Torches required in some areas.

Open: 19 May - 2 September.

Directions

L'Escala is northeast of Girona on the coast between Palamós and Roses. From A7/E15 autostrada take exit 5 towards L'Escala on GI 623. Turn north 2 km. before reaching L'Escala towards Sant Marti d'Ampúrias. Site well signed.
GPS: N42:09.659 E03:08.087

Charges guide

Per person	€ 3,50 - € 5,00
child (2-10 yrs)	€ 3,00 - € 3,25
pitch incl. electricity	€ 14,00 - € 42,00
incl. water and drainage	€ 17,50 - € 51,00
dog	€ 3,20 - € 4,40

All plus 7% VAT.

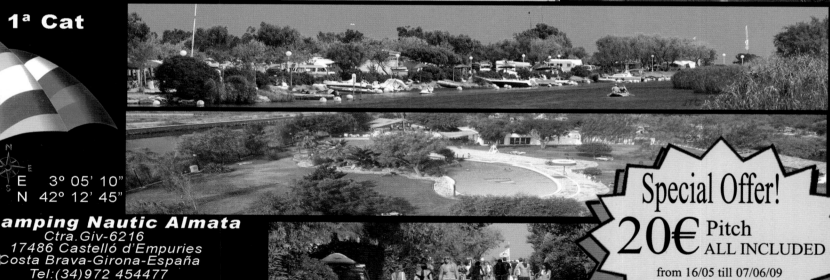

1ª Cat
E 3º 05' 10"
N 42º 12' 45"
amping Nautic Almata
Ctra.Giv-6216
17486 Castelló d'Empuries
Costa Brava-Girona-España
Tel:(34)972 454477
Fax:(34)972 454686
info@almata.com
www.almata.com
Special Offer!
20€ Pitch
ALL INCLUDED
from 16/05 till 07/06/09
Minimum 5 nights
www.almata.com

ES80150 Camping Caravaning La Laguna

Apdo 55, E-17486 Castelló d'Empúries (Girona)
Tel: **972 450 553**. Email: **info@campinglaguna.com** www.alanrogers.com/ES80150

La Laguna is a relaxed, spacious site on an isthmus within a Catalan national maritime park, on the migratory path of many different birds. It has direct access to a sandy beach and the estuary of the river Muga. The owners continue to spend much time and effort on improvements. The double lagoons are a most attractive feature. The 773 pitches (with just 40 mobile homes) are shaded and clearly marked on grass and sand, all with 6/10A electricity. There are also 37 fully serviced pitches. An attractive bar/restaurant overlooks the lagoons and there are two swimming pools (one is heated in low season). A disco operates across the road from reception, keeping the noise away from the main site. A large riding school operates (May - Sept) and there are many other activities. The beach frontage is large and has a sailing school. It is said to be possible to cross over to Empuria Brava when the tide is out. There are many pleasant walks in this area and this a good site for family holidays.

Facilities

Five toilets blocks, placed to avoid long walks. All have been completely rebuilt and provide solar heated water. Laundry room. Bar, restaurant and takeaway. New supermarket. Swimming pools (1/4-26/10). Football. Tennis (free in low seasons). ATM. Minigolf. Windsurfing and sailing schools (July/Aug). Fishing. Miniclub. New play area. Bicycle hire. Riding. Animation programme and competitions. Satellite TV. Internet access and WiFi.
Off site: Boat launching. Golf 15 km. Birdwatching.

Open: 29 March - 25 October.

Directions

Castelló d'Empuries is north of Girona and east of Figueras on the coast. From AP7/E15 take exit 3 south or exit 4 north (note there is no exit 3 north) and then N11 to the C260 towards Roses. At Castelló d'Empúries follow camping signs and a 4 km. unmarked road will take you to the site.
GPS: N42:14.238 E03:07.284

Charges 2009

Per person	€ 5,15 - € 8,95
child (3-10 yrs)	€ 4,15 - € 6,65
pitch	€ 9,55 - € 17,90

Discounts for longer stays and pensioners in low season. No credit cards.

ES80080 Camping Joncar Mar

Ctra Figueres s/n, E-17480 Roses (Girona)

Tel: **972 256 702**. Email: **info@campingjoncarmar.com** **www.alanrogers.com/ES80080**

Family owned since 1977, Jonca Mar is a mature, all year site with basic facilities. Its strength is its location with the beach promenade just outside the gate, and the many resort leisure facilities and local cultural attractions readily available to customers. The site is divided by a minor road and most leisure facilities are positioned on one side of the site. There are no views and the site has some apartment blocks around the periphery. Pitches are small (60 sq.m) with 6A electricity, and the mobile home area in one corner of the site is extremely cramped. Some pitches require long electricity leads. Long stay customers have arranged unpleasant systems of hoses draining into road drains. The modest pool has a shallow area at right angles at one end for children (no lifeguard). The pool is overlooked by a restaurant area offering an uncomplicated 'eat all you can' fixed evening buffet menu, which is open to the street and thus non-camping customers. We met a few regular, low season British customers who stated that this was a two star site in a five star location, but they seemed happy. The site offers a very basic, no frills service.

Facilities

Two dated, refurbished toilet blocks are well positioned . No formal facilities for disabled visitors but one toilet/shower with a wider door. One washing machine. Small shop. Small bar and buffet restaurant. Swimming pool. Basic play area. TV in bar. Limited animation programme. Internet. Torches useful. Off site: Nearest beach 50 m. Bicycle hire 100 m. Riding 3 km. Golf 20 km.

Open: All year.

Directions

From AP7/E15 take exit 3 south or exit 4 north (there is no exit 3 northbound) and then the N11 to the C260 and on to Roses. Site is well signed before you enter the town - follow camping signs initially. GPS: N42:15.983 E03:09.813

Charges guide

Per person	€ 5,90 - € 6,10
pitch incl. electricity	€ 10,90 - € 16,25

ES80310 Camping La Gaviota

Ctra de la Platja s/n, E-17470 Sant Pere Pescador (Girona)

Tel: **972 520 569**. Email: **info@lagaviota.com** **www.alanrogers.com/ES80310**

La Gaviota is a delightful, small, family run site at the end of a beach access road. This ensures a peaceful situation with a choice of the pleasant L-shaped pool or direct beach access to the fine clean beach and slowly shelving access to the water. Everything here is clean and smart and the Gil family are very keen that you will enjoy your time here. There are 165 touring pitches on flat ground with shade and 6A electricity supply. A lush green feel is given to the site by many palms and other semi-tropical trees and shrubs. The restaurant and bar are very pleasant indeed and have a distinct Spanish flavour. The cuisine is reasonably priced but perfectly prepared and served by friendly staff. All facilities are at the reception end of this rectangular site with extra washing up areas at the far end. The guests here were happy and enjoying themselves when we visited. English is spoken.

Facilities

One smart and clean toilet block is near reception. All WCs are British style and the showers are excellent. Superb facilities for disabled visitors. Two excellent family rooms. Washing machine. Gas supplies. Supermarket. Pleasant bar and small, delightful restaurant. Swimming pool. Playground. Games room. Limited animation. Beach sports and windsurfing. Internet. Torches useful. Off site: Boat launching 2 km. Riding 4 km. Golf 15 km.

Open: 20 March - 25 October.

Directions

From the AP7/E15 take exit 4 onto the N11 north towards Figueras and then the C260 towards Roses. At Castelló d'Empúries take the GIV 6216 and continue to Sant Pere Pescador. Site is well signed in the town. GPS: N42:11.341 E3:06.506

Charges 2009

Per person	€ 2,60 - € 3,70
child (under 10 yrs)	€ 1,20 - € 2,60
pitch incl. electricity	€ 16,70 - € 41,70

Spain

ES80120 Kawan Village Mas Nou

Ctra Mas Nou no. 7, E-17486 Castelló d'Empúries (Girona)

Tel: **972 454 175**. Email: **info@campingmasnou.com** **www.alanrogers.com/ES80120**

Some two kilometres from the sea on the Costa Brava, this is a surprisingly tranquil site in two parts on either side of the access road. One part contains the pitches and toilet blocks, the other houses the impressive leisure complex. There are 450 neat, level and marked pitches on grass and sand, a minimum of 70 sq.m. but most 80-100 sq.m. and 300 with electricity (10A). The leisure complex is across the road from reception and features a huge L-shaped swimming pool with a paddling area. A formal restaurant has an adjoining bar, pleasant terrace crêperie and rotisseria under palms. A barbecue/rotisseria in another part of the site offers takeaway meals (in season). The site owns the large souvenir shop on the entrance road. There are many traditional bargains here and it is worth having a good look around as the prices are extremely good. Lots of time and money goes into the cleanliness of this site and it is good very for families. Ask about the origin of the site coat of arms. The Bay of Roses and the Medes islands have a natural beauty and a visit to Dali's house or the museum (the house is fascinating) will prove he was not just a surrealist painter.

Facilities

Three excellent, fully equipped sanitary blocks include baby baths, good facilities for disabled visitors. Washing machines. Supermarket and other shops. Bar/restaurant. Takeaway. Swimming pool with lifeguard (from 1/5). Tennis. Minigolf. Miniclub (July/Aug). Play area. Electronic games. Off site: Riding 1.5 km. Fishing or bicycle hire 2 km. Beach 2.5 km. Aquatic Park. Romanica tour of famous local churches.

Open: 4 April - 27 September.

Directions

From A7 use exit 3. Mas Nou is 2 km. east of Castelló d'Empúries, on the Roses road, 10 km. from Figueras. Do not turn left across the main road but continue to the roundabout and return.
GPS: N42:15.935 E03:06.150

Charges 2009

Per person	€ 2,50 - € 4,80
child (4-11 yrs)	free - € 3,40
pitch	€ 14,70 - € 28,00
electricity	€ 3,20 - € 4,50
dog	free - € 2,20

Camping Cheques accepted.

ES81020 Camping Resort Mas Patoxas Bungalow-Park

Ctra C31 Palafrugell - Pals km 339, E-17256 Pals (Girona)
Tel: **972 636 928**. Email: **info@campingmaspatoxas.com** **www.alanrogers.com/ES81020**

This is a mature and well laid out site for those who prefer to be apart from, but within easy travelling distance of, the beaches (5 km.) and town (1 km). It has a very easy access and is set on a slight slope with wide avenues on level terraces providing over 400 grassy pitches of a minimum 72 sq.m. All have electricity (5A) and water; many have drainage as well. There are some very pleasant views and shade from a variety of mature trees. Both bar and restaurant terraces give views over the pools and distant hills. The air-conditioned restaurant/bar provides both waiter service meals and takeaway food to order (weekends only mid Sept - April) and entertainment takes place on a stage below the terraces during high season. The restaurant menu is varied and very reasonable. We were impressed with the children's miniclub activity when we visited. There is a large, supervised irregularly shaped swimming pool with triple flume, a separate children's pool and a generous sunbathing area at the poolside and on the surrounding grass.

Facilities

Three modern sanitary blocks provide controllable hot showers, some washbasins with hot water. Baby bath and three cabins for children. No specific facilities for disabled people. Laundry facilities. New supermarket (15/3-30/9). Restaurant/bar, pizzeria and takeaway (all 15/3-30/9). Swimming pool (1/5-30/9). Tennis. Entertainment in high season. Fridges for rent. Gas supplies. Torches useful in some areas. Off site: Bus service from site gate. Bicycle hire or riding 2 km. Fishing or golf 4 km.

Open: 12 January - 16 December.

Directions

Site is east of Girona and about 1.5 km. south of Pals at km. 339 on the C31 Figueres-Palamós road, just north of Palafugel.
GPS: N41:57.311 E03:09.478

Charges guide

Per unit incl. 2 persons and electricity	€ 15,00 - € 42,00
extra person	€ 3,60 - € 5,75
child (1-7 yrs)	€ 3,00 - € 4,00
dog	€ 2,10 - € 3,20

Plus 7% VAT. Special low season offers.

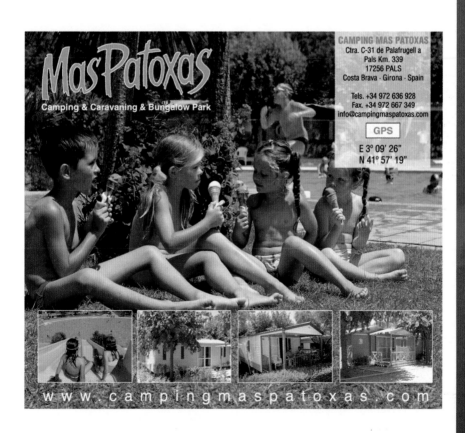

ES81030 Camping El Maset

Playa de Sa Riera, E-17255 Begur (Girona)
Tel: **972 623 023**. Email: **info@campingelmaset.com** **www.alanrogers.com/ES81030**

A delightful little gem of a site in lovely surroundings, El Maset has 107 pitches, of which just 20 are slightly larger for caravans or motorcaravans, the remainder suitable only for tents. The owner of some 40 years, Sr Juan Perez is delightful and his staff are very helpful. The site entrance is steep and access to the caravan pitches can be quite tricky. However, the owner's son will tow your caravan to your pitch. All these pitches have electricity, water and drainage with some shade. Tent pitches are more shaded on attractive rock-walled terraces on the hillside. Access to these seems quite straightforward, with parking for cars not too far away – of necessity the pitches are fairly small. All steep terraced pitches are safely fenced for children. For a small site the amenities are quite extensive, including an unusual elliptical shaped swimming pool. A bar and very homely restaurant offering excellent food, with a terrace giving very pleasant views over the pool and towards the other side of the valley. This small site provides the standard of service normally associated with the very best of the larger sites. It is situated in the tiny resort of Sa Riera with access to the beach (300 m), in a beautiful protected bay with traditional fishing boats taking up one end of the sand. Begur, with its beautiful, small, quite unspoilt bay and beach, is 10 minutes by car.

Facilities

Good sanitary facilities in three small blocks are kept very clean. Baby facilities. Washing machines and dryers. Unit for disabled campers but the ground is steep. Bar/restaurant, takeaway (all season). Shop. Swimming pool (all season). Solarium. Play area. Area for football and basketball. Excellent games room. Internet access and free WiFi. Dogs are not accepted. Off site: Beach and fishing 300 m. Golf and bicycle hire 1 km. Riding 8 km.

Open: Easter - 24 September.

Directions

From the C31 Figueres - Palamós road south of Pals, north of Palafrugell, take GI653 to Begur. Site is 2 km. north of the town; follow signs for Playa de Sa Riera and site (steep entrance). GPS: N41:58.116 E03:12.601

Charges guide

Per person	€ 5,35 - € 7,49
child (1-10 yrs)	€ 3,21 - € 5,35
pitch incl. electricity	€ 15,28 - € 19,28

ES80600 Camping La Ballena Alegre 2

E-17470 Sant Pere Pescador (Girona)
Tel: **902 510 520**. Email: **infb2@ballena-alegre.com** **www.alanrogers.com/ES80600**

La Ballena Alegre 2 is partly in a lightly wooded setting, partly open, and has some 1,800 m. of frontage directly onto an excellent beach of soft golden sand (cleaned daily). They claim that none of the 1,432 pitches is more than 100 m. from the beach. The site has won Spanish tourist board awards and is keen on ecological fitness. The grass pitches are individually numbered and there is a choice of size (up to 100 sq.m). Electrical connections (5/10A) are available in all parts and there are 91 fully serviced pitches. It is a great site for families.

Facilities

Seven well maintained toilet blocks are of a very high standard. Launderette. Motorcaravan services. Gas supplies. Supermarket. Restaurant. Self-service restaurant and bar. Takeaway. Swimming pool complex. Jacuzzi. Tennis. Watersports centre. Fitness centre. Bicycle hire. Playgrounds. Organised activities, sports, entertainment, etc. ATM. WiFi. Off site: Fishing 300 m. Riding 2 km.

Open: 15 May - 20 September.

Directions

From A7 Figueres - Girona autopista take exit 5 to L'Escala GI 623 for 18.5 km. At roundabout take sign to Sant Marti d'Empúries and follow site signs. GPS: N42:09.194 E03:06.749

Charges guide

Per unit incl. 2 persons	€ 24,50 - € 54,00
extra person	€ 3,75 - € 4,50

No credit cards.

ES80500 Camping Aquarius

2015
2008

Playa s/n, E-17470 Sant Pere Pescador (Girona)

Tel: **972 520 003**. Email: **camping@aquarius.es** **www.alanrogers.com/ES80500**

A smart and efficient family site, Aquarius has direct access to a quiet sandy beach that slopes gently and provides good bathing (the sea is shallow for quite a long way out). One third of the site has good shade with a park-like atmosphere. There are 435 pitches with electricity (6/16A). Markus Rupp and his wife are keen to make their visitors' experience a happy one and even issue flags to denote the number of years they have stayed at the site. The site is ideal for those who really like sun and sea, with a quiet situation. Mr Rupp has a background in architecture and a wealth of knowledge on the whole Catalan area and culture.

Facilities

Attractively tiled, fully equipped, large toilet blocks provide some cabins for each sex. Excellent facilities for disabled people, plus baths for children. Superb new block has underfloor heating and features family cabins with showers and basins. Laundry facilities. Gas supplies. Motorcaravan services. Full size refrigerators. Supermarket. Pleasant restaurant and bar with terrace. Takeaway. Children's play centre (with qualified attendant), playground and games hall. TV room. 'Surf Center'. Minigolf. Bicycle hire. Barbecue and dance once weekly when numbers justify. ATM. Internet access. WiFi. Dogs are accepted in one section. (Note: no pool). Off site: Fishing and boat launching 3 km. Riding 6 km. Golf 15 km.

Open: 15 March - 31 October.

Directions

Sant Pere Pescador is south of Perpignan on coast between Roses and L'Escala. From the AP7/E15 take exit 4 onto N11 north towards Figueras and then the C31 towards Torroella de Fluvia. Take the Vilamacolum road east and continue to Sant Pere Pescador. Site is well signed in town.
GPS: N42:10.614 E03:06.478

Charges guide

Per person	€ 3,00 - € 3,85
child (under 12 yrs)	free - € 2,65
pitch	€ 8,05 - € 38,70
electricity	€ 3,15 - € 6,30
animal	€ 2,80 - € 3,70

All plus 7% VAT. No credit cards.
Discounts for pensioners on longer stays.

ES80690 Camping Neus

Cala Montgó, E-17130 L'Escala (Girona)

Tel: **972 770 403**. Email: **info@campingneus.cat** **www.alanrogers.com/ES80690**

Camping Neus is a mature site which is undergoing an ongoing renovation programme. It is set on the edges of a forest under mature pines with 190 pitches arranged on sets of terraces. The pitches vary in size and 160 have 4A electricity. The site facilities are mainly close to the reception building. A small pool with a circular paddling pool is welcome after a hot day's sightseeing and other site amenities include a tennis court and bar/restaurant. The nearest beach at Cala Montgó is 850 m. away and easily accessible on foot. A range of activities is on offer there, including sea kayaking and diving (introductory courses available in the site's pool).

Facilities

Bar. Restaurant. Takeaway. Shop. Play area. Swimming pool. Paddling pool. Entertainment and activities in peak season. Club for children. Off site: Nearest beach 850 m. Fishing. Kayaking. Diving.

Open: 29 May - 13 September.

Directions

Take exit 5 from the AP7 and the GI623 to L'Escala. Continue to Riells and Montgó. Site is on the right shortly before reaching Cala Montgó.
GPS: N42:06.294 E3:09.490

Charges 2009

Per unit incl. 2 persons and electricity	€ 21,00 - € 40,50
extra person	€ 3,00 - € 5,00

CAMPING
neus
L'ESCALA
milà
Small and cosy campsite, 850m from the beach of Cala Montgó l'Escala, with plenty of shade. Large sites (100m2).
www.campingneus.cat
42°10' 50,7"N 3° 15' 83,8"E
COSTA BRAVA

Spain

BOOK THIS SITE
CALL 01580 214000
...we'll arrange everything
The Travel Service

ES80730 Camping Empordá

E-17258 L'Estartit (Girona)

Tel: **972 750 649**. Email: **info@campingemporda.com** **www.alanrogers.com/ES80730**

L'Empordá is a fairly small, family site located 1 km. from the resort of L'Estartit and a similar distance from the nearest beach. This site has been recommended by our Spanish agent and we hope to undertake a full inspection in 2009. Pitches here are of a good size and generally grassy. There are also chalets available for rent. The main appeal of this site will no doubt be the fine beach, 5 km. long, gently shelving and with great views towards the beautiful Medes islands. L'Empordá has a good range of amenities, including a good sized swimming pool and separate children's pool. In high season, the site organises a variety of activities, including aerobics, aquagym and evening entertanment including karaoke and discos.

Facilities

Bar. Restaurant. Takeaway. Shop. Play area. Swimming pool. Children's pool. Entertainment and activities in peak season. Children's club. Chalets for rent. Off site: Nearest beach 1 km. L'Estartit 1 km. Minigolf. Tennis. Fishing.

Open: 15 March - 28 September.

Directions

From the AP7 take Palamos exit and take the C66 towards Palamós. Then take the GI 642 towards Parlava and the GI 643 towards Torroella de Montgri. Lastly, take the GI 641 towards L'Estartit and site is well signed shortly before arriving at the resort centre. GPS: N42:02.944 E3:11.031

Charges guide

Per unit incl. 2 persons and electricity	€ 16,00 - € 26,40
extra person	€ 2,80 - € 5,30
child (3-10 yrs)	€ 1,80 - € 3,90

ES80720 Camping Les Medes

Paratge Camp de L'Arbre, E-17258 L'Estartit (Girona)

Tel: **972 751 805**. Email: **campinglesmedes@cambrescat.es** **www.alanrogers.com/ES80720**

Les Medes is different from some of the 'all singing, all dancing' sites so popular along this coast and the friendly family of Pla-Coll are rightly proud of their award winning site and provide a very warm welcome. With just 172 pitches, the site is small enough for the owners to know their visitors and, being campers themselves, they have been careful in planning their top class facilities and are aware of environmental issues. The level, grassy pitches range in size from 60-80 sq.m. depending on your unit. All have electricity (5/10A) and the larger ones (around half) also have water and drainage. All are clearly marked in rows, but with no separation other than by the deciduous trees which provide summer shade. A cheery children's pool with fountains is behind the unusually shaped pool ringed by palms. This is part of an attractively landscaped feature with a false island, producing a relaxing atmosphere in front of the old Catalan farmhouse buildings.

Facilities

Two modern spacious sanitary blocks can be heated and are extremely well maintained. Top class facilities for disabled people and baby baths. Motorcaravan services. Bar with snacks (all year). Good value restaurant (1/4-31/10). Shop. Swimming pool (1/5-15/9). Indoor pool with sauna, solarium (15/9-15/6). WiFi. Bicycle hire. Dogs only accepted at certain times – check with the site. Off site: Riding 400 m. Fishing 800 m. Beach 800 m.

Open: All year excl. November.

Directions

Site is signed from the main Torroella de Montgri - L'Estartit road GE641. Turn right after Camping Castel Montgri, at Joc's hamburger/pizzeria and follow signs. GPS: N42:02.900 E03:11.273

Charges 2009

Per unit incl. 2 persons	€ 21,05 - € 37,95
extra person	€ 3,95 - € 7,90

No credit cards.

ES81010 Camping Playa Brava

Avenida del Grau 1, E-17256 Platja de Pals (Girona)
Tel: **972 636 894**. Email: **info@playabrava.com** **www.alanrogers.com/ES81010**

This is a pleasant site with an open feel which has access to a large sandy beach and a freshwater lagoon. On both you can enjoy watersports and you may launch your own boat. The ground is level and very grassy with shade provided for the 500 pitches by a mixture of conifer and broad-leaf trees. Electricity is provided (5A) and about a third of the pitches (75-85 sq.m) have water and drainage. The air of spaciousness continues around the large swimming pool. There are no fences but huge grass sunbathing areas, the whole being overlooked by the restaurant terrace. The restaurant is very pleasant and offers a most reasonable menu of the day including wine. An energetic entertainment programme runs during July and August. There are many interesting things to explore in the area including La Bisbal – famous for the ceramics, Dali's museum, the Roman ruins at Empuries Girona and many more. This is a green and pleasant family site.

Facilities

Five modern, fully equipped toilet blocks include facilities for disabled visitors. Washing machines and dryers. Motorcaravan service point. Bar/restaurant. Takeaway. Supermarket. Swimming pool. Tennis. Minigolf. Play area on grass. Fishing. Watersports on river and beach, including sheltered lagoon for windsurfing learners. Internet access. Satellite TV. ATM. Gas supplies. Torches required in some areas. Dogs are not accepted. Off site: Two 18-hole golf courses 1 km. Bicycle hire 3 km. Riding 5 km.

Open: 14 May - 18 September.

Directions

From the AP7/E15 at Girona take exit 6 towards Palamós on the C66. This road changes number to the C31 near La Bisbal. 7.5 km. past La Bisbal, exit to Pals on the GI 652. Follow signs for Platja de Pals. At El Masos take the 6502 east to the coast. Travel through Sa Piera (site signed). Site on left just before road ends. GPS: N42:00.106 E03:11.621

Charges guide

Per person	€ 2,00 - € 3,00
child (2-9 yrs)	free - € 2,00
senior (over 60 yrs)	free - € 3,00
pitch incl. electricity	€ 23,00 - € 38,00

All plus 7% VAT. No credit cards.

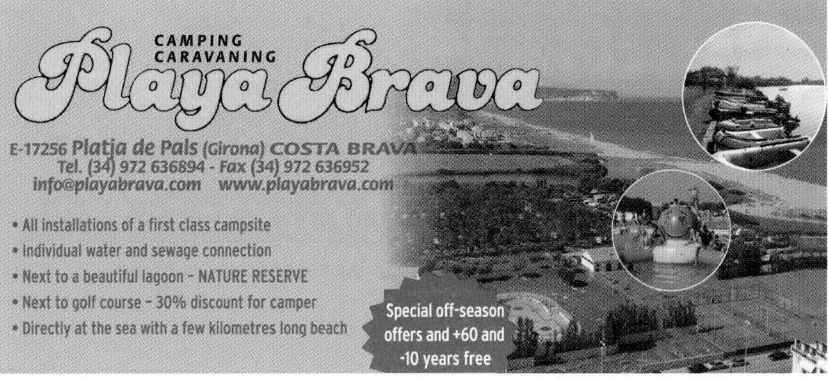

ES81750 Yelloh! Village Mas Sant Josep

Ctra Santa Cristina - Platja d'Aro km 2, E-17246 Santa Cristina d'Aro (Girona)
Tel: **04 66 73 97 39 (FR)**. Email: **info@yellohvillage-mas-sant-josep.com** **www.alanrogers.com/ES81750**

This is a very large well appointed site in two parts. The main side is centred around charming historic buildings, including a beautiful, but mysterious, locked and long unused chapel. Nearby are excellent lagoon style pools with a palm decorated island and a large complex including a bar, restaurant, takeaway foods and entertainment areas. The sporting facilities and fitness areas across the minor road are superb. Here there is another swimming pool and many sport and training possibilities. There are 868 pitches with 200 for touring units in a separate area with shade from established trees.

Facilities

Three older style toilet blocks and the facilities for tourers are better than the long stay areas but all had graffiti when seen. Facilities for disabled visitors and baby rooms. Washing machines. Motorcaravan service point. Supermarket. Bars, restaurant, snack bar and takeaway. Swimming pools. Tennis. Spa room and gym. Animation programme. Internet. ATM. Bicycle hire. Off site: Riding 2 km. Nearest beach 3 km. Fishing 3 km. Golf 6 km.

Open: 29 February - 7 December.

Directions

Site is at Santa Christiana d'Aro, 3 km. from the sea at San Feliu. From AP7 E15 (Girona - Barcelona) take exit 7 and C65 San Filiu road. Site is well signed at the Sant Christina d'Aro roundabout 3 km. from San Filiu. GPS: N41:48.670 E03:01.093

Charges guide

Per unit incl. 2 persons and electricity	€ 17,00 - € 44,00
extra person (over 1 yr)	€ 6,00 - € 7,00

ES81000 Camping Inter-Pals

Avenida Mediterrania, E-17256 Platja de Pals (Girona)

Tel: **972 636 179**. Email: **interpals@interpals.com** **www.alanrogers.com/ES81000**

Set on sloping ground with tall pine trees providing shade and about 500 metres from the beach, Inter-Pals has 625 terraced pitches. It is sister site to no. ES81700 Valldaro. Arranged on level terraces, mostly with shade, some of the terraced pitches have views of the sea through the trees. The main entrance and its drive resembles a pretty village street as the bungalows are set on both sides of the street which is lined with traditional lamp posts. Continuing the village theme is a row of shops where you will find most campers' needs. The formal restaurant with good value menu and choice of takeaway overlooks the pools. The site is close to Platja de Pals which is a long sandy unspoilt stretch of beach, a discreet area, part of which is now an official naturist beach. The pretty town of Pals is close by along with a good golf course. The site will assist with touring plans of the area.

Facilities

Three well maintained toilet blocks include facilities for disabled campers. Laundry facilities. Gas supplies. Fridge/TV rental. Shops. Restaurant/bar. Pizzeria. Café/bar. Swimming pool. Tennis. Playground. Activities and entertainment in high season. Excursions. ATM. Internet access. Some breeds of dog are excluded (check with site). Mini adventure park. Off site: Fishing 200 m. Bicycle hire 500 m. Golf 1 km. Riding 10 km.

Open: 1 April - 27 September.

Directions

Site is on the road leading off the Torroella de Montgri - Bagur road north of Pals and going to Playa de Pals (Pals beach).
GPS: N41:58.520 E03:11.590

Charges 2009

Per person	€ 4,15 - € 6,30
child (3-12 yrs)	€ 3,00 - € 3,70
pitch	€ 19,10 - € 33,20

No credit cards. Camping Cheques accepted.

ES81700 Camping Valldaro

Apdo 57, avenida Castell d'Aro 63, E-17250 Platja d'Aro (Girona)

Tel: **972 817 515**. Email: **info@valldaro.com** **www.alanrogers.com/ES81700**

Valldaro is 600 m. back from the sea at Platja d'Aro, a small, bright resort with a long, wide beach and plenty of amusements. It is particularly pleasant during out of peak weeks. Like a number of other large Spanish sites, Valldaro has been extended and many pitches have been made larger, bringing them up to 85 sq.m. There are now almost 1,200 pitches with 544 for touring units. The site is flat, with pitches in rows divided up by access roads. You will probably find space here even at the height of the season. The newer section has its own vehicle entrance (the nearest point to the beach) and can be reached via a footbridge; it is brought into use at peak times. It has some shade and its own toilet block. There are 400 permanent Spanish pitches and 150 mobile homes and chalets to rent, but these are in separate areas and do not impinge on the touring pitches.

Facilities

Four sanitary blocks are of a good standard and are well maintained. Child-size toilets. Washbasins (no cabins) and adjustable showers (temperature perhaps a bit variable). Two supermarkets and general shops. Two restaurants. Large bar. Swimming pools. New outdoor jacuzzi. Tennis. Playgrounds. Sports ground. Children's club. Organised entertainment in season. Hairdresser. Internet. WiFi area (charge to use). Satellite TV. Gas supplies. Off site: Beach 1.5 km. Fishing, bicycle hire and golf 1 km. Riding 4 km.

Open: 3 April - 27 September.

Directions

From Girona on the AP7/E15 take exit 7 to Sant Feliu on C65. On C65 at km. 313 take exit to Platja d'Aro (road number changes here to C31). In 200 m. at roundabout take GI662 towards Platja d'Aro. Site is at km. 4. GPS: N41:48.856 E03:02.622

Charges 2009

Per unit incl. 2 persons	€ 20,00 - € 44,60
extra person	€ 4,10 - € 6,75
child (3-12 yrs)	€ 2,70 - € 3,80

No credit cards. Camping Cheques accepted.

ES80900 Camping Cypsela

Ctra de Pals - Platja de Pals, E-17256 Platja de Pals (Girona)

Tel: **972 667 696**. Email: **info@cypsela.com** **www.alanrogers.com/ES80900**

This impressive, de-luxe site with lush vegetation and trees is very efficiently run. The main part of the camping area is pinewood, with 569 clearly marked touring pitches of varying categories on sandy gravel, all with electricity and some with full facilities. The 228 'Elite' pitches of 120 sq.m. are impressive. Cypsela is a busy, well administered site, only 2 km. from the sea, which we can thoroughly recommend, especially for families. The site has good quality fixtures and fittings, all kept clean and maintained to a high standard. All your needs will be catered for here. The site has many striking features, one of which is the sumptuous complex of sports facilities and amenities near the entrance. This provides a fine large swimming pool, a good children's pool and playgrounds, two excellent squash courts, a tennis court, fitness room, and other entertainment rooms. These include a children's playroom with miniclub and organised entertainment (including video screen), an amusements room with pool tables, football tables, video games, and a luxurious air conditioned lounge. The 'Les Moreres' is a pleasant al fresco restaurant offering a varied menu plus good wines (it can become very busy). Another air conditioned indoor restaurant offers a similar excellent service. You have the choice of a smart bar or the air conditioned cocktail bar. If you wish to travel to the beach there is a regular free bus service from the site. The gates are closed at night. Several tour operators use the site (257 pitches).

Facilities

Four sanitary blocks are of excellent quality with comprehensive cleaning schedules and solar heating. Three have washbasins in cabins and three have amazing children's rooms. Superb facilities for disabled people. Serviced launderette. Supermarket and other shops. Restaurant, cafeteria and takeaway. Bar. Hairdresser. Swimming pools. Tennis. Squash. Minigolf. Skating rink. Fitness room. Solarium. Air conditioned social/TV room. Comprehensive animation programme in season. Games room. Business and internet centre. Gas supplies. ATM. Dogs are not accepted. Off site: Bicycle hire 150 m. Golf 1 km. Fishing 2 km.

Open: 15 May - 21 September.

Directions

Platja de Pals is southeast of Girona on the coast. From the AP7/E15 at Girona take exit 6 towards Palamós on the C66. This road changes number to the C31 near La Bisbal. 7.5 km. past La Bisbal, exit to Pals on the GI 652. Follow signs for Platja de Pals. At El Masos take the 6502 for 1 km. Main entrance for Cypsela is on the left between the white metal fencing. GPS: N41:59.100 E03:10.740

Charges guide

Per person	€ 6,00
child (2-10 yrs)	€ 4,60
pitch acc. to season and services	€ 22,80 - € 61,50

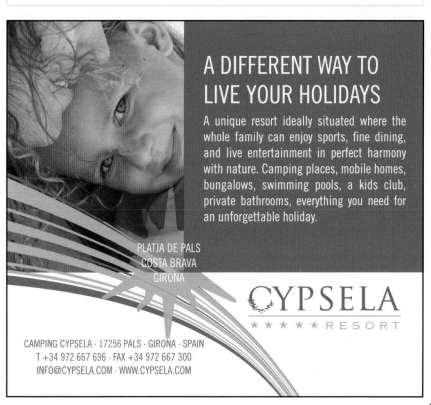

ES81040 Camping Begur

Ctra d'Esclanya km 2, E-17255 Begur (Girona)

Tel: **972 623 201**. Email: **info@campingbegur.com** **www.alanrogers.com/ES81040**

The owners here have made a massive investment in making the site a pleasant place to spend some time. There are some good supporting facilities including a new pool complex at its centre which has been well designed with terraces and sunbathing area. The touring areas are protected from the sun by mature trees which are all numbered. The 317 pitches are informally arranged on sloping sandy ground (chocks useful). Most pitches have electricity (10A), water and drainage.

Facilities

Two modern toilet blocks are fully equipped and include really large showers. Excellent facilities for disabled campers. Baby bath. Laundry facilitites. Motorcaravan services. Bar and snacks. Swimming pools. Boules. Weight training room. Play area. Some animation and children's entertainment in high season. Little farm with ponies, goat and chickens. Internet access. Off site: Restaurant and supermarket just outside gate. Beaches 1.5 km. Fishing 3 km. Golf 10 km. Riding 15 km.

Open: 3 April - 27 September.

Directions

From Girona take road east to La Bisbal and Palafrugell then Begur. Turn south towards Fornells, the site is well signed 3 km. south of Begur. GPS: N41:56.998 E03:11.934

Charges 2009

Per person	€ 3,30 - € 6,20
child (3-10 yrs)	€ 1,60 - € 3,30
pitch incl. electricity	€ 11,80 - € 20,00
fully serviced	€ 13,70 - € 22,60

No credit cards.

ES81600 Camping Cala Gogo

Ctra San Feliu - Palamós km 46.5, Platja d'Aro, E-17251 Calonge (Girona)

Tel: **972 651 564**. Email: **calagogo@calagogo.es** **www.alanrogers.com/ES81600**

Cala Gogo is a large traditional campsite with a pleasant situation on a wooded hillside with mature trees giving shade to most pitches. The 619 shaded touring pitches varying in size are in terraced rows, some with artificial shade, all have 10A electricity and 250 have water and drainage. There may be road noise in eastern parts of the site. Some pitches are now right by the beach, the remainder are up to 800 m. uphill, but a tractor train takes people between the centre of site and beach.

Facilities

Seven toilet blocks are of a high standard and are continuously cleaned. Some washbasins in private cabins. Two private cabins for hire. New laundry room. Motorcaravan services. Gas supplies. Supermarket. General shop. Restaurants and bars. Swimming and paddling pools (lifeguards). New playground. Crèche and babysitting service (charged). Sports centre. Sports and entertainment. Bicycle hire. Kayaks. Fishing. Internet access and WiFi. Dogs are not accepted mid June - end August. Off site: Golf 5 km. Riding 10 km. Aqua Park.

Open: 25 April - 27 September.

Directions

The town of Sant Antoni de Calonge is southeast of Girona. Leave the AP7/E15 at exit 6. Take C66 towards Palomos which becomes the C31. Use the C31 (Girona - Palomos) road to avoid Palomas town. Take the C253 coast road. Site is at km. 46.5 (4 km. south of Palomas). GPS: N41:49.850 E03:04.948

Charges 2009

Per unit incl. 2 persons and electricity (5A)	€ 18,20 - € 46,15
extra person	€ 3,60 - € 7,15
child (3-12 yrs)	€ 1,10 - € 3,60

ES81300 Camping Internacional de Calonge

Ctra San Feliu/Guixols - Palamós, E-17251 Calonge (Girona)

Tel: **972 651 233**. Email: **info@intercalonge.com** **www.alanrogers.com/ES81300**

This spacious, well laid out site has access to the fine beach by a footbridge over the coast road, or you can take the little road train as the site is on very sloping ground. Calonge is a family site with two good sized pools on different levels, a paddling pool plus large sunbathing areas. The site's 800 pitches are on terraces and all have electricity (5A) with 167 available for winter use. A large proportion are suitable for touring units (the remainder for tents) being set on attractively landscaped terraces. Access to some pitches may be a little difficult.

Facilities

Generous sanitary provision in new or renovated blocks include some washbasins in cabins. One block is heated in winter. Laundry facilities. Motorcaravan services. Gas supplies. Shop, Bar/restaurant, Patio bar (pizza and takeaway) (all 15/3-19/10). Swimming pools (15/3-12/10). Playground. Electronic games. Rather noisy disco two nights a week (but not late). Bicycle hire. Tennis. Hairdresser. ATM. Internet. Torches necessary in some areas. Off site: Fishing 300 m. Supermarket 500 m. Golf 3 km. Riding 10 km.

Open: All year.

Directions

Site is on the inland side of the coast road between Palamós and Platja d'Aro. Take the C31 south to the 661 at Calonge. At Calonge follow signs to the C253 towards Platja d'Aro and on to site which is well signed. GPS: N41:50.000 E03:05.050

Charges guide

Per person	€ 3,65 - € 7,55
child (3-10 yrs)	€ 1,85 - € 4,25
pitch incl. electricity	€ 14,80 - € 33,25

All plus 7% VAT. No credit cards.

ES80740 Camping Illa Mateua

Avenida de Montgó 260, E-17130 L'Escala (Girona)

Tel: **972 770 200**. Email: **info@campingillamateua.com** **www.alanrogers.com/ES80740**

If you prefer a quieter site out of the very busy resort of L'Escala then this site is an excellent option. This large, family run site has a dynamic owner Marti, who speaks excellent English. The site is divided by the beach access road and has its own private access to the very safe and unspoilt beach. There are 358 pitches, all with electricity (10A), some on sloping ground although the pitches themselves tend to be flat. Established pine trees provide shade for most places with more coverage on the western side of the site. Non-stop maintenance ensures that all facilities at this site are of a high standard. There are three swimming pools, the largest with an idyllic and most unusual setting on the top of a cliff overlooking the Bay of Roses. A CCTV security system monitors the pools and general security from a purpose built centre.

Facilities

Modern, fully equipped sanitary blocks are kept very clean. Washing machines and dryers. Shop, extensive modern complex of restaurants, bars and takeaways (all open all season). Swimming pools (1/5-20/9). Pool bar. Play areas. Fishing. Kayak hire. Organised activities for children in high season. ATM. Private access to beach. Off site: Cala Montgó beach 100 m. with a charming bay of soft sand offering all manner of watersports, pretty restaurants and a disco in season. Road train service to town centre from outside site. Riding 2 km. Golf 10 km.

Open: 18 March - 15 October.

Directions

Leave autopista A7 at exit 5 heading for Viladimat, then L'Escala. Site is well signed from town centre. Follow signs for Montgó and site is south of town beside the coast. GPS: N42:06.631 E3:09.925

Charges guide

Per person	€ 3,10 - € 5,60
child (3-10 yrs)	€ 2,20 - € 3,90
pitch	€ 15,50 - € 30,00
electricity	€ 3,40

Plus 7% VAT.

No credit cards.

ES81200 Kim's Camping

Font d'en Xeco, E-17211 Llafranc (Girona)

Tel: **972 301 156**. Email: **info@campingkims.com** **www.alanrogers.com/ES81200**

This attractive, terraced site (to which the owner has been welcoming guests for 50 years) is arranged on the wooded slopes of a narrow valley leading to the sea and there are many trees including huge eucalyptus. There are 350 grassy and partly shaded pitches, 240 used for touring units, all with electricity (5A). Many of the larger pitches are on a plateau from which great views can be enjoyed. The terraced pitches are connected by winding drives, narrow in places. This is a pleasant place for holidays where you can enjoy the bustling village and beach, while staying in a quieter environment. The site has an excellent swimming pool (with lifeguard) and children's pool, a bar, and a pleasant restaurant with 'al fresco' eating. An entertainment programme is provided. The site is under 1 km. from the resort of Llafranc. There is an outstanding view along the coastline and of the Pyrenees from Cap Sebastian close by. English and Dutch is spoken by the very friendly management and staff.

Facilities

All sanitary facilities are spotlessly clean and include a small new block and excellent toilet facilities for disabled visitors. Laundry facilities. Motorcaravan services. Gas supplies. Well stocked shop. Bar. Bakery and croissanterie. Café/restaurant (15/6-10/9). Swimming pools. Play areas. Children's club. TV room. Excursions. Visits arranged to sub-aqua schools (high season). Torches required. WiFi. Mobile homes to rent. Off site: Beach, fishing, sailing and bicycle hire 500 m. Riding 3.5 km. Golf 9 km.

Open: Easter - 30 September.

Directions

Llafranc is southeast of Palafrugell. Turn off the Palafrugell - Tamariu road at turn (GIV 6542) signed Llafranc, Club de Tennis. Site is on right 1 km. further on. GPS: N41:54.032 E03:11.361

Charges guide

Per person	€ 2,67 - € 6,42
child (3-10 yrs)	€ 1,07 - € 3,21
pitch incl. electricity	€ 12,84 - € 27,80

Discounts for long stays and for senior citizens.

ES82000 Camping Cala Llevadó

Ctra GI-682 de Tossa a Lloret pk. 18,9, E-17320 Tossa de Mar (Girona)

Tel: **972 340 314**. Email: **info@calallevado.com** **www.alanrogers.com/ES82000**

For splendour of position Cala Llevadó can compare with almost any in this book. A beautifully situated cliff-side site, it has fine views of the sea and coast below. It is shaped something like half a bowl with steep slopes. High up in the site with a superb aspect, is the attractive restaurant/bar with a large terrace overlooking the pleasant swimming pool. There are terraced, flat areas for caravans and tents (with electricity) on the upper levels of the two slopes, with a great many individual pitches for tents scattered around the site. Some of these pitches have fantastic settings and views. Many of the 577 touring pitches are available for caravans with 10/16A electricity. There are a few tour operator pitches (45) and 26 bungalows.

Facilities

Four very well equipped toilet blocks are immaculately maintained and well spaced around the site. Baby baths. Laundry facilities. Motorcaravan services. Gas supplies. Fridge hire. Large supermarket. Restaurant/bar (5/5-28/9). Swimming and paddling pools. Three play areas. Botanic garden. Entertainment for children (4-12 yrs). Sailing, water ski and windsurfing school. Fishing. Excursions. Internet access and WiFi. Torches definitely needed in some areas. Off site: Bicycle hire 3 km.

Open: 1 May - 30 September, with all services.

Directions

Leave the AP7/E15 at exit 7 to the C65 Sant Feliu road and then take C35 southeast to the GI681 to Tossa de Mare. Site is signed off the GI682 Lloret - Tossa road at km. 18.9, about 3 km. from Tossa. GPS: N41:42.769 E02:54.374

Charges 2009

Per person	€ 5,65 - € 9,45
child (4-12 yrs)	€ 3,25 - € 5,05
pitch incl. car	€ 9,55 - € 19,45
electricity	€ 4,55 - € 5,00

ES82100 Camping Tucan

Ctra de Blanes - Lloret, E-17310 Lloret de Mar (Girona)

Tel: **972 369 965**. Email: **info@campingtucan.com** **www.alanrogers.com/ES82100**

Situated on the busy Costa Brava near Lloret de Mar, Camping Tucan is well placed to access all the attractions of the area. Views over the mountains are mixed with views of the nearby town. The 250 good size pitches all have electricity, and are laid out in a herringbone pattern with areas dedicated to singles, families with young children and couples who enjoy the quiet. Pitches are on terraces, flat surfaced with gravel and many are shaded. Camping Tucan is a lively site with a variety of activities on offer including an animation programme for children and modest entertainment at night. Activities on the site centre around the pleasant pool, bar, restaurant and terrace all of which are close to reception. There is a separate, largely independent facility for young people at the rear of the site.

Facilities

Two modern toilet blocks include washbasins with hot water and facilities for disabled visitors, although access is difficult. All very clean when seen. Washing machine. Gas supplies. Shop. Busy bar and good restaurant. Takeaway. Swimming pools and indoor solarium. Playground and fenced play area for toddlers. TV in bar. Bicycle hire. Animation in high season. Miniclub. Off site: Town 500 m. Nearest beach 600 m. Riding 1 km. Golf 4 km.

Open: 3 April - 27 September.

Directions

From A7/E4, A19 or N11 Girona - Barcelona roads take an exit for Lloret de Mar. Site is 1 km. west of the town, well signed and is at the base of the hill off the roundabout. The entrance can get congested in busy periods. GPS: N41:41.832 E02:49.310

Charges 2009

Per person	€ 4,95 - € 8,50
child (1-9 yrs)	€ 3,50 - € 5,70
pitch incl. electricity	€ 12,90 - € 21,95

BOOK THIS SITE
CALL 01580 214000
...we'll arrange everything
The Travel Service

2015

ES83920 Camping El Garrofer

Ctra 246 km 39, E-08870 Sitges (Barcelona)
Tel: **938 941 780**. Email: **info@garroferpark.com** **www.alanrogers.com/ES83920**

This large pine covered site, alongside fields of vines, is 800 m. from the beach close to the pleasant town of Sitges. This is an attractive resort with seaside entertainments and is well worth exploring. The site has over 500 pitches of which 380 with 6A electricity are for tourers, including 28 with water used for large motorcaravans. Everything is kept clean and the pitches are tidy and shaded. The amenity buildings are along the site perimeter next to the road which absorbs most of the road noise. The permanent pitches are grouped in a completely separate area. A varied menu is offered in the cosy restaurant with a small terrace. Everything is cooked to perfection and complemented with the wines of the Penedes DO made hereabouts (the restaurant has a local reputation and is used by non campers – the menu of the day is great value). A traditional bar is alongside and from here you can see the pretty mosaic clad play area (the 'Gaudi touch' which is also evident elsewhere). An ambitious animation programme is conducted for children in summer. Late evening Salsa classes were offered for adults when we visited. A small pool is welcome on hot summer days or you can walk to the very pleasant beach (ten minutes from a gate at the back of the site). Open most of the year the site offers all manner of adventure activities (extra charge) which may be organized through reception and there are many things to see here – we especially recommend a visit to Monserrat.

Facilities

Two of the three sanitary blocks have been refurbished and provide roomy showers and special bright facilities for children. Separate baby room with bath. Good facilities for disabled campers. Laundry. Bar/restaurant. Shop (reception in low season). Swimming pool. Golf packages. Practice golf. Tennis. Play area for older children and fenced play area for toddlers. Bicycle hire. Boules.
Off site: Bus from outside site to Barcelona. Golf, riding and fishing 500 m.

Open: 17 January - 17 December.

Directions

From the A16/C32 autopista take exit 26 towards Vilanova and St Pere Ribes. From Tarragona, go under the autopista, around roundabout and back to the roundabout on the other side to pick up site sign (towards Sitges). Follow C-246a to km. 39. Look for the flags. GPS: N41:14.011 E01:46.867

Charges guide

Per person	€ 2,85 - € 5,00
pitch incl. electricity	€ 14,98 - € 19,70

Plus 7% VAT.

ES84820 Camping La Pineda de Salou

Ctra Costa Tarragona - Salou km 5, E-43481 La Pineda (Tarragona)
Tel: **977 373 080**. Email: **info@campinglapineda.com** **www.alanrogers.com/ES84820**

La Pineda is just outside Salou towards Tarragona and this site is just 300 m. from the Aquapark and 2.5 km. from Port Aventura, to which there is an hourly bus service from outside the site entrance. There is some noise from this road. The site has a fair-sized swimming pool adjoining a smaller, heated one, open from mid June, behind large hedges close to the entrance. A large terrace has sun loungers, and various entertainment aimed at young people is provided in season. The 366 flat pitches are mostly shaded and of about 70 sq.m. All have 5A electricity.

Facilities

Sanitary facilities are mature but clean. Facilities for disabled visitors. Washing machines. Shop (1/7-31/8). Restaurant and snacks (1/7-31/8). Swimming pools (1/7-31/8). Bar (all season). TV room. Bicycle hire. Playground. Entertainment (1/7-30/8). Off site: Beach 400 m.

Open: All year.

Directions

From A7 just southwest of Tarragona take exit 35 and follow signs to La Pineda and Port Aventura then site signs appear. GPS: N41:05.310 E01:10.947

Charges guide

Per person	€ 5,00 - € 7,70
pitch incl. electricity	€ 21,10 - € 41,00

2008

ES83900 Camping Vilanova Park

Ctra de l'Arboc km 2.5, E-08800 Vilanova i la Geltru (Barcelona)
Tel: **938 933 402**. Email: **info@vilanovapark.es** **www.alanrogers.com/ES83900**

Sitting on the terrace of the bustling but comfortable restaurant at Vilanova Park, it is difficult to believe that in 1908 this was a Catalan farm and then, quite lacking in trees, it was known as 'Rock Farm'. Since then imaginative planting has led to there being literally thousands of trees and gloriously colourful shrubs making a most attractive, large campsite, with an impressive range of high quality amenities and facilities open all year. There are 344 marked pitches for touring units in separate areas. All have 6A electricity, 185 also have water and some larger pitches (100 sq.m) also have drainage. The terrain, hard surfaced and mostly on very gently sloping ground, has many trees and considerable shade. At present there are 786 pitches with a significant proportion occupied by bungalows and chalets carefully designed to fit into the environment. The site is used by tour operators (190 pitches). The really good amenities include a new second pool higher up in the site with marvellous views across the town to the sea and an indoor pool, sauna, jacuzzi and gym. Here there is also a second, more intimate restaurant for that special romantic dinner overlooking the twinkling evening lights. The original pool has water jets and a coloured floodlit fountain playing at night, which complement the dancing and entertainment taking place on the stage in the courtyard overlooking the pool. An unusual attraction is a Nature Park and mini-zoo with deer and bird life. There is a good excursion programme to Barcelona, Monserrat and Bodegas Torres for wine tasting. There is also a transfer service from both Barcelona and Reus airports should you fancy taking advantage of the off season offers in the site's own accommodation.

Facilities

All toilet blocks are of excellent quality, can be heated and have washbasins (over half in cabins) with free hot water. Serviced laundry. Motorcaravan services. Supermarket. Souvenir shop. Restaurants. Bar with simple meals. Swimming pools (outdoor 1/4-15/10, indoor all year). Wellness centre including sauna, jacuzzi and gym. Play areas. Sports field. Games room. Bicycle hire. Tennis. ATM and exchange facilities. Off site: Fishing 4 km. Golf 5 km. Good train service from Vilanova to Barcelona, not so good the other way (to Tarragona). Vilanova 4 km.

Open: All year.

Directions

Site is 4 km. northwest of Vilanova i la Geltru towards L'Arboc (BV2115). From the A7 Tarragona - Barcelona take exit 29 onto C15 to Vilanova, then C31 El Vendrell road (Km. 153) then onto BV2115. GPS: N41:13.942 E01:41.455

Charges 2009

Per person	€ 4,00 - € 10,00
child (4-12 yrs)	€ 3,20 - € 6,00
pitch incl. electricity	€ 15,50 - € 25,00
incl. water	€ 18,50 - € 28,00

Camping Cheques accepted.

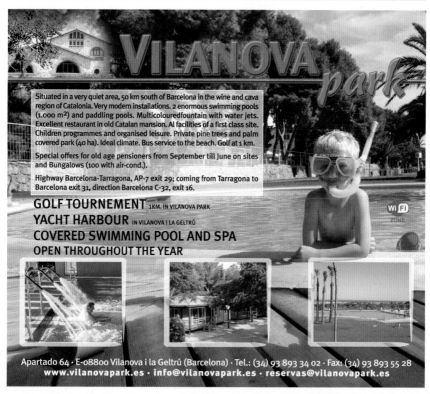

BOOK THIS SITE
CALL 01580 214000
...we'll arrange everything
The Travel Service

ES84810 Camping Cambrils Park

Avenida Mas Clariana s/n., E-43850 Cambrils (Tarragona)

Tel: **977 351 031**. Email: **mail@cambrilspark.es** **www.alanrogers.com/ES84810**

This is a superb site for a camping holiday providing for all family members, whatever their ages. A drive lined with palm trees and flowers leads from a large, very smart round reception building at this impressive modern site. Sister site to no. ES8480, it is set 500 metres back from the excellent beach in a generally quiet setting with outstanding facilities. The 684 slightly sloping, grassy pitches of around 90 sq.m. are numbered and separated by trees. All have 10A electricity, 55 have water and waste water connections, some having more shade than others. The marvellous central lagoon pool complex with three pools and water slides is the main focus of the site with a raised wooden 'poop deck' sunbathing area with palm surrounds that doubles as an entertainment stage at night. There is a huge bar/terrace area for watching the magnificent floodlit spectacles, along with an excellent restaurant in the old farmhouse with an adjacent takeaway. By day there is a small bar at a lower level in the pool where you can enjoy a cool drink from submerged stools, plus a drier version on the far side or just relax on the spacious grass sunbathing areas. A fabulous jungle theme children's pool is nearer the entrance – they love it, especially the elephants! An extra pool for adults has been added here, along with a snack bar. There are tour operator pitches and attractive thatched chalets.

Facilities

Four excellent sanitary buildings provide some washbasins in cabins, superb units for disabled visitors and immaculate baby sections. Huge serviced laundry. Motorcaravan services. Car wash. Restaurant. Takeaway. Huge supermarket, souvenir shop and 'panaderia' (freshly baked bread and croissants). Swimming pools. Minigolf. Tennis. Multisport court. Pétanque. Animation and entertainment all season. Miniclub. Internet café. Medical centre. ATM. Gas supplies. Dogs are not accepted.
Off site: Beach 500 m. Fishing, bicycle hire 400 m. Riding 3 km. Port Aventura theme park 4 km. Golf 7 km.

Open: 7 April - 8 October.

Directions

Site is about 1.5 km. west of Salou. From the A7 take exit 35 and at roundabout take signs for Cambrils. Follow new dual carriageway around the back of Salou and site is signed at last roundabout towards Cambrils. GPS: N41:04.584 E01:06.527

Charges guide

Per person	€ 6,00
child (4-12 yrs)	€ 4,00
pitch incl. electricity	€ 15,00 - € 49,00
incl. water and waste water	€ 15,00 - € 52,00

All plus 7% VAT. Special offers.
Camping Cheques accepted.

ES84830 Camping Tamarit Park

N340 km 1172, Tamarit, E-43008 Tarragona (Tarragona)

Tel: **977 650 128**. Email: **tamaritpark@tamarit.com** **www.alanrogers.com/ES84830**

This is a marvellous, beach-side site, attractively situated at the foot of Tamarit castle at one end of a superb one kilometre long beach of fine sand. Parts are landscaped with lush Mediterranean palms and shrubs; other areas have natural pine shade, all home to mischievous red squirrels. The 694 pitches, 50 of which are virtually on the beach, are marked out on hard sand and grass and some are attractively separated by green vegetation which provides good shade. There are about 120 tour operator pitches, a number of seasonal pitches and about 120 bungalows. All pitches have electricity (6A). Long electricity leads and metal awning pegs may be required in places but wide internal roads give good access for even the largest of units (American motorhomes accepted). Catering includes a beach-side waiter service restaurant with superb views and a terrace with tables just a few metres from the sea. A vast, attractively designed, lagoon-type swimming pool with bar and sun terrace has recently been added. The site is approached by a long access road, rather narrow but with passing places, reached across a bridge (6 m) over the railway line (there is train noise on the site). Security is provided but the very low wall which is the site beach boundary must be viewed with caution.

Facilities

Sanitary blocks (one heated) are modern and tiled, providing good facilities. An unfortunate economy feature in the showers is push-button controlled hot water with tap controlled cold, leading to a confusing mix of temperatures. Private bathrooms to rent. Laundry facilities. Motorcaravan services. Gas supplies. Shop, bar/restaurant and takeaway. Swimming pool (15/5-15/10). Tennis. Pétanque. Minigolf. Playground. Animation programme in season. Fishing. Internet access. Barbecues not permitted on pitches.
Off site: Riding 1 km. Bicycle hire 2 km. Golf 8 km.

Open: 30 March - 15 October.

Directions

From A7 take exit 32 towards Tarragona and continue for 4.5 km. At roundabout (km. 1172) turn back towards Atafulla and Tamarit and after 200 m. turn right to Tamarit (beside Caledonia Bungalow Park). Take care over railway bridge, then immediately sharp right. Site on left after 1 km.
GPS: N41:07.943 E01:21.652

Charges guide

Per person	€ 5,00
child (4-12 yrs)	free - € 4,00
pitch acc. to size and season	€ 18,00 - € 52,00
dog	€ 2,00 - € 4,00

All plus 7% VAT. Discounts for students, pensioners, large families and longer stays in low season.

ES85080 Camping Poboleda

Placa de les Casetes s/n, E-43376 Poboleda (Tarragona)

Tel: **977 827 197**. Email: **poboleda@campingsonline.com** **www.alanrogers.com/ES85080**

Time stands still at this unique site hidden away in a corner of the village, watched over by La Morera de Montsant, a peak of the Serra del Montsant. Situated among olive groves, yet almost in the heart of the lovely old village of Poboleda, it is an idyllic site for tents, small caravans and motorcaravans. Large units may have problems negotiating the narrow village streets. The 151 pitches of 80 sq.m. are set under olive and almond trees. Fairly level and 70 with 4A electricity, they provide a peaceful haven broken only by the peal of church bells or bird song. The young manager is enthusiastic and proud of the facilities offered which are quite unexpected and special. Behind the modern reception is a traditional, comfortably furnished room with piano and TV, which doubles as a peaceful cool area for relaxing if it is too hot on the terrace. Here you can have breakfast or order a drink. The village is on the doorstep for other needs. The mellow terraced pool area is a lovely surprise and very welcome, as is the tennis court. There is plenty to do, walking or climbing, visiting the region's vineyards and enjoying the local cuisine. A must to visit is the monastery of Poblet nearby.

Facilities

One small block, open all year, is fully equipped, as is a larger block open for high season. Shower for children. Facilities for disabled people (key). Laundry service. Breakfast can be ordered. Bar. Swimming pool (24/6-11/9). Tennis. Boules. Reception has postcards and basic items. Off site: Beach and Port Aventura 30 km. Bicycle hire 10 km. Fishing 12 km.

Open: All year.

Directions

Bypass Reus on the N420. After Borges del Camp pick up C242, signed Alforja. Continue over Coll d'Alforja. Watch for left turn (T702) for Poboleda. Continue for 6 km. to village. Watch for tent signs and follow carefully through narrow streets. Not advised for large units. GPS: N41:14.000 E00:50.410

Charges guide

Per person	€ 5,67
pitch incl. electricity	€ 15,67 - € 20.67

ES84700 Camping La Siesta

Calle Ctra Norte 37, E-43840 Salou (Tarragona)

Tel: **977 380 852**. Email: **info@camping-lasiesta.com** **www.alanrogers.com/ES84700**

The palm bedecked entrance of La Siesta is only 250 m. from the pleasant sandy beach and close to the life of the resort of Salou. The site is divided into 470 pitches which are large enough and have electricity (10A), with smaller ones for tents. Many pitches are provided with artificial shade and within some there is one box for the tent or caravan and a shared one for the car. There is considerable shade from the trees and shrubs that are part of the site's environment. In high season, the siting of units is carried out by the friendly management. Young campers are located separately to the rear of the site. The town is popular with British and Spanish holidaymakers and has just about all that a highly developed Spanish resort can offer.

Facilities

Three bright and clean sanitary blocks provide very reasonable facilities. Motorcaravan services. Supermarket. Various vending machines. Self-service restaurant and bar. Dancing some evenings untill 23.00. Swimming pool (300 sq.m. open all season). Playground. Medical service daily in season. ATM point. Off site: Shops, restaurants and bars near. Port Aventura is close. Bicycle hire 200 m.

Open: 14 March - 3 November.

Directions

Leave A7 at exit 35 for Salou. Site is signed off the Tarragona - Salou road and from the one way system in the town of Salou. Keep a sharp eye for the small signs. GPS: N41:04.662 E1:08.334

Charges guide

Per person	€ 4,60 - € 8,80
pitch incl. electricity	€ 6,55 - € 21,60

All plus 7% VAT. No credit cards.

ES84800 Camping & Bungalows Sanguli

Prolongacion Calle, Apdo 123, E-43840 Salou (Tarragona)

Tel: **977 381 641**. Email: **mail@sanguli.es** **www.alanrogers.com/ES84800**

Sanguli is a superb site boasting excellent pools and ambitious entertainment. Owned, developed and managed by a local Spanish family, it provides for all the family with everything open when the site is open. There are 1,041 pitches of varying size (75-90 sq.m) and all have electricity. About 155 are used by tour operators and 205 for bungalows. A wonderful selection of trees, palms and shrubs provides natural shade. The good sandy beach is little more than 100 metres across the coast road and a small railway crossing (a little noise). Although large, Sanguli maintains a quality family atmosphere due to the efforts of the very keen and efficient staff. The owners are striving to achieve the 'Garden of Eden' that is their dream. There are three very attractive pool areas, one (heated) near the entrance with a grassy sunbathing area partly shaded and a second deep one with water slides that forms part of the excellent sports complex (with fitness centre, tennis courts, minigolf and football practice area). The third pool is the central part of the amphitheatre area at the top of the site which includes an impressive Roman style building with huge portals, containing a bar and restaurant with terraces. An amphitheatre seats 2,000 campers and treats them to very professional free nightly entertainment (1/5-30/9). All the pools have adjacent amenity areas and bars. A real effort is made to cater for the young including teenagers with a 'Hop Club' (entertainment for 13-17 year olds), along with an internet room. Located near the centre of Salou, the site can offer the attractions of a busy resort while still being private and it is only 3 km. from Port Aventura. This is a large, professional site providing something for all the family, but still capable of providing peace and quiet for those looking for it.

Facilities

The quality sanitary facilities are constantly improved and are always exceptional, including many individual cabins with en-suite facilities. A new block also has excellent facilities for babies. All are kept very clean. Launderette with service. Motorcaravan services. Bars and restaurant with takeaway. Swimming pools. Jacuzzi. Fitness centre. Sports complex. Fitness room (charged). Playgrounds. Miniclub, teenagers' club. Internet room. Upmarket minigolf. First-aid room. Gas supplies. Off site: Fishing and bicycle hire 100 m. Riding 3 km. Golf 6 km.

Open: 14 March - 2 November.

Directions

On west side of Salou about 1 km. from the centre, site is well signed from the coast road to Cambrils and from the other town approaches.
GPS: N41:04.500 E01:06.960

Charges guide

Per person	€ 6,00
child (4-12 yrs)	€ 4,00
pitch incl. electricity	€ 15,00 - € 44,00
incl. water	€ 15,00 - € 52,00

All plus 7% VAT.
Special long stay offers for senior citizens.

ES85350 Camping-Pension Cala d'Oques

Via Augusta s/n, E-43890 Hospitalet del Infante (Tarragona)

Tel: **977 823 254**. Email: **eroller@tinet.org** **www.alanrogers.com/ES85350**

This peaceful and delightful site has been developed with care and dedication by Elisa Roller over 30 years or so and she now runs it with the help of her daughter Kim. Part of its appeal lies in its situation beside the sea with a wide beach of sand and pebbles, its amazing mountain backdrop and the views across the bay to the town and part by the atmosphere created by Elisa, and staff – friendly, relaxed and comfortable. There are 255 pitches, mostly level and laid out beside the beach, with more behind on wide, informal terracing. Electricity is available although long leads may be needed in places. Odd pine and olive trees are an attractive feature and provide some shade. The restaurant with its homely touches has a super menu and a reputation extending well outside the site (the excellent cook has been there for many years) and the family type entertainment is in total contrast to that provided at the larger, brasher sites of the Costa Daurada. Gates provide access to the pleasant beach with useful cold showers to wash the sand away. Torches are needed at night.

Facilities

Toilet facilities are in the front part of the main building. Clean and neat, there is hot water to showers (hot water by token but free to campers - a device to guard against unauthorised visitors from the beach). New heated unit with toilets and washbasins for winter use. Additional small block with toilets and washbasins at the far end of the site. Motorcaravan service point. Restaurant/bar and shop (1/4-30/9). Play area. Kim's kids club. Fishing. Internet access and WiFi. Gas supplies. Torches required in some areas. Off site: Village facilities, incl. shop and restaurant 1.5 km. Bicycle hire or riding 2 km.

Open: All year.

Directions

Hospitalet del Infante is south of Tarragona, accessed from the A7 (exit 38) or from the N340. From the north take first exit to Hospitalet del Infante at the 1128 km. marker. Follow signs in the village, site is 2 km. south, by the sea.
GPS: N40:58.666 E00:54.203

Charges guide

Per unit incl. 1 person	€ 13,65 - € 24,75
extra person	€ 4,55 - € 8,25
child (0-10 yrs)	free
electricity	€ 3,30 - € 3,90

Discounts for seniors and for longer stays.
No credit cards.

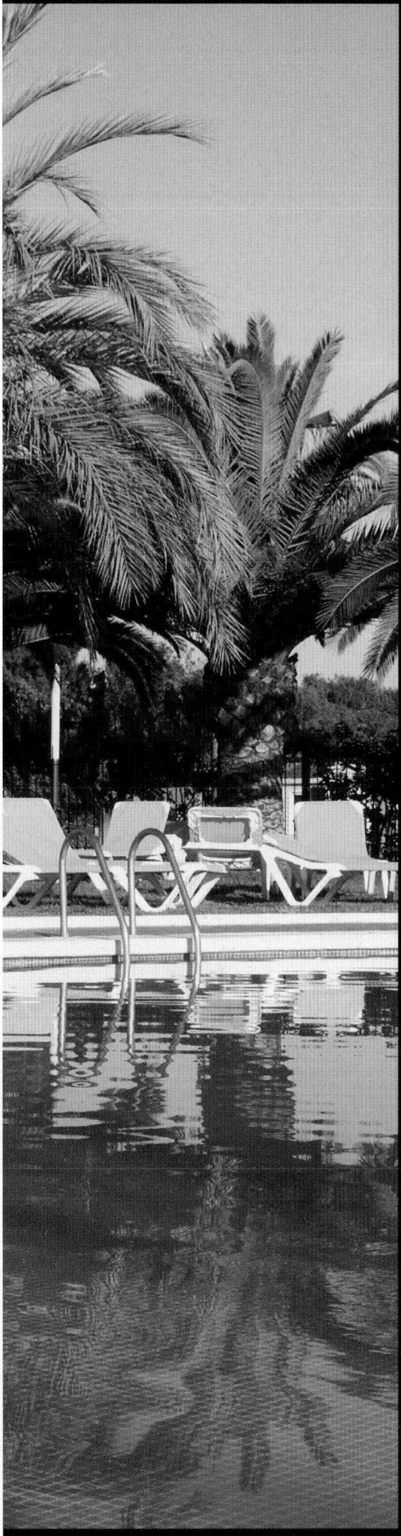

ES84100 Camping Playa Bará

Ctra N340 km 1183, E-43883 Roda de Bará (Tarragona)

Tel: **977 802 701**. Email: **info@barapark.es** **www.alanrogers.com/ES84100**

This is a most impressive, family owned site near the beach, which has been carefully designed and developed. On entry you find yourself in a beautifully sculptured, tree-lined drive with an aroma of pine and woodlands and the sound of waterfalls close by. Considering its size, with over 850 pitches, it is still a very green and relaxing site with an immense range of activities. It is well situated with a 50 m. walk to a long sandy beach via a tunnel under the railway (some noise) to a new promenade with palms and a quality beach bar and restaurant. Much care with planning and in the use of natural stone; palms, shrubs and flowering plants gives a pleasing tropical appearance to all aspects of the site. The owners have excelled themselves in the design of the impressive terraced Roman-style pool complex, which is the central feature of the site. This complex is really amazing. Sunbathe on the pretty terraces or sip a drink whilst seated at the bar stools submerged inside one of the pools or enjoy the panorama over the sea from the rooftop spa. An extremely well equipped gym with an instructor and a massage service. A separate attractive amphitheatre seats about 2,000 people and is used to stage very professional entertainment in season. Pitches vary in size and are being progressively enlarged; the older ones terraced and well shaded with pine trees, the newer ones more open, with a variety of trees and bushes forming separators between them. All have electricity (5A) and a sink with water. Arrive early to find space in peak weeks.

Facilities

Excellent, fully equipped toilet blocks include private cabins and facilities for children and new block for disabled visitors. Private facilities to hire. Superb launderette. Motorcaravan services. Supermarket and several other shops. Full restaurant. Large bar with simpler meals and takeaway. Three other bars and pleasant bar/restaurant on beach. Swimming pools. Jacuzzi/hydro-massage. Fronton and tennis (floodlit). Junior club. Sports area. Windsurfing. Gym. Minigolf. Fishing. Entertainment centre. Cocktail bar/disco. ATM. Hairdresser. Internet. Medical centre. Flights and excursions. WiFi.
Off site: Bicycle hire 2 km. Riding 6 km. Golf 8 km.

Open: 7 March - October, with all amenities.

Directions

From the A7 take exit 31. Site entrance is at the 1183 km. marker on the main N340 just opposite the Arco de Bara Roman monument from which it takes its name. GPS: N41:10.200 E01:28.100

Charges guide

Per person	€ 3,00 - € 9,70
child (1-9 yrs)	€ 2,00 - € 6,80
pitch	€ 6,80 - € 19,70
electricity	€ 3,30

All plus 7% VAT. Low season reductions for pensioners and all sports charges reduced by 90%. No credit cards.

ES84200 Kawan Village Stel

Ctra N340 km 1182, E-43883 Roda de Bará (Tarragona)

Tel: **977 802 002**. Email: **rodadebara@stel.es** **www.alanrogers.com/ES84200**

Camping Stel is situated between the pre-Littoral mountains and the sea. The rectangular site is between the N340 road and the excellent beach, with the railway running close to the bottom of the site. Beach access is gained through a gate and under the railway – there is rail noise on the lower pitches. The pitches are generally in rows with hedges around the rows but at the lower end of the site the layout is less formal. Many pitches have individual sinks. There is a separate area where no radio or TV is allowed ensuring peace and quiet. The main facilities are grouped around the pools which are very pleasant with a large flume to an extension of the main pool (heated all season), an octagonal paddling pool and pleasant grass area carefully set out with palms. The central complex containing all the services is impressive with a large bar, terrace and snack area overlooking the pools. A small restaurant is behind the bar. Just outside the gate is the famous Roman Arc de Bara which sits astride the original road.

Facilities

Four clean, fully equipped, sanitary blocks. One offers excellent facilities for children and disabled campers and four high standard private cabins. Baby baths. Large launderette. Motorcaravan service area. Supermarket and tourist shop. Bar/restaurant and snack bar. Swimming pool, jacuzzi and paddling pool (4/4-28/9). Sport field. Bicycle hire. Miniclub and activities for adults (high season). Internet room (10 units). Hairdresser. ATM. Dogs are not accepted. Torches useful. Off site: Fishing from beach. Golf and riding 4 km.

Open: 4 April - 30 September.

Directions

Site is at 1182 km. marker on the N340 near Arc de Bara, between Tarragona and Vilanova. GPS: N41:10.181 E1:27.881

Charges guide

Per person	€ 7,35 - € 7,75
child (3-10 yrs)	€ 5,75 - € 6,05
pitch incl. electricity	€ 23,15 - € 28,45
incl. water and drainage	€ 27,90 - € 37,70

All plus 7% VAT.
Camping Cheques accepted.

ES85300 Playa Montroig Camping Resort

Apdo 3, N340 km 1136, E-43300 Montroig (Tarragona)

Tel: **977 810 637**. Email: **info@playamontroig.com** **www.alanrogers.com/ES85300**

What a superb site! Playa Montroig is about 30 kilometres beyond Tarragona set in its own tropical gardens with direct access to a very long soft sand beach. The main part of the site lies between the sea, road and railway (as at other sites on this coast, there is some train noise) with a huge underpass. The site is divided into spacious, marked pitches with excellent shade provided by a variety of lush vegetation including very impressive palms set in wide avenues. There are 1,950 pitches, all with electricity and 330 with water and drainage. Some 48 pitches are directly alongside the beach. They are somewhat expensive and extremely popular. The site has many outstanding features: an excellent pool complex near the entrance has two pools (one heated for children). A quality restaurant serves traditional Catalunian fare (seats 150) and overlooks an entertainment area where you may watch genuine Flamenco dancing and buffet food is served (catering for 1,000). A large terrace bar dispenses drinks or if you yearn for louder music there is a disco and smaller bar. If you prefer international food there is yet another eating option in a very smart restaurant (seats 500). Above this is the 'Pai-pai' Caribbean cocktail bar where softer music is provided in an intimate atmosphere. Activities for children are very ambitious – there is even a ceramics kiln. 'La Carpa', a spectacular open air theatre, is an ideal setting for daily keep fit sessions and the professional entertainment provided. If you are 5-11 years old you can explore the 'Tam-Tam Eco Park', a 20,000 sq.m. forest zone where experts will teach about the natural life of the area. You can even camp out for a night (supervised) to study wildlife (a once weekly activity). Adults are also allowed in to separate barbecues and other evening fun. Bathing, windsurfing, surfboarding two diving rafts and many beach sports are available on the beach. This is an excellent site and there is insufficient space here to describe all the available activities. We recommend it for families with children of all ages and there is much emphasis on providing activities outside the high season. Member of 'Leading Campings Group'.

Facilities

Fifteen sanitary buildings, some small, but of very good quality with toilets and washbasins, others really excellent, air conditioned larger buildings housing large showers, washbasins (many in private cabins) and separate WCs. Facilities for disabled campers and for babies. Several launderettes. Motorcaravan services. Good shopping centre. Restaurants and bars. The 'Eurocentre' equipped for entertainment (air conditioned). Fitness suite. Eco-park. TV lounges (3). Beach bar. Playground. Free kindergarten with multilingual staff. Skate-boarding. Jogging track. Sports area. Tennis. Minigolf. Organised activities. Windsurfing and water skiing courses. Surfboard and pedalo hire. Boat mooring. Hairdressers. Bicycle hire. Internet café. Gas supplies. Dogs are not accepted.
Off site: Riding and golf 3 km.

Open: 1 March - 31 October.

Directions

Site entrance is off main N340 nearly 30 km. southwest from Tarragona. From motorway take Cambrils exit and turn west on N340 at 1136 km. marker. GPS: N41:01.975 E00:58.153

Charges guide

Per unit incl. 2 persons and electricity	€ 16,00 - € 69,50
premium pitch	€ 29,00 - € 109,10
extra person	€ 5,80 - € 6,90
child (1-9 yrs)	free - € 5,30

All plus 7% VAT.
Discounts for longer stays and for pensioners.

See advertisement on the back cover.

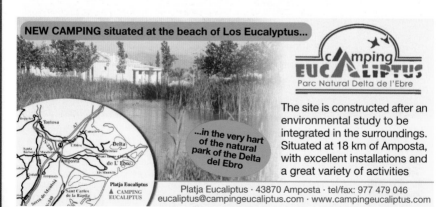

ES84790 Camping Playa Cambrils Don Camilo

Ctra Cambrils - Salou km 1,5, E-43850 Cambrils (Tarragona)

Tel: **977 361 490**. Email: **camping@playacambrils.com** **www.alanrogers.com/ES84790**

Almost completely canopied by trees which provide welcome shade on hot days, the site is 300 m. from the beach across a busy road. It is mature and has had some recent renovations. The small (60 sq.m) pitches are on flat ground, divided by hedges. There are many permanent pitches and half the site is given up to chalet style accommodation. Large units are placed in a dedicated area where the trees are higher. The pool complex includes a functional glassed restaurant and bar with a distinct Spanish flavour reflected in the menu and tapas available all day. As this is a popular site with Spanish families it is a good place to practise your language. The pool is long and narrow with separate children's pool and a large paved area for soaking up the sun. Entertainment for children is organised by a good animation team. A big building at one end of the site consists of the supermarket, an attended electronic games room and a large play room.

Facilities

One modern sanitary building, and one large plus one small refurbished block offer reasonable facilities with British style WCs and free showers in separate buildings. Facilities for disabled campers. Laundry facilities. Supermarket (April - Sept). Bar/snacks and separate restaurant (April - Sept). Swimming pool. Playground. Animation in high season. Miniclub. Off site: Resort town has a range of shops, bars and restaurants. Bicycle hire 500 m. Fishing and golf 1 km. Riding 1.5 km.

Open: 15 March - 12 October.

Directions

Leave AP7 autopista at exit 37 and head for Cambrils and then to the beach. Turn left along beach road. Site is 1 km. east of Cambrils Playa and is well signed as you leave Cambrils marina.
GPS: N41:03.892 E01:05.021

Charges guide

Per person	€ 2,50 - € 4,80
child (under 9 yrs)	€ 1,70 - € 3,65
pitch	€ 11,60 - € 27,60

No credit cards.

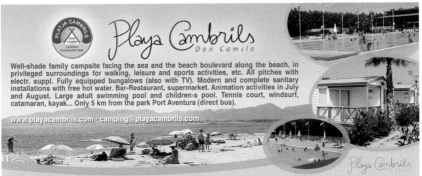

ES85550 Camping Eucaliptus

Platja Eucaliptus s/n, E-43870 Amposta (Tarragona)

Tel: **977 479 046**. Email: **eucaliptus@campingeucaliptus.com** **www.alanrogers.com/ES85550**

Ideally situated in the Delta del Ebro national park, a unique area of wetland (320 sq.m.) and close to the golden sands of Platja Eucaliptus. Arriving at Camping Eucaliptus is like finding an oasis after the extraordinary drive through miles of flat marshland and rice fields. There are 264 small, level, shady grass pitches, 156 for touring, all with electricity. The site is well maintained and three modern buildings near the entrance house the reception, toilet block, shop, bar and restaurant. The terrace overlooks the pleasant pool area with lawned gardens for sunbathing and the campsite's own lagoon. There is access to the beach through a gate at the back of the site where care must be taken with children as there is an open irrigation channel.

Facilities

The single toilet block is kept very clean and includes open style washbasins and good sized shower cubicles. Baby bath. Good facilities for disabled people. Laundry facilities. Dog shower. Well stocked shop. Gas supplies. Large bar with satellite TV. Good restaurant and snack bar with takeaway (all season). Play area. Swimming and paddling pools (1/6-15/9). Bicycle hire. Attractive barbecue area with covered seating. Off site: Fishing 300 m. Boat launching 8 km. Small town of Sant Jaume.

Open: 27 March - 27 September.

Directions

From the A7 take exit 41, signed Amposta, N340. Immediately after crossing river Ebro leave N340 signed Els Muntells and Sant Jaume. On entering Sant Jaume turn right over canal, signed Els Muntells. At T-junction turn left. Site on right in 6 km. GPS: N40:39.395 E00:46.771

Charges guide

Per person	€ 4,40 - € 5,95
pitch incl. car	€ 10,10 - € 12,20
electricity (5A)	€ 4,05 - € 4,30

ES85400 Kawan Village La Torre del Sol

Ctra N340 km 1136, E-43300 Montroig (Tarragona)

Tel: **977 810 486**. Email: **info@latorredelsol.com**

www.alanrogers.com/ES85400

A pleasant banana tree-lined approach road gives way to avenues of palms as you arrive at Torre del Sol. This is a very large site occupying a good position in the south of Catalunya with direct access to the soft sand beach. The site is exceptionally well maintained by a large workforce. There is good shade on a high proportion of the 1,500 individual, numbered pitches. All have electricity and are mostly of about 70-80 sq.m. Strong features here are 800 m. of clean beach-front with a special Mediterranean type of pitch, and the entertainment that is provided all season. Part of the site is between the railway and the sea so there is some train noise. The cinema doubles as a theatre to stage shows all season. A complex of three pools, thoughtfully laid out with grass sunbathing areas and palms has a lifeguard. There is wireless internet access throughout the site. There is usually space for odd nights but for good places between 10/7-16/8 it is best to reserve (only taken for a stay of seven nights or more). We were impressed with the provision of season-long entertainment, and to give parents a break, children were in the safe hands of the animation team who ensure they enjoy the novel 'Happy Camp' and various workshops. There is a separate area where the team will take your children to camp overnight in the Indian reservation.

Facilities

Four very well maintained, fully equipped, toilet blocks include units for disabled people and babies. Washing machines. Gas supplies. Large supermarket, bakery and souvenir shops. Full restaurant. Takeaway. Bar with large terrace where entertainment is held daily. Beach bar. Coffee bar and ice cream bar. Pizzeria. Open roof cinema. 3 TV lounges. Well soundproofed disco. Swimming pools (two heated). Solarium. Sauna. Two large jacuzzis. Sports areas. Tennis. Squash. Language school (Spanish). Minigolf. Sub-aqua. Bicycle hire. Fishing. Windsurfing school; sailboards and pedaloes for hire. Playground, crèche and Happy Camp. Fridge hire. Library. Hairdresser. Business centre. WiFi. Car repair and car wash. No animals permitted. No jet skis accepted. Off site: Beach fishing. Riding 3 km. Golf 4 km.

Open: Easter - 20 October.

Directions

Entrance is off main N340 road by 1136 km. marker, about 30 km. from Tarragona towards Valencia. From motorway take Cambrils exit and turn west on N340. GPS: N41:02.224 E00:58.487

Charges guide

Per unit incl. 2 persons and electricity	€ 19,70 - € 61,15
extra person	€ 3,25 - € 9,35
child (0-10 yrs)	free - € 7,45

Discounts in low season for longer stays.
Camping Cheques accepted.

ES86150 Kiko Park Oliva

E-46780 Oliva (Valencia)

Tel: **962 850 905**. Email: **kikopark@kikopark.com** **www.alanrogers.com/ES86150**

Kiko Park is a smart site nestled behind protective sand dunes alongside a 'blue flag' beach. There are sets of attractively tiled steps over the dunes or a long boardwalk near the beach bar (good for prams and wheelchairs) to take you to the fine white sandy beach and the sea. The 180 large pitches all have electricity and the aim is to progressively upgrade all these to serviced 'super' pitches. There are plenty of flowers, hedging and trees adding shade, privacy and colour. A pool complex provides a spa, whirlpool, solarium, gym and a pool bar. An award winning restaurant with architecture that reminds one of a ship is near the tropical style beach-bar, both overlooking the marina, beautiful beach and sea. This is an excellent site for watersports enthusiasts.

Facilities

Four modern sanitary blocks are very clean with large showers, washbasins (a few in cabins), British style WCs and excellent facilities for disabled visitors (who will find a large part of this site flat and convenient). Laundry facilities. Motorcaravan services. Gas supplies. Supermarket. Restaurant. Bar with TV. Beach-side bar and restaurant (all year). Swimming pools and gym. Playground. Watersports facilities. Diving school in high season (from mid June). Entertainment for children from mid June. Pétanque. Bicycle hire. Off site: Golf 5 km.

Open: All year.

Directions

From A7 north of Benidorm take exit 61 to the town and then the beach; site is at the northwest end. GPS: N38:55.896 W0:05.808

Charges guide

Per person	€ 3,21 - € 6,53
child (under 10 yrs)	€ 2,68 - € 5,78
pitch	€ 10,60 - € 32,40
dog	€ 0,80 - € 2,68
electricity (per kWh)	€ 3,75

ES86250 Kiko Park Rural

Ctra Embalse Contreras km 3, E-46317 Villargordo del Cabriel (Valencia)

Tel: **962 139 082**. Email: **kikoparkrural@kikopark.com** **www.alanrogers.com/ES86250**

Approaching Kiko Park Rural, you will see a small hilltop village appearing in a landscape of mountains, vines and a jewel-like lake. Kiko was a small village and farm and the village now forms the campsite and accommodation. Amenities are contained within the architecturally authentic buildings, some old and some new. The 76 pitches (with 6A electricity and water) all have stunning views, as do the pools. Generous hedge plantings have been made which already afford some privacy. The new Valencia - Madrid rail link will cut through the valley, due for 2009.

Facilities

Three toilet blocks are very well equipped, including excellent facilities for disabled people. Motorcaravan services. Gas. Well stocked shop. Excellent restaurant. Pleasant bar. Swimming and paddling pools. Very good playground. Bicycle hire. Animation in high season. Many adventurous activities can be arranged, including white water rafting, gorging, orienteering, trekking, bungee and riding. Large families and groups catered for.
Off site: Fishing, canoeing and windsurfing on the lake. Village 3 km.

Open: All year.

Directions

From autopista A7/E15 on Valencia ring road (near the airport) take A3 to west. Villagordo del Cabriel is 80 km. towards Motilla. Take the village exit and follow signs through village and over a hill - spot the village on a hill 2 km. away. That is the campsite! GPS: N39:31.800 W01:26.400

Charges guide

Per person	€ 4,75 - € 5,95
child (up to 10 yrs)	€ 3,60 - € 4,10
pitch	€ 4,75 - € 13,45

ES85600 Camping Playa Tropicana

Playa Tropicana, E-12579 Alcossebre (Castelló)
Tel: **964 412 463**. Email: **info@playatropicana.com** **www.alanrogers.com/ES85600**

Playa Tropicana is a unique site which will strike visitors immediately as being very different. It has been given a tropical theme with scores of 'Romanesque' white statues around the site including in the sanitary blocks. The site has 300 marked pitches separated by lines of flowering bushes under mature trees. The pitches vary in size (50-90 sq.m), most are shaded and there are electricity connections throughout (some need long leads). There are 50 pitches with shared water and drainage on their boundaries. The site has a delightful position away from the main hub of tourism, alongside a good sandy beach which shelves gently into the clean waters. To gain access to this it is necessary to cross a promenade in front of the site, which also has statues. It is in a quiet position and it is a drive rather than a walk to the centre of the village resort. The theme extends into an excellent restaurant where, in high season, you may dine on the upper terrace with uninterrupted sea views. A variety of entertainment is provided and there is also a children's club and social room with films and soft drinks bar in high season. The site has several large water features by the high quality restaurant (some are very cheeky!). Aviaries are housed in a corner of the site.

Facilities

Three sanitary blocks delightfully decorated, fully equipped and of excellent standard, include washbasins in private cabins. Baby baths and facilities for disabled people. Washing machine. Motorcaravan services. Gas supplies. Large supermarket. Superb restaurant, a little expensive. (Easter - late Sept). Swimming pool (18 x 11 m) and children's pool. Playground. Bicycle hire. Children's club. Fishing. Torches necessary in some areas. No TVs allowed in July/Aug. Dogs are not accepted. Off site: Fishing and watersports on the beaches. Riding and boat launching 3 km. Golf 40 km.

Open: All year.

Directions

Alcoceber (or Alcossebre) is between Peñiscola and Oropesa. Turn off N340 at 1018 km. marker towards Alcossebre on CV142. Just before entering town proceed through two sets of traffic lights and turn right immediately after the second set, follow the road to the coast and site is 2.5 km. The entrance sliding gate faces the coast road and incorporates a pedestrian gate. Avoid alternative route given by GPS. GPS: N40:13.320 E00:16.020

Charges guide

Per unit incl. 2 persons and electricity	€ 19,00 - € 63,00
extra person	€ 4,00 - € 8,00
child (1-10 yrs)	€ 3,00 - € 7,00

Many discount schemes out of season.
Camping Cheques accepted.

2016

ES85800 Bonterra Park

Avenida de Barcelona 47, E-12560 Benicasim (Castelló)

Tel: **964 300 007**. Email: **info@bonterrapark.com** **www.alanrogers.com/ES85800**

If you are looking for a town site which is not too crowded and has very good facilities, this one may be for you. It is a 300 m. walk to a good beach – and parking is not too difficult. The site has 320 pitches (70-90 sq.m), all with electricity (6/10A) and a variety of bungalows, some attractively built in brick. There are dedicated 'green' pitches for tents. Bonterra has a clean, neat appearance with tarmac roads, gravel covered pitches, palms, grass and a number of trees which give good shade. Overhead sunshades are provided for the more open pitches in summer. There is a little road and rail noise. The site has an attractive pool complex including a covered pool for the winter months. The beach is good for scuba diving or snorkelling – hire facilities are available at Benicasim. This is a well run, Mediterranean style site with English spoken by reception staff. It is usefully located for visiting attractions such as the Carmelite monastery at Desierto de las Palmas, 6 km. distant or the historic town of Castellon.

Facilities

Four attractive, well maintained sanitary blocks provide some private cabins, washbasins with hot water, others with cold. Baby and dog showers. Facilities for disabled campers. Laundry. Motorcaravan services. Restaurant/bar. Shop. Swimming and paddling pools. Covered, heated pool (all year). Playground (some concrete bases). Tennis. Multisport court. Gym. Disco. Bicycle hire. Miniclub. Satellite TV. Internet access (WiFi). Off site: Town facilities. Sandy beach and fishing 500 m. Riding 3 km. Boat launching 5 km. Golf 10 km. Nature Park.

Open: All year.

Directions

Site is on the quiet old main road running through Benicasim. From either direction leave the N340 at km. 987. At roundabout turn left and travel for about 1.5 km. to site on the left (white painted walls). Look for two supermarkets, one 200 m. before site and a second directly opposite. Site is well signed. GPS: N40:03.416 E00:04.464

Charges guide

Per person	€ 3,75 - € 5,51
child (0-9 yrs)	€ 3,21 - € 4,49
pitch acc. to type and season	€ 8,72 - € 38,31
electricity	€ 3,75 - € 6,21

All plus 7% VAT. Less in low season and special long stay rates excl. July/Aug.

ES87550 Camping Caravanning Moraira

Camino Paellero 50, E-03724 Moraira-Teulada (Alacant)

Tel: **965 745 249**. Email: **campingmoraira@campingmoraira.com** **www.alanrogers.com/ES87550**

This small hillside site with some views over the town and marina is quietly situated in an urban area amongst old pine trees and just 400 metres from a sheltered bay. Terracing provides shaded pitches of varying size, some really quite small (access to some of the upper pitches may be difficult for larger units). Some pitches have water and drainage and a few have sea views. There are electricity connections. An attractive irregularly shaped pool with paved sunbathing terrace is below the small bar/restaurant and terrace. The pool has observation windows where you can watch the swimmers, and is used for sub-aqua instruction. The site runs a professional diving school for all levels (the diving here is good and the water warm, even in winter). A sandy beach is 1.5 km. A large, painted water tower stands at the top of the site. The reception building is being extended to provide a range of new facilities.

Facilities

The high quality toilet block, with polished granite floors and marble fittings, is built to a unique and ultra-modern design with extra large free hot showers (hot water may be variable during the winter). Washing machine and dryer. Motorcaravan services. Bar/restaurant and shop (1/7-30/9). Small swimming pool (not all year). Sub-aqua with instruction. Tennis. Torches may be required.
Off site: Shops, bars and restaurants within walking distance. Beach 1.5 km. Fishing 400 m. Bicycle hire 1 km. Golf 8 km.

Open: All year.

Directions

Best approach is from Teulada. From A7 exit 63 take N332 and in 3.5 km. turn right (Teulada and Moraira). In Teulada fork right to Moraira. At junction at town entrance turn right signed Calpe and in 1 km. turn right into road to site on bend immediately after Res. Don Julio.
GPS: N38:41.520 E00:08.400

Charges guide

Per person	€ 6,42
child (4-9 yrs)	€ 4,82
pitch incl. electricity	€ 20,45

All plus 7% VAT. Less 15-60% in low season.

ES87540 Camping Jávea

Ctra Cabo de la Nao km 1, Apdo 83, E-03730 Jávea (Alacant)

Tel: **965 791 070**. Email: **info@camping-javea.com** **www.alanrogers.com/ES87540**

The 200 metre long access road to this site is a little unkempt as it passes some factories, but all changes on the final approach with palms, orange and pine trees, the latter playing host to a colony of parakeets. English is spoken at reception. The boxed hedges and palms surrounding this area with a backdrop of hills dotted with villas presents an attractive setting. Three hectares provides space for 214 numbered pitches with 183 for touring units. Flat, level and rectangular in shape, the pitches vary in size 60-80 sq.m. (not advised for units with an overall length exceeding 7 m).

Facilities

Two very clean, fully equipped, sanitary blocks include two children's toilets plus a baby bath. Two washing machines. Fridge hire. Small bar and restaurant where in high season you purchase bread and milk. Large swimming pool with lifeguard and sunbathing lawns. Play area. Boules. Electronic barriers (deposit for card). Caravan storage. WiFi. Tennis. Off site: Sandy beach 3 km. Old and New Jávea within easy walking distance with supermarkets and shops catering for all needs.

Open: All year.

Directions

Exit N332 for Jávea on A134, continue in direction of Port (road number changes to CV 734). At roundabout (Lidl supermarket) turn right signed Arenal Platges and Cabo de la Nao. Straight on at next roundabout to camping sign and slip road in 100 m. If you miss slip road go back from next roundabout. GPS: N38:47.000 E00:10.190

Charges guide

Per person	€ 5,22 - € 5,80
pitch incl. electricity	€ 15,92 - € 19,50

ES87430 Camping Marjal

Ctra N332 km 73,4, E-03140 Guardamar del Segura (Alacant)

Tel: **966 727 070**. Email: **camping@marjal.com** **www.alanrogers.com/ES87430**

Marjal is located beside the estuary of the Segura river, alongside the pine and eucalyptus forests of the Dunas de Guardamar natural park. The fine sandy beach can be reached through the forest (800 m). This is a new site with a huge lagoon-style pool and a superb sports complex. There are 212 pitches on this award winning site, all with water, electricity, drainage and satellite TV points, the ground covered with crushed marble, making the pitches clean and pleasant. There is some shade and the site has an open feel with lots of room for manoeuvring. Reception is housed in a delicately coloured building complete with a towering Mirador, topped by a weather-vane depicting the 'Garza Real' (heron) bird which frequents the local area and forms part of the site logo. The large leased restaurant overlooks the pools and the river that leads to the sea in the near distance. This situation is shared with the taperia (high season) and bar with large terraces fringed by trees, palms and pomegranates. The impressive pool/lagoon complex (1,100 sq.m) has a water cascade, an island bar plus bridge, one part sectioned as a pool for children and a jacuzzi. The extensive sports area is also impressive with qualified instructors who will customise your fitness programme whilst consulting the doctor. No effort has been spared here, the quality heated indoor pool, light-exercise room, sauna, solarium, beauty salon, fully equipped gym and changing rooms, including facilities for disabled visitors, are of the highest quality. Aerobics and physiotherapy are also on offer. All activities are discounted for campers. A programme of entertainment is provided in season.

Facilities

Three excellent heated toilet blocks have free hot water, elegant separators between sinks, spacious showers and some cabins. Each block has high quality facilities for babies and disabled campers, modern laundry and dishwashing rooms. Car wash. Well stocked supermarket. Restaurants. Bar. Large outdoor pool complex (1/6-31/10). Heated indoor pool (low season). Fitness suite. Jacuzzi. Sauna. Solarium. Aerobics and aquarobics. Play room. Minigolf. Floodlit tennis and soccer pitch. Bicycle hire. Games room. TV room. ATM. Business centre. Internet access. Off site: Beach 800 m. Riding or golf 4 km.

Open: All year.

Directions

On N332 40 km. south of Alicante, site is on the sea side between 73 and 74 km. markers.
GPS: N38:06.560 W00:39.280

Charges guide

Per person	€ 3,00 - € 8,50
child (4-12 yrs)	free - € 5,50
dog	€ 2,20 - € 3,20

ES86810 Camping Villasol

Avenida Bernat de Sarria, E-03503 Benidorm (Alacant)

Tel: **965 850 422**. Email: **camping-villasol@dragonet.es** **www.alanrogers.com/ES86810**

Benidorm is increasingly popular for winter stays and Villasol is a genuinely good, purpose built modern site. Many of the 309 well separated pitches are arranged on wide terraces which afford views of the mountains surrounding Benidorm. All pitches (80-85 sq.m.) have electricity and satellite TV connections, with 160 with full services for seasonal use. Shade is mainly artificial. Reservations are only accepted for winter stays of over three months (from 1 Oct). There is a small indoor pool, heated for winter use, and a very attractive, large outdoor pool complex (summer only) overlooked by the bar/restaurant and restaurant terrace.

Facilities

Modern toilet blocks provide free, controllable hot water to showers and washbasins and British WCs. Good facilities for disabled campers. Laundry facilities. Good value restaurant. Bar. Shop. Swimming pools, outdoor and indoor. Playground. Evening entertainment programme. Dogs are not accepted. Off site: Fishing and bicycle hire 1.3 km. Golf 8 km.

Open: All year.

Directions

From autopista exit 65 (Benidorm) and turn left at second set of traffic lights. After 1 km. at another set of lights turn right, then right again at next lights. Site is 400 m. GPS: N38:32.280 W00:07.140

Charges guide

Per person	€ 5,30 - € 6,90
pitch incl. electricity	€ 14,80 - € 22,50

All plus 7% VAT.
Good discounts for longer stays in winter.

ES86830 Camping Benisol

Avenida de la Comunidad Valenciana s/n, E-03500 Benidorm (Alacant)

Tel: **965 851 673**. Email: **campingbenisol@yahoo.es** **www.alanrogers.com/ES86830**

Camping Benisol is a well developed and peaceful site with lush, green vegetation and a mountain background. Mature hedges and trees afford privacy to each pitch and some artificial shade is provided where necessary. There are 298 pitches of which around 115 are for touring units (60-80 sq.m). All have electrical hook-ups (4/6A) and 75 have drainage. Some daytime road noise should be expected. The site has an excellent restaurant serving traditional Spanish food at great prices, with a pretty, shaded terrace overlooking the pool with its palms and thatched pool bar.

Facilities

Modern sanitary facilities, heated in winter and kept very clean, have free, solar heated hot water to washbasins, showers and sinks. Laundry facilities. Gas supplies. Restaurant with terrace and bar (all year, closed 1 day a week). Shop. Swimming pool (Easter - Nov). Small, old style play area. Minigolf. Jogging track. Tennis. Golf driving range. ATM. Off site: Riding 1 km. Bicycle hire 3 km. Fishing (sea) 3 km. Golf 14 km. Bus route.

Open: All year.

Directions

Site is northeast of Benidorm. Exit N332 at 152 km. marker and take turn signed Playa Levant. Site is 100 m. on left off the main road, well signed. GPS: N38:33.540 W00:05.820

Charges guide

Per person	€ 4,95 - € 5,25
pitch incl. electricity	€ 16,05 - € 20,90

All plus 7% VAT. Less 15-60% in low seasons.
No credit cards.

2016 OK

ES87420 Camping Internacional La Marina

Ctra N332 km 76, E-03194 La Marina (Alacant)

Tel: **965 419 200**. Email: **info@campinglamarina.com** **www.alanrogers.com/ES87420**

Efficiently run by a friendly Belgian family, La Marina has 381 pitches of seven different types and size ranging from about 50 sq.m. for tents to 100 sq.m. with electricity (10/16A), TV, water and drainage. Artificial shade is provided and the pitches are extremely well maintained on level, well drained ground with a special area allocated for tents in a small orchard. The lagoon swimming pool complex is absolutely fabulous and has something for everyone (with lifeguards). William Le Metayer, the owner, is passionate about La Marina and it shows in his search for perfection. A magnificent new, modern building houses some superb extra amenities. These include a relaxed business centre with internet access, a tapas bar decorated with amazing ceramics (handmade by the owner's mother) and a quality restaurant with a water fountain feature and great views of the lagoon. There is also a conference centre and an extensive library, with the whole of the lower ground floor dedicated to children with a play area and a 'cyber zone' for teenagers. With a further bar and a soundproofed disco, the building is of an exceptional, eco-friendly standard. A fine fitness centre and covered, heated pool (14 x 7 m) are close by. A pedestrian gate at the rear of the site gives access to the long sandy beach through the coastal pine forest that is a feature of the area. We recommend this site very highly whatever type of holidaying camper you may be. Member of 'Leading Campings Group'.

Facilities

The elegant sanitary blocks offer the very best of modern facilities. Heated in winter, they include private cabins and facilities for disabled visitors. Laundry facilities. Motorcaravan services. Gas. Supermarket. Bars. Restaurant (all year). Swimming pools (1/4-15/10). Indoor pool. Fitness centre. Sauna. Play rooms. Extensive activity and entertainment programme. Sports area. Tennis. Huge playground. Hairdresser. Bicycle hire. Off site: Fishing 500 m. Boat launching 5 km. Golf 7 km. Riding 15 km. Hourly bus service from outside the gate. Theme parks.

Open: All year.

Directions

Site is 2 km. west of La Marina. Leave N332 Guardamara de Segura - Santa Pola road at 75 km. marker if travelling north, or 78 km. marker if travelling south. Site is well signed. GPS: N38:07.779 W00:38.974

Charges 2009

Per person	€ 5,35 - € 8,00
child (under 10 yrs)	€ 3,75 - € 5,50
pitch incl. electricity, acc. to type and season	€ 22,58 - € 46,61
dog	free - € 2,14

Seven grades of pitch. Good discounts for longer stays 16/9-14/6, excluding Easter.

ES86870 Camping Cap Blanch

Playa de Cap Blanch 25, E-03590 Altea (Alacant)

Tel: **965 845 946**. Email: **capblanch@ctv.es** **www.alanrogers.com/ES86870**

This well run, small site has plenty of character. It is open all year and is very popular for winter stays. Alongside the beach road, it has direct access to the pebble beach and is within a few hundred yards of all Albir's shops and restaurants. The 250 pitches on flat, hard gravel are of a good size and well maintained with 5A electricity. The site tends to be full in winter and is very popular with several nationalities, especially the Dutch. For winter stays, it would pay to get there before Christmas as January and February are the peak months.

Facilities

The refurbished sanitary block can be heated and provides good facilities including some washbasins in cabins, baby facilities and a room for disabled visitors (both these accessed by key). Motorcaravan services. Gas supplies. Laundry. Bar and restaurant. Takeaway. Playground. Tennis. Boules. Fitness centre. Organised entertainment and courses. ATM. Off site: Restaurants, shops and commercial centre close. Golf 500 m. Bicycle hire 1 km. Riding 5 km.

Open: All year.

Directions

From N332, north or south, watch for sign Playa del Albir and proceed through Albir to the coast road. Site is on north side of Albir, well signed. GPS: N38:34.646 W0:03.871

Charges guide

Per person	€ 3,90 - € 6,00
child (3-12 yrs)	€ 3,25 - € 5,00
pitch incl. electricity	€ 11,70 - € 18,00

VAT included. Less 10-35% for low season stays 7-30 days, special rates for long stays.

ES87520 Camping Naturista El Portus

El Portus, E-30394 Cartagena (Murcia)

Tel: **968 553 052**. Email: **elportus@elportus.com** **www.alanrogers.com/ES87520**

Set in a secluded south facing bay fringed by mountains, El Portus is a fairly large naturist site enjoying magnificent views and with direct access to a small sand and pebble beach. This part of Spain enjoys almost all year round sunshine. There are some 400 pitches, 300 for tourers, ranging from 60-100 sq.m, all but a few having electricity (6A). They are mostly on fairly level, if somewhat stony and barren ground. El Portus has a reasonable amount of shade from established trees and nearly every pitch has a view. Residential units are situated on the hillside above the site. In season, a large supervised swimming pool and paddling pool are sheltered with landscaping and grass areas for sunbathing. At other times there is a smaller heated pool above the camping area that has a retractable dome cover. One of the bar/restaurants is open all year. Mobile homes, chalets and new, fully equipped, modern studios with superb views are available to rent. El Portus has a positive Spanish atmosphere in high season and is popular through the winter months with all nationalities including many British. This is a relaxed site with welcoming, English speaking reception staff.

Facilities

Five acceptable toilet blocks, all unisex, are of varying styles and fully equipped. Opened as required, they are clean and bright. Unit for disabled visitors. Washing machines. Motorcaravan services. Well stocked shop. Bar with TV and library. Restaurants. Swimming pools (June - Sept). Wellness centre. Play area. Tennis. Pétanque. Yoga. Scuba-diving club (high season). Windsurfing. Spanish lessons. Small boat moorings. Entertainment programme all season. Off site: Fishing from beach. Golf 28 km.

Open: All year.

Directions

Site is on the coast, 10 km. west of Cartagena. Follow signs to Mazarron then take E22 to Canteras. Site is well signed for 4 km. If approaching through Cartagena, exit the town on N332 following signs for Canteras. GPS: N37:35.100 W01:04.030

Charges guide

Per person	€ 7,00
pitch incl. 6A electricity	€ 22,20

Plus 7% VAT.
Camping Cheques accepted.

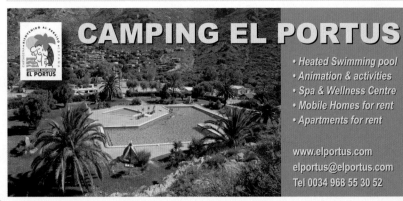

ES87530 Caravaning La Manga

Autovia Cartagena - La Manga Salida 11, E-30386 La Manga del Mar Menor (Murcia)

Tel: **902 021 352**. Email: **lamanga@caravaning.es** **www.alanrogers.com/ES87530**

This is a very large well equipped 'holiday style' site with its own beach and both indoor and outdoor pools. With a good number of typical Spanish long stay units, the length of the site is impressive (1 km) and a bicycle is very helpful for getting about. The 1,000 regularly laid out, gravel touring pitches (100 or 110 sq. m) are generally separated by hedges which also provide a degree of shade. Each has 10A electricity supply, water and the possibility of satellite TV reception. This site's excellent facilities are ideally suited for holidays in the winter when the weather is very pleasantly warm. If you are suffering from aches and pains try the famous local mud treatment. Reception will assist with bookings. November daytime temperatures usually exceed 20°C. La Manga is a 22 km. long narrow strip of land, bordered by the Mediterranean on one side and by the Mar Menor on the other. There are sandy beaches on both sides and considerable development in terms of hotels, apartments, restaurants, night clubs, etc. in between – a little reminiscent of Miami Beach! The very end of the southern part is great for 'getting away from it all' (take a picnic for the beach and be sure to go over the little bridge for privacy). The campsite is situated on the approach to 'the strip' enjoying the benefit of its own semi-private beach with impressive tall palm trees alongside the Mar Menor which provides shallow warm waters, ideal for families with children.

Facilities

Nine clean toilet blocks of standard design, well spaced around the site. Laundry. Gas supplies. Large well stocked supermarket. Restaurant. Bar. Snack bar. Pool complex (April - Sept). Indoor pool, gym (April - Oct), sauna, jacuzzi and massage service. Outdoor fitness course. Open air cinema (July/Aug). Tennis. Pétanque. Minigolf. Play area. Watersports school. Internet café (also WiFi). Winter activities. Off site: Golf, bicycle hire and riding 5 km.

Open: All year.

Directions

Use exit 11 from MU312 dual carriageway towards Cabo de Palos, signed Playa Honda (site signed also). Cross road bridge and double back on yourself. The site entrance is clearly visible beside dual carriageway. GPS: N37:37.467 W00:44.665

Charges guide

Per pitch incl. 2 persons	€ 18,85 - € 33,00
extra person	€ 3,85 - € 4,80

All plus 7% VAT. Camping Cheques accepted.

ES87450 Camping La Fuente

Camino de La Bocamina, E-30626 Banos de Fortuna (Murcia)

Tel: **968 685 125**. Email: **info@campingfuente.com** **www.alanrogers.com/ES87450**

Located in an area known for its thermal waters since Roman and Moorish times and with just 87 pitches and six bungalows, La Fuente is a gem. Unusually winter is high season here. The main attraction here is the huge hydrotherapy centre where the water is constant at 36°C all year. The pool can be covered in inclement weather. The site is in two sections, one where pitches are in standard rows and the other where they are in circles around blocks. The hard, flat pitches are on shingle (rock pegs advised), have 10A electricity and 53 have their own mini sanitary unit.

Facilities

All pitches have their own facilities including a unit for disabled campers. Washing machines and dryers. High quality restaurant shared with accommodation guests. Snack bar by pool. Supermarket. Bicycle hire. Communal barbecues. Jacuzzi. Off site: Spa town, massage therapies, hot pools 500 m. Fortuna, shops, bars, restaurants 3 km.

Open: All year.

Directions

From A7/E15 Alicante - Murcia road take C3223 to Fortuna then follow signs to Banos de Fortuna. The site with its bright yellow walls can be easily seen from the road and is very well signed in the town. GPS: N38:12.409 W01:06.439

Charges guide

Per person	€ 3,25
pitch incl. electricity	€ 9,50 - € 11,50

ES87480 Camping Los Madriles

Ctra de la Azohia km 4.5, E-30868 Isla Plana (Murcia)

Tel: **968 152 151**. Email: **camplosmadriles@terra.es** **www.alanrogers.com/ES87480**

An exceptional site with super facilities, Los Madriles is run by a hard working team, with continual improvements being made. Twenty kilometres west of Cartegena, the approach to the site and the surrounding area is fairly unremarkable, but the site is not. A fairly steep access road leads to 313 flat, good to large size terraced pitches, each having electricity, water and a waste point. Most have shade from large trees with many benefiting from panoramic views of the sea or behind to the mountains. The site has huge rectangular and lagoon style pools with water sprays and jacuzzis.

Facilities

Four sanitary blocks and one small toilet block provide excellent facilities, including services in one block for disabled campers. Private wash cabins. Washing machines and dryers. Motorcaravan services. Car wash. Supermarket, restaurant/snack bar and bar (all open all season but hours are limited). Swimming pools with jacuzzi. Boules. Play areas. Animals are not accepted. Off site: Town close by. Beach 800 m. and fishing 800 m. (Licence required, purchase in Puerto Mazarron). Boat launching 3 km. Riding 6 km. Golf 20 km.

Open: All year.

Directions

From E15/A7 take exit 845 and follow RM3 in direction of Cartagena, Fuente Alamo and Mazarron (do not turn into Mazarron). Continue towards Puerto Mazarron and take N332 (Cartagena). On reaching coast continue with N332 (Cartagena and Alicante). At roundabout turn right towards Isla Plana and La Azohia. Site is well signed and on the left in 5 km. GPS: N37:34.410 W01:11.470

Charges guide

Per person	€ 4,50 - € 5,50
pitch incl. electricity	€ 17,00 - € 20,00

ES87630 Camping Cabo de Gata

Ctra Cabo de Gata s/n, Cortijo Ferrón, E-04150 Cabo de Gata (Almería)

Tel: **950 160 443**. Email: **info@campingcabodegata.com** **www.alanrogers.com/ES87630**

This medium sized site can be regarded as a very pleasant, all year campsite offering facilities to a good standard. Very popular with British visitors through the winter, it is located within the Cabo de Gata-Nijar natural park and set in open farmland, yet is only a 1 km. walk from a fine sandy beach. The 250 gravel pitches are level and of a reasonable size, with 6/16A electricity and limited shade from maturing trees or canopies. There are specific areas for very large units and seven chalets for rent. A modern, airy reception is adjacent to internet facilities, whilst the nearby irregularly shaped swimming pool in close proximity to the bar/restaurant are both first class. To the west, Salinas de Acosta and the lighthouse at Faro de Gata (fine views). The salinas are renowned for their bird life and from one of the hides large flocks of pink flamingo and many other species can be seen. Almeria has many quality shops and the Alcazaba (955 A.D.), whilst a short drive away near Tabernas, are Mini Hollywood and the whitewashed village of Nijar, noted for its basketry and rugs.

Facilities

Two, well maintained, clean toilet blocks provide all the necessary sanitary facilities. including British type WCs, washbasins and free hot showers. Facilities for disabled campers. Restaurant, bar and shop (all year). Swimming pool. Tennis. Small playground. Library. Bicycle hire. English spoken. Entertainment programme. Off site: Nearest beach 1 km. Bus 1 km. Fishing 1 km. Golf 10 km. Riding 15 km.

Open: All year.

Directions

From A7-E15 take exit 460 or 467 and follow signs for Retamar via N344 and for Cabo de Gata. Site is on the right before village of Cabo de Gata. The final stretch of road is in a poor state of repair. GPS: N36:48.113 W2:14.683

Charges guide

Per person	€ 5,50
pitch incl. electricity	€ 16,20 - € 16,80

Camping Cheques accepted.

ES92760 Camping Reina Isabel

Ctra Granada - La Zubia, km. 4, E-18140 La Zubia (Granada)

Tel: **958 590 041**. Email: **info@reinaisabelcamping.com** **www.alanrogers.com/ES92760**

Reina Isabel can be found just 3 km. from the centre of Granada and just 1 km. from the entrance to the spectacular Sierra Nevada National Park. The site is open for an extended season and is well located for winter sports holidays in the Sierra Nevada. There are 51 shady touring pitches here (each around 70 sq.m), all with electrical connections. A number of chalets and apartments are also available for rent. A regular bus service operates to the city centre and to other places of interest, notably the Alhambra palace. On-site facilities include a swimming pool and bar/restaurant. Granada is, by any standard, a fascinating city. Apart from the Alhambra, the palace of Charles V and the UNESCO listed ancient Arab quarter, El Albayzin, are well worth a visit, along with much else in the city. The Sierra Nevada is made up of some of Spain's most stunning mountain scenery and is ideal walking and mountain biking country.

Facilities

Bar/restaurant. Shop. Swimming pool. Play area. Chalets and apartments for rent. Off site: Bus stop with regular service to the city centre (20 minutes). Sierra Nevada ski resort 29 km.

Open: All year.

Directions

Site is south of Granada. Leave A44 motorway at exit 132 and head east on A395. Follow signs to La Zubia, joining the southbound Calle de Laurel de la Reina. Site is clearly signed from here.
GPS: N37:07.474 W3:35.175

Charges guide

Per unit incl. 2 persons and electricity	€ 18,95 - € 23,00
extra person	€ 4,60

ES92900 Camping El Balcon de Pitres

Ctra Orgiva - Ugijar km 51, E-18414 Pitres (Granada)

Tel: **958 766 111**. Email: **info@balcondepitres.com** **www.alanrogers.com/ES92900**

A simple country site perched high in the mountains of the Alpujarras, on the south side of the Sierra Nevada, El Balcon de Pitres has its own rustic charm. Many thousands of trees planted around the site provide shade. There are stunning views from some of the 175 level grassy pitches (large units may find pitch access difficult). The garden is kept green by spring waters, which you can hear and sometimes see, tinkling away in places. The Lopez family, have built this site from barren mountain top to cool oasis in the mountains in just fifteen years. It is a wonderful relaxing place to cool down, away from the heat of the coast.

Facilities

Two toilet blocks provide adequate facilities but the steeply sloping site is unsuitable for disabled campers and thus there are no facilities for them. Snack bar. Bar. Shop (closed Tuesdays). Swimming pools (extra charge). Bicycle hire. Torches useful. Off site: Fishing. Canyoning. Trekking. Parascending. Quad bikes.

Open: All year.

Directions

Site is about 30 km. northeast of Motril. Heading south on A44 (E902) exit 164 (Lanjaron) onto E348 towards Orgiva. Fork left at sign (A4132) Pampaneira 8 km. Continue to Pitres (7 km). Site signed. (Steep and winding roads).
GPS: N36:55.911 W03:19.961

Charges guide

Per person	€ 5,00
child	€ 3,50
pitch incl. car	€ 9,50 - € 11,50
electricity (2A)	€ 3,00

2016

ES92850 Camping Las Lomas

Ctra de Sierra Nevada, E-18160 Güejar-Sierra (Granada)

Tel: **958 484 742**. Email: **laslomas@campings.net** **www.alanrogers.com/ES92850**

This site is high in the Güéjar–Sierra and looks down on the Patano de Canales reservoir. After a wonderful drive to Güéjar-Sierra, you are rewarded with a site boasting excellent facilities. It is set on a slope but the pitches have been levelled and are quite private, with high separating hedges and many mature trees giving good shade (some pitches are fully serviced, with sinks and most have electricity). The large bar/restaurant complex and pools have wonderful views over the lake and a grassed sunbathing area runs down to the fence (safe) looking over the long drop below. A new feature is luxury rooms for rent, including one with a superb spa which is for hire by the hour. Any infirm visitors will need a car to get around as the inclines are extreme.

Facilities

Pretty sanitary blocks (heated in winter) provide clean facilities. First class facilities for disabled campers and well equipped baby room (key at reception). Spa for hire. Motorcaravan services. Good supermarket. Restaurant/bar. Swimming pool. Play area. Minigolf. Many other activities including parascending. Barbecue. Internet access. Torches useful. Off site: Buses to village and Granada (15 km). Tours of the Alhambra organised. Useful site for winter skiing.

Open: All year.

Directions

Heading south towards Granada on A44 (E902 Jaén - Motril) take exit 132 onto A395 (Alhamba - Sierra Nevada). After 4 km. marker, exit 5B (Sierra Nevada). At 7 km. marker, exit right onto slip road. At junction turn left (Cenes de la Vega - Güéjar-Sierra). In 200 m. turn right on A4026. In 1.6 km. turn left (Güéjar-Sierra). Drive uphill, past dam and site is on right in 2.8 km. GPS: N37:09.644 W3:27.233

Charges guide

Per person	€ 4,00 - € 6,00
child (2-10 yrs)	€ 3,50 - € 4,50
pitch	€ 12,00 - € 14,00

VAT included.

ES92800 Camping Sierra Nevada

Avenida Madrid 107, E-18014 Granada (Granada)

Tel: **958 150 062**. Email: **campingmotel@terra.es** **www.alanrogers.com/ES92800**

This is a good site either for a night stop or for a stay of a few days while visiting Granada and for a city site it is surprisingly pleasant. Quite large, it has an open feeling and, to encourage you to stay a little longer, an irregular shape pool with a smaller children's pool open in high season. There is some traffic noise around the pool as it is on the road boundary. With 148 pitches for touring units (10/20A electricity), the site is in two parts with more mature trees and facilities to the northern end.

Facilities

Two very modern sanitary blocks, with excellent facilities, including cabins, very good facilities for disabled people and babies. Washing machines. Motorcaravan services. Gas supplies. Shop (15/3-15/10). Swimming pools with lifeguards and charge of € 1.50 (15/6-15/9). Bar/restaurant by pool. Tennis. Pétanque. Large playground. Doctor lives on site. Off site: Fishing 10 km. Golf 12 km. Bus station 50 m. from site gate.

Open: 1 March - 31 October.

Directions

Site is just outside the city to north, on road to Jaén and Madrid. From autopista, take Granada North - Almanjayar exit 123 (close to central bus station). Follow road back towards Granada and site is on the right, well signed. From other roads join the motorway to access the correct exit.
GPS: N37:12.241 W03:37.022

Charges guide

Per person	€ 5,70
child (3-10 yrs)	€ 4,85
pitch incl. electricity (10A)	€ 17,00

Runner up Alan Rogers Awards 2008

ES92950 Camping Don Cactus

Ctra N340 km 343, Playa de Carchuna, E-18730 Carchuna-Motril (Granada)

Tel: **958 623 109**. Email: **camping@doncactus.com** **www.alanrogers.com/ES92950**

Situated between the main N340 and the beach, this family run campsite is pleasantly surprising with clever planning and ongoing improvements. It is a comfortable site of 320 pitches (280 for touring). The flat pitches vary in size with electricity, some also with water and satellite TV connections, and are arranged along avenues with eucalyptus trees (which keep the mosquitoes away apparently) for shade. This quieter section of the coast is beautiful with coves and access to larger towns if wished. The friendly reception staff are very helpful with tourist advice and can arrange trips if needed.

Facilities

The large toilet block is dated but clean and provides British style WCs, showers and plenty of washbasins. Laundry facilities. Beach showers. Well stocked shop. Bar, restaurant and takeaway (all year). Swimming pool (in high season € 1.50 per day). Tennis. Play area. Summer activities for children. Outdoor fitness centre for adults. Pets corner. ATM. Internet point. Dogs are not accepted in July/Aug. Barbecues only in special area. Caravan storage. Off site: Bus service 500 m.

Open: All year.

Directions

From Motril - Carchuna road (N340/E15) turn towards the sea at km. 343. (site signed, but look at roof level for large green tent on the top of the building!). Travel about 600 m. then turn east to site on left. GPS: N36:41.743 W03:26.609

Charges guide

Per person	€ 6,00
pitch incl. electricity (5A)	€ 18,30

Low season discounts for longer stays.
Camping Cheques accepted.

ES88000 Camping Marbella Playa

Ctra N340 km 192,8, E-29600 Marbella (Málaga)

Tel: **952 833 998**. Email: **recepcion@campingmarbella.com** **www.alanrogers.com/ES88000**

This large site is 12 kilometres east of the internationally famous resort of Marbella with public transport available to the town centre and local attractions. A sandy beach is about 150 metres away with direct access. There are 430 individual pitches of up to 70 sq.m. with natural shade (additional artificial shade is provided to some), and electricity (10/20A) available throughout. Long leads may be required for some pitches. The site is busy throughout the high season but the high staff/customer ratio and the friendly staff approach ensures a comfortable stay. A large swimming pool complex with a restaurant/bar provides a very attractive feature.

Facilities

Four sanitary blocks of mixed ages, are fully equipped and well maintained. Three modern units for disabled visitors. Laundry service. Large supermarket. Bar, restaurant and café (all open all year). Supervised swimming pool (free: April - Sept). Playground. Children's activities. Torches advised. Off site: Bus service 150 m. Fishing 100 m. Golf and bicycle hire 5 km. Riding 10 km. Beach 200 m.

Open: All year.

Directions

Site is 12 km. east of Marbella. Access is close to the 193 km. point on the main N340. Signed Elviria, then camping signs. GPS: N36:29.476 W04:45.795

Charges guide

Per person	€ 3,42 - € 5,67
pitch incl. electricity	€ 7,57 - € 20,67

All plus 7% VAT. Reductions (up to 50%) for long stays and senior citizens outside 1/6-16/9.

ES88020 Kawan Village Cabopino

NO

Ctra N340 km 194,7, E-29604 Marbella (Málaga)

Tel: **952 834 373**. Email: **info@campingcabopino.com** **www.alanrogers.com/ES88020**

This large, mature site is alongside the main N340 Costa del Sol coast road, 12 km. east of Marbella and 15 km. from Fuengirola. The Costa del Sol is also known as the Costa del Golf and fittingly there is a major golf course alongside the site. The site is set amongst tall pine trees which provide shade for the sandy pitches (there are some huge areas for large units). The 300 touring pitches, a mix of level and sloping (chocks advisable), all have electricity (10A), but long leads may be required for some. There is a separate area on the western side for groups of younger guests.

Facilities

Five mature but very clean sanitary blocks provide hot water throughout (may be under pressure at peak times). Washing machines. Bar/restaurant and takeaway (all year). Shop. Outdoor pool (1/5-15/9) and indoor pool (all year). Play area. Some evening entertainment. ATM. Charcoal barbecues are not permitted. Off site: Beach and golf 200 m. Fishing, bicycle hire and riding within 1 km.

Open: All year.

Directions

Site is 12 km. from Marbella. Approaching Marbella from the east, leave the N340 at the 194 km. marker (signed Cabopino). Site is off the roundabout at the top of the slip road. GPS: N36:29.610 W04:44.630

Charges guide

Per unit incl. 2 persons and electricity	€ 20,95 - € 33,00

Discounts outside high season and for over 7 days.
Camping Cheques accepted.

ES90810 Camping Villsom

Ctra Sevilla - Cadiz km 554,8, E-41700 Sevilla (Sevilla)

Tel: **954 720 828** **www.alanrogers.com/ES90810**

This city site was one of the first to open in Spain and it is still owned by the same pleasant family. The administrative building consists of a peaceful and attractive bar with patio and satellite TV (where breakfast is served) and there is a pleasant, small reception area. It is a good site for visiting Seville with a frequent bus service to the centre. Camping Villsom has around 180 pitches which are level and shaded. A new hotel (Spanish style) of nine rooms has been added and new facilities for disabled visitors are planned. It is important to book if you intend to visit this site in peak weeks. It is not suitable for large motorhomes and there are few places for large caravans, but book.

Facilities

Sanitary facilities require modernisation in some areas. Some washbasins have cold water only. Laundry facilities. Small shop selling basic provisions. Bar with satellite TV (open July/Aug). Swimming pool (June - Sept). Putting. Drinks machine. Off site: Bus stop close. Most town facilities including restaurant, supermarket, cinema and theatre.

Open: All year.

Directions

On main Seville - Cadiz NIV road travelling from Seville take exit at km. 553 signed Dos Hermanos - Isla Menor. Go under road bridge and turn immediately right (Isla Mentor) to site 80 m. on right. From Cadiz take same signed exit and at roundabout take fourth exit to go over main road and then down a slip road to go under bridge, then as above. GPS: N37:16.641 W05:56.210

Charges guide

Per person	€ 4,45
child	€ 4,01
pitch incl. car	€ 9,40 - € 11,50
electricity	€ 3,05

All plus 7% VAT.

ES88590 Camping Roche

N340 km 19,5, Carril de Pilahito, E-11140 Conil de la Frontera (Cádiz)

Tel: **956 442 216**. Email: **info@campingroche.com** **www.alanrogers.com/ES88590**

Camping Roche is situated in a pine forest near white sandy beaches in the lovely region of Andalucia. It is a clean and tidy, welcoming site. Little English is spoken but try your Spanish, German or French as the staff are very helpful. A family site, it offers a variety of facilities including a sports area and swimming pools. The restaurant has good food and a pleasant outlook over the pool. Games are organised for children. A recently built extension provides further pitches, a new toilet block and a tennis court. There are now 240 pitches which include 104 bungalows to rent. There are pleasant paths in the area for mountain biking and this is an ideal base for visiting the cities of Seville and Cádiz.

Facilities

Three toilet blocks are traditional in style and provide simple, clean facilities. Washbasins have cold water only. Washing machine. Supermarket. Bar and restaurant. Swimming and paddling pools. Sports area. Tennis. Play area. Off site: Bus stops 3 times daily outside gates.

Open: All year.

Directions

From the N340 (Cádiz - Algeciras) turn off to site at km. 19,5 point. From Conil, take El Pradillo road. Keep following signs to site. From CA3208 road turn at km 1 and site is 1.5 km. down this road on the right. GPS: N36:18.653 W6:06.761

Charges guide

Per person	€ 6,00
pitch incl. electricity	€ 19,00

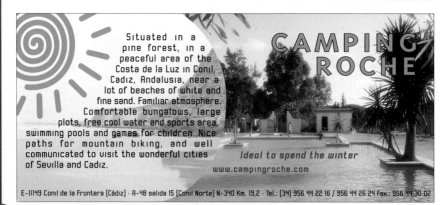

ES88650 Camping Playa Las Dunas

Paseo Maritimo, Playa de la Puntilla s/n, E-11500 El Puerto de Santa Maria (Cádiz)

Tel: **956 872 210**. Email: **info@lasdunascamping.com** **www.alanrogers.com/ES88650**

This site lies within the Parque Natural Bahia de Les Dunes and is adjacent to the long and gently sloping golden sands of Puntilla beach. This is a pleasant and peaceful site (though very busy in August) with some 539 separate marked pitches, 260 for tourers, with much natural shade and ample electrical connections (10A). Motorcaravans park in an area called the Oasis which is very pretty. The tent and caravan pitches, under mature trees, are terraced and separated by low walls. This is a spacious site with a tranquil setting and is popular with people who wish to 'winter over' in peace.

Facilities

Immaculate modern sanitary facilities with separate facilities for disabled campers and a baby room. Laundry facilities are excellent. Gas supplies. Bar/restaurant (all year). Supermarket (high season). Very large swimming pool and paddling pool (1/7-31/8). Play areas. Night security all year. Barbecues not permitted 15/5-15/10. Off site: Beach 100 m. Fishing 500 m. Bicycle hire, riding and golf 2 km. Municipal sports centre. Local buses for town and cities visits and a ferry to Cadiz.

Open: All year.

Directions

Site is 5 km. north of Cadiz off the N443. Take road to Puerto Santa Maria, site is very well signed throughout the town (small yellow signs high on posts). From south, turn left into town just after large bridge. Keeping sea inlet on your left, follow road for about 1 km. Site on right opposite beach. GPS: N36:35.340 W6:14.304

Charges guide

Per person	€ 4,03 - € 4,47
pitch incl. electricity (5A)	€ 9,13 - € 11,53

ES88730 Camping La Aldea

El Rocio, E-21750 Almonte (Huelva)

Tel: **959 442 677**. Email: **info@campinglaaldea.com** **www.alanrogers.com/ES88730**

This impressive site lies just on the edge of the Parque Nacional de Donana, southwest of Sevilla on the outskirts of El Rocio. The town hosts a fiesta at the end of May with over one million people attending the local shrine. They travel for days in processions with cow drawn or motorized vehicles to attend. If you want to stay this weekend book well in advance! The well planned, modern site is well set out and the 246 pitches have natural shade from trees or artificial shade and 10A electricity. There are 52 serviced pitches with water and sewage connections. There are also pitches for tents and bungalows for rent. The facilities are new, large and very clean. A waiter service restaurant (where the Spanish eat) provides lovely local food. The staff are welcoming and helpful. Expeditions on horseback or by 4 x 4 vehicle can be arranged in the national park.

Facilities

Two sanitary blocks provide excellent facilities including provision for disabled visitors. Motorcaravan service point. Swimming pool (May - Oct). Restaurant and bar in separate new complex. Shop. Internet connection. Playground. Off site: Bus stop 5 minutes walk. Huelva and Sevilla are about an hour's drive. Beach 15 km.

Open: 6 January - 25 December.

Directions

From main Huelva - Sevilla road E1/A49 take exit 48 and drive south through Almonte to outskirts of El Rocio. Site is on left just past 25 km. marker. Go down to the roundabout and back up to be on the right side of the road to turn in. GPS: N37:08.495 W6:29.463

Charges guide

Per person	€ 5,00 - € 6,50
child	€ 4,00 - € 5,00
pitch incl. car	€ 8,00 - € 12,00
electricity	€ 5,00

Less 10-15% for low season stays over 3 days.

ES90800 Camping Municipal El Brillante

Avenida del Brillante 50, E-14012 Córdoba (Córdoba)
Tel: **957 403 836**. Email: **elbrillante@campings.net** **www.alanrogers.com/ES90800**

Córdoba is one of the hottest places in Europe. If you really want to stay in the city, then this large site is a good choice. It has 120 neat pitches of gravel and sand, the upper pitches covered by artificial and natural shade but the lower, newer area with little. The site becomes very crowded in high season. The entrance is narrow and may be congested – there is a lay-by just outside and it is easier to walk in initially. The newer area has 32 fully serviced pitches and an area for a few large motorhomes. The site is on the north side of the river with a canal running through the centre.

Facilities

The toilet blocks include facilities for babies and disabled people. Motorcaravan services. Gas supplies. Shop (all year). Bar and restaurant (1/7-30/9). Swimming pool (15/6-15/9). Play area. Off site: Bus service to city centre from outside site. Commercial centre 300 m. (left out of site, right at traffic lights).

Open: All year.

Directions

From the NIV/E25 road from Madrid, take exit km. 403 (middle of three exits for Córdoba). Follow signs for Mosque/Cathedral into city centre. Pass it (on right) and turn right onto main avenue. Right fork where road splits. Follow signs for site/district of El Brillante. Site on right. GPS: N37:53.000 W4:45.998

Charges 2009

Per unit incl. 2 persons and electricity	€ 26,00
extra person (over 10 yrs)	€ 5,80

No credit cards.

ES90270 Camping Parque Natural de Monfragüe

2017.

Ctra Plasencia - Trujillo km 10, E-10680 Malpartida de Plasencia (Cáceres)
Tel: **927 459 233**. Email: **contacto@campingmonfrague.com** **www.alanrogers.com/ES90270**

Situated on the edge of the Monfragüe National Park, this well managed site owned by the Barrado family, has fine views to the Sierra de Mirabel and surrounding countryside. Many of the 130 good-sized grass pitches are on slightly sloping, terraced ground. Scattered trees offer a degree of shade, there are numerous water points and 10A electricity. It would prove difficult to find a more suitable location for those that savour tranquillity. On rare occasions a goods train travels along the nearby railway line. Created as a National Park in 1979, Monfragüe is recognised as one of the best locations in Europe for birdwatching. During our visit we saw Spanish imperial eagles, eagle owl, griffon, black and Egyptian vultures, black and red kites, azure-winged magpies, purple gallinule, purple heron, black-eared wheatear, bee-eater, blue rock thrush and the more rare black stork to name but a few. Nearby Plasencia has a medieval aqueduct, fine cathedral and the town's original twin ring of walls containing 68 towers. To the south, are the historical towns of Merida, Cáceres and Trujillo.

Facilities

Large modern toilet blocks, fully equipped, are very clean. Facilities for disabled campers and baby baths. Laundry. Motorcaravan service point. Supermarket/shop. Restaurant, bar and coffee shop. TV room with recreational facilities. WiFi. Swimming and paddling pools (June - Sept). Play area. Tennis. Bicycle hire. Riding. Animation for children in season. Barbecue areas. Guided safaris into the Park for birdwatching. Off site: Large supermarket at Plasencia.

Open: All year.

Directions

From the north on the N630 take the EX-208 road (previously C524) Plasencia - Trujillo; site on left in 6 km. From the south turn right just south of Plasencia on EX-108 (previously C511) in direction of Malpartida de Plasencia. Right at main junction onto EX-208 to site. GPS: N39:56.370 W06:05.040

Charges guide

Per person	€ 4,00
child (3-12 yrs)	€ 3,50
pitch	€ 7,00 - € 7,50

VAT included. Camping Cheques accepted.

ES90860 Cáceres Camping

Ctra N630 km 549,5, E-10005 Cáceres (Cáceres)

Tel: **927 233 100**. Email: **info@campingcaceres.com** **www.alanrogers.com/ES90860**

Recommended by our agent in Spain, we plan to conduct a full inspection of this all-year site in 2009. Cáceres Camping is quite a small site, located to the west of the interesting city of Cáceres, a World Heritage site. There are 130 pitches here, and, unusually, each has a chalet providing a shower, washbasin and toilet. The pitches are of a reasonable size (80 sq.m) and are well shaded. A range of leisure facilities is provided, including a swimming pool and a separate children's pool. Cáceres is a city with much interest, and a fascinating history. Cave paintings on the city outskirts date back 30,000 years! The city is capital of High Extremadura and close by, the Montanchez mountain range offers many opportunities for walking and cycling.

Facilities

Individual toilet blocks. Bar, restaurant, cafeteria and takeaway meals. Supermarket. Swimming pool.
Off site: City centre 2 km. Golf, walking and cycling opportunities.

Open: All year.

Directions

From the east (E90 motorway) take the N521 to Cáceres. Continue on this road to the west of the city. At the large roundabout sign for 'Campo de Futbol Principe Felipe' is the entrance to the site.
GPS: N39:29.340 W06:24.768

Charges guide

Per person	€ 4,00
child	€ 3,00
pitch	€ 12,00
electricity	€ 3,20

ES90280 Camping Las Villuercas

Ctra Villanueva, E-10140 Guadalupe (Cáceres)

Tel: **927 367 139** **www.alanrogers.com/ES90280**

This rural site nestles in an attractive valley northwest of Guadalupe. The 50 pitches (25 with 10A electricity) are level and of a reasonable size; although large units may experience difficulty in getting into the more central pitches. With an abundance of mature trees most pitches offer some degree of shade. A river runs alongside the site and the ground can be muddy in very wet periods. The site is co-located with hostel accommodation. The restaurant provides excellent food at low prices and leads to a pretty patio with elevated views of the pools.

Facilities

The single toilet block is older but very clean, one area for women and one for men, providing British type WCs, washbasins and showers (hot water is from a 40 litre immersion heater which could be overwhelmed in busy periods). Facilities for disabled visitors. Laundry facilities. Restaurant. Bar. Swimming pools. Shop. Tennis. Small playground. Barbecue area. No English spoken.
Off site: Riding 2 km. Fishing 3 km.

Open: 1 March - 30 November.

Directions

From NV/E90 Madrid - Mérida exit at Navelmoral de la Mata. Follow south to Guadalupe on CC713 (83 km). Site is 2 km. from Guadalupe (near Monastery). From further southwest take exit 102 off main E90/NV (northeast of Merida). Follow signs (Guadalupe). Go through a few villages and near 72 km. marker turn left to site, 100 m. on right.
GPS: N39:27.600 W05:19.320

Charges guide

Per person	€ 3,21
pitch	€ 4,28 - € 5,88
electricity	€ 2,67

No credit cards.

ES90870 Camping Mérida

Ctra NV Madrid - Portugal km 336,6, E-06800 Mérida (Badajoz)

Tel: **924 303 453**. Email: **proexcam@jet.es** **www.alanrogers.com/ES90870**

Camping Mérida is situated alongside the main N-V road to Madrid, the restaurant, café and pool complex separating the camping site area from the road where there is considerable noise. The site has 80 good sized pitches, most with some shade and on sloping ground, with ample electricity connections (long leads may be needed) and hedges with imaginative topiary. No English is spoken, but try out your Spanish. Reception is open until midnight. Camping Mérida is ideally located to serve both as a base to tour the local area or as an overnight stop en route.

Facilities

The central sanitary facility includes hot and cold showers, British style WCs. Gas supplies. Small shop for essentials. Busy restaurant/cafeteria and bar, also open to the public. Medium sized swimming and paddling pools (May - Sept). Bicycle hire. Play area (unfenced and near road). Caravan storage. Torches useful. Off site: Town 5 km.

Open: All year.

Directions

Site is alongside NV road (Madrid - Lisbon), 5 km. east of Mérida, at km. 336.6. From east take exit 334 and follow camping signs (doubling back). Site is actually on the 630 road that runs alongside the new motorway. GPS: N38:56.143 W06:18.306

Charges guide

Per person	€ 4,06
pitch incl. car and electricity	€ 22,74

All plus VAT.

ES90900 Camping El Greco

Ctra CM4000 km 0,7, Puebla de Montalban, E-45004 Toledo (Toledo)

Tel: **925 220 090**. Email: **campingelgreco@telefonica.net** **www.alanrogers.com/ES90900**

Toledo was the home of the Grecian painter and the site that bears his name boasts a beautiful view of the ancient city from the restaurant, bar and superb pool. The friendly, family owners make you welcome and are proud of their site which is the only one in Toledo (it can get crowded). The 150 pitches are of 80 sq.m. with electrical connections and shade from strategically planted trees. Most have separating hedges that give privacy, with others in herringbone layouts that make for interesting parking in some areas. The river Tagus stretches alongside the site which is fenced.

Facilities

Two sanitary blocks, both modernised include facilities for disabled campers and everything is of the highest standard and kept very clean. Laundry. Motorcaravan services. Swimming pool (15/6-15/9, charged). Restaurant/bar (1/4-30/9) with good menu and fair prices. Small shop in reception. Playgrounds. Ice machine. Off site: Fishing in river. Golf 10 km. Riding 15 km. An hourly air-conditioned bus service runs from the gates to the city centre, touring the outside of the walls first.

Open: All year.

Directions

Site is on C4000 road on the edge of the town, signed towards Puebla de Montelban; site signs also in city centre. From Madrid on N401, turn off right towards Toledo city centre but turn right again at the roundabout at the gates to the old city. Site is signed from the next right turn. GPS: N39:51.900 W04:02.820

Charges 2009

Per person	€ 6,10
pitch incl. electricity	€ 15,55 - € 15,85

ES90980 Camping Rio Mundo

Ctra Comarcal 412 km 205, Mesones, E-02449 Molinicos (Albacete)

Tel: **967 433 230**. Email: **riomundo@campingriomundo.com** **www.alanrogers.com/ES90980**

This typically Spanish site is situated in the Sierra de Alcaraz (south of Albacete), just off the scenic route 412 between Elche de la Sierra and Valdepenas. The drive to this site is through beautiful scenery (well worth the drive) and although from the west the main road is winding in some places, it should cause no problems if driven carefully. Shade is provided either by trees or by artificial means for the 100 pitches and electricity is supplied to the centre ones. It is a beautiful setting with majestic mountains and wonderful countryside which begs to be explored.

Facilities

One toilet block has been upgraded and provides clean modern facilities. Basic toilet facilities for disabled people. Washing machine. Small shop for basics. Outside bar serving snacks with covered seating area. Takeaway. Another bar by the swimming pool. Playground. Pétanque. Barbecue area. Off site: Riding 7 km.

Open: 18 March - 12 October.

Directions

Site is just off the 412 road which runs west to east between the A30 and 322 roads south of Albacete. Turn at km. 205 on the 412, 5 km. east of village of Riopar and west of Elche de la Sierra. From here follow signs to site. The road narrows to one lane for a few hundred yards but keep straight on for 1-2 km. to site. GPS: N38:29.347 W02:20.781

Charges guide

Per person	€ 3,80 - € 5,00
pitch incl. electricity	€ 11,40 - € 17,45

ES90910 Camping Internacional Aranjuez

Soto del Rebollo, s/n antigua NIV km 46,8, E-28300 Aranjuez (Madrid)

Tel: **918 911 395** www.alanrogers.com/ES90910

Aranjuez, supposedly Spain's version of Versailles, is worthy of a visit with its beautiful palaces, leafy squares, avenues and gardens. This useful, popular and well equipped site is therefore excellent for enjoying the unusual attractions or for an en-route stop. It is 47 km. south of Madrid and 46 km. from Toledo. The site is alongside to the River Tajo in a park-like situation. There are 178 touring pitches, all with electricity (10A), set on flat grass amid tall trees. The site has recently been acquired by the owners of La Marina (ES87420) who are working hard to make improvements. Two little tourist road trains run to the palaces daily. You can visit the huge, slightly decaying Royal Palace or the Casa del Labrador (farmer's cottage) which is a small neo-classical palace in unusual and differing styles. It has superb gardens commissioned by Charles II. Canoes may be hired and there is a lockable moat gate to allow access to the river. Security is good with CCTV around the river perimeter.

Facilities

The largest of three modern, good quality sanitary blocks is heated in winter and well equipped with some washbasins in cabins. Laundry facilities. Gas supplies. Small shop, bar and restaurant (all year) with attractive riverside patio (also open to the public). Takeaway. TV room. Swimming and paddling pools (15/6-15/9). Play area. Bicycle hire. Canoe hire. Torch useful. Off site: Within easy walking distance of palace, gardens and museums. Riding 5 km. Golf 20 km.

Open: All year.

Directions

From the M305 look for 8 km. marker on the outskirts of town. Follow campsite signs - these lead back onto the M305 (going north now) and site is signed off right at 300 m. on first left bend. Follow signs down the narrow road for 400 m. From the south ensure that you have the M305 to Madrid (other roads are signed to Madrid. If in doubt ask as it is very confusing if the M305 road is missed. GPS: N40:02.556 W3:5.970

Charges guide

Per person	€ 4,28 - € 5,88
child (3-10 yrs)	€ 3,21 - € 4,81
pitch incl. electricity	€ 14,44 - € 19,84

Plus 7% VAT. Camping Cheques accepted.

Visit Aranjuez, the Spanish Versailles!
Camping Internacional Aranjuez
WiFi ZONE
C/ Soto del Rebollo, s/n
E-28300 Aranjuez (Madrid) SPAIN
Telf.: (+34) 91 891 13 95
Fax: (+34) 91 892 04 06
info@campingaranjuez.com
www.campingaranjuez.com

ES92100 Camping Pico de la Miel

Ctra NI Madrid - France km 58, E-28751 La Cabrera (Madrid)

Tel: **918 688 082**. Email: **pico-miel@picodelamiel.com** www.alanrogers.com/ES92100

Pico de la Miel is a very large site 60 km. north of Madrid. Mainly a long-stay site for Madrid, there is a huge number of established, fairly old statics. There is a small separate area for touring units. The pitches are on rather poor, sandy grass, some with artificial shade. Others, not so level, are under sparse trees and there are yet more pitches for tents (ground could be hard for pegs). The noise level from the many Spanish customers is high and you will have a chance to practise your Spanish!

Facilities

Dated but clean tiled toilet block, with some washbasins in cabins. It can be heated. En-suite unit with ramp for disabled visitors. Motorcaravan services. Gas supplies. Shop. Bar/restaurant and takeaway (1/6-30/9). Excellent swimming pool complex (15/6-15/9). Tennis. Playground. Off site: Bicycle hire and riding 200 m. Fishing 8 km.

Open: All year.

Directions

Site is well signed from the N1. Going south or north use exit 57 and follow site signs. When at T-junction, facing a hotel, turn left. (Exit 57 is closer to site than exit 60). GPS: N40:51.547 W03:37.034

Charges guide

Per person	€ 5,80
pitch incl. electricity	€ 10,00 - € 18,20
car	€ 5,80

All plus 7% VAT. Less 10-25% for longer stays.

ES92000 Caravanning El Escorial

Apdo 8, Ctra M600, km 3,5, E-28280 El Escorial (Madrid)

Tel: **918 902 412**. Email: **info@campingelescorial.com** **www.alanrogers.com/ES92000**

There is a shortage of good sites in the central regions of Spain, but this is one (albeit rather expensive). El Escorial is very large, there are 1,358 individual pitches of which about 600 are for touring, with the remainder used for permanent or seasonal units, but situated to one side of the site. The pitches are shaded (ask for a pitch without a low tree canopy if you have a 3 m. high motorcaravan). There are another 250 pseudo 'wild' spaces for tourists on open fields, with good shade from mature trees (long cables may be necessary for electricity).

Facilities

One large toilet block for the touring pitches, plus two smart, small blocks for the 'wild' camping area, are all fully equipped with some washbasins in cabins. Baby baths. Facilities for disabled campers. The blocks can be heated. Large supermarket (1/3-31/10). Restaurant/bar and snack bar (all year; w/ends only in low season). Disco-bar. Swimming pools (15/5-15/9). Three tennis courts. Two well equipped playgrounds on sand. ATM. Off site: Town 3 km. Riding or golf 7 km.

Open: All year.

Directions

From the south go through town of El Escorial, and follow M600 Guadarrama road. Site is between the 2 and 3 km. markers north of the town on the right. From the north use A6 autopista and exit 47 to M600 towards El Escorial town. Site is on the left. GPS: N40:37.440 W04:05.940

Charges guide

Per person	€ 3,25
pitch incl. electricity	€ 22,90

VAT included. No credit cards.

ES90190 Camping La Pesquera

Ctra de Caceres - Arrabal, E-37500 Ciudad Rodrigo (Salamanca)

Tel: **923 481 348** **www.alanrogers.com/ES90190**

This modest site has just 54 pitches and is located near the Rio Agueda looking up to the magnificent fortress ramparts of Ciudad Rodrigo. Entry to the site is through a municipal park with a large play area. Whilst the site is small it can take even the largest units, the centrally located facilities have all been refurbished to a high standard, the pitches are flat and grassy and the roads are well maintained gravel. The pitches are shaded by trees by day and there is site lighting at night although you may find torches useful due to the tree canopy. The reception and a small bar which serves snacks in summer is near the front of the site.

Facilities

Attractive ochre stone sanitary building with British style WCs and free hot showers. Facilities for disabled campers. Washing machine. Basics sold from bar in high season. Bar/snacks (April - Sept). Playground and barbecue area outside gates. Torches useful. Off site: River fishing 1 km. Riding 5 km. Superb walking area.

Open: 25 April - 30 September.

Directions

Site is southwest of Salamanca close to Ciudad Rodrigo. From the E80 N260, any direction, take the 526 to Coria. Site is alongside river directly off the road and well signed. GPS: N40:35.940 W6:31.980

Charges guide

Per person	€ 3,20
child (up to 12 yrs)	€ 3,00
pitch incl. electricity	€ 6,60 - € 9,40

ES92420 Camping El Acueducto

Avenida D Juan de Borbón 49, E-40004 Segovia (Segovia)

Tel: **921 425 000**. Email: **informacion@campingacueducto.com** **www.alanrogers.com/ES92420**

Located right on the edge of the interesting city of Segovia with lovely views across the open plain with mountains in the background, this is a family run, typically Spanish site. The grass pitches are mostly of medium size, although a few pitches near the gate would have room for larger units. Reception is small but the owner is helpful and speaks good English. El Acueducto is well positioned for discovering Segovia. About 5 km. Segovia is deeply and haughtily Castilian, with plenty of squares and mansions from its days of Golden Age grandeur, when it was a royal resort.

Facilities

Two traditional style toilet blocks provide basic facilities and are kept clean. Laundry room. Small shop for basics. Bar. Two swimming pools. Large play area. Off site: Large restaurant nearby. Bus service into city centre. Madrid is within driving distance.

Open: 1 April - 30 September.

Directions

From the north on N1 (Burgos - Madrid) take exit 99 on N110 towards Segovia. On outskirts of city take third exit onto N603 signed Madrid. Pass one exit to Segovia and take second signed Segovia and La Granja. At roundabout turn right and site is 500 m. on the right. GPS: N40:55.875 W4:05.546

Charges guide

Per person	€ 5,00 - € 5,40
pitch incl. electricity (5A)	€ 19,50 - € 20,40

ES90260 Camping El Burro Blanco

Camino de las Norias s/n, E-37660 Miranda del Castañar (Salamanca)

Tel: **923 161 100**. Email: **el.burro.blanco@hotmail.com** **www.alanrogers.com/ES90260**

Set on a hill side, within the Sierra Peña de Francia and with views of the romantic walled village of Miranda del Castañar and its charming, crumbling castle, this site has been developed by a Dutch team; husband and wife Jeff and Yvonne and their friend Paul. There are a total of 31 level touring pitches, all between 80 and 120 sq.m. and 25 have electricity. The pitches are set in 3.5 hectares of natural woodland. Owners of large caravans and motorhomes should contact the site first.

Facilities

One central modern sanitary facility, fully equipped includes a baby bath. Two washbasins have hot water. Out of season part of the unit is closed and therefore facilities are unisex. Launderette. Gas supplies. Library with book swap and small bar. Off site: Restaurants, bars, shops and ATM in village 600 m. Municipal swimming pool nearby. River swimming and fishing 1.5 km. Riding 15 km.

Open: 1 April - 1 October.

Directions

From north - south take Salamanca - Coria road southwest for about 70 km. through Vecinos, Linares de Rio Frio towards Coria (numbers change but keep on this main road). From east - west take Bejar - Ciudad Rodrigo road south towards Cepeda/Coria. Road to Miranda del Castañar is 7 km. northeast of village of Cepeda. Turn off main road (Miranda). After 1.2 km. downhill towards town look for left turn onto concrete road. Follow road for 1.1 km. and site is on right. GPS: N40:28.488 W05:59.931

Charges guide

Per person	€ 4,80
pitch incl. electricity (2-10A)	€ 9,50 - € 12,80

Plus 7% VAT. No credit cards.

ES90290 Kawan Village El Astral

Camino de Pollos 8, E-47100 Tordesillas (Valladolid)

Tel: **983 770 953**. Email: **info@campingelastral.es** **www.alanrogers.com/ES90290**

The site is in a prime position alongside the wide River Duero (safely fenced). It is homely and run by a charming man, Eduardo Gutierrez, who has excellent English and is ably assisted by brother Gustavo and sister Lola. The site is generally flat with 154 pitches separated by thin hedges. They vary in size from 60 - 200 sq.m. with mature trees providing shade. There is an electricity pylon tucked in one corner of the site but this is hardly noticeable. This is a friendly site ideal for exploring the area.

Facilities

One sanitary block including two cabins with WC, bidet and washbasin. Facilities for disabled campers. Baby room. Washing machines. Motorcaravan services. Supermarket. Bar. Restaurant. Swimming and paddling pools (1/6-15/9). Playground. Tennis (high season). Minigolf. Internet and WiFi. Local bus service. Animation in high season. Torches useful. Off site: River fishing 100 m. Golf 10 km.

Open: 1 March - 31 October.

Directions

Tordesillas is 28 km. southwest of Valladolid. From all directions, leave the main road towards Tordesillas and follow signs to campsite or 'Parador' (a hotel opposite the site). GPS: N41:29.779 W05:00.312

Charges 2009

Per person	€ 4,30 - € 6,60
pitch incl. electricity	€ 11,10 - € 18,50

Plus 7% VAT. Camping Cheques accepted.

ES90230 Camping Camino de Santiago

2017

Avenida Virgen del Manzano s/n, E-09110 Castrojeriz (Burgos)

Tel: **947 377 255**. Email: **info@campingcamino.com** **www.alanrogers.com/ES90230**

This tranquil site lies to the west of Burgos on the outskirts of Castrojeriz, a small unspoilt Spanish rural town. In a superb location, almost in the shadow of the ruined castle high on the hillside. The 50 marked pitches are level, grassy and divided by hedges, with electricity (5A) and drainage available to all. There are new mobile homes and bungalows to rent and some permanent pitches. Mature trees provide shade and there is an orchard in one corner of the site. English is spoken here.

Facilities

Adequate sanitary facilities with showers, British and Turkish style WCs, and washbasins with cold water only. These facilities are in older style, but are well maintained and clean. Washing machine. Bar/restaurant and takeaway. Swimming pool. Bicycle hire. Small library. Internet access and WiFi. Games room. Tennis. Play area. Bicycle hire. Barbecue area. Off site: Fishing and riding 17 km.

Open: 1 March - 30 November.

Directions

From the N120/A231 (Leon - Burgos), turn on BU404 (Villasandino, Castrojeriz). Turn left at crossroads on southwest side of town, then left at site sign. From A62 (Burgos - Valladolid) turn north at Vallaquirán on Bu400/401 to Castrojeriz. Turn sharp right at filling station and as above. GPS: N42:17.484 W04:07.899

Charges guide

Per person	€ 4,50
pitch incl. car and electricity	€ 11,00 - € 12,00

All plus 7% VAT.

ES90240 Camping As Cancelas

Rue do 25 de Xullo 35, E-15704 Santiago de Compostela (A Coruña)

Tel: **981 580 476**. Email: **info@campingascancelas.com** **www.alanrogers.com/ES90240**

The beautiful city of Santiago has been the destination for European Christian pilgrims for centuries and they now follow ancient routes to this unique city, which is a national monument. The As Cancelas campsite is excellent for sharing the experiences of these pilgrims in the city and around the magnificent cathedral. It has 125 marked pitches (60-90 sq.m), arranged in terraces and divided by trees and shrubs. On a hillside overlooking the city, the views are good, but the site has a steep approach road and access to most of the pitches can be a challenge for large units. Electrical hook-ups (5A) are available, the site is lit at night and a security guard patrols. There are many legendary festivals and processions here, the main one being on July 25th, (especially when the Saint's birthday falls on a Sunday). Examine for yourself the credibility of the fascinating story of the arrival of the bones of Saint James at Compostela ('field of stars'), and discover why the pilgrims carry a scallop shell on their journey. There are many pilgrims' routes, one commencing from Fowey in Cornwall.

Facilities

Two modern toilet blocks are fully equipped, with ramped access for disabled campers. The quality and cleanliness of the fittings and tiling is good. Laundry with service wash for a small fee. Small shop. Restaurant. Bar with TV. Swimming pool and children's pool (unsupervised). Small playground. Internet access. Off site: Regular bus service to the city from near football ground 200 m. from site. Huge commercial centre (open late and handy for off season use) 20 minutes walk downhill.

Open: All year.

Directions

From motorway AP9-E1 take exit 67 and follow signs for 'Casco Historico' and 'Centro Ciudad' then follow site signs. GPS: N42:53.360 W08:31.450

Charges guide

Per person	€ 4,50 - € 5,90
child (up to 12 yrs)	€ 2,70 - € 4,50
pitch	€ 4,50 - € 19,00
electricity	€ 4,10

All plus VAT.

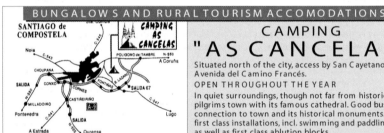

ES89420 Camping Los Manzanos

Avenida de Emilia Pardo Bazan, E-15179 Santa Cruz (A Coruña)

Tel: **981 614 825**. Email: **info@camping-losmanzanos.com** **www.alanrogers.com/ES89420**

Los Manzanos has a steep access drive down to the site, which is divided by a stream into two sections linked by a bridge. Pitches for larger units are marked and numbered, 85 with electricity (12A) and, in one section, there is a fairly large, unmarked field for tents. Some aircraft noise should be expected as the site is under the flight path to La Coruña (but no aircraft at night). The site impressed us as being very clean, even when full, which it tends to be in high season. Some interesting huge stone sculptures create focal points and conversation pieces.

Facilities

One good toilet block provides modern facilities including free hot showers. Small shop with fresh produce daily (limited outside June - Sept). High quality restaurant/bar (July/Aug). Swimming pool with lifeguard, free to campers (15/6-30/9). Playground. Barbecue area. Bungalows for rent. Off site: Bus service at end of entrance drive. Beach and fishing 800 m. Bicycle hire 2 km. Golf and riding 8 km.

Open: Easter - 30 September.

Directions

From AP9 take exit 7, signed O Burgo and carry on through town. At roundabout (signed airport to left), go straight ahead. Continue and immediately at entry to underpass take slip road and turn right into NV1. Take next left (Santa Cristina/Santa Cruz) and follow AC173. In Santa Cruz turn right and follow sign to site for 0.8 km. Site on left.
GPS: N43:20.945 W08:20.140

Charges guide

Per person	€ 5,90
pitch incl. electricity	€ 15,10 - € 17,10

All plus 7% VAT.

ES89400 Camping Los Cantiles

Ctra N634 km 502,7, E-33700 Luarca (Asturias)

Tel: **985 640 938**. Email: **cantiles@campingloscantiles.com** **www.alanrogers.com/ES89400**

Luarca is a picturesque little place with a pretty inner harbour and two sandy beaches, and Los Cantiles is two kilometres to the east of town on a cliff top that juts out into the sea, giving excellent views from some pitches and the sound of the waves to soothe you to sleep. The site is well maintained and is a pleasant place to stop along this under-developed coastline. The 150 pitches, 105 with electricity, are mostly on level grass, divided by huge hedges of hydrangeas and bushes.

Facilities

Two modern, fully equipped sanitary blocks (one in low season which is heated in winter) are kept very clean. Facilities for disabled people and babies. Laundry. Freezer service. Gas supplies. Small shop (open all year for basics). Bar with hot snacks (1/7-15/9). Day room for backpackers with tables, chairs and cooking facilities (own gas). Off site: Indoor swimming pool, sauna and fitness centre, plus a bar/restaurant and shop 300 m. Luarca 2 km. Beach and fishing 700 m. Riding 4 km.

Open: All year.

Directions

Luarca is 85 km. west of Gijon. From A8 Oviedo - La Coruña exit at 467 onto N634 for Luarca. After km. 502 east of Luarca, turn right at petrol station and follow signs to site for 2.5 km. Last 150 m. is narrow. GPS: N43:32.953 W06:31.459

Charges guide

Per person	€ 4,20
pitch	€ 8,10 - € 9,70
electricity (3/6A)	€ 2,00 - € 2,50

Plus 7% VAT. No credit cards.

ES89450 Camping Lagos de Somiedo

Valle de Lago, E-33840 Somiedo (Asturias)

Tel: **985 763 776** **www.alanrogers.com/ES89450**

This is a most unusual site in the Parque Natural de Somiedo. Winding narrow roads with rock overhangs, hairpin bends and breathtaking views (for 8 km) bring you to the lake and campsite at an elevation of 1,200 m. This is a site for 4 x 4s, powerful small campervans and cars – not for medium or large motorhomes, and caravans are not accepted. There are 210 pitches (just 4 with electric hook-up), undefined in two open meadows. There is a cool wind here most of the time.

Facilities

There are British style toilets and free hot water to clean hot showers and washbasin. Facilities for babies and children. Washing machine. Combined reception, small restaurant, bar and reference section. Shop for bread, milk and other essentials, plus local produce and crafts. Horses for hire, trekking. Lectures on flora, fauna, history and culture. Fishing (licence required). Barbecue area. Small play area. Gas supplies. No caravans accepted. A torch at night is essential. Off site: The very small village is 500 m. and it maintains the Spanish customs and traditions of this area.

Open: 1 April - 30 September.

Directions

From N634 via Oviedo turn left at 442 km. marker on AS-15 (Parque Natural de Somiedo). At 9 km. marker past village of Longoria, turn left on AS-227. At 38 km. marker, turn left into Pol de Somiedo, signed Centro Urbano. Follow signs for Valle de Lago and El Valle; 8 km. of hairpin bends from Pola, passing Urria on left, brings you to the valley. Site is signed on right. GPS: N43:06.320 W06:10.110

Charges guide

Per person	€ 5,35
pitch incl. car	€ 11,23
motorcaravan incl. electricity	€ 11,77

All plus 7% VAT. No credit cards.

ES89550 Camping Caravaning Arenal de Moris

A8 Salida 337, E-33344 Caravia Alta (Asturias)

Tel: **985 853 097**. Email: **camoris@teleline.es** **www.alanrogers.com/ES89550**

This smart, well run site is close to three fine sandy beaches so gets very busy at peak times. It has a backdrop of the mountains in the nature reserve known as the Sueve which is important for a breed of short Asturian horses, the 'Asturcone'. The site has 330 grass pitches (269 for touring units) of 40-70 sq.m. and with 200 electricity connections available (5A). With little shade, some pitches are terraced with others on an open, slightly sloping field with views of the sea.

Facilities

Three sanitary blocks provide comfortable, controllable showers (no dividers) and vanity style washbasins, laundry facilities and external dishwashing (cold water). Supermarket. Bar/restaurant. Swimming pool. Tennis. Play area in lemon orchard. English is spoken. Off site: Fishing 200 m. Golf 5 km. Riding, bicycle hire and sailing 10 km. Bar and restaurants in village 2 km. Beach 200 m.

Open: 1 June - 17 September.

Directions

Caravia Alta is 50 km. east of Gijón, Leave the A8 Santander - Oviedo motorway at km. 337 exit, turn left on N632 towards Colunga and site is signed to right in village, near 16 km. marker. GPS: N43:28.349 W05:10.999

Charges guide

Per person	€ 5,20 - € 5,40
pitch incl. car	€ 13,05 - € 13,70
electricity	€ 4,00 - € 4,40

ES89610 Camping El Helguero

Ctra Santillana - Comillas, E-39527 Ruiloba (Cantabria)

Tel: **942 722 124**. Email: **reservas@campingelhelguero.com** **www.alanrogers.com/ES89610**

This site, in a peaceful location surrounded by tall trees and impressive towering rock formations, caters for 240 units (of which 100 are seasonal) on slightly sloping ground. There are many marked pitches on different levels, all with access to electricity (6A), but with varying amounts of shade. There are also attractive tent and small camper sections set close in to the rocks and some site owned chalets. The site gets very crowded in high season, so it is best to arrive early if you haven't booked.

Facilities

Three well placed toilet blocks, although old, are clean and all include controllable showers and hot and cold water to all basins. Facilities for children and disabled visitors. Laundry facilities. Motorcaravan services. Small supermarket (July/Aug). Bar/snack bar plus separate more formal restaurant. Swimming pool (caps compulsory). Playground. Activities and entertainment (high season). ATM. Torches useful in some places. Off site: Bus service 500 m. Bar/restaurants in village (walking distance). Beach, fishing, sailing, golf and riding, all 3 km.

Open: 1 April - 30 September.

Directions

Site is 45 km. west of Santander. From A8 (Santander - Oviedo) take km. 249 exit (Cabezón and Comillas) and turn north on CA135 towards Comillas, At km. 7 turn right on CA359 to Ruilobuca and Barrio la Iglesia. After village turn right up hill on CA358 to site on right (note: signs refer to 'Camping Ruiloba'). GPS: N43:22.973 W04:14.880

Charges 2009

Per person	€ 4,50 - € 5,35
pitch incl. electricity	€ 8,55 - € 15,30

Camping Cheques accepted.

ES89620 Camping La Isla Picos de Europa

Picos de Europa, E-39570 Potes-Turieno (Cantabria)

Tel: **942 730 896**. Email: **campicoseuropa@terra.es** **www.alanrogers.com/ES89620**

La Isla is beside the road from Potes to Fuente Dé, with many mature trees giving good shade and glimpses of the mountains above. Established for over 25 years, a warm welcome awaits you and a most relaxed and peaceful atmosphere exists here. The 121 unmarked pitches are arranged around an oval gravel track under a variety of trees. Electricity is available to all, although some need long leads. A small bar and restaurant are beside a small river which runs through the site.

Facilities

Single, clean and smart sanitary block retains the style of the site. Washbasins with cold water. Washing machine. Gas supplies. Freezer service. Small shop and restaurant/bar (all season). Small swimming pool (caps compulsory; 1/5-30/9). Play area. Barbecue area. Fishing. Bicycle hire. Riding. Off site: Shops, bars and restaurants plus Monday morning market in Potes 4 km. Fuente Dé and its spectacular cable car ride 18 km.

Open: 1 April - 30 October.

Directions

From A8/N634 (Santander - Oviedo) take km. 272 exit for Unquera (end of motorway section). Take N621 south to Panes and up spectacular gorge (care needed if towing) to Potes. Take CA165 to Funte Dé and site is on the right, 3 km. beyond Potes. GPS: N43:08.999 W04:41.998

Charges guide

Per person	€ 3,75 - € 4,05
pitch incl. electricity (6A)	€ 6,15 - € 13,80

All plus VAT. Low season reductions.

ES90000 Camping Playa Joyel

2016.

Playa de Ris, E-39180 Noja (Cantabria)

Tel: **942 630 081**. Email: **playajoyel@telefonica.net** **www.alanrogers.com/ES90000**

This very attractive holiday and touring site is some 40 kilometres from Santander and 80 kilometres from Bilbao. It is a busy, high quality, comprehensively equipped site by a superb beach providing 1,000 well shaded, marked and numbered pitches with 3A electricity available. These include 80 large pitches of 100 sq.m. Some 250 pitches are occupied by tour operators or seasonal units. This well managed site has a lot to offer for family holidays. With much activity in high season it gets crowded.

Facilities

Six excellent, spacious and fully equipped toilet blocks include baby baths. Large laundry. Motorcaravan services. Supermarket. General shop. Kiosk. Restaurant and takeaway (1/7-31/8). Bar and snacks. Swimming pools, bathing caps compulsory (20/5-15/9). Entertainment with a soundproof pub/disco (July/Aug). Gympark. Tennis. Playground. Riding. Fishing. Natural animal park. Hairdresser (July/Aug). Medical centre. Torches necessary in some areas. Animals are not accepted. Off site: Bicycle hire and sports complex including an indoor pool 1 km. Sailing and boat launching 10 km. Riding and golf 20 km.

Open: Easter - 27 September.

Directions

From A8 (Bilbao - Santander) take km. 185 exit and N634 towards Beranga. Almost immediately turn right on CA147 to Noja. In 10 km. turn left at multiple campsite signs and go through town. At beach roundabout turn left and continue to site at end of road. GPS: N43:29.369 W03:32.220

Charges 2009

Per person	€ 4,20 - € 6,40
pitch	€ 15,00 - € 27,30
electricity	€ 3,60 - € 4,70

No credit cards.
Camping Cheques accepted.

ES90350 Camping Portuondo

Ctra Gernika - Bermeo, E-48360 Mundaka (Bizkaia)

Tel: **946 877 701**. Email: **recepcion@campingportuondo.com** **www.alanrogers.com/ES90350**

This well kept site has a lovely restaurant, bar and terrace taking full advantage of the wonderful views across the ocean and estuary. Set amongst gardens, the pitches are mainly for tents and smaller vans, but there are eight large pitches at the lower levels for caravans and motorhomes. The access to these is a little difficult as the road is steep and there is no turning space. In high season (July/Aug) it is essential to ring to book a space. In high season the site is popular with surfers and young people.

Facilities

Two fully equipped toilet blocks can be heated and include mostly British WCs and a smart baby room. Washing machines and dryers. Shop (15/6-15/9). Bar and two restaurants, all open to public (28/1-14/12). Takeaway (15/6-15/9). Swimming pools (15/6-15/9). Barbecue area. Torches may be useful. Off site: Fishing 100 m. Beaches 500 m. bracing walk. Surfing on Mundaka beach 500 m. Boat launching 1 km. Shops, bars and restaurants 2 km. Riding 8 km. Bicycle hire 10 km. Golf 40 km. Buses to Bilbao and Gernika (every 30 mins) 300 m.

Open: 28 January - 16 December.

Directions

From the A8 (San Sebastián - Bilbao) take exit 18. Follow signs for Gernika on BI635. Continue on the BI2235 (Bermeo). Site is on right approaching Mundaka. Note: a wide approach may be necessary as this is a sharp right turn with a steep access. No turn left to site. GPS: N43:23.951 W02:41.766

Charges guide

Per person	€ 5,10 - € 5,70
pitch incl. electricity	€ 14,40 - € 15,20

From mid June to end August one week minimum reservation is required.

ES90430 Camping Caravanning Errota el Molino

E-31150 Mendigorria (Navarra)

Tel: **948 340 604**. Email: **info@campingelmolino.com** **www.alanrogers.com/ES90430**

This is an extensive site set by an attractive weir near the town of Mendigorria, alongside the river Arga. It takes its name from an old disused water mill (molino) close by. The site is split into separate permanent and touring sections. The touring area is a new development with good-sized flat pitches with electricity and water for tourers, and a separate area for tents. Many trees have been planted but there is still only minimal shade. The friendly owner Anna Beriain will give you a warm welcome. Reception is in the lower part of a long building along with the bar/snack bar which has a shaded terrace, a separate restaurant and a supermarket. The upper floor is dormitory accommodation for backpackers. The site has a sophisticated dock with boat launching and watersport competitions in season with a safety boat present. The site is very busy during the festival of San Fermín (bull running) in July in Pamplona. Tours of the local bodegas can be organised to sample Navarra wines.

Facilities

The well equipped toilet block is very clean and well maintained, with cold water to washbasins. Facilities for disabled campers. Washing machine. Large restaurant, pleasant bar. Supermarket. Superb new swimming pools for adults and children (1/6-15/9). Bicycle hire. Riverside bar. Weekly animation programme (July/Aug) and many sporting activities. Squash courts. Internet access. River walk. Pedaloes and canoes for hire. Torches useful.
Off site: Bus to Pamplona 500 m. Riding 15 km. Golf 35 km.

Open: All year (excl. 23 December - 4 January).

Directions

Mendigorria is 30 km. southwest of Pamplona. From A15 San Sebastian - Zaragoza motorway, leave Pamplona bypass on A12 towards Logon. Leave at km. 23 on NA601 to hill top town of Mendigorria. At crossroads turn right towards Larraga and down hill to site. GPS: N42:37.497 W01:50.533

Charges guide

Per person	€ 4,70 - € 5,00
child	€ 3,95 - € 4,22
pitch incl. car and electricity	€ 12,90 - € 13,80

Plus 7% VAT. Discounts outside high season. Camping Cheques accepted.

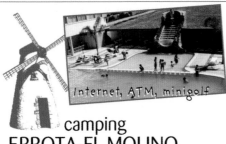

ES90470 Camping Ezcaba

E-31194 Eusa (Navarra)

Tel: **948 330 315**. Email: **info@campingezcaba.com** **www.alanrogers.com/ES90470**

Camping Ezcaba is a small site located 5 km. north of Pamplona, on the banks of Ulzama river. This all year site has been recommended by our Spanish agent and we hope to undertake a full inspection in 2009. Pitches here are large and grassy and there is a number of mobile homes available for rent. The site becomes very busy for the Festival of San Fermin in Pamplona, possibly Spain's most famous fiesta and best known for the running of the bulls through the city's narrow streets. The site has a swimming pool and a restaurant specialising in local cuisine. Ezcaba is well located for exploring the magnificent Navarra countryside and maybe sample some of its fine wines.

Facilities

Bar. Restaurant. Takeaway food. Shop. Play area. Swimming pool. Entertainment and activities in peak season. Mobile homes and chalets for rent.
Off site: Pamplona 7 km. Parque Natural de Bertiz 38 km. Fishing. Walking and cycle trails.

Open: All year.

Directions

From Pamplona take the northbound N121A towards Irun and the French border. Shortly after leaving the city, turn left to join the NA 4210 and then the NA 4211 to Eusa. Site is clearly signed from here. GPS: N42:51.509 W1:37.466

Charges guide

Per person	€ 4,90
child	€ 4,10
pitch	€ 5,35 - € 7,70
electricity	€ 4,28

ES90420 Camping Etxarri

Paraje Dambolintxulo s/n, E-31820 Etxarri-Aranatz (Navarra)

Tel: **948 460 537**. Email: **info@campingetxarri.com** **www.alanrogers.com/ES90420**

Situated in the Valle de la Burundi the site is a peaceful oasis with superb views of the 1,300 m. high San-Donator Mountains. The approach to the constantly improving site is via a road lined by huge 300-year-old oak trees, which are a feature of the site. Reception is a purpose built chalet with a touring reference library (mostly in Spanish). There are 100 pitches of average size on flat ground (50 for tourers) with 6A electricity to all and water to 25. The site gets very crowded during the Fiestas de San Fermín (bull-running) in Pamplona early in July. It is essential to make a reservation if you wish to stay.

Facilities

Toilet facilities are good and include a baby bath and facilities for disabled visitors. Laundry. Gas supplies. Essential supplies kept in high season. Bar (1/4-30/9). Restaurant and takeaway (1/6-15/9). Large new swimming and paddling pools (15/6-15/9) also open to the public and can get crowded. Bicycle hire. Minigolf. Play area. Off site: Bus and trains nearby. Bars, restaurants and shops 2 km. Golf, fishing, riding all 20 km. Pamplona 40 km.

Open: 1 April - 1 October.

Directions

Etxarri-Aranatz is 40 km. northwest of Pamplona. From A8 (San Sebastian - Bilbao) take A15 towards Pamplona, then 20 km. northwest of Pamplona, take A10 west towards Vitoria/Gasteix. At km. 19 take NA120 to and through town following site signs. Turn left after crossing railway to site at end of road. GPS: N42:54.780 W02:04.800

Charges 2009

Per person	€ 4,80
pitch	€ 7,45 - € 10,26
electricity	€ 5,00

ES90600 Camping Peña Montañesa

Ctra Ainsa - Francia km 2, E-22360 Labuerda (Huesca)

Tel: **974 500 032**. Email: **info@penamontanesa.com**

www.alanrogers.com/ES90600

A large site situated quite high up in the Pyrenees near the Ordesa National Park, Peña Montañesa is easily accessible from Ainsa or from France via the Bielsa Tunnel (steep sections on the French side). This site has grown very quickly and may at times be a little hard pressed, although it is very well run. It is divided into three sections opening progressively throughout the season and all have shade. The 288 pitches on fairly level grass are of about 75 sq.m. and 10A electricity is available on virtually all.

Facilities

A newer toilet block, heated when necessary, has free hot showers but cold water to open plan washbasins. Facilities for disabled visitors. Small baby room. An older block in the original area has similar provision. Laundry facilities. Bar. Restaurant. Takeaway. Supermarket. Outdoor swimming pool (1/4-31/10). Indoor pool (all year). Playground. Boules. Bicycle hire. Riding. Rafting. Only gas barbecues are permitted. Torches required in some areas. Off site: Fishing 100 m. Skiing in season. Canoeing near.

Open: 1 March - 10 December.

Directions

Site is 2 km. from Ainsa, on the road from Ainsa to France. GPS: N42:26.112 E00:08.171

Charges guide

Per person	€ 3,60 - € 6,80
child (1-9 yrs)	€ 3,10 - € 5,70
pitch	€ 13,00 - € 21,60
electricity	€ 5,15

All plus 7% VAT.

ES90620 Kawan Village Boltaña

Ctra N260 km 442, E-22340 Boltaña (Huesca)

Tel: **974 502 347**. Email: **info@campingboltana.com**

www.alanrogers.com/ES90620

Nestled in the Rio Ara valley, surrounded by the Pyrenees mountains and below a tiny but enchanting, historic, hill top village, is the very pretty, thoughtfully planned Camping Boltaña. Generously sized, grassy pitches have good shade from a variety of trees and a stream meanders through the campsite. The landscaping includes ten charming rocky water gardens and a covered pergola doubles as an eating and play area. Angel Moreno, the owner of the site, is a charming host and has tried to think of everything to make his guests comfortable.

Facilities

Two modern sanitary blocks include facilities for disabled visitors and laundry facilities. Supermarket. Bar (1/7-31/8). Swimming pools (1/6-15/9). Playground. Barbecues. Animation for children (high season). Pétanque. Guided tours, plus hiking, canyoning, rafting, climbing, mountain biking and caving. Torches useful in some parts.
Off site: Local bus service.

Open: 15 January - 15 December.

Directions

South of the Park Nacional de Ordesa, site is about 50 km. from Jaca near Ainsa. From Ainsa travel northwest on N260 toward Boltaña (near 443 km. marker) and 1 km. from Boltaña turn south toward Margudgued. Site is well signed and is 1 km. along this road. GPS: N42:25.811 E00:04.729

Charges 2009

Per person	€ 6,50
pitch incl. electricity	€ 22,00

Camping Cheques accepted.

ES91250 Kawan Village Lago Barasona

Ctra N123a km 25, E-22435 La Puebla de Castro (Huesca)

Tel: **974 545 148**. Email: **info@lagobarasona.com**

www.alanrogers.com/ES91250

This site, alongside its associated ten room hotel, is beautifully positioned on terraces across a road from the shores of the Lago de Barasona (a large reservoir), with views of hills and the distant Pyrenees. The very friendly, English speaking owner is keen to please and has applied very high standards throughout the site. The grassy, fairly level pitches are generally around 100 sq.m. with 35 high quality pitches of 110 sq.m. for larger units. All have electricity (6/10A), many are well shaded and some have great views. This site will suit families looking for quality and choice in their camping.

Facilities

Two toilet blocks in modern buildings have high standards and hot water throughout including cabins (3 for ladies, 1 for men). Bar/snack bar and two excellent restaurants (all season). Shop (1/4-30/9). Swimming pools (1/6-30/9). Tennis. Mountain bike hire. Canoe, windsurfing motor boat and pedalo hire. Miniclub (high season). New wellness centre (open all year). Lake swimming, fishing, canoeing, etc. Walking (maps provided). Money exchange. Mini-disco. Off site: Riding 4 km.

Open: All year.

Directions

Site is on the west bank of the lake, close to km. 25 on the N123A, 6 km. south of Graus (about 80 km. north of Lleida/Lerida). Travelling from the south, the site is on the left from a roundabout and slip road. GPS: N42:08.498 E00:18.915

Charges 2009

Per unit incl. 2 persons and electricity	€ 23,00 - € 35,00
extra person	€ 4.50 - € 6.50

Camping Cheques accepted.

BOOK THIS SITE CALL 01580 214000 ...we'll arrange everything The Travel Service

BOOK THIS SITE CALL 01580 214000 ...we'll arrange everything The Travel Service

MAP 8

With giant lakes and waterways, rich forests, majestic mountains and glaciers, and vast, wide open countryside, Sweden is almost twice the size of the UK but with a fraction of the population.

CAPITAL: STOCKHOLM

Tourist Office

Swedish Travel and Tourism Council
Sweden House, 5 Upper Montagu Street,
London W1H 2AG
Tel: 020 7108 6168
Email: info@swetourism.org.uk
Internet: www.visit-sweden.com

The beautiful southwest region, otherwise known as the 'Swedish Lake and Glass country', is easily accessible by ferry or overland from Norway. The area is dominated by two great lakes, Vänern and Vättern, Europe's second and third largest lakes. There are also many fine beaches with picturesque harbours and historic ports such as Gothenburg, Helsingborg and Malmö, which is now linked by a bridge to Copenhagen. Stockholm, the capital, is a delightful place built on fourteen small islands on the eastern coast. It is an attractive, vibrant city, with magnificent architecture, fine museums and historic squares. Moving northwards into central and northern Sweden, you'll discover beautiful forests and around 96,000 lakes, which are perfect for ice skating (in winter!) and you may even see moose and reindeer. Today Sweden enjoys one of the highest standards of living in the world and a quality of life to go with it.

Population

9 million

Climate

Sweden enjoys a temperate climate thanks to the Gulf Stream. There is generally less rain and more sunshine in the summer than in Britain.

Language

Swedish. English is fairly widely spoken.

Telephone

The country code is 00 46.

Money

Currency: The Krona
Banks: Mon-Fri 09.30-15.00. Some city banks stay open until 17.30/18.00 on Thursdays (regions may vary).

Shops

Mon-Fri 09.00-18.00.
Sat 09.00-13.00/16.00. Some department stores remain open until 20.00/22.00.

Public Holidays

New Year; Epiphany; Easter Mon; Labour Day; Ascension; Whit Sun; Constitution Day June 6; Mid-summer Festival; All Saints; Christmas Dec 24-26.

Motoring

Roads are generally much quieter than in the UK. Dipped headlights are obligatory. Away from large towns, petrol stations rarely open 24 hours but most have self service pumps (with credit card payment). Buy diesel during working hours, it may not be available at self service pumps.

SW2630 Röstånga Camping & Bad

Blinkarpsvägen 3, S-260 24 Röstånga (Skåne Län)

Tel: **043 591 064**. Email: **nystrand@msn.com** **www.alanrogers.com/SW2630**

Beside the Söderåsen National Park, this scenic campsite has its own fishing lake and many activities for the whole family. There are 100 large, level, grassy pitches with electricity (10A) and a quiet area for tents with a view over the fishing lake. The tent area has its own service building and several barbecue places. A large holiday home and 14 pleasant cabins are available to rent all year round. A pool complex adjacent to the site provides a 50 metre swimming pool, three children's pools and a water slide, all heated during peak season. A one day visit is free for campers. Activities are arranged on the site in high season, including a children's club with exciting activities such as treasure hunts and gold panning, and for adults aqua-aerobics, Nordic walking and tennis. The Söderåsen National Park offers hiking and bicycle trails. The friendly staff will be happy to help you to plan interesting excursions in the area.

Facilities

Four good, heated sanitary blocks with free hot water and facilities for babies and disabled visitors. Laundry with washing machines and dryers. Kitchen with cooking rings, oven and microwave. Motorcaravan service point. Small shop at reception. Bar, restaurant and takeaway. Minigolf. Tennis. Fitness trail. Fishing. Canoe hire. Children's club. Off site: Swimming pool complex adjacent to site (one visit free for campers). Many golf courses nearby. Motor racing track at Ring Knutstorp 8 km.

Open: 31 March - 29 October.

Directions

From Malmö: drive towards Lund and follow road no. 108 to Röstånga. From Stockholm: turn off at Østra Ljungby and take road no. 13 to Röstånga. In Röstånga drive through the village on road no. 108 and follow the signs. GPS: N55:59.795 E13:16.803

Charges guide

Per pitch	SEK 130 - 165
electricity	SEK 35

Camping Cheques accepted.

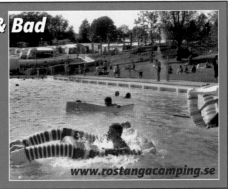

SW2640 First Camp Båstad-Torekov

Flymossa Vagen 5, S-260 93 Torekov (Skåne Län)

Tel: **043 136 4525**. Email: **torekov@firstcamp.se** **www.alanrogers.com/SW2640**

Part of the Kronocamping chain, this campsite is 500 m. from the fishing village of Torekov, 14 km. west of the home of the Swedish tennis WCT Open at Båstad on the stretch of coastline between Malmö and Göteborg. Useful en route from the most southerly ports, it is a very good site and worthy of a longer stay for relaxation. It has 510 large pitches (390 for touring units), all numbered and marked, mainly in attractive natural woodland, with some on more open ground close to the shore. Of these, 300 have electricity (10A) and cable TV, 77 also having water and drainage.

Facilities

Three very good sanitary blocks with free hot water and facilities for babies and disabled visitors. Laundry. Cooking facilities and dishwashing. Motorcaravan service point. Bar. Restaurant, pizzeria and snack bar with takeaway (15/-5/8). Shop and kiosk. Minigolf. Sports fields. Play areas and adventure park for children. Bicycle hire. TV room. Beach. Fishing. WiFi on 50% of pitches. Off site: Tennis close. Golf 1 km. Riding 3 km. Games, music and entertainment in high season.

Open: 11 April - 28 September.

Directions

From E6 Malmö - Göteborg road take Torekov/Båstad exit and follow signs for 20 km. towards Torekov. Site is signed 1 km. before village on right. GPS: N56:25.858 E12:38.433

Charges guide

Per pitch incl. electricity and TV connection	SEK 200 - 340
tent pitch	SEK 155 - 255

SW2706 Lisebergs Camping Askim Strand

Marholmsvagen, S-436 45 Askim (Hallands Län)

Tel: **031 286 261**. Email: **askim.strand@liseberg.se**

www.alanrogers.com/SW2706

Within easy reach of the city, this is a very pleasantly located site, close to a long gently sloping beach which is very popular for bathing. As a result the area behind the campsite is populated by many holiday homes and cabins. A very open site with very little shade, it has 266 mostly level, grassy pitches all with 10A electricity, plus two areas for tents. Many pitches are fairly compact, although there are some larger ones. The key card entry system operates the entrance barrier and access to the buildings and there is a night security guard (June-Aug).

Facilities

Two heated sanitary buildings, the larger one fairly new, the smaller recently refitted. Both are maintained to a high standard and provide all the usual facilities, including a good suite for small children, laundry, kitchens with cooking facilities, and a unit for disabled visitors. Hot water is free. Motorcaravan services. Snack bar (July). Playground. TV room. Bicycle hire. Off site: Small shop just outside the site. Göteborg city. Golf 2 km.

Open: 20 April - 2 September.

Directions

About 10 km. south of Göteborg, take exit signed Mölndal S and ports (Hamnar). Take the Rv 159 towards Frolunda, and watch for a slip-road to the right. After 200 m. turn left at the roundabout, signed Askim, and follow signs to campsite. GPS: N57:37.699 E11:55.231

Charges guide

Per pitch	SEK 165 - 345

Only pitches with electricity available for high season.

SW2645 Kawan Village FirstCamp Mölle

S-260 42 Mölle (Skåne Län)

Tel: **042 347 384**. Email: **molle@firstcamp.se**

www.alanrogers.com/SW2645

FirstCamp Mölle is a family campsite with a fine location at the foot of the Kullaberg, which marks the point where the Atlantic divides into the Kattegatt and Øresund. The site is open all year. There are 250 pitches, generally of a good size and 220 with electrical connections. The nearby Kullaberg Nature Park is dramatic and well worth a visit. The region is also well known for its ceramics and many potters and artists have settled in the area. On-site amenities include a heated paddling pool and water games complex. The nearest beach is 1.5 km. distant; popular for kayaking and fishing.

Facilities

Two modern sanitary blocks with free hot water and facilities for disabled visitors. Family shower rooms. Laundry facilities. Kitchen. Motorcaravan services. Restaurant with bar and cafeteria. Shop. Minigolf. Sports pitch. Heated paddling pool. Entertainment and children's activity programme (high season). Bicycle hire. TV room. WiFi. Cabins for rent. Off site: Nearest beach 1.5 km. Kayaking 2 km. Golf 4 km. Kullaberg Nature Park 1 km. Mölle lighthouse 6 km. Höganäs ceramics 8 km.

Open: All year.

Directions

From Helsingborg take the E4 north and then join road 111 towards Höganäs. Pass through this town and follow signs to Mölle and site. From the north take exit 33 on E6 towards Höganäs. Follow signs to site. GPS: N56:16.252 E12:31.798

Charges guide

Per pitch	SEK 150 - 285
electricity	SEK 45
tent pitch	SEK 110 - 240

SW2655 Tingsryds Camping

Mårdslyckesand, S-362 91 Tingsryd (Kronobergs Län)

Tel: **047 710 554**. Email: **tingsryd.camping@swipnet.se**

www.alanrogers.com/SW2655

A pleasant, well managed site by Lake Tiken, Tingsryds Camping is well placed for Sweden's Glass District. The 200 large pitches are arranged in rows divided by trees and shrubs, with some along the edge of a lakeside path (public have access). All have electricity (10/16A) and there is shade in parts. The facilities are housed in buildings near the site entrance, with the reception building having the restaurant, café, bar and a small shop. Adjacent to the site is a small beach, grassy lying out area, playground and lake swimming area and three tennis courts.

Facilities

Heated sanitary facilities are in two well maintained buildings, one including showers, mostly with curtains (on payment, communal undressing), the other a campers' kitchen with hobs and dining area. Facilities for disabled visitors. Laundry. Motorcaravan services. Shop (1/5-15/9). Restaurant and cafe (1/5-15/9). Minigolf. Playground. Boules. Lake swimming. Canoe hire. Fishing. Bicycle hire. Off site: Golf 15 km.

Open: 5 April - 20 October (full service 24/5-19/8).

Directions

Site is 1 km. from Tingsryd off road no. 120, well signed around the town. GPS: N56:31.723 E14:57.688

Charges guide

Per pitch	SEK 120 - 195
incl. electricity	SEK 160 - 235

SW2650 Skånes Djurparks Camping

Jularp, S-243 93 Höör (Skåne Län)

Tel: **041 355 3270**. Email: **info@grottbyn.se** **www.alanrogers.com/SW2650**

This site is probably one of the most unusual we feature. It is next to the Skånes Djurpark – a zoo park with Scandinavian species – and has on site a reconstructed Stone Age Village. The site is located in a sheltered valley and has 110 large, level grassy pitches for caravans and motorhomes all with 10A electricity and a separate area for tents. The most unusual feature of the site is the sanitary block – it is underground! The fully air-conditioned building houses a superb and ample complement of facilities. Well placed for the Copenhagen - Malmo bridge or the ferries, this is also a site for discerning campers who want something distinctly different. The site also has a number of underground, caveman style, eight bed (dormitory type) holiday units which can be rented by families or private groups (when not in use by schools on educational trips to the Stone Age Village). They open onto a circular courtyard with a barbecue and camp fire area and have access to the kitchens and dining room in the sanitary block. There are good walks through the nature park and around the lakes, where one can see deer, birds and other wildlife.

Facilities

The underground block includes roomy showers, two fully equipped kitchens, laundry and separate drying room and an enormous dining/TV room. Facilities for disabled people and baby changing. Cooking facilities. Laundry. A small new block and motorcaravan service point are planned. Small shop and café (15/6-15/8). Small heated family swimming pool (15/6-15/8). Playground. Stone Age Village. Off site: Restaurant just outside the entrance. Fishing 1.8 km. Bicycle hire 5 km. Riding and golf 8 km.

Open: All year (full services 15/6-10/8).

Directions

Turn off no. 23 road 2 km. north of Höör (at roundabout) and follow signs for Skånes Djurpark. Campsite entrance is off the Djurpark car park. GPS: N55:57.620 E13:32.285

Charges 2009

Per pitch	SEK 190
electricity	SEK 40 - 50

SW2665 Jönköping Swecamp Villa Björkhagen

Friggagatan 31, S-554 54 Jonkoping (Jönköpings Län)

Tel: **036 122 863**. Email: **villabjorkhagen@swipnet.se** **www.alanrogers.com/SW2665**

Overlooking Lake Vättern, Villa Björkhagen is a good site, useful as a break in the journey across Sweden or visiting the city during a tour of the Lakes. It is on raised ground overlooking the lake, with some shelter in parts. There are 280 pitches on well kept grass which, on one side, slopes away from reception. Some pitches on the other side of reception are flat and there are 200 electrical (10A), 100 cable TV and 40 water connections available. Jönköping is one of Sweden's oldest trading centres with a Charter dating back to 1284 and several outstanding attractions.

Facilities

Heated sanitary facilities were clean when we visited but looking rather tired. They include hot showers on payment (some in private cubicles) and a sauna, plus provision for disabled visitors and babies. Laundry. Motorcaravan services. Gas supplies. Well stocked shop (all year). Bar and restaurant (1/6-16/9). Playground. TV room. Minigolf. Off site: Pool complex 500 m. Fishing 500 m. Golf 1 km. Riding 7 km.

Open: All year (full services 1/6-16/9).

Directions

Site is well signed from the E4 road on eastern side of Jönköping. Watch carefully for exit on this fast road. GPS: N57:47.221 E14:13.077

Charges guide

Per unit incl. all persons	SEK 185 - 235
electricity	SEK 30 - 35

Prices may be increased if there is a local exhibition. Camping Cheques accepted.

SW2670 Grannastrandens Familjecamping

Box 14, S-563 21 Granna (Jönköpings Län)

Tel: **039 010 706** www.alanrogers.com/SW2670

This large, lakeside site with modern facilities and busy continental feel, is set below the old city of Gränna. Flat fields separate Gränna from the shore, one of which is occupied by the 25 acres of Grännastrandens where there are 450 numbered pitches, including a tent area and some seasonal pitches. About 230 pitches have electricity (10A). The site is flat, spacious and very regularly laid out on open ground with only a row of poplars by the lake to provide shelter, so a windbreak may prove useful against any onshore breeze. Part of the lake is walled off to form a swimming area.

Facilities

The large, sanitary block in the centre of the site has modern, well kept facilities including British style WCs, some with external access, washbasins, and free hot showers, some in private cubicles. Laundry facilities. Provision for disabled people. A further small, older block is by reception. Cooking facilities. Motorcaravan services. Shop (15/6-20/8). TV room. Playground. Lake swimming area. Boating and fishing. Off site: Café outside site (1/5-31/8) or town restaurants close. Golf 6 km.

Open: 1 May - 30 September.

Directions

Take Gränna exit from E4 road (no camping sign) 40 km. north of Jönköping. Site is signed in the centre of the town, towards the harbour and ferry. GPS: N58:01.657 E14:27.482

Charges guide

Per pitch	SEK 160
incl. electricity and satellite TV connection	SEK 200

SW2705 Lisebergsbyn Karralund

Olbersgatan 9, S-416 55 Goteborg (Västra Götalands Län)

Tel: **031 840 200**. Email: **karralund@liseberg.se** www.alanrogers.com/SW2705

Well positioned for visiting the city, this busy, well maintained site has 190 marked pitches, 152 with electricity (10A) and cable TV, 42 hardstandings, and several areas for tents. Pitches do vary in size, some are fairly compact and there are no dividing hedges, consequently units can be rather close together. Additionally there are cabins for rent, a budget hotel and a youth hostel. All this makes for a very busy site in the main season, which in this case means June, July and August. An advance telephone call to check for space is advisable.

Facilities

Two heated sanitary buildings, the larger one fairly new, and a smaller, older one with limited facilities, are well maintained and cleaned. They provide all the usual facilities, with controllable hot showers, a good suite for small children, laundry, kitchens, and a complete unit for disabled visitors. Motorcaravan services. Shop. Playground. TV room. Off site: Göteborg city.

Open: All year (full services 9/5-28/8).

Directions

Site is about 2.5 km. east of city centre. Follow signs to Lisebergsbyn and campsite symbol from E20, E6 or Rv 40. GPS: N57:42.293 E12:01.790

Charges guide

Per pitch	SEK 190 - 245
electricity	SEK 50
tent and car	SEK 225

Only pitches with electricity available in high season.

SW2675 Västervik Lysingsbadet

Lysingsvägen, S-593 53 Västervik (Kalmar Län)

Tel: **049 088 920**. Email: **lysingsbadet@vastervik.se** www.alanrogers.com/SW2675

One of the largest sites in Scandinavia, Lysingsbadet has unrivalled views of the 'Pearl of the East Coast' – Västervik and its fjords and islands. There are around 1,000 large, mostly marked and numbered pitches, spread over a vast area of rocky promontory and set on different plateau, terraces, in valleys and woodland, or beside the water. It is a very attractive site, and one which never really looks or feels crowded even when busy. There are 83 full service pitches with TV, water and electricity, 163 with TV and electricity and 540 with electricity only, the remainder for tents.

Facilities

Ten modern toilet blocks of various ages house a mix of showers, basins and WCs. All are kept very clean. Several kitchens. Four laundry rooms. All facilities and hot water are free. Key cards operate the barriers and gain access to sanitary blocks, pool complex and other facilities. Motorcaravan services. Supermarket (15/5-31/8). Restaurant and café/takeaway (12/6-138). Swimming pool complex (1/6-31/8). Golf. Minigolf. Bicycle and boat hire. Fishing. Entertainment and dances in high season. Playgrounds. Bus service. Off site: Riding 10 km.

Open: All year.

Directions

Turn off E22 for Västervik and follow signs for Lysingsbadet. GPS: N57:44.294 E16:40.119

Charges guide

Per pitch	€ 17,00 - € 30,00
incl. electricity	€ 22,00 - € 36,00
incl. electricity, TV	€ 24,00 - € 38,00

SW2680 Krono Camping Saxnäs

S-386 95 Färjestaden (Kalmar Län)

Tel: **048 535 700**. Email: **info@kcsaxnas.se** **www.alanrogers.com/SW2680**

Well placed for touring Sweden's Riviera and the fascinating and beautiful island of Øland, this family run site, part of the Krono group, has 420 marked and numbered touring pitches. Arranged in rows on open, well kept grassland dotted with a few trees, all have electricity (10A), 320 have TV connections and 112 also have water. An unmarked area without electricity can accommodate around 60 tents. The site has about 130 long stay units and cabins for rent. The sandy beach slopes very gently and is safe for children. Reception is efficient and friendly with good English spoken.

Facilities

Three heated sanitary blocks provide a good supply of roomy shower cubicles, washbasins, some washbasin/WC suites and WCs. Facilities for babies and disabled visitors. Well equipped laundry room. Good kitchen. Hot water is free. Motorcaravan services. Shop (1/5-30/8). Pizzeria, licensed restaurant and café (all 1/5-30/8). Bar (1/7-31/7). Playgrounds. Bouncy castle. Boules. Fishing. Canoe hire. Bicycle hire. Minigolf. Family entertainment and activities. Football. Off site: Golf 500 m. Riding 2 km.

Open: 17 April - 11 September.

Directions

Cross Øland road bridge from Kalmar on road no. 137. Take exit for Øland Djurpark/Saxnäs, then follow campsite signs. Site is just north of the end of the bridge. GPS: N56:41.236 E16:28.909

Charges guide

Per pitch	SEK 110 - 235
incl. electricity	SEK 160 - 285
incl. electricity/TV connection	SEK 170 - 295

Weekend and weekly rates available.

SW2690 Krono Camping Böda Sand

S-380 75 Byxelkrok (Kalmar Län)

Tel: **048 522 200**. Email: **bodasand@kronocampingoland.se** **www.alanrogers.com/SW2690**

Krono Camping Böda Sand is beautifully situated at the northern end of the island of Øland and is one of Sweden's largest and most modern campsites. Most of the 1,300 pitches have electricity (10/16A) and TV connections, 130 have water and waste water drainage. The pitches and 123 cabins for rent are spread out in a pine forest, very close to the fabulous 10 km. long, white sand beach. Here you will also find a restaurant, kiosks, toilets and beach showers, and a relaxation centre with an indoor/outdoor pool. The reception, the toilet blocks and the services at this site are excellent.

Facilities

Seven heated sanitary blocks provide a good supply of roomy shower cubicles, washbasins, some washbasin suites and WCs. Facilities for babies and disabled visitors (key at reception). Well equipped laundry rooms. Excellent kitchens. Motorcaravan services. Supermarket and bakery. Pizzeria, café, pub and restaurant. Takeaway. Bicycle hire, pedal cars and pedal boat hire. WiFi. Minigolf. 9-hole golf course. Indoor/outdoor swimming pool (on the beach). Trim trails. Family entertainment and activities.

Open: 1 May - 1 October.

Directions

From Kalmar cross the Øland road bridge on road no. 137. On Øland follow road no. 136 towards Borgholm and Byxelkrok. Turn left at the roundabout north of Böda and follow the campsite signs to Krono camping Böda Sand.
GPS: N57:16.462 E17:02.911

Charges guide

Per pitch	SEK 155 - 235
incl. electricity	SEK 195 - 285

SW2710 Lidköping SweCamp Kronocamping

Läckögatan, S-531 54 Lidköping (Västra Götalands Län)

Tel: **051 026 804**. Email: **info@kronocamping.com** **www.alanrogers.com/SW2710**

This high quality, attractive site provides 423 pitches on flat, well kept grass. It is surrounded by some mature trees, with the lake shore as one boundary and a number of tall pines have been left to provide shade and shelter. There are 374 pitches with electricity (10A) and TV connections and 91 with water and drainage also, together with 60 cabins for rent. The site takes a fair number of seasonal units. There is a small shop and a fully licensed restaurant with conservatory seating area.

Facilities

Excellent, modern sanitary facilities are in two blocks with underfloor heating. Hot water is free. Make up and hairdressing areas, baby room and facilities for disabled people. Private cabins. Good kitchens. Motorcaravan services. Small shop. Restaurant. Minigolf. Playgrounds. TV room. Games and amusements room. Bicycle hire. Play field. Lake swimming, fishing and watersports.
Off site: Swimming pool adjacent. Riding 4 km. Golf 6 km. The castle of Läckö, Kinnekulle, Spiken's fishing harbour.

Open: All year (full services 8/6-15/8).

Directions

From Lidköping town junctions follow signs towards Läckö then pick up camping signs and continue to site. GPS: N58:30.889 E13:08.390

Charges guide

Per pitch	SEK 170 - 210
incl. electricity/TV connection	SEK 190 - 250

SW2715 Gröne Backe Camping & Stugor

Södra Moränvägen, S-668 32 Ed (Västra Götalands Län)

Tel: **053 410 144**. Email: **gronebackecamping@telia.com** **www.alanrogers.com/SW2715**

In the heart of the beautiful Dalsland region, this pleasant, well shaded (mostly pine) site is open all year. It is well laid out, mostly overlooking the Lilla Le lake, and there is easy access from road no. 164. There are 180 pitches for caravans or motorcaravans, most with electricity (10A) and special areas for tents. Also on the site are 11 cabins for rent and 40 seasonal pitches. This pleasant, friendly family site is easy to find and the location makes it ideal for a longer stay.

Facilities

Three heated toilet blocks, two in the centre, one at reception, provide washbasins both vanity type and in cubicles. Showers (on payment). Baby rooms. Facilities for disabled visitors. Laundry. Cooking facilities. Motorcaravan services. Small shop. Café. Internet and WiFi. Playground. Minigolf. Sports field. Canoes, rowing boats, bicycles and pedal cars for hire. Beach. Off site: Village. Moose ranch. Canodal (large canoe centre). Tresicklan National Park.

Open: All year.

Directions

Site is on road no. 164 at Ed, and is well signed. GPS: N58:53.965 E11:56.092

Charges guide

Per pitch	SEK 135 - 230

SW2720 Tidaholm-Hökensås Semesterby och Camping

Hakangen, S-522 91 Tidaholm (Västra Götalands Län)

Tel: **050 223 053**. Email: **info@hokensas-semesterby.com** **www.alanrogers.com/SW2720**

Hökensås is located just west of Lake Vättern and south of Tidaholm, in a beautiful nature reserve of wild, unspoiled scenery. This pleasant campsite is part of a holiday complex that includes wooden cabins for rent. It is relaxed and informal, with over 200 pitches either under trees or on a more open area at the far end, divided into rows by wooden rails. These are numbered and electricity (10A) is available on 135. Tents can go on the large grassy open areas by reception. This site is a find for all kinds of people who enjoy outdoor activities.

Facilities

The original sanitary block near reception is supplemented by one in the wooded area, both refurbished. Hot showers in cubicles with communal changing area are free. Separate saunas for each sex and facilities for disabled visitors and babies. Campers' kitchen at each block. Laundry facilities. Small shop. Good angling shop. Licensed restaurant with takeaway. Playground. Minigolf. Lake swimming. Fishing. Off site: Town of Tidaholm and Lake Hornborga. Fishing 2 km. Riding 10 km.

Open: All year (full services 20/6-11/8).

Directions

Approach site from no. 195 western lake coast road. at Brandstorp, about 40 km. north of Jönköping, turn west at petrol station and camp sign signed Hökensås. Site is about 9 km. up this road. GPS: N58:05.890 E14:04.480

Charges guide

Per pitch (more for Midsummer celebrations)	SEK 125 - 140
electricity	SEK 20 - 21,45

SW2725 Hafsten Swecamp Resort

Hafsten 120, S-451 96 Uddevalla (Västra Götalands Län)

Tel: **052 264 4117**. Email: **info@hafsten.se** **www.alanrogers.com/SW2725**

This privately owned site on the west coast is situated on a peninsula overlooking the magnificent coastline of Bohuslän. Open all year, it is a lovely terraced site with a beautiful, shallow and child-friendly sandy beach and many nature trails in the vicinity. There are 180 touring pitches, all with electricity (10A), 70 of them with water and drainage. In all, there are 300 pitches including a tent area and 60 cottages of a high standard. There are plenty of activities available including canoeing, fishing, horse riding, minigolf, tennis and clay pigeon shooting.

Facilities

Two heated sanitary buildings provide the usual facilities. Showers are on payment. Kitchen with good cooking facilities. Dining room. Laundry facilities. Units for disabled visitors. Motorcaravan services. Shop. Restaurant, takeaway and pub. Troubadour evenings. TV room. Relaxation centre with sauna and jacuzzi (charged). Water slide (charged). Internet access (WiFi). Riding. Minigolf. Tennis. Playground. Boat hire. Off site: Nordens Ark (animal park) 40 km. Havets hus (marine museum) 30 km. Golf 13 km. Shopping centre 13 km.

Open: All year.

Directions

From the E6, north Uddevalla, at Torpmotet exit take the 161 road (Lysekil). At Rotviksbro roundabout take the 161 road (Orust). The site exit is located further on road 2 km. on the left. Follow signs for 4 km. It is a narrow, one way road for motorcaravans and caravans. GPS: N58:18.881 E11:43.400

Charges guide

Per pitch	SEK 150
incl. electricity	SEK 195

No credit cards.
Camping Cheques accepted.

SW2730 Ekuddens Camping

Strandbadet, S-542 00 Mariestad (Västra Götalands Län)

Tel: **050 110 637**. Email: **a.appelgren@mariestad.mail.telia.com** **www.alanrogers.com/SW2730**

Ekuddens occupies a long stretch of the eastern shore of Lake Vänern to the northwest of the town, in a mixed woodland setting, and next door to the municipal complex of heated outdoor pools and sauna. The lake, of course, is also available for swimming or boating and there are bicycles, tandems and canoes for hire at the tourist information office. The spacious site can take 350 units and there are 230 electrical hook-ups (10A). Most pitches are under the trees but some at the far end of the site are on more open ground with good views. The site becomes very busy in high season.

Facilities

Sanitary facilities are in three low wooden cabins, all clean and well maintained. Free hot showers in cubicles. Facilities for disabled visitors. Baby changing rooms. Kitchens. Shop. Licensed bar. Takeaway (high season). Playground. Minigolf. TV. Entertainment in high season. Lake swimming, boating and fishing. Off site: Swimming pools adjacent. Bicycle 3 km. Golf 4 km. Riding 7 km.

Open: 1 May - 15 September (full services 15/6-15/8).

Directions

Site is 2.5 km. northwest of the town and well signed at junctions on the ring road. From the E20 motorway take exit for Mariestad S. and follow signs in the direction of Marieholm.
GPS: N58:42.943 E13:47.723

Charges guide

Per unit	SEK 120 - 160
electricity	SEK 40

SW2735 Daftö Feriecenter

S-452 97 Stromstad (Västra Götalands Län)

Tel: **052 626 040**. Email: **info@dafto.com** **www.alanrogers.com/SW2735**

This extremely high quality, open all year site, is beautifully situated on the west coast, 5 km. south of the small 'summer town' of Strömstad. A very large site, some parts are terraced, other areas are open, some parts are shady. In total there are 650 pitches with 350 for touring, all with electrical hook-ups (10A, CEE plugs). In addition there are 125 modern, very well equipped chalets of various sizes. Daftö Feriecenter is a family campsite with all kinds of activities for children such as beach volleyball, theatre, competitions, treasure hunting and a 'Jolly Roger' playground.

Facilities

Four toilet blocks of excellent quality with washbasin cubicles, showers, family rooms, a children's bathroom, sun beds, saunas and make up rooms. Units for disabled visitors. Kitchen. Laundry facilities. Large shop. Fully licensed restaurant. Heated pool (peak season). Games and TV rooms. Minigolf. Bicycle hire. Football field. Children's club. Boat excursions and seal safaris. Internet and WiFi for hire. Off site: Ferry to Norway (Sandefjord) from Strömstad. Rock carvings at Tanum 25 km. The Koster islands (ferry from Strömstad). Golf at Strömstad.

Open: All year excl. 22/12-6/1.

Directions

Daftö is 5 km. south of Strömstad on road 176. It is signed. GPS: N58:54.256 E11:12.007

Charges guide

Per pitch incl. electricity (max. 5 persons)	SEK 200 - 330
incl. water and drainage	SEK 200 - 340
tent incl. 2 persons	SEK 140 - 265

SW2740 Laxsjons Camping och Friluftsgard

S-660 10 Dals Långed (Västra Götalands Län)

Tel: **053 130 010**. Email: **office@laxjon.se** **www.alanrogers.com/SW2740**

In the beautiful Dalsland region, Laxsjöns is an all year round site, catering for winter sports enthusiasts as well as summer tourists and groups. On the shores of the lake, the site is in two main areas – one flat, near the entrance, with hardstandings and the other on attractive, sloping, grassy areas adjoining. In total there are 300 places for caravans or motorcaravans, all with electricity, plus more for tents. Leisure facilities on the site include minigolf, trampolines and a playground.

Facilities

The main toilet block has hot showers (on payment), washbasins in cubicles, WCs and a hairdressing cubicle. With a further small block at the top of the site, the provision should be adequate. Facilities for disabled visitors. Laundry with drying rooms for bad weather. Cooking rooms for tenters. Restaurant (high season). Shop. Minigolf. Playground. Lake for swimming, fishing and boating.

Open: All year (full services 22/6-15/8).

Directions

From Åmål take road no. 164 towards Bengtfors, then the 172 towards Billingsfors and Dals Långed. Site is signed about 5 km. south of Billingsfors, 1 km. down a good road. From the south, (Uddevalla) take road 172. From the west (Strömstad) take the 164 towards Bengtfors and 5 km. south of Billingsfors turn right towards Långed for 1 km.
GPS: N58:57.172 E12:15.140

Charges guide

Per pitch	SEK 130 - 175
electricity (10/16A)	SEK 35

SW2750 FirstCamp Årjäng

Sommarvik, S-672 91 Årjäng (Värmlands Län)

Tel: **057 312 060**. Email: **arjang@firstcamp.se** **www.alanrogers.com/SW2750**

This is a good site in beautiful surroundings with some of the 350 pitches overlooking the clear waters of the Västra Silen lake in peaceful countryside. The numbered pitches are arranged in terraces on a hillside interspersed with pines and birches, with half set aside for static units and 20 for tents. The remaining touring pitches all have 10A electricity hook-ups and 40 also include water and drainage. The site also has 60 chalets for rent. This site makes an ideal base to explore this scenic region in summer or winter when skiing is an additional attraction.

Facilities

Five sanitary units provide shower cubicles (hot showers on payment), washbasins, toilets, family bathrooms, facilities for disabled persons and baby changing. All are clean and acceptable but may be stretched in high season. Campers' kitchens. Laundry facilities. Motorcaravan services. Small shop (1/5-1/10). Bar, restaurant and takeaway 15/6-20/8. Good play areas. Bicycle hire. Internet access. 'Quick stop' pitches for overnight stays. Youth hostel and conference centre. Off site: Indoor pool 3 km. Riding 5 km. Golf 9 km.

Open: All year.

Directions

Site is well signed on road 172.3 km. south of its junction with the E18 close to Årjäng. GPS: N59:22.059 E12:08.377

Charges guide

Per tent pitch	SEK 200
pitch incl. electricity and water	SEK 200 - 300

SW2755 Alevi Camping

Fastnäs 53, S-680 51 Stöllet (Värmlands Län)

Tel: **056 386 050**. Email: **info@alevi-camping.com** **www.alanrogers.com/SW2755**

Alevi Camping is a small, welcoming site with 60 large pitches, five cabins and two tepees for hire. Open all year, the site is situated on the bank of the river Klarälven, the longest river in Sweden. With its own beach this is a perfect place for swimming, fishing, canoeing and rafting. The site, which had its first season in 2006, offers large level pitches all with electricity (4/10A). The county of Värmland is famous for its lakes, rivers and forests. There, if you are lucky, you can see the 'big four' predators of Scandinavia – wolf, bear, wolverine and lynx.

Facilities

One new sanitary block with free hot water. Unisex toilets and showers. Washbasins, both vanity style and in cubicles. Facilities for babies and disabled visitors. Family room. Good campers' kitchen. Motorcaravan services. Reception with small shop, restaurant, takeaway. TV room. Canoes and bicycle hire. River beach. Barbecue area. Sauna. Playground. Fishing. Skiing in winter. Off site: Supermarket 10 minutes by car.

Open: All year.

Directions

Site is between Ekshärad and Stöllet on road no. 62. Follow signs. GPS: N60:17.116 E13:24.404

Charges guide

Per unit incl. 5 persons	SEK 130 - 140
incl. private sanitary facilities	SEK 210 - 230
electricity	SEK 35 - 65
dog	SEK 10

SW2760 Frykenbadens Camping

Frykenbaden, S-665 91 Kil (Värmlands Län)

Tel: **055 440 940**. Email: **frykenbaden@telia.com** **www.alanrogers.com/SW2760**

Frykenbaden Camping is in a quiet wooded area on the southern shore of Lake Fryken, taking 200 units on grassy meadows surrounded by trees. One area nearer the lake is gently sloping, the other is flat with numbered pitches arranged in rows, all with electricity (10A). Reception, a good shop, restaurant and takeaway are located in a traditional Swedish house surrounded by lawns sloping down to the shore, with minigolf, a play barn and playground, with pet area also close by. Frykenbadens Camping is a quiet, relaxing place to stay, away from the busier lakes.

Facilities

The main sanitary block is of good quality and heated in cool weather with showers on payment, open washbasins, a laundry room and room for families or disabled people. A further small block has good facilities. Well equipped camper's kitchen. Shop. Snack bar, restaurant and takeaway. Minigolf. Play barn and playground. Lake swimming. Canoes and bicycles for hire. Off site: Golf 1 km. Go-karts, riding, jogging track 4 km.

Open: All year (full services 19/6-15/8).

Directions

Site is signed from the no. 61 Karlstad - Arvika road, then 4 km. towards lake following signs. GPS: N59:32.775 E13:20.479

Charges guide

Per pitch	SEK 110 - 150
electricity	SEK 40

SW2780 Gustavsvik Camping

Sommarrovägen, S-702 30 Ørebro (Ørebro Län)

Tel: **019 196 950**. Email: **camping@gustavsvik.se** **www.alanrogers.com/SW2780**

Gustavsvik is one of the most modern and most visited camping and leisure parks in Sweden. It is ideally situated almost half way between Oslo and Stockholm or Gothenburg and Stockholm, at the junction of the E18 and E20 roads. This large campsite provides 720 marked and numbered pitches partly shaded by birch and pine trees, 488 with electrical connections, 440 with cable TV and 56 with water and waste water drainage. There are also three partly shaded areas for tents. The leisure park includes adventure golf, a mini zoo, pools, water slide, a swimming lake and a private fishing lake.

Facilities

Two excellent heated toilet blocks including washbasins with dividers, free hot showers, family rooms, facilities for disabled visitors and children. Kitchens. Dining area. Laundry facilities. Motorcaravan service points. Shop. Restaurant and pub. Takeaway. TV room and playroom. Arcade with games room. Internet room. Adventure golf. Football. Swimming pool with waterslide. Swimming lake. Fishing lake. Mini zoo. Bicycle hire. Off site: Pool complex adjacent. Golf. Ørebro city. Marieberg shopping centre.

Open: 15 April - 6 November (full services 10/6-14/8).

Directions

Site is 1 km. south of Ørebro town centre. Follow signs from E18/E20 or main road 50/51.
GPS: N59:15.246 E15:11.488

Charges guide

Per pitch	SEK 190 - 305

SW2800 Glyttinge Camping

Berggårdsvägen, S-584 37 Linköping (Østergötlands Län)

Tel: **013 174 928** **www.alanrogers.com/SW2800**

Only five minutes by car from the Ikea Shopping Mall and adjacent to a good swimming pool complex, Glyttinge is a most attractive site with a mix of terrain – some flat, some sloping and some woodland. A top quality site with enthusiastic and friendly management, it is maintained to a very high standard and flowers, trees and shrubs everywhere give it a garden like atmosphere. There are 222 good size, mostly level pitches of which 120 have electricity (10A) and 35 are fully serviced. There is a fenced and very safe children's play area and tricycles, pedal cars, scooters and carts for hire.

Facilities

The main, central toilet block is modern and exceptionally well equipped and maintained. It has showers in cubicles, washbasin and WC suites. Separate facilities for disabled visitors. Baby rooms. Laundry. Solarium. Superb kitchen and dining/TV room, fully equipped. Motorcaravan services. Small shop (15/6-15/8). Minigolf. Football. Bicycle hire. Playground. Off site: Swimming pool complex adjacent (15/5-25/8). Riding and golf 3 km. Fishing 5 km.

Open: 27 April - 1 October.

Directions

Exit E4 Helsingborg - Stockholm road north of Linköping at signs for Ikea and site. Turn right at traffic lights and camp sign and follow signs to site.
GPS: N58:26.282 E15:32.692

Charges guide

Per pitch	SEK 140 - 165
electricity	SEK 35

Low season discounts for pensioners.

SW2805 Kawan Village First Camp Kolmården

S-618 34 Kolmården (Østergötlands Län)

Tel: **011 398 250**. Email: **kolmarden@firstcamp.se** **www.alanrogers.com/SW2805**

This is a family site, located on Bråviken Bay on the Baltic coast 160 km. south of Stockholm. Open all year, the site is just 4 km. from Kolmården Zoo, one of Sweden's most popular family attractions. There are 300 pitches of which 180 have electrical connections (10A). Some pitches have sea views and there is also a large beautiful wooded area for tents and 99 cabins of various standards for rent. A good range of amenities includes a 120 m. water slide and a children's playground. Adjacent to the site is a handicraft village and the Sjöstugans restaurant.

Facilities

Three sanitary blocks (two heated) provide a good supply of showers, washbasins and toilets. Baby rooms and facilities for disabled visitors. Good kitchen. Hot water is free throughout. Laundry rooms. Sauna. Motorcaravan services. Shop (1/5-15/9). Snack bar. Adjacent licensed restaurant and bar. Takeaway. Playground. Water slide. Family entertainment and children's activities (high season). Minigolf. Sea fishing. WiFi. Chalets for rent. Off site: Kolmården Zoo 4 km. Riding 2 km. Golf 18 km.

Open: All year.

Directions

From the E4 motorway take Kolmården exit (no. 126) 23 km.north of Norrköping. Follow signs for Kolmården and site is well signed.
GPS: N58:39.566 E16:24.053

Charges guide

Per pitch	SEK 145 - 195
electricity	SEK 45

SW2820 Skantzö Bad & Camping

S-737 27 Hallstahammar (Västmanlands Län)

Tel: **022 024 305**. Email: **skantzo@hallstahammar.se** **www.alanrogers.com/SW2820**

A very comfortable and pleasant municipal site just off the main E18 motorway from Oslo to Stockholm, this has 200 large marked and numbered pitches, 162 of these with electricity (10A). The terrain is flat and grassy, there is good shade in parts and the site is well fenced. There are 23 alpine style cabins for rent with window boxes of colourful flowers. Reception is very friendly. There is direct access to the towpath of the Strömsholms Kanal and nearby is the Kanal Museum.

Facilities

One sanitary block is maintained and equipped to a high standard, including free hot showers (in cubicles with washbasin), facilities for disabled people and baby changing. Another unit has been added and both are heated. Campers' kitchen. Laundry facilities. Motorcaravan services. Barbecue grill area. Cafeteria and shop (18/5-19/8). Playground. Swimming pool and waterslide (20/5-21/8). Minigolf. Tennis. Bicycle and canoe hire. Fishing. Off site: Golf 6 km. Strömsholms Kanal.

Open: 1 May - 30 September.

Directions

Turn off E18 at Hallstahammar and follow road no. 252 to west of town centre and signs to campsite. GPS: N59:36.647 E16:12.925

Charges guide

Per pitch	SEK 130 - 160
electricity	SEK 40

SW2825 Camping Herrfallet

S-732 92 Arboga (Västmanlands Län)

Tel: **058 940 110**. Email: **reception@herrfallet.se** **www.alanrogers.com/SW2825**

Open all year, Herrfallets Camping is situated on a peninsula, a designated nature reserve, on Lake Hjälmaren, one of Sweden's large lakes. There is a 1 km. long sandy beach on the site and the atmosphere is friendly and 'green'. All the 135 touring pitches have electricity hook-ups (10A) and the area is neatly laid out overlooking the lake where you can hire boats, canoes, pedal boats and go fishing. Fishing is free. You can explore the beautiful and peaceful surroundings by bike which you hire at reception. There are 45 large cottages of an excellent standard and 5 a bit smaller.

Facilities

Two sanitary blocks, one basic for the summer season, one new with central heating. Open washbasins, showers (charged). Provision for disabled visitors. Fully equipped kitchen and laundry facilities. Baby room. Motorcaravan service point. Sauna cottage with shower and relaxing room. Lapland hut (Sami style) for barbecue parties (charged). Shop (peak season). Restaurant and bar. Takeaway. Pedal car, pedal boat, bicycle, canoe and boat hire. Fishing (free). Minigolf. Football field. Fitness trail. Playground. Internet. Off site: Arboga (old town with medieval festival in July) 15 km. Golf 15 km.

Open: All year (full services 27/5-28/8).

Directions

Follow signs from the E20/E18. Turn off at Sätra exit towards Arboga and cross the river. Follow signs towards Herrfallet/Västermo. 15 km. from Arboga. GPS: N59:16.884 E15:54.306

Charges guide

Per pitch	SEK 170
incl. electricity (10A)	SEK 200

SW2840 Stockholm Swecamp Flottsbro

S-141 22 Huddinge (Stockholms Län)

Tel: **085 353 2700**. Email: **info@flottsbro.se** **www.alanrogers.com/SW2840**

Flottsbro is a neat, small site with good quality facilities and very good security system (including a night guard), located some 18 km. south of Stockholm. There are 80 large numbered pitches for caravans and motorhomes and a separate unmarked area for tents. Pitches are arranged on level terraces, 52 with electricity (10A), but the site itself is sloping and the restaurant is at the bottom with all the ski facilities and further good sanitary facilities. Campers have keys to the barrier and toilet blocks. The site has a small lakeside beach with grass area and a playground.

Facilities

Two modern sanitary facilities include free showers, a suite for disabled people, baby facilities and a family bathroom. Excellent campers' kitchen. Washing machine, dryer (charged for). Shop (high season). Restaurant. Minigolf. Frisbee. Jogging track. Canoe hire. Playground. Off site: Large supermarket and rail station are 10 minutes by car. Golf and riding 15 km. Stockholm 15 km.

Open: All year.

Directions

Turn off the E4 - E20 at Huddinge onto road no.259. After 2 km. turn right and follow signs to Flottsbro. GPS: N59:13.826 E17:53.291

Charges guide

Per pitch	SEK 115 - 160
incl. electricity	SEK 180 - 220

SW2842 Bredäng Camping Stockholm

Stora Sällskapets väg, S-127 31 Skärholmen (Stockholms Län)

Tel: **089 770 71**. Email: **bredangcamping@telia.com** **www.alanrogers.com/SW2842**

Bredängs is a busy city site, with easy access to Stockhom city centre. Large and fairly level, with very little shade, there are 380 pitches, including 115 with hardstanding and 204 with electricity (10A), and a separate area for tents. Reception is open from 07.00-23.00 in the main season (12/6-20/8), reduced hours in low season, and English is spoken. A Stockholm card is available, or a three-day public transport card. Stockholm has many events and activities, you can take a circular tour on a free sightseeing bus, various boat and bus tours, or view the city from the Kaknäs Tower (155 m). The nearest Metro station is five minute walk, trains run about every ten minutes between 05.00 and 02.00, and the journey takes about twenty minutes. The local shopping centre is five minutes away and a two minute walk through the woods brings you to a very attractive lake and beach.

Facilities

Four heated sanitary units of a high standard provide British style WCs, controllable hot showers, with some washbasins in cubicles. One has a baby room, a unit for disabled people and a first aid room. Cooking and dishwashing facilities are in three units around the site. Laundry facilities. Motorcaravan services and car wash. Well stocked shop and fully licensed restaurant (both 1/5-8/9). Sauna. Playground. Bicycle hire. Off site: Fishing 500 m.

Open: 15 April - 10 October.

Directions

Site is about 10 km. southwest of city centre. Turn off E4/E20 at Bredängs signpost and follow clearly marked site signs. GPS: N59:17.736 E17:55.389

Charges guide

Per person	SEK 95 - 120
pitch	SEK 190 - 240
electricity	SEK 40

Discounts for pensioners in low season.

SW2836 Mora Parkens Camping

Box 294, S-792 25 Mora (Dalarnas Län)

Tel: **025 027 600**. Email: **moraparken@mora.se** **www.alanrogers.com/SW2836**

Mora, at the northern end of Lake Silijan is surrounded by small localities all steeped in history and culture. On the island of Sollerön, south of Mora, is evidence of a large Viking burial ground. Traditional handicrafts are still alive in the region. Mora is lively, friendly and attractive. The campsite which is good for family holidays is only 10 minutes walk from the town. The camping area is large, grassy, open and flat. It is bordered by clumps of trees and a stream. The staff are pleasant and helpful.

Facilities

Four fully equipped toilet blocks. Campers' kitchen. Laundry. Shop. Restaurant/bar. Sauna. Fishing. Minigolf. Playground. Canoe hire. Internet access. Off site: Swimming pools. Zorn Museum. Orsa Bear Park. Dalhalla (limestone quarry) musical stage. Nustriäs.

Open: All year.

Directions

Follow signs to centre of town. Campsite is clearly signed from the town centre and is next to Zorngården and Zorn museum. GPS: N61:00.512 E14:31.907

Charges guide

Per pitch incl. electricity	SEK 155 - 235
tent	SEK 85

Full services mid June - mid August.

SW2845 Svegs Camping

Kyrkogränd 1, S-842 32 Sveg (Jämtlands Län)

Tel: **068 013 025** **www.alanrogers.com/SW2845**

On the 'Inlandsvägen' route through Sweden, the town centre is only a short walk from this neat, friendly site. Two supermarkets, a café and tourist information office are adjacent. The 80 pitches are in rows, on level grass, divided into bays by tall hedges, and with electricity (10/16A) available to 70. The site has boats, canoes and bicycles for hire, and the river frontage has a barbecue area with covered seating and fishing platforms. Alongside the river with its fountain, and running through the site is a pleasant well lit riverside walk.

Facilities

In the older style, sanitary facilities are functional rather than luxurious, providing stainless steel washing troughs, controllable hot showers with communal changing areas, and a unit for disabled visitors. Although a little short on numbers, facilities will probably suffice at most times as the site is rarely full. Kitchen and dining room with TV, four full cookers and sinks, plus more dishwashing sinks outside under cover. Laundry facilities. TV room. Minigolf. Canoe, boat and bicycle hire. Fishing.

Open: All year.

Directions

Site is off road 45 behind the tourist information office in Sveg. Site is signed.
GPS: N62:01.964 E14:21.869

Charges guide

Per pitch	SEK 150
electricity	SEK 25

SW2850 Ostersunds Camping

Krondikesvagen 95, S-831 46 Ostersund (Jämtlands Län)

Tel: **063 144 615**. Email: **ostersundscamping@ostersund.se** **www.alanrogers.com/SW2850**

Østersund lies on Lake Storsjön, which is Sweden's Loch Ness, with 200 sightings of the monster dating back to 1635, and more recently captured on video in 1996. Also worthy of a visit is the island of Frösön where settlements can be traced back to prehistoric times. This large site has 254 pitches, electricity (10A) and TV socket available on 131, all served by tarmac roads. There are also 41 tarmac hardstandings available, and over 220 cottages, cabins and rooms for rent. Adjacent to the site are the municipal swimming pool complex (indoor and outdoor pools), with cafeteria, a Scandic hotel with restaurant, minigolf, and a Statoil filling station.

Facilities

Toilet facilities are in three units, two including controllable hot showers (on payment) with communal changing areas, suites for disabled people and baby changing. The third has four family bathrooms each containing WC, basin and shower. Two kitchens with full cookers, hobs, fridge/freezers and double sinks (all free of charge), and excellent dining rooms. Washing machines, dryers and free drying cabinet. Very good motorcaravan service point suitable for all types of unit including American RVs. Playground. Off site: Østersund, Frösön.

Open: All year.

Directions

Site is south of the town on the road towards Torvalla. Turn by Statoil station and site entrance is immediately on right. It is well signed from around the town. GPS: N63:09.565 E14:40.413

Charges guide

Per pitch	SEK 135 - 170
electricity	SEK 40

SW2853 Snibbens Camping & Stugby och Vandrarhem

Hälledal 527, S-870 16 Ramvik (Västernorrlands Län)

Tel: **061 240 505** **www.alanrogers.com/SW2853**

Probably you will stop here for one night as you travel the E4 coast road and stay a week. It is a truly beautiful location in the area of 'The High Coast' listed as a World Heritage Site. During high season Snibbens is a busy, popular site but remains quiet and peaceful. Besides 30 bungalows for rent there are 50 touring places, each with 16A electricity, set amongst delightful scenery on the shores of Lake Mörtsjön. The welcoming owners take you to your grass pitch set amongst spacious trees.

Facilities

Excellent, spotlessly clean facilities include controllable showers and partitioned washbasins. Baby changing facilities. Two kitchens with hot plates, microwaves and a mini oven. Laundry room. Small shop (15/6-20/8). Rowing boats and pedaloes for hire. Minigolf. Free fishing for site guests. Youth hostel. Off site: Small supermarket 800 m. Golf 20 km.

Open: 30 April - 15 September.

Directions

Travelling north on the E4 and immediately prior to Höga Kusten bridge (one of the largest in Europe) take road 90 signed Kramfors. Site is directly off road 90 on left in 3 km, well signed.
GPS: N62:47.943 E17:52.188

Charges guide

Per pitch	SEK 140
incl. electricity	SEK 155

SW2855 Flogsta Camping

S-872 80 Kramfors (Västernorrlands Län)

Tel: **061 210 005**. Email: **flogsta@basterang.se** **www.alanrogers.com/SW2855**

Kramfors lies just to the west of the E4, and travellers may well pass by over the new Höga Kusten bridge (one of the largest in Europe), and miss this friendly little site. This area of Ådalen and the High Coast, reaches as far as Ørnsköldsvik. The attractive garden-like campsite has 50 pitches, 21 with electrical connections (10A), which are arranged on level grassy terraces, separated by shrubs and trees into bays of 2-4 units. All overlook the heated outdoor public swimming pool complex and attractive minigolf course. The non-electric pitches are on an open terrace nearer reception.

Facilities

Sanitary facilities comprise nine bathrooms, each with British style WC, basin with hand dryer, shower. Laundry facilities. More WCs and showers are in the reception building with a free sauna. A new toilet block has a sauna and outside hot tub. A separate building houses a kitchen, with hot-plates, fridge/freezer and TV/dining room (all free). The reception building has a small shop and snack bar. Playground. Snowmobile hire.
Off site: Fishing 10 km. Golf and riding 15 km.

Open: All year.

Directions

Signed from road 90 in the centre of Kramfors, the site lies to the west in a rural location beyond a housing estate and by the Flogsta Bad, a municipal swimming pool complex.
GPS: N62:55.537 E17:45.385

Charges guide

Per pitch	SEK 100 - 125

SW2857 Strömsund Swecamp

S-833 24 Strömsund (Jämtlands Län)

Tel: **067 016 410**. Email: **stromsund.turism@stromsund.se** **www.alanrogers.com/SW2857**

A quiet waterside town on the north - south route 45 known as the Inlandsväen, Strömsund is a good place to begin a journey on the Wilderness Way. This is route 342 which heads northwest towards the mountains at Gäddede and the Norwegian border. Being on the confluence of many waterways, there is a wonderful feeling of space and freedom in Strömsund. The campsite is set on a gentle grassy slope backed by forest. Another part of the site, across the road, overlooks the lake. Cabins are set in circular groups of either six or seven. The site is owned by the town council.

Facilities

Excellent facilities include two toilet blocks, one on each side of the road. Both contain showers, toilets, washbasins with dividers and underfloor heating. Facilities for disabled visitors. Laundry. Large campers' kitchen with cooking rings, microwave and sinks. Motorcaravan service point. Bicycle, canoe, pedalo and boat hire. Play area. Off site: Municipal pool is next to the site.

Open: All year.

Directions

Site is 700 m. south of Strömsund on route 45.
GPS: N63:50.787 E15:32.023

Charges guide

Per pitch	SEK 120
electricity	SEK 30 - 50

Full services mid June - mid August.

SW2860 First Camp Umeå

S-906 54 Umeå (Västerbotens Län)

Tel: **090 702 600**. Email: **umea@firstcamp.se** **www.alanrogers.com/SW2860**

An ideal stopover for those travelling the E4 coastal route, or a good base from which to explore the area, this campsite is 6 km. from the centre of this university city. It is almost adjacent to the Nydalsjön lake, which is ideal for fishing, windsurfing and bathing. There are 450 grassy pitches arranged in bays of 10-20 units, 320 with electricity (10A or 16A), and some are fully serviced. Outside the site, adjacent to the lake, are football pitches, an open air swimming pool, minigolf, mini-car driving school, beach volleyball and a mini farm.

Facilities

The new large, heated, central sanitary unit includes controllable hot showers with communal changing areas. (Facilities stretched in high season). Kitchen. Large dining room. TV. Laundry facilities. Shop (25/5-21/8). Fully licensed restaurant. WiFi. Walk-on chess. Playgrounds. Bicycle hire. Rowing boat hire. Fishing in the lake. Canoes and pedal cars for hire. Adventure golf. Off site: Riding adjacent. Golf 18 km.

Open: All year (full services 25/5-12/8).

Directions

A camping sign on the E4 at a set of traffic lights 5 km. north of the town directs you to the site. Direction also indicates Holmsund and Vassa.
GPS: N63:50.596 E20:20.432

Charges guide

Per pitch	SEK 160 - 220
incl. electricity	SEK 170 - 260

SW2865 Camp Gielas

Järnvägsgatan 111, S-933 34 Arvidsjaur (Norrbottens Län)

Tel: **096 055 600**. Email: **gielas@arvidsjaur.se** **www.alanrogers.com/SW2865**

A modern municipal site with excellent sporting facilities on the outskirts of the town, Gielas is well shielded on all sides by trees, providing a very peaceful atmosphere. The 160 pitches, 81 with electricity (10A) and satellite TV connections, are level on sparse grass and accessed by tarmac roadways. The sauna and showers, sporting, gymnasium and Internet facilities at the sports hall are free to campers. Also on site is a snackbar. The lake on the site is suitable for boating, bathing and fishing. There is a swimming pool and a 9-hole golf course nearby, and hunting trips can be arranged.

Facilities

Two modern, heated sanitary units provide controllable hot showers and a unit for disabled visitors. Well equipped kitchens (free). Washing machine and dryer. The unit by the tent area also has facilities for disabled people and baby changing. Snack bar. Tennis. Minigolf. Play areas. Sauna. Sporting facilities. Boat and canoe hire. Pedal cars. Lake swimming. Fishing. Winter golf course on snow on site. Off site: Golf 200 m. Bowling centre and riding 500 m. Bicycle hire 2 km.

Open: All year.

Directions

Site is on road 95 3 km. south of town centre. GPS: N65:34.955 E19:11.412

Charges guide

Per pitch	SEK 150

SW2870 Jokkmokks Camping Center

Box 75, S-962 22 Jokkmokk (Norrbottens Län)

Tel: **097 112 370**. Email: **campingcenter@jokkmokk.com** **www.alanrogers.com/SW2870**

This attractive site is just 8 km. from the Arctic Circle. Large and well organised, the site is bordered on one side by the river and with woodland on the other, just 3 km. from the town centre. It has 170 level, grassy pitches, with an area for tents, plus 59 cabins for rent. Electricity (10A) is available to all touring pitches. The site has a heated open air pool complex open in summer (no lifeguard). There are opportunities for snow-mobiling, cross-country skiing in spring, or ice fishing in winter.

Facilities

Heated sanitary buildings provide mostly open washbasins and controllable showers - some are curtained with a communal changing area, a few are in cubicles with divider and seat. A unit by reception has a baby bathroom, a fully equipped suite for disabled visitors, games room, plus a very well appointed kitchen and launderette. A further unit with WCs, basins, showers plus a steam sauna, is by the pool. Shop, restaurant and bar (in summer). Takeaway (high season). Swimming pools (25 x 10 m. main pool with water slide, two smaller pools and paddling pool). Sauna. Bicycle hire. Playground and adventure playground. Minigolf. Football field. Games machines. Free fishing. Off site: Riding 2 km.

Open: All year (for groups on request).

Directions

Site is 3 km. from the centre of Jokkmokk on road 97. GPS: N66:35.698 E19:53.562

Charges guide

Per caravan or motorcaravan	SEK 120 - 150
hiker and small tent	SEK 70
car and small tent	SEK 90
electricity	SEK 30

MAP 1

A small, wealthy country, best known for its outstanding mountainous scenery, fine cheeses, delicious chocolates, Swiss bank accounts and enviable lifestyles. Centrally situated in Europe it shares its borders with four countries: France, Austria, Germany and Italy, each one having its own cultural influence on Switzerland.

CAPITAL: BERN

Tourist Office

Switzerland Tourism
Switzerland Travel Centre,
30 Bedford Street, London WC2E 9ED
Tel: 020 7420 4900 Fax: 020 7845 7699
Email: info.uk@switzerland.com
Internet: www.myswitzerland.com

The landscape of Switzerland boasts mountains, valleys, waterfalls and glaciers. The Bernese Oberland is probably the most visited area, with picturesque villages, lakes and awe inspiring peaks, including the towering Eiger, Mönch and Jungfrau. The highest Alps are those of Valais in the southwest where the small busy resort of Zermatt gives access to the Matterhorn. The southeast of Switzerland has densely forested mountain slopes and the wealthy and glamorous resort of St Moritz. Zurich in the north is a German speaking city with a wealth of sightseeing, particularly in the old town area with its 16th- and 17th-century houses. Geneva, Montreux and Lausanne on the northern shores of Lake Geneva make up the bulk of French Switzerland, with vineyards that border the lakes and medieval towns. The southernmost canton, Ticino, is home to the Italian speaking Swiss, with the Mediterranean style lakeside resorts of Lugano and Locarno.

Population

7.1 million

Climate

Mild and refreshing in the northern plateau. South of the Alps it is warmer, influenced by the Mediterranean. The Valais is noted for its dryness.

Language

German in central and eastern areas, French in the west and Italian in the south. Raeto-Romansch is spoken in the southeast. English is spoken by many.

Telephone

The country code is 00 41.

Money

Currency: Swiss franc
Banks: Mon-Fri 08.30-16.30. Some close for lunch.

Shops

Mon-Fri 08.00-12.00 and 14.00-18.00.
Sat 08.00-16.00. Often closed Monday mornings.

Public Holidays

New Year; Good Fri; Easter Mon; Ascension; Whit Mon; National Day 1 Aug; Christmas 25 Dec. Other holidays are observed in individual Cantons.

Motoring

The road network is comprehensive and well planned. An annual road tax is levied on all cars using Swiss motorways and the 'Vignette' windscreen sticker must be purchased at the border (credit cards not accepted), or in advance from the Swiss National Tourist Office, plus a separate one for a towed caravan or trailer.

CH9380 Bergcamping Heiti

CH-3785 Gsteig bei Gstaad (Bern)

Tel: **033 755 11 97**. Email: **info@bergcamping.ch** **www.alanrogers.com/CH9380**

Bergcamping Heiti is a brand new site opened in June 2007 and located 10 km. from the stylish resort of Gstaad. The site has been recommended by our Swiss agent and we plan to undertake a full inspection in 2009. Bergcamping Heiti is open all year and has 50 grassy pitches suitable for summer and winter use. There is also a number of traditional wooden chalets available for rent. The toilet block is fully heated and has a drying room for skiers and walkers. A new 'wellness' suite is planned and this will include a sauna, whirlpool and beauty salon. The site is situated at the foot of the Col du Pillon and a wide choice of walking and mountain biking routes are available. A little further afield, Les Diablerets offers the opportunity for both summer and winter skiing. The nearby village of Gsteig is five minutes by foot and has a good selection of shops and restaurants.

Facilities

Heated toilet blocks. Washing machines and dryers. Drying room. Small shop. Restaurant. Bar. Play area. Off site: Gsteig with a wide choice of shops, restaurants and bars 500 m. Gstaad 10 km. Many walking paths and cycle trails. Summer and winter skiing.

Open: All year.

Directions

From Gstaad, follow signs to Col du Pillon. Continue to Gsteig. Turn left here after the church and the site can be found 500 m further to the left.
GPS: N46:22.800 E07:16.200

Charges guide

Per person	CHF 4,30
child (0-15 yrs)	CHF 2,15
pitch	CHF 12,00 - 17,00
electricity	CHF 3,00

CH9330 TCS Camping Thunersee

CH-3770 Gwatt (Bern)

Tel: **033 336 4067**. Email: **camping.gwatt@bluewin.ch** **www.alanrogers.com/CH9330**

Thunersee is an ideal site for those who wish to explore this part of the Bernese Oberland and who would enjoy staying on a small site in a quiet area, away from the larger sites and town atmosphere of Interlaken. There are 85 numbered, but unmarked pitches for tourists, most with 4A electricity available, and about the same number of static units. There are hard access roads but cars must be parked away from the pitches. Although there are some trees, there is little shade in the main camping area. Direct access to the lake is available for swimming and boating.

Facilities

Single, modern, well constructed sanitary block, fully equipped with hot water provided for washbasins in cabins (cold otherwise). Facilities should be adequate in high season. Room for disabled visitors. Washing machine and dryer. Motorcaravan services. Well stocked shop. Restaurant. Lake swimming and boating. Off site: Many cycle tracks.

Open: 1 April - early October.

Directions

From Berne - Thun - Interlaken autoroute, take exit Thun-Süd for Gwatt and follow signs for Gwatt. Site is signed near town centre to the left.
GPS: N46:43.649 E07:37.656

Charges guide

Per person	CHF 6,20 - 8,20
child (6-16 yrs)	CHF 3,10 - 4,10
caravan or motorcaravan and electricity	CHF 19,00 - 24,00
dog	CHF 3,00 - 4,00

CH9430 Camping Lazy Rancho 4

Lehnweg 6, CH-3800 Interlaken (Bern)

Tel: **033 822 8716**. Email: **info@lazyrancho.ch** **www.alanrogers.com/CH9430**

This super site is in a quiet location with fantastic views of the dramatic mountains of Eiger, Monch and Jungfrau. Neat, orderly and well maintained, the site is situated in a wide valley just 1 km. from Lake Thun and 1.5 km. from Interlaken. The English speaking owners lovingly care for the site and will endeavour to make you feel very welcome. Connected by tarmac roads, the 155 pitches, of which 90 are for touring units, are on well tended level grass (some with hardstanding, all with 10A electricity). 23 pitches also have water and waste water drainage. This is a quiet friendly site, popular with British visitors. The owners offer advice on day trips out, and how to get the best bargains which can be had on the railway.

Facilities

Two good sanitary blocks are both heated with free hot showers, good facilities for disabled customers and a baby room. Laundry. Camper's kitchen with microwave, cooker, fridge and utensils. Motorcaravan service point. Well stocked shop. TV and games room. Play area. Small swimming pool. Bicycle hire (June-Aug). WiFi. Off site: Cycle trails and way-marked footpaths. Riding 500 m. Golf and bicycle hire 1 km. Lake Thun for fishing 1.5 km. Boat launching 1.5 km. Interlaken (free regular bus service 400 m. from site) and leisure centre 2 km.

Open: 1 April - 15 October.

Directions

Site is on north side of Lake Thun. From road 8 (Thun - Interlaken) on south side of lake take exit 24 Interlaken West. Follow towards lake at roundabout then follow signs for campings. Lazy Rancho is Camp 4. The last 500 m. is a little narrow but no problem. GPS: N46:41.163 E07:49.838

Charges 2009

Per unit incl. 2 persons and electricity	CHF 26,50 - 44,70
extra person	CHF 6,00 - 6,60
child (6-15 yrs)	CHF 3,50 - 3,80
dog	CHF 3,00

Payment also accepted in euros.

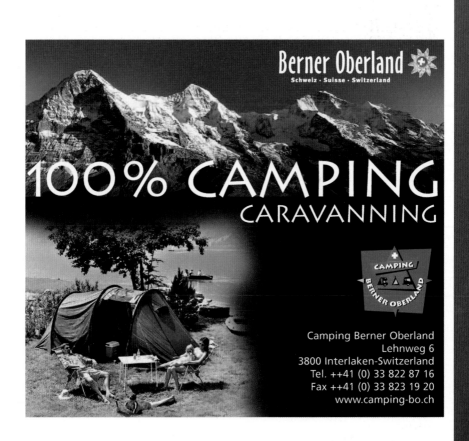

CH9370 Camping Rendez-vous

CH-3718 Kandersteg (Bern)

Tel: **033 675 1534**. Email: **rendez-vous.camping@bluewin.ch** **www.alanrogers.com/CH9370**

Camping Rendez-vous is an all year site located at an altitude of 1,200 m, just outside the delightful mountain village of Kandersteg. This site has been recommended by our Swiss agent and we plan to conduct a full inspection in 2009. There are 80 terraced touring pitches here and a further 20 pitches are occupied by chalets. The pitches are grassy and many have fine views over the surrounding mountain scenery. Although there are few amenities on site, Kandersteg is nearby and is an important mountain resort with shops and restaurants, as well as a railway station and cable car.

Facilities

Heated toilet block. Washing machines and dryers. Small shop. Restaurant at site entrance. Play area. Off site: Kandersteg with a wide choice of shops, restaurants and bars 2 km. Oeschinensee cable car. Railway station and cable cars. Many walking paths and cycle trails.

Open: All year.

Directions

From the north, take the N6 Bern - Spiez motorway and take the Kandersteg exit. Follow signs to Kandersteg (25 km) and the site is well signed (to the left) in the village. GPS: N46:29.814 E7:41.022

Charges 2009

Per unit incl. 2 persons	CHF 20,60 - 34,60
electricity per kWh	CHF 0,60
extra person	CHF 6,30
child (1-16 yrs)	CHF 3,00

CH9055 TCS Camping Fanel

CH-3236 Gampelen (Bern)

Tel: **032 313 2333**. Email: **camping.gampelen@tcs.ch** **www.alanrogers.com/CH9055**

This Swiss Touring Club site is particularly suited to families with children. From the terrace of a well provisioned self service restaurant there is a view of the small swimming pool and the large grass area that leads to the gently shelving waters of the lake and a small wooden jetty. The site has 900 pitches (150 for tourists) which means that it could become quite busy at weekends and holidays. The level, grass pitches have electricity and some young trees provide shade. This quiet site is located in a protected nature area, a habitat for beavers, wild boar and foxes.

Facilities

Three modern, well maintained toilet blocks with free showers and washbasins in cabins. Facilities for disabled people. Baby room. Laundry room with washing machines and dryers. Motorcaravan service point. Modern, well appointed self service restaurant with takeaway. Shop. Gas supplies. Internet access. Play area. Bicycle hire. Archery.

Open: 1 April - 1 October.

Directions

Site is on the northeast shore of Lake Neuchatel. From A1 exit 29 (Murten) or exit 30 (Kerzers) travel north towards Neuchatel as far as village of Gampelen where site is well signed. GPS: N47:00.407 E07:02.420

Charges guide

Per person	CHF 7,00 - 8,00
child	CHF 3,50 - 4,00
pitch incl. electricity	CHF 20,50 - 34,00
dog	CHF 3,00 - 4,00

CH9440 Camping Jungfraublick

Gsteigstrasse 80, Matten, CH-3800 Interlaken (Bern)

Tel: **033 822 4414**. Email: **info@jungfraublick.ch** **www.alanrogers.com/CH9440**

The Berner Oberland is one of the most scenic and well known areas of Switzerland with Interlaken probably the best known summer resort. Situated in the village of Matten, Jungfraublick is a delightful, medium sized site with splendid views up the Lauterbrunnen valley to the Jungfrau mountain. The 90 touring pitches 60-90 sq.m. with electricity connections are in regular rows on level, well cut grass. A number of fruit trees adorn but offer little shade. The 30 static caravans are to one side of the tourist area and do not intrude. There is some traffic noise from the main road.

Facilities

Fully equipped sanitary facilities and provision for disabled visitors. Showers are on payment, as is hot water for dishwashing. Washing machines and dryers. Motorcaravan services. Shop for basics (from 1/6). Small swimming pool (12 x 8 m) open mid June - end Aug. according to the weather. Heated rest room with TV and electronic games. Barbecues must be off the ground. Off site: Wilderswil train station 10 minutes walk. Bicycle hire 700 m. Town 1 km. Golf, riding and fishing 4 km.

Open: 1 May - 20 September.

Directions

Take the exit Nr. 25 from the N8 motorway, turn towards Interlaken. Site is within 500 m. on left. GPS: N46:40.345 E07:52.058

Charges guide

Per unit incl. 2 persons and electricity (6A)	CHF 24,30 - 50,40
extra person	CHF 7,60 - 8,60
child (4-16 yrs)	CHF 3,50 - 4,20
dog	CHF 3,00

CH9460 Camping Jungfrau

CH-3822 Lauterbrunnen (Bern)

Tel: **033 856 2010**. Email: **info@camping-jungfrau.ch** **www.alanrogers.com/CH9460**

This friendly site has a very imposing situation in a steep valley with a fine view of the Jungfrau at the end. It is a popular site and, although you should usually find space, in season do not arrive too late. A fairly extensive area with grass pitches and hard surfaced access roads. All 391 pitches (250 for touring) have shade in parts, electrical connections (13A) and 50 have water and drainage also. About 30% of the pitches are taken by seasonal caravans and it is used by two tour operators. The von Allmen family own and run the site and provide a warm welcome (English is spoken). You can laze here amid real mountain scenery, though it does lose the sun a little early. There are naturally many more active things to do – mountain walks or climbing, trips up the Jungfrau railway or one of the mountain lifts or excursions by car.

Facilities

Three fully equipped modern sanitary blocks can be heated in winter and also provide facilities for disabled visitors. Baby baths. Laundry facilities. Motorcaravan services. Supermarket. Self-service restaurant with takeaway (May - end Oct). General room with tables and chairs, TV, jukebox, drink machines, amusements. Playgrounds and covered play area. Excursions and some entertainment in high season. Mountain bike hire. Internet point. ATM. Drying room. Ski store. Off site: Free bus to ski station (in winter only).

Open: All year.

Directions

Go through Lauterbrunnen and fork right at far end before road bends left, 100 m. before church. The final approach is not very wide.
GPS: N46:35.284 E07:54.646

Charges guide

Per person	CHF 9,20 - 10,90
child (6-15 yrs)	CHF 4,40 - 5,10
pitch incl. electricity (plus meter in winter)	CHF 23,00 - 25,00
car	CHF 3,50
dog	CHF 3,00

Discounts for camping carnet and for stays over 3 nights outside high season.

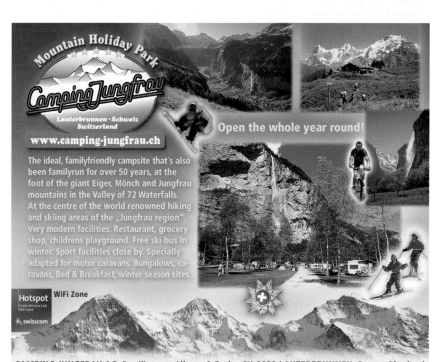

CH9360 Camping Grassi

CH-3714 Frutigen (Bern)

Tel: **033 671 1149**. Email: **campinggrassi@bluewin.ch** **www.alanrogers.com/CH9360**

This is a small site with about half the pitches occupied by static caravans, used by their owners for weekends and holidays. The 70 or so places available for tourists are not marked out but it is said that the site is not allowed to become overcrowded. Most places are on level grass with two small terraces at the end of the site. There is little shade but the site is set in a river valley with trees on the hills which enclose the area. Electricity is available for all pitches but long leads may be required in parts. It would make a useful overnight stop en-route for Kandersteg and the railway station where cars can join the train for transportation through the Lotschberg Tunnel to the Rhône Valley and Simplon Pass, or for a longer stay to explore the Bernese Oberland.

Facilities

The well constructed, heated sanitary block is of good quality. Washing machine and dryer. Gas supplies. Motorcaravan services. Rest room with TV. Kiosk (1/6-31/8). Play area and play house. Mountain bike hire. Fishing. Bicycle hire. WiFi. Off site: Shops and restaurants 10 minutes walk away in village. Riding 2 km. Outdoor and indoor pools, tennis and minigolf in Frutigen. Skiing and walking.

Open: All year.

Directions

Take Kandersteg road from Spiez and leave at Frutigen Dorf exit from where site is signed. GPS: N46:34.925 E07:38.431

Charges guide

Per unit incl. 2 persons and electricity	CHF 19,80 - 26,80
extra person	CHF 6,40
child (1-16 yrs)	CHF 1,50 - 3,20
dog	CHF 1,50

CH9496 Alpencamping

Brünigstrasse 47, CH-3860 Meiringen (Bern)

Tel: **033 971 3676**. Email: **info@alpencamping.ch** **www.alanrogers.com/CH9496**

Alpencamping is a small family site located close to Meiringen, an important winter sports resort and hiking centre in the summer. This all-year site in central Switzerland has been recommended by our Swiss agent and we plan to undertake a full inspection in 2009. There are 54 touring pitches here. These are flat and grassy and all have electrical connections. A further 32 pitches are occupied by residential units. This is a simple site with few amenities but there is a centrally located wash block and a small shop for essentials. A larger supermarket is five minutes walk away.

Facilities

Heated toilet block. Washing machine and dryer. Small shop. Play area. Off site: Meiringen with a wide choice of shops, restaurants and bars 500 m. Reichenbach Falls. Brienzersee Lake. Many walking paths and cycle trails. Summer and winter skiing.

Open: All year excl. November.

Directions

From Bern take the A6 motorway towards Interlaken and Thun. At Interlaken, join the A8 towards Spiez. Continue on road 11 to Meiringen, from where the site is well signed. GPS: N46:43.986 E08:10.417

Charges 2009

Per unit incl. 2 persons	CHF 27,00 - 38,40
electricity (low season 0.45 per kWh)	CHF 3,50
extra person	CHF 7,00 - 8,00
child (6-15 yrs)	CHF 4,00 - 4,50
dog	CHF 2,50

CH9410 Camping Stuhlegg

Stueleggstr. 7, CH-3704 Krattigen (Bern)

Tel: **033 654 2723**. Email: **campstuhlegg@bluewin.ch** **www.alanrogers.com/CH9410**

On the outskirts of the village of Krattigen, Camping Stuhlegg is a quiet and attractive site, located well above the lake and with beautiful, wide-ranging views over the lake to the mountains beyond. The 65 touring pitches are arranged on grassy terraced areas, some for motorcaravans having hardstanding. A few young trees provide shade. The friendly bar and bistro is also popular as a meeting point for the villagers, which gives a touch of local colour. This is a site where you can enjoy the fresh mountain air and scenery and relax. The site owner, Herr Schweizer, speaks excellent English. He is only too willing to advise on activities and excursions that can be undertaken in the region. In addition, the Krattigen guest information booklet is available in English and is a wealth of diverse information. Here you can discover where in the village good home Swiss cooking can be tried, what boat, train and bus excursions are available, museums to visit or where the William Tell play, in Swiss German, can be seen.

Facilities

Two modern sanitary facilities, the one near the entrance is heated, the other at the top of the site is for summer use and unheated. They contain all the usual facilities, showers operate with either coins or with tokens. Laundry room. Baby bath. Motorcaravan service point. Shop. Bar (all year) and bistro with takeaway (closed Nov). Swimming pool. TV room. Play area. Internet point. Off site: Plenty of footpaths in the immediate area. Bicycle hire 800 m. Riding, golf and fishing 4 km.

Open: All year.

Directions

Site is almost halfway between Spiez and Interlaken on the southern side of the Thunersee. Leave A8 at exit 20 and follow signs for Krattigen. Site is signed at top of village to the right (north). GPS: N46:39.475 E07:43.076

Charges 2009

Per unit incl. 2 persons and electricity	CHF 24,00 - 33,00
extra person	CHF 5,00 - 6,00
child	CHF 4,00 - 4,60
dog	CHF 3,00

CH9420 Camping Manor Farm 1

CH-3800 Interlaken-Thunersee (Bern)

Tel: **033 822 2264**. Email: **manorfarm@swisscamps.ch** **www.alanrogers.com/CH9420**

Manor Farm has been popular with British visitors for many years, as this is one of the traditional touring areas of Switzerland. The flat terrain is divided entirely into 525 individual, numbered pitches which vary considerably both in size (60-100 sq.m) and price with 10A electricity available and shade in some places. There are 144 equipped with electricity, water, drainage and 55 also have cable TV connections. Around 30% of the pitches are taken by permanent or letting units and a tour operator's presence.

Facilities

Six separate heated toilet blocks include free hot water for baths. Twenty private units for rent. Laundry facilities. Motorcaravan services. Shop (1/4-15/10). Restaurant adjoining (1/3-30/11). Snack bar with takeaway (July/Aug). TV. Playground and paddling pool. Minigolf. Bicycle hire. Sailing and windsurfing school. Lake swimming. Boat hire. Fishing. Activity and entertainment in high season. Excursions. Off site: Golf 500 m. (handicap card). Riding 3 km. Free bus to swimming pools.

Open: All year.

Directions

Site is 3 km. west of Interlaken along the road running north of the Thunersee towards Thun. Follow signs for 'Camp 1'. From A8 (bypassing Interlaken) take exit 24 marked 'Gunten, Beatenberg', which is a spur road bringing you out close to site. GPS: N46:40.516 E07:48.550

Charges guide

Per person	CHF 5,00 - 10,00
child (6-15 yrs)	CHF 2,40 - 4,80
pitch incl. electricity	CHF 10,50 - 43,00

CH9480 Camping Gletscherdorf

Gletscherdorf 31, CH-3818 Grindelwald (Bern)

Tel: **033 853 1429**. Email: **info@gletscherdorf.ch** **www.alanrogers.com/CH9480**

Set in a flat river valley on the edge of Grindelwald, one of Switzerland's well known winter and summer resorts, Gletscherdorf enjoys wonderful mountain views, particularly of the nearby north face of the Eiger. The site has 120 pitches, 60 for touring units. Most are marked and have electricity connections (10A), with a few others in an overflow field. There is a good community room with tables and chairs. This is, above all, a very quiet, friendly site for those who wish to enjoy the peaceful mountain air, walking, climbing and exploring with a mountain climbing school in Grindelwald.

Facilities

Excellent small, heated, fully equipped, sanitary block. Washing machines and dryer. Motorcaravan services. Gas supplies. Small shop for basic food items. Torches useful. Dogs are not accepted. Off site: Bicycle hire or golf 1 km. Indoor pool 1 km. Town shops and restaurants within walking distance.

Open: 1 May - 20 October.

Directions

To reach site, go into town and turn right at site signs after town centre; approach road is quite narrow and steep down hill but there is an easier departure road. GPS: N46:37.264 E08:02.718

Charges guide

Per person	CHF 7,50
child (6-15 yrs)	CHF 3,50
pitch	CHF 6,00 - 18,00

CH9450 TCS Camping Seeblick

Campingstrasse 14, CH-3806 Bönigen (Bern)

Tel: **033 822 1143**. Email: **camping.boenigen@tcs.ch** **www.alanrogers.com/CH9450**

This small, quiet site, bordered on two sides by Lake Brienz, is only 1.5 kilometres from the centre of Interlaken and the autoroute exit. It is therefore a useful site, not only to spend time on and enjoy the views, but also as an ideal base to tour this picturesque region, dominated by the Eiger and Jungfrau mountains. Almost all the 107 pitches are available for tourists. On level grassy ground and under tall trees, all have electricity. With magnificent views over the lake, gates give direct access to a footpath and to the lake shores.

Facilities

A well maintained, modern sanitary block has free showers and some washbasins in cabins. Facilities for disabled people. Baby room. Washing machine and dryer. Motorcaravan service point. Small shop sells gas and provides essentials. Informal bar and snack bar with takeaway food. Small solar heated swimming pool, and paddling pool. Play area.

Open: 31 March - 1 October.

Directions

Site is beside the Brienzersee in the eastern suburbs of Interlaken. From A8 take exit 26 (Interlaken Ost) and follow signs for Bönigen and then site signs. GPS: N46:41.480 E07:53.610

Charges guide

Per person	CHF 6,00 - 7,80
child	CHF 3,00 - 3,90
pitch with electricity	CHF 21,00 - 24,00
dog	CHF 3,00 - 4,00

Camping Cheques accepted.

CH9510 Camping Aaregg

Seestrasse 26, CH-3855 Brienz am See (Bern)

Tel: **033 951 1843**. Email: **mail@aaregg.ch** **www.alanrogers.com/CH9510**

Brienz in the Bernese Oberland is a delightful little town on the lake of the same name and the centre of the Swiss wood carving industry. Camping Aaregg is an excellent site situated on the southern shores of the lake with splendid views across the water to the mountains. There are 60 static caravans occupying their own area and 240 tourist pitches, all with electricity (10A). Of these, 16 are larger with hardstandings, water and drainage also and many of these have good lake views. Pitches fronting the lake have a surcharge. The trees and flowers make an attractive and peaceful environment. An excellent base from which to explore the many attractions of this scenic region, and is a useful night stop when passing from Interlaken to Luzern. Nearby at Ballenberg is the fascinating Freilichtmuseum, a very large open-air park of old Swiss houses which have been brought from all over Switzerland and re-erected in groups. Traditional Swiss crafts are demonstrated in some of these.

Facilities

New very attractive sanitary facilities built and maintained to first class standards. Showers with washbasins. Washbasins (open style and in cubicles). Children's section. Family shower rooms. Baby changing room. Facilities for disabled visitors. Laundry facilities. Motorcaravan services. Pleasant restaurant with terrace and takeaway in season. Play area. English is spoken.

Open: 1 April - 31 October.

Directions

Site is on road B6 on the east of Brienz. Entrance between BP and Esso filling stations, well signed. From the Interlaken-Luzern motorway, take Brienz exit and turn towards Brienz, site then on the left. GPS: N46:44.833 E08:02.833

Charges guide

Per person	CHF 10,00
child (6-16 yrs)	CHF 5,00
pitch incl. electricity	CHF 14,00 - 24,00
dog	CHF 3,00

Low season less 10%.

CH9570 Camping Eienwäldli

Wasserfallstraße 108, CH-6390 Engelberg (Unterwalden)

Tel: **041 637 1949**. Email: **info@eienwaeldli.ch** **www.alanrogers.com/CH9570**

This super site has facilities which must make it one of the best in Switzerland. It is situated in a beautiful location 3,500 feet above sea level, surrounded by mountains on the edge of the delightful village of Engelberg. Half of the site is taken up by static caravans which are grouped together at one side. The camping area is in two parts – nearest the entrance there are 57 hardstandings for caravans and motorcaravans, all with electricity (metered) and beyond this is a flat meadow for about 70 tents.

Facilities

The excellent toilet block, heated in cool weather, has free hot water in washbasins (in cabins) and (on payment) showers. Washing machines and dryers. Shop. Café/bar. Small lounge. Indoor pool complex. Ski facilities. Playground. Torches useful. TV. Internet access. Golf. Off site: Golf driving range and 18-hole course near. Fishing and bicycle hire 1 km. Riding 2 km.

Open: All year.

Directions

From N2 Gotthard motorway, leave at exit 33 'Stans-Sud' and follow signs to Engelberg. Turn right at T-junction on edge of town and follow signs to 'Wasserfall' and site. GPS: N46:48.564 E08:25.420

Charges guide

Per person	CHF 8,00
pitch incl. electricity (plus meter)	CHF 14,00 - 16,50

Credit cards accepted (surcharge).

CH9425 Camping Alpenblick

Seestrasse 130, Unterseen, CH-3800 Interlaken (Bern)

Tel: **033 822 77 57**. Email: **info@alpenblick-camping.ch** **www.alanrogers.com/CH9425**

Alpenblick is an all year site, located at the heart of the Bernese Oberland just 100 m. from Lake Thun. Susanne Knecht and George Zehntner took over the site in 2006 and have made a number of improvements, including a smart new toilet block. There are 100 touring pitches and a further 70 'residential' pitches. Touring pitches are grassy and all have electrical connections. There are also several teepees available for rent. One of these is used for socialising in the evening with the opportunity to barbecue food as well as occasional fondue evenings. All campers here receive a special tourist card with many benefits including free local bus transport. This is, of course, a superb area for cycling and walking. The lake is very popular for all manner of water sports and cruisers depart from a point very close to Alpenblick. The site's bistro specialises in local food such as 'schnitzelbrot' and bread is baked daily in the kitchen.

Facilities

Shop with daily delivery of fresh bread. Bistro. Teepee for socializing and events. Playground. Basketball. Teepees for rent. Off site: Nearest lake beach 100 m. Walking and cycle routes. Fishing. Riding. Boat trips on Lake Thun. Neuhaus lakeside restaurant and windsurfing school. Golf.

Open: All year.

Directions

Approaching from Thun and Bern on Road no. 8 leave at exit 24 (Interlaken West). Head north towards Neuhaus and follow signs to Camping no. 2. GPS: N46:40.800 E07:49.037

Charges guide

Per person	CHF 5,60 - 7,20
child (6-16 yrs)	CHF 3,50 - 3,80
pitch	CHF 12,00 - 22,00
electricity	CHF 4,00

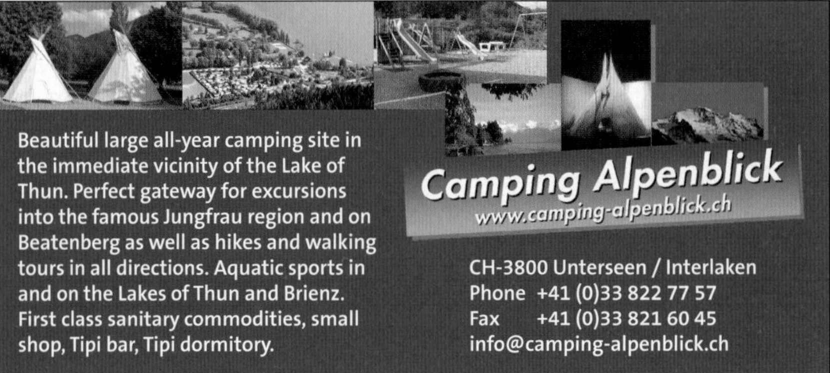

Beautiful large all-year camping site in the immediate vicinity of the Lake of Thun. Perfect gateway for excursions into the famous Jungfrau region and on Beatenberg as well as hikes and walking tours in all directions. Aquatic sports in and on the Lakes of Thun and Brienz. First class sanitary commodities, small shop, Tipi bar, Tipi dormitory.
Camping Alpenblick
www.camping-alpenblick.ch
CH-3800 Unterseen / Interlaken
Phone +41 (0)33 822 77 57
Fax +41 (0)33 821 60 45
info@camping-alpenblick.ch

CH9500 Camping Hofstatt-Derfli

Hofstatt, CH-6085 Hasliberg Goldern (Bern)

Tel: **033 971 3707**. Email: **welcome@derfli.ch** **www.alanrogers.com/CH9500**

This attractive new site has been created by a goldsmith and her husband. Small and family run, with 45 pitches, it is in a quiet location, over 1,000 metres high at the end of a small village in the Berner Oberland. One innovation is the one metre high mushrooms – with their white dotted red tops they are difficult to miss. They provide the electrical supply points for the 35 touring pitches and site lighting. The grass pitches are level, some with gravel hardstanding for motorcaravans and the gently sloping site is partly surrounded by trees with mountain top views across the valley.

Facilities

Well maintained, all the year round, sanitary facilities are housed in the main building. Showers controllable and free, some washbasins in cabins. Facilities for disabled visitors. Baby areas. Kitchen to rent in community room. Laundry facilities. Motorcaravan service point, Small shop. Play area. Bicycle hire. Ski and snowboard room, ski lifts at 1.5 and 2 km. New hot tub. Off site: Shop and restaurant 300 m. in village. Lots of scenic walking in the region.

Open: 15 May - 25 October, 25 December - 15 April.

Directions

Site is 25 km. east-northeast of Interlaken. From A8 exit 30 (Unterbach) follow signs for Luzern and Brünig Pass. At the top Brünig Pass follow signs for Hasliberg (you may spot a dwarf on a swing). Head towards Hasliberg Goldern where site is signed at bottom end of village on the right. GPS: N46:44.264 E08:11.797

Charges 2009

Per unit incl. 2 persons	CHF 26,00 - 36,00
electricity per kWh	CHF 0,55
extra person	CHF 8,00 - 9,00

No credit cards.

CH9495 Camping Balmweid

Balmweidstrasse 22, CH-3860 Meiringen (Bern)

Tel: **033 971 5115**. Email: **Info@camping-meiringen.ch** **www.alanrogers.com/CH9495**

This good, family run site is peaceful, just south of the village of Meiringen on the route to the Grimsel Pass and Susten Passes. With a backdrop of steep cliffs it has good views of the adjacent mountains and forest-covered slopes. It provides 180 pitches of which 120 are for tourers, 64 with 10A electricity. Whilst this is a good site on which to base a longer stay, it is also useful as an overnight stop en-route to the Grimsel Pass or for a rest having faced the challenges that the Pass has to offer.

Facilities

The excellent and well maintained heated sanitary block in the reception building has WCs, showers and washbasins. Facilities for disabled visitors. Washing machines and dryer. Motorcaravan service point. Restaurant and shop. TV Room. Playground. Covered communal grill area. Internet access.

Open: All year.

Directions

From Meiringen the site is well signed to the south. At roundabout turn left and then left again in about 200 m. From Bern and Interlaken just go straight on at the roundabout signed 'Grimsel'.
GPS: N46:43.539 E08:10.335

Charges guide

Per person	CHF 7,00 - 8,00
child (3-16 yrs)	CHF 1,00 - 4,00

CH9110 TCS Camping Seeland

CH-6204 Sempach-Stadt (Luzern)

Tel: **041 460 1466**. Email: **camping.sempach@tcs.ch** **www.alanrogers.com/CH9110**

Lucerne is a very popular city in the centre of Switzerland and Camping Seeland makes a peaceful base from which to visit the town and explore the surrounding countryside or, being a short way from the main N2 Basel - Chiasso motorway, is a convenient night stop if passing through. This neat, tidy site has 200 grass pitches for tourists, all with electricity (6A), a few with gravel hardstanding on either side of hard roads under trees with further places on the perimeter in the open. There are about 235 static caravans. A small river runs through the site with a connecting covered bridge.

Facilities

Three good quality sanitary blocks have the usual facilities including excellent facilities for disabled visitors and a baby room. Washing machine and dryer. Motorcaravan service point. Excellent self-service bar/restaurant with terrace overlooking the play area, lake and surrounding hills. Shop. Children's paddling pool and playground. Fishing. Lakeside beach. Off site: Shops and restaurants in the village. Tennis courts, boat and bicycle hire, minigolf and golf club. Hot air ballooning, river rafting and archery can be arranged. Windsurfing school nearby.

Open: 31 March - 1 October.

Directions

From the N2 take exit 21 for Sempach and follow signs for Sempach and site.
GPS: N47:07.529 E08:11.397

Charges guide

Per person	CHF 6,40 - 8,20
child (6-15 yrs)	CHF 3,20 - 4,10
caravan or motorcaravan incl. electricity	CHF 20,00 - 34,50
dog	CHF 3,00 - 4,00

Camping Cheques accepted.

CH9115 TCS Camping Steinibachried

CH-6048 Horw-Luzern (Luzern)

Tel: **041 340 3558**. Email: **camping.horw@tcs.ch** **www.alanrogers.com/CH9115**

Situated in the southern suburbs of Luzern and with easy autoroute access, this site is a very convenient base for visiting what is quite deservedly a popular tourist area. The level, grassed site provides 100 touring pitches with electricity, separated into rows by trees and hedges. It is dominated by the Pilatus mountains, over 2,000 metres high. The peaks and mountain top restaurants offer fantastic views and can be reached by cable car on the steepest cog railway in the world from Alpnachstad. Access to the lake from the site is over a wooden walkway which passes through a small protected nature area.

Facilities

Single, well maintained toilet block to one end of tourist area. Showers are free, some washbasins in cabins. Facilities for disabled visitors. Baby room. Washing machine and dryer. Motorcaravan service point. Gas supplies. Small shop. Bar with terrace. Convenient self service restaurant with takeaway. New play area.

Open: 31 March - 1 October.

Directions

Site is 4 km. south of the centre of Luzern and borders the Vierwaldstatter See. Leave motorway 2 at exit 28 Luzern/Horw. Site is signed at roundabout towards Horw-Sud.
GPS: N47:00.711 E08:18.660

Charges guide

Per person	CHF 6,00 - 8,00
child (6-15 yrs)	CHF 3,00 - 4,00
pitch incl. electricity	CHF 18,00 - 24,00
dog	CHF 3,00 - 4,00

CH9130 Camping Vitznau

CH-6354 Vitznau (Luzern)

Tel: **041 397 1280**. Email: **info@camping-vitznau.ch** **www.alanrogers.com/CH9130**

Camping Vitznau is situated in the small village of the same name, above and overlooking Lake Luzern, with splendid views across the water to the mountains on the other side. It is a small, neat and tidy site very close to the delightful village on the narrow, winding, lakeside road. The 160 pitches for caravans or motorhomes (max length 8 m) have 15A electricity available to most and all have fine views. They are on level, grassy terraces with hard wheel tracks for motorcaravans and separated by tarmac roads. There are separate places for tents.

Facilities

The single, well constructed sanitary block provides free hot showers (water heated by solar panels). Laundry facilities. Gas supplies. Motorcaravan services. Shop. General room for wet weather. Games room. Small heated swimming pool and children's splash pool (1/5-30/9). Off site: Village restaurants about five minutes walk. Fishing or bicycle hire within 1 km. Watersports near. Golf 15 km.

Open: 1 April - 31 October.

Directions

Site is signed from the centre of Vitznau. GPS: N47:00.403 E08:29.174

Charges 2009

Per unit incl. 2 persons and electricity	CHF 35,00 - 54,00
extra person	CHF 8,00 - 10,00
child (4-14 yrs)	CHF 4,00 - 5,00
dog	CHF 4,00 - 5,00

CH9820 Camping Pradafenz

Girabadaweg 34, CH-7075 Churwalden (Graubünden)

Tel: **081 382 1921**. Email: **camping@pradafenz.ch** **www.alanrogers.com/CH9820**

In the heart of the village of Churwalden on the Chur - St Moritz road, Pradafenz makes a convenient night stop and being amidst the mountains, is also an excellent base for walking and exploring this scenic area. At first sight, this appears to be a site for static holiday caravans but three large rectangular terraces at the front take 50 touring units. This area has a hardstanding of concrete frets with grass growing through and 'super-pitch' facilities of electricity (10A), drainage, gas and TV sockets. A flat meadow is also available for tents or as an overflow for caravans.

Facilities

New sanitary block is well appointed and heated. It includes some washbasins in cabins. Baby room. Another two blocks are in the tourist section. Washing machines, dryers and separate drying room. Motorcaravan services. Gas supplies. Small restaurant.WiFi. Off site: Restaurants and shops 300 m. in village. Municipal outdoor pool 500 m. Riding 3.5 km. Golf 5 km. Fishing 4 km. Bicycle hire 200m.

Open: 1 June - 31 October, 15 December - 18 April.

Directions

Churwalden is 10 km. south of Chur. From Chur take road towards Lenzerheide. It is initially a fairly long, steep climb with one tight hairpin. In centre of Churwalden turn right in front of the tourist office towards the site. GPS: N46:46.632 E09:32.500

Charges 2009

Per unit incl. 2 persons	CHF 28,00 - 32,00
electricity (winter, 0.50 per kWh)	CHF 2,50
extra person	CHF 8,00
child (2-16 yrs)	CHF 5,00 - 6,50

CH9830 Camping Sur En

CH-7554 Sur En/Sent (Graubünden)

Tel: **081 866 3544**. Email: **wb@bluewin.ch** **www.alanrogers.com/CH9830**

Sur En is at the eastern end of the Engadine valley, about 10 km. from the Italian and Austrian borders. The area is, perhaps, better known as a skiing region, but has summer attractions as well. This level site is in an open valley with little shade. They say there is room for 120 touring units on the meadows where pitches are neither marked nor numbered; there are electricity connections for all (6A). As you approach on road 27 and spot the site way below in the shadow of a steeply rising, wooded mountain, the drop may appear daunting. However, as you drive it becomes reasonable.

Facilities

The modern, heated sanitary block is good with some extra facilities in the main building. Washing machine and dryer. Motorcaravan services. Shop and good restaurant (15/12-15/4 and 1/5-31/10) with covered terrace. Takeaway (high season). Swimming pool (1/6-15/10). Bicycle hire. Fishing. Entertainment in July/Aug.
A symposium for sculptors is held during the second week in July. Excursions arranged in high season. Off site: Golf 8 km. Bus service to Scuol for train to St Moritz.

Open: All year.

Directions

Sur En is 28 km. east of Davos. It is signed from the 27 road about halfway between Susch and Scuol. The road is a steady, winding descent. Cross covered timber bridge (3.8 m) to site.
GPS: N46:49.060 E10:21.570

Charges guide

Per person	CHF 5,00 - 5,80
child (6-16 yrs)	CHF 2,50 - 2,90
pitch	CHF 11,10 - 15,00
electricity	CHF 2,80

CH9850 TCS Camping Neue Ganda

CH-7302 Landquart (Graubünden)

Tel: **081 322 3955**. Email: **camping.landquart@tcs.ch** **www.alanrogers.com/CH9850**

Situated close to the Klosters, Davos road and the nearby town of Landquart, this valley campsite provides a comfortable night-stop near the A13 motorway. The 80 touring pitches are not marked or separated but are all on level grass off a central tarmac road through the long, narrow wooded site. All pitches have 6/10A electricity. The many static caravans are mostly hidden from view situated in small alcoves. A modern, timber clad building at the entrance houses all the necessary amenities.

Facilities

The toilet block is extremely well appointed and can be heated. Facilities for disabled visitors. Baby room. Washing machine and dryer. Drying room. Motorcaravan services. Restaurant. Shop. Internet access. Off site: Rambling. Cycling tours. Tennis, riding and canoeing nearby. Fishing 2 km.

Open: 6 April - 23 October, 19 December - 20 March.

Directions

From A13 motorway take Landquart exit 14 and follow road to Davos. 800 m. after crossing large bridge, go down slip-road where site is signed on right. At the bottom turn left under road and follow signs right towards site.
GPS: N46:58.140 E09:35.360

Charges guide

Per person	CHF 5,40 - 6,60
pitch	CHF 15,60 - 17,80
electricity	CHF 4,00

Camping Cheques accepted.

CH9855 Camping Cavresc

CH-7746 Le Prese (Graubünden)

Tel: **081 844 0797**. Email: **camping.cavresc@bleuwin.ch** **www.alanrogers.com/CH9855**

Le Prese is on the Tirano to St Moritz road, south of the Bernina Pass. Camping Cavresc is on grassy meadows in the Valposchiano valley and, with its southern climate, peaceful ambience and beautiful views, is a very good, newly built site with ultramodern sanitary facilities. There are 36 flat, level pitches, all with 10A electricity and water, plus a large area for tents. There is no shade. If the campsite reception is unmanned, walk back into town, as the Sertori family who own the site also run the small well stocked supermarket. Le Prese is close to Italy and the Poschiavo Lake.

Facilities

The excellent toilet block is very well maintained. Showers on payment. Facilities for disabled visitors. Washing machine and dryer. Motorcaravan services. Restaurant/bar. Small shop. Swimming pool (high season). There are plans for outdoor ice skating to be added. Off site: Le Prese 250 m. Windsurfing and sailing and of course skiing.

Open: All year.

Directions

Le Prese is 6 km. south of Poschiavo. Coming from Italy on road no. 29, the site is towards the southern end of the town. Turn right towards Pagnoncini/Cantone and site is on right in about 100 m. Go over a humpback bridge at the entrance.
GPS: N46:17.330 E10:04.510

Charges guide

Per person	CHF 10,00 - 12,00
pitch	CHF 6,00 - 15,00
electricity	CHF 4,00

CH9860 Camping Plauns

Morteratsch, CH-7504 Pontresina (Graubünden)

Tel: **081 842 6285**. Email: **plauns@bluewin.ch** **www.alanrogers.com/CH9860**

This is a mountain site in splendid scenery near St Moritz. Pontresina is at the mouth of the Bernina Pass road (B29) which runs from Celerina in the Swiss Engadine to Tirano in Italy. Camping Plauns, some 4 km. southeast of Pontresina, is situated in the floor of the valley between fir clad mountains at 1,850 m. above sea level. There are about 250 pitches for tourists in summer, all with electricity, some in small clearings amongst tall trees and some in a larger open space. In winter the number is reduced to 40. They are neither numbered nor marked and size depends on the natural space between the trees.

Facilities

Three fully equipped toilet blocks, one old and two new, modern and excellent, and can be heated in cool weather. Some washbasins in private cabins and showers on payment. Facilities for disabled visitors. Laundry facilities. Shop. Grill-snack. TV room. Internet access. Bicycle hire. Playground. Torch useful. Off site: Restaurant 1 km. Entertainment programme offered at nearby Pontresina.

Open: 1 June - 15 October, 15 December - 15 April.

Directions

Site is on B29, the road to Tirano and Bernina Pass, about 4 km. southeast of Pontresina - well signed.
GPS: N46:27.420 E09:56.040

Charges guide

Per person	CHF 10,40
child (6-15 yrs)	CHF 4,00 - 6,50
pitch	CHF 9,00 - 15,00
electricity (6-13A)	CHF 3,00 - 4,50

CH9865 TCS Camping Fontanivas

Via Fontanivas 9, CH-7180 Disentis (Graubünden)

Tel: **081 947 4422**. Email: **camping.disentis@tcs.ch** **www.alanrogers.com/CH9865**

Nestled in the Surselva valley with superb views of the surrounding mountains, this is an attractive site with its own lake. Surrounded by tall pine trees, the site is owned by the Touring Club of Switzerland, the Swiss version of the AA, and provides flat, level pitches, almost all with 13A electricity. There are plenty of opportunities for walks, nature trails and cycle rides, whilst the more adventurous can enjoy themselves canyoning, rafting, hang-gliding or mountain biking. The Medelser Rhine near Disentis is known to be the richest place in gold in the country.

Facilities

The excellent sanitary block is well maintained with free showers and hairdryers. Facilities for disabled visitors. Baby room. Washing machine and dryer. Motorcaravan services. Shop. Restaurant/bar. Play room. Bicycle hire. Fishing. Caravans and tent bungalows to rent. Off site: Disentis 2 km. Indoor pool.

Open: 27 April - 30 September.

Directions

The site is 2 km. south of Disentis. From Andermatt take the Oberalppass to Disentis. In town at T-junction turn right towards Lukmanier. Site is at bottom of hill on the left, past the droopy power cables. GPS: N46:41.814 E08:51.197

Charges guide

Per person	CHF 6,20 - 7,20
pitch	CHF 14,80 - 18,80
electricity	CHF 4,50

Camping Cheques accepted.

CH9160 TCS Camping Rheinwiesen

Haupt Strasse, CH-8246 Langwiesen (Schaffhausen)

Tel: **052 659 3300**. Email: **camping.schaffhausen@tcs.ch** **www.alanrogers.com/CH9160**

Rheinwiesen is a friendly site in a very pleasant setting on the banks of the Rhine, with some tall trees, amongst which are some attractive willows. It is level and grassy, the first half quite open and the rest of the touring area wooded, with numbered pitches (mostly small – up to 70 sq.m), many under tall trees. There are many day visitors in summer as the site is ideally placed for swimming, canoeing and diving in the Rhine. Whilst here, you would not want to miss the impressive waterfalls at Schaffhausen, 150 m. wide and 25 m. high.

Facilities

For tourers, there is an old but clean building which might be under pressure at the busiest times. Washing machine and dryer. Bar/snack bar with covered terrace for burgers etc. open daily. Bread to order, some essentials kept. Pool room also used as wet weather rest room. Two shallow paddling pools, with play area close by. Dogs are not accepted at any time. Off site: Shop 500 m.

Open: 27 April - 29 September.

Directions

From Schaffhausen head east towards Kreuzlingen (road no. 14) for about 2.5 km. Site is signed just before Langwiesen. If coming from the east, note the tight turn into the site. GPS: N47:41.240 E08:39.350

Charges guide

Per person	CHF 5,60 - 7,20
pitch	CHF 14,00 - 17,00
electricity (4A)	CHF 3,00

Camping Cheques accepted.

CH9175 Camping Giessenpark

CH-7310 Bad Ragaz (St Gallen)

Tel: **081 302 3710**. Email: **giessenpark@bluewin.ch** **www.alanrogers.com/CH9175**

The luxury spa resort of Bad Ragaz nestles in the Rhine valley and Giessenpark surrounds this site, which is located in a forest. There are 86 flat, level gravel pitches of which 52 are for touring, all with access to electricity (10A). The Rhine and the extensive park are within a minutes walk and add to the peaceful nature of the site. The local authority swimming pool is close to the site, which is open from mid May to mid September. There is also a children's pool in a very large play area about 200 m. from the site.

Facilities

Good, modern toilet is well maintained with free showers. Facilities for disabled visitors. Baby room. Sinks with hot water for laundry and dishwashing. Washing machine and dryer. Motorcaravan services. Shop (limited). Restaurant. Off site: Bad Ragaz 1 km. Golf and bicycle hire 1 km. Riding 3 km.

Open: All year.

Directions

From the A13 take Bad Ragaz exit and follow Bad Ragaz signs. In town, go over small bridge and turn right immediately, then right again after 300 m. following signs towards the site.
GPS: N47:09.999 E09:29.699

Charges guide

Per unit incl. 2 persons and electricity	CHF 38,80
extra person	CHF 11,90

No credit cards.

CH9185 Camping Fischerhaus

Promenadenstrasse 52, CH-8280 Kreuzlingen (Thurgau)

Tel: **071 688 4903**. Email: **camping.fischerhaus@bluewin.ch** **www.alanrogers.com/CH9185**

Camping Fischerhaus is tucked behind the town's light industrial estate and next to Lake Constance. It provides 250 pitches of which 150 are for tourers, all with 10A electricity supply. The seasonal pitches are grouped together near reception and the lakeside, although from the site it is hardly visible. The touring pitches are grass, level and located towards the back of the site, a short walk from the main sanitary block. The town of Kreuzlingen is a short walk away along the banks of the lake past a marina.

Facilities

The main sanitary block, near reception, has WCs, showers and facilities for disabled visitors. The second block, near the area used by tourers, just has WCs. Washing machines and dryer. Small shop for basics. Restaurant and bar overlooking lake. Playground. Fishing. Dogs are not accepted. Off site: Swimming pool adjacent.

Open: 20 March - 26 October.

Directions

Site is at the east side of Kreuzlingen on the banks of Lake Constance. It is well signed from all directions as is the adjoining swimming pool.
GPS: N47:38.824 E09:11.875

Charges guide

Per person	CHF 9,00
child (6-16 yrs)	CHF 4,50

CH9180 Camping Buchhorn

Philosophenweg 17, CH-9320 Arbon (Thurgau)

Tel: **071 446 6545**. Email: **info@camping-arbon.ch** **www.alanrogers.com/CH9180**

This small site is directly beside Lake Bodensee in the town's parkland. The site has some shade but few of the touring pitches are by the water's edge. An overflow field used for tents is next door. There are many static caravans but said to be room for 100 tourists. Pitches are on a mixture of gravel and grass, on flat areas on either side of access roads, most with 6A electricity. Cars may have to be parked elsewhere. A railway runs directly along one side. A single set of buildings provide all the site's amenities.

Facilities

Toilet facilities are clean and modern, and should just about suffice in high season. Washing machine, dryer and drying area. Fridge. Shop (basic supplies, drinks and snacks all season). General room. Playground. Dogs are not accepted. Off site: Tennis 150 m. Town swimming lido 400 m. Watersports and steamer trips are available on the lake, walks and marked cycle tracks around it. Nature reserve nearby.

Open: April - October.

Directions

On Arbon - Konstanz road 13. From the A1 take the Arbon West exit and head towards the town. Straight on at the lights and turn left just after the town sign. Turn left again and head towards the warehouses. Turn right and the site is straight ahead.
GPS: N47:30.960 E09:26.040

Charges guide

Per person	CHF 8,00
child (6-16 yrs)	CHF 3,50

CH9000 Camping Waldhort

Heideweg 16, CH-4153 Reinach bei Basel (Basel-Land)

Tel: **061 711 6429**. Email: **info@camping-waldhort.ch** **www.alanrogers.com/CH9000**

This is a satisfactory site for night halts or for visits to Basel. Although there are almost twice as many static caravan pitches as spaces for tourists, this site, on the edge of a residential district, is within easy reach of the city by tram. It is flat, with 210 level pitches on grass with access from the tarmac road which circles round inside the site. Trees are now maturing to give some shade. All pitches have electricity (10A). Owned and run by the Camping and Caravanning Club of Basel, it is neat, tidy and orderly and there is usually space available. An extra, separate camping area has been added behind the tennis club which has pleasant pitches and good sanitary facilities.

Facilities

The good quality, fully equipped, central sanitary block includes facilities for babies and disabled people. Washing machine and dryer. Kitchen with gas rings. Fridge for ice packs. Motorcaravan services. Small shop with terrace for drinks. Play area with two small pools. Swimming pool and tennis next to site.

Open: 1 March - 25 October.

Directions

Take Basel - Delémont motorway spur, exit for Reinach-Nord and follow site signs.
GPS: N47:29.954 E07:36.119

Charges 2009

Per unit incl. 2 persons and electricity	CHF 36,00
extra person	CHF 9,00
child (6-14 yrs)	CHF 5,00
dog	CHF 3,00

Electricity included.

CH9010 TCS Camping Lido Solothurn

Glutzenhopstraße 1, CH-4500 Solothurn (Solothurn)

Tel: **032 621 8935**. Email: **camping.solothurn@tcs.ch** **www.alanrogers.com/CH9010**

The Swiss Camping Club site is like many in their ownership with excellent facilities and pleasant location. There are 166 level, grass pitches including 116 for touring units, all with electricity and 12 also have water and drainage. A small marina adjoining the site is under the same ownership. The site is close to the large town of Solothurn, on the banks of the Aare. Although it is behind the town's football stadium and close to some high-rise flats, there are pleasant views of the local hills.

Facilities

Two extremely well maintained sanitary blocks. Washing machines and dryer. Motorcaravan service point. Small shop for basics. Restaurant overlooking marina. Playground. Small, unheated children's pool. Internet access. Off site: Large municipal swimming pool 200 m. Solothurn and the River Aare. The stork colony at Altreu.

Open: 1 March - 3 January.

Directions

Site is on the western outskirts of Solothurn. From A5 motorway at Solothurn Sud take exit 32 and follow sign for Solothurn, then Zentrum then Biel. Site on Soloturn-Biel road near football stadium.
GPS: N47:12.780 E07:31.740

Charges guide

Per person	CHF 6,20 - 7,80
child (6-15 yrs)	CHF 3,10 - 3,90
pitch incl. electricity	CHF 20,00 - 29,50
dog	CHF 3,00 - 4,00

Camping Cheques accepted.

CH9890 Camping Campofelice

Via alle Brere 7, CH-6598 Tenero (Ticino)

Tel: **091 745 1417** **www.alanrogers.com/CH9890**

The largest site in Switzerland, it is bordered on the front by Lake Maggiore and on one side by the Verzasca estuary, where the site has its own harbour. Campofelice is divided into rows, with 1,030 individual pitches of average size on flat grass on either side of hard access roads. Mostly well shaded, all pitches have electricity connections (10A) and some also have water, drainage and TV connections. Pitches near the lake cost more (these are not available for motorcaravans) and a special area is reserved for small tents. English is spoken at this good, if rather expensive site. Sporting facilities are good and there are cycle paths in the area, including into Locarno. The beach by the lake is sandy, long and wider than the usual lakeside ones. It shelves gently so that bathing is safe for children.

Facilities

The six heated toilet blocks are of excellent quality. Washing machines and dryers. Motorcaravan services. Gas supplies. Supermarket. Restaurant. Tennis. Minigolf. Bicycle hire. Playground. Doctor calls. Dogs are not accepted Off site: Fishing 500 m. Water skiing and windsurfing 1 km. Boat hire 5 km. Riding 6 km. Golf 8 km.

Open: 26 March - 26 October.

Directions

On the Bellinzona - Locarno road 13, exit Tenero. Site is signed at roundabout. GPS: N46:10.114 E08:51.355

Charges guide

Per unit incl. 2 persons and electricity	CHF 44,00 - 82,00
extra person	CHF 8,00 - 10,00

Some pitches have min. stay regulations.

CH9880 Camping Lido Mappo

Via Mappo, CH-6598 Tenero (Ticino)

Tel: **091 745 1437**. Email: **camping@lidomappo.ch** **www.alanrogers.com/CH9880**

Lido Mappo lies on the lakeside at the northeast tip of Lake Maggiore, about 5 km. from Locarno, and has views of the surrounding mountains and hills across the lake. The site is attractively laid out in rows of individual, numbered pitches, half for tents and half for caravans and mostly split up by access roads or hedges. The pitches (358 for touring) vary in size, those by the lake costing more and most are well shaded. Electricity (10-16A) is available on all pitches. With helpful English speaking staff, this is a quiet site with its own narrow, mainly sandy beach.

Facilities

The five, recently renovated toilet blocks can be heated in cool weather and are always well kept. They include individual washbasins, all in cabins for women and some for men. Facilities for disabled visitors. Baby room. Laundry and cooking facilities. Motorcaravan services. Supermarket. Restaurant/bar. Takeaway. TV room. Large playground. Lake swimming. Fishing. First aid post. Dogs are not accepted. Off site: Bicycle hire nearby. Riding 3 km. Golf 5 km.

Open: 27 March - 18 October.

Directions

On Bellinzona - Locarno road 13, exit Tenero site is signed at roundabout. GPS: N46:10.625 E08:50.570

Charges 2009

Per unit incl. 2 persons and electricity	CHF 33,00 - 53,00

Less 5% for stays over 10 days and 10% over 21 days.

CH9950 TCS Camping Piodella

CH-6933 Muzzano (Ticino)

Tel: **091 994 7788**. Email: **camping.muzzano@tcs.ch** **www.alanrogers.com/CH9950**

This modernised site, on the edge of Lake Lugano facing south down the lake must rank as one of the best in Switzerland. There are 265 numbered pitches (212 for touring units) all with 10A electricity and 26 with water connections. There is shade in the older part nearest the lake and young trees in the new area. Cars must be parked in the car park, not by your pitch. The site is a short way from the airport so there may be some aircraft noise. Well placed for exploring Lugano, southern Switzerland and northern Italy, or simply to enjoy the facilities of the site.

Facilities

The original refurbished toilet block and a splendid new one which includes a baby room and a bathroom for disabled visitors, are heated in cool weather. Washing machines and dryers. Motorcaravan services. Gas supplies. Shop. Bar/restaurant with pleasant terrace. Swimming pools (May-mid Oct). Day and TV rooms. Playground. Two tennis courts. Marina. Off site: Bicycle hire 2 km. Riding 4 km. Golf 5 km.

Open: All year excl. 24 October - 10 December.

Directions

Piodella is on Bellinzona - Ponte Tresa road; take motorway exit 49 Lugano-Nord for Ponte Tresa and turn left at T-junction in Agno. Follow signs for Piodella or TCS at roundabout. Site is at south end of the airport. GPS: N45:59.755 E08:54.503

Charges guide

Per person	CHF 7,80 - 9,80
child (6-15 yrs)	CHF 3,90 - 4,90
pitch incl. electricity	CHF 24,00 - 44,60

CH9970 TCS Camping Parco al Sole

CH-6866 Meride (Ticino)

Tel: **091 646 4330**. Email: **camping.meride@tcs.ch** **www.alanrogers.com/CH9970**

Meride is a small village in the extreme south of Switzerland with the Italian border close on three sides. A little remote, Parco al Sole is on a slight slope 1 km. before the village, with mountain views. There is space for 64 small units, with electricity connections (10A) available for 40, and 16 static caravans. The pitches are not numbered or marked out and caravans are placed between tall trees or on an open space. When the site is busy units could be crowded. Cars are parked by the entrance.

Facilities

A good quality sanitary block with the usual facilities, free hot water and a baby room. 'Grotto Café' with log fire during cool weather with drinks and simple meals. Basic food supplies. Heated swimming pool (1/61-30/8) and paddling pool. Playground. Some animation is organised in high season. TV and videos (in café).

Open: 1 May - 25 September.

Directions

From N2 motorway take exit 52 for Mendrisio towards Stabio, Varese. Head to Rancate then Basazio, Arzo and Meride. Site signed (6 km. from motorway exit). Road to site is narrow. Any problems follow signs for camping Serpiano until village of Meride. GPS: N45:53.332 E08:56.930

Charges guide

Per person	CHF 6,20 - 7,80
caravan or tent incl. electricity	CHF 17,80 - 22,10
motorcaravan incl. electricity	CHF 21,70 - 26,10

Camping Cheques accepted.

CH9520 Camping du Botza

Route du Camping 1, CH-1963 Vétroz (Valais)

Tel: **027 346 1940**. Email: **info@botza.ch** **www.alanrogers.com/CH9520**

Situated in the Rhône Valley at a height of 460 m. and not far from the autoroute, this is a pleasant site with views of the surrounding mountains. It is set in a peaceful wooded location, even though it is close to an industrial zone. There are 125 individual touring pitches, ranging in size (60-130 sq.m) all with 4A electricity, many with some shade and 25 with water and drainage. Considerable investment has taken place in making the site environmentally friendly with solar power used to heat the pool and sanitary blocks and a large recycling facility. The gates are locked at night.

Facilities

Some private cabins in the heated sanitary block. Washing machines and dryers. Shop. Pizzeria. Swimming pool, completely renovated in 2008, (15/5-1/9). Playground. Tennis court. Internet access. WiFi. Off site: Many walks alongside small streams nearby. Good cycle track. Riding 2 km. Golf 8 km. The historic town of Sion is 8 km.

Open: All year.

Directions

From the A9/E62 between Sion and Martigny, take exit 25 Conthey/Vétroz and go south towards 'zone industrial', after 200 m. turn right to 'Camping 9.33 Botza' and follow signs. Site is 2.5 km. from autoroute exit. GPS: N46:12.210 E07:16.440

Charges 2009

Per unit incl. 2 persons and electricity	CHF 25,40 - 36,70
extra person	CHF 5,00 - 8,20
child (6-16 yrs)	CHF 2,50 - 4,10

CH9600 Camping Rive-Bleue

Bouveret Plage, CH-1897 Bouveret (Valais)

Tel: **024 481 2161**. Email: **info@camping-rive-bleue.ch** **www.alanrogers.com/CH9600**

At the eastern end of Lac Léman with mountain views, the main feature of this site is the very pleasant lakeside lido only a short walk of 300 m. from the site and with free entry for campers. It has an 'Aquaparc' pool with a water toboggan and plenty of grassy sunbathing areas, a bathing area in lake, boating facilities with storage for sailboards, canoes, inflatables etc, sailing school, pedaloes for hire. The site has 220 marked pitches on well kept flat grass, half in the centre with 6A electricity, the other half round the perimeter.

Facilities

Two decent toilet blocks have washbasins with cold water in the old block, hot in the new, and preset free hot showers. Covered area for cooking with electric rings and barbecue. Drying room. Motorcaravan services (Euro-relais). Shop, restaurant by beach (both all season). Bicycle hire. Fishing.

Open: 1 April - 1 October.

Directions

Leave motorway 5, south of Montreux, at exit 16 (Villeneuve) and follow signs for Evian. Just after passing town sign for Le Bouveret, turn right, north, and follow Aquaparc and site signs. GPS: N46:23.194 E06:51.610

Charges guide

Per person	CHF 8,10 - 9,90
child (6-16 yrs)	CHF 5,60 - 6,70
motorcaravan or caravan and car incl. electricity	CHF 14,30 - 17,50

CH9640 Camping de la Sarvaz

Route de Fully, CH-1913 Saillon (Valais)

Tel: **027 744 1389**. Email: **info@sarvaz.ch** **www.alanrogers.com/CH9640**

The Rhône valley in Valais with its terraced vineyards provides a beautiful setting for this site. Family owned and run, Camping de la Sarvaz provides excellent facilities and would be a good base for relaxing or for the more energetic walking, cycling, climbing or skiing. The site adjoins a restaurant/bar. It has 57 level touring pitches all with electricity, 19 of which have water and drainage. Lovely mountain views surround the site and there are nine chalets to rent. An inflatable pool is available from May to September. English is spoken.

Facilities

New, heated sanitary facilities are of very high standards, very well maintained. Free showers. Additional toilets on the first floor. Facilities for disabled people. Baby room. Washing machine and dryer. Motorcaravan services. Shop (all season). Restaurant/bar (all season, not Mondays and Tuesdays). Good play area. Internet access. Off site: Saillon 2 km. with Thermal centre and spa facilities.

Open: 4 February - 31 December.

Directions

From the A9 take exit 23 for Saxon/Saillon. Follow signs to Saillon then turn right towards the site, which is 3 km. from the autoroute exit. GPS: N46:09.593 E07:10.053

Charges guide

Per unit incl. 2 persons and electricity	CHF 37,50 - 44,50
extra person	CHF 8,00
child (6-16 yrs)	CHF 4,00

CH9655 TCS Camping les Neuvilles

Rue de Levant 68, CH-1920 Martigny (Valais)

Tel: **027 722 4544**. Email: **camping.martigny@tcs.ch** **www.alanrogers.com/CH9655**

Easily accessible from the autoroute (A9) and close to the town centre, this site has a total of 225 pitches. There are 185 for touring units, all with electricity and most on level, grassy ground (some slope slightly). A number of trees provide some shade, although the site is fairly open allowing views of the surrounding mountains. Being close to the autoroute and located in an industrial area, the site can be quite noisy, especially noticeable during the night and mornings. With its ease of access, it makes a convenient night stop when travelling along the Rhône Valley.

Facilities

Two sanitary buildings, one close to the entrance the other at the far end. Showers are large and free, some washbasins in cabins, some with only cold water. Facilities for disabled people. Baby room. Cooking rings. Washing machines and dryers. Motorcaravan service point. Shop. Bar and snack bar. TV room. Play area and paddling pool. Bicycle hire. Off site: Entry to the municipal swimming pool is free. Riding 1 km. Fishing 3 km.

Open: 1 February - 15 November.

Directions

From A9 exit 22 (Martigny) follow signs for Expo. After leaving the autoroute, at first roundabout, site is signed. GPS: N46:05.822 E07:04.726

Charges guide

Per person	CHF 6,80 - 7,80
child	CHF 3,40 - 3,90
pitch incl. electricity	CHF 18,70 - 24,20
dog	CHF 3,00 - 4,00

CH9660 Camping des Glaciers

CH-1944 La Fouly (Valais)

Tel: **027 783 1735**. Email: **camping.glaciers@st-bernard.ch** **www.alanrogers.com/CH9660**

Camping des Glaciers at 1,600 m. above sea level is set amidst magnificent mountain scenery in a quiet, peaceful location in the beautiful Ferret Valley. The site offers some pitches in an open, undulating meadow and the rest are level, individual plots of varying sizes in small clearings, between bushes and shrubs or under tall pines. All of the 170 places have 25A electricity. The charming lady owner, Mme Darbellay, who has run the site for over 35 years, is fluent in six languages and always ready to welcome you to this peaceful haven and to give information on the locality.

Facilities

Three sanitary units of exceptional quality and heated when necessary (the site reports a new unit built in 2008). Hot water is free in all washbasins (some in cabins), showers and sinks. British style WCs. Washing machines and dryers in each block, one block has a drying room, another a baby room. Gas supplies. Motorcaravan services. Small shop. Recreation room with TV. Playground. Torches may be useful. Off site: Shop and restaurant 500 m. Bicycle hire 500 m. Riding 8 km.

Open: 15 May - 30 September.

Directions

Leave Martigny - Gd St Bernard road (no. 21) at Orsieres and follow signs (Ferret valley or La Fouly). Site is signed on right at end of La Fouly village. GPS: N45:56.008 E07:05.620

Charges 2009

Per unit incl. 2 persons and electricity	CHF 27,50 - 33,50
extra person	CHF 7,00
child (2-12 yrs)	CHF 4,00
dog	CHF 2,00

CH9670 Camping de Molignon

CH-1984 Les Haudères (Valais)

Tel: **027 283 1240**. Email: **info@molignon.ch** **www.alanrogers.com/CH9670**

De Molignon, surrounded by mountains, is a quiet, peaceful place 1,450 m. above sea level; although there may be some road noise, the rushing stream and the sound of cow bells are likely to be the only disturbing factor in summer. The 100 pitches for tourists (75 with 10A electricity) are on well tended, level terraces leading down to the river. Good English is spoken by the owner's son who is now running the site. The uphill drive from Sion in the Rhône Valley is enhanced by the Pyramids of Euseigne, through which the road passes via a short tunnel.

Facilities

Two fully equipped sanitary blocks, heated in cool weather, with free hot showers. Baby room. Washing machines and dryer. Kitchen for hikers. Motorcaravan services. Gas supplies. Shop for basic supplies (15/6-15/9). Restaurant. Heated swimming pool with cover for cool weather (6 x 12 m). Sitting room for games and reading. Playground. Guided walks, climbing, geological museum, winter skiing. Fishing. Off site: Tennis and hang-gliding near. Bicycle hire 1 km. Riding 15 km. Langlauf in winter.

Open: All year.

Directions

Follow signs southwards from Sion for the Val d'Herens through Evolène to Les Haudères where site is signed on the right at the beginning of the village. GPS: N46:05.670 E07:29.849

Charges guide

Per person	CHF 6,70
child (4-16 yrs)	CHF 3,80
pitch incl. electricity	CHF 12,80 - 17,90
dog	CHF 3,00

Less 10% in low season.

CH9720 Camping Bella-Tola

Waldstrasse 57, CH-3952 Susten-Leuk (Valais)

Tel: **027 473 1491**. Email: **info@bella-tola.ch** **www.alanrogers.com/CH9720**

An attractive site with good standards, Bella-Tola is on the hillside above Susten (east of Sierre) with good views over the Rhône valley. Extensive terracing has been carried out and most of the pitches are now terraced and flat. All of the 180 individually numbered pitches have electricity connections. The fullest season is 10/7-10/8, but they say that there is usually room somewhere. Used by tour operators (20%). Guests are requested to comply with environmental rules by sorting rubbish as directed. The site boasts a good sized heated swimming pool and children's pool (both free to campers) which, like the restaurant and bar overlooking them, are also open to non-campers and so more crowded at weekends and holidays. In the low rain climate of the Valais the pool is naturally much used.

Facilities

Three good quality modern sanitary blocks should be quite sufficient, with some washbasins in cabins. Free hot water in washbasins, showers and sinks for clothes and dishes, plus baby rooms. Facilities for disabled visitors. Washing machines, dryers and irons. Motorcaravan services. Shop. Newly renovated restaurant/bar. Takeaway (July-Aug). Swimming pool (heated 29/5-20/9). General room with TV. Films and guided walks in July/Aug. Torches advised. WiFi (free). Off site: Riding and tennis. Golf 4 km.

Open: 20 May - 5 October.

Directions

Travelling eastwards from Sierre along main road, small site road is to the right (south) just after entering Susten (site signed).
GPS: N46:17.937 E07:38.194

Charges guide

Per unit incl. 2 persons and electricity	CHF 38,60 - 49,60
extra person	CHF 10,00
child (2-16 yrs)	CHF 5,00 - 7,00
dog (max 1)	CHF 2,80

Less 25% on person and pitch fees outside July/Aug.

CH9680 TCS Camping Bois de Finges

CH-3960 Sierre (Valais)

Tel: **027 455 0284**. Email: **camping.sierre@tcs.ch** **www.alanrogers.com/CH9680**

This site is situated in the middle of the 'Bois des Finges' pine forest on a rocky wooded hillside. It is attractive and well maintained with much to offer for the naturalist. With 100 pitches cut out of the hillside, some are difficult to access but the manager will help. They can take units of up to 7 metres but mainly smaller units and tents in some parts. All pitches are screened by trees and 62 have 4A electricity (long leads useful). Staff are welcoming and helpful but little English is spoken. Useful for an overnight stop. There is road noise from a quarry opposite.

Facilities

Two very clean and well maintained wooden toilet blocks are fully equipped. Freezer, washing machine and dryer. Motorcaravan service point. Well stocked but limited shop and snack bar. Outdoor heated pool (6 x 12 m) and paddling pool. Well appointed play area. Tennis. Bicycle hire. Barbecues are not permitted. Torches are useful. Off site: Sierre 1 km. Walking and hiking area. Fishing (licence required) 900 m. Golf and riding 3 km.

Open: 15 April - 3 October.

Directions

Leave motorway at exit 29, Sierre East. Follow sign for Sierre. Site is signed on the right (TCS) within 200 m. GPS: N46:17.633 E07:33.472

Charges guide

Per person	CHF 6,00 - 7,00
child	CHF 3,00 - 3,50
pitch incl. electricity	CHF 16,90 - 23,70
dog	CHF 3,00 - 4,00

Camping Cheques accepted.

CH9730 Camping Gemmi

Briannenstrasse 4, CH-3952 Susten-Leuk (Valais)

Tel: **027 473 1154**. Email: **info@campgemmi.ch** **www.alanrogers.com/CH9730**

The Rhône Valley is a popular through route to Italy via the Simplon Pass and a holiday region in its own right. Gemmi is a delightful small, friendly site in a scenic location with 65 level pitches, all with 16A electricity, on well tended grass amidst a variety of trees, some of which offer shade. 40 pitches also have water and drainage. The pleasant, friendly owner speaks fluent English, maintains high standards and has established a campsite mainly for tourists with few resident static units. A site more suitable for the mature camper.

Facilities

A modern sanitary block, partly heated, is of excellent quality and kept very clean. It includes some washbasins in cabins. Eight private bathrooms for hire on a weekly basis. Washing machines and dryers. Motorcaravan services. Well stocked shop. Small bar/restaurant where snacks and a limited range of local specialities are served. Terrace bar and snack restaurant. Playground. Tennis. Internet access. Swimming and walking near.
Off site: Golf 500 m. Riding 2 km. Fishing 6 km.

Open: 19 April - 18 October.

Directions

From east (Visp), turn left 1 km. after sign for Agarn Feithieren. From west (Sierre), turn right 2 km. after Susten at sign for Camping Torrent and Gemmi.
GPS: N46:17.880 E07:39.544

Charges guide

Per person	CHF 7,00 - 9,00
child	CHF 3,50 - 6,50
pitch incl. electricity	CHF 12,00 - 14,00
dog	CHF 2,00

CH9740 Camping Attermenzen

CH-3928 Randa (Valais)

Tel: **027 967 1379**. Email: **rest.camping@rhone.ch** **www.alanrogers.com/CH9740**

Randa, a picturesque Valais village, at 1,409 m. is a beautiful location for a campsite and ideal for those wishing to visit Zermatt only 10 km. away. Reception is open from mid June to mid September, otherwise call at the restaurant (closed on Tuesdays). Unmarked pitches are on an uneven field with some areas that are fairly level and 6A electricity is within easy reach. A paradise for walking, mountaineering, climbing and mountain biking and surrounded by famous 4,000 m. peaks, such as the Dom and Weisshorn, this site also offers modern facilities with a restaurant and bar next door.

Facilities

The sanitary block is of a good standard and well maintained with free showers. Washing machine. Shop (June-Sept). Gas supplies. Restaurant/bar. Takeaway.
Off site: Zermatt 10 km.

Open: All year.

Directions

From A9 at Visp turn right at roundabout (Zermatt). Go through the 3.3 km. long tunnel and follow road towards Zermatt. Go through Stalden and turn right at roundabout (Zermatt). Site is about 1 km. after Randa village on the left.
GPS: N46:05.129 E07:46.860

Charges guide

Per person	CHF 6,00
pitch	CHF 9,00
electricity	CHF 4,00

CH9790 Camping Augenstern

Postfach 16, CH-3998 Reckingen (Valais)

Tel: **027 973 1395**. Email: **info@campingaugenstern.ch** **www.alanrogers.com/CH9790**

The village of Reckingen is about halfway between Brig and the Furka/Grimsel passes. You can still get the train with car and caravan, or motorcaravan from Oberwald to Andermatt to avoid the steep climbs and descents of the Furka Pass, but in doing so you will miss some unforgettable scenery. This family run site, at 1,326 m. provides 100 flat, level pitches for touring units, all with 10A electricity and not much shade. It provides an excellent base for walking, climbing or cycling as well as rafting on the Rhone in the summer or skiing in the winter.

Facilities

The toilet block is good and is well maintained. Showers on payment. Motorcaravan services. Shop in high season. Restaurant/bar with satellite TV. Bicycle hire. Off site: Large swimming pool complex 200 m. Reckingen 500 m. Riding 800 m.

Open: 16 May - 17 October, 15 December - 15 March.

Directions

From the no. 19 road turn south in Reckingen next to church. Go down hill, along one-way street and over railway (carefully!) and bridge. Over next bridge and right to end of lane past swimming pool.
GPS: N46:27.900 E08:14.658

Charges guide

Per person	CHF 7,50 - 9,50
pitch	CHF 9,50 - 11,50
electricity	CHF 4,00 - 7,00

CH9785 Camping Eggishorn

CH-3984 Fiesch (Valais)

Tel: **027 971 03 16**. Email: **info@camping-eggishorn.ch** **www.alanrogers.com/CH9785**

The Valais is a deservedly popular region lying at the heart of the Swiss Alps. This site is open all year and has been recommended by our Swiss agent. There are 178 sunny pitches, some of which are occupied by chalets (available for rent). Pitches are on flat ground with fine views of the surrounding mountain scenery. All have electrical connections (16A) and some have TV and radio connections. The site's restaurant specialises in local cuisine and other amenities include a small shop and a heated toilet block with special facilities for disabled visitors. Camping Eggishorn is just 400 m. from the village centre and the Fiesch cable car. The cable car conveys passengers to the Eggischorn summit with unprecedented views of the Aletsch glacier (a world heritage site) and no less than 46 mountain peaks over 4,000 m. In winter, this is an important skiing region with a cross-country circuit just 100 m. from the site and downhill skiing on the Fiescheralp.

Facilities

Heated toilet blocks. Motorcaravan services. Small shop. Bar. Restaurant. Playground. Small lake. River adjacent. Chalets for rent. Off site: Village centre 400 m. Cable car 400 m. Tennis 300 m. Golf 14 km. Cross-country skiing 100 m. Ski lift 400 m. Hang gliding 100 m.

Open: All year.

Directions

Head east on the A9 motorway until its end at Sierre and continue on the E62 as far as Brig. Continue along the Rhone valley (road no. 19) to Fiesch and the site is signed from here.
GPS: N46:24.599 E08:08.365

Charges guide

Per unit incl. 2 persons and electricity	CHF 44,00 - 48,00
extra person	CHF 13,00
child (0-15 yrs)	CHF 6,00
dog	CHF 3,00

CH9300 Camping Le Bivouac

Route des Paccots 21, CH-1618 Châtel-Saint Denis (Fribourg)

Tel: **021 948 7849**. Email: **info@le-bivouac.ch** **www.alanrogers.com/CH9300**

A pleasant little site in the mountains north of Montreux, Le Bivouac has its own small swimming pool and children's pool. Most of the best places here are taken by seasonal caravans (130) and there are now only about 30 pitches for tourists. Electrical connections (10A) are available and there are five water points. The site is also open for winter sports caravanning and all the sanitary facilities are heated. Entertainment is organised for adults and children in high season. This is a good centre for walking and excursions and there is a friendly welcome from the owner M. Fivaz.

Facilities

The good toilet facilities in the main building include preset, free hot water in washbasins, showers and sinks for laundry and dishes. Baby room. Gas supplies. Shop (1/7-31/8). Bar (1/6-30/9). Swimming pool (1/6-15/9). Room for general use adjoining. Fishing. Off site: Bicycle hire 3 km. Riding 10 km. Bus passes the gate.

Open: 1 April - 30 September.

Directions

From motorway 12/E27 (Bern - Vevey) take Châtel St Denis exit no. 2 and turn towards Les Paccots (1 km). Site is on left up hill. GPS: N46:31.508 E06:55.097

Charges guide

Per person	CHF 5,00 - 6,00
child (6-16 yrs)	CHF 3,00 - 4,00
pitch	CHF 15,00
electricity	CHF 4,00

No credit cards. Less 10% on showing this guide. Euros are accepted.

CH9040 Camping des Pêches

Route du Port, CH-2525 Le Landeron (Neuchâtel)

Tel: **032 751 2900**. Email: **info@camping-lelanderon.ch** **www.alanrogers.com/CH9040**

This recently constructed, touring campsite is on the side of Lake Biel and river Thienne, and close to the old town of Le Landeron. The site is divided into two sections, one side of the road for static caravans, and on the other is the modern campsite for tourists. The 220 pitches are all on level grass, numbered but not separated, a few with shade, all with electricity (10A) and many conveniently placed water points. All the facilities are exceptionally well maintained and in pristine condition during our visit throughout a busy holiday weekend.

Facilities

The spacious, modern sanitary block contains all the usual facilities including a food preparation area with six cooking rings, a large freezer and refrigerator. Payment for showers is by card. Baby room. Laundry facilities. Motorcaravan service point. Community room and small café in reception building. Playground. Bicycle hire. TV and general room. Off site: Fishing 300 m. Swimming pool 300 m. (16/5-1/9; charged). Golf and riding 7 km.

Open: 1 April - 15 October.

Directions

Le Landeron is signed from the Neuchâtel - Biel motorway, exit 19 and site is well signed from the town. GPS: N47:03.177 E07:04.184

Charges guide

Per person	CHF 8,00
child (6-16 yrs)	CHF 4,00
pitch incl. car and electricity	CHF 8,50 - 16,50

CH9270 Camping De Vidy

Chemin du Camping 3, CH-1007 Lausanne (Vaud)

Tel: **021 622 5000**. Email: **info@campinglausannevidy.ch** **www.alanrogers.com/CH9270**

The ancient city of Lausanne spills down the hillside towards Lake Geneva until it meets the peaceful park in which this site is situated. The present owners have enhanced its neat and tidy appearance by planting many flowers and shrubs. Hard access roads separate the site into sections for tents, caravans and motorcaravans, with 10A electrical connections in all parts, except the tent areas. Pitches are on flat grass, numbered but not marked out, with 260 (of 350) for tourists. 20 are fully serviced and some large pitches near the lake are suitable for American type motorhomes.

Facilities

Two excellent sanitary blocks, one heated, have mostly British, some Turkish style WCs, hot water in washbasins, sinks and showers with warm, pre-mixed water. Facilities for disabled people. A third small block has been added. Motorcaravan services (Euro-Relais). Gas supplies. Shop and self-service bar/restaurant (1/5-30/9). Takeaway (high season). Playground. Evening entertainment in high season. Internet point. Lake swimming. Fishing. Off site: Bus service into Lausanne. Boat excursions on the lake.

Open: All year.

Directions

Site is left of road to Geneva, 500 m. west of La Maladière. Take autobahn Lausanne-Süd, exit no.3 La Maladière, and at this roundabout almost turn back on yourself following signs for CIO and camping. At traffic lights turn left, then on for site. Take care at La Maladière roundabout (large trolley buses). GPS: N46:30.960 E06:35.940

Charges guide

Per unit incl. 2 persons and electricity	CHF 31,00 - 32,00
extra person	CHF 7,50
child (6-15 yrs)	CHF 5,50
dog	CHF 2,00

No credit cards.

CH9900 Camping Delta

Via Respini 7, CH-6600 Locarno (Ticino)

Tel: **091 751 6081**. Email: **info@campingdelta.com** **www.alanrogers.com/CH9900**

Camping Delta is actually within the Locarno town limits, only some 800 m. from the centre, and it has a prime position right by the lake, with bathing direct from the site, and next to the municipal lido and sports field. Boats can be put on the lake and the site also has some moorings on an estuary at one side, with a jetty. It has 300 pitches on flat ground of 60-100 sq.m. of which 255 are available for touring units. They are marked out at the rear but have nothing between them. Delta is a well run and well situated site. Locarno is host to an International Film Festival, classical and jazz concerts and exhibitions.

Facilities

The single toilet block has been completely renovated in 2008. Washing machine and dryer. Motorcaravan services. Small supermarket. Restaurant/bar with limited menu. Fitness centre. Playgrounds. Baby sitting. Badminton. Amusements. Entertainment and excursions. Children's animation programme. Fishing. Bicycle hire. Internet access. Kayaks and electric bikes for hire. Dogs are not accepted. Off site: Golf 500 m. Riding 3.5 km.

Open: 1 March - 31 October.

Directions

From central Locarno follow signs to Camping Delta, Lido or Stadio along the lake. Beware that approaching from south there are also Delta signs which lead you to Albergo Delta in quite the wrong place. GPS: N46:09.334 E08:48.016

Charges 2009

Per unit incl. 2 persons and electricity	CHF 48,00 - 98,00
extra person	CHF 11,00 - 18,00
child (3-15 yrs)	CHF 6,00

CH9240 TCS Camping Le Petit Bois

CH-1110 Morges (Vaud)

Tel: **021 801 1270**. Email: **camping.morges@tes.ch** **www.alanrogers.com/CH9240**

This excellent TCS campsite is on the edge of Morges, a wine-growing centre with a 13th-century castle, on Lake Geneva about 8 km. west of Lausanne. Flowers, shrubs and trees adorn the site and the neat, tidy lawns make a most pleasant environment. There are 170 grass pitches for tourists, all with 6A electricity and laid out in a regular pattern from wide hard access roads on which cars stand. There are eight larger pitches for motorcaravans with electricity, water and drainage. The friendly managers speak good English, and will advise on local attractions.

Facilities

Two well built, fully equipped, modern toilet blocks include hot water in half of the washbasins, sinks and showers. Separate block with excellent baby room and cosmetics room. Facilities for disabled visitors. Washing machines, dryers and irons. Motorcaravan services. Restaurant and takeaway. Shop. Playground. Boules. Bicycle and scooter hire. Small general room. Internet point. Entertainment (high season). Picnic area. Fishing. Bicycle hire. Off site: Swimming pool adjacent. Small harbour. Town centre. Tennis.

Open: 23 March - 21 October.

Directions

Leave A1 autoroute (Lausanne - Geneva) at exit 15 (Morges-ouest). Turn towards town and signs for site. GPS: N46:30.274 E06:29.350

Charges guide

Per person	CHF 6,00 - 7,40
child	CHF 3,00 - 3,70
pitch incl. electricity	CHF 23,10 - 32,30
dog	CHF 3,00 - 4,00

Camping Cheques accepted.

Open All Year

The following sites are understood to accept caravanners and campers all year round. Please refer to the site's individual entry for details.

Andorra
AN7143 Xixerella
AN7145 Valira

Austria
AU0035 Alpin Seefeld
AU0040 Zugspitze
AU0045 Ötztal
AU0055 Arlberg
AU0065 Seehof
AU0070 Hofer
AU0090 Zillertal-Hell
AU0100 Toni
AU0102 Stadlerhof
AU0155 Prutz
AU0160 Zell am See
AU0170 Kranebitten
AU0180 Woferlgut
AU0220 Krismer
AU0262 Oberwötzlhof
AU0405 Ramsbacher
AU0440 Schluga
AU0475 Brunner am See
AU0502 Im Thermenland
AU0515 Katschtal

Belgium
BE0530 Waux-Hall
BE0555 Klein Strand
BE0560 Lombarde
BE0580 Memling
BE0590 De Gavers
BE0655 Lilse Bergen
BE0670 Clusure
BE0675 Spineuse
BE0700 Spa d'Or
BE0710 Vallée de Rabais
BE0725 Val de L'Aisne
BE0732 Floreal La Roche
BE0735 Petite Suisse
BE0740 Eau Rouge
BE0780 Wilhelm Tell
BE0782 Jocomo Park
BE0788 Hengelhoef
BE0792 Zavelbos
BE0794 Molenheide

Czech Republic
CZ4640 Areal Jadran
CZ4700 Jaroslav Kohoutek
CZ4770 Dlouhá Louka
CZ4795 Cisarska Louka
CZ4845 Busek Praha
CZ4850 Sokol Troja
CZ4880 Roznov

Denmark
DK2015 Ådalens
DK2020 Mogeltonder
DK2044 Hampen Sø
DK2046 Trelde Næs
DK2140 Jesperhus
DK2150 Sølyst
DK2215 Odense
DK2255 Feddet

Finland
FI2850 Rastila
FI2970 Nallikari

France
FR06080 Cigales
FR16060 Marco de Bignac
FR47110 Cabri
FR65080 Lavedan
FR69010 Lyon
FR77020 Chêne Gris
FR85930 Forges
FR86040 Futuriste
FR88040 Lac de Bouzey
FR88130 Vanne de Pierre

Germany
DE3002 Schlei-Karschau
DE3003 Wulfener Hals
DE3008 Klüthseecamp
DE3010 Röders Park
DE3021 Am Stadtwaldsee
DE3025 Alfsee
DE3030 Tecklenburg
DE3055 Prahljust
DE3065 Bärenbache
DE3070 Süd-See
DE3080 Hardausee
DE3180 Sonnenwiese
DE3185 Münster
DE3202 Grav-Insel
DE3210 Biggesee
DE3212 Wirfttal
DE3215 Goldene Meile
DE3222 Moselbogen
DE3242 Schinderhannes
DE3254 Harfenmühle
DE3255 Am Königsberg
DE3256 Hunsrück
DE3260 Bad Dürkheim
DE3280 Teichmann
DE3406 Kleinenzhof
DE3415 Adam
DE3420 Oberrhein
DE3427 Schwarzwälder Hof
DE3432 Bonath
DE3436 Bankenhof
DE3437 Hochschwarzwald
DE3439 Freiburg
DE3440 Kirchzarten
DE3445 Belchenblick
DE3450 Münstertal
DE3452 Alte Sägemühle
DE3455 Gugel's
DE3490 Hegau
DE3610 Nürnberg
DE3685 Allweglehen
DE3697 Dreiqueller
DE3710 Bayerischer Wald
DE3720 Naabtal
DE3820 Havelberge
DE3836 Erzgebirgsblick
DE3847 Auensee
DE3855 Oberhof

Greece
GR8000 Batis
GR8330 Ionion Beach
GR8525 Chrissa
GR8560 Ramnous
GR8590 Athens
GR8595 Nea Kifissia
GR8685 Gythion Bay
GR8695 Finikes

Hungary
HU5095 Vulkán Resort
HU5150 Fortuna
HU5155 Római
HU5165 Zugligeti Niche
HU5210 Diófaház
HU5255 Martfü
HU5260 Jonathermál
HU5300 Kek-Duna
Dunafoldvar

Italy
IT60420 Alba d'Oro
IT60530 Fusina
IT62000 Olympia
IT62030 Sexten
IT62080 Gamp
IT62085 Sass Dlacia
IT62420 Orta
IT64010 Dei Fiori
IT64110 Miraflores
IT66050 Mugello Verde
IT66100 Panoramico
IT66670 Finoria
IT67915 Foci
IT68890 Costa Verde
IT69190 Scarabeo
IT69230 Jonio
IT69300 Marinello
IT69350 Rais Gerbi

Liechtenstein
FL7580 Mittagspitze

Luxembourg
LU7670 Ardennes
LU7770 Val d'Or
LU7850 Fuussekaul
LU7880 Trois Frontières

Netherlands
NL5500 Pannenschuur
NL5540 Katjeskelder
NL5560 Wijde Blick
NL5600 Delftse Hout
NL5620 Duinrell
NL5630 Koningshof
NL5640 Kijkduinpark
NL5665 Zeeburg
NL5735 Tempelhof
NL5760 Kuilart
NL5790 Kuierpadtien
NL5910 Hertenwei
NL5960 Wielerbaan
NL5985 Beerze Bulten

NL6090	Lauwersoog
NL6153	Witterzomer
NL6425	Twee Bruggen
NL6510	Schatberg
NL6520	BreeBronne
NL6540	Rozenhof
NL6930	Schoneveld

Norway

NO2320	Odda
NO2375	Lærdal
NO2385	Sandvik
NO2400	Jolstraholmen
NO2432	Harstad
NO2460	Prinsen
NO2475	Saltstraumen
NO2490	Skjerneset
NO2505	Magalaupe
NO2510	Håneset
NO2515	Gjelten Bru
NO2525	Østrea Æra
NO2545	Rustberg
NO2590	Sandviken
NO2610	Neset
NO2615	Olberg

Portugal

PO8030	Rio Alto
PO8100	Sao Pedro-Moel
PO8130	Guincho
PO8170	São Miguel
PO8175	Zmar
PO8200	Valverde
PO8202	Turiscampo
PO8210	Albufeira
PO8220	Quarteira
PO8230	Olhao
PO8370	Cerdeira
PO8400	O Tamanco
PO8430	Sagres
PO8480	Foz do Arelho

Slovakia

SK4910	Turiec
SK4980	Levocská Dolina

Slovenia

SV4150	Kamne
SV4340	Ljubljana Resort
SV4440	Terme Ptuj

Spain

ES80080	Joncar Mar
ES81300	Calonge
ES83900	Vilanova Park
ES84820	Pineda de Salou
ES85080	Poboleda
ES85350	Cala d'Oques
ES85600	Playa Tropicana
ES85800	Bonterra
ES86150	Kiko
ES86250	Kiko Rural
ES86810	Villasol
ES86830	Benisol
ES86870	Cap Blanch
ES87420	Marina
ES87430	Marjal
ES87450	Fuente
ES87480	Madriles
ES87520	El Portus (Naturist)
ES87530	Manga
ES87540	Javea
ES87550	Moraira
ES87630	Cabo de Gata
ES88000	Marbella Playa
ES88020	Cabopino
ES88590	Roche
ES88650	Playa Las Dunas
ES89400	Cantiles
ES90240	As Cancelas
ES90270	Monfrague
ES90470	Ezcaba
ES90600	Peña Montañesa
ES90800	El Brillante
ES90810	Villsom
ES90860	Cáceres
ES90870	Merida
ES90900	El Greco
ES90910	Aranjuez
ES91250	Lago Barasona
ES92000	El Escorial
ES92100	Pico-Miel
ES92760	Reina Isabel
ES92850	Lomas
ES92900	El Balcon
ES92950	Don Cactus

Sweden

SW2645	Mölle
SW2650	Skånes
SW2665	Björkhagen
SW2675	Västervik Swe
SW2705	Lisebergsbyn
SW2710	Lidköping
SW2715	Gröne Backe
SW2720	Hökensås
SW2725	Hafsten
SW2740	Laxsjons
SW2750	Sommarvik
SW2755	Alevi
SW2760	Frykenbaden
SW2805	Kolmårdens
SW2825	Herrfallet
SW2836	Mora Parkens
SW2840	Flottsbro
SW2845	Svegs
SW2850	Ostersunds
SW2855	Flogsta
SW2857	Strömsund
SW2860	Umeå
SW2865	Gielas
SW2870	Jokkmokks

Switzerland

CH9175	Giessenpark
CH9270	Vidy
CH9360	Grassi
CH9370	Rendez-vous
CH9380	Heiti
CH9410	Stuhlegg
CH9420	Manor Farm
CH9425	Alpenblick
CH9460	Jungfrau
CH9495	Balmweid
CH9520	Du Botza
CH9570	Eienwäldli
CH9670	Molignon
CH9740	Attermenzen
CH9785	Eggishorn
CH9830	Sur En
CH9855	Cavresc

Quick reference - Dogs

Dogs

For the benefit of those who want to take their dogs with them or for people who do not like dogs at the sites they visit, we list here those sites that have indicated to us that they do not accept dogs. If you are, however, planning to take your dog we do advise you to check first – there may be limits on numbers, breeds, etc. or times of the year when they are excluded.

Never – these sites do not accept dogs at any time:

Croatia

CR6731 Valalta (Naturist)
CR6736 Valdaliso

France

FR17010 Bois Soleil
FR66590 Bois du Valmarie
FR84020 Bélézy (Naturiste)
FR85020 Jard
FR85210 Ecureuils

Germany

DE3005 Schnelsen Nord
DE3233 Holländischer Hof

Hungary

HU5090 Füred

Italy

IT60030 Pra' Delle Torri
IT60065 Tenuta Primero
IT60100 Capalonga
IT60150 Il Tridente
IT60200 Union Lido
IT60210 Italy
IT60220 Portofelice
IT60330 Malibu Beach
IT60340 Waikiki
IT60370 Jesolo
IT60400 Garden Paradiso
IT60460 Miramare Punta Sabb.
IT60550 Isamar
IT60560 Miramare (Chioggia)
IT60650 Tahiti
IT62630 Bella Italia
IT62660 Gasparina
IT63570 Cisano & San Vito
IT63580 Delle Rose
IT63590 Serenella
IT64010 Dei Fiori
IT66450 Delle Piscine
IT66710 Argentario
IT66810 Capalbio
IT68000 Europe Garden
IT68190 Settebello
IT68200 Baia Domizia
IT68650 Riva di Ugento

Netherlands

NL5555 Oase
NL5675 Vliegenbos
NL5680 Noordduinen
NL5980 Roos
NL6285 Wildhoeve
NL6630 Spegelt
NL6790 Kienehoef
NL6870 Lakens
NL6872 Bakkum
NL6925 Weltevreden
NL6952 Julianahoeve
NL6960 Klepperstee
NL6980 Krabbeplaat

Portugal

PO8170 São Miguel

Spain

ES80900 Cypsela
ES81010 Playa Brava
ES81030 El Maset
ES84200 Stel (Roda)
ES84810 Cambrils
ES85300 Playa Montroig
ES85400 Torre del Sol
ES85600 Playa Tropicana
ES86810 Villasol
ES87480 Madriles
ES90000 Playa Joyel

Switzerland

CH9160 Rheinwiesen
CH9180 Buchhorn
CH9185 Fischerhaus
CH9480 Gletscherdorf
CH9880 Lido Mappo
CH9890 Campofelice
CH9900 Delta

Maybe – accepted but with certain restrictions:

Austria

AU0060 Natterer See
AU0090 Zillertal-Hell
AU0227 Camp Grän
AU0400 Arneitz

Belgium

BE0580 Memling

France

FR40250 Grands Pins

Germany

DE3232 Family Club
DE3250 Warsberg
DE3440 Kirchzarten
DE3442 Herbolzheim
DE3465 Wirthshof
DE3686 Waging

Italy

IT62100 Steiner
IT62460 Isolino
IT62485 Conca d'Oro
IT62540 Lido
IT66060 Europa
IT66310 Mareblu
IT66600 Maremma
IT66750 Cieloverde
IT68130 Porticciolo
IT68890 Costa Verde
IT69230 Jonio
IT69300 Marinello
IT69350 Rais Gerbi
IT69960 Mariposa

Netherlands

NL5560 Wijde Blick
NL6000 Vechtdalcamping

Portugal

PO8370 Cerdeira

Spain

ES80720 Medes
ES80800 Delfin Verde
ES81600 Cala Gogo
ES85800 Bonterra
ES92950 Don Cactus

Travelling

When taking your car (and caravan, tent or trailer tent) or motorcaravan to the continent you do need to plan in advance and to find out as much as possible about driving in the countries you plan to visit. Whilst European harmonisation has eliminated many of the differences between one country and another, it is well worth reading the short notes we provide in the introduction to each country in this guide in addition to this more general summary.

Of course, the main difference from driving in the UK is that in mainland Europe you will need to drive on the right. Without taking extra time and care, especially at busy junctions and conversely when roads are empty, it is easy to forget to drive on the right. Remember that traffic approaching from the right usually has priority unless otherwise indicated by road markings and signs. Harmonisation also means that most (but not all) common road signs are the same in all countries.

Your vehicle

Book your vehicle in for a good service well before your intended departure date. This will lessen the chance of an expensive breakdown. Make sure your brakes are working efficiently and that your tyres have plenty of tread (3 mm. is recommended, particularly if you are undertaking a long journey).

Also make sure that your caravan or trailer is roadworthy and that its tyres are in good order and correctly inflated. Plan your packing and be careful not to overload your vehicle, caravan or trailer – this is unsafe and may well invalidate your insurance cover (it must not be more fully loaded than the kerb weight of the insured vehicle).

CHECK ALL THE FOLLOWING:

- **GB sticker.** If you do not display a sticker, you may risk an on-the-spot fine as this identifier is compulsory in all countries. Euro-plates are an acceptable alternative within the EU (but not outside). Remember to attach another sticker (or Euro-plate) to caravans or trailers. Only GB stickers (not England, Scotland, Wales or N. Ireland) stickers are valid in the EU.
- **Headlights.** As you will be driving on the right you must adjust your headlights so that the dipped beam does not dazzle oncoming drivers. Converter kits are readily available for most vehicle, although if your car is fitted with high intensity headlights, you should check with your motor dealer. Check that any planned extra loading does not affect the beam height.
- **Seatbelts.** Rules for the fitting and wearing of seatbelts throughout Europe are similar to those in the UK, but it is worth checking before you go. Rules for carrying children in the front of vehicles vary from country to country. It is best to plan not to do this if possible.
- **Door/wing mirrors.** To help with driving on the right, if your vehicle is not fitted with a mirror on the left hand side, we recommend you have one fitted.
- **Fuel.** Leaded and Lead Replacement petrol is increasingly difficult to find in Northern Europe.

Compulsory additional equipment

The driving laws of the countries of Europe still vary in what you are required to carry in your vehicle, although the consequences of not carrying a required piece of equipment are almost always an on-the-spot fine.

To meet these requirements we suggest that you carry the following:

- FIRE EXTINGUISHER
- BASIC TOOL KIT
- FIRST AID KIT
- SPARE BULBS
- TWO WARNING TRIANGLES – two are required in some countries at all times, and are compulsory in most countries when towing.
- HIGH VISIBILITY VESTS – now compulsory in France, Spain, Italy and Austria (and likely to become compulsory throughout the EU) in case you need to walk on a motorway.

Insurance and Motoring Documents

Vehicle insurance

Contact your insurer well before you depart to check that your car insurance policy covers driving outside the UK. Most do, but many policies only provide minimum cover (so if you have an accident your insurance may only cover the cost of damage to the other person's property, with no cover for fire and theft).

To maintain the same level of cover abroad as you enjoy at home you need to tell your vehicle insurer. Some will automatically cover you abroad with no extra cost and no extra paperwork. Some will say you need a Green Card (which is neither green nor on card) but won't charge for it. Some will charge extra for the Green Card. Ideally you should contact your vehicle insurer 3-4 weeks before you set off, and confirm your conversation with them in writing.

Breakdown insurance

Arrange breakdown cover for your trip in good time so that if your vehicle breaks down or is involved in an accident it (and your caravan or trailer) can be repaired or returned to this country. This cover can usually be arranged as part of your travel insurance policy (see below).

Documents you must take with you

You may be asked to show your documents at any time so make sure that they are in order, up-to-date and easily accessible while you travel. These are what you need to take:

- **Passports** (you may also need a visa in some countries if you hold either a UK passport not issued in the UK or a passport that was issued outside the EU).
- **Motor Insurance Certificate**, including Green Card (or Continental Cover clause)
- **DVLC Vehicle Registration Document** plus, if not your own vehicle, the owner's written authority to drive.
- **A full valid Driving Licence** (not provisional). The new photo style licence is now mandatory in most European countries).

Personal Holiday insurance

Even though you are just travelling within Europe you must take out travel insurance. Few EU countries pay the full cost of medical treatment even under reciprocal health service arrangements. The first part of a holiday insurance policy covers people. It will include the cost of doctor, ambulance and hospital treatment if needed. If needed the better companies will even pay for English language speaking doctors and nurses and will bring a sick or injured holidaymaker home by air ambulance.

An important part of the insurance, often ignored, is cancellation (and curtailment) cover. Few things are as heartbreaking as having to cancel a holiday because a member of the family falls ill. Cancellation insurance can't take away the disappointment, but it makes sure you don't suffer financially as well. For this reason you should arrange your holiday insurance at least eight weeks before you set off.

Whichever insurance you choose we would advise reading very carefully the policies sold by the High Street travel trade. Whilst they may be good, they may not cover the specific needs of campers, caravanners and motorcaravanners.

Telephone 01580 214006 for a quote for our European Camping Holiday Insurance with cover arranged through Green Flag Motoring Assistance and Inter Group Assistance Services, one of the UK's largest assistance companies. Alternatively visit our website at www.insure4campers.com.

Travelling continued

European Health Insurance Card (EHIC)

Make sure you apply for your EHIC before travelling in Europe. Eligible travellers from the UK are entitled to receive free or reduced-cost medical care in many European countries on production of an EHIC. This free card is available by completing a form in the booklet 'Health Advice for Travellers' from local Post Offices. One should be completed for each family member. Alternatively visit www.dh.gov.uk/travellers and apply on-line. Please allow time to send your application off and have the EHIC returned to you.

The EHIC is valid in all European Community countries plus Iceland, Liechtenstein, Switzerland and Norway. If you or any of your dependants are suddenly taken ill or have an accident during a visit to any of these countries, free or reduced-cost emergency treatment is available - in most cases on production of a valid EHIC.

Only state-provided emergency treatment is covered, and you will receive treatment on the same terms as nationals of the country you are visiting. Private treatment is generally not covered, and state-provided treatment may not cover all of the things that you would expect to receive free of charge from the NHS.

Remember an EHIC does not cover you for all the medical costs that you can incur or for repatriation - it is not an alternative to travel insurance. You will still need appropriate insurance to ensure you are fully covered for all eventualities.

Travelling with children

Most countries in Europe are enforcing strict guidelines when you are travelling with children who are not your own. A minor (under the age of 18) must be accompanied by a parent or legal guardian or must carry a letter of authorisation from a parent or guardian. The letter should name the adult responsible for the minor during his or her stay. Similarily, a minor travelling with just one of his/her parents, must have a letter of authority to leave their home country from the parent staying behind. Full information is available at www.fco.gov.uk.

Important: Travel Health Alert

UK HOLIDAYMAKERS COULD BE AT RISK OF DEADLY EUROPEAN VIRUS

Thousands of British tourists risk contracting a potentially life-threatening disease in Europe this summer.

The **'Tick Alert'** campaign has been launched warning UK travellers about Tick Borne Encephalitis (TBE), a viral disease contracted via the bite of an infected tick. It can lead to meningitis and, in serious cases, result in paralysis and death.

The warning identifies 16 central and eastern European countries where the TBE infected tick population is officially endemic and therefore poses a high risk to visitors who have not been immunised or taken bite prevention precautions.

According to figures from the Foreign Office, the number of UK tourists visiting central and eastern Europe rose by 38 per cent to 558,000 last summer.

This includes many of the new popular European holiday destinations such as Croatia, the Czech Republic, Estonia, Latvia, Lithuania, Slovenia and Slovakia, where there is a growing adventure travel market.

TBE-infected ticks are found typically in rural and forest areas during the late spring and summer months. At-risk groups include all visitors to rural areas of endemic countries, particularly those participating in outdoor activities such as trekking, hiking, climbing, cycling and camping.

A number of measures can be taken to reduce the risk of infection: these include using an insect repellent, wearing protective clothing to cover all areas of exposed skin, regularly inspecting for tick bites and carefully removing any found. The disease can also be transmitted by the ingestion of unpasteurised milk which should be avoided.

However, the Foreign Office advises that visitors to TBE endemic regions seek inoculation advice from their local surgery or clinic – well before travelling.

Immunisation against TBE is available as a paid-for travel vaccine from specialist travel health clinics and at GP surgeries and healthcare centres.

Further information on the endemic regions of Europe and latest advice for travellers is available at www.masta-travel-health.com/tickalert.

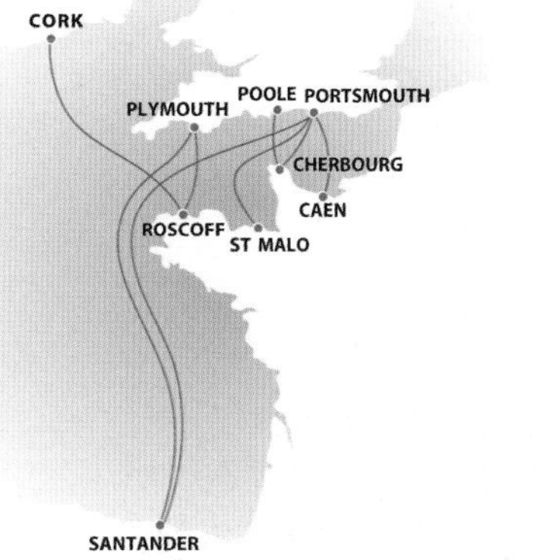

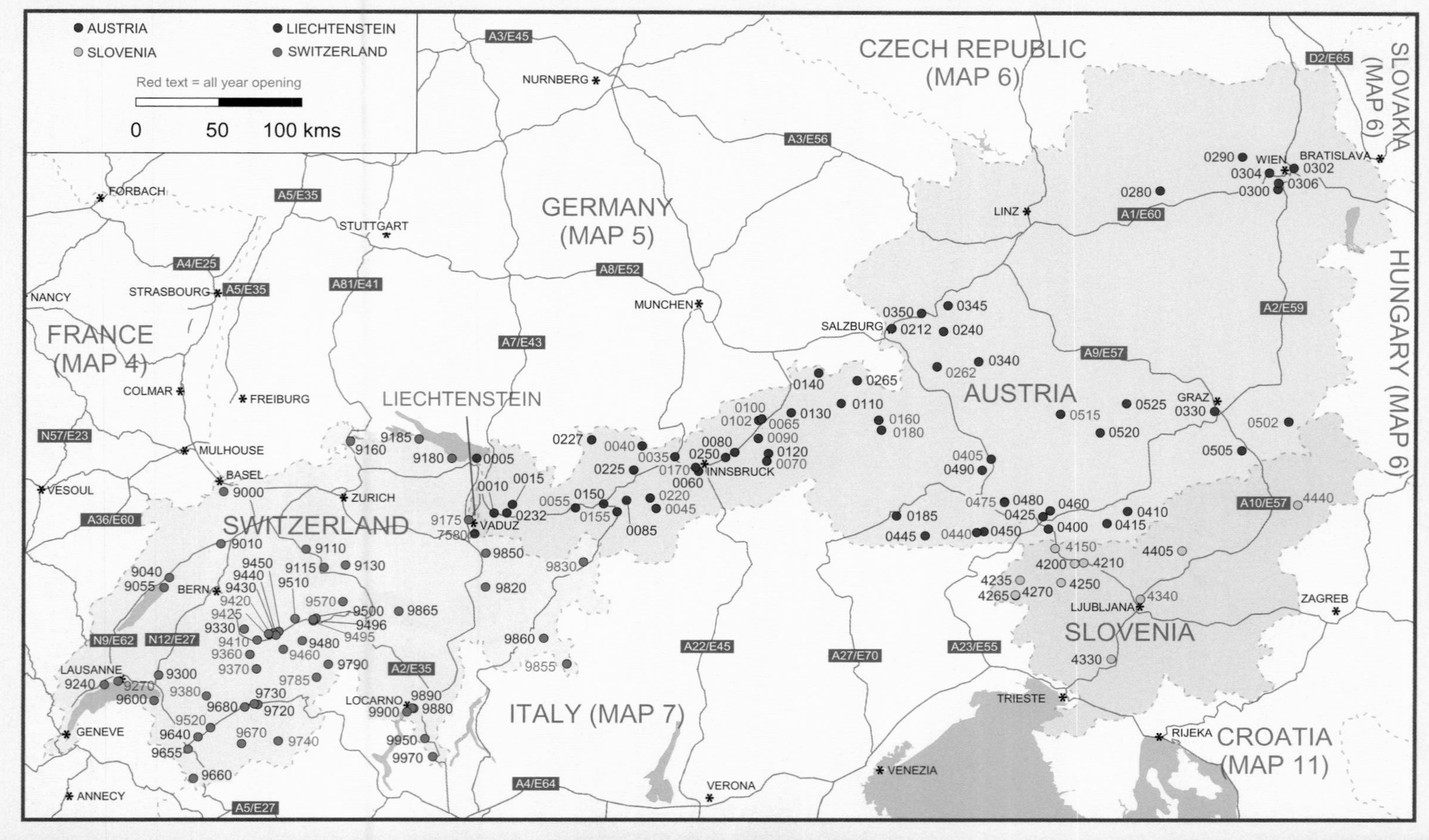

● AUSTRIA
● LIECHTENSTEIN
○ SLOVENIA
● SWITZERLAND
Red text = all year opening
0 50 100 kms
FRANCE (MAP 4)
GERMANY (MAP 5)
CZECH REPUBLIC (MAP 6)
SLOVAKIA (MAP 6)
HUNGARY (MAP 6)
CROATIA (MAP 11)
ITALY (MAP 7)
SWITZERLAND
LIECHTENSTEIN
AUSTRIA
SLOVENIA
NANCY
FORBACH
STRASBOURG
COLMAR
MULHOUSE
FREIBURG
STUTTGART
NURNBERG
MUNCHEN
SALZBURG
LINZ
WIEN
BRATISLAVA
GRAZ
VESOUL
BASEL
ZURICH
BERN
LAUSANNE
GENEVE
ANNECY
LOCARNO
VADUZ
INNSBRUCK
VERONA
VENEZIA
TRIESTE
LJUBLJANA
RIJEKA
ZAGREB

Please refer to the numerical index (page 565) for campsite page references

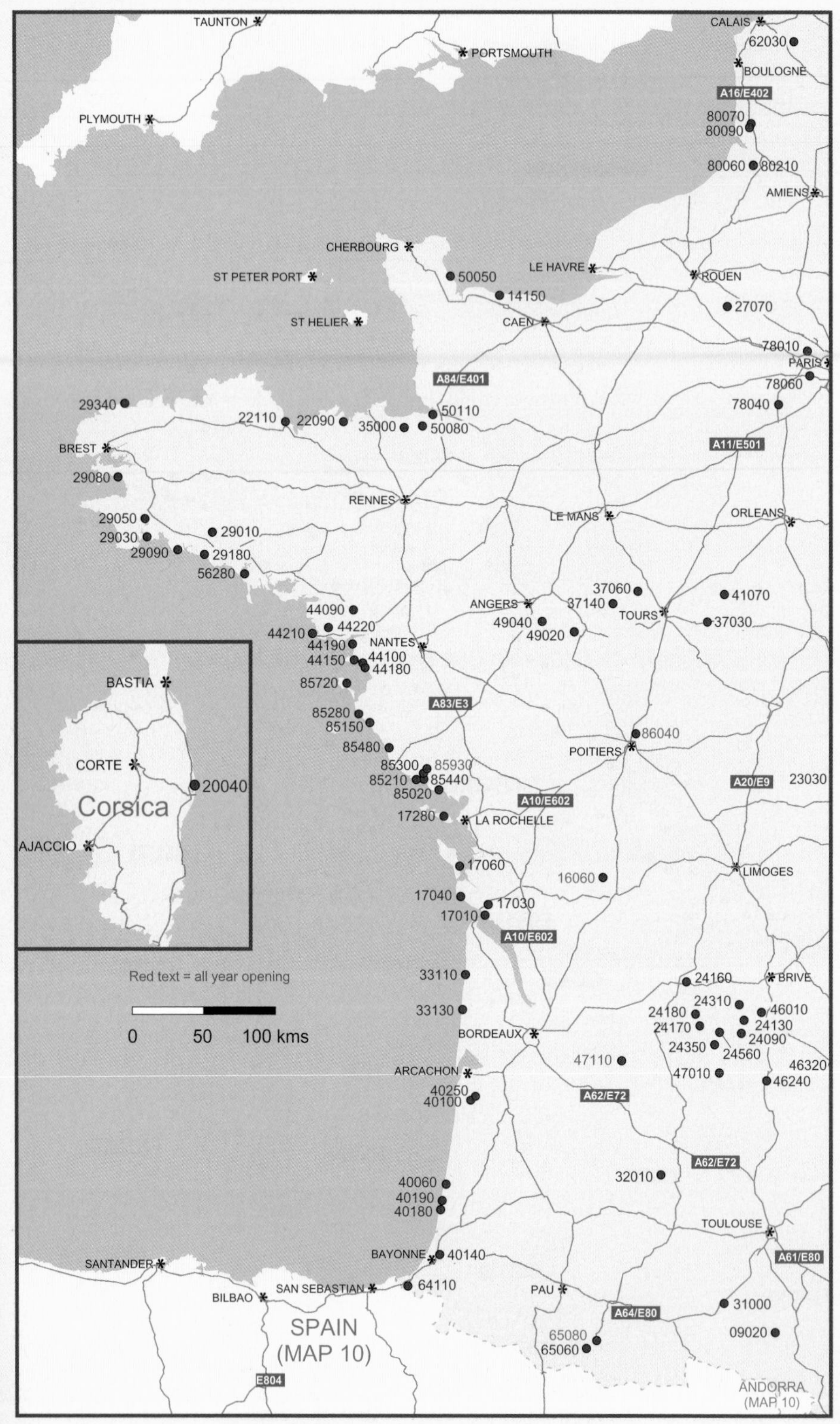

Please refer to the numerical index (page 565) for campsite page references

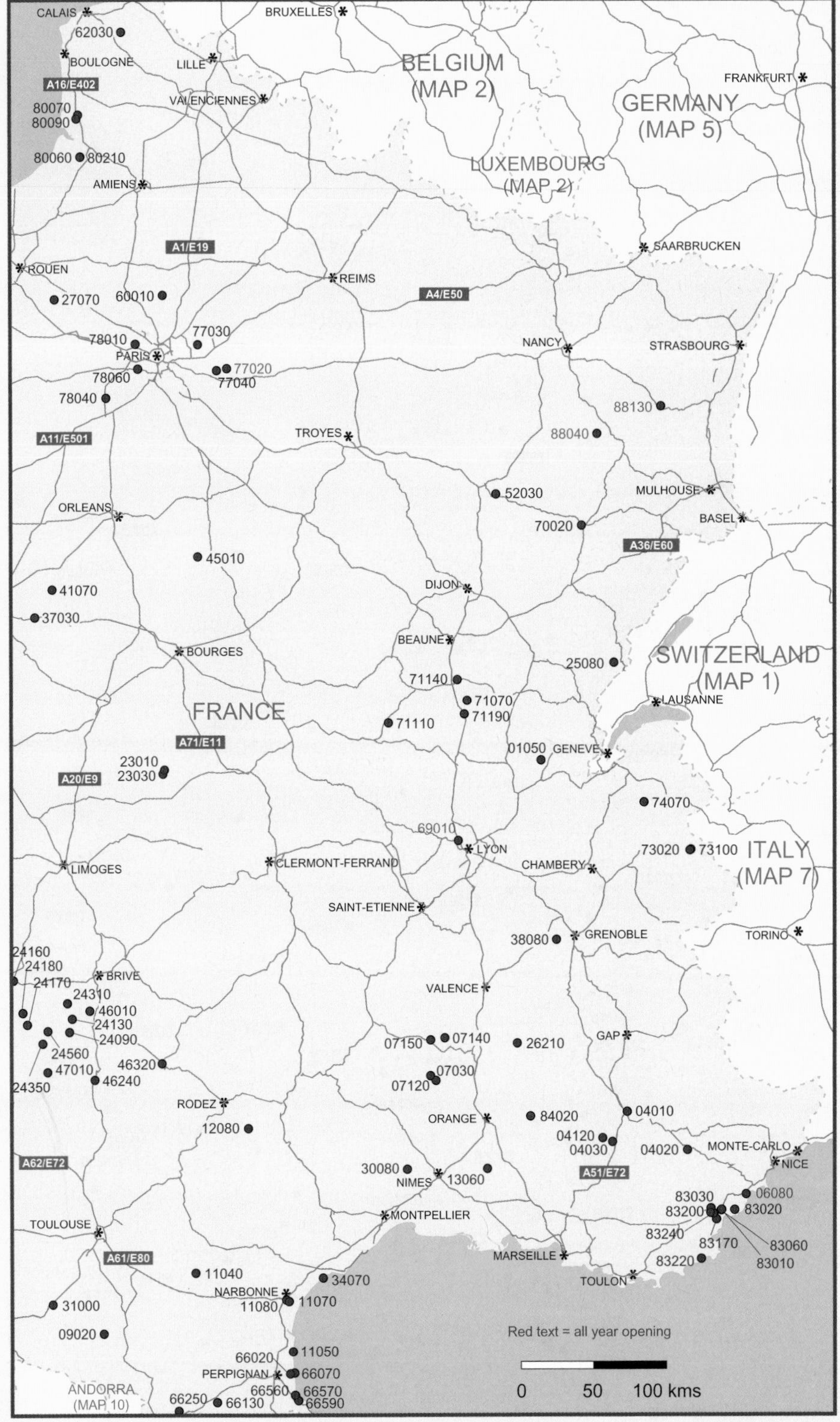

Please refer to the numerical index (page 565) for campsite page references

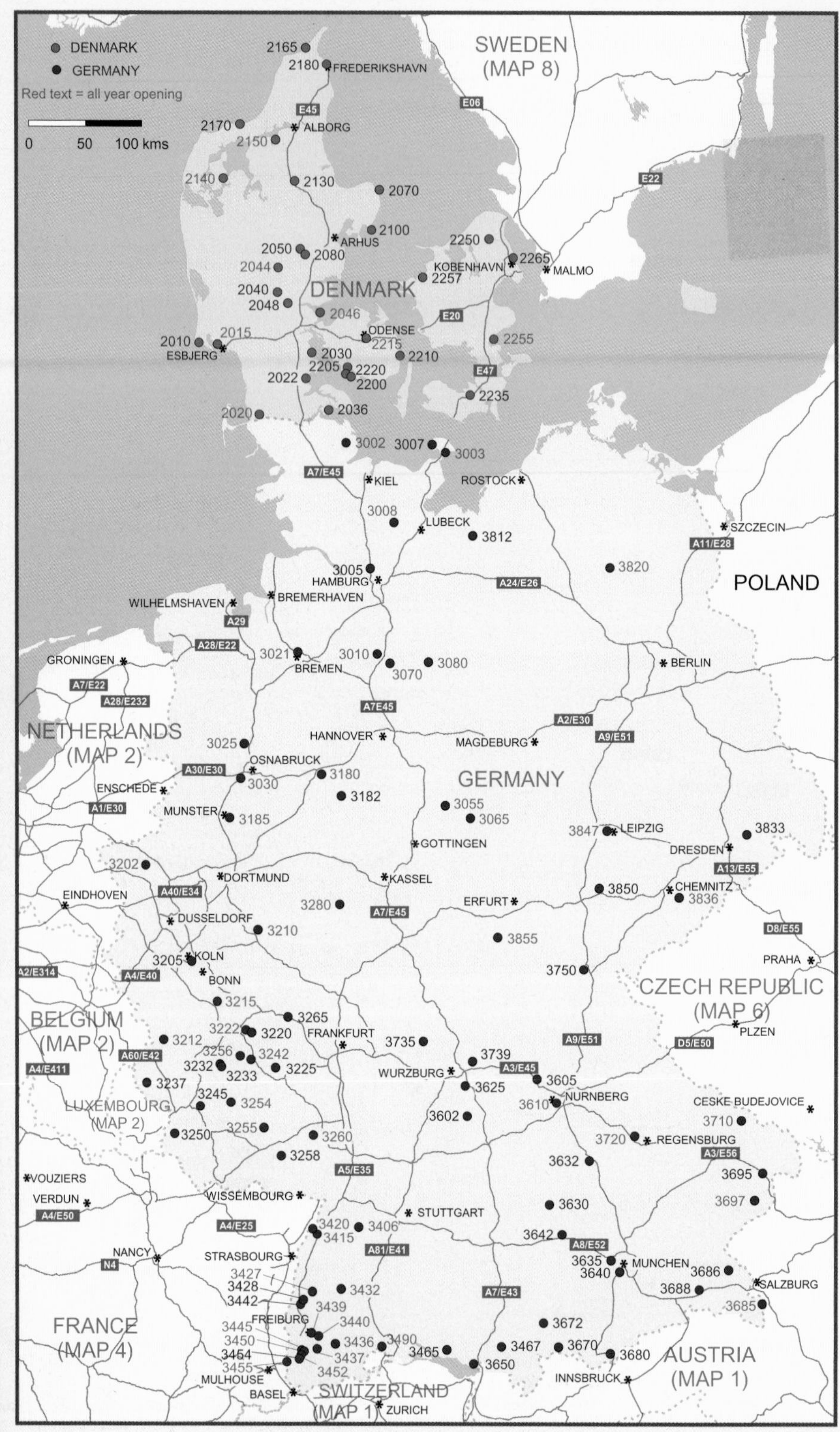

Please refer to the numerical index (page 565) for campsite page references

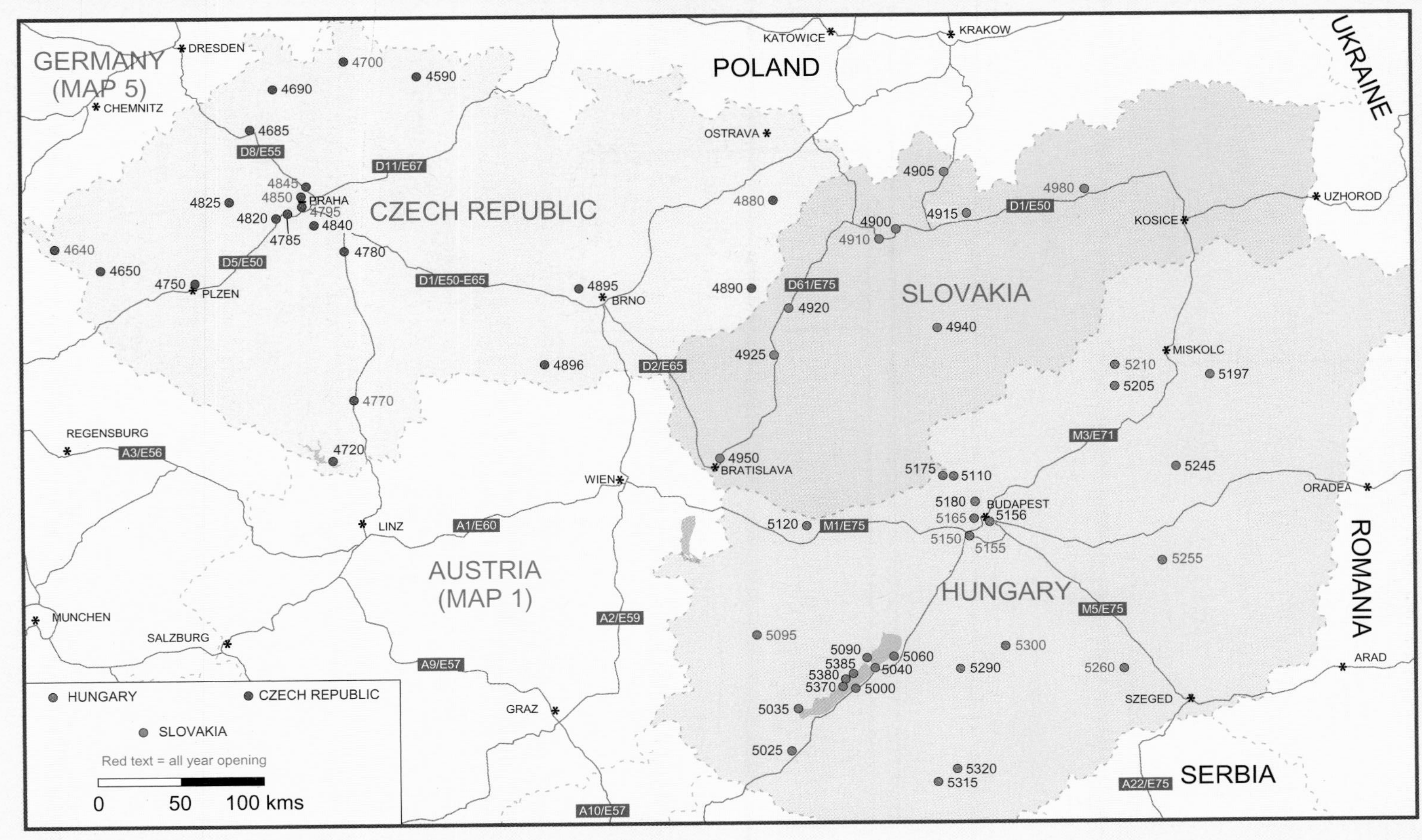

Please refer to the numerical index (page 565) for campsite page references

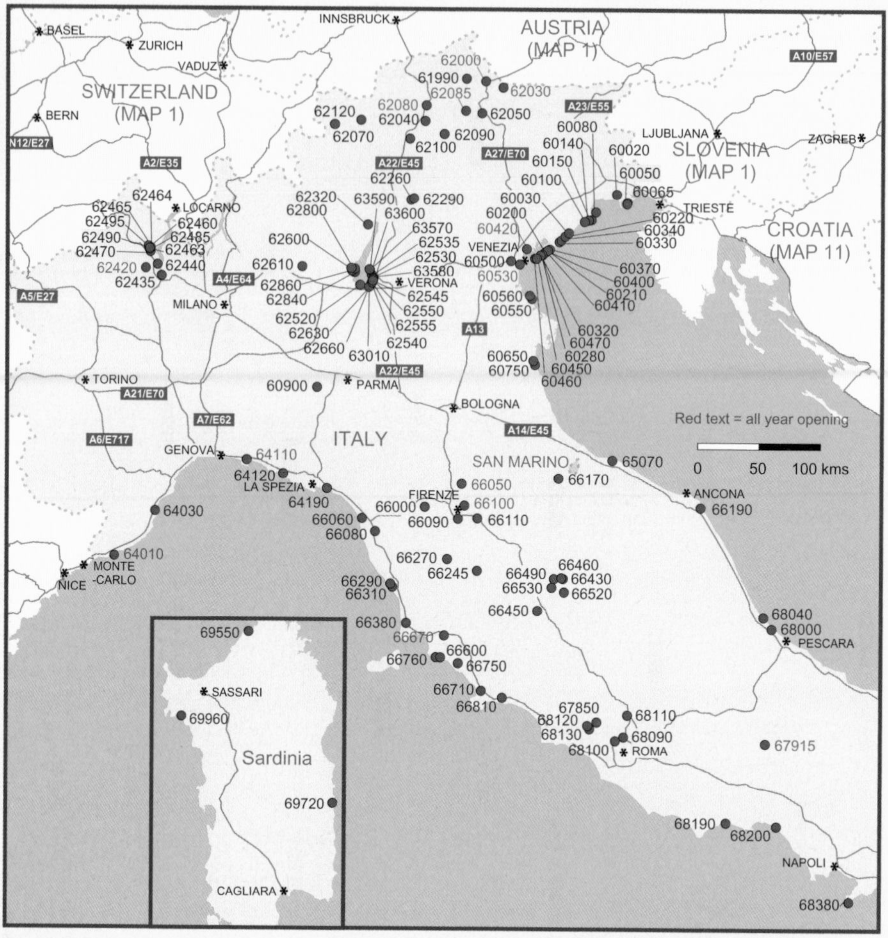

BASEL
ZURICH
VADUZ
INNSBRUCK
AUSTRIA (MAP 1)
SWITZERLAND (MAP 1)
BERN
N12/E27
A2/E35
LOCARNO
62464
62465
62495
62490
62470
62460
62485
62463
62420
62440
62435
A5/E27
A4/E64
MILANO
62000
61990
62030
62085
62080
62050
62120
62040
62070
62090
62100
A22/E45
62260
A23/E55
A27/E70
60080
60140
60150
60100
60020
60050
60065
LJUBLJANA
SLOVENIA (MAP 1)
ZAGREB
A10/E57
TRIESTE
60220
60340
60330
CROATIA (MAP 11)
62320
62800
63590
62290
63600
63570
62535
62530
62600
62610
63580
VERONA
62860
62840
62545
62550
62520
62630
62555
62540
62660
63010
60030
60200
60420
VENEZIA
60500
60530
60560
60550
60370
60400
60210
60410
60320
60470
60280
60650
60750
60450
60460
A13
TORINO
A21/E70
A22/E45
60900
PARMA
BOLOGNA
A7/E62
A6/E717
A14/E45
Red text = all year opening
0 50 100 kms
ITALY
GENOVA
64110
64120
LA SPEZIA
64190
SAN MARINO
65070
66170
66050
ANCONA
66190
FIRENZE
66000
66100
66090
66110
64030
66060
66080
64010
NICE
MONTE -CARLO
66270
66245
66460
66490
66430
66530
66520
66290
66310
66450
68040
68000
PESCARA
66380
66670
66600
66760
66750
66710
66810
67850
68110
68120
68130
68090
68100
ROMA
67915
68190
68200
NAPOLI
68380
69550
SASSARI
69960
Sardinia
69720
CAGLIARA

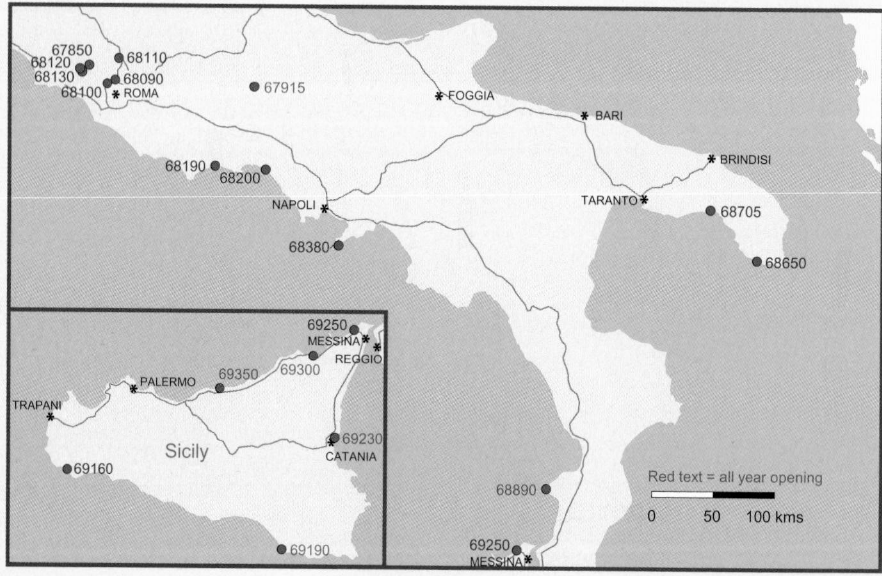

Please refer to the numerical index (page 565) for campsite page references

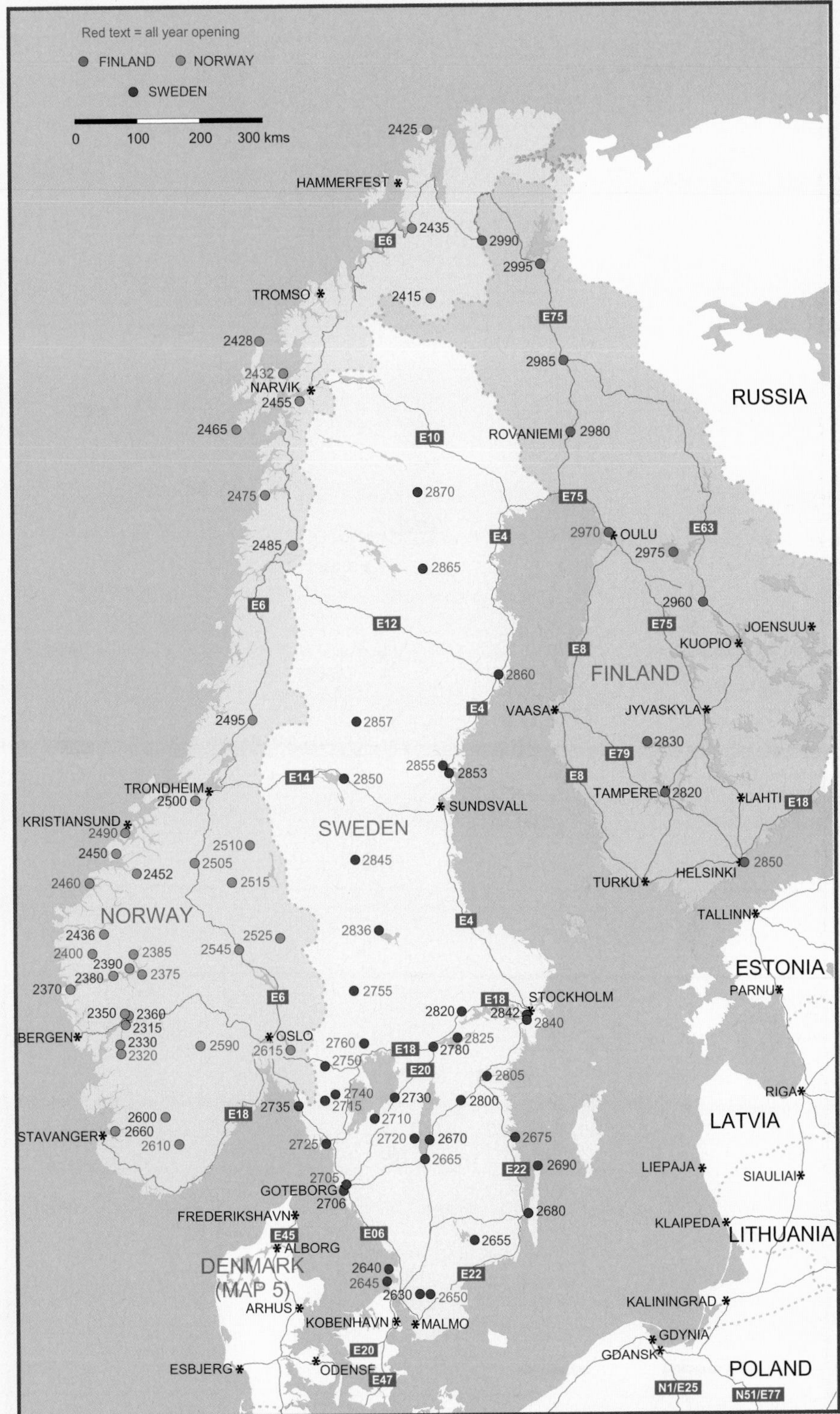

Please refer to the numerical index (page 565) for campsite page references

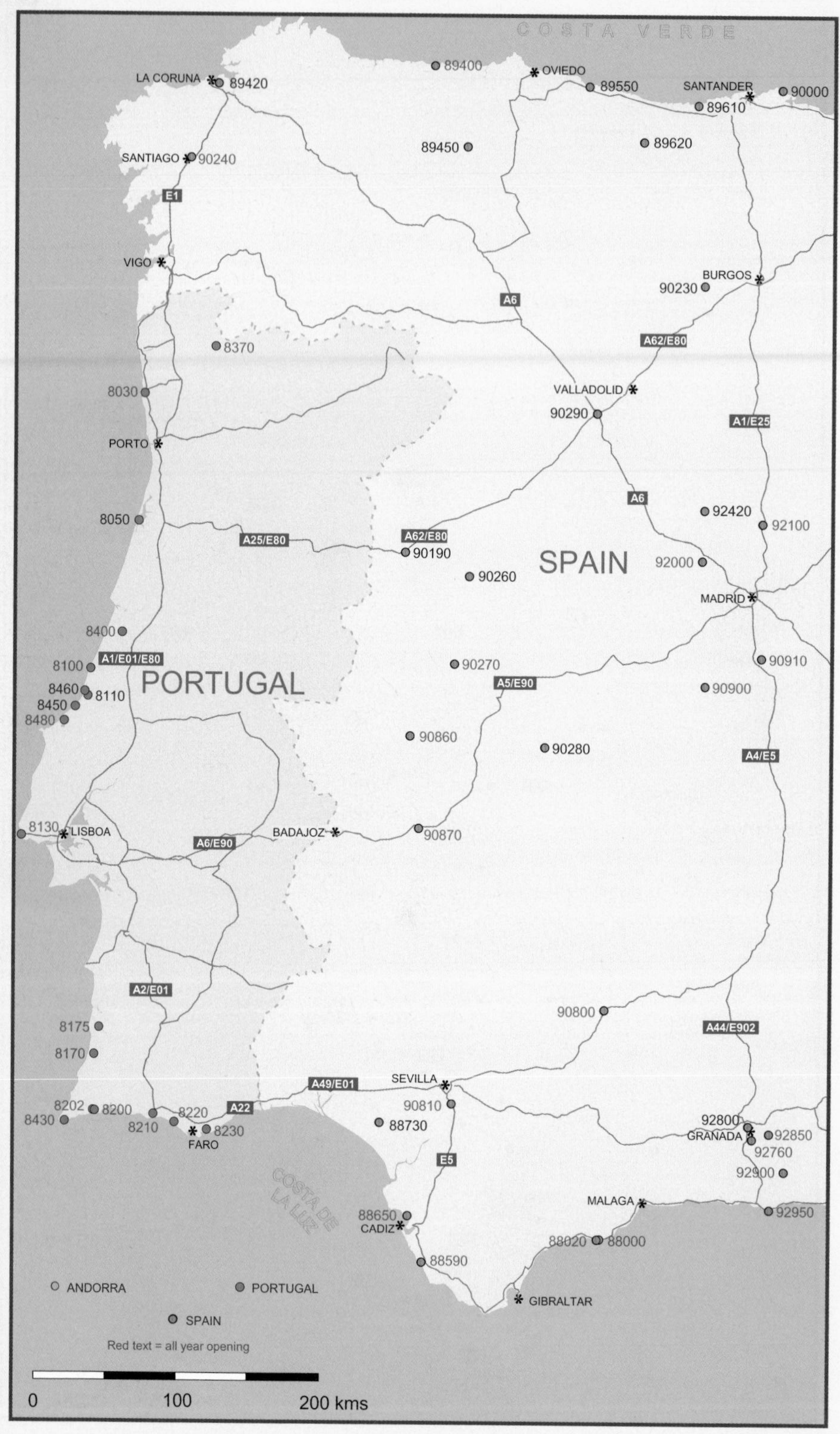

Please refer to the numerical index (page 565) for campsite page references

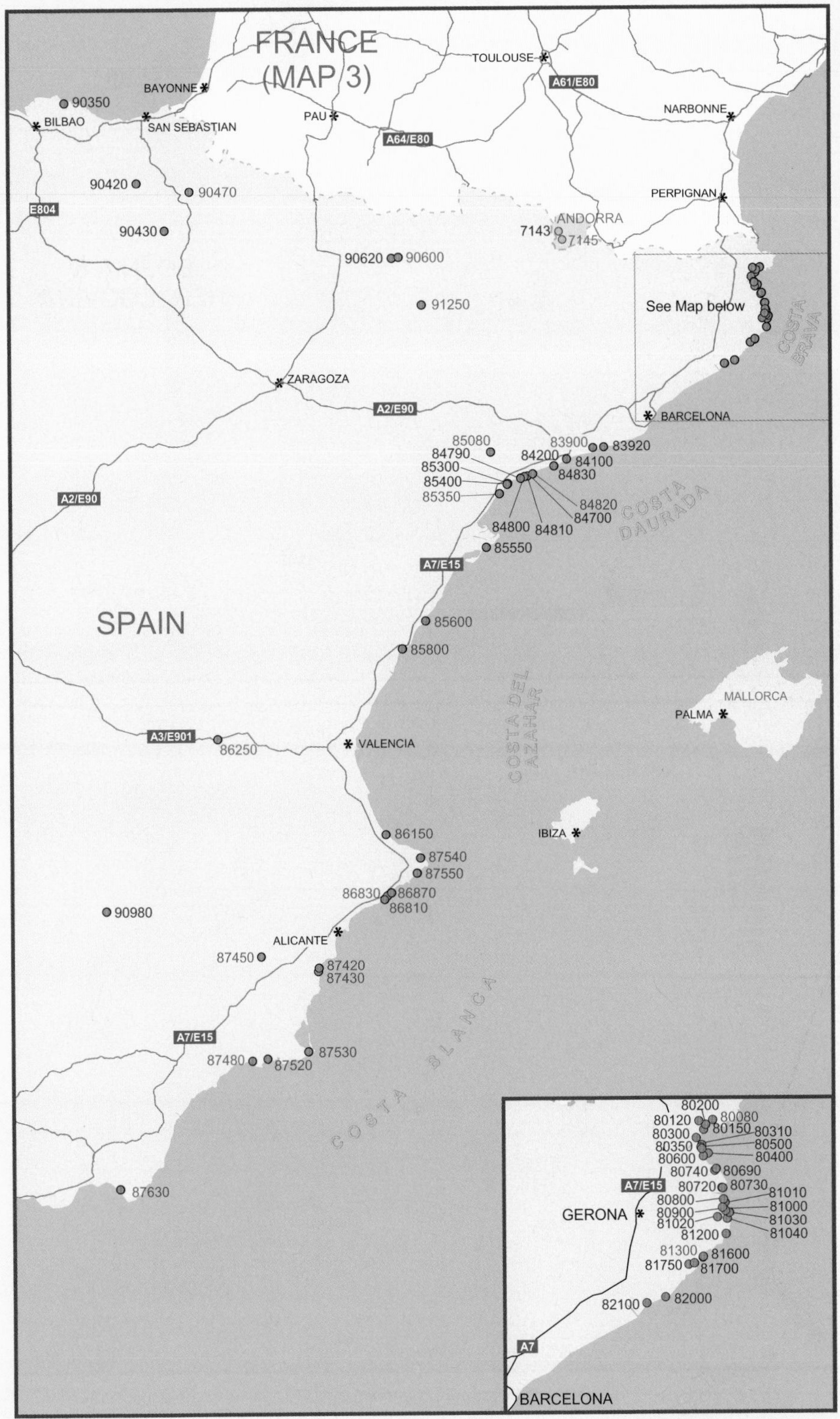

Please refer to the numerical index (page 565) for campsite page references

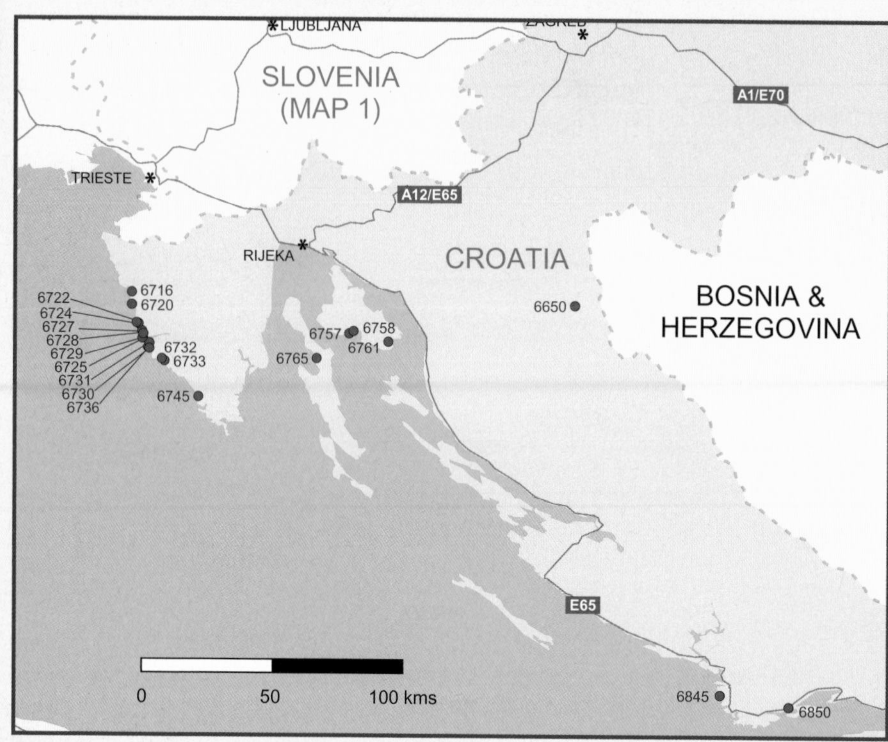

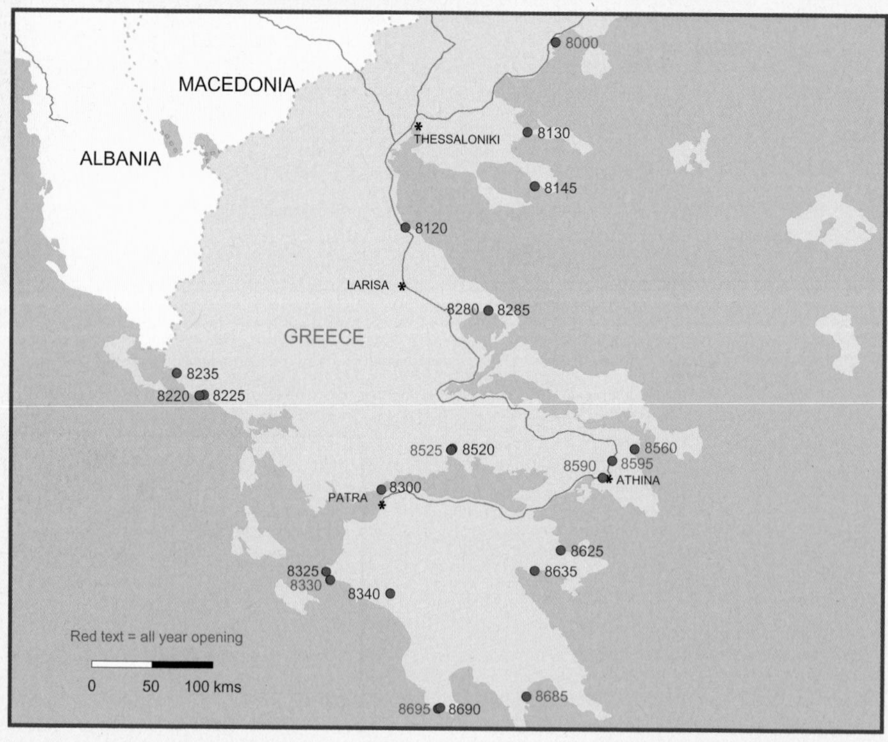

Please refer to the numerical index (page 565) for campsite page references

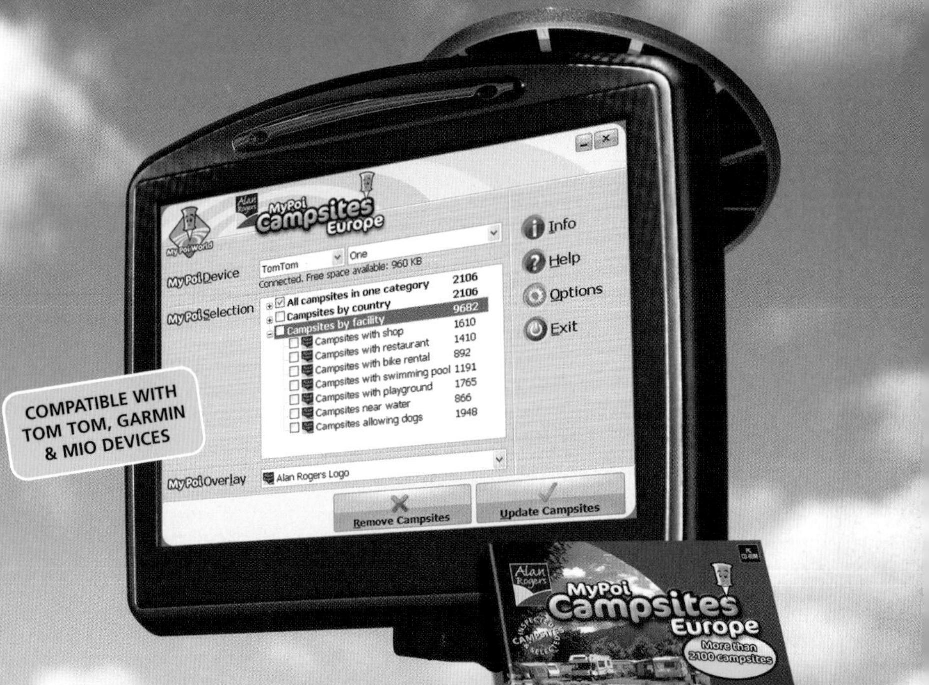

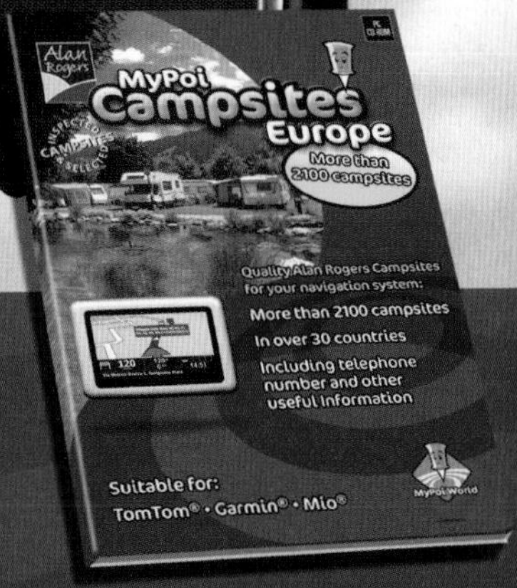

NEW from Alan Rogers

Sat Nav
To Your Campsite

Fed up with vague signs, indistinct directions and ambiguous road markings?

Navigating to continental campsites can be a complicated affair. That's why Alan Rogers have teamed up with MyPoi World to create a sure-fire solution.

Easily navigate to over 2,100 campsites in more than 30 European countries, including the UK. All campsites are 'inspected and selected' by Alan Rogers, giving you real peace of mind.

It's easy to use, with intuitive search criteria, making your journey a real pleasure.

- **Select campsites by name, location or type of facilities**
- **Includes campsite phone number**
- **Identifies pet-friendly campsites**
- **Identifies presence of pool, shop, bar, restaurant etc**
- **Identifies if campsite is situated close to water**

Alan Rogers

www.**alanrogers**.com

More information - and download option

MyPoi World

Town and Village Index

Town and Village Index continued

Index by Campsite Number

Liechtenstein

Luxembourg

Netherlands

Norway

Index by Campsite Number continued

Index by Country and Campsite Name

Index by Country and Campsite Name continued

Liechtenstein

Luxembourg

Netherlands

Norway

Index by Country and Campsite Name continued

Acknowledgements

We would like to thank the following national and regional Tourist Boards for supplying photographs for use in this guide:

Andorra Tourist Office
Toerisme Vlaanderen
Croatian National Tourist Board
Danish Tourism Board
Bayern Tourismus
Hungarian Tourist Board
Italian Tourist Board
Liechtenstein Tourist Board
Luxembourg Tourist Office
Netherlands Tourist Board
Norwegian Tourist Board
Portuguese National Tourism Office
Slovakia Travel
Turespana
Costa Brava Girona Tourist Board
Sweden Travel & Travel Tourism Council
Switzerland Tourism